"Steve Wellum has already made a significant contribution in the area of biblical-theological methodology: a progressive covenantalism that emphasizes the covenants as the framework for the proper understanding of the whole of Scripture. With this new book, he makes another important contribution based upon progressive convenantalism: a systematic theology that arises out of that covenantal framework to express doctrinal truth about the triune God and his ways so that the church grows in faith and obedience and expands into the whole world through the gospel of Jesus Christ. *Systematic Theology* is a *tour de force*!"

—**Gregg R. Allison**, professor of Christian theology, The Southern Baptist Theological Seminary

"*Systematic Theology* is solidly evangelical, thoroughly biblical, informed by major church history voices, written to serve the church, and shaped by an overarching progressive covenantalism. Wellum's engagement with other thinkers combined with his articulation of matters related to theological method and Christian worldview development are superb. This comprehensive volume reflects decades of study, research, and teaching, and it will provide insightful, thoughtful, and edifying guidance for a generation of students, pastors, church leaders, and seasoned theologians as well."

—**David S. Dockery**, distinguished professor of theology, Southwestern Baptist Theological Seminary, and president, International Alliance for Christian Education

"Wellum proves himself to be extremely adept at summarizing and synthesizing biblical material, understanding the history of Christian theology, grasping various philosophical schools of thought, and is passionate about bringing his work to bear on contemporary life and practice. This theology is thoroughly Christian and trinitarian, steeped in ancient Christian theological reflection, committed to the best of the Reformation, and convictionally Baptist. It is satisfying to see a first-rate theological mind engage in the theological task. I am excited to see such a robust and forthright new systematic theology come to see the light of day. It is simply excellent, and I look forward to its reception and influence."

—**Bradley G. Green**, professor of theological studies, Union University, and professor of philosophy and theology, The Southern Baptist Theological Seminary

"Stephen Wellum has given us the best systematic theology from the perspective of 'progressive covenantalism.' An alternative to both classic Reformed covenant theology and dispensationalism, Wellum casts a wide vision for this 'third way' of interpreting Scripture. Although I remain persuaded of the former perspective, I found Wellum's arguments edifying, challenging and at many points an advance in serious evangelical engagement with Scripture's own theological framework. Plus, he writes for the church and that aim is evident throughout all of the topics."

—**Michael Horton**, J. Gresham Machen Professor of Systematic Theology and Apologetics, Westminster Seminary, California

"Wellum's *Systematic Theology* is biblically faithful, pastorally wise, culturally adept, and methodologically astute. Wellum addresses the basic philosophical challenges that loom behind theologizing today, yet most fundamentally he is a Baptist theologian who formulates doctrine exegetically, covenantally, and canonically. While other systematics do good work, this volume is the systematic theology I've been waiting for. It moves to the top of the heap."

—**Jonathan Leeman**, editorial director, 9Marks

"We hold in our hands a volume that will become a standard textbook for evangelical seminaries. It will be referenced for decades to come because it truly is a theology driven by the biblical storyline, grounded in church history, and related to contemporary issues. It shows both the maturity of a seasoned professor and precision of a well-published scholar. Pastors, students, and professors alike will want to learn from it."

—**Christopher W. Morgan**, dean and professor of theology, School of Christian Ministries, California Baptist University

"Steve Wellum is one of the most astute and brilliant theologians of our day and now we are treated to his *magnum opus*. This volume is a profound systematic theology that draws on biblical theology, historical theology, and philosophy in formulating a coherent and articulate presentation of Christian doctrine. In my mind no one has done this better today than Steve Wellum. He emphasizes that systematic theology is practical—it is theology applied to all of life. We all live, whether we know it or not, based on our systematic theology. Thus, this is a life-changing book that is a must read both for the academy and for the church."

—**Thomas R. Schreiner**, James Buchanan Harrison Professor of New Testament Interpretation, and associate dean, The Southern Baptist Theological Seminary

"In *Systematic Theology*, Stephen Wellum not only engages in the task of doing theology, he also does so as an expression of worship to God. In this exceptional volume, Wellum presents the storyline of the Bible and then masterfully moves from biblical to systematic theology in light of historical theology. And for Wellum, the goal of discerning doctrinal truth from Scripture is good but not ultimate. Theology and doctrine are for knowing and worshipping God rightly and to live obediently and joyfully under Christ's lordship. This is theology of the church, in the church, and for the church. Take up and read. Learn of God. And ultimately, worship our Creator-Covenant Lord."

—**Gregory C. Strand**, executive director of theology and credentialing, EFCA, and adjunct professor of pastoral theology, Trinity Evangelical Divinity School

"According to the law of supply and demand, the need for evangelical systematic theologies is not as great as it was twenty years ago—thanks be to God. Yet Wellum's volume, the first of a promised pair, stands out from the pack, for two reasons. First, it is unashamedly Baptist. Second, and more importantly, Wellum's systematic theology takes its marching orders from biblical theology. The whole of part three lays out his distinctive progressive covenantal theological framework. The 'system' that emerges is one that centers on and magnifies the being and works of the triune God in creating and caring for the world. Readers will find here clearly argued, biblically grounded theological thinking about God and all things in relation to God for the edification of the people of God."

—**Kevin J. Vanhoozer**, research professor of systematic theology, Trinity Evangelical Divinity School

SYSTEMATIC THEOLOGY

SYSTEMATIC THEOLOGY

FROM CANON TO CONCEPT

VOLUME ONE

STEPHEN J. WELLUM

Systematic Theology, Volume 1

Published by B&H Academic
Brentwood, Tennessee

ISBN: 978-1-4336-7644-4

Dewey Decimal Classification: 230
Subject Heading: DOCTRINAL THEOLOGY \ CHRISTIANITY--DOCTRINES

Cover design by Brian Bobel. Cover images: Icon of Jesus Christ with Open Bible, sourced from kadmy/iStock; The Last Supper by Willem Jacob Herreyns, sourced from sedmak/iStock; and Crucifixion Of Jesus, chromolithograph from 1886, sourced from ZU_09/iStock.

Printed in the United States of America

3 4 5 6 7 8 9 10 • 29 28 27 26 25 24

To my theological colleagues, past and present, at The Southern Baptist Theological Seminary, who have sharpened my thinking, carried out robust theological discussion, and exhibited grace even in areas of disagreement. I am thankful for your partnership in the gospel as we have sought to take seriously our sober and joyous responsibility to teach the next generations of Christian ministers to remain faithful to Scripture alone and to know and proclaim the glory of our triune God in the face of our Lord Jesus Christ.

CONTENTS

Preface xi
Introduction xv

Part 1: Introduction to Systematic Theology

Chapter 1: Systematic Theology: Nature and Importance 3
Chapter 2: Systematic Theology: Cultural Context 31
Chapter 3: Systematic Theology: The Foundation 79
Chapter 4: Systematic Theology: The Method 107

Part 2: The Revelation of the Triune God Who Speaks

Chapter 5: God and His Word: Divine Speech 151
Chapter 6: Natural or General Revelation 191
Chapter 7: What is Scripture? Three Views of Biblical Authority 219
Chapter 8: Why Receive Scripture as God's Word Written? 255
Chapter 9: The Inspiration of Scripture 289
Chapter 10: The Infallibility and Inerrancy of Scripture 311
Chapter 11: The Sufficiency and Clarity of Scripture 335
Chapter 12: The Canon of Scripture 365

Part 3: The Biblical-Theological Framework of Scripture

Chapter 13: Creation, Fall, Redemption, and New Creation 393
Chapter 14: *Kingdom* through Covenant: Progressive Covenantalism 431
Chapter 15: Competing Biblical-Theological Systems in Evangelical Theology 485

Part 4: From Biblical Theology to Theological Formulation

Chapter 16: The God Who Is There: Contemporary Discussion 535
Chapter 17: The Triune Covenant Lord: Theological Overview 569
Chapter 18: The Attributes of Our Triune God 593
Chapter 19: The Triune God of All Glory 671
Chapter 20: The Triune God Who Plans All Things: The Divine Decree 725
Chapter 21: The Triune God Who Creates: Creation 785
Chapter 22: The Triune God Who Sustains and Rules: Providence (Part 1) 861
Chapter 23: The Triune God Who Sustains and Rules: Providence (Part 2) 895

Name Index 937
Subject Index 942
Scripture Index 955

PREFACE

When I first agreed to write a systematic theology many years ago, I underestimated how difficult and daunting such a project would be. The weight and responsibility of communicating faithfully the whole counsel of God to the church for our time is no small task. In fact, to think that one person can do such a thing is already a problem! Who is sufficient for such a task, apart from the constant encouragement of others, dependence on those who have gone before, and a constant reliance on the grace and help of our triune God?

Systematic theology is best understood as "faith seeking understanding," and it requires an accurate understanding of God's word, centered in the knowledge of God, and the application of Scripture to every area of life. Theology must stand on the shoulders of the theological giants who have gone before; it is never done in a vacuum. Moreover, theology must also address the needs of our current day, so that we can fulfill our calling as the church to "demolish arguments and every proud thing that is raised up against the knowledge of God, and to take every thought captive to obey Christ" (2 Cor 10:4b–5). Apart from faith and sound theology, the church is always in constant danger of being "tossed by the waves and blown around by every wind of teaching, by human cunning with cleverness in the techniques of deceit" (Eph 4:14), instead of being rooted and grounded in our Lord Jesus Christ, in whom is "hidden all the treasures of wisdom and knowledge" (Col 2:3), and to know is life eternal (John 17:3). No wonder, the writing of a systematic theology for the church in our day is both a daunting task and an amazing joy and privilege. As such, I could not have finished this first volume of a projected two volume systematic theology apart from the help of many people too numerous to thank.

My understanding of the gospel and sound theology was first taught to me by my parents, family members, faithful pastors too numerous to mention, and by my teachers during my seminary years at Trinity Evangelical Divinity School—all of whom faithfully sought to know, proclaim, and apply the truth of Scripture without compromise. In addition, I want to thank my wife, Karen, and our children, Joel, Justin, Joshua, Janae, and Jessica, who endured my teaching theology in the home and seeking to make it relevant to their lives as the baton was passed to them to remain faithful to the triune God of the gospel as they seek to honor him in their marriages and families.

Also, I want to thank my students over the years, starting over twenty-seven years ago, first at the Associated Canadian Theological Schools in western Canada, and since then in various theological institutions in North America, Ireland, and other international countries. However, special thanks go to my students at The Southern Baptist Theological Seminary where I have served since 1999. Over the years, my students have greatly encouraged me to persevere and to get this work done. Their strong support to finish this work has been much appreciated. Even more: their desire to know God and his Word and to think theologically in every area of life has been such an encouragement to me as a teacher, and I am so thankful to the Lord for the opportunity he has given me to teach and the train the next generation of gospel ministers to be faithful in their theology and lives. Today, what is needed are faithful pastors and strong local churches, and I am encouraged by many of my students who are such pastors in the churches they have been called to serve, teach, and minister.

I must also thank the administration and trustees of Southern Seminary, and especially Dr. Albert Mohler. Dr. Mohler has led the seminary well by modeling vigilance in holding to sound doctrine, and also demanding this of his faculty. Also, apart from the generous sabbatical policy of the seminary, it would have been difficult to finish this first volume. I am thankful for the investment of Southern in theological education for the church, along with the Southern Baptist Churches who faithfully and sacrificially support their seminaries. My prayer is that our Convention of churches and our seminaries will never cease to uphold the full authority of Scripture, sound orthodox theology, and to proclaim the unsearchable riches of Christ.

This book is dedicated to my colleagues, both past and present, who have served alongside me in the teaching of systematic theology. I have benefited from all of my colleagues at Southern Seminary who have sharpened and challenged me to faithful biblical and theological teaching, but I especially want to acknowledge those in systematic theology who have served as colleagues in gospel ministry. Although we may disagree at some points, there is remarkable unity in the glorious truths of Christian theology, and a deep desire to pass sound theology on to the next generation. It has been a joy and privilege to serve alongside Bruce Ware, Gregg Allison, Kyle Claunch, and previously Oren Martin, Tyler Wittman, Chad Brand, and Craig Blaising. All of my colleagues have taught and sharpened me, and encouraged me in the doing of theology for the glory of our triune God and the good of the church. Thank you, gentlemen, for being fellow partners in the gospel, and may we remain faithful to the high calling that is ours to know God and his Word and to theologize correctly.

My prayer is that this work will encourage many in their understanding of God's Word and to think rightly about our great and glorious God. We live in challenging days for the church, and what is needed is faithfulness to the whole counsel of God so that gospel ministry may continue, God may be glorified, and Christ proclaimed. *Soli Deo gloria.*

INTRODUCTION

Systematic theology is *not* optional for the church. In fact, theology is the very lifeblood of the church and thus necessary for her life and health. At the center of theology's task is the knowledge of our triune God as our Creator, Redeemer, and covenant Lord, along with the application of his word to our lives. For us, who are created and redeemed by God, there is no higher calling than to know the only true God in and through our Lord Jesus Christ (John 17:3).

Theology, which is disciplined thought about God and all things in relation to him, is not reserved for academic theologians; it is the calling and responsibility of all Christians. As the "queen of the sciences," theology is the culminating discipline that uses sanctified reason to understand the whole of Scripture and to apply its teaching to every area of our lives. Theology allows us to "to think God's thoughts after him" to the praise of his glory and for the good of the church. In fact, apart from sound theology, we do not think rightly about God, the self, or the world. Although everyone has some kind of theology, our task is to make sure that our theology is true to Scripture and faithful to "the faith that was delivered to the saints once for all" (Jude 3).

Theology is needed in every era but especially today. Since its beginning, the church has always been in danger of theological and spiritual drift, and theology's task is to keep her from being "tossed by the waves and blown around by every wind of teaching" (Eph 4:14). Theology is called to expound and defend the truth of God's word so that the church continues to love and proclaim the unsearchable riches of Christ to the nations (Col 1:28–29) in every cultural context. But today, the need seems even greater. On every side, many evangelicals are experiencing a collective identity crisis. Why? I am sure there are many reasons, but certainly one of them is due to the waning conviction that theology is an objective discipline grounded in the triune God who is truly there and who has authoritatively made himself known to us. For many years, as David Wells has repeatedly warned the evangelical church in the West, we have traded theological faithfulness for "pragmatic success."[1] As a result, disciplined biblical and theological thinking has taken second place to other cultural concerns, so much so that even critics of evangelicalism are noticing some massive changes within contemporary evangelicalism.[2] For this reason, if the evangelical church is not careful, she is in danger of surrendering her conviction that an objective theology is possible (because Scripture *is* God's authoritative and trustworthy word) and is desirable.

However, the conviction of this work is the opposite of some of these current trends. With the historic and "catholic" church, I am convinced that the triune God is actually there and that he has revealed himself in his authoritative word, and hence that theology is both possible and absolutely necessary for the life and health of the church. But what makes this work distinctive in contrast to other works of theology? Five comments are in order.

First, in many ways this work is saying nothing new, and I consider this its strength. This work is not seeking to be novel, but instead faithful to Scripture and classic, orthodox theology. As such, I gladly affirm the "catholic" confessions of the church as true (e.g., the Apostles' Creed, Nicaea, Chalcedon), and I am convinced that the "old paths" are what the church needs today, especially in the doctrinal areas of theology proper and Christology.

Second, this book is committed to the truth of the Reformation *solas* (e.g., *sola Scriptura, sola gratia, sola fide, solus Christus, soli Deo Gloria*) and what the Reformers recaptured in terms of these central gospel truths. Furthermore, I am convinced that at the heart of Reformation theology is the supremacy of the triune God of glory as the independent, self-sufficient, holy Creator, Lord, and Redeemer. On this point, this work is thoroughly committed to Reformed

[1] See David F. Wells, *The Bleeding of the Evangelical Church* (Carlisle: Banner of Truth, 2021); cf. Wells, *No Place for Truth or Whatever Happened to Evangelical Theology?* (Grand Rapids: Eerdmans, 1993); Wells, *The Courage to Be Protestant: Reformation Faith in Today's World*, 2nd ed. (Grand Rapids: Eerdmans, 2017).

[2] For example, see David Gushee, "The Deconstruction of American Evangelicalism," *Baptist News Global*, October 11, 2021, https://baptistnews.com/article/the-deconstruction-of-american-evangelicalism/#.YWR-8trMKUk. Gushee, a critic of evangelicalism, notes some recent trends within evangelicalism away from theology to more cultural concerns.

theology as the view that is most faithful to who God is as the sovereign Lord worthy of all of our worship, love, and obedience.

Third, this book is unashamedly Baptist, although specific Baptist distinctives as they pertain to the church will be developed in volume 2. However, it is evident even in this volume that I am convinced that a proper view of the covenants and God's new covenant work in Christ requires an uncompromising commitment to Baptist distinctives and convictions.

Fourth, as already stated, my Baptist convictions are due to my understanding of how God unfolds his eternal plan through the biblical covenants. In this regard, this book offers an alternative to classic Reformed covenant and dispensational theology, and in their place, I affirm "progressive covenantalism" as the best way of "putting together" the Bible's metanarrative from Genesis to Revelation.

Fifth, this work is convinced that systematic theology arises from the entire canon of Scripture, but not merely as isolated texts that may be organized in a variety of ways. Instead, theology arises out of the Bible's own presentation and covenantal framework, which is why theology must be *intratextual* and not *extratextual*. By the former, I mean that theology must be true to the Bible's own structures and categories and thus function as our authoritative "lens" by which we look at the world. This is in contrast to extratextual theologies that function as "authoritative" grids imposed on Scripture, thus reinterpreting the Bible according to an external framework outside of Scripture and not vice versa. This extratextual "method of correlation" is destructive of orthodox theology and must be rejected in order to be faithful to the Bible's own theological framework. Scripture, precisely because it is *God's* first-order authoritative word, presents its own God-given worldview, which must serve as the spectacles by which we draw theological conclusions *and* interpret the world. Otherwise, the Bible becomes merely a "wax nose" beholden to the latest conceptual scheme, which sadly we have repeatedly witnessed in theologies from the Enlightenment until today that have departed from historic Christianity.

This project is divided into two volumes. In part 1 of this volume, we discuss crucial prolegomena issues by setting the theological task in our present context and arguing for the necessity of a theology "from above." Since theology is never done in a vacuum, specific focus is on the exposition and defense of Christian theology as an objective, true discipline. We do so by unpacking the foundations (*principia*) for such a theology, namely, the triune God who exists and his authoritative speech given to us in Scripture. In part 2, the doctrine of revelation as God's divine speech contained first in nature and then supremely in Scripture is developed in detail. Since our theology is dependent on God's self-revelation, it is crucial that our theological conclusions arise from the entirety of Scripture. For this reason, in part 3, we spend time unpacking the Bible's covenantal story from creation to the new creation and from Adam to Christ so that the Bible informs our theological conclusions as a coherent, unified story of God's eternal plan centered in Christ. Then in part 4, we begin to do theology by moving from biblical theology to theological formulation. We begin where Scripture begins, namely, the glory of our triune God. Theology proper is first discussed in terms of who God is in himself (*ad intra*) before we discuss God in his external works (*ad extra*) as our Creator and providential Lord.

In volume 2, by God's grace, we will continue to do theological formulation from the Bible's own covenantal story by completing the other loci of systematic theology: the doctrines of humanity and sin, the person and work of Christ, salvation, the church, and last things.

My earnest prayer is that in some small way this work will encourage the evangelical church to think theologically in every area of life for God's glory and the life and health of the church. We live in challenging times, which are witnessing much theological drift, and I am convinced that what is needed is not novel theologies indebted to the Zeitgeist, but theologies that retrieve the "old paths" and that, in doing so, remain faithful to God's holy word. What is needed is not less theology but more; not the lowest common denominator theology, but robust theology that takes God at his word and glories in Christ Jesus as Lord!

Soli Deo Gloria

PART 1

Introduction to Systematic Theology

CHAPTER 1

Systematic Theology: Nature and Importance

Introduction

Theology means different things to people. For some it is an academic discipline that describes various theologians and their theologies and is thus only for professors or pastors, but not for the everyday Christian. For others, theology is a speculative, esoteric discipline that often leads us away from Scripture and that is detrimental for a vibrant relationship with the Lord. Others think of theology, especially "systematic" theology, as imposing "systems" on Scripture, thus removing it from Scripture and making it less than "biblical."

Whatever people may think theology is, in the church, sadly, it has fallen on hard times. The evidence for this claim is not hard to find. On a biennial basis since 2014, Lifeway and Ligonier have conducted "The State of Theology" poll.[1] When basic theological questions are asked of self-identified evangelicals, it is evident that many are lacking even a rudimentary theological understanding. For example, in the 2020 poll, 96 percent of evangelicals agreed that "there is one true God in three persons: God the Father, God the Son, and God the Holy Spirit." Yet 30 percent of these same people affirmed that "Jesus was a great teacher, but he was not God," and 65 percent agreed that "Jesus was the first and greatest being created by

[1] "The State of Theology," https://thestateoftheology.com.

God"—a contradiction of the first statement. However we try to make sense of these paradoxical answers, they minimally reveal that our churches are lacking basic doctrinal knowledge.

However, this should not surprise us. We have privileged religious experience and pragmatics over disciplined thinking about Scripture. For many, theology is a hard "sell," especially in the age of social media, where careful thought is replaced by images and tweets. Theology has little "cash value"; what we want are instant answers to meet our felt needs. And we especially fear divisions within the church that often occur when careful theological thinking confronts false teaching.[2]

It is imperative that these "popular" misconceptions of theology are corrected by replacing them with a proper understanding of theology. As we begin our study, the purpose of this chapter is to define what systematic theology really is. We will do so by first reflecting on what systematic theology is in Scripture before identifying some of its basic elements and its relation to the other theological disciplines. Our aim is to demonstrate that systematic theology is *not* optional for the church; it is fundamental to our thinking rightly about God, the self, and the world. Theology is basic to Christian discipleship, and it is the culminating discipline, which leads to worldview formation. Theology is not a discretionary exercise; it is essential for the life and health of the church, and whether we realize it or not, everyone has some kind of theology. But the most significant question for us is whether our theology is true to Scripture or not. If it is not, this is serious since wrong ideas about God and Scripture result in disastrous consequences. Ultimately, what is at stake is the issue of truth and whether the church is faithful to Scripture's command to "demolish arguments and every proud thing that is raised up against the knowledge of God" and to "take every thought captive to obey Christ" (2 Cor 10:4b–5).

Theology *and* Scripture

Historically, systematic theology has been viewed as the "queen of the sciences." As the "queen," she is the beautiful capstone and culmination of all the disciplines, especially the theological disciplines. Properly understood, theology is the "study of the triune God," who is our Creator

---

[2] See David Wells, *No Place for Truth* (see Introduction, n. 1); Wells, *God in the Wasteland: The Reality of Truth in a World of Fading Dreams* (Grand Rapids: Eerdmans, 1994); Wells, *Losing Our Virtue: Why the Church Must Recover Its Moral Vision* (Grand Rapids: Eerdmans, 1999); and Wells, *Above All Earthly Pow'rs: Christ in a Postmodern World* (Grand Rapids: Eerdmans, 2005).

and Lord and thus the source and standard of all knowledge and truth (Prov 1:7; Isa 46:8–10; Rom 11:33–36). In fact, the summum bonum of knowledge is the knowledge of God. In fact, all human knowledge, whether in creation or Scripture, is grounded in God's speech and self-disclosure. For humans to know anything, we are dependent on God's initiative to make himself known to us.[3] For this reason, theology is not something reserved for the academic theologian, pastor, or spiritually-minded Christian. Rather, it is the calling and responsibility of all humans to know God as their Creator and Lord. And this is especially true for God's redeemed people, who are re-created in Christ Jesus to know the only true God (John 17:3).

At its heart, systematic theology is the obedient task of the church to use renewed reason by reflecting faithfully on the whole of Scripture and to apply its teaching to every area of life. In other words, theology is the discipline that seeks "to think God's thoughts after him"—for the praise of his glory and the good of the church.[4] Viewed this way, theology obeys what God commands his people to do.

For example, think of our Lord's command in the Great Commission (Matt 28:18–20). Under the authority of King Jesus, we are to "make disciples of all nations," baptizing them in the name of the triune God and "teaching them to observe everything I have commanded you." To obey our Lord's command requires careful biblical and theological thinking; knowing the Scripture; thinking rightly about who the Father, Son, and Spirit are; and faithfully applying all of Scripture to people's lives. This is what theology *is*. Paul exhorts Timothy to "pay close attention to [his] life and [his] teaching," which has life-and-death implications (1 Tim 4:16). He is commanded to "be diligent to present [himself] to God as one approved, a worker who doesn't need to be ashamed, correctly teaching the word of truth" (2 Tim 2:15). Titus is exhorted to hold "to the faithful message as taught, so that he will be able both to encourage with sound teaching and to refute those who contradict it" (Titus 1:9). All of these exhortations require that theology be done. One must first understand Scripture to have correct

---

[3] John Calvin, *Institutes of the Christian Religion*, ed. John T. McNeill, trans. Ford Lewis Battles, 2 vols. (Philadelphia: Westminster Press, 1960), 1.1.1 (1:35), astutely notes the interrelated nature of the knowledge of God and of ourselves. In fact, we cannot know who we are apart from the knowledge of who God is.

[4] Viewing theology as "thinking God's thoughts after him" is a helpful summary of the entire theological task. On this point, see Greg L. Bahnsen, *Van Til's Apologetic: Readings and Analysis* (Phillipsburg: P&R, 1998), 220–60.

teaching (or doctrine), and one must refute error by applying the teaching of Scripture properly. However, it is not only leaders in the church who must know sound theology; all believers must be "ready at any time to give a defense (*apologia*) to anyone who asks you for a reason for the hope that is in you" (1 Pet 3:15). To obey this command, all believers must first know sound teaching in order to defend it against various objections. All of this requires rigorous and sound biblical and theological instruction.

So what, then, is systematic theology? In its most basic sense, systematic theology is the orderly, comprehensive "study of the triune God" and all things in relationship to him (Gk. *theos* [God] + *logos* [words, study of]). John Webster states it this way: Christian theology is the work of renewed, biblical reasoning to consider a twofold object:[5] "first, God in himself in the unsurpassable perfection of his inner being and work as Father, Son and Spirit and his outer operations, and, second and by derivation, all other things relative to him."[6] B. B. Warfield defined theology in a similar way: "Theology . . . is that science which treats of God in himself and in his relations" to humans and the world.[7] An older term to describe systematic theology is "dogmatic theology." In this work, we will use these terms interchangeably, although technically dogmatic theology refers to "core biblical doctrines officially established in a church's confessional statements,"[8] and as such reflects the conclusions of a particular community or tradition's biblical reasoning from Scripture.

If this is what systematic theology is, we can now see why there is no higher calling or study. The Westminster Shorter Catechism begins with the famous question, "What is the chief end of man?" Its answer: "Man's chief end is to glorify God, and to enjoy him forever." In Scripture,

---

[5] John Webster, *The Domain of the Word: Scripture and Theological Reason* (New York: T&T Clark, 2012), 115.

[6] John Webster, *God without Measure*, vol. 1, *God and the Works of God* (New York: T&T Clark, 2016), 3. Elsewhere, Webster unpacks the nature of theology in terms of theology's object and cognitive principles: "The Holy Trinity is the ontological principle of Christian systematic theology. Its external or objective cognitive principle is the divine Word, by which . . . God's incommunicable self-knowledge is accommodated to saints. The internal or subjective cognitive principle is the redeemed intelligence of the saints. Systematic theology is thus ectypal knowledge. . . . Its matter is twofold: God, and all things in God." Webster, "Principles of Systematic Theology," *IJST* 11, no. 1 (2009): 56.

[7] B. B. Warfield, "Theology a Science," in *Selected Shorter Writings*, ed. John E. Meeter, 2 vols. (Phillipsburg: P&R, 1973), 2:207.

[8] Joel R. Beeke and Paul M. Smalley, *Reformed Systematic Theology*, 3 vols. (Wheaton, IL: Crossway, 2019–2021), 1:42.

central to our glorifying God is the knowledge of God. In fact, the purpose of our being created is to know and love God as his image-bearers and covenant people (Matt 22:37–40). Think of how the new covenant relationship is described between God and his people: "And no longer shall each one teach his neighbor and each his brother, saying, 'Know the LORD,' for they shall all know me, from the least of them to the greatest, declares the LORD" (Jer 31:34a ESV). There is no higher calling and nothing more urgent than for humans, as God's creatures, and especially for God's redeemed people in Christ, to know our triune God in all of his majesty, beauty, and holy splendor (Ps 89:16; Isa 11:9; John 17:3). The life and health of the church is directly dependent on our knowledge of God and thus the doing of theology.

In fact, as Herman Bavinck rightly reminds us, theology is really nothing but the knowledge of God, which is then applied to every area of life. Bavinck writes:

> So, then, the knowledge of God is the only dogma, the exclusive content, of the entire field of dogmatics [theology]. All the doctrines treated in dogmatics—whether they concern the universe, humanity, Christ, and so forth—are but the explication of the one central dogma of the knowledge of God. All things are considered in light of God, subsumed under him, traced back to him as the starting point. Dogmatics is always called upon to ponder and describe God and God alone. . . . It is the knowledge of him alone that dogmatics must put on display.[9]

The assumption undergirding such a view of theology is that it is an objective discipline or science, grounded in the triune God who is truly there and who has made himself known to us. This understanding of theology stands in contrast to "liberal" theology that broadly views theology as the study of "religion" or "faith"—a "subjectivist" idea. Friedrich Schleiermacher's understanding of theology is a good example of this. For Schleiermacher, theology is the analysis of the religious consciousness, the feeling of absolute dependence.[10] As we will note in chapters 2–3, the problem with such a view is that theology is made *independent* of Scripture, and its source is not directly grounded in God's divine speech but in one's personal experience

---

[9] Herman Bavinck, *Reformed Dogmatics*, ed. John Bolt, trans. John Vriend, 4 vols. (Grand Rapids: Baker Academic, 2003–2008), 2:29.

[10] Friedrich Schleiermacher, *The Christian Faith*, ed. H. R. Mackintosh and J. S. Stewart (1830; New York: T&T Clark, 1999), 3–128.

mediated through the communion of saints. But personal experience, even mediated through the church, is never the final authority for the theologian. In fact, this view of theology suspends the question of objective truth. "Religion" is more about our experience of and search for the divine. But for such a view, God becomes an aspect of human experience, a view contrary to historic Christian theology. Theology is not about us finding a way to talk about God from the fabric of human experience; instead, it is about the triune God choosing to make himself known to us.

In addition, John Frame defines systematic theology as "the application of God's Word by persons to all areas of life."[11] The focus on "application" is important because it reiterates what people often forget about theology, namely, that theology applies to every area of our lives. If we combine the definitions of Webster and Frame, we can say that systematic theology is the study of the triune God and all things in relationship to him and that it involves the application of God's word to all areas of life.[12] Furthermore, Frame's introduction of "application" into the definition of theology not only helps us think about what theology is but also how it is done. Although we will say more about theological method in chapter 4, at this point, working with our definition of theology, we can say that the doing of systematic theology minimally involves two steps.

First, theology requires that we *apply* God's word. This not only assumes that Scripture, as God's word written, is first order and thus foundational for our theology but also that a right reading of Scripture is central to the doing of theology. The Bible is more than a collection of isolated texts from ancient history. Instead, Scripture is God's unfolding revelation of his eternal plan that moves from creation to the new creation, centered in the coming of Christ. Thus, a correct reading of Scripture requires that individual texts be located in relation to the Bible's unfolding covenantal story and ultimately in light of the entire canon fulfilled in Christ. Careful attention must be given to the Bible's own presentation of its content, categories, and teaching, which, as we will note below, involves the doing of *biblical theology*.

In this regard, Charles Hodge's well-known definition of theology requires modification, as does Wayne Grudem's definition that is dependent on Hodge. For example, Hodge defines theology as "the exhibition of the facts of Scripture in their proper order and relation,

---

[11] John Frame, *The Doctrine of the Knowledge of God* (Phillipsburg: P&R, 1987), 76.

[12] See Frame, 81–88.

with the principles or general truths involved in the facts themselves, and which pervade and harmonize the whole."[13] Likewise, Wayne Grudem defines theology as the study that answers the question, "'What does the whole Bible teach us today?' about any given topic," which involves "collecting and understanding all the relevant passages in the Bible on various topics and then summarizing their teachings clearly so that we know what to believe about each topic."[14]

No doubt there is truth in what Hodge and Grudem say. Systematic theology does seek to know what the entirety of Scripture teaches on any given topic, hence the term "systematic." Yet, the problem with such definitions is that they fail to do justice to what Scripture actually is. Scripture is not a theological dictionary or a storehouse of propositions and facts, although it is thoroughly propositional. Instead, Scripture is first-order God-given language that is composed of many literary forms that require careful interpretation, *and* it is an unfolding revelation given to us over time, a point we will develop in chapter 4. Theology, then, does not simply collect texts and arrange them properly as if we could remove texts out of their immediate and overall canonical context. Instead, Scripture, as God's unfolding revelation over time, comes to us in a specific order and within its own interpretive framework. Texts have to be interpreted and made sense of in light of their redemptive-historical context and ultimately in terms of a closed canon. Our task is to understand individual texts in light of the entirety of Scripture and then to "put together" Scripture and all that it teaches "on its own terms."[15]

Another way of stating this is that Scripture is a word-act revelation. It not only recounts God's mighty actions in history; it is also God's interpretation of his redemptive acts through human authors and thus true, objective, and authoritative. For this reason, Scripture's own interpretations and descriptions are infallible, and they serve as our "interpretive framework" or "spectacles" for thinking about God, the world, and ourselves.[16] Thus, *to apply* Scripture first entails that we interpret Scripture correctly as an entire canon.

---

[13] Charles Hodge, *Systematic Theology*, 3 vols. (1852; repr., Grand Rapids: Eerdmans, 1982), 1:19.

[14] Wayne Grudem, *Systematic Theology*, 2nd ed. (Grand Rapids: Zondervan, 2020), 1 (emphasis removed).

[15] For a similar critique of Charles Hodge's use of Scripture and theological method, see Bavinck, *Reformed Dogmatics*, 1:93–94.

[16] See Calvin, *Institutes*, 1.6.1–4 (1:69–74).

Second, theology requires that we apply Scripture *to all areas of life*. This entails that theology is more than repeating Scripture; instead, theology has a "constructive" element to it. This "constructive" element not only "puts together" all that Scripture teaches; it also involves application to every area of life. For this reason, theology is foundational for worldview formation, as it seeks to integrate God's revelation in nature and Scripture as an exercise of "faith seeking understanding." As we take the Bible's first-order description, we seek *to understand* Scripture in terms of application, logical implications, and metaphysical entailments. No doubt, we do so with help from the past, but we also seek to apply Scripture to the issues of our day in order to teach the church sound doctrine and refute the errors of both the past and present age. God has not given us his word for only one aspect of our lives; God's word applies to every area of life, just as Christ's Lordship is over everything. Abraham Kuyper captured this point well with his famous words: "There is not a square inch in the whole domain of our human existence over which Christ, who is Sovereign over *all*, does not cry: 'Mine!'"[17]

We will return to this point in subsequent chapters, but let me briefly illustrate what this second step looks like in the doing of Christology. To answer the question of who Jesus is, we first turn to the entire canon of Scripture. After we do so, we discover that the Jesus of the Bible is utterly unique; he is God the Son from eternity, who, in the incarnation, added a human nature to himself (John 1:1, 14). Yet, this biblical presentation raises some legitimate *theological* questions that require understanding and theological construction, even the use of extra-biblical language, concepts, and judgments. For example, how should we think of the relation between Jesus as the Son and the Father and Spirit? Or, how should we understand the relationship between the Son's deity and humanity given the Creator-creature distinction (Phil 2:6–11)? Or, how do we make sense of Jesus's statement that he does not know certain things if he is God the Son and thus omniscient (Mark 13:32)? To answer these questions, the "constructive" element of theology is done, which seeks to "understand" Scripture and "put together" the biblical teaching in such a way that accounts for all the biblical data. It is not enough to repeat Scripture, we must also "make sense" of it in order to disciple believers in the truth and to obey Scripture's exhortation to always be ready to give a reasoned defense for what we believe.

---

[17] Abraham Kuyper, "Sphere Sovereignty," in *Abraham Kuyper: A Centennial Reader*, ed. James D. Bratt (Grand Rapids: Eerdmans, 1998), 488.

In the end, the purpose of theology is to help God's people understand Scripture better so that we can rightly know God's word, apply it to our lives, and fulfill our calling as the church to know God and to make him known.[18] As Christians, we are called to bring all of our life, language, and thought into conformity with God's word. As we do so, we also formulate a well-thought-out biblical worldview so that we obey Scripture's command, "Do not be conformed to this age, but be transformed by the renewing of our mind" (Rom 12:2).

Theology *in* Scripture

With this basic idea of what systematic theology is in place, let us now turn to a biblical example of theology being done before our eyes. Sometimes it is easier to grasp what theology is by seeing it practiced, and this also has the added advantage of letting Scripture serve as the paradigm for our thinking about what theology is and how it is to be done. No doubt, in Scripture there are many examples of the doing of theology, yet Paul's Athenian address is most instructive for us today for a variety of reasons (Acts 17:16–32).[19]

First, Paul's reasoning illustrates that theology is *biblical* in that it is grounded in the Bible's unfolding story from creation to Christ. Even more: the Bible's content, categories, and theological framework serve as the interpretive matrix by which he explains the gospel, interprets the world, diagnoses the human problem, gives its solution in Christ, and applies the truth of Scripture to his hearers. Second, building on the first point, Paul's reasoning illustrates that theology presents a well-thought-out *worldview* or philosophy, that is, a total perspective on life, or a grand metanarrative, which allows him to interpret and critique all other theologies or worldviews. Scripture's own description of reality provides the "spectacles" by which Paul thinks and acts. Theology, then, is not only "constructive" in describing and explaining the Bible's message; it is also "apologetic" in that it calls non-Christians to repent of their thinking and suppression of the truth and to turn to the only source of truth, the triune God of Scripture and his word. Third, Paul's reasoning illustrates that theology is *contextual*; that is, it addresses a specific context and people, and it is applied to that context with precision and power. Theology is not

[18] See Frame, *Doctrine of the Knowledge of God*, 76–85.

[19] My discussion of Acts 17 is indebted to D. A. Carson, "Athens Revisited," in *Telling the Truth: Evangelizing Postmoderns*, ed. D. A. Carson (Grand Rapids: Zondervan, 2000), 384–98.

merely interested in giving us a list of timeless propositions; it is interested in applying God's authoritative word to specific people and bringing God's truth to bear on every area of life.

Each of these points is important to understand what theology is and how it is to be done. Yet, the third point links what Paul is doing in his day to ours and encourages us to do likewise. Why? For this reason: in many ways, our present cultural context is parallel to what Paul faced in Athens in the first century, and how he approaches the theological task is instructive for us. As we will discuss in chapter 2, our present context is pluralistic, postmodern, secular, and post-Christian. Central to the thinking of our age is a denial of objective truth largely due to the embrace of viewpoints that cannot account for a proper ground of said truth, in contrast to Christian theology. Specifically in the West, this has resulted in the acceptance of a multiplicity of worldviews other than Christianity and a corresponding biblical and theological illiteracy along with a rising syncretism. Our context is similar to what Paul faced at Athens except for the post-Christian aspect. This is why Paul's Athenian address and biblical reasoning is so instructive for us; he teaches us how to present the truth of the gospel in terms of an entire biblical-theological framework rooted in the Bible's story, which illustrates for us the theological task.

To underscore this point, think about *how* Paul in the book of Acts proclaims the truth of the gospel—including an entire theology—depending on his audience. Normally, when Paul went to a city, he first went to the synagogue, where he reasoned with the Jews and God-fearers, and his proclamation of the gospel followed a basic pattern: he reasoned from the OT that Jesus is the promised Messiah, who in his life, death, resurrection, ascension, and in his sending of the Holy Spirit at Pentecost had ushered in the long-awaited kingdom of God and new covenant era (see Acts 13:5, 14–41, 44–45; 14:1; 17:2, 10, 17). Paul could begin this way because he and his Jewish audience had a common theology. They both believed the OT, and thus when Paul spoke about "God," "Messiah," "covenants," "sin," and so on, he spoke to people with a common worldview.

At Athens, however, Paul's audience and context were quite different. The Athenians did not accept the OT; they were steeped in idolatry, pluralistic in their outlook, and ignorant of the biblical teaching and worldview necessary to understand even the most rudimentary truths that Paul needed to communicate. Paul's preaching of Christ and the entire biblical worldview in the midst of the Areopagus, therefore, had a different starting place and structure than his preaching in the synagogues.

In Athens, Paul's gospel reasoning did not immediately begin with Jesus as the Messiah. Instead, he first built a biblical *and* theological frame of reference so that his proclamation of Christ would make sense *on the Bible's own terms* and *within its own categories*. This is not to deny that Paul and the Athenians had natural revelation in common (a point Paul makes clear in Rom 1). However, the point is that the Athenians, in suppressing the truth, could not fully understand Paul's message apart from placing it within the conceptual framework of Scripture.[20] Later on, we will identify this approach as *intratextual*, or "theology from above"; that is, theology's starting point is from the standpoint of God's revelation to us. Paul knows that his presentation of Christ only makes sense *within* the Bible's view of reality (metaphysics) grounded in a specific theory of knowledge (epistemology), which results in a specific view of moral obligation (ethics). The Athenians interpret and explain the world and themselves by an alien worldview framework due to a suppression of the truth of natural revelation, or what we will identify as an extratextual conceptual scheme. Paul does not start on some neutral ground where both he and the Athenians have a common epistemological agreement. No doubt, the Athenians are image-bearers of God like Paul and commonly share in the created order, but their interpretation of the world is dependent on their overall philosophy. This is why Paul first sets the entire Christian position as true over against the opposing non-Christian views; only *then*, and only from *within* the biblical worldview as governed by the "spectacles" of Scripture, does Paul proclaim Jesus as Lord and Savior.

This is instructive for us, especially in thinking about what theology is. In fact, in Paul's gospel presentation, he develops the two interrelated steps mentioned above. First, Paul lays down six building blocks that are foundational to the biblical worldview and essential to the correct exposition and defense of Jesus's identity as the Christ. In laying down these building blocks, he erects the Bible's own interpretive framework, by which he interprets the world. And it is from *within this theological framework* that Paul proclaims the message of the gospel. Paul also makes the second step: he applies Scripture by setting the biblical view over against

[20] On this point, see the interaction between C. Kavin Rowe and Matthew Levering in Rowe, "God, Greek Philosophy, and the Bible: A Response to Matthew Levering," *Journal of Theological Interpretation* 5 (2011): 69–80; and Levering, "God and Greek Philosophy in Contemporary Scholarship," *Journal of Theological Interpretation* 4 (2010): 169–85; and the helpful discussion in Steven J. Duby, *God in Himself: Scripture, Metaphysics, and the Task of Christian Theology* (Downers Grove: IVP Academic, 2019), 63–72.

its competitors, and in this case, he does so by calling his audience to repentance and faith in Christ as the only Lord and Savior. Before we apply what Paul is doing to our thinking on the nature of the theological task, let us look briefly at these six building blocks, which are essential to making sense of the Bible's view of the world and within which theology is done.

First, Paul begins with the triune God of creation, where all Christian theology must begin (v. 24). He frames his entire discussion of Christ and the gospel within a theistic universe, and he immediately establishes the most fundamental fact of reality, the Creator-creature distinction. As he explains to the Athenians, this world is not the result of blind chance (in contrast to Epicureans and naturalism) or the evolution of a world spirit (in contrast to Stoicism and pantheism), but it is the creation of one sovereign, personal God, who alone reigns as the Lord of heaven and earth.

Second, Paul establishes the nature of the God of creation as the one who is independent and self-sufficient (divine aseity). God is one (singularity and simplicity) and thus by definition in a different category than everything else. God alone is the source of all existence, the standard of truth, and the criterion of goodness. As such, God gives humans all things, but he receives nothing from us to help him rule as the Lord of all history and providence (vv. 25–26). For this reason, God cannot be bribed or cajoled; he judges justly and righteously, with his own will and character as the standard of justice, morality, and goodness. If we receive anything from him, it is not because we deserve it; instead, it is solely due to his sovereign choice to act in grace.

Third, Paul explains that God is a talking God who takes the initiative to make himself known to us, creating us in his image ("offspring"), and sovereignly locating us in our exact places so that we may know him as Lord of heaven and earth (vv. 26–29). The Athenians had constructed an idol to the "unknown god," but Paul is clear that God is known and ought to be worshipped as God. Our *not* knowing God is our fault, not his, which raises the issue of the human problem as sin *before* the known Creator and Lord. God is not removed from this world and unknown; instead, he is active in it to reveal himself in truth (vv. 25, 28). In fact, due to creation, which all people have in common, God is universally known. As such, there is no real ignorance of him. In addition, God is known to his covenant people by his specific revelation of himself in word and deed, which Paul is now proclaiming.

Fourth, Paul establishes the basis for human responsibility in not knowing God in truth. By starting with the doctrine of God and then placing humans in their proper frame of reference,

Paul demonstrates that by nature and by choice we are alienated from God and justly condemned because we have turned from the truth about our Creator and Lord and his universe. This is why humans stand guilty under divine judgment and are in need of redemption (vv. 30–31). As image-bearers of God, descended from one man (v. 26), we not only have a common creation but also a common problem: we have *all* willfully rebelled against the one God, who alone gives us our very life and breath. We are without excuse. But apart from this framework, it is difficult to account for such truths. Whether in the first or the twenty-first century, one of the great challenges we face in presenting the truth of Scripture, who Jesus is, and why we need him is communicating a biblical sense of human depravity before *this* God.

Fifth, given the theocentric nature of the universe and humanity's rebellion, Paul declares that all people are commanded to repent before the coming day of God's final judgment (vv. 29–31). Note how discussion of final judgment is placed in an overall context that makes sense of it on the Bible's own terms. On that day, all humans, given their common creation and common problem, will stand before the one true and living God in either repentance or rebellion. If there is hope at all, it will not be found in us, either individually or corporately; it is only found in God the righteous, who must act in sovereign grace to provide salvation for us. Since God is one, the only Creator and Lord, he alone can redeem, and he alone must initiate. In the end, and in keeping with his character, God will act in both judgment on the rebels and grace toward the repentant.

Sixth, after constructing the Bible's basic theological framework as tied to its overall storyline, Paul finally arrives at a point where he is able to proclaim Jesus as a man (yet more than a mere man) whom God raised from the dead to judge the world in righteousness (v. 31).

For our purposes, as we reflect on how Paul's address instructs us regarding the nature of the theological task, it is crucial to note how much time Paul spends in first constructing the Bible's own *theological categories* before he preaches Christ. Why? Because the Jesus of the Bible can only be understood as the unique and incomparable Lord and Savior by first placing him *within* the theology and worldview of Scripture, not the extratextual framework of the Athenians. For example, just think of Paul's emphasis on Christ's bodily resurrection. For the Greeks, bodily resurrections were impossible and undesirable.[21] But within the

---

[21] See David G. Peterson, *The Acts of the Apostles*, PNTC (Grand Rapids: Eerdmans, 2009), 486–505.

biblical conceptual scheme and worldview in which Paul has placed Jesus, a bodily resurrection is not only possible but also entirely plausible and desirable. After all, given who God is, it is entirely reasonable to think that the Creator and Lord is actively involved in history and able to bring about the bodily resurrection of Christ. In fact, given who God is and God's choice to save a fallen humanity, it makes total sense that the only one who can redeem us is utterly unique. By first erecting the biblical worldview of God, self, and the world, Paul is able to communicate Christ's true identity *within* the theology and plausibility structures of Scripture. Conversely, apart from the Bible's worldview, Jesus's identity will inevitably be misunderstood, distorted, and rejected as implausible. D. A. Carson captures this crucial point:

> The good news of Jesus Christ—who he is and what he accomplished by his death, resurrection, and exaltation—is simply incoherent unless certain structures are already in place. You cannot make heads or tails of the real Jesus unless you have categories for the personal/transcendent God of the Bible; the nature of human beings made in the image of God; the sheer odium of rebellion against him; the curse that our rebellion has attracted; the spiritual, personal, familial, and social effects of our transgression; the nature of salvation; the holiness and wrath and love of God. One cannot make sense of the Bible's plot line without such basic ingredients; one cannot make sense of the Bible's portrayal of Jesus without such blocks in place.[22]

Carson's point is important. However, it is not only noteworthy for grasping Jesus's identity or for doing Christology; it is also critical in the construction of *all* Christian doctrines. Biblical truth does not come to us in a vacuum; it comes to us embedded within the specific theology of Scripture. Or, as J. I. Packer reminded us, "theology is a seamless web, a circle within which everything links up with everything else through its common grounding in God."[23] As a web, biblical truths are interrelated, and to understand Christian doctrine, one must locate doctrines *within* the content, categories, and framework of Scripture. This is why Paul's Athenian address is an important illustration of systematic theology in practice.

---

[22] Carson, "Athens Revisited," 386.

[23] J. I. Packer, "Encountering Present-Day Views of Scripture," in *The Foundation of Biblical Authority*, ed. James Montgomery Boice (Grand Rapids: Zondervan, 1978), 61.

Specifically, it demonstrates that the doing of theology consists of the two interrelated steps discussed previously.

First, theology begins by constructing the biblical worldview, or what we have labelled the "biblical-theological framework" rooted in the Bible's unfolding covenantal storyline. In so doing, it begins where Scripture begins: first, the triune God within himself (*ad intra*) and then the triune God in action outside of himself (*ad extra*) in creation, providence, redemption, and consummation. In tracing out the Bible's covenantal story from creation to the new creation, centered in Christ, theology presents the Bible's view of reality, knowledge, and ethics. And it is from *within* the entire canon that doctrines are formulated according to Scripture's presentation of them. In this first step, the role of biblical theology is vital since it allows us "to interpret the biblical texts 'on their own terms'" and guarantee that our doctrine is from all of Scripture.[24]

Second, theology applies Scripture to every area of life. As an exercise in "faith seeking understanding," theology seeks to "make sense" of the biblical teaching on specific points on the Bible's own terms. In so doing, theology also gives us a well-thought-out worldview grounded in the Bible's overarching metanarrative, by which we interpret and critique all other views. Theology, then, gives us *truth* as it applies Scripture to all areas of life—salvation, science, psychology, marriage, children, ethics, and so on. In the end, systematic theology is the high calling of every Christian and the sacred responsibility of the church to learn anew "to think God's thoughts after him" and to be both "hearers" and "doers" of the word (Jas 1:22–25).

The Discipline of Systematic Theology

We have described systematic theology as the discipline that the church undertakes to apply renewed reason to the study of the triune God and all things in relation to him. In this section, we want to develop further the nature of systematic theology by describing first four elements that constitute the discipline and, second, its relationship to the other theological disciplines and why systematic theology is the capstone and culmination of those disciplines.

[24] Kevin J. Vanhoozer, "Exegesis and Hermeneutics," in *New Dictionary of Biblical Theology* (hereafter, *NDBT*), ed. T. Desmond Alexander and Brian S. Rosner (Downers Grove: InterVarsity, 2000), 52.

The Elements of Systematic Theology

As a discipline, systematic theology submits to the magisterial authority of Scripture, attends to the ministerial authority of the historical witness of the church, and then engages perennial and contemporary issues. As such, at least four elements constitute the discipline.

First, systematic theology is *grounded and warranted* by Scripture alone (*sola Scriptura*). Given that Scripture is God's word written, it alone is first order, the epistemological warrant and foundation for our theology. All of our theological conclusions, what we say about God, ourselves, and the world, must be true to Scripture. To be "biblical" is not to "proof text" Scripture, that is, to interpret texts out of context. Instead, it is to interpret texts first in their immediate context, then in terms of the Bible's unfolding covenantal story, and finally in light of the entire canon fulfilled in Christ. Furthermore, *sola Scriptura* means that Scripture is our final, sufficient authority, not our only ("*solo*") authority.[25] There are other "ministerial" authorities, such as historical and philosophical theology, which serve a vital role. Yet as important as these authorities are, they are never sufficient: Scripture alone is the final, "magisterial" authority, the "ruling rule" (*norma normans*) for all of our theological formulations.

Second, systematic theology is historically *informed*. As Winston Churchill wisely reminded us, "Those that fail to learn from history are doomed to repeat it." This is not only true in the political realm but also in the study of theology. Our present context is pluralistic, postmodern, and secular. With the loss of an agreed-on metanarrative and the rejection of cultural traditions, we are committed to what C. S. Lewis dubbed "chronological snobbery." We are bent on self-destruction; anything from the past is rejected as biased and oppressive, including the wisdom of the past.[26] This mentality has sadly crept into the church, contrary to how the church has viewed the importance of tradition. The Reformers, for example, were not committed to theological iconoclasm, but theological retrieval; they did not reject tradition but sought to reform it in light of Scripture. As Carl Trueman notes,

---

[25] On this point, see Matthew Barrett, *God's Word Alone: The Authority of Scripture* (Grand Rapids: Zondervan, 2016).

[26] See Carl R. Trueman, *The Rise and Triumph of the Modern Self: Cultural Amnesia, Expressive Individualism, and the Road to Sexual Revolution* (Wheaton: Crossway, 2020), 73–102.

"Sacred text and ecclesiastical history were agreed-on authorities for both [Catholics and Protestants]. The question was not whether they were to be rejected but how they were to be understood."[27]

Historical theology and the confessional tradition of the church serve a critical "ministerial" role in our theologizing; we ignore them at our peril. We do not approach Christian theology *de novo*; rather, we stand on the shoulders of giants and learn from the past's mistakes *and* from its constructive dogmatic formulations. Theology must listen to its forefathers and not simply think that its only creed is the Bible. We stand within the tradition of the church and of the "faith that was delivered to the saints once for all" (Jude 3).

In this regard, we need to distinguish between different kinds of tradition. On the one end, there is the Roman Catholic Church that argues for two sources of divine revelation: Scripture and tradition (Tradition II).[28] According to this view, Scripture is not sufficient to determine correct interpretation or to establish doctrine; Christ has established the magisterium of the church for that purpose.[29] On the other end is "biblicism," or "*solo*" *Scriptura*. This view argues that we can interpret the Bible and establish doctrine without the benefit of tradition: "No creed but the Bible" (Tradition 0).[30] However, the more consistent view, held by the church fathers and the Reformers, is Tradition I. There is only one source of revelation, namely Scripture, but tradition as given in the "rules of faith" provides a "single exegetical tradition of interpreted Scripture."[31] In other words, Scripture is the final authority, yet tradition often rightly interprets Scripture and makes theological judgments true to Scripture. In the laboratory of history, theological ideas are tested for their faithfulness to Scripture, and doctrinal formulations that have received "catholic" (universal) consent are rightly viewed as "rules of faith" for the church.

---

[27] Trueman, 91.

[28] See Heiko A. Oberman, *Forerunners of the Reformation: The Shape of Late Medieval Thought*, trans. Paul L. Nyhus (London: Lutterworth, 1967), 58.

[29] See Gregg R. Allison, *Roman Catholic Theology and Practice: An Evangelical Assessment* (Wheaton: Crossway, 2014), 71–116.

[30] See Alister McGrath, *Reformation Thought: An Introduction*, 2nd ed. (Oxford: Blackwell, 1993), 144–45.

[31] See Heiko A. Oberman, *The Dawn of the Reformation: Essays in Late Medieval and Early Modern Thought* (Grand Rapids: Eerdmans, 1992), 280.

This is why the Reformers did not reject the early church councils, given their "catholicity."[32] Nicaea, Chalcedon, and the Christological conclusions of Constantinople II and III were viewed as faithful to the entirety of Scripture, albeit in *theological* language, as the church sought to conceptualize ("faith seeking understanding") and defend (apologetics) what Scripture teaches. These early councils established the parameters for trinitarian and Christological orthodoxy as "ruled rules" (*norma normata*) for the church.

Within evangelical theology today, there is a healthy emphasis on "retrieval theology."[33] Retrieval theology is "theological discernment that looks back in order to move forward."[34] It does more than repeat; it reforms—by Scripture and the tradition. This renewed emphasis in evangelical theology on the role of tradition is strongly encouraged. Yet it is also true that "retrieval" works best in the doctrinal areas of "catholic" agreement (e.g., Trinity, Christology) associated with Nicaea and Chalcedon given that they accurately reflect the teaching of Scripture. However, in other doctrinal areas where disagreement still resides (e.g., the nature of sin, the atonement, soteriology, ecclesiology, and some aspects of eschatology), tradition is instructive but not sufficient. In these latter areas, where our confessions materially differ, we are reminded that tradition is "ministerial," but Scripture is "magisterial." In fact, even in areas of "catholic" agreement (Trinity and Christology), there are still areas of disagreement that can only be resolved by testing our exegesis and theological formulations with Scripture. For this reason, systematic theology is *informed* by tradition, but Scripture alone is our *final* authority.

Third, systematic theology is *contextual*, as it engages *perennial and contemporary issues*. Given that theology involves the application of Scripture to every area of life, it must bring God's truth to bear on the battles of our present day while learning from the past. It is true that "there is nothing new under the sun," yet old battles take on new forms, and theology seeks to apply God's unchanging truth to a changing world. For example, think of debates today over what a human

---

[32] The early church councils include Nicaea (325), Constantinople (381), Ephesus (431), Chalcedon (451), Constantinople II (553), and Constantinople III (680–81).

[33] See Gavin Ortlund, *Theological Retrieval for Evangelicals* (Wheaton: Crossway, 2019); Scott R. Swain and Michael Allen, *Reformed Catholicity: The Promise of Retrieval for Theology and Biblical Interpretation* (Grand Rapids: Baker Academic, 2015); John Webster, "Theologies of Retrieval," in *The Oxford Handbook of Systematic Theology*, ed. John Webster, et al. (Oxford: Oxford University Press, 2008).

[34] Kevin J. Vanhoozer, *Biblical Authority after Babel: Retrieving the* Solas *in the Spirit of Mere Protestant Christianity* (Grand Rapids: Brazos Press, 2016), 23.

is, given our culture's embrace of postmodern and secular thought, and our ability to "manufacture" humans, or consider how our culture has embraced changing ideas of human sexuality. Although the Reformation certainly knew of homosexuality and condemned it, transgenderism, along with our culture's attempt to redefine maleness, femaleness, and marriage were not crucial debates in their day. However, given our cultural context, theology cannot avoid these issues.

This is why knowing the "culture" is important for theology, but contrary to the thinking of some, "culture" does not serve as a source for our theology.[35] Instead, as Paul taught us in Acts 17, theology addresses our current context by setting Scripture's own description of reality over against non-Christian views, and we interpret and critique the culture from *within* the biblical worldview. This is not to deny that due to natural revelation and common grace, non-Christians know various truths, but it does deny that non-Christians *consistent with their worldview* rightly understand and interpret the world, especially when it comes to diagnosing the human problem and offering any solutions to it.

Fourth, systematic theology is *practical*; it must to be lived out by the church. We must "walk our talk." Since theology is a whole-person response to God's word, it is not enough merely to confess what we believe; we must also apply God's word to every area of our thinking and lives. When our Lord Jesus diagnosed the condition of the Ephesian church, he was pleased with their orthodoxy and consistent application of the truth, but he rebuked them for their loss of their "first love" (Rev 2:2–5). God calls his people both to know the truth and to live out the truth before a watching world, to exhibit simultaneously the holiness and love of God as they stand against the "spirit of our age," and to make all of their thought captive to Christ for his glory, the good of the church, and their witness in the world.[36]

Systematic Theology in Relation to the Other Theological Disciplines

Systematic theology is the "queen of the sciences," the capstone and culmination of all the disciplines, especially the theological disciplines. As such, biblical, historical, and philosophical

---

[35] In contrast to many in the post-conservative camp, such as Stanley J. Grenz and John R. Franke, *Beyond Foundationalism: Shaping Theology in a Postmodern Context* (Louisville: Westminster John Knox Press, 2001).

[36] See Francis A. Schaeffer, *The Mark of the Christian*, in *The Complete Works of Francis A. Schaeffer: A Christian Worldview*, 5 vols. (Wheaton: Crossway, 1982), 4:183–204.

studies contribute to the overall theological task of applying renewed reason to the study of the triune God and all things in relationship to him. Let us briefly discuss the various theological disciplines to discover why they are necessary for doing systematic theology.

Exegetical Theology

This discipline is identified with biblical studies, which seeks to interpret specific books of Scripture. The goal of exegesis is to discover God's intent through the human authors by grasping the intent of the authors in their text by grammatical/literary-historical exegesis. This involves understanding the rules of the original language used by the author, analyzing the book's literary structure, including its genre, and placing the book in its historical setting. A commentary is the fruit of such exegetical work. Since theology involves the application of God's word, exegetical theology is foundational to knowing what Scripture says.

Biblical Theology

In recent days, the term *biblical theology* has become somewhat of a buzzword; however, there is little agreement on exactly what it is and how to do it. Yet, it is vitally important to the doing of theology since it is the theological discipline that seeks to understand the entire canon as "the whole plan of God" (Acts 20:27). One cannot draw legitimate theological conclusions from Scripture apart from the doing of biblical theology; it provides the *biblical* warrant for theology. Given its importance for theology, and given the fact that people mean different things by it, let me explain what biblical theology is and how it functions in this work.[37]

Biblical theology is the theological discipline that seeks to understand the canon of Scripture "on its own terms." Or, as Brian Rosner states, biblical theology is "theological interpretation of Scripture in and for the church. It proceeds with historical and literary sensitivity and seeks

---

[37] For a helpful overview of the history of biblical theology, see C. H. H. Scobie, "History of Biblical Theology," in *NDBT*, 11–20. For helpful discussions regarding diverse conceptions of biblical theology, see Edward W. Klink III and Darian R. Lockett, *Understanding Biblical Theology: A Comparison of Theory and Practice* (Grand Rapids: Zondervan, 2012); and Graeme Goldsworthy, *Christ-Centered Biblical Theology: Hermeneutical Foundations and Principles* (Downers Grove: IVP Academic, 2012).

to analyze and synthesize the Bible's teaching about God and his relations to the world on its own terms, maintaining sight of the Bible's overarching narrative and Christocentric focus."[38]

As a discipline, biblical theology is *not* presuppositionless. It approaches Scripture according to its own claim; namely, Scripture is *God's* word written. Moreover, biblical theology presupposes the central truths of historic Christianity; hence it is a *theological* discipline. Since Scripture is *God's* word, it assumes that despite its diversity, Scripture is a unified revelation. And given that Scripture has come to us over time, Scripture is a *progressive* unfolding of God's plan across a specific redemptive-historical storyline demarcated by the biblical covenants. As an exegetical method, it is sensitive to literary, historical, and theological dimensions of various corpora, as well as to the interrelationships between the *earlier* and *later* texts in Scripture, thus relating the "parts" of Scripture to the "whole." By doing so, it allows us to discern *God's intention*, which is most *fully* given in terms of the canon. Furthermore, biblical theology is interested in reading Scripture *on its own terms* (intratextual), that is, in light of its own content, categories, and structure, not by superimposing "outside" (extratextual) categories on it. For this reason, biblical theology provides the *biblical* warrant from the whole Bible for our theological conclusions.

In thinking about biblical theology, it is vital to distinguish an "evangelical biblical theology" from an Enlightenment or "classic liberal biblical theology," often identified with Johann Philipp Gabler (1753–1826).[39] As we will discuss more in chapter 2, during the Enlightenment there was a growing tendency to approach Scripture *critically*, uncoupled from historic Christian theology. The result: Scripture was viewed "as any other book," open to

---

[38] Brian Rosner, "Biblical Theology," in *NDBT*, 10 (italics removed from original). Similar to Rosner, Jeremy Treat offers the following definition: "*Biblical theology is faith seeking understanding of the redemptive-historical and literary unity of the Bible in its own terms, concepts, and contexts*" (emphasis original). Treat, *The Crucified King: Atonement and Kingdom in Biblical and Systematic Theology* (Grand Rapids: Zondervan, 2014), 35; Cf. D. A. Carson, "Systematic Theology and Biblical Theology," in *NDBT*, 89–104.

[39] Gabler is viewed as the "father of biblical theology" from his inaugural lecture at the University of Altdorf on March 30, 1787, "An Oration on the Proper Distinction between Biblical and Dogmatic Theology and the Specific Objectives of Each." Yet, Gabler is better identified as the "father of classic liberal biblical theology." On this point, see J. V. Fesko, "On the Antiquity of Biblical Theology," in *Resurrection and Eschatology: Theology in Service of the Church*, ed. L. G. Tipton and J. C. Waddington (Phillipsburg: P&R, 2008), 443–77.

criticism, and *not* God's unified, true revelation. Thus, when Gabler defined biblical theology as an inductive, historical, and descriptive discipline, he used the term "historical" in a historical-*critical* sense. For him, "historical" did not mean that we read Scripture as *God's* word, accurately describing God's unfolding plan in redemptive history. Instead, Scripture is to be read by virtue of Enlightenment presuppositions, which, from the outset, denied Scripture's authority and trustworthiness.

As this view of biblical theology developed into the next century, practitioners increasingly made use of the historical-critical method, which assumed *methodological* naturalism.[40] Over time, the end result of this approach was Scripture's fragmentation and a biblical theology governed by *critical* methodologies and theological views foreign to historic Christian theology. Consequently, this view of biblical theology emphasized more "diversity" than "unity" in Scripture, and ultimately, it came to an end.[41] In the twentieth century, there were attempts to overcome the Enlightenment restrictions on Scripture. In theology, the work of Karl Barth is notable. Barth is often viewed as the forerunner of the post-liberal school, a school that attempts to read Scripture as a unified canon, but which does not fully embrace Scripture's reliability and thus renders the theological task problematic. In biblical studies there was also the "Biblical Theology Movement."[42] Although its goal was to overcome the negative results of historical criticism, it too failed because it did not return to the theology of historic Christianity.[43]

Today in non-evangelical theology, there are a variety of options that attempt to read Scripture as a unified whole, but most of them are weak on Scripture and reject consistent

---

[40] "Methodological naturalism" is the view that approaches our study of history (including our study of the Bible) and science without considering God's involvement in the world and divine action as represented by divine revelation and miracles. Methodological naturalism does *not* necessarily require a commitment to atheism, even though it is consistent with it. Deism and panentheism also assume methodological naturalism given their denial of divine action in an effectual, supernatural sense.

[41] See Hans Frei, *The Eclipse of Biblical Narrative: A Study in Eighteenth and Nineteenth Century Hermeneutics* (New Haven: Yale University Press, 1980). In the nineteenth century, "biblical theology" was eventually identified with "classic liberalism" as represented by various schools of thought associated with such people as F. C. Baur, J. Wellhausen, the history of religions school, and so on.

[42] For a survey of this movement, see Gerhard F. Hasel, "The Nature of Biblical Theology: Recent Trends and Issues," *AUSS* 32, no. 3 (1994): 211–14; and James Barr, "Biblical Theology," in *Interpreter's Dictionary of the Bible: Supplementary Volume*, ed. K. Crim (Nashville: Abingdon, 1976), 104–6.

[43] On this point, see Langdon Gilkey, "Cosmology, Ontology, and the Travail of Biblical Language," *JR* 41 (1961): 194–205.

Christian presuppositions.[44] This is why an "evangelical biblical theology" is often viewed as impossible given evangelicals' denial of Scripture's unity and embrace of historical criticism. In fact, Geerhardus Vos, the pioneer of an "evangelical biblical theology," warned us that such a biblical theology is impossible apart from historic Christian theology, on which it stands.[45]

However, in this work, we are not only convinced that an "evangelical biblical theology" is possible, but that it also provides the *biblical* warrant for our theologizing. Working from historic Christian theological convictions, especially in regard to the doctrines of God and Scripture, we believe that biblical *and* systematic theology are possible because the triune God is there, has spoken, and, in his speech, has given us an authoritative, unified word that is the foundation for our reasoning rightly about God and all things in relation to him (Heb 1:1–2).

Historical Theology, Philosophy, and Apologetics

We have already discussed the "ministerial" role that *historical theology* and the confessional standards serve in the doing of theology. We do not approach Christian theology as blank

---

[44] One thinks of the movement known as "Theological Interpretation of Scripture" (TIS). This movement is fairly diverse and encompasses evangelicals and non-evangelicals alike. For the non-evangelicals, generally speaking, commitment to the Bible's unity is not due to Scripture's self-attestation but to the church's decision to choose these texts as Scripture. For example, think of the canonical approach of Brevard Childs, who chooses to read texts in their final form and canonical shape. However, as Paul Noble astutely argues, unless Childs grounds his preference for final form and canonical shape in the doctrine of inspiration and divine authorship, it is a view hanging in midair. Noble, *The Canonical Approach: A Critical Reconstruction of the Hermeneutics of Brevard S. Childs* (Leiden: Brill Academic, 1995). For a critique of post-liberalism and its view and use of Scripture, see Kevin J. Vanhoozer, *The Drama of Doctrine: A Canonical Linguistic Approach to Christian Doctrine* (Louisville: Westminster John Knox, 2005). As helpful as TIS is in its attempt to recapture the voice of Scripture for the church, given that it is composed of such a diverse number of people with such divergent views of Scripture, one wonders how long it can be sustained without a return to orthodox theological convictions. On this point, see D. A. Carson, "Theological Interpretation of Scripture: Yes, But . . .," in *Theological Commentary: Evangelical Perspectives*, ed. R. Michael Allen (London: T&T Clark, 2011), 187–207.

[45] See Geerhardus Vos, *Biblical Theology: Old and New Testaments* (Grand Rapids: Eerdmans, 1948); Geerhardus Vos, *Pauline Eschatology* (Phillipsburg: P&R, 1979); Geerhardus Vos, *Redemptive History and Biblical Interpretation: The Shorter Writings of Geerhardus Vos*, ed. Richard B. Gaffin Jr. (Phillipsburg: P&R, 2001). On Vos's contribution to biblical theology, see Fesko, "On the Antiquity of Biblical Theology," 449–53.

slates; rather, we stand in a received tradition that is crucial to our dogmatic formulations. However, historical theology is not the only discipline that serves as a handmaid to theology. This is also true of philosophy, apologetics and, by extension, the discipline of science, which focuses on God's revelation in nature.[46]

Philosophy is the discipline that attempts to answer the most fundamental questions we face. Historically, philosophers have sought the "basic principles" by which to explain and interpret a total account of reality (metaphysics), a final criterion of truth (epistemology), and a normative moral standard (ethics).[47] These *basic* principles are such that no further explanation or proof is needed for them; they are logically fundamental, and they function as *presuppositions* by which we interpret the world and our place in it. In fact, anyone who thinks about this world, ultimate reality, meaning, truth, human nature, moral values, and so on is doing philosophy and, as such, has a worldview. The important question is whether we are doing philosophy well and on what epistemological grounds.[48]

From a Christian view, philosophy is *not* a neutral discipline. In thinking about our most basic and ultimate commitments, the philosopher reasons about the world either upon the foundation of God and his word or views human reason as self-sufficient, having the ability to interpret experience apart from divine revelation (Rom 1:18–21; Col 2:6–8). To do philosophy as a Christian, one does it under the authority of God's revelation in Scripture and creation, although the emphasis is more on natural revelation. It is difficult to draw a sharp distinction between a Christian theology and philosophy; ultimately, it is a matter of emphasis and terminology.[49]

The study of philosophy is important for theology. Although every philosophy assumes a specific worldview and must be evaluated as such, due to natural revelation and common grace, philosophers have developed, for example, systems of logic, critical distinctions in the analysis of causality, language, and so on that are useful for theology *if* they are placed within an overall Christian theology. Philosophy helps theology critically analyze arguments, avoid conceptual confusions, and constructively understand Scripture by offering definitions of terms and

---

[46] God's revelation in creation will be discussed in chapter 6.

[47] See Frame, *Doctrine of the Knowledge of God*, 85.

[48] See Bahnsen, *Van Til's Apologetic*, 51.

[49] See Cornelius Van Til, *A Survey of Christian Epistemology* (Philadelphia: P&R, 1969), xiv–xv.

concepts (e.g., what a nature and person is, analysis of various definitions of freedom, etc.).[50] Philosophers have argued well for the need for universals in metaphysics, epistemology, and ethics—all important for theology. But the history of philosophy has also revealed the basic antithesis between Christian and non-Christian thought, that "ideas have consequences," and that the attempt to ground human knowledge apart from God and his revelation is futile.[51]

This is why apologetics is necessary. As Frame defines it, apologetics is the discipline that applies "Scripture to unbelief,"[52] and as such it functions as an important subset of theology. Theology supplies to apologetics its presuppositions and the truth that it defends. It is part of the theological task to "take every thought captive to obey Christ" (2 Cor 10:5), to defend the truth of the gospel, and to call all people to submit their thinking and lives to Christ.

The Goal of Systematic Theology

What is the goal of theology? Ultimately, it is to enable the church to know and worship our triune Creator-covenant Lord rightly, to live obediently and faithfully under Christ's lordship, and unashamedly to witness to and defend the life-changing truth of the gospel.

First, theology's task is to know and love God according to his word (Matt 22:37–38). As Bavinck succinctly states: "God, and God alone, is man's highest good."[53] Yet, one cannot fully know God apart from the doing of theology, which requires careful, renewed biblical reasoning. As we grow in our understanding of Scripture and theology, we grow in our knowledge of

---

[50] On this point, the role of "analytic theology" is important. See Oliver D. Crisp, *Analyzing Doctrine: Toward a Systematic Theology* (Waco: Baylor University Press, 2019).

[51] Bavinck has some helpful comments on the role of philosophy in theology:

> The question here is not whether theology should make use of a specific philosophical system. Christian theology has never taken over any philosophical system without criticism and given it the stamp of approval. . . . [Theology] is not per se hostile to any philosophical system and does not, a priori and without criticism, give priority to the philosophy of Plato or of Kant, or vice versa. But it brings along its own criteria, tests all philosophy in general. In other words, it arrives at scientific knowledge only by thinking. The only internal principle of knowledge, therefore, is not faith as such, but believing thought, Christian rationality. (*Reformed Dogmatics*, 1:608–9)

[52] Frame, *Doctrine of the Knowledge of God*, 87.

[53] Herman Bavinck, *The Wonderful Works of God* (Philadelphia: Westminster Seminary Press, 2019), 1.

God. In the end, there is no greater knowledge. Charles Spurgeon captured this truth well in contrast to non-Christian thought:

> It has been said by someone that "the proper study of mankind is man." I will not oppose the idea, but I believe it is equally true that the proper study of God's elect is God; the proper study of a Christian is the Godhead. The highest science, the loftiest speculation, the mightiest philosophy, which can ever engage the attention of the child of God, is the name, the nature, the person, the work, the doings, and the existence of the great God whom he calls his Father.[54]

First, theology's goal and purpose are to know God; indeed, to reason with Paul on "the depth of the riches / and the wisdom and the knowledge of God!" and how all things are "from him and through him / and to him. . . . To him be the glory forever. Amen" (Rom 11:33, 36).

Second, theology's task is to enable the church to understand and apply Scripture rightly in order to live faithful and obedient lives under Christ's lordship. But again, one cannot fulfill this goal apart from the doing of theology. In the church's preaching and teaching, we apply the truth of the gospel to people's lives, equipping "the saints . . . [building] up the body of Christ, until we all reach unity in the faith and in the knowledge of God's Son" (Eph 4:12–13). But even to know what the gospel is, who Jesus is, and what he has done for us requires sound theology. In fact, faithful preaching and teaching *is* theology in practice.

For one to rightly build up the church so that she is no longer "tossed by the waves and blown around by every wind of teaching" (Eph 4:14) requires careful biblical exposition and constructive canonical application (2 Tim 4:1–5). Apart from theology, we have no message to preach and no gospel to apply. Even in thinking about the Scripture's application to our lives, we are keenly aware that we cannot randomly apply texts without carefully thinking how those texts apply to us given where we live in redemptive history. Given that God has revealed his plan over time, theology must wrestle with how the parts fit with the whole and how the whole applies to us today in light of Christ's work. Thus, for example, to counsel people from Scripture regarding God's providence in their lives and why there is suffering and evil in the world, or to help people in their questions regarding their marriages, the assurance of salvation, or how to live as God's new covenant people in relation to the state all requires theology.

---

[54] Cited in J. I. Packer, *Knowing God*, 20th anniversary ed. (Downers Grove: InterVarsity, 1993), 17.

And unless we do theology, the goal of enabling those in the church to live godly lives will be thwarted, with potentially disastrous consequences, as evidenced by some of the false teaching the apostles had to confront in the NT era and to which the church had to respond throughout church history.

Third, theology's task is to enable the church to witness to and defend the truth of the gospel. The Lord of the church has called his people to proclaim the unsearchable riches of Christ to the nations (Matt 28:18–20; Col 1:28–29). But to proclaim who Jesus is as God the Son incarnate, the meaning of his death "for our sins" (1 Cor 15:1–3), and so on, requires systematic theology. In church history, people have differed on these central gospel points, so to know what Scripture rightly teaches, we have to engage in faithful theological formulation and careful refutation of false views that threaten the truth (Gal 1:6–10; 1 John 4:2–3; 5:5–10). Just because someone claims to be "biblical" does not mean they are. All heresies appeal to Scripture, but not rightly. It is incumbent on the church to know the truth *and* defend it (Titus 1:9; 1 Pet 3:15–16).

The apostle Paul viewed gospel ministry as the positive proclamation of Christ *and* the "demolishing of arguments" that stand contrary to Christ (2 Cor 10:5). Theology's task is to enable the church in every generation to do likewise and to embolden the church to say with Paul: "I am not ashamed of the gospel, because it is the power of God for salvation to everyone who believes" (Rom 1:16). What is needed, then, is not a minimalist theology, but a comprehensive and thoroughly biblical one. For unless we have such a theology, church history has taught us that we will easily be swept away by the "wisdom" of our age. Given our tendency to embrace error faster than the truth, the church must remain vigilant. Theology's goal is to enable the church to expound the truth and to reject error. Without careful theology being done, taught, and embraced, the church will drift aimlessly from the truth of God.

In the end, the goal of theology is for God's redeemed people to know, contemplate, and delight in the sheer glory of God. As John Owen wrote many years ago: "Evangelical theology has been instituted by God in order that sinners may once again enjoy communion with God himself, the All-Holy One. . . . The ultimate end of true theology is the celebration of the praise of God, and his glory and grace in the eternal salvation of sinners."[55]

---

[55] John Owen, *Biblical Theology: The History of Theology from Adam to Christ*, trans. Stephen P. Westcott (Orlando: Soli Deo Gloria, 1994), 6.4 (618–19).

Concluding Reflection

Systematic theology is not an option for the church; it is necessary for her spiritual health and well-being. In this chapter, we have described what theology is and why it is essential to our thinking rightly about God, ourselves, and the world. In the end, we are called to faithfulness under the lordship of Christ. Our triune God calls us to love him with our minds and hearts, which is true life for us. Theology matters to achieve these ends.

Yet one of the challenges we face today is that the historic view of theology as an objective science that yields true knowledge of God is considered impossible. In the next chapter, we will look at some of the reasons why this is the case so we can understand our context. Theology is never done in a vacuum, and it is important to recognize that there is no greater challenge to theology than the battle over truth.

CHAPTER 2

Systematic Theology: Cultural Context

Introduction

We have defined what systematic theology is and why it is essential for the life of the church. We have assumed that theological formulations yield true and objective, although finite, knowledge of God. The foundation for this view is that our triune Creator-covenant Lord has made himself known to us in creation, the incarnate Word, and Scripture. Theology is grounded in divine revelation, with Scripture serving as theology's authoritative, final, and sufficient epistemological warrant. All of this is necessary because God is God; humans are creatures, and now fallen creatures; and apart from God's true and reliable speech to us, the transcendental condition for theology evaporates. For this reason, historic Christian theology is a theology "from above," namely, a theology done from the vantage point of divine revelation. What is also important to note is that this view of theology is true for all branches of the church, whether East or West, Roman Catholic or Protestant, despite significant differences between them.

However, since the Enlightenment, this understanding of the nature of theology has changed, especially in the West. Theology is no longer viewed as the "queen" of the sciences. Given various shifts in intellectual history over the last three centuries, the historic view of theology is no longer seen as possible. In this chapter, we want to explain *why* this is so.

Why spend time doing this? Why not simply assume the historic view and turn immediately to the theological task? For this reason: systematic theology is never done in a vacuum. Theology is always done in a specific context, as it *applies* Scripture to all areas of life, as "we take every thought captive to obey Christ" (2 Cor 10:5). Theology does not merely articulate doctrines in timeless propositions; theology also helps the church "interpret this present time" (Luke 12:56). The theological task is not only to formulate doctrine correctly but also to defend the truth in light of our specific challenges (1 Pet 3:15), thus helping the church faithfully to know and to proclaim the "whole plan of God" (Acts 20:27) for God's glory.

David Wells makes this exact point in *Above All Earthly Pow'rs*. He notes that theology is now done within a twofold reality: first, "the disintegration of the Enlightenment world and its replacement by the postmodern ethos"; second, the increase of religious pluralism.[1] These two intellectual *and* cultural developments have posed some serious implications for theology, the most significant being the need to defend the objective truth of Christianity and specifically the uniqueness and exclusivity of Jesus Christ. Wells insists that our theology must not remain merely internal to the church; theology must also help the church to meet the challenges it faces in presenting the truth of God's word and the glory of Christ Jesus to a skeptical age that regards the truth claims of Scripture and theology as implausible.[2]

Wells's point is noteworthy as we think about the context in which we do theology. Today, for example, in contrast to the medieval and Reformation eras, the conditions of belief, or the plausibility structures, of our culture have changed.[3] No longer does "our time" assume many of the basic truths of Christian theology. Instead, the secularization and pluralization of the West has altered the way people think, or, as Charles Taylor articulates, it has changed our

---

[1] Wells, *Above All Earthly Pow'rs*, 5, cf. 60–262 (see chap. 1, n. 2). "Pluralism" is being used in the philosophical/religious sense: the view that "any notion that a particular ideological or religious claim is intrinsically superior to another is *necessarily* wrong. . . . No religion has the right to pronounce itself right or true, and others false, or even (in the majority view) relatively inferior." D. A. Carson, *The Gagging of God: Christianity Confronts Pluralism* (Grand Rapids: Zondervan, 1996), 19 (emphasis original).

[2] See Wells, *Above All Earthly Pow'rs*, 6–12.

[3] See Peter L. Berger, *The Sacred Canopy: Elements of a Sociological Theory of Religion* (Garden City: Doubleday, 1967).

"social imaginary,"[4] or worldview. In fact, Taylor traces out the cognitive impact of secularization on our society and its impact on the plausibility of believing in Christianity by arguing that the West has experienced three different sets of conditions of belief pivoting around the Enlightenment. Before the Enlightenment, people found it *impossible not to believe* in the basic truths of Christianity, especially the existence of God. However, starting with the Enlightenment, it became *possible not to believe* in the basic truths of Christianity, especially beliefs centered in the existence of God and his importance for our lives. Now, 300 years later, due to the rise of postmodern pluralism, most people find it *impossible to believe* in the objective truths and ultimate concerns of Christianity, especially in the significance of God for their lives.

What Taylor has discerned in Western thought impacts how systematic theology is viewed in terms of its plausibility, credibility, and logical coherence. In addition, the current conditions of belief challenge us with how best *to do* theology in light of the past *and* our present context in order to present the truth of God's word faithfully to a skeptical, pluralistic world. As such, before we do theology, we must address our current context for at least two principal reasons.

First, it is imperative to grasp that our disagreement with current thought is not piecemeal; it is over entire worldviews/theologies, or "social imaginaries." Unless we realize this, the church tends to drift towards syncretism in our theological method *and* conclusions. Too often we are held captive by the current Zeitgeist "rather than Christ" (Col 2:8).

In fact, what we discover is that those who drink from the wells of current thought inevitably substitute a theology "from above" with one "from below." What this entails is an embrace of an epistemological warrant outside of *sola Scriptura*, usually involving a commitment to historical-critical research and/or the reigning conceptual scheme of the day, which entails a different way of viewing God, self, and the world. Scripture is not approached and read on its own authority (intratextual); instead, it is read within the limits of an authority "outside" of it (extratextual). These "outside" authorities may differ. For some, it is human

---

[4] Charles Taylor, *A Secular Age* (Cambridge, MA: Belknap Press, 2007), 171–72, cf. 159–211. A "social imaginary" is distinguished from a "social theory" because (1) it is the way people *intuitively* "imagine" the world, which is not always expressed in theoretical terms; (2) it is shared by large groups of people, not merely a few; and (3) it provides what is viewed as plausible or legitimate for a society. In this way, it is similar to a "worldview."

rationality; for others, it is religious experience (individual or communal), the "assured" results of biblical scholarship, or, today, critical theory. But whatever form it takes, it always leads to a theology "from below," which renders the church's theological task implausible, incoherent, and unfaithful.

Second, unless we understand *why* many today find historic systematic theology implausible, we will fail to help the church fight *the* battle of our day, which is the battle over whether objective truth is possible and over its epistemological warrant. In previous eras of the church, this was not the central issue, but today it is. Faithfulness to the *truth* of the gospel demands that we understand why this is the case. At this point, we need to heed the words often attributed to Martin Luther, which nicely reflect his stand for the truth:

> If I profess with the loudest voice and clearest exposition, every portion of the truth of God except precisely that little point which the world and the devil are at that moment attacking, I am not confessing Christ, however boldly I may be professing Christianity. Where the battle rages the loyalty of the soldier is proved; and to be steady on all the battle-field besides is mere flight and disgrace to him if he flinches at that one point.[5]

Exhorted by Scripture *not* to be "conformed to this age, but transformed by the renewing of . . . [our] minds" (Rom 12:2) *and* to enable the church to proclaim and defend the *truth* of the gospel, we need to probe the "social imaginary" that operates today, shaping the way people think, which has led many to conclude that historic theology is impossible and thus irrelevant. In the next two chapters, before we turn to knowing the triune God and all things related to him, we need to know *why* many view the task of historic theology as implausible, do some demolition work, *and* construct the Bible's own structure of belief, thus giving the epistemological warrant for theology as an objective science and discipline. To do this, we need to trace the roots of our current Zeitgeist, which is the focus of this chapter. Specifically, we need to outline the "seeds/ideas" that were sown years ago and have now bloomed in our time.

---

[5] See Carl Wieland, "Where the Battle Rages—A Case of Misattribution" at https://creation.com/battle-quote-not-luther. Wieland notes that these words reflect Luther's thinking, but are probably not his.

How will we proceed? In two steps: first, we will give a brief history of "catholic" agreement on the nature of theology. Despite theological differences within Christianity, until the modern age, *all* branches of Christian theology assumed that systematic theology was possible. Second, we will trace the ideas that resulted in a change of plausibility structures regarding the possibility of historic theology so that we can learn from history and not repeat its mistakes.

Catholic Agreement: A Brief History

In theory, until the eleventh century the church was united, identified as "catholic" Christianity. Although there were growing theological differences that resulted in the Great Schism (the division between the East and West in 1054) and the Great Western Schism in the sixteenth century (division between the Roman Church and the Protestants), all agreed that systematic theology resulted in a finite but objective, true knowledge of God. As Edward Farley admits, despite differences within "catholic" Christianity, there was "one historical form of Christianity for which the doctrinal development of the church in the patristic period remains decisive."[6] Significantly, what united all branches of the church was a common "criteriology" grounded in the "Scripture Principle," which served as the norm and source for doctrinal formulations. By the "Scripture Principle," Farley means the "catholic" view of Scripture: "scripture contains a unique deposit of divine revelation—a deposit whose special qualities are due to its inspired origins, and which is to be handed down through the ages by an authoritative teaching tradition."[7]

In fact, the dogmatic formulations of the ecumenical councils were warranted by the Church's commitment to Scripture as God's first-order word-revelation.[8] The Church's

---

[6] Edward Farley, *Ecclesial Reflection: An Anatomy of Theological Method* (Philadelphia: Fortress, 1982), 3.

[7] See Edward Farley and Peter C. Hodgson, "Scripture and Tradition," in *Christian Theology: An Introduction to its Traditions and Tasks*, ed. Peter C. Hodgson and Robert H. King, 2nd ed. (Philadelphia: Fortress, 1985), 62. On the view of Scripture in the Patristic era, see Geoffrey W. Bromiley, "The Church Fathers and Holy Scripture," in *Scripture and Truth*, ed. D. A. Carson and John D. Woodbridge (Grand Rapids: Zondervan, 1983), 199–220.

[8] The main councils that gave trinitarian and Christological orthodoxy were Nicaea, 325; Constantinople, 381; Ephesus, 431; Chalcedon, 451; Constantinople II, 553; and Constantionople III, 680–81.

confession of the Trinity, the deity of Christ, and the incarnation were not viewed as departures from Scripture, but faithful expositions of it. In contrast to Adolf von Harnack, who argued that the councils distorted Scripture due to an acute Hellenization, or even N. T. Wright, who thinks that the councils left the biblical narratives behind,[9] the early councils represent a correct reading of the entirety of Scripture, albeit in *theological* language, as the church sought to conceptualize and defend what Scripture teaches. Although there were differences, the "catholic" Church agreed that theological conclusions were objectively true and more than mere "rules of grammar" that "regulate" how the Church speaks about God, self, and the world.[10] That view of theology comes later.

In the East, Orthodoxy developed. Churches used to identify as Eastern Orthodox by being in communion with the patriarchate of Constantinople (Istanbul), but given various political developments, this communion has broken up into a number of groups. However, churches are Eastern Orthodox as they continue to commune with a larger body of Orthodox Churches, which include churches of Greece, Cyprus, Bulgaria, Romania, Serbia, Russia, and Georgia; the ancient patriarchates of Antioch, Jerusalem, and Damascus; and smaller churches around the world.[11] Here are some of its distinctives.

1. *Authority*. Authority is derived from the "tradition" of the church, which includes Scripture and the decisions of the seven ecumenical councils.[12] Although there is a strong place for tradition, it "never supplant[s] or contradict[s], the written biblical canon."[13] For this reason, the East believes that theological conclusions result in a finite yet true knowledge of God.

---

[9] N. T. Wright, "Historical Paul and 'Systematic Theology,'" in *Biblical Theology: Past, Present, and Future*, ed. Carey Walsh and Mark W. Elliott (Eugene: Cascade, 2016), 157–60.

[10] This is the postliberal view. See George A. Lindbeck, *The Nature of Doctrine: Religion and Theology in a Postliberal Age* (Philadelphia: Westminster, 1984), 30–45, 112–138.

[11] On Eastern Orthodoxy, see Gerald Bray, "Eastern Orthodox Theology," in *New Dictionary of Theology* (hereafter *NDT*), ed. Martin Davie et al., 2nd ed. (Downers Grove: IVP Academic, 2016), 277–79; Donald Fairbairn, *Eastern Orthodoxy through Western Eyes* (Louisville: Westminster John Knox, 2002).

[12] In addition to the first four councils universally accepted by all branches of Christianity, the East accepts three more councils: Constantinople II (553), Constantinople III (680–81), and Nicaea II (787).

[13] A. Chrysostomos, *Contemporary Eastern Orthodox Thought* (Belmont, MA: Büchervertriebsanstalt, 1982), 104.

2. *The Triune God and Christology.* Nicene trinitarianism and Chalcedonian Christology are affirmed. But the East rejects the West's addition of the *filioque* clause, which speaks of the Spirit proceeding from the Father *and the Son.* This results in some differences with the West regarding the relations and ordering (*taxis*) of the triune persons within God (*ad intra*), yet there is overall agreement on the doctrine of the Trinity.[14]

3. *Sin.* Sin is viewed differently than in the West, specifically in contrast to Augustinian and Reformed theology.[15] Adam does not function as our covenant head, nor is his sin imputed to us. Total depravity is denied, and sin as a violation of God's law is deemphasized. Sin is less about our guilt before God than about effecting death, thus requiring resurrection and immortality. However, there is agreement that sin and its effects require God to act in grace to redeem us in Christ Jesus and that apart from Christ and his work there is no salvation.

4. *Salvation.* Since sin's effects are not total, the application of Christ's work to us is more synergistic than monergistic.[16] In salvation, Christ's atonement is substitutionary, but it is not understood as penal substitution. In the incarnation, death, and resurrection, Christ recapitulates Adam, frees us from death, and secures our immortality. Salvation is less about our legal justification before God than our "union with Christ" and our sanctification/transformation (*theosis*, "deification") into the image and likeness of God.

5. *The Church.* In contrast to Roman Catholicism, the East rejects the "primacy" of Rome. Instead, each bishop is viewed as a "first among equals." However, like Rome, the East has a strong sacramental theology: it affirms baptismal regeneration and communion for infants, but it rejects Rome's view of transubstantiation. Instead, it affirms that the Eucharist is a "mystery whose purpose is to bear witness to the life of the Church and the reality of the coming age."[17]

In the West, the Roman Church emerged. It separated from the Eastern churches due to its claim to be *the* "Catholic" (universal) church, a view tied to its belief in apostolic succession

---

[14] We will return to this discussion in part 4, chapter 18, on the Trinity.

[15] See Andrew Louth, "An Eastern Orthodox View," in *Original Sin and the Fall: Five Views*, ed J. B. Stump and Chad Meister (Downers Grove: IVP Academic, 2020), 78–100.

[16] Synergism (Gk: *syn*, "with"; *ergon*, "work"): God and humans cooperate in the application of salvation. Monergism (Gk: *monos*, "alone"; *ergon*, "work"): God alone acts to redeem, first in unconditional election and then in effectual grace that applies Christ's work to us by the Holy Spirit.

[17] Fairbairn, *Eastern Orthodoxy through Western Eyes*, 26.

from Peter to the Roman papacy.[18] In common with the East, Rome accepts the first four ecumenical councils and the Christological conclusions of the later ones. The Fourth Lateran Council (1215), the Council of Trent (1545–63), Vatican I (1868–70), and Vatican II (1962–65) also forge Rome's theology. Here are some of Rome's theological distinctives:

1. *Authority*. Rome argues for two sources of divine revelation: Scripture (which includes the Apocrypha) and tradition. Scripture is God's authoritative word, but it is not sufficient to determine correct interpretation or to establish doctrine; Christ has established the magisterium of the church for that purpose. This allows for doctrinal development "beyond" Scripture, focused on papal authority due to apostolic succession and supported by the magisterium. In fact, when the Pope speaks ex cathedra on doctrine and morals, he can define doctrine, hence the embrace of such dogmas as transubstantiation and the Immaculate Conception and Assumption of Mary. However, Scripture and tradition together result in theological conclusions that yield an objective knowledge of God.

2. *The Triune God and Christology*. Nicene trinitarianism and Chalcedonian Christology are affirmed. But, in contrast to the East, and in agreement with Protestant theology, Rome accepts the *filioque* clause, added to the Nicene Creed at the Council of Toledo (589) and officially endorsed in 1017. This was one of the reasons for the Great Schism in 1054.

3. *Sin*. Rome's view of sin is tied to its view of "nature-grace," which is on a continuum of lower to higher. Nature (lower) is a channel of God's grace (higher), and grace elevates and perfects nature. In Adam's sin, due to our organic relationship to him, we lost our original righteousness, viewed as a superadded gift, with a consequent disruption of reason's governance of our passions, resulting in our being dominated by our lower, emotional and physical nature. Yet Adam's sin did not eradicate the original nature-grace relationship; it only marred it so that "nature still possesses a capacity to receive, transmit, and cooperate with grace."[19] Thus, by God infusing grace into nature, beginning with our baptism and continuing through the sacraments, humans become participants with God as grace elevates us by making us righteous by the transformation of our nature.[20]

---

[18] On Roman Catholicism, see D. H. K. Hilborn, "Roman Catholic Theology," in Davie et al., *NDT*, 783–85; L-A. Dyer Williams, "Roman Catholicism," in *Evangelical Dictionary of Theology* (hereafter *EDT*), ed. Daniel J. Treier and Walter A. Elwell, 3rd ed. (Grand Rapids: Baker Academic), 757–60.

[19] Allison, *Roman Catholic Theology and Practice*, 47 (see chap. 1, n. 29).

[20] See Aquinas, *Summa Theologica*, pt. 2.1, q. 109, art. 5, in St. Thomas Aquinas, *Summa Theologica*, 5 vols. (Notre Dame: Christian Classics, 1948).

4. *Salvation*. Salvation is possible because of Christ's atoning sacrifice for us, usually understood along Anselm's satisfaction theory of the cross. In Christ's substitutionary death for us, he paid for our past/original sin. But regarding our present and future sins, we are justified, that is, *made* righteous, not declared righteous, by a combination of Christ's merit and our sacramental incorporation into Christ via the church. By receiving the sacraments, Christ's work is applied to us, and we are infused with divine grace, thus transforming our natures and enabling us to cooperate with God to merit eternal life, hence synergism. In contrast to Protestant theology, justification is not God's declaration that we are righteous in Christ as our covenant and legal head. Instead, justification is the process by which we are made righteous by the infusion of grace mediated through the sacraments.

5. *Church*. Rome's sacramental theology is organically tied to its view that the Roman Church is the continuation of the incarnation, mirroring Christ as a divine-human reality, thus acting as a "second Christ."[21] Through the Roman Church's priestly order, Christ dispenses grace to us in embodied forms, that is, the seven sacraments (baptism, confirmation, penance, the Eucharist, holy orders, marriage, and extreme unction). The sacraments function ex opere operato—"as objectively conferring grace by their very enactment, rather than according to the condition of those ministering or receiving them."[22] For this reason, Rome teaches that there is no salvation outside of the Catholic church, although this belief underwent modification in Vatican II, allowing Protestants and others to be viewed as separated brethren, even extending this to non-Christian religions, thus leading to a strong affirmation of inclusivism.

In the West, the Protestant Reformation in the sixteenth century led to a break from the Roman Church.[23] It was a reform effort to call the church back to the first things of the gospel, centered in the glory of the triune God and his sovereign grace to redeem us in Christ alone. The best way to characterize Reformation distinctives is by its *solas* ("alones"): *sola Scriptura* (Scripture alone), *sola gratia* (grace alone), *sola fide* (faith alone), *solus Christus* (Christ alone), and *soli Deo Gloria* (to God alone be the glory).

---

[21] Allison, *Roman Catholic Theology and Practice*, 56–57.

[22] Hilborn, "Roman Catholic Theology," 784.

[23] On Reformation theology, see R. T. Jones, "Reformation Theology," in Davie et al., *NDT*, 737–41.

1. *Authority. Sola Scriptura* is central to the Reformation and a departure from Rome and even the East. The Reformers did not reject the importance of tradition, yet Scripture is the final, sufficient authority for our theology. As important as tradition is, if it is not warranted by Scripture, it must be rejected; hence, the Reformers rejected beliefs such as purgatory, transubstantiation, the veneration of Mary, and the role of the saints. Also, tied to *sola Scriptura*, the Reformers rejected Rome's hierarchical view of the church and apostolic succession, thus undercutting a two-sourced view of divine revelation.

2. *The Triune God and Christology*. Consistent with all branches of Christian theology, the Reformers affirmed Nicene trinitarianism and Chalcedonian Christology, yet more consistently applied *solus Christus* in terms of the finality and sufficiency of Christ's work, which we receive by sovereign grace and faith alone.

3. *Sin*. Following Augustine, the magisterial Reformers (Martin Luther, Ulrich Zwingli, and John Calvin) insisted that Adam's sin resulted in our total depravity, which necessitates monergism: our triune God must initiate, in unconditional election, the provision of the divine Son as our Mediator and by effectual grace unite us to Christ by the Holy Spirit. The Reformers also rejected the nature-grace view of Rome. For them, as Herman Bavinck notes, "grace serves, not to take up humans into a supernatural order, but to free them from sin. Grace is opposed not to nature, only to sin."[24] Grace is not viewed as an aid to humans in their pursuit of deification; rather, "grace is the beginning, the middle, and the end of the entire work of salvation; it is totally devoid of human merit."[25]

4. *Salvation*. Salvation is found in Christ *alone*, but for the Reformers, this entailed the rejection of Rome's sacramental theology and an affirmation of Christ's all-sufficient work as our covenant head, representative, and substitute. Christ does not merely pay for our past sins by penal substitution; he also pays for all present and future sin. Because Jesus is God the Son incarnate, by his obedient life and death, *he* has fully paid for our sin: there is nothing we can add to his work. Instead, by grace through faith, we are united to Christ by the Spirit's effectual work and declared just before God since Christ's righteousness is ours by imputation. As Protestant theology developed, previous debates within the church over monergism and synergism arose, known today as "Calvinism" and "Arminianism."

---

[24] Bavinck, *Reformed Dogmatics*, 3:577 (see chap. 1, n. 9).

[25] Bavinck, 3:579.

5. *Church*. For the Reformers, the church does not function as a "second Christ" or dispense grace via the sacraments due to its hierarchical structure. Instead, as God's people, who all function as priests ("the priesthood of all believers"), the church proclaims the gospel of God's sovereign grace, which we receive by faith alone in Christ alone. There are only two sacraments of the church: baptism and the Lord's Supper. However, these sacraments do not confer grace; instead, they are a *means* of grace to believers. Yet, among the Reformers, and especially in the development of later Protestant theology, there were a number of disputes regarding the nature of the Lord's Supper and who is to be baptized, leading to debates over infant baptism. As Protestant theology developed, these debates also wrestled with the nature of the church: whether the church is a "mixed" (believers and unbelievers; Reformed, Presbyterian) or a "regenerate" people (Baptist, Believers' Church).

Although this survey of different branches within Christian theology has been brief, our main point is this: despite significant differences in the "catholic" Church, *all* branches assumed that systematic theology resulted in a finite but true, objective knowledge of God. Yet, this belief has changed. We now turn to the reasons for this change.

Ideas Have Consequences: The Changing of Social Imaginaries

The times have changed. The "social imaginary" today is not the same as in previous eras of the church. Life is not viewed in terms of a transcendent, created, teleological order; instead, a secularized, immanent frame governs the way we look at the world, which directly impacts *what* we think theology is and, if it is done, *how* it is done. *Why* this change?

No doubt, skepticism regarding the truth of the gospel has existed in every age of the church. But in the West, its full-blown assault begins in the Enlightenment and continues today unabated. Why? Although the answer is complex, it is primarily due to worldview shifts, where the truth of "ideas have consequences" has been on display.[26] A generation ago, Francis Schaeffer labored to teach this truth as he traced the development of Western thought. His goal was to help the evangelical church know why the concept of truth was under attack, with its growing consequences in our views of God, humans, sin, salvation,

---

[26] See Richard M. Weaver, *Ideas Have Consequences* (Chicago: University of Chicago Press, 1948).

ethics, and the state.[27] Schaeffer knew that history is like a laboratory where "ideas" are tested for good or for ill. And he knew that to understand our intellectual present, we must connect it with our intellectual past; otherwise, the church will drift towards syncretism and potentially undermine the gospel.

With this same goal in mind, let us explain *why* historic theology is now viewed with skepticism by tracing some of the shifts in "ideas" that have resulted since the Enlightenment. Although the intellectual history is complicated, our aim is to avoid reductionism and to help the church better articulate and defend the doing of systematic theology today. We will argue (1) that the Enlightenment sowed the seeds of skepticism that have been cultivated in modernity and postmodernity; (2) that these seeds resulted in the rejection of *sola Scriptura*, which, in turn (3) has rejected a theology "from above"; and (4) that the epistemological and philosophical trajectory starting in the Enlightenment must be rejected and replaced with historic Christian theology.

The Enlightenment and the Implausibility of Historic Systematic Theology

The Enlightenment (*Aufklärung*) (1560–1780) witnessed momentous changes in epistemology and methodology that affected every sector of society, but it was not monolithic.[28] It was the fruit of seeds sown in the Renaissance, notably in the Humanist movement.[29] Yet ideas in the Enlightenment resulted in a profound departure from the conviction that Scripture and the confessions give us true, objective knowledge of God. Looking back, the Enlightenment served as the disintegration of the medieval-Reformation worldview and the gradual *secularization* of Western thought, what morphed into what we identify today as "modernism."[30] In

---

[27] For example, see Francis A. Schaeffer, "The God Who Is There," and "Escape from Reason," in *The Francis A. Schaeffer Trilogy* (Wheaton: Crossway, 1990); Schaeffer, *How Should We Then Live? The Rise and Decline of Western Thought and Culture* (Wheaton: Crossway, 2005).

[28] See S. N. Williams, "Enlightenment, The," in Davie et al., *NDT*, 290–92.

[29] On Humanism as an intellectual movement, see James A. Herrick, *The Making of the New Spirituality: The Eclipse of the Western Religious Tradition* (Downers Grove: InterVarsity, 2003), 49–54; also cf. Carl R. Trueman, "The Renaissance," in *Revolutions in Worldview: Understanding the Flow of Western Thought*, ed. W. Andrew Hoffecker (Phillipsburg: P&R, 2007), 178–205.

[30] See, e.g., W. Andrew Hoffecker, "Enlightenments and Awakenings: The Beginnings of Modern Culture Wars," in Hoffecker, *Revolutions in Worldview*, 240–80. Referring to the medieval-Reformation

noting the significance of this era, Alister McGrath observes, "With the benefit of hindsight, the Enlightenment can be said to have marked a decisive and irreversible change in the political, social, and religious outlook of Western Europe and North America."[31]

The Enlightenment did not arise in a vacuum. As Stanley Grenz reminds us, "[the Enlightenment] came as the outgrowth of various social, political, and intellectual factors that led up to and transpired during this traumatic era in human history."[32] Europe was embattled in religious wars between Protestants and Roman Catholics, and there was a desire to arbitrate these debates by rational means. In fact, many Enlightenment thinkers came to believe that human rationality was the only way to resolve these theological disputes, and as a result, many began to assert that theology also derived from reason and was therefore open to critical examination.

The phrase "Age of Reason" describes the *nature* of the Enlightenment. But we must not think that reason was inoperative prior to this era. Reason has always played a crucial role in theology, as evidenced in the work of Athanasius, Augustine, Anselm, Aquinas, and so on. In the Enlightenment, however, reason was elevated from a ministerial instrument to a magisterial rule, especially over Scripture and tradition. McGrath states it this way: "The ability of reason to judge revelation was affirmed. As human reason was omnicompetent, it was argued that it was supremely qualified to judge Christian beliefs and practices, with a view to eliminating any irrational or superstitious elements."[33] Immanuel Kant reflects this mindset in his 1784 article "What is Enlightenment?" For Kant, the "enlightened" person is the one who "dares to reason" without dependence upon the authorities of the past. In such a context, the previous motto of theology, "faith seeking understanding," changes to "I believe what I can understand."[34]

---

worldview is not to deny the major differences within this era. The main point is simply that despite the differences in this era (which were numerous), the era was united in its belief in objective truth and that a normative Christian theology was possible.

[31] Alister E. McGrath, *The Making of Modern German Christology, 1750–1990*, 2nd ed. (Eugene: Wipf & Stock, 2005), 14.

[32] Stanley J. Grenz, *A Primer on Postmodernism* (Grand Rapids: Eerdmans, 1996), 63.

[33] McGrath, *Making of Modern German Christology*, 21. Herman Reimarus in Germany and the *philosophes* in France illustrate this point. Both placed reason above revelation and introduced a critical spirit, which required the reconstruction of Christian theology.

[34] Grenz, *Primer on Postmodernism*, 62.

By elevating human rationality to a position of supreme authority, the Enlightenment began to undermine Christian orthodoxy. The new ways of thinking could not support even the basic view that God had revealed truth about himself, humans, and the world in Scripture.[35] The significance of this challenge is evident if we contrast the epistemology and theological framework of the Reformers (reflecting much of historic theology) with the Enlightenment.

First, the Reformers held to a "revelational epistemology," which necessitated that human reason functions under the magisterial authority of Scripture. Objective truth and knowledge are not grounded in humans or the world, but in the comprehensive plan/decree of the triune God. Humans, as creatures and image-bearers, are dependent on God, metaphysically *and* methodologically,[36] as illustrated by John Calvin in his *Institutes*, where he insists that without the knowledge of God, there is no knowledge of the self.[37] As such, humans come to know truth by reasoning from divine revelation (both general and special), and Scripture is the "spectacles" by which we rightly interpret God, the self, and the world. Although Scripture is not an exhaustive revelation, because it is God-given, it gives us a true "God's-eye point of view."

Second, the Reformers practiced a theology "from above"; that is, all theological formulations are constructed from Scripture. For example, in Christology, the Reformers never separated the "Jesus of history" from the "Christ of faith," as would occur later in Enlightenment thought. Scripture's presentation and description of the historical Jesus were taken to be true, reliable, and theologically significant. As Hans Frei observed, the Reformers believed that the Gospel narratives actually corresponded to the real world as "history-like narratives."[38] Thus, the Reformers, along with "catholic" theology, had no problem affirming Christ's preexistence, virgin conception, and bodily resurrection and making universal and metaphysical conclusions about his identity and work. Their understanding of Jesus, along with all dogmatic formulations, was of one piece with their entire theological understanding of God, self, and the

---

[35] See John M. Frame, *A History of Western Philosophy and Theology* (Phillipsburg: P&R, 2015), 214–50.

[36] For this point, see Kevin J. Vanhoozer, "Human Being, Individual and Social," in *The Cambridge Companion to Christian Doctrine*, ed. Colin E. Gunton (Cambridge: Cambridge University Press, 1997), 158–59.

[37] See Calvin, *Institutes*, 1.1.1 (1:35) (see chap. 1, n. 3).

[38] Frei, *Eclipse of Biblical Narrative*, 17–50 (see chap. 1, n. 41).

world, and in truth, it could not be understood apart from the entire presentation of Scripture and its worldview.

However, in the Enlightenment, this solid epistemological-theological/metaphysical ground for theology was challenged by new ways of thinking in science, religion, and hermeneutics. Yet, the first and most significant place it was challenged was in epistemology. In the Enlightenment's "turn to the subject," Calvin's maxim is reversed: "There is no knowledge of God *except through knowledge of the self*."[39] By giving human subjectivity a foundational status in knowing, a seed is sown that runs through every discipline and that introduces skepticism regarding the plausibility of historic Christian theology. Let us now turn to this point.

Enlightenment Epistemology: "The Turn to the Subject"

Many crucial thinkers sowed ideas that changed the plausibility structures of the West, but two individuals stand out: one at the beginning of the Enlightenment era and the other at the end. Both philosophers are known for their famous "turns to the subject."

First, René Descartes (1596–1650) is a key figure who moved the medieval-Reformation era to a modern mindset, especially through the influence of his *Discourse on the Method* (1637).[40] Working against Pyrrhonism and its skepticism, which threatened our ability to know anything with certainty, Descartes devised a method to discover objective truth. However, instead of starting with God as the ground for his philosophy, Descartes stripped away all of his beliefs about God, the world, and the self. He was left with only one truth he could not doubt: he existed as a thinking subject. From that starting point, Descartes's famous "cogito, ergo sum" (I think, therefore I am) served as the foundation for building all knowledge in every field of inquiry.

On the surface, Descartes's use of the cogito argument may seem innocent, but it is not. In fact, Descartes was not the first to use this kind of argument; Augustine used it before him. However, Descartes's use of the argument was a significant departure from Augustine. Andrew Hoffecker states it this way: "Cartesian rationalism effectively inaugurated the 'modern self' or the 'subjective turn,' a shift from knowledge as objectively rooted in biblical

[39] Vanhoozer, "Human Being, Individual and Social," 159 (emphasis mine).

[40] René Descartes, *Discourse on Method and Related Writings* (London: Penguin, 1999).

revelation (both general and special) to knowledge as authenticated and demonstrated by human reason."[41] As such, Descartes's turn to the self is vastly different from Augustine's cogito centered on God:

> Augustine formulated the *cogito* in the *context* of objective Christian belief, in which knowing God took preeminence. Certainty of his own existence served the higher end of knowing God. His *cogito* formed but a small part of thought that would center on God, who alone is self-existent and self-sufficient.
>
> Descartes's use of the *cogito*, on the other hand, launched the whole project of modernity. Self-authenticating, rational self-sufficiency was the basis of Cartesian foundationalism. No matter what form epistemology took in the ensuing seventeenth- and eighteenth-century discussions, its formulators used assumptions that furthered Descartes's break from the past.[42]

The result of Descartes's new method was to displace God with the human subject as the ground for his philosophy, which set the agenda for all future philosophical discussion. True knowledge would now be authenticated and demonstrated by human reason and perception, which might not correspond to biblical revelation. Descartes's view, now known as "classical foundationalism" (which includes the epistemological schools of Continental rationalism and British empiricism),[43] contended that our *derived beliefs* are justified only if they are supported by an *infallible foundation*, that is, "basic beliefs" that need no justification. Under this system, however, many beliefs—like memory beliefs, belief from logical induction, and, most significantly, belief in God—would not qualify as knowledge.[44] And many Enlightenment philosophers urged this kind of agnosticism, with Immanuel Kant questioning the legitimacy of the entire metaphysical project (including theology) as objective knowledge.

---

[41] Hoffecker, "Enlightenments and Awakenings," 254.

[42] Hoffecker, 254.

[43] Continental Rationalism is identified with René Descartes (1596–1650), Baruch Spinoza (1632–77), and Gottfried Leibniz (1646–1716); British Empiricism is identified with John Locke (1632–1704), George Berkeley (1685–1753), and David Hume (1711–76).

[44] See, e.g., Nicholas Wolterstorff, *Reason within the Bounds of Religion*, 2nd ed. (Grand Rapids: Eerdmans, 1988); Alvin Plantinga and Nicholas Wolterstorff, eds., *Faith and Rationality: Reason and Belief in God* (Notre Dame: University of Notre Dame Press, 1983).

Immanuel Kant (1724–1804) is the second pivotal figure that doubled-down on Descartes's "turn to the subject" and by doing so greatly impacted modern philosophy and theology. By the end of the Enlightenment era, Kant sought to salvage the Enlightenment project by offering a via media between Continental rationalism and British empiricism and an answer to David Hume's (1711–76) destructive skepticism against epistemology, science, and religion. Kant identified his "new" approach to epistemology as a "Copernican revolution" that radicalized Descartes's methodological turn to center *all* knowledge in the human subject.

For Kant, rationalism seemed arbitrary and speculative, while a consistent empiricism led to Hume's conclusion that since basic ideas such as substance, causality, and the self are not empirically verified, they have no "rational" warrant.[45] Hume's conclusion was disturbing; if he was correct, then the Enlightenment project was greatly mitigated. In response, Kant proposed a further "turn to the self" by reversing the traditional understanding of the relationship between the subject (mind) and the object (world) in the knowing process. Instead of our minds passively conforming to objects outside of them, they actively schematize or "construct" the sense data from the world (contra rationalism) to conform the objects of the world to our a priori categories (contra empiricism).

As Kant worked out his "constructivist" view of human knowledge in *Critique of Pure Reason*, he made a strict distinction between objects present in our experience ("phenomena") and objects lying beyond our experience ("noumena").[46] Why? Because the a priori categories of the mind do not work beyond the sense world: mental categories without sense experience are *empty*; sense experience without categories is *blind*. As such, the human mind cannot know anything objectively beyond the range of immediate experience, and attempts to do so inevitably result in irresolvable contradictions and antinomies. Humans can *only* know the phenomena; we have no *direct* knowledge of the noumena. The result: *All* metaphysical knowledge is excluded, including the knowledge of God and the self. Of such realities, we must remain metaphysically and theologically agnostic.[47] Ideas of God, self, and

---

[45] For a description and critique of Hume, see James N. Anderson, *David Hume* (Phillipsburg: P&R, 2019).

[46] Immanuel Kant, *Immanuel Kant's Critique of Pure Reason*, trans., Norman K. Smith (London: Macmillan, 1929).

[47] Kant allows only a moral theology: "Now I maintain that all attempts to employ reason in theology in any merely speculative manner are altogether fruitless and by their very nature null and void, and

the world are only *regulative*, not *constitutive*, meaning that "we are not to regard [them] as actually existing, but . . . 'as if' they existed in our experience."[48] In this way, Kant makes room for "faith/theology." But note: it is a "faith/theology" that does *not* result in an objective knowledge of God.

The consequences of Kant's ideas for theology are profound. Over the years, Kantianism has changed through criticism and reconsideration. For example, his critics have rightly charged that Kant overstepped his own philosophy by claiming to know that *all* humans have the same mental categories, which assumes some kind of *universal* human nature. Kant accounted for this by his deism, but when later thinkers embraced Darwin, Kant's earlier view was impossible to sustain. However, what was retained was Kant's "constructivism" and rejection of metaphysical knowledge but now via mental categories tied to language that are the product of social evolution. Human autonomy is primary; knowledge of metaphysics is impossible; and if "theology" is allowed, it can make no claim to metaphysical/theological knowledge.

For Kant, revelation, miracles, and direct divine activity in human history, and objective truth statements about God, Christ, and humans are reduced to the unknowable. Since God is a *noumenal* reality, we can never *know* if God is sovereign, that he is the Creator, or whether he has disclosed himself to us.[49] And even if God has revealed himself to us in the world, such "revelation" is always subjected to a natural explanation supplied by the categories and active construction of the human mind. Such "theology" is limited to the confines of *methodological* naturalism, and Scripture is interpreted within an *extratextual* framework foreign to Scripture. In the place of historic theology is some kind of "reconstructed" theology.

In fact, Kant illustrates such a "reconstructed" theology in *Religion within the Limits of Reason Alone*.[50] Theology, stripped of its metaphysical truth claims, is reduced to preserving human freedom and morality. For Kant, religion provides the ultimate goal of morality,

---

that the principles of its employment in the study of nature do not lead to any theology whatsoever. Consequently, the only theology of reason which is possible is that which is based upon moral laws or seeks guidance from them." *Immanuel Kant's Critique of Pure Reason*, 528.

[48] Frame, *History of Western Philosophy and Theology*, 266.

[49] For Kant, God is only "known" as a postulate of practical reason as the one who upholds the imperatives of the moral law, but no metaphysical knowledge of God is possible.

[50] Immanuel Kant, *Religion within the Limits of Reason Alone*, trans. Theodore M. Greene and Hoyt H. Hudson (New York: Harper & Row, 1960).

where it speaks of a powerful moral Lawgiver whose will ought to be the human's final end. But in such a view, Jesus is not God the Son incarnate, but the moral exemplar of a morally perfect humanity who reminds us that we can attain moral perfection in this life. Since we are not the authors of this idea, we may say that it has symbolically come down to us "from heaven" and has "assumed our humanity," but we are *not* to think that Christ's incarnation is actually true to history or that Christ reveals to us a true knowledge of God otherwise unattainable by reason.

For many theologians who follow the Kantian project, especially those identified with "classic liberalism" in the nineteenth century, such as Friedrich Schleiermacher (1768–1834), Albrecht Ritschl (1822–89), and his successors, every Christian dogma is "reconstructed" to fit within the confines of Enlightenment thought. As knowledge is limited to our experience of the world, it becomes plausible to think that only science, not theology, is capable of justification. Or, if theology is viewed as a science, it is grounded in the experience of God within human experience. Many who follow after such theologians eventually view theology as a *sub*-rational discipline open to critical assessment by science.[51] But, of course, this view simply begs the question of *which* science? Is it a science grounded in the triune Creator or in a deistic and/or naturalistic worldview? After all, the discipline of science is not presuppositionless; like theology, science is dependent upon worldview commitments. So what kind of science did the Enlightenment assume?

Enlightenment Science: Applying Methodological Naturalism to Theology[52]

The impact of science on the Enlightenment worldview is significant. Christian theology is *not* against science, properly understood. In fact, one can make a strong case that Christian theology provided the necessary preconditions for an empirical science.[53] The Enlightenment,

---

[51] See John S. Feinberg, *No One Like Him: The Doctrine of God* (Wheaton: Crossway, 2001), 84–95.

[52] "Methodological naturalism" is the view that for any study of the world to be rational, including history and theology, all cause-effect relationships are naturalistic and thus explained without reference to divine extraordinary action in the world. By definition, this view rejects the possibility of God's miraculous action in the world.

[53] See Nancy R. Pearcey and Charles B. Thaxton, *The Soul of Science: Christian Faith and Natural Philosophy* (Wheaton: Crossway, 1994); and our discussion of this point in part 4, chapter 21.

however, combined the view that God created the world in a rational, orderly, and knowable fashion (deism) with the belief in human autonomy. The result: the scientific method was now applied to *all* disciplines of knowledge, including metaphysics, theology, history, and ethics. As James Sire notes: "If this way of obtaining knowledge about the universe was so successful, why not apply the same method to knowledge about God?"[54]

In this regard, Isaac Newton (1642–1727) is important in the Enlightenment and beyond. Newton was interested in both theological and scientific questions, but it was his view of the physical universe that transformed the thinking of the age. Newton's universe was an orderly, grand machine whose movements could be known because it followed specific observable laws. Yet, while Newton was a committed theist, his successors were not. They looked at the same orderly universe but then separated God from his creation. For them, the universe was "a vast machine or a watch designed so wisely by a watchmaker that it runs on its own without outside intervention . . . according to Newton's laws."[55]

This mechanistic view of the world paved the way for the rise of deism and a *methodological* naturalism. When coupled with the "turn to the subject," this set the stage for a growing rejection of historic theology. According to the deistic view, if God acts at all in the world, it is only by upholding the laws of nature that he established; God does not act extraordinarily in the world. Thus, belief in "God" remained, but not in the triune God of Scripture and all the theological entailments that follow. The Enlightenment, then, rendered implausible God's unique action in the world. As such, the Scripture's teaching that God has planned all things from eternity and now in creation, providence, and redemption is working out his plan in history to redeem a people for himself, to judge human sin, and to usher in a new creation by the person and work of Christ seemed highly unlikely. In fact, any theology that is not circumscribed completely by the scientific method is simply rejected as impossible.[56] As we will note below, as deism gives way to Darwinian naturalism, this mindset is only entrenched.

---

[54] James W. Sire, *The Universe Next Door: A Basic Worldview Catalogue*, 4th ed. (Downers Grove: InterVarsity, 1997), 47.

[55] Hoffecker, "Enlightenments and Awakenings," 247.

[56] On this point, see James R. Edwards, *Is Jesus the Only Savior?* (Grand Rapids: Eerdmans, 2005), 13.

Enlightenment Religion: Replacing Trinitarian Theism with Deism

We have already noted the rise of deism during the Enlightenment, a view of the God-world relation that is far different from trinitarian theism and the Bible's Creator-creature distinction. Deism, as Frederick Copleston notes, is not a *school* of thought or even an organized *religion*. Rather, it is a view associated with some influential thinkers who (while disagreeing at points) formed a basic *system* of thought that helped to change people's thinking from a theistic view to a more secular mindset.[57] Deism views religion as *natural* rather than revealed and *super*natural. And despite the diversity of religions, all religions are reducible to common, universal truths that are discoverable by reason alone.

Deism as a *system* affirmed four basic points in contrast to historic Christian theology.[58] First, a transcendent "God" created the universe, but he is not sovereign over or active in it. Second, because God created the world, the universe is rational and law-governed, but it is a *closed* system, which entails *no extraordinary* divine agency in history. Third, humans are valuable and inherently good; there was no historic Adam or fall. However, humans are also part of nature's closed system, which begins to raise questions about human dignity, significance, and freedom. On this third point, Jean-Jacques Rousseau (1712–78) was a seminal thinker.[59] Rousseau denied the doctrine of original sin. Humans are not born fallen, thus needing God to act in sovereign grace to redeem us in Christ. Instead, we are born innocent, and our problem is due to the corruptive influences of culture. What is needed, then, is not regeneration by the Spirit and justification before God but for humans to express their inner desires, to act in "self-determining freedom" devoid of an external standard,[60] and to throw off the oppressive shackles of society.[61] Fourth, the nature of religion is to order moral behavior. "Theology" is not about formulating speculative dogmas, such as the Trinity, Christology, and so on. Instead, theology is to help people live moral lives and to make a better world by social transformation.

---

[57] See Frederick Copleston, *A History of Philosophy*, new rev. ed., vol. 5, *The British Philosophers from Hobbes to Hume* (Garden City: Doubleday, 1963), 162–63.

[58] See Sire, *Universe Next Door*, 48–55.

[59] See Trueman, *Rise and Triumph*, 105–28 (see chap. 1, n. 26).

[60] See Charles Taylor, *The Ethics of Authenticity* (Cambridge, MA: Harvard University Press, 1991), 27.

[61] In volume 2, we will return to this discussion and contrast a *theological* anthropology with our culture's view.

Not surprisingly, deism, coupled with the Enlightenment's "turn to the subject," radically altered people's thinking about the plausibility of historic theology in at least two areas. First, God's extraordinary action in history is rejected, thus calling into question the uniqueness of Christianity, especially regarding the person and work of Christ. Think of how Jesus's unique identity and significance is tied to God's action in history: incarnation, life, death, and resurrection. But deism rejects these unique, extraordinary events as impossible, thus leaving us with an entirely different Jesus. In such a view, Scripture's own presentation of *who* Jesus is and *what* he does cannot be taken on its own terms, thus rendering incomprehensible the incarnation, along with the biblical link between sin and its solution in a divine-human Redeemer.

Second, deism's rejection of the possibility of "revealed religion"—according to its presupposed worldview—entails a rejection or redefinition of every doctrine of Christianity. Gone is the Trinity, divine agency in redemptive history, a historic Adam, original sin, the incarnation, Christ's substitutionary atonement, and the forgiveness of sins. In the place of orthodoxy is a reconstructed natural theology circumscribed by the limits of human rationality. Furthermore, *sola Scriptura* disappears, which results in uprooting the epistemological warrant for systematic theology. Not surprisingly, this period of time witnesses a sustained attack on biblical authority, a point to which we now turn, given the foundational ground Scripture serves for historic theology.

Enlightenment Hermeneutics: Reading the Bible "Like Any Other Book"[62]

Given Enlightenment "ideas," we also witness corresponding consequences in how the Bible is viewed, interpreted, and used for various theological conclusions. Presuppositions matter to the *way we think*, and the way we think affects *how* we approach *and* read Scripture. Specifically, we will outline how the combination of rationalism and deism affected how people received and interpreted Scripture with the rise of biblical criticism and the historical-critical method.

The Rise of Biblical Criticism. For the first time since Constantine, this era witnessed the open rejection of Christian dogma, from outside the church and even from those who

[62] This is an expression taken from Benjamin Jowett (1817–1893), who in an influential article in *Essays and Reviews* (1860) argued that the Bible should be treated like any other book and thus be subject to criticism.

professed to be within the church. A critical examination of the Bible began in earnest and culminated in yet another major shift away from the previous era. Prior to this time, differences in the Pentateuch or between the Gospels were acknowledged, but it was assumed that such differences could be harmonized. With the epistemological revolution well under way in the Enlightenment, however, many abandoned an attitude of trust and confidence toward the Bible as God's word. These "enlightened" hermeneuts began to criticize the reliability of the OT and the Gospels, especially dismissing the miracles, the fulfillment of prophecies, and how the NT authors used the OT. Many attribute the rise of this "biblical criticism" to the work of Richard Simon (1638–1712) and Baruch Spinoza (1632–77);[63] but two of the most significant biblical critics in the eighteenth century were Herman Reimarus (1694–1768) and Gotthold Lessing (1729–81).[64]

First, C. Stephen Evans notes two assumptions that Reimarus taught that drove biblical criticism: first, he viewed Scripture "as ordinary historical documents, with no presumption of divine inspiration or even reliability;"[65] second, he approached the text with suspicion, assuming that "to learn what really happened one must look through the texts and not take them at face value."[66] As applied to the Gospels, the "Jesus of history" vs. "Christ of faith" distinction began in earnest, which assumed that Scripture was "like any other book" and not the God-given, reliable interpretation of the historical Jesus.

Second, Lessing's singular contribution to biblical criticism was his doubting the epistemic value of history, especially regarding the uniqueness of Christ. Prior to the Enlightenment, the church universally argued that the identity and significance of Jesus was based upon specific historical events: the virgin conception, miracles, death, and resurrection. In fact, the church claimed that it was these historical events that established Jesus's *unique identity* and warranted his *universal significance* for all people. On this point, Christianity is different from

---

[63] See John Woodbridge, "Some Misconceptions of the Impact of the Enlightenment," in *Hermeneutics, Authority, and Canon*, ed. D. A. Carson and John Woodbridge (Grand Rapids: Zondervan, 1986), 253–57.

[64] See McGrath, *Making of Modern German Christology*, 28–35; Colin Brown, *Jesus in European Protestant Thought, 1778–1860* (Grand Rapids: Baker, 1985), 1–55.

[65] C. Stephen Evans, *The Historical Christ and The Jesus of Faith: The Incarnational Narrative as History* (Oxford: Oxford University Press, 1996), 18.

[66] Evans, 18.

all other religions since the essence of non-Christian religions is not found in their historical claims. As John Frame notes, "What is important about [non-Christian] religions is certain general truths that they propose for belief. These truths do not depend on any historical events. . . . If these religions are true, they are true in all times and places, indeed timelessly."[67] But not so with Christianity; its truthfulness is tied to history, from creation to Christ. But Lessing challenged this claim by doubting the uniqueness and the universality of theology's historical claims.

Lessing argued that Enlightenment epistemology inserted "an ugly, broad ditch" between the particular facts of history and the universal truths of reason.[68] As such, true knowledge cannot be attained through historical religions, specifically Christianity. In Christology, Lessing introduced the problem of how to start with the NT's presentation of Jesus as a historical figure and then move to his *universal* significance for all people and all times. For Lessing, a historically-mediated knowledge of God is unjust, and historical persons and events cannot yield universal truths: the "scandal of historical particularity" cannot be overcome.[69] This idea has now become known as "Lessing's ugly ditch." The Enlightenment allowed only reason to provide the basis for establishing necessary and universal truths; the "accidental truths of history can never become the proof of the necessary truths of reason."[70]

For Lessing, this unbridgeable divide has a chronological and metaphysical aspect to it. Regarding the former, Lessing acknowledged that to know the historical Jesus, we are dependent upon written accounts based upon human testimony. However, he questioned the *accuracy* of these accounts given the time gap between our time and theirs. Further, Lessing argued that human testimony cannot make a past event credible unless we have a present experience of the exact same kind of event. Thus, not having firsthand experience of resurrection, we should not believe the NT's affirmation that Jesus rose from the dead because it "rests upon

[67] Frame, *History of Western Philosophy and Theology*, 222.

[68] G. E. Lessing, "On the Proof of the Spirit and Power," in *Lessing's Theological Writings*, comp. and trans. Henry Chadwick, A Library of Modern Religious Thought (Stanford: Stanford University Press, 1956), 53, 55.

[69] McGrath, *Making of Modern German Christology*, 32.

[70] Lessing, "On the Proof," 53.

the authority of others, rather than the authority of our own experience and rational reflection upon it."[71]

Regarding the latter, Lessing insisted that historical facts alone cannot yield *universal* significance. Historical facts are accidental and contingent; the only truths that are universal are truths of reason, not history. For us to know the universal significance of a historical fact, it would first have to be part of a universal plan and then we would have to know that plan. But apart from a "God's-eye viewpoint," we cannot draw universal/metaphysical/theological conclusions from historical facts alone. Thus, Christianity's uniqueness, specifically centered in Christ, is undermined, and with it, the assumption that historic theology is possible.

The Hermeneutic of Historical Criticism and the Bible. What people like Reimarus and Lessing birthed was institutionalized as an entire hermeneutic within biblical studies. Even today, the starting point for biblical and theological studies, despite attempts to read Scripture as a unified canon, is that the Bible is unreliable and subject to critical evaluation. Describing biblical scholarship, Evans puts it "bluntly and simply . . . we have become unsure whether the events happened, and uncertain about whether we can know that they happened, even if they did."[72]

The rise of biblical criticism, then, has led to the rule(s) of the historical-critical method, which subjects the Bible to historical-critical analysis by the use of various tools (e.g., source, form, and redaction criticism). The use of the tools may differ; some scholars are less skeptical of the historicity of the Bible than others (ironically, making the "assured results of scholarship" unsure). But *the governing assumption* is that the Bible is not completely reliable. Thus, for example, in Christology, the "Jesus of history" is assumed *not* to be identical with the "Jesus of the Bible." Much could be said about the specifics of the method, but our concern is to describe the controlling philosophical assumptions that undergird it, which will allow us to see why the historical-critical method renders problematic the historic conception of theology.

---

[71] McGrath, *Making of Modern German Christology*, 30. Regarding miracles, for example, Lessing explains that "since the truth of these miracles has completely ceased to be demonstrable by miracles still happening at the present time, since they are no more than reports of miracles . . . I deny that they can and should bind me in the least to a faith in the other teachings of Jesus." Lessing, "On the Proof," 53–55.

[72] Evans, *Historical Christ*, 13.

What are the governing principles of the historical-critical method? They are as follows: (1) the principle of methodological doubt, (2) the principle of analogy, and (3) the principle of correlation.[73] The first principle states that all historical judgments (including biblical ones) are only statements of probability and, as such, are always open to doubt, criticism, and revision. The next two principles work in tandem to determine a text's historical accuracy. The principle of analogy assumes that all historical events are in principle qualitatively similar; the principle of correlation views all historical phenomena as existing in a causal nexus. All historical events, then, are interrelated, interdependent, and qualitatively similar.

With these three principles in place, only one question can legitimately lead to a proper judgment regarding a text's historical accuracy: Given the causal nexus of history, is the supposed historical event analogous to our present experience? If analogous, we have warrant for historicity; if not analogous, however, we have no warrant to think that the event actually occurred. As applied to Scripture, Ernst Troeltsch is honest about the result: "Jewish and Christian history are thus made analogous *to all other history*,"[74] thus denying from the outset anything unique about Scripture, especially the uniqueness and exclusivity of Christ.

However, as many critics of the historical-critical method have observed, the method presupposes a *methodological* naturalism that rejects trinitarian theism and agency by definition. It assumes from the outset a theology "from below" as opposed to a theology "from above." But this is precisely the problem. One cannot simply impose one's method on Scripture without first arguing for its truthfulness. Nevertheless, when we contrast the historical-critical method with historic Christian theology, we discover two incompatible worldviews at work. Even a quick glance at the first principles of the historical-critical method demonstrates their incompatibility with the self-presentation of Scripture. Van A. Harvey identifies two principles: "(1) No critical historian can make use of supernatural intervention as a principle of historical explanation because this will shatter the continuity of the causal nexus, and (2) no event can be regarded as a final revelation of the absolute spirit, since every manifestation of truth and value is relative and historically conditioned."[75]

---

[73] See Ernst Troeltsch, "Historical and Dogmatic Method in Theology (1898)," in *Religion in History*, trans. James Luther Adams and Walter E. Bense (Minneapolis: Fortress, 1991), 11–32.

[74] Troeltsch, "Historical and Dogmatic Method," 14 (emphasis added).

[75] Van A. Harvey, *The Historian and the Believer: The Morality of Historical Knowledge and Christian Belief* (Philadelphia: Westminster, 1966), 29–30.

Van Harvey's admission simply confirms that presuppositions matter to the *way we think*, and the way we think affects *how* we approach *and* read Scripture. The rise of biblical criticism represents a momentous shift in how the Bible was approached and how theology was practiced. As adopted and practiced, it changed the plausibility structures regarding the possibility of historic theology. Troeltsch is a good example of this. He regarded historical criticism as a complete overturn of the medieval-Reformation worldview (or, better, historic theology): biblical criticism is "a new scientific mode of representing man and his development, and, as such, shows at all points an absolute contrast to the Biblico-theological views of later antiquity."[76] Troeltsch also made this point by characterizing the rise of biblical criticism as leavening the whole of theological methodology: if the critical assumptions are admitted at one point, it changes everything and finally destroys "the dogmatic form of method that has been used in theology."[77]

All of this explains *why* the "ideas" sown in the Enlightenment changed people's thinking about the nature and possibility of theology. The result was a redefinition of theology constrained within the extratextual worldview of the Enlightenment.[78] However, the consequence of such a view was the inability to say anything true, universal, and metaphysical about any doctrine, a point to which we now turn.

A Redefinition of Theology: The Consequences of Enlightenment-Modernist Ideas

What consequences followed for theology from Enlightenment-Modernist ideas? At least two: first, a revelational epistemology was jettisoned for a theology "from below," warranted by human reason, experience, and historical-critical reconstruction. Second, a redefinition occurred of every point of doctrine of the Christian faith. An example of the first are the famous "quests for the historical Jesus," while an illustration of the second is the rise of "classic liberal" theology. Let us look at each of these in turn.

---

[76] Ernst Troeltsch, "Historiography," *Encyclopedia of Religion and Ethics*, ed. James Hastings, vol. 6 (New York: Charles Scribner's Sons, 1912–1915), 718.

[77] Cited in Edgar Krentz, *The Historical-Critical Method* (Philadelphia: Fortress, 1975), 55.

[78] See Hans W. Frei, *Types of Christian Theology*, ed. George Hunsinger and William C. Placher (New Haven: Yale University Press, 1992). An "extratextual" approach gives priority to a foreign ideology "outside" (*extra*) Scripture so that Scripture and theological claims are valid only within it.

Quests for the Historical Jesus: Historical Criticism Applied. The "quests for the historical Jesus" nicely illustrate the effects of the historical-critical method on theology.[79] The goal of the quests was to recover the "Jesus of history," who is *not* identical with the "Jesus of the Bible," by using the historical-critical method to peel back the biblical layers of legend and myth. The starting point and conclusion of the quests represent a sharp turn away from the doing of historic theology.[80]

The Old Quest (1778–1906) assumed that the Bible is wholly unreliable and proceeded to reconstruct the "historical" Jesus without reliance on and almost without reference to the biblical presentation.[81] During an interim period (1906–53) that some call the "No Quest," theologians disregarded historical facts about Jesus as necessary for the Christian faith. The best example of this is Rudolf Bultmann, who simply replaced (demythologized) the NT's "mythological" framework with an existential structure, asking only, "What is man?"[82] This

[79] The specific developments within and the individuals associated with the quests are detailed in many places. See Colin Brown, *Jesus in European Protestant Thought*; McGrath, *Making of Modern German Christology*; N. T. Wright, *Christian Origins and the Question of God*, vol. 2, *Jesus and the Victory of God* (Minneapolis: Fortress, 1997). The taxonomy of the quests is from N. T. Wright's description in *Christian Origins and the Question of God*, 2:1–124.

[80] As Albert Schweitzer observes regarding the quests, "The historical investigation of the life of Jesus did not take its rise from a purely historical interest; it turned to the Jesus of history as an ally in the struggle against the tyranny of dogma. Afterwards when it was freed from this *pathos* it sought to present the historic Jesus in a form intelligible to its own time." *The Quest of the Historical Jesus: A Critical Study of its Progress from Reimarus to Wrede*, trans. William Montgomery (New York: Macmillan, 1968), 3. N. T. Wright agrees:

> Let us be clear. People often think that the early "lives of Jesus" were attempting to bring the church back to historical reality. They were not. They were attempting to show what historical reality really was, in order that, having glimpsed this unattractive sight, people might turn away from orthodox theology and discover a new freedom. One looked at the history in order then to look elsewhere, to the other side of Lessing's "ugly ditch," to the eternal truths of reason unsullied by the contingent facts of everyday events, even extraordinary ones like those of Jesus. (Wright, *Christian Origins and the Question of God*, 2:17–18)

[81] The Old Quest received its name from the English title of Schweitzer's book, *Quest of the Historical Jesus*. The Old Quest starts with Reimarus, ends with Schweitzer, and includes a veritable who's who in biblical studies: e.g., David Strauss (1808–74), F. C. Baur (1792–1860), Albrecht Ritschl (1822–89), Adolf von Harnack (1851–1930), William Wrede (1859–1906), Wilhelm Bousset (1865–1920).

[82] Rudolf Bultmann, *New Testament and Mythology and Other Basic Writings*, ed. and trans. Schubert Miles Ogden (Philadelphia: Fortress, 1984), 5–6; cf. Bultmann, *Jesus Christ and Mythology* (New York: Scribner, 1958), 11–21.

anthropocentric framework was more congenial to modern thought and consistent with the assumed primacy and power of human reason in Enlightenment hermeneutics.

The New Quest (1953 to present) focuses on the sayings of Jesus in Scripture.[83] It is less pessimistic about discovering the "historical Jesus," but it still agrees with the other quests that the Gospels contain the subjective interpretations of the early church, not God's authoritative interpretation of who Jesus is through the biblical authors. But they argue that we can sift through the subjectivity using extratextual rules (e.g., consistency and multiple attestation, the criteria of dissimilarity, various linguistic and cultural tests) to determine what the historical Jesus really said. Finally, at the same time, the Third Quest (early 1980s to present) applies its own versions of historical-critical criteria that take the NT texts more seriously as literary documents set within the Jewish context of early Christianity.[84] But these conciliatory efforts still come with *critical* commitments that deny the full reliability of Scripture and, thus, its ability to identify the historical Jesus with complete accuracy and authority.

The quests serve as an example of the impact of the Enlightenment on Scripture and theology as historically conceived. If Enlightenment assumptions are adopted, not only is the *revealed* Jesus of the Bible replaced by a "mythical, desupernaturalized Jesus,"[85] but nothing *theological*, that is, metaphysical, can be said about him. Merely human historical research can never yield an objective and infallibly true interpretation of Jesus's identity and significance. Correctly identifying Jesus rather requires God himself to give us both the historical facts and the theological interpretation of those facts.

The Rise of Classic Liberalism: A Redefinition of Theology. The second consequence of Enlightenment ideas was the rise of "classic liberal" theology.[86] This movement arose in

---

[83] For example, see Ernst Käsemann, "The Problem of the Historical Jesus," in *Essays on New Testament Themes*, trans. W. J. Montague (1964; repr., London: SCM Press, 2012), 15–47; James M. Robinson, *A New Quest of the Historical Jesus and Other Essays* (Minneapolis: Augsburg, 1983); Norman Perrin, *Rediscovering the Teaching of Jesus* (New York: Harper & Row, 1976).

[84] N. T. Wright is a major figure in the Third Quest. Cf. Ben F. Meyer, *The Aims of Jesus* (Eugene: Wipf & Stock, 2002); J. D. G. Dunn, *Christianity in the Making*, vol. 1, *Jesus Remembered* (Grand Rapids: Eerdmans, 2003).

[85] B. B. Warfield, *The Person and Work of Christ* (Phillipsburg: P&R, 1950), 22.

[86] See Gary Dorrien, *The Making of American Liberal Theology: Imagining Progressive Religion 1805–1900* (Louisville: Westminster John Knox, 2001); Frame, *History of Western Philosophy and Theology*, 214–328; T. A. Noble, "Liberal Theology," in Davie et al., *NDT*, 514–16.

the West, mainly, but not exclusively, within Protestant theology. It arose first in Germany among students and followers of Friedrich Schleiermacher (1768–1834) and Georg Hegel (1770–1831), and then it is primarily associated with Albrecht Ritschl (1822–89), Adolf von Harnack (1851–1930), Wilhelm Herrmann (1846–1922), and, in North America, Walter Rauschenbusch (1861–1918).

This view accepts the Kantian limitations on theology and opts for a theology "from below," that is, grounded in human experience and the historical-critical reconstruction of the Bible. George Lindbeck labels this theology "experiential-expressivist" since theology is done by reflecting on a "common core experience" that is present in all humans and religions with Christianity serving as the "highest" expression.[87] One consequence of this theology, especially for those who accept the Kantian limits, is that it no longer claims to have an "objective" truth about God, self, and the world grounded in God's external word. Instead, it only results in "subjective" conclusions since "revelation" is located in human religious experience. Theology is less about dogma in the historic sense; instead, its main concern is with ethical, social, and political action.

Although classic liberal theology is diverse, there are some common features—all of which depart from orthodoxy and leave us with a redefined Christianity.

First, classic liberal theology was committed to reconstructing Christian belief in light of current knowledge, whether it was current philosophical, scientific, or psychological theories. Its motive was to make Christianity relevant to its "cultured despisers." Yet its "method of correlation" was thoroughly extratextual; that is, the Bible only served as an "authority" for theology as it was interpreted by the standard of human religious experience and the current thought of the day.

Second, it also rejected doctrinal belief on the basis of *sola Scriptura*. The Bible was merely a fallible human book birthed by the religious community that reflects the worldview of the ancient world. Given our common religious experience, the Bible is useful for the church, but only as "corrected in the light of human reason and experience."[88] Thus, all the results of historical criticism were applied to biblical studies, seeking to discern what in Scripture was true and what false. In the Bible we can still find a *timeless core* that is true in any age, but the task of

[87] Lindbeck, *The Nature of Doctrine*, 31–32.

[88] T. A. Noble, "Liberal Theology," 515. Cf. W. A. Hoffecker, "Schleiermacher, Friedrich Daniel Ernst," in Treier and Elwell, *EDT*, 780–81.

biblical scholarship is to separate the "husk" of cultural ideas from the "kernel" of the "essence of Christianity." Indeed, much of "liberal" scholarship was preoccupied with the quests for the historical Jesus and discerning how to speak of Jesus's ongoing *value* for us despite the fact that he was a mere human and not the eternal Son made flesh.

Third, classic liberalism rejected the Creator-creature distinction of orthodox theology and along with it the triune Creator-covenant Lord for an evolutionary, panentheistic view of the God-world relationship.[89] Darwin's evolutionary theory grounded divine immanence at the expense of God's transcendence, explaining how God was involved in the world but not sovereign over it. For classical liberal theologians, God is the soul/life of the world, and as such, God is found in all of life, not merely revelatory events. However, as with deism, panentheism embraces *methodological* naturalism and rejects any kind of effectual, extraordinary divine action.

Fourth, classic liberal theology also rejected the need for God to initiate in sovereign grace to provide a Redeemer from sin. Indeed, classical liberal theologians' view of God does not even allow this to be possible. Further, humans are innately good; our problem is due to the corrupting influences of society. What is needed is the transformation of society by social and political action. By bringing the kingdom of God to this earth, we can build a utopian society of peace and prosperity for all.

Fifth, theological liberalism led to a radical revision of every doctrine of the Christian faith, and as such, it resulted in the construction of a different religion. Even though old theological language was used, what was meant by the terms was contrary to historic theology. Talk of the Trinity, incarnation, atonement, sin, salvation, and so on, continued, but redefined and reconstructed. What resulted was a renewed emphasis on "universalism and pluralism,"[90] within a theology characterized by the lack of "the supernatural, a purely human Jesus, and a gospel of works-righteousness, based on a merely human Scripture."[91]

Responses to "Classic Liberal" Theology. At the beginning of the twentieth century, classic liberal theology made deep inroads into Protestant churches in Europe and North America,

---

[89] "Panentheism" is the view that the world, or "all" (*pan*), is "in" (*en*) "God" (*theos*), thus denying the Creator-creature distinction. "God" is greater than the world but not distinct from it. Both God and the world are eternal and dependent on each other. We will discuss this view more in part 4, chapter 16.

[90] T. A. Noble, "Liberal Theology," 515.

[91] Frame, *History of Western Philosophy and Theology*, 302.

redefining the Christian faith root and branch. Yet, given its embrace of "modern" thought and its doing of a theology "from below" grounded in common human religious experience, it could not escape the charge of Ludwig Feuerbach (1804–72) and the other "masters of suspicion":[92] theological liberalism had reduced "theology to anthropology."[93] In fact, any theology that uncouples itself from its foundation in the triune God and his divine speech will find it difficult to avoid this charge. In addition, its naïve optimism and denial of human depravity was hard to square with two World Wars. As such, it came under severe attack, although its extratextual methodology continues today in different forms tied to the rise of postmodernism, which we will discuss below.

As a consequence, at the beginning of the twentieth century, theological liberalism was rejected by historic Protestant theology and from within its own movement, as evidenced in the rise of neo-orthodoxy. However, it was only in the first rejection of liberalism that there was a consistent return to theology as historically conceived. Let us discuss each of these responses in turn.

First, there was the response of historic Protestant theology in Europe and in North America. In Europe, for example, liberalism was rejected by the work of various Dutch theologians, such as Abraham Kuyper (1837–1920), Herman Bavinck (1854–1921), and Geerhardus Vos (1862–1949), in the discipline of biblical theology, the latter spending most of his teaching career in the United States.

In North America, theological liberalism was rejected by Princeton Theological Seminary, associated with the names of Archibald Alexander (1772–1851), Charles Hodge (1797–1878), A. A. Hodge (1823–86), and B. B. Warfield (1851–1921). This response eventually resulted in the Fundamentalist-Modernist controversies in the 1920s and 1930s and the publication of a collection of twelve pamphlets between 1910 and 1915 called *The Fundamentals,*[94] which defended historic Protestant theology. Specifically, Christians came together from a variety of denominations and identified five core fundamentals of Christian theology that were viewed as

---

[92] The "masters of suspicion" refer to the atheistic challenge against Christian theology as represented by Ludwig Feuerbach (1804–72), Karl Marx (1818–83), Friedrich Nietzsche (1844–1900), and Sigmund Freud (1856–1939).

[93] Ludwig Feuerbach, *The Essence of Christianity,* trans. George Eliot (Buffalo, NY: Prometheus Books, 1989), 336.

[94] See the collection in Charles L. Feinberg, ed., *The Fundamentals for Today* (Grand Rapids: Kregel, 1961).

non-negotiable: Biblical authority and inspiration, the Trinity, Christ's deity and bodily resurrection, the virgin birth, the substitutionary atonement of Christ as the only ground for our justification before God, and the historical reality of Christ's miracles. As a result of the debate over theological liberalism, whole Protestant denominations split, new ones were formed, and new institutions were established, most notably, Westminster Theological Seminary, in Philadelphia, and Fuller Theological Seminary, in California, with a corresponding but later fight for theological orthodoxy among the Southern Baptists in the 1980s–1990s.

A crucial book in the midst of the debate was J. Gresham Machen's *Christianity and Liberalism*, which demonstrated that "classic liberal" theology was a different religion than historic Christianity.[95] Out of these debates eventually arose the growth of "evangelicalism," which saw its mission as to expound, defend, and proclaim the truth of historic Christianity and to recapture territory lost to theological liberalism. In this response, a robust biblical and systematic theology was recaptured. It was placed on the foundation of a revelational epistemology, which once again resulted in a return to a theology "from above" in contrast to "from below."

Second, there was a response to theological liberalism from within its ranks, known by a number of names: dialectical theology, crisis theology, and sometimes neo-orthodox theology. This movement was strongest from the 1920–1960s, and it is most commonly associated with Karl Barth (1886–1968), although initially there were others who identified with the movement, such as Rudolph Bultmann (1884–1976), Friedrich Gogarten (1887–1967), and Emil Brunner (1889–1966). Barth's commentary on Romans (1919) was the beginning of the movement—what Karl Adam said was "the bomb that fell on the playground of the theologians."[96] In the early phase of Barth's thinking, he denied any point of contact between God's revelation and humans. In contrast to liberalism, Barth argued that theology is not warranted because it establishes truths from religious experience, history, or the natural order. Instead, theology is warranted only because God has first spoken to us by his word. Barth's concern about theological liberalism echoed Feuerbach's concern but for different reasons: liberalism had turned theology into anthropology, and all theologies "from below" are not true theologies in any historic meaning of the word.

---

[95] J. Gresham Machen, *Christianity and Liberalism* (Grand Rapids: Eerdmans, 1923).

[96] Cited in Terry Cross, *Dialectic in Karl Barth's Doctrine of God* (New York: Peter Lang, 2001), 82.

However, Barth soon broke with Bultmann and Gogarten since "they based their dialectical theology on human existence in dialectic with God, whereas Barth's dialectic was rooted in the event of revelation and its judgment on human existence and experience."[97] Although Bultmann rejected "classic liberal" theology, he continued its theology "from below" by rejecting the authority of Scripture, the Trinity, the deity of Christ, and the bodily resurrection and embracing methodological naturalism and historical criticism, even "classifying any talk of miracles, angels or demons, or indeed of God's action in the world as 'myth.'"[98] For Bultmann, the Bible interprets Jesus within the mythological framework of the ancient world, but since this framework is wrong, theology must "demythologize" Scripture by stripping away its ancient interpretive framework and replace it with a framework amendable to the modern age. For Bultmann, the extratextual interpretive framework within which the core message of the Bible must be placed is the existentialist philosophy of Martin Heidegger. The result of Bultmann's thought was not a return to orthodox theology grounded in the interpretive framework of Scripture, but the revival of a neo-liberalism that denied that historic Christian theology is possible and that opened the door to the embrace of pluralism and postmodernism.

Barth, on the other hand, did not go the path of Bultmann. Instead, he sought to return to historic theology but in a "new" way based on a Christocentric theism.[99] Yet, Barth continued to affirm the results of historical criticism, which meant that Scripture was fallible. For Barth, God's being is revealed in his acts, specifically the acts that constitute the life and ministry of Christ.[100] In continuity with historic theology, theology is "from above": God must reveal himself to be known, hence a reversal of Kant's approach. Theology begins with God's free and gracious initiative to reveal himself to us in Christ.[101] However, in contrast with historic theology, Barth denied the truth of natural revelation *and* that Scripture *is* the Word of God in a direct sense.

---

[97] T. Bradshaw, "Dialectical Theology," in Davie et al., *NDT*, 256.

[98] T. A. Noble, "Liberal Theology," 515.

[99] See Kevin J. Vanhoozer, *First Theology: God, Scripture and Hermeneutics* (Downers Grove: InterVarsity, 2002), 143–44.

[100] On this point, see George Hunsinger, *How to Read Karl Barth: The Shape of His Theology* (Oxford: Oxford University Press, 1991), 30.

[101] See Karl Barth, *Church Dogmatics*, ed. G. W. Bromiley and T. F. Torrance, 14 vols. (Edinburgh: T&T Clark, 1936–1975), I/1, 150 (hereafter *CD*).

For Barth, God's word "is no mere thing; it is the living, personal and free God,"[102] who communicates to us freely but never in such a way that he is available to us directly. God's word, in other words, "is not a deposit of truth upon which the church can draw, or a set of statements which can be consulted. The word of God is an act which God undertakes. God's word is that complex but unitary event in which God has spoken, speaks and will speak, an event which encounters us through the human means of Scripture and its proclamation in the church."[103] For Barth, God's word *revealed* is Jesus Christ, who is God's direct and objective revelation.[104] Scripture is God's Word *written*, but only *indirectly* as a human, fallible word that witnesses to Christ. But although Scripture is distinguished from God's objective word (Christ), the Bible can *become* revelation by God's free choice in the event of witnessing to Christ.[105] In this way, we have access to Christ through *indirect* means (God's Word written and proclaimed) *and* only due to God's free decision to act and reveal him to us. God's self-revelation is not ours for the taking; it only comes to us as an event by God's free decision to act and make it so.[106]

Barth's view is an improvement on classic liberal theology, and his work is viewed as the forerunner to the postliberal school that attempts to receive Scripture as the church's book and to read Scripture as a unified canon. Yet Barth's view of divine revelation and its relationship to Scripture is unstable, a point we will return to in part 2. Although Barth attempts to do a theology "from above," his rejection of the Bible's view of inspiration, authority, and reliability inevitably requires extratextual criteria to determine its truthfulness, which renders the theological task problematic on the Bible's own terms.

Postmodernism and the Impossibility of Historic Systematic Theology

In Western culture, most acknowledge an important shift from a modern to a postmodern society. The seeds sown in the Enlightenment, although developed in different ways, continued to shape the way modernity thought about reality and knowledge of it. By the early part of the twentieth century, ideas forged in modernism were worked out, which resulted

[102] Barth, *CD* I/1, 198.

[103] John Webster, *Karl Barth* (New York: Continuum, 2000), 55.

[104] See Barth, *CD* I/2, 1–25.

[105] On this point, see Barth, *CD* I/1, 112–13.

[106] See Barth, 149.

in a further change of plausibility structures. The result, as Taylor noted, was that it now became *impossible* to believe in the objective truths and ultimate concerns of the Christian worldview. The exact nature of the shift and its implications for theology remain debated, but most acknowledge that something significant has occurred.[107] Even the term "postmodernism" is difficult to define because of its diverse use. For our purposes, however, an exact definition is not required; we only need to focus on its key ideas that have resulted in a new "social imaginary."

"Postmodernism" breaks from the Enlightenment's confidence in the reality of objective truth and/or our ability to know it. The French sociologist Jean-François Lyotard first used the term to signal an important shift in epistemology and cultural values.[108] Lyotard described the postmodern condition as skepticism of our ability to gain universal truth: "incredulity toward metanarratives."[109] The prefix *post* refers to a move away from the "modern" ideals of rationality and progress.[110] Specifically, postmodernism rejects three conditions of modern knowledge: "(1) the appeal to metanarratives as a foundationalist criterion of legitimacy, (2) the outgrowth of strategies of legitimation and exclusion, and (3) a desire for criteria of legitimacy in the moral as well as the epistemological domain."[111] In brief, postmodernism is suspicious of "grand narratives" and universal, objective truth by which we can validate some things (e.g., ideas, events, people) and invalidate others.

While this mindset sounds like a radical departure from modernism, postmodernism is best viewed as the logical extension of the autonomous "turn to the subject/self" that first occurred in Descartes and then was radicalized in Kant's "constructivist" epistemology. Postmodern thought continues to embrace evolutionary naturalism that rejects a created order planned and determined by God. In addition, it teaches that our "construction" of the world is tied to

---

[107] See Myron B. Penner, ed., *Christianity and the Postmodern Turn: Six Views* (Grand Rapids: Brazos Press, 2005).

[108] Sire, *Universe Next Door*, 213.

[109] Jean-François Lyotard, *The Postmodern Condition: A Report on Knowledge*, trans. Geoff Bennington and Brian Massumi, Theory and History of Literature 10 (Minneapolis: University of Minnesota Press, 1984), 24.

[110] Kevin J. Vanhoozer, "Theology and the Condition of Postmodernity: A Report on Knowledge (of God)," in *The Cambridge Companion to Postmodern Theology*, ed. Kevin J. Vanhoozer (Cambridge: Cambridge University Press, 2003), 7.

[111] Vanhoozer, 9.

contingent language systems that cannot describe reality "as it objectively is" (i.e., noumena). As such, postmodern thought continues to embrace Kant's limitations on our ability to know objective, universal truth, especially regarding metaphysics, ethics, and theology. Although postmodernity critiques the hubris of earlier thought, by starting with human autonomy and not the triune God of Scripture, it offers no better alternative to modernism. Instead, the "postmodern condition" is only able to offer a philosophy/theology "from below" and no epistemological warrant for objective truth: "no longer can we aspire to the knowledge of angels, much less a God's-eye point of view."[112] And, sadly, the consequences of the view do not foster "tolerance" of all ideas as claimed; rather, it only offers intolerance *and* an outright, even hostile rejection of historic Christian theology.

Two ideas of postmodernity reveal why its "social imaginary" rejects the possibility of a theology "from above." First, "knowledge" is merely a subjective human construction "relative to the interests and purposes of the institutions (e.g., the state, the academy, society) out of which such claims emerge,"[113] and it is the means by which political power is exerted.[114] Second, "God" is merely the non-personal and developmental dynamics of a changing world (i.e., an embrace of panentheism). Let us look at each of these in turn.

Postmodern Epistemology: A "Constructivist" View of Knowledge

Epistemology again provides one of the key ways by which we can see the most fundamental intellectual shifts from historic Christianity to the modern and now postmodern world.[115] Historic theology is grounded in a revelational epistemology: truth is universal and objective because the triune Creator-covenant Lord is the source and standard of truth, whose decree and plan includes everything (Eph 1:11). In other words, God's knowledge is *archetypal* while human knowledge is *ectypal*; that is, our knowledge is a subset of God's knowledge. Thus, due

---

[112] Vanhoozer, 10.

[113] Kevin J. Vanhoozer, "Postmodern Theology," in Davie et al., *NDT*, 689.

[114] For example, see Herbert Marcuse, "Repressive Tolerance," in Robert Paul Wolff, Barrington Moore Jr., and Herbert Marcuse, *A Critique of Pure Tolerance* (Boston: Beacon, 1970), 81–123. On these points, see Thomas Sowell, *The Quest for Cosmic Justice* (New York: Simon & Schuster, 1999).

[115] For a helpful discussion of these shifts, see John S. Feinberg, *Can You Believe It's True? Christian Apologetics in a Modern and Postmodern Era* (Wheaton: Crossway, 2013), 37–76.

to divine revelation in nature and Scripture, it is possible for humans to have finite, objective, and true knowledge.

In the modern era, philosophy took a decisive "turn to the subject." Human reason, under the limits of classical foundationalism, sought for objective truth independent of divine revelation. Modernism believed that if autonomous human reason followed the correct methods, it could offer a "metanarrative" to explain reality, knowledge, and behavior. Coupled with this epistemological rationalism was methodological naturalism, and together they formed an entire social imaginary that necessitated a total redefinition of Christian theology.

Now in its "constructivist" "turn to the self," postmodernism rejects foundationalism, not by returning to a revelational epistemology, but by pressing the assumptions of rationalism to their logical end. Building on Kant's "constructivist" view of the mind and on evolutionary naturalism, postmodernism denies the modern assumption of a universal, common human nature and set of mental categories, thus elevating the subjectivity of the self to first-order status. The result: the acquisition of objective truth and knowing reality "as it really is" is simply impossible. What remains are only forms of coherentism, pragmatism, or raw political power.[116] This is not to say that postmodernism rejects all rationality. Instead, what is impossible is universal reason given the finitude of humans. As Kevin Vanhoozer states it: "What counts as rational is relative to the prevailing narrative in a society or institution."[117] For this reason, postmodernism is associated with the attempt to "deconstruct" anyone who thinks that they have a universal viewpoint.

Central to postmodern thought is the attempt to undo the link between language and reality—"logocentrism"—that once characterized Western thought, indebted to Christian theology. Living off the borrowed capital of Christianity, the modern era continued its logocentrism. However, in the postmodern era, the grounding for logocentrism became difficult to sustain. In place of a referential view of language, postmoderns substituted a constructivist view.[118] Rather than conceiving of the mind as a "mirror of nature" consistent with a correspondence theory of truth, postmoderns insist that humans view reality through the lens of language and culture. Reality is a "social construct," or as Taylor suggests, postmoderns adopt a

---

[116] See Feinberg, *Can You Believe It's True?*, 37–76; and James Lindsay and Helen Pluckrose, *Cynical Theories* (Durham: Pitchstone Publishing, 2020), 45–66.

[117] Vanhoozer, "Theology and the Condition of Postmodernity," 10.

[118] See Kevin J. Vanhoozer, *Is There a Meaning in This Text? The Bible, the Reader, and the Morality of Literary Knowledge* (Grand Rapids: Zondervan, 1998), 43–147.

"poiesis" view of reality in contrast to a "mimetic" view.[119] The latter is the Christian view: the self and the world are planned, created, and ordered by God, and the human task is *to discover* what God has made and conform to it. In other words, our high calling as humans is "to think God's thoughts after him." The former is postmodern: the self and the world are not created and ordered by God; rather, they are the result of blind, impersonal forces. Our human task, then, is *to create or construct* ourselves according to our dictates, which from a Christian view is the height of sin and rebellion against God.

As these ideas are lived out, and since "objective" authorities are simply "subjective" constructs "designed by the powerful to intimidate and to harm the weak,"[120] "overthrowing them" is our "highest" calling, entailing that we are to throw off the restraints of any "external" authority, especially the authority of God and his created/natural order. And given the postmodern turn to the self, what Taylor calls "expressive individualism," the idea that "each of us finds our meaning by giving expression to our own feelings and desires,"[121] is now center stage. Not surprisingly, what emerges in postmodern thought is the priority of the psychological "self" and the "construction" of our own identities unrestrained by any external authority. Yet, with the "death of God," what also emerges is the power of the "state," where there is no longer *lex rex* (God's law over the king), but the reverse.[122] As postmodern thought is inevitably politicized, freedom is not the result, but a growing totalitarianism, which is on full display around the world. In such thinking, Calvin's view as reflective of historic theology, namely, that a true knowledge of the self, indeed true freedom and liberty of the self, is first grounded in the knowledge of God because the triune God is the source and standard of truth, is viewed as simply impossible, even dangerous.

---

[119] Taylor, *A Secular Age*, 97–99.

[120] Trueman, *Rise and Triumph*, 50. Cf. Pluckrose and Lindsay, who note that in "postmodern thought, language is believed to have enormous power to control society and how we think and thus is inherently dangerous." As a result, "since discourses are believed to create and maintain oppression, they have to be carefully monitored and deconstructed." *Cynical Theories*, 39–40.

[121] Trueman, 46; Cf. Taylor, *A Secular Age*, 473–504. Alasdair MacIntyre calls this "emotivism": "all evaluative judgments and more specifically all moral judgments are *nothing but* expressions of preference, expressions of attitude or feeling." *After Virtue: A Study in Moral Theory*, 2nd ed. (London: Duckworth, 1985), 11–12.

[122] See Samuel Rutherford, *Lex, Rex, or The Law and the Prince* (1644; repr., Harrisonburg, VA: Sprinkle, 1982).

On these points, Friedrich Nietzsche (1844–1900) is a crucial forerunner of current thought. In his attempt to take "the death of God" seriously, he concluded that the universe has no inherent meaning, that there are no universal moral norms, and that knowledge is simply the "will to power." Nietzsche applied Kant's constructivist view stripped of its deism and argued that the desire to schematize, to impose order and form on the multiplicity of impressions and sensations is the will to power. Truth is simply the invention of the philosophers, yet humans adopt "useful fictions" that serve as "truths." And as these "truths" have proved their utility, they become embedded in language. But we must not think that our language mirrors reality. All truths are fictions, and all fictions are merely subjective interpretations, and in the end, humans are called "to seek our own greatness" and to "reject moral and religious ideas that restrict the full expression of our will to power."[123] The "turn to the subject" is now complete; the world and all that is in it are now viewed totally "from below" or within an "immanent frame,"[124] which is "preoccupied with the self-actualization and fulfillment of the individual."[125]

Jacques Derrida (1930–2004) also applied to philosophy "the death of logocentrism." Derrida's "deconstructive" project sought to reveal that humans do not have objective truth by applying Kant's constructivism to a world "produced" by evolutionary naturalism. Derrida argues, against Descartes, that the self cannot know its own mind; our consciousness is not pure. Instead, the self is located in a world "produced" by blind, buzzing confusion and limited to a particular sociopolitical context and thus "determined" by its language, culture, and time. As we interpret the world, there is no access to "reality-as-it-really-is" (noumena) independent of our social-linguistic "constructions"; no interpretation rises to the level of a God's-eye viewpoint, and no *one* language "map[s] the contours of ultimate reality."[126] The result: the traditional study of metaphysics and theology is simply impossible. In place of comprehensive theories, all we have are relative confessions about how things look to us. All we have is subjectivity; we have no access to what is real, true, or good. Thus, Derrida and postmodern

---

[123] Frame, *History of Western Philosophy and Theology*, 332. This thought continues in Michel Foucault and the Frankfurt School associated with "critical theory." See Christopher Watkin, *Michel Foucault* (Phillipsburg: P&R, 2018); and Trueman, *Rise and Triumph*, 225–68.

[124] Taylor, *A Secular Age*, 539–93.

[125] Trueman, *Rise and Triumph*, 80.

[126] Vanhoozer, "Postmodern Theology," 689; Cf. Christopher Watkin, *Jacques Derrida* (Phillipsburg: P&R, 2017).

thinkers reject the "natural," that is, nature as created and ordered by God, and ironically, with the "death of God," what is also at stake is the "death of humanity."

Postmodern thought, as represented by thinkers such as Derrida, Lyotard, and Michel Foucault is now "applied" in a decidedly "critical theory" direction, resulting in the privileging of social constructions of identity and the application of raw political power. In this regard, the influence of Karl Marx (1818–83) is significant both in the larger culture and in theology.[127] Gone is any appeal to the God of Scripture to ground human knowledge and the idea of a created, natural order. The result: the attempt to reconstruct society by throwing off any remnant of the past, especially Christianity, and to rebuild society on the "subjective" ground of a socially constructed human self. As the postmodern turn has rejected the possibility of historic theology, it has done so by establishing an opposing extratextual "metanarrative," thus resulting in a worldview clash of life-and-death proportions. As with modernism, and now with postmodernism, the attempt to correlate theologies "from below" with historic Christianity's theology "from above" is doomed to failure, a point we will return to in the next chapter.

Postmodern Science: Naturalism, but . . .

The movement from a modern to a postmodern outlook has also brought a corresponding change in science: "it is naturalism, but . . ."[128] According to the predominant scientific paradigm of modernism, the world is a closed system of causal laws. Today, however, science has switched paradigms to quantum and relativity theories that view the world as integrated, contingent, and continuously changing. John Feinberg helpfully summarizes this change in perspective:

> In contrast to Newtonian physics, which saw the universe as composed of static, changeless bits of matter that interact according to set natural laws, the new science claims that things in our world are interrelated in a continuous process of change and becoming. Even in the most solid bits of matter (at the atomic and subatomic levels) things are not static but in motion. . . . Moreover, as opposed to Newtonian physics which held that physical things interact according to set physical laws, quantum

[127] On Marx, see Trueman, *Rise and Triumph*, 176–84, 225–64; Cf. William D. Dennison, *Karl Marx* (Phillipsburg: P&R, 2017).

[128] This phrase and concept is taken from Feinberg, *No One Like Him*, 104.

physics claims that there is a certain indeterminacy at least at the atomic and subatomic levels of existence.[129]

At the same time that scientific paradigms have changed, evolutionary theory remains entrenched. As in the modern era, the establishment of evolution as a basic presupposition comes as a necessary part of the larger move to an a priori definition of science that rules out any consideration of the supernatural and non-material. With the acceptance of quantum mechanics and relativity theory, however, some believe the door has opened for a return to an affirmation of God acting in our world.[130] Even so, most postmoderns still view the universe as a closed system, hence their application of methodological naturalism to all academic disciplines. The primary reason for this adherence to naturalism is a refusal to return to a trinitarian theism, which can rationally account for the miraculous. If postmoderns have a conception of God, it has turned in a decidedly panentheistic direction.[131]

Although the concept of panentheism is not monolithic, the most rigorous theological view of it thinks of "God" as the universe in constant progression (opposed to permanence), with historical events as the basic building blocks (instead of substances).[132] This kind of panentheism pictures all reality as a series of events, each of which has two poles. The mental or primordial pole is all the possibilities that actual entities can become; the physical or consequent pole is the world, God's body, which is the progressive realization of the various possibilities. In this metaphysical scheme, God is viewed as an event who is *in* everything, thus rejecting the Creator-creature distinction and making God correlative with the world. God and the world are not identical, but neither are they distinct; they are mutually dependent without one being subordinate to the other. The world is viewed as a moment within the divine life, and since God is immanent to the world, he is undergoing a process of self-development and growth. God is not the transcendent, sovereign Creator and Lord; instead, he is (in) the natural processes of evolution by which the world and history take shape.

---

[129] Feinberg, 104–5.

[130] See, for example, Evans, *Historical Christ*, 137–69.

[131] See John W. Cooper, *Panentheism, the Other God of the Philosophers: From Plato to the Present* (Grand Rapids: Baker Academic, 2006); also see Kevin J. Vanhoozer, *Remythologizing Theology: Divine Action, Passion, and Authorship* (Cambridge: Cambridge University Press, 2010), 81–138.

[132] See John B. Cobb Jr. and David R. Griffin, *Process Theology: An Introductory Exposition* (Philadelphia: Westminster Press, 1976).

This evolutionary view of God fits well with current "scientific" conceptions of the world, and it supports many familiar postmodern beliefs: "a God who is immanent and relational; a God whose very being interpenetrates all things and hence underscores the connectedness of all things; a God who is not static but is constantly changing as he responds to our needs; and a God to whom we can contribute value as well as one who enhances our existence."[133] John Feinberg rightly reminds us that this "process" conception of God "poses a formidable threat to traditional Christian understanding of God, and it also offers a way to synthesize various non-evangelical postmodern notions about God."[134] In fact, a panentheistic view of God looms large in non-evangelical theology today. And even within evangelical theology, movements such as "open theism" have embraced some tenets of panentheism, which renders the historic understanding of theology problematic, along with redefining almost every doctrinal area.[135]

Postmodern Hermeneutics: Reading the Bible as an "Indeterminate" Authority

Building on our discussion of postmodern epistemology, we now turn to the role of language and the place of hermeneutics in current thought. If the modern era is identified with the "subjective turn," the postmodern era may be identified with the "linguistic turn." Inconsistent with its own starting points, modernity assumed that reason is universal and impervious to differences of culture and language; postmodernity is more consistent on this point. Applying Kant's "constructivism," postmoderns insist that our mental categories impose themselves on the world, thus continuing the distinction between phenomena and noumena. Yet postmoderns reject Kant's view that our mental categories are universal and necessary; instead, they are linguistic and arbitrary. It follows, then, "that there is no commonly agreed way of interpreting reality. The distinctions that make up the 'natural order'

---

[133] Feinberg, *No One Like Him*, 142.

[134] Feinberg, 142.

[135] On open theism, see Clark H. Pinnock et al., *The Openness of God: A Biblical Challenge to the Traditional Understanding of God* (Downers Grove: InterVarsity, 1994); John Sanders, *The God Who Risks: A Theology of Divine Providence* (Downers Grove: InterVarsity, 1998); Thomas Jay Oord, *The Uncontrolling Love of God: An Open and Relational Account of Providence* (Downers Grove: InterVarsity, 2015). We will discuss open theism in part 4, ch. 16.

are neither 'natural' nor 'given' but rather artificial and man-made. There is no such thing as an absolute, God's-eye point of view on reality, only a number of finite and fallible human perspectives."[136]

Postmodernism's linguistic turn and artificial (self-constructed) view of reality has produced a constructivist approach to meaning and the biblical texts. Despite differences in hermeneutics in the Christian tradition, Christian theology has always prioritized the literal sense tied to discovering God's intent in and through the human authors of Scripture. As such, Scripture has a determinate authority. As Calvin stated, "It is the first business of an interpreter to let his author say what he does say, instead of attributing to him what we think he ought to say."[137] Modernism rejected the Bible's inspiration and reliability and sought to discover "what really happened" *behind* the text, but still had the same goal of interpreting the text according to the author's intent.[138] Both historic theology and the modern eras held to hermeneutical realism: "the position that believes meaning to be prior to and independent of the process of interpretation."[139] The postmodern era, however, approaches the Bible with hermeneutical *non*-realism; the reader brings meaning to the text in the process of interpretation. As such, this constructivist approach guarantees universal subjectivity, and it renders the Bible's authority indeterminate. In fact, in postmodern thought, biblical authority has more to do with the community than with the text itself, hence the loss of *sola Scriptura*. Vanhoozer helpfully summarizes postmodern hermeneutical philosophy:

> Hermeneutic philosophers no longer consider knowledge as the result of a disinterested subject observing facts, but rather as an interpretive effort whereby a subject rooted in a particular history and tradition seeks to understand the strange by means

---

136 Vanhoozer, *Is There a Meaning?*, 49; Pluckrose and Lindsay note that "*all* claims to truth are value-laden constructs of culture. This is called *cultural constructivism* or *social constructivism*. The scientific method, in particular, is not seen as a better way of producing and legitimizing knowledge than any other, but as one cultural approach among many, as corrupted by biased reasoning as any other" (emphasis original). *Cynical Theories*, 32.

137 Preface to John Calvin's *Commentary on Romans*, cited in Vanhoozer, *Is There a Meaning?*, 47.

138 Vanhoozer explains the difference between intent and truth: "In historical critical exegesis, then, the original sense is authoritative, not in the sense of being necessarily true, but insofar as it remains the norm for establishing the meaning of a passage (which may be true or false)." *Is There a Meaning?*, 48.

139 Vanhoozer, 48.

> of the familiar. Instead of "uninterpreted fact" serving as grist for the mill of "objective reason," both fact and reason alike are what they are because of their place in history and tradition. Hermeneutics is a cousin to historical consciousness; the realization that we do not know things directly and immediately suggests that knowledge is the result of interpretation. Reality is a text to be interpreted, mediated by language, history, culture, and tradition.[140]

Postmodernism, then, agrees with modernism's rejection of the Bible's universal authority but for different reasons. Modernism denies the text's truthfulness and thus rejects its authority. Postmodernism reads Scriptures but only according to the reader's or community's interpretive experience, thus rejecting its inherent authority. Rather than reading Scripture as objectively true, the postmodern hermeneutic transforms the text into "an echo chamber in which we see ourselves and hear our own voices."[141] The modernist critic reads the Bible according to the author's intent but then rejects the Bible's historical and theological claims. The postmodernist interpreter argues that "the text has no stable or decidable meaning, or that what meaning is there is biased and ideologically distorted. The result is that the Bible is either not recognized as making claims or, if it is, that these claims are treated as ideologically suspect."[142] Either way, the result of modernism or postmodernism is that the concept of Scripture as the *norma normans* (ruling rule) for all of our theological formulations is rendered impossible.

Postmodern Consequences: The Impossibility of Historic Christian Theology

If Enlightenment-modernist thought rendered historic systematic theology implausible, then postmodern thought renders it impossible—*if* viewed according to their respective worldviews and plausibility structures. For different reasons, they both leave us with a theology "from below," constructed from the fabric of human experience, whether individual or communal, and within the confines of a methodological naturalism. In both ways, as D. A. Carson noted a number

---

[140] Vanhoozer, 20.
[141] Vanhoozer, 20.
[142] Vanhoozer, 24.

of years ago, God has been "gagged," thus leading to a redefinition of theology.[143] At stake is whether theology is a discipline that renders true, objective knowledge of the triune God.

Although classic liberal theology attempted to maintain the "uniqueness" of Christ as the highest expression of God-consciousness and moral virtue, its "experiential-expressivist" ground undermined the true uniqueness and absoluteness of Christianity. Yet, most postmodern theology has doubled down on modern ideas by radicalizing them, which has resulted in a plethora of *theologies*, all of which embrace some form of theological pluralism. Within a postmodern view of God, self, and the world, there is no place for an authoritative, fully trustworthy first-order word that yields a God's-eye interpretation of his mighty acts in redemptive history. Nor is there a place for the Jesus of the Bible, who is God the Son incarnate, our *exclusive, unique, and all-sufficient* Lord and Savior. Postmodern thought still leaves us on the wrong side of Lessing's ditch, and today Troeltsch's view dominates, namely, that Christ is no different in kind or degree from other religious leaders or religions. In this view, it is impossible to say anything certain or unique about Jesus, let alone any point of Christian doctrine.

Within postmodern thought, a variety of "neo-liberal" theologies have emerged—liberation-Marxist, feminist, LGBTQ, and so on. Some have tried to categorize these theologies as deconstructive, reconstructive, liberationist, post-conservative, and so on.[144] However, the best way to categorize them is as extratextual in contrast to intratextual. The former category refers to theologies that continue the trajectory of modern/postmodern thought by embracing the "method of correlation" and interpreting Scripture within a conceptual scheme "outside" (*extra*) of Scripture. Such theologies are "from below," although the "below" may differ. For example, for some the *extra* may be a specific philosophical or scientific view or simply the privileging of human religious experience as interpreted by some current conceptual scheme. However, regardless of what the extratextual view is, when combined with Scripture, it always results in syncretism, something Scripture forbids (2 Cor 10:5; Col 2:8–10). Such theologies are a departure from and rejection of historic Christian theology and, as Machen wrote many years ago, represent a theology in antithesis to historic Christianity.

---

[143] See Carson, *Gagging of God.*

[144] For examples of postmodern theologies, see Vanhoozer, *Cambridge Companion to Postmodern Theology*; Terrence W. Tilley, *Postmodern Theologies: The Challenge of Religious Diversity* (Maryknoll: Orbis, 1995).

Instead, what is needed is a return to what Paul taught us at Athens as we noted in chapter 1. Theology must be intratextual, that is, a theology "from above" that starts with the triune God and his spoken word both in nature and Scripture. Priority is given to the language, self-description, categories, and framework of Scripture as the "spectacles" by which we view the world and make theological conclusions. Scripture functions as our final authority and interpretive grid by which we view the world. It is only on this epistemological ground that we can say anything objectively true about God, self, and the world. Yet not all intratextual theologies are equal.

Some within post-liberalism claim, along with some post-conservatives, to be intratextual. Both views are often seen as the continuation of Barth's attempt to overcome the restrictions of "modernism."[145] They attempt to return to a revelational ground for theology and, as such, are identified as intratextual or, in the words of George Lindbeck, "cultural-linguistic." Instead of translating Scripture into an extratextual view, these theologies seek to "redescribe reality within the scriptural framework."[146] Theological statements and doctrines function as second-order rules of grammar by which the church establishes the "language-game" of Christian thinking, speaking, and living. But, in contrast to historic theology, theological language does not make direct truth claims. Instead, it functions more like Kantian "regulative" principles to govern the church's thought and life. However, this is problematic.

If doctrinal statements do not make direct truth claims, then is our theology true to reality? One reason why post-liberalism adopts this view is their weakened view of Scripture's reliability. Like Barth, post-liberalism has a thinned view of Scripture, and hence, it never fully escapes the problem bequeathed by modern/postmodern thought. If Scripture is not reliable, how does it function as a sufficient warrant for our theology, and how does it warrant truths of universal significance? Once again, Lessing's ugly ditch rears its head, demanding that we have

[145] Post-liberalism is often identified with the Yale school associated with such people as Hans Frei and George Lindbeck. See George Hunsinger, "Postliberal Theology," in Vanhoozer, *Cambridge Companion to Postmodern Theology*, 42–57. Post-conservative theology is similar to post-liberal, but instead of emerging out of the main line Protestant denominations, it emerged out of evangelicalism. For examples, see Grenz and Franke, *Beyond Foundationalism* (see chap. 1, n. 35); cf. Roger E. Olson, *Reformed and Always Reforming: The Postconservative Approach to Evangelical Theology* (Grand Rapids: Baker Academic, 2007).

[146] Grenz and Franke, *Beyond Foundationalism*, 46.

some kind of extratextual criteria to determine what is true. But what exactly is that criteria? As Michael Horton notes, "Like the earlier biblical theology movement, narrative theology [post-liberalism] seems divided between (intratextual) faith and (extratextual) doubt, a characteristically modern dilemma."[147] Such a view renders problematic its claim to be intratexual, something that is essential for a normative theology "from above."

Concluding Reflection: The Church's Need in Every Generation

Ideas have consequences, especially ideas central to one's entire theology or worldview. Historic Christian theology has always been viewed as an objective discipline, indeed as the "queen" of the sciences, that yields a finite but true, objective knowledge of God, self, and the world. But from the Enlightenment era to our own day, this view of theology is now considered impossible. Why? As we have outlined, it is due to a change of "ideas" tied to entire worldview shifts.

Rather than simply bemoan the situation, we need to take this intellectual history seriously. This is not only the world in which we minister and proclaim the truth of the gospel, but it also teaches us that what is needed is not conformity to our Zeitgeist, but a self-conscious rejection of it. The way forward is not doing a theology "from below" fashioned after the current views of God, self, and the world. Instead, we need to follow Paul's example at Athens: to pursue a theology "from above" as we seek to bring our entire thought captive to Christ on the Bible's own terms.

In every generation, the church must learn to articulate, defend, and proclaim the truth from a revelational ground and not a modern or postmodern one. Apart from doing so, we will cease to speak rightly of God, and we will have little to say to our world. Truth is only possible on *theological* grounds tied to God and his word. In fact, the modern/postmodern epistemologies leave us with an "authority" crisis, which ultimately reduces to internal contradictions, self-refutations, and societal disaster. Today, *the* pressing battle is whether there is a foundation for objective truth. Current thought leaves us with little ground to stand on. However, for the church, we do not do theology based on changing human traditions; instead, we do theology on the only true and sure foundation: the triune God and his incarnate and spoken word (Col 2:8–9; Heb 1:1–3). To this subject, we now turn.

---

[147] Michael S. Horton, *Covenant and Eschatology: The Divine Drama* (Louisville: Westminster John Knox, 2002), 169.

CHAPTER 3

Systematic Theology: The Foundation

Introduction

In the last chapter, we discussed why so many in our day reject the historic understanding of systematic theology as an objective discipline that yields true knowledge of God, self, and the world. Rather than bemoan the situation, as David Wells reminds us, we need to recognize the fact that Christian theology is now done amidst the disintegration of the Enlightenment world and its replacement by the postmodern ethos and pluralism.[1] As modernism first took hold and then gave way to a postmodern mindset, a distrust of Scripture and all that it teaches gradually arose. The entire "social imaginary" of Christianity was gradually replaced by views opposed to historic theology by extratextual conceptual schemes that resulted in a change of plausibility structures. No longer was Scripture viewed as the final authority for establishing theological truth claims; instead, if theology is done at all, *sola Scriptura* was replaced by other criteria governed by a variety of extratextual viewpoints. Whether we like it or not, this is the cultural context in which we live, do theology, and, as the church, proclaim the truth of the gospel.

[1] Wells, *Above All Earthly Pow'rs* (see chap. 1, n. 2).

Our survey of the last four centuries of intellectual history was not for the sake of curiosity. Instead, it was done first to learn lessons to help us do theology today. The study of history not only sets the context of our time; it also helps us avoid the pitfalls of the past. As we stand on the shoulders of those who have gone before us, we learn both what *to do* and what *not to do*. The church is always in danger of compromise and syncretism, and to heed the warnings of Scripture to build our lives and thinking on Christ and not on false ideologies of our day (Rom 12:2; Col 2:6–8), we must learn from the past so that we do not repeat its mistakes. Second, given that so many view the task of historic theology as impossible, it is incumbent on us to explain the foundation on which we build (1 Pet 3:15). If we reject theologies "from below" as destructive of theology, then where do we start? What is the foundation for a theology "from above"?

So before we turn to theological formulation, we need to construct the Bible's own structure of belief, thus giving the epistemological warrant for theology as an objective science. This will then lead to the next chapter: a discussion of theological method. Given that God and his word are the foundation for our theology, how should we read Scripture so that we are warranted in our move from the biblical text (canon) to theological and dogmatic formulation (concept)?[2]

Learning from Intellectual History to Avoid Its Mistakes

There are at least two lessons to learn from our survey of intellectual history.

First, the central debate today is whether truth is possible and, if it is, its grounding. In previous eras of the church, this was *not* the principal issue, but today it is. As the plausibility structures have changed, people no longer think that objective truth is possible to attain, and sadly this mindset has also seeped into the church.[3]

---

[2] For the use of "canon" and "concept," see Kevin J. Vanhoozer, "From Canon to Concept: 'Same' and 'Other' in the Relation between Biblical and Systematic Theology," *SBET* 12, no. 2 (1994): 96–124.

[3] For example, in the State of Theology (2020) poll (https://thestateoftheology.com), 23% of self-identified evangelicals agreed with the statement "Religious belief is a matter of personal opinion; it is not about objective truth," in contrast to 54% of the general public.

Evangelical theology cannot ignore these cultural trends if it is to remain faithful to the truth of God and his word in our generation. No doubt, every era of the church has faced skeptics and critics, but what we see today, especially in the West, is a skepticism tied to a post-Christian culture, resulting from an intentional shift away from a Christian view of the world. The current rejection of historic theology is directly related to the larger intellectual and cultural shifts that have occurred in our society over centuries, resulting in the questioning of Scripture and replacing revealed theology with extratextual constructed views of reality. As this occurred, the plausibility structures changed, which made belief in the uniqueness and normativity of Christian theology seem impossible, irrelevant, and now even intolerant. Thus, the first lesson to learn from our survey of intellectual history is that the church is in a worldview clash with opposing views *and* that historic theology must start self-consciously from the Bible's own view of God, self, and the world and *not* the social imaginaries of our age. The debate today is not over merely this or that point, but over entire worldviews and visions of reality.[4]

Years ago, Francis Schaeffer made this exact point, which is even more prescient today:

> The present chasm between the generations has been brought about almost entirely by a change in the concept of truth. . . .
>
> The tragedy of our situation today is that men and women are being fundamentally affected by the new way of looking at truth, and yet they have never even analyzed the drift which has taken place. Young people from Christian homes are brought up in the old framework of truth. Then they are subjected to the modern framework. In time they become confused because they do not understand the alternatives with which they are being presented. Confusion becomes bewilderment, and before long they are overwhelmed. This is unhappily true not only of young people, but of many pastors, Christian educators, evangelists and missionaries as well.

---

[4] Steven Cowan and James Spiegel capture the basic sense of a "worldview": "A worldview is a conceptual scheme or intellectual framework by which a person organizes and interprets experience. More specifically, a worldview is a set of beliefs, values, and presuppositions concerning life's most fundamental issues. You might say it is a *perspective* on reality. Like tinted glasses, a worldview 'colors' the way we see things and shapes our interpretation of the world. And, it must be emphasized, *everyone* has a worldview." *The Love of Wisdom: A Christian Introduction to Philosophy* (Nashville: B&H Academic, 2009), 7.

So this change in the concept of the way we come to knowledge and truth is the most crucial problem, as I understand it, facing Christianity today.[5]

One implication of the worldview clash we face is that the church must learn to think in terms of entire viewpoints in antithesis to each other. As Schaeffer also perceptively noted,

> Today we have a weakness in our educational process in failing to understand the natural associations between the disciplines. We tend to study all our disciplines in unrelated parallel lines. This tends to be true in both Christian and secular education. This is one of the reasons why evangelical Christians have been taken by surprise at the tremendous shift that has come in our generation. We have studied our exegesis as exegesis, our theology as theology, our philosophy as philosophy; we study something about art as art; we study music as music, without understanding that these are things of man, and the things of man are never unrelated parallel lines.[6]

So what is the first lesson to learn? Our battle today is over entire worldviews, which demands that theology must start from the Bible's own view of reality, knowledge, moral norms (intratextual), and not from some extratextual conception of the world.

Second, we must learn that the reason *why* we must think in terms of entire worldviews is because worldviews/theologies are "package" deals. Beliefs within a worldview are not isolated; instead, they are part of an entire network of beliefs that are mutually (inter)dependent on each other. In fact, this is precisely what we discovered in our survey of intellectual history. Theology is never done in a piecemeal and neutral way—it relies on an entire nexus of theological-philosophical commitments. Theological conclusions depend on and presuppose entire theological visions, not isolated parts. J. I. Packer stated it this way: "theology is a seamless robe, a circle within which everything links up with everything else through its common grounding in God."[7] Every theological doctrine already assumes, implicitly or explicitly, an entire theology. This insight is not new, but in light of the last 400 years, it should be more evident to us, and it is a vital lesson to learn.

---

[5] Francis A. Schaeffer, *The God Who Is There*, in *Complete Works of Francis A. Schaeffer*, 1:5–6 (emphasis his) (see chap. 1, n. 36).

[6] Francis A. Schaeffer, *Escape from Reason*, in *Complete Works of Francis A. Schaeffer*, 1:211.

[7] Packer, "Encountering Present-Day Views," 61 (see chap. 1, n. 23).

We can explore the integrated nature of entire theological visions in two complementary ways: (1) by examining the presuppositions of those who departed from orthodoxy, which resulted in a whole set of assumptions that together opposed historic theology; (2) by examining how historic theology hangs together as a whole in contrast to the extratextual views of the modern/postmodern world.

First, in our survey of intellectual history and its effects on historic theology, we discovered that a crucial reason for its rejection was due to a priori shifts in worldview: the Enlightenment's "turn to the subject" and embrace of deism, the espousal of historical criticism along with its methodological naturalism, the later acceptance of a naturalistic-evolutionary view of reality, and postmodernism's "linguistic turn" and rejection of all metanarratives. These shifts in worldview turned in one direction—away from historic Christian theology—thus questioning such theology's plausibility, coherence, and legitimacy. When the defining beliefs of the modern/postmodern view are scrutinized, each can be seen as an implicit or explicit rejection of the truthfulness of historic Christianity and the worldview supporting it.

For this reason, the methodology of most modern/postmodern theologies is extratextual; that is, they are theologies done according to an ideology/worldview "outside" of Scripture. If Scripture is appealed to, it is "correlated" with the priority of the extratextual viewpoint. No doubt, these "outside" views vary, and some may be more amenable to the Christian view as they live off the borrowed capital of historic Christianity, but in the end, methodologically, they embrace the "method of correlation" central to non-orthodox theologies. If ultimate authority is given to these extratextual views, historic Christian theology is inevitably viewed as impossible, and some form of syncretism follows, with the priority and authority never going to Scripture. The end result: theology "from above" is replaced by a theology "from below."

Second, by contrast, historic theology is intratextual, grounded in a revelational epistemology. It follows the example of Paul at Athens, who does theology from *within* the Bible's theological framework, content, and categories, which serve as the interpretive matrix by which he explains God, self, and the world. He does not embrace "outside" systems to explain who God is, the nature of the human problem, and the glorious gospel centered in Christ. Instead, Scripture's own description of reality, given by divine revelation, provides the "spectacles" by which Paul theologizes, thinks, and applies the truth of God to every aspect of life.

Furthermore, the Bible's view of reality is a unit or "package." From Genesis to Revelation, a specific view of God is given—the triune Creator-covenant Lord—which results in a specific view of the God-world relationship, the authority of Scripture, divine action, providence, history, teleology, humans, sin, the moral order, eschatology, and so on. In fact, the Bible's own presentation necessitates a specific metaphysics, epistemology, and ethics, in contrast to other worldviews. And every aspect of the Bible's teaching hangs together as a unit *and* is necessary to make sense of any and all theological formulations grounded in Scripture.

Until the significance of this point is understood, we will not articulate properly the warrant for historic theology and make headway against opposing views. For example, think of our theological understanding of who Jesus is as the divine Son, the second person of the Trinity, who has assumed our human nature to redeem us as our Mediator and new covenant head. Such a Christology, as given by Scripture and confessed by the Councils of Nicaea and Chalcedon, does not emerge from nowhere. It reflects a theology "from above": a theology that starts with a specific conception of Scripture as God's word written, an authoritative and accurate God's-eye interpretation of who Jesus is. It also warrants its conclusion by placing Jesus *within* the Bible's entire canonical presentation of him, grounded in a specific view of the Creator-creature distinction, providence, divine agency, humanity, sin, and so on. Even Robert Funk, the founder of the Jesus Seminar who rejected Chalcedonian Christology, had to admit that, "Jesus' divinity goes together with the old theistic way of thinking about God,"[8] which is another way of speaking of the Bible's view of God. Thus, any attempt to remove Jesus from the Bible's presentation or to accept certain parts and reject others only leads to a denial of the Jesus of the Bible and puts in his place a subjective, arbitrary, and false construction of Jesus's identity.

What is true in Christology is true of every doctrine. For historic theology to be viewed as *possible*, its entire worldview must be articulated and defended as an entire "package." It must not be combined or syncretized with "outside" frameworks; instead, it must stand on its own authority with each part contributing to the whole. What we learn from our survey of intellectual history is that historic theology stands on its own worldview/theology against non-Christian thought. As Cornelius Van Til reminded us a number of years ago:

[8] Robert W. Funk, "The Coming Radical Reformation: Twenty-one Theses," *The Fourth R* 11, no. 4 (July–August 1998), http://www.westarinstitute.org/resources/the-fourth-r/the-coming-radical-reformation/.

> The fight between Christianity and non-Christianity is, in modern times, no piecemeal affair. It is the life and death struggle between two mutually opposed life and world-views. The non-Christian attack often comes to us on matters of historical, or other, detail. It comes to us in the form of objections to certain teachings of Scripture, say, with respect to creation, etc. It may seem to be simply a matter of asking what the facts have been. Back of this detailed attack, however, is the constant assumption of the non-Christian metaphysics of the correlativity of God and man. He who has not been trained in systematic theology will often be at a loss as to how to meet these attacks.[9]

Evangelical theology must be a theology "from above." *Sola Scriptura* is no mere slogan; it is the foundation for a normative theology that yields a finite, but true, objective knowledge of God, self, and the world. We must not walk the path of theologies "from below" since their ultimate warrant is not the triune God and his spoken, trustworthy word. Given the importance of this point, let us now turn to describe the Bible's own epistemological warrant for theology as an objective science by turning to a discussion of the foundation of theology.

The Foundation of Systematic Theology: The Triune God Who Speaks

What makes systematic theology possible? The triune God who speaks. The Reformed tradition lays down two foundations (*principia*) for theology: the essential foundation (*principium essendi*) and the cognitive foundation (*principium cognoscendi*)—the triune God[10] *and* his word,[11] specifically Scripture, although word also refers to natural revelation.[12]

---

[9] Cornelius Van Til, *In Defense of the Faith*, vol. 5, *An Introduction to Systematic Theology* (Phillipsburg: P&R, 1982), 6–7.

[10] See part 4, chapters 17–19.

[11] See part 2, chapters 5–12.

[12] See Richard A. Muller, *Post-Reformation Reformed Dogmatics*, 4 vols. (Grand Rapids: Baker Academic, 2003), 2:162–66. In addition, *principium cognoscendi* is often divided into two categories: God's self-revelation in nature and Scripture (*principium cognoscendi externum*, "external cognitive foundation") and the Spirit's illumination of the truth (*principium cognoscendi internum*, "internal cognitive foundation"). See Bavinck, *Reformed Dogmatics*, 1:213–14 (see chap. 1, n. 9).

Think first about the triune Creator-covenant Lord who is the foundation for truth, knowledge, and thus theology.[13] It almost sounds like a truism, but it is not: the ground for truth is the God of Scripture, not a generic theism or mere monotheistic conception of God.

From the opening verses of Scripture, God is presented in a category all by himself (sui generis): he alone is uncreated, independent, self-contained, self-sufficient, the holy One who creates and rules all things by his word (Gen 1–2; Exod 3:1–15; Lev 11:44; Pss 50:12–14; 93:2; Isa 40:17–29; Acts 17:24–25; cf. John 1:1). This truth establishes the central distinction of all theology: the Creator-creature distinction, which eliminates any pantheistic or panentheistic views of the God-world relationship: God alone is God (Deut 4:35, 39; 1 Kgs 8:27; Pss 7:17; 9:2; 21:7; 97:9; Isa 6:1; 45:18–22; Rev 4:3). It also denies any notion of deism, which rejects God's agency in human history; God is transcendent *and* immanent with his creation. As Creator, God is the covenant Lord who is fully present and related to his creatures; he freely, sovereignly, and purposefully sustains and governs all things according to his eternal plan (Pss 33:9–11; 139:1–10; Acts 17:28; Eph 1:11; 4:6), but he is not part of his world or developing with it.

As Creator and Lord, God rules with perfect power, knowledge, and righteousness (Pss 9:8; 33:5; 96:10–13; 139:1–4, 16; Isa 46:9–11; Jer 11:20; Acts 4:27–28; Rom 11:33–36). As the God who knows and plans all things according to his own will (Isa 46:9–13), he is the source and standard of truth (Isa 40:13–14). God has created humans to know him and a world that reflects his universal, comprehensive plan (Ps 19:1–6; Acts 17:24–28; Rom 1:18–32). All of creation is revelatory of him and it is impossible for humans to function except within the environment of revelation.

As covenant Lord, God acts in, with, and through his creatures to accomplish his plan and purposes (Eph 1:11). As personal, God commands, loves, and judges in a manner consistent with himself and according to the covenant relationships that he establishes with his creatures. As we move through redemptive history, God discloses himself not merely as unipersonal but as tri-personal, a being-in-relation, a unity of three persons: Father, Son, and Spirit (e.g., Matt 28:18–20; John 1:1–4, 14–18; 5:16–30; 17:1–5; 1 Cor 8:5–6; 2 Cor 13:14; Eph 1:3–14).

---

[13] For the phrase, "Covenant Lord," see John M. Frame, *The Doctrine of God* (Phillipsburg: P&R, 2002), 1–115.

Theologians have sought to capture the majestic sense of God's triune lordship by the term *aseity* (*a se*, "from himself"), tied to God's simplicity. God is not composed of parts; instead, he is the *one* God who is indivisible in nature *and* as triune has fullness of being and life within himself (*ad intra*, within God). God is not dependent on anything outside of himself, nor is he correlative to the world. But, as John Frame rightly reminds us, God's aseity is more than a metaphysical concept; it also has epistemological and ethical implications. God is self-existent, self-attesting (his omniscience and eternal plan are "from himself" and not dependent on the world; God is the standard of truth), and self-justifying (his will and nature is "from himself"; God is the absolute standard of goodness).[14] Moreover, only the Bible teaches that the universe is created and ruled by *this* kind of God, who serves as the transcendental ground for existence, knowledge, and moral norms. The triune God is the only ground for "absolute rationality" since "in him, i.e., with respect to his own Being, apart from the world, fact and interpretation of fact are coterminous,"[15] which entails that God alone has a truly universal, exhaustive, comprehensive knowledge of all things—a God's-eye viewpoint.[16]

Yet, for theology to be possible, the triune God who is there must also reveal himself to us, first in the creation of a world and second in terms of divine speech. In terms of the latter, God's speech is necessary to know him and all things related to him in a true and warranted way, and the entirety of Scripture teaches that God speaks to us through human words. Hebrews 1:1–2 captures this truth well: "Long ago God spoke to the fathers by the prophets at different times and in different ways. In these last days, he has spoken to us by his Son."

---

[14] Frame, *Doctrine of God*, 602.

[15] Van Til, *In Defense of the Faith*, 5:10.

[16] Bavinck develops this point in terms of God's trinitarian nature. He argues that the Trinity alone makes sense of God's relationship to the creation and his revelation of himself. The world is not "mere happenstance" (contrary to deism), nor is it "the outcome of divine self-development" (contrary to pantheism). Instead, the world is the creation of the triune God, who within himself (*ad intra*) has a complete, absolute fullness of knowledge and self-communication between the triune persons, which results in God's free acts of creation and revelation (*ad extra*). "All things come from the Father; the 'ideas' of all existent things are present in the Son; the first principles of all life are in the Spirit. Generation and procession in the divine being are the immanent acts of God, which make possible the outward works of creation and revelation. . . . this also explains why all the works of God *ad extra* are only adequately known when their trinitarian existence is recognized." *Reformed Dogmatics*, 2:332–33.

In fact, apart from the triune God *and* his initiative to speak to us, the universe would not exist (Gen 1:1–3) and we would have no objective foundation for the knowledge of God, truth, and the doing of a normative theology. As for God's speech, as we will develop in part 2, it involves both creation/nature (natural revelation) and Scripture (special revelation). Since God has created the universe according to his eternal plan by his word and his Spirit (Gen 1:1–2; John 1:1–2), the world is ordered, designed, and revelatory of God. As such, our knowledge of creation/nature is a revelational knowledge. However, although creation is revelatory of God and necessary to know him (Ps 19:1–6; Rom 1:18–32), a point we will discuss in part 2, God never intended for us to know him by natural revelation alone. To know God's nature, character, will, and promises, to enter into covenant relationship with him, we need divine speech in a verbal and written form. We need God to disclose who he is, what his eternal plan is all about, and how we fit into that plan for God's glory (1 Cor 2:11; cf. Rom 11:33–36).[17]

In fact, theology can only speak of the universal, objective significance of any fact of history, or of theological/metaphysical truths, *if* those "facts" are located within the eternal plan of the triune God who not only creates and rules all things according to his plan but also reveals his plan to us. The only answer to Lessing's ugly ditch, or the subjectivism of postmodern thought, is the triune God who knows and plans all things and speaks to us in an authoritative, trustworthy way.[18] Thus, to know God and to do theology in a normative way, divine speech is necessary, and thankfully God has not left us to mere human subjectivity. Although the entire "catholic" church has taught this, the Reformation comprehensively developed this point: the "foundation of all true knowledge of God is God's own revelation. There can be no true knowledge of God, indeed, no knowledge of God at all, if God does not manifest himself to his creatures."[19]

---

[17] See James N. Anderson, "Presuppositionalism and Frame's Epistemology," in *Speaking the Truth in Love: The Theology of John M. Frame*, ed. John J. Hughes (Phillipsburg: P&R, 2009), 431–59. Anderson discusses how natural and special revelation combine for a full-blown "revelational epistemology" as the foundation for truth and theology.

[18] Carl F. H. Henry, *God, Revelation, and Authority*, 6 vols. (Waco: Word, 1976), 1:323–43.

[19] Muller, *Post-Reformation Reformed Dogmatics*, 2:153; cf. Calvin, *Institutes*, 2.12.1 (see chap. 1, n. 3).

For this reason, the Reformed tradition speaks of the *necessity* of God's self-revelation, and states that systematic theology is grounded in a "revelational epistemology."[20] In light of our survey of intellectual history and the need to respond to the challenges of our day, it is important to develop the *necessity* of divine speech in at least three ways: (1) as the answer to our present cultural moment with its loss of a ground for objective truth, (2) as the foundation for a normative theology, and (3) as necessary due to God's incomprehensibility. In the last area, since the triune God is sui generis, the distance between the Creator and creature, eternity and time, one who is infinite in being, knowledge, and perfection, and humans, who are finite and now fallen, is vast. How, then, can finite, fallen creatures know God apart from his initiative to speak to us? Let us now develop the *necessity* of divine revelation or communicative agency in these three ways.

The Necessity of Divine Revelation for the Possibility of Truth

This point is crucial for the church to maintain today. As our survey of intellectual history demonstrated, our time, at least in the West, is characterized by a massive loss of truth, largely due to our rejection of Christian theology, the "turn to the subject," and the embrace of evolutionary naturalism. As such, the grounding for objective truth has evaporated, and in its place, "truth" is now merely subjective, perspectival, and provisional. By making finite human reason (let alone *fallen* human reason) the ultimate standard instead of God as the archetype of knowledge, the grounds for objective truth have been rendered impossible for us. Sadly, this has not resulted in peace and tranquility, but an increased soft totalitarianism as all claims for objective truth are rejected as intolerant.[21]

The reason for this loss of warrant for objective truth is not hard to understand if we think of the consequences of the modern/postmodern worldview. Without the triune God as the normative standard of knowledge and his revelation to us, humans, as finite and fallen creatures, cannot serve as that standard. Our knowing is always finite (and thus ectypal), but it may be objectively true because it is caused by and dependent on God's universal knowledge.

[20] See Muller, *Post-Reformation Reformed Dogmatics*, 2:161–82.

[21] See Rod Dreher, *Live Not By Lies: A Manual for Christian Dissidents* (New York City: Sentinel, 2020).

For this reason, the *transcendental* condition for truth and theology is the same: the triune God who speaks.[22] But, sadly, this is what the modern/postmodern view rejects. And, ironically, the omnicompetence of human reason in the Enlightenment has given way to "reason" turning in on itself and now unable to warrant why finite humans can know things that are universal and objectively true.

As we discovered in thinkers such as Immanuel Kant, Charles Darwin, Friedrich Nietzsche, and Jacques Derrida, "ideas" were sown that eventually undercut the ground for objective truth. The "self," as merely a finite subject, is located in a world "produced" by chance and limited to a particular sociopolitical context, thus "determined" by its language, culture, and time. As "we" interpret the world ("we" who are only the product of impersonal forces), there is no access to "reality-as-it-really-is" (noumena) independent of our social-linguistic "constructions." Further, we have no confidence that the world/object we study is designed, ordered, or purposed. This is why our finite interpretations cannot provide adequate warrant to say we know anything that is universal and objective; as such, the traditional study of metaphysics, epistemology, and ethics dissipates, let alone the study of theology. All that remains are human "constructs" within an immanent frame that is devoid of any archetypal grounding in God. As the "death of God" was taken seriously, logocentrism was undermined, and with it the *guarantee* that reason operates correctly and that language corresponds to the world.[23] The end result: "the True, the Good, and the Beautiful are *all* in the eyes of their human beholders. There is no privileged or absolute viewpoint, no authoritative voice to end the discussion."[24]

From a Christian view, this is not surprising. The foundation for truth is not located in the human subject, but in the triune God who speaks. Human thinking, unless grounded in God and his revelation, is merely subjective, a product of chance that has no ability to warrant

---

[22] The term "transcendental" refers to the task of discovering the preconditions for something to be possible. In this context, "transcendental condition" refers to "the triune God who speaks" as the necessary precondition for the possibility of objective truth and a normative theology. On this point, see Kevin J. Vanhoozer, "Christ and Concept: Doing Theology and the 'Ministry' of Philosophy," in *Doing Theology in Today's World: Essays in Honor of Kenneth S. Kantzer*, ed. John D. Woodbridge and Thomas E. McComiskey (Grand Rapids: Zondervan, 1991), 99–145. On the nature of transcendental arguments, see Bahnsen, *Van Til's Apologetic*, 496–529 (see chap. 1, n. 4); Robert Stern, ed. *Transcendental Arguments: Problems and Prospects* (Oxford: Oxford University Press, 1999).

[23] See Alvin Plantinga's epistemological argument against evolutionary naturalism.

[24] Vanhoozer, "Christ and Concept," 129 (emphasis original).

the ideas of "universality, causal connections, or moral prescriptions,"[25] and the "facts" that we study are simply the product of randomness and chance. If God's omniscience and plan does not determine the relationship of every particular event to another, then "the way things are in the world and what happens there are random and indeterminate . . . there is no intelligible basis for holding that any experience is like any other experience, there is nothing objectively common to the two of them . . . thus they are meaningless and indescribable."[26] Even "laws" of science, logic, and morality are left hanging in midair. How is anything "universal and law-abiding when every event is isolated and random?" Humans can never know that universality is objective, and "if universality is subjective (internal to man's thinking), then it is arbitrarily imposed by man's mind on his experience without warrant."[27]

Christian theology is the opposite of today's thinking. Instead, it starts with the triune God who knows and plans all things, who creates a world to reveal himself, and who makes humans in his image to know him.[28] Humans are not a tabula rasa or "constructors" of our own reality. Instead, we are created in God's image to know God and the world *he* has constructed according to his plan; hence we are "to think God's thoughts after him."[29] Universal, objective truth is first grounded in God as the archetype; human thinking is only ectypal. Yet, because God knows, plans, and creates all things according to his plan, "God's thinking is what gives unity, meaning, coherence, and intelligibility to nature, history, reasoning, and morality."[30] Human knowing is to receive what God has revealed in both nature and Scripture. Even human knowledge gained from empirical research and logical reasoning is still thinking thoughts "on the creaturely level which God originally thought (or thinks) as Creator and providential Governor of the world, and to reach such truths by means of the intellectual tools He has granted us as His image bearers."[31] Apart from such a view, the warrant for objective truth is gone.

---

[25] Bahnsen, *Van Til's Apologetic*, 112.

[26] Bahnsen, 110 n. 64.

[27] Bahnsen, 110 n. 65.

[28] For a critique of non-Christian epistemologies, see Bahnsen, *Van Til's Apologetic*, 311–404; and Bavinck, *Reformed Dogmatics*, 1:214–33.

[29] See Bahnsen, *Van Til's Apologetic*, 220–46.

[30] Bahnsen, 223.

[31] Bahnsen, 224.

The Necessity of Divine Revelation for a Normative Theology

If theology walks the same path of modern/postmodern thought, it too will lose its identity and integrity as a normative discipline; it will forever be reduced to anthropology, psychology, sociology, and philosophy.[32] In fact, this is the problem with all *extratextual* theologies (modern or postmodern); they surrender the full authority and reliability of Scripture (*sola Scriptura*), embrace the "method of correlation," and do theology from the standpoint of some conceptual scheme "outside" of Scripture, usually with a commitment to the worldview assumptions of historical criticism. But the end result is inevitable: theology is reduced to subjectivity and it relinquishes its distinct identity, method, and claim to objective truth.

In our survey of Western thought, "classic liberalism" was an example of this, with Friedrich Schleiermacher serving as its paradigm example. Schleiermacher made the human feeling of absolute dependence to be theology's foundation, rather than an external, authoritative written word. For him, theology is the "science of faith," that is, human feeling. But it was only a matter of time before such a view became indistinguishable from the psychology of religion.[33]

Two further problems illustrate why theologies "from below" (as diverse as they are) render unviable a normative theology. Both of these examples are from Christology, but they also are true for every doctrinal area. Moreover, both examples illustrate why historic theology necessitates a fully authoritative *and reliable* Scripture for its epistemological warrant. Why? For this reason: if Scripture is unreliable in its "facts" and "theological interpretation" of the facts at any point, then any statement of Scripture may be false. And if any statement of Scripture may be false, the only way to determine what is true ("facts" and "interpretation") is by criteria outside of Scripture, which entails that Scripture is no longer a necessary and sufficient authority for our theology, thus rendering a theology "from above" problematic.[34]

---

[32] On this point, see Vanhoozer, "Christ and Concept," 99–110.

[33] On this point, see Vanhoozer, 110.

[34] This argument is *not* reducible to the fallacious argument that error in *some* places means error in *all* places, contra Stephen T. Davis, *The Debate About the Bible: Inerrancy Versus Infallibility* (Philadelphia: Westminster John Knox, 1977), 66–82. Instead, the argument is that if the Bible is unreliable at any point, we must *first* determine what is true by criteria *outside of Scripture* before Scripture can function in our theology. But then the "outside" criteria become more authoritative than Scripture. The problem is not remedied by appealing to a trusting attitude toward Scripture or the inward witness of the Holy Spirit or holding that God can achieve his revelatory purposes even if Scripture errs at some points. For

First, consider the "facts" of Scripture: if Scripture is not fully authoritative and reliable, it cannot serve as the necessary and sufficient condition to warrant our theological formulations. For example, think of the doctrinal area of Christology. In our survey of intellectual history, we noted how theologies "from below," especially those that pursued the "quests for the historical Jesus," assumed that the "Jesus of history" was *not* identical with the "Jesus of the Bible." However, the problem was establishing the criteria, and warrant *outside of Scripture* to determine which "parts" of the Gospels are accurate so they can function in our Christological formulation. What exactly are those "outside" criteria and who decides? Human rationality? Religious experience? The "assured" results of biblical scholarship?

Recently, in wrestling with this problem, Francis Watson has proposed an interesting but finally unsuccessful via media between a theology "from above" and one "from below." Watson admits that, "For Christians, Jesus' true identity is established above all by the fourfold canonical Gospel. It is within this sacred textual space that we discover who Jesus is and who we are in relation to him."[35] Yet Watson also thinks the "Jesus of history" is *not* identical with the "Jesus of the Bible"; in fact, the Gospels are a combination of historical facts and "legendary motifs created by early Christian storytellers."[36] Thus, while Watson admits that we need to identify Jesus within the "narrative framework of the Gospels,"[37] it does not appear that he believes the Gospels are *God-given* and thus factually and theologically reliable in their presentation of Jesus. Instead, the Gospels are the product of *the church's* interpretation of Jesus, which mixes recollections of Jesus's life and death with early Christian legends.[38] Eventually, Watson's proposal leaves us with the same problem of criteria and warrant. The attempt to have both "from

---

the former view, see Stephen T. Davis, "What Do We Mean When We Say, 'The Bible is True'?," in *But Is It All True? The Bible and the Question of Truth*, ed. Alan G. Padgett and Patrick R. Keifert (Grand Rapids: Eerdmans, 2006), 86–103; for the latter, see Kevin Diller, *Theology's Epistemological Dilemma: How Karl Barth and Alvin Plantinga Provide a Unified Response* (Downers Grove: IVP Academic, 2014), 270–79. One must still appeal to "outside" criteria to determine what is true in Scripture, which begs the question as to what *the* criteria is. But Scripture, *on its own say so*, cannot function as theology's *final, sufficient authority* for our theological formulations.

[35] Francis Watson, "*Veritas Christi*: How to Get from the Jesus of History to the Christ of Faith without Losing One's Way?," in *Seeking the Identity of Jesus: A Pilgrimage*, ed. Beverly Roberts Gaventa and Richard B. Hays (Grand Rapids: Eerdmans, 2008), 96.

[36] Watson, 100.

[37] Watson, 104.

[38] See Watson, 106–11. On this point, Watson aligns with the postliberal tradition.

above" and "from below" aspects to ground Christology fails at just this point. If Scripture is somewhere unreliable, then Scripture *on its own say so* cannot ground our Christological formulation as a necessary and sufficient criterion.

Second, thinking about the "interpretation" of the facts of Scripture, if Scripture is not God's authoritative and fully reliable word, it cannot serve as the necessary and sufficient condition to warrant anything theological and universal in our theological formulations. Again, think about Christology. To say anything theological/metaphysical about Jesus, as the church has done at Nicaea and Chalcedon, the Bible's entire God-given, authoritative interpretive framework must be true. Orthodox Christology requires the life-giving soil of Scripture to grow. We can only establish Jesus's universal significance and his metaphysical identity as God the Son incarnate by interpreting him *in the Bible's framework* and not an extratextual one. If Jesus is removed from the categories and content of Scripture, starting with the triune Creator-covenant Lord, a specific view of creation, providence, humans, sin, covenant relationships, and so on, he will lose his true identity as the divine Son who has become human for us and our salvation. In the end, Jesus simply becomes an enigma to us, susceptible to various imaginative and arbitrary constructions. This is the problem for those who think that historical "facts" about Jesus, even the fact of his bodily resurrection, carry their own meaning apart from placing Jesus and his resurrection within the overall theological framework of Scripture.

For example, Wolfhart Pannenberg is an illustration of this problem for Christology.[39] He contends that historical "facts," warranted by historical-critical research, are self-interpreting and allow us to say something *theological* (universal, metaphysical) about Christ, yet he is not consistent on this point. Pannenberg also knows that to say something theological, the "fact" of Christ's resurrection must be placed within the "apocalyptic framework" of later Judaism.[40] Why? Because unless the "fact" of Jesus's resurrection is placed in this universal framework, we cannot infer from the resurrection alone that Jesus is unique. It is only when historical research is placed in this "universal" framework that we can draw theological conclusions about Christ.

---

[39] See Wolfhart Pannenberg, *Jesus: God and Man*, 2nd ed., trans. Lewis L. Wilkins and Duane A. Priebe (Philadelphia: Westminster John Knox, 1977); Pannenberg, *Systematic Theology*, trans. Geoffrey W. Bromiley, 3 vols. (Grand Rapids: Eerdmans, 1992), 1:277–396.

[40] Pannenberg, *Jesus: God and Man*, 98.

Pannenberg is correct on this point: to say anything *theological* about Jesus, we must place him within a universal frame of reference; otherwise, we have not overcome Lessing's ditch. Yet the universal framework he requires is from Scripture, which he thinks is *not* fully reliable. But how can Scripture be appealed to on its own say so if, at points, it is inaccurate? For example, what if the apocalyptic framework he needs to warrant his theological conclusions is merely the mythological construction of Judaism and the early church? If so, then it carries no authority for Christology, and Rudolf Bultmann's demythologization project rears its ugly head.

Colin Gunton asks these same questions of Pannenberg. Gunton insists that even if we grant that Pannenberg's Christology affirms the divine significance of Jesus, it is difficult to see how he has done so consistent with his method. As Gunton argues, to locate historical facts within the Bible's interpretive framework without warranting it entails that he is "*either* presupposing some dogmatic beliefs ('context of meaning') and thus not arguing genuinely from below at all; *or* failing to establish what is wanted, namely, the divinity of Jesus."[41] Gunton also charges Pannenberg with confusing two separate questions: "the first is that about the significance of Jesus within the context of interpretation—what he meant to his contemporaries. The second is that concerning his significance now."[42] As Gunton rightly insists, what must be warranted is the truth of the Bible's framework of meaning *for us today*, but given Pannenberg's rejection of Scripture's full authority, how can he do so apart from criteria "outside" of Scripture?

The lesson to learn is this: We can only warrant the theological/metaphysical claim that Jesus is the divine Son incarnate and that he has universal significance by placing him within the framework, categories, and teaching of an authoritative, reliable Scripture. Orthodox Christology is rooted in a specific conception of God, Scripture, humans, and so on, and apart from that theology, it cannot stand. In the end, whether it is Christology or any other doctrine, we must articulate *and* defend the theological system on which it stands, along with Scripture as more than basically reliable. For a normative theology, we need more than the "facts" of Scripture; we also need "God's interpretation" of those facts, which alone yields a true, universal, and theological account.

---

[41] Colin E. Gunton, *Yesterday and Today: A Study of Continuities in Christology*, 2nd ed. (London: SPCK, 1997), 21 (emphasis original).

[42] Gunton, 21.

Once again, this is why the triune God who speaks in an authoritative, reliable written word, is the *transcendental condition* for the doing of theology in an objective, normative fashion. Without *God's* speech "from above," theology loses its uniqueness and truthfulness, and it is set adrift to wander into the mire of pluralism. Evangelical theologians must reject *all* theologies "from below." Only a theology "from above" can provide the warrant for a normative theology for the church and remain true to God and his word. It is simply not possible to construct a biblical, true, and objective theology out of the fabric of human experience by historical-critical reconstruction tied to various extratextual worldviews, whatever they may be.

Yet, many within the post-conservative, postliberal tradition attempt to do so. In eschewing biblical inerrancy, the problem of criteria and warrant for a normative theology resurfaces.[43] For example, Stanley Grenz (and John Franke) insisted that evangelicals wrongly made biblical inerrancy our "foundation" for theology similar to the Enlightenment's grounding knowledge in "foundationalism" or classic liberal theology's grounding theology in religious experience.[44] In replacement of Scripture as our theological foundation, Grenz proposes a "non-foundationalism" rooted in three sources: Scripture, tradition, and culture. Thus, the "norming norm" for theology is the Holy Spirit speaking through *all* three sources, with primacy given to the "biblical message." But it is crucial to note that Grenz does *not* identify the "biblical message" one-to-one with Scripture.[45] Instead, Scripture is viewed as "appropriated discourse" that allows for a distinction between what human authors say and what God says and affirms.[46] Just because God "appropriates" Scripture as his own does not entail that he

---

[43] For example, this is a problem for William Abraham's work, *Canon and Criterion in Christian Theology* (Oxford: Oxford University Press), 1998; *Crossing the Threshold of Divine Revelation* (Grand Rapids: Eerdmans, 2006); and "Post(modern) Biblical Historiography: An Interim Report from the Front Lines," in *The Voice of God in the Text of Scripture*, ed. Oliver D. Crisp and Fred Sanders (Grand Rapids: Zondervan, 2016), 146–63. In *Canon and Criterion*, Abraham argues that the canon (primarily Scripture) is not the epistemological criterion for theology. Scripture is *not* divine speech or revelation, but the product of "acts of revelation," and we "know" by the witness of the Spirit, dependent on historical reconstruction and personal religious experience. But this reduces theology to subjectivity since the Spirit's work is not tied directly to the full authority and reliability of Scripture: the Spirit's work is "a divine witness within" (*Crossing the Threshold*, 186).

[44] See Grenz and Franke, *Beyond Foundationalism* (see chap. 1, n. 35).

[45] Grenz and Franke, 70–71.

[46] "Appropriated discourse" is from Nicholas Wolterstorff, *Divine Discourse: Philosophical Reflections on the Claim that God Speaks* (Cambridge: Cambridge University Press, 1995). Wolterstorff also thinks

agrees with everything said. Thus, when the Spirit speaks through Scripture, the Spirit's intention goes *beyond* the intention of the authors, so "exegesis alone can[not] exhaust the Spirit's speaking to us through the text."[47]

Much could be said in response to Grenz's proposal for evangelical theology, but in the end, it renders a theology "from above" problematic.[48] First, it mistakenly equates Enlightenment "foundationalism" or liberalism's "religious experience" with Scripture as the foundation for theology. But a "revelation foundation" is *not* grounded in the finite human subject as in modern/postmodern thought; instead, it is grounded in the triune God who speaks.[49] Second, Grenz introduces hermeneutical subjectivism into the theological task in how the Spirit communicates to the church through Scripture. Since Scripture is *not* viewed as first order, objective, divine speech that is fully reliable, the Spirit's speaking through the Bible, tradition, and culture shifts the locus of authority from Scripture to the community. This is especially the case since the Spirit's speaking goes *beyond* the intention of the biblical authors, which raises the question, "Whose community, which interpretation?"[50] The distinction between text and interpretation is blurred; biblical authority is redefined, along with the objectivity of theology tied to God and his first-order, authoritative word as the "norming norm" for theology.[51]

Instead, what is needed for a normative theology is the triune God who speaks and especially who speaks in an authoritative, reliable Scripture. Scripture is not merely a human word; it is God's divine speech through human authors. As such, its worldview, content,

---

that God "appropriates" the discourse of biblical authors without necessarily agreeing with them at every point. For a critique of Wolterstorff, see Horton, *Covenant and Eschatology*, 156–64 (see chap. 2, n. 147).

[47] Grenz and Franke, *Beyond Foundationalism*, 74.

[48] For example, see my "Postconservatism, Biblical Authority, and Recent Proposals for Re-doing Evangelical Theology: A Critical Analysis," in *Reclaiming the Center: Confronting Evangelical Accommodation in Postmodern Times*, ed. Paul Helseth, Millard Erickson, et al. (Wheaton: Crossway, 2004), 161–97.

[49] See Frame, *Doctrine of the Knowledge of God*, 128–29 (see chap. 1, n. 11), who makes the same point.

[50] Horton, *Covenant and Eschatology*, 214.

[51] For a similar critique, see Kevin J. Vanhoozer, "On the Very Idea of a Theological System: An Essay in Aid of Triangulating Scripture, Church and World," in *Always Reforming: Explorations in Systematic Theology*, ed. A. T. B. McGowan (Leicester: Apollos, 2006), 143–47.

and categories are first order and foundational for our theological formulations. Scripture is God's interpretation of reality, including his own redemptive acts in history; hence, it is a true, objective, and authoritative interpretation. No doubt, Scripture is not an exhaustive revelation, but it is true, and as such, it is the "spectacles" by which we view God, self, and the world. Scripture not only describes accurately a certain segment of redemptive history; it also serves as our interpretive grid by which we view the world. For this reason, as we will discuss in the next chapter, theological formulation moves from Scripture's first-order interpretive framework as given across the Bible's covenantal storyline to second-order theological/doctrinal construction.

The bottom line is this: Because the triune God is there and has spoken, the "True," "Good," and the "Beautiful" are not merely in the eyes of their human beholders; they are grounded in God and his word. A normative theology, then, is not only possible; it is our highest calling as we seek to know, love, and obey our triune God for his glory and our good (Matt 22:36–40).

The Necessity of Divine Revelation and God's Incomprehensibility

So far we have argued for the necessity of divine revelation for the possibility of truth and a normative theology. But it is also necessary due to the nature of the triune God, specifically, God's incomprehensibility. Since the triune God is sui generis, the distance between the Creator and creature, eternity and time, one who is uncreated, simple, independent, self-sufficient, infinite in being, knowledge, and perfection, and humans, who are finite and now fallen, is vast. How can finite, fallen creatures know God apart from his own initiative to speak to us and make himself known?

"Incomprehensibility" is the theological term that seeks to capture the biblical presentation of the triune God in all of his uniqueness, transcendence, and majestic glory.[52] In historical theology, however, some have used the concept of God's incomprehensibility to conclude wrongly that God is so different from us that our knowledge of him is only by the "way of negation" (*via negativa*). Some who walk this path say they are doing apophatic theology, that is, describing God by emphasizing the limitations of human language and only saying what

---

[52] See Muller, *Post-Reformation Reformed Dogmatics*, 3:164–70.

God is *not.*[53] In this view, God is beyond definition and description; incomprehensibility, then, entails that God is unintelligible and unknowable.

However, Scripture rejects that God is unintelligible and unknowable. Instead, it teaches that God is incomprehensible *and* knowable due to his creation of humans in his image and self-revelation to us. God alone knows himself and his eternal decree perfectly, comprehensively, and exhaustively: God's being and knowledge is *archetypal.* Yet, due to God's free and gracious choice to create us and to reveal himself to us, our knowledge of him is *ectypal*, that is, revealed but limited, sufficient, and objectively true.[54] The same God who is our Creator and Lord is also the covenant Lord who is fully present to his creatures: he freely and sovereignly sustains and governs all things to his desired end (Ps 139:1–10; Acts 17:28; Eph 1:11; 4:6). He rules with complete and exhaustive knowledge, control, and holy justice (Pss 33:5; 139:1–4, 16; Isa 40:12–31; 46:9–11; Dan 4:34–35; Acts 2:23–24; Rev 4:11) so that he is known by us due to his creation and word-revelation so that we are without excuse (Ps 19; Acts 17:24–28; Rom 1:18–32). As Lord, God acts in, with, and through his creatures to accomplish his plan and purposes (Rom 11:33–36). As personal, God, who alone is Creator and Lord, creates, rules, and redeems so that his image-bearers will know him in covenant relationship. Indeed, as we move through redemptive history, the triune God makes himself known uniquely in the incarnation of the Son; and in Christ Jesus, we are redeemed, reconciled, justified, and brought into the fellowship of the triune God (John 1:1–18; 14–16; 17:1–5; 1 Cor 1:9; Eph 1:3–14; Rev 21–22).

---

[53] See Bavinck, *Reformed Dogmatics*, 2:27–52.

[54] On the distinction between archetypal and ectypal theology, see Muller, *Post-Reformation Reformed Dogmatics*, 1:225–38. Reformed theology identified different kinds of ectypal theology throughout redemptive history. First, there is the "theology of union," which Christ possesses according to his human nature. Christ's human knowledge is created and finite (Luke 2:52), but due to the hypostatic union and the work of the Spirit, his human knowledge surpasses all other creatures. Second, there is the "theology of revelation," which we possess now in varying degrees due to God's revelation both in nature and in Scripture. Under this category, we can talk about the knowledge of angels and of humans. In terms of humans, there are three basic forms of human knowledge—"before the fall (*ante lapsum*); after the fall (*post lapsum*) but informed by grace, that is, the theology of pilgrims on earth (*theologia viatorum*); and theology of the blessed in heaven (*theologia beatorum*)." *Post-Reformation Reformed Dogmatics*, 1:235. In addition, the "theology of pilgrims" can be divided into natural and supernatural knowledge. For a further discussion of these points see Franciscus Junius, *A Treatise on True Theology*, trans. David C. Noe (Grand Rapids: Reformation Heritage Books, 2014), 107–20; Duby, *God in Himself*, 31–43 (see chap. 1, n. 20).

For this reason, the triune God who is beyond our comprehension can also be known by us. In fact, this is why revelation is necessary. We would not have an objective, true, and certain knowledge of God in himself apart from his self-revelation.[55] No doubt, as finite creatures (and now fallen), we can never *fully* understand who and what God is. God is beyond our full comprehension and description. Yet God is not unintelligible. God's incomprehensibility is best understood in the sense that he is *unfathomable*. As the triune God, his being is utterly unique and thus unfathomable. As the God who knows and plans all things, his thoughts are too deep to fathom and plumb. In fact, even in our future, glorified condition in the eternal state, as finite creatures who remain creatures, we will never *fully* plumb the depths of God's knowledge and being (Job 38:1–42:6; Pss 145:3, 7; 139:6; Isa 40–48; 55:8–9; 1 Cor 2:9–16). As the Reformed tradition has rightly taught, "The finite cannot contain the infinite" (*finitum non capax infiniti*).

In thinking about God's incomprehensibility, especially his knowledge, it is important to remember that God's thoughts are not merely quantitatively greater than ours; they are also *qualitatively* different. His knowledge is the *archetype* of all knowledge. We can say that the "objects" of God's thoughts (in terms of what God created according to his plan) and human thoughts are the same, yet the process and content of God's thinking is entirely different.[56]

For example, God's thinking is original, creative, and truly constructive; ours is not. Our thinking and knowledge are only the *ectype* of his exhaustive, complete knowledge. In fact, God's thinking and speech creates worlds and brings all things to pass (Gen 1:1, 3, 6, 9, 14, 20, 24; Eph 1:11). Our thoughts are never creative; they are only receptively reconstructive of God's prior thinking, knowledge, and construction of the world.

God's thoughts are also criteriological; that is, they are the standard of truth. What God thinks and plans determines what is true, and morally speaking, his will and nature are the absolute standard of goodness. For this reason, God is the standard of truth and moral norms (Gen 18:25; Matt 4:4). God's thinking represents perfect coherence because he is the source and standard of truth and his knowledge is "from himself," which is why human thinking is

[55] Francis Turretin, *Institutes of Elenctic Theology*, ed. James T. Dennison, Jr. and trans. George Musgrave Giger, 3 vols. (Phillipsburg; P&R, 1992), 1:16.

[56] See Bahnsen, *Van Til's Apologetic*, 220–46.

governed by logical consistency. The law of contradiction, for example, is simply the expression on a created level of the internal coherence of God's nature, will, and plan. Our ability to reason logically is warranted by God's thinking, which not only creates reality to be what it is but also creates the human subject with rational faculties to know God and his world.[57] Nothing in human thought is like this.

Moreover, God's thoughts produce in us a quality of awe, in contrast to human knowledge. At the human level, the more we grow in understanding, the less awe we have of our teachers and those from whom we learned. But the opposite is the case with God. The more we know, the more we realize that God's knowledge is unfathomable and beyond searching out; indeed, we discover how much we do not know (Job 38:1–42:6).

However, although we cannot know God *fully* (exhaustively), we may know him *truly* (objectively) because of his choice to reveal himself to us both in nature and Scripture. Due to God's gracious self-revelation, the incomprehensible God is known by us. Our knowledge of him is never exhaustive, even in eternity, yet it is objectively true if it corresponds to his self-revelation. Christian theology stands in contrast to current postmodern thought that wrongly leaves us with an either-or due to its "turn to the subject"—*either* humans have exhaustive, objective knowledge (which is not possible), *or* we only have finite, subjective, arbitrarily constructed knowledge (which is affirmed). Christian theology completely rejects this way of thinking. Instead, we affirm that *finite* humans may have true, objective knowledge because, as creatures, our knowledge is caused by and dependent upon God's exhaustive knowledge. Thus, the foundation of human knowledge is first grounded in God's being (*principium essendi*) and, second, his self-revelation to us (*principium cognoscendi*).

Also, it is important to note that specific divine speech was necessary *before* the fall; it is not merely a post-fall phenomenon. God spoke to humans before the fall (Gen 1:28; 2:15); the necessity of a word-revelation was *not* solely due to human sin. In fact, regardless of sin, due to our finitude, God still needs to speak for us to understand God, self, and the world correctly. God's revelation in creation and Scripture are intended to function together. Cornelius Van Til states it this way: "Revelation in nature and revelation in Scripture are mutually

---

[57] On this point, see James N. Anderson and Greg Welty, "The Lord of Noncontradiction: An Argument for God from Logic," *Philosophia Christi* 13, no. 2 (2011): 321–38.

meaningless without one another and mutually fruitful when taken together."[58] For example, God's command not to eat of the tree of the knowledge of good and evil identifies our human task to rule over creation in obedience to God. One cannot truly understand what sin is apart from Adam willfully disobeying God's *explicit* command (Gen 3:17; Rom 5:14). No doubt, now that sin has entered the world, our need for God's special revelation to redeem us is more necessary than ever. But pre-redemptive special revelation is the presupposition of redemptive special revelation.[59]

Thus, from a Christian view, human "reason" is never magisterial but always ministerial; it was never meant to function outside of God's spoken word. Ideally, both go together, and it is only as a result of the fall that they are separated. Furthermore, it is why systematic theology is always "from above," grounded in divine revelation.

The Locus of Divine Revelation

Apart from the triune God who speaks, we have no universal, objective grounds for knowledge of God, self, and the world. But where is God's revelation found? This is the question of "locus." In theology, we make a distinction between where God speaks "generally" (universally) or "naturally" *and* where God speaks in a "special" (specific), supernatural, and salvific manner, normally associated with God's mighty actions, our Lord Jesus Christ (the incarnate Word), and Scripture (the Word written). In part 2, we will develop these two categories further.

However, for our purpose here, it is important to note that both natural and special revelation are necessary to know God and to do theology, even though natural revelation is insufficient for our salvation and our primary focus is on the incarnate and written word. As the *Belgic Confession* reminds us: creation is set "before our eyes like a beautiful book, in which all creatures, small and great, are as letters to make us ponder the invisible things of God: God's eternal power and divinity, as the apostle Paul says in Romans 1:20."[60] Yet we also need special revelation to know God. And because Scripture *is* God's word written, its language, even

---

[58] Cornelius Van Til, "Nature and Scripture," in *The Infallible Word*, ed. N. B. Stonehouse and Paul Woolley (Phillipsburg: P&R, 1946), 269.

[59] See Cornelius Van Til, *A Christian Theory of Knowledge* (Phillipsburg: P&R, 1969), 30.

[60] Belgic Confession, art. 2, at https://www.crcna.org/welcome/beliefs/confessions/belgic-confession #toc-article-2-the-means-by-which-we-know-god.

though human and finite, is divinely chosen, true, and adequate to reveal who God is. As God describes himself across the entire canon of Scripture, appropriate and adequate speech is chosen so that we have an understanding of the nature of the incomprehensible God. No doubt, our knowledge of God is never exhaustive, but on the basis of revelation, we do know God truly. Also, throughout redemptive history, God has entered into covenant relationship with his people, and at each point, he has given us a written word so that we may have total trust in all that he has promised and revealed (Deut 5:22, 32; 29:9; 30:15–16; Josh 1:7–8; John 20:31). Now in Christ—the Word incarnate—*all* of God's promises have reached their fulfillment (Heb 1:1–2), resulting in a closed canon. In Christ, the entirety of Scripture is for our instruction so that the church may be built up in truth and sound doctrine. The standard by which the church knows God, does theology, and evaluates all ideas, is Scripture. The only proper response to God's word is to trust and obey since to disbelieve or disobey Scripture is to disbelieve or disobey God (Isa 66:1–2).

Our Knowledge of God is Analogical

Scripture, as God's word written, gives us true, finite knowledge about God. However, it is important to remember that *all* biblical language in reference to God is true but analogical.[61] What this entails is that we must not confuse "literal" speech about God with univocal speech nor "non-literal" speech with analogical speech. Instead, under the larger category of analogical predication (i.e., language applied to God and humans is similar but different), we should place both "literal" and "non-literal" speech about God. In other words, both "literal" and "non-literal" language in Scripture about God is analogical. This allows us to consistently maintain the Creator-creature distinction and to affirm that *all* biblical language about God is analogical, accommodated, and God-chosen *human* speech about him that truly communicates who he is, but not exhaustively.

In "literal" speech, words and phrases are used in an ordinary and normal sense tied to convention unless some contextual clue suggests otherwise. For example, God *is* love; this is a "literal" description of God. "Non-literal" speech, which includes figurative and metaphorical language, uses words and phrases in a non-ordinary way intended by the speaker or author. For

[61] See Duby, *God in Himself*, 232–91.

example, "God is a Shepherd" and "God is a rock" are "non-literal," or "metaphorical," descriptions of God. However, both literal and non-literal speech about God—"God exists," "God is holy," "God is love," "God is a Shepherd," "God is a rock"—are analogical and not univocal. So, to say God is holy, God is love, or God is a rock is to affirm that God is love, holy, and a rock in a way similar *and* different from humans or created realities. But if we equate "literal" with univocal and say that God is love or God is holy in exactly the same way that humans love or are holy, we make a fundamental theological mistake: we reduce the Creator to the creature and undermine the biblical teaching of God's incomprehensibility and uniqueness. All biblical language in reference to God is true, but it's never one-for-one with the creature; it's always analogical predication. Thus, in all of the Bible's descriptions of God, whether they are "literal" or "non-literal," the Creator-creature distinction must be preserved.

This point is crucial in our interpretation of Scripture, and it must govern how we understand *all* biblical language about God. It must also govern how we rightly theologize about who God is: his nature, attributes, works, and relation to the world. This requires that in our knowing God from Scripture, we must pay careful attention to all that Scripture says and in the way that Scripture says it. God is the incomprehensible Creator and Lord, yet he is also the triune-personal God who has disclosed himself to us in a covenantal context and in real history. Because Scripture is God-given, the very language that God employs to describe himself is accurate, true, and reliable, yet not exhaustive, univocal, or equivocal, but analogical. What is needed to know God rightly is to let all of Scripture speak for itself in its own categories, presentation, and across the entire canon. When we do so, we can be assured that our incomprehensible, glorious, triune God is known truly by us, yet for all eternity, we will never exhaust who God is in all of his majesty, transcendence, and covenant love and faithfulness in Christ Jesus.

Concluding Reflection

What is the foundation for truth and theology? Truth and all normative theology are only possible because of the triune God who in himself is the source and standard of life, truth, and goodness and because of his sovereign and gracious choice to reveal himself to us. Apart from these two foundations—the triune God (*principia essendi*) and his word-revelation (*principium cognoscendi*)—truth and theology are impossible.

If we try to substitute these two *principia* for something else located in the created realm, whether in the self, the world, or some idolatrous construct of "god," the reality of objective truth and theology crumbles before our eyes (Rom 1:18–32). In faithfulness to our triune God who speaks and out of love and obedience to our Lord Jesus Christ, and in order to avoid futility in this life and judgment in the life to come, evangelical theology must self-consciously reject all theologies "from below" and unashamedly practice a theology "from above."

As Christ's church, we are called to the supreme privilege by God's sovereign grace to engage in the joy, privilege, and responsibility of "faith seeking understanding." By reflecting on the entirety of God's speech and bringing all of life and thought captive to God's word, we glorify our triune Creator-covenant Lord, we fulfill the purpose of our creation and redemption, and we serve to proclaim the glory of Christ to this poor, lost, and fallen world. As we do so, we see the church grounded in the truth, equipped to stand strong and to avoid the quicksand of false ideas that stand in opposition to Christ and that are coming to naught.

But given that theology is grounded in divine revelation and uniquely in *sola Scriptura*, it is imperative that we rightly read and apply God's word, which leads to questions of hermeneutics, theological method, and theological interpretation of Scripture, a subject to which we now turn.

CHAPTER 4

Systematic Theology: The Method

Introduction

The foundation for systematic theology is the glorious triune God who speaks, who alone is the source and standard of life, truth, and goodness (Exod 3:14–15; Isa 46:9–13; Acts 17:24–25; 1 Tim 6:16). The task of theology is to know God and all things in relation to him as we apply his word, known both in creation and uniquely in Scripture, to every area of life (Deut 6:1–8; Matt 22:37–38). Theology enables the church to understand and apply Scripture rightly in order to live faithful and obedient lives under Christ's Lordship (Col 2:6–10) and to witness to and defend the truth of the gospel as we proclaim the unsearchable riches of Christ to the nations (Matt 28:18–20; 1 Cor 1:18–31; 2 Cor 10:3–5; Col 1:28–29; 2 Tim 4:1–5; 1 Pet 3:15–16).

Theology is grounded and warranted by *sola Scriptura* as the "ruling rule" (*norma normans*). As noted in chapter 1, *sola Scriptura*, in the Reformation sense, means that Scripture is our final, sufficient authority, *not* our only authority. Other theological disciplines serve a "ministerial" function as "ruled rules" (*norma normata*), but Scripture alone is the final, "magisterial" authority for all theological formulations, which entails doing a theology "from above."

Doing theology minimally involves two interrelated steps. First, theology requires that we "put together" all that Scripture teaches on a specific subject the way that Scripture does, which involves the task of exegesis and biblical theology. The Bible is not a collection of isolated texts; Scripture is God's first-order, unfolding revelation of his eternal plan, forged across a specific storyline from creation to the new creation, centered in our Lord Jesus Christ. Thus, a correct reading of Scripture demands that we pay careful attention to the Bible's own presentation before drawing theological conclusions. Second, theology does not merely repeat Scripture; it seeks "to understand" Scripture in terms of application, logical implications, and metaphysical entailments as a "constructive" exercise in "faith seeking understanding." Theology constructs and defends sound doctrine so that the church is not "blown around by every wind of teaching" (Eph 4:14), but is instead "rooted and built up in [Christ]" (Col 2:7).

But more needs to be said, especially regarding the first step that raises the crucial question: What does it mean to be *biblical* in our theology?[1] How do we rightly exegete biblical texts and draw correct theological conclusions? At the heart of systematic theology is the attempt to "take every thought captive to obey Christ" (2 Cor 10:5). But how do we *know* that our theological formulations are faithful to Scripture? This question might seem strange to ask, especially for evangelicals. Many believe that the task of doing theology is fairly obvious: simply the collection and organization of biblical texts. Yet, a moment's reflection reminds us that this is not the case.

For example, think of Paul's exhortation to Timothy: "Be diligent to present yourself to God as one approved, a worker who doesn't need to be ashamed, correctly teaching the word of truth" (2 Tim 2:15). This is not only an exhortation to read Scripture correctly; it is also a warning that we may fail in the task! Also, we know that all theologies are *not* equally biblical. Just because one appeals to Scripture does not necessarily warrant the view. After all, historical theology is replete with heresies that claim to be biblical but are not, as evidenced by the dogmatic standards of Nicaea and Chalcedon. Scripture is *not* a "wax nose" that can be twisted

[1] What it means to be "biblical" was impressed on me by Kevin Vanhoozer at Trinity Evangelical Divinity School. For his answer to the question, see *Drama of Doctrine* (see chap. 1, n. 44); and his more recent, "Analytics, Poetics, and the Mission of Dogmatic Discourse," in *The Task of Dogmatics: Explorations in Theological Method*, ed. Oliver D. Crisp and Fred Sanders (Grand Rapids: Zondervan, 2017), 23–48; and "Staurology, Ontology, and the Travail of the Biblical Narrative: Once More unto the Biblical Theological Breach," *SBJT* 23 (2019): 7–33.

to fit a plurality of views, even conflicting readings of Scripture. So, how do we know that our theological proposals are *true* to Scripture and *true* to "the faith that was delivered to the saints once for all?" (Jude 3). This question is not an insignificant one given that the triune God of all glory has spoken, and as such, *his* word deserves, indeed, demands our complete attention, faithful reading, and careful application. Also, given our present cultural context, which denies the reality of truth, if we claim to have a normative theology, we must account for how our theological views are *true*.

In what follows, some reflections are given on how to be *biblical* in our interpretation *and* application of Scripture in the doing of systematic theology. The issue of theological method is vast, yet it is essential to describe how we envision the *theological* interpretation of Scripture *and* the doing of theology according to Scripture. The basic point is this: our reading and application of Scripture must be according to what it *is*. This entails that our theological method is dependent on a *theology* of Scripture, which should not surprise us given the intertwined, mutually dependent nature of theology.[2] Thus, to answer questions of theological interpretation and method, we must first ask: What *is* the Bible? The answer to this question impacts how one views theological interpretation *and* method. We will answer the question in two steps. First, we will reflect on how to approach and interpret Scripture "on its own terms," thus accounting for how we are *biblically* warranted in our theological conclusions. Second, we will reflect on how we move from "canon to concept," that is, to theological formulation.[3]

Approaching and Reading Scripture Theologically

Biblical interpretation must be true to the *nature* of Scripture. Minimally, we can think of what Scripture is in two ways: (1) what Scripture claims for itself, that is, its self-attestation; and (2) how Scripture has come to us. We find that (1) Scripture is God's speech through human authors and that (2) Scripture has come to us *over time*, centered in Christ. Let us turn to both of these points to offer reflections on how to approach and interpret Scripture according to a

---

[2] Craig A. Carter makes this same point. *Interpreting Scripture with the Great Tradition: Recovering the Genius of Premodern Exegesis* (Grand Rapids: Baker Academic, 2018), 31–59.

[3] From "canon to concept" are from Vanhoozer, "From Canon to Concept," 96–124 (see chap. 3, n. 2).

theology of Scripture before we apply our discussion to how we move from "canon to concept" for the life and health of the church.

What is Scripture? A Brief Theology of Scripture

Two points will summarize what Scripture *is*. What follows is only a summary of a theology of Scripture with some important implications for our interpretation of Scripture. A full account of the doctrine of Scripture is reserved for part 2.

1. Scripture Is God's Word Written through the Agency of Human Authors

To approach Scripture correctly, we begin with its own claim for itself: Scripture is God's word written, the unfolding of his eternal plan, the product of God's mighty action through the word and by the Spirit, whereby human authors freely wrote exactly what God intended them to write without error (2 Tim 3:15–17; 2 Pet 1:20–21; cf. Matt 4:4; John 10:35).

In fact, as we read Scripture from beginning to end, this claim is pervasive, yet since the Enlightenment, not everyone has accepted this view of Scripture, especially those who embraced worldview assumptions in opposition to Scripture, as discussed in chapter 2. As such, some insist that the human character of Scripture entails error. Others argue that the Bible is only a record of God's revelation, while others suggest that Scripture gives us no doctrine of inspiration that demands that we identify its human writings with God's own word. However, all of these views fail because they inevitably deny the Bible's view of itself, a point we will return to in part 2.

What impact does Scripture's self-attestation have on our interpretation of it? Two answers may be given consistent with Scripture and historic Christian theology.

First, since Scripture is *God's* word from the triune Creator-sovereign Lord, we expect a coherent unity across the canon despite its diversity, which reveals God's eternal plan and purposes for this fallen world. Kevin Vanhoozer describes Scripture as "a unified communicative act, that is, as the complex, multi-levelled speech act of a single divine author,"[4] which entails that we interpret Scripture as a *unified* revelation that demands our complete trust. As

[4] Vanhoozer, "Exegesis and Hermeneutics," 61 (see chap. 1, n. 24).

a result, we interpret all of Scripture's "parts" in light of the "whole," which finds its overall unity in the unfolding of God's plan centered in Christ (Eph 1:9–10; Heb 1:1–2). Contrary to postliberal theology, Scripture's canonical unity is not due to an ecclesiastical decision to choose these books as Scripture. Instead, its unity is due to the triune God who reveals himself so that the Bible's content and categories are first-order and foundational in our doctrinal formulations.

Second, since Scripture is God's word through human authors, we discover God's intent through the writing(s) of the human author(s) by reading the texts according to grammatical-literary-historical exegesis and reading books in their final form. We attend to what the human authors communicate to us because "what Scripture says [human authors], God says," and vice versa.[5] Our goal in exegesis is to remain true to authorial intent; otherwise, we run the risk of standing over Scripture instead of under it. As John Calvin stated, "It is the first business of the interpreter to let his author say what he does say, instead of attributing to him what we think he ought to say."[6] For this reason, throughout the ages and especially in the Reformed tradition, Scripture is read with a commitment to *sensus literalis*, that is, the reading of Scripture according to authorial intention, both in terms of the human author(s) and the divine author.[7]

This point also leads us to a "whole-Bible" or canonical reading of Scripture since each biblical author's text is a necessary "part" of the "whole," and it cannot be fully understood apart from the whole. We must not read Scripture in a "thin" way, that is, as isolated texts apart from the whole. Instead, we must read texts in a "thick" way, that is, in light of the entire canon of Scripture.[8] Due to divine inspiration, we discover God's intent through the writing(s) of the biblical authors, but given the diversity of authors over time, what each author writes must be interpreted in terms of the entire Bible. No doubt, God may say more than each author had in mind, but God's intent is never less than the human author's intent. And it is only by reading Scripture in light of the canon that we discover its true meaning;

---

[5] B. B. Warfield, *The Inspiration and Authority of the Bible* (Phillipsburg: P&R, 1980).

[6] John Calvin, "Preface to Romans," cited in Vanhoozer, *Is There a Meaning?*, 47 (see chap. 2, n. 118).

[7] See Iain Provan, *The Reformation and the Right Reading of Scripture* (Waco: Baylor University Press, 2017), 1–312.

[8] On a "thin" vs. "thick" reading of Scripture, see Vanhoozer, "Exegesis and Hermeneutics," 61–62.

God's ultimate intent, purposes, and plan; and how Scripture applies to us today in light of Christ's coming. This point is simply the application of the Reformation principle, "Scripture must interpret Scripture."

It is also another way of thinking about the "fuller sense" (*sensus plenior*) of Scripture. This term bears different meanings, so it requires careful definition.[9] Greg Beale suggests that the "fuller sense" means that "the Old Testament authors did not exhaustively understand the meaning, implications, and possible applications of all that they wrote,"[10] yet because they wrote under divine inspiration, what they wrote was God-given, true, and authoritative. However, the earlier authors probably did not fully grasp where God's plan was going given that God had not yet disclosed all of the details of his eternal plan. Thus, as more revelation is

---

[9] For a discussion of *sensus plenior*, see Raymond E. Brown, *The Sensus Plenior of Sacred Scripture* (Baltimore: St. Mary's University, 1955), 88–122; Douglas J. Moo and Andrew D. Naselli, "The Problem of the New Testament's Use of the Old Testament," in *The Enduring Authority of the Christian Scriptures*, ed. D. A. Carson (Grand Rapids: Eerdmans, 2016), 702–46; G. K. Beale, "Did Jesus and His Followers Preach the Right Doctrine from the Wrong Texts?," in *The Right Doctrine from the Wrong Texts: Essays on the Use of the Old Testament in the New*, ed. G. K. Beale (Grand Rapids: Baker, 1994), 392–93. Many advocates of a "fuller sense" insist that this "sense" is *not* what the human author intended and thus not discoverable by grammatical-historical exegesis. I reject this view. What is needed is God's intent discovered through human author(s) unfolded over time and "fully" known at the canonical level. God intends more than the individual authors knew, yet God does not contravene what the earlier authors intended; instead, he builds on it through later authors.

[10] Beale, "Did Jesus and His Followers Preach?," 393; see also Moo and Naselli, "Problem of the New Testament's Use," 702–46. Moo and Naselli note that

> the canonical approach decreases and may eliminate the questionable division between the human and divine authors, intentions in a given text. This approach does not appeal to the divine author's meaning that is deliberately concealed from the human author in the process of inspiration (a *sensus occultus*); it appeals to the meaning of the text itself that takes on deeper significance as God's plan unfolds (a *sensus praegnans*). When God breathes out his words through human authors, he surely knows what the ultimate meaning of their words will be, but he has not created a *double entendre* or hidden a meaning in the words that we can uncover only through special revelation. The "added meaning" that the text takes on is the product of the ultimate canonical shape, although often we can clearly perceive it only if God reveals it. . . . We can often verify the "fuller sense" that the NT discovers in the OT by reading OT texts as the NT authors do: as part of a completed, canonical whole. "Problem of the New Testament's Use," 736.

given through later authors, more of God's plan is discovered and we grasp better where that plan is going.

This is why the NT's interpretation of the OT is decisive: later texts yield greater clarity and understanding. The NT shows us how the OT is fulfilled in Christ and that he is the proper referent of OT texts. Although the NT's interpretation of the OT expands the OT author's meaning by seeing new implications and applications, later texts do *not* contravene the integrity of the earlier texts. Instead, as Beale notes, the NT "develop[s] them in a way which is consistent with the Old Testament author's understanding of the way in which God interacts with his people" in previous eras of redemptive history.[11] Thus, Scripture interprets Scripture; the later parts "draw out and explain more clearly the earlier parts,"[12] and theological conclusions are derived from the entirety of Scripture, not merely one part of it. In fact, a canonical reading is not optional; it is demanded by what Scripture *is*.

2. Scripture Is God's Word-Act Revelation Written over Time

Scripture is best understood as a "word-act" revelation. Although we will develop this point in part 2, this simply means that Scripture *is* God's own authoritative interpretation of his redemptive acts through the agency of human authors. For this reason, Scripture is *God's* true, authoritative interpretation of his redemptive plan, which entails that the Bible's own description of reality on *its* terms, that is, within the Bible's own framework, presentation, categories, and content (*intratextual*), is first order and indispensable. Scripture's interpretive framework is our spectacles by which we view the world, unlike all extratextual theologies.[13]

---

[11] Beale, "Did Jesus and His Followers Preach?," 393. Michael D. Williams rightly argues that allegorical interpretations that discover an entirely "other" sense are preventable "not by denying the reality of the fuller sense but by insisting that the fuller sense be established only as an extension of the original sense and solely on the basis of subsequent biblical revelation." *Far as the Curse Is Found: The Covenant Story of Redemption* (Phillipsburg: P&R, 2005), 81–82.

[12] Beale, "Did Jesus and His Followers Preach?," 393; see also Vanhoozer, *Is There a Meaning?*, 307–452.

[13] Remember "intratextual" means to interpret Scripture *on its own terms*, that is, its own claim for itself, and according to its own framework, presentation, structures, and content. "Extratextual" is to interpret Scripture in light of an "outside" worldview that is viewed as more authoritative than Scripture.

This point is also underscored by noting that Scripture is a *progressive revelation*, or a revelation written over time.[14] Part of the Bible's own self-presentation is that redemption and revelation occur over time, and this has substantial implications for our reading and application of Scripture, as we will note below. Due to God's choice, he has unveiled his eternal plan step-by-step, starting in creation and reaching its fulfillment in Christ's two advents. Scripture, as God's interpretation of his redemptive acts, also involves historical progression. In this way, as Scripture unfolds God's plan centered in Christ, the overall point of Scripture is both Christocentric and Christotelic (God's entire plan reaches its *telos* in Christ). Ardel Caneday captures this point well:

> Throughout the biblical storyline, God is the leading actor but also the scriptwriter, the director, the producer of this grand drama, and the creator and owner of the universal theater in which the drama unfolds. The Bible's storyline spans the history of God's redemption of his creation. Integral to this history of redemption are progressive sequences of God's revelation that reach their completion and fulfillment in the revelation of Jesus Christ.[15]

Hebrews 1:1–2 magnificently captures this point. "Long ago," the author writes, "God spoke to the fathers by the prophets," and he did so "at different times and in different ways." God's word-act revelation took place over time, and as it was given, it anticipated more to come. In fact, this is the point that the author makes by his use of "at different times and in different ways" (*polumerōs kai polutropōs*). Not only was the OT revelation repetitive, it was also incomplete. In God's unfolding plan, we gradually "see" that it is moving forward to Christ's coming. As William Lane rightly notes, "The fragmentary and varied character of God's self-disclosure under the old covenant awakened within the fathers an expectation

---

[14] "Progressive" refers to the unfolding of God's covenantal plan over time but not in the sense that an earlier era was inferior and the later era has progressed or has reached a superior stage. The latter idea is associated with classic liberalism and its evolutionary and Hegelian understanding of religion, including its interpretation of Christianity.

[15] Ardel B. Caneday, "Biblical Types: Revelation Concealed in Plain Sight to be Disclosed—'These Things Occurred Typologically to Them and Were Written Down for Our Admonition,'" in *God's Glory Revealed in Christ: Essays on Biblical Theology in Honor of Thomas R. Schreiner*, ed. Denny Burk, James M. Hamilton Jr., and Brian Vickers (Nashville: B&H Academic, 2019), 144.

that he would continue to speak to his people. . . .The ministry of the prophets marked the preparatory phase of that history."[16] But now, "in his Son" (*en huiō*, v. 2), the last days the OT predicted are here in Christ, in whom all of God's revelation and redemptive purposes culminate. Christ is the final, definitive, and complete revelation; he is qualitatively different from the prophets who preceded him. This does not diminish the OT's authority; rather, it stresses that it was incomplete as it pointed forward to its intended fulfillment in Christ.[17] Just as redemption occurs *over time* and culminates in Christ, so Scripture is an unfolding word-act revelation centered in Christ.

The Nature of Scripture and Theological Interpretation

How does our *theology* of Scripture affect our interpretation of it and warrant our theological formulations? To answer this question, first, let us focus on some of the hermeneutical implications of Scripture as God's word-act revelation given to us *over time*, and then let us address the issue of reading Scripture in context, in fact, in *three* contexts that are basic to a correct theological interpretation of Scripture.

1. Interpreting Scripture as a Word-Act Revelation over Time

The fact that revelation, alongside redemption, occurs over time entails that we read Scripture by carefully tracing out God's unfolding plan—the task of biblical theology. As discussed in chapter 1, biblical theology is the exegetical and theological discipline that attempts to interpret Scripture on its own terms and to put together the entire canon in terms of its redemptive-historical progression. Scripture consists of many authors, books, and literary forms that require

---

[16] William L. Lane, *Hebrews 1–8*, WBC 47a (Dallas: Thomas Nelson, 1991), 11.

[17] This fits with 1 Pet 1:10–12. The prophets investigated "what time and circumstances" (*eis tina ē poion kairon*) as they anticipated the coming of Christ. Yet the full significance of what was written becomes clearer as the Bible's story unfolds. Each biblical author may not have understood the Bible's whole story, to which his life and writing is a contribution, but in its own context, what he did and wrote communicated something of that overall plan. Yet because of the promises of God, the biblical authors knew that what they were writing was also pointing forward in the story to its resolution. See Thomas R. Schreiner, *1, 2 Peter, Jude*, NAC 27 (Nashville: B&H, 2003), 71–76.

careful interpretation. Yet what unites the Bible's diversity is God's unfolding plan, starting in creation, accounting for the fall, unpacking God's redemptive promises through his covenants, and culminating in Christ's coming and the dawning of the new creation. As D. A. Carson reminds us, despite the Bible's diversity, "the fact remains that the Bible as a whole document tells a story, and, properly used, that story can serve as a metanarrative that shapes our grasp of the entire Christian faith."[18] For interpretation, this entails that we read Scripture in such a way that we account for the Bible's unfolding story and how each text ("part") fits in the overall plan of God centered in Christ ("whole").

In addition, it is also crucial that we interpret Scripture in terms of its own presentation, categories, and content (*intratextual*). This involves not only an unfolding storyline but also the Bible's own description of reality, which involves specific metaphysical commitments. In his work on theological method, Michael Horton emphasizes these same points. Given the nature of Scripture, Horton suggests that a proper theological method must be "redemptive-historical-eschatological" so that our reading of Scripture and drawing theological conclusions is according to the Bible's own "intrasystematic categories."[19]

For Horton, the terms *eschatological*, *redemptive-historical*, and *covenant* capture Scripture's own intrasystematic categories. By "eschatological," Horton means more than a mere doctrinal topic. Instead, it is the lens by which we read Scripture and do our theology. Scripture itself comes to us as a redemptive revelation starting in creation and unfolding in God's eternal plan. As such, the very "form" and "shape" of Scripture is "eschatological." This is why Horton is uncomfortable with George Lindbeck's labelling evangelical theology as "cognitive-propositionalist."[20] Scripture is more than a storehouse of facts or propositions; Scripture unfolds a *plot*, a divine interpretation of the drama of redemption, that is eschatological and Christological, and, thus, our interpretation and application of Scripture must reflect this. With the term *redemptive-historical*, Horton is referring to Scripture's own presentation of itself as "the organic unfolding of the divine plan in its execution through word (announcement), act (accomplishment), and word (interpretation)."[21] Given that redemption is progressive and

---

[18] Carson, *Gagging of God*, 194 (see chap. 2, n. 1).

[19] See Horton, *Covenant and Eschatology*, 1–19, 147–276 (see chap. 2, n. 147). Horton's use of *intrasystematic categories* is similar to my use of *intratextual*.

[20] See Lindbeck, *Nature of Doctrine* (see chap. 2, n. 10).

[21] Horton, *Covenant and Eschatology*, 5.

unfolding, so is revelation since revelation is God's own interpretation of his mighty actions through human authors.

Horton draws a number of important implications for our interpretation of Scripture and the doing of theology, but our focus here is on one of them tied to the idea of progressive revelation. Our reading of Scripture and our doing theology must attend to the historical unfolding of redemptive history that is organically related to and centered in Christ. The very "form" and "shape" of Scripture reminds us that God did not disclose himself in one exhaustive act but in an organic, progressive manner, and in fact, it is this organic quality of revelation that serves to explain the diversity of Scripture. Our reading of Scripture and drawing theological conclusions, as a result, must be very careful not to proof-text without considering where each text is located in God's unfolding plan and how each text contributes to the whole story now seen in light of its fulfillment in Christ.[22] This observation leads to the importance of reading Scripture in context, in fact, in *three* contexts.

2. Interpreting Scripture as a Closed Canon: The Three Contexts of Biblical Interpretation

Given that Scripture is God's word written through human authors unfolding God's eternal plan, to interpret it correctly requires that we read it according to three contexts, or three horizons: textual, epochal, and canonical.[23] This follows from the fact that God's revelation is progressive. As biblical authors build on each other, we discover how each text contributes to God's overall plan centered in Christ, which allows us to avoid an incorrect form of "proof-texting," namely, taking texts out of context. In biblical interpretation and theological formulation, "context" is king; in fact, three contexts are crucial to putting together the entire Bible. Let us briefly discuss each of these "contexts" for a proper biblical-theological interpretation of Scripture.[24]

---

[22] Horton, 1–19, 147–276.

[23] See Richard Lints, *The Fabric of Theology* (Grand Rapids: Eerdmans, 1993), 259–311.

[24] Reading Scripture according to three horizons/contexts is not new. In fact, it is what all Christians have done, at least implicitly though not consistently, in their reading and application of the biblical text. For others who advocate this approach, see Richard B. Gaffin Jr., "The Redemptive-Historical View," in *Biblical Hermeneutics: Five Views*, ed. Stanley E. Porter and Beth M. Stovell (Downers Grove:

The Textual or Immediate Context. Since we cannot read the Bible all at once, our reading of Scripture begins with any text in its immediate context (entire book).[25] Our task in interpretation is to discover God's intent through the human author by grasping what the author has communicated in his text according to grammatical/literary-historical exegesis. Here we seek to discern the human author's given intent by placing the text (book) in its historical setting; understanding the rules of language; and analyzing the syntax, textual variants, word meanings, and the literary structure, including its literary form. By paying careful attention to the text, we discover what authors are seeking to communicate. Standard books in hermeneutics cover these areas, and the reader is referred to these books.[26] However, our interpretation of Scripture does not terminate here; it leads to the epochal context.

The Epochal Context. This context is reading the text by locating it in God's unfolding plan. Since Scripture is given *over time*, texts do not come to us in a vacuum; instead, they are embedded in a larger context of what has come *before* them. As God communicates through biblical authors, these same authors write in light of what has preceded them. The label *epochal* is not used to convey that God has different plans; it simply reminds us that God's revelation of his plan occurs over time. As God speaks through authors, there is a unity in his plan but also development as he enacts and reveals his plan, which reaches fulfillment in Christ Jesus.

Also, by locating texts in God's unfolding plan, we are able to see the "intertextual" links between earlier and later revelation.[27] As later authors refer to earlier texts, they build on them, not only in terms of greater understanding of God's plan but also by identifying God-given

---

IVP Academic, 2012), 89–110; Carson, *Gagging of God*, 190 n. 133; Horton, *Covenant and Eschatology*, 147–80; Vanhoozer, "Exegesis and Hermeneutics," 60–62.

[25] The textual/immediate context is the entire book in its final form. For some books this is a bit more complicated due to their being part of *one* book. For example, Genesis is one book, but it is really part of a larger book: the Pentateuch. The textual horizon for Genesis or Leviticus is the entire Pentateuch. The same is true of the Psalter. Each individual psalm needs to be interpreted as a text that is part of *one* book, the Psalter.

[26] For example, see Jason S. DeRouchie, *How to Understand and Apply the Old Testament* (Phillipsburg: P&R, 2017); Andrew David Naselli, *How to Understand and Apply the New Testament* (Phillipsburg: P&R, 2017).

[27] *Intertextual* refers to how later authors build on previous revelation but do not contravene the original sense. This differs from Richard Hays, *Echoes of Scripture in the Letters of Paul* (New Haven: Yale University Press, 1989), 154–61. He argues that Paul read the OT in light of Christ but not always true to the OT's "original sense."

"patterns" between earlier and later "persons, events, and institutions" within the plan—what is identified as "typology." As God unveils his plan, including the unveiling of God-given patterns (types), his plan moves forward until it reaches its telos in Christ. As later authors draw out these God-given types (as features of divine revelation), they do not arbitrarily make connections that contravene earlier texts; rather, they develop these patterns according to God's patient unfolding of his design, which spans the ages.[28] Only by reading texts first in their immediate context and then in relation to where these texts are in God's unfolding plan do we begin to grasp God's redemptive plan and how we fit into it. Individual texts do not become fragmented, and the road from "text" to "reader" is *not* a matter of one's intuition, preference, or prejudice.

As we read texts in their textual and epochal contexts, we understand God's unfolding plan. Given how Scripture has come to us, it is crucial not to bypass how later authors build on earlier ones, moving too quickly from texts to canon. If we move too quickly from the textual to the canonical horizon, individual texts become fragmented, and we miss how they are part of the Bible's storyline that prepares us for Christ. We may even draw conclusions for ourselves today in ways that do not follow how God's plan unfolds and reaches its fulfillment in Christ. In fact, some of our theological differences center on this point: circumcision to baptism, Israel to church, and the land promise. Theological conclusions must be made in light of the entire canon, but it is important that texts "fit" in Scripture as they do within God's unfolding dramatic plan.

Must we be precise regarding the epochal differences in Scripture?[29] This question is a major debate within biblical theology. Scripture divides redemptive history in a number of ways. Most agree that the major epochal division is between the OT era and the fulfillment of

---

[28] On this point, see Beale, "Did Jesus and His Followers Preach?," 391–98; Cf. Carson, "Systematic Theology and Biblical Theology," 98 (see chap. 1, n. 38).

[29] An important debate in biblical theology is whether we ought to read Scripture, specifically the OT, by the ordering of the Hebrew Canon. For example, Stephen G. Dempster insists that we do. *Dominion and Dynasty: A Biblical Theology of the Hebrew Bible*, NSBT 15 (Downers Grove: InterVarsity, 2003), 15–51; Cf. James M. Hamilton Jr., *God's Glory in Salvation through Judgment: A Biblical Theology* (Wheaton: Crossway, 2010), 59–65. I am sympathetic with this approach; however, one potential problem is the difficulty of establishing *the* official order of the OT canon since there are a variety of orderings. Regardless of whether *the* official order of the OT canon can be established (for which a strong case can be made), minimally the actual practice of NT authors is to interpret OT texts in relation to where

God's plan in Christ. But there are also other crucial biblical divisions. For example, in Rom 5:12–21, Paul divides all of human history under two heads: Adam and Christ. Under these two heads, Paul further subdivides redemptive history by the following epochs: Adam (vv. 12–13), from Adam to Moses (vv. 14–17), from Moses and the giving of the old covenant to Christ (vv. 18–21). Or, in Acts 7:1–53, Stephen identifies three distinct periods: the age of the patriarchs (vv. 2–16); the Mosaic age, which included within it the time of the exodus and conquest of the Promised Land (vv. 17–45a); and the age of the monarchy (vv. 45b–53). Or, in the genealogy in Matthew 1, Matthew divides up redemptive history into three distinct periods: Abraham to David (vv. 2–6a), Solomon to the exile (vv. 6b–11), and the exile to the coming of Christ (vv. 12–17).

This is not an esoteric point. To be "biblical" requires that we ask the "structure" question so that we read Scripture according to its own intrasystematic categories and presentation. This entails that to read Scripture properly is more than merely getting the author's meaning right or tracing large "themes" across the canon. No doubt, our reading of Scripture will carefully unpack how themes such as temple, land, sacrifice, priest, and so on, unfold in Scripture. But before we do, we must first ask whether God has put together his plan and revealed it to us in such a way that there is a correct *structuring* or *backbone* to the Bible's story that must be understood so that we are true to Scripture's *own terms*. In other words, is there a specific *structure* that the Bible has that each part fits within and contributes to the larger whole?

Over the years, Christians have wrestled with this question and answered it in different ways. My contention is that there is a specific structure or backbone to the Bible's story and God's unfolding plan that is essential to follow in order to read and apply Scripture rightly, namely, the *progression of the biblical covenants*. If this is correct, then to be "biblical," we must interpret texts both in terms of their threefold context *and* in relationship to their covenantal location (creation/Adam, Noah, Abraham, Israel, David, and the Prophets who predict the dawning of the new covenant). In other words, if our interpretation of Scripture is true to "*its* terms," we cannot ignore how the progression of the biblical covenants unveil God's plan now fulfilled in Christ.

---

they are covenantally located in history, and thus it is crucial to read texts in light of *earlier* and then *later* texts (hence epochal and canonical horizons), as we discuss below.

In Scripture, the covenants are not window dressing. Instead, they are God's chosen means to unfold his plan, the backbone to the Bible's storyline, and thus *hermeneutically* significant. The progression of the covenants is the Bible's own way of structuring God's redemptive plan. To not attend to how the covenants relate to each other and culminate in Christ will result in a failure to grasp the narrative plot structure of the Bible and inevitably lead to crucial theological mistakes. On this point, think about how many debates in Scripture center on changes that have occurred in redemptive history due to the inauguration of the new covenant in Christ: Jew-Gentile (Acts 10–11; Rom 9–11; Eph 2:11–22); the Judaizers (Gal 2–3); the conclusions of the Jerusalem Council (Acts 15); and today, debates over the application of the OT to us today, the Sabbath, the nature of the church, baptism, the promised land, eschatology, and so on. All of these debates cannot be resolved unless we think through the progression of the biblical covenants.

In this regard, Graeme Goldsworthy's *Christ-Centered Biblical Theology* is helpful in thinking through the Bible's "own terms," especially the Bible's own structure, yet it needs to be supplemented by thinking through how the covenants serve as the backbone of the Bible's metanarrative.[30] As Goldsworthy contrasts various approaches to biblical theology within evangelical theology, he rightly observes that a crucial question that divides various biblical theologies is this: "What is the Bible's own internal structure which determines how it should be put together and read so that we are reading the Bible *on its own terms*?" Goldsworthy is asking the right question. But given the lack of consensus among evangelicals on how the Bible is put together, what exactly is the Bible's own structure, if there is one at all? Goldsworthy proposes that the "Robinson-Hebert" view best reflects the Bible's structure. His book is devoted to defending this view—a view he adopts from his former professor and colleague Donald Robinson at Moore Theological College in Sydney, Australia, and Gabriel Hebert.

After Goldsworthy summarizes the various proposals of leading evangelical biblical theologians,[31] he spends most of his time analyzing the Geerhardus Vos–Edmund Clowney

---

[30] See Goldsworthy, *Christ-Centered Biblical Theology*, 19–110 (see chap. 1, n. 37); also cf. Goldsworthy, *Preaching the Whole Bible as Christian Scripture: The Application of Biblical Theology to Expository Preaching* (Grand Rapids: Eerdmans, 2000).

[31] Goldsworthy discusses the following biblical theologians: Geerhardus Vos, Edmund Clowney, Dennis Johnson, Willem VanGemeren, William Dumbrell, Sidney Greidanus, Charles Scobie, Craig Bartholomew and Michael Goheen, Gerhard Hasel, and Elmer Martens.

approach, which divides redemptive history into various epochs. Goldsworthy's main critique is that the Vos-Clowney epochal divisions are *not* consistent with the Bible's own structure. For example, he states, "both Vos and Clowney nominate the period from Moses to the coming of Christ as the last great epoch of the Old Testament."[32] But Goldsworthy questions whether this is how the OT divides redemptive history and whether this accounts for the watershed revelation associated with David and Solomon, let alone prophetic eschatology, which focuses on the return from exile, the restoration of the people, and the anticipation of the renewal of all things.[33]

Instead, Goldsworthy, following Matthew 1, suggests that the unfolding of the "kingdom" is the backbone of the Bible's plotline, yet his epochal divisions look a bit arbitrary upon closer examination. For example, Goldsworthy argues that the Bible moves from creation to new creation in three main stages: (1) the basic biblical history from creation to Abraham and then to David and Solomon, (2) the eschatology of the later writing Prophets, and (3) the fulfillment of all things in Christ. Goldsworthy argues that the first stage of biblical history offers the rationale and setting for the calling of Abraham and the covenant with Israel, *and* it establishes the typological patterns which are later developed in the Prophets and fulfilled in Christ. Furthermore, he argues that the high point of the first stage is found in David and Solomon and in the building of the temple, which represents God's presence among his people, an echo back to Eden. The second stage begins with Solomon's apostasy. Biblical history from this time on is primarily one of judgment that is overlaid with the prophetic promises that the Day of the Lord will come and bring final blessing and judgment. In this stage, the typological patterns laid down in the earlier history are recapitulated as they project a greater future fulfillment. In the final stage, the fulfillment of the previous stages now takes place in Christ who fulfills all the previous patterns in himself in an "already-not-yet" fashion.

Goldsworthy is not only asking the right questions; he is also helpfully describing the Bible's "own terms" in regard to the Bible's own *internal* structure. However, a question that emerges is how he warrants his redemptive-historical, epochal divisions from Scripture and thus avoids the charge of being arbitrary. Is there a way of accounting for the Bible's own internal structure and incorporating the insights of Goldsworthy? Yes, if we follow the *progression*

[32] Goldsworthy, *Christ-Centered Biblical Theology*, 112.

[33] See Goldsworthy, 111–69, for his critique of Vos-Clowney and his alternative proposal.

of the covenants as the backbone to the Bible's story and place the concept of the "kingdom" within the unfolding covenants. Beginning in Gen 1–11, what frames these chapters is God's creation covenant first made with Adam and upheld in Noah. As God's promise of redemption from Gen 3:15 is given greater clarity through the subsequent covenants with Abraham, Israel, and David, we can make better sense of how God's redemptive plan progressively unfolds in promise, prophecy, and type. We can also make sense of how the typological patterns unfold and how the Prophets recapitulate and project these patterns forward, if we link these typological patterns to the progression of the covenants culminating in the arrival of the new covenant. Thus to follow the Bible's own "intrasystematic" categories is to follow the unfolding of God's kingdom through covenantal progression. This captures the Bible's own *internal* structure in a non-arbitrary way and thus gives textual warrant to the various epochal divisions in God's plan.

For theological interpretation, this requires that the biblical covenants are not simply part of the Bible's content or another theme. Instead, the covenants are central to the Bible's own internal structure and foundational to grasping God's unfolding plan from creation to Christ. Apart from thinking through the progression of the covenants and seeing how all of Scripture reaches its fulfillment in Christ and the new covenant, we will miss what is central to Scripture *and* potentially misapply Scripture, which inevitably results in faulty theological conclusions.

However, an important question must be asked: Is it hermeneutically and theologically significant to place texts within their epochal/covenantal context? Does Scripture warrant this? The answer is *yes*. For example, in Rom 4 Paul argues that Abraham serves as the paradigm, for Jews *and* Gentiles, of one who was justified by grace through faith apart from works. Warrant for this claim comes from Gen 15:6, where God declares Abraham righteous because Abraham believed the promises of God. But in order to demonstrate that God's declaration of justification is for both the Jew and the Gentile, Paul then argues that in Abraham's life this declaration took place *before* he was circumcised (Gen 17 comes *after* Gen 15), thus demonstrating that Abraham's justification was *not* due to his circumcision but to faith alone in God's promises. For this reason, Abraham is the paradigm of faith for Jews *and* Gentiles in the new covenant. This is not to say that circumcision was insignificant in the Old Testament. Circumcision was the covenant sign given in the Abrahamic covenant and continued in the Mosaic covenant. But, given its epochal location in Abraham's life, the Judaizers were theologically wrong to argue that Gentiles, now that Christ has ratified the new covenant, must first be circumcised to enter into the new covenant. Paul's argument against the Judaizers is that they have misread

Scripture. To claim that Gentiles must be circumcised to know God in the new covenant is not true of Abraham, *and* it fails to grasp how circumcision functions across the covenants to reveal our need for a circumcised heart.[34] Now that Christ has come, circumcision's role as a covenant sign in the previous covenants is fulfilled (1 Cor 7:19). However, Paul's argument only works if circumcision is instituted *after* Gen 15, thus illustrating that our interpretation of texts must take seriously what comes *before* and *after* them in order to draw correct biblical conclusions.

Galatians 3–4 also illustrates this point but even more so in terms of covenantal location in God's unfolding plan. Paul counters the Judaizers who, like many conservative Jews, "saw in the law given at Sinai not only a body of instruction but a hermeneutical key to the rest of Scripture."[35] The Judaizers viewed the law covenant as permanent, not as a temporary means to bring us to Christ and the new covenant. This is why they insisted that for Gentiles to become Christians, they *had* to be circumcised per the law covenant. Paul argues that the Judaizers' hermeneutic is wrong. Christians are *not* under the law *as a covenant.*[36] Instead, Jews and Gentiles are united to Christ by faith apart from the Mosaic covenant (vv. 1–6). Paul warrants his argument from Scripture. He first appeals to Gen 15:6 to demonstrate that Abraham was justified by grace through faith (vv. 6–9). True children of Abraham are *all* who have faith in Christ, regardless of their nationality. Also, Jews and Gentiles now receive *all* the promised blessings of Abraham because of Christ, who is Abraham's promised singular seed (v. 16).[37] Moreover, God's declaring Abraham righteous was *before* the establishment of the Mosaic covenant (vv. 15–29). From this, Paul draws two further conclusions. First, the Mosaic law's coming after Abraham did not nullify the previous promise that Abraham's true offspring, identified as believing Jews and Gentiles, would inherit the promised blessings via Christ. Second, given the placement of the law covenant in God's plan, God never intended for it to redeem us. What, then, was the law covenant's purpose? Multiple answers could be given, but Paul focuses on

---

[34] On this point, see John D. Meade, "Circumcision of Flesh to Circumcision of Heart: The Typology of the Sign of the Abrahamic Covenant," in *Progressive Covenantalism: Charting a Course between Dispensational and Covenant Theologies*, ed. Stephen J. Wellum and Brent E. Parker (Nashville: B&H Academic, 2016), 127–58.

[35] Carson, "Systematic Theology and Biblical Theology," 98.

[36] See Brian S. Rosner, *Paul and the Law: Keeping the Commandments of God*, NSBT 31 (Downers Grove: InterVarsity, 2013).

[37] See Jason S. DeRouchie, "Father of a Multitude of Nations: New Covenant Ecclesiology in OT Perspective," in Wellum and Parker, *Progressive Covenantalism*, 7–38.

one: the Mosaic law functioned as a guardian over Israel *until* Christ came (vv. 21–24). Now that Christ has come, the law, *as a covenant*, is fulfilled, and, in Christ, the Abrahamic promise (grounded in Gen. 3:15) is given to believing Jews and Gentiles together as heirs (vv. 25–29).[38]

These two texts illustrate how important it is to put together God's plan by locating texts and covenants in relation to what *preceded* and *followed* them.[39] We risk theological error if we do not carefully think about texts in their epochal-covenantal location by failing to see how the *parts* of God's plan fit with the *whole*. In fact, this was one of the reasons why many Jewish people, along with the Judaizers, misunderstood Scripture and failed to see how Christ is the fulfillment of the previous covenants. If they had properly located the covenants in God's plan, they should have known that the old covenant was temporary and that, along with all of the other covenants, it prophetically anticipated the ratification of a new covenant and the inauguration of a new creation in Christ.[40]

The Canonical Context. The final context is the canonical, namely, texts read and applied in light of Christ.[41] Scripture is *God's* unified speech act, so texts *must* be interpreted canonically due to Christ's coming and the completion of revelation in the NT era.[42] We cannot interpret individual texts properly if we ignore the canonical level since the canon is where the "whole"

---

[38] See Douglas Moo, *Galatians*, BECNT (Grand Rapids: Baker, 2013), 195–272.

[39] Hebrews gives more examples of this point, i.e., texts must be read by virtue of their placement in the Bible's story (e.g., Heb 2:5–18 and its use of Ps 8; Heb 3:7–4:11 and its use of Ps 95; Heb 7 and its use of Gen 14 and Ps 110; Heb 8 and its use of Jer 31:31–34). For example, in Heb 7, the author concludes that the OT viewed the Levitical priesthood as temporary because God announced later another priest in a different order (Heb 7:11, 28; cf. Ps 110). In Heb 8, the author argues that the old covenant was temporary because God promised later a new covenant (Jer 31). See Thomas R. Schreiner, *Commentary on Hebrews* (Nashville: B&H, 2015), 85–93, 120–49, 205–55.

[40] See D. A. Carson, "Mystery and Fulfillment," in *Justification and Variegated Nomism*, vol. 2, *The Paradoxes of Paul*, ed. D. A. Carson, et al. (Grand Rapids: Baker, 2004), 410–12. Carson argues that Paul understands the significance of the law covenant by paying strict attention to its place in the Pentateuch's storyline. When Paul does so, he almost treats the law covenant as a parenthesis (Gal 3:15–4:7). Carson states, "The promise to Abraham that in his seed all the nations of the earth would be blessed antedates Moses and the giving of the law by centuries, and that promise cannot be annulled by the giving of the law (3:17), regardless of how much space is given over to the law in the sacred text, or how large a role it played in the history of Israel." "Mystery and Fulfillment," 412.

[41] See Moo and Naselli, "Problem of the New Testament's Use," 736, for their helpful comments on how the canonical horizon brings resolution between the human and divine author.

[42] See Vanhoozer, "Exegesis and Hermeneutics," 61.

plan is fully grasped and what the earlier revelation anticipated. As Vanhoozer notes, it is only when Scripture is interpreted canonically that we are reading it in a truly "biblical" manner—"according to its truest, fullest, *divine* intention."[43] In fact, to read the Bible canonically corresponds to what Scripture *is*. That is why "to read the Bible as unified Scripture is not just one interpretative interest among others, but the interpretative strategy that best corresponds to the nature of the text itself, given its divine inspiration."[44] The canon is best viewed as

> a great hall of witnesses in which different voices all testify to the Lord Jesus Christ. Over and above the laws and promises, the warnings and commands, the stories and the songs, is an all-embracing act, that of witnessing to what God was and is doing in Christ. . . . Thanks to their overarching canonical context, the smaller communicative acts are caught up and reoriented to the larger purpose of "making wise unto salvation."[45]

As texts are located in the Bible's covenantal story and interpreted in light of the culmination of God's plan in Christ, we rightly interpret Scripture in the way God intended.

What does it mean to be "biblical"? Consistent with Scripture's self-attestation and its nature as a word-act/progressive revelation, a three-context interpretation of the canon is the proper, *theological* way to read Scripture, summarized as a grammatical/literary-historical-canonical method of interpretation. To interpret Scripture and to draw theological conclusions accurately, we must interpret texts in light of their covenantal and canonical context. This allows us to read Scripture according to its own intrasystematic categories, framework, and presentation so that in the end, our drawing of theological conclusions from Scripture is biblical.[46]

---

[43] Vanhoozer, 61.

[44] Vanhoozer, 61.

[45] Vanhoozer, 62.

[46] On this point, see Lints, *Fabric of Theology*, 268–89. Lints rightly insists that our reading of Scripture, if it is on the Bible's "own terms," must follow the "interpretive matrix of the Scriptures," which is not searching "for doctrinal models and keys that fit the Bible's complex locks and open them up to the reader" (270). Rather, it is unpacking the *Bible's own structure* and making sure that "the conceptual categories of the theological framework adequately reflect the phenomena of Scripture" (270) in terms of its specific content *and* its structure (see 270–74). Our understanding of the interpretive framework may have to be modified in light of exegesis, however. But, as Lints notes, "the fact that this framework is properly subject to reform should in no way be taken to imply that the Scriptures themselves contain data that may be organized in any number of conflicting fashions or indeed that there are a variety of competing frameworks in the Scriptures themselves" (288).

3. Further Reflections on the Canonical Context

How does Scripture "on its own terms" link the canon together? What are its intrasystematic structures? To answer this question, much could be said, but minimally the canon is "glued" together by the plot movements of the Bible's story: creation, fall, redemption, new creation, *and* the Bible's *covenantal* unfolding.[47] In thinking about the latter, two further points are important.

First, the "promise-fulfillment" motif unfolded through the biblical covenants. This motif is central to how Scripture glues the epochs of redemptive history together and how Christ is revealed in all of Scripture (cf. Acts 13:32–33). A case can be made for Gen 3:15 being viewed as the first "gospel" promise (*protevangelium*) that anticipates the coming of a Redeemer, the "seed of the woman"—an enigmatic promise that is given more definition as God's plan unfolds across time.[48] This motif establishes the continuity between God's covenant promises and his fulfillment of those promises in Christ. Furthermore, when one thinks of promise fulfillment, it is impossible to think of God's promises apart from the covenants. By covenantal progression, Scripture speaks of the continuity of God's plan (tied to his promises) and its ultimate fulfillment in Christ and the ratification of a new covenant.

Second, one way that the "promise-fulfillment" motif is developed is by the presence of typology, which is also unveiled by covenantal progression. To speak of "typology" is to raise a whole host of debates over what it is and how it works. As Paul Hoskins reminds us, "Studies in biblical typology have been complicated by the use of the terms 'typology' and 'type' where no definitions of these terms are given."[49] Yet, regardless of the debate over typology, getting at

---

[47] We will develop these points in part 3 when the Bible's framework and storyline are discussed.

[48] Contrary to R. W. L. Moberly, "Christ in All the Scriptures? The Challenge of Reading the Old Testament as Christian Scripture," *Journal of Theological Interpretation* 1 (2007): 82–85. In response to Moberly, see C. John Collins, *Genesis 1–4: A Linguistic, Literary, and Theological Commentary* (Phillipsburg: P&R, 2006), 155–59; T. Desmond Alexander, "Further Observations of the Term 'Seed' in Genesis," *TynBul* 48 (1997): 363–67.

[49] Paul M. Hoskins, *Jesus as the Fulfillment of the Temple in the Gospel of John* (Eugene: Wipf & Stock, 2006), 18. Hoskins describes two different views of typology within current biblical studies: a traditional view, which believes that the correspondence between type and antitype is God-given, intentional, and predictive, versus a critical view, which is skeptical about the predictive and prospective significance of the types (18–36). I affirm the traditional view. For a defense of the view, see Richard Davidson, *Typology in Scripture: A Study of Hermeneutical TUPOS Structures* (Berrien Springs: Andrews University Press, 1981); G. K. Beale, *Handbook on the New Testament Use of the Old Testament: Exegesis*

the character of typology is vital to understanding Scripture and to drawing many theological conclusions. With that in mind, let us make a few brief comments about typology.

The Nature of Typology. First, we must distinguish typology from "allegory."[50] The difference is that typology is grounded in *history*, the *text*, and *intertextual* development, where various "persons, events, and institutions" are intended by God to correspond to each other, while allegory assumes none of these things. As a literary form, an allegory is an extended metaphor, similar to a parable. Nevertheless, by allegorizing a text by not grounding it in authorial intent, which is intertextually warranted, "allegorical interpretation" depends on some kind of extratextual grid to warrant its explanation. As Vanhoozer notes, allegorical interpretation is represented by the interpretive strategy for declaring "*this* (word) means *that* (concept)"[51] with *that* being determined by something "outside" the text. When one investigates the six explicit NT texts that employ explicit terminology of typology (Rom 5:14; 1 Cor 10:6, 11; 1 Pet 3:21; Heb 8:5; 9:24), a consistent picture emerges that clearly distinguishes it from allegory.

Second, what is the nature of typology? To answer this question, let us first define what typology is and then explain some of its key features. Typology is the study of OT redemptive-historical

---

and Interpretation (Grand Rapids: Baker, 2012), 13–25; cf. Moo and Naselli, "Problem of the New Testament's Use," 702–46; Lints, *The Fabric of Theology*, 304–10. For the critical view, see David L. Baker, *Two Testaments, One Bible: The Theological Relationship between the Old and New Testaments*, 3rd ed. (Downers Grove: InterVarsity, 2010), 169–89.

[50] See Brent E. Parker, "Typology and Allegory: Is There a Distinction? A Brief Examination of Figural Reading" *SBJT* 21, no. 1 (2017): 57–83. Contrary to Mitchell L. Chase, *40 Questions about Typology and Allegory* (Grand Rapids: Kregel Academic, 2020), 193–300. Chase incorrectly posits typology and allegory as examples of "figural reading." This leads him to place typology and allegory in the realm of hermeneutics with the focus on "typological" and "allegorical *interpretation*" as "reading strategies." Aside from conflating typology and allegory, or allegorizing the text of Scripture in some of the examples he provides, Chase also wrongly argues that Scripture has more than one sense, with literal and nonliteral senses (201). For a helpful corrective, see Caneday, "Biblical Types," 135–55.

[51] Vanhoozer, *Is There a Meaning?*, 119 (emphasis original). For many, Gal 4:24–26 is a text in which it is difficult to know whether Paul is employing an allegorical interpretation or using typology. For a helpful analysis, see A. B. Caneday, "Covenant Lineage Allegorically Prefigured: 'What Things Are Written Allegorically' (Galatians 4:21–31)," *SBJT* 14, no. 3 (2010): 50–77. Caneday argues that *allegory* is present, but not due to Paul's interpretative prowess. Rather, the Genesis *text* is allegorical in that the characters in the historical narrative are invested with symbolic representations and significance due to God's plan that reaches fulfillment in Christ.

"types" (persons, events, institutions) that God designed/planned to correspond to, and predictively prefigure, their intensified "antitype," the antitype being the fulfillment of the type in NT redemptive history.[52] Two points develop this understanding of typology:

1. Types are a feature or species of divine revelation rooted in *history* and the *text*.[53] Types involve an *organic* relationship or analogical correspondences between "persons, events, and institutions" in one epoch ("type"), which anticipates its fulfillment in a later epoch ("antitype"). As Lints reminds us, "The typological relation is a central means by which particular epochal and textual horizons are linked to later horizons in redemptive revelation. It links the present to the future, and it retroactively links the present with the past. It is founded on the organic connection of God's promises with his fulfillment of those promises."[54]

2. Types are *prophetic* and *predictive*.[55] A type is not prophetic as a direct verbal prediction. Instead, types are more indirect in the sense of predictions built on models/patterns that God intends but that become unveiled as later texts reinforce those patterns and reach fulfillment in Christ. Types are part of the "mystery" theme, tied to God's unfolding plan.[56]

---

[52] This definition is compiled from Davidson, *Typology in Scripture*, 397–408. Also see similar definitions in Beale, *Handbook on the New Testament*, 14; and Graham A. Cole, *He Who Gives Life: The Doctrine of the Holy Spirit* (Wheaton: Crossway, 2007), 289.

[53] See Caneday, "Biblical Types," 143–50; Brent E. Parker, "The Israel-Christ-Church Relationship," in Wellum and Parker, *Progressive Covenantalism*, 39–68.

[54] Lints, *Fabric of Theology*, 304. The emphasis on history is important since it distinguishes a traditional view from a critical view. For the critical view, the historicity of the types is not essential. For a traditional view, the correspondence between type and antitype is not a mere literary reality; it is also rooted in historical realities. See Hoskins, *Jesus as Fulfillment of the Temple*, 27; Carson, "Mystery and Fulfillment," 404.

[55] The predictive/prospective nature of typology distinguishes a traditional view from a critical view. For the critical view the discovery of typological patterns is based on analogies that later NT authors retrospectively make—a "construction" by later authors that is *not* intended by OT author(s). It rejects the idea that *from the vantage point of the OT*, especially the prophets who pick up earlier typological patterns, types were predictive. See R. T. France, *Jesus and the Old Testament: His Application of Old Testament Passages to Himself and His Mission* (Grand Rapids: Baker, 1982), 38–43. Within the critical view, some think that the NT authors were creating "new" meaning due to divine inspiration, while others think that the NT authors were distorting the meaning of the OT texts. Regardless, the critical view rejects the predictive/prospective nature of typology. For the former view, see Richard Longenecker, *Biblical Exegesis in the Apostolic Period*, 2nd ed. (Grand Rapids: Eerdmans, 1999), 124–34.

[56] On "mystery," see G. K. Beale and Benjamin L. Gladd, *Hidden but Now Revealed: A Biblical Theology of Mystery* (Downers Grove: InterVarsity, 2014).

Given the indirectness of types, they require careful exegesis in their immediate contexts, and a type may not be fully recognized as a type until later authors pick up the discernable pattern. Yet types, in an ontological sense, are *in* the text, exegetically discovered. But in the epistemological sense, we come to know types as God-intended patterns as *later* OT authors repeat a pattern before it reaches its fulfillment in Christ.[57]

In thinking about the nature of typology, it is crucial to note that this view of typology is theologically dependent on a specific view of God and divine providence.[58] How so? While the type has significance for its own time, its greater significance is directed toward the future; it testifies to something greater than itself that is still to come. But the future antitype is *guaranteed* to come because God has planned it from eternity and in history; he sovereignly guarantees that the prophetic fulfillment of the original type will occur in Christ. The relationship, then, between type and antitype is *not* arbitrary—a mere analogy or a human construction; instead, it is an organic relationship intended by God so that specific types actually reveal and point forward to their fulfillment in Christ. Apart from this view of God, the traditional view of typology hangs in midair. This is *not* to say that everyone associated with the OT type understood and knew the pattern to be pointing forward. Rather, it is to say that when the type is discovered to be a type (at some point along the trajectory of its repeated pattern in redemptive history), it is then correctly "seen" as such and as *divinely*-intended.[59]

---

[57] Types are *predictive/prospective* by nature (ontology) because they are divinely designed. Yet, epistemologically, they are *retrospective* as *later* authors recognize the types as God-intended patterns. If the types are retrospective in the ontological sense, then they are not God intended but subjective human constructions. Instead, redemption *and* revelation are divinely planned and progressive. As later OT authors reflect on earlier texts, they begin to "see" how God's plan is unfolding. The NT authors, then, pick up the OT trajectory and reveal how the types reach their fulfillment in Christ (Heb 1:1–3). Greater clarity is the result of God's unfolding redemption and revelation.

[58] On this point, see Beale, "Did Jesus and His Followers Preach?," 394–95; and Lints, *Fabric of Theology*, 306–10.

[59] Typological patterns are discovered *exegetically* by interpreting texts in their textual, epochal, and canonical contexts. On the criteria for determining what a legitimate type is, see G. K. Beale, "Finding Christ in the Old Testament," *JETS* 63 (2020), 25–50; Beale, *Handbook of the New Testament*, 19–25; and Richard Davidson, "The Eschatological Hermeneutic of Biblical Typology," *TheoRhēma* 6, no. 2 (2011): 5–48. In the immediate context where the type is first introduced, there are clues in the text which signal its importance. The significance of the type might not be grasped immediately, but by intertextual development *within the OT* (e.g., later authors pick up the typological patterns, thus creating a trajectory) and then in terms of the entire canon, readers begin to grasp the significance of the

Characteristics of Typology

How do types work in Scripture? Typology exhibits a threefold character:

1. Types involve repetition of a person, event, or institution so that they are repeated in later persons, events, or institutions. This is how the pattern is discovered. Ultimately, types reach their antitypical fulfillment in Christ with a spillover effect to his people. In this way, typological patterns have a Christological and eschatological orientation given that Christ brings "the last days" era of the Prophets to fulfillment (Heb 1:1–3). Not all typological patterns are directly Christocentric (e.g., the antitype of Peter's flood typology is not Christ, but water baptism and final judgment [1 Pet 3:18–22]); nevertheless, Brent Parker rightly insists that "all OT types have a Christotelic emphasis as they are qualified by their relationship to Jesus, his redemptive work, and the consummation of the new heavens and the new earth."[60] All typological patterns, then, either converge or are mediated through Christ and his work.

For example, Adam is a type of Christ (Rom 5:14; 1 Cor 15:21–49), the covenant head of the old creation. In God's plan, Adam anticipates the coming of Jesus, the last Adam, and the head of the new creation. How do we know this? In the immediate context of Gen 1–3, there are exegetical clues that speak of Adam's significance. Then through the covenants "other Adams" take on Adam's role (e.g., Noah, Abraham, Israel, and David). But none of these "Adams" are the fulfillment although they "predict" the last Adam to come. Also, in Christ and his work, the last Adam, we, as his people, are restored to our Adamic role as image-sons in relation to God and the creation (Heb 2:5–18). Thus, *through the covenants*, Adam, as a type, takes on greater definition until the last Adam comes with a spillover effect to Christ's people.

Or think of the nation of Israel. As God's son (Exod 4:22–23), Israel takes on Adam's role in the world and anticipates the coming of the true Son, the true Israel/servant/vine—our Lord Jesus Christ (see Isa 5:1–7; Hos 11:1; Matt 2:15; John 15:1–17). Again, since types find their fulfilment first in Christ and not in us, we as God's people participate in the

---

type and how it fits in God's overall plan, which reaches its fulfillment in Christ with application to his people, the church.

[60] Brent E. Parker, *The Israel-Christ-Church Typological Pattern: A Theological Critique of Covenant and Dispensational Theologies* (PhD diss., The Southern Baptist Theological Seminary, 2017), 72.

typological pattern only by virtue of our covenantal union with Christ. Thus, in the case of Israel, Christ is first the "true Israel," and in him, we, the church, are the eschatological people of God. The church is *not* the antitypical fulfillment of Israel in the first sense; Christ alone fills that role. Yet in Christ, the true Son/Israel, we are the beneficiaries of his work. In relationship to Christ, we are adopted sons (Gal 3:26–4:7), the "Israel of God" (Gal 6:16), Abraham's spiritual offspring (Gal 3:29), restored to what God created us to be (Eph 4:20–24). In this way, the new covenant promise given to the "house of Israel" and the "house of Judah" (Jer 31:31) is applied to the church. Christ, as the antitypical fulfillment of Israel, takes on Israel's role, and by faith in union with him, his work becomes ours as his new covenant people.

2. Types have a "lesser to greater" (a fortiori) quality as the type reaches its fulfillment in the antitype.[61] For example, as one moves from Adam or David to the prophets, priests, and kings to the last Adam, the true Davidic King, the great High Priest, the antitype is *always* greater than the previous types. Yet, escalation across time does *not* occur incrementally from the original type to each installment and then to Christ as if there were a straight line of increase; escalation only fully occurs in Christ's coming. The previous types point forward to the greater one to come (Rom 5:14), but the *greater* aspect is realized only in Christ and then his people. For example, Adam is a type of Christ, and "other Adams" arise, yet these "Adams" disobey. It is only in the last Adam that perfect obedience results. And what is true of Adam is also true of other typological patterns whether they are various persons (Moses, Israel, David, prophets, priests, and kings), events (the exodus), or institutions (sacrificial system, tabernacle/temple).

This observation is important since the a fortiori quality of types is one of the ways Scripture reveals our Lord's unique identity and warrants the greater new covenant era. Due to Christ's incarnation and work, discontinuity occurs between the old and new in God's plan, as God intended. When the antitype arrives in history, or better, when it is inaugurated, the previous types reach their telos, and the entire "last days" era results in various changes from the old. For this reason, the fulfillment inaugurated by Christ (the "already"), although it still awaits the consummation (the "not yet"), has resulted in greater realities directly linked

---

[61] For a discussion of escalation in typology, see Parker, *Israel-Christ-Church Typological Pattern*, 69–79.

to the inauguration of the kingdom, the dawning of the new covenant era, and the arrival of the new creation.[62]

3. Types are also developed *through covenantal progression*. For example, Adam and "other Adams" are associated with the covenants of creation, Noah, Abraham, Israel, and David. In these covenant heads, Adam's role continues; each one anticipates Christ, who by his obedience secures our redemption.[63] Or think of the promise to Abraham regarding his "seed." As the seed promise unfolds, it does so in Isaac, Israel, the Davidic king, and ultimately in Christ with application to the church.[64] Or think of how Moses, who is foundational for the institution of prophets and who inaugurates the priestly role under the old covenant, is developed in terms of an entire institution of prophets and priests, which ultimately culminates in Christ.[65] More examples could be given: David and his sons, the tabernacle-temple structure, the exodus event, which anticipates a greater exodus to come (Exod 15:14–17; Isa 11:15–16; 40:3–5; Hos 2:14–15; 11:1, etc.). *All* of these types are tied to the covenants and progress through them to Christ and the new covenant. In this way, OT history is eschatological and prophetic not merely in terms of verbal predictions but in types/patterns associated with the covenants, which anticipate and predict the dawning of the end of the ages in the coming of the Lord of Glory. This is why the entire NT is Christological in focus; Jesus is the one that the covenants and prophets anticipate (e.g., Matt 5:17–18; 11:11–15; Rom 3:21, 31). Apart from wrestling with how types function in the covenants to lead us to Christ, we fail to discern how the "parts" fit with the "whole," and we are less than "biblical" in our reading of Scripture.[66]

---

[62] On inaugurated eschatology, see Thomas R. Schreiner, *New Testament Theology: Magnifying God in Christ* (Grand Rapids: Baker, 2008), 41–116.

[63] See Gen 1–3; 5:1–2; 9:1–17; 12:1–3; Exod 4:22–23; 2 Sam 7:5–16; Ps 8; Rom 5:12–21; Heb 2:5–18.

[64] See Gen 12:1–3; 17:1–22; Exod 1:1–7; 2 Sam 7:5–16; Gal 3:16, 29. See T. Desmond Alexander, "Seed," in *NDBT*, 769–73 (see chap. 1, n. 24); DeRouchie, "Father of a Multitude of Nations," 7–38.

[65] See Exod 19–20; 24; 32–34; Lev 8–9; Deut 18:14–22; 34:10–12; John 1:14–18; Heb 1:1–3; 3:1–6.

[66] This is in contrast to Chase, *40 Questions*, 54–55. Chase mentions the covenantal stream of biblical types, but he does not develop what he says. The many examples he offers of typological patterns are often disconnected from the covenants, thus he does not demonstrate how types function within the covenantal backbone of Scripture.

What does it mean to be *biblical*? How do we approach *and* interpret Scripture on its own terms so that we are biblically warranted in our doctrinal conclusions? Our brief reflections on the interpretation of Scripture from a theology of Scripture have sought to answer this question. The hermeneutical questions must be asked given our commitment to *sola Scriptura*. The triune God who speaks is the foundation for theology; as such, we must know what he has said, in the way he has said it, across the entire canon. But systematic theology is more than the repetition of Scripture or even the doing of biblical theology. Theology is "faith seeking understanding," as the church applies the entirety of God's word to every area of life by formulating doctrine and a whole worldview for God's glory, the life and health of the church, and the proclamation and defense of the unsearchable riches of Christ.

From Canon to Concept: The Formulation of Christian Doctrine

To recap: systematic theology minimally involves *two* intertwined steps.

First, theology requires *understanding* all that Scripture says on its own terms on a specific subject, which involves exegesis and biblical theology, as discussed above. It is vital to note that this first step is not independent of theology since one's *theological* interpretation already presupposes a theology of God and Scripture given the web-like nature of theology. Yet, in this first step, theology works from Scripture's first-order, God-given interpretive framework as the "lens" by which we think about God, self, and the world. Our task is to "think God's thoughts after him," which demands a careful reading of Scripture according to the three contexts forged across the Bible's covenantal storyline. Our goal is to let Scripture speak for itself as our triune Creator-covenant Lord discloses who he is, who we are as created but now fallen image-bearers, and how God's redemptive plan has reached its fulfillment in Christ. For this reason, theology is grounded in *sola Scriptura* as our final authority and epistemological warrant. The theologian's task is to account for *all* that Scripture teaches in the way that Scripture teaches it.

Second, faithful to Scripture, theology is also "constructive" and "apologetic" as it formulates doctrine for the church to know, love, and obey God; to enable Christians to bring their lives and thought into conformity with God's word; and to witness and defend the truth of the gospel before a watching world as the church brings every area of her life under Christ's lordship.

Theology's *constructive* work seeks to "put together" and "make sense" of all that Scripture teaches in terms of application, logical coherence, and metaphysical entailments in light of the church's tradition and contemporary questions, as it draws out theological judgments for today, consistent with the Bible's own presentation across the entire canon. In chapter 1, we briefly illustrated the constructive task of theology in the doing of Christology. To answer the question of who Jesus is, we must first turn to the entire canon of Scripture. After we do, we discover that the Jesus of the Bible is unique; he is the eternal divine Son who, by assuming a human nature, is now God the Son *incarnate* (John 1:1–18). Yet, as we reflect on *all* that Scripture teaches about Jesus, legitimate theological questions are raised that require careful biblical and theological reasoning, as later summarized by the Chalcedonian definition (along with Nicaea).

What is true of Christology is also true of every doctrine. In fact, inseparably joined to Christology is theology proper, specifically the doctrine of the Trinity. As in Christology, so also in trinitarian formulation, theology thinks through *all* that God says about himself in Scripture: God alone is the *one* true and living God, uncreated, independent, self-sufficient, the holy and sovereign Creator and Lord (Exod 3:14–15; Deut 6:4; Jer 10:1–16; Rev 4:11). But again, as we reflect on God's unfolding revelation, specifically that God is uniquely *one*, the promise of the coming Messiah/Son, who is both human yet also identified with the Lord in name and action (Pss 2; 110; Isa 9:6–7; Phil 2:9–11), who also has the Spirit *of God* (Isa 11:1–3; 42:1; 61:1–3), and so on, we cannot think of the *one* true and living God apart from the Father, Son, and Holy Spirit (Matt 28:19; 1 Cor 8:6; 2 Cor 13:14). As we attempt to understand *all* that Scripture teaches on God's *oneness* and *threeness*, legitimate theological questions arise that require careful biblical reasoning and theological formulation. How do we "make sense" of how God is simultaneously one and three without diminishing either? What *language* do we employ to describe this truth? If the Father, Son, and Spirit are the *one* God, how do we understand the nature of his oneness? A generic unity? A numerical identity as expressed by divine simplicity? And if the three are one because they share or subsist in the same identical divine "nature," how do we distinguish the Father, Son, and Spirit without surrendering divine unity and singularity? How do we "put together" *all* that Scripture teaches, grounded in the most fundamental distinction of Christian theology, namely, the Creator-creature distinction? To answer these questions that *Scripture itself raises*, theological *construction* and doctrinal formulation is necessary in order to remain true to God's self-revelation.

Or think of how Scripture speaks of our triune God's rule over and relationship to his world: divine providence. If we take seriously the sweep of the entire canon, Scripture teaches that God is the Creator and sovereign Lord of history; he has created us in his image as significant, free, and responsible creatures; and God's decree/plan and purposes are never thwarted (Gen 1:1–2; Isa 46:9–13; Dan 4:34–35; Eph 1:11). But as we reflect on *all* of the biblical teaching, legitimate theological questions arise: What is meant by God's sovereignty? Is God's eternal plan based on his own choice, or is it conditioned or dependent on his foreknowing our human choices? If the former, then what is the relationship between God's plan and agency and human agency? If God decrees everything in a guaranteed way, including our human choices, then how are they free and responsible? If the latter, then how is God truly *a se* (independent, self-sufficient) in his perfect knowledge and eternal plan? We cannot answer these questions merely by repeating Scripture or, worse, ignoring all that Scripture teaches. Instead, *theological construction* must be done as we wrestle with the relationship between God's decree/plan, his primary agency in all things, and the reality of our human choices or secondary actions. Indeed, not to think carefully about these matters according to Scripture only results in a failure to "think God's thoughts after him" and, in our lives, potentially disastrous consequences. God has given us his word of truth to apply to our lives so that we will know him correctly and grow in our trust, love, and obedience to him as the sovereign Lord of providence and grace. There is simply no higher calling for his people!

As we do theology, it is also true that all of us approach Scripture with preconceived ideas indebted to historical theology, our backgrounds, and cultural influences. None of us are "blank slates" (tabula rasa); instead, for example, as in the case of divine providence, we approach Scripture with various views of divine sovereignty, human freedom, and so on. Yet, given our view of Scripture as God-given, first-order, and objective truth, we are not caught in a vicious hermeneutical circle. Instead, by God's work in our lives, uniquely by the Spirit in regeneration and illumination, Scripture is able to correct our pre-understandings by careful exposition, thought, prayer, obedience, and reliance on those who preceded us. Our task is to return to Scripture again and again and faithfully formulate, as in the case of divine providence, the nature and scope of God's sovereign rule, the nature of human freedom, and the relationship between the Creator and creature. But given *sola scriptura*, our theological formulations must *not* pick and choose certain biblical truths over other truths. We must let Scripture on its own terms unpack the doctrinal area we are thinking through, and even if tensions arise between the biblical teaching, our reason must never reinterpret or eliminate biblical data simply because we do not fully grasp how it all fits together, a point we will return to below.

Systematic theology's apologetic work also defends the truth, coherence, and logical consistency of biblical teaching against the "wisdom" of this age that stands in rebellious opposition to the God of truth (1 Cor 1:18–31; 2 Cor 10:5). As theology *applies* Scripture to every area of life under Christ's lordship—history, science, philosophy, ethics, psychology, and so on—it formulates a well-thought-out worldview and defends it against all non-Christian thought. From the earliest years until today, the church has set forth the truth to be believed *and* defended it against its critics who build their lives on the quicksand of "human tradition . . . rather than Christ" (Col 2:8). In fact, following Scriptural commands, theology's task is to demonstrate why Scripture is God's word and why its teaching is logically consistent/coherent (1 Pet 3:15–16). No doubt, no theologian is able to explain *how* all of the biblical data fits together; an exhaustive theology is not possible given the fact that God has not revealed everything to us, let alone our creaturely finitude and now our sin.[67] However, theology is required to demonstrate why Scripture and its doctrinal formulations are not contradictory, a point we will return to below.

We can even say that systematic theology is *critical*, as it evaluates ideas and theological proposals both within and outside of the church.[68] Within the church, theology is critical by analyzing alternative theologies that continue to divide the church, such as covenant vs. dispensational theology, Calvinism vs. Arminianism, a mixed vs. regenerate view of the church, or different millennial views. Since those within the church appeal to Scripture, there are two ways to evaluate differences among us: first, in terms of the view's fit with Scripture and, second, in terms of whether the view in question is consistent with other areas of our theology that we know to be true. In these ways, theology is the discipline that seeks to arbitrate differences within the church with the goal of reaching "unity in the faith" (Eph 4:13), teaching "sound teaching" (Titus 1:9), and conforming our life and thought to God's word (Rom 12:1–2).

---

[67] As discussed in chapter 3, this is the archetype-ectype distinction in theology and epistemology. On this point, see Paul Helm, *John Calvin's Ideas* (Oxford: Oxford University Press, 2004), 11–34; Cf. Muller, *Post-Reformation Reformed Dogmatics*, 1:229–38 (see chap. 3, n. 12).

[68] The term *critical* is *not* used as it is often used today to refer to various "critical theories," such as "critical race theory." Instead, it is used in the older sense of the evaluation and critique of ideas/theologies/worldviews.

Outside the church, theology takes on an *apologetic* function as it first sets forth the faith to be believed and defended by critiquing and evaluating all views that reject the truth of God's word. As we do so, we are following the exhortation of Scripture to defend the truth by reason and argumentation.

In thinking about the constructive-apologetic endeavor of systematic theology, two important issues need to be addressed: the use of extrabiblical language *and* the role of reason and logic in drawing theological conclusions from Scripture. Let us look at each of these in turn.

The Use of Extrabiblical Language and Concepts in Theological Formulation

Given the constructive-apologetic nature of theology, the use of extrabiblical language and concepts in our doctrinal formulations has been an issue from the beginning. For example, in trinitarian and Christological formulation, the early church wrestled with how to understand coherently God's oneness and threeness; the relations of the Father, Son, and Spirit; and subsequently how to make sense of the relationship between the Son's deity and humanity in the incarnation given the Creator-creature distinction. But debates over the use of extrabiblical language were not isolated to these doctrinal areas; every doctrinal area must address this issue. For example, in divine providence, to speak of human "freedom" requires the use of concepts from philosophy in the construction and defense of the doctrine. So, throughout church history, theology has wrestled with two related issues: *whether* we can and should use extrabiblical terminology in our doctrinal formulations, and if so, *which* terms/concepts advance the constructive and apologetic tasks.

First, is it legitimate to use *extrabiblical* language/concepts to explain the biblical teaching? Why not simply repeat Scripture? After all, if we must not interpret Scripture from an extratextual viewpoint, then why is the use of extrabiblical language/concepts legitimate?[69] In fact, the Arians early on argued this point: the church was *unbiblical* in utilizing extrabiblical language, such as *homoousios*, to speak of the full deity of the Son in relation to the Father. But

---

[69] Note the distinction between extratextual and extrabiblical. The former refers to a worldview "outside" of Scripture that is more authoritative than Scripture and by which Scripture is interpreted. The latter refers to language or concepts that are not found in Scripture but that convey the meaning of Scripture correctly. In this work, the use of extrabiblical language is affirmed, while extratextual viewpoints having priority over Scripture are rejected.

the Arians were not the only ones to argue this point: later on, this same argument was made by Socinians, various classic liberals, and even today's open theists. In the nineteenth century, Adolf von Harnack famously charged that the church was guilty of "acute Hellenization," specifically in trinitarian and Christological formulation.[70]

What was the church's response? It was this: the use of extrabiblical concepts is not only acceptable but also necessary given the nature of systematic theology. Theology is not simply the repetition of Scripture; it is the *application* of Scripture by "making sense" of what Scripture teaches both in construction and defense. As such, as Herman Bavinck notes, "Christian theology . . . [has] always defended it as proper and valuable."[71] Yet, as Bavinck also insists, "the use of these terms is not designed to make possible the introduction of new—extrabiblical or antibiblical—dogmas, but, on the contrary, to defend the truth of Scripture against all heresy. . . . They mark the boundary lines within which Christian thought must proceed in order to preserve the truth of revelation."[72] This last observation is important: extrabiblical concepts are legitimate and necessary in theology *as long as* they faithfully represent and communicate the Bible's own "biblical-canonical judgments."[73] For this reason, at Nicaea and Chalcedon, the church employed extrabiblical terms/concepts, such as "Trinity," "nature" (Gk. *ousia*; Latin, *essentia*), "person" (Gk. *hypostasis*; Latin, *persona*), and so on. However, the church did so because these words/concepts accurately and faithfully communicated, explained, and clarified the biblical teaching.[74]

---

[70] Bavinck, *Reformed Dogmatics*, 2:296, (see chap. 1, n. 9).

[71] Bavinck, 2:296.

[72] Bavinck, 2:297; see John Owen, *The Works of John Owen*, ed. William H. Goold, 16 vols. (Carlisle: Banner of Truth, 1965), 2:377–79.

[73] See Vanhoozer, *Biblical Authority after Babel*, 126 (see chap. 1, n. 34).

[74] It is also important to reject the Greek vs. Hebrew language dichotomy that prevails in much of this discussion. This distinction goes back to the "Biblical Theology Movement" in the 1940s and 1950s. It was preoccupied with biblical words and language, and its proponents believed that word studies and etymologies gave access to the distinctive mentality and theology of the biblical authors. On the basis of word studies, it was then argued that the biblical notions of divine action, time, etc., were dynamic and concrete in contrast to the static and abstract concepts of the Greeks. However, James Barr thoroughly dismantled this argument and put this false dichotomy to rest. Barr, *The Semantics of Biblical Language* (Eugene: Wipf & Stock, 2004). All of this is to say that the early church did not distort Scripture with its use of extrabiblical language.

Second, since the use of extrabiblical words/concepts is legitimate and necessary in doctrinal construction, which ones do we employ without distorting biblical teaching? This is not an easy question to answer; extrabiblical language is never neutral because words have a history, are tied to particular cultures, and carry philosophical and theological baggage.

For example, think of the linguistic freight the early church faced in its trinitarian and Christological debates. To account for the biblical data and to think rightly about the triune God, the church had to make a crucial "person-nature" distinction. Scripture demanded that the church speak of the *threeness* of the Father, Son, and Spirit yet without undermining God's *oneness*. But what words can be used to make this distinction? Every word chosen inevitably carries with it linguistic baggage. So when the church employed *hypostasis* and *ousia* to make the "person-nature" distinction, the problem they faced was that these words were synonyms in Greek, which either meant the church was affirming tritheism or modalism, both a denial of biblical teaching. Thus, to communicate properly what Scripture taught, the church in the fourth century had to uncouple these words, something contrary to Hellenistic thought. In fact, by uncoupling these words, the church demonstrated that Scripture, not Greek thought, is "magisterial" in her theological formulation, the opposite of an "acute Hellenization."[75] As a result, the church was able to articulate the doctrine of the Trinity, namely, that God is three "persons" (*hypostases*) subsisting in one "nature" (*ousia*), which then carried over into Christology: Jesus is one "person"—the eternal Son, the second person of the Godhead—who assumed our human nature and now subsists in two "natures."[76]

But, as noted above, the use of extrabiblical words/concepts was not limited to theology proper and Christology; it impacts every doctrinal area. For example, think again of divine providence and the challenge of defining human freedom. Scripture teaches that humans are "free"; that is, we make choices according to our desires, and we are held responsible by God for our choices. Yet nowhere does Scripture define what human freedom is. The Bible's teaching on the nature of freedom is underdetermined. As theology moves from "canon to concept," it is necessary to define what "freedom" is by the use of extrabiblical concepts/definitions. But as we do, theology must reject concepts of freedom which redefine or eliminate

---

[75] See Turretin, *Institutes of Elenctic Theology*, 1:253–60 (see chap. 3, n. 55).

[76] See Aaron Riches, *Ecce Homo: On the Divine Unity of Christ* (Grand Rapids: Eerdmans, 2016), 1–152.

biblical teaching. Not all definitions of "freedom" are equal; each definition must be judged by Scripture in terms of whether it is consistent with the overall biblical teaching, a point we will return to throughout this work as the debate over the nature of freedom has direct impact on most doctrinal areas.[77]

What is crucial to note is that the church made these theological *judgments* because of her commitment to Scripture. The principle for using extrabiblical words/concepts in theological formulation is that whatever words are chosen, they must accurately represent and communicate the biblical teaching. The criterion by which extrabiblical language was judged legitimate is Scripture, and the goal in its use is not inventiveness but faithfulness.[78]

This principle is important as we think about the "ministerial" role of other disciplines in the doing of theology, especially the incorporation of knowledge from natural revelation. Think of the discipline of philosophy, for example, specifically the study of metaphysics. Metaphysics is a branch of philosophy that studies God's world or "created reality."[79] As noted in chapters 1 and 3, metaphysics is not independent of Scripture since God's revelation in nature and Scripture go together according to God's plan, knowledge, and action. Moreover, due to God's revelation in creation *and* common grace, non-Christian metaphysicians have made true observations about the created world despite their overall worldviews not being grounded in God and his word. Yet, since metaphysics (or any discipline) is not neutral,

---

[77] We will discuss various conceptions of "freedom" throughout this work since the nature of freedom directly impacts almost every doctrine, especially God's decree, aseity in knowledge, providence, Scripture, Christology, and the Calvinist-Arminian debates, etc. In the current theological/philosophical discussion, there are two basic views of human freedom: libertarian and compatibilistic. Both views argue that humans are free and responsible for their actions but not in the same way. When one considers these two views, even if we grant that both are metaphysically "possible," both cannot be true since they entail different conclusions in almost every doctrinal area. Given *sola Scriptura*, we can arbitrate which view is more acceptable in two ways: first, which view fits best with the biblical data and, second, which view fits best with other truths we know from Scripture without diminishing, redefining, or undermining them. For a discussion of these views of freedom, see Feinberg, *No One Like Him*, 625–76 (see chap. 2, n. 51); Scott Christensen, *What About Free Will? Reconciling Our Choices with God's Sovereignty* (Phillipsburg: P&R, 2016), 12–54, 75–92, 238–43.

[78] On this point, see David S. Yeago, "The New Testament and the Nicene Dogma: A Contribution to the Recovery of Theological Exegesis," in *The Theological Interpretation of Scripture: Classic and Contemporary Readings*, ed. Stephen Fowl (Oxford: Blackwell, 1997), 87–102.

[79] Duby, *God in Himself*, 188–231 (see chap. 1, n. 20).

theologians must evaluate which ideas from it are consistent with and true to God's revelation in creation by the standard of Scripture.

This is not to claim that Scripture is a textbook on every discipline or that *all* human knowledge is derived from Scripture. Instead, Scripture gives us a framework by which we interpret natural revelation and adjudicate ideas from other disciplines. The Bible's framework is not the technical vocabulary of philosophers; nonetheless, Scripture has its own philosophical view, including metaphysics. Therefore, in theology we apply metaphysical concepts, such as the "person-nature" distinction in theology proper and Christology, but because of the Bible's Creator-creature distinction, we apply these "created" metaphysical concepts to God analogically and not univocally. Steven Duby reminds us of this point: "Christian theologians using concepts like 'being' will have to acknowledge that God is not limited within a field of being shared by other (divine or created) entities."[80] Why? For this reason: Scripture is our "magisterial" authority, authorizing our use of metaphysical concepts from "created realities" consistent with the teaching of Scripture.

Scripture, then, speaks on *all* matters—not as an exhaustive account—but by revealing the overall framework that can be rendered conceptually, allowing for some "concepts" and ruling out others. Our use of natural revelation is crucial in theology, including extrabiblical concepts, but only under the authority of Scripture. Scripture does not say everything about specific things, but it does say something about everything, and what it says is authoritative.[81] For theology, Scripture is the epistemological warrant, while other disciplines serve an important ministerial role. But we must never forget the order: Scripture warrants *all* of our theological formulations, and where differences lie, the ministerial disciplines are invaluable but not sufficient.

Drawing Logical Conclusions from Scripture in Theological Formulation

In addition to the issues surrounding the use of extrabiblical language in theology is the crucial discussion of the role of reason and logic in drawing theological conclusions from Scripture.

---

[80] Duby, 216.

[81] See Cornelius Van Til, *Apologetics* (Phillipsburg: P&R, 1976), 2: "[Scripture] speaks of everything either directly or by implication."

Systematic theology, as an exercise in "faith seeking *understanding*," involves the proper use of renewed reasoning for God's glory and our eternal good.[82] As creatures, and now redeemed image-bearers in Christ being sanctified by the Holy Spirit, we were created and now re-created to love God with all that we are, including the use of our minds (Matt 22:37). In fact, our growth in grace is organically related to the use of our minds, as we engage ideas and arguments (2 Cor 10:5) and "put together" all that Scripture teaches, by the renewing and transforming work of the Spirit (Rom 8:5–11; 12:1–2), according to Scripture (Eph 1:17–19; Col 1:9–13).

This is a key point to remember, especially today. As we outlined in chapter 2, our culture's "turn to the subject" elevated human reason by undermining it. By rejecting Christian theology, the pursuit of objective truth has been replaced by an obsession with the inward, subjective, and psychologized self.[83] In such a context, the church needs to recapture a proper and right use of the mind, reason, and pursuit of truth in accordance with God's word-revelation. The doing of systematic theology is indeed biblical and theological reasoning of the highest order.[84]

However, an important question still remains: What is the proper use of reason in theology? How do we draw logical conclusions that are faithful to Scripture? And given the constructive-apologetic nature of theology, how do we respond to charges of irrationality from both *outside* and *within* the church? For example, from critics outside the church, theology is often charged with logical incoherence. Whether it was the Arians early on; Socinians in the Reformation era; or Jehovah's Witnesses, Islam, and postmodern secularists today, doctrines such as the Trinity, Christology, divine providence, the problem of evil, original sin, and so on have all been charged with incoherence and contradiction.

But the charge of incoherence also takes place from *within* the church. As Christians differ on various theological proposals, each side accuses the other of irrationality. This often occurs, for example, in Calvinist-Arminian polemics. If Calvinists affirm that God ordains *all* things, including human choices and evil, Arminians insist that such a view *logically* entails that God

---

[82] Obviously, systematic theology is more than biblical *reasoning* since it is a whole-person response to God's revelation, which includes our minds, hearts, emotions, etc. On this point, see Beeke and Smalley, *Reformed Systematic Theology*, 1:55–67, 145–58 (see chap. 1, n. 8).

[83] See Trueman, *Rise and Triumph* (see chap. 1, n. 26).

[84] For helpful reflections on theology as "biblical reasoning," see Webster, *Domain of the Word*, 115–32 (see chap. 1, n. 5).

is responsible for evil, that we cannot fight against evil since God ordained it, that God needs evil for his own glory, and that humans have no free will. [85] Calvinists respond by denying that these conclusions logically follow and, in return, insist that if Arminians were consistent in their theology, logical inconsistencies would result.[86] These charges raise a methodological question of significance: How is logical consistency demonstrated in our theological formulations?

Our answer to this question begins with a basic point. To draw logical conclusions, we must first have sufficient data. Our premises, derived from Scripture, must be true, but we must also have enough data to appeal to, otherwise determining what is logical is difficult. For example, think of divine providence and the relationship between divine and human agency. To draw logical conclusions about this relationship, we need a correct understanding of divine sovereignty, human freedom, and how they relate to each other—all of which assumes that we have enough data to conclude what is logical or not. This may seem like an obvious point, but it is precisely at this point that complications arise.

Although Scripture is true, infallible, and inerrant, it is *not* exhaustive in its explanations and teaching, especially in our illustration of divine providence. After all, just read the book of Job and notice that God does not give Job a detailed answer to all of his questions. In fact, repeatedly God says to Job that his judgment is simply wrong because he does not know enough.[87] Or think of the well-known statement from Deuteronomy: "The hidden things belong to the LORD our God, but the revealed things belong to us and our children forever" (29:29).

For this reason, theology rightly distinguishes between archetypal and ectypal knowledge, grounded in the Creator-creature distinction. As noted in chapter 3, archetypal knowledge refers to God's perfect knowledge whereby he knows himself and all things exhaustively, including all propositional truths and possibilities and their logical relations. God knows his plan for every detail of creation and history and the relations between all events and objects.

---

[85] See Bruce A. Little, "Evil and God's Sovereignty," in *Whosoever Will: A Biblical-Theological Critique of Five-Point Calvinism*, ed. David L. Allen and Steve W. Lemke (Nashville: B&H, 2010), 280, 284, 287–94, 296–97.

[86] See Scott Christensen, *What About Evil? A Defense of God's Sovereign Glory* (Phillipsburg: P&R, 2020), 84–115.

[87] On this point, see D. A. Carson, *How Long O Lord? Reflections on Suffering and Evil*, 2nd ed. (Grand Rapids: Baker Academic, 2006), 135–57.

His understanding is total and without error; he alone has a "God's-eye viewpoint." This is why for God there are no "mysteries" or, better, "unknowns." God knows completely *how* he exists as three persons subsisting in one divine nature, or *how* he created the universe *ex nihilo*, or *how* the divine Son subsists and acts simultaneously in two natures without confusion or change, or *how* his ordination of all things is perfectly compatible with human responsible action.

However, our knowledge as creatures is only ectypal, that is, knowledge caused by and dependent on God's exhaustive knowledge. Thankfully, in contrast to our postmodern society, we, as finite creatures, can have true, objective knowledge since our knowledge is grounded in God's perfect knowledge, yet even the knowledge we receive from Scripture is limited.[88] In fact, in eternity, the archetype-ectype distinction will never be erased. Thus, although God plans and knows all things, he has not revealed everything to us, but what he has revealed to us is true and sufficient although it is not exhaustive. This is why *for us* "mysteries/unknowns" are inevitable in our theological formulations, but such unknowns are *not* contradictions.

With these basic points in place, let us now discuss three further points that help us answer the question of how to draw logical conclusions in our theological formulations.[89]

First, given our ectypal knowledge, when we draw logical conclusions from Scripture, we must make sure that *all* of our premises are warranted by Scripture *and* in the manner Scripture presents them. Once again think about the relationship between divine sovereignty and human freedom. Our first task is to account for and maintain simultaneously *all* that Scripture teaches about this relationship without picking or choosing one set of truths over another.

---

[88] Theologically and apologetically, it is crucial to contrast a Christian concept of "mystery/unknowns" in *our knowledge* from a postmodern one. In theology, "unknowns" are acceptable and *not* destructive of objective truth since our knowledge is grounded in the triune God who speaks (*principium essendi* and *principium cognoscendi*). Although we only have finite knowledge, *if* our knowledge corresponds and coheres with God's self-revelation both in creation and supremely in Scripture, it is objective and true. However, for postmodern, secular thought, there is no universal, objective God's-eye viewpoint that grounds knowledge and truth. As such, *all* human knowing is finite and reduces to perspectivalism, subjectivity, and relativism. Ultimately, the argument for the Christian worldview is that apart from the triune God who speaks, human knowledge is rendered internally self-contradictory.

[89] For a detailed treatment, see James Anderson, *Paradox in Christian Theology* (Eugene: Wipf & Stock, 2007).

What does Scripture teach about this relationship? Although we will return to this subject in part 4 (chapters 22–23), we are convinced that Scripture teaches at least four truths about the relationship between divine sovereignty and human freedom: (1) God is completely sovereign in his rule of the world, including his rule of sin and evil, so that nothing is done outside of his foreordained plan and/or permission. (2) God is perfectly good, holy, righteous, and just; God is not responsible for sin and evil or an accomplice of it. (3) Human creatures are free and morally responsible for their choices and actions, but their freedom never limits God's sovereign rule over the world. And (4) sin and evil are real but also foreordained by God for his ultimate glory.

Assuming that these four truths are faithful to Scripture, the theological task, then, is to "make sense" of *how* these four truths "fit" together with proper application to our lives without redefining or eliminating any of the biblical data. The full exercise of our reason is required but in such a way that our conclusions simultaneously uphold all of the four truths.[90] In other words, we cannot appeal to God's sovereignty to eliminate human freedom, nor can we appeal to human freedom to redefine or limit God's sovereign rule over all things, including humans. In the same way, we must also let biblical truths *function* in our theology as they do in Scripture. For example, God's sovereign choice in election does *not* function in Scripture to eliminate human responsibility, or diminish our evangelistic desire, or rob us of our assurance—all points that Arminian theology claims unconditional election logically entails. Rather, in Scripture, unconditional election functions to ground our assurance (Rom 8:28–39), stir us to evangelistic action (2 Tim. 2:10), and lead us to praise (Eph 1:4–6). Thus, in our drawing theological conclusions from Scripture, our conclusions must account for *all* that Scripture teaches.

Second, given our ectypal knowledge, it is not surprising that in our theologizing tensions arise as we seek to understand *how* all the biblical teaching fits together. Since God has not exhaustively revealed everything to us, "unknowns" inevitably result. This is not to say that everything in theology is a "mystery" or "unknown." As such, in our theologizing we

---

[90] Grudem offers this helpful rule to follow in our drawing logical conclusions from Scripture in our theological construction: "we are free to use our reasoning abilities to draw deductions from any passage of Scripture so long as these deductions do not contradict the clear teaching of some other passage of Scripture" (italics removed). *Systematic Theology*, 18 (see chap. 1, n. 14).

should not appeal to "mystery" too quickly. It is only after we have done our exegesis of the relevant passages and follow how Scripture unpacks the tensions between the biblical data that we should appeal to "mystery" on matters that Scripture does not fully address. Yet, after this is done, *if* our exegesis is correct, we must learn to live with *biblically* derived tensions/mysteries. So, for example, in theologizing about divine providence, we must maintain that God foreordains all things, including our human choices, yet his decree does not remove our responsible and free action despite the tensions this creates in our attempt to "wrap" our minds around this.

How do we *know* that our reasoning is correct? Because Scripture teaches *all* of these truths and *if* our theological formulation maintains *all* of the biblical truths simultaneously, it is correct. But someone objects: This seems "unreasonable" or "illogical" to me. *How* can God foreordain all things, including our future free actions, and they still be free? Answer: *if* we have understood Scripture correctly, then in terms of the *how*, we are not completely sure; however, our reasoning is warranted because Scripture teaches it. Our warrant for knowing what is *logically* possible is Scripture, yet given our ectypal knowledge, we should not expect that we can fully answer every *how* question. On some matters, we simply do not know enough. God has not fully disclosed to us how all of these areas fit together, and even if he had, as finite creatures, we would not be able to grasp all the nuances of it. So for the critic to insist that it is illogical or irrational to assert what Scripture teaches *and* that such a metaphysical state of affairs is not possible, the critic must assume that he has a kind of exhaustive knowledge that only God has!

Third, although "unknowns" are inevitable and acceptable in our theological formulations, we must reject contradictions. Why? Our doctrine of God and his archetypal knowledge requires it. For God, there are no contradictions; he is the triune Lord who plans and knows all things. Moreover, even though Scripture is not exhaustive, it is *his* word and thus true and noncontradictory. So as we exegete Scripture and draw theological conclusions, we have confidence that Scripture is coherent and logically consistent, yet, in construction *and* defense, we must also demonstrate that there is no necessary contradiction in our theological formulations even if we cannot fully explain every "how" and "why."

Systematic theology, then, works hard to understand *all* that Scripture teaches in the way Scripture teaches it, without leaving anything out. Also, as the data is put together, extrabiblical concepts consistent with Scripture may be employed to demonstrate that there is no necessary contradiction in our theological conclusions. However, it is not the job of theology to explain exhaustively *how* everything fits together; instead, theology constructs and defends biblical teaching by demonstrating its coherency and logical consistency on the Bible's own terms.

In the end, the test of whether our theological formulations are *biblical* is whether they account for *all* of Scripture *and* whether they lead us to affirm and not contradict other areas in our theology that we know are true to Scripture. In fact, as we evaluate and arbitrate other theological viewpoints within the church in a number of doctrinal areas, these two tests are central to the critical task of theology: (1) Does our theological view account for all of Scripture? (2) Are the theological entailments of my view consistent with Scripture?

Concluding Reflection

The task of theology is to know the triune God and all things in relation to him as we apply his word to every area of life. The church has the high calling of embracing the role of renewed reason to make proper (faithful and logical) theological conclusions from Scripture, moving from canon to concept, which is the essential act in formulating doctrines and coordinating them into a fully integrated worldview. By doing so, the church is enabled to understand and apply Scripture rightly in order to live faithful and obedient lives under Christ's lordship for the glory of God, the good of the church, and the proclamation and defense of the truth of the gospel to the nations.

In part 1, we have focused on *what* systematic theology is and *why* and *how* the church must undertake the theological task. As we have concluded part 1 with some reflections on theological method, we now turn to the doing of theology. In part 2, we turn to a more detailed exposition of God's speech in nature and Scripture, the foundation for systematic theology, which we have only briefly mentioned. Then in part 3, we outline the Bible's covenantal storyline from creation to Christ, what we have described as the first of two intertwined steps in the doing of theology, although even in doing so a theology is already at work. In part 4, we turn to the second step of theological formulation as we think through the doctrinal loci of systematic theology that arise from the Bible's own presentation, framework, and unfolding plan, which discloses the glory of our triune God centered in Christ Jesus our Lord.

PART 2

The Revelation of the Triune God Who Speaks

CHAPTER 5

God and His Word: Divine Speech

Introduction

What is the warrant for objective truth and the possibility of theology as a normative discipline? What is the transcendental condition for both? As we argued in part 1, it is the triune God (*principium essendi*) who speaks (*principium cognoscendi*). Both "foundations" (*principia*) are necessary for truth and theology, and both are interrelated and inseparable.

In terms of the former, truth and theology are not grounded in any concept of "god" but only in the God of Scripture, the triune Creator-covenant Lord, who alone is uncreated, independent, self-sufficient, and self-attesting. It is only *this* God who knows and plans all things (Isa 46:8–10; Eph 1:11), and as such, his knowledge is "from himself" (*aseity*), not dependent on or correlative to the world. For this reason, the triune God is the source and standard of truth, and he alone has a truly universal, exhaustive, comprehensive knowledge of all things—a God's-eye viewpoint (archetype). In terms of the latter, because God has sovereignly and freely spoken the universe into being ex nihilo, resulting in an ordered, designed, purposed universe, *and* he has spoken to us in a verbal and written form, we have true knowledge of God's plan and promises and the world around us. As we "think God's thoughts after him," although we cannot know God, self, and the world exhaustively, we can know them truly (ectype), thus warranting objective truth and a normative theology.

As we now turn to the specifics of a theology of divine revelation, we must keep together the doctrine of the God–revelation relationship, or, more succinctly, the God-word relationship. The *necessity* of divine speech assumes a specific theology proper and vice versa. In the doctrine of Scripture, as this relationship is unpacked, we discover that one cannot talk about what Scripture is apart from the God who gave it, and that different views of God inevitably result in different views of Scripture. In fact, theologians have wrestled with which area of theology comes first: God or Scripture.[1] We will start with the doctrine of revelation, but throughout, we will assume a theology proper represented by pro-Nicene trinitarianism and the Reformed tradition since the God-word and the God-world relationship are inseparably intertwined.

The word "revelation" is from the Latin, *revelatio*, and its basic concept is "to unveil, uncover, bring to light, disclose, and/or make known that which is previously hidden, veiled, and/or unknown."[2] The object revealed can be a "person, information, feelings, thoughts, and action."[3] In the case of God, revelation conveys the idea that God chooses to disclose or unveil something of his being, thoughts, and promises to "rational beings to whom the revelation is made and who are capable of appropriating it."[4] Revelation, then, is making known previously hidden truths, especially regarding the nature of God and his eternal plan. In contrast to neo-orthodox theology and current theology that is indebted to it, revelation is both propositional and personal. As we will develop below, when God discloses himself to us, *he* speaks and reveals information about himself, us, and the world, and in so doing, we know truth about these areas and we know *him*.[5]

---

[1] For example, Bavinck, *Reformed Dogmatics*, vol. 1 (see chap. 1, n. 9); and Beeke and Smalley, *Reformed Systematic Theology* (see chap. 1, n. 8), discuss divine revelation and Scripture prior to theology proper. However, John M. Frame, *Systematic Theology: An Introduction to Christian Belief* (Phillipsburg: P&R, 2013); and Robert Letham, *Systematic Theology* (Wheaton: Crossway, 2019) discuss theology proper first.

[2] John S. Feinberg, *Light in a Dark Place: The Doctrine of Scripture* (Wheaton: Crossway, 2018), 38. Also see a discussion of the biblical concept of divine revelation in Robert W. Yarbrough, "Revelation," in *NDBT*, 732–38 (see chap. 1, n. 24).

[3] Feinberg, 38.

[4] Louis Berkhof, *Introduction to Systematic Theology* (repr., Grand Rapids: Baker, 1979), 117.

[5] See Guy P. Waters, *For the Mouth of the Lord Has Spoken: The Doctrine of Scripture* (Fearn, Ross-shire, UK: Christian Focus, 2020), 13–18. For a discussion of current theology and the propositional vs. personal revelation divide, see John M. Frame, *The Doctrine of the Word of God* (Phillipsburg: P&R, 2010), 3–104.

Where does God reveal himself to us? This is the question of the *locus* of divine revelation. Historically, theology has distinguished between where God reveals himself "generally" (universally) or "naturally" and where God speaks in a "special" (specific), salvific, and supernatural manner, associated with God's mighty actions, our Lord Jesus Christ (the incarnate Word), and Scripture (the written word). More simply, these categories are often reduced to "natural/general" or "special" revelation. Before we develop these categories in more detail in this chapter and the next, it is important first to think about what Scripture says about the "word of God," especially given diverse and confused understandings of it. In modern/postmodern theology, especially theology indebted to neo-orthodoxy, the discussion of divine revelation has been significant, along with important consequences for the doctrine of Scripture.[6]

In this chapter we will begin our discussion of divine revelation in three steps. First, we will explain what Scripture says about divine speech (the "word of God") and the God-word relation. Second, we will draw some preliminary theological reflections about the God-word and the God-world relation as traditionally discussed under the category of "special revelation." Third, we will outline some of the reasons why people deny Scripture's view of the God-word-world relation, specifically applied to Scripture. Our discussion in this chapter is foundational to our treatment of God's "word" in natural/general revelation in chapter 6, and the development of the doctrine of Scripture in chapters 7–12.

The Triune God and His Word

The Nature of God's Word

What does Scripture say the "word of God" is?[7] Scripture speaks more about the *word* of God than *revelation*, although there is diverse terminology for both and they are organically

---

[6] See Avery Dulles, *Models of Revelation* (Garden City: Image Books, 1983). Dulles considers five models of revelation in theology, both inside and outside of evangelical theology: (1) revelation as doctrine, (2) revelation as history, (3) revelation as inner experience, (4) revelation as dialectical presence, (5) revelation as new awareness. Each of these views of revelation assumes a specific God-word-world relationship, which also leads to different conceptions of Scripture. For a historical treatment of the doctrine of revelation, see H. D. McDonald, *Theories of Revelation: An Historical Study 1700–1960* (Grand Rapids: Baker, 1979).

[7] My discussion is indebted to and following John M. Frame, *Perspectives on the Word of God* (Phillipsburg: P&R, 1990), 9–35; and Frame, *Doctrine of the Word*, 47–100; cf. Andrew G. Shead, *A*

related. In the OT, the main term for "revelation" conveys the idea of "to reveal," "to uncover," and "to appear" (Heb. *gālāh*). In the NT the main terms are similar: "to manifest," "to make visible," or "to make known" (Gk. *apokalyptō* and *phaneroō*).[8] Yet, other Hebrew and Greek words convey the idea of "to unveil, reveal, make known," all of which communicates the idea of God taking the initiative to make himself known by his own self-communication.[9] However, *word* of God emphasizes more God's self-communication, while *revelation* highlights the content disclosed by God's speech. No doubt, the two concepts are often used interchangeably, but *word* is more common and it is linked to the idea of divine speech. What, then, is the "*word* of God?"

Most Christians intuitively answer the question by saying, "the Bible." In fact, as John Frame reminds us, this is how the Westminster Larger Catechism answers question 3: "What is the Word of God?" Answer: "The holy Scriptures of the Old and New Testaments are the Word of God, the only rule of faith and obedience."[10] Of course, this answer is true, but the concept of the "word of God" in Scripture is more than merely "the Bible," which technically is "God's word *written*." To illustrate this point, Frame suggests that we substitute "the

---

Mouth Full of Fire: The Word of God in the words of Jeremiah, NSBT 29 (Downers Grove: InterVarsity, 2012), 265–90.

[8] See *NIDOTTE* 1:861; *TDNT* 3:576–77. See Gen 35:7; Lev 18:6–19; 20:11; Num 22:31; Deut 29:29; 1 Sam 2:27; 3:21; Prov 11:13; 20:19; 25:9; Isa 53:1; Dan 2:22; Amos 3:7; Matt 10:26; Mark 4:22; John 2:11; 17:6.

[9] In the OT, we have the language of "the Lord appeared" using the passive form of the verb translated "to see" (*niphal* of *raah*) (Gen 12:7; 17:1; 18:1; 26:2, 24; Lev 9:23; Num 14:10; 16:19). We also have the words, "to say" (*amar*), "to speak" (*diber*), and the noun "word" (*dābār*). "Thus says (*amar*) the Lord," is used over 400 times to refer to God's authoritative communication (*NIDOTTE* 1:444). In the NT, alongside *apokalyptō*, we have the words for "speak" (*laleō*) (John 14:25; 15:11; 16:1; Heb 1:1–2), "to say" (*legō*), and the related noun for "word" (*logos*) (*NIDOTTE* 3:134–35) and *rhēma*, all of which convey the idea of verbal communication (*NIDOTTE* 4:207; Rom 10:17; Eph 6:17). "Appearing" (*epiphaneia*) is another word that communicates the idea of disclosing and bringing to light (*TDNT* 9:9; Luke 1:79; Acts 17:20; Titus 2:11). Beeke and Smalley summarize the biblical data this way: "The terminology of divine communication in the Old and New Testaments revolves around three major foci: first, the idea of a verbal message from God in a form that human beings can receive, understand, and repeat; second, the idea of a gracious revelation of hidden, divine truth that man cannot discover on his own; third, the idea of an intrusion of eternal glory into our ordinary, mundane existence." Beeke and Smalley, *Reformed Systematic Theology*, 1:181; cf. Bavinck, *Reformed Dogmatics*, 1:324–25.

[10] See Frame, *Doctrine of the Word*, 47.

Bible" for "word" in Psalm 147:15–18. As we read, "He sends his command throughout the earth; his *word* ["the Bible"] runs swiftly" (v. 15), or "He sends his *word* ["the Bible"] and melts them; he unleashes his winds, and the water flows" (v. 18), we realize that this substitution does not quite fit. Or try making a similar substitution in John 1:1, 14: "In the beginning was the Word, and the Word was with God, and the Word was God. . . . The Word became flesh and dwelt among us." To replace "Word" with "the Bible" is not a suitable replacement.

So if the "*word* of God" cannot simply be substituted in every place by "the Bible," then what is it? As Frame answers this question, he observes that "God's word is, certainly, the sum total of his communications, everything that he has said, is saying, and will say."[11] But it is also more than this since God's *word* is inseparable from God's own being. Indeed, *the Word* is also a title for the divine Son (John 1:1–2, 14), and it is by his *word* that God accomplishes his *ad extra* works of creation, providence, redemption, and judgment. To make this point, Frame first defines "the word of God" as "God's 'self-expression,'"[12] and then specifies the various forms of self-expression that Scripture describes as divine speech.[13] Let us follow his overall presentation to understand better how Scripture defines God's *word* and its implications for understanding God within himself (*ad intra*) and God's self-communication to us (*ad extra*).

First, the "word of God" is the *power* by which God acts and accomplishes all of his plans and purposes according to his will (Acts 2:23; Eph 1:11).[14] Since God's word is tied to *him*, it is never a "blind force" or "raw power," but it is a power that makes things happen and that expresses God's being, wisdom, and glory (Ps 104:24). Furthermore, since God's word is *his*

---

[11] Frame, 48.

[12] Frame, *Perspectives*, 10–16. In *Doctrine of the Word*, 49, Frame gives this definition: the "word of God" is (1) God himself, understood as communicator, and (2) the sum total of his free communications with his creatures."

[13] See D. A. Carson, *The Gospel According to John*, PNTC (Grand Rapids: Eerdmans, 1991), 114–17. Carson discusses the meaning of *logos* in relation to the concept of the "word of God" in the OT. Carson, like Frame, offers the following definition: God's word "is his powerful self-expression in creation, revelation and salvation" (116). As applied to the divine Son, this is a significant way of speaking of the Son's oneness with the Father in sharing the same, identical divine nature (John 1:1ac) yet also that he is distinct from the Father (1:1b).

[14] Bavinck, *Reformed Dogmatics*, 1:401.

powerful self-expression, it is always *meaningful* due to the fact that God is a personal being. God's word as power is not contrary to his word as a communication of linguistic content; both go together. Here is a list of some of God's works that are all done by his *powerful* word.[15]

1. God *created* all things by his word (Gen 1:3; John 1:1–3; Heb 11:3). When God first speaks, "he speaks not to rational beings, but to inanimate objects,"[16] and by his word, he "calls things into existence that do not exist" (Rom 4:17b).

2. God *rules* providentially over his creation and commands things to happen by his word (Gen 1:9, 11, 22; 8:21–22; Job 37:12; Pss 18:15; 33:11; 147:15–18; Matt 8:27; Heb 1:3).

3. God *judges* the universe by his word of power (Gen 3:14–19; 6:7; Isa 30:30; 66:6; Matt 7:21–27; 25:31–46; John 12:48; 2 Pet 3:7) and also graciously *redeems* us by that same word (Gen 18:14; Isa 43:1; Luke 1:37; 7:1–10; John 6:63, 68; Rom 1:16; Phil 2:16; 1 John 1:1). In Luke 7:7–9, Christ simply has to "say the word" (*eipe logō*), and the centurion's servant is healed.

4. God effectually calls people savingly to himself by his word (Isa 62:2; 65:15; Acts 2:39; Rom 1:6–7; 8:28; 1 Cor 1:2, 24, 26). God's *word* has power to make alive people who were spiritually dead in their sins, thus resulting in resurrection life (Rom 6:1–4; Eph 2:1–7).

5. Even before God's external acts, God *planned* all things from eternity according to his word. It is difficult to think of God's decree (Eph 1:11) apart from divine power and speech. In Reformed theology, related to God's decree is the "covenant of redemption" (*pactum salutis*), by which the triune persons agree to plan and execute the redemption of the elect, as one act but according to distinctive roles (Gen 1:26; Pss 2:7–9; 110; Matt 11:25–27; John 5:20; 17:1–26; Acts 2:33–36; John 4:34; 6:38f; Rev 13:8). However we think of the shared communication within God himself, the *pactum salutis* certainly assumes some kind of communication.

In these acts, God's *powerful* word is at work, which also includes verbal meaning, since in most of these acts, God's *word* includes linguistic content. Due to God's eternal plan, which involves some kind of communication, the universe is created, ordered, and designed by God's word, and history unfolds according to that plan (Gen 1:1; Acts 2:22; Col 1:16–17; Eph 1:11; 2 Tim 1:8–10; Heb 1:3; Rev 13:8). The power of God's word is "nothing less than his own

---

[15] Thinking of divine speech especially in the context of the category of "speech-act" is helpful since it brings together "God saying" and "God doing" since "saying too is a doing and that persons can do many things by 'saying.'" Vanhoozer, *First Theology*, 130, cf. 159–203 (see chap. 2, n. 99).

[16] Frame, *Doctrine of the Word*, 50.

omnipotence,"[17] which shows itself in creation, providence, redemption, and judgment. By God's powerful word, he is able to accomplish all that he has planned as the sovereign Lord (Isa 55:11).

Also, we begin to see that God's word is associated with the power of God's Spirit (1 Thess 1:5) since Scripture closely links God, his word, and his Spirit (Heb. *ruach*; Gk. *pneuma*) (Gen 1:2 [John 1:1–3]; Num 11:25; 24:3–4; Ps 33:6; Luke 1:67; 2:25–32; John 3:34–35). This linkage between God, his word, and his Spirit are important for making sense of the relations between the divine persons in the doctrine of the Trinity, both within God (*ad intra*) and in his external works (*ad extra*).

Second, the "word of God" is God's *authoritative* and thus *meaningful speech* because it is from God's own self-sufficient being.[18] As Frame notes, "Authority is a function of the *meaning* of language,"[19] and God's word is powerful *and* meaningful. The difference between "power" and "authority" is that "God's power determines what *will* happen, while God's authority determines what *ought* to happen,"[20] which also shows itself in the distinction between God's "decretive" and "preceptive" will. That there is a difference between these two, namely, that God sometimes decrees to happen what his precepts and revealed will forbid (e.g., Luke 22:22; Acts 2:23; 4:28), underlies the doctrine of providence, the divine sovereignty–human freedom relationship, and especially the problem of evil. God has decreed the entire plan of redemption centered in Christ (Eph 1:11; Rev 13:8), which includes our sin, but God also holds humans responsible for their actions. We will return to the doctrine of providence in chapters 22–23, but here the vital point to highlight is that God's word includes "both the exertions of God's power and the expressions of God's authoritative will."[21] In creation, God speaks in power and the universe comes to be. But as Frame observes, God does so by the use of intelligible speech, "giving names to things that interpret their function. In Genesis 1:5, 8, 10, God 'calls' (*qara'*) things by names: Day, Night, Heaven, Earth, Seas. . . . In verses 27–28 he defines by his word the nature and task of mankind."[22] Indeed, this is analogous to the task that God gives to

[17] Frame, 53.

[18] Bavinck, *Reformed Dogmatics*, 1:401–2.

[19] Frame, *Doctrine of the Word*, 54.

[20] Frame, *Perspectives*, 12.

[21] Frame, 12.

[22] Frame, *Doctrine of the Word*, 55.

Adam—to rule over creation by naming the animals and "creat[ing] a system of meaningful words that would indicate the nature and characteristics of the animals."[23]

When God speaks to humans, announcing his will for their lives, he does so with *authority*, and his speech acts are meaningful, thus cognitive in nature. In fact, all the issues of life depend on our response to divine speech. Frame writes: "When God shares his love with us, we have the obligation to treasure it. When he questions us, we should answer. When he expresses his grace, we are obligated to trust it. When he tells us his desires, we should conform our lives to it. When he shares his knowledge and intentions, we ought to believe that they are true."[24] Indeed, from creation to the new creation, God speaks, and humans, as God's creatures created for a covenant relationship, are to respond in faith, love, trust, and obedience.

As we walk through Scripture, this truth is evident. Adam's first recorded experience was God speaking to him by a command, and his entire life and future depended on his response to that word (Gen 2:16–17). After the fall, Adam's only hope for salvation was God keeping his word of promise (Gen 3:15). Noah had to take God at his word to know that divine judgment was coming. Abraham's faith, a paradigm for faith throughout Scripture (Rom 4; Gal 3:6–9; Heb 11:8–19; Jas 2:21–24), was wholehearted trust in God's word, tied to God's covenant promises (Gen 12:1–3). Israel under the Law covenant was called to trust and obey all that God promised and commanded by his word (Deut 6; Josh 1:8–9; Pss 1; 119). After the old covenant, God also spoke through the prophets (Deut 18:15–22; Jer 1:6–19; Ezek 13:2f, 17), whose word was to be believed as authoritative and true because the prophets spoke from the Lord.

Then supremely in the NT, Jesus comes as the fulfillment of the OT (Matt 5:17–20), obeying all of its precepts and commands and thereby confirming its absolute authority.[25] Even more: as God the Son/Word incarnate (John 1:1, 14), Jesus speaks words of authority that are to be received, believed, and obeyed. Indeed, apart from receiving and obeying his word, we have no life and salvation; instead, we stand under his authoritative word of judgment (Matt 7:21ff, 28f; Mark 8:38; Luke 8:21; 9:26ff; John 6:63, 68; 8:47; 12:47–50; 14:15, 21, 23f; 15:7, 10, 14; 17:6, 17; 1 Tim 6:3; 1 John 2:3–5; 3:22; 5:2f; 2 John 6; Rev 12:17; 14:12).

---

[23] Frame, 55.

[24] Frame, 56.

[25] See Matthew Barrett, *Canon, Covenant, and Christology: Rethinking Jesus and the Scriptures of Israel*, NSBT 51 (Downers Grove: InterVarsity, 2020), 297–315.

From Jesus, the apostles are commissioned, and by the work of the Spirit, their words are also authoritative and true and thus to be believed and obeyed (John 14:23–26; 15:26–16:16; Rom 2:16; 1 Cor 2:10–13; 4:1; 2 Cor 4:1–6; 12:1, 7; Gal 1:1, 11–16; 1 Thess 4:2; Jude 17–19). God's word is powerful and authoritative because it is *his* word. For this reason, it is to be heard, obeyed, and trusted since it alone is true. God's word will never fail and it will never lead us astray (John 10:35).

Third, the "word of God" is God's *personal presence* with us. Even in human language it is difficult to separate a speaker from his words. Today, appeal is made to speech-act theory (a subset of the philosophy of language) to make this point.[26] In human communication, we use words/sentences (locutions), but intention is tied to what we *do* with our sentences (illocutions), which then assumes a certain kind of response (perlocutions). In other words, we do not merely say words; instead, we *do* something with our words, such as assert, command, promise, or warn. As such, speakers intend something by their speech, which is directly tied to the speaker who utters the speech. For example, think of a wedding ceremony. When a man and a woman say the words, "I do," these are not simply words. They are promises that enact the covenant relationship of marriage. The couple is *doing* or *intending* something by their words, which are inseparable from them; each one is held legally accountable for their words. In a far greater way, what is true of humans is true of God: God cannot be separated from his words.[27] To obey God's word is to obey *him*; to reject his word is to reject *him* (Isa 66:2). God is present in his word: "whenever God speaks, he himself is there with us" as the omnipresent Lord.[28] Frame lists a number of ways that God's word is united to himself:[29]

1. God's word reveals *him* (Deut 4:5–8; 2 Tim 3:15).

2. God's Spirit is present with his word. As noted above, in Scripture there is a close correlation between word and Spirit, ultimately grounded within God himself (Gen 1:2; Ps 33:6; Isa 34:16; 59:21; John 6:63; 16:13; Acts 2:1–4; 1 Thess 1:5; 2 Thess 2:2). This correlation is

---

[26] See John R. Searle, *Speech Acts: An Essay in the Philosophy of Language* (Cambridge: Cambridge University Press, 1974); cf. Vanhoozer, *First Theology*, 159–203.

[27] See Timothy Ward, *Words of Life: Scripture as the Living and Active Word of God* (Nottingham: InterVarsity Press, 2009), 22–50; cf. Gregg R. Allison and Andreas J. Köstenberger, *The Holy Spirit* (Nashville: B&H Academic, 2020), 309–11.

[28] Frame, *Doctrine of the Word*, 63.

[29] See Frame, *Perspectives*, 14–15; and Frame, *Doctrine of the Word*, 64–68.

crucial in the doctrine of Scripture, where human words are said to be "God-breathed" (*theopneustos*) and thus *God's* word (2 Tim 3:16) by the agency of the Spirit (2 Pet 1:21).

3. God's nearness is also the nearness of the word (Deut 4:5–8; 30:11–14; Rom 10:6–8).

4. All of God's *acts* are performed by speech. As such, *he* is present in his acts by his word. God is a spirit and not a physical being, but he is nevertheless present with us by his word. For example, God is present in his acts accomplished by his divine speech: creation (Gen 1:3; Pss 33:6, 9; 148:5; John 1:3; Heb 1:2; 11:3; 2 Pet 3:5–7), providence (Gen 1:9, 11, 22; 8:21f; Pss 18:15; 28:3–9; 145:15f; 119:89–91; 148:8; Job 37:12; 33:11f; Matt 8:27; Heb 1:3; 2 Pet 3), redemption (Gen 3:15; 12:1–3; Ps 111:9; Isa 43:1; 62:2; 65:15; Luke 7:1–10; Rom 1:16; Phil 2:16; 1 John 1:1; 2 Tim 1:10), and judgment (Gen 3:17ff; 6:7; 11:6f; Ps 46:6; Isa 30:30; 66:6; Ezek 1:1; 3:22; Hos 6:5; John 5:21–30; Rev 20:11–15).

5. A crucial way that God is distinguished from idols as the true and living God is by divine speech, thus linking divine speech, or God's word, to the very being of God (1 Kgs 18:24, 26, 29, 36; Pss 115:5–9; 135:15–18; Jer 10:1–16; Hab 2:18–20; 1 Cor 12:2). God, unlike the idols, is by nature the triune God who speaks.

6. The word of God is described in terms of divine attributes, thus linking *word* to God. For example, God's word is wonderful (Ps 119:129), righteous (Ps 119:7), faithful (Ps 119:86), upright (Ps 119:137), pure (Ps 119:140), true (Ps 119:142; cf. John 17:17), eternal (Ps 119:89, 160), omnipotent (Gen 18:14; Isa 55:11; Luke 1:37), perfect (Ps 19:7ff), and holy (Deut 31:26; 2 Tim 3:15). Not surprisingly, because God's word is linked to *him*, it is also an object of worship (Pss 9:2; 34:3; 56:4, 10; 68:4; 119:48, 120, 161–168; 138:2; Isa 66:5).

Also, the "word of God" is correlated to the "name of God." God's "name" is his whole self-revelation (Exod 3:14; 34:5–7; Pss 7:17; 9:10; 18:49; 68:4; 74:18; 105:1; Isa 25:1; 26:8; 56:6; Zech 14:9; Mal 3:16; John 8:58), which is evident in Exod 33–34. As Moses pleads to see God's glory (33:18), God graciously reveals himself by the proclamation of his "name:" the LORD, the God of *hesed* (covenant faithfulness or "grace") and *emet* (truth) (34:5–7). This episode reaches its ultimate fulfillment in the revelation of Christ's glory, the eternal Word/Son made flesh, who dwells or tabernacles among us, full of "grace and truth" (John 1:14–18).

7. The triune persons are distinguished by their personal relations of origin, which are revealed in their role in divine speech.[30] The Word is the divine Son (John 1:1), who shares the

[30] Bavinck, *Reformed Dogmatics*, 1:402.

same divine nature with the Father and Spirit (John 1:1c) and yet is distinguished from them as the Word (John 1:1b). Although every external act of God is one, we can still distinguish the divine persons' role in God's speaking due to their eternal, immanent personal relations.[31] For this reason, as Frame notes, the divine persons' role in divine speech "is not the only scriptural way of representing the trinitarian distinctions, but it is one significant way."[32] The unbegotten Father is the one who initiates by speaking through the Son and by the Spirit (Gen 1:1; Ps 29; Isa 40:26; 43:1; 62:2; 65:15; Eph 3:14–15); the Son, who is from the Father, is the Word spoken (John 1:1; Col 1:15–16; Heb 1:1–3); and the Spirit, who is from the Father and Son, and who is the breath (Heb. *ruach*; Gk. *pneuma*) that accompanies the Word and brings to completion all of God's acts (Gen 1:2; Ps 33:6; 1 Thess 1:5; 2 Tim 3:16; 2 Pet. 1:21). All of this is to say that when we encounter God's *word*, we encounter God himself in his triune glory.[33]

8. God's word does only what God can do as fully present with us. Hebrews 4:12–13 teaches this point by highlighting the inseparable relation between God and his word. In v. 12 we are told that "the word of God is living and effective and sharper than any double-edged sword. . . . able to judge the thoughts and intentions of the heart," something only God can do. But in this context, the word referred to is Scripture, thus correlating Scripture's words to God's own authority, power, and presence. In v. 13, we discover why this is the case: to be confronted by God's word is to be confronted by God himself: "No creature is hidden from him, but all things are naked and exposed to the eyes of him to whom we must give an account." Such a connection refuses to dichotomize Scripture and its propositional content from God's revelation of himself since they are inseparable: to speak of God's word is to speak of God himself.

Care must be exercised as we put together the biblical teaching on "the word of God." As Frame suggests, God's word is the sum total of his free communications with his creatures. Yet we must also link God's word to God: God's word is inseparable from *him*. God is the speaking God, by his very nature, over against the non-speaking idols. "When we encounter the word of God, we encounter God. When we encounter God, we encounter his word. We cannot

---

[31] See Allison and Köstenberger, *The Holy Spirit*, 255–94.

[32] Frame, *Doctrine of the Word*, 66.

[33] See Mark D. Thompson, *The Doctrine of Scripture: An Introduction* (Wheaton: Crossway, 2022), 66–70.

encounter God without the word, or the word without God. God's word and his personal presence are inseparable . . . whenever God's Word is spoken, read, or heard, God himself is there."[34] However, this is not to say that "word" is simply a synonym for "God"; the two cannot be simply substituted for one another in every context. For example, God does things *by* the word, so there is a close relationship but a difference between the "word" and "God himself."

These distinctions are important to remember, especially regarding the doctrine of Scripture. To identify "word" closely with God's being does not make Scripture necessary to God's being. By nature, God is a communicative being as expressed in the two eternal, necessary processions of the Son from the Father and the Spirit from the Father and Son. But it is *not* necessary for God to speak *to creatures*. If it was, then the creation would be necessary to God—a contradiction of divine aseity and an undermining of the Creator-creature distinction. In God's *ad extra* works, speaking the universe into existence and speaking to his creatures is a *free* act of God, not necessary to him. Thus, Scripture, along with all *ad extra* divine speech, is *free* speech. Nevertheless, Scripture as God's word *written* through the agency of human authors is the product of God's sovereign and free communicative agency that ties this *human* word with God's word, and as such, it carries all of the power and authority of God himself (Heb 4:12–13).

In summary, what then is the nature of the "word of God?" It is God's own powerful, authoritative self-communication, which is inseparable from him; and in God's works, communicative of God's rule, wisdom, grace, and truth. By God's powerful word, the universe is created and God enacts his plans and purposes. By God's authoritative word, he governs and rules over all things, and his word is the only absolute standard of truth, knowledge, and moral norms. By God's word he is present and supremely so in Christ, God's eternal Word/Son made flesh (John 1:1, 14). In Christ, the divine Word not only speaks God's authoritative word, he also has come to take up residence among us through the human nature he has assumed (John 14:9) without change to himself as God the Son, who has and will always share the one identical divine nature with the Father and Spirit. Indeed, where God is, the word is, and vice versa. By God's initiative and grace, we know God only by his word; hence the triune God must speak to us if we are to know him in truth and to experience life in covenant relationship.

---

[34] Frame, *Doctrine of the Word*, 68.

The Media of God's Word

How does God's word get from him to us? What are the created "means by which God reveals and gives himself to people"?[35] This is the question of "media," and the answer to the question also explains the various "modes" of revelation, that is, the different ways God has spoken to us.[36]

In Scripture, God's word always comes to us mediated through some creaturely means, even when revelation seems "direct." For example, Frame illustrates this point by referring to God's speech to Israel at Mt. Sinai (Exod 19–20). The people heard God's voice "directly," but even here God's speech was mediated through human language, the normal earthly atmosphere to transmit the sounds to the eardrums of the people, and so on.[37] As such, God's word never lacks "media" when it is spoken to us. But what kinds of media are there? Primarily, Scripture teaches that God speaks or reveals himself to us through *acts/events* and *words*.

Before we look at these two media, a crucial point needs to be made. God's speech through created means does not limit his ability to communicate to us, contrary to the thought of much modern/postmodern theology. As Frame notes, "God is never prevented by the limitations of creation, or the finitude of people, from saying what he wants to say to them. Rather, the media are God's chosen instruments for bringing his absolute power, authority, and presence to the attention of finite hearers."[38] This point is crucial to remember in our discussion of Scripture. Many non-orthodox views of Scripture insist that the Bible's "humanity" limits God's ability to communicate truly and accurately to us. The thought is that if God speaks through finite and fallen humans, mistakes must occur.[39] But as Frame rightly insists, this is

---

[35] Bavinck, *Reformed Dogmatics*, 1:328.

[36] In this section, I am following Frame's presentation in *Doctrine of the Word*, 71–104; Frame, *Perspectives*, 19–35; Thompson, *Doctrine of Scripture*, 70–97.

[37] Frame, *Doctrine of the Word*, 71–72.

[38] Frame, 73; Peter Jensen notes that the biblical authors "are not in the slightest embarrassed by the human involvement in the transmission of revelation. For them, God uses human nature without abusing it to accomplish his ends." *The Revelation of God* (Downers Grove: InterVarsity, 2002), 39.

[39] Neo-orthodoxy, post-liberalism, and post-conservative theology reflect this view. On the post-conservative side, for example, see Peter Enns, *Inspiration and Incarnation: Evangelicals and the Problem of the Old Testament*, 2nd ed. (Grand Rapids: Baker Academic, 2015); Kenton L. Sparks, *God's Word in Human Words: An Evangelical Appropriation of Critical Biblical Scholarship* (Grand Rapids: Baker Academic, 2008); Sparks, *Sacred Word, Broken Word: Biblical Authority and the Dark Side of Scripture*

a non sequitur for at least the following reasons: first, it is not necessary for humans to err; second, Christ was fully human and he did not err; third, this view assumes that human language is incapable of truly referring to God (which is not a biblical assumption); and fourth, the opposite is actually the case, namely, the humanity of Scripture is not a liability, but its perfection.[40] The glory of Scripture is that God speaks to us in ordinary language that is true and reliable because it is *his* word.[41]

Event Media or Act Revelation

God reveals himself through what he *does* in our world or through various acts/events. In this media, God gloriously reveals his power and sovereignty, but it is not separated from God's authority and presence. What kind of "acts" does Scripture say God "speaks" in and through?

1. *Nature and history* (Gen 9:12–17; Deut 4:26; 30:19; 31:28; 32:1; Pss 19; 46:8–10; 65; 104; 147:15–18; 148:5–8; Acts 14:17; 17:26–28; Rom 1:18–32). Historically, this mode of revelation has been placed under the category of "natural/general" revelation, a topic we will return to in chapter 6. At this point, we simply note that God speaks to *all* people *in* creation and history. No doubt, God's speech in natural revelation does not consist in literal words, yet, as Frame notes, "it is an infallible *medium* of such divine words. As such, natural revelation conveys to us God's power, authority, and presence."[42] Although natural revelation is not salvific, and God never intended it to function apart from his spoken, verbal revelation, it does reveal God to us, and every event that takes place in history is part of God's plan and thus is revelatory. In fact, as we noted in chapter 3, apart from the triune God who speaks creation into existence and governs all the events of history according to his plan, we have no confidence that the world/object we study, let alone ourselves, is designed, ordered, or purposed. The "facts" of history simply become a series of meaningless events apart from some kind of finite human "construction" to give it

(Grand Rapids: Eerdmans, 2012); Gregory A. Boyd, *Inspired Imperfection: How the Bible's Problems Enhance its Divine Authority* (Minneapolis: Fortress, 2020).

[40] For these points and more, see Frame, *Doctrine of the Word*, 73–74.

[41] On this point, see Bavinck, *Reformed Dogmatics*, 1:442–48.

[42] Frame, *Doctrine of the Word*, 78 (emphasis original).

coherence and meaning, which reduces to mere subjectivity. If God's plan and decree does not determine the relationship of every particular event to another, then the way things are in the world are simply indeterminate. But because the triune God creates by his word and plans the events of history, nature and history reveal something of God's being, glory, and purposes.

2. *Human constitution* (Gen 1:26–28). This mode of revelation, as with the previous one, is normally discussed under the category of "natural" revelation. Again, our point here is to note that Scripture views our creation in God's image as part of natural revelation. By God's word, he has created humans to reflect something of God himself, albeit at a finite level and only by analogy. But given our creation, "even unbelievers cannot escape the revelation of God in their own persons, any more than they can escape God's revelation in the facts of creation external to them. God's reality is stamped on every fact; it is found wherever we look, outward or inward."[43]

3. *Redemptive history and God's mighty acts* (Exod 7:5; 14:18, 31; 15; Deut 8:11–18; Pss 66:5–7; 77:11–20; 106; 135; 136; 145:4, 12; Mark 2:10–12; John 2:11; Acts 2:22; 7:2–53; Rom 1:4; 2 Cor 12:12; Heb 2:1–4). Historically, this mode of revelation has been placed under the category of "special" revelation. It is different from the previous "acts" since these "mighty acts" are characterized by God's *extraordinary* agency (what Scripture labels as "signs," "wonders," and "powers," or we identify as "miracles"); they are particular and not universally accessible; and their purpose is salvific. As God's mighty acts, they reveal God's sovereign rule, authority, and presence.[44] These "acts" consist of both saving grace and divine judgment. In the NT, every event centered in Christ's incarnation, life, death, resurrection, ascension, and Pentecost is a mighty act (Matt 1:23; John 1:1–18). Unlike natural revelation, God's mighty acts are salvific because through them, God accomplishes our redemption in Christ and brings judgment to this world. But similar to natural revelation, God never intended for his mighty acts to function apart from God's word revelation, which interprets and explains the true meaning of what God is revealing and doing in his mighty signs and wonders, a point we will return to below.[45]

---

[43] Frame, *Perspectives*, 30.

[44] Bavinck, *Reformed Dogmatics*, 1:336–40; cf. Feinberg, *Light in a Dark Place*, 80–84.

[45] Frame, *Doctrine of Word*, 80–81.

Word Media or Word-Revelation

God's word also comes to us through the media of "words," specifically, God's own voice *and* through human words. Historically, this mode of divine speech is viewed as "special" revelation due to its extraordinary, particular, and salvific nature. Although God's power, authority, and presence are revealed in all of his "acts," they are uniquely revealed in word media. Why? Because in this media, "*word* of God" takes on a narrower meaning, that is, a verbal-linguistic sense, so that God speaks *through human words in a cognitive fashion*. As such, God's nature, plan, promises, will, and presence are unveiled and known in a true, objective, propositional, and sufficient manner, hence the priority of God's word-revelation over natural revelation, even though both are God's revelation. Also, as with all of God's speech, when God speaks *through* human words in a cognitive manner, fallibility does not inevitably result, as many assume almost without argument. Why? The answer to this question depends on one's view of God and the entire God-word-*world* relationship, a discussion we will return to below.

Here are several types of "word media" or modes of divine speech.

1. *The divine voice*. Sometimes God speaks "directly" to people (Gen 2:16; Exod 19; 20; 33:11; Num 12:6–8; Deut 5:28–31; 1 Sam 3:4–14; Matt 3:17; 17:5; Luke 9:35; John 12:28; Acts 9:4; 10:19; 13:2; Gal 1:11–17). In the OT, when God spoke at Sinai, the people were terrified by God's presence, authority, and power (Exod 19–20; cf. Heb 12:18–21). Also in this category is God's word *to* the prophets and the entire teaching ministry of Christ, but not when God speaks *through* the prophets or the apostles. But as Frame importantly notes, "In the divine voice, God 'accommodates' himself to his hearers. . . . Nevertheless, this accommodation does not diminish in any way the authority with which God speaks (or, indeed the power and presence of his word)."[46] In other words, though adapted to our understanding, the divine voice carries with it all the power and authority of God. The divine voice addressed to us has no less power or authority than the word spoken by God to himself in eternity.[47]

2. *The divine voice and God's presence*. Building on God's direct speech to us, God also reveals himself by presenting himself to us. When God speaks to his people, even if there is no visible form (Deut 4:15), he is surely there. But Scripture also teaches that God has made

---

[46] Frame, *Perspectives*, 23.

[47] See Feinberg, *Light in a Dark Place*, 84–87.

himself present to us in various theophanies, which are described in a number of ways. For example, sometimes they are simply divine appearances without any further description (Gen 12:7; 17:1, 22; 26:24; 35:9; Exod 6:2). Other times, God appears in a dream (Gen 20:3; 28:12ff; 31:24; 1 Kgs 3:5; 9:2), or in a prophetic vision (1 Kgs 22:19ff; Isa 6; Ezek 1; Luke 2:9; 2 Pet 1:17), or in clouds of smoke and fire (Gen 15:17; Exod 3:2; 19). Probably the most striking theophany is the Messenger/Angel of the Lord (*malak Yhwh*) who appeared to Hagar (Gen 16:6–13), to Abraham (Gen 18; 22:11–12), to Jacob (Gen 32:29–30), to Moses (Exod 3:2–6), to Joshua (Josh 5:14–15), to Gideon (Judg 6:11–14), and to David (1 Chr 21:16, 18, 27). Although people have disputed whether this figure is the pre-incarnate divine Son or not, it seems to be a true personal appearance of God distinct from God (Exod 23:20–23; 33:14f; Isa 63:8–9) but also one with him in name, power, redemption, and blessing (Gen 16:10–13; 18:3; 22:12; 31:13; 32:28, 30; 48:16; Exod 3:2–8; 14:19; 23:20–23; Isa 63:8–9; Judg 6:21; 13:3).[48] As Bavinck notes, following the redemption from Egypt, the "messenger of Yhwh" recedes from view as God dwells among his people in the temple (1 Kgs 8:10; 2 Chr 7:1; Pss 68:17; 74:2; 132:13; 135:21). But this theophany is incomplete; it awaits a more glorious dwelling of God with his people, finally fulfilled in Christ (Isa 2:21; Zech 1:8–12:3; Mal 3:1; cf. Matt 1:18; 11:27; John 1:14; 14:9; Col 1:15; 2:9).[49]

The idea of God's personal presence in revelation leads us to think supremely of our Lord Jesus Christ, the divine Word/Son incarnate (John 1:1, 14). The prophets speak God's word; Christ is the *Word* of God (John 1:1–2; 1 John 1:1), Immanuel (Matt 1:18). The incarnate Son mediates all other forms of God's word (Matt 11:25–28; John 14:6), and he is proof that God's word is true. In Christ, the Father not only speaks *through* the Son, but the Father's speech *is* the Son. In and through Christ, the Father by the Spirit creates and rules over all things (John 1:3, 10; 1 Cor 8:6; Col 1:16; Heb 1:2). He is the content of Scripture (Luke 24:25–27; John 5:45–47; 1 Cor 10:4), the final prophet (Luke 4:17–21; John 3:34ff; 5:20; 7:16; 8:28; 12:47–49; 17:8; 19:24, 31; Acts 3:22ff; 7:37), the last Adam who is the pattern of our glorified humanity (Matt 11:29; 16:24; John 13:35; 1 Cor 11:1; 1 Pet 2:21; 1 John 3:16).

---

[48] See Andrew Malone, *Knowing Jesus in the Old Testament: A Fresh Look at Christophanies* (Nottingham: Inter-Varsity Press, 2015); Vern S. Poythress, *Theophany: A Biblical Theology of God's Appearing* (Wheaton: Crossway, 2018).

[49] On this point, see Bavinck, *Reformed Dogmatics*, 1:328–29.

Thus, we may say that God, in the Son, is present whenever God speaks to us.[50] In Christ, all of God's speech, tied to his entire covenantal revelation, has been fulfilled and demonstrated to be true (Heb 1:1–3).

3. *God's word through the prophets and apostles.* In the prophetic word, God speaks not only in human language, but *through* a human messenger in such a way that there is an identity between God's speech and their words while preserving the Creator-creature distinction. Thus, what the prophet says by his own words is also God's word (Exod 4:10–16; Deut 18:15–22; Jer 1:6–19). This is why the test of whether the prophet truly speaks God's word is that his word is completely true and accurate (Deut 13:1–5; 18:18–22). If the word of the prophet is false, it is *not* the word of God. For this reason, views of Scripture that weaken divine authority *through* human prophets or apostles cannot be sustained. This is not only true of Moses as a paradigm of the prophets (Num 12; Deut 18:15–22; 34:10–12), but it is also true of the other OT prophets (1 Kgs 17:1; Jer 1:4–12) and the apostles (Acts 11:27–28; 13:1–3; 21:9–14). In the NT, an apostle is one whom Jesus appointed to bring the gospel to the world (John 14:23–26; 16:13f), and apostles claim a divine source for their message (John 14:26; 15:26–27; 16:13; 1 Cor 2:10–13; 4:1; Gal 1:1, 11f, 16; 2:2; Eph 3:3).[51] Thus, there is no biblical warrant for thinking that there is a decrease in authority from the divine voice to the prophetic utterance, contrary to the assumptions of much of current non-orthodox theology.[52] God's speech is infallible and perfect, and its truthfulness is undiminished as it is mediated through humans. What accounts for this? As we will note below, what accounts for it is our understanding of the God-word-*world* relationship, specifically the biblical teaching of God's sovereign *extraordinary* agency in and through the prophets and apostles, which does not remove their freedom but *guarantees* that their word is God's word.

4. *God's word written: Scripture.* At this point, we are now able to speak of God's *word* as it applies to Scripture. God's word not only comes *through* the words of the prophets-apostles, but it is also identified with specific texts (collected as a canon) written by the prophets-apostles by inspiration (2 Tim 3:15–17; 2 Pet 1:21). God's *written* word is the result of God's triune

---

[50] Bavinck, *Reformed Dogmatics,* 1:328–30; cf. Feinberg, *Light in a Dark Place*, 99–105.

[51] Bavinck, *Reformed Dogmatics,* 1:330–36.

[52] See Ward, *Words of Life*, 32–38.

agency through the human authors of Scripture so that their human texts are God's word, a point we will develop below and in subsequent chapters on the doctrine of Scripture. From the beginning, especially due to God's establishing a covenant relationship with his people, God has always intended for his word to be more than spoken through prophets-apostles; he intended it to be written and thus permanent for his people. This is why Scripture is our final, sufficient, and "magisterial" authority for our knowledge of God, self, and the world—the "ruling rule" (*norma normans*) for all of our theological formulations and our life as the church. As Frame rightly reminds us,

> The concept of a written word of God, bearing the full authority of God, is not a product of twentieth-century fundamentalism, or seventeenth-century rationalism, or medieval scholasticism, or post-apostolic defensiveness, or pharisaic legalism. It is embodied in the very constitution of the people of God and is assumed throughout Scripture. Modern theologians have opposed this idea by saying that the word of God is too transcendent or too dynamic to be kept in a book. Barth argued on such grounds that revelation cannot be "preserved." But in Scripture God explicitly calls upon his people to preserve the word from one generation to another (Deut. 6:6ff; Jude 3). There is a "tradition," a permanent "body of truth" to be handed down (1 Cor. 15:2f; 2 Thess. 2:15; 3:6; 1 Tim. 6:20; 2 Tim 1:12ff; 2:2; 2 Pet. 2:21).[53]

Furthermore, just as the authority and truthfulness of God's word is not diminished from the divine voice to the words of the prophets-apostles, there is no decrease in authority in a written word. From Genesis to Revelation, Scripture is *God's* word written, which cannot be broken (John 10:35): "The grass withers, the flowers fade, / but the word of our God remains forever" (Isa 40:8). Also, as our Lord Jesus Christ teaches, who is God the Son/Word incarnate: "Don't think that I came to abolish the Law or the Prophets. I did not come to abolish but to fulfill. For truly I tell you, until heaven and earth pass away, not the smallest letter or one stroke of a letter will pass away from the law until all things are accomplished" (Matt 5:17–18).

[53] Frame, *Perspectives*, 25–26.

Preliminary Theological Reflections on the God-Word/Scripture Relationship

The Unity and Message of God's Word

As we have thought about the various ways God's word comes to us, it is legitimate and important to distinguish "act-revelation" from "word-revelation." But we must also remember that both are the single, unified revelation of God, mutually dependent on each other, although priority must ultimately be given to God's cognitive speech through human authors, which functions as our final and sufficient authority.

For example, in the exodus, God performs his mighty *acts*, but for Israel, God must explain the meaning of the event in *words*, and for us, the event is now part of written Scripture. Or the giving of the law covenant (or any covenant) involves divine speech, but it also involves God's mighty action to redeem his people and to constitute them as his covenant people. Or, in the incarnation of the divine Son and his entire life and ministry, every action is a divine act, yet it is necessary for our Lord to speak to us to know him in truth, and we only have "access" to him today by Scripture, which functions as God's first-order exposition and interpretation of him. Even natural revelation, which is God's word through "acts," was never intended to be sufficient on its own. In Eden, Adam was to investigate the world and thus learn something about God and the world, but he did not do so independent of God speaking directly to him. God's speech to Adam was to enable him to interpret nature accurately, as evidenced in God's command (Gen 2:15–17). For us today, natural revelation truly reveals God (although it is now more complicated due to sin and the abnormality of the created order), and it serves an important function in our knowledge of God, self, and the world, but it does not stand alone. "All truth is God's truth," but one must not isolate natural revelation from God's interpretation of the world by his word-revelation.

All of this is to say there is a *unity* to God's word. Whether it is in the natural order, or in specific mighty acts and words spoken by God through humans and written permanently for our instruction in Scripture, God's word comes to us in power and authority. And through his word, God sovereignly and graciously reveals himself to us in order that we may know him. Even for humans who stand in rebellion to their Creator, God's word, even in creation, is inescapable and sufficient to condemn (Rom 1:18–32). The triune God is not absent from his universe; he is known by his word (Acts 17:24–31).

In fact, the overall message of God's word is the declaration that the triune God is Lord.[54] Scripture, from beginning to end, is first and foremost about God and secondarily about us. God's word declares his own name and glory and how *he*, who needs nothing, has graciously chosen to share himself with his creatures, specifically his people, to the praise of his glorious grace and our eternal good (Job 38–41; Ps 115:1; Isa 44:6–8; Rom 11:33–36; Eph 1:3–14; 2:1–10). God's word expresses his lordship in many ways, from creation to the new creation, as we see God's eternal plan worked out on the stage of human history, centered in the fulfillment of God's purposes in our Lord Jesus Christ (Eph 1:9–10; Col 1:15–20; Heb 1:1–3), with the ultimate goal that God's triune glory be magnified (1 Cor 15:26–28; Rev 21–22).[55] God's self-revelation by his speech, then, ensures that *his* word accomplishes all of his purposes, including his glorification through the redemption and covenant instruction of his people (Isa 40:68; 55:11; John 10:14–30; 17:17; Heb 12:22–29) and the judgment and defeat of sin and death (John 5:19–30; 1 Cor 15:26–28; Rev 20:11–15). All that God does, beginning with his self-revelation, he does to manifest his own glory, which we, as his people, are the beneficiaries of by sovereign grace.

Bavinck captures well the purpose of God's self-revelation by his word. Supremely, "the final goal is God himself. . . . God reveals himself for his own sake: to delight in the glorification of his own attributes." But God has chosen to glorify himself through his creation of a world and specifically humans who "bring to manifestation the glory of God's name before the eyes of God." To accomplish this end, especially in light of sin, God must "re-create the whole person after God's image and likeness and thus transform that person into a mirror of God's attributes and perfections." As such, the purpose of God's word and self-revelation is not only to redeem "human beings in their totality" but also "the whole world in its organic interconnectedness, from the power of sin and again to cause the glory of God to shine forth from every creature."[56]

---

[54] See Frame, *Doctrine of the Word*, 3–11, 145–66.

[55] On God's glory as the ultimate end of God's plan and purposes, see Christensen, *What About Evil?*, 249–346 (see chap. 4, n. 86).

[56] Bavinck, *Reformed Dogmatics*, 1:346.

The Distinction between Natural and Special Revelation

Although there is a *unity* to God's word, it may also be distinguished in terms of "act-revelation" and "word-revelation." Historically, the former is identified as "natural/general" revelation, specifically nature, history, and the human constitution. The latter is categorized as "special" revelation, explicitly God's mighty acts ("miracles") and everything under the word-media category (e.g., the divine voice, theophany, Jesus as the Word incarnate, divine speech through the prophets-apostles, and Scripture as God's word written). Although both forms of revelation go together and mutually require one another, there are at least two reasons why we need to distinguish them.

First, given the entrance of sin into the world (Gen 3), natural and special revelation has become separated. Apart from God's redemptive promise (Gen 3:15) and God's initiative in grace to redeem a people for himself as reflected in the biblical covenants, humans as covenant-breakers stand outside of God's specific spoken and written word, and all they have is natural revelation apart from coming into contact with God's people (Rom 3:1–2; Eph 2:11–12). As we will discuss in the next chapter, God's word in creation is true knowledge and thus sufficient to condemn people (Rom 1:18–32), but it is not enough to know God in a full, complete sense, especially in salvation. Also, given the noetic effects of sin (i.e., effects of sin on our minds and thinking), fallen humanity apart from God's saving grace now distorts and misinterprets natural revelation. This is not to say that unbelievers do not know truths from the natural order. Instead, it is to say that unbelievers only know various truths from creation due to common grace and living off the borrowed capital of natural revelation. For these reasons, it is important to discuss natural revelation on its own to become clear as to its purpose, the kind of knowledge it yields, its built-in limitations, and the reminder that God never intended for it to stand alone. This is especially significant in debates over whether natural revelation is enough to yield a saving knowledge of God, as affirmed by the view known as "inclusivism." It is also important in our evaluation of non-Christian thought, its truthfulness, and its value for a Christian worldview and its usefulness in theology. "All truth is God's truth," but natural revelation on its own is not sufficient, and especially when Scripture addresses specific matters, Scripture, as special revelation, has priority over non-Christian interpretations of God, self, and the world.

Second, the dividing line between historic theology and what we identified as *extratextual* theologies is whether "special" revelation is in fact true, whether God's authoritative, true, and reliable *word* is actually given to us through human authors in a written text, that is, Scripture, or whether all we have is natural revelation, reduced to natural theology. And depending on one's view of Scripture, either Scripture is viewed as God's word in an indirect sense that somehow witnesses to God, allowing for him to be present in it, but that as a text/canon is human and contains errors (the view of neo-orthodoxy). Or Scripture is viewed merely as a human book that arises out of the religious consciousness of Israel and the church, thus having "authority" if it agrees with a more "authoritative" *extratextual* view (the view of classic liberalism and its postmodern expressions). We will discuss these non-orthodox views of Scripture in chapter 7. Our point here is that the debate over whether special revelation is actually true, reliable, and authoritative is the dividing line between historic Christian theology and its non-orthodox, *extratextual* alternatives. As such, it is important to distinguish the two forms of revelation and to expound and defend the reality and truth of God's *special* revelation, a point to which we now turn.

Special Revelation as a Word-Act Revelation

The concept of "special" revelation includes God's *extraordinary* acts, in contrast to his *ordinary* acts of sustaining and ruling over nature by his word (Col 1:17; Heb 1:3), and everything under the word-media category—the divine voice, theophany, Jesus as the Word/Son incarnate, God's speech through the prophets and apostles in oral form, and God's speech through the agency of human authors by inspiration, which results in God's word written. Special revelation assumes a specific concept of God and divine action: God is Lord over his world, *and* he is able to act in it by *extraordinary* (supernatural) and *effectual* agency. This is why deistic, panentheistic, and pantheistic conceptions of God reject the possibility of special revelation.

If we combine God's mighty acts and speech, special revelation is best understood as a "word-act" revelation by which God makes himself known through the communication of truth and life by the imparting of truth through particular *acts* and *words*, specifically in the covenant word of Scripture and the Lord Jesus Christ.[57] In terms of Scripture, God has revealed

[57] Special revelation as a "word-act" revelation rejects reductionistic views of revelation, such as (1) revelation as only historical "acts" *behind* the texts of Scripture that the Bible in fallible human language tries to explain; (2) revelation as a "word" of address to human subjectivity, but not communicating objective truths from God who is the source and standard of truth; (3) revelation as dialectical presence by which Scripture witnesses to Jesus Christ as the objective revelation of God, but Scripture

himself in a *progressive* manner with a *Christological* focus. In Christ, the Word incarnate, all of God's self-revelation unites (2 Cor 1:20; Eph 1:9–10; Heb 1:1–3). Unlike natural/general revelation, special revelation is *particular*, not *universal*, and it is *salvific*. It is only by God's mighty acts in history to redeem his people, and by his word interpretation of his actions and the giving of his covenant promises, that redemption is accomplished and applied by grace alone (*sola gratia*), through faith alone (*sola fide*), in Christ alone (*solus Christus*).

Scripture as a Word-Act Revelation: God's Word Written

To think of Scripture as a "word-act" revelation is to say that it is *special* revelation committed to writing. In other words, Scripture is God's *word* through the agency of human authors so that what Scripture says (the human texts, canon), God says. No doubt, Scripture is not the sum total of special revelation. As John reminds us, "there are also many other things that Jesus did, which, if every one of them were written down, I suppose not even the world itself could contain the books that would be written" (John 21:25). Jesus himself is special revelation, and Scripture does not record all he said and did. In fact, Scripture is not an exhaustive revelation of everything God knows and has said by his divine voice, in our Lord Jesus Christ, and through prophets and apostles. But Scripture *is* special revelation, God's *word* through human authors, our written covenant constitution, objectively true in all its communication, and sufficient for our knowledge of God, self, and the world because it is a product of God's redemptive, *extraordinary* activity. Scripture as a "word-act" revelation can be developed in three steps.

First, we have seen that all of God's acts are due to his word and thus revelatory of him, his plan, and his purposes. God has disclosed himself in history, especially in his *mighty* acts. In the OT, as noted above, the great redemptive act of God was the Exodus (Exod 6–15). In the

---

does so as a human, fallible witness (e.g., Karl Barth). We will discuss Karl Barth's view of the "word of God" and Scripture in chapter 7. The first view is represented by, for example, the Biblical Theology Movement as represented by Oscar Cullmann (1902–1999), G. E. Wright (1909–1974), and even Wolfhart Pannenberg (1928–2014). See G. E. Wright, "God Who Acts," in *God's Activity in the World*, ed. Owen C. Thomas (Chico: Scholars Press, 1983), 25. The second view is represented by, for example, Friedrich Schleiermacher (1768–1834) and Rudolf Bultmann (1884–1976). See Hans Werner Bartsch, ed., *Kerygma and Myth: A Theological Debate*, trans. Reginald H. Fuller (London: SPCK, 1953).

NT, the gospel recites God's acts in history centered in the divine Son incarnate (Acts 2:22–36; 3:11–26; 10:34–48; 13:16–41; 1 Cor 15:3–11). The NT proclaims that what God had promised in ages past, what the OT prophets anticipated, God has now brought to fulfillment in the life, death, and resurrection of Christ—the greatest display of God's mighty acts. For this reason, expressions of fulfillment are everywhere in the NT (Mark 1:15; Luke 4:21; Gal 4:4).

Second, as crucial as it is to affirm that God acts in an *extraordinary* manner in history in order to redeem his people and to reveal himself, God's redemptive acts are never left to speak on their own. God's "acts" by word are never separated from God's verbal communication. Word *and* act always accompany each other; both are due to God's communicative agency. Also, just as redemption is historically successive, so is revelation; God's revelatory word interprets God's redemptive acts. For example, Exodus 15:1–18 interprets the events of the Red Sea crossing; the act by itself is not self-interpreting. Geerhardus Vos stressed this point: "without God's acts the words would be empty, without his words the acts would be blind."[58]

In fact, Scripture gives a general pattern to how "word-act" functions in redemption and revelation. There is first a preparatory word, then the divine act, followed by the interpretive word. For example, in the giving of the law covenant a preparatory word is given (Exod 19), then the divine act of giving the law (Exod 20), followed by an interpretative explanation of the law (Exod 21). This same order is true of the Bible as a whole. The OT is the predictive word that anticipates the coming of the Lord and his Messiah; the Gospels recount the mighty acts surrounding the incarnation, life, death, and resurrection of the divine Son; and the remainder of the NT explains all that Christ has achieved and its implications for God's people as we live in light of the ratification of a new covenant and the fulfillment of the OT prophetic word.

---

[58] Vos, "The Idea of Biblical Theology as a Science and as a Theological Discipline," in *Redemptive History and Biblical Interpretation*, 10 (see chap. 1, n. 45). See also George Ladd, who rightly finds that the "events themselves . . . are not self-explanatory; there was always a divinely initiated prophetic or apostolic word of interpretation. That Jesus died is an objective fact that even the Pharisees could affirm. That Jesus died *for our sins* is no less an 'objective' fact; but it is a theological event occurring within the historical fact which could be understood only from the prophetic word of interpretation. Revelation, therefore, occurred in the complex of event-Word." G. E. Ladd, "Biblical Theology, Nature of," in *The International Standard Bible Encyclopedia*, ed. Geoffrey W. Bromiley, rev. ed., 4 vols. (Grand Rapids: Eerdmans, 1979), 1:506.

Third, Scripture as God's *word* is the product of God's *extraordinary* divine communicative agency (2 Tim 3:15–17; 2 Pet 1:21); it is not the product of mere "natural" causes, and as such, it is not "like any other book." Scripture not only records and describes God's mighty actions and words in history; Scripture itself *is* the product of God's supernatural agency through human authors. Scripture *is God's word* by virtue of divine action in *inspiration* so that the biblical authors' freely written texts are what God wants written and *his* intended speech to us. Indeed, Scripture is *God's* own interpretation of his own redemptive acts through the biblical authors. For this reason, although Scripture is not an exhaustive revelation, it is *God's* first-order, true, authoritative, and sufficient word for our theology and lives.

As we will develop in chapters 8–12, Scripture *is* God's covenant document to us. Scripture as a whole is rightly "the Book of the Covenant" (Exod 24:7; 2 Chr 34:14–31; 2 Cor 3:6, 14).[59] It is God's written word to govern his people, and it has the authority of God himself. As a covenant document, Peter Jensen notes, God's people "have never been without his rule through his word; and these words may be found in the Scriptures. To see the Bible as merely a human artefact, a testimony to the human experience of the divine, but without the authority of God, is to misunderstand its nature."[60] As a covenant document, uniquely tied to God's promises, "[Scripture] gives us information about the plan and purposes of God."[61] In fact, apart from God's word, we would not know God's being, plan, and promises in a true, warranted sense. And given who God is, God has promised to keep his word, which assumes that his word is completely trustworthy (Heb 6:17–18). In this way, the gospel of our Lord Jesus Christ "is inherently related to the truthfulness of Scripture. When we receive the gospel, we receive God's word of promise, and we believe that his word is true and that it is what it says it is."[62] Within the divine economy of redemption, the triune God has given us his word to communicate his promises and presence to us, and by the Spirit's work, to create new life within us.[63]

---

[59] Jensen, *Revelation of God*, 81.

[60] Jensen, 83.

[61] Jensen, 83.

[62] Barrett, *God's Word Alone*, 160–61 (see chap. 1, n. 25); cf. Jensen, 195.

[63] See Mark D. Thompson, *A Clear and Present Word: The Clarity of Scripture* (Downers Grove: InterVarsity, 2006), 136.

Furthermore, given what Scripture is, our reading of Scripture and theological formulation must correspond to the Bible's own terms in order to remain true to *God's* own explanation of his mighty acts, as discussed in chapter 4. We must carefully follow the Bible's own presentation, language, content, structure, and categories since theological truth comes to us *within* a framework *that is God-given*; therefore, we must be intratextual in our interpretation of Scripture and our theology must be done "from above."

The God-Word/Scripture Relationship

In reflecting on the God-word relationship as it applies to Scripture, three points may be stated.

First, Scripture is the product of the triune God, who by nature is a communicative being. Within God's eternal life, there are ordered relations between the divine persons, as expressed in communication and love (John 5:26; 17:5). The divine processions, that is, the eternal, ordered, and incommunicable relations between the persons, consists in the Father's begetting the Son, the Son's being begotten, and the Spirit proceeding from the Father and the Son. These relations of origin—paternity, filiation, and spiration—"identify God's perfect life" and "ground the work of the Son and Spirit in the history of salvation."[64] In God's *ad extra* works, "God *enacts* his perfection,"[65] while remaining fully himself. In choosing to create and to speak to his creatures and, after the fall, to redeem a people for himself, God freely acts to communicate himself by his *word* since all of "God's external works are communicative."[66]

As we think of God's action in giving us Scripture, the divine persons act inseparably yet with specific acts terminating on specific persons consistent with their ordered relations.[67] In the case of Scripture, the Father speaks through the Son and by the Spirit, but it is the Spirit who brings to completion God's communicative act of inspiration (2 Tim 3:15–16; 2 Pet 1:21), even though the entire Godhead is at work.[68] Thus, in God's self-

---

[64] Vanhoozer, *Biblical Authority After Babel*, 51 (see chap. 1, n. 34).

[65] John Webster, "God's Perfect Life," in *God's Life in Trinity*, ed. Miroslav Volf and Michael Welker (Minneapolis: Fortress, 2006), 147.

[66] See Webster, *Domain of the Word*, 7 (see chap. 1, n. 5).

[67] See Allison and Köstenberger, *The Holy Spirit*, 273–94.

[68] See Allison and Köstenberger, 312–15, for a description of the completing work of the Spirit in inspiration.

revelation, as John Webster notes, it "is not merely the communication of arcane information, as if God were lifting the veil on some reality other than himself and indicating it to us. Revelation is an event or mode of relation; it is God's self-presentation to us."[69] Also, as Matthew Barrett observes, "God's communication to us is the very means by which we have communion with him (1 John 1:3; 4:13). This means that the Bible is not just any type of revelation; it is the superlative written articulation of the triune God himself in redemptive history."[70]

Second, to say that Scripture *is* God's word written is to identify it as a *locus* of divine speech, namely, ongoing triune communicative action both in the production of Scripture (inspiration) and the understanding of Scripture (illumination).[71] Although God speaks to Adam before the fall, God's written word after the fall is specifically tied to our redemption, and thus Scripture is part of the triune economy of saving grace. In fact, as God unfolds his plan from creation to the new creation, God's trinitarian nature is disclosed. As the Creator-covenant Lord communicates who he is through his covenant word in the OT, the unveiling of the divine Son takes place, who in the incarnation fulfills all of God's covenant promises. Due to the Son's work, the Father and Son pour out the Spirit at Pentecost so that through the apostles new covenant Scripture is written (i.e., the NT). Thus, the giving and receiving of Scripture is due to the communicative agency of the triune God, planned in eternity, and enacted in human history.

Third, Scripture is *human* because it is the product of human authors. In this sense it has a "natural history." But because Scripture is the product of divine *extraordinary* agency, its humanity does not compromise its status as God's word. In providence, God normally acts in *ordinary* ways, sustaining and governing all things, and, in relation to Scripture, calling and preparing the human authors of Scripture. But in the writing of Scripture, God is uniquely

---

[69] John Webster, *Word and Church: Essays in Christian Dogmatics* (New York: T&T Clark, 2016), 27.

[70] Barrett, *God's Word Alone*, 163.

[71] Kevin J. Vanhoozer describes Scripture as "triune discourse: something (covenantal) someone (Father, Son and Spirit) says to someone (the church) about something (life with God)." "Triune Discourse: Theological Reflections on the Claim that God Speaks (Part 2)," in *Trinitarian Theology for the Church: Scripture, Community, Worship*, ed. Daniel J. Treier and David Lauber (Downers Grove: IVP Academic, 2009), 64.

at work: the Father communicates the wisdom and truth embodied in the Son to the authors of Scripture by the Spirit (inspiration). Thus, one cannot explain Scripture merely in human terms, although it is human. Scripture is the result of God's gracious choice and sovereign action. J. I. Packer captures this point in his description of Scripture: Scripture is "God the Father preaching God the Son in the power of God the Holy Ghost. God the Father is the giver of Holy Scripture; God the Son is the theme of Holy Scripture; and God the Spirit, as the Father's appointed agent in witnessing to the Son, is the author, authenticator, and interpreter of Holy Scripture."[72]

The God-Word/Scripture-World Relationship

Building on the last point, the best theological or dogmatic location for comprehending the nature of Scripture is triune divine agency in extraordinary providence, not Christology.[73] Nor, contrary to classic liberalism and much of modern/postmodern theology, do we understand the nature of Scripture in terms of a series of naturalistic causes with God merely immanently involved, as understood by the God-world relationship of panentheism.

Instead, Scripture is located within a specific theology proper, namely, the triune Lord and God's economy of grace and salvation. And because Scripture is from God, it is not merely a human book. Scripture is the product of God's gracious, sovereign, supernatural agency, and as such, it has his authority. As we have noted above, in Scripture, there is no evidence that as one moves from God's divine voice to the prophets and apostles and then to a written text authored by finite, fallen human beings that God's authority is decreased, diminished, or

---

[72] J. I. Packer, *God Has Spoken* (Grand Rapids: Baker, 1979), 97.

[73] Scripture is not best understood by Christology given the nature of the hypostatic union. See Webster, *Domain of the Word*, 13:

> God's use of creaturely auxiliaries in the prophetic and apostolic word is *toto caelo* different from the union of divine and human natures in the incarnate Son. Scripture does not have a divine nature; the scriptural text is not substantially united to the divine Word; there is no *unio personalis* in inspiration. And so there can be no communication of divine properties to the Bible, no scriptural *genus maiestaticum*. Scripture is prophetic and apostolic speech; God gives his Word to the prophets and apostles, but God does not become their words.

compromised. God's speech accomplishes his plan. And God accomplishes his purposes in and through human texts so that they communicate precisely what God wants communicated (2 Pet 1:21). Webster captures something of this point when he writes: "[God] draws their acts [Scripture] into his own act of self-utterance, so that they become the words of the Word, human words uttered as a repetition of the divine Word, existing in the sphere of the divine Word's authority, effectiveness and promise."[74]

Getting right the God-word-world relationship is crucial in our grasping what Scripture is and "constructing" a biblical doctrine of Scripture. Scripture as God's word written requires an explicit theology proper and a definite understanding of the God-world relationship. As we will note below and in subsequent chapters, we can only sustain a high view of Scripture with a proper understanding of God's sovereign rule over the world in relation to human authors. In other words, underneath our doctrine of Scripture is a specific *theology* of divine providence along with a certain understanding of the divine sovereignty–human freedom relationship.

Denials of Special Revelation and the God-Word/Scripture-World Relationship

As discussed previously, the dividing line between historic theology and all extratextual theologies (whether of the modern or postmodern varieties) is over whether *special* revelation exists or all we have is natural revelation. And if special revelation is a fact, then *is* Scripture the "word of God" in a direct or indirect sense? If the latter, then Scripture is at best a witness to God's word and, at worst, only human texts that arise out of the religious consciousness of Israel and the church. For both options, Scripture is inevitably unreliable due to its humanity and only "authoritative" as interpreted by a more "authoritative" criterion external to it, which varies depending on one's extratextual worldview. On both accounts, Scripture as the epistemological warrant for objective truth and a normative theology is undermined.

Such views of Scripture are reflected in much of non-orthodox theology, although there is a spectrum regarding how the identity between God's word and the human texts is construed, a point we will return to as different views of Scripture are discussed in chapter

---

[74] Webster, *Domain of the Word*, 8.

7. But in the end, what results is either a denial of special revelation as outlined above or a compromise of it. Why do people reject the biblical concept of special revelation and Scripture as God's word written, especially given the serious consequences that are at stake?[75] Numerous reasons could be given, but we want to discuss four main ones, with specific focus on the last one since it is the main *theological* reason, tied to one's construal of the God-world relationship.

The Issue of "Science" and Origins

With a wide acceptance of the macro-theory of evolution, whether in its naturalistic or theistic form, many believe that Scripture's teaching on creation and the origins of the universe is no longer "literally" true; that is, Scripture is not giving us a true account of what actually happened. Instead, Scripture is describing the origins of the universe similar to the thought of the ancient Near East, and as such, Scripture is viewed more in terms of "legend," "saga," or "myth." If we think the Bible is "revelation," it is only a human word seeking to describe what happened in the categories of its day (which we now know are false), but not an authoritative *word from God*, and not a true account of historical events and God's creation of the world and of humans.[76] Today, much discussion centers on the historicity of Adam as the progenitor of humanity and whether the "fall" occurred in history.[77]

Much could be said in response, but two brief comments are in order. First, our disagreement is not with the discipline of science. In fact, as we will note in chapters 13 and 21, the Bible's view of God, self, and the world is what actually provides the epistemological warrant for the discipline of science and the study of the world. Frame is correct in his assertion:

---

[75] See Bavinck, who discusses many in his day rejecting special revelation as a result of historical-critical scholarship and the acceptance of *extratextual* worldviews, reasons that are still with us today. *Reformed Dogmatics*, 1:414–48.

[76] For example, see James Barr, *The Bible in the Modern World* (London: SCM, 1973). Those who identify with post-conservative theology also hold a similar view. For example, see Enns, *Inspiration and Incarnation*, 13–60; Sparks, *God's Word in Human Words*, 57–72; and the BioLogos group (https://biologos.org/).

[77] See Matthew Barrett and Ardel B. Caneday, eds., *Four Views on the Historical Adam* (Grand Rapids: Zondervan, 2013).

> Science itself presupposes the absolute personal God of the Bible to validate the relative uniformity of nature and the possibility of intelligible thought about the world. If the universe is fundamentally impersonal, there is no reason why we should feel obligated to seek truth rather than error, or any reason why we should think our intellectual faculties capable of finding truth.[78]

Instead, our disagreement is at the worldview level and over an entire explanation of reality, including origins and whether the triune personal God is the Creator or whether the universe is the result of time, chance, and impersonal natural processes. As such, our critique must evaluate the truth of the macro-theory of evolution as an entire worldview, whether in its naturalistic or theistic form.[79]

Second, in our interpretation of the biblical text, we must remember that Scripture is *human*, that is, its communication is "ordinary," but because it is *God's* word, it is true and reliable. In this regard, Bavinck offers some helpful comments. He stresses the Bible's "organic" view of inspiration, namely, that God's speech through human authors is not intended to be a technical account, but a true, ordinary description. God's revelation is not "abstractly supernatural but has entered into the human fabric" as "the human has become an instrument of the divine; the natural has become a revelation of the supernatural; the visible has become a sign and seal of the invisible."[80] Unlike historical criticism that fails to understand the purpose of Scripture and demands that Scripture offer an exact precision and knowledge of various sciences,[81] Scripture is a book "for the whole of humanity in all of its ranks and classes, in all of its generations and peoples. But for that very reason too it is not a scientific book in a strict sense. . . . It does not speak the exact language of science and the academy but the language of observation and daily life."[82] Scripture looks at the world in terms of observation or phe-

---

[78] Frame, *Doctrine of the Word*, 199. Cf. Pearcey and Thaxton, *Soul of Science* (see chap. 2, n. 53).

[79] We will return to this discussion in chapter 21 (the doctrine of creation), but the amount of literature critiquing the macro-theory of evolution is voluminous. For example, see Stephen C. Meyer, *Return of the God Hypothesis: Three Scientific Discoveries that Reveal the Mind Behind the Universe* (New York: HarperOne, 2021); J. P. Moreland et al., eds., *Theistic Evolution: A Scientific, Philosophical, and Theological Critique* (Wheaton: Crossway, 2017).

[80] Bavinck, *Reformed Dogmatics*, 1:442–43.

[81] Bavinck, 1:444–45.

[82] Bavinck, 1:445.

nomena, and, as Bavinck continues, "for that reason it speaks of 'land approaching,' of the sun 'rising' and 'standing still,' of blood as the 'soul' of an animal, of the kidneys as the seat of sensations, of the heart as the source of thoughts, etc.,"[83] but this does not deny its truthfulness. In fact, as Bavinck reminds us, if Scripture had spoken in the language of the academy or in precise scientific terms, "it would have stood in the way of its own authority. If it had decided in favor of the Ptolemaic worldview, it would not have been credible in an age that supported the Copernican system. Nor could it have been a book for life, for humanity."[84] Rather, Scripture is God speaking to us through ordinary language that employs the language of observation, which always remains true alongside the "scientific" theories that wax and wane.[85]

Historical Criticism

Some have also questioned the *uniqueness* of the biblical writings, and thus their truthfulness, undermining the historic view of special revelation and specifically the reliability of Scripture. Many contend that the OT shows signs of dependence on ancient Near Eastern thought patterns (e.g., circumcision, covenantal treaties, creation accounts, etc.).[86] The "history-of-religions" approach to Scripture and theology viewed the biblical writings as merely "natural" products of their time, tied to the vicissitudes of history.[87] Others have insisted that historical criticism has demonstrated that the biblical documents do not yield a coherent, unified canon. Scripture, as a collection of diverse historical texts, is only "unified" by Israel and/or the church choosing these texts as their "canon," but there is no inherent unity due to divine inspiration; the texts are merely fallible *human* texts that reflect mutually contradictory viewpoints.[88]

---

[83] Bavinck, 1:446.

[84] Bavinck, 1:446.

[85] On this point, see Vern S. Poythress, *Interpreting Eden: A Guide to Faithfully Reading and Understanding Genesis 1–3* (Wheaton: Crossway, 2019); cf. Andrew S. Kulikovsky, *Creation, Fall, Restoration: A Biblical Theology of Creation* (Fearn, Ross-shire, UK: Mentor, 2009); Collins, *Genesis 1–4* (see chap. 4, n. 48).

[86] See Enns, *Inspiration and Incarnation*, 13–60.

[87] On this school and thought, see Bavinck, *Reformed Dogmatics*, 1:439–42.

[88] See for example, J. D. G. Dunn, *Unity and Diversity in the New Testament: An Inquiry into the Character of Earliest Christianity*, 3rd ed. (London: SCM, 2006).

James Barr likened the advent of the historical-critical method to a "Copernican revolution," arguing that those who ignore the conclusions of the critical methods are like those who continue to affirm a geocentric view of the universe.[89] Due to the embrace of the historical-critical method in biblical studies, Scripture is viewed as a fallible book, not the product of God's communicative agency resulting in an authoritative and trustworthy word. Thus, the aim of historical criticism is to reconstruct what happened "behind" the text and who wrote the text and to try to determine whether it happened by using critical tools, such as form, source, and redaction criticism. From the outset, historical criticism assumes a *methodological* naturalism that excludes any appeal to *extraordinary* agency to account for what Scripture is. Barr admits this point: "We do not have any idea of ways in which God might straightforwardly communicate articulate thoughts or sentences to men; it just doesn't happen."[90] So, as Kevin Vanhoozer notes, "The Bible may involve 'God' inasmuch as it contains descriptions of religious experience. However, while the Bible may teach *of* God, [it] cannot say it is 'taught *by* God.'"[91]

Much could be said in response, but three brief comments are offered. As argued in chapter 2, the historical-critical method relies on extratextual assumptions (e.g., the principles of doubt, analogy, and correlation) and is governed by *methodological* naturalism that "begs the question." In other words, from the outset, a "naturalistic" approach to Scripture is assumed to be true, which, first, must be demonstrated and, second, fails to account for what Scripture is on its own terms and within its own worldview presentation. As Vanhoozer notes, "naturalistic approaches to Scripture ascribe no causal agency to God in relation to Scripture or anything else,"[92] but this is precisely what is in dispute. Second, Scripture can be repeatedly shown to be historically reliable on the matters it touches. Although more needs to be said in terms of an overall apologetic defense of the truthfulness of Scripture, this is an important point to remember.[93] Third, the discipline of biblical theology has demonstrated

---

[89] James Barr, *Fundamentalism* (London: SCM, 1977), 173; cf. Sparks, *God's Word in Human Words*.

[90] Barr, *Bible in the Modern World*, 17.

[91] Kevin J. Vanhoozer, "Holy Scripture," in *Christian Dogmatics: Reformed Theology for the Church Catholic*, ed. Michael Allen and Scott R. Swain (Grand Rapids: Baker Academic, 2016), 32.

[92] See Vanhoozer, "Holy Scripture," 31–32

[93] For example, see Craig L. Blomberg, *The Historical Reliability of the New Testament: Countering the Challenges to Evangelical Christian Beliefs* (Nashville: B&H Academic, 2016); James K. Hoffmeier

that Scripture does have a unified, coherent message and that the biblical documents are not mutually contradictory, especially when we read Scripture within its worldview framework and theological teaching.

Cultural and Moral Arguments

Probably the most "popular" current reasons for the denial of special revelation and the authority and trustworthiness of Scripture are based on the Bible's teaching on specific moral issues. In the West, we have undergone a change of "plausibility structures" away from the belief in Christian theology. This has opened the floodgate to moral subjectivism and "constructivism," pluralism, and cultural relativism and the embrace of a whole host of "critical theories" that now view traditional Christian morality as intolerant and oppressive. Criticisms arise against specific people in Scripture who did grievous wrongs and as such, Scripture's claim that it is God's word is denied. This also results in a rejection of specific doctrinal convictions, such as the universal reality of sin, divine wrath, judgment, and the exclusivity of the Christ for salvation.[94]

In response, two brief points may be given. First, Scripture does not endorse the actions of every person in Scripture. In fact, Scripture is clear that even the best in Scripture have sinned (Rom 3:23) and that there is only one righteous person, namely, our Lord Jesus Christ. Second, as Frame notes, a major problem with those who reject Scripture based on "moral" arguments is they often do so "in the absence of a theistic foundation for ethics."[95] If people reject Scripture due to its teaching on human sexuality, then what is their epistemological warrant for doing so? Within the biblical worldview, the triune God

---

and Dennis R. Magary, ed., *Do Historical Matters Matter to Faith? A Critical Appraisal of Modern and Postmodern Approaches to Scripture* (Wheaton: Crossway, 2012); Steven B. Cowan and Terry L. Wilder, eds., *In Defense of the Bible: A Comprehensive Apologetic for the Authority of Scripture* (Nashville: B&H Academic, 2013).

[94] In post-conservative circles, it is now fashionable to pit the teachings of Jesus against the OT and argue that God did not command the destruction of the Canaanites; instead, the human authors thought that God had commanded it, but they were wrong. For example, see Boyd, *Inspired Imperfection*, 85–165.

[95] Frame, *Doctrine of the Word*, 186.

is the absolute standard for ethics, and apart from demonstrating that the entire Christian position is false, a rejection of Scripture based on the moral sensibilities of our culture is simply question begging.

Different Theologies of the God-Word-World Relationship

An often-neglected reason why special revelation, specifically Scripture as God's word written, is rejected is *theological.* For many years, Kevin Vanhoozer has contended that "one's doctrine of Scripture depends on one's doctrine of God and the God-world relationship."[96] If one accepts unbiblical views of the God-world relationship, inevitably our doctrine of Scripture goes awry, and the warrant for Scripture as *God's* word written is undermined. Evidence for this claim is found in numerous authors, but the work of Edward Farley is especially incisive. Let us outline his argument in *Ecclesial Reflection* that illustrates this point.[97]

Farley divides his book into two parts: first, a critical analysis of the presuppositions that underlie the criteria, norms, and authorities of classical Christianity (i.e., Protestantism, Roman Catholicism, and Eastern Orthodoxy), known as the "Scripture Principle"; and, second, his constructive proposal. Our primary focus is on part 1 since it is here that Farley describes the "classical" view of Scripture and the *theology* that undergirds it.

For Farley, the "classical" view is really the biblical view as discussed above: Scripture *is* God's word. There is a direct identity between the human texts of Scripture *and* God's word. What God says, Scripture says, and vice versa. "Scripture contains a unique deposit of divine revelation—a deposit whose special qualities are due to its inspired origins."[98] There is no decrease in authority and truthfulness because Scripture is human. Human authors communicate in their texts, but their texts are God's word, precisely what God wanted communicated.

---

[96] Vanhoozer, "Holy Scripture," 34; also see Vanhoozer, *First Theology*, 127–58. In fact, Vanhoozer emphasized this point repeatedly during my studies at Trinity Evangelical Divinity School in the late 1980s.

[97] Farley, *Ecclesial Reflection* (see chap. 2, n. 6). See Farley's summary of his work in Farley and Hodgson, "Scripture and Tradition," 61–87 (see chap. 2, n. 7); also see David H. Kelsey, *The Uses of Scripture in Recent Theology* (Philadelphia: Fortress, 1975), who points out the importance of one's theology proper for Scripture.

[98] Farley and Hodgson, "Scripture and Tradition," 62.

If this is the "classical" view of Scripture, then what is the *theology* that warrants it? Farley answers this question by stating two presuppositions that are necessary for the classical view.

First, there is the presupposition of "salvation history." Salvation history "interprets the past, present, and future of a particular people (Israel, the church) as a sequential story whose development and outcome is determined by God."[99] The last phrase is significant because it highlights a specific theology proper grounding the salvation-historical presupposition. What is this view of God? Farley identifies it as the "royal metaphor"—God is the sovereign Lord who is able to exert causality over world affairs so that he can *guarantee* his will through creaturely means, such as miracles ("acts") and acts of inspiration ("words"). As Farley notes, "God, the infinitely powerful world sovereign, is always able to accomplish the divine will either indirectly through the contingencies of nature and the finite purposes of human beings or, when necessary, by means of a direct causality that assures the attainment of divinely purposed ends."[100]

Second, there is the presupposition of "the principle of identity."[101] This principle explains how anything creaturely, such as Scripture, is also "*God's* word," given the Creator-creature distinction. Farley's answer: there is "an identity between what God wills to communicate and what is in fact brought to expression in the interpretative act of a human individual or community."[102] When these two presuppositions are combined, we now have the *theology* that explains why the classical view affirms a *direct identity* between human texts *and* God's word. Since God is the sovereign Lord, he is able to exert causality to accomplish his will through creaturely means. As such, "if God wills to communicate information about divine things, God has the means to ensure that the information is correctly received and handed on."[103] This is why we can attribute "infallibility and inerrancy to what appears to be human and creaturely."[104]

Farley's excavation captures well the theology that warrants the classical view of Scripture, but does he accept it? No. Why? Farley raises a number of concerns, but primarily he rejects

---

[99] Farley and Hodgson, 64–65. Cf. Farley, *Ecclesial Reflection*, 28–29.

[100] Farley and Hodgson, 65.

[101] Vanhoozer, *First Theology*, 146–48, calls this the "identity thesis."

[102] Farley and Hodgson, "Scripture and Tradition," 66. Note: Farley means a cognitive, not ontological identity.

[103] Farley and Hodgson, 66; cf. Farley, *Ecclesial Reflection*, 37–39.

[104] Farley, *Ecclesial Reflection*, 39.

the classical view because he cannot accept its underlying *theology*. He insists that the theology of the classical view gives rise to an inescapable dilemma: either God controls all things or he does not. If God controls all things (which the classical view assumes), then the question of theodicy arises: the horrors of history have the same relation to God's causality as salvific events.[105] So, given the problem of evil, Farley rejects that God is sovereign over the world and thus able to guarantee his will through creaturely means and, consistently, the classical view of Scripture. Instead, he opts for a panentheistic conception of the God-world relationship; that is, God and the world are mutually correlated and dependent; God acts in all things by persuasive love but his action is never effectual; God cannot guarantee his will due to human freedom.

In Farley's theological analysis of the classical view of Scripture, he leaves us with a choice: either we accept the classical view *and* its theological understanding of the God-world relation, or we reject the classical view and embrace a different theology of the God-world relationship by opting for a loving, persuasive God who cannot effectively act in the world or guarantee what the human authors write.[106] Farley chooses the latter, which results in a view that Scripture is a *human*, fallible word and not identical with divine speech. Even if one disputes that these are the only options, Farley's analysis is significant for three reasons.

First, it confirms that the doctrine of Scripture *and* theology proper are organically related, especially in terms of the God-word-world relationship. This entails that a classical, or better, a biblical view of Scripture is only sustainable by a specific understanding of God and his sovereign rule over the world in relation to human authors, identified with a compatibilistic view of divine providence.[107] This is why the classical view has argued for a *concursive* theory over against, for example, a dictation theory of inspiration. "Concursus" is from the doctrine of divine providence that unpacks the relationship between divine and

---

[105] See Farley, 155–57.

[106] See Farley, 157. Farley is certainly not the only theologian to reject the "royal metaphor" and opt for a panentheistic view of the God-world relationship. In many ways, within non-orthodox and non-evangelical theology, the dominant view of God today is panentheistic. On this point, see Vanhoozer, *Remythologizing Theology* (see chap. 2, n. 131); cf. Peter C. Hodgson, who discusses some of the reasons why modern/postmodern theology has embraced a more panentheistic view. *God in History: Shapes of Freedom* (Nashville: Abingdon Press, 1989), 11–50.

[107] A compatibilistic view of divine providence will be discussed in part 4, especially chapters 22–23. It is also discussed in relation to the doctrine of inspiration in chapter 9.

human agency and argues for dual agency in God's sovereign rule over the world. All of *this* theology is necessary to account for the biblical view of Scripture. Conversely, if one rejects or modifies this theology of the God-world relationship, a different view of Scripture inevitably follows.

Second, it confirms that the theological/dogmatic location for Scripture is in theology proper, specifically triune agency in extraordinary providence in the economy of grace and salvation. Scripture is *human* because it is the result of the writings of human authors, but the Bible is also the result of God's *extraordinary* action in and through the human authors. This is why God is able to guarantee what he wants written, yet as we will argue in subsequent chapters, a proper understanding of the God-world relationship, specifically the divine sovereignty-human freedom relationship, does not entail Farley's conclusions about the problem of evil.

Third, it demonstrates that the primary reason for a denial of special revelation, specifically Scripture, is *theological*. No doubt, as we have noted above, other reasons may be given. But what is chiefly at stake in debates about Scripture are theology-proper debates. Why is this point important? Given current attempted revisions in the doctrine of God within evangelical theology as illustrated by the debate over open theism, these "revisions" have direct consequences on our view of Scripture. Debates regarding the God-world relationship, specifically the relationship between divine sovereignty and human freedom, not only affect soteriology (e.g., election, effectual grace) but also our doctrine of Scripture, indeed, every area of our theology.

For example, Clark Pinnock, a well-known open theist, insists that "God is present, not normally in the mode of control, but in the way of stimulation and guidance."[108] It is no surprise that Pinnock has a difficult time giving the theological warrant for Scripture's full authority and reliability. After all, if God is present only by "stimulation and guidance," how does God *guarantee* that finite, fallible human authors write texts that are objectively true and yield a normative theology of God, self, and the world?[109] In fact, as God's sovereign agency in relation to human authors is weakened, the unbiblical assumption often emerges in people's thinking, namely, that if finite, fallen humans write Scripture, then it must necessarily be unreliable

---

[108] Clark Pinnock with Barry Callen, *The Scripture Principle*, 2nd ed. (Grand Rapids: Baker Academic, 2006), 131.

[109] We will return to this point in our discussion of open theism in part 4, chapter 16.

and not identical to God's word. Kenton Sparks, for example, operates with this assumption without argument. He assumes that God cannot guarantee what the biblical authors write, so he embraces a faulty view of "accommodation" defined as "God's adoption in inscripturation of the human audience's finite and fallen perspective. Its underlying conceptual assumption is that in many cases God does not correct our mistaken human viewpoints but merely assumes them in order to communicate with us."[110] In another book, Sparks says it even more starkly: "Scripture was written by godly but fallen human authors who sometimes thought and wrote ungodly things."[111] We will return to some of the implications of such a view in chapter 7, but at this point we simply note that Scripture as our final authority for a normative theology is undercut, and the magisterial authority of some extratextual worldview must operate over Scripture. As Sparks admits, given his view, "Scripture's natural meaning sometimes runs contrary to the Gospel and, where it does, begs for a hermeneutical explanation."[112] But what is the standard by which Sparks determines what the gospel is if it runs contrary to Scripture?

Concluding Reflection

In this chapter, we have traversed a lot of territory. We have explained what Scripture teaches about the "word of God" and unpacked the God-word relationship. Building on this discussion, we have drawn some preliminary theological reflections about special revelation, specifically focusing on Scripture as God's word written. Since the dividing line between historic theology and extratextual, non-orthodox theologies centers on whether God has given us an authoritative, true, and reliable word through human authors, we mentioned some of the reasons why people deny that Scripture is God's word. Most significant in our discussion is getting right a correct theology of the God-word-world relationship in order to grasp what Scripture is and to formulate a biblical doctrine of Scripture. So far everything we have said is foundational to the doctrine of revelation. We are now in a position to turn to the subject of God's speech in natural revelation in chapter 6 and to a more detailed exposition of the doctrine of Scripture in chapters 7–12.

---

[110] Sparks, *God's Word in Human Words*, 230–31.

[111] Sparks, *Sacred Word, Broken Word*, 46–47.

[112] Sparks, 48.

CHAPTER 6

Natural or General Revelation

Introduction

Our triune God has graciously made himself known to us in his mighty *acts* and *words*, or what historically has been identified as "natural" and "special" revelation. Although these forms of divine speech go together and mutually require each other, it is important to distinguish them for the sake of discussion. Since the fall, natural and special revelation have been separated for some, especially those outside of God's redemptive covenant promises. Even today, there are many who do not yet have access to Scripture and the gospel message, although everyone has access to divine speech through creation. So what exactly is the purpose, content, role, and limits of natural revelation in God's self-disclosure and the divine economy?

This question is significant in two areas. First, does natural revelation result in a *saving* knowledge of God for those without Scripture? Second, what is the relation between the truth discovered in "nature" and "Scripture," and which one has priority? Let us turn to the subject of natural revelation in four steps: a definition; historical perspectives; biblical warrant; and its theological significance and relationship to special revelation, specifically Scripture.

Definition of Natural/General Revelation

"Natural," or "general," revelation is the knowledge that God gives of himself to all peoples at all times and in all places since it is given through the creation, our human constitution and conscience, and by the ordinary experience of living in the world.[1] It communicates truth to us, especially regarding God and his moral demands, and it serves as the backdrop to special revelation. In the divine economy, it functions together with God's word-revelation, but due to sin, there is a separation of the two for those who stand outside God's redemptive covenants. On its own, it communicates a true, inescapable knowledge of God in terms of God's nature, attributes, and glory, but not a saving knowledge of God since it carries no redemptive promise and divine action to save. Instead, in our sin and suppression of God's revelation in creation, it leaves us without excuse and under God's righteous judgment.[2] But properly used, natural revelation communicates to us the knowledge of God, ourselves, and the world, although it was never intended to function apart from special revelation.

Historical Perspectives

In thinking about the purpose, content, and role of natural revelation, there have been a number of views in history. We will look at four views, but the first view is the historic or classical one, while the other views are either departures from or distortions of it.

1. Natural Revelation as a True and Limited but Non-salvific Knowledge of God

Despite significant differences regarding how much Christians should accept non-Christian thought as true, there has been a consistent view of natural revelation in church history.[3] The classic view is that natural and special revelation is *from God* so that truth is *one* and known in a

[1] The term "general" means "universal" since, in contrast to special revelation, which is "particular," it is given to all peoples at all times and in all places, and as such, it is inescapable.

[2] On natural/general revelation, see Bruce A. Demarest, *General Revelation: Historical Views and Contemporary Issues* (Grand Rapids: Zondervan, 1982); Beeke and Smalley, *Reformed Systematic Theology*, 1:195–263 (see chap. 1, n. 8); Bavinck, *Reformed Dogmatics*, 1:283–322 (see chap. 1, n. 9).

[3] For a helpful resource on theology's interaction with non-Christian thought, see Frame, *History of Western Philosophy and Theology* (see chap. 2, n. 35).

twofold way: by the study of "nature" and "Scripture." Also, the traditional view is that natural revelation on its own is not salvific. We do not discover God's promises in nature, nor does the natural order produce a Redeemer to act as our covenant representative and substitute. Salvation only comes by God's gracious initiative and action to redeem us by the Father's sending his Son and the work of the Spirit, along with a saving promise—all of which is achieved in history but is not the result of the natural order. Instead, after the fall, the true but limited knowledge of God given in creation is willfully rejected so that apart from God's saving grace, we stand justly condemned. On these points, Herman Bavinck asserts, "Christian theologians are unanimous."[4]

For example, Tertullian argued that God's revelation in creation is true and clear such that it results in our just condemnation: "this is the crowning guilt of men, that they will not recognize One, of whom they cannot possibly be ignorant."[5] Also, in affirming the value of natural revelation, he never viewed it as sufficient in itself since special revelation was necessary for salvation and for us to know God and his will in a greater and more authoritative manner.[6] Athanasius agreed: Against the pagans he argued that "creation almost raises its voice against them, and points to God as its Maker and Artificer, who reigns over creation and over all things, even the Father of our Lord Jesus Christ. . . . the proof of this is not obscure, but is clear enough in all conscience to those the eyes of whose understanding are not wholly disabled."[7] John of Damascus says the same thing: God's existence is known in creation. God "did not leave us in absolute ignorance. For the knowledge of God's existence has been implanted by Him in all by nature. This creation, too, and its maintenance, and its government, proclaim the majesty of the Divine nature."[8] From Romans 1, Augustine insisted that all people know that God exists and are responsible for their not honoring and obeying God.[9]

---

[4] Bavinck, *Reformed Dogmatics*, 1:312.

[5] Tertullian, *Apology* 17 (*ANF* 3:32).

[6] Tertullian, *Apology* 18 (*ANF* 3:32).

[7] Athanasius, *Contra Gentes* 27.3, 5 (*NPNF*[2] 4:18); cf. also Athanasius 28.1 (*NPNF*[2] 4:18). He argues that creation testifies to the God of Scripture and not just any conception of God: a God who is "self-sufficient and self-contained," thus underscoring the Creator-creature distinction in contrast to non-Christian thought.

[8] John of Damascus, *The Orthodox Faith* 1.1 (*NPNF*[2] 9.2:1).

[9] Augustine, *On the Spirit and the Letter* 19 (*NPNF*[1] 5:91).

In the medieval era, Anselm and Thomas Aquinas insisted on the significance of natural revelation for truth and theology. In his *Proslogion*, Anselm, in his famous ontological argument, argued for God's existence from natural revelation, but his argument is also dependent on Scripture. Anselm assumes the biblical view of God, but in an exercise of "faith seeking understanding," he seeks to demonstrate by reason that one cannot think of "being" apart from God as the foundation of all being and rational thought. Douglas Kelly explains Anselm's argument:

> Unless we presuppose God as the one than whom no greater can be conceived, then we cannot make sense of anything else. . . . Some kind of 'ontological' presupposition seems necessary for any and every comprehensive system of reasoning. . . . Systems of thought that reject the Holy Trinity need some other ultimate reference point to make their system work; some necessary thing.[10]

Anselm, then, is not offering an argument distinct from Scripture; instead, he is arguing from the biblical conception of God and insisting that one cannot account for ultimate reality and human rationality apart from his existence.[11]

Thomas Aquinas, the pinnacle theologian of the medieval era, continued the tradition of viewing natural revelation as resulting in a true but insufficient knowledge of God. His famous five ways offered rational arguments from creation for belief in God.[12] Some have interpreted Aquinas as separating natural and special revelation, or reason and faith. No doubt, there is a tendency for this to occur in later Catholic theology, which reaches its full separation in the Enlightenment, but it is debatable whether it occurs in Aquinas.[13] Aquinas views natural and special revelation as *one* truth that may be approached in terms of the natural and revealed, or reason and faith, but these two ways of reasoning do not conflict with one another. However, as later Catholic theology weakened the effects of sin on the will, human reason was increasingly

---

[10] Douglas F. Kelly, *Systematic Theology*, vol. 1, *The God Who Is: The Holy Trinity* (Fearn, Ross-shire, UK: Christian Focus, 2008), 74–75.

[11] See Frame, *History of Western Philosophy and Theology*, 128–40.

[12] Aquinas, *Summa Theologica*, pt. 1, q. 2, art. 3, answer (see chap. 2, n. 20).

[13] On these points, see Richard A. Muller, "Reading Aquinas from a Reformed Perspective: A Review Essay," *CTJ* 53, no. 2 (2018): 255–88.

viewed as functioning independently of special revelation, thus leading to a gradual separation of natural from special revelation.[14]

The Reformers and the post-Reformed tradition taught the same view of natural revelation except they strongly emphasized the "noetic" effects of sin on the mind (*nous*).[15] Although "reason" and the "conscience" ought to know God from creation, due to sin, we reject the truth, thus requiring the Spirit's work in us and the "spectacles" of Scripture to see things rightly.[16] Although we suppress the truth, God testifies to himself through the world he created, rules, and sustains so that *all* people are without excuse (Rom 1:20; cf. Acts 14:17). In fact, Calvin argued that humans cannot make sense of themselves apart from the knowledge of God.[17] In this sense, belief in God is "basic," tied to our being created in God's image and living in God's world that bears witness of him. Calvin writes: "The final goal of the blessed life, moreover, rests in the knowledge of God. Lest anyone, then, be excluded from access to happiness, he . . . revealed himself and daily discloses himself in the whole workmanship of the universe. As a consequence, men cannot open their eyes without being compelled to see him."[18]

The Reformed tradition teaches the same truth. Franciscus Junius (1545–1602) argues that natural revelation results in objective truth about God, but due to sin, we distort what we know, thus requiring the work of the Spirit and Scripture.[19] Stephen Charnock (1628–1680) also speaks of the truth that natural revelation testifies to: "Every plan, every atom, as well

---

[14] In later Roman Catholic theology, a strong distinction is made between "natural reason" and "divine faith" (e.g., Vatican I, 1870). With a weakened view of sin, Catholic thought insisted that "reason" can think rightly about the "natural" realm while "faith" is reserved for theology but that "faith" supplements "reason." In the Enlightenment this separation of "reason" and "faith" led to a denial of the need for special revelation at all, thus making natural revelation solely a natural theology apart from Scripture. See Frame, *Doctrine of the Word*, 144–60 (chap. 5, n. 5); Demarest, *General Revelation*, 25–42, 75–114.

[15] For a development of Reformation thought on natural revelation, see Beeke and Smalley, *Reformed Systematic Theology*, 1:237–41.

[16] Calvin, *Institutes*, 1.6.1 (see chap. 1, n. 3).

[17] Calvin begins his *Institutes* (1.1.1) with a biblical epistemology: we cannot know ourselves apart from knowing God. As creatures, we are not autonomous. As we come into the world, God's revelation is inescapable.

[18] Calvin, *Institutes*, 1.5.1.

[19] Junius, *Treatise on True Theology*, 141–58 (see chap. 3, n. 54); cf. Turretin, *Institutes of Elenctic Theology*, 1:6–16 (see chap. 3, n. 55).

as every star, at the first meeting, whispers this in our ears, 'I have a Creator; I am witness to a Deity.'"[20] But, similar to the Reformers, the Reformed tradition strongly emphasizes the noetic effects of sin so that apart from God's grace—common and saving—we reason incorrectly about God (Eph 4:17). A right use of reason requires the Spirit's work in regeneration and illumination. Arguments from nature to provide rational grounds for belief in God are warranted, but they do not function independent of Scripture, nor do they yield a saving knowledge of God.

Thus, despite differences within the tradition, the classic view is that natural revelation gives a true and limited but non-salvific knowledge of God. Both natural and special revelation are from God and mutually dependent on each other: natural revelation serves as the backdrop to special, and special revelation presupposes natural. Since *all* people know God from creation, and creation establishes an objective order to reality, there is a legitimate point of contact we have with all people, despite human sin, a point we will return to below.

2. Natural Revelation as Natural Theology Independent of Scripture

In the Enlightenment, natural revelation morphed into a full-blown "natural theology," which functioned independently of special revelation, specifically Scripture.[21] Theologically, natural revelation is the *content* of what God reveals of himself through creation, but "natural theology" is an entire *method*, dependent on whole worldview assumptions, that "attempt[s] to attain an understanding of God's existence, nature and relationship with the universe by means of rational reflection, without appealing to special revelation."[22]

Natural theology comes into its own with the deists and then continues in the classic liberal tradition associated with methodological naturalism, the historical critical method, and a growing embrace of panentheism. As we discussed in chapter 2, the deists argued that God's universal revelation of himself in creation was "fully sufficient for man's religious needs."[23] Within humans, God has placed reason and conscience, and by the use of reason and following

---

[20] Stephen Charnock, *The Existence and Attributes of God*, 2 vols. (1853; repr., Grand Rapids: Baker, 1979), 1:43.

[21] See Demarest, *General Revelation*, 75–114.

[22] S. Wilkens, "Natural Theology," in Davie et al., *NDT*, 603 (see chap. 2, n. 11).

[23] Demarest, *General Revelation*, 79.

one's conscience, one is able to formulate a "universal religion of reason and nature,"[24] without any need for Scripture. In fact, Scripture, as a historical revelation, is inferior since only reason and nature can yield the universal truths of reason. In addition, deists denied a biblical view of sin, and viewed humans as basically good, thus denying any need for salvation from God; what mattered was living a moral life according to one's conscience.

In classic liberal theology, Friedrich Schleiermacher denied the Creator-creature distinction and argued for panentheism. "God" is experienced in the depths of the human soul, that is, in the religious feeling (*Gefühl*) of absolute dependence, which theology brings to cognitive thought. However, this theology "from below," in its rejection of the authority of Scripture, is closer to a natural than revealed theology, except that the data reflected on is human religious experience rather than "nature."[25] As the modern world gives way to the postmodern, theologies "from below" continue but are now tamed by a denial of objective truth and the embrace of post-Kantian "constructivist" epistemologies. But in the end, Karl Barth's stinging rebuke of classic liberalism remains true for such views: normative theology has been turned into anthropology.

3. Natural Revelation as Theologically Insignificant: Karl Barth

In contrast to historic theology, Barth was skeptical about our ability to know God from creation. Barth famously affirmed a strong "Nein!" to natural revelation, especially natural theology. He insisted that humans have no inherent capacity to know God apart from God's free decision to reveal himself to us. Fallen humans have no direct epistemic access to God by our observation of the world. Why did Barth argue this? Barth's rejection of natural revelation is tied to his overall theology and theological method and the historic context in which he lived. Here are some key ideas from his theology that explain why he rejected natural revelation in contrast to historic theology.

Barth's theology is a Christocentric theism.[26] For Barth, God's being is revealed in his acts, specifically in Christ.[27] In agreement with orthodoxy, God must reveal himself to be known,

---

[24] Demarest, 79.

[25] Demarest, 157–200; cf. Bavinck, *Reformed Dogmatics*, 1:306–07.

[26] See Vanhoozer, *First Theology*, 143–44 (see chap. 2, n. 99).

[27] Hunsinger, labels this "actualism." "Negatively, this means that God's being cannot be described apart from the basic act in which God lives. . . . Positively, the description means that God lives in a set

but God is not known by natural *and* special revelation, only the latter. On this point, Barth was influenced by Anselm's "faith seeking understanding," although Anselm affirmed the truth of natural revelation.[28] For Anselm, theology was not about requiring proof but understanding what the church already believed. In Barth's use of Anselm, faith begins by hearing God's word in Christ, and this alone makes theology possible.

This view of theology was a development from the "early Barth."[29] Although people debate about how much change occurred in Barth's theology, his earlier theology is more "dialectical"; that is, God can only be spoken about in a paradoxical fashion given his "wholly otherness." We have no natural capacity to know God; we are incapable of making direct assertions about him. But in Anselm, Barth found a way to say something positive about God in Christ.[30] Theology's task is not to establish the object of inquiry on "common ground" independent of God's word; rather, theology starts with God's free decision to reveal himself to us in Christ. In fact, all that we know about God's action in creation and history is due to God's self-revelation in Christ.[31]

Barth's theology directly opposed classic liberalism.[32] Instead of some "natural" point of contact between God's revelation and humans, God must first initiate to speak to us. Theology is not grounded in religious experience, history, or the natural order. We do not know God

---

of active relations. The being of God in act is a being in love and freedom." *How to Read Karl Barth*, 30 (see chap. 2, n. 100).

[28] See Barth's work on Anselm: *Anselm: Fides Quaerens Intellectum* (Richmond, VA: John Knox Press, 1960).

[29] There is much debate on this point. Hans Urs von Balthasar argued for an "early" and "later" Barth. Balthasar, *The Theology of Karl Barth: Exposition and Interpretation*, trans. Edward T. Oakes (San Francisco: Ignatius, 1992). Bruce L. McCormack denies it. See McCormack, *Karl Barth's Critically Realistic Dialectical Theology: Its Genesis and Development 1909–1936* (Oxford: Clarendon, 1995). For a similar, more nuanced view to McCormack, see John Webster, *Barth* (New York: Continuum, 2000), 22–24; cf. McCormack, "Barth, Karl (1886–1968)," in Davie et al., *NDT*, 103–7.

[30] See Webster, *Barth*, 22–24, 51–53. One implication of Barth's constructive method is that instead of moving from the general (philosophical systems tied to natural reason) to the particular (theology), Barth now does theology from the particular to the general. Cf. Hunsinger, *How to Read Karl Barth*, 32–35; Barth, *CD* II/1, 602 (see chap. 2, n. 101).

[31] See Barth, *CD* I/1, 150.

[32] Barth argued that classic liberalism had turned theology into anthropology and revelation into natural theology.

from a cognitive ability in us, but only from *his* revelation.[33] Thus, instead of working from "abstract metaphysical or anthropological foundations for theology"—an "analogy of being"—Barth moves from Christ to speak about creation and humans.[34] But Barth's view also differs from historic theology.[35] In place of natural *and* special revelation for our knowledge of God, self, and the world, Barth offers his understanding of "God's word" given to us in Christ.[36]

But what exactly is "God's word"? Historically, God's word is given in nature, Scripture, and Christ. But for Barth, God's word is not given in creation since it "is no mere thing; it is the living, personal and free God,"[37] who is never available to us directly. God's word "is not a deposit of truth upon which the church can draw, or a set of statements which can be consulted. The Word of God is an act which God undertakes. God's Word is that complex but unitary event in which God has spoken, speaks and will speak, an event which encounters us through the human means of Scripture and its proclamation in the church."[38]

Barth, in fact, argues for three forms of God's word: the Word revealed (Christ), the word written (Scripture), and the word preached.[39] But only Christ is the direct Word; the other forms are *indirect*. We only have access to Christ through *indirect* means, and even in these other forms, we only know Christ by God's free decision to reveal him to us. God's word only comes to us by God's *free* decision to act and make it so.[40]

Barth's view of divine freedom helps explain why he rejects natural revelation (and the historic view of Scripture). For Barth, God's freedom requires that his word is not objectively given through any creaturely means; otherwise, it would be universally present and become a mere object of human inquiry.[41] This is why Barth rejects natural revelation (and refuses to identify Scripture *as* God's word). If humans have a "natural/innate" capacity to know God, then our

---

[33] See Webster, *Barth*, 53–55.

[34] Webster, "Barth, Karl," 105.

[35] See Duby, *God in Himself*, 108–112 (see chap. 1, n. 20).

[36] See Keith L. Johnson, "Natural Revelation in Creation and Covenant," in *Thomas Aquinas and Karl Barth: An Unofficial Catholic-Protestant Dialogue*, ed. Bruce L. McCormack and Thomas Joseph White (Grand Rapids: Eerdmans, 2013), 141–44; cf. Duby, *God in Himself*, 110.

[37] Barth, *CD* I/1, 198.

[38] Webster, *Barth*, 55.

[39] See Barth, *CD* I/1, 88–124.

[40] See Barth, 149.

[41] See Barth, 158.

knowledge of God is separate from God's free and gracious act in Christ. And, as Barth insists, "even if we only lend out a little finger to natural theology, there necessarily follows the denial of the revelation of God in Jesus Christ."[42] Also, given our sin, there is no point of contact in us other than what God creates in us.[43] We do not know God from creation apart from Christ and God's decision to make creation real in him.[44] In fact, creation must be viewed in light of humanity's gracious election in Christ,[45] since, as Michael Horton reminds us, "there is no point in eternity or time where we encounter God apart from the redeeming grace of Jesus Christ."[46]

For Barth, then, "nature" is not independent of God's revelation in Christ. Creation does not reveal theological truths and moral norms independent of Christ. Reasoning apart from God's revelation in Christ is arbitrary, as evidenced by classic liberalism's appeal to "natural" law to justify Nazi Germany. Although Barth later allowed for God's word to come through "secular parables of truth," and thus a qualified role for natural revelation, they still had to be tested in light of Christ.[47] There is "no continuing voice of creation that is independent of God's work in Christ,"[48] and as such, the most significant point of contact we have with God is in God's electing action in Christ.[49]

4. Natural Revelation as a True and Limited but Salvific Knowledge of God: Inclusivism

In The State of Theology (2020) poll, 42 percent of evangelicals agreed that "God accepts the worship of all religions, including Judaism, Christianity, and Islam."[50] This is in direct contrast

---

[42] Barth, *CD* II/1, 173.

[43] See Barth, *CD* I/1, 236–41.

[44] See James J. Cassidy, *God's Time for Us: Barth's Reconciliation of Eternity and Time in Jesus Christ* (Bellingham, WA: Lexham Press, 2016), 55–100.

[45] See David VanDrunen, *Natural Law and the Two Kingdoms: A Study in the Development of Reformed Social Thought* (Grand Rapids: Eerdmans, 2010), 320–24.

[46] Michael S. Horton, "Covenant, Election, and Incarnation," in *Karl Barth and American Evangelicalism*, ed. Bruce L. McCormack and Clifford B. Anderson (Grand Rapids: Eerdmans, 2011), 119.

[47] Barth *CD* IV/3.1, 139.

[48] VanDrunen, *Natural Law and the Two Kingdoms*, 325.

[49] See Johnson, "Natural Revelation in Creation and Covenant," 148–56, for a more sympathetic understanding of the role of natural revelation in Barth's later theology.

[50] https://thestateoftheology.com/

to historic theology, which has argued for an "exclusivist" view of salvation in Christ, which denies that God accepts the worship of all religions. Salvation is in Christ alone, and we receive his work in this life by grace through faith in God's specific covenant promises. In fact, this statement reflects the view of *inclusivism* rather than historic theology.[51]

"Inclusivism" is the view that Christ alone is Savior, but for those who have never heard the gospel, it is *not* necessary to believe in Christ in this life to benefit from his work.[52] At this point, a distinction is made between the *ontological* and *epistemological* grounds of salvation. For the former, Christ and his work is the only ground of salvation. But for the latter, it is possible for someone to benefit from Christ's work without knowing it. For example, think of the person who has never heard of Christ, whether in the OT era or today. They may be a "believer" in God (as were OT saints), but they are not "Christians" since they have no explicit faith in Christ. Such a person is saved by Christ's work, even "by grace through *faith*," but their *faith* is more generic, not specifically in Christ.[53] Thus, in the world, there are numerous "seekers" of God who have never heard the gospel but who throw themselves on God's mercy due to the Spirit's work in them, and at death they discover that God has saved them in Christ.[54]

But what does inclusivism have to do with natural revelation? In order to make *theological* sense of their view, inclusivists affirm two truths tied to natural revelation, both of which are departures from historic theology. First, natural revelation must result in a *saving* knowledge of God. Why? For this reason: Jesus alone is Savior (John 14:16), but not

---

[51] For the various views and a defense of "exclusivism," see Christopher W. Morgan and Robert A. Peterson, ed., *Faith Comes by Hearing: A Response to Inclusivism* (Downers Grove: IVP Academic, 2008).

[52] For evangelical inclusivism, see John Sanders, *No Other Name: An Investigation into the Destiny of the Unevangelized* (Grand Rapids: Eerdmans, 1992); Clark H. Pinnock, *A Wideness in God's Mercy: The Finality of Jesus Christ in a World of Religions* (Grand Rapids: Zondervan, 1992); Terrance L. Tiessen, *Who Can Be Saved? Reassessing Salvation in Christ and World Religions* (Downers Grove: InterVarsity, 2004).

[53] See Sanders, *No Other Name*, 224–25; Pinnock, *A Wideness in God's Mercy*, 105–6, 157–68; Tiessen, *Who Can Be Saved?*, 165–203. Appeal is made to "holy pagans," such as Enoch, Melchizedek, Naaman, Cornelius, etc., who were saved by the gracious work of the Spirit in them apart from explicit faith in Jesus. Pinnock asserts: "The Bible does not teach that one must confess the name of Jesus to be saved. . . . The issue God cares about is the direction of the heart, not the content of theology" (158).

[54] Tiessen argues for an at-death experience, while Pinnock argues for a post-mortem opportunity. Tiessen, *Who Can Be Saved?*, 216–29; Pinnock, *A Wideness in God's Mercy*, 168–72.

everyone has heard about him, and God desires that none perish (1 Tim 2:4; 2 Pet 3:9). God *must* make accessible to *all* people a *saving* knowledge that is *universal*, which is only given in natural revelation (which also includes non-Christian religions).[55] Otherwise, God does not *truly* desire that everyone be saved unless he gives all people equal access to salvation.[56] Natural revelation, then, is the means by which God meets us everywhere: there is no "natural knowledge of God that is not at the same time gracious revelation and a potentially saving knowledge."[57]

Second, inclusivists must explain how God's *saving* grace is given in natural revelation and how *saving faith* results from it. On this point, appeal is made to the "pneumatological proposal." This proposal centers on the personal relations within the Trinity, specifically the relations between the Son and the Spirit.[58] Contrary to pro-Nicene trinitarianism, this proposal inverts the Son-Spirit "ordering" (*taxis*) in the divine missions.[59] Instead of the Father *and the Son* sending the Spirit so that the Spirit's work is inseparable from theirs *and* the Spirit is the one who *applies* Christ's work,[60] this proposal reverses the *taxis* by making the Son's work a subset of the Spirit's work.[61] Why do this? It allows inclusivists to explain how the Spirit is *universally* at work apart from bringing people to faith in Christ. Prior to and geographically larger than the Son's mission, the Spirit is universally and graciously at work in the world. Since

---

[55] For God's use of non-Christian religions, see Clark H. Pinnock, "An Inclusivist View," in *Four Views on Salvation in a Pluralistic World*, ed. Dennis L. Okholm and Timothy R. Phillips (Grand Rapids: Zondervan, 1996), 99–100. Pinnock argues that "God *may* use religion . . . for evoking faith and communicating grace" (100).

[56] As an open theist, Pinnock argues that God's grace *must* be available to all people, thus erasing the distinction between common and saving grace. He states: "If God really loves the whole world and desires everyone to be saved, it follows logically that everyone must have access to salvation." *A Wideness in God's Mercy*, 157.

[57] Clark Pinnock, *The Flame of Love: A Theology of the Holy Spirit* (Downers Grove: InterVarsity, 1996), 187.

[58] See Pinnock, *Flame of Love*, 192–98.

[59] On this point, see Keith E. Johnson, *Rethinking the Trinity and Religious Pluralism: An Augustinian Assessment* (Downers Grove: IVP Academic, 2011), 93–140.

[60] The italics represent the *filioque* clause, which reflects a *taxis* between the divine persons *ad intra* (i.e., the divine processions) that is revealed in God's actions *ad extra* (i.e., the divine missions). Pinnock rejects the *filioque* clause and argues for a social understanding of the relations of the divine persons. *Flame of Love*, 21–48, 196–97.

[61] Pinnock, *Flame of Love*, 192.

the Spirit is everywhere, God's good gifts are graciously given, even to people who have never heard of Christ. By the Spirit, God reaches out to sinners in "nature," working in them to bring them to a *saving, generic faith* in God, and after death they discover that they were saved all along "by grace through faith" in Christ.

Biblical Warrant for Natural Revelation

Scripture teaches that God's being, authority, and power are disclosed through the created order. Although that order has been deeply scarred by human sin and its effects (Gen 3:18; Rom 8:19–22), creation continues to reveal God's nature and his moral will for his creatures. Since the created order is accessible to all peoples at all times and in all places, it is a *universal* revelation. As David proclaims, "The heavens declare the glory of God, / and the sky proclaims the work of his hands. / Day after day they pour out speech; / night after night they communicate knowledge" (Ps 19:1–2). Or, as Paul reminds the Gentiles who are outside of God's covenants (Eph 2:11–12), they are responsible for God's revelation of his nature, glory, and will in creation. *Outside* of all people, creation flashes like neon lights testifying to God's glory, and *within* each person, we have an intuitive sense that we are creatures of God, made to know and glorify him, hence the reason why idolatry is so heinous and culpable (Acts 14:15–18; 17:22–31). Our turning from God to our construction of idols is not innocent; it is a willful act of defiance, and Scripture's verdict is clear: "The fool says in his heart, 'There's no God'" (Ps 14:1).

The classic text that addresses the purpose, content, role, and limitations of natural revelation is Romans 1. Paul locates the text in the context of two revelations (*apokalyptetai*): the revelation of the "righteousness of God" in the gospel (1:17) and the "wrath of God" against "all ungodliness and unrighteousness of men" (1:18). Before Paul discusses the glory of the former, he establishes the reality of the latter.[62] As Paul moves from "plight to solution," his argument from 1:18–3:20 is that *all* people are justly under divine wrath for their suppression of the truth (1:18). This exchange of the truth first began with Adam (Gen 3; Rom 5:12–21), and it continues in all people (3:23) until it reaches its culmination in final judgment. Apart from

[62] On relationship of the two "revelations," see Thomas R. Schreiner, *Romans*, 2nd ed., BECNT (Grand Rapids: Baker Academic, 2018), 83–86.

God's sovereign and gracious initiative to redeem us in Christ, there is no hope for humanity.[63] As Paul unpacks our universal plight, he begins with the Gentile before he turns to the Jew. But how are Gentiles justly under divine wrath if they are outside God's special word-revelation? Israel was guilty for her rejection of "the spoken words of God" (3:2), but what about Gentiles? Paul's answer: Although not everyone has special revelation, God holds all people responsible for their response to God's authoritative, true, and clear revelation of himself *outside* of them and *within* them.

First, God has universally made himself known to us in creation so that all people know him. Paul states: "since what can be known about God is evident (*phaneron*, "manifest") among them, because God has shown (*ephanerōsen*) it to them. For his invisible attributes, that is, his eternal power and divine nature (*dynamis kai theiotēs*), have been clearly seen (*kathoratai*) since the creation of the world, being understood (*nooumena*) through what he has made" (vv. 19–20). God is not silent; he has inescapably revealed himself to all people. By observing the creation, we know the God who created it, who sustains it, and who is present in it as Creator and Lord.[64]

This is confirmed in v. 21: "For though they knew God" (*dioti gnontes ton theon*). This is more than a vague awareness of God but knowledge of the one true God (*ton theon*), in contrast to our false constructions of "god." Paul insists that "the non-Christian has definite beliefs about God that are true, and he possesses full and overwhelming warrant for those beliefs."[65] Also, it is significant that *all* people have this knowledge of God by simply observing the world; it is not the result of "careful deduction and reasoning . . . instead this knowledge of God is a reality for all people, not simply for those who possess unusually logical minds."[66]

No doubt, God does not reveal everything about himself in creation; it "falls far short of what is necessary to establish a relationship with him,"[67] thus the need for a word-revelation.

---

[63] Paul confirms that God's wrath from Genesis 3 is ongoing until the end by his use of past tenses in Rom 1:24, 26, 28 (*paredōken*, "handed over"). As Schreiner notes, "the moral desolation of human society from the beginning of the world (v. 20) and continuing up to the present day is a manifestation of God's wrath." *Romans*, 92.

[64] David G. Peterson, *Commentary on Romans* (Nashville: B&H, 2017), 114.

[65] Bahnsen, *Van Til's Apologetic*, 181 (see chap. 1, n. 4).

[66] Schreiner, *Romans*, 93–94.

[67] Douglas J. Moo, *The Epistle to the Romans*, NICNT (Grand Rapids: Eerdmans, 1996), 106–7.

But even though what God reveals is limited, it is a true revelation that results in all people possessing the truth of God and leaving them "without excuse" (*anapologētous*) (v. 20). God's revelation in creation demands a correct response, but tragically in our sin, we do not properly respond.[68] Rather, we "suppress" the truth (v. 18) and "exchange" it for a lie (v. 25), and rather than glorifying God and giving him thanks (v. 21), we corrupt our thinking and our very being (vv. 21–22). We refuse to obey God's moral demands that we rightly know (vv. 23–32), and thus we are justly condemned.

What is the result? Humans who were created to love, obey, and know their Creator and Lord have become idolaters (vv. 22–23). There is no evidence in this text that apart from God's saving initiative and special revelation that the knowledge given in creation is salvific.[69] The purpose of this text is to demonstrate why Gentiles are *all* under sin, which is confirmed in the conclusion of this section (3:9–20). "The argument is not that *most* people are under the power of sin, but that *all* people, without exception, are under the dominion of sin."[70] For this reason, God is just to reveal his wrath on human sin since we are receiving what we deserve.[71] In fact, Paul stresses three times that God *actively* gives us over (*paredōken*, vv. 24, 26, 28) in judgment. "The meaning is not simply that God withdrew from the wicked the restraining force of His providence and common grace . . . but that He positively gave men over" to their own lusts,[72] thus reaping greater judgment on them, which has occurred since Genesis 3.

Significantly, what Paul gives as evidence of our suppression of the truth is our rebellious desire to overturn the structures, order, and boundaries of the created order. Paul first illustrates this in the sexual realm. God created humans as male and female with ordered boundaries (Gen 1:27). But in our sin, we attempt to "construct" our own reality, as evidenced in homosexuality.[73] In Scripture, *all* sexual sin is idolatry: we substitute the Creator's order for our own, which leads to futility and the destruction of what is good, proper, and just. Paul continues speaking of sin in terms of the violation of the great commandment, that is, not

---

[68] Peterson, *Romans*, 115.

[69] Schreiner, *Romans*, 92–93.

[70] Schreiner, 93.

[71] S. Lewis Johnson Jr., "'God Gave Them Up:' A Study in Divine Retribution," *BSac* 129 (1972): 124–33.

[72] Johnson, 128; cf. Peterson, *Romans*, 119–20; Moo, *Romans*, 110–11.

[73] Schreiner, *Romans*, 102–6; Peterson, *Romans*, 122–26; Moo, *Romans*, 113–18.

loving God and our neighbor. Paul even describes being disobedient to parents because marriage and the family is the foundational building block of human society and God's created order. In creation, God alone is the proper object of worship and love, but he has also created human dignity, sexuality, the family, and private property to rule over creation. Yet in our sin and idolatry, humans attempt to turn God's good order on its head, which is the height of rebellion, anarchy, and utter foolishness.

Second, God's revelation is also within us. God has created us as rational, moral creatures whose moral demands are stamped on us. The classic text used to prove this point is Rom 2:14–15: "So, when Gentiles, who do not by nature have the law, do what the law demands, they are a law to themselves even though they do not have the law. They show that the work of the law is written on their hearts. Their consciences confirm this." The common interpretation of this text is that God has written his moral demands on all people apart from special revelation.[74] Although this interpretation has a long pedigree, it probably refers to Gentile *Christians*,[75] who have come under the new covenant. But regardless of which interpretation is adopted, the truth that *all* people know of God's moral demands *from within* is taught throughout Scripture.[76]

For example, Rom 1:32 teaches this truth. Leading up to v. 32, Paul has established that our thinking has become "worthless" and our "senseless hearts were darkened" (v. 21). Although "claiming to be wise, [we] became fools" (v. 22), and God's judgment on our sin was to give us over to distorted passions as evidenced in our trying to turn the created order on its head (vv. 23–31). In our minds, we have become "corrupt" (v. 28), which speaks of internal, moral distortion. In fact, we use the good gifts of reason and conscience not for God's glory or the good of others but instead to be "arrogant, proud, boastful, inventors of evil, disobedient to parents, senseless, untrustworthy, unloving, and unmerciful" (30–31), which climaxes in

---

[74] See Moo, *Romans*, 148–57.

[75] A. B. Caneday, "Judgment, Behavior, and Justification according to Paul's Gospel in Romans 2," *Journal for the Study of Paul and His Letters* 1, no. 2 (2011): 153–92; S. J. Gathercole, "A Law unto Themselves: The Gentiles in Romans 2.14–15 Revisited," *JSNT* 85 (2002): 27–49; cf. Schreiner, *Romans*, 128–34.

[76] For example, think of how Scripture speaks of a "good" or "clear" conscience, which presupposes that we all have a conscience with moral significance (e.g., 1 Tim 3:9; 2 Tim 1:3; Heb 13:18; 1 Pet 3:16, 21).

a devastating statement of moral perversity in v. 32. There is a "continuing moral awareness within fallen humanity that God exists and is a righteous Judge,"[77] in fact, we know "God's just sentence (*to dikaiōma tou theou*)—that those who practice such things deserve to die—they not only do them, but even applaud others who practice them." This is a remarkable verse. "God's just sentence" is the same expression used of the Mosaic Law (Rom 2:26; 8:4), but here it is applied to Gentiles who do not have the Law.[78] This assumes that *all* people, "without specifically having the Mosaic law, are aware of the moral requirements contained in that law."[79] This makes perfect sense since central to God's moral demand is love for God as our Creator and love for our neighbor. Humans were created to know and love God and to rule over the world in relation to each other. Written into our very being are God's moral requirements that we rightly know. "Natural law" as the moral content of natural revelation is inescapable.[80] In fact, Paul states that we know God's moral demands so well that we also know that a violation of them deserves God's judicial sentence of death. But instead of repenting of our sin, we encourage more people to join us in it. "The hatred of God is so entrenched that people are willing to risk future judgment in order to carry out their evil desires."[81] For this reason, God's judgment of *all* people's sin is just, right, and good.

Other texts also confirm this truth. In speaking of Gentiles, Paul says that our sin "sears" and "defiles" our consciences (1 Tim 4:2; Titus 1:15), resulting in "futile" thinking, "darkened" understanding, and "calloused" hearts (Eph 4:17–19). All of this assumes that God's moral demands are known by us but willfully rejected, and even more: we know that we stand under God's judgment. In fact, as we look at humanity, this is precisely what we see. Regardless of how hard we try, we cannot deny an objective moral sense. Even the most hardened relativist acts "as if" moral norms exist. In place of the God of truth, we construct our own "moral" and "religious" systems, yet our attempt to suppress and exchange the truth is futile and dangerous.[82]

---

[77] Beeke and Smalley, *Reformed Systematic Theology*, 1:202.

[78] Peterson, *Romans*, 129–30.

[79] Schreiner, *Romans*, 108.

[80] By "natural law" I mean the moral content of natural revelation, not the "theory" of how to discern what the moral content is. The latter involves arguments tied to entire worldview assumptions, which need their own justification.

[81] Schreiner, *Romans*, 109.

[82] For a helpful discussion of these points, especially regarding a theology of other religions, see Daniel Strange, *Their Rock is Not Like Our Rock: A Theology of Religions* (Grand Rapids: Zondervan, 2014).

The Theological Significance of Natural Revelation

Natural Revelation Results in a True Knowledge of God[83]

Scripture teaches that the triune God who has planned from eternity, created the universe, and rules over it is revealed in what he has made, including the human conscience (Ps 19:1–6; Acts 14:17; 17:22–31; Rom 1:18–32). The knowledge of God in creation is best viewed as an effect of divine revelation, not an independent discovery or deduction of humans,[84] and as such, it is not a potential but an actual knowledge that is universally known and inescapable. For this reason, all people are held accountable for not knowing God (Rom 1:18–20).[85]

What is exactly known? Natural revelation results in a true but limited knowledge of God, the self, and the world. For example, we do not know of God's promises, his plan, his triune nature, but we do know that God alone is God and all else is his creation, hence the Creator-creature distinction. We know that God exists as the one true and living personal God, the eternal, invisible, self-sufficient (*a se*), powerful, all-wise Creator and Lord of history (Ps 104:24; Acts 17:24–27; Rom 1:20). In creation, God's power, glory, authority, and presence are known. Also, in knowing that God is the Creator and Lord of history, we know that this world is not accidental but planned, designed, and ordered.

---

[83] See Demarest, *General Revelation*, 227–62; cf. Beeke and Smalley, *Reformed Systematic Theology*, 1:205–7. This is in contrast to theologians such as Karl Barth who either reject or at best minimize the true knowledge of God, self, and the world that results from natural revelation.

[84] See Duby, *God in Himself*, 72–103.

[85] Natural revelation yields an *actual* knowledge of God. Often a distinction is made between an "implanted" natural knowledge of God prior to an "acquired" natural knowledge of God that comes from discursive reasoning. In terms of the former, it is "innate" or "implanted" but not in a Greek, idealist, or cartesian sense. Instead, God has created us with not only intellectual capacities (against the view that the mind is a tabula rasa) but also an implanted natural knowledge of God. No doubt, this "implanted" knowledge is mediated in the sense of being caused by the stimulus of the external world and our internal constitution, but "it is apprehended immediately without argumentation, computation, or self-conscious reasoning" (Bahnsen, *Van Til's Apologetic*, 184). As such, the knowledge of God is immediately perceived; hence, it is inescapable and undeniable, although sadly, since the fall, we suppress this knowledge. For a discussion of "implanted" and "acquired" natural knowledge of God in historical theology, see Duby, *God in Himself*, 72–103; Muller, *Post-Reformation Reformed Dogmatics*, 1:270–310 (see chap. 3, n. 12).

History is not a series of meaningless events, and although we might not know the specifics of God's plan from creation, we know that the created order and history has meaning, purpose, and design.

From creation, we also know that humans are creatures of dignity who ought to worship and obey God and that idolatry is culpable foolishness (Rom 1:20–23, 32). Creation testifies that God is the source of moral norms and that these objective norms require our obedience (Rom 1:32). Minimally, God's moral standard reflected in creation is love of God and our neighbor. From creation, we know that we are creatures of dignity; that male and female are created and ordered; that the proper use of our sexuality is in heterosexual, monogamous marriage; we know the value of the family and the dignity of work, property, and respect for others. In all these areas, tragically in our sin, we suppress the truth and attempt to overturn God's good order and design, which results in idolatry and distorted reason, even though we know that our actions deserve judgment (Rom 1:24–32).

Natural revelation, then, "is a clear and personal revelation of the true God, which makes authoritative demands on human beings."[86] We *know* God exists and we *know* something of his nature and moral demands. This knowledge is not merely the result of inferential or discursive reasoning; instead, *all* people know God by direct contact with his creation and within them. Even without a discursive argument, "all men see and recognize the signature of their Creator in the world that He created and controls, as well as in themselves as His created image."[87] Our knowledge from creation is caused by contact with the world and our own internal constitution and can be known even apart from self-conscious reasoning.

Since all people suppress the truth of natural revelation, God must act in sovereign grace to remove our suppression of it, to give us new hearts, to reveal his redemptive promises, and to bring people to faith in God's promises centered in Christ. Thus, a right use of reason depends on the Spirit-illuminated word in order to acknowledge the glory of our Creator in his creation. Yet rational arguments can and must be made from creation to all people, appealing to what we have in common, namely, the created order and universal moral norms, yet these arguments do not ultimately function independent of Scripture.

---

[86] Frame, *Systematic Theology*, 538 (see chap. 5, n. 1).

[87] Bahnsen, *Van Til's Apologetic*, 184.

Natural Revelation Stabilizes Human Society by Providing to All People Common Notions

Despite human sin and due to God's common grace, natural revelation stabilizes human society by providing a check on our rebellious "constructs" of the world, especially in the moral realm. Creation reveals God's created order, design, and boundaries, which are not easily eradicated, although we try to do so (Rom 1:18–32). Combined with common grace, natural revelation gives common notions to all people, including a moral sense of obligation whereby good and evil are distinguished, evil is held in check, and human life in general functions tolerably even in a fallen, abnormal world. For example, God's creation of marriage, the family, and societal authorities—all tied to the created order—helps limit our tendency to self-destruction. But, sadly, when these creation orders are dismantled and our consciences are seared, societies internally collapse, and often in history, anarchy leads to totalitarianism by the state.

However, natural revelation and common grace reveal who God is *and* his moral demands, which are common to all people. Surrounded by God's objective order and his moral demands written on our consciences, despite our attempt to eradicate these truths, we can appeal to people's intuitive sense that human life is precious (Gen 1:26–28; cf. Gen 9:6). From here appeal can be made to argue for the sanctity of human life, and thereby abortion, infanticide, and euthanasia may be opposed. Similarly, people know that humans are designed in terms of the complementarity of the sexes; hence, people "know" that a proper use of our sexuality is to function within the permanency of heterosexual marriage. All misuses of our sexuality, whether fornication, adultery, divorce, homosexuality, polygamy, or bestiality, are distortions of God's creation of male and female and what is best for a well-functioning human society. Sin has corrupted our appeal to natural revelation, but nonetheless, due to common grace, God's created order and moral demands cannot be easily dismissed.

Natural Revelation Is a True but Non-salvific Knowledge That Renders All People Guilty

God's being, authority, and moral will are universally revealed through the created order, but in our sin, we suppress the truth and exchange it for a lie, which renders us guilty before God. For this reason, God is perfectly just in condemning us even if we have never heard the gospel, contrary to the view of "inclusivism."[88] Although there are varieties of inclusivism, and it is an integrated view dependent on an entire theology, at least four points of response are in order.[89]

First, Romans 1 gives us no confidence that humans respond positively to natural revelation apart from God's saving grace *and* special revelation. The logic of Romans 1 is to drive us to the work of Christ and explicit saving faith in that work.

However, Terrance Tiessen, along with other inclusivists, attempts to counter this point. They contend that natural revelation *may* lead to a saving, generic "faith" in God. But what exactly is this? Tiessen suggests that a person may look at creation and respond with a "spirit of thankfulness for what [God] has made and provided for us."[90] Also, he thinks that Rom 2:14–16 teaches that a person may live a life consistent with God's law, thus showing that those who only have natural revelation may have *saving* faith.[91] He admits that if people suppress the truth of nature, they are without excuse, but he then suggests that Romans 1 does not say that "*everyone* ultimately and *finally* does this."[92] So, *if* there is a positive response to natural revelation, it is the result of the Spirit's work and an example of saving faith.[93]

There are at least two problems with this line of argument.

1. Tiessen's (and other inclusivists') reading of Romans 1–2 is incorrect.[94] No doubt, Paul does not *explicitly* address the issue of whether someone positively responds to natural revelation. Yet, the text precludes this possibility. The function of Romans 1 is to explain why *all* people are under divine wrath, namely, because they have *not* responded positively to natural revelation.

2. We may imagine someone afflicted by conscience who cries out to God for mercy. But again, this is *not* what Rom 2:14–16 teaches. Either this text refers to a hypothetical situation that is never realized, or it refers to Gentile *Christians* who have responded to special

[88] Inclusivism is found both outside and within evangelical theology. Our focus is on the latter.

[89] For a more detailed response, see my "Saving Faith: Implicit or Explicit?," in Morgan and Peterson, *Faith Comes by Hearing*, 142–83, along with the other essays in the book.

[90] Tiessen, *Who Can Be Saved?*, 144.

[91] Tiessen, 144–45. This is not a works salvation, but a faith that shows itself in obedience to God's law.

[92] Tiessen, 141.

[93] See Tiessen, 142.

[94] See Moo, *Romans*, 123–25.

revelation.[95] Nowhere does Paul say that "Gentiles apart from the gospel can be saved by meeting the demands of the law, or by doing good works."[96] Making logical possibilities to be actualities is illegitimate, especially when it runs counter to the entire argument of Romans 1–3.

Second, many inclusivists insist that God's love entails that God's presence is always a gracious presence and since God desires that all be saved, then logically God *must* provide universal access to salvation. Since people do not have equal access to special revelation, then the knowledge of God from natural revelation *must* be salvific, or God may possibly allow a post-mortem opportunity for people to respond to Christ. In response, three points need to be given:

1. Inclusivists have inverted the biblical presentation of sin, responsibility, and judgment. Humans are judged on what we know from creation and our rejection of the truth of God-given in creation. Thus, we are under divine judgment due to *our* sin, and it is not God's fault that we do not have equal access to special revelation. In other words, humans are not judged for not hearing the gospel; we are judged for our sin against God and our suppression of the truth. Although there is greater responsibility in having special revelation, and special revelation is the solution to our problem, natural revelation is a true revelation of God and our rejection of it results in our *just* condemnation.

2. Scripture teaches that God is love, but he is also holy, just, righteous, and so on. Inclusivists tend to privilege divine love at the expense of everything else Scripture teaches about God. Also, given divine simplicity, we cannot elevate one divine attribute over others: God is all that he is in his glorious perfection, and his entire self-sufficient being stands in all of its fullness, upholding his own glory in relation to his creatures in salvation and judgment. Although God is love, his love is, first, love within himself before it is love for his creation. As such, God's love is not dependent on his creation, although he chooses to love his creation and especially his people.

3. Building on the previous point, God's presence is not always a saving, gracious presence. God is present in the fullness of his triune being. In relation to sin, God's entire being

---

[95] On Rom 2:14–16, see Schreiner, *Romans,* 128–35; Moo, *Romans,* 148–57; also see Douglas J. Moo, "Romans 2: Saved Apart from the Gospel?," in *Through No Fault of Their Own? The Fate of Those Who Have Never Heard,* ed. William V. Crockett and James G. Sigountos (Grand Rapids: Baker, 1991), 137–45.

[96] Moo, "Romans 2," 145.

upholds his glory and brings judgment on sin. In relation to his gracious decision to redeem us in Christ, God displays his grace consistent with his holy justice. Yes, God takes no pleasure in the death of the wicked, and he desires all to be saved, but this does not entail *either* universalism *or* a limitation of God's knowledge and power. Scripture can speak of God's presence and relation to the world in different ways while maintaining his self-sufficient fullness, just as it can speak of God's will in different ways without making his desire that none perish (2 Pet 3:9) contrary to his decreeing all things, including salvation and judgment (Eph 1:11). In the end, many inclusivists offer a stunted view of God that does not reflect all that Scripture teaches.

Third, the "pneumatological proposal" that seeks to explain how the Spirit universally and graciously works through creation to bring those who have never heard the gospel to *saving, generic* faith is not biblical. Why? At least two reasons may be given.

1. This proposal inverts the Son-Spirit personal relations in Scripture. As we noted in chapter 4, *theological* conclusions must be true to the Bible's own presentation forged through the covenants. If we investigate the Son-Spirit relation in Scripture, it is contrary to this proposal. For example, in the OT the "Spirit of God" occurs around 100 times, mostly in reference to God's mighty actions and presence. But as we work through the covenants and we move to the Prophets and the anticipation of the new covenant, we discover that the coming Messiah (Son) not only has the Spirit in fullness (Isa 11:1–3; 42:1; 61:1–2; cf. Luke 4:14–21; John 1:32–34); he also pours out the Spirit on his people (Ezek 36:25–27; Joel 2; cf. John 7:39; Acts 2). As such, it is impossible to think of the Spirit's work unfolded across the canon divorced from the Son (Messiah) and the glorification of the Son by bringing people to faith in him. Inclusivists are not correct to think of the Spirit's work "prior to and geographically larger" than the Son's.

2. In light of the previous point, we always see the Spirit's work tied to gospel realities. In the NT, the Spirit's work is to testify to Christ, to convict the world of sin, righteousness, and judgment so that people will believe in Jesus (John 16:7–11). To contend that the Spirit may work in us graciously so that we "believe" in God, but not in Christ as the object of our faith, is foreign to the work of the Spirit as described in the NT. In fact, when the NT speaks of faith, it is never faith in the abstract or divorced from the proper object of saving faith, namely, Christ.

Fourth, the appeal to OT holy pagans or even OT believers in Israel who have saving faith apart from faith in Christ is illegitimate. At least three points may be made.

1. When appeal is made to holy pagans and the work of grace in them, including their religious traditions, inclusivists fail to discern where these people are located in redemptive

history. For example, OT believers within Israel are under the Mosaic covenant, not natural revelation alone. Or OT holy pagans either come under the covenant (Rahab, Ruth), or they know of special revelation because of their contact with God's people. In all these cases, *saving* faith is never tied to natural revelation but always to God's covenant promises that are all centered in Christ (Gen 3:15; 15:6). None of these people are exercising a generic "faith" in an undefined "God." In addition, now in light of Christ's coming, it is unthinkable that the Spirit of God is bringing people to faith apart from Christ (e.g., Cornelius).

2. What is true, saving faith in Scripture? Saving faith is always in relationship to its proper object and thus has specific content that is always tied to special revelation. Even the first "gospel" promise given in Gen 3:15 is specific and Christological. The "saving" faith inclusivism defends is not remotely related to biblical faith.

3. Scripture clearly teaches that in order to receive salvation, one must repent of one's sin and believe the good news centered in the promises of God, tied to the special revelation covenants, and now that he has come, explicitly in Christ (John 5:23; 14:6; Acts 4:12). Since Scripture is ambiguous on this point, Ronald Nash is correct to warn about the dangers of inclusivism when he writes: "I believe it is reckless, dangerous, and unbiblical to lead people to think that the preaching of the gospel (which I insist must contain specifics about the person and work of Christ) and personal faith in Jesus are not necessary for salvation."[97] Instead, what is needed is for the church to proclaim the gospel to the ends of the earth so that by God's grace, people who have never heard the gospel will hear and respond.

Natural Revelation Is Not the Same as Natural Theology[98]

Natural revelation is God's revelation of himself and his moral will in creation and in humans, which results in a true knowledge that leaves *all* people without excuse. Natural *theology* consists of discursive arguments that seek to demonstrate that the existence and nature of God is rationally warranted from the observation of the world.[99] Most of the arguments "begin with

---

[97] Edwards, *Is Jesus the Only Savior?*, 126 (see chap. 2, n. 56).

[98] Bahnsen, *Van Til's Apologetic*, 182–86.

[99] Letham, *Systematic Theology*, 55–56 (see chap. 5, n. 1). See Bavinck who distinguishes natural revelation from natural theology if "natural theology" is viewed solely as a product of human reason. He states:

observations about the *natural* world (e.g., that there is motion, or that there is order in nature) and then draw inferences about the *supernatural* existence or character of God."[100] In these arguments, natural theology assumes various philosophical assumptions (e.g., metaphysical, epistemological, and methodological), which require specific worldview commitments.

Although Scripture teaches that God is known from creation, this is not necessarily the same as natural theology. Just as natural law *theory* is not exactly the same as "natural law," that is, the moral content revealed by natural revelation, since *theories* assume philosophical commitments that require defense before they are simply assumed. So natural *theology* is best viewed as an entire *method* that is not the same as natural *revelation*. For example, in Romans 1, Paul does not argue that the created realm gives brute facts that merely makes *possible* a natural knowledge of God as the eventual *conclusion* of their reasoning, provided people rationally reflect upon it correctly. Instead, Romans 1 teaches something much stronger. From natural revelation *all* people have no excuse because God's revelation of himself is a conduit of constant, inescapable, information about God. *All* people possess an *actual* knowledge of God from the outset of their reasoning, which explains the universal moral sense that all people possess. God's revelation is everywhere, and apart from him, the basis for a warranted human knowledge is difficult to sustain. Thus, appeal to what people "know" from nature is not vacuous but crucial since all people in all places, even in their sin, know God and something of his moral will from creation. Scripture is claiming that without the God of Scripture and the revelation of himself in creation, humans could not account for the preconditions of all intelligible experience that they must take for granted but that only the Christian position

---

> There is no such thing as a separate natural theology that could be obtained apart from any revelation solely on the basis of a reflective consideration of the universe. The knowledge of God that is gathered up in so-called natural theology is not the product of human reason. Rather, natural theology presupposes, first of all, that *God* reveals himself in his handiwork. It is not humans who seek God but God who seeks humans, also by means of his works in nature. That being the case, it further presupposes that it is not humans who, by the natural light of reason, understand and know this revelation of God. . . . Accordingly, Christians follow a completely mistaken method when, in treating natural theology, they, as it were, divest themselves of God's special revelation in Scripture and the illumination of the Holy Spirit, discuss it apart from any Christian presuppositions, and then move on to special revelation.

Reformed Dogmatics, 2:74.

[100] Bahnsen, *Van Til's Apologetic*, 184.

warrants. *This* "transcendental" argument for God's existence and nature is not the same form of argument made by natural *theology*, but it is much closer to what natural revelation reveals and communicates.[101]

Natural Revelation Is Important to Remember in Evangelism and Missions[102]

Due to natural revelation, *all* people everywhere know truth about God, themselves, and the world so that no one has an excuse. This fact is significant for evangelism and missions. Every person you meet is surrounded by God's revelation of himself *outside* and *inside* them. Even if the truth is suppressed, it cannot be eradicated; our point of contact with them is as broad and deep as creation itself. Humans, in other words, cannot live in this world apart from constantly butting up against reality—a reality that reveals God. Ultimately, our witness and apologetic are that humans cannot escape their Creator and Lord and that in their exchange of the truth for a lie, they live in an irrational world of their own "making" that in the end leads to futility.

In our rebellious "construction" of idols, we know better (Acts 17:28–29). In our denial of moral norms, we inconsistently act as if such norms exist. We say that life is without meaning, design, and purpose, but we cannot consistently live this out. We affirm a "constructivist" view of knowledge, but we know that nature, humans, language, and, indeed, reality have a "givenness" that cannot be denied (Rom 1:32). We insist that humans are merely animals, but we desperately desire significance, justice, and love. Thus, no matter whom we talk to, given that all people live in God's created order, including our own human constitution, we have a point of contact to speak the truth of the gospel to them. For evangelism and missions, this is important to remember: the glorious triune God we proclaim is *known* by all people, and their suppression of the truth is never consistent. In fact, all non-Christian worldviews live off the "borrowed capital" of natural revelation and what Scripture teaches. As Frame rightly notes, "The non-Christian's suppression of the truth is never complete. He can never completely eradicate the truth from his consciousness. If he could, he could not live at all. For this is God's world, and all the world's structures, order, and meaning is God's work."[103]

---

[101] On this point, see Bahnsen, 496–529.

[102] Beeke and Smalley, *Reformed Systematic Theology*, 1:210–11.

[103] Frame, *History of Western Philosophy and Theology*, 614.

Natural Revelation Is Not Sufficient on Its Own

As we have noted, God never intended for natural revelation to function apart from special revelation. Before the fall, Adam, as a creature and image-bearer, knew God, himself, and the world in the context of God's revelation in nature and divine speech. In fact, Adam was created to know God and to be in natural religious fellowship with God as his covenant creature, or what Scripture speaks of as true righteousness and holiness (Eph 4:24). In entering into covenant relationship with Adam, God had to speak to Adam (Gen 2:15–17), and Adam in relation to God would have discovered many truths directly from God apart from his study of nature (e.g., his own age, the age of the earth, etc.). No doubt, after the fall, divine speech was even more necessary since *all* people now suppress the truth of creation, *and* if God chooses to redeem, he must act to redeem us.[104] Also, as God's moral demand is known from natural revelation, special revelation is needed to make it cogent; it is not sufficient in itself. For example, one can appeal to "nature" to argue for human dignity or a heterosexual sexual ethic, but moral conclusions require an "ought" that is not derived from the "is" of description or observation.[105] Persuasive moral reasoning requires more than what we observe from nature alone, yet natural revelation provides the backdrop and framework for such arguments when combined with special revelation.

Why do we need special revelation in addition to natural revelation? Whether it is before or after the fall, since humans are finite creatures, God must speak directly to supplement and interpret natural revelation. We were not created to figure out everything on our own. Divine speech shortens the learning curve, and even if we had endless time to investigate the world, our knowledge would only remain finite. After the fall, divine speech continues to be necessary but with greater urgency. Due to our suppression of the truth, we need a divine word to correct our distorted misinterpretations of natural revelation. And if we are to be justified before God, redeemed from the bondage of sin and death, and reconciled to a state of favor in covenant relationship with our Creator and Lord, we need a divine word of promise along with God's mighty actions to save—none of which is derived from natural revelation alone. So before and

---

[104] See John M. Frame, *The Doctrine of the Christian Life* (Phillipsburg: P&R, 2008), 951–52. For a similar point, see Bavinck, *Reformed Dogmatics*, 1:308–14, 1:359–62, 2:74.

[105] See Frame, 954, who observes that many natural-law arguments do not escape the "naturalistic fallacy," i.e., "an attempt to reason from fact to obligation, from 'is' to 'ought.'"

after the fall, we need the "spectacles" of God's word to rightly interpret God, self, and the world and, more significantly, to know, glorify, and adore our glorious triune God.

As we will develop in subsequent chapters, a crucial implication of this point is that Scripture must take precedence over what we think we know from natural revelation, especially when Scripture speaks directly on the matter. God has given us the "two books of nature and Scripture," and "all truth is God's truth," but when Scripture speaks directly on a subject, the "two books" do not carry equal weight. Scripture is not a textbook on all matters, and in terms of the natural order, we must investigate the world to discover what God has created and designed. Scripture's main purpose is to know God salvifically in Christ Jesus, yet Scripture provides the overall framework by which we view the world and interpret all things. As important as natural revelation is, it is not sufficient for a full understanding of God, self, and the world.

Concluding Reflection

In this chapter, we have focused on the purpose, content, role, and limits that natural revelation serves in God's self-disclosure and the divine economy. We are now in a position to develop the doctrine of Scripture in chapters 7–12, the cognitive foundation of theology, which allows us to speak of God and all things related to him in a normative way. Yet unfortunately, there is much confusion today regarding what Scripture *is*, which is the subject of the next chapter.

CHAPTER 7

What is Scripture? Three Views of Biblical Authority

Introduction

Scripture is *special* revelation committed to writing, a point we began to develop in chapter 5. In other words, Scripture *is* God's word through the agency of human authors so that what Scripture says (the human texts, canon), God says. Due to triune, extraordinary action through the biblical authors (i.e., inspiration), Scripture is objectively true in all of its diverse communication and sufficient for our knowledge of God, self, and the world.

At least this has been the historic view of Scripture. But since the Enlightenment, some who have broadly identified with Christianity have sought to modify this view, as noted in chapter 2. As such, today there are competing views of Scripture, especially by theologies committed to some form of modern or postmodern thought. In these views, *if* special revelation is affirmed, there is ambiguity regarding the precise relation between the human texts of Scripture and God's word/speech. Is it a direct, indirect, or non-direct identity relation?

Given that in our current context different views of Scripture are held that are not equal, it is crucial to distinguish *and* evaluate these views according to Scripture and historic theology. Given that Scripture is our final authority, the "ruling rule" (*norma normans*) for our theology, we need to know what we are confessing and defending in contrast to other views. So with this in mind, we will discuss a spectrum of three views of Scripture current today. We will set the historic view of Scripture over against two other views that vie for our attention, especially iterations of the "neo-orthodox" view since many evangelicals think it is the most viable option, a viewpoint we reject. This will allow us in subsequent chapters to expound the classical view of Scripture as the view that evangelical theology needs to continue to embrace and defend for the health of the church and the glory of the triune God who has given us his word.

The "Received View": The Classical View of Scripture[1]

The "received view" refers to the historic or classical view of Scripture that has been consistently held throughout church history until the rise of the Enlightenment and the "modern" era. Specifically, it refers to the view of Scripture held by the magisterial Reformers and post-Reformation Reformed theology and its contemporary restatements by evangelical theology as represented by the International Council on Biblical Inerrancy (ICBI),[2] which spanned numerous denominations,[3] including Baptists, Presbyterians,

[1] The title "Received View" is from Vanhoozer, *First Theology*, 127–58 (see chap. 2, n. 99). It refers to the historic or classical view of Scripture that has been handed down ("received") through church history until the rise of the Enlightenment and the "modern" age. Specifically, it refers to the exposition and defense of Scripture in the Reformation and post-Reformation eras and its current restatements by "old Princeton" (e.g., B. B. Warfield, A. A. Hodge, Geerhardus Vos), the Reformed Dutch tradition (e.g., Herman Bavinck, Abraham Kuyper), Westminster Theological Seminary (e.g., J. Gresham Machen, E. J. Young, John Murray, Cornelius Van Til), and in evangelical theology by the International Council on Biblical Inerrancy (ICBI) and literature that arose from ICBI, such as the Chicago Statement on Inerrancy and Hermeneutics. In Southern Baptist theology, this has also been the historic position. See L. Rush Bush and Tom J. Nettles, *Baptists and the Bible*, 40th anniversary ed. (Fort Worth: Seminary Hill Press, 2020).

[2] See Richard A. Muller, *Post-Reformation Reformed Dogmatics*, vol. 2 (see chap. 3, n. 12).

[3] For information on ICBI (1977–87), see Boice, *Foundation of Biblical Authority*, 9–12 (see chap. 1, n. 23); and https://www.alliancenet.org/international-council-on-biblical-inerrancy.

Lutherans, and others.[4] In the SBC, it is represented by the current version of the *Baptist Faith and Message*.[5]

There are at least three components of the "received view": propositional revelation, verbal-plenary inspiration, and infallibility and inerrancy. Central to the classical view is the "identity thesis": Scripture *is* God's word. In other words, there is a "direct" identity between what God communicates by divine words/speech and what the human authors communicate in their texts. As discussed in chapter 5, all views of Scripture are dependent on a theology proper, specifically a view of the God-world relation. This is also true of the received view. Its theology assumes that God is sovereign over his world, including the free and responsible choices of his creatures. God is able to *guarantee* that what the biblical authors write is what he wants written, which is best explained by a compatibilistic view of divine providence. Scripture is human but it is also the product of triune *extraordinary* communicative agency so that what Scripture says, God says.

Propositional or Cognitive Revelation

To affirm that Scripture is "propositional revelation" is not to minimize all the ways that God speaks to us through the biblical texts. Historically, the term was employed to counter neo-orthodoxy's overemphasis on revelation as "personal," especially in Christ, the Word

---

[4] Here is a sample of some of the literature. For "old Princeton," see A. A. Hodge and B. B. Warfield, *Inspiration* (1881; repr., Grand Rapids: Baker Books, 1979); Warfield, *Inspiration and Authority* (see chap. 4, n. 5); and for the Dutch tradition, see Bavinck, *Reformed Dogmatics*, 1:323–494 (see chap. 1, n. 9). For some of the literature from ICBI, see Boice, *Foundation of Biblical Authority*; Norman Geisler, ed., *Inerrancy* (Grand Rapids: Zondervan, 1980); Norman Geisler, ed., *Biblical Errancy: An Analysis of its Philosophical Roots* (Grand Rapids: Zondervan, 1981); Earl D. Radmacher and Robert D. Preus, eds., *Hermeneutics, Inerrancy, and the Bible* (Grand Rapids: Zondervan, 1984). Also see Gordon Lewis and Bruce Demarest, eds., *Challenges to Inerrancy: A Theological Response* (Chicago: Moody Press, 1984); Carson and Woodbridge, ed., *Scripture and Truth* (see chap. 2, n. 7); Carson and Woodbridge, *Hermeneutics, Authority, and Canon* (see chap. 2, n. 63). In recent days, see Ward, *Words of Life* (see chap. 5, n. 27); Frame, *Doctrine of the Word* (chap. 5, n. 5); Carson, *Enduring Authority* (see chap. 4, n. 9); Feinberg, *Light in a Dark Place* (see chap. 5, n. 2).

[5] See https://bfm.sbc.net/bfm2000/#i-the-scriptures.

incarnate, which we will discuss below. But as discussed in chapter 5, Scripture teaches that God's *word* is his own communication, which includes both cognitive content and his personal presence. Thus to affirm "propositional revelation" is to stress that God reveals himself *verbally*, *cognitively*, and *truthfully* in Scripture. Scripture is not merely the means by which we "encounter" God; it also gives us the *knowledge* of God, self, and the world in an objective and warranted way.

Also, as noted in chapter 5, God speaks to us directly through prophets and apostles and through the biblical authors in their written texts. God's authoritative speech and its truthfulness are not diminished from the divine voice to the written word; instead, God communicates himself, his plan, promises, and purposes to us, which yield cognitive truth and knowledge. The emphasis is on "God's self-communication through the revealed truths formulated in the canon."[6] No doubt, God also reveals himself in his mighty "acts," but Scripture is more than a record of what God has done in redemptive history that he has left us to interpret apart from a word-revelation. Instead, Scripture is a "*word*-act" revelation; *God's* own interpretation of his redemptive acts through the biblical authors. This is why Scripture *is* God's authoritative word. J. I. Packer states it this way:

> Leave man to guess God's mind and purpose, and he will guess wrong; he can know it only by being told it. Moreover, the whole purpose of God's mighty acts is to bring man to know Him by faith; and Scripture knows no foundation for faith but the spoken word of God, inviting our trust in Him on the basis of what He has done for us. . . . Therefore, verbal revelation—that is to say, propositional revelation, the disclosure by God of truths about Himself—is no mere appendage to His redemptive activity, but a necessary part of it.[7]

Furthermore, to affirm "propositional revelation" is not to deny God's revelation of himself in other "speech acts" and in diverse literary forms. God does many things with human language besides assert truths, which is what propositions are.[8] In addition to assertions, God

[6] Vanhoozer, *First Theology*, 133.

[7] J. I. Packer, *"Fundamentalism" and the Word of God: Some Evangelical Principles* (London: InterVarsity Fellowship, 1958), 92. On propositional revelation, also see the extensive discussion in Henry, *God, Revelation, and Authority*, 3:455–81 (see chap. 3, n. 18).

[8] On this point, see Vanhoozer, *First Theology*, 130–39.

gives us questions, promises, riddles, parables, hymns, warnings, commands, laments, stories, and letters. All of these speech acts are authoritative but in different ways. For example, when Scripture communicates God's truths, that is, his "assertives," we are to believe them without question; when Scripture gives us God's "directives," they are either to be obeyed directly as God's commands or by reflective observance as in the wisdom literature; when Scripture gives us "promises," we are to completely trust them; when Scripture contains "expressives," as in the psalms and hymns of Scripture, we are to share and participate in their normative response to God's glory.[9] As speech acts are reflected in the literary forms of Scripture (e.g. narratives, prophetic writings, psalms, proverbs, apocalyptic, etc.), each literary form must be appreciated for what it is and properly interpreted.[10] But, in the end, no matter what speech act or literary form/genre we are dealing with, Scripture communicates God's objective truth to us.

Verbal-Plenary Inspiration

To affirm verbal-plenary inspiration is to insist that what the Bible says in its entirety, right down to its words, sentences, and literary forms, God says. Even more, it is to affirm that *everything* in Scripture is what God wanted written, his intended speech to us. "Plenary" means "all," while "verbal" refers to the words/language of the text. The affirmation, then, is that there is a *direct* identity between the human *words* of the biblical text and God's *word* and communicative intent.

B. B. Warfield explains the concept of verbal-plenary inspiration this way: "Inspiration is that extraordinary, supernatural influence (or, passively, the result of it), exerted by the Holy Ghost on the writers of our Sacred Books, by which their words were rendered also

---

[9] See Frame, *Doctrine of the Word*, 56; Kevin J. Vanhoozer, "The Semantics of Biblical Literature: Truth and Scripture's Diverse Literary Forms," in Carson and Woodbridge, *Hermeneutics, Authority, and Canon*, 53–104.

[10] On this point, see Barry G. Webb, "Biblical Authority and Diverse Literary Genres," in Carson, *Enduring Authority*, 577–614; cf. Kevin J. Vanhoozer, "Augustinian Inerrancy: Literary Meaning, Literal Truth, and Literate Interpretation in the Economy of Biblical Discourse," in *Five Views on Biblical Inerrancy*, ed J. Merrick and Stephen M. Garrett (Grand Rapids: Zondervan, 2013), 199–224.

the words of God, and, therefore, perfectly infallible."[11] Many critics of the "received view" charge its view of "inspiration" as necessitating a dictation theory of inspiration.[12] But this charge reflects more the *theology* of the critic, specifically their view of the God-world relationship. As discussed in chapter 5, if one rejects a strong view of divine providence and its concomitant understanding of the divine sovereignty–human freedom relationship, then the affirmation that God is able *to guarantee* what the human authors write becomes highly problematic. But the theological undergirding of the classical view assumes a view of dual agency where God's sovereign actions are compatible with human actions, and God's purposes are not thwarted.[13]

For this reason, the received view of Scripture affirms a *concursive* theory of inspiration. It does not deny that a few sections of Scripture are given by dictation, such as the writing of the Decalogue on the two tablets of stone (Exod 32:15–16). However, Scripture as a whole, even the Pentateuch, which includes the Decalogue, is not dictated. Scripture is written by human authors, and their texts reflect their language, style, and free agency. Yet Scripture is not merely the product of human authors; it is simultaneously the product of triune, *extraordinary* agency in and through the biblical authors so that what they write freely is precisely what God intended to communicate, right down to the words, sentences, and literary forms. In the writing and production of Scripture, God was sovereignly at work, superintending the process of composing the Scriptures so that the end result manifests his divine intention without overriding the intentions of the human authors. Warfield captures this point with these words:

> The fundamental principle of this conception [concursus] is that the whole of Scripture is the product of divine activities which enter it, however, not by superseding the activities of the human authors, but confluently with them; so that the Scriptures are the joint product of divine and human activities, both of which penetrate them at every point, working harmoniously together to the production of a writing which is not divine here and human there, but at once divine and human in every part, every

---

[11] Warfield, *Inspiration and Authority*, 420; also see J. I. Packer, "Scripture," in *New Dictionary of Theology*, ed. Sinclair B. Ferguson et al. (Downers Grove: InterVarsity, 1988), 629.

[12] See Henry, *God, Revelation, and Authority*, 4:138–42.

[13] We will discuss this in more detail in chapters 21–22, on divine providence.

> word and every particular. According to this conception, therefore, the whole Bible is recognized as human, the free product of human effort, in every part and word. And at the same time, the whole Bible is recognized as divine, the Word of God, his utterances, of which he is in the truest sense the Author.[14]

Infallibility and Inerrancy

As a consequence of divine inspiration, the classical view insists that Scripture is infallible and thus completely trustworthy in all that it affirms, teaches, and communicates. If Scripture truly *is* God's word, and there is no evidence that the authority and truthfulness of God's speech is diminished from the divine voice to the communication of the prophets and apostles in their written texts, then it follows that Scripture has the authority of God himself. In other words, the Bible's authority is not merely functional but intrinsic to it.[15] Scripture is not only without error in all that it teaches and asserts; it is also our final and sufficient authority in all matters of faith and practice. Out of this follows the proper affirmation of *sola Scriptura*. Scripture is our final, sufficient, and magisterial authority for our knowledge of God, self, and the world. It is the "ruling rule" (*norma normans*) for all of our theological formulations and our life as the church.

The Neo-Orthodox View

Although the term "neo-orthodoxy" can refer to a number of people, we are using it here to refer to the view of Karl Barth (1886–1968). We discussed the "neo-orthodox" response to theological liberalism in chapter 2 and Barth's view of natural revelation in chapter 6. Our focus here is on his view of Scripture, which continues to influence theological discussion. Barth's view represents a half-way house (via media) between the received view and the continuation of theological liberalism in modern/postmodern theology. Some have argued that Barth and his theology is the way forward for evangelical theology. For this reason, it is important

---

[14] See Warfield, "The Divine and Human in the Bible," in *Selected Shorter Writings*, 2:547 (see chap. 1, n. 7).

[15] See J. I. Packer, "Scripture," in *NDT*, 628 (see chap. 2, n. 11).

to discuss Barth's view of Scripture given its ongoing influence and embrace by many who fit under the broad categories of post-liberal and post-conservative theology.[16]

Karl Barth's View of Scripture

In contrast to the received view, Barth rejects that there is a *direct* identity between the human texts/words of Scripture and the "word of God." Thus, Barth denies that Scripture *is* God's word written, assuming a different understanding of the God-word relation, as discussed in chapter 5. Instead, Barth argues for an *indirect* identity or relation between Scripture and God's word, resulting in a departure from the received view. Barth's view consists of two interrelated components. Let us look at each of these in turn.

1. Scripture Is a "Witness" to the "Word of God"

What is central to Barth's view is his concept of God's word. For Barth, the "word of God" is a description of the triune God in action, in self-revelation. Although he affirms that "God's Word means that God speaks,"[17] and that God's speaking is supremely in Christ—indeed, to say "revelation" is to say "the Word became flesh"[18]—for Barth, God's word "is no mere thing; it is the living, personal and free God," who communicates to us but never *directly*. John Webster nicely captures Barth's view: God's word "is not a deposit of truth upon which the church can draw, or a set of statements which can be consulted. The Word of God is an act which God undertakes. God's Word is that complex but unitary event in which God has spoken, speaks and will speak, an event which encounters us through the human means of Scripture and its proclamation in the church."[19]

To understand better Barth's concept of God's word, we must locate it in his larger theology. As we mentioned in chapter 6, Barth's theology is rightly viewed as a Christocentric

[16] See Bernard Ramm, *After Fundamentalism: The Future of Evangelical Theology* (New York: Harper & Row, 1983), who argued that Barth's theology was the way forward for evangelicals to respond to modernity.

[17] Barth, *CD* I/1, 132 (see chap. 2, n. 101).

[18] Barth, 132.

[19] Webster, *Barth*, 55 (see chap. 6, n. 29).

theism.[20] For Barth, God's being is revealed in his acts, specifically the acts that constitute the life and ministry of Jesus Christ.[21] Thus, for God to be known, he must reveal himself. But, as noted in the last chapter, Barth denies the reality of natural revelation and reduces all revelation to the category of special revelation, specifically that given in Christ as the Word incarnate. So for Barth, there is no knowledge of God without faith, and conversely, no faith and theology apart from hearing God's Word, Jesus Christ.

As noted in the last chapter, there is an ongoing debate regarding how much development occurred in Barth's theology from an earlier "dialectical" phase, which could say little about God, to a more mature theology that could say something positive about God in light of Christ. But regardless of this debate, Barth insists that God is only known, and theology is only possible, due to God's own free and gracious initiative to speak to us in Christ, who alone is God's *Word*. But this raises a question: If the "Word of God" is directly Jesus Christ, then what is Scripture, and how is it related to God's Word? Historic theology has argued that Scripture *is* God's word, but Barth is not comfortable with this identification, at least in terms of how the received view has understood this identification.[22] So what is the relationship between God's word and Scripture? To answer this question, we must turn to Barth's view of the three forms of God's *word*: the word revealed, the word written, and the word preached.[23]

First, there is God's Word *revealed*, namely, Jesus Christ, who is God's direct and objective revelation, the Word made flesh.[24] In this sense, revelation is both a historical and unrepeatable

---

[20] See Vanhoozer, *First Theology*, 143–44.

[21] In chapter 6, we noted that Hunsinger labelled this "actualism" in Barth's theology. Hunsinger, *How to Read Karl Barth*, 30 (see chap. 2, n. 100).

[22] On this point, see David Gibson, "The Answering Speech of Men: Karl Barth on Holy Scripture," in Carson, *Enduring Authority*, 268–77. Gibson notes that Barth can affirm that Scripture *is* God's word: "the Bible cannot come to be God's Word if it is not this already." *The Göttingen Dogmatics*, vol. 1, ed. H. Reiffen, trans. G. Bromiley (Grand Rapids: Eerdmans, 1991), 219. But for Barth, this is understood in an indirect sense and as the Spirit of God enabling the reader to encounter God in the text. And as Gibson notes, for Barth, "At every point he is *against* a concept of 'inspired-ness' inhering in the biblical text, and *for* a concept of inspiration as something that happened then but also has to happen now" (277).

[23] See Barth, *CD* I/1, 88–124.

[24] See Barth, *CD* I/2, 1–25.

event[25] and "once-for-all."[26] "Revelation in fact does not differ from the person of Jesus Christ nor from the reconciliation accomplished by Him,"[27] and it is to him that Scripture witnesses.

Second, there is God's word *written*, that is, Scripture, which is an *indirect* revelation or *witness* to Christ.[28] Scripture is *not* directly God's word; it is only a witness to Christ. Barth insists: "A witness is not absolutely identical with that to which it witnesses. . . . In the Bible we meet with human words written in human speech, and in these words, and therefore by means of them, we hear of the lordship of the triune God."[29] But although Scripture is distinguished from God's Word in Christ, the Bible can *become* revelation by God's sovereign and free choice in the event of witnessing to Christ,[30] a point we will discuss below. For Barth, then, Scripture is a human, fallible word that indirectly witnesses to Christ. Not even the Bible can "freeze" God's past revelation. Only as God acts, only as God causes the Bible to be his word, only as he speaks through it, can we say the Bible *is* God's word in a dynamic sense.[31]

Third, there is God's word *preached*,[32] which, like Scripture, is also an *indirect* revelation. In our proclamation of Scripture, God acts and bears witness to Christ. And when God acts to do so, we not only hear the preached word as God's word but also *experience* God with us.

Given Barth's view of the "word of God" in its three forms, there is a necessary distinction between Scripture (i.e., human texts) and divine revelation (i.e., the word of God). Scripture is a *witness* to God's *word*, but it is not identical with it. Barth writes: "Again it is quite impossible that there should be a direct identity between the human word of Holy Scripture and the Word of God, and therefore between the creaturely reality in itself as such and the reality of God the Creator. It is impossible that there should have been a transmutation of the one into the other or an admixture of the one with the other."[33] But in arguing that Scripture only witnesses to Christ, Barth is *not* saying that Scripture is dispensable. On the contrary, he insists that the Bible is indispensable for the church even though the human authors of

[25] Barth, *CD* I/1, 116.
[26] Barth, *CD* I/2, 12.
[27] Barth, *CD* I/1, 119.
[28] See Barth, 99–111.
[29] Barth, *CD* I/2, 463.
[30] On this point, see Barth, *CD* I/1, 112–13.
[31] See Barth, 109.
[32] See Barth, 88–99.
[33] Barth, *CD* I/2, 499.

Scripture were not infallible in what they wrote. The biblical authors' indispensable importance for the church is that they bore witness to Christ, and thus, as Barth argues, "we are tied to these texts."[34]

However, although Barth has the highest respect for Scripture, his view requires its fallibility. For Barth, God's word is directly identified with Christ, but God cannot communicate his word through human speakers and authors without error necessarily occurring, an assumption that is not taught by Scripture. Why does he argue this way? As we will note below, it is due to his understanding of the God-world relation. But regardless, Barth rejects the infallibility and inerrancy of Scripture, contrary to the classical view.

For example, Barth writes:

> The men whom we hear as witnesses speak as fallible, erring men like ourselves. What they say, and what we read as their word, can of itself lay claim to be the Word of God, but never sustain that claim. We can read and try to assess their word as a purely human word. It can be subjected to all kinds of immanent criticism, not only in respect of its philosophical, historical and ethical content, but even in its religious and theological.[35]

Or, in his discussion of the biblical narratives, specifically Genesis, Barth writes: "We have to face up to them and to be clear that in the Bible it may be a matter of simply believing the Word of God, even though it meets us, not in the form of what we call history, but in the form of what we think must be called saga or legend."[36] Or, regarding specific errors, Barth writes: "There are obvious and overlapping contradictions—e.g., between the Law and the prophets, between John and the Synoptists, between Paul and James."[37] Barth continues in

---

[34] Barth, 492. Barth argues that the uniqueness of the biblical authors is that they were commissioned servants of the Lord (491). They enjoyed a special and singular position in their relation to the Word of God by virtue of "the specific historical situation in which they are confronted by this Word, by the particular service to which the Word called and equipped them." Karl Barth, *Evangelical Theology: An Introduction* (Grand Rapids: Eerdmans, 1963), 26. Thus, the Bible has priority because we are tied to their witness. See Barth, *Evangelical Theology*, 31–33; also see John Baillie, *The Idea of Revelation in Recent Thought* (New York: Columbia University Press, 1956), 109–33.

[35] Barth, *CD* I/2, 507; cf. Barth, 65, for a similar sentiment.

[36] Barth, 509.

[37] Barth, 509.

his discussion of the biblical authors: "For within certain limits and therefore relatively they are all vulnerable and therefore capable of error even in respect of religion and theology."[38] Or, lastly, "The prophets and apostles as such, even in their office, even in their function as witnesses, even in the act of writing down their witnesses, were real, historical men as we are, and therefore sinful in their action, and capable and actually guilty of error in their spoken and written word."[39]

To summarize Barth's view, we only have access to God's Word in Christ through the two indirect forms of revelation: Scripture and preaching. But even in these forms, we only have Christ due to God's free decision to act and reveal him to us. God's revelation of himself is not ours for the taking; it only comes to us as an event by God's free decision to act and make it so.[40] Barth's emphasis on divine freedom is crucial. In fact, it helps explain why Barth thinks that when God speaks to us through the human authors of Scripture, fallibility is introduced. Barth seems to think that in order for God's revelatory action to remain free,[41] it cannot be given objectively through creaturely means. God must take the initiative to make himself the object of human thought and speech by taking form, "and this taking form is His self-unveiling."[42] But even in the form God assumes in his self-revelation (including the incarnation), God is still free to reveal or not to reveal himself; God must act to give himself. The alternative, Barth thinks, is a denial of God's freedom. Why? Because if we identify the form with God's revelation, humans would be able to control God; God's word would be universally present and under human control and thus a mere object of human inquiry.[43] This is

---

[38] Barth, 510.

[39] Barth, 529; cf. Barth, 529–33. Many have noted that Barth is better in *practice* than in *theory*. For example, Barth rarely, if ever, appeals to errors in Scripture to dismiss an exegetical point. See Ben Rhodes, "Barth's Theology of Scripture in Dogmatic Perspective," in *Freedom Under the Word: Karl Barth's Theological Exegesis*, ed. Ben Rhodes and Martin Westerholm (Grand Rapids: Baker, 2019), 48.

[40] See Barth, *CD* I/1, 149.

[41] Barth defines the Godhead in terms of freedom. He writes: "Godhead in the Bible means freedom, ontic and noetic autonomy." Barth, *CD* I/1, 307. Also see Barth's extensive treatment of this subject in Barth, *CD* II/1, 297–321. By ontic autonomy, Barth means that God alone is self-sufficient, and uniquely is the source of his own being. That is why God is dependent upon, or in need of, no one. Moreover, by God's noetic absoluteness, Barth means what he has asserted from the very beginning: God cannot be known except by and in his own acts of self-revelation.

[42] Barth, *CD* I/1, 316.

[43] For a denial that the word of God is universally present and ascertainable, see Barth, 158.

why, as Kevin Vanhoozer notes, "Barth is reluctant to attach the predicate 'divine' to any other creaturely reality, even the Scriptures, for fear of detracting from God's being in the event of Jesus Christ: to suggest that some worldly object or activity is 'the same as' God's Word is basically to say that it is God."[44]

For this reason, Barth cannot say in the same way as the received view that Scripture *is* God's word. God as the Lord is free to act whenever and wherever he chooses, and thus he has free control over the wording of Scripture; God is not under our control.[45] Barth writes:

> He [God] can use it or not use it. He can use it in this way or in that way. He can choose a new wording beyond that of Holy Scripture. What Holy Scripture proclaims as His Word can be proclaimed in a new wording as His Word so long as it is He Himself who speaks in this wording. Furthermore, the personal character of God's Word means, not its deverbalising, but the posing of an absolute barrier against reducing its wording to a human system or using its wording to establish and construct a human system. It would not be God's faithfulness but His unfaithfulness to us if He allowed us to use His Word in this way. This would mean His allowing us to gain control over His Word, to fit it in with our own designs, and thus to shut up ourselves against Him to our own ruin. God's faithfulness to His Church consists in His availing Himself of His freedom to come to us Himself in His Word and in His reserving to Himself the freedom to do this again and again.[46]

Thus, for Scripture to become revelation for us, God must graciously act. Only by God's free decision does Scripture *become* God's word, which leads to the second aspect of Barth's view.[47]

2. Scripture Is a "Witness" to God's Word That May "Become" God's Word

By a free act of God, the fallible human witnesses to Christ may *become* the "word of God" as the Spirit graciously decides to appropriate them for the purpose of self-revelation. The human texts of Scripture, then, are not objectively identified with God's word so that what

---

[44] Vanhoozer, *Remythologizing Theology*, 207 (see chap. 2, n. 131).

[45] Barth, *CD* I/2, 527.

[46] Barth, *CD* I/1, 139. Also see Barth, *CD* I/2, 512–13.

[47] See Barth, *CD* I/2, 530; cf. McCormack, "Being of Holy Scripture," 55–75.

Scripture says, God says. Rather, by God's free agency, these human texts may *become* God's word so that Christ is present with us in some kind of dynamic, existential sense. But even in God's action, the texts remain what they are: fallible witnesses to Christ. And, as Barth admits, we do not decide when and where God chooses to act through Scripture. But because God has done so in the past, we have confidence that he will do it repeatedly again. Barth writes:

> Of the book [Bible] as we have it, we can only say: We recollect that we have heard in this book the Word of God; we recollect, in and with the Church, that the Word of God has been heard in all this book and in all parts of it; therefore we expect that we shall hear the Word of God in this book again, and hear it even in those places where we ourselves have not heard it before. Yet the presence of the Word of God itself, the real and present speaking and hearing of it, is not identical with the existence of the book as such. But in this presence something takes place in and with the book, for which the book as such does indeed give the possibility, but the reality of which cannot be anticipated or replaced by the existence of the book. A free divine decision is made. It then comes about that the Bible, the Bible *in concreto*, this or that biblical context, i.e., the Bible as it comes to us in this or that specific measure, is taken and used as an instrument in the hand of God, i.e., it speaks to and is heard by us as the authentic witness to divine revelation and is therefore present as the Word of God.[48]

What does Barth mean by the "inspiration" of Scripture? In contrast to the classical view, inspiration is not God's action by which the human authors are "carried along" (2 Pet 1:21) so that their texts are God's intended word to us (2 Tim 3:16). Instead, "inspiration" is the special activity of the Spirit on the biblical authors, commissioning them for their specific task of witnessing to Christ, but it is not the production of an authoritative text in its words, sentences, and literary forms.[49] For Barth, *verbal inspiration* is the continuous, dynamic activity of God by which he chooses to use fallible human words to witness to Christ: "Verbal inspiration does not mean the infallibility of the biblical word in its linguistic, historical and theological character

---

[48] Barth, *CD* I/2, 530.

[49] Barth, 520–21.

as a human word. It means that the fallible and faulty human word is as such used by God and has to be received and heard in spite of its human fallibility."[50]

To summarize: for Scripture to become revelation for us, God must act freely and graciously. Only by God's free decision does Scripture *become* God's Word. As to when, where, and how Scripture shows itself to us in this event, only God decides.[51] For Barth, to affirm God's freedom is to say, as John Frame notes, that "God does not place his words on paper. For God to inspire words in this way would compromise his freedom and sovereignty; God himself could not abrogate such words once he has spoken them."[52] Also, since God is the one who acts whenever and wherever he chooses, inspiration is not a unique divine action in the past that guarantees the truth of the text. No doubt, God has used Scripture in the past to witness to Christ, and thus, we believe that God will do so in the future. But to say Scripture *is* God's word is to displace Christ and to force God to honor a word spoken in the past. Even worse, it would mean that those who "have" the texts in their possession would have God under their control.

A Current Example of Barth's Influence in Post-Liberalism

Karl Barth's influence on current theology is strong, especially for those who fit under the broad category of "post-liberalism." For example, his influence is seen in Katherine Sonderegger's, "Holy Scripture as Sacred Ground."[53] In agreement with the classical view and Barth, Sonderegger views Scripture as utterly *unique*. Yet, in contrast to the "received view" and in agreement with Barth, she is hesitant to think of divine inspiration in terms of a resulting product that yields authoritative *content* without error; these ideas are too indebted to modernist influences.[54] Instead, she attempts to hold together the Bible's uniqueness *and* its errors, thus transcending the old debates of whether Scripture is inerrant or fallible.[55] So what category

---

[50] Barth, 533. On this point, see Gibson, "Answering Speech of Men," 282–86.

[51] See Barth, 531.

[52] Frame, *Doctrine of the Word*, 622; cf. Frame, 422–39.

[53] Katherine Sonderegger, "Holy Scripture as Sacred Ground," in Crisp and Sanders, *Task of Dogmatics*, 131–43 (see chap. 4, n. 1).

[54] See Sonderegger, 136–37.

[55] See Sonderegger, 137.

does Scripture belong in? She proposes the category of "uniqueness": "It [the Bible] stands utterly alone, sovereign, majestic. It stands at the beginning of all our theological ways simply because there is nothing like it—really nothing at all."[56]

But what exactly does this mean *if* Scripture is fallible? In Sonderegger's explanation, she is clearly indebted to Barth.[57] Scripture is unique because in it we encounter God not because of "some truth it contains" or due to "particular events, histories, and peoples,"[58] but because Scripture is holy and in it we meet God. The Bible, then, "is a *mode of Divine Presence*."[59] Scripture is authoritative because through it we experience God's presence. "We do not know God, nor encounter Him, nor worship Him apart from Him. He is the Gracious Opener of our heart and mind to His Reality, His Hidden Majesty. Just this, *mutatis mutandis*, is the Doctrine of Inspiration of Holy Scripture."[60] In fact, Sonderegger explains what she means by "inspiration."

> Inspiration . . . is the name we give to the meeting of God in the Bible. Like the Fiery Presence of God in the burning bush, we encounter the Fire who is God in the thornbush, we remove our sandals, we turn aside from our daily path and task. . . . We do not properly ask in what way God is in the bush, nor what parts of the shrub are bearers of God, or God's Holy Name, nor whether we simply know the Name now. . . . The One Lord burns there, and the creature remains. That is the miracle of Divine Presence, the miracle of the Bible as Holy Scripture. Because inspiration just is the encounter with one's Maker and Lord in Holy Scripture; there is no need, no room, in truth for discrete categories such as Revelation or Inerrancy or Conversion . . . the Bible is this Fiery Thornbush. That is why we meet God there.[61]

There is no doubt that Sonderegger's view is indebted to Barth. Scripture is a human word, and inspiration has less to do with the production of an authoritative text than with God choosing to be present with us through Scripture despite its fallibility. Scripture is unique

---

[56] Sonderegger, 137.

[57] See Sonderegger, 137–39.

[58] Sonderegger, 141.

[59] Sonderegger, 141 (emphasis original).

[60] Sonderegger, 141.

[61] Sonderegger, 141–42.

because it is precisely in *this* book that we encounter God. As Sonderegger states, we turn to the Bible "not because we learn of these things in its pages, but because we meet God there. . . . Not in virtue of the content, then, but in virtue of the Divine Presence is the Bible the Unique Ground of all theology, of all Christian prayer and contrition and praise."[62]

Current Examples of Barth's Influence in Post-Conservative Theology

Stanley Grenz and John Franke[63]

At the turn of the century, Stanley Grenz and John Franke represented a view known as post-conservative theology—a movement that arose out of evangelicalism that sought to rethink the nature of theology in light of the postmodern critique of modernism.[64] In their various works, they argued that evangelical theology was too "modernist." Specifically, evangelicals wrongly attempted to ground theology in an unassailable *foundation*, namely, an inerrant Bible "as the source book of information for systematic theology."[65] Evangelicals were committed to doing theology by appealing to the "propositions" of Scripture as objective, true statements of reality. Ironically, Grenz and Franke argued, classic liberalism and evangelical theology were both "modernist" but for different reasons. The former sought to ground theology in the foundation of "universal" religious experience while the latter grounded theology in an "inerrant" Bible.

Grenz and Franke's alternative proposal was a non-foundational theology that finds its truth "in God, who is the ground of the unity of truth," but in this life, "our human knowledge is never complete or absolutely certain."[66] Objective truth is only known by God and,

---

[62] Sonderegger, 143.

[63] See Grenz and Franke, *Beyond Foundationalism* (see chap. 1, n. 35); Stanley J. Grenz, "Nurturing the Soul, Informing the Mind: The Genesis of the Evangelical Scripture Principle," in Bacote, Miguélez, and Okholm, *Evangelicals and Scripture*, 21–41; John R. Franke, "Reforming Theology: Toward a Postmodern Reformed Dogmatics," *WTJ* 65 (2003): 1–26; John R. Franke, "Response to Trueman and Gaffin," *WTJ* 65 (2003): 331–43; John R. Franke, "Scripture, Tradition and Authority: Reconstructing the Evangelical Conception of *Sola Scriptura*," in Bacote, Miguélez, and Okholm, *Evangelicals and Scripture*, 192–210; John R. Franke, "Recasting Inerrancy: The Bible as Witness to Missional Plurality," in *Five Views on Biblical Inerrancy*, 259–87.

[64] See Olson, *Reformed and Always Reforming* (see chap. 2, n. 145).

[65] Grenz and Franke, *Beyond Foundationalism*, 13.

[66] Grenz and Franke, 44.

for us, only known in the future. Doctrines are only "regulative" in the Kantian sense, that is, rules of grammar that establish the "language game" of theology, but such language, at least in the present, does not yield objective truth about the world; we do not have access to the "world-in-itself."[67]

Historically, as we discussed in chapter 3, classic orthodox theology, including evangelical theology, has argued that the triune God who speaks is the source and standard for truth and theology and that Scripture *as* God's word written is first-order, objective, and true. Although Scripture is not an exhaustive revelation, because it *is* God's word, it is objectively true. And *if* our doctrines (which are second-order interpretations) are true to Scripture, they are objectively true. However, Grenz and Franke, like Barth, are reluctant to identify Scripture with God's word in a direct way, hence their rejection of inerrancy as the foundation for their theology. Instead, what is *basic* for theology is not *sola Scriptura* as God's first-order divine speech, but "the Christian-experience-facilitating interpretative framework, arising as it does out of the biblical narrative."[68] This Christian interpretative framework is a *combination* of our shared interpreted experience of God in Christ that arises from Scripture that theology reflects on. In fact, there are three sources for theology: Scripture, tradition, and culture. And it is through all three sources that the Spirit speaks to the church as we make "regulative" theological statements about God, self, and the world, but these theological statements are not objective truth claims.

Obviously, Grenz and Franke's proposal for theology raises questions about their view of Scripture. If Scripture is not directly identified with God's word as first-order, objective, and true, then what is it? Here we see the unmistakable influence of Karl Barth. In agreement with Barth, they affirm that Scripture is a human, fallible *witness* to God's self-revelation in Christ.[69] God alone is truth, but Scripture is *not* identical with divine speech. It is human speech that is accommodated to the limited capacities of humans, but in such a way that Scripture is not first-order divine speech but second-order human speech that is "contingent on the contexts and situations that give rise to particular vocabularies that shape and are shaped by the

[67] See Grenz and Franke, 45–46. On this point, they are following the post-liberal approach of George A. Lindbeck, *The Nature of Theology* (Philadelphia: Westminster Press, 1984).

[68] Grenz and Franke, *Beyond Foundationalism*, 49.

[69] See Franke, "Recasting Inerrancy," 268–29.

social circumstances in which they arise."[70] Thus, *biblical* language "lacks the capacity and universality required to provide a description of God or ultimate truth that can be thought of as absolute."[71] But, also similar to Barth, God is able to take what is human, finite, and fallible and speak in and through Scripture. In this way, Scripture *becomes* God's word, and it is authoritative because "it is the vehicle through which the Spirit speaks. In other words, the authority of the Bible, as the instrument through which the Spirit speaks, is ultimately bound up with the authority of the Spirit. Christians acknowledge the Bible as Scripture because the Spirit has spoken, now speaks, and will continue to speak with authority through the canonical texts of Scripture."[72] Scripture, then, does not have an inherent authority due to divine inspiration; instead, it has authority due to the Spirit's speaking in and through it.

But is the Spirit's speaking through Scripture identical with Scripture? What is the relation between what the human authors say and the Spirit's speaking, especially given that the text is the product of finite, fallible humans? Similar to Barth, and contrary to the "received view," they do not posit a "one-to-one correspondence between the revelation of God and the Bible, that is, between the Word of God and the words of scripture."[73] For them, the relationship is indirect and fluid. To make sense of this *indirect* relationship, they employ three ideas.

First, they adopt Nicholas Wolterstorff's "appropriated discourse" model.[74] This entails that God "appropriates" the discourse of the biblical authors as his own without necessarily agreeing with them at every point given human finitude and fallibility, hence the *indirect* relationship.

Second, in contrast to Wolterstorff, they adopt a "textual-sense interpretation" over against an "authorial-discourse interpretation." In an authorial-discourse view, God's speaking is tied to the text by the way of the intention of the biblical authors. But Grenz and Franke, in contrast to traditional hermeneutics (specifically grammatical-historical-literary exegesis), opt for a textual-sense interpretation. This entails that the meaning of the text is not tied directly to the author's intent because once the text is created, it is separated from the author. Appealing to Paul Ricoeur, they state their view this way:

---

[70] Franke, 267.

[71] Franke, 267.

[72] Franke, 271; Grenz and Franke, *Beyond Foundationalism*, 65.

[73] Grenz and Franke, *Beyond Foundationalism*, 70–71; cf. Franke, "Recasting Inerrancy," 271–72.

[74] See Wolterstorff, *Divine Discourse* (see chap. 3, n. 46).

> Although an author creates a literary text, once it has been written, it takes on a life of its own. The author's intention has been 'distanced' from the meanings of the work, although the ways in which the text is structured shape the meanings the reader discerns in the text. In a sense, the text has its own intentions, which has its genius in the author's intention but is not exhausted by it.[75]

Third, building on the previous points, Grenz and Franke propose that the Spirit's speaking *through* Scripture is related to Scripture but *not* identified with the author's intention in the text. For this reason,

> exegesis alone can[not] exhaust the Spirit's speaking to us through the text. Although the Spirit's illocutionary act is to appropriate the text in its internal meaning (i.e., to appropriate what the author said), the Spirit appropriates the text with the goal of communicating to us in *our* situation, which, while perhaps paralleling in certain respects that of the ancient community, is nevertheless unique.[76]

Also,

> in appropriating the biblical text, the Spirit speaks, but the Spirit's speaking does not come through the text in isolation. Rather, we read the text cognizant that we are the contemporary embodiment of a centuries-long interpretive tradition within the Christian community (and hence we must take seriously the theological tradition of the church). And we read realizing that we are embedded in a specific historical-cultural context (and hence we must pay attention to our culture). In this process of listening to the Spirit speaking through the appropriated text, theology assists the community of faith in discerning what the Spirit is saying and in fostering an appropriate obedient response to the Spirit's voice.[77]

But, again, the Spirit's speaking is *not* identical with Scripture itself, hence their rejection of *sola Scriptura* and the possibility of theology as a normative discipline.

---

[75] Grenz and Franke, *Beyond Foundationalism*, 74.
[76] Grenz and Franke, 74–75.
[77] Grenz and Franke, 74–75.

This is further complicated since they also think that the Spirit speaks as one voice through Scripture, tradition, and culture. But if the Spirit speaks through these three *sources* (all of which are second-order), then how do we avoid subjectivism in our theology? We cannot appeal to Scripture alone as the epistemological warrant for theology. Their solution is to tie the Spirit's speaking to the community and not the individual. But this raises more questions: Which community? And what happens when communities disagree with each another? Since Scripture is not our final court of appeal, how do we know if we have heard the Spirit's voice correctly, especially if the Spirit's speaking is not identical with Scripture? In fact, how do we arbitrate theological differences if there is no objective, normative standard?[78]

Gregory Boyd[79]

In a recent book on Scripture, Greg Boyd, a well-known open theist, is another example of a post-conservative who is influenced greatly by Barth's view of Scripture.

First, Boyd agrees with Barth that Jesus Christ is the direct, "the one and only Word of God,"[80] and that Scripture is an indirect witness to him. "Scripture is breathed by God not to function as a revelation *in its own right*, but to rather serve as a *witness to* the one revelation of the triune God in Jesus Christ."[81] *Second,* as a *human* document, by itself, Scripture is fallible. It reflects the thought of authors who are culturally conditioned, prone to error in their historical, theological, and ethical content.[82] *Third,* although the Bible is written by fallible humans, it can become "a divinely inspired witness to the Word of God only when God sovereignly decides for it to do so. When this happens, Scripture *can*, in a secondary and derivative sense, be identified as 'God's Word.'"[83] When this occurs, God is making himself known to us through the fallibility of the word written.

---

[78] See Grenz and Franke, 67–68, 92.

[79] See Boyd, *Inspired Imperfection* (see chap. 5, n. 39).

[80] Boyd, 63–71.

[81] Boyd, 55 (emphasis original).

[82] Boyd, 57–62.

[83] Boyd, 55 (emphasis original).

However, Boyd also critiques Barth's dynamic conception of inspiration. Boyd thinks that when God speaks through Scripture to us, there is "an abiding quality to Scripture";[84] that is, the fallible words of Scripture remain so that we can view them as God's word. Furthermore, unlike Barth, Boyd proposes that we view Scripture as analogous to Christ's cross. In the cross, "despite the fact that the sin and curse that Jesus bore were antithetical to God's true eternal nature, they nevertheless *contribute to* the self-revelation that God breathes through them."[85] By analogy, "why should we not expect to find sinful, cursed, and erroneous material *contributing to* the God-breathed story of God that bears witness to and culminates in the cross?"[86] In other words, God takes the fallible, culturally conditioned human texts and uses them to point to Christ.

Boyd's view of Scripture also adopts a specific understanding of progressive revelation and divine accommodation, both of which are contrary to the "received view" and more in line with Barth.[87] For Boyd, *progressive* revelation is not God's unfolding revelation that is true but incomplete; instead, it is God using the false, culturally conditioned views of humans and correcting them as history unfolds. Along a similar line, divine accommodation is not God speaking to us in human language that is finite but true; instead, it is God allowing Scripture to remain with all of its errors but still using it to witness to Christ. In fact, given Boyd's weakened view of the divine sovereignty–human freedom relationship, God *cannot guarantee* that the biblical authors are free from error unless he dictates the text. All that God can do is use the imperfections of the texts to witness to Christ.[88]

Of course, given Boyd's view, some crucial authority and hermeneutical questions arise, similar to any view that maintains Scripture's fallibility. For example, what is the standard by which one knows what is false in Scripture and what God actually agrees with? If, as Boyd says, "we should read Scripture with the awareness that sometimes the surface meaning of a passage will not reflect what God is truly like; it will rather reflect the way God's fallen and culturally

---

[84] Boyd, 77. See Boyd's entire critique of Barth on 72–81.

[85] Boyd, 95.

[86] Boyd, 95.

[87] Boyd, 125–39. However, it needs to be admitted that Barth would have rejected Boyd's view of open theism.

[88] Boyd, 107–8.

conditioned ancient people viewed God,"[89] then what is our criterion for determining this? It certainly cannot be Scripture on its own terms given its fallibility, cultural myopia, and imperfection. Inevitably Boyd's view requires an extratextual standard that is more authoritative than Scripture, but what exactly is that standard, and what warrants its authority? Boyd's answer is to appeal to the God revealed in the cross. But the problem is that we do not have access to Christ and his cross apart from Scripture and its teaching, a point we will return to below.

Kenton Sparks[90]

In many ways, Kenton Sparks's view of Scripture is influenced by Barth, but in contrast to Barth, he is more willing to affirm Scripture's fallibility both in theory and practice. Sparks identifies with post-liberalism,[91] affirms the "authority" of Scripture in some sense, but in the end is closer to the classic liberal view that continues today in higher critical studies. Sparks repeatedly wants to remind us of the Bible's "dark side" in terms of its faulty ethics, thinking, and theology. In fact, he makes the outrageous claim that the Bible supports slavery, genocide, misogyny, and child abuse, to name a few, without ever wrestling with how these texts function in the Bible's covenantal storyline and canonical presentation.[92] Yet Sparks also says that the Bible is a "wonderful book, a divinely given book that powerfully witnesses to and participates in God's saving work in our cosmos" as it points us to Christ.[93] On this point, Sparks is similar to Barth. He acknowledges that God knows all things,[94] but given that Scripture is human, God is unable to keep humans from error given Sparks's weakened view of divine providence, which is similar to that of Boyd. Also, he argues that the Bible's special status is not tied to its authors, "but rather from its divinely-ordained relationship to the incarnate word."[95] Scripture, then, only has authority by virtue of its witness to Christ. In every other way, God

[89] Boyd, 145.

[90] Sparks, *God's Word in Human Words* (see chap. 5, n. 39); Sparks, *Sacred Word, Broken Word* (see chap. 5, n. 39).

[91] Sparks, *Sacred Word, Broken Word*, 6.

[92] Sparks, 11.

[93] Sparks, 8.

[94] Sparks, 143–46.

[95] Sparks, 62–63.

accommodates himself to the error of the human authors, and it is up to us to discern the truth from the error in Scripture.

In contrast to Boyd, who wants to draw an analogy between the cross and Scripture, Sparks draws the analogy between the problem of evil and Scripture.[96] Sparks is a theistic evolutionist who thinks that God created the world fallen. As such, the world includes both good and evil, including finite, fallen creatures, who are now in need of redemption. In our fallenness, humans make mistakes, morally and theologically, which is also true of the biblical authors. In fact, Sparks insists, contrary to orthodox Christology, that Christ assumed a fallen human nature, which entails that Jesus believed culturally-conditioned, false ideas that we now know are wrong due to advances in science and secular knowledge. Sparks insists that "Orthodoxy only demands that Jesus was sinless, not that his teachings were wholly insulated from the human condition."[97] So what is true of God's creation of the world to include both good and evil and Christ's assumption of a fallen human nature that allowed him to err is also true of Scripture since "the human beings who wrote Scripture erred as all humans do."[98] "Scripture was written by godly but fallen human authors who sometimes thought and wrote ungodly things."[99]

But given Sparks's view, how does he determine what is true from false or good from evil in Scripture since it includes both. After all, Scripture itself is "in need of redemption,"[100] and "Scripture's natural meaning sometimes runs contrary to the Gospel and, where it does, begs for a hermeneutical explanation."[101] But what exactly is the extratextual criterion Sparks appeals to? He is convinced that "God infallibly achieves his redemptive aims through the fallible words of human authors,"[102] but how does he know this if Scripture is mistaken? He appeals to giving Christ priority in our interpretation of Scripture, but given his Christology, this makes little sense. In the end, he assumes some kind of extratextual standard that allows him to pick and choose what is "true" and "good" in Scripture, but what exactly is the warrant

[96] Sparks, 22.
[97] Sparks, 27.
[98] Sparks, 29.
[99] Sparks, 46–47.
[100] Sparks, 88.
[101] Sparks, 48.
[102] Sparks, 49.

for that standard? No doubt, Sparks appeals to a canonical reading along with a trajectory reading of development within Scripture,[103] but all of this is independent of Scripture. As he states, "Scripture was not intended to stand alone as *the* criterion by which theological and ethical judgments are made. Hence, Christian theology, as it reads and seeks to follow Scripture, must be ready to move beyond Scripture in some cases."[104] This is done by following the Spirit's voice in natural revelation, tradition, and religious experience, which in the end is a version of some form of extratextual theology indebted to his concept of science and modern/postmodern thought.[105]

Peter Enns[106]

In a similar way to Sparks's view, Enns affirms that Scripture is God's word but not in the sense that Scripture is fully authoritative, reliable, first-order, and true in all that it teaches and is thus our final authority for our theology. Instead, Scripture is a human, fallible, contradictory, and culture-bound word reflecting the thinking and beliefs of the ancient world that, despite its error, somehow reveals Christ to us, who is the true Word of God. In fact, the "unity" of the Bible is ultimately found in Christ himself. Despite the Bible's diversity, contradictions, and errors,

> the written word bears witness to the incarnate Word, Christ. . . . He is the one through whom heaven and earth—including the Bible itself—were created, and he is the one in whom Israel's story reaches its climax. The Bible bears witness to Christ *by*

---

[103] Sparks, 112–17. Sparks appeals to the work of William J. Webb, *Slaves, Women and Homosexuals: Exploring the Hermeneutics of Cultural Analysis* (Downers Grove: InterVarsity, 2001). Webb argues for a "trajectory hermeneutic" in Scripture by which we compare and contrast biblical teaching with the culture and ultimately draw ethical and theological conclusions from Scripture that go "beyond" the actual teaching of Scripture in its textual, epochal, and canonical context.

[104] Sparks, *Sacred Word, Broken Word*, 117.

[105] Sparks, 118–31.

[106] Enns, *Inspiration and Incarnation* (see chap. 5, n. 39); Enns, "Inerrancy, However Defined, Does Not Describe What the Bible Does," in *Five Views on Biblical Inerrancy*, 83–116; also see Peter Enns, *The Bible Tells Me So: Why Defending Scripture Has Made Us Unable to Read It* (New York: HarperOne, 2014); Enns, *How the Bible* Actually *Works* (New York: HarperOne, 2019).

> *Christ's design*. He is over the Bible, beyond it, separate from it, even though the Bible is *his* word and thus bears witness to him.[107]

Similar to the previous examples, Enns draws an analogy to make sense of what Scripture is. But in his case, he draws an incarnation analogy.[108] It is not uncommon in theology to speak of Scripture as analogous to the full deity and humanity of Christ. Herman Bavinck, for example, speaks of the dual nature of Scripture as divine and human, but importantly, unlike Enns, he never concludes that God is unable to keep the human authors from error.[109] But, in contrast to historic theology, Enns insists that the humanity of Scripture entails that God accommodates to the errors of the biblical authors and that Christ in his humanity also erred,[110] at least in the sense that he held to culturally-bound, false ideas of the world.[111] In the end, Enns leaves us with the same problems as all fallibility views. For Scripture to function as an "authority," it cannot do so by itself. It requires an extratextual standard to evaluate what is true and false in Scripture.

Criticism of Neo-Orthodox, Post-Liberal, and Post-Conservative Views of Scripture

What should we think about the neo-orthodox view of Scripture, a view that continues to influence theology today? Many today think that Barth's view is a viable via media between the "received" and the "liberal" view that continues today in much of postmodern theology.[112] However, there are serious problems with the view, and as such, it needs to be rejected. Already in chapter 5, and in subsequent chapters, the biblical and theological grounds for the historic view of Scripture have been developed and will be developed more fully. But presently I offer five problems with the neo-orthodox view of Scripture and some of its current iterations.

First, the view creates a distance between Scripture (i.e., the human texts) and the "*word* of God" that has no biblical warrant. In all versions of the view, God is infallible, the biblical texts as human are necessarily fallible, and there is no direct identity between God's speech/word

---

[107] Enns, *Inspiration and Incarnation*, 98 (emphasis original).
[108] Enns, 5–6.
[109] See Bavinck, *Reformed Dogmatics*, 1:434–48.
[110] Enns, *Inspiration and Incarnation*, 95–99.
[111] Enns, 174–78.
[112] For a discussion of "classic liberalism" and "postmodern" theology, see chapter 2.

and Scripture. As Guy Waters notes, "To say that the Bible may *become* the Word of God and, in that respect, is the Word of God, is different from saying that the Bible *is* the Word of God without qualification."[113] This is why the neo-orthodox view does not affirm that Scripture is *God's* first-order, authoritative, and true revelation through human authors. God's word is one thing and Scripture is another, and the relation between them is only *indirect.*

However, as discussed in chapter 5, Scripture identifies God's word with the biblical texts, a point we will return to in chapters 8–10.[114] The triune God is Creator and Lord, independent and self-sufficient, the source and standard of truth, and when he speaks through created means, there is no evidence that he is limited in his ability to communicate to us. As we move from God's divine voice, to the prophets and apostles, and then to a written text authored by finite, fallen humans, God's word is not diminished, corrupted, or less authoritative and true. No doubt, God, as *archetype* accommodates his speech to us through ordinary human language (ectype), but divine accommodation, in contrast to the neo-orthodox view, does not result in fallibility.[115] God's word accomplishes his plan and purposes, and the very media he uses to speak to us, including human prophets, apostles, and their written texts brings God's word to us in *his* power, authority, and presence. For this reason, what the prophet and apostles say and write *is* God's word (Exod 4:10–16; 20:1–4; 24:3–4; Deut 13:1–5; 18:15–22; Isa 40:8; 66:2; Jer 1:6–19; John 14:25–26; 15:26–27; 16:12–15; 1 Cor 2:10–13; 14:37; Gal 1:1; 2 Thess 3:14; 2 Tim 3:15–17; 2 Pet 1:21; 3:15–16). In fact, in Christ, God the Son/Word incarnate, all of God's word is fulfilled, thus underscoring its authority and truthfulness (Matt 5:17–20; 11:25–28; John 5:19–47; 8:12–30; 14:6; 2 Cor 1:20).[116] This is why Mark Thompson, for

---

[113] Waters, *For the Mouth*, 258–59 (chap. 5, n. 5). Interestingly, N. T. Wright, *The Last Word* (San Francisco: HarperSanFrancisco, 2005) has the same problem. He argues that the authority of Scripture is "the authority of the triune God, exercised somehow *through* Scripture" (23), which seems to create a wedge between God's word and the biblical text. For a critique of Wright, see John M. Frame, "N. T. Wright and the Authority of Scripture," in *Did God Really Say? Affirming the Truthfulness and Trustworthiness of Scripture*, ed. David B. Garner (Phillipsburg: P&R, 2012), 107–27.

[114] See Shead, *A Mouth Full of Fire*, 273–81 (see chap. 5, n. 7); cf. Gibson, "The Answering Speech of Men," 286–88, who makes this point.

[115] The neo-orthodox view and its current iterations adopt a view of divine accommodation that is not true to Scripture and historical orthodoxy. On this point, see Glenn S. Sunshine, "Accommodation Historically Considered," in Carson, *Enduring Authority*, 238–65.

[116] On this point, see Barrett, *Canon, Covenant, and Christology*, 297–315 (see chap. 5, n. 25).

example, in light of what Jesus says about himself and the truthfulness of his word, questions whether "Barth really [was] Christological enough,"[117] a point we will return to in chapter 8.

Second, the neo-orthodox view and its current restatements assume for different reasons that the humanity of Scripture requires, even necessitates, fallibility. But all of the reasons given assume a flawed understanding of the God-world relationship as discussed in chapter 5, which we will return to below. However, before we address the issue of the God-world relation underlying this view of Scripture, there are at least three further problems with this assumption. First, following the Bible's distinction between creation and fall, we cannot equate human nature with fallenness apart from the historic fall. In other words, fallenness is not intrinsic to humanity. Second, in a proper appeal to Christology, our Lord did not sin or err in his office as mediator for us. Some of the current forms of the neo-orthodox view, especially in Sparks and Enns, require Christ in his humanity to be a man of his time and thus fallible in his views of God, self, and the world, which we may "correct" by some extratextual authority. But this Christology is not sustainable as it fails to account for Christ's deity, trinitarian relations, and the work of the Spirit on Christ's humanity, let alone a proper understanding of the hypostatic union.[118] Third, Scripture does not teach that human language, albeit finite, is incapable of truly referring to God and communicating accurately what God intends to be said. In fact, throughout Scripture, the opposite is taught. The humanity of Scripture is not its liability, but its perfection. The beauty of Scripture is that God speaks to us in ordinary language that is true and reliable because it is *his* word. Indeed, the only reason why one thinks that this is impossible leads to the next point, namely, a discussion of the God-world relation that underlies this view of Scripture.

Third, why does the neo-orthodox view and its iterations insist that the humanity of Scripture requires, even necessitates, fallibility? The answer to this question goes back to its *theology* of the God-world relation, which varies depending on the specific restatement of the view. But despite the variances, the conclusion is the same: God *cannot* guarantee that Scripture (i.e., human texts) *is* God's word written, a conclusion opposite to the "received view."

---

[117] Mark D. Thompson, "Barth's Doctrine of Scripture," in *Engaging with Barth: Contemporary Evangelical Critiques*, ed. David Gibson and Daniel Strange (New York: T&T Clark, 2008), 185.

[118] See the Christology section in volume 2 and Christ's view of Scripture in chapter 8. Cf. Barrett, *Canon, Covenant, and Christology*, 297–315.

For example, Barth's view of the God-world relation is dependent on his understanding of divine freedom. God's being is absolute freedom, and he is only known in his acts centered in Christ. Our only access to Christ is by indirect forms of revelation, such as Scripture and preaching. In these forms, including the incarnation, God must continually choose to reveal himself, and in the event of revelation and its reception by us, the forms reveal Christ. But the forms never become the objective word of God. If they did, Barth fears that the Creator-creature distinction would be compromised, and God would not be free in his acts. In a similar way, John Franke argues that the Bible's human texts are *indirectly* God's word by appealing to Barth's unveiling-veiling dialectic. This is why he insists that the Bible's authority is the Spirit's continually speaking *through* Scripture, but is not necessarily tied one-to-one with the biblical texts.[119]

However, the problem with Barth's view is that Scripture does not construe God's freedom and divine sovereignty as he does. Barth agrees that the triune God is a speaker, but then he divorces God's speech from his word, specifically his word through prophets and apostles, and written Scripture. As we discussed in chapter 5, all of God's *ad extra* actions are done by speech. And by his speech, God commands, informs, warns, forgives, calls, comforts, and promises. These speech acts cannot be separated from *him*. In fact, it is by staying true to his word that God reveals himself to be who he is. As God *extraordinarily* acts through the biblical authors, Scripture is both an act and a testament (i.e., word-act revelation) by which God makes himself known and keeps his word. In this way, the canon of Scripture is a collection of diverse speech acts that together identify and render who God is. But is it the case that if God *freely* chooses to reveal himself in such a way that God's freedom is compromised? Barth says, "yes." Scripture says, "no." As Frame rightly argues, "there is something odd about saying that an inerrant

[119] See Franke, "Response to Trueman and Gaffin," 341–43. However, Franke also confuses Barth's dialectic with Reformed theology's archetype/ectype distinction. In Reformed theology, this distinction stresses the Creator-creature distinction: God as Creator and Lord is the source and standard of truth, and human knowledge is a subset of God's knowledge due to divine revelation. But this distinction was never used to affirm that the human words of Scripture are not God's word or that they are fallible. Instead, due to triune, communicative, extraordinary agency, what the authors of Scripture write is precisely what God wants written, and thus, is his word. Scripture is human, but it is also God's own speech in human language. Thus, all biblical language in all of its diversity—because it is God who authorizes it—must be accurate and true, even though it does not give us access to the kind of knowledge that God has. Scripture is sufficient for the purposes God intended.

canonical text places God under our control";[120] Scripture never draws any such inference.[121] In fact, Scripture teaches that, as Frame states,

> God makes covenant promises, by which he *binds himself*. In Christ, all these promises are Yes and Amen (2 Cor. 1:20). God cannot lie or deny himself (2 Tim. 2:13; Titus 1:2; Heb. 6:18). Therefore, his Word abides forever (Isa. 40:8). These divine words constitute a body of truth, a "tradition" (2 Thess. 2:15; 3:6), a faith that was "once for all entrusted to the saints" and for which we are to contend earnestly (Jude 3). . . . Moreover, the biblical writers do not reason that these divine promises compromise God's sovereignty! On the contrary, God's sovereignty is expressed through the irresistible power of his Word . . . God's Word is an instrument of his sovereign rule. It is precisely the case that his sovereignty would be compromised if he did *not* speak such words.[122]

But not everyone who holds to a view of Scripture indebted to Barth holds to his theology of the God-world relation. For example, Greg Boyd argues that the humanity of Scripture requires, even necessitates, fallibility due to *human* freedom. God accommodates himself to the false, culturally conditioned views of humans because he *cannot* keep the human authors free from error due to his weakened view of divine sovereignty. God can only *guarantee* that the biblical authors will write correctly *if* he removes their libertarian freedom and dictates the text. But since God has not dictated the text, Scripture is necessarily fallible due to its humanity. Boyd's view of the human fallibility of Scripture is still tied to his understanding of the God-world relation, as is Barth's, but for different reasons.[123] But, as we will argue in subsequent chapters, both Barth's and Boyd's understanding of the God-world relation is not biblical.

---

[120] Frame, *Doctrine of the Word*, 623.

[121] See Steven J. Duby, "Free Speech: Scripture in the Context of Divine Simplicity and Divine Freedom," *ITQ* 82, no. 3 (2017):197–207. Duby makes this case by appealing to divine simplicity and a more classical view of the God-world relation in contrast to Barth's view of divine freedom and its implications for Scripture.

[122] Frame, *Doctrine of the Word*, 623–24.

[123] See Boyd, *Inspired Imperfection*, 107–8.

Fourth, regardless of the iterations of the neo-orthodox view of Scripture, each one faces similar hermeneutical problems. The biblical texts are fallible, culturally conditioned, mere "witnesses" to God's word, but somehow God is able to take these fallible words and reveal himself to us. But how do we *know* in a warranted way what God is communicating to us if *his* word is not identical with Scripture? Barth tries to preserve the unity of God's speech in the act of taking up Scripture to witness to Christ, but the unity is in the event, *not* Scripture itself.[124] Grenz and Franke argue that the Bible has authority because the Spirit speaks *through* it, but again, the Spirit's speaking is not directly tied to the text (which is also true of Sparks and Enns). That is why exegesis alone cannot discover what the Spirit is speaking.[125] Scripture on its own terms cannot serve as the final court of appeal. For Grenz and Franke, this is furthered by their embrace of a "textual-sense" interpretation model. Since the text now takes on a life of its own apart from the author's illocutions, a serious problem emerges: How does one know what the illocutionary acts of the Spirit are, especially when it is possible for the Spirit to speak independently of the human authors' illocutionary acts?[126]

In all views that do not identify God's word with Scripture, Scripture cannot be appealed to as an objective, final authority. In other words, we cannot warrant our hearing of the Spirit's voice by Scripture itself. But if this is so, then how do we know we are not simply hearing what *we want* to hear? Ultimately, this view of Scripture locates authority in the hearer/reader or, for Grenz and Franke, the community. The locus of authority has shifted from Scripture to the community. But Michael Horton rightly reminds us of the dangers of such a view: "much of modern theology (*especially* Protestant theology) has turned repeatedly to 'what the Spirit is saying to us today' while neglecting or in many cases rejecting rather significant sections of scripture. This done, one can either turn to his or her own inner light or to an authoritative magisterium"[127]—or to a community of believers. But that raises a further question: Which community and which tradition do we listen to? It is a sad fact of church history that there are

[124] See Barth, *CD* I/1, 113–14.

[125] See, once again, Grenz and Franke, *Beyond Foundationalism*, 74–75.

[126] Vanhoozer, *First Theology*, 198, makes this same criticism.

[127] Horton, *Covenant and Eschatology*, 210 (see chap. 2, n. 147).

a variety of church traditions on many central points of doctrine. So, to whom do we listen since every community thinks it is hearing faithfully the Spirit's voice?[128]

In the end, this view of Scripture undercuts our ability to *know* what God says in a warranted, true, objective manner. In the place of an authoritative, God-given text, human subjectivity is crowned. And as J. I. Packer noted years ago, if God's word is not directly identified with Scripture, this "opens the door to allegorizing and turns God's gift of insight into Scripture into the bestowal of uncheckable private revelations."[129] Also, once our interpretations cannot appeal to the objectivity of the text, we are left inevitably with some kind of "canon within a canon" for hearing God's voice, determined not by Scripture but by an extratextual standard. The practical result is this view calls into question the reliability of God's word and his promises. Indeed, "if God is not bound to the intention of the human author, on what basis have God's people expected—or may expect now—His promises in the Bible to come to fulfillment?"[130] Ultimately, we are left with a plurality of meanings in Scripture, errors, and subjectivity, which undercuts the ground for a normative theology, which leads us to the last problem.

Fifth, a neo-orthodox view of Scripture and its iterations undercuts the epistemological grounds for a normative theology. The triune God may serve as the foundation for theology (which neo-orthodoxy confesses), but without a reliable and true word from him, we have no objective, true, warranted speech from him. As we discussed in chapter 3, the foundation for a normative theology is the triune God *who speaks* and who speaks in an authoritative, true, and reliable way that we may know. In the end, the neo-orthodox view requires extratextual criteria to determine its truthfulness, which renders the theological task problematic *on the Bible's own terms*. No longer can Scripture serve as its own self-attesting authority sufficient in itself to warrant our theological conclusions apart from external verification. The transcendental condition for a true, objective knowledge of God is an authoritative, true word-revelation. Apart from such a view of Scripture, theology loses its identity and integrity as a normative discipline, which is precisely the problem with the neo-orthodox view, which is a serious problem indeed!

---

[128] See Kevin J. Vanhoozer, "The Voice and the Actor: A Dramatic Proposal about the Ministry and Minstrelsy of Theology," in *Evangelical Futures: A Conversation on Theological Method*, ed. John G. Stackhouse, Jr. (Grand Rapids: Baker, 2000), 85–87. Vanhoozer raises these same kinds of questions.

[129] Packer, "Encountering Present-Day Views," 73 (see chap. 1, n. 23).

[130] Waters, *For the Mouth*, 264.

The Classic Liberal and Postmodern View of Scripture[131]

On the other end of the spectrum from the "received view" is the classic liberal view of Scripture, which continues today in various forms of postmodern theology. This view rejects both the classic view, with its direct identity between God's word and Scripture, and neo-orthodoxy's indirect identity in favor of a "non-identity" relationship.[132] We can outline the "liberal" view under three headings: revelation, inspiration, and authority.

First, the "liberal" view rejects propositional revelation. It denies that Scripture *is* God's word that yields a true, objective knowledge of God. Instead, it opts for a view of revelation rooted in human experience, today mostly grounded in the God-world relation of panentheism. Hence, God does not reveal propositions about himself; instead, he makes himself known in the religious dimension of common human experience.[133] What this entails, then, is that the Bible is simply the record of human attempts both to understand this revelatory experience and transmit it to the people of God through its religious traditions. The Bible, in other words, should not be viewed as a movement from God to humans or the product of God's sovereign, extraordinary agency in and through human authors. "Modern/postmodern" learning, with its rival descriptions of natural, social, and historical processes indebted to methodological naturalism that either arises from a deistic or panentheistic framework, rejects from the outset the Bible as a document of propositional authority.[134] Thus, John Barton explains, "what is writ-

---

[131] For example, see Friedrich Schleiermacher, *The Christian Faith*, ed. H. R. Mackintosh and J. S. Stewart (1830; repr., New York: T&T Clark, 1999); Barr, *Bible in the Modern World* (see chap. 5, n. 76); Barr, *Beyond Fundamentalism: Biblical Foundations for Evangelical Christianity* (Philadelphia: Westminster Press, 1984); David Tracy, *Blessed Rage for Order* (New York: Seabury Press, 1975); Tracy, *The Analogical Imagination* (New York: Crossroad, 1981); John Barton, *People of the Book? The Authority of the Bible in Christianity* (Louisville: Westminster John Knox Press, 1988); Darrell Jodock, *The Church's Bible: Its Contemporary Authority* (Minneapolis: Fortress Press, 1989).

[132] The phrase "non-identity" is from Vanhoozer, *First Theology*, 133–34.

[133] See Tracy, *Blessed Rage for Order*, 91–171.

[134] In fact, Barr goes so far as to say that because of the acceptance of the modern worldview, he has difficulty even conceiving of something such as propositional revelation. He states,

> The real problem, as it seems to me, is that we have no access to, and no means of comprehending, a communication or revelation from God which is antecedent to the human tradition about him and which then goes on to generate that very tradition. In attempting to found the status of scripture upon such antecedent revelation [propositional revelation] we are

ten in the Bible, with rare exceptions such as certain prophetic oracles, is presented as human words about God, not as words of God to humanity. . . . The Bible is people's reflection on their relationship with the known God: the knowledge, or revelation if you like, lies behind it rather than in it."[135]

Second, the "liberal" view rejects verbal inspiration as historically conceived. Instead, it views "inspiration" as expressing the belief that in *some way* the Bible comes from God, "that he has in some sense a part in its origin, that there is a linkage between the basic mode through which he has communicated with man and the coming into existence of this body of literature."[136] Of course, the great problem for such a view is trying to define the exact nature of this relationship. James Barr's proposal is that we understand it in exactly the same way as God relates to his people today.[137] In fact, that is why Barr identifies the locus of inspiration in *ecclesiology*, not theology proper. In other words, as the people of God acted selectively and critically to sort through their religious traditions and then handed their traditions on to the next generation, God was somehow in contact with his people and present through the whole process, again usually understood along the lines of panentheism. "Inspiration," then, for Barr, "is a way of affirming that God was present in his community in the Spirit as it formed and shaped the traditions that became Scripture."[138] Thus, inspiration has more to do with the readers of Scripture than its authors. Inspiration refers to the Bible's capacity to mediate God's saving intention to the world. God is not the author of Scripture; he is the illuminator of persons who wrote and compiled what they believed to be of enduring value.

Third, the "liberal" view affirms a *functional* view of authority. It rejects Scripture's infallibility and inerrancy. In fact, these are impossible concepts. From beginning to end, the Bible is a human, fallible text created by religious geniuses who are seeking to communicate in words

---

explaining what is obscure by what is quite unknown. I am not saying that there is nothing there; only that (a) its status is too obscure for us to base anything upon, and (b) consideration of it thus becomes a speculative exercise in which we are not called to engage. *Bible in the Modern World*, 121.

[135] Barton, *People of the Book?*, 56.

[136] Barr, *Bible in the Modern World*, 17.

[137] See Barr, 17–18.

[138] Barr, *Beyond Fundamentalism*, 128.

their subjective experiences of God.[139] Scripture's authority, then, is tied to what it does, not what it is. The Bible, as a human document, is the instrument of faith, not its object. As such, Scripture is only authoritative when it shows itself fruitful in the life of the believing community as gauged by some kind of external standard outside of Scripture. Scripture, in the end, is one of the great religious classics of humanity that can be studied as any other book, and it does not yield a true, objective knowledge of God nor a normative theology.

Much could be said against the "liberal" view of Scripture. But ultimately it is a view that stands outside of the historic Christian faith. It assumes an entirely different theology/worldview, and as such, it needs to be rejected as a different religion. For example, first, it rejects what Scripture says about itself. Second, it embraces a different view of God and the God-world relation: initially, deism in the Enlightenment and, now, an evolutionary naturalism. Third, it embraces historical criticism that is grounded in *methodological* naturalism, which stands in direct opposition to historic Christian theology. Fourth, hermeneutically speaking, given Scripture's fallibility, if Scripture is appealed to at all, it is only "authoritative" in light of an external standard, which ultimately is a rejection of Scripture as *God's word*.

Concluding Reflection

Here, then, is a basic spectrum of views of Scripture in our day. Although the "liberal" view has been with us since the Enlightenment, it stands outside of Christian orthodoxy, and it simply needs to be rejected. However, as we noted, some people think that the neo-orthodox view is a viable option for theology today, a view we also reject. For some of the reasons given, it is our contention that it is only the "received view" that is true to Scripture, historic theology, and the transcendental condition for a normative theology. In chapters 8–12, we now turn to the task of expounding and defending the classical view as the only option for theology. We will do so in two steps. First, we will establish that the "received view" is not only true to the tradition of the church but, more significantly, that it is true to Scripture itself by discussing the importance of the self-attestation of Scripture. Second, we will expound further the classical view by unpacking the following theological terms: inspiration, inerrancy, sufficiency, perspicuity, and canon.

---

[139] Jodock, *The Church's Bible*, 58–62; Barr, *Bible in the Modern World*, 25; Barton, *People of the Book?*, 45–46.

CHAPTER 8

Why Receive Scripture as God's Word Written?

Introduction

Why should evangelicals continue to embrace the "received view" in contrast to other views of Scripture, especially current views associated with the influence of neo-orthodoxy? Two answers may be given, but the second is the most significant.

First, the "received view" is the classic view of Scripture throughout church history, and as such, it is the default position. Given its place in the tradition, one needs overwhelming reasons to overturn it; in fact, the burden of proof is on those who desire to do so. No doubt, "tradition" is not the ultimate warrant for any doctrine's truthfulness, yet, as D. A. Carson wisely comments, "Thoughtful Christians who sincerely want to base their beliefs on the Scriptures will be a little nervous if the beliefs they think are biblical form no part of the major streams of tradition throughout the history of the church."[1] Second, and most importantly, evangelicals should continue to affirm without hesitation the "received view" because it is what Scripture teaches about itself in terms of its own "self-attestation." Let us look at both of these in turn.

[1] D. A. Carson, "Recent Developments in the Doctrine of Scripture," in Carson and Woodbridge, *Hermeneutics, Authority, and Canon*, 18 (see chap. 2, n. 63).

The "Received View" as the Historic View of the Church

Until fairly recently, evangelicals and non-evangelicals alike have agreed that the "received view," including an affirmation of the Bible's inerrancy, has been the historic view of the church. For example, Kirsopp Lake, a NT scholar during the Fundamentalist-Modernist controversies of the 1920s–30s, is a good example of this. In an important statement, Lake admits the following:

> It is a mistake, often made by educated men who happen to have little knowledge of historical theology, to suppose that Fundamentalism is a new and strange form of thought. It is nothing of the kind: it is the partial and uneducated survival of theology that was once universally held by all Christians. How many were there, for instance, in the Christian churches, in the eighteenth century, who doubted the infallible inspiration of all Scripture? A few, perhaps, but very few. No, the Fundamentalist may be wrong; I think he is. But it is we who have departed from the tradition, not he, and I am sorry for the fate of anyone who tries to argue with a Fundamentalist on the basis of authority. The Bible and the corpus theologicum of the church is on the Fundamentalist side.[2]

However, since the late 1970s, this view has been challenged by a revisionist historiography, which now, in many places, is embraced without question. A new generation of historians has argued that the conservative view of Scripture, as represented by ICBI,[3] is an aberration of the tradition, something the church has not always believed. In fact, the so-called received view is the product of the "scholastic" theology (viewed negatively) of the post-Reformation era and old Princeton, especially Charles Hodge, A. A. Hodge, and B. B. Warfield. As such, it is more of a "Modernist" invention than the historic position of the church and even of Scripture itself!

One of the best-known works to espouse this view was Jack Rogers and Donald McKim's *The Authority and Interpretation of the Bible.*[4] In this book, they offered a broad sweep of

---

[2] Kirsopp Lake, *The Religion of Yesterday and Tomorrow* (Boston: Houghton Mifflin, 1925), 61–62.

[3] ICBI is the International Council on Biblical Inerrancy, which resulted in the "Chicago Statement on Inerrancy and Hermeneutics," mentioned in chapter 7.

[4] Jack B. Rogers and Donald K. McKim, *The Authority and Interpretation of the Bible: An Historical Approach* (San Francisco: Harper & Row, 1979).

mostly Western church history and argued that the "traditional" view of Scripture is that the Bible is fully authoritative and "infallible" in "faith and practice," but beyond these areas, the Bible is *not* necessarily inerrant.[5] In fact, a belief in biblical inerrancy is "modern"; it is not what the church has believed in previous centuries. In addition, in terms of *accommodation*, they contended that "the Bible was to be interpreted as a document in which God had accommodated his ways and thoughts to our limited, human ways of thinking and speaking."[6] Scripture, then, is fallible except in areas of "faith and practice." Here is a summary of their overall argument.

1. The church fathers did *not* think that inerrancy applied to all areas that Scripture touches, including history and science. Instead, they understood that the *purpose* of the Bible was to lead people to a saving knowledge of God, hence infallibility only applied to "faith and practice."

2. The Reformers (Martin Luther, John Calvin) affirmed that the Bible was infallible in its *saving function*, but they were *not* concerned about *factual errors*. Instead, Luther argued that Scripture is reliable in accomplishing righteousness in the believer, not truthfulness in all areas.

3. The Reformation's view of divine accommodation was that God spoke to us through the "false" ideas of the biblical author's culture, not that God spoke to us in ways appropriate for our understanding yet truthfully on all matters Scripture addresses.[7] However, similar to Karl Barth, due to the internal witness of the Spirit, God is able to speak to us today through a fallible word.

4. A belief in ICBI's view of "inerrancy" is an innovation in church history. Its seeds were sown in the post-Reformation era by Francis Turretin, John Owen, and others, and it reached full bloom in "old Princeton." At Princeton, the Bible was viewed as truthful in *all* areas, and for the first time, inerrancy was restricted to the *original autographs*.

---

[5] Rogers and McKim, 127.

[6] Rogers and McKim, xvii.

[7] This view of accommodation is more akin to Socinianism than Calvin. For Calvin's view, see Calvin, *Institutes*, 1.13.1 (see chap. 1, n. 3). On this point, see Glenn S. Sunshine, "Accommodation Historically Considered," in Carson, *Enduring Authority*, 238–65 (see chap. 4, n. 9). As noted in chapter 7, this view of accommodation is also the view adopted by post-liberalism and post-conservatism.

5. Thus, the concept of inerrancy, as extending to factual details, was not part of the tradition, including for the Reformers. Inerrancy is the result of "modernist" influences tied to the embrace of "classical foundationalism" and an empirical inductive methodology.[8]

Rogers and McKim's book won huge support from post-liberals and post-conservatives, yet their work was seriously flawed, as demonstrated by John Woodbridge in *Biblical Authority*,[9] along with numerous historical essays published by the ICBI. Woodbridge argued the following:

1. Rogers and McKim accused conservatives of reading B. B. Warfield into John Calvin and the church fathers, but the truth is that they read Karl Barth into Calvin and the church fathers.

2. Their book was based on the flawed work of Ernest Sandeen,[10] who wrongly argued that inerrancy tied to the original autographs was first affirmed at old Princeton by A. A. Hodge and B. B. Warfield, and thus was an innovation. "Inerrancy," Sandeen argued, was an apologetic strategy as these men sought to respond to conclusions of higher criticism. But, as Woodbridge demonstrated, there is no evidence for Sandeen's view.

3. Rogers and McKim misunderstood some of their sources, and they quoted other sources with prejudicial selectivity. Repeatedly, they succumbed to an "ahistoricism" that neglected the church's sustained attempt to guard both the form of the message and the message itself. In other words, inerrancy, even in the original autographs, and biblical truthfulness have always been the view of the church, even if "inerrancy" as a word was not always

---

[8] The idea that inerrancy is the result of "modernist" influences is embraced by post-liberalism/post-conservativism, as we noted in chapter 7 in our discussion of Stanley Grenz, John Franke, Kenton Sparks, Peter Enns, and Greg Boyd.

[9] John D. Woodbridge, *Biblical Authority: A Critique of the Rogers/McKim Proposal* (Grand Rapids: Zondervan, 1982). Also see, Paul Kjoss Helseth, *"Right Reason" and the Princeton Mind: An Unorthodox Proposal* (Phillipsburg: P&R, 2010). On Reformation and post-Reformation theology, see Muller, *Post-Reformation Reformed Dogmatics*, vol. 1 (see chap. 3, n. 12); Peter A. Lillback and Richard B. Gaffin, Jr., eds., *Thy Word is Still Truth: Essential Writings on the Doctrine of Scripture from the Reformation to Today* (Phillipsburg: P&R, 2013). Also see the historical essays in the following: Carson, *Enduring Authority*, 43–317; Carson and Woodbridge, ed., *Scripture and Truth*, 199–279 (see chap 2., n. 7); Carson and Woodbridge, *Hermeneutics, Authority, and Canon*, 237–94; Geisler, *Inerrancy*, 357–446 (see chap. 7, n. 4); John D. Hannah, ed., *Inerrancy and the Church* (Chicago: Moody, 1984); Gregg R. Allison, *Historical Theology: An Introduction to Christian Doctrine* (Grand Rapids: Zondervan, 2011), 59–119.

[10] Ernest Sandeen, *The Roots of Fundamentalism: British and American Millenarianism, 1800–1930* (Chicago: University of Chicago Press, 1970).

used. Here are some selected examples from church history that demonstrate the error of their view.[11]

- *Clement of Rome* (c. 100) in reference to the OT: "You have searched the Scriptures, which are true, which were given by the Holy Spirit; you know that nothing unrighteous or counterfeit is written in them."[12]
- *Irenaeus* (125–202). After repeatedly quoting Scripture, he writes: "We should leave things of that nature to God who created us, being most properly assured that the Scriptures are indeed perfect, since they were spoken by the Word of God and His Spirit."[13]
- *Tertullian* (150–225): "The statements of Holy Scripture will never be discordant with truth."[14]
- *Justin Martyr* (100–165) denied that Scripture contradicts itself: "Since I am entirely convinced that no Scripture contradicts another, I shall admit rather that I do not understand what is recorded, and shall strive to persuade those who imagine that the Scriptures are contradictory, to be rather of the same opinion as myself."[15]
- *Augustine* (354–430). He addresses the inerrancy of Scripture in numerous places.
    1. Augustine argues that if we were to admit there was one error in the sacred text, the result would be to call into question its authority. The reason for this consequence is that any statement of Scripture that imposed a difficult belief or duty could then be explained in terms of error. He states,

        > It seems to me that the most disastrous consequences must follow upon our believing that anything false is found in the sacred books: that is to say that the men by whom the Scripture has been given to us, and committed to writing, did put down in these books anything false. . . . If you once admit into such a high sanctuary of authority one false statement, . . . there will not be left a single sentence of those books which, if appearing to any one difficult

[11] For these examples and many more, see the resources in n. 9.

[12] Clement of Rome, *Letter of the Romans to the Corinthians* 45 (*ANF* 1:17).

[13] Irenaeus, *Against Heresies* 2.28.2 (*ANF* 1:399).

[14] Tertullian, *A Treatise on the Soul* 21 (*ANF* 3:202).

[15] Justin Martyr, *Dialogue with Trypho, a Jew* 65 (*ANF* 4:230).

> in practice or hard to believe, may not by the same fatal rule be explained away, as a statement in which, intentionally, . . . the author declared what was not true.[16]

2. Augustine in another place writes,

    > I have learned to yield this respect and honor only to the canonical books of Scripture: of these alone do I most firmly believe that the authors were completely free from error. And if in these writings I am perplexed by anything which appears to me opposed to truth, I do not hesitate to suppose that either the manuscript is faulty, or the translator has not caught the meaning of what was said, or I myself have failed to understand it.[17]

3. Augustine responds to the charge that the Gospels are contradictory or conflicting with each other. He writes: "And in order to carry out this design to a successful conclusion, we must prove that the writers in question do not stand in any antagonism to each other. For those adversaries are in the habit of adducing this as the primary allegation in all their vain objections, namely that the evangelists are not in harmony with each other."[18]
4. Augustine even addressed the issue of accommodation. As John Woodbridge contends, for Augustine accommodation meant Scripture was written in ordinary language, that is, the language of appearance, but this did not entail error as in Socinian theology, the view taught by Rogers and McKim and current forms of post-liberalism/post-conservativism. For Augustine, "the Bible may describe the natural world simply, but truthfully as it is."[19]

- *Anselm* (1033–1109): "For I am sure that if I say anything which is undoubtedly contradictory to Holy Scripture, it is wrong."[20]

---

[16] Augustine, *Letters of St. Augustine* 28.3 (*NPNF*[1] 1:251–52).

[17] Augustine, *Letters of St. Augustine* 82.1.3 (*NPNF*[1] 1:350).

[18] Augustine, *Harmony of the Gospels* 1.7.10 (*NPNF*[1] 6:81).

[19] John D. Woodbridge, "Evangelical Self-Identity and the Doctrine of Biblical Inerrancy," in *Understanding the Times: New Testament Studies in the 21st Century*, ed. Andreas J. Köstenberger and Robert W. Yarbrough (Wheaton: Crossway, 2011), 112–13.

[20] Anselm, *Why God Became Man* 1.18, in *Anselm of Canterbury: The Major Works*, ed. Brian Davies and G. R. Evans (Oxford: Oxford University Press, 1998), 298.

- *Thomas Aquinas* (1225–74): In commenting on the Bible's truthfulness that impacts our reading of it: "It is plain that nothing false can ever underlie the literal sense of Holy Writ."[21]
- *Johannes Eck* (1496–1543). Eck interacted with Erasmus, who suggested that Matthew may have made a mistake. Eck writes: "Listen, dear Erasmus: do you suppose any Christian will patiently endure to be told that the evangelists in their Gospels made mistakes?"[22] Eck continues arguing the same point Augustine argued a millennium earlier: even if *one* word was wrongly substituted for another by a biblical author (something Erasmus suggested), Scriptural authority would be affected. Thus, long before the nineteenth century, people like Eck, following Augustine, argued for the full reliability of Scripture.
- *Martin Luther* (1483–1546). The Reformation debate with the Roman Catholic Church was more over the *sources* of authority than the *nature* of authority. Nevertheless, Luther could write for the Bible's full authority and reliability. Repeatedly, for Luther, as Robert Preus demonstrates, "the notion of an authoritative but *errant* Word of God would have been utter nonsense."[23] Preus offers numerous citations that prove this point: "He who adheres to the Scriptures will find that they do not lie or deceive"; "Scripture cannot err"; "The Scriptures have never erred"; "If Scripture seems to err, it is our fault for not understanding it properly or yielding to it"; "Scripture agrees with itself everywhere"; "It is impossible that the Scriptures should contradict themselves; it only appears that way to the senseless and the obstinate."[24] For Luther, *sola Scriptura* meant that the tradition, the church fathers, and the councils may err, but Scripture never errs.
- *William Whitaker* (1548–95). He writes:

  > But, say they [the Roman Church], the church never errs; the pope never errs. We shall shew both assertions to be false in the proper place. We say that scripture

---

[21] Thomas Aquinas, *Summa Theologica*, pt. 1, q. 1, art. 10 (see chap. 2, n. 20).

[22] Letter 769, from Johann Maier von Eck, February 2, 1518, in *The Correspondence of Erasmus* (Toronto: University of Toronto Press, 1979), 5:289.

[23] Robert D. Preus, "The View of the Bible Held by the Church: The Early Church Through Luther," in Geisler, *Inerrancy*, 379.

[24] Cited in Preus, 379–80.

> never errs, and therefore judge that interpretation to be the truest which agrees with scripture. What have we to do with churches, or councils, or popes, unless they can show that what they define is in harmony with the scriptures?[25]

- *Francis Turretin* (1623–87). In the writing of Scripture, Turretin argued that the biblical authors

  > were so acted upon and inspired by the Holy Spirit (as to the things themselves and as to the words) as to be kept free from all error and that their writings are truly authentic and divine. . . . The prophets did not fall into mistakes in those things which they wrote as inspired men (*theopneustōs*) and as prophets, not even in the smallest particulars; otherwise faith in the whole of Scripture would be rendered doubtful.[26]

- *Richard Baxter* (1615–91): "No error or contradiction is in it [Scripture], but what is in some copies, by failure of preservers, transcribers, printers, and translators."[27]
- *Richard Simon* (1638–1712). On the first page of *Critical History of the Old Testament*, Simon generalized about the current belief of Christians and Jews concerning the reliability of Scripture in 1678. He writes:

  > One is not able to doubt that the truths contained in Holy Scripture are infallible and of a divine authority, since they come immediately from God, who in doing this used the ministry of men as his interpreters. Is there anyone, either Jew or Christian, who does not recognize that this Scripture being the pure Word of God, is at the same time the first principle and the foundation of Religion. But in that men have been the depositories of Sacred Books, as well as all other books, and that the first Originals had been lost; it was in some measure impossible that a number of changes occurred, due as much to the length of time passing, as to the negligence of copyists. It is for this reason St. Augustine recommends before all things to those who wish to study Scripture

[25] William Whitaker, *A Disputation on Holy Scripture, against the Papists, Especially Bellarmine and Stapleton*, trans. and ed. William Fitzgerald (1588; repr., Morgan, PA: Soli Deo Gloria, n.d.), 476.

[26] Turretin, *Institutes of Elenctic Theology*, 1:62, 1:69 (see chap. 3, n. 55).

[27] Cited in Warfield, "Inerrancy of the Original Autographs," in *Selected Shorter Writings*, 2:586 (see chap. 1, n. 7).

> to apply themselves to the Criticism of the Bible and to correct the mistakes of their copies.[28]

Here we not only have a general statement about what all Jews and Christians believe about Scripture in 1678 but also the continuation of the need for "textual criticism" as a legitimate endeavor.

- *A. A. Hodge* (1823–1886) and *B. B. Warfield* (1851–1921). They write:

  > the historical faith of the Church has always been that all the affirmations of Scripture of all kinds, whether of spiritual doctrine or duty, or of physical or historical fact, or of psychological or philosophical principle, are without any error when the *ipsissima verba* of the original autographs are ascertained and interpreted in their natural and intended sense.[29]

  They continue in their summary of the Reformation tradition:

  > It is not questionable that the great historic churches have held these creed definitions in the sense of affirming the errorless infallibility of the Word. This is everywhere shown by the way in which all the great bodies of Protestant theologians have handled Scripture in their commentaries, systems of theology, catechisms and sermons. And this has always been pre-eminently characteristic of epochs and agents of reformation and revival. All the great world-moving men, as Luther, Calvin, Knox, Wesley, Whitefield and Chalmers, and proportionately those most like them, have so handled the Divine Word.[30]

- More names could be added (e.g., Benjamin Keach, John Gill, Andrew Fuller, J. P. Boyce, Basil Manly Jr., Abraham Kuyper, Herman Bavinck, J. Gresham Machen, etc.). But the point is that from the first century to the twenty-first, the "received view" is the "classical" view.
- This truth is also confirmed in the confessional standards of the church, such as the *Belgic Confession* (1561), the *Westminster Confession of Faith* (1647), and the *London Baptist Confession* (1689). For example, the *Westminister Confession* and the *London*

[28] Richard Simon, *Histoire critique du Vieux Testament* (Rotterdam: Reinier Leers, 1685), 1. Cited in Woodbridge, "Evangelical Self-Identity and the Doctrine of Biblical Inerrancy," 116.

[29] A. A. Hodge and B. B. Warfield, *Inspiration* (1881; repr., Grand Rapids: Baker, 1979), 28.

[30] Hodge and Warfield, *Inspiration*, 33.

> *Baptist Confession* are similar in their affirmation of a high view of Scripture, along with the Roman Catholic Church, despite debates over the role of tradition and the magisterium. Currently, the *Baptist Faith and Message* also affirms what the church has confessed over time.[31]

Although Rogers and McKim were thoroughly answered, revisionist historiography remains. Since their work, the "modernist" charge continues by those who insist that the Princetonians were unduly influenced by Thomas Reid's common-sense realism philosophy. Charles Hodge was isolated as the problem. As the story goes, Hodge was too "inductivist" in his methodology, only focusing on the "facts" and "truths" of Scripture at the expense of knowing God.[32] But once again, this "newer" version of the thesis fails. However much common-sense realism affected the Princetonians (which has been greatly exaggerated), it certainly did not affect the early church or European theologians (e.g., Herman Bavinck and Abraham Kuyper).[33] Interestingly, the Dutch school rejected Thomas Reid's view and critiqued Hodge's theological method. Yet they still held to the same view of Scripture.[34] For example, Bavinck distinguished his theological method from Hodge's "inductive" method. Scripture as a word-act revelation "does not merely convey the facts that we have to explain, but itself clearly illumines those facts."[35] But despite Bavinck's rejection of Hodge's epistemology and method, he held to the same view of Scripture.[36]

In summary, why is this discussion significant? At least three points need to be made.

---

[31] See *Westminster Confession of Faith* (1647) (1.1–10); *London Baptist Confession* (1689) (1.1–10); *Baptist Faith and Message* (2000) (1) at https://bfm.sbc.net/bfm2000/#i; and the current *Roman Catholic Catechism* (1.1.2, article 3.2) at https://www.vatican.va/archive/ENG0015/__PP.HTM.

[32] See George M. Marsden, *Fundamentalism and American Culture: The Shaping of Twentieth Century Evangelicalism 1870–1925* (New York: Oxford University Press, 1980).

[33] See Bradley N. Seeman, "The 'Old Princetonians' on Biblical Authority," in Carson, *Enduring Authority*, 195–237.

[34] Richard B. Gaffin Jr., *God's Word in Servant-Form: Abraham Kuyper and Herman Bavinck on the Doctrine of Scripture* (Jackson, MS: Reformed Academic Press, 2008).

[35] Bavinck, *Reformed Dogmatics*, 1:94 (see chap. 1, n. 9).

[36] Regrettably, Rogers and McKim's discredited view continues without warrant. See Grenz and Franke, *Beyond Foundationalism*, 23–24, 35–37, 60–63 (see chap. 1, n. 35); cf. John R. Franke, "Recasting Inerrancy: The Bible as Witness to Missional Plurality," in Merrick and Garrett, *Five Views on Biblical Inerrancy*, 261–64 (see chap. 7, n. 10); Dennis R. Bratcher, "Thinking about the Bible Theologically: Inerrancy, Inspiration, and Revelation," in *Rethinking the Bible*, ed. Richard P. Thompson and Thomas Jay Oord (Nampa, ID: SacraSage, 2018), 49–50.

First, it can be demonstrated that the "received view" is the historic view of Scripture held in every age of the church except in our most recent age. Regardless of the influence of diverse epistemologies on theology (e.g., Platonism, Aristotelianism, common-sense realism, etc.), Christians have articulated the same view of Scripture. Why? Because despite those influences, the church has remained faithful to Scripture's own testimony, a point we will return to below.

Second, although tradition does not establish the truth of Scripture, it does establish what the church has believed. This is important because if one insists that the "received view" cannot be maintained today, one has to first admit that one is walking away from the tradition of the church, *and* the burden of proof is on those who reject the historic position of the church.

Third, building on the last point, since the "received view" is *the* view of the church, then to continue to use the label "Christian," "evangelical," or even "Baptist" and deny the tradition is dishonest. Instead, the honesty of a Kirsopp Lake is preferred. He knew that his rejection of the "received view" was against the tradition of the church. Unfortunately, today, too many people want to identify with historic Christianity and then surrender its key points. One is free to do so, but the burden of proof is on that person to explain why and on what theological grounds they do so. Even more, they need to give a rational accounting for their own theology and worldview and demonstrate how they can warrant objective truth and a normative theology. If they cannot, as J. Gresham Machen rightly argued, we are dealing with different theologies and worldviews.

So why should evangelicals, including Baptists, continue to embrace the "received view"? The first answer: it is the historic view of the church. But this answer is not sufficient. Tradition is never our ultimate epistemological warrant; only Scripture is, a point to which we now turn.

The "Received View" and the Self-Attestation of Scripture

Scripture as a "Self-Attesting" Authority

Throughout the ages, the church has consistently affirmed that Scripture *is* God's Word written, the product of triune communicative action whereby human authors freely wrote what God intended to be written and without error. Why has the church claimed this for Scripture? For this reason: this is what Scripture claims for itself. The Bible, then, is not authoritative because the church has desired it to be or conferred authority on it. Rather Scripture is received as God's word because it is the word of the triune Creator and Lord, who plans and knows all things and, through the agency of human authors, speaks with all authority and power.

This is what is meant by the "self-attestation" of Scripture, and although the "received view" is the historic view of the church, Scripture as a self-attesting authority is uniquely a Reformation argument.[37] The Roman Church affirmed that Scripture is God's word, but it rejected the self-attestation of Scripture and its corollary, *sola Scriptura*. At stake was whether Scripture is authoritative "in and of itself (*in se* and *per se*) [so that] no external authority, whether church or tradition, need be invoked in order to ratify Scripture as the norm of faith and practice."[38] Rome sought to authorize Scripture *ultimately* by appeal to the magisterium. However, the Reformers authorized Scripture by appeal to Scripture.[39] But the self-attestation of Scripture was not merely a dispute between the theology of Rome and the Protestant Reformers; it is also of vital importance *for Christian theology* for at least three reasons.

First, if Scripture does not claim to be God's word, we cannot make it so by conferring an alien authority on it.[40] Our belief about what Scripture *is* must be consistent with its own claims. In theology and apologetics, when we evaluate the claim of any worldview, we must first begin with its specific claims (including its metaphysic, epistemology, and ethic). The same is true for Christianity. If we are to understand *and* evaluate the claims of Christian theology, we must first let the Bible identify itself given that it is the cognitive foundation (*principium cognoscendi*) for our worldview. When we do, we discover that Scripture, on its

---

[37] Calvin, *Institutes*, 1.7.5. The term for "self-attestation" is *autopistos*, i.e., "trustworthy in and of itself." See Richard A. Muller, *Dictionary of Latin and Greek Theological Terms* (Grand Rapids: Baker, 1985), 54.

[38] Muller, *Dictionary of Latin and Greek*, 54.

[39] See Martin Luther, *What Luther Says: An Anthology*, ed. Ewald M. Plass, 3 vols. (St. Louis: Concordia, 1959), 1:85–90, 405. Calvin (*Institutes*, 1.7.1) writes: "A most pernicious error widely prevails that Scripture has only so much weight as is conceded to it by the consent of the church. As if the eternal and inviolable truth of God depended upon the decision of men!" The church does not confer authority on Scripture; instead, it *recognizes* Scripture's inherent authority due to divine inspiration (Calvin, *Institutes*, 1.7.2). As Calvin continues: "Our opponents [the Roman Catholic Church] locate the authority of the church outside God's Word; but we insist that it be attached to the Word, and do not allow it to be separated from it" (*Institutes*, 4.8.13).

[40] See John Murray, "The Attestation of Scripture," in Stonehouse and Woolley, *Infallible Word*, 17–40 (see chap. 3, n. 58); James M. Grier Jr., "The Apologetic Value of the Self-Witness of Scripture," *Grace Theological Journal* 1 (1980): 71–76.

own terms, claims to be the word of the triune Creator and Lord. And as God-given, the Bible bears the marks of divine origin as God's true and sufficient word to know him, ourselves, and the world. This does *not* entail that simply a claim to divine speech makes it legitimate, a point we will discuss below. But it is to say that in evaluating the truth of Christianity and its epistemological foundation, we must first begin with Scripture's self-attestation. Furthermore, if Scripture *does* make such a claim for itself, given the nature of the claim, we cannot simply dismiss it without giving reasons why the biblical claim is false. In fact, the nature of the claim to dismiss it already assumes that the person has grounds to do so, which is the precise point at dispute.

Second, given the God-word relation as discussed in chapter 5, Scripture's claim for itself is also a witness to a *specific* view of God. Who is the God of the Bible? He is the one who is in a category all by himself as the triune Creator and Lord, independent and *a se* in his existence, knowledge, and ground to moral norms. As such, *this* God by nature is alone able to witness to himself. No finite created thing is self-attesting; only God is. Thus, only God can identify *his* word and speak for his creatures on his own authority (cf. Heb 6:13). To think otherwise is to elevate some created thing to the status of God himself and to deny Scripture's own teaching regarding the Creator-creature distinction. In fact, it is to appeal to something "outside" (i.e., extratextual) of *God's* word as more authoritative than *him*, hence people think that this "outside" standard can stand in judgment of Scripture. But just as Job learned his understanding was not equal to God's knowledge (Job 38–41), we must learn that appeals to philosophy, science, archaeology, current scholarship, or my own "constructed" (subjective) identity are never *ultimate*; these things are only finite and without objective universal warrant.

In other words, given the scriptural claim that is inseparably tied to the *specific* God of the Bible (in contrast to a generic theism, panentheism, or some other conception of "god"), a message claiming to be from *him* has to be self-attesting since *his* word, of necessity, is the *ultimate* authority that authorizes itself.[41] Certainly more needs to be said in our defense of Scripture and the Christian worldview, but not less. Calvin beautifully captures this point when he insists that "God alone is a fit witness of himself in his Word. . . . Scripture is indeed

[41] See Van Til, *Survey of Christian Epistemology*, 29–30 (see chap. 1, n. 49); cf. Grier, "Apologetic Value of the Self-Witness of Scripture," 73.

self-authenticated."[42] Or, as Bavinck rightly notes, Scripture as our *principium* ("first principle") must be "believed on its own account, not on account of something else . . . Scripture's authority with respect to itself depends on Scripture."[43] For this reason, the Protestant confessions clearly affirm the self-attestation of Scripture and insist that it is the *ultimate* reason why we believe Scripture to be what it is. For example, the *London Baptist Confession* (1689) (1.4), following the *Westminster Confession of Faith* (1.4), states: "The authority of the Holy Scripture, for which it ought to be believed, depends not upon the testimony of any man or church; but wholly upon God (who is truth itself), the author thereof; therefore it is to be received because it is the Word of God." Scripture's self-attestation is organically related to the God that Scripture attests to.

Third, given that Scripture is the cognitive foundation for all of our theological formulations, any doctrine of the Christian faith, *including our doctrine of Scripture*, must be warranted by Scripture, not merely Scripture in some narrow sense or some isolated texts taken out of context, but the entire, unified word of God centered in Christ.[44] Greg Bahnsen captures this point well: "The substantial message of the Bible taken as a whole as God's word (its content)—not simply the claim that it is God's word—is referred to when 'the testimony' is said to be authorized by the divine testimony itself."[45] No doubt, this leads to a kind of "circularity" in our doctrine of Scripture, but this is to be expected. When it comes to *ultimate* criterions in anyone's worldview, an argument of this sort is unavoidable, and if we think otherwise, we are not honest with how epistemological warrant functions in worldview discussions.[46] As already stated in previous chapters, Christian theology is like a seamless robe

---

[42] Calvin, *Institutes*, 1.7.4–5.

[43] Bavinck, *Reformed Dogmatics*, 1:458.

[44] This point has been affirmed throughout church history. For example, Thomas Aquinas makes clear that sacred doctrine only appeals to other authorities in a probable way, but appeal is made to "the authority of the canonical Scriptures as an incontrovertible proof. . . . For our faith rests upon the revelation made to the apostles and prophets, who wrote the canonical books, and not on the revelations (if any such there are) made to other doctors." Aquinas, *Summa Theologica* (Notre Dame: Christian Classics, 1948), 1:6.

[45] Bahnsen, *Van Til's Apologetic*, 202 (see chap. 1, n. 4).

[46] On the issue of "circularity," see John M. Frame, *Apologetics: A Justification of Christian Belief* (Phillipsburg: P&R, 2015), 10–18; D. A. Carson, "Approaching the Bible," in *New Bible Commentary: 21st Century Edition*, ed. Gordon J. Wenham et al. (Downers Grove: InterVarsity, 1994), 9–10; Grier, "Apologetic Value of the Self-Witness of Scripture," 75–76.

or an organic whole grounded in theology proper. Since God is the final court of appeal, our ultimate appeal for Scripture is to *God's* word. Otherwise, as Michael Kruger notes, "To deny circularity when it comes to an ultimate authority is to subject oneself to an infinite regress of reasons."[47] God's word of necessity must be our *ultimate* criterion for warranting *any* theological doctrine, including our doctrine of Scripture.[48] In the Reformation, an affirmation of the self-attestation of Scripture stood contrary to the view of the Roman Church, and today, it stands contrary to all extratextual theologies that think they can warrant Scripture by something external to it, whatever that "outside" criterion may be.

From this discussion a significant entailment follows. Given the Scriptural claim for itself, biblical authority and inerrancy necessarily follow.[49] Why? For this reason: how can Scripture serve as theology's *ultimate* warrant if it is not trustworthy? *If,* at any point, Scripture is false in its "facts" and "word/theological interpretation" of the facts, then *any* statement of Scripture *may be false.* And if any statement of Scripture may be false, the only way to determine what is true is by a standard *outside* of Scripture. But if this is so, then Scripture is no longer the necessary *and* sufficient authority for our theology. It is no longer the warrant for any doctrine based on the Bible's *own say so.* In the end, we have to say that the Bible teaches this point, but this point is *ultimately* warranted by something "outside" of Scripture. This is why Reformed theology has always insisted that *sola Scriptura* entails biblical authority *and* inerrancy. No wonder our doctrine of Scripture is so important and foundational to the entire theological enterprise!

What about Other Claims to Divine Authority?

From our previous discussion, an obvious question arises: What about other claims to divine authority? This is an important and legitimate question, and three points need to be considered.

First, we must remember that *not* all claims to divine authority are equal. In fact, as we study other worldviews/religions, very few of them make any claim close to what Scripture

[47] Michael J. Kruger, "The Sufficiency of Scripture in Apologetics," *TMSJ* 12 (2001): 81, n. 31.

[48] Of course, this whole discussion has a bearing on apologetic methodology. For a helpful discussion of this applied to apologetics, see Bahnsen, *Van Til's Apologetic.*

[49] See chapter 3 for a discussion of this point. For a similar argument, see Nigel M. de S. Cameron, "The Logic of Biblical Authority," in *The Challenge of Evangelical Theology: Essays in Approach and Method*, ed. Nigel M. de S. Cameron (Edinburgh: Rutherford House, 1987), 1–16.

claims. For example, in Hinduism or Buddhism, their "holy" books do not claim to give objective, universal truth that yields a normative theology. Why? For this reason: their view of the god-word relation (or, their entire metaphysic, epistemology, and ethic) cannot substantiate such a claim. On *their* own terms, they deny any concept of the Creator-creature distinction, which results in a "god" who is not triune and who cannot plan, know, and govern all things, thus rendering a strong epistemological claim impossible. The only religions that even come close to making a strong truth claim are those views that live off the "borrowed capital" of Christianity (e.g., Islam, and various cults—Mormonism, Jehovah's Witnesses, etc.), hence the reason they are rightly viewed as Christian "heresies." However, even though these views make a similar *formal* claim (i.e., the Qur'an is Allah's word or the Book of Mormon is God's final revelation), when we investigate each view's specific *material* content, we discover that they cannot "make good" on their claims *on their own terms*. Claims to divine authority are inseparably tied to each worldview's specific theology. When the entire worldview package is investigated, including its claim to divine authority, we quickly discover that these "other" authority claims are *internally* contradictory, which renders their claim false.[50] Islam is an example of this point, which leads to our next point.

Second, Islam makes a similar "formal" claim to divine authority as Christianity, grounded in its monotheistic concept of Allah.[51] Islam claims that the Qur'an is from Allah and, thus, is a self-attesting authority. So how do we arbitrate between the self-attesting claims of Christianity and Islam? The answer: we press further into the specific material claims that Islam makes and ask whether Islam can "make good" on its *own* claims. When we do, we discover that their claim to divine authority is internally contradictory and thus self-defeating.

---

[50] An "internal" contradiction results when a worldview's own claims cannot be substantiated, which is the strongest way to evaluate the truthfulness of a worldview *on its own terms*.

[51] In our discussion of Islam, we cannot explain the entire theology of Islam, which is necessary if we are to adequately compare and contrast it with Christianity. In our discussion, we are simply pointing out a crucial *internal* problem for Islam, which renders it self-defeating. For an exposition and critique of Islam, see Norman L. Geisler and Abdul Saleeb, *Answering Islam: The Crescent in Light of the Cross* (Grand Rapids: Baker, 1993); James R. White, *What Every Christian Needs to Know About the Qur'an* (Minneapolis: Bethany House, 2013); Nabeel Qureshi, *No God But One: Allah or Jesus?* (Grand Rapids: Zondervan, 2016); and Matthew Bennett, *40 Questions About Islam* (Grand Rapids: Kregel, 2020); Ayman S. Ibrahim, *A Concise Guide to the Quran: Answering Thirty Questions* (Grand Rapids: Baker Academic, 2020).

Why? If we take seriously the material claims of the Qur'an, we will have to question its truthfulness. For example, Islam claims that the Qur'an is the final revelation of three previous revelations—the Law of Moses (Torah), the Psalms of David, and the Gospel of Jesus.[52] Although we could discuss how Islam's view of the Bible is already false,[53] our point here is that when you compare the Qur'an to the Bible, the Qur'an contradicts the Bible on significant historical and theological details, which renders Islam's claim to divine authority internally incoherent.[54] One cannot assert that the previous revelations are from God and then have the final revelation contradict them. Islam's "formal" claim of divine authority is ultimately undercut by its "material" content.

How does Islam respond to its own "internal" problem? Usually, Islam responds by claiming that the Bible has been corrupted. But there are serious problems with this claim. First, the Qur'an never actually claims that the text of the Bible has been corrupted, only that it has been misinterpreted, hence the Qur'an can appeal to Christians to go back to Scripture. Second, there is no evidence that the Bible has been corrupted, thus making it an arbitrary claim that cannot be substantiated historically. Third, the sheer logic of this kind of corruption makes no sense even within the context of Muslim theology. Obviously, what we have stated only scratches the surface, but our point is that even if there are other claims to divine authority, this does not entail that all claims to divine authority are legitimate. We must still

[52] For this claim in the Qur'an, see surahs (chapters) 2:40–41, 136; 4:150–152, 163; 5:43–47, 68; 10:95; 21:7; 62:5.

[53] For example, there is no "Gospel of Jesus" as if Jesus, like Muhammad, was given a dictated word from God. In the NT, we have four Gospels that explain who Jesus is. What this reveals is that a Christian view of Scripture, divine revelation, inspiration, and so on is *not* the same as Islam. Although there is a "formal" claim of divine authority for both views, even the "formal" claim means something entirely different for Christianity and Islam.

[54] For example, on historical details, the Qur'an contradicts the Bible. Here are three examples: (1) one of Noah's sons died in the flood (11:42–43; cf. 21:76); (2) Miriam is confused with Mary, Jesus's mother (19:27–33); and (3) Jesus was not crucified (4:157)! On theological details, the Qur'an denies (1) the Trinity (4:166–172; 5:68–77; 5:116; 29:46), (2) Christ as the eternal Son (9:30; 21:24–26), and (3) Christ's deity (5:116). On these theological points, it is evident that the Qur'an has little to no knowledge of the doctrine of the Trinity or Christology, even though it postdates the orthodox definitions of both of these doctrines at Nicaea (325) and Chalcedon (451). But note: in these crucial mistakes, the Qur'an demonstrates that its "claim" to divine authority is self-defeating.

evaluate the material content of a worldview's claims *on its own terms*. In the case of Islam, despite the "formal" similarity of the authority claim, "materially" it is rendered internally self-defeating.[55]

Third, is there a positive case that can be made to demonstrate the authority and truthfulness of Scripture other than merely claiming it is a self-attesting authority? The answer is yes, but it will begin with self-attestation for the reasons noted above. Yet the Bible's claim is not merely "formal"; it also has "material" content. The question, then, is whether the Bible can "make good" on its claims, unlike Islam. On this point, at least three points need to be said.

1. Our defense of Scripture is part of an overall worldview argument. To defend the Bible's view of itself also requires a defense of the Bible's view of God, creation, providence, miracles, humans, sin, redemption, and so on since we cannot make sense of the Bible's claim of *divine* authority, inspiration, or human authorship without an entire *theology* in place. Again, this should not surprise us. Worldviews/theologies come to us as whole "packages" and not isolated pieces.

2. Given that Christian theology is a "package," our overall defense of Scripture is that without the entire "package" (i.e., specific view of God, self, and the world and the metaphysic, epistemology, and ethic it assumes), we could not account for what we must assume to reason at all. In other words, without the entire worldview, the preconditions for knowledge, truth, logic, morality, human dignity, and so on, would be unwarranted, a point we noted briefly in chapter 3.

3. Building on these points, the positive case for Scripture minimally involves three mutually dependent and interrelated steps. First, we begin with the Bible's *formal* claim for itself. Second, we demonstrate that the Bible can make good on its *material* claims. One crucial claim, as we will discuss below, is that Scripture claims to be God's unified revelation from creation to Christ. This is why a significant argument for Scripture is that it is written over a 1,500-year span by some forty different authors, yet it is a unified message centered in Christ. In part 3, we will develop the Bible's overall metanarrative, which further demonstrates this point. But here we note that, unlike Islam, Christians did not jettison the OT because it did not fit with the "new" revelation in Christ. Instead, Jesus, the apostles, and the church received

---

[55] The self-defeating claim for Islam can also be demonstrated for Mormonism and other claims to divine authority. For example, see James R. White, *Is the Mormon My Brother? Discerning the Differences between Mormonism and Christianity* (Port St. Lucie, FL: Solid Ground Books, 2008).

the OT *as Scripture* and argued that it was intended by God to reveal, anticipate, and predict the coming of the Messiah Jesus, hence canon included the OT *and* the NT. Third, we show that the Bible can "make good" on its *historical* claims unlike other "holy" books."[56]

More can be said. However, our point is that our *ultimate* reason for believing that Scripture *is* God's word is due to its self-attestation, and not all claims to divine authority are equal. Furthermore, although self-attestation is the ultimate reason why we believe Scripture to be what it is, this does not entail that we do not defend the Bible's claim about itself to be true. But as we do, we must do so consistent with the Bible's own terms, theology, and teaching. In the remainder of this chapter, we will develop the Bible's claim for itself, which is foundational to our subsequent exposition of the doctrine of Scripture. However, not surprisingly, some have challenged that Scripture is a self-attesting word. So, we will first look at that challenge before we conclude that it is wrong since Scripture, from beginning to end, if read on its own terms, claims to be God's authoritative word written.

A Challenge and Defense of the Self-Attestation of Scripture

The Challenge

Historical critics, tied to their embrace of methodological naturalism and rejection of historic Christian theology, have always challenged whether Scripture claims to be God's word. In recent years, James Barr represents this kind of criticism. In his dismissive manner, Barr writes:

> According to conservative arguments, it is not only Jesus who made "claims"; the Bible made "claims" about itself. The book of Daniel "claims" to have been written by a historical Daniel some time in the sixth century BC; the book of Deuteronomy "claims" to have been written by Moses; and more important still, the Bible as a whole "claims" to be divinely inspired. All this is nonsense. There is no "the Bible" that "claims" to be divinely inspired, there is no "it" that has a "view of itself." There is only this or that source, like 2 Timothy or 2 Peter, which makes statements about certain

---

[56] On the historical reliability of Scripture, see Blomberg, *Historical Reliability of the New Testament* (see chap. 5, n. 93); Hoffmeier and Magary, *Do Historical Matters Matter?* (see chap. 5, n. 93); Cowan and Wilder, *In Defense of the Bible* (see chap. 5, n. 93).

> other writings, these rather undefined. There is no such thing as "the Bible's view of itself" from which a fully authoritative answer to these questions can be obtained. This whole side of traditional conservative apologetic, though loudly vociferated, just does not exist; there is no case to answer.[57]

What is our response? First, Barr has a point if we merely limit the Bible's witness to a few random texts. For example, Paul, in 2 Tim 3:16, is referring to the OT, not the entire Christian canon. Evidence must be given that 2 Timothy (and then the entire NT) *is* Scripture to prove that *this text* gives Scripture's view of itself. But, second, even with this admission, Barr is simply wrong. Scripture's view of itself is not found in a few texts (e.g., 2 Tim 3:16; 2 Pet 1:21); it pervades the entire canon. When we let Scripture speak for itself, as Sinclair Ferguson correctly insists, there is a "canonical self-consciousness" from Genesis to Revelation. From the opening pages of the OT, we are presented with the eternal triune Lord who speaks with authority (Gen 1:1–2:3). As God establishes covenants with Adam, Noah, Abraham, and then Israel, he gives his word to his people, which is to be believed and obeyed (Deut 5:22, 32; 29:9; 30:15–16; Josh 1:7–8). As redemptive history unfolds, the covenant-making and keeping God continues to reveal himself through the prophets, which reaches its glorious fulfillment in Messiah Jesus (Heb 1:1–2). In Christ—God the Son incarnate—God's final Word is spoken (John 1:1–3; 14–18). From all of God's activity in redemptive history, God clearly intends to rule his people, whether in the OT or the NT era, through a written constitution, which is *his* word. Let us unpack this truth in four steps.[58]

The Defense: Scripture's Pervasive Witness to Itself

First, the OT displays a canonical self-consciousness; a recognition that what is written is given by God through his prophets to rule and direct his people. This is indicated, as

---

[57] Barr, *Fundamentalism*, 78 (see chap. 5, n. 89).

[58] My discussion is indebted to Sinclair B. Ferguson, "How Does the Bible Look at Itself?," in *Inerrancy and Hermeneutic*, ed. Harvie M. Conn (Grand Rapids: Baker, 1988), 47–66. For more on Scripture's self-attestation, see E. J. Schnabel, "Scripture" in *NDBT*, 34–43 (see chap. 1, n. 24); Frame, *Doctrine of the Word*, 105–39 (chap. 5, n. 5); Barrett, *God's Word Alone*, 153–220 (see chap. 1, n. 25); Barrett, *Canon, Covenant, and Christology* (see chap. 5, n. 25); Bavinck, *Reformed Dogmatics*, 1:389–402; cf. Warfield, *Inspiration and Authority* (see chap. 4, n. 5).

Meredith Kline notes, by the fact that covenants are accompanied by written documentation, which is precisely what we discover (see Deut 5:22, 32; 29:9; 30:9–10, 15–16; 31:24–29; Josh 1:7–8; 8:34).[59]

Kline, along with many others, correctly insists that in the covenant relationship of the OT, a written document is not peripheral to the covenant but central to it. To violate the document is to violate the covenant and to disobey God (Deut 6:24–25; 8:11; 31:19–22). Also, the King who enters into covenant relationship with Israel is the sovereign LORD, who alone is independent, *a se*, and the source and standard of knowledge. And in entering into covenant relationship with Israel, God gives them *his* word. In the document, God speaks as author, giving his own name in the usual location for the name of the great king (Exod 24:12; 31:18; 32:15–16; 34:1; Deut 4:13; 10:4), which emphasizes God's authorship of the document. This fact is underscored by the statement that the document was "inscribed by the finger of God" (Exod 31:18). Eventually, as the Law is located in the Pentateuch written by Moses, God's word is identified with Moses's writing, thus highlighting the identity between God's word and the text. As redemptive history unfolds, God constantly brings his people back to his covenantal word (Deut 32). It is God's song of witness against the nation (Deut 31:19) since God's word is holy, wonderful, righteous, eternal, pure, and true (Deut 31:26; Ps 119:7, 89, 129, 140, 142, 160). For this reason, no one is to add to or subtract from God's word (see Deut 4:2; 12:32; cf. Josh 1:7; Prov 30:6; cf. Rev 22:19–20); God's word is meant to be heard and obeyed as a permanent, written word.

But as redemptive history unfolds, God also adds new words to this covenant document (Deut 18:14–22), which results in a canonical sense. Over time, God continues to speak through the prophets, and their written texts are added to the "book of the covenant," which entails a growing canon *and* the idea of *progressive* revelation. We see this in Joshua. He is to follow the "book of instruction" (Josh 1:7–8), but at the end of his life, he adds words to the previous covenant words "in the book of the law of God" (Josh 24:25–28). John Frame captures the significance of this point: "As with the words of Moses, the words of Joshua are God's

---

[59] Meredith G. Kline, *The Structure of Biblical Authority* (Grand Rapids: Eerdmans, 1972), 21–68; cf. Peter J. Gentry, "MasPs[a] and the Early History of the Hebrew Psalter: Notes on Canon and Text," in *Studies on the Intersection of Text, Paratext, and Reception: A Festschrift in Honor of Charles E. Hill*, ed. Gregory R. Lanier and J. Nicholas Reid (Leiden: Brill, 2021), 240–42.

words, put with the other words of God with the ark, in God's sanctuary, with a stone as God's witness against Israel. Thus a pattern is established for additions to the canon."[60]

This pattern continues with the OT prophets. God told, for example, Isaiah, Jeremiah, Ezekiel, and Daniel to write down what he revealed to them (Isa 8:1–2; 30:8–11; 51:16; 59:21; Jer 1:9; 3:6; 5:14; Ezek 3:26; Dan 9:2). The prophetic books, then, are an extension of God's authoritative, covenantal word. As Ferguson notes, "The Old Testament grows from this root. Out of this flows, in part, the Chronicler's covenantal, canonical interpretation of history and the confidence of the prophetic 'This is what the Sovereign Lord says.' New Scripture is written in the confidence that it is 'Scripture' only because of its inherent relationship to what God has already given."[61] In fact, within the OT, authors refer to each other (Isa 34:16–17; Jer 25:13; 30:2; 51:60–61; Dan 9:1–2), as they quote other OT authors (Jer 26:17–18 with Mic 3:12–13; Isa 2:4 with Mic 4:1–5; Isa 11:9 with Hab 2:14), and treat their human writings as *God's* word.

Also, the historical books are written by the prophets (1 Chr 29:29; 2 Chr 9:29; 20:34). They serve as commentaries on God's covenant relationship with Israel while anticipating a greater, new covenant to come. The wisdom literature (Job, Proverbs, Ecclesiastes, Song of Songs) is also tied to the covenants, specifically the Davidic king. Repeatedly, these books stress that wisdom is from God (Prov 2:6–8) and to gain wisdom, we must fear God (Prov 1:7; 9:10; Eccl 12:13–14; cf. Ps 1). Agreeing with the prophets, Proverbs reminds us that "Every word of God is pure. . . . Don't add to his words, / or he will rebuke you, and you will be proved a liar" (30:5–6).

But in the OT, the words *and writings* of the prophets are no mere human words and texts. Think of the tests of the prophets that determine whether a prophet truly speaks and writes from God. In Deut 13:1–5 and 18:20–22, two tests are given. First, does the prophet speak in the name of the Lord or a false god? If the prophet teaches contrary to what God has spoken, he is a false prophet (Deut 13:1–2; 18:20). This assumes a body of truth that has been given and which is completely authoritative and true. Second, do the prophet's words come true (Deut 13:1–5; 18:22)? If not, then he is a false prophet because God's word, spoken through the prophets, *must* always be true (Isa 44:6–8). False prophets do not speak from God; their

[60] Frame, *Doctrine of the Word*, 110.

[61] Ferguson, "How Does the Bible Look at Itself?," 50.

word and predictions are false. For true prophets, God puts his own word in their mouths and they speak the truth (Num 22:35; 23:5, 12, 16; Jer 1:9, 14; Isa 51:16; 59:21; Ezek 3:4).

Thus, within the OT, there is a pervasive God-given "canonical consciousness," contrary to the assertion of James Barr. The OT is not the mere product of human authors and the Israelite community. Instead, the growing OT canon is the "book of the covenant" (Exod 24:7; 2 Kgs 23:2–3, 21; 2 Chr 34:14–31) that God gives to his people as *his* word. Indeed, as the covenant LORD, God's word is tied to God himself, the one who makes and keeps his promises to his people (cf. Heb 6:13–20). In fact, as God's word is given over time, God promises the coming of a new covenant (Jer 31:29–34)—a word he will surely keep (2 Sam 7:12–14; 1 Chr 17:11–14).[62] God's word never fails because *he* is always true to it (Isa 40:6–8): God's word can always be believed and wholly trusted. As God declares through Ezekiel: "I the LORD have spoken, and I have done it" (Ezek 37:14 NIV). God's people are to live by God's word (Pss 1:1–2; 12:6–7; 19:7–11; Prov 30:5; Hab 2:4), and to believe all that God has said through Moses, the prophets, and the entire OT canon. Since God is perfect in every way, so is his word.

Second, in the NT, there is an unmistakable recognition of a God-given canon (the OT) that Jesus identifies as the "Law of Moses, the Prophets, and the Psalms" (Luke 24:44). In the NT, Jesus and the apostles view and use the OT as normative. Evidence for this is abundant; we only list some of the data. We begin by thinking about Jesus's view of the OT. Our Lord Jesus Christ, who *is* the eternal Word/Son made flesh (John 1:1, 14)—truth incarnate (John 14:6; Col 2:9)—views the OT, written by humans, as God's word. Here is some of the evidence.[63]

1. Jesus views the OT as of divine origin. For example, think about our Lord's citation of the OT. Sometimes the author is cited: Moses (Matt 8:4; 19:8; John 5:45), Isaiah (Matt 15:7; Mark 7:6), David (Matt 22:43–45), and Daniel (Matt 24:15). But more commonly the citation assumes a normative status to the OT: "it is written" (Matt 4:4–10; 11:10; 21:3; 26:34, 31), "Scripture says" (Matt 21:42; Mark 12:10; Luke 4:21; John 7:38; 10:35), and "God says" or "the Holy Spirit says" (Matt 15:4; 19:4–5; 22:43; Mark 12:26, 36). In these latter citations,

---

[62] See part 3 for a development of these points.

[63] For a more detailed discussion, see John Wenham, *Christ and the Bible*, 3rd ed. (Grand Rapids: Baker, 1994); Craig L. Blomberg, "Reflections on Jesus's View of the Old Testament," in Carson, *Enduring Authority*, 669–701.

Jesus assumes a specific body of literature that is *from God*. In fact, Jesus affirms that the human authors wrote from God by the Spirit, thus grounding their authority. For example, in Matt 22:43–45, Jesus quotes Psalm 110 to speak of *his* identity as the divine Son and David's Lord, but David, as a prophet, wrote "by the Holy Spirit," hence its divine authority (cf. Acts 1:16; 2:30–31; 4:25). Also, as Jesus quotes the OT as fulfilled in *him*, he underscores his unique, divine identity *and* teaches that the OT "Scripture" (*graphē*) is from God (Matt 21:42 [Ps 118:22–23]; 26:54 [Zech 13:7–9]; Luke 4:16–19 [Isa 61:1–2]; John 7:38–39 [Zech 14:8; cf. Isa 44:3; 55:1; 58:11]).

2. Jesus can speak of "Scripture" and "God" interchangeably so that what Scripture says, God says. In chapter 5, we noted how the *word* of God, given in Scripture, is also described in terms of *God* (Ps 119:19–20, 31, 41–42, 46–48, 86, 89, 140, etc.). Jesus teaches this same point. In Matt 4:4, in quoting Moses's words (Deut 8:3), Jesus says that they are "from the mouth of God." Or, in Matt 19:4–6, Jesus quotes the OT (Gen 1:27; 2:24) but in such a way that God is the one who said it, not merely Moses, although it is Moses's word given in the Pentateuch.

3. Jesus, the divine Son, comes to redeem us by his obedient life, death, and resurrection as our new covenant head and last Adam. In his humanity, the Son submits to the OT precisely because it is *God's* word. In his temptations (Matt 4:1–11), he submits to Scripture and not Satan, in contrast to the first Adam. When he is accused of breaking the law, he corrects them in terms of what the OT teaches (John 7:21–24). Repeatedly, Jesus challenges the religious leaders with their lack of understanding and obedience to the OT. Constantly he asks them: "Haven't you read in the law?" (Matt 12:5; 19:4–6); "What did Moses command you?" (Mark 10:3); "Have you never read in the Scriptures?" (Matt 21:42); etc. (see Matt 12:3; 22:31; Luke 10:26; 20:17; John 8:17). Jesus viewed his entire work as fulfilling the OT, an OT that in every detail is given by God and is to be obeyed without question. In John 10:34–35, Jesus quotes Ps 82:6 and asserts that "Scripture cannot be broken," underscoring again the total authority and trustworthiness of the OT. In looking at such data, Matthew Barrett rightly concludes: "We cannot claim to believe in the authority of Jesus and then reject the authority of Scripture. Our trust in Jesus is intrinsically and inseparably connected to our trust in Scripture."[64]

---

[64] Barrett, *God's Word Alone*, 246.

The apostles have the same view of the OT as our Lord. For them the OT is written by human authors, but it is also God's word. Here is some of the evidence to demonstrate this point.

1. The apostles view the OT as of divine origin, although written by human authors. For example, they, like Jesus, use the expressions "that which is spoken by the prophets" (Matt 1:22; 2:15, 17, 23; 3:3, et al.), or "by God," or "by the Holy Spirit" (Matt 1:22; 2:15; Luke 1:70; Acts 1:16; 3:18; 4:24–26; 28:25). When Paul speaks of the OT, he always speaks of "Scripture" (Rom 4:3; 10:11; 11:2; 1 Tim 5:18, et al.), which assumes its total authority. Paul can even "personalize" Scripture as a stand-in for God, thus what Scripture says, God says (Acts 13:34–35 [Isa 55:3; Ps 16:10]; Gal 3:8 [Gen 12:1–3], 22; 4:30; Rom 9:17 [Exod 9:16]). Or, the author of Hebrews often refers to "God" or "Holy Spirit" as the primary author in replacement of the human authors; Scripture is *from God* (Heb 1:5–14; 3:7; 4:3, 5; 5:6, 7; 7:21; 8:5, 8; 10:16, 30; 12:26; 13:5).

2. The apostles' use of the OT demonstrates that they believe it *is* God's word. When the apostles argue for the truth of the gospel and who Jesus is as the incarnate Son and promised Messiah, they appeal to the OT as having complete authority to warrant their conclusions. For example, they say: "it is written" or "according to Scripture" (Matt 2:5; Mark 1:2; Acts 13:35; Rom 1:17; 3:4; 4:18; 1 Cor 6:16; 15:3–4; Gal 3:16; Eph 4:8; Heb 1:7–10; 3:7, 15), or the "words of God" (Acts 7:38; Rom 3:2; Heb 5:12; 1 Pet 4:11), or the "perfect law" (Jas 1:25; 2:8). Also, as Bavinck notes, for the apostles "the OT is the foundation of doctrine, the source of solutions, the end of all argument. The OT is fulfilled in the New."[65] Bavinck illustrates this point by referring to events in Christ's coming that fulfill the Scripture (e.g., Matt 1:22; Mark 14:49; 15:28; Luke 4:21; 24:44; John 13:18; 19:24, 36; Acts 1:16) even in small details (Matt 21:16; Luke 22:37; John 15:25; 17:12; 19:28). The apostles also appeal to the OT to ground doctrine and life (Rom 4; Gal 3; 1 Cor 15). In fact, Paul's argument in Gal 3:16 turns on the OT's use of the singular rather than the plural—seed, not seeds (cf. Matt 22:45).[66] As Barrett rightly concludes, Paul assumes "that inspiration is both verbal *and* plenary."[67]

---

[65] Bavinck, *Reformed Dogmatics*, 1:395.

[66] See Thomas R. Schreiner, *Galatians*, ZECNT (Grand Rapids: Zondervan, 2010), 229–30.

[67] Barrett, *God's Word Alone*, 253.

3. The apostles assume that the entire OT canon is *from God*, hence they argue that Christ is the long-awaited Messiah who fulfills God's covenantal promises (Acts 2, 4). In proclaiming Christ, Paul calls the people back to the OT. Paul demonstrates that, in Christ, God has kept all of his promises (Acts 13:16–52 [Isa 55:3; Pss 2:7; 16:10; Hab 1:5]; cf. Rom 1:3–4; 2 Cor 1:20) and that God intended the entire OT for the instruction of the church (Rom 15:4).[68] John Frame notes the importance of this:

> Here, Paul says that the Scriptures, though written centuries before his time, were written for the specific purpose of instructing and encouraging believers of the first century A.D. There are, of course, many ancient books that have the ability to instruct people centuries later. . . . But none of these ancient writings were composed *for the purpose* of instructing people of later ages.[69]

This can only be true if the apostles believe that Scripture is *from God*. In fact, if we place 2 Tim 3:15–17 in this context, Paul's reference to "Scripture" (*graphē*) is a reference to the entire OT as normative and binding on the church. Although the OT was written long ago, it has one overall message: to make us wise to salvation in Christ. It can only do so because it is God's breathed-out word and thus for our instruction. Simply put: "To the authors of the New Testament, the Old Testament is God's Word."[70]

Third, in the NT, there is a consciousness among the authors that the authority of their own writing is on par with the OT and also, due to the content of the revelation, *greater*—not in an inspiration sense, but due to the coming of the Word made flesh. After all, in Christ, the divine Son assumed our human nature and brought to fulfillment the eternal plan of redemption. Previously, the prophets spoke and wrote God's word, but our Lord is the *Word* of God (John 1:1–2, 14), which the NT directly bears witness to (Eph 3:2–6). The era that our Lord has inaugurated is the "last days" and the dawning of the new creation. Due to Christ's coming

[68] On this point, see Peter F. Jensen, "God and the Bible," in Carson, *Enduring Authority*, 477–96. Jensen rightly argues that the entire covenantal structure of Scripture, tied to promise and fulfillment, not only assumes that there is a word of God written (the OT) but that in Christ all of God's promises have now reached their fulfillment, which assumes the OT's authority and its utter truthfulness.

[69] Frame, *Doctrine of the Word*, 123.

[70] Ferguson, "How Does the Bible Look at Itself?," 50.

and the fullness of revelation in him, the prophetic word is now confirmed to be completely truthful (2 Pet 1:19; cf. Heb 1:1–3). In this sense, then, the apostles know that their writings, which are the new covenant documents that expound the full revelation in Christ for the church, are fully authoritative, true, and "greater" than the OT revelation. On this point, the apostles are following Jesus's own self-understanding and authority.

For example, think of Jesus's self-identity in relation to the OT in Matt 5:17–20. Much has been written on how best to interpret Jesus's words.[71] The best option stresses the antithesis between "abolish" and "fulfill": Jesus is claiming that he "fulfills" the Law and the Prophets in that they point forward to him.[72] "Fulfill" has the same meaning as its use elsewhere in Matthew, where emphasis is placed on the prophetic nature of the OT and how the OT anticipates Jesus through typological persons, events, and institutions. Thus, as D. A. Carson notes, Jesus is not claiming to abolish the OT as Scripture; instead, he is claiming that "the OT's real and abiding authority must be understood through the person and teaching of him to whom it points and who so richly fulfills it."[73] The continuity of the Law and the Prophets is established with reference to Jesus himself. The Christological claim is staggering. Jesus says *he* is the eschatological goal of the OT, the one the OT was predicting and in whom all of God's plans and promises are realized. *He* is the OT's sole authoritative interpreter, and thus *he* has the authority of God himself.

Jesus makes the same point in Matthew 11. As he speaks of his relation to John the Baptist, he begins by focusing on John's greatness: "Truly, I tell you, among those born of women no one greater than John the Baptist has appeared, but the least in the kingdom of heaven is greater than he" (v. 11). But note: Jesus is defining John's greatness in terms of himself! John is great since he has the supreme privilege, as the last of the OT prophets, to identify the Messiah. No other previous prophet had this privilege. But, as Jesus continues, those least in the kingdom are greater than John because they live after John and thus know more about Jesus. They, unlike John, know more about Jesus's cross work and, as such, have a greater witness than John.

---

[71] For a discussion of the various options, see D. A. Carson, *Matthew*, 2nd ed., EBC 9 (Grand Rapids: Zondervan, 2010), 171–80; R. T. France, *The Gospel of Matthew*, NICNT (Grand Rapids: Eerdmans, 2007), 177–91.

[72] For a defense of this view, see Carson, *Matthew*, 173–79; cf. France, *Matthew*, 182–84.

[73] Carson, *Matthew*, 175.

But again note: this only makes sense if Jesus sees himself as the focal point of history, the one who brings all of God's plans and purposes to fulfillment, thus the apostles view the content of the revelation in Christ as "greater" than the prophets.

Jesus teaches the same point in Luke 24.[74] Two of Jesus's disciples are confused regarding his death and reports of his resurrection. They were not thinking of a crucified messiah, but Jesus takes them back to the OT to show them otherwise. By rehearsing the OT plotline from the OT canon—the Law, Prophets, and Psalms—Jesus *opens* the authoritative Scriptures (v. 32) and explains to them what was *truly there*, namely that the messiah *had* to suffer, die, and be raised. Jesus does not read into the OT something that was not there. Instead, he explains what was there and he brings clarity to their failure to discern the OT properly.[75] What was *there* all along—in seed and shadow form—is now unveiled. Yet, as Ardel Caneday notes, "Jesus expounds the Scriptures not backward by projecting Messiah back onto the OT or by reinterpreting the text, but forward by proceeding through the OT and climaxing upon himself to demonstrate that at many times and in numerous ways it foretells of both Messiah's suffering and glory."[76]

Building on Jesus's teaching, the NT teaches that the OT finds its fulfillment in Christ. Hebrews 1:1–3 best captures this point. "Long ago," the author writes, "God spoke to our ancestors by the prophets," and he did so "at different times and in different ways." God's speech is given over time, and it points forward to something *greater*. In fact, the phrase "at different times and in different ways" makes this point. The OT revelation is authoritative and true but incomplete. But now, "in Son" (*en huiō*, v. 2), the last days the OT predicted are here in Christ, in whom *all* of God's revelation and redemptive purposes culminate. The NT is clear: there is no reduction of the OT's authority; instead, it

---

[74] Jesus teaches these same truths in John's Gospel. "You search the Scriptures because you think that in them you have eternal life; and it is they that bear witness about me, yet you refuse to come to me that you may have life" (5:39–40 ESV). See Carson, *Gospel According to John*, 259–67 (see chap. 5, n. 13).

[75] B. B. Warfield: "The OT is like a fully furnished but dimly lit room which when light is brought into it, nothing is added that was not already there, but the light dispels dark shadows and things shrouded begin to emerge with clarity even as shadows linger." *Biblical Doctrines* (Grand Rapids: Baker, 1981), 141.

[76] Caneday, "Biblical Types," 152 (see chap. 4, n. 15).

was given by God through the prophets to point beyond itself to God's full self-disclosure in his Son.[77]

A number of important points follow from the NT teaching. First, as Matthew Barrett argues,

> The works and words of Christ substantiate the claim that God's word through the Prophets is divine in origin (inspiration), trustworthy in nature (inerrancy), perspicuous in its saving message (clarity) and effective in its truth claims (sufficiency). To be even more accurate, the *person* of Christ—whether Christ is who he says he is—verifies that God's word through the Prophets does not return to him void.[78]

For this reason, the NT authors are aware that the end of the ages has dawned in Christ and in him the OT has reached its fulfillment, terminus, and telos. This does not mean the previous writings of the prophets are not inspired or authoritative; they certainly are. As our Lord teaches, the OT is not done away with; instead, it is fulfilled, meaning it has reached its intended, purposed end. The OT is now made complete, which is proof that God's covenantal word is true. Thus, Christ himself is proof of the OT's verbal and plenary inspiration. In Christ, the Father not only speaks through the Son, but the Father's speech is the Son. He is the content of Scripture (Luke 24:25–27; John 5:45–47), the final self-disclosure of God, who brings the prophetic word to pass. Jesus is proof that God's covenantal word is true and *God's* promises have not failed: "For every one of God's promises is 'Yes' in him. Therefore, through him we also say 'Amen' to the glory of God" (2 Cor 1:20).

Second, due to God's climactic revelation in Christ, it follows that a NT will be written. Barr is right that 2 Tim 3:16 refers to the OT and not the NT. But Paul is also aware that the OT is now fulfilled in Christ, and that the apostles are writing new covenant documents in continuity with the OT. This is why the apostles are conscious that their writings are on par

---

[77] See 1 Pet 1:10–12. The prophets investigated "what time and circumstances" (*eis tina ē poion kairon*) as they anticipated the coming of Christ. Yet, the full significance of what was written becomes clearer as the Bible's story unfolds. Each biblical author may not have understood the Bible's whole story to which his life and writing is a contribution, but in its own context, what he did and wrote communicated something of that overall plan. Yet because of the promises of God, the biblical authors knew that what they were writing was also pointing forward in the story to its resolution. See Schreiner, *1, 2 Peter, Jude*, 71–76 (see chap. 4, n. 17).

[78] Barrett, *Canon, Covenant, and Christology*, 294.

with the OT, indeed, are "greater" in explaining and declaring who Jesus is and what he has accomplished in his new covenant work. The apostles know that their writings are "a deliberate addition to the [OT] canon in order to bring it to completion in the light of Christ's coming."[79] As such, the NT canon is not only demanded by Christ's coming and the inauguration of the "last days"; it is also closed (Heb 1:1–2).[80] In the "Son-revelation" (*en huiō*), God's word must be believed, trusted, and obeyed.[81] In Christ, God's OT revelation is now complete; there is no more revelation beyond it, and in the writing of the NT, we have both an authoritative *and sufficient* word.

Fourth, in the NT, although it is still being written, the apostles know that their writings are "Scripture" that are bringing the OT to completion. No doubt, we do not have texts that mention the division of the NT canon as the OT is mentioned, for instance, Luke 24:44. Yet, given God's climactic revelation in Christ, the apostles knew that their writings were unveiling the full implications of Christ's person and work, as fulfilled in the dawning of the new creation and the ratification of a new covenant (Heb 1:1–3; cf. Rom 16:25–27; 1 Cor 2:6–16; 10:1–13; 2 Cor 3; Gal 1:6–9; Eph 1:3–14; 1 Pet 1:10–12).

In fact, in Christ's office as our new covenant head and mediator, Jesus, as the great prophet (Acts 3:22–23; Heb 3:1–6), priest (Heb 2:17–18; 4:14–10:18), and king (Phil 2:9–11; Col 1:15–20; Heb 1:4–14), calls the apostles to a unique and foundational role: to bear witness to him (Matt 10:1–15; Mark 3:13–19; Luke 6:12–16), to lay the foundation for the church (Acts 2:42; Eph 2:20), and to write the new covenant documents (2 Cor 3). As Jesus prepared for his death, he taught his disciples that *he, as the Son, and the Father* would pour out the Holy Spirit so that they would have authority to explain who and what Jesus did (see John 13–17, especially 14:26; 15:26–27; 16:5–15). As Jesus was from the Father and spoke authoritative words from him (John 5:19–47; 12:47–50), the Father and Son will send the Spirit to guide the apostles to understand the fullness of God's revelation in Christ (John 15:26). Carson writes: "The Spirit's ministry in this respect was not to bring qualitatively new revelation, but

[79] Ferguson, "How Does the Bible Look at Itself?," 51.

[80] For this same point, see Carson, "Approaching the Bible," 1–3.

[81] For a sample of such texts see Matt 7:21–29; Mark 8:38; Luke 8:21; 9:26ff; John 6:63, 68–69; 8:47; 12:27ff; 14:15, 21, 23–24; 15:7, 10, 14; 17:6, 17; Rom 1:16–17; 2:16; Col 4:16; 1 Thess 4:2; 5:27; 2 Thess 3:14; 1 Tim 6:3; 2 Pet 3:16; Rev 12:17; 14:12.

to complete, to fill out, the revelation brought by Jesus himself."[82] This is why Pentecost is no minor event; it is the culminating event of Christ's first coming work. Due to Christ's cross, resurrection, and ascension, the Father and Son pour out the *promised* Holy Spirit on the apostles and the church (Acts 2:32–36), uniquely equipping the apostles for their foundational role for the church, especially in writing Scripture.

In this way, our Lord, after his departure, extends his prophetic ministry in the apostles. The apostles' teaching is like the prophets of old but now speaking God's word about the Son by the Spirit—"recall the words previously spoken by the holy prophets and the command of our Lord and Savior given through your apostles" (2 Pet 3:2). Peter has no problem identifying the apostles as equal with the prophets and saying that Jesus himself, the Lord of Glory, speaks through the apostles so that to receive their word is to receive *his* word.[83] As the apostles proclaim Christ, they, like the OT prophets, call the people to hear and obey God's word (e.g., Acts 2:14–41; 3:12–26; 13:16–41). Throughout Acts, we are reminded that the apostolic gospel is the "word of God" (Acts 6:2, 7; 8:4; 10:36, 44; 13:5, 46; 17:13; 18:11), the "word of the Lord" (Acts 8:25; 13:44–49; 15:25, 36; 16:32; 19:10, 20), and that those who believe it receive "the word of God" (Acts 11:1; cf. 12:24). The apostles are the extension of Christ's ministry and work; there is simply no dichotomy between them (cf. Eph 2:17). But Christ's prophetic ministry through the apostles does not end in their oral proclamation; it also extends to their writings by triune agency appropriated by the work of the Spirit. The Father sends the Son; the Son speaks from the Father; the Father and Son send the Spirit; the Spirit bears witness to the Son, who not only "carried along" the OT prophets, but now the NT apostles, who do not speak their own words but the word of Christ (2 Pet 1:20–21). As a result of the Spirit's work in the apostles, the texts they write are "God-breathed" (2 Tim 3:16–17), as inspired as the OT Scriptures. Just as the OT was the word of God in the words of humans, so is the NT. In other words, the production of the apostolic writings is due to triune extraordinary agency in and through human authors, thus rendering their texts as God's word written, fully authoritative and true. This is not to insist that every book of the NT was directly written by an apostle, but, as we will discuss in chapter 12, one criterion to know whether a NT book was inspired

---

[82] Carson, *John*, 505 (see chap. 5, n. 13).

[83] See Schreiner, *1, 2 Peter, Jude*, 370–71.

was whether it emerged from the apostolic circle given the foundational role of the apostles in the church (Eph 2:20).

Not surprisingly, the NT authors view their writings as authoritative and on par with the OT. For example, Paul knows that the Thessalonians are Christians because they received Paul's apostolic preaching as from the Holy Spirit (1 Thess 1:5; 4:8), indeed, "not as a human message, but as it truly is, the word of God" (1 Thess 2:13). Thus, to obey the words of the apostles is to obey the words of Christ (2 Thess 3:14).[84] Or think of how Paul quotes from Deut 25:4 *and* Luke 10:7 and identifies both as "Scripture" (1 Tim 5:18).[85] Or Peter refers to Paul's writings as "Scripture" and thus God's word (2 Pet 3:15–16). Even the public reading of the apostolic writings in the church confirms that just as Israel read the OT in the synagogues (Luke 4:17–20; Acts 13:15; 15:21), so the church read the growing NT books *as Scripture* (Col 4:16; 1 Thess 5:27; 2 Cor 10:9; 1 Tim 4:13).

One can also see this canon consciousness emerge in the opening and closing sections of the book of Revelation. It is assumed that Revelation will be read in public to the church (1:3). Both reader and hearer are promised "blessing," that is, divine, covenantal blessing. Also, the book ends with the warning to not add or subtract from it (22:18–19), which echoes the same warning of the OT (Deut 4:2, 5, 14, 40; 12:32). These final words reflect the apex of canon consciousness in the NT, which links it with God's OT covenantal word.[86] In all these ways, Scripture views itself as supremely authoritative speech and writing precisely because it is *God's* word.

Concluding Reflection

As we read Scripture on its own terms, we conclude that it makes a pervasive claim about itself: Scripture *is* God's word written. James Barr and others are incorrect when they assert that Scripture never attests to its own divine origin and inspiration.[87] People who make such claims

---

[84] See Waters, *For the Mouth*, 92–93 (chap. 5, n. 5).

[85] See George W. Knight, *Commentary on the Pastoral Epistles*, NIGTC (Grand Rapids: Eerdmans, 1992), 234.

[86] See Ferguson, "How Does the Bible Look at Itself?", 52.

[87] For example, see Craig D. Allert, *A High View of Scripture? The Authority of the Bible and the Formation of the New Testament Canon* (Grand Rapids: Baker Academic, 2007), 147–72. Allert makes

are already working with some kind of *extratextual* viewpoint, usually tied to the embrace of historical criticism and some form of modern or postmodern epistemology that undergirds it.

However, Scripture will not allow such viewpoints. From Genesis to Revelation, Scripture claims to be the product of triune communicative agency in and through human authors. And given who the triune God is, Scripture speaks with absolute authority. Even though Scripture is written by human authors, its message, truth, and reliability are not lessened. B. B. Warfield was correct to say that what Scripture says, God says. Thus, to disbelieve or disobey Scripture is to disbelieve or disobey God (Luke 24:25; John 17:17; 2 Thess 3:14; 2 Cor 13:2–3), and the only fitting response to God's word is to receive it, believe it, and gladly obey it (Isa 66:2).

To speak of the self-attestation of Scripture is no minor point. It is the *ultimate* warrant for why we receive Scripture as God's word. Also, our theology of Scripture emerges from it (i.e., the doctrines of inspiration, inerrancy, sufficiency, clarity, and canon), topics we will turn to in chapters 9–12. Furthermore, to receive Scripture on its own authority is what distinguishes historic theology from its non-orthodox alternatives, or what we have identified as intratextual versus extratextual theologies. But also, practically speaking, for the health and life of the church, Scripture's self-attestation entails that God's people do not stand over Scripture but under it as we seek to read and apply *all* of God's word to our lives for God's glory and our good.

---

a similar claim to Barr by arguing that the Bible does not give a precise and pervasive view of its own inspiration and thus a view of itself.

CHAPTER 9

The Inspiration of Scripture

Introduction

Scripture's own self-testimony is that it is God's word written by the agency of human authors. But how do we explain or account for the relation between God's word and the words of the human authors? The *theological* term that accounts for this relation is *inspiration*, and in this chapter we will define and explain what *inspiration* means as it pertains to what Scripture *is*.

However, before we do so, it is crucial to note that the term *inspiration* is used differently in theology than in common usage, which unfortunately people sometimes confuse. In ordinary use, we think of inspiration as something "inspiring" or "moving"—a functional, dynamic, or subjective use of the word. Often, the term is used of artists or writers who perform or write something "inspiring." When the word is used in this way, it refers either to the greatness of their work or its effect on us. But this is not the theological meaning or use of the word.

"Inspiration" is the translation of *theopneustos* in 2 Tim 3:16, which means—"God-breathed." In biblical thinking, *inspiration* is not used in a subjective sense, nor does it even convey the idea of God's "in-breathing" (either into the authors or into the text of Scripture). Instead, the word is used in an objective sense to refer to God's mighty action of "breathing out" the text (Scripture) so that the human author's text *is* God's word. What is stressed, then, is *not* the manner of Scripture's coming into being, *but its divine source*. Just as God spoke the universe into existence (Gen 1:1), he has spoken and "breathed-out" Scripture through human authors (2 Tim 3:16). Thus, to speak of the "inspiration" of Scripture is to affirm two truths simultaneously: first, Scripture *is* God's word because of triune communicative agency appropriated by the Spirit upon the human authors (2 Pet 1:20–21); and, second, the text written by the human authors is "God-breathed" (2 Tim 3:16–17).

A Definition and Exposition of Inspiration

A working definition of "inspiration" is as follows: inspiration is the extraordinary or supernatural work of the triune God in and through the Holy Spirit on the human authors of Scripture so that their freely composed writings are what God intended them to write in order to communicate his truth, and as such, they are completely authoritative and trustworthy.[1] Let us develop, unpack, and defend this definition in *four* steps.

1. Inspiration Accents God's Triune Action, Appropriated by the Spirit, on the Human Authors, Who Freely Write According to Their Own Style and Abilities and *the Nature of the Resultant Text.*

This double emphasis is taught in two classic texts that together give us our doctrine of inspiration: (1) 2 Pet 1:20–21, which speaks of God's sovereign action in the human authors; and (2) 2 Tim 3:16, which speaks of the God-breathed text that results from God's action. Let us look at each of these important texts in turn.

Second Peter 1:20–21: "Above all, you know this: No prophecy of Scripture comes from the prophet's own interpretation (*idias epiluseōs*), because no prophecy ever came by the will of man; instead, men spoke from God as they were carried along (*pheromenoi*) by the Holy Spirit."

---

[1] For a similar definition, see, Hodge and Warfield, *Inspiration*, 17–18 (see chap. 7, n. 4); Warfield, *Inspiration and Authority*, 131–66, 420 (see chap. 4, n. 5); Paul D. Feinberg, "The Meaning of Inerrancy," in Geisler, *Inerrancy*, 277–87 (see chap. 7, n. 4); Sinclair B. Ferguson, "How Does the Bible Look at Itself?," in Conn, *Inerrancy and Hermeneutic*, 54–56 (see chap. 8, n. 58); Feinberg, *Light in a Dark Place*, 111–228 (chap. 5, n. 2).

The stress of this text, which focuses on the first aspect of "inspiration," is on God's triune action appropriated by the Holy Spirit *in* and *on* the human authors of Scripture. In context, Peter is reminding the church that the truth of the glory of Christ was not built on "cleverly contrived myths" (v. 16). On the contrary, the apostles were "eyewitnesses of his [Christ's] majesty." Peter then recounts his experience of seeing first-hand the glory of Christ's transfiguration and hearing the voice of God the Father speaking about the divine Son as proof of this point (Matt 17:5; Mark 9:7; Luke 9:35). But Peter also wants the church to know that in Christ's incarnation and his entire work, the truthfulness of Scripture, that is, the prophetic word of the OT and its proper interpretation, is confirmed (v. 19).[2] Minimally, Peter is thinking of the Prophets, but given his use of *graphē* (vv. 20–21), he is probably referring to the entire OT and the prophecies regarding the coming of Messiah Jesus.[3] It is this prophetic word, confirmed by our Lord, to which Peter points the church, and the church is bound to this word until Jesus returns again at the end of the age (v. 19).[4] Once again, we see how NT authors strongly underscore the ongoing authority and significance of the OT.

In v. 20, there is a legitimate debate over whether "one's own" (*idias*) refers to the prophet or the reader of prophecy. In context, the latter is better. The point is that the meaning of the OT is not open to the subjective interpretation of its readers.[5] Instead, "the readers must pay attention to the prophetic word as it is interpreted by the apostles, for the Old Testament prophecies are not a matter of personal interpretation but have been authoritatively interpreted by the apostles."[6] In fact, v. 21 provides the ground for v. 20. The interpretation of the apostles is authoritative not because of their inherent brilliance, but solely due to the work of the Spirit in them. As Tom Schreiner notes, in this verse "Peter brings together two themes: both the origin of prophecy and its subsequent interpretation stem from God himself."[7]

As this text pertains to inspiration, Peter reminds us that the origin of prophecy is from God and not the will of humans. Prophecy originates in God, and as the prophets speak and then write their prophecies as literary documents, God is the source of these prophecies. But

---

[2] Schreiner, *1, 2 Peter, Jude*, 320 (see chap. 4, n. 17).

[3] Schreiner, 319.

[4] Waters, *For the Mouth*, 83 (chap. 5, n. 5).

[5] Schreiner, *1, 2 Peter, Jude*, 322–23.

[6] Schreiner, 323.

[7] Schreiner, 324.

how does God *guarantee* that what the prophets say and, subsequently, what they write is *from God* and thus authoritative and true? Peter answers this question: the prophets were "carried along" (*pheromenoi*) by the Holy Spirit (v. 21), which B. B. Warfield rightly interprets: "Speaking thus under the determining influence of the Holy Spirit, the things they spoke were not from themselves, but from God."[8] Here Peter is stating what we have seen that all of Scripture teaches, namely, Scripture is simultaneously authored by God and humans.

As we think of Scripture's dual authorship, Peter does not spell out the precise relationship between the two. But Peter's use of "to carry along" (Gk. *pherō*, "to bear along") implies an *effectual* work, much stronger than mere guidance.[9] For this reason, "inspiration" is more than the leading of the Spirit that occurs in *ordinary* providence; rather, it is an act of *extraordinary* divine agency, which involves a sovereign, "constraining" influence of the Spirit. However, as we will discuss below, this *extraordinary* action of the Spirit in and through the authors does *not* necessitate a dictation theory of inspiration, but it does assume a specific *theology* of the divine sovereignty–human freedom relationship. The words and texts the prophets spoke and wrote are *from God* and thus fully authoritative and true, but they are also their own words. A close look at the writings of the prophets confirms this point. There is no evidence that the prophet's abilities and personalities disappear; each prophet freely writes in his own style, yet it is also God's word. Scripture does not teach that if God is the author, then humans are not, or vice versa. And, as argued in chapter 5, God's speech *through* the prophets results in no loss of authority. What the prophet says and writes *is* God's word,[10] a point strongly emphasized in 2 Timothy 3.

Second Timothy 3:16–17: "All Scripture is inspired by God (*pasa graphē theopneustos*) and is profitable for teaching, for rebuking, for correcting, for training in righteousness, so that the man of God may be complete, equipped for every good work."

The stress of this text, which focuses on the second aspect of "inspiration," is on God's sovereign action by the Holy Spirit in the human author *that results in a "God-breathed" text.* The context of the passage is Paul's exhortation to Timothy, his young pastor-apprentice, on

---

[8] Warfield, *Inspiration and Authority*, 136.

[9] See Warfield, 136–37; cf. Schreiner, *1, 2 Peter, Jude*, 324. In Acts 27:15, *pherō* describes a ship being driven along by the wind in its sails, thus emphasizing the strong, active use of the verb.

[10] On this point, see Douglas J. Moo, *2 Peter, Jude*, NIV Application Commentary (Grand Rapids: Zondervan, 1996), 78–89.

how to live in the "last days" (3:1), that is, the time span between the first and second coming of Christ. After warning Timothy of the challenges of the "last days," Paul encourages Timothy not only to follow his example (v. 10–14) but more significantly to follow the "holy Scriptures" (a reference to the OT) because they are all you need for faith in Christ (v. 15), to lead the church as the "man of God," and to equip God's people for life and godliness (vv. 16–17). But why follow Scripture? Paul's answer: "All Scripture is God-breathed" (*pasa graphē theopneustos*). Three exegetical points are necessary to grasp what Paul is teaching about Scripture.

First, what is the meaning of *pasa graphē*? In the NT, *graphē* is found over fifty times, and it always refers to the sacred writings of the OT.[11] This is why it does not have an article before it; it functions as a technical term for the entire OT. *Pasa* may be translated either by "all" or "every." As Paul Feinberg notes, "the distinction between 'all Scripture' and 'every Scripture' is the difference between reference to the whole body of the Old Testament (see Gal. 3:8) and particular passages of Scripture (see Acts 8:35),"[12] but either way it does not affect the main point.[13] Yet "all" is a better reading given that *pasa* is used with *graphē* (functioning as a collective and proper noun), thus referring to "Scripture as a whole."[14] The emphasis, then, is not that every OT text is profitable but that the entirety of the OT is profitable because "the whole of the Old Testament has its origin in God speaking its words."[15]

The second issue is the meaning of *theopneustos*, which only appears here in the NT.[16] *Theopneustos* is a verbal adjective, a compound of *theos* (God) and *pneō* (to breathe).[17] Adjectives of this class either have the meaning of a perfect passive participle, or they express possibility, but Warfield has demonstrated that it is the former.[18] Thus, *theopneustos* focuses on the production

---

[11] George W. Knight, *The Pastoral Epistles*, NIGTC (Grand Rapids: Eerdmans, 1992), 445; Paul Feinberg, "The Meaning of Inerrancy," 277.

[12] Feinberg, "Meaning of Inerrancy," 277.

[13] Knight, *The Pastoral Epistles*, 445.

[14] See Philip H. Towner, *The Letters to Timothy and Titus*, NICNT (Grand Rapids: Eerdmans, 2006), 585–87; Knight, *The Pastoral Epistles*, 445–48; Feinberg, "Meaning of Inerrancy," 277.

[15] Waters, *For the Mouth*, 81.

[16] On the meaning of *theopneustos*, see Towner, *Letters to Timothy and Titus*, 589; Robert W. Yarbrough, *The Letters to Timothy and Titus*, PNTC (Grand Rapids: Eerdmans, 2018), 429–30.

[17] Knight, *Pastoral Epistles*, 446; Feinberg, "Meaning of Inerrancy," 278.

[18] Warfield, *Inspiration and Authority*, 275; cf. Knight, *Pastoral Epistles*, 446; Feinberg, "Meaning of Inerrancy," 278.

of Scripture: the Bible is the product of the "spirated breath of God." For this reason, Scripture is viewed as God's speech (Gal 3:8, 22; Rom 9:17) since God is the ultimate author of what is recorded (Acts 13:32–35), and the entire OT is the "very words of God" (Rom 3:2). Here is the exegetical warrant, along with the next point, for the "received view" in contrast to the neo-orthodox view: Scripture *is* God's word, and what God says, Scripture says.[19]

The third issue is the relationship between *graphē* and *theopneustos*. *Theopneustos* functions as a predicate adjective rather than an attributive adjective, thus "Scripture is God-breathed."[20] As Feinberg notes, Paul places the emphasis *on the OT text* as "God-breathed," *not* the authors as "God-breathed."[21] This point is crucial for a proper understanding of the doctrine of inspiration. Biblical authors were finite and fallen, and even Peter needed to be corrected by Paul (Gal 2). But Paul's point is that "inspiration" does not pertain to the writers, *but to the text of Scripture*. Thus, to speak of "inspiration," we are referring to God's triune action by which the Holy Spirit has acted in and through human authors so that what they write is a "God-breathed" text.

Conclusions of These Texts for the Doctrine of Inspiration[22]

We may draw at least *five* important conclusions from these texts for the doctrine of inspiration.

First, inspiration has to do with the *text* of Scripture, not with the subjective interiority of the writers.[23] Scripture *is* God-breathed, not merely a witness to Scripture, hence the neo-orthodox view, along with its current iterations, is incorrect.[24]

---

[19] See Warfield, *Inspiration and Authority*, 299–348.

[20] Knight, *Pastoral Epistles*, 446. Knight argues that if *theopneustos* is attributive, i.e., "God-breathed Scripture," it would imply that Paul did not regard all "Scripture" as God-breathed, which is contrary to Paul's view of the OT (447).

[21] Feinberg, "Meaning of Inerrancy," 278–79.

[22] See Feinberg, 279–83, for these conclusions.

[23] Andrew T. B. McGowan fails to see this point. He argues that authority is in God and not Scripture, but this fails to account for how Scripture is God-breathed, and that inspiration is not merely God approving of the words of Scripture, but these human words are actually his intended speech. *The Divine Authenticity of Scripture: Retrieving an Evangelical Heritage* (Downers Grove: InterVarsity, 2008), 43–44.

[24] For example, see Grenz and Franke, *Beyond Foundationalism*, 65–66 (see chap. 1, n. 35). In their discussion of 2 Tim 3:16, they argue that the stress of *theopneustos* is on "the surpassing value of

Furthermore, to affirm that inspiration pertains to the *text* of Scripture, it is best to think of the text in its final form. How some biblical books were composed is complicated and in some cases unknown. For example, Moses is the author of the Pentateuch, but it seems that a later editor(s) added the ending to the book (Deut 34), possibly Ezra after the return from exile and as the OT canon was formalized.[25] Or think of the Psalter. It consists of numerous authors (e.g., Moses, David, Solomon, sons of Korah, etc.), yet after the exile, it was "put together" as an entire book with a deliberate order, structure, and overall message.[26] Or think of how Luke did research for his gospel (Luke 1:1–4) and how the Gospel authors depend on each other in the composition of their gospels.[27] Yet, in the composition of each biblical book, God is sovereignly at work in and through the biblical authors and even later editors at every stage of the writing, but ultimately inspiration pertains to the final form of the text.

Second, if the *text* is God-breathed, then Scripture's *form* and *content* are the result of divine inspiration, which has important implications for hermeneutics. The Bible is not a theological dictionary, but a collection of books of various literary forms that unpacks a specific redemptive storyline, which together are God's word. Also, inspiration applies to *all* and to *every* Scripture.

---

the Spirit-energized scriptures and not on some purported 'pristine character of the autographs.' The church, in short, came to confess the authority of Scripture because the early believers experienced the power and truth of the Spirit of God through these writings. They knew these documents were 'animated with the Spirit of Christ.'" But this misses the entire point of the text! Paul stresses the *objective* nature of the text that results from the Spirit's work. Scripture then is not merely a human word that the Spirit energizes; Scripture itself *is God's word.* Interestingly, there is no exegesis of 2 Tim 3:16 in Peter Enns or Greg Boyd. Sparks, in *Sacred Word, Broken Word* (see chap. 5, n. 39), discusses 2 Tim 3:16 but gets it wrong. He argues that *theopneustos* says nothing about "*how* the transaction between God and the human authors took place" (56) and then says that the primary point of the text is about the benefits of Scripture. But Sparks knows better since one page later he admits that that the emphasis in 2 Tim 3:16 is "on the inspired *text*" and not the authors (57, his emphasis). But if this is the case, then his understanding of God's action in inspiration requires a doctrine of God with greatly reduced sovereignty since God is unable to keep human authors from writing fallibly.

[25] See Stephen G. Dempster, "An 'Extraordinary Fact': Torah and Temple and the Contours of the Hebrew Canon, Part 1 and 2," *TynBul* 48 (1997): 23–56, 191–218.

[26] See James M. Hamilton Jr., *Psalms*, vol. 1, EBTC (Bellingham: Lexham Academic, 2021), 1–70; Adam D. Hensley, *Covenant Relationships and the Editing of the Hebrew Psalter* (Edinburgh: T&T Clark, 2019).

[27] See Craig L. Blomberg, *The Historical Reliability of the Gospels*, 2nd ed. (Downers Grove: IVP Academic, 2007).

The Scripture, in its parts and its whole, is God's word, and thus authoritative, reliable, and true. Feinberg rightly concludes that since inspiration pertains to the text of Scripture, we cannot make a "distinction between those things that are either Christological, salvific, or necessary for faith and practice, and those things that are historical, scientific or incidental."[28] Such a distinction is unsustainable, and in practice the two cannot be separated. Furthermore, it requires an extratextual criterion to know what is reliable and what is not in Scripture.[29]

Third, these two texts combined entail that "inspiration" is understood as an *extraordinary* act of providence, not merely an ordinary one. As we will note below, God calls and prepares the biblical authors by "ordinary" means, but the emphasis in these texts is on *God's* supernatural action as the primary cause of inspiration. This is why Warfield insists that by inspiration "these books become not merely the word of godly men, but the immediate word of God Himself."[30]

Fourth, due to inspiration, Scripture is a *unified* word-act revelation, unfolding God's eternal plan centered in Christ. The unity of Scripture, as John Webster notes, "is not to be located at the level of authorial intention, as if in some esoteric way the prophets and apostles knew themselves to be contributors to a collective whole."[31] No doubt, each author is carried along by God's Spirit so that they write God's word. But the Bible's unity is due to God's speaking through each author and in terms of the entire canon. Also, the Bible's unity is not a "function of canonization, as if the church's establishment of a list of authorized texts created (rather than recognized) the unity of these texts,"[32] as affirmed by Roman Catholic theology and even within post-liberalism.

---

[28] Feinberg, "Meaning of Inerrancy," 280.

[29] Sparks admits this point. Instead of affirming what Scripture explicitly teaches about inspiration, he appeals to diverse processes that produced Scripture. *Sacred Word, Broken Word*, 58. In the end, he says, "we simply do not understand how [inspiration] worked. Inspiration affirms that the Bible is God's authoritative word and that we should read it with seriousness, but conceptually speaking this does not tell us with precision either *what* we should expect from the Bible or *how* we should read it," which for him entails that "God speaks to us through the finite and fallen perspectives of human authors, and, thereby, through the limited and fallen horizons of human cultures and audiences." *Sacred Word, Broken Word*, 59. However, the problem is that his description of inspiration is not what Scripture teaches.

[30] Warfield, *Inspiration and Authority*, 158.

[31] Webster, *Domain of the Word*, 17–18 (see chap. 1, n. 5).

[32] Webster, 18.

Fifth, when we think of inspiration, we must also affirm triune agency.[33] As we discussed in chapter 5, Scripture is the product of the triune God, who by nature is a communicative being. God's external actions are "one and indivisible," although specific acts terminate on specific divine persons. In the case of Scripture, inspiration is a triune act of the Father speaking through the Son and by the Spirit, with the Spirit as the person who brings to completion God's action in and through the human authors.[34] The Spirit's role is to bear witness to Christ (John 16:13–14). He speaks what he hears from the Father and the Son and glorifies both by bearing witness to the Son. Kevin Vanhoozer states it this way: "The Father initiates communicative action, the Son executes it, and the Spirit carries it out to completion."[35] In *inspiration*, God is active in producing Scripture, but God is not finished with it once it is produced. God is also active in *illumination*. The two are not the same, yet both are essential "components in the divine economy of communication."[36]

2. God's Act of Inspiration Is Given No Final Explanation Other Than It Is an Act of Our Triune God in and through the Human Authors.

Texts such as 2 Peter 1 and 2 Timothy 3 state what inspiration is, but they do not describe *how* God acted in the authors. This is why the *means* or *mode* of inspiration is determined exegetically in an a posteriori manner, that is, by an examination of the phenomena of Scripture.

From Scripture, we know that it came to us through a variety of *modes* (e.g., dreams, visions, research, and even dictation). Some texts are given directly by God ("Thus says the Lord"); others are the product of historical research and thoughtful interpretation (e.g., Luke 1:1–4, Chronicles' interpretation of Israel's history from a covenantal perspective, and the wisdom literature). Scripture also includes poetry, which required hard literary labor. Although Scripture consists of diverse *modes* of revelation, two truths characterize the *manner* of inspiration.

---

[33] See Vanhoozer, "Triune Discourse (Part 2)," 50–78 (see chap. 5, n. 71).

[34] Calvin, *Institutes*, 1.13.18 (see chap. 1, n. 3): "To the Father is attributed the beginning of the activity, . . . to the Son . . . the ordered disposition of all things; but to the Spirit is assigned the power and efficacy of that activity."

[35] Vanhoozer, "Triune Discourse (Part 2)," 61.

[36] Vanhoozer, 73.

First, God's *ordinary* providential superintending of the lives and circumstances of the biblical authors. As B. B. Warfield argued, "If God wished to give His people a series of letters like Paul's, He prepared a Paul to write them, and the Paul He brought to the task was a Paul who simultaneously would write just such letters."[37] This is not to say that the biblical authors were sinless or had knowledge of divine realities on their own. As Francis Turretin reminds us,

> The prophets did not fall into mistakes in those things which they wrote as inspired men (*theopneutōs*) and as prophets, not even in the smallest particulars. . . . But they could err in other things as men . . . because the influence of the Holy Spirit was neither universal nor uninterrupted, so that it might not be considered an ordinary excitation or merely an effect of nature. . . . The apostles were infallible in faith, not in practice; and the Spirit was to lead them into all truth so that they might not err, but not into all holiness that they might not sin.[38]

Second, Scripture is the result of triune, *extraordinary* action in the authors by the Spirit. The Holy Spirit's work in the human authors is sovereign and supernatural (2 Pet 1:20–21) so that what they write *is* God's word (2 Tim 3:16). God not only governs their lives in equipping them to write; he also teaches them the words they use (see 1 Cor 2:13). Hence, Scripture, due to its inspiration, down to its very words, is both human and divine, the very Word of God.

The "concursive theory of inspiration," or what Bavinck calls "organic inspiration,"[39] best accounts for the phenomena of Scripture, in contrast to other theories.[40] "Concursive" is from

---

[37] Warfield, *Inspiration and Authority*, 155.

[38] Turretin, *Institutes of Elenctic Theology*, 1:69 (see chap. 3, n. 55).

[39] See Herman Bavinck, *Reformed Dogmatics*, 1:435–48 (see chap. 1, n. 9).

[40] See Barrett, *God's Word Alone*, 225–26 (see chap. 1, n. 25). Barrett discusses some common theories of inspiration given throughout church history. Also see Bavinck, *Reformed Dogmatics*, 1:428–35. For example, there is (1) *the intuition theory* that thinks the biblical authors, like other religious leaders, had some kind of intuition or religious instinct, thus setting their writings apart, relatively speaking; (2) *the illumination theory*, which says the Spirit "influenced" the authors, heightening their religious insight, but this minimizes the sovereign, effectual work of God in and through the human authors guaranteeing that their word *is* God's word; (3) *the dynamic theory*, which sees the Spirit directing the human author to have specific ideas or concepts that he expresses in his own style, but inspiration does not pertain to the actual words of Scripture; and (4) *the dictation theory*, which holds that God dictated the text to the authors. Critics of the "received view" have argued that the dictation theory is required to maintain a strong view of inspiration and its corollary, inerrancy. In the church fathers,

concursus, a term used in the doctrine of providence that undergirds the relation between divine and human agency. *Concursus* affirms that in a single action or event, both God and humans act and the relation between them is non-competitive, tied to the Creator/creature distinction. God is the primary cause/agent and humans are secondary causes/agents.[41] In providence, God's action is *ordinary*; that is, in all secondary, contingent acts, God also acts by sustaining, governing, and ruling. But his action is sometimes *extraordinary*. In the latter, God acts supernaturally through secondary causes/agents, but he does not remove the reality of secondary causes/agents. This is known as "dual agency," or in the case of Scripture, "dual authorship."[42] In the case of inspiration, the concursive theory is tied to extraordinary providence and the divine sovereignty–human freedom relationship, whereby the triune God by "the Spirit's efficient causality [acts] through the human authors as instrumental causes without overriding their own personality or freedom of action."[43]

In giving us Scripture, God's first primary causal work is to call, sanctify, and gift the human authors so that by divine appointment they become God's chosen instruments to write Scripture. As Warfield mentioned, God is at work preparing the authors of Scripture in their prophetic and apostolic offices. Also, the prophets and apostles are redeemed men so that in regeneration and sanctification, God has renewed them.[44] But in the act of inspiration, there is an extraordinary work of the Holy Spirit (who is the Lord and giver of life) in the human authors so that Scripture is truly a divine-human word. In fact, John Webster reminds us that

---

there were dictation tendencies, but also affirmation of the role of the human authors. However, in the Reformation and post-Reformation eras, with sustained reflection on the divine sovereignty–human freedom relationship and an affirmation of dual agency, *concursus* was embraced in a more consistent manner (e.g., Calvin, *Institutes*, 1.7.5, 4.8.8). For a helpful discussion of this point, see Allison, *Historical Theology*, 59–69 (see chap. 8, n. 9).

[41] See Muller, *Dictionary of Latin and Greek*, 76 (see chap. 8, n. 37). The laws of nature are also secondary causes but impersonal, in contrast to moral agents (human and angelic).

[42] See Henri A. G. Blocher, "God and the Scripture Writers: The Question of Double Authorship," in Carson, *Enduring Authority*, 497–541 (see chap. 4, n. 9).

[43] Kevin J. Vanhoozer, "Triune Discourse: Theological Reflections on the Claim that God Speaks (Part 1)," in Treier and Lauber, *Trinitarian Theology for the Church*, 32 (see chap. 5, n. 71).

[44] See John Webster, "On the Inspiration of Holy Scripture," in *Conception, Reception, and the Spirit: Essays in Honor of Andrew T. Lincoln*, ed. J. G. McConville and L. K. Pietersen (Eugene: Cascade, 2015), 242–43.

we can describe three divine acts in the human authors of Scripture:[45] first, God's work of illumination so that God's truth is revealed to them (1 Cor 2:7–13); second, a Spirit-given impulse to write so that the human authors' will and understanding is *intrinsically* effected by the Spirit "as an augmentation of creaturely powers, and not merely as an extrinsic efficient cause;"[46] and third, the Spirit supplies the message, words, and form of the writings so that *their* word is also *God's* word. Verbal inspiration, then, "is not an extrinsic compelling, but an interior forming movement of the Spirit, 'organic' rather than 'mechanical' in character,"[47] but it is also the result of God's sovereign and extraordinary action to give us his word.

As one unpacks the biblical view of inspiration, we quickly discover that we cannot account for it *theologically* apart from theology proper and a specific grasp of the God-world relation. In chapter 5, we noted how Edward Farley correctly perceived the organic relation between the "received view" and a specific view of the divine sovereignty–human freedom relationship. However, Farley surrendered a biblical view of *concursus* with his embrace of panentheism and wrongly concluded that God's sovereign action in providence is always of an extraordinary nature, hence his inability to answer the problem of evil.[48] But in a proper view of the God-world/human freedom relation, God's action in providence is ordinary *and* extraordinary. In the case of Scripture, God's *guaranteed* action in the human authors is more direct, immediate, and supernatural than in ordinary providence. Unless we make these careful distinctions, we lose the uniqueness of inspiration, and we fail to account for the complexity of the divine sovereignty–human freedom relationship.[49]

---

[45] Webster, "On the Inspiration of Holy Scripture," 244–47; cf. Webster, *Domain of the Word*, 14–16.

[46] Webster, "On the Inspiration of Holy Scripture," 246.

[47] Webster, *Domain of the Word*, 17.

[48] A similar problem occurs for those who depart from a Reformed view of the divine sovereignty–human freedom relation. In so emphasizing a libertarian view of human freedom and thus undermining dual agency and *concursus*, it is not surprising that in inspiration, God cannot *guarantee* that the human authors will write without error. For example, this problem is evident in Sparks, *Sacred Word, Broken Word*, 56–58. Also see Dennis R. Bratcher, "Thinking about the Bible Theologically: Inerrancy, Inspiration, and Revelation," in Thompson and Oord, *Rethinking the Bible*, 51–52, 57–62 (see chap. 8, n. 36).

[49] In part 4, chapter 23, we will examine this more in our discussion of divine providence and the problem of evil.

3. Inspiration Characterizes All of Scripture, Not Just Certain Parts of It.

Inspiration rejects any notion of a "canon within a canon," as if certain portions of Scripture are more God-breathed than others. As we discussed in chapter 8, one proof of this truth is the NT authors' quotation of the OT. It is estimated that there are around 300 quotations and 1,500 allusions from the OT. This is significant, as Sinclair Ferguson reminds us, because "the random, rather than selective, use of Scripture is manifest. If any part is God-breathed, then the whole is God-breathed."[50]

Theologians have sought to capture this *allness* of inspiration by the words *verbal* and *plenary*. *Verbal* captures the truth that inspiration does not pertain merely to the general ideas, teaching, or moral truths of the authors but to their very words and sentences, while *plenary* emphasizes that every part of Scripture is God-breathed, even those parts we tend to ignore! Verbal-plenary inspiration does *not* mean that we can read the Bible like a theological dictionary, divorced from the author's intention given in their literary work as communicated in their sentences, paragraphs, and choice of literary forms. Nor does verbal-plenary inspiration entail that we can know what God communicates to us apart from the three contexts of Scripture, as discussed in chapter 4. Instead, verbal-plenary inspiration affirms that *all* of Scripture is God-given, even to its very *words*. This is why the study of textual criticism is so important. Since inspiration pertains to what is originally given, then it is incumbent on the church to know what the original text was since it is *this* text, in its final form, that is God's inspired word.

One last point: in thinking about the entirety of Scripture as God-breathed, it is important to distinguish the concept of progressive revelation from inspiration. Revelation, on the one hand, is progressive and cumulative; it unfolds God's eternal plan from creation to the new creation through the progression of the covenants, reaching its fulfillment in Christ (cf. Heb 1:1–3). Inspiration, on the other hand, is *not* subject to degrees, unfolding, or development. At each stage of revelation, God graciously gives us his inspired word so that his people always have his trustworthy and sufficient word. No doubt, in light of Christ's coming, the NT gives us a completion to revelation, but equally the OT and the NT are the inspired word of God. This does not mean all parts of Scripture are as directly applicable to the church as other parts now that Christ has come. For example, it is not surprising that the Gospels, Romans,

---

[50] Ferguson, "How Does the Bible Look at Itself?", 57.

Ephesians, and Galatians have played a more significant role in the theology and life of the church than the Song of Solomon. Yet, all the parts of the canon are equally inspired for our "teaching, rebuking, correcting, and training in righteousness" (2 Tim 3:16 NIV). By analogy, each book of Scripture functions like the instruments of a symphony orchestra: some may be more prominent than others, but each contributes to the harmony of the whole. Discerning the whole counsel of God requires listening to the entire canon and applying *all* that God has said and doing due diligence to how each part fits within the whole of Scripture, especially now in light of the closed canon.

4. Inspiration Does Not Remove the Need to Interpret Scripture Correctly.

No text of Scripture discloses its meaning to us apart from actual exegesis, yet the same triune God who "was active in producing [Scripture] . . . is active again whenever it is read and received with understanding."[51] Although it is necessary to distinguish "inspiration" from "illumination," we must never separate them. The purpose of Scripture is to make us wise to salvation in Christ Jesus by uniting us to him by grace through faith and to make us his new covenant people. But this does not occur unless we understand the truth of God's word and believe all of God's promises in Christ, which is also the gracious work of the Holy Spirit in us. Our belief in the Bible's inspiration does not remove the hard work of interpretation.[52]

Criticisms of the Doctrine of Inspiration

Inspiration, Dictation, and the God-Scripture-World Relation

Given the Bible's view of inspiration, critics have often questioned its logical coherence. Repeatedly critics ask the question, assuming a negative answer, How is it logically possible for God to *guarantee* that humans will freely write exactly what *he* wants written, infallibly and without error, unless a dictation theory of inspiration is embraced?[53] After all, the biblical

---

[51] Vanhoozer, "Triune Discourse (Part 2)," 64.

[52] See chapter 11 for a discussion of this point regarding the clarity/perspicuity of Scripture.

[53] Repeatedly, the "received view" is charged with requiring the dictation theory of inspiration. See e.g., Sparks, *Sacred Word, Broken Word*, 56–57; Boyd, *Inspired Imperfection*, 106–24 (see chap. 5, n. 39).

authors are finite and fallen, and if they write *freely* (usually defined in a libertarian sense), how does God keep them from error unless he removes their freedom? It seems that to affirm a biblical view of inspiration requires either the acceptance of a dictation view or its denial and the embrace of a weakened view of Scripture. But, as the critic rightly notes, to affirm a dictation theory is disastrous since the phenomena of Scripture will not allow it. As we read Scripture, the human authors give no evidence of being stenographers; rather, they write freely, utilizing their own gifts and abilities. But if this is so, then we must reject a dictation view, which only seems to leave us with one option: we must embrace a weakened view of Scripture similar to neo-orthodoxy and its current iterations. In response, two points need to be made.

First, the critic correctly insists that Scripture gives little evidence of dictation except in a few places (Exod 31:18). The human authors write their books freely exercising their gifts and abilities.[54] In fact, as noted above, God used a variety of *modes* in giving us Scripture (e.g., direct revelation, dreams, historical research, thoughtful reflection, etc.). For this reason, the "received view" has insisted on a "concursive theory" in order to account for what Scripture teaches about inspiration and the dual authorship of the Bible.

Second, the critic wrongly insists that the biblical view of inspiration is logically incoherent and that it must be replaced by a weakened view of Scripture. No doubt, Scripture never explains fully *how* our triune God by the Spirit so superintended and *guaranteed* that the writing of the biblical authors is *his* infallible and inerrant word, but Scripture certainly gives us the *theology* to account for it. But this requires that we receive Scripture on its own terms *and* according to its own teaching of *theology proper*, specifically the God-world relation as expressed in the divine sovereignty–human freedom relationship.

As we will develop in our discussion of the doctrine of God and divine providence in part 4 (chapters 22–23), it is nigh impossible to account for *all* that Scripture teaches regarding the God-world relation without affirming at least four truths simultaneously. First, our triune God is the one who plans and knows all things and, as such, is sovereign over his world, including

---

For a refutation of this charge and a correct view of the God-world relation, see Henry, *God, Revelation, and Authority*, 4:138 (see chap. 3, n. 18); Packer, *"Fundamentalism" and the Word of God*, 78–79 (see chap. 7, n. 7); Warfield, "Inspiration," in *Selected Shorter Writings*, 2:614–36 (see chap. 1, n. 7).

[54] For a discussion as to why the dictation theory of inspiration is contrary to the biblical evidence and thus why it should be rejected, see I. H. Marshall, *Biblical Inspiration* (Grand Rapids: Eerdmans, 1982), 32–33.

the free actions of his creatures (Pss 115:2–3; 139:16; Isa 14:24–26; 46:9–11; Dan 4:34–35; Acts 17:24–26; Eph 1:11). Second, humans are free and morally responsible, yet their freedom does not thwart God's plan and sovereign rule over the world (Josh 24:14–15; Prov 16:9; 19:21; 21:1; Ezek 18:30–32). Third, in providence, God acts as the primary cause accomplishing his plan, but in doing so, he does not remove the reality of secondary causes/agents (Gen 50:19–20; Isa 10:5–17; Acts 2:23; 4:23–31). Furthermore, as noted above, God's first primary causal work is to call, sanctify, and gift the human authors so that by divine appointment they become God's chosen instruments to write Scripture, and in the act of inspiration, there is an extraordinary work of the Holy Spirit in the human authors so that Scripture is truly a divine-human word. Fourth, God is perfectly good (Deut 32:4; Hab 1:13; 1 John 1:5).

With these biblical truths in place, the doctrine of inspiration, a strong view of *concursus*, dual agency, the sanctifying and gifting work of the Spirit in and through the human authors, and dual authorship make perfect sense. But if one rejects these truths, one is unable to account for the Bible's teaching on inspiration, which is precisely the critic's problem. In fact, when the critic charges that the biblical view of inspiration requires a dictation theory, he reveals that he is assuming a different God-world relationship than Scripture actually teaches. At dispute then is not the logical coherence of inspiration but, more significantly, the doctrine of God that underlies it. Years ago, B. B. Warfield made this exact point. After describing the biblical view of *concursus* and rejecting a dictation theory, he argued that the *theological* basis for *concursus*

> is the Christian conception of God as immanent in his modes of working as well as transcendent. It is this theory, as has already been pointed out, that underlies the church doctrine of inspiration and constitutes, indeed, the church doctrine of the mode of inspiration. It was the conception of the greatest of the Fathers (e.g., Augustine) and of the Reformers, and it remains the conception of the great body of modern theologians.[55]

---

[55] Warfield, "Inspiration," in *Selected Shorter Writings*, 2:649. Warfield mentions various theologians in his day who held to *concursus*: Louis Gaussen, Basil Manly, Charles Hodge, A. A. Hodge, William Shedd, etc. For Warfield's discussion of *concursus* and the divine-human authorship of Scripture tied to his theology proper, see Anthony N. S. Lane, "B. B. Warfield and the Humanity of Scripture," *VE* 16 (1984): 77–94.

This is why we argued in chapter 5 that the theological/dogmatic location for Scripture is *triune divine agency* in providence in the *extraordinary* sense. If one rejects this, then the theological accounting for how God can *guarantee* what the human authors wrote freely in *his* word is found wanting.[56]

On this point, that is, a biblical view of inspiration requiring a specific view of the divine sovereignty–human freedom relationship, we also part company with Nicholas Wolterstorff.[57] Wolterstorff is to be commended for writing a masterful philosophical treatise on Scripture as divine discourse. In contrast to many today, he argues for a strong view of divine authorship, and he rightly insists that the Bible as divine speech is the result of double agency. Humans write Scripture, and God speaks through their writings in two ways. First, God *deputizes* the biblical authors to speak on his behalf similar to an ambassador speaking on behalf of his head of state.[58] Second, God *appropriates* the author's writings and thus speaks through them.[59] But, given his dismissal of what he calls a theory of divine origination, i.e., inspiration,[60] he argues, similar to Karl Barth, that there is a distinction between what the biblical authors say and what God says.[61] Thus, the biblical authors say things that God does not agree with or intend for them to say. For example, God did not command the Israelites to kill the Canaanites, although the biblical authors thought he did. But in creating a wedge between what the human authors say and God intends to say, Wolterstorff requires extratextual criteria to determine what to believe from Scripture. And as Michael Horton suggests, he needs a standard outside of Scripture to determine exactly "what God could or couldn't have said . . . [but] what God 'could' or 'couldn't' do (especially in terms of what is loving) differs widely, depending on one's

---

[56] This is another reason why the dogmatic location for Scripture is not Christology. As Henri Blocher states: "Confessing Chalcedon, Christology deals with *one* Person and *two* natures classically conceived as *distinct substances*." But "Bibliology deals with the cooperation of *two* persons and *one act*, speech-act, with qualities one should not think of as substances! . . . God speaks through his human 'mouth': his speech-act is precisely what he causes the prophet or apostle, through the Spirit's assistance, to do in his name." "God and the Scripture Writers," 532.

[57] See Wolterstorff, *Divine Discourse* (see chap. 3, n. 46).

[58] Wolterstorff, 45.

[59] Wolterstorff, 41.

[60] See Wolterstorff, 283–84, where he distinguishes divine discourse from divine inspiration.

[61] Wolterstorff, 206–7.

perspective."[62] In the end, although Wolterstorff views Scripture as divine speech, it is consistent with what Scripture says about itself, namely, what the human authors say (Scripture says), God says and intends.

The heart of Wolterstorff's problem is his weak view of *concursus* and dual agency. Wolterstorff embraces a libertarian view of freedom, which necessarily weakens God's sovereignty, thus making it difficult for him to affirm that what the biblical authors write is precisely what God intended to say.[63] According to Scripture's self-attestation, God does not simply deputize or appropriate discourse; he *authors* it. The human words of the Bible are the means by which God authoritatively and truthfully speaks to us.[64] What Scripture says, God says. The human authors are divinely commissioned witnesses, but they speak and write exactly what God wants said. God works in and through the biblical authors in an *extraordinary* way without removing their freedom so that what they write *is* his word.

In summary, the lesson to learn is this. We cannot account for the Bible's view of inspiration apart from the Bible's view of God. As noted in chapter 5, debates over the doctrine of Scripture are fundamentally debates over the doctrine of God. Blocher rightly insists that what is needed is classical "Trinitarian monotheism" with a high view of God's sovereignty and divine authorship. He writes:

> Trinitarian monotheism confesses both the fullness of God's being and distinction of Creator and creature. This foundation is required for fully affirming the being of creatures, above all the Image-creature made for fellowship with the Father of spirits, and for its gracious promotion or glorification. The One God—Father, Son/Word, and Holy Spirit—is able to "breathe out" the discourse of human authors as his own.[65]

Limited Inspiration?

Before we conclude, we need to mention a wrongheaded view that argues that "inspiration" only applies to matters of salvation, not truthfulness in all matters. Appeal is made to 2 Tim

---

[62] Horton, *Covenant and Eschatology*, 162 (see chap. 2, n. 147).

[63] See Wolterstorff, *Divine Discourse*, 119–23.

[64] For a similar point, see Blocher, "God and the Scripture Writers," 519–23.

[65] Blocher, 541.

3:16–17, and the argument is this: if the *purpose* of Scripture is to lead us to salvation, then it is futile to link inspiration with truthfulness and authority.[66] There are two problems with this view.

First, there is an error in categories. When we speak of inspiration, we need to distinguish the following categories of inspiration: the "mode" (dreams, research, thoughtful reflection, dictation), the "means" (authors write in different literary forms), the "purpose" (Scripture is given to make us wise to salvation in Christ), and the "result" (due to triune agency by the Spirit in and through the human authors, what Scripture says, God says). But this argument conflates "purpose" with "result," thus confusing what Scripture says inspiration actually is as the objective work of God in and through human authors.

Second, it is also impossible to separate matters of history, science, and so on, from matters of "faith and practice."[67] God's plan of redemption is enacted on the stage of human history, and the specifics of history matter to the truthfulness of Christian theology. For example, if Christ did not die on the cross and, in history, rise bodily from the dead, our theology is false (1 Cor 15:12–19). In other words, the Bible speaks about what we are to believe in the context of creation, history, and God's redemptive work for us in history—all of which must correspond to reality. Unlike other religions, our salvation is dependent on history and specific events happening as Scripture describes them. God's revelation includes his mighty acts in history (which must occur) along with his word interpretation of those events. A "limited" view of inspiration simply leaves us with a fallible Scripture that cannot serve as our standard for truth nor as the foundation for a normative theology.

Concluding Reflection

Scripture's own self-testimony is that it is God's word written by the agency of human authors. "Inspiration" is the *theological* concept that accounts for the relation between God's word and the words of the human authors. But it is also the warrant for the Reformation's affirmation of *sola Scriptura*. Scripture *alone* is our *final* authority by which we know God, ourselves, and the

[66] See Richard Coleman, "Reconsidering 'Limited Inerrancy,'" *JETS* 17 (1974): 207–14. For a response, see Vern S. Poythress, "Problems for Limited Inerrancy," *JETS* 18/2 (1975): 93–102; and Feinberg, *Light in a Dark Place*, 303–7.

[67] See Frame, *Doctrine of the Word*, 177–78 (chap. 5, n. 5).

world and by which we preach, teach, command, warn, and exhort the church and all people because Scripture *is* God's word. Other books can teach us much. Church tradition is helpful and necessary. But in matters of truth, doctrine, life, and moral demand, Scripture *alone* is our final authority. The question by which the church must live is: Where stands it written?

Many people throughout church history have illustrated what it means to live under God's word and not stand over it, but none better than Martin Luther at the Diet of Worms (1521). By this time, Luther had caused quite a stir in Europe, which the Pope had underestimated. Initially, the Pope thought that Luther's protest would disappear, but this was not the case. So at the Diet of Worms, Luther was called before the religious establishment to recant his writings. Luther demonstrated his commitment to *sola Scriptura* in his famous words:

> Unless I am convinced by the testimony of the Scriptures or by clear reason (for I do not trust either in the pope or in councils alone, since it is well known that they often err and contradict themselves), I am bound by the Scriptures I have quoted and my conscience is captive to the Word of God. I cannot and will not recant anything . . . here I stand, may God help me, Amen.[68]

What was illustrated in Luther's life, the Reformation, and throughout church history is a commitment to Scripture for what it is: God's word written. It alone must command our total trust and confidence because it is God's gracious means by which we come to know *him* as our glorious triune Creator, Lord, and Redeemer. In the Reformation, as David Wright describes, *sola Scriptura* was "Scripture's freedom to rule as God's Word in the church, disentangled from papal and ecclesiastical *magisterium* (authoritative teaching office) and tradition."[69] For the evangelical church today, Scripture must continue to be our final authority for our theology, thinking, and lives. We must test everything by it and critique all thought according to it. We must never be held captive by the so-called knowledge of the world apart from bringing our thought captive to Christ (2 Cor 10:3–5; Col 2:8–10). We must not add to Scripture or subtract from it (Deut 4:2; 12:32; Rev 22:18–19), whether by so-called new revelations generated from our own subjectivity or human traditions. Scripture alone must govern our lives, for it gives us the words of life, the promises of God, and the knowledge of our glorious Lord and Savior.

---

[68] "Luther at the Diet of Worms, 1521," in *LW* 32:112.

[69] David F. Wright, "Protestantism," in Treier and Elwell, *EDT*, 704 (see chap. 2, n. 18).

Many of our Protestant confessions have captured what Scripture is and its import for the church. We conclude with the beautiful statement of the *London Baptist Confession* (1689) (1.1):

> The Holy Scripture is the only sufficient, certain, and infallible rule of all saving knowledge, faith, and obedience, although the light of nature, and the works of creation and providence do so far manifest the goodness, wisdom, and power of God, as to leave men inexcusable; yet they are not sufficient to give that knowledge of God and His will which is necessary unto salvation. Therefore it pleased the Lord at sundry times and in diversified manners to reveal Himself, and to declare (that) His will unto His church; and afterward for the better preserving and propagating of the truth, and for the more sure establishment and comfort of the church against the corruption of the flesh, and the malice of Satan, and of the world, to commit the same wholly unto writing; which makes the Holy Scriptures to be most necessary, those former ways of God's revealing His will unto His people being now completed.

CHAPTER 10

The Infallibility and Inerrancy of Scripture

Introduction

The subject of inerrancy is of vital significance in our discussion of the doctrine of Scripture. But it is crucial to note that it cannot be dichotomized from our previous discussion of inspiration as if one can affirm the latter without the former. The Bible's trustworthiness is a consequence of its verbal-plenary inspiration. Scripture is free from error in all its teaching and communicative intent because it is the product of the triune God, who cannot err. As discussed in previous chapters, we cannot separate God from his word, specifically his word spoken through prophets and apostles. And as the triune Lord who plans and knows all things (Eph 1:11), who cannot lie (Num 23:19), and who cannot change his mind (1 Sam 15:29; Heb 6:18), the *graphē* that God "breathes out" (2 Tim 3:16) is reliable and true. E. J. Young captures this point: "There is no such thing as inspiration which does not carry with it the correlate of infallibility. A Bible that is fallible—and we speak of course of the original—is a Bible that is not inspired. A Bible that is inspired is a Bible that is infallible. There is no middle ground."[1]

Inerrancy has been the hallmark of evangelical theology. In response to the classic liberalism of the "modern" age, evangelicals were known for their confession and defense of

[1] Edward J. Young, *Thy Word is Truth: Some Thoughts on the Biblical Doctrine of Inspiration* (Grand Rapids: Eerdmans, 1957), 109.

inerrancy,[2] as reflected by the *Chicago Statement on Biblical Inerrancy*, and in the Southern Baptist Convention by *The Baptist Faith and Message*.[3] Historically, although the term "infallibility" was more common than "inerrancy" given the unfortunate decoupling of infallibility from inerrancy, the latter term was introduced more recently to emphasize what the church has always confessed: Scripture *is* God's word written, and thus it is inerrant.

Today, many within post-liberalism and post-conservatism not only complain that "inerrancy" is an overly negative term; they also claim that it is logically inadequate. As the argument goes, since much of Scripture is not propositional in nature, technically, "inerrancy" only applies to propositions or assertions, not to other speech acts, such as commands, promises, exclamations, questions, and so on.[4] Technically speaking, this is correct, but it also misses the point. "Inerrancy" was *not* used to convey the idea that every conceivable speech-act in Scripture must be susceptible to the term "inerrant" as we mean it for assertions. Everyone acknowledges that Scripture consists of many diverse speech-acts, yet the point of inerrancy was to affirm that the Bible is "wholly true" in all that it affirms, including all of its speech-acts, specifically its propositions and assertions. This is why, historically, infallibility always included within it the concept of inerrancy.

For this reason, we need to keep together infallibility *and* inerrancy, as the church has done, and not separate them as some have done recently.[5] Yet, technically speaking, in order to account for all of Scripture's speech acts and literary forms, Kevin Vanhoozer's proposal is helpful: "The term *infallible*—in the sense of 'not liable to fail'—remains useful as the broader term for biblical authority, with *inerrancy* a vital subset (that is, not liable to fail *in its*

---

[2] In 1947, Fuller Seminary, and in 1949, the Evangelical Theological Society, were formed to defend the full authority and inerrancy of Scripture. Prior to them, in 1929, Westminster Theological Seminary, continuing the tradition of "old Princeton," also was formed for the same reason. In the SBC, the conservative resurgence was also concerned to recover the Bible's full authority and inerrancy.

[3] See *Chicago Statement on Biblical Inerrancy* at https://www.alliancenet.org/the-chicago-statement-on-biblical-inerrancy. For the *Baptist Faith & Message*, see https://bfm.sbc.net/bfm2000/.

[4] For a description of this argument, see Kevin J. Vanhoozer, "The Semantics of Biblical Literature: Truth and Scripture's Diverse Literary Forms," in Carson and Woodbridge, *Hermeneutics, Authority, and Canon*, 53–104 (see chap. 2, n. 63); Vanhoozer, "Augustinian Inerrancy: Literary Meaning, Literal Truth, and Literate Interpretation in the Economy of Biblical Discourse," in Merrick and Garrett, *Five Views on Biblical Inerrancy*, 203–4 (see chap. 7, n. 10); also cf. Frame, *Doctrine of the Word*, 167–200 (chap. 5, n. 5).

[5] On this point, see our discussion of the "Rogers and McKim proposal" in chapter 8.

assertions)."[6] Furthermore, as we account for Scripture's diverse literary forms and the specific truth claims each literary form makes,[7] Vanhoozer is again helpful when he insists that the concept of "error" is also "context-dependent:" "What might count as an error in the context of scientific historiography (or the natural sciences) might not count as an error in the context of less exacting, 'ordinary' forms of discourse."[8]

All of this is true and necessary to define inerrancy correctly. Thus, when all the nuances are made, we should never separate the concepts of "infallibility" and "inerrancy" since as Guy Waters notes, "If the Bible is incapable of deceiving us, it must be free from deceptions of any kind."[9] Inerrancy and infallibility together affirm that Scripture as *God's* word is completely true and reliable. Even more, as Waters continues: "Inerrancy is a 'necessary inference' from the character of the God who authored the Bible,"[10] which entails that a denial of inerrancy is indeed theologically significant.

Unfortunately, in the current discussion of inerrancy within evangelical theology, there is now a spectrum within which three groups that have emerged.[11] First, there is the group represented by the ICBI, who considers inerrancy to be a watershed issue for the church and that a departure from it has serious consequences for one's entire theology.[12] Second, there is the group who affirms inerrancy but insists that church unity is more important than dividing over it. Third, there is the group who rejects inerrancy and contends that it is an innovation due to the influence of "modernism" on evangelical theology. Today, this last group identifies with post-conservative or post-liberal theology and replaces the "received view" with a more neo-orthodox view of Scripture, as discussed in chapter 7.

---

[6] Vanhoozer, "Augustinian Inerrancy," 203–4 (emphasis original). See Frame, *Doctrine of the Word*, 168–69, who concurs.

[7] See Barry G. Webb, "Biblical Authority and Diverse Literary Genres," in Carson, *Enduring Authority*, 577–614 (see chap. 4, n. 9).

[8] Vanhoozer, "Augustinian Inerrancy," 210 n. 33.

[9] Waters, *For the Mouth*, 104 (chap. 5, n. 5); cf. Ward, *Words of Life*, 132–33 (see chap. 5, n. 27).

[10] Waters, *For the Mouth*, 105.

[11] This breakdown is from Harold O. J. Brown, "The Inerrancy and Infallibility of the Bible," in *The Origin of the Bible*, ed. Philip W. Comfort et al. (Wheaton: Tyndale, 2003), 40. These groups are also evident in Merrick and Garrett, *Five Views on Biblical Inerrancy*. R. Albert Mohler Jr. and Kevin Vanhoozer fit in group 1 (possibly Vanhoozer fits in group 2); Michael Bird, in group 2; and Peter Enns and John Franke, in group 3.

[12] I agree with this group regarding the significance of inerrancy for theology.

Given the significance of inerrancy for our understanding of Scripture *and* our view of God, we must formulate it carefully. Inerrancy must be able to account for the Bible's actual content, including ordinary language, human author's idiosyncrasies, unique grammatical constructions, issues of precision in recording that reflect the times and culture of the Bible, genre issues, and so on. But when our formulation of inerrancy is done, we must remember that behind it is the larger question of whether our triune God has spoken and is able to speak in an authoritative and trustworthy manner. Let us now turn to the topic of inerrancy by focusing on three areas: first, a definition and exposition of inerrancy; second, various clarifications or nuances of inerrancy; and third, specific arguments for inerrancy.

A Definition and Exposition of Inerrancy

Our working definition of inerrancy will employ Paul Feinberg's definition from the ICBI literature. After stating it, we will expound and develop its basic meaning. What is inerrancy? "Inerrancy means that when all the facts are known, the Scriptures in their original autographs and properly interpreted will be shown to be wholly true in everything that they affirm, whether that has to do with doctrine or morality or with the social, physical, or life sciences."[13]

"When All the Facts Are Known . . ."

This phrase is important because it reminds us of a number of truths.

First, it reminds us that not all the problems regarding inerrancy are fully resolved at the present time. Our affirmation of inerrancy does not imply, and has never implied, that we know how to resolve every apparent inconsistency in Scripture. In fact, we are under no obligation to do so in order to believe in inerrancy. No doubt, we are more than willing to resolve difficulties where possible, convinced that when all the facts are known, Scripture will be shown

---

[13] Paul D. Feinberg, "Meaning of Inerrancy," in Geisler, *Inerrancy*, 294 (see chap. 7, n. 4). For other definitions of inerrancy, see Frame, *Doctrine of the Word*, 169; Vanhoozer, "Augustinian Inerrancy," 207: Inerrancy means that "the authors speak the truth in all things they affirm (when they make affirmations), and will eventually to be seen to have spoken truly (when right readers read rightly)."

to be wholly true and never false. But we affirm inerrancy not because we can answer all of the difficulties, but because of Scripture's self-attestation plus the larger worldview argument that, apart from a true and reliable word from God, we have no ultimate epistemological warrant for objective truth and a normative theology. We will return to this last point at the end of the chapter when we discuss specific arguments for inerrancy.

Second, this phrase also admits that some of our interpretations of Scripture and the "facts" that seemingly contradict Scripture may need correction to "see" how apparent problems may be resolved. Scripture's reliability is not dependent on the reliability of our interpretations of it.[14]

Third, this phrase also acknowledges, especially in the study of history and archaeology, that *more* evidence is still waiting to be unearthed. No doubt, some historical data may have been lost forever, but other evidence still awaits further discovery. In fact, repeatedly the Bible's historical trustworthiness has been questioned, but later discoveries overturned the earlier skepticism. Many examples could be given, but here are a few from the OT and the NT.[15]

Evidence of the Historical Reliability of the OT[16]

1. *The Hittite Civilization* (Gen 10:15). Prior to 1906, the Hittite civilization was unknown in non-biblical history. But due to the work of Hugo Winckler, Scripture was confirmed to be true.

2. *The Horites* (Gen 36:20; Deut 2:12, 22). The Bible tells us that the Horites from Seir were driven out of the land by Esau's descendants, but this was unconfirmed outside of Scripture. But in 1995, they were discovered under the Egyptian term *Hurru*. The capital city, Urkesh, was discovered beneath the Syrian town of Tell Mozan. Their estimated date is c. 2300–2200 BC.

---

[14] See Vanhoozer, "Augustinian Inerrancy," 223–24. Vanhoozer strongly makes this point.

[15] The literature on the historical accuracy of Scripture is legion. For example, see Cowan and Wilder, *In Defense of the Bible* (see chap. 5, n. 93); Hoffmeier and Magary, *Do Historical Matters Matter?* (see chap. 5, n. 93); Walter C. Kaiser Jr. *The Old Testament Documents: Are They Reliable and Relevant?* (Downers Grove: InterVarsity, 2001); K. A. Kitchen, *On the Reliability of the Old Testament* (Grand Rapids: Eerdmans, 2003); Blomberg, *Historical Reliability of the New Testament* (see chap. 5, n. 93); Paul Barnett, *Is the New Testament Reliable?*, 2nd ed. (Downers Grove: InterVarsity, 2003); Peter J. Williams, *Can We Trust the Gospels?* (Wheaton: Crossway, 2018).

[16] These examples are taken from Kaiser, *The Old Testament Documents*, 97–108. For more examples, consult the resources in n. 15.

3. *Belshazzar* (Dan 5). Daniel says that Belshazzar was reigning at the time of Babylon's fall. But available cuneiform records said that Nabonidus was the king, thus contradicting the Bible. But Daniel was correct since we have now discovered that Nabonidus spent the last days of his reign residing in Arabia, leaving the rule of Babylon to his eldest son, Belshazzar.

4. *Sargon* (Isa 20:1). Isaiah says that Sargon was king of Assyria, which no one could verify. But in 1843, Paul Emile Botta discovered a new capital city, twelve miles northeast of Nineveh, where Sargon began a building project in 717 BC. After his death, his son, Sennacherib, moved the capital. Sargon (722–705 BC) is now one of the best known of the Assyrian monarchs.

5. *Ophir*. The Bible says that Solomon's ships sailed to and brought back huge amounts of gold from Ophir (1 Kgs 9:28). But where was this city? In 1956 it was found at the coastal site of Tell Qasile (north of Tel Aviv). It was not only a real location but also a major source of gold.

6. *Numbers 33 and the Transjordanian route*. Most said that the Bible's detailed description of this route was inaccurate. But Charles Krahmalkov demonstrated that the Israelites' invasion route described in Num 33:45b–50 was in fact an official, heavily trafficked Egyptian road through the Transjordan in the Late Bronze Age.

The list could go on. Given the discovery of more "facts," we now have confirmation of what before was lacking. For example, we have confirmed the existence of Balaam, David, Ahab, Jehu, Hezekiah, Menahem, and so on. Missing people and places have been found, and in each case the reliability of Scripture was confirmed. This does not mean that history and archaeology have solved every problem, but repeatedly Scripture has been demonstrated to be true.

Evidence of the Historical Reliability of the NT

1. *The Work of William Ramsay* (1851–1939). William Ramsay was a NT scholar, archaeologist, and biblical critic. His research led him to the conviction that Luke-Acts was historically reliable, as proven by external attestation. For example, he discovered that Luke was well acquainted with the political arrangements in the provinces of Asia as evidenced by these kinds of details in the book of Acts, which people previously disputed:[17]

---

[17] See William M. Ramsay, *St. Paul the Traveler and the Roman Citizen* (London: Hodder & Stoughton, 1910); *The Bearing of Recent Discovery on the Trustworthiness of the New Testament* (London:

- Luke correctly spoke of Sergius Paulus by the title of proconsul (13:7).
- Philippi was accurately described as a Roman colony whose officials were *stratagoi* (16:38).
- At Thessalonica the reference to the politarchs (17:6) is now well attested.
- In Ephesus the officials were correctly identified as the Asiarchs (19:31).
- At Malta, the *protos* (28:7) was the "chief official."
- Luke was correct about the census account in Luke 2:1–4.

2. *Intersections of Scripture with Extrabiblical Sources.*[18]

- King Herod and the killing of the boys (Matt 2:16; Macrobius, *Saturnalia* 2.4.11).
- The revolt of Judas (Acts 5:37; Josephus, *Jewish War* 2.118).
- Emperor, prefect, high priest (Luke 3:1–2; Josephus, *Jewish War* 2.169; Josephus, *Jewish Antiquities* 18.113–117).
- Execution of Jesus (Mark 15:15; Tacitus, *Annals* 15.44).
- Death of Agrippa I (Acts 12:20–23; Josephus, *Jewish Antiquities* 19.344–349).
- James, the brother of Jesus (Acts 21:17–18; Josephus, *Jewish Antiquities* 20.200).
- Felix and Drusilla (Acts 24:24; Josephus, *Jewish Antiquities* 20.131–143; Tacitus, *History* 5.9; Tacitus, *Annals* 12.54).

"The Scriptures in Their Original Autographs . . ."

This phrase is probably the most contentious. In fact, Bart Ehrman says that this issue was one of the main reasons he departed from an evangelical view of Scripture.[19] Others think that since we do not have the originals, we should not make it part of our definition of inerrancy, or it is dismissed as solely an "American" debate.[20] Nonetheless, most definitions of

---

Hodder & Stoughton, 1915); *Was Christ Born At Bethlehem? A Study on the Credibility of St. Luke* (London: Hodder & Stoughton, 1905).

[18] These examples are taken from Barnett, *Is the New Testament Reliable?*, 165–75.

[19] Bart D. Ehrman, *Misquoting Jesus: The Story Behind Who Changed the Bible and Why* (New York: HarperCollins, 2005), 5–11.

[20] For example, see Michael F. Bird, "Inerrancy is Not Necessary for Evangelicalism Outside the USA," in *Five Views of Biblical Inerrancy*, ed. Merrick and Garrett, 145–73.

inerrancy include it for good reasons. Let us unpack the significance of this phrase by making five points.[21]

First, the church has always affirmed the significance of the original autographs. In chapter 8, we gave some examples, but early on Augustine expresses this view in his letter to Jerome:

> I have learned to yield this respect and honor only to the canonical books of Scripture: of these alone do I most firmly believe that the authors were completely free from error. And if in these writings I am perplexed by anything which appears to me opposed to truth, I do not hesitate to suppose that either the manuscript is faulty, or the translator has not caught the meaning of what was said, or I myself have failed to understand it.[22]

In the early church, the practice of "textual criticism" was operative, that is, the attempt to remove copyists' errors from extant copies—all of which assumed the reliability of the originals. This attitude continued until the Enlightenment and continues today, but with the rise of "higher criticism," the idea of "originals" was dismissed.

Second, the question of original autographs is the result of inscripturation. God's *written* word is a gracious gift. In contrast to oral revelation, a written revelation results in "greater durability, fixity, purity, and catholicity. A written document is capable of universal distribution through repeated copying, and yet it can be preserved in various kinds of depositories

---

[21] My discussion is indebted to Greg L. Bahnsen, "The Inerrancy of the Autographa," in Geisler, *Inerrancy*, 151–93. On what constitutes an "original autograph," see Timothy N. Mitchell, "Myths about Autographs," in *Myths and Mistakes in New Testament Textual Criticism*, ed. Elijah Hixson and Peter J. Gurry (Downers Grove: IVP Academic, 2019), 26–47; Mitchell, "Where Inspiration is Found: Putting the New Testament Autographs in Context," *SBJT* 24.3 (2020): 83–101. I am following Mitchell's definition, especially in regard to the NT: the autograph is "the text of the completed authorial work the moment in which it was released by the author for circulation and copying, not earlier draft versions or layers of composition." "Where Inspiration is Found," 96. The autograph, then, is the "final" form of the text. In the OT, it is more complicated, as evidenced by the Pentateuch and the Psalter. For the former, the autograph would refer to the Pentateuch in its final form (including Deut 34 and possibly some later editorial seams). Prior to this, the Pentateuch is what Moses wrote prior to the later additions. For the latter, the autograph is the Psalter in its final form, not the individual psalms. This does not mean that the writers of the individual psalms did not write under the inspiration of the Spirit, but the reference to original autographs refers to the final form/text of the Psalter.

[22] Augustine, *Letters of St. Augustine* 82.1.3 (*NPNF*[1] 1:350).

from generation to generation."[23] In fact, God *intended* for his covenant word to be *written* down. But as Abraham Kuyper recognized, a written word does *not* make it immune from the "vicissitudes of history."[24] The transmission of Scripture allows for the possibility of differences between what was originally written and its copies and translations. But this raises the crucial question: Does Scripture teach that *inspiration* applies to the final form of the original *and to its copies*, or only to the former? In chapter 9, we argued that 2 Tim 3:16 applies to the original final form of the text, not to its copies (apographs) or translations. Inspiration is an *extraordinary* act that results in a "God-breathed" text, but there is no evidence that this unique act continues in every copyist or translator. If so, we must distinguish between the originals and their transmission.

Third, Scripture assumes the reality of original autographs and their significance, which is best seen by maintaining two biblical truths simultaneously.[25] On the one hand, Scripture affirms the full authority of copies and translations of Scripture. For example, the king is to copy the Torah and to obey it (Deut 17:18; cf. 1 Kgs 2:3). Or, as Ezra reads a copy of God's word and translates it, it is received as fully authoritative (Ezra 7:14; Neh 8:8). When the NT authors quote from the OT, they often used the Septuagint (LXX), the Greek translation of the Hebrew texts, but although it was a translation from copies, it was viewed as Scripture (Luke 4:16–21; John 5:39; Acts 17:2, 11; 2 Tim 3:15–16). The reason this is possible is because although the original manuscript (autograph) no longer existed, the *message/text* given by the original still continues in the copies.[26] Loss of the original autograph does not entail the loss of the original *message/text*. Thus, biblical writers could use copies and translations and view them as authoritative. In fact, since our Lord never questioned the reliability of the OT text, we have warrant to think that the first century text of the OT adequately corresponded to the original.

On the other hand, although copies and translations were viewed as authoritative, they are only so as they accurately reflected what was originally written.[27] Repeatedly, Scripture brings God's people back to the message/text that was first given. For example, Israel was commanded to do what God "commanded their fathers by Moses" (Judg 3:4), which calls them back to the

[23] Bahnsen, "The Inerrancy of the Autographa," 155.

[24] Cited in Bahnsen, 155.

[25] See Bahnsen, 159–71.

[26] See Bahnsen, 161.

[27] Bahnsen, 161–62.

original message that was first given. Isaiah's prophecy was to be a witness forever (Isa 8:1; 30:8), which assumes that the original message is the standard text for the future. And similar to the OT, the NT works with the same assumption. Copies of the OT are authoritative as they reflect the original text. For example, Jesus quotes from a copy of Isaiah but views it as the word of the Lord (Matt 1:22 [Isa 7:14]), or from Deuteronomy as from "the mouth of God" (Matt 4:4), which assumes that his present text corresponds to the original. Also, as we have discussed, 2 Tim 3:16 focuses on the *origin* of Scripture and thus the original. The reason why the sacred writings known to Timothy, which was probably the LXX, could make him wise unto salvation is because the present texts he was reading reflected what was originally given by God.

In fact, in the OT, four occasions demonstrate that inspiration and inerrancy are located in the original autographs.[28] Each example is a kind of textual restoration that reproduces the original. For example, in Exodus 32–34, the first tablets written by God (32:15–16) were destroyed by Moses (32:19). The rewriting of the words (34:1, 27–28) was to be done "according to the first writing" (Deut 10:2, 4); the second text, or copy, had to reflect exactly the *original* words. In Jeremiah, King Jehoiakim destroyed the original scroll that Jeremiah had dictated to Baruch, but God instructed Jeremiah to make a new copy according to the first one (36:28). Or think of how every time the king took his throne, he was to copy the Torah and obey it (Deut 17:18), but the copy is only authoritative as it reflects the original. In 2 Kings 22 (2 Chr 34), the Torah was recovered in the temple. It seems that the original was lost but that copies of the Law were in the hands of some of the priests and the prophets. King Josiah began to follow the Torah (2 Chr 34:3–7), but then a more complete version of it is found, which alarmed Josiah because it included parts absent from the other copies (2 Kgs 22:8, 13; 2 Chr 34:14). Since the new discovery reflected more accurately the original, it replaced the copies. This illustrates how the original corrects the subsequent copies *if* those copies did not adequately reflect the original. In other words, "The sufficiency of a copy is proportionate to its accurate reflection of the original. Deviation from the autograph jeopardizes the profit of a copy for doctrinal instruction and for direction in righteous living."[29] These examples demonstrate that Scripture itself distinguished originals from copies, thus locating the authority of the text in the original.

---

[28] See Bahnsen, 165–67.

[29] Bahnsen, 167.

The normative status of the originals is also affirmed in other ways.[30] We are not to alter the text of God's word (Deut 4:2; 12:32; Prov 30:6; Rev 22:18–19). The conflicts between Jesus and human tradition assume the normativity of the original message (Mark 7:1–13; Matt 5:43; 19:7; cf. 2 Cor 4:2). Paul instructs Christians not to tamper with God's word (2 Cor 4:2). Paul also wrote his letters by means of an amanuensis (Rom 16:22), but to avoid any forgery, he added his own authenticating signature to his letters so that the church knows what precisely comes from him (2 Thess 3:17; cf. 1 Cor 16:21; Gal 6:11; Col 4:18).

In summary, "it stands written" holds together the twin biblical truths we have discussed. The use of the perfect tense underscores the truth that something has been completed but its effects continue.[31] In terms of Scripture, the original autographs have been written and *that message* continues in the copies (and translations). But these texts are only authoritative if the present copies reflect what was originally given. Bahnsen nicely captures this point:

> New Testament arguments based on a phrase (as in Acts 15:13–17), a word (as in John 10:35), or even the difference between the singular and plural form of a word (as in Gal. 3:16) in the Old Testament would be completely emptied of genuine force if two things were not true: (1) that phrase, word, or form must appear in the present copies of the Old Testament, or else the argument falls to the ground . . . and (2) that phrase, word, or form must be assumed to have been present in the original text of the passage cited, or else the argument loses its authoritative foundation in the Word of God (i.e., such an element of the text would have no more authority than the word of any mere human at best and would be an embarrassing scribal error at worst). If the New Testament authors are not appealing through their extant copies to the original text, their arguments are futile.[32]

Fourth, there is also a significant *theological* reason for restricting inerrancy to the originals. Given that God has not promised that the unique act of inspiration continues in the transmission of Scripture, we have no warrant to think it has. Is this strange? As E. J. Young noted years

[30] See Bahnsen, 167–69.

[31] Bahnsen, 169.

[32] Bahnsen, 169.

ago, there is nothing strange about thinking that an *infallible* text has been *fallibly* transmitted unless Scripture explicitly teaches so.[33] Furthermore, as Young continues,

> If the Scripture is "God breathed," it naturally follows that only the original is "God-breathed." If holy men of God spoke from God as they were borne by the Holy Spirit, then only what they spoke under the Spirit's bearing is inspired. It would certainly be unwarrantable to maintain that copies of what they spoke were also inspired, since these copies were not made as men were borne of the Spirit. They were therefore not "God-breathed" as was the original.[34]

Thus given these truths about the inspiration and transmission of Scripture, theologically speaking, the restriction of inerrancy to the originals is also necessary to allow us "*to consistently confess the truthfulness of God*."[35] Why? For this reason: only with an inerrant autograph can we avoid attributing error to Scripture and *to God*. As argued in previous chapters, God and his word cannot be separated. This is why Young is rightly shocked by those who seem so cavalier about the originals: "Amazing indeed is the cavalier manner in which modern theologians relegate this doctrine of an inerrant original Scripture to the limbo of the unimportant,"[36] as "the veracity of God and the perfection of the Godhead are involved in that doctrinal outlook."[37] Ultimately, the foundation of theological knowledge is dependent on a reliable and trustworthy revelation from God. If the originals are errant, and thus not reliable, it is impossible to know the *extent* of error in them since who can say when an errant text from God stops making mistakes? But if the errors are due to the Bible's *transmission*, then in principle it can be corrected by textual criticism. Without the inerrancy of the originals, our knowledge of truth and theology is dependent on some kind of extratextual authority, not on Scripture alone. Our epistemological starting point for objective truth and a normative theology vanishes, and our position succumbs to the self-defeating view of modern/postmodern theology.

But someone objects. If we do not have the originals in our possession but only the copies, then what *practical* difference does it make? All the difference in the world! Just because

---

[33] Young, *Thy Word Is Truth*, 39–61.

[34] Young, 55–56.

[35] Bahnsen, "The Inerrancy of the Autographa," 179 (emphasis original).

[36] Young, *Thy Word Is Truth*, 89–90.

[37] Bahnsen, "The Inerrancy of the Autographa," 180.

we do not possess the inerrant originals does not entail that it does not matter if they ever existed. Cornelius Van Til illustrated this point by a thought experiment. Imagine crossing an overflowing river by a bridge that was under water a couple of inches. Although you cannot "see" the bridge, you cannot cross the river without it.[38] By analogy, we cannot "see" the originals, yet unless original inerrant texts undergird our present copies and in principle we can correct most transmission errors by textual criticism, Scripture as our *final* authority disappears. The value of our present Bibles is dependent on the inerrant originals. Or we could state it another way: since Scripture is inerrant in the originals, when the original *message* is identified through textual criticism, we have objective truth. But if errors are in the originals, when the original *message* is identified through textual criticism, it is only *possibly true*. This is why, theologically, original inerrancy allows us to confess consistently the truthfulness of God.

Fifth, although we do not possess the originals, we know that our present copies adequately reflect the originals despite textual variants since none of them affect any point of doctrine. Our confidence in the Bible's reliable transmission is warranted by the truth that our triune covenant Lord intends for his people to know him by his word and by the results of textual criticism.[39]

In thinking about textual criticism, regarding the OT, our Hebrew text is the Masoretic text, preserved by Jewish scholars known as the Masoretes (AD 500–1000). The oldest complete manuscript we have is Leningrad B19a (c. 1008–1009). We know that the copying techniques of these scholars were meticulous, and this was confirmed by the discovery of the Dead Sea Scrolls in 1946. At the Dead Sea, there were around 800 scrolls or parts, and in some cases, entire texts of the OT. The significance of this find was that it gave us OT texts from the first and second century BC. This allowed us to compare the transmission of the OT text, and overall, we have confidence that it was reliably transmitted. In looking at texts and variants, it is not easy to say exactly what percentage we have of the original, but Bruce Waltke estimates

---

[38] See Van Til, *In Defense of the Faith*, 5:153 (see chap. 3, n. 9).

[39] On the transmission of the OT, see Kaiser, *The Old Testament Documents*, 40–49; Paul D. Wegner, "Has the Old Testament Text Been Hopelessly Corrupted?," in Cowan and Wilder, *In Defense of the Bible*, 119–38. On the transmission of the NT, see Hixson and Gurry, *Myths and Mistakes*; Daniel B. Wallace, "Has the New Testament Text Been Hopelessly Corrupted?," in Cowan and Wilder, *In Defense of the Bible*, 139–63.

that it is around ninety percent, and of the remaining ten percent, the variants do not affect any doctrinal issue.[40]

For the NT, given that it is written later and given the number of manuscripts that allow us to know how reliable the transmission has been, our confidence is even greater. We have over 5,000 Greek manuscripts containing all or part of the NT. In addition, we have around 8,000 manuscript copies of the Vulgate (Latin translation by Jerome [382–405]) and more than 350 copies of the Syriac versions of NT (c. 150–250; most of the copies are from the 400s). Besides this, a good portion of the NT can be reproduced from citations of the church fathers prior to Nicaea (325). The dates of our NT manuscripts range from c. AD 125 (P52, which is a fragment of John 18:31–33, 37–38), to the Chester Beatty papyri (c. 200, which includes major portions of the NT), to Codex Vaticanus (c. 325–350, which contains the entire NT). What all the data shows is that the NT we currently possess has been accurately copied. Zachary Cole summarizes the data this way: "The macrostructure of the New Testament is remarkably stable, especially in comparison to other ancient works. Though textual variation exists, it is usually at the micro rather than the macro level."[41] As with the OT, where textual variations exist, no doctrine is at issue, and we have full confidence that God has remarkably and faithfully preserved his word.[42]

"Properly Interpreted in All That Scripture Affirms . . ."

One cannot talk about inerrancy without also addressing various issues of hermeneutics.

First, at the pedantic level, we must correctly interpret the text before we claim it is false. Our false interpretations do not count against the truth of Scripture. Also, this assumes that we have correctly identified what the text is and the kind of truth claim authors make in their texts. As Kevin Vanhoozer reminds us, "There is a difference between 'sentence meaning' and 'speaking meaning.' It is therefore not enough to speak about the *semantics* of biblical literature (its propositional content, sentence meaning); we must also account for the *pragmatics* (kinds

[40] Bruce K. Waltke, "Old Testament Textual Criticism," in *Foundations for Biblical Interpretation*, ed. David S. Dockery et al. (Nashville: B&H, 1994), 157.

[41] Zachary J. Cole, "Myths about Copyists," in Hixson and Gurry, *Myths and Mistakes* 151.

[42] See Barnett, *Is The New Testament Reliable?*, 43–47; cf. Williams, *Can We Trust the Gospels?*, 111–22.

of communicative action, speech act meaning)."[43] This distinction is important because it helps us discern what authors are doing or intending in their texts. Reading Scripture for the "literal sense" (*sensus literalis*) instead of "literalistically" is to follow the intention of the author as given in their specific texts along with its literary form. Only then can we determine what the author is actually saying and intending to say, which allows us to determine the kind of truth claim the author is making. "We must specify the author's communicative intent in order rightly to say what he is *doing* with his words."[44]

For example, in Matt 13:31–32, was Jesus affirming that the mustard seed is the smallest of all seeds as a scientific fact, or "was he *drawing an analogy* that his hearers would have understood, in order to communicate a nonbotanical truth?"[45] In context, Vanhoozer correctly argues that "Jesus was not *affirming* as scientific fact the proposition semantically expressed by his sentence. The subject matter of Jesus' authoritative teaching was not mustard seeds but the kingdom of God. . . . Jesus was not making a *literalistic* truth claim (about mustard seeds), but he was speaking the *literal* truth (about the kingdom)."[46] Or we could say it as Frame does.[47] Jesus is not making an incorrect statement. He is using ordinary language to communicate truth to his audience in the specific context of Israel. There is nothing that suggests that Jesus was making a statement to reflect the larger context of a universal scientific fact. To demand that kind of "precision" is to misunderstand what Jesus is communicating in his context.

Second, the issue of "precision" raises the question of cultural context and the issue of accommodation. As we have noted in previous chapters, there are different conceptions of "accommodation," and it is important to distinguish the historic view from current views. The historic view (e.g., Augustine, Calvin, etc.) is that God has communicated to us *truly* but in language accommodated to our understanding. Related to this, especially for issues of precision, Scripture communicates to us in the language of "appearances" (e.g., the sun rising and setting). Scripture is purposely not a "scientific" textbook, for the "assured" results of science change as we learn more about the world, and if God spoke in precise scientific language, most people would not understand it. Instead, Scripture is written in ordinary, phenomenal language

---

[43] Vanhoozer, "Augustinian Inerrancy," 218.

[44] Vanhoozer, 219–20.

[45] Vanhoozer, 219.

[46] Vanhoozer, 221.

[47] Frame, *Doctrine of the Word*, 187.

suited to communicate truth to us. But this view of accommodation rejects the Socinian view embraced by many today, that God "accommodates" his speech to the faulty and wrong ideas of the day. Rather than affirming that biblical language is ordinary but truthful in its communicative intent, the Socinian view leaves us with an errant Bible that needs to be corrected by the "assured" results of the current "knowledge" of the day. Such a view must be rejected.[48]

Third, we must distinguish between what the Bible describes and what it affirms/approves. It may seem strange to say that Scripture includes "false" teaching in it, but it is true. Yet not in a way that Scripture affirms or endorses it. Think of Job's friends. Most of what they said to Job was wrong, but it is described for us, and by reading the entire book of Job, we know what is true. Or think of the description of various behaviors in the OT, many of which God rejects or are not universally applicable. But we know this from reading Scripture as a canon, and we cannot jump to the conclusion that Scripture is endorsing a specific behavior just because it describes it.

Fourth, a correct interpretation of Scripture also raises the issue of harmonizations. Given the truth of inerrancy, it is legitimate to reconcile two seemingly contradictory texts, but carefully. For example, the Gospels are not exhaustive accounts of our Lord Jesus, so information is purposely not given. Hermeneutically, each Gospel stands on its own to determine what God is saying through each author, but valid questions arise in comparing the Gospels. In Matthew, at the empty tomb there was one angel (28:2–3), but in Luke there are two (24:4–8). Which is it? Or did Jesus heal one (Luke 8:26–39) or two demoniacs (Matt 8:28–34)? Did Jesus cleanse the temple at the beginning of his ministry (John 2:12–25), or the end (Matt 21:12–17), or both? All of these issues have been answered at length, but the point here is that before we charge the Scripture with an error or contradiction, we must first interpret it correctly.[49]

"Whether in Doctrine or Morality or in the Social, Physical, or Life Sciences . . ."

Inerrancy is not limited to matters of "faith and practice," but it applies to all areas of knowledge that Scripture addresses. It is impossible to create a neat dichotomy between the

---

[48] For a discussion of these issues, see Glenn S. Sunshine, "Accommodation Historically Considered," in Carson, *Enduring Authority*, 238–65.

[49] For a discussion of these issues and why they are not contradictory or an example of error, see Blomberg, *Historical Reliability* (see chap. 5, n. 93).

theological and the factual given the glorious truth that God acts to bring about our redemption in history. Think of Christ's life, death, resurrection, ascension, and Pentecost—all of these "acts" are in history (1 Cor 15:3–8), and apart from them actually occurring, our theology hangs in midair and is false. This is why, as we have discussed in other chapters, Jesus and the apostles regarded the OT and its history as revelatory of God's plan now fulfilled in Christ (Acts 7:1–53; 13:16–41). Scripture is true in every area that it addresses, and inerrancy applies to each of these areas.

Clarifications Regarding the Meaning of Inerrancy[50]

At this point, we need to discuss a number of nuances of inerrancy for the sake of clarity. This is necessary because our concept of inerrancy must be consistent with Scripture; we must not impose false criteria on Scripture and then claim Scripture errs. Let us discuss four areas.

First, as noted above, God speaks to us in the ordinary language of everyday speech, or what is sometimes called phenomenological language. Inerrancy does not deny this; it requires it. So, the Bible speaks of the sun rising and setting (Gen 19:23; Matt 5:45; Luke 4:40), but this does not require that Scripture is endorsing a geocentric view of the world. Scripture does *not* purport to be an astronomical textbook; it speaks to us in ordinary language that describes reality from the perspective of ordinary experience, which, even in light of a heliocentric view, we continue to speak the same way. The issue of ordinary language also raises two further issues.

1. *Inerrancy and Precision.* The amount of precision is context dependent and tied to the intention of the author. Precision must be defined in relation to Scripture's time period,

---

[50] See Feinberg, "Meaning of Inerrancy," 299–302. He lists eight points of clarification: (1) inerrancy does not demand strict adherence to the rules of grammar; (2) inerrancy does not exclude the use either of figures of speech or of a given literary genre; (3) inerrancy does not demand historical or semantic precision; (4) inerrancy does not demand the technical language of modern science; (5) inerrancy does not require verbal exactness in the citation of the Old Testament by the New; (6) inerrancy does not demand that the *Logia Jesu* (the sayings of Jesus) contain the *ipsissima verba* (the exact words) of Jesus, only the *ipsissima vox* (the exact voice); (7) inerrancy does not guarantee the exhaustive comprehensiveness of any single account or of combined accounts where those are involved; (8) inerrancy does not demand the infallibility or inerrancy of the non-inspired sources used by biblical writers.

context, and the author's intention. As noted, we read Scripture according to the "literal sense," which means according to the intention of the author. Only then can we determine what the author is actually saying, which allows us to determine the kind of truth claim he is making. So, in ordinary language, authors do not always intend to give "precise" descriptions. A reporter can say that 8,000 people were killed without implying that he had counted everyone, and if, after counting, we discover it was only 7,990 who died, this does not count against inerrancy. Joel Beeke and Paul Smalley offer the illustration of the bat. In Leviticus a bat is classified as a "fowl" (*'oph*) along with a hawk and owl (11:13–19). This is not false since "fowl" "refers to flying animals, not a class in modern biological taxonomy."[51]

2. *Inerrancy and Literary Forms*. The amount of precision demanded of Scripture must account for the standards of the time *and* the author's intention in the literary form he employs. For example, think of the Gospels. They are not strict biographies, but *theological* accounts. As such, the Gospels do not give us strict chronologies, nor are they exhaustive. In fact, John reminds us of this fact (John 21:25). This is why the Gospels sometimes present a different order to the events (Matt 4:5–10 vs. Luke 4:5–12); each one is written from a different perspective. But none of this entails contradictions between them. Inerrancy has to do with *truthfulness*, not with the degree of precision with which events are reported.[52] In the OT, this is also true. For example, the historical books recount Israel's history from complementary perspectives that are both true (Samuel-Kings and Chronicles).[53] Thus, when David takes a census of the people, in Chronicles it says that Satan incited David to do it (1 Chr 21:1), while in Samuel it is the Lord who incited him (2 Sam 24:1). This is not contradictory; instead, it is unpacking different aspects of the relation between divine sovereignty and human freedom, which also includes the actions of Satan as evidenced in Job.[54]

---

[51] Beeke and Smalley, *Reformed Systematic Theology*, 1:374 (see chap. 1, n. 8).

[52] Contrary to Sparks, *Sacred Word, Broken Word*, 92 (see chap. 5, n. 39). He thinks of the Bible as giving us "primitive science and anthropology." In contrast to Sparks, see Frame, *Doctrine of the Word*, 171–74.

[53] In contrast to Enns, *Inspiration and Incarnation*, 72–74, 95–99 (see chap. 5, n. 39). Enns interprets these differences as God accommodating himself to cultural standards, which introduces the concept of error.

[54] Ward, *Words of Life*, 141. Read Job 1:12 with vv. 13–19 with v. 21. In the same actions, God, Satan, and humans are active.

Second, inerrancy includes the diverse use of language, including analogical language in reference to God. Biblical authors write in terms of their cultural standard of precision and linguistic patterns. For example, Scripture employs various figures of speech (hyperbole [Matt 2:3], synecdoche [Gal 1:16], personification [Gal 3:8], and metonymy [Rom 3:30]), along with diverse literary forms. The "exact correspondence to reality" must be determined by the kind of literary form it is. We must not impose on Scripture our preconceived views. Thus, references to God "high and lifted up" do not reflect an ancient view of a three-decker universe. Rather, it follows a consistent use of analogical language in reference to God that correctly preserves the Creator-creature distinction. God's arm, hand, and fingers (Exod 6:1, 6; 8:19), along with his change of mental states, and so on, are not reflecting a primitive view but God's gracious communication to us in ways that we can understand. None of this counts against inerrancy.

Third, Scripture is inerrant even though it includes loose and free quotations, as repeatedly occurs in the NT's use of the OT.[55] The method by which a person quotes the words of another is culturally dependent. In the West, we quote a person's exact words; otherwise, we are charged with plagiarism, but this was not the standard of the ancient world. At the time of the NT, Greek had no quotation marks or equivalent kinds of punctuation, and an accurate citation of a person only required an accurate representation of the *content* of what was said. For example, when the Gospels quote Jesus, we must distinguish *ipsissima verba* (Jesus's exact words) from *ipsissima vox* (Jesus's voice, or the content of his message). Also, in the NT, we have translations of what Jesus said (probably in Aramaic) into the Greek. All that is required for inerrancy is that the *content* is true to what was originally said.[56] In inspiration, the Spirit's work through the authors is to keep them from error. We must define inerrancy according to the Bible's own standards tied to the author's intention and the literary form of the book, not our preconceived conceptions of what we think Scripture ought to be.

Fourth, inerrancy also includes unusual grammatical constructions. Some of the language of Scripture is elegant, while other texts are less so. Although Scripture is written

---

[55] On the NT's correct use of the OT, see Moo and Naselli, "Problem of the New Testament's Use," 702–46 (see chap. 4, n. 9).

[56] Ward, *Words of Life*, 92.

under inspiration, the freedom and abilities of the authors are not eclipsed. Also, rules of grammar merely describe the "normal" usage of any language. Skilled writers break "rules" of grammar all the time precisely to communicate their intent. Frame rightly notes, "In natural languages, there are many variations in grammar, style, and accent."[57] The biblical authors are no different. After all, the NT is written in Koine Greek, which was the language of ordinary people. What is crucial for inerrancy is the communication of *truthfulness* in speech.

Arguments for Inerrancy

The Biblical Argument

1. *The Self-Attestation of Scripture.* Given what Scripture claims for itself, it is inerrant (Matt 5:17–20; John 10:34–35). In fact, as we look at the biblical claim through the eyes of Jesus and the apostles, they not only believed that the OT was God's unified revelation now fulfilled in Christ (Luke 24:44) but also that even in its small details, to the jot and tittle (Matt 5:17–18), Scripture is true and accurate. All of God's promises and patterns are fulfilled in Christ's person and work (Matt 26:54–56; Mark 14:27 [Zech 13:7]; John 5:39, 46–47; 19:23–24 [Ps 22:18], 36–37 [Exod 12:46; Zech 12:10]). The OT, in every detail, prepares us for Christ, and in fact, Jesus grounds our conviction that God's word through the prophets is completely trustworthy.

2. *The Biblical Tests for a Prophet* (Deut 13:1–5; 18:20–22). For a prophet to speak truly from God, his word has to be (1) completely true, (2) consistent with what God has already revealed, and (3) completely accurate in terms of the future. In other words, a true prophet is one whose word is completely trustworthy because it is *from God.* If this is true of the prophet's oral word, it must also be true of the prophet's *written* word. For Scripture to be *God's* word it must be inerrant.

3. *Scripture's Witness to Its Truthfulness in All Matters.* Scripture does not claim inerrancy only in matters of "faith and practice" but in all areas. First, think of how our Lord regarded the historical details of the OT as true to reality.

---

[57] Frame, *Doctrine of the Word*, 174.

- Adam and Eve as the first historical people (Matt 19:4–6; Mark 10:6).
- Abel as the first martyr (Matt 22:35).
- Noah and the flood (Matt 24:37–38).
- The destruction of Sodom and Lot's wife turned to salt (Luke 17:26–32).
- Abraham (John 8:56).
- Moses as the author of the Law (Luke 24:44; John 7:19).
- Moses's lifting up the serpent in the wilderness (John 3:14).
- David's eating the consecrated bread in the temple (Matt 12:3–4).
- The queen of the south visiting Solomon (Matt 12:42).
- Elijah being sent to the widow of Zarephath (Luke 4:25–26).
- Naaman being cleansed of leprosy (Luke 4:27).
- Isaiah as the author of the book of Isaiah (John 12:38–41).
- Jonah in the great fish (Matt 12:40–41).
- All of the historical narratives from Abel to Zechariah son of Berekiah (Matt 23:25).[58]
- The apostles also regarded the OT as completely true in its promises and historical details.[59]
- The NT refers to people, places, and events as historical (Heb 7:2 [Melchizedek]; 1 Pet 3:20 [Noah and the flood]; 2 Pet 2:5–6 [Sodom and Gomorrah]; Jude 7 [Sodom and Gomorrah]).
- The NT believes that the promises and patterns of the OT are all fulfilled in Christ and the new covenant age (Acts 2:17; 3:22; 7:37; 8:32; 1 Cor 5:7; 10:4; Gal 3:13; 4:21; Heb 7–8).

4. *The NT Use of Scripture*. Think first of Jesus's use of Scripture. He makes entire arguments from the OT that rest on a single word (Matt 22:43–45 [Ps 110:1]; John 10:34–35 [Ps 82:6]) or the tense of a verb (Matt 22:32). For example, in Matthew 22, Jesus accepts the superscriptions of the Psalms as reliable, and he identifies David as the author. But David did not speak on his own, but "in the Spirit," thus as an authoritative prophet. But given that David is the author, he is referring to someone other than himself, a crucial Messianic point.

---

[58] For these examples and more, see Barrett, *God's Word Alone*, 274–76 (see chap. 1, n. 25); Craig L. Blomberg, "Reflections on Jesus' View of the Old Testament," in Carson, *Enduring Authority*, 680.

[59] See Barrett, *God's Word Alone*, 280.

An entire theology rests on the authorship of this psalm and David's use of "my Lord."[60] Or, in John 10, Jesus refers to Psalm 82 and assumes that Scripture cannot be "annulled, set aside, or deprived of its force."[61] Jesus views Scripture as inerrant. Or think of Paul's appeal to the singular use of "seed," specifically in the Abrahamic covenant (Gen 15:3; 17:8; 22:18; cf. 3:15), to argue that Jesus is the promised Messiah (Gal 3:16). All of these uses of the OT assume that the text is inerrant; otherwise, it is difficult to understand the point in these arguments. If they are not assuming that the text is completely reliable, one could simply respond by saying, "The text may be wrong." But this is not the assumption of Jesus and the NT authors as they appeal to the OT.

5. *The Nature and Character of God.* God is the God of truth and covenant faithfulness (Exod 34:6). God cannot lie (Num 23:19; 1 Sam 15:29; Titus 1:2); indeed, it is "impossible for God to lie" (Heb 6:18). Also, Paul emphatically declares that only God is trustworthy (Rom 3:4). If the Scripture has its origin *from God*, then his character stands behind it (cf. John 17:17).[62] In chapter 5, we unpacked how God and his word are inseparable: God is truth and so is his word (Ps 119:43, 142, 151, 160). Ultimately, our view of Scripture is bound up with our view of God. In Scripture, the triune God plans and knows all things (Eph 1:11), and as alone *a se*, he is the source and standard of truth (Pss 139:1–4, 16; 147:5; Prov 30:5–6; Isa 40:28; 46:10–11; John 17:17). In his speaking through the prophets and the apostles and in their written texts, there is no loss of authority or truthfulness. Given this, if the Bible contains falsehood, it entails that God is either not sovereign to keep human authors from error (which is an unbiblical view), or he is not omniscient and thus unable to know and reveal objective truth (which is also unbiblical). Either way, a denial of inerrancy has serious implications for our doctrine of God and especially one's understanding of the God-Scripture relationship.[63]

---

[60] Note how in the NT, the apostles follow Jesus in his understanding of the author of Psalm 110 as David, its application to him, and testimony of the OT to Messiah's divine identity (see Acts 2:34–35; 1 Cor 15:25; Eph 1:20; Heb 1:3, 13; 5:6–10; 7:10–28; 8:1; 10:12–13; 12:2).

[61] Donald Macleod, "Jesus and Scripture," in *The Trustworthiness of God: Perspectives on the Nature of Scripture*, ed. Paul Helm and Carl R. Trueman (Grand Rapids: Eerdmans, 2002), 77.

[62] See Carl R. Trueman, "The God of Unconditional Promise," in Helm and Trueman, *The Trustworthiness of God*, 178: "Scripture is trustworthy because the God of Scripture is trustworthy."

[63] We will develop this point in part 4 when we discuss current revisions of theology proper in evangelical theology.

The Historical Argument

As we discussed in chapter 8, the church has always held to the inspiration, infallibility, and inerrancy of Scripture until recent times. Inerrancy is not an innovation; it is the classic view of the church. As such, the burden of proof is on those who want to depart from it.

The Epistemological Argument

Over a millennium and half ago, Augustine gave us the basic form of what today is known as the epistemological argument for inerrancy. Augustine argued that if there is one error in Scripture, it would call into question its authority. Why? He explains: "If you once admit into such a high sanctuary of authority one false statement, . . . there will not be left a single sentence of those books which, if appearing to any one difficult in practice or hard to believe, may not by the same fatal rule be explained away, as a statement in which, intentionally, . . . the author declared what was not true."[64] In other words, if the Bible errs at any point, it allows the possibility that *any* statement *may be false*. If so, one must determine exactly where Scripture is correct from where it is not; otherwise, one can dismiss what Scripture says as one of those places it errs.

What Augustine argues in rudimentary form is vitally important and often missed by those who reject inerrancy. To deny inerrancy is ultimately to undermine *sola Scriptura* since Scripture can no longer function as theology's *final self-attesting* authority. If Scripture errs at *any* point, we need some *extratextual* criterion to confirm if that one point is the error. Or we could state it this way: without inerrancy we cannot agree with the children's hymn—"Jesus loves me this I *know* [i.e., justified true belief], *because the Bible tells me so*"—since we will need some kind of justification to *know* that what Scripture teaches on *this* specific point is true. But what exactly is this independent criterion to determine Scripture's truthfulness if it is not Scripture itself? Human reason? Religious experience? The "assured" results of science, philosophy, psychology, sociology, and so on? However, the problem with these so-called solutions is that they are not self-attesting; instead, they reflect finite thought, which in the end cannot yield objective truth. They require their own justification! But apart from the Creator, there is

[64] Augustine, *Letters of St. Augustine* 28.3 (*NPNF*[1] 1:251–52).

no *transcendental* ground for objective truth. For this reason, not only Scripture is necessary, but a certain kind of Scripture from a specific view of God is necessary, namely, Scripture as *God's* word that is fully authoritative *and inerrant*.

Concluding Reflection

For the Christian worldview and theology, the affirmation of inerrancy is no small matter. Without the full authority of Scripture, including its inerrancy, we have no epistemological warrant to affirm that God has truly spoken definitively and objectively. Indeed, apart from inerrancy, the possibility of a normative theology evaporates. In many ways, we have come full circle from our discussion of current thought in chapter 2 and the foundation for objective truth and theology in chapter 3. As we argued there, we argue here: the foundation for truth and theology is the triune God who is there and who speaks, and who speaks in a *truthful* way.

Today, our postmodern society is in the midst of a "crisis of authority," which is largely due to its rejection of Christian theology and its replacement with the self-defeating idols of our day that are grounded in created things rather than the triune Creator and Lord. Whether our culture is wrestling with the issues of philosophy, ethics, economics, politics, social justice, or what have you, it has no grounds for objective truth as it has embraced a "constructivist" view of "knowledge," which reduces to subjectivity and some form of relativism. But when objective truth is lost and human subjectivity reigns, given the depravity of the human heart, history warns us that disaster follows. Apart from God's restraining common grace and the salt-and-light effect of the church, we can only expect what history has repeatedly illustrated: nothing but heartache, tyranny, and statism, which will result in the destruction of human value, freedom, and liberty.

The church, especially given our context, must not follow the culture and its mindset. We must gladly confess that our triune God is there and has spoken a word that is trustworthy. We must proclaim that universal objective truth and morality are *true* but only because the source and standard of truth is our glorious triune Creator, Lord, and Redeemer. As the church, we must gladly confess and embrace *sola Scriptura*, not as some outdated confession of the Reformation, but as true to Scripture and our joy and delight. More than this: we must read and obey all that Scripture teaches since apart from God's word, we have no sure, reliable, and *true* word.

CHAPTER 11

The Sufficiency and Clarity of Scripture

Introduction

In Scripture, there is an inseparable relationship between God and his Word. Within God's eternal life, he is a communicative being in the eternal necessary relations of the Father, Son, and Holy Spirit. By his free and sovereign choice, God created the universe and communicated to his creatures by his word, and after the fall, he accomplished redemption for his people. Indeed, all of God's external works are "communicative."[1] By his powerful authoritative word, God enacts his eternal plan and rules over all as the absolute standard of truth and goodness. Furthermore, God is present with us by his word, supremely in Christ, God's eternal Word made flesh (John 1:1, 14), but also in his spoken and written word through his inspired prophets and apostles. Due to God's extraordinary agency, *his* word is identified with the text of Scripture (2 Tim 3:16), written by human authors who were "carried along" by the Spirit of God (2 Pet 1:21) so that what the authors wrote is what God wanted written. For this reason, Scripture *is* God's covenant word to us that is fully authoritative, infallible, and inerrant. God's word is given to us so that we may know him, believe his promises, obey his commands,

[1] Webster, *Domain of the Word*, 7 (see chap. 1, n. 5).

know ourselves, and supremely enjoy him forever in covenant relationship as his people. But more needs to be said about Scripture in terms of its properties or attributes.[2] As God's word, Scripture is also *sufficient* and objectively *clear* or *perspicuous*.[3]

Scripture is "sufficient" because as *God's* word to his people, it is precisely what God wants us to know to be in covenant relationship with him. For all things necessary to know and glorify God and to experience redemption in Christ, Scripture is *enough*. Nothing needs to be added to it; Scripture is our final and sufficient norm for our knowledge of God and relationship to him—the "ruling rule" (*norma normans*) for our theology and life as the church.

Scripture is also objectively "clear" because it is *God's* word. Scripture's perspicuity is an attribute of Scripture; it is *not* the consequence of our interpretation of it.[4] Within God's eternal life, Father, Son, and Spirit share the same identical divine nature, which entails an "eternal and unencumbered intra-Trinitarian fellowship" and "unambiguous triune communication."[5] As David Garner explains, "for perfect unity to exist within the Godhead, intra-Trinitarian communication must occur with unobstructed purity and seamless fluidity. Thus, divine intra-Trinitarian communication is internally and eternally perspicuous, for God is infinite in his self-understanding; the omni-competent Spirit knows 'the thoughts of God' (1 Cor. 2:11b)."[6] Since this is true of God *ad intra*, in God's *ad extra* actions, which he effectively accomplishes by divine speech, including the inspiration of Scripture, God does not fail to communicate his plan and promises to us with clarity. God's speech through human language does not obscure his communication because it is *his* word. Also, God has created humans in his image to be in covenant relationship with him; human language is not a barrier to knowing God. Instead, it is a designed and created gift to fulfill our calling to rule as God's

---

[2] Historically, Protestant theology has spoken of four "attributes" of Scripture: necessity, authority, sufficiency, and clarity. In chapter 3, we addressed the necessity of divine revelation in nature and supremely in Scripture. In chapters 7–10, we have addressed the authority of Scripture in terms of its meaning and its grounding in inspiration, infallibility, and inerrancy. In this chapter, we now address the sufficiency and clarity of Scripture.

[3] "Perspicuity" is from the Latin *perspicuitas*, meaning "clarity of thought, lucidity." Muller, *Dictionary of Latin and Greek* , s.v. "perspicuitas," 228 (see chap. 8, n. 37).

[4] On this point, see Wayne Grudem, "The Perspicuity of Scripture," *Them* 34, no. 3 (2009): 295.

[5] David B. Garner, "Did God Really Say?," in Garner, *Did God Really Say?*, 147 (see chap. 7, n. 113).

[6] Garner, 147.

image-bearers over the world.[7] For this reason, the clarity of Scripture follows from the nature of Scripture and the God who gave it: "The clarity of Scripture is connected to the clarity of God's speech."[8] God accommodates his speech to us, but God's speech is always clear. In fact, given the God-word relation, if Scripture is unclear, ultimately "God's character and purpose [are] at stake."[9] Mark Thompson makes this point by appealing to Benedict Pictet: "Those who deny the clarity of Scripture are faced with an unenviable dilemma: '[E]ither God *could not* reveal himself more plainly to men, or he *would not*. No one will assert the former, and the latter is most absurd; for who could believe that God our heavenly Father has been unwilling to reveal his will to his children . . . ?'"[10]

For these reasons, "sufficiency" and "clarity" follow from the nature of Scripture, which in turn follows from the triune God, who has chosen to communicate to us by his word. When God speaks to us through human authors, Scripture, as Thompson notes, is not an "abstraction from God's being and in particular his determination to be known."[11] To affirm the sufficiency and clarity of the Bible is to affirm what Scripture claims for itself and the triune God who gave it. God's word is enough to know him and to live for his glory as his people, which also assumes a clear word. Divine authority, as John Frame notes, demands an understandable word since God "creates obligations in its hearers; obligations to believe what it says, to do what it commands, to write it on our hearts, and so on. The clarity of God's Word means that we have no excuse for failing to meet those obligations."[12] Otherwise, God is ineffective in his communication to us, and biblical authority is robbed of its meaning. But as Heb 4:12 reminds us, God's word is effective, successfully achieving God's intended purpose.

Let us now develop in more detail "sufficiency" and "clarity" respectively in three steps: first, by outlining their biblical warrant; second, defining and expounding their meaning; and third, discussing some current challenges to these significant attributes of Scripture.

---

[7] See Richard B. Gaffin Jr., "Speech and the Image of God: Biblical Reflections on Language and its Uses," in *The Pattern of Sound Doctrine: Systematic Theology at the Westminster Seminaries*, ed. David Van Drunen (Phillipsburg: P&R, 2004), 191.

[8] Barrett, *God's Word Alone*, 304 (see chap. 1, n. 25).

[9] Mark D. Thompson, "The Generous Gift of a Gracious Father: Toward a Theological Account of the Clarity of Scripture," in Carson, *Enduring Authority*, 617 (see chap. 4, n. 9).

[10] Thompson, 617.

[11] Thompson, 618.

[12] Frame, *Doctrine of the Word*, 206 (chap. 5, n. 5).

The Sufficiency of Scripture

Sufficiency is an attribute or property of Scripture due to divine inspiration. Scripture's purpose is to give God's people all that we need to know him and his saving promises in Christ and to live as his covenant people.[13] For this purpose, Scripture is enough. Sometimes its sufficiency has been called its "perfection."[14] But regardless of the term used, the concept is the same: Scripture is complete, and thus, "The whole counsel of God concerning all things necessary for His own glory, man's salvation, faith and life, is either expressly set down or necessarily contained in the Holy Scripture."[15] The point is that all things necessary for salvation and for living the Christian life are given to us in Scripture.

Biblical Warrant for Sufficiency

Scripture is God's covenant word given to rule his people and to equip us for every good work. By God's word, we are enabled to fulfill the purpose of our existence: to know and glorify God. By God's word, we know what God has chosen to reveal about his plan, will, and promises, and we are instructed in what is true, good, and beautiful: "Your word is a lamp to my feet and a light to my path" (Ps 119:105); "The instruction of the LORD is perfect, / renewing one's life; / the testimony of the LORD is trustworthy, / making the inexperienced wise" (Ps 19:7); "Sanctify them by the truth; your word is truth" (John 17:17). God's word is enough.

For this reason, we are forbidden to add to or subtract from Scripture (Deut 4:1–2; 12:32; cf. Prov 30:5–6). In fact, if we think we can add to God's word, as Frame observes, it is tantamount to claiming "that [our] words have the authority of God himself."[16] This is why false prophets who claimed to speak in God's name were put to death; they spoke their own word

---

[13] The Reformation distinguished between "the formal and material sufficiency of Scripture." The former means that Scripture's authority is not conferred on it by individuals or the church, but "from God alone." The latter refers to Scripture "contain[ing] everything needed for Christian faith and life." Ward, *Words of Life*, 112, 110 (see chap. 5, n. 27).

[14] For example, see Turretin, *Institutes of Elenctic Theology*, 1:134–43 (see chap. 3, n. 55); also see John Murray, "The Finality and Sufficiency of Scripture," in *Collected Writings of John Murray*, 4 vols. (Carlisle: Banner of Truth, 1976), 1:16–22.

[15] *London Baptist Confession* (1689), 1.6; cf. *WCF*, 1.6.

[16] Frame, *Doctrine of the Word*, 224.

(Deut 18:20). Only God's word has the authority to be believed and obeyed without question. God's word gives life to his people even more than food: "Man does not live on bread alone but on every word that comes from the mouth of the LORD" (Deut 8:3), which assumes the authority and sufficiency of God's word. Importantly, Jesus emphasizes this same point as the divine Son, who assumed our humanity to become the last Adam and true Israel to obey his Father's will for us by living his entire life according to Scripture (Matt 4:4; cf. Gal 4:4–7).

The same emphasis on hearing and obeying God's word for saving faith, life, and godliness continues in Joshua (Josh 1:6–9) and throughout the OT. Indeed, the first task of the king is to copy God's word so that he can "read from it all the days of his life" and by doing so "learn to fear the LORD his God, to observe all the words of this instruction, and to do these statutes" (Deut 17:18–19). It is only by obeying God's word that he will know God and be able to rule God's people according to truth. This same emphasis is found throughout the entire OT (e.g., Pss 1; 119). Scripture is enough to revive the soul, make wise the simple, rejoice the heart, enlighten the eyes, warn about sin, and reward obedience (Ps 19:7–11).

In the NT, Paul insists that faith in Christ alone is the only way sinners are justified before God, which is only known by the gospel message given in Scripture (Rom 10:13–17). The purpose of Scripture is to lead us to faith in God's covenant promises in Christ Jesus (John 20:31; 1 John 5:13; cf. 2 Tim 3:15). Also, our growth in Christ, Peter teaches, only comes from God's word: "Like newborn infants, desire the pure milk of the word, so that by it you may grow up into your salvation" (1 Pet 2:2). Peter reminds us that God has given us "everything required for life and godliness through the knowledge of him who called us by his own glory and goodness" (2 Pet 1:3). In the context of the text, the knowledge of God is tied to God's OT promises, which are now fulfilled in the person and work of Christ (2 Pet 1:4, 16–21), to which both the prophets and the apostles testify (2 Pet 3:2). Likewise, Paul reminds us that everything written in the OT was for OT believers *and* the church, as God's new covenant people (Rom 15:4; cf. 1 Cor 10:1–12; 1 Pet 1:10–12). Thus, the entire canon of Scripture is sufficient for us.

This same point is taught in 2 Tim 3:16: "Scripture is not merely helpful but is *the* source we turn to for all of life as a Christian."[17] Scripture is enough to lead us to salvation in Christ (3:15). And it is enough for life and godliness: "teaching" (what we ought to believe, sound doctrine), "rebuking," "correcting," "training in righteousness" (how we ought to live and how

[17] Barrett, *God's Word Alone*, 342.

we may be pleasing to God) so that Timothy as "the man of God," and by extension all Christians,[18] "may be complete, equipped for every good work" (3:16–17). Scripture is all Timothy needs to discharge his duties. In fact, this point is even stronger if we remember the context of Paul's instruction. As Paul is at the end of his life (4:6–8), he warns Timothy that although Christ has inaugurated the "last days" that he will gloriously consummate, the entire inter-advental age will be characterized by the triumph of the gospel *and* the suffering of the church. Timothy, then, must carefully instruct the church, be vigilant in his teaching, "exercise self-control in everything, endure hardship, do the work of an evangelist, fulfill [his] ministry" (4:5). But how is Timothy to "hold on to the pattern of sound teaching," "guard the good deposit" (2 Tim 1:13–14), confront false teachers, and lead the church well? The answer: Preach and teach God's word "in season and out of season" (4:2). Timothy is not to look to the latest trend or fad; instead, he is to read, obey, and teach God's word, which is sufficient.

One important last point: a proper grasp of sufficiency must also account for progressive revelation and the closing of the canon in Christ. In Christ, the "last days" are inaugurated, fulfilling the prophetic word (Luke 24:44; Heb 1:1–3). Although at every stage of redemptive history, Scripture was "sufficient" for God's people, it was also incomplete. As God unfolds his plan, more revelation is added, building on what was given and pointing forward to more to come. Repeatedly, God forbids the adding of human "tradition" to his word, but this did not exclude the addition of new revelation *from him* through the prophets. But now that Christ has come, what the OT revealed and predicted is here, and God's word is complete; thus, the canon has closed. Fulfillment in Christ results in more understanding of God's redemptive plan. The OT is no longer open-ended; the patterns/types are now fulfilled in Christ. The prophetic word is made complete by the apostolic word (2 Pet 3:2). Until Christ returns, no further word is needed. This entails that "sufficiency" is now defined canonically.[19]

Frame makes this point by distinguishing between "general" and "particular" sufficiency. By "general" he means that "at any point of redemptive history, the revelation given at the time is sufficient."[20] After the fall, for example, God revealed a saving promise (Gen 3:15) that

---

[18] See Waters, *For the Mouth*, 158 n. 31 (chap. 5, n. 5).

[19] On this point, see Herman Ridderbos, *Redemptive History and the New Testament Scripture* (Phillipsburg: P&R, 1988); and Richard B. Gaffin Jr., "The New Testament as Canon," in Conn, *Inerrancy and Hermeneutic*, 165–83 (see chap. 8, n. 58).

[20] Frame, *Doctrine of the Word*, 226.

pointed forward to Christ, but it was sufficient for that time. As redemptive history unfolds, more revelation is given, which is sufficient for that time, even as more revelation is anticipated. However, with the coming of Christ, the new covenant documents of the apostles bring the canon to a close. There is no additional revelation beyond the NT, until Christ returns, which Frame labels "particular" sufficiency.[21]

This redemptive-historical sense of "sufficiency" is vital for our interpretation, application, and drawing theological conclusions from Scripture, a point we will discuss in part 3.[22] Biblical texts must never be taken out of context but read and applied in light of the entire canon. Due to Christ's coming, we know more fully who God is, his plan, and his will for our lives. On the Bible's own terms, we know that not all Scriptural commands apply to the church in exactly the same way as they did in previous epochs. This is not because previous commands were inferior; rather, they served a specific purpose in God's plan, which is now applied to us in Christ.[23] But to think of more revelation beyond Christ is unthinkable. As Frame states, "God himself will not add to the work of Christ, and so we should not expect him to add to the message of Christ."[24] Not surprisingly, the NT ends with the exhortation to not add to or subtract from God's word (Rev 22:18–19). Although this text first applies to Revelation, it also has application to the entire canon of Scripture now closed in Christ. We do not go beyond what is written.

Again, this point is important for doing theology and applying the entire canon to the church. It also goes against those who want to go "beyond" Scripture by applying today what the NT forbids. For example, some argue that Paul's teaching on male headship in marriage, the family, and the church was "true" for the first century, but not today, similar to how various OT commands no longer apply to the church.[25] But this view is incorrect. Specifically, it

---

[21] Frame, 226–27.

[22] On this point, see Waters, *For the Mouth*, 174–77.

[23] For example, under the old covenant, Israel was commanded to obey specific food laws, offer sacrifices, etc. Also, circumcision functioned as a covenant sign starting in the Abrahamic covenant and continuing through the Mosaic. But now, as new covenant believers, we are no longer under the old covenant *as a covenant*, which means that most of its commands are no longer binding on us, and what does "carry over" must be viewed in light of its fulfillment in Christ and the larger creation, fall, redemption, new-creation structures of Scripture. On this point, see part 3.

[24] Frame, *Doctrine of the Word*, 228.

[25] See Webb, *Slaves, Women and Homosexuals* (see chap. 7, n. 103); I. Howard Marshall, *Beyond the Bible: Moving from Scripture to Theology* (Grand Rapids: Baker Academic, 2004); cf. Gary T. Meadors,

does not recognize that the closing of the canon entails that the ethical application of the NT is normative for us. No doubt, we go "beyond" some of the commands of the OT, but only because God intended for those commands to reach their fulfillment in Christ, which the NT explains for us. In other words, within the Bible's own covenantal unfolding, "Scripture interprets Scripture," and we do not go beyond what the NT teaches since it brings to completion and closure God's authoritative word for the church.

Definition and Exposition of Sufficiency

Definition of Sufficiency

The classic definition of sufficiency arises from the Reformation and post-Reformation eras due to the affirmation of *sola Scriptura* against the Roman Catholic Church.[26] Rome denied that the Bible was sufficient apart from the Church's interpretation of it and the Church's

---

ed., *Four Views on Moving Beyond the Bible to Theology* (Grand Rapids: Zondervan, 2009). For example, Webb argues that Paul's prohibition of women serving as authoritative teachers in the church in 1 Tim 2:11–15 was legitimate for *his* time but it is not required for the church today. Paul's command is on a "trajectory" that, if followed, takes us "beyond" the NT. Webb thinks that this "trajectory" is warranted by how the NT views slavery. The NT does not outright reject slavery; instead, it is on a trajectory that takes us "beyond" the teaching of the NT. *Slaves, Women and Homosexuals*, 236-44. This view is highly problematic. First, it does not follow the Bible's own creation, fall, redemption, new-creation structures, which locates the complementarian role differences between men and women in marriage, the family, and the church in creation order that does not change across redemptive history. Furthermore, it fails to recognize that slavery is not part of the created order but is only the result of the fall, thus an unsuitable warrant to apply to male and female relationships in marriage and the church. Second, it does not account for the sufficiency of Scripture in terms of the closing of the canon and the normativity of the NT teaching for the church regardless of whether we live in the first or twenty-first century. The Bible, on its own terms, teaches us what applies and does not apply to the church, but we never go "beyond" what the NT teaches and commands as if Scripture is not sufficient for the faith and practice of the church.

[26] Prior to the Reformation, sufficiency was affirmed in the early church. For example, see Irenaeus, *Against Heresies* 3.1 (in *ANF*, 1:414): "We have learned from none others the plan of our salvation, than from those through whom the Gospel has come down to us, which they did at one time proclaim in public, and, at a later period, by the will of God, handed down to us in the Scriptures, to be the ground and pillar of our faith"; Vincent of Lerins, *Commonitory* 2.5 (*NPNF*[2] 11:132): "the canon of Scripture is complete, and sufficient of itself for everything, and more than sufficient"; Clement of Alexandria, *Stromata* 7.16 (*ANF* 2:551): in commenting on the teaching of Scripture, Clement states, "It has no need of proof, nor is it capable of being corrected. Rather, it is the standard by which everything else is

authority to formulate dogma that can go "beyond" Scripture. Rome argued that Christ had granted authority to the magisterium of the Church by apostolic succession, which the Reformers rightly denied.[27] As such, the definition of sufficiency arising out of the Reformed tradition, especially in the *Westminster Confession of Faith* (1646) and its similar statement in the 1689 *London Baptist Confession* is difficult to improve on. The latter Confession defines *sufficiency* this way:

> The whole counsel of God concerning all things necessary for His own glory, man's salvation, faith and life, is either expressly set down or necessarily contained in the Holy Scripture: unto which nothing at any time is to be added, whether by new revelation of the Spirit, or traditions of men. Nevertheless, we acknowledge the inward illumination of the Spirit of God to be necessary for the saving understanding of such things as are revealed in the Word, and that there are some circumstances concerning the worship of God, the government of the church, common to human actions and societies, which are to be ordered by the light of nature and Christian prudence, according to the general rules of the Word, which are always to be observed.[28]

Given the importance of sufficiency in historical theology and its continued significance today, let us build on the historic definition and explain what sufficiency is and is not.

Exposition of Sufficiency

First, sufficiency is defined in terms of Scripture's *purpose*; it does not claim that Scripture is an exhaustive revelation or that there is no knowledge outside of Scripture. Scripture is sufficient for "all things necessary for His own glory, man's salvation, faith and life."

---

evaluated"; and Athanasius, *Against the Heathen* 1 (*NPNF*[2] 4:4): Athanasius affirmed that "the sacred and inspired Scriptures are sufficient to declare the truth."

[27] See Allison, *Historical Theology*, 147–58 (see chap. 8, n. 9); Waters, *For the Mouth*, 179–90; Barrett, *God's Word Alone*, 347–63.

[28] *London Baptist Confession* (1689), 1.6; cf. *WCF*, 1.6. For a current statement of sufficiency, see Beeke and Smalley, *Reformed Systematic Theology*, 1:396 (see chap. 1, n. 8): "The doctrine of the sufficiency of the Holy Scriptures declares that everything necessary for saving faith and spiritual life is taught in the Bible. There is no warrant or need for the church to base its doctrine or directives on anything else, be it church tradition, the opinions of men, or the wisdom of the world."

Thus, to know God (who he is, his triune being and nature), to understand the nature of the gospel (what sin is, what salvation is), what saving faith is (what God's promises are), who Jesus is as God the Son incarnate and what he has done for us, and how we are justified before God (the nature of conversion and salvation), it is necessary to look in Scripture alone. Scripture is enough for *this* purpose: for formulating sound doctrine and rejecting false teaching (1 Cor 15:1–3; Gal 1:6–9; Col 2:8–10). Scripture is also sufficient to know God's will for our lives and how rightly to apply Scripture to our lives in every circumstance that we find ourselves in.

However, Scripture is *not* an exhaustive revelation on all matters. Scripture is a true but finite revelation, but it does not give us a complete knowledge on all subjects. There are at least two ways that Scripture is not exhaustive. First, God has not told us everything about how he created the world, how he sovereignly governs history, the nature of the Trinity and the incarnation, and so on: all of this requires careful theological reflection and the allowance of "unknowns" in our theology. But what is given is sufficient for our doctrine and life as God's people.

An additional way to think of Scripture's limitations is that "it is not a textbook of philosophy, economics, political science, or biology, to give a few examples."[29] Notice how the Confession's definition speaks of truths from "the light of nature," that is, natural revelation that is not included in Scripture yet yields true knowledge because it is *from God*. As noted in previous chapters, natural and special revelation require each other, although priority is given to special revelation where it addresses specific topics directly. But natural revelation yields true "extrabiblical" knowledge that sufficiency does not deny. In fact, even to read and apply Scripture requires knowledge of biblical languages, textual criticism, the study of history, and so on. As Frame notes, Scripture does not mention current ethical issues, such as cloning or various uses of genetic engineering; we need to know what these are from the study of science. But Scripture does provide "the ultimate norms" so we are able to make proper ethical decisions. "Scripture contains all the words of God that we need for any area of life, and all ultimate norms come from divine words."[30] Sufficiency, then, does not exclude extrabiblical knowledge, but in its overall teaching, Scripture provides the interpretative framework by which we utilize knowledge from nature. Frame continues, "These sciences [extrabiblical knowledge] enable us

---

[29] Waters, *For the Mouth*, 170.

[30] Frame, *Doctrine of the Word*, 231.

to understand Scripture, but they must themselves be carried on in accord with Scripture."[31] Extrabiblical knowledge must be distinguished from extratextual viewpoints. The former is God's natural revelation that serves its purpose alongside Scripture; the latter refers to entire worldviews that interpret God, self, and the world contrary to Scripture.[32]

Second, sufficiency does *not* eliminate the need for careful biblical and theological reasoning to understand God's word. The definition captures this point: "The whole counsel of God . . . is either expressly set down or necessarily contained in the Holy Scripture" or, as the *WCF* states, "is either expressly set down in Holy Scripture, or by good and necessary consequence may be deduced from Scripture." Drawing theological conclusions from Scripture is direct and indirect. As we discussed in chapter 4, the Bible is not a theological dictionary; it is God's word written over time, which requires a careful reading of Scripture by putting together texts within Scripture's own theological framework, structures, and categories. Doctrinal formulation is rarely decided by one text; it requires multiple texts located in an entire canon. For example, thinking rightly about the Trinity requires an entire Bible. Or, thinking biblically about Christology requires putting together other biblical truths regarding God, humans, sin, the biblical covenants, and so on.[33] Obviously, not every deduction by "good and necessary consequence" is legitimate. As we will discuss in part 3, covenant theologians appeal to this point to defend infant baptism even though there is no clear text in the NT that teaches it. Yet this does not curtail the fact that our reading and application of Scripture requires the proper use of reason.[34]

Third, sufficiency does *not* set aside the significance of tradition and historical theology in our reading and application of Scripture. These theological disciplines serve a crucial

---

[31] Frame, 232.

[32] On these points, see Waters, *For the Mouth*, 171–79; Frame, *Doctrine of the Word*, 228–33. Also refer to the discussion in chapter 2 of how modern and postmodern thought operate with *extratextual* views contrary to Scripture.

[33] See Frame, *Doctrine of the Word*, 230–33. Waters has a helpful discussion of the use of reason in our reading Scripture. He discusses four representative texts that illustrate how various biblical authors draw necessary deductions from Scripture (Matt 22:29–32 [Exod 3:6]; 1 Cor 10:25–26 [Ps 24:1–2]; Acts 2:25–32 [Ps 16]; Heb 1:6 [Deut 32:43]). *For the Mouth*, 163-69.

[34] Frame discusses why logical deductions of Scripture do not add to Scripture. Instead, they "make the implicit content explicit" by "bringing out meaning that is already there in the text." Frame concludes: "So (a) the 'content of Scripture' includes all the logical implications of Scripture, (b) the logical implications of Scripture have the same authority as Scripture, and (c) logical deductions from Scripture do not add anything to Scripture." *Doctrine of the Word*, 222.

ministerial role in our doing of theology. Instead, sufficiency means that we are not to view the "traditions of men" as an equal or rival authority to Scripture. In the Reformation, this statement rejected the Roman Catholic view of tradition. Rome argued for two sources of divine revelation: Scripture and tradition, thus denying that Scripture was sufficient to determine its own meaning or to establish doctrine. Christ had established the magisterium for that purpose. But this is what the Reformers rightly rejected. We are not to add to Scripture any human tradition that is not expressly taught in Scripture or legitimately deduced from it. To do so is to put human traditions on par with *God's* word, which Scripture forbids (e.g., Mark 7:5–13; Col 2:8–10). But if historical theology correctly interprets and makes true theological conclusions from Scripture (which occurred at Nicaea and Chalcedon), then these "ruled rules" (*norma normata*) function as authorities for theology under the *magisterial* authority of Scripture.

Fourth, sufficiency acknowledges the need for the Spirit's illuminating work to understand, believe, and obey the saving message of Scripture. Just as there is an inseparable relation between God and his word, there is also an inseparable relation between Scripture and the appropriated work of the Spirit, both in his work of inspiration (2 Tim 3:16) and illumination (1 Cor 2:9–12). We cannot truly understand and believe God's word without the regenerating and illuminating work of the Spirit. Yet the Spirit's speaking *through* Scripture, contrary to many of the iterations of a neo-orthodox view, is not "independent" of the human authors of Scripture. We will return to this point below in our discussion of clarity.

Furthermore, sufficiency denies that the Spirit adds "new revelations" to Scripture now that the entire canon is closed. In the context of the Reformation, the Reformers rejected the "enthusiasts," who claimed to have "new" revelations from the Spirit, similar to claims of some current charismatics. But Scripture denies that there are any "new" revelations of the Spirit in addition to or that go beyond Scripture. Due to Christ's coming, the apostles and NT prophets constitute the foundation on which the church is built (Eph 2:20), and with the writing of the NT, this unique era is now ended. Until Christ comes again, Scripture is enough, and we should not expect any new revelations of the Spirit apart from what is already given in Scripture.[35]

[35] In volume 2, in our discussion of ecclesiology, or the doctrine of the church, we will discuss the issue of whether the extraordinary spiritual gifts continue.

Challenges to Sufficiency

The perennial challenge to sufficiency is the tendency to add to or subtract from God's word. Let us think of two ongoing challenges.

First, there is the ongoing challenge of Roman Catholic theology.[36] At the Council of Trent (1545–63), Rome argued for two sources of divine revelation: Scripture and tradition, thus making tradition, passed on from Peter to his successors via the magisterium of the church (consisting of the Pope, bishops, and councils), equal to Scripture. Later, at the Second Vatican Council (1962–65), there was a slight change: Scripture and tradition come from *one* source of divine revelation that is committed to the church, but practically it resulted in the same view.[37] In the end, Rome affirms dogmas/traditions that are *not* warranted by Scripture and, in fact, lead to its denial (e.g., the bodily assumption of Mary, the Immaculate Conception, the veneration of Mary and her role as co-mediatrix, etc.). At its heart, Rome's problem is their unbiblical view of apostolic succession and the role of the church in the divine economy. Instead of arguing that God's word creates the church, they reverse the relationship. In addition, Rome wrongly views the church as the continuation of the incarnation, mirroring Christ as a divine-human reality and acting as an *altera persona Christi*, a "second Christ."[38] As a "second Christ," the church mediates God's grace to people and speaks with divine authority. But biblically, the foundation for theology is God's word centered in Christ and the gospel. In the divine economy, the church is not a "second Christ," but God's new covenant people, redeemed by grace, and as such, her very life is dependent upon God's word. As Herman Bavinck rightly states, "The church with its tradition may be the rule of faith (*regula fidei*); it is not its foundation (*fundamentum fidei*). That distinction belongs only to Scripture alone."[39]

Second, there is the ongoing challenge to integrate correctly "natural" revelation and Scripture so that extrabiblical data does not become an *extratextual* grid by which Scripture's authority is relativized and so that the extrabiblical data does not become a "new revelation" more authoritative than Scripture. This challenge has a number of facets to it. It often begins

---

[36] See Allison, *Roman Catholic Theology and Practice* (see chap. 1, n. 29).

[37] *The Documents of Vatican II*, ed. Walter Abbott, trans. Joseph Gallagher (New York: American, 1966), 115–17.

[38] Allison, *Roman Catholic Theology and Practice*, 56–57.

[39] Bavinck, *Reformed Dogmatics*, 1:452–53 (see chap. 1, n. 9).

with the slogan "All truth is God's truth," but if not careful, it privileges "knowledge" from natural revelation over Scripture. Obviously, this is a difficult issue since Scripture is *not* an exhaustive revelation. And since "natural" revelation is *of God*, the issue is not whether to make use of it, but *how* to do so. Scripture may not be a textbook on everything, but it does "speak of everything either directly or by implication."[40] Scripture provides the overall theological framework to make sense of God, self, and the world, even though it does not address every issue in detail. Thus, our interpretation of natural revelation must be consistent with the overall teaching of Scripture, especially in areas that the Bible specifically addresses, albeit briefly.

For example, think of the science issues surrounding the question of human origins and the naturalistic evolutionary theory. Although Scripture is not a textbook on all of these matters, it does address how the universe came to exist, and it teaches that Adam and Eve were the first humans. But Peter Enns (and others) views the evolutionary theory as settled science, which in turn leads him to reinterpret Scripture in light of what he views as "scientific knowledge." This leads him to assert that Paul's beliefs about a historical Adam and a historical fall were culturally accommodated and thus wrong (e.g., Rom 5:12–21; 1 Cor 15:21–28).[41] But for Enns, the "assured results of science" have now become an extratextual hermeneutical grid over Scripture by which we determine what is true and false in Scripture. Natural and special revelation go together, but when Scripture explicitly teaches what an extratextual view denies and we opt for the latter, we have added a false human tradition to Scripture undermining biblical authority and sufficiency.

This also happens with other disciplines that use extrabiblical "knowledge" to deny biblical teaching. For example, various ideas from psychology, gender identity theory, and critical race theory function as entire interpretive schemes that interpret God, self, and the world in

---

[40] Van Til, *Apologetics*, 2 (see chap. 4, n. 81). What Van Til means is that Scripture gives us an overall theological interpretive framework by which we view the world and every discipline. It is only on the basis of Christian theology that disciplines outside of Scripture are even possible. Although Scripture does not speak of everything and we gain knowledge by natural revelation, it is also true that "there is nothing in this universe on which human beings can have full and true information unless they take the Bible into account." *Apologetics*, 2.

[41] Peter Enns, *The Evolution of Adam: What the Bible Does and Doesn't Say about Human Origins* (Grand Rapids: Brazos, 2012), 79–148. In response, see Hans Madueme and Michael Reeves, eds., *Adam, the Fall, and Original Sin: Theological, Biblical, and Scientific Perspectives* (Grand Rapids: Baker Academic, 2014).

light of their overall worldview. When these extratextual grids are "correlated" with Scripture, what often happens is that biblical concepts, terms, and thought are redefined. "Male and female" no longer have consistent borders tied to creation order, thus prohibiting the LGBTQ agenda, or "systemic" racism takes on ideological-political overtones that are contrary to the Bible's teaching on original sin and total depravity. Although Scripture is not a psychology book, it does imply a theological psychology, and as such, it addresses us as image-bearers, created as male and female and united as one human race despite our ethnic differences. All of this establishes a norm for sexual ethics and ways of viewing race, ethnicity, and so on that is not susceptible to the latest in secular thought. But what often occurs in this "method of correlation" with such "knowledge" is that it becomes the interpretive grid by which biblical teaching is denied. This can also occur when we elevate our personal "experiences" or even the leading of the "Spirit" in ways that contradict the teaching of Scripture. In all these ways, biblical authority and sufficiency is undermined.[42]

The Clarity/Perspicuity of Scripture[43]

Biblical Warrant for Clarity/Perspicuity

In the OT, God intends for his people to know him by his covenant word. God's word was not given to the elite but to the entire people of God, and God expected his people to understand it. Think of how parents are commanded to teach their children (Deut 6:4–9). Or how when Moses assembled the entire nation to hear God's word, he assumed they could understand and obey it (Deut 31:9–13). Also, as discussed in chapter 5, God is present by his word (Deut 4:5–8;

[42] On some of these points, see Trueman, *Rise and Triumph* (see chap. 1, n. 26); Nancy R. Pearcey, *Love Thy Body: Answering Hard Questions about Life and Sexuality* (Grand Rapids: Baker, 2018); Scott David Allen, *Why Social Justice Is Not Biblical Justice* (Grand Rapids: Credo, 2020); Thaddeus J. Williams, *Confronting Injustice without Compromising Truth: 12 Questions Christians Should Ask about Social Justice* (Grand Rapids: Zondervan, 2020); Douglas R. Groothius, *Fire in the Streets* (Washington, DC: Salem Books, 2022); cf. Thomas Sowell, *Race and Culture: A World View* (New York: Basic Books, 1994); and Sowell, *The Quest for Cosmic Justice* (see chap. 2, n. 114).

[43] See Barrett, *God's Word Alone*, 307–15; Thompson, "Generous Gift," 624–38; Waters, *For the Mouth*, 204–12; Frame, *Doctrine of the Word*, 201–9; Grudem, "The Perspicuity of Scripture," 291–93; D. A. Carson, *Collected Writings on Scripture* (Wheaton: Crossway, 2010), 179–93; see also Thompson, *Clear and Present Word* (see chap. 5, n. 63).

30:11–14; cf. Rom 10:6–8). God's word is not far from the people but near, and it is meant to reveal, not conceal. "The accessibility of the words that God gives to his people throughout the Old Testament arises in this context of God's determination to be known by those he has claimed as his own and God's gift of human language as critical to the process of making himself known."[44]

This same emphasis is throughout the OT (Josh 1:7–9; Pss 1:2; 19:7–11). Scripture keeps us from walking in darkness; it is a lamp for our feet and a light for our path (Pss 36:7–9; 119:105). God's word gives understanding to the simple (Ps 119:130), and it will never fail to accomplish its purpose (Isa 55:10–11). God's word is given to his people to be understood.

In the NT, the clarity of Scripture is taught in our Lord's teaching. Jesus never blames the OT for not being clear; it is quite the opposite. Jesus assumes that the OT can be rightly understood. Jesus sees himself as the fulfillment of the "Law and the Prophets" (Matt 5:17–20), but he indicts the religious leaders for not understanding this point. In fact, Jesus's correction of the religious leaders assumes, as Thompson argues, "at least formal willingness to allow behavior to be corrected by the Scriptures and an assumption that their meaning is not beyond those who read them or hear them read."[45] This point is also assumed in Jesus's constant appeal to the OT. When Jesus is challenged by the religious leaders, he appeals to Scripture—"Have you not read . . . ?"—to make his point, indeed to indict them for not knowing what the OT "clearly" teaches (Matt 12:1–8; 19:3–9; 22:31–32). In Jesus's rebuke, he knows that the leaders have read these texts, but *they* have failed to understand them. Yet, for Jesus's indictment to be effective, it assumes that their reading of the OT should have resulted in a correct understanding. "In the end, it wasn't because the words were obscure that the Pharisees failed to obey the Scriptures or the Sadducees were without hope. There were other, moral failures involved."[46] We can also see this in Jesus's interaction with Nicodemus. Jesus expects Nicodemus to know what the OT says about him and the coming of the new covenant age (John 3:10). The same is true of Jesus's rebuke of the two men on the way to Emmaus—"How foolish you are, and how slow to believe all that the prophets have spoken!" (Luke 24:25).

Jesus also appeals to the OT to settle all theological questions and disputes. Jesus repeatedly begins his teaching with "It is written" and then quotes the OT as settling the dispute (Matt

[44] Thompson, "Generous Gift," 635.

[45] Thompson, 624.

[46] Thompson, 625.

4:4, 7, 10; 21:13; 26:31; Luke 24:46; John 6:45; 8:17), which assumes that the OT meaning is clear. As Thompson points out, "Jesus's teaching about the sufficiency of Scripture—even prior to the inclusion of the New Testament documents—carries with it similar assumptions that the meaning of the text is intelligible to its readers."[47] In Jesus's parable about the rich man and Lazarus (Luke 16:19–31), he appeals to the sufficiency and clarity of the OT more than a personal encounter with someone who has come back from the dead! As Thompson concludes, "Moses and the prophets are clear enough for the rich man's brothers to be accountable for the choices that they make."[48]

However, as with sufficiency, clarity also requires an awareness of progressive revelation. Jesus appeals to the OT as clear but incomplete without him (Matt 5:17–20; Luke 24). The OT was clear on its own terms, but God intended for it to point beyond itself. Yet, Jesus still assumes that refusal to come to him was culpable. The OT rightly speaks of him (John 5:39–40), but full clarity comes in light of the entire canon. In other words, the OT becomes "clearer" due to the progress of revelation, especially regarding its central message centered in Christ (John 2:21–22; 7:37–39). This is why Thompson distinguishes "between the clarity of Jesus' teaching in its original setting (i.e., in the midst of his teaching ministry, before the cross and resurrection, the giving of the Spirit and the completion of the canon) and the clarity of Jesus' teaching in its canonical context (including the completed Gospel records and the apostolic proclamation)."[49] The canonical context results in further clarity and understanding.

One last point is also important to understand the clarity of Scripture: Jesus's use of parables. As Thompson and Frame note, Jesus uses parables to communicate to his hearers. But the use of parables also carries with it "a double edge that cannot be understood apart from the discriminating purpose of God."[50] On the one hand, parables clearly communicate the truth to God's people, but on the other hand, they also obscure the truth to those outside the kingdom (Mark 4:11–12; cf. Isa 6:9–10). Why is this important? For this reason: it reminds us that the problem of clarity is not with Scripture but with its readers![51] Apart from the regenerating and illuminating work of the Spirit, readers do not properly receive, understand, and obey God's word.

---

[47] Thompson, 626.

[48] Thompson, 626.

[49] Thompson, 631.

[50] Thompson, 628; cf. Frame, *Doctrine of the Word*, 204–6.

[51] See Thompson, 628–29; Frame, *Doctrine of the Word*, 204–5.

Thompson captures this point: "Revelation in the fullest sense (i.e., including its reception) remains a sovereign act of God, inseparable from a saving relation to the Son (Matt 11:27)."[52]

As we move from the Gospels to the rest of the NT, Scripture's clarity continues to be taught. For example, NT letters were written to the entire church, not merely to church leaders (1 Cor 1:2; Gal 1:2; Phil 1:1). Paul assumes that the common person can understand Scripture, and he encourages the sharing of his letters with other churches (Col 4:16), along with their public reading (2 Cor 1:13; Eph 3:4; 1 Tim 4:13; Jas 1:1, 22–25; 1 Pet 1:1; 2:2; 2 Pet 1:19; 1 John 5:13). Or think of how Paul addresses children, assuming that they can understand what he is saying (Eph 6:1–3; cf. 2 Tim 3:14–15a); or how Scripture was written for Jewish people who knew the OT and Gentiles who did not (Acts 13:46; 18:6; 22:21). This assumes that both can understand Scripture with due diligence. Even the purpose of Scripture assumes its clarity (2 Tim 3:16–17).

As in the OT and in Jesus's teaching, the NT authors also teach that the Spirit's work is necessary to illuminate readers to receive, believe, and understand Scripture. The inseparable God-word relation also shows itself in the inseparable word-Spirit relation (Gen 1:2–3; Num 11:25, 29; Joel 2:28; Matt 22:44; Acts 1:16; 4:25; Heb 3:7; 10:15–17). The Spirit who produced Scripture through the apostles (John 14:26; 16:13–15; 2 Tim 3:16; 2 Pet 1:21) also enables us to receive it. The problem is not with Scripture; clarity is a property of the text. The problem is in the reader. Apart from the Spirit's work, those outside of Christ—the "natural person"—do not "accept the things of the Spirit of God, for they are folly to him and he is not able to understand them because they are spiritually discerned" (1 Cor 2:14; cf. 2 Cor 3:14, 17).

Definition and Exposition of Clarity/Perspicuity

Definitions of Clarity/Perspicuity

Similar to sufficiency, the classic statement of "clarity/perspicuity" comes from the Reformation due to debates regarding the clarity of Scripture with the Roman Catholic Church.[53]

---

[52] Thompson, 629.

[53] As with sufficiency, Scripture's clarity was also affirmed prior to the Reformation. For example, Irenaeus, *Against Heresies* 2.27.1–2 (*ANF*, 1:398): the truths of the Gospel "fall [plainly] under our observation, and are clearly and unambiguously in express terms set forth in the Sacred Scriptures. . . .

> All things in Scripture are not alike plain in themselves, nor alike clear unto all; yet those things which are necessary to be known, believed, and observed for salvation, are so clearly propounded, and opened in some place of Scripture or other, that not only the learned, but the unlearned, in a due sense of ordinary means, may attain to a sufficient understanding of them.[54]

The historical context of this definition is the Reformation polemics with the Roman Catholic Church. In this context, the "clarity" of Scripture meant that the church magisterium does not function as the infallible interpreter of Scripture, but Scripture itself is sufficiently perspicuous that ordinary believers can understand its main message if they exercise due diligence. Martin Luther, in *The Bondage of the Will* (1525), reflects the Reformation view. In his response to Erasmus, Luther argued *against* Rome's view that the magisterium has the final say in the interpretation of Scripture. Instead, Scripture's ultimate interpreter is the Spirit speaking through Scripture, thus giving us the crucial hermeneutical principle: "Scripture interprets Scripture."

Erasmus objected to the "clarity" of Scripture by appealing to theology proper! Since God is transcendent and he conceals things (Deut 29:29), the church must tell us what Scripture means. Also, since Christians differ on interpretations, how could Scripture be clear? Luther responded with an important distinction between "external and internal" clarity.[55] The former refers to "clarity" as an attribute of Scripture itself, while the latter refers to what must occur

---

The entire Scriptures—the Prophets and the Gospels—can be clearly, unambiguously, and harmoniously understood by all, although all do not believe them." Or Tertullian, *On the Resurrection of the Flesh* 21 (*ANF*, 3:560), in referring to reading portions of Scripture: "(since some passages are more obscure than others), it cannot but be right . . . that uncertain statements should be determined by certain ones, and obscure ones by such as are clear and plain"; Augustine, *On Christian Doctrine* 2.9.14 (*NPNF*[1] 2:539):

> For among the things that are plainly laid down in Scripture are to be found all matters that concern faith and the manner of life. . . . After this, when we have made ourselves to a certain extent familiar with the language of Scripture, we may proceed to open up and investigate the obscure passages, and in doing so draw examples from the plainer expressions to throw light upon the more obscure, and use the evidence of passages about which there is no doubt to remove all hesitation in regard to the doubtful passages.

[54] *London Baptist Confession of Faith* (1689), 1.7 is the same as the earlier *WCF* (1647), 1.7.

[55] See Thompson, "Generous Gift," 637; cf. Provan, *Reformation and the Right Reading*, 11–12 (see chap. 4, n. 7).

in the reader to understand the Bible rightly—the Holy Spirit must open our minds to understand it (1 Cor 2:14). Thus, we misunderstand Scripture not because of it, but because of our finitude and sin. For the Christian and the church, we never read Scripture "in the absence of its primary author. Scripture is never read, never studied, never commented upon, behind God's back as it were."[56] In the divine economy, the Spirit gives us Scripture *and* enables us to receive and read it correctly.

Building on the classic definition of the "clarity/perspicuity" of Scripture that emerged from the Reformed tradition, Mark Thompson offers a more current definition that is helpful: "The clarity of Scripture is that quality of Scripture which, arising from the fact that it is ultimately God's effective communicative act, ensures the meaning of each biblical text, when viewed in the context of the canonical whole, is accessible to all who come to it in faith and dependent upon the Holy Spirit."[57]

Exposition of Clarity/Perspicuity

First, the clarity of Scripture does not mean that all texts of Scripture are equally clear and easy to comprehend.[58] Think of Peter's statement about Paul's writings (2 Pet 3:16). Peter reminds us that "some things" in Paul's letters are "difficult to understand" (*dusnoēta*) but not beyond understanding (*anoēta*), which assumes that they are understandable but effort is required. This is why the confession states: "All things in Scripture are not alike plain in themselves, nor alike clear unto all." Why is this so? Many reasons could be given.

God has disclosed himself to us *in history* that is tied to real people, cultures, and languages. This entails that we have to grapple with Scripture and do our homework. Furthermore, God also has an infinite mind and he is properly incomprehensible. God has not exhaustively revealed everything to us, and even if he had done so, finite creatures, let alone fallen creatures, would not be able to understand it. But what God has revealed is sufficiently clear for the knowledge of God centered in Christ. In addition, God has chosen to reveal himself over time.[59] This means

---

[56] Thompson, "Generous Gift," 638.

[57] Thompson, 617–18.

[58] On this point, see Turretin, *Institutes of Elenctic Theology*, 1:144; Bavinck, *Reformed Dogmatics*, 1:450.

[59] Thompson, "Generous Gift," 638–39; Garner, "Did God Really Say?," 154–59.

that more "difficult" texts (e.g., 1 Cor 15:29; 1 Pet 3:19) must be interpreted in light of clearer texts, hence the Reformation principle of "Scripture interpreting Scripture," or the "analogy of Scripture."[60] Progressive revelation also entails that not every doctrinal truth is given in one text. Think of the doctrine of the Trinity or the person of Christ. God has disclosed his triune nature and the identity of the divine Son over time. Thus, the proper context of our interpretation of Scripture is the canon along the lines of the three horizons/contexts discussed in chapter 4. Given what Scripture is and how it has come to us, we must not treat texts in isolation. Despite the diversity of Scripture, there is an overall unity to it, but this unity is "seen" at the canonical level. Scripture, then, never contradicts itself, but clarity properly understood requires the entire canon now brought to fulfillment in Christ (Heb 1:1–3). But as Garner correctly cautions, the progress of revelation does not mean that "God's revelation lacked clarity at any stage,"[61] although the OT was incomplete as it anticipated the fulfillment of God's promises in Christ. Instead, "the content of [God's] speech becomes fuller, in Christ attaining its fullness. . . . Thus, revelation is clear at each stage according to the wise purposes of God, and the eschatological revelation in Jesus Christ, the Son of God, completes these redemptive purposes."[62]

Second, Scripture is clear but not without effort and the help of others, or what Iain Provan calls "perspicuity and perspiration!"[63] This is why the definition includes "the due sense of ordinary means." Since Scripture is complex and tied to history, this means that we have to know something about historical backgrounds, biblical languages, and how literary forms work in that time period. This requires study and diligence, following the example of Ezra (Ezra 7:10). As we read Scripture, there are difficult matters to grasp, but it is not impossible (2 Pet 3:15–16).

---

[60] The "analogy of Scripture" is also known as the "analogy of faith" (*analogia fidei*), namely, Scripture must interpret Scripture. The former is a better expression since the latter may be confused with the Roman Catholic teaching that "the analogy of faith" means that "biblical passages must not be set in opposition either to one another, or to the faith and teaching of the Roman Catholic Church." Provan, *Reformation and Right Reading*, 11. Instead, the use of "analogy of Scripture" makes clear that the "rule of faith" "is Scripture itself, and not something external to it" (11).

[61] Garner, "Did God Really Say?," 155.

[62] Garner, 156.

[63] Provan, *Reformation and Right Reading*, 305–7; cf. Grudem, "The Perspicuity of Scripture," 295–98.

This is why we need help from others. We need lexicons, concordances, grammars, and translations. We need teachers who write commentaries to explain Scripture to us (Acts 8:30–31). Exegetes, teachers, pastors, and theologians are gifts to the church for her edification (Eph 4:7–16; 1 Tim 3:2). But we must not think of them as mediators, in contrast to how prophets, priests, and kings functioned under the OT covenants. Nor should we think of them as a "magisterium" that determines the right meaning of Scripture as in Roman Catholic theology.[64] Instead, they are gifts given by the Lord of the church to help God's people read and apply Scripture better. They also help defend the Bible against specialized attacks (2 Tim 2:25; Titus 1:9).

All of this highlights the important role of historical theology and tradition.[65] *Sola Scriptura* is not *solo Scriptura*: we are to listen to the past and to learn from our forefathers in the faith. Tradition and confessions serve a vital "ministerial" role in our reading of Scripture and the doing of theology that we ignore to our peril. We do not approach the Bible or theology *de novo*. We stand on the shoulders of those who have gone before us. We stand within a tradition that has interpreted Scripture and drawn theological conclusions, and we learn from them.

Third, "clarity" does not mean that there are no longer theological disputes within the church. Clarity is a property of *Scripture*, not a property of its readers, a common mistake made by those too influenced by postmodern thought.[66] Clarity affirms that Scripture is *able* to be understood, *not* that it will *always* be understood rightly by us. Clarity is not dependent on the individual or communal reader. If it was, then "God himself [would be] contingent upon his listeners for the clarity of his own speech."[67] Yet, as Thompson admits, "Personal preferences,

---

[64] See the fourth session of the Council of Trent (April 8, 1546), which argues that we are not to interpret Scripture contrary to the magisterium of the church. See Philip Schaff, ed., *Creeds of Christendom*, 3 vols. (Grand Rapids: Baker, 1977), 2:83. In evangelical theology, we must also avoid what J. I. Packer called a "new papalism—the infallibility of the scholars." Packer, *God Has Spoken*, 21 (see chap. 5, n. 72).

[65] For a more detailed discussion of this relationship, see Provan, *Reformation and Right Reading*, 289–302.

[66] See Grudem, "The Perspicuity of Scripture," 295; Garner, "Did God Really Say?," 143. Contrary to James Callahan, *The Clarity of Scripture: History, Theology, and Contemporary Literary Studies* (Downers Grove: InterVarsity, 2011), 11, 25, 50, who fails to distinguish the nature of Scripture (clarity as a property of Scripture) from our understanding of Scripture. He confuses what Luther distinguished, i.e., the external and internal clarity of Scripture.

[67] Barrett, *God's Word Alone*, 317.

cultural blind spots and allegiance to the community of which the reader is a part—or to an interpretative tradition associated with that community—all have the potential for distorting our reading."[68] In fact, one of the benefits of retrieving the past is to listen to others since they help us expose our own biases and encourage us to warrant our theological conclusions from Scripture. However, even though theological disputes within the church remain, we must also acknowledge significant points of agreement so that there is a recognizable *Christian* theology (e.g., Nicaea, Chalcedon, etc.) and a "faith that was delivered to the saints once for all" (Jude 3).

Fourth, Scripture is clear to us but not without our willingness to obey it.[69] In Scripture, the relationship between understanding and obedience is tight. For example, a right understanding is to lead us to obedience (Ps 119:34), while obedience is necessary to understand Scripture (1 Cor 3:1–3; Heb 5:11–6:12). As we grow in grace and obey God's word, we gain more understanding. To understand Scripture, we must be hearers *and* doers of God's word (Jas 1:22–25).

Fifth, Scripture is clear but not without the illumination of the Holy Spirit.[70] In the OT, the Psalmist cries to God for understanding (Ps 119:18, 27, 34, 73), which in the divine economy is associated with the appropriated work of the Holy Spirit (2 Cor 3:14–16; 4:3–4). In this regard, the classic text is 1 Cor 2:2–16.[71] In 1 Corinthians 2, two contrary options are often given in thinking about the Spirit's role in hermeneutics. According to the first option, the text says nothing about the Spirit's role in our *understanding* of Scripture but only about the Spirit's role in *significance* (i.e., our *applying* Scripture). But according to the second option, the text teaches that apart from the Spirit we cannot *understand* Scripture, almost as if clarity is not a property of Scripture, but only a property of the reader. However, this text teaches neither of these options.

The context of the text begins in 1:18. Paul is discussing the "wisdom of the cross" over against the "isms" of Corinth and the wisdom of the world. The message of the cross, although

---

[68] Thompson, "Generous Gift," 642.

[69] Grudem, "The Perspicuity of Scripture," 298.

[70] See John Webster, "Illumination," *Journal of Reformed Theology* 5 (2011): 325–40; cf. Grudem, "The Perspicuity of Scripture," 299–300.

[71] See D. A. Carson, *The Cross and the Christian Ministry: An Exposition of Passages from 1 Corinthians* (Grand Rapids: Baker, 1993), 43–66; Anthony C. Thiselton, *The First Epistle to the Corinthians*, NIGTC (Grand Rapids: Eerdmans, 2000), 224–86.

rejected by the world, is the very demonstration of *God's* wisdom (1:18–25). In chapter 2, Paul is continuing to expound on the "wisdom of the cross." As he does, he gives three important contrasts. First, he contrasts "those who receive God's wisdom" and "those who do not" (2:6–10a). The "mature" (2:6) refers to all Christians against "the rulers of this age" (2:6), that is, all those who embrace the mindset of the world in opposition to God (e.g., the scholar, philosopher, and political rulers [1:20, 26; 2:6]). To Christians, Paul proclaims God's "wisdom in a mystery" (2:7), which is the revelation of God's eternal plan that was prophesied in the OT yet veiled, but which now is revealed in Christ and his cross. *This* is what is now unveiled to believers by the Spirit (2:10), and Christians (the "mature") have only come to understand the OT properly because of the Spirit's illuminating work. In other words, God has acted *publicly* in Christ and his cross, but there must also be a *private* work of God, by his Spirit, in the mind and heart of the individual. In fact, this is what distinguishes the believer (the "mature") from the unbeliever (the "people/rulers of this age"). If Christians "see" the truth of the gospel, it is due to God's work of grace by the Spirit.

This point is reinforced in the second contrast: a contrast between the Spirit of God and the "spirit" of the world (2:10b–13). In 2:10, Paul says that the message of the cross ("it") is revealed to Christians ("us") by the Spirit (2:13), which again refers to the work of the Spirit *in* us; otherwise, the message of the cross does not make sense. Then there is the third contrast between the "natural" person (i.e., the non-Christian) and the "spiritual" person (i.e., the Christian born of the Spirit) (2:14–16). Paul says two things about those who do *not* have the Spirit. They do *not* accept the things that come from the Spirit because they are foolish to them. They may grasp truths at a certain level, but not in terms of embracing them as wisdom, life, and truth. In this, Paul insists that humans *cannot* understand the gospel because it is spiritually discerned. This statement is the complement of 2:12. There we were told that the Spirit was given to believers so that we may understand what God has freely given us. Here Paul rules out the possibility that anyone could possibly understand this without the Spirit's aid.

Why is this text important? For this reason: it underscores the need for the Spirit's work in regeneration and illumination to understand truly the gospel message of Scripture. No doubt, this text is not first concerned with the mechanics of how people come to understand their Bibles and do hermeneutics. Paul's primary focus is on the fundamental message of the cross and how it cannot be fully understood apart from the regenerative work of the Spirit. But as we apply this text to hermeneutics, it teaches us that ultimately to understand Scripture requires the Spirit's work in regeneration and illumination. In other words, in hermeneutics, there is a crucial *spiritual* component tied to "understanding." If we do not understand Scripture, the fault is *not* in Scripture; it is clear. Instead, the fault lies in us, which only the Spirit of God can remedy. So, how should we think of the word-Spirit relationship theologically?[72] Here are *two* points:

1. The work of the Holy Spirit is first in the *production* of Scripture, which involves a number of aspects. First, as God the Spirit, *he* was involved in formulating the eternal plan of creation and redemption inseparably with the Father and the Son; Scripture is a part of that plan.[73] Second, "the Spirit was the author of revelation, the one who revealed God's truth to the prophets (Isa 61:1–4; Acts 2)."[74] Third, the Spirit sovereignly superintended "inspiration," which resulted in God's word written (1 Cor 2:9–10; 2 Tim 3:16; 2 Pet 1:21). In inspiration, the Spirit speaks in and through what the authors write. No doubt, the human authors may not understand all the implications of what they write, but the Spirit's speaking *through* Scripture is not separated from what the human author communicates in his text, as we discussed in chapter 7.

2. The work of the Holy Spirit is also involved *internally*, that is, the "internal testimony of the Spirit" that enables readers to receive, believe, understand, and obey Scripture, tied to the Spirit's work in regeneration and illumination (Rom 8:14–17; 1 Cor 2:10–16; 1 Thess 1:5; 2:13; 1 John 2:27; 5:9).[75] In thinking about the Spirit's "internal" work to illuminate Scripture so that we are enabled *to understand* it, in contrast to much of postmodern theology, we should not think of the Spirit creating new meaning independent of what Scripture says. Rather, as Vanhoozer states: "the Spirit's role in bringing about understanding is to witness to what is other than himself (meaning accomplished) and to bring its significance to bear on the reader (meaning applied)."[76] In other words, the Spirit's speaking in and through Scripture is *singular*, grounded in the text itself due to divine inspiration, and in illumination the Spirit bears witness to it. In so doing, the Spirit *illumines* by impressing the meaning of the text on the reader

---

[72] This discussion is indebted to Frame, *Doctrine of the Word*, 615–40; Vanhoozer, *Is There a Meaning?*, 413–15 (see chap. 2, n. 118).

[73] Frame, *Doctrine of the Word*, 615.

[74] Frame, 615.

[75] Frame, 615–16.

[76] Vanhoozer, *Is There a Meaning?*, 413, italics removed.

so that we understand the author's intent for what it is—"warnings, promises, commands, assertion—together with their implicit claim on our minds and hearts."[77] In illumination, then, the Spirit does *not* change or go beyond the meaning of the text; instead, he enables us to understand what is already there, which is rightly identified with the "literal sense" (*sensus literalis*). No doubt, involved in illumination is the Spirit's prior work of regeneration and his ongoing work of sanctification. "Negatively," as Vanhoozer notes, "the Spirit progressively disabuses us of those ideological or idolatrous prejudices that prevent us from receiving the message of the text. . . . Positively, the Spirit conforms our interests to those of the text."[78] But, in the end, the Spirit's work in illumination is not to create new meanings but to drive home what the text says in all of its authority and power.

Challenges to Clarity/Perspicuity

The constant challenge to "clarity/perspicuity" is the tendency to obscure Scripture's meaning, which results in the inability to affirm *sola Scriptura*. It also results in the need for some kind of "infallible magisterium" to tell you what Scripture means (either of the Roman Catholic variety or what J. I. Packer dubbed the "new papalism" of infallible scholars).[79] In the end, this results in a denial of *God's* authority and *his* ability to communicate clearly to us, along with the loss of the transcendental condition for a normative theology. Throughout church history, this tendency has surfaced in different ways, some more serious than others, but all of which needs to be avoided if we are truly going to honor our triune God who so graciously has given us his word. Let us look at some of the ways clarity has been obscured throughout the ages.

First, in the early church, clarity/perspicuity was affirmed, but it was undercut by the rise of the allegorical method of interpretation. At the heart of the allegorical method is interpreting biblical texts for meanings "other" (Gk. *allos*, "other") than what they seem to say: "This text means *that*," with *that* being determined by something "outside" the text.[80] If the method is consistently applied, the meaning of Scripture is no longer determined *on its own terms*, that is, by what God says through the human authors, which is *in* their texts. Instead, the meaning

---

[77] Vanhoozer, 413.

[78] Vanhoozer, 413; cf. Webster, "Illumination," 337–40.

[79] See Packer, *God Has Spoken*, 25.

[80] Vanhoozer, *Is There a Meaning?*, 114; cf. Provan, *Reformation and Right Reading*, 151–225.

of Scripture is determined by some kind of extratextual system that allows you to know what the *that* is, which in the end is the real authority, not the "literal sense" of Scripture.

Fortunately, in the early church, and even the medieval era, the allegorical method was not consistently applied, although it was often used to derive all kinds of fanciful interpretations.[81] Not only was the *that* controlled by the "rule of faith," which was derived from Scripture, but also larger theological constraints that tethered the use of the method. Most acknowledged, from Irenaeus to Augustine and from Aquinas to the Reformers, that the "literal" sense, that is, what the biblical authors intended to communicate in their texts (their speech acts and use of literary forms), was the primary sense.[82] Indeed, as Augustine emphasized in *On Christian Doctrine*, the *literal* sense established doctrine, and "other senses" are only allowed if the text does not teach either a doctrinal truth or the love of God and neighbor.[83] But although the allegorical method and its appeal to multiple senses were not consistently applied, Scripture's clarity was undercut. As D. A. Carson notes, "the commitment to multiple levels of meaning became systematic, and as the full apparatus of patristic and medieval scholarship was applied, and vernacular Latin was gradually dissipated, the accessibility and thus the perspicuity of Scripture faded a little farther into the distance."[84] In this context, the Reformation recaptured *sola Scriptura* along with a proper view of "clarity" and a commitment to read Scripture according to its *sensus literalis*.[85]

Second, in the Reformation, the "perspicuity" debate was related to whether Scripture *alone* is our final authority and thus able to be understood apart from an infallible magisterium. Today, this debate continues between Protestant and Roman Catholic theology. And despite Rome's protestations, there is no biblical warrant for apostolic succession from Peter

---

[81] Some of the reasons why some embraced the allegorical method was due to the perceived difficulties in Scripture. Allegory was used to soften and make sense of difficult texts, even offensive ones, such as God's command to destroy peoples in the OT by Israel. In addition, allegory sought to demonstrate to Jewish people how Christ was in the OT; thus, a strong motive to show how all of Scripture speaks of Christ was also behind the use of the method. However, this is unnecessary if we read Scripture *on its own terms* and as a progressive revelation unfolding God's eternal plan centered in Christ. On this point, see chapter 4 and part 3.

[82] Provan, *Reformation and Right Reading*, 151–225.

[83] See Vanhoozer, *Is There a Meaning?*, 117.

[84] Carson, *Collected Writings on Scripture*, 182.

[85] Provan, *Reformation and Right Reading*, 283–345.

to the present pope or for the magisterium's authority to establish the correct reading of Scripture, along with dogma in addition to (and even contrary to) Scripture. The Roman view, in the end, reduces to some form of extratextual theology that eclipses the sufficiency and clarity of Scripture.[86]

Third, in the modern/postmodern eras, "clarity" has basically been eclipsed, along with the very possibility of a normative word from God. In chapters 2 and 5, we discussed some of the reasons for this, largely due to a shift in worldviews away from historic Christianity and the embrace of a theology "from below." In the "modern" era, the rejection of trinitarian theism for deism and panentheism, the turn away from a revelational epistemology to a "turn to the subject" as represented in classical foundationalism, and the embrace of the historical-critical method with its corresponding presupposition of methodological naturalism undermined biblical authority. Gerhard Maier nicely captures this point:

> The representatives of the higher-critical method have given sharp opposition to the orthodox thoughts concerning the *perspicuitas* (clarity) and *sufficientia* (sufficiency) of the Scriptures. They have obscured the clarity by their "proof" of contradictions in the Bible, and they have clung to and deepened the obscurity by means of their fruitless search for a canon in a canon. . . . To the degree that their views asserted themselves, a division set in between Scripture and the congregation . . . they have also destroyed the certainty of faith. If it is uncertain *where* the living God is speaking, then I no longer know *who* is speaking.[87]

In the postmodern era, the situation has not changed; it has only doubled down. In the place of classical foundationalism, a "constructivist" view of knowledge is now embraced. Deism has given way to a full-blown panentheism, and the meaning of Scripture is no longer "in" the text determined by God's speech through the human authors. Instead meaning is located in the reader's or community's interpretive experience, thus rejecting any notion that "clarity" is a property of Scripture. Gone is the attempt to read Scripture according to its "literal

---

[86] For a critique of the Roman Catholic view, see Waters, *For the Mouth*, 219–29; Barrett, *God's Word Alone*, 329–31, 347–66.

[87] Gerhard Maier, *The End of the Historical-Critical Method*, trans. Edwin W. Leverenz and Rudolph F. Norden (St. Louis: Concordia, 1977), 48–49.

sense"; instead, the allegorical method has returned, but now uncoupled from any determinate theological constraint. As a result, any concept of *sola Scriptura* is rendered impossible.[88]

Ultimately what is at stake are two different worldviews, and it is the modern/postmodern view which must be rejected as a total unit.[89] What is needed is a theology "from above" that affirms unashamedly the truth that the glorious triune God of Scripture is there and he has not remained silent. Given who *he* is and his choice to communicate to us, *sola Scriptura* is not only plausible but absolutely necessary. And, given who our triune God is, since *he* has something to say, as Thompson reminds us, "he is very good at saying it,"[90] which if understood within the larger framework of the Christian worldview and theology, entails the "clarity" of Scripture.

Concluding Reflection

As we conclude our discussion of the attributes of Scripture, biblical authority as reflected in "sufficiency and clarity" has numerous practical consequences for the church. By Scripture, we test all beliefs; we do not believe anything that Scripture does not warrant either directly or by implication. By Scripture, we test our own personal experiences to make sure we do not live in a world of our making. By Scripture, we know what God demands of us, and we are not left in the dark. We know that nothing is required of us that is not taught in Scripture. We know that all we need for life and godliness is given to us so that we may grow in grace and the knowledge of our Lord Jesus Christ. In our churches, we do not have to guess what the mission of the church is, how we should govern ourselves, and how we should relate to the world. Scripture is our light and lamp, and it will never lead us astray.

John Murray, in reflecting on the finality and sufficiency of Scripture, challenges us with these points. He first notes that "our dependence upon Scripture is total."[91] Without it, we have no normative and sure word from God. He continues by saying that because of what Scripture is, we must apply it to our lives "in all its fullness, richness, wisdom, and power,"[92] which demands careful exposition and application. He reminds us that too often we do not

---

[88] See Vanhoozer, *Is There a Meaning?*, 43–195.

[89] See Carson, *Collected Writings on Scripture*, 186–93.

[90] Thompson, *Clear and Present Word*, 170.

[91] Murray, "The Finality and Sufficiency of Scripture," in *Collected Writings*, 1:20.

[92] Murray, 1:21.

value Scripture. Instead, "we have resorted to other techniques, expedients, and methods of dealing with the dilemma that confronts us all. . . . Some of us may have relied upon our heritage, our tradition. . . . Some, on the other hand, may be so enamored of modernity."[93] But what the church desperately needs is to teach, expound, apply, and defend "the Word of the living and abiding God deposited for us in Holy Scripture." "We must bring forth from its inexhaustible treasures, in exposition, proclamation, and application—application to every sphere of life—what is the wisdom and power of God for man in this age . . . [and] for man in every age." It is only then that the church will awaken from her lethargy, call upon the Lord, and fulfill her calling to be God's new covenant people living between the ages, as she proclaims the unsearchable riches of Christ and calls all people to repentance and faith in Christ. Only then will the church be relevant, for she will be proclaiming God's word "in the unction and power of the Spirit."[94]

---

[93] Murray, 1:21.
[94] Murray, 1:22.

CHAPTER 12

The Canon of Scripture

Introduction

So far, we have discussed the nature of Scripture by focusing on its authority, inspiration, inerrancy, sufficiency, and clarity—all of which are important in expounding a *theology* of Scripture. But one issue remains: given that only certain books are "God-breathed" (2 Tim 3:16), which ones are they? This is the issue of canon.

The word "canon" is a Semitic loanword in Greek (*kanōn*) that originally meant "reed" but came to mean a "measuring reed," "rule," or "standard."[1] When the term was later applied to Scripture by the church in the fourth century, the word took on a technical sense of referring to a list of books that are inspired Scripture, in contrast to other human documents. Thus to speak of the "canon" of Scripture is to refer to a closed collection of books that alone are God's word and fully authoritative and sufficient to define the "rule of faith" or theology for the church.[2] Before the term *canon* was more commonly used, other terms were used by Jews

[1] David G. Dunbar, "The Biblical Canon," in Carson and Woodbridge, *Hermeneutics, Authority, and Canon*, 300 (see chap. 2, n. 63); Roger Beckwith, "The Canon of Scripture" in *NDBT*, 27 (see chap. 1, n. 24).

[2] This occurred in AD 367 in Athanasius's famous Festal letter, which included a list of canonical books, our present NT. For a discussion of Athanasius's letter, see Edmon L. Gallagher and John D.

and Christians to refer to Scripture: "Holy Scriptures" (Rom 1:2; 2 Tim 3:15; Philo; Josephus), "the Holy Books," and the "Law and the Prophets" (1 Macc 12:9; 2 Macc 15:9). The terms *Old Testament* and *New Testament* began to be applied by Christian writers to collections of Scriptures in the second to early third century.[3]

When we think of "canon," we must distinguish between the concept of "Scripture" functioning as God's word given to his people that is more open-ended since new books may be added to it ("canon 1") and an official list of books that signify that the "canon" is now closed ("canon 2").[4] Too often *canon* is only used in the latter sense, which entails that we do not have a "canon" until a specific list is drawn up.[5] For example, if this definition of "canon" is applied to the NT, then there is no "canon" until the end of the fourth century, which is patently false. The church always was ruled by the OT canon, which was already in existence prior to Christ, and it was ruled by the word of our Lord through the apostolic writings that were recognized immediately as Scripture. In other words, God's people, whether Israel or the church, never existed apart from God's authoritative word, although over time, lists eventually delineated a specific collection of inspired books, something God's people *recognized* from the very beginning of their existence.

Why is the issue of canon important? At least four reasons may be given.

First, since the only epistemological warrant for truth and a normative theology is the triune God who speaks, we must know where God has authoritatively spoken. On this point, Protestant theology disagrees with Roman Catholicism. The Roman Church adds the "Apocrypha" to the canon and views it as God's word. This major point of contention between

---

Meade, *The Biblical Canon Lists from Early Christianity: Texts and Analysis* (Oxford: Oxford University Press, 2017), 118–29.

[3] Beckwith, "Canon of Scripture," 28.

[4] For these distinctions, see Stephen G. Dempster, "Canons on the Right and Canons on the Left: Finding a Resolution in the Canon Debate," *JETS* 52:1 (2009): 50–51. Dempster borrows these distinctions from Gerald T. Sheppard, "Canon," in *The Encyclopedia of Religion*, ed. Mircea Eliade (New York: Macmillan, 1987), 3:62–69.

[5] For this "exclusive" view of canon, which is too reductionistic, see Lee Martin McDonald, *The Formation of the Christian Biblical Canon* (Peabody: Hendrickson, 1995), 13–21; Eugene Ulrich, "The Notion and Definition of Canon" in *The Canon Debate*, ed. Lee Martin McDonald and James A. Sanders (Peabody: Hendrickson, 2002), 21–35; Allert, *A High View of Scripture?*, 49–51 (see chap. 8, n. 87).

Protestantism and Catholicism is important. If the Apocrypha is Scripture, then it must govern the thought and life of God's people, but if it is not, then it must not function as authoritative for our theology.

Second, canon is important in answering the question of whether there is on-going revelation, especially after the coming of our Lord Jesus Christ, a major point of dispute between various cults (e.g., Mormonism), and even Islam, which views itself as a continuation of the Bible.

Third, as noted in previous chapters, a closed canon has consequential implications for hermeneutics and theological method. A closed canon allows us to read *all* of Scripture in light of Christ, to make better sense of how the "parts" fit with the "whole," and it drives us to draw our theological conclusions from the whole of Scripture, not merely its parts.

Fourth, due to ongoing historical-critical scholarship that continues to question biblical authority by raising questions of authorship, the dates of books, textual transmission, and so on, questions regarding the formation of the canon have resurfaced today. Also, given recent discoveries of the Dead Sea Scrolls and the Nag Hammadi Library, which recovered biblical manuscripts from the OT and NT *and* Gnostic and Apocryphal texts, further questions about which books belong in the canon and why are being asked anew, even in the popular media. For example, talk of the *Gospel of Thomas*, the *Gospel of Judas*, and multiple works like these, along with attacks on historic Christianity by such people as Elaine Pagels[6] and Bart Ehrman[7] have challenged the idea of a normative, fixed canon of Scripture. In such novels as *The DaVinci Code*, we are told that there was no NT canon until the fourth or fifth century.[8] In addition, we are told that when the church did produce a canon, it had nothing to do with God's sovereign work among his people to recognize his word; instead, it was the result of

---

[6] Elaine Pagels, *The Gnostic Gospels* (New York: Random House, 1979); Pagels, *Beyond Belief: The Secret Gospel of Thomas* (New York: Random House, 2003).

[7] Bart D. Ehrman, *Lost Christianities: The Battles for Scripture and the Faith We Never Knew* (New York: Oxford University Press, 2002); Ehrman, *Misquoting Jesus* (see chap. 10, n. 19); Ehrman, *Lost Scriptures: Books that Did Not Make It Into the New Testament* (New York: Oxford University Press, 2005); Ehrman, *Forged: Writing in the Name of God—Why the Bible's Authors Are Not Who We Think They Are* (New York: HarperOne, 2011).

[8] For example, see David L. Dungan, *Constantine's Bible: Politics and the Making of the New Testament* (Philadelphia: Fortress Press, 2006), 132–33; Geoffrey M. Hahneman, *The Muratorian Fragment and the Development of the Canon* (Oxford: Clarendon, 1992), 129–30.

political power struggles that eventually were won by the "strong," which then imposed their "orthodox" view on their enemies, namely, the "heretics."[9] None of this is true, but it has raised anew the issue of the canon and especially how the church came to recognize Scripture to be God's word.

One last comment: in thinking about the "canon," we need to distinguish two issues: the theological and the historical. The *theological* is thinking about the relation between "authority" and "canon." Which comes first? Scripture's own inherent authority that God's people recognize? Or do God's people *confer* authority on the books thus making them Scripture? The *historical* answers the question of *when* Israel and the church recognized what we know as the thirty-nine books of the OT and the twenty-seven books of the NT. And, furthermore, why did Israel and the church reject other books as non-canonical? Let us look at each of these in turn.[10]

Theological Issues Regarding the Canon

There are at least three significant theological issues regarding the canon.

First, do God's people recognize Scripture's inherent authority, or do we confer authority on Scripture? In the Reformation, and within evangelical theology, Scripture's authority

[9] This is the thesis of Walter Bauer, *Orthodoxy and Heresy in Earliest Christianity* (Tübingen: Mohr, 1934), now with a postmodern twist. Cf. Ehrman, *Lost Christianities*, 159–257. For a critique of Bauer's thesis, see Andreas Köstenberger and Michael J. Kruger, *The Heresy of Orthodoxy* (Wheaton: Crossway, 2010).

[10] For helpful resources, see Roger T. Beckwith, *The Old Testament Canon of the New Testament Church, and Its Background in Early Judaism* (Grand Rapids: Eerdmans, 1986); Beckwith, "Canon of Scripture," 27–34; Stephen Dempster, "Canons on the Right and Canons on the Left," 47–77; Dempster, "The Old Testament Canon, Josephus, and Cognitive Environment," in Carson, *Enduring Authority*, 321–61 (see chap. 4, n. 9); Dempster, "From a Smoking Canon to Burning Hearts: The Making of the Hebrew Bible," *SBJT* 24.3 (2020): 25–52; Michael J. Kruger, *Canon Revisited: Establishing the Origins and Authority of the New Testament Books* (Wheaton: Crossway, 2012); Kruger, *The Question of Canon: Challenging the Status Quo in the New Testament Debate* (Downers Grove: InterVarsity, 2013); Kruger, "Deconstructing Canon: Recent Challenges to the Origins and Authority of the New Testament Writings," in Garner, *Did God Really Say?*, 49–70 (see chap. 7, n. 113). Also see D. A. Carson, Douglas J. Moo, and Leon Morris, *An Introduction to the New Testament* (Grand Rapids: Zondervan, 1992), 487–500; Ridderbos, *Redemptive History*, (see chap. 11, n. 19); and Dunbar, "Biblical Canon," 299–360.

is tied to the God whose word it is.[11] In other words, Scripture is authoritative because it is *God's* self-attesting word (due to inspiration). For this reason, we must distinguish the *nature* of canonicity from its *recognition* as a canon. The authority of canonical books exists independently of their being recognized as authoritative by any individual or group. The triune God renders Scripture *authoritative*; we recognize that authority, but we do not confer authority on Scripture. Accordingly, the canon is not the product of the Christian church or the Jewish community. The church has no authority to control, create, or define God's word; rather, Scripture controls, creates, and defines the church. Authority is inherent in Scripture; the church simply confesses this to be the case. This crucial truth about the canon is found throughout Scripture, but it is stated well by Paul: "If anyone thinks that he is a prophet or spiritual, he should recognize that what I write to you is the Lord's command" (1 Cor 14:37). What is primary is God speaking through Paul, or in the case of Scripture, the Bible's own inherent authority, which is then recognized by God's people.

Second, by affirming that Scripture has inherent authority that the church recognizes, such an understanding opposes the Roman Catholic view and even some current Protestant views. Let us look at each of these in turn.

1. *The Roman Catholic View*. Roman Catholic theology often quotes Augustine in favor of their view: "I should not believe the gospel except as moved by the authority of the Catholic Church."[12] Their interpretation of Augustine is that the Roman Catholic Church, as the ongoing incarnation of Christ on earth through its magisterium, creates and brings into existence Scripture. Apart from the church declaring these books to be Scripture, they would not be authoritative. This is not to say that Rome denies that Scripture is *of God*, and as J. T. Lienhard acknowledges, "No Catholic would want to say that the authority of the Bible derives simply from the decree of a council."[13] However, within Catholic theology, there is an intertwined relationship between Scripture, tradition, and the magisterium. In the end, the authority of the church, as understood as the continuing incarnation of Christ on earth or the "whole Christ" (*totus Christus*) acting as one person by the moving influence of the Holy Spirit, precedes

[11] See Richard B. Gaffin Jr., "The New Testament as Canon," in Conn, *Inerrancy and Hermeneutic*, 171–72 (see chap. 8, n. 58).

[12] Augustine, *Against the Epistle of Manichaeus* 5 (*NPNF*[1] 4:131).

[13] J. T. Lienhard, *The Bible, the Church, and Authority* (Collegeville, MN: Liturgical, 1995), 72.

Scripture; hence, Rome rejects *sola scriptura*.[14] Scripture is crucial for the church's "well-being" (*bene esse*). However, when it comes to the church's "being" (*esse*), namely, its very existence, Scripture is unnecessary since the church produced Scripture. This is why the church can survive even if Scripture vanishes.[15]

However, there are a number of problems with this view.[16] First, Augustine's statement is not saying what Rome claims. As John Calvin noted, Augustine, in addressing the false teaching of Manichaeism, is not claiming that God's word is dependent on the church as the ultimate source of the authority for why he believes in Christ. Instead, Augustine is speaking in reference to Christians, not non-Christians. "He is simply teaching that there would be no certainty of the gospel for unbelievers to win them to Christ if the consensus of the church did not impel them."[17] As such, Augustine is simply arguing that the gospel message comes *through* the church, but it is a message she has received *from God* and on *his* authority. Second, Augustine's statement is confirmed by Scripture. Throughout redemptive history, God, by his word, creates his people, not vice versa. In fact, as Michael Kruger reminds us, even Jesus and the apostles had a canon, the OT, which ruled their thinking and lives (Luke 24:44; Rom 15:4; 1 Cor 10:6; 2 Tim 3:15–16).[18] And after our Lord ascended, the writings of the apostles, who were called by Christ and borne along by the Spirit to proclaim and to write the truth of the gospel, were received and recognized by the church *as God's word*, not merely a human word (1 Thess 2:13; 2 Pet 3:16). Thus, "the Scriptures themselves never give the impression that their authority was 'derivative' from the church, or from some future ecclesiastical decision."[19] As the NT is written by inspiration, Robert Saucy is correct to say that "the apostolic word thus continues in the church through the authoritative Scriptures and not in an authoritative teaching office of the church."[20] J. I. Packer captures the priority of God's word over the church, and the fact that Scripture's authority is not dependent on the church but vice versa, when he

---

[14] See Karl Rahner, *Foundations of Christian Faith* (New York: Crossroads, 1997), 373.

[15] On this point, see Bavinck, *Reformed Dogmatics*, 1:452–72 (see chap. 1, n. 9); cf. Barrett, *God's Word Alone*, 353 (see chap. 1, n. 25).

[16] For a more detailed response, see Kruger, *Canon Revisited*, 38–48.

[17] Calvin, *Institutes*, 1.7.3 (see chap. 1, n. 3).

[18] Kruger, *Canon Revisited*, 44–45.

[19] Kruger, 45.

[20] Robert Saucy, *Scripture: Its Power, Authority, and Relevance* (Nashville: Nelson, 2001), 236.

writes: "The Church no more gave us the New Testament canon than Sir Isaac Newton gave us the force of gravity. God gave us gravity . . . Newton did not create gravity but recognized it."[21]

2. *Current Protestant Discussion.* Unfortunately, some current Protestant thought, similar to Rome, but for different reasons, also contends that the "canon" and its authority are dependent on the church (and Israel).[22] The argument is that "the church existed before the Bible,"[23] thus making the canon dependent on the church.[24] In fact, Scripture is viewed as a human creation; it is not self-attesting.[25]

But this view too is problematic. On the one hand, it is not true to Scripture's self-testimony. As discussed in previous chapters, the OT recognizes texts that are *Scripture* and authoritative ("canon 1"), which is also true of the NT. No doubt, it takes time to draw up official lists ("canon 2"), and this occurs at a specific time in the history of Israel and the church, but God's people have never been without his word. "The church is always the *creatura verbi* ('creation of the Word')."[26] On the other hand, the church has never existed apart from Scripture. In fact, our Lord, the apostles, and then the church from its inception received the OT as *Christian* Scripture, along with the growing NT (Matt 5:17–20; Luke 24:25–27, 44; Rom 3:2; 2 Tim 3:15–17; 2 Pet 1:20–21).[27] In the post-apostolic eras, the church was built on the OT and the NT apostolic writings given the apostles, foundational, God-given role for the church as they wrote the "word" interpretation of the mighty "acts" of Christ (Heb 1:1–3). As Iain Provan notes, the "rule of faith" for the early church was not independent of Scripture but a summary of it, which explained "the grand biblical narrative and its leading themes, beginning in Genesis and ending with the apostolic teaching that is more fully unpacked in

---

[21] Packer, *God Has Spoken*, 109 (see chap. 5, n. 72).

[22] See Allert, *A High View of Scripture?*

[23] Allert, 76.

[24] Allert, 68.

[25] For example, see Allert, 59. This is especially the case for people like James Barr, who operate within the *extratextual* restrictions of the historical-critical method. Barr bluntly states: "The decision[s] to collect a group of chosen books and form a 'Scripture,' are all human decisions," which entails that the canon is not of God but the result of human religious "construction." Barr, *Bible in the Modern World*, 120 (see chap. 5, n. 76).

[26] Kruger, "Deconstructing Canon," 69. For a similar point, see Provan, *Reformation and the Right Reading*, 32–37 (see chap. 4, n. 7).

[27] On this point, see chapter 8.

the writings that ultimately became part of the NT."[28] Scripture created the church, and the church recognized what was God-given.

Third, the *theological* or dogmatic discussion of the canon is best located under *triune divine agency* in providence. In our discussion of inspiration, we located it under God's extraordinary agency in providence, thus resulting in *human* texts being identified with *God's* word. As noted, this divine action is not merely ordinary but extraordinary, a triune act appropriated to the Spirit. The *recognition* of authoritative Scripture by God's people is also best located under providence as God, in history, establishes a covenant relationship with his people for his own glory. But in our *recognition* of Scripture, both the categories of *extraordinary* and *ordinary* providence are involved. In terms of the former, God's people recognize Scripture due to the "inward testimony of the Spirit" (which involves the supernatural work of regeneration and illumination). In terms of the latter, God, as the Lord of history (Eph 1:11), works out all things for his own glory and the good of his people (Rom 8:28). Our Lord's intention is to build his church by *his* word and we know that "the gates of Hades will not overpower it" (Matt 16:18). We are assured that our *recognition* of the canon will occur—which, in retrospect, is now a matter of historical record. To think otherwise is to deprive the church of the sure word of God, and it is to deny the triune God who intends that we know him by his word (John 17:17). In turn, it would also undermine our confidence in God's promises and leave us with skepticism about our knowledge of God. Richard Gaffin emphasizes this point when he writes: "The New Testament is not a collection that 'just happened,' a kind of brute fact hanging there on the horizon of the past. Rather, it is the historical phenomenon by which God, the sovereign Architect and Lord of history, asserts and maintains himself as canon, that is, by which his supreme authority comes to expression."[29]

The Historical Recognition of the Canon

How and when did Israel and the church come to recognize Scripture *as Scripture*? Scripture's authority comes first, but how did God lead his people to recognize his word? In what

---

[28] Provan, *Reformation and the Right Reading*, 45. For a larger discussion of the "rule of faith" in the early church, see Provan's helpful discussion on 44–53.

[29] Gaffin, "New Testament as Canon," 171.

follows, a summary of the historical record is given, first in terms of the OT canon and then the NT canon.

The OT Canon

We have noted previously that within the OT there is a "canonical self-consciousness," namely, that God has spoken and given us *his* covenant word through Moses and the Prophets. We also noted how covenants are bound up with written documentation and that in redemptive history divine revelation follows a "word-act" pattern, which the people received as God's word. Over time, as God gave his word, first through Moses, and then the Prophets, Scripture was added to Scripture to form an overall canon. But on the historical front, under the providential hand of God, how did Israel come to recognize Scripture and eventually conclude that the OT canon was closed? Let us answer this question by emphasizing *three* points.

First, many argue that the OT (the Tanak) was canonized in three stages: the "Pentateuch" (Torah), the "Prophets" (Nevi'im), and finally the "Writings" (Ketuvim). Furthermore, the last stage was not complete until the end of the first century AD, at the Council of Jamnia, or, for some, even until the second or third century AD.[30] This would entail that in the time of Christ and the post-apostolic era, there was no defined OT canon for Israel or the church. But despite this view being the "consensus" in current scholarship, it is incorrect for a variety of reasons. The historical data demonstrates that there was a closed OT canon prior to our Lord's coming, even possibly back to the time of Ezra (fifth century BC), although some of the historical data is complicated. But this claim can be demonstrated by thinking about the *external* or historical data and also the *internal* evidence within the OT itself.

In terms of the *external* or *historical* data, we can say the following.

1. At the Council of Jamnia (c. AD 90), we discover that two books from the Writings were discussed in regard to their canonical status (Ecclesiastes and Song of Solomon). But the debate was not whether these books should be put into the canon; instead, it was whether they should remain in the canon, which assumes their prior canonical status. Thus, there is

---

[30] For this "consensus" view, or what Stephen Dempster calls the "minimalist" view, see Armin Lange and Emmanuel Tov, ed., *Textual History of the Bible: The Hebrew Bible*, vol. 1a, *Overview Articles* (Leiden: Brill, 2016); Lee Martin McDonald, *The Formation of the Biblical Canon*, 2 vols. (New York: T&T Clark, 2021).

"no evidence that Jamnia assigned canonical status to any book not previously recognized, or rejected any book previously accepted."[31] An analogous situation occurred with Martin Luther. Luther questioned the canonical status of James, but it had already been received as canonical for centuries.

2. There is strong evidence that pre-Christian Judaism believed that prophecy had ceased, thus bringing to closure the prophetic writings. For example, 1 Macc 9:23–27 (c. 100 BC) laments the cessation of divine revelation through the prophets.[32] Also, those at Qumran wrote commentaries only on biblical books. This suggests that they viewed them in a category different from other books. Also, 2 Macc 2:1–15 tells us that Judas Maccabeus collected the books as a collection after the war, which had a threefold division,[33] following the example of Nehemiah and Ezra, which may mean that the OT canon was stabilized at the end of the fifth century BC.

3. The existence of the Pseudepigrapha (from 400 BC–AD 100) is an indirect witness to a closed canon.[34] Why? For this reason: "authors appeal to authoritative figures in order to claim divine inspiration,"[35] instead of appealing to their own authority. This assumes that specific books are divinely inspired and that prophetic revelation has ceased, hence their writing literature in the names of these prophets.[36]

4. There is also the evidence for a closed OT canon from Bava Batra 14b, a baraita, that is, a tradition "external" to the Mishnah quoted in the Babylonian Talmud.[37] It is dated to

---

[31] Carson, Moo, Morris, *Introduction to the New Testament*, 488; cf. Provan, *Reformation and the Right Reading*, 67–68.

[32] Also see 1 Macc 4:46; 14:41; cf. 2 Bar 85:1–3; 1Q Serek Hayahad 9:11–12.

[33] On the threefold division, see Stephen G. Dempster, "Torah, Torah, Torah: The Emergence of the Tripartite Canon," in *Exploring the Origins of the Bible: Canon Formation in Historical, Literary, and Theological Perspective*, ed. Craig A. Evans and Emmanuel Tov (Grand Rapids: Baker, 2008), 116–17.

[34] The Pseudepigrapha are Jewish writings, similar to the Apocrypha, written before the coming of Christ. For example, they include such literature as 1 Enoch, the Letter of Aristeas, the Testament of Levi, Jubilees, the Psalms of Solomon, the Assumption of Moses, and the Martyrdom of Isaiah. On this literature, see Beckwith, *Old Testament Canon*, 17–19.

[35] Peter J. Gentry and Andrew M. Fountain, "Reassessing Jude's Use of Enochic Traditions," *TynBul* 68, no. 2 (2017): 277.

[36] On this point, see Dempster, "The Old Testament Canon, Josephus, and Cognitive Environment," 344–45.

[37] See Stephen G. Dempster, "From a Smoking Canon," 30.

the first or second century AD (no later than AD 240), and its significance is that it lists the exact books of the OT (twenty-four) in their specific ordering and according to a threefold division: Torah, Prophets, and Writings.[38] Since this tradition goes back to an earlier time, it is strong evidence that before the coming of Christ, there was a specific collection of books in the temple organized in a specific order according to a threefold division.

5. Philo (c. 25 BC–AD 50) (*De Vita Contemplativa* 3.25) refers to a tripartite division of the OT canon in the first century AD, which assumes that the OT was a closed number of books organized in a specific way before the coming of Christ.

6. This is also confirmed in the early second century BC in Ben Sira's "Praise of the Fathers." In that work, he lists people associated with the OT as if they were commonly known, and "he describes the twelve Minor Prophets not as individuals but as a booked entity: The Twelve Prophets."[39] This implies that there is a defined collection of books. In fact, two generations later, Ben Sira's grandson translated this book into Greek and describes it as a meditation on divine revelation divided into the Law, the Prophets, and the Writings.[40]

7. Josephus (c. AD 37–100) is another strong witness to a closed canon and its threefold division in first-century Judaism. Josephus assumes that prophecy has ceased since about 400 BC.[41] In addition, he lists twenty-two books as authoritative Scripture that contain the same content as Bava Batra's twenty-four books and the thirty-nine books of our Bibles (*Against Apion* 1.37–43).[42] Josephus views these texts as having divine authority, and since prophecy

---

[38] It assumes the Torah and then states that the Rabbis taught "the order of the Prophets (Nevi'im) is—Joshua and Judges, Samuel and Kings, Jeremiah and Ezekiel, Isaiah, and the Twelve Minor Prophets. . . . The order of the Writings (Ketuvim) is—Ruth and the Book of Psalms, and Job, and Proverbs, Ecclesiastes, Song of Songs, and Lamentations, Daniel, and the Scroll of Esther, Ezra, and Chronicles." Cited in Dempster, "From a Smoking Canon," 30.

[39] Dempster, "From a Smoking Canon," 34.

[40] See Dempster, "Canons on the Right and Canons on the Left," 59–61; cf. Dempster, "Torah, Torah, Torah," 107–14.

[41] Dempster, "From a Smoking Canon," 33; cf. Provan, *Reformation and the Right Reading*, 61–62.

[42] Josephus mentions twenty-two books, while others speak of twenty-four books (2 Esd 14:44–48). These numbers reflect the same books but different arrangements of the books. Beckwith, explains the differences:

> The Jews reckoned Samuel, Kings, Chronicles, Ezra-Nehemiah and the twelve Minor Prophets together as one book each, giving a total of twenty-four books (instead of the familiar thirty-nine). But this figure was often reduced to twenty-two, to assimilate it to the number of letters

has ceased, he does not expect further additions. Also, Josephus seems to imply that the entire OT was completed in the fifth century BC under the leadership of Ezra and Nehemiah. The twenty-two books that Josephus lists are the Torah (the five books of Moses); from Moses to Artaxerxes (c. 465 BC), he lists the thirteen books of the prophets (Joshua, Judges and Ruth, Samuel, Kings, Chronicles, Ezra and Nehemiah, Esther, Job, Isaiah, Jeremiah, Ezekiel, the Minor Prophets, Daniel). The remaining four books contain hymns to God and precepts for life (probably a reference to Psalms, Songs, Proverbs, Ecclesiastes). Josephus then states that from Artaxerxes to his time, no other books have been written that fit into the category of the twenty-two books, thus clearly distinguishing OT books from the Apocrypha and other intertestamental writings. Josephus then writes: "We have given practical proof of our reverence for our own Scriptures. For, although such long ages have now passed, no one has ventured either to add, or to remove, or to alter a syllable; and it is an instinct with every Jew, from the day of his birth, to regard them as the decrees of God, to abide by them, and, if need be, cheerfully to die for them."[43]

In addition to the external or historical evidence for a closed canon prior to the coming of Christ, there is also *internal* evidence. This internal evidence demonstrates how authoritative Scriptures ("canon 1") were stitched together to form a closed collection of books that are to be received and read together as an entire canon ("canon 2"). Here is some of the *internal* data.

1. For Chronicles, Ziporah Talshir demonstrated that the author is aware of the Torah in its final shape, the Prophets, and the collection of the Psalter. She argues that Chronicles functions as the bookend from Genesis to the exile in 2 Kings, thus bringing closure to the previous

---

> in the Hebrew alphabet, by appending Ruth to Judges and Lamentations to Jeremiah. For the benefit of his Greek readers, Josephus provides a simple arrangement for the twenty-two books, putting all those with historical content into Moses and the Prophets (consisting of five and thirteen books respectively), and leaving just 'hymns to God and precepts for human life' in the final section of four books (*Against Apion* 1:7f, or 1:37–43). "Canon of Scripture," 29.

Also note Origen (184–253 AD), Epiphanius (315–403 AD), and Jerome (347–420 AD) mention that in Jewish tradition people speak of a twenty-two and twenty-four book canon, depending on how the books are combined (see Gallagher and Meade, *Biblical Canon Lists*, 83–98, 156–70, 197–215).

[43] Josephus, *Against Apion* 1.42.

writings.[44] In other words, Chronicles is deliberately functioning as the closure to the previous writings of the Torah, the Prophets, and the Writings.

2. Within the OT, one can see evidence of authoritative books (canon 1) being put together to form an entire collection of books (canon 2) so that, prior to Christ's coming, a closed, tripartite canon is in place. This is confirmed in the NT, a point we will return to.[45] As we look at how the canon is deliberately organized, we discover that the Torah (Pentateuch) is first closed by the concluding section of Deuteronomy 34, which stresses the importance of Moses (Num 12; Deut 18:15–18). The closing verses of chapter 34 also anticipate a prophetic revelation that begins from Joshua as he carries on the ministry of Moses through the Minor Prophets. At the end of Malachi, which ends the Prophets section of the canon (following the order of Bava Batra), a reference is made to a coming prophet like Moses, namely, Elijah, which picks up Deuteronomy 18 and 34. This deliberate allusion to the Torah and to Moses is strong internal evidence that Scriptures are being put together as an entire collection.[46] In the Writings, one can make a strong case that Ruth and Psalms 1–2 function as the overall introduction to the entire section, which also picks up the importance of David and the Davidic covenant.[47] The Psalter is deliberately organized into five sections analogous to the Pentateuch. Chronicles ends the Writings, and it serves as the bookend to Genesis and the Pentateuch. As noted, within the Writings there is a strong focus on the Davidic king, and the genealogies of Chronicles are linked to the genealogies of Genesis, starting with Adam. As Dempster reflects on how OT Scriptures are deliberately organized into a unified canon, he rightly argues that "this seriously calls into question the view that the notion of a canon of Scripture belongs to the later period of Judaism." In fact, "there is no reason why the canonisation process should not have been completed by the time of the Maccabees."[48]

---

[44] See Ziporah Talshir, "Several Canon-Related Concepts Originating in Chronicles," *ZAW* 113 (2001): 386–403.

[45] For the evidence for this claim, see Dempster, "Extraordinary Fact," 23–56, 191–218 (see chap. 9, n. 25). Cf. Dempster, *Dominion and Dynasty*, 15–51 (see chap. 4, n. 29).

[46] See Dempster, "Extraordinary Fact: Part 1," 49–56; and Dempster, "Extraordinary Fact: Part 2," 191–200.

[47] Dempster, "Extraordinary Fact: Part 2," 204–14. In part 3, we will discuss the importance of the Davidic covenant for understanding the Bible's metanarrative centered and fulfilled in Christ.

[48] Dempster, 216.

3. Also, based on internal clues within the canon (e.g., Deut 34; Josh 1:1–9; Mal 4:4–6; Ruth 4:18–22; Pss 1–2; 2 Chron 36:22–23), there is confirmation that the OT canon is what Bava Batra 14b listed.[49] No doubt, other "orderings" of the OT exist, yet this tradition "is the oldest and most illuminating."[50] Over time, the ordering of the OT books is simplified or the books are rearranged "according to literary character and chronology, as law, histories, poetical and wisdom books, prophecies (though not always in that order, and with the histories sometimes subdivided)."[51] But the ancient ordering of Bava Batra is the traditional way of organizing the OT canon, all prior to Christ's coming. As the curtain of history opens on the first century AD, an OT canon is in place—with a specific number and order of books—which is recognized by the Jewish people. Not surprisingly, Jesus assumes such a canon in his interaction with the Jewish leaders and in his teaching from the OT (e.g., Matt 23:35; Luke 24:44).

In summary, as we look at the external and internal evidence for a closed OT canon, the "consensus" view that the OT canon was closed somewhere from 500 BC (Law and Prophets) to about AD 200 (Writings) cannot be sustained. In fact, to say that the OT was closed much later than the first century BC is hard to justify, and it is probably best to think that the text of the OT in terms of its content, arrangement, and stabilization was fixed at the end of the fifth century BC by Ezra and Nehemiah, but certainly no later than the second century BC.[52]

Second, in the NT, there is *confirming* evidence that the OT canon was recognized as closed. Here is some of the data for this claim.

1. Jesus and the Jewish leaders did not dispute over the extent of the OT canon. No doubt, Jesus and the NT authors correct traditional Jewish theology, yet they appeal to what both sides have in common, namely the OT (e.g., Mark 7:6–7, 10–13; 11:17; 12:10–11, 24; Luke 4:16–21; John 6:45; 10:34–35; 15:25; Acts 17:2–3, 11; 18:28; 24:14–15; 26:22; Rom 3:1–2; Gal 3).

2. In Luke 24:44, Jesus refers to the OT as "the Law of Moses, the Prophets, and the Psalms"—the traditional designation of the tripartite division of the Hebrew canon, which we have seen was already accepted in the Jewish community prior to Christ's coming.

---

[49] Dempster, 215–18.

[50] Beckwith, "Canon of Scripture," 32.

[51] Beckwith, 32.

[52] Carson, Moo, Morris, *Introduction to the New Testament*, 490. On the stabilization of the OT text, see Peter J. Gentry, "The Text of the Old Testament," *JETS* 52.1 (2009): 19–45.

3. Jesus's statement in Matt 23:35 is significant. Jesus not only assumes an OT canon, but a specific order to it. When Jesus mentions "the blood of righteous Abel to the blood of Zechariah, son of Berechiah," Abel is from Genesis 4 while Zechariah is from 2 Chron 24:20–22. Chronologically, Zechariah was not the last one to be killed, but Jesus's statement is referring to the recognized OT canon as given in Bava Batra 14b. In the Hebrew ordering of the OT canon, Genesis begins the canon, while Chronicles ends it. Thus, Jesus's statement is another way of saying "from beginning to end" (from Genesis to Chronicles) of a recognized canon.[53]

4. The NT quotes from every section of the OT canon (Torah, Prophets, and Writings), and almost every book of the OT (roughly 300 times). As it does, Jesus and the apostles frequently quote the OT *as Scripture* (*graphē*)—an acknowledgement of the unique, revelatory status of these books. Furthermore, the quotation patterns of the NT line up with the shape of the OT canon.

> New Testament writers quote every book in the Pentateuch (in its Jewish, not Samaritan, form), and from many of the other canonical books, from both the Prophets (Kings, Isaiah, Jeremiah, Ezekiel, and the Minor Prophets) and the Writings (Psalms, Job, Proverbs, Daniel, Chronicles). Even some Old Testament books not certainly quoted in the New may be alluded to (e.g., Josh. 1:5 in Heb. 13:5; Judges in Heb. 11:32).[54]

5. Paul insists that "the Scriptures" were written for our instruction and encouragement as Christians (Rom 15:3–6; cf. 1 Cor 10:11; 2 Tim 3:14–17; 1 Pet 1:10–12; Heb 11:39–40), thus assuming the existence of a fixed, recognized OT canon.

6. The NT authors distinguish between OT books that are Scripture (*graphē*) and others that are not. Thus, quotations from Cleanthes (Acts 17:28), Menander (1 Cor 15:33), Epimenides (Titus 1:12), or *1 Enoch* (Jude 14–15) are *not* introduced as authoritative Scripture. This is crucial in considering the status of the Apocrypha and whether it should be viewed as Scripture.

---

[53] There is debate over the precise identity of Zechariah son of Berechiah. It is probably a reference to Zechariah son of Jehoiada (2 Chron 24:20–22). On the resolution to his identity, see Carson, *Matthew*, 545 (see chap. 8, n. 71).

[54] Carson, Moo, Morris, *Introduction to the New Testament*, 491.

7. Regarding the Apocrypha,[55] the NT never cites it *as* Scripture. No doubt, copies of the Septuagint (LXX) from the fourth and fifth centuries AD include most of the Apocryphal books, but it is widely recognized that these codices provide little evidence of what first century Jews in Palestine thought or what Jewish people believed outside of Israel. Importantly, Philo (early first century AD), an Alexandrian Jewish philosopher, quotes OT books as divinely inspired, but he does not do so for the Apocrypha.[56] As Beckwith notes,

> the Jews of course read these books [Apocrypha], and so did the early Christians, but the idea that they were Scripture is a purely Christian phenomenon, of slow and irregular development, and always opposed by the greatest scholars, such as Origen and Jerome. The NT never quotes the Apocrypha as Scripture, and the earliest Christian OT lists and biblical manuscripts contain few or none of them.[57]

In fact, as Beckwith continues,

> A better case could be made out for the canonicity of the so-called Pseudepigrapha (books under false names), such as *1 Enoch* and *Jubilees*, which were cherished by the Essenes at Qumran; two of which are mentioned in the NT epistle of Jude. The Dead Sea Scrolls, however, never actually treat these books as Scripture, and the Essenes seemed to have regarded them as an interpretative appendix to the standard canon, not as part of it.[58]

---

[55] The Apocrypha are Jewish writings (c. early second century BC through the first century AD). The Jewish community never accepted these writings *as Scripture*, and this was also true of the church except for the Roman Catholic Church, which made these books part of the canon at the Council of Trent (1546). On the Apocrypha, see Provan, *Reformation and the Right Reading*, 29–32, 75–78. The Apocrypha includes such books as: Tobit, Judith, 1–2 Maccabees, the Wisdom of Solomon, Ecclesiasticus (also known as Sirach or Ben Sira), the *Additions to Esther*, Baruch, the *Epistle of Jeremiah*, the *Song of the Three*, Susanna, and Bel and the Dragon. Sometimes the Apocrypha also includes books identified with the Pseudepigrapha, such as 1 and 2 Esdras, the *Prayer of Manasseh*, and *3–4 Maccabees*.

[56] Beckwith, "Canon of Scripture," 29.

[57] Beckwith, 29. Also see John D. Meade, "Myths about Canon: What the Codex Can and Can't Tell Us," in Hixson and Gurry, *Myths and Mistakes*, 253–77 (see chap. 10, n. 21).

[58] Beckwith, "Canon of Scripture," 29.

8. But what about Jude's use of *1 Enoch* and other extra-canonical Jewish traditions? Does he regard them as Scripture? Peter Gentry and Andrew Fountain have persuasively argued from the literary structure of Jude that Jude is *not* appealing to *1 Enoch* as Scripture, but as an illustration from extra-canonical history, which also occurs in Jude 9–10 and Jude 14–15.[59] In fact, Jude's appeal to these Enochic traditions functions to overturn the thought of those who appeal to Jewish tradition to blame evil in this world on angels rather than humans. Thus, "Jude is using the Jewish Enochic traditions to counter their own assertion that evil in the world is due to angelic impurity. Rather, evil is due to human rebellion against God, as taught in Genesis 3,"[60] thus rejecting Jewish tradition that blamed evil's origin on angels. Jude, then, is not appealing to *1 Enoch* as Scripture, nor does he view it as other OT books.

All of this data confirms that there was a specific OT canon in place before Christ's coming. The Bible of the early church was the OT. As such, the church was never without God's word to instruct, teach, and correct (2 Tim 3:15–17). Furthermore, the OT canon (Tanak) contained the same content of books as we presently have in our Bibles, albeit in a different order.

Third, regarding the Apocrypha, some additional points need to be made that explain why the church did not recognize them as Scripture and why Rome's acceptance of them is incorrect.

1. The Apocrypha do not claim the same kind of self-attesting authority as the OT. For example, the author of 2 Macc 15:38 writes, "If it is poorly done and mediocre, that was the best I could do," (RSV) which is quite a contrast to the Prophets of the OT, who claim that their writings are God's word. Also, in 1 Macc 9:27, the author recognizes that prophetic revelation has ceased, thus distinguishing his own writing from normative Scripture.

2. There is no evidence that the Jewish people recognized the Apocrypha as Scripture.

3. The Apocrypha were not considered as Scripture by Jesus and the NT authors. The NT never quotes it *as Scripture*, and the earliest Christian OT lists and biblical manuscripts contain few or none of them.

---

[59] In a chiastic structure, Jude refers to *1 Enoch* in Jude 14–15 and the *Assumption of Moses* in Jude 9–10, thus distinguishing them as examples from extra-canonical sources versus the OT. See Gentry and Fountain, "Reassessing Jude's Use," 283–85.

[60] Gentry and Fountain, 286.

4. The Apocrypha contain teachings inconsistent with Scripture, thus disqualifying them. For example, the Apocrypha include various fables and legends that have no historical warrant.[61] Judith wrongly identifies Nebuchadnezzar as king of the Assyrians (1:1, 7). Tobit endorses the use of burning the liver of a fish to turn away demons because they cannot cope with its smell. Tobit claims to have been alive when Jeroboam revolted (931 BC) and when Assyria conquered Israel (722 BC), which is not possible (1:3–5; 14:11). There is also the endorsement of prayers and atonement for the dead (2 Macc 12:39–46), which has no other biblical warrant. And the Wisdom of Solomon possibly teaches that the world was created from pre-existent matter (7:17), which contradicts the teaching of Genesis 1 and renders problematic the God-world relationship.

5. Overall, the acceptance of the Apocrypha was more of a Christian phenomenon, a slow, irregular, and adverse development. No two Septuagint codices contain the same Apocrypha books, and it seems that the Apocrypha functioned more as service books for people. Among the church fathers, there was no uniform acceptance of the Apocrypha, although it was cited by Augustine and others. However, at the Council of Laodicea (AD 360), it was rejected. Origen, Jerome, and Athanasius, in his Festal letter (AD 367), also rejected it. It was not until the Council of Trent (1546) that Rome officially recognized the Apocrypha and anathematized all who rejected it.[62] But the reasons for doing so are not warranted.

The NT Canon

One cannot approach the closing of the NT canon in exactly the same way as the OT, that is, by appealing to a later revelation to confirm it. That would require a later corpus beyond the NT to authenticate it. This is impossible since the canon is now closed (both OT and NT) by the NT writings. However, even so, it is worth noting how some later documents in the NT refer to some earlier ones *as Scripture* (*graphē*) (1 Tim 5:18 [quoting Deut 25:4 and Luke 10:7]; 2 Pet 3:16). As the NT was being written, it was already being *recognized* by the church

[61] See Bel and the Dragon.

[62] *Canons and Decrees of the Council of Trent*, 4th session (April 8, 1546), *Decree Concerning the Canonical Scriptures*, in Schaff, *Creeds of Christendom*, 2:80 (see chap. 11, n. 64).

as Scripture on par with the OT canon. As we rehearse the historical data that leads to a closed NT canon, and thus the entire Bible (canon 2), *four* points are significant.

First, we cannot think of the NT canon apart from our Lord, who is the final revelation of God and who fulfills the OT in his person and new covenant work (Heb 1:1–3). Our Lord is the Word made flesh, the one the entire OT pointed forward to and anticipated, and any concept of a NT canon immediately is tied to him.[63] As God spoke in the past and gave covenant writings, so in Christ, and through the apostles, we have NT covenant writings for the church that completes God's unfolding word-act revelation until Christ returns.

For this reason, the role of the apostles is crucial in giving us the NT canon. Without doubt, our Lord called the apostles to lay the foundation of new covenant revelation for the church, and their ministry is seen as an extension of his ministry (John 14:26; 16:12–15; 20:21; cf. Eph 2:20) by the regenerative and illuminating work of the Spirit. *And* in an extraordinary way, their texts were "breathed-out" by the Spirit as they were "carried" along and spoke God's word (2 Tim 3:16; 2 Pet 1:20–21). Although the apostles were human, by the Spirit's work in them, they were conscious that they were writing God's word (1 Cor 14:37–38; 1 Thess 1:4; 2:13).

In fact, the apostles view their writings as on par with the writings of the OT prophets (2 Pet 3:2). Even more: the apostles viewed "divine revelation in two distinct phases or epochs,"[64] thus establishing the warrant for a NT alongside the OT, or what is known as a bi-covenantal canon. As apostles, and by the Spirit, they spoke with the authority of Christ himself (e.g., Gal 1:1) as "ministers of a new covenant" (2 Cor 3:6). And as Eph 2:20 teaches, NT prophets and apostles served a foundational role in explaining God's final self-disclosure in his Son (cf. 1 Cor15:1–2),[65] which is now given in their writings.[66] Kruger captures this point well: the NT

---

[63] Gaffin, "New Testament as Canon," 172–81.

[64] Kruger, *Canon Revisited*, 207–9.

[65] Gaffin, "New Testament as Canon," 175.

[66] The NT canon flows organically from the OT tied to the person and work of Christ. Christopher Seitz states it this way: "The New is not a phase of development that grounds the Old but rather a statement of the Old's abiding sense and final meaning, perceived now afresh within its own plain-sense deliverance and helping to interpret and ground the New's meaning and final purpose as well." *The Goodly Fellowship of the Prophets: The Achievement of Association in Canon Formation* (Grand Rapids: Baker, 2009), 132.

books are "the *product* of Christ's redemptive work in history . . . they are the outworking of the authority Christ gave to his apostles to lay down the permanent foundation for the church."[67]

This is why a key criterion for the recognition of new covenant Scriptures is whether they are apostolic. The book did not necessarily have to be written by an apostle, although most were, but it had to have "authoritative apostolic *tradition*."[68] Luke was not an apostle, but he attributed his content to those who "were eyewitnesses and ministers of the word" (Luke 1:2). The author of Hebrews makes a similar claim, linking his work to Christ and the apostles (Heb 2:3).

Second, we must distinguish between the NT canon as an official list (canon 2) and authoritative "Scripture" *functioning* as a recognized authority (canon 1). Otherwise, we will succumb to the false idea that the early church took a long time to recognize the authority of the NT documents. This is simply not true. Long before a specific *list* was made (technically in AD 397 at the Third Council of Carthage), the NT writings were *recognized as Scripture*. By the end of the first century and early second century, most of the NT books were accepted by the church as divinely authoritative, and all of them were accepted in large parts of the church.[69] As Kruger correctly notes, by the middle of the second century, "we see a solid core of New Testament books fully received as Scripture and operating with the highest level of authority for early Christians."[70] This includes the four Gospels, Acts, the thirteen Pauline letters, 1 Peter, and 1 John. Indeed, most of the rest of the NT canon was in place by the time of Eusebius (early fourth century), who gives us a specific list of books.

This should not surprise us given the early years of the church. One of the reasons a *list* of books was eventually made was due to pressures from heretical groups who either denied certain books that the church already recognized or began to make their own list of "authoritative" books. Thus, due to the pressures from heretical groups associated with Marcion (ca. 85–160) and the Montanists (late second century), the church had to delineate exactly which

---

[67] Kruger, *Canon Revisited*, 110 (emphasis original).

[68] Kruger, "Deconstructing Canon," 61 (emphasis original).

[69] This fact is analogous to the church's affirmation of Christ's deity. Long before the official confession that the Son was "of the same nature" (*homoousios*) as the Father at Nicaea (AD 325), the church believed, taught, and proclaimed the full deity of the Son (John 1:1, 18; 8:58; 20:28; Rom 9:5; Phil 2:6–11; Col 1:15–17; Heb 1:1–3, etc.).

[70] Kruger, "Deconstructing Canon," 55; cf. Kruger, *Canon Revisited*, 195–232.

books were inspired. Marcion, for example, rejected the OT canon and only accepted an edited version of Luke's Gospel and ten letters of Paul, excluding the Pastorals. To guard against such error, the church began to draw up public lists, first to state the OT canon then the specific NT writings. Also, the church had to do this because of Montanism. This movement, similar to more radical forms of the charismatic movement, elevated "new" prophecies and revelations to a level of supreme authority, and as a result, the church had to delineate clearly where God had spoken.[71] But long before these pressures arose to go public with a specific list of books, what we know as the NT was already functioning as Scripture in the church and recognized as such.

Here is a basic summary of key points in the church's recognition of Scripture from the first century to the official lists drawn up at the end of the fourth century:

1. *The First Century*. The NT was written over a fifty-year period (c. 45–95). The churches made copies of the NT writings (Col 4:16), and apostolic letters were circulating among the churches in the late 60s (2 Pet 3:15–16). The same is true of the Gospels. Although we do not have a closed list, all of these NT books were recognized as God's word, on par with the OT (2 Pet 3:2). At the end of the first century, the writings of the "apostolic fathers" emerge, which are dependent on the Gospels and the Pauline letters (e.g., *1 Clement* 42.1–2; 47.1–3).

2. *The Second Century*.[72] Ignatius, Polycarp, and Papias make references to the Gospels and Paul's letters.[73] In addition, Justin Martyr (c. 100–165) refers to the Gospels as "memoirs of the apostles" (*1 Apol.* 33, 66; *Dial.* 100–7, 133) and quotes them as authorities on par with the OT (*1 Apol.* 67; *Dial.* 100.1; 103.6, 8).[74] Tatian (c. 120–180), a student of Justin Martyr, compiled the *Diatesseron*, which combined all four Gospels into one narrative. By the middle of the second century, there was widespread agreement regarding the four Gospels. Also, Irenaeus (writing c. 170–180) regards the following books as Scripture: the four Gospels, Acts, Paul's letters (minus Philemon), Hebrews, James, 1 Peter, 1–2 John, and Revelation.[75]

---

[71] Dunbar, "Biblical Canon," 328–33.

[72] See Kruger, *Canon Revisited*, 210–232; Dunbar, "Biblical Canon," 323–42.

[73] Kruger, *Canon Revisited*, 214–25.

[74] Dunbar, "Biblical Canon," 333–34.

[75] See Michael J. Kruger, "The New Testament Canon," in *A Biblical-Theological Introduction to the New Testament*, ed. Michael J. Kruger (Wheaton: Crossway, 2016), 563; Dunbar, "Biblical Canon," 334–37.

By the end of the century, the Muratorian list (c. 170–200, from Rome) gives us a canon similar to our present one (it lists twenty-two books).[76] The list is fragmentary but it includes all four Gospels, Acts, Paul's thirteen letters, 1–2 John, Jude, and Revelation. What is not mentioned is Hebrews, James, 1–2 Peter, and 3 John. All Gnostic, Marcionite, and Montanist writings are rejected. Yet there is mention of the *Apocalypse of Peter* and the Wisdom of Solomon, but there is good evidence they were not recognized as canonical.[77]

In looking at how the NT books were grouped in the manuscript collections, David Trobisch argues that there is a self-conscious attempt to tie specific books together as a unified whole, which shows evidence of a canon consciousness. For example, the four Gospels are grouped together, along with Paul's letters, Acts and General Epistles, and Revelation.[78] Also, the titles to Paul's letters were based on the addressee and not on authorship. Trobisch argues that this means that Paul's letters were part of a larger collection from the same author, and not mere individual letters that circulated; hence, there was no need to identify them by the author since they were part of one collection.[79] The titles of Paul's letters were also numbered (e.g., 1 and 2 Corinthians, 1 and 2 Timothy, etc.), but such numbering is only necessary if multiple letters to the same addressee are part of a larger collection.[80] This demonstrates that there was a conscious attempt to create a fixed order of documents that functioned as a canon, which Trobisch suggests occurred as early as the second century.[81]

3. *The Third Century*. The early church fathers (e.g., Irenaeus, Clement of Alexandria, Origen) refer to many NT books as authoritative for the church.[82] Most important is Codex Claromontanus (which is a list of books regarded as authoritative in North Africa or Egypt). It lists all twenty-seven of our NT books, but also includes some disputed books such as the *Apocalypse of Peter*, the *Epistle of Barnabus*, the *Shepherd of Hermas*, and the *Acts of Paul*.

---

[76] On the date of the Muratorian list as second century, see Charles E. Hill, "The Debate over the Muratorian Fragment and the Development of the Canon," *WTJ* 57 (1995): 437–52.

[77] See Kruger, *Canon Revisited*, 230–31.

[78] See David Trobisch, *The First Edition of the New Testament* (Oxford: Oxford University Press, 2000).

[79] Trobisch, 26.

[80] Trobisch, 39–40.

[81] Trobisch, 40.

[82] See Kruger, *Canon Revisited*, 265–87; cf. Dunbar, "Biblical Canon," 340–42. Also see Meade, "Myths about Canon," 253–77.

4. *The Fourth Century*. At the Third Council of Carthage (397), we have an official list of the twenty-seven books that constitute the NT canon (canon 2), although canon 1 had functioned since the end of the first century. Here are some key developments in this century.

Eusebius of Caesarea (c. 260–340), in his famous *Ecclesiastical History*, draws up a list of recognized NT books dependent on Clement and Origen.[83] In his list he utilizes four categories: "recognized," "disputed," "rejected," and "heretical" books.[84] Under "recognized," which are undisputed by the church, he lists the four Gospels, Acts, Paul's letters (which includes Hebrews), 1 Peter, 1 John, and, with some reservation, Revelation. In the "disputed" category, he lists James, Jude, 2 Peter, 2 and 3 John. In the "rejected" category, he lists the *Acts of Paul*, the *Shepherd of Hermas*, the *Apocalypse of Peter*, *Barnabas*, the *Didache*, and the *Gospel of the Hebrews*. In the "heretical" category, he lists such works as the *Gospel of Peter* and the *Gospel of Thomas*, etc. When we add the "recognized" with the "disputed," we have our present NT.

In addition to Eusebius, we have a list of NT books from North Africa from around AD 360 (Cheltenham manuscript). It includes all our NT books except Hebrews, James, and Jude. Then, Athanasius, in his Festal letter (AD 367), gives his list, which is identical to our present NT. At the Third Council of Carthage (AD 397), the list is made official.

Third, the *criteria* used by the early church to recognize inspired Scripture were threefold. The church fathers first looked for *apostolicity*, that is, whether the text was written by an apostle or by someone within the apostolic circle. Of the twenty-seven NT books, only four were not written by an apostle: Mark (who was identified with Peter), Luke-Acts (which was identified with Paul), and Hebrews (which was sometimes associated with Paul, but it was anonymous and identified with the apostolic circle). Importantly, the Muratorian list rejected the reading of the *Shepherd of Hermas* in public since "it was too recent and therefore cannot find a place 'among the prophets, whose number is complete, or among the apostles' ('the prophets' here refers to the Old Testament books, and the 'the apostles' to the New)."[85] The church fathers also rejected any document under the suspicion of pseudonymity (written

[83] Dunbar, "Biblical Canon," 316.

[84] Eusebius, *Ecclesiastical History* 3.25 (*NPNF*^{2} 1:155–57); cf. Kruger, *Canon Revisited*, 266–80.

[85] Carson, Moo, and Morris, *Introduction to the New Testament*, 494–95.

by someone other than the claimed author) because it could not be identified properly with the apostles.

A second requirement for canonicity was the book's *orthodoxy*. Did it conform to the *rule of faith* (*regula fidei*), that is, to the apostolic gospel received and passed on to the churches (cf. Gal 1:8–9; Col 2:8; 1 Tim 6:3; 1–2 John). On this basis, false gospels, such as the *Gospel of Thomas* or the *Gospel of Judas*, were rejected.

The third criterion for canonicity was *catholicity*. Did the book enjoy widespread and continuous usage in the churches? Obviously, this criterion required the passage of time to be useful, and it helps explain why time elapsed before the church universally recognized all the NT books. One of the reasons Hebrews was delayed in being accepted in the West was because it was anonymous, and in fact it was more quickly accepted in the East, where many (wrongly) thought it was written by Paul.

Fourth, we must also remember that despite any church hierarchy, the universal church came to recognize the same books of the NT. This may be the "official" recognition of the NT, but in truth, the church came to *recognize* Scripture as *God's* word due to its self-attestation by the work of the Spirit. The church did not confer authority on the books; rather, the church came to *recognize* the full revelation in Christ and the new covenant documents that bore witness to him. D. A. Carson, Douglas Moo, and Leon Morris capture this point well:

> The locus and source of all authoritative new-covenant revelation rests, finally, in the Son. The apostles, in the narrower sense of the term, were viewed as those who mediated such revelation to the rest of the church; but precisely because that revelation was tied to the Jesus who appeared in real history, an implicit closure was built into the claim. There could not be an unending stream of "revelations" about Jesus if those revelations were detaching themselves from the Jesus who presented himself in real history and who was confessed by the first eyewitnesses and apostles. Thus there was both extraordinary authority and implicit closure from the very beginning. . . . In short, that God is a self-disclosing, speaking, covenant-keeping God who has supremely revealed himself in a historical figure, Jesus the Messiah, establishes the necessity of the canon and implicitly, its closure. The notion of canon forbids all self-conscious attempts to select only part of the canon as the governing standard of the Christian church: that would be to decanonize canon, a contradiction in terms.

> Because the canon is made up of books whose authority ultimately springs from God's gracious self-revelation, it is better to speak of recognizing the canon than establishing it.[86]

Concluding Reflection

As we conclude our discussion of the doctrine of Scripture, let us recognize that this is no mere academic discussion. As D. A. Carson warned the evangelical church years ago, "A high view of Scripture is of little value to us if we do not enthusiastically embrace the Scripture's authority."[87] What the church needs in every era, including our own, is not merely an affirmation of biblical authority but obedience to it. The motivation behind theological liberalism has always been to make the Bible "relevant" to the culture. Sadly, within evangelicalism, too often we adopt the same mindset.

Scripture *is* God's word to his covenant people. Apart from God's authoritative speech, we have no epistemological warrant to know God, ourselves, and the world in a normative way. Even more, apart from God's word, we know nothing of his promises, who he is, and what he has done for us. Our hope in life and death is in knowing the triune God by grace through faith in Christ and being made alive and progressively transformed by the Holy Spirit. All of these great realities are impossible apart from the message and truth of Scripture.

As we turn from discussion of the *foundation* of theology, the triune God *and* his word, we now begin to put into practice our theological method by seeking to read and apply God's word. In part 3, we begin to lay out the biblical-theological framework that Scripture gives so that, in part 4, we are able to draw theological conclusions and formulate doctrine with the goal of knowing our triune Creator and Redeemer in the face of our Lord Jesus Christ for his glory and the good of the church.

---

86 Carson, Moo, Morris, 496, 499.

87 D. A. Carson, "Recent Developments in the Doctrine of Scripture," in Carson and Woodbridge, *Hermeneutics, Authority, and Canon*, 46.

PART 3

The Biblical-Theological Framework of Scripture

CHAPTER 13

Creation, Fall, Redemption, and New Creation

Introduction

The Bible is a large book that consists of many topics and diverse literature and spans centuries. However, given that Scripture is *God's* Word written, despite being written by multiple authors and addressing various subjects, it is one grand metanarrative whose central message is about what our triune Creator-covenant God planned in eternity and executed in time to glorify himself by the redemption of his people, the judgment of sin, and the making all things new in Christ Jesus (Rom 11:33–36; Eph 1:9–10; Col 1:15–20). From Genesis to Revelation, the Bible's message is first and foremost about the triune God. It is centered in his name and glory and how *he*, who needs nothing, has sovereignly and graciously chosen to share himself with his creatures, specifically his people, to the praise of his glorious grace and our eternal good (Eph 2:1–10).

In light of God's authoritative self-disclosure to us, the task of systematic theology is "to think God's thoughts after him" as we apply all that Scripture says to our lives on any given topic. As discussed in part 1, the first step in "putting together" what Scripture teaches is to think through its own God-given, first-order interpretive framework as the lens by which we think about God, self, and the world. All theological formulation must be done "from above," namely, from within Scripture's own presentation (intratextual), thus making sure our theology is true to the Bible's own teaching and categories. Scripture is *not* a collection of random texts that can be organized in any way we desire. Instead, Scripture is God's own interpretation of his mighty acts (word-act revelation) unfolding his eternal plan that moves from creation to the new creation along a specific covenantal storyline centered in Christ Jesus our Lord. As such, Scripture already gives us a specific theology and worldview, and our "making sense" of it, that is, the constructive task of theology, must be true to the Bible's own biblical-theological framework.

For example, think of the doing of Christology. David Wells perceptively notes that in order to understand who the Jesus of the Bible is and what he has accomplished for us, we must first locate him within the larger framework of Scripture. Why? For this reason: the entire canonical presentation of Christ is the "interpretive framework within which [Jesus's] birth, death, and resurrection assume their proper meaning."[1] In fact, apart from placing Jesus in this framework, we will not have the *biblical* Jesus but a Jesus of our own imagination. As such, D. A. Carson correctly reminds us that even with all of its diverse teaching, "the Bible as a whole document tells a story, and, properly used, that story can serve as a metanarrative that shapes our grasp of the entire Christian faith."[2]

Of course, this raises the question of how best to "put together" the Bible's own framework, out of which doctrinal formulation occurs. We have noted that this is the role of biblical theology in the theological task, yet biblical theology is not presuppositionless; it already assumes some kind of theology at work, hence the web-like nature of systematic theology. However, given that Scripture is first-order, our construction of the Bible's framework can be corrected by Scripture as we submit our minds and hearts to God's word and stand on the shoulders of those who have preceded us. With this in mind, we can outline the Bible's long and layered story in at least two ways. First, we can capture the Bible's theological framework by unpacking its four major plot movements: creation, fall, redemption, and new creation, which is the focus of this chapter. Second, and complimentary to the Bible's plot movements, we can construct Scripture's interpretive framework by thinking through the unfolding of God's eternal plan from creation to the new creation through the progression of the biblical covenants, which is the concentration of the next chapter. Both of these approaches are aspects of each other and

[1] David F. Wells, *The Person of Christ: A Biblical and Historical Analysis of the Incarnation* (Westchester, IL: Crossway, 1984), 32.

[2] Carson, *Gagging of God*, 194 (see chap. 2, n. 1).

necessary to understand the Bible's overall story and worldview, and thus they are foundational for making sure our doctrinal formulations arise from and are true to Scripture.

Understanding the Bible's Theological Framework by Its Plot Movements

An extremely important way that Christians have captured the overall framework of Scripture is by thinking through the Bible's plot movements: creation, fall, redemption, and new creation. This is the "wide-angle" lens that gives shape to the Bible's metanarrative and holds together all the smaller parts and stories. By thinking through these plot movements, we can grasp the broadest contours of the biblical framework and contrast the Bible's worldview with other views. This way of putting together Scripture is also helpful for at least two further reasons.

First, by starting with creation and culminating in the new creation, we confirm that the Bible's own claim to be God's unified, coherent revelation is indeed true. As we noted in part 2, despite being written over the course of 1,500 years and by numerous authors, Scripture provides many reasons why it is God's Word but especially the "majesty of [its] style, the consent of all the parts, [and] the scope of the whole (which is to give all glory to God)."[3] As Francis Schaeffer said in one of his lectures on why the Bible is unique in contrast to other religious books: "It [the Bible] begins at the beginning and goes to the end."[4] In other words, from Genesis to Revelation, we discover God's unfolding plan decreed in eternity past, initiated in creation, worked out through history, and now awaiting its consummation at Christ's return. By unpacking the Bible's plot movements, we discover the glory of our triune God, the promise maker and keeper, who is "heading up" everything in Christ (Eph 1:9–10) for his own glory and the good of his people.

Second, it allows Scripture to function as the lens by which we interpret and view the world. Everyone has a worldview whether one realizes it or not.[5] Despite differences regard-

---

[3] *London Baptist Confession* (1689), 1.5.

[4] This is a paraphrase of what Francis Schaeffer said since I do not have his exact quotation.

[5] On worldview discussion, see Sire, *Universe Next Door*, 17 (see chap. 2, n. 54); Sire, *Naming the Elephant: Worldview as Concept* (Downers Grove: IVP Academic, 2004); David K. Naugle, *Worldview: The History of the Concept* (Grand Rapids: Eerdmans, 2002).

ing the definition of a worldview, at its core, it is "a set of basic beliefs, values, and presuppositions concerning life's most fundamental issues" that affects "the way we see things and shapes our interpretation of the world."[6] In fact, worldviews are often expressed in terms of an overall story that seeks to explain why we are here (origins), what reality is (metaphysics), whether truth and knowledge is possible (epistemology), and whether certain actions are right or wrong (ethics).[7] Since the task of theology is to apply Scripture to all of life, to proclaim the gospel to the nations, and to challenge the unbelief of people who stand opposed to the truth of God's word, we must learn to compare and contrast a Christian view of the world with non-Christian views.

But where do we start? Taking our cue from Paul in Athens, we start by presenting the truth of Scripture in terms of an entire biblical framework rooted in the Bible's metanarrative. As we do, we set the Christian view over against other views by unpacking its truth, coherence, unity, and beauty as we call all people to repent and believe. But we also challenge the non-Christian with the fact that their view *on its own terms* is internally incoherent, and apart from living off the borrowed capital of the Bible, it cannot account for reality and the world as it is.[8] One way of contrasting the Christian view with non-Christian views is by thinking through the Bible's plot movements of creation, fall, redemption, new creation.[9]

1. *Creation*. Every worldview must explain the question of origins: Why is there something rather than nothing? The answer given to the "origins" question not only determines what one's worldview is, it also governs how the basic questions of life are answered. In other words, ideas about ultimate reality determine how we view God, ourselves, the world, the

---

[6] Cowan and Spiegel, *The Love of Wisdom*, 7 (see chap. 3, n. 4).

[7] See Michael W. Goheen and Craig G. Bartholomew, *Living at the Crossroads: An Introduction to Christian Worldview* (Grand Rapids: Baker Academic, 2008), 4–5, 18. Goheen and Bartholomew explain how worldviews are tied to overall stories. Cf. Sire, who explains how worldviews are expressed in stories. *Universe Next Door*, 16–19.

[8] On this point, see our discussion of Paul in Athens in part 1, chapter 1. The basic apologetic approach employed here is known as presuppositionalism. For a discussion of this view with some helpful application to the apologetic task, see Bahnsen, *Van Til's Apologetic* (see chap. 1, n. 4); Frame, *Apologetics* (see chap. 8, n. 46); Greg L. Bahnsen, *Against All Opposition: Defending the Christian Worldview* (Powder Springs, GA: The American Vision, 2020).

[9] See Nancy Pearcey, *Total Truth: Liberating Christianity from Its Cultural Captivity* (Wheaton: Crossway, 2004), 25–26, 82–87, 123–50. Pearcey works through the categories of creation, fall, and redemption and then employs it in her critique of non-Christian worldviews.

meaning of history, the possibility of objective truth and morality, what we can hope for, the role of the state, and so on. Likewise, the Christian view grounds everything in what is ultimate, which for us is the triune God in all of his glory. In a Christian view of creation/origins, everything begins with God in himself, who then, according to his plan, creates *ex nihilo*, rules, and redeems.

2. *Fall.* Every worldview must also explain the question of the human problem: What is wrong with humans and the world? And if what is wrong lies with us, has it always been so? And if it has always been so, is there a real solution to our problem? In answering this question, the issue of origins resurfaces since ideas of what is ultimate and explanations of what is wrong with humans are organically related. On this point, the biblical worldview is in a category all by itself since the Bible's explanation for the human problem is tied to its view of God, creation, and history, and it is the only view that takes the human problem seriously and offers a true solution to it.

3. *Redemption.* The question raised by redemption is, Is there a solution to the human problem? How can the world be set right? Is there such a thing as justice, and how is it to be implemented? Is the solution to our problem found in God or in humans as epitomized by the state? Most people acknowledge that there is something wrong with humans and the world, but the answers given are directly determined by one's view of origins/creation and the nature of the human problem/fall. Ideas about God, self, and the world have consequences, especially regarding what people think the solution is to the ills of this world. The same is true of the Christian worldview, although it is completely different from all non-Christian views given our view of God, creation, and the fall. In fact, it is only the Bible that gives a sure hope of a solution to our problem since our hope is grounded in the triune Creator-covenant Lord who alone can redeem, transform, and make all things right in Christ Jesus.

4. *New Creation.* The question raised here is, What may we hope? Where is history going? Is the future optimistic or pessimistic? Utopian or dystopian? And on what grounds may we hope? Non-Christian answers to these questions follow from their answers to the previous questions, and the same is true of the Christian worldview. At the heart of the Bible's answer to what we may hope are God's unfailing promises in Christ, grounded in his own initiative to redeem a people for himself, to execute judgment on all sin in righteousness and justice, and to make all things right in a consummated new creation for all eternity.

With this basic overview in place, let us now develop the Bible's plot movements with the goal of sketching the broad contours of the Bible's framework in order to contrast the biblical worldview with other views and lay the foundation on which our doctrinal formulations arise.

Creation

It is impossible to overestimate the magnitude of the doctrine of creation for theology and the Christian worldview. Many Christians are naturally interested in the doctrine of salvation. However, creation is not only where the Bible's story begins, it is also foundational to all theological formulation. Without a proper theology of creation, there is no understanding of the Christian worldview as the Bible describes it. Creation establishes a unique theistic, covenantal, and eschatological framework by which we understand God, self, and the world, with the glorious God of Scripture as the ground and foundation.[10] Let us look at each of these in turn.

The Triune Creator-Covenant Lord

The Bible's story begins with creation *ex nihilo* (out of nothing) by the sovereign/absolute-personal God—the triune covenant Lord:[11] "In the beginning God created the heavens and the earth" (Gen 1:1). From the opening verses of Scripture, we discover that the true and living God is *categorically different* in existence and nature than his creation: he alone is eternal, uncreated, independent, the holy One who creates and rules all things by his word—the God who speaks and calls all things into existence (Gen 1–2; Pss 50:12–14; 93:2; Rev 4:11). This truth establishes the most fundamental distinction of the Christian worldview: the Creator-creature distinction, which in turn establishes a specific view of the God-world relationship. God alone is God; all else is creation that depends totally on him for life and all things, and he shares his glory with no one (Isa 42:8; Acts 17:24–25). Thus, from the outset, Scripture rejects all naturalistic, dualistic, deistic, polytheistic, pantheistic, and panentheistic views of

---

[10] On the importance of Genesis 1–3 in the Bible's storyline, see D. A. Carson, "Genesis 1–3: Not Maximalist, Not Minimalist, But Seminal," *TJ* 39 (2018): 143–63.

[11] The term "covenant Lord" is from Frame, *Doctrine of God*, 1–115 (see chap. 3, n. 13).

the world.[12] All such views deny the Creator-creature distinction and thus deny the God of Scripture, who alone is to be worshipped, trusted, and obeyed. The Bible's answer as to why there is something rather than nothing is due to God's decision to enact his plan by first creating the world as the stage of history and the theater of his own glory, which he is now bringing to its planned telos for his own glory.

But it is also crucial to remember that when the Bible speaks of the "beginning," there was a "before" the beginning. As Christopher Watkin notes: "To begin with the Bible's own 'In the beginning . . .' would risk skipping over the fact that 'before' the beginning of creation (for want of a better way of putting it!) there was God, and that in a number of places the Bible gives us details about the sort of existence enjoyed by God before he created the world."[13] Thus, *before* creation, Scripture speaks of the triune God in himself (*ad intra*) apart from creation and then, due to God's decision to create, God in relation to the world (*ad extra*).[14] But *before* there was ever a universe, God existed in total perfection, blessedness, and shared love and communion. God is not correlative to the world and dependent on it. Instead, within God there is a blessed self-sufficiency (aseity); hence, God is "essentially distinct from the world, yet having a blessed life of his own" as "the absolute Being, the eternal One, who is and was and is to come . . . the ever-living and ever-productive One."[15] God is not a blank unity; rather, he is an indivisible unity of persons, the triune Lord.

No doubt, we cannot discern God's triune nature from Genesis 1–2 alone; we come to know it by God's self-disclosure over time. As God makes himself known in redemptive history, we learn that he is not a unipersonal being but a unity of three persons who share and subsist in the one indivisible divine nature: Father, Son, and Spirit (Matt 28:18–20; John

---

[12] See Frame, *History of Western Philosophy and Theology*, 14–19 (see chap. 2, n. 35).

[13] Christopher Watkin, *Thinking through Creation: Genesis 1 and 2 as Tools of Cultural Analysis* (Phillipsburg: P&R, 2017), 16.

[14] In systematic theology, this is the crucial distinction between *theologia* and *oikonomia*. The former refers to the knowledge of God in himself apart from creation (*ad intra*) in the perfection and blessedness of his eternally ordered relations as Father, Son, and Holy Spirit. The latter refers to the knowledge of God due to his external works (*ad extra*) in creation, revelation, providence, redemption, and judgment. In our discussion of theology proper in part 4, we will discuss this in more detail. For a helpful discussion of this distinction, see Duby, *God in Himself*, 11–58 (see chap. 1, n. 20); cf. John Webster, *God without Measure*, 1:213–24 (see chap. 1, n. 6).

[15] Bavinck, *Reformed Dogmatics*, 2:331 (see chap. 1, n. 9).

1:1–18; 5:16–30; 17:1–5; 2 Cor 13:14). In fact, the triune nature of God is disclosed with the unveiling of who the Messiah is as God's Son (2 Sam 7:14; Pss 2; 45; 72; 110), along with the Spirit of God, who is inseparable from the Messiah/Son (Isa 11; 42; 61).[16] But in light of God's self-revelation across the canon, we know that *before* creation, God has always existed in triune perfection.

For example, think of how John opens his gospel in speaking about the eternal Father-Son/Word relation: "In the beginning was the Word, and the Word was with (*pros*, "face to face") God, and the Word was God" (1:1). Both "God/Father" and the "Word/Son" are God (1:1c) *and* there is a shared eternal relation of love and communion between them (1:1b). This is confirmed by what Jesus, the divine Son, says about this fullness of life, love, and communication: "Now, Father, glorify me in your presence with that glory I had with you before the world existed" (17:5), and then a bit further, "Father, I want those you have given me to be with me where I am, so that they will see my glory, which you have given me because you loved me before the world's foundation" (17:24). Here we also discover that tied to this glory shared is a divine plan that grounds God's free and sovereign decision to create and ultimately to redeem a people for himself (1 Cor 2:6–7; Eph 1:3–14; Titus 1:1–3; 1 Pet 1:19–20; Rev 13:7–8).

As we will discuss in part 4, chapter 21, God's eternal plan is known as his decree, which is "the internal work of the Triune God (*opera Dei interna*)."[17] In God's decree, he freely foreordains all that comes to pass, including creation, providence, redemption, and judgment, thus moving and directing "the external works of the Triune God (*operationes Dei externae*)."[18] Within the divine decree, there is a "covenant of redemption" (*pactum salutis*) which speaks of God manifesting his glory to redeem a people for himself by the initiation of the Father, through the appointment of the Son as our mediator, and by the work of the Spirit, who applies Christ's work to us. In this plan, we discover that the ultimate end (telos) of God's decree is to direct all things to their fulfillment in Christ (Eph

---

[16] See Fred Sanders, *The Triune God* (Grand Rapids: Zondervan, 2016), 37–153. We will develop this point in part 4, chapter 18.

[17] Scott R. Swain, "Covenant of Redemption," in Allen and Swain, *Christian Dogmatics*, 107 (see chap. 5, n. 91). See Christensen, *What About Evil?*, 152–78 (see chap. 4, n. 86).

[18] Swain, "Covenant of Redemption," 107.

1:10–12; Col 1:15–20) so that God receives all glory and praise for his marvelous works in creation and redemption.

From a worldview perspective, this entails that history is not a series of meaningless events that the human mind "constructs" at will, contrary to much of modern and postmodern thought. Instead, history is the outworking of God's eternal plan, which he has ordained for his own glory, an overflow of his own delight within himself. Scott Christensen states it this way: "The unfallen world gives a glimpse of divine glory in its perfections, beauty, harmony, and order as somewhat ideally intended,"[19] but in God's plan even creation was intended to lead to "the final state of creation," which is "better than its initial state."[20] Even though God has ordained the reality of secondary agents and causes, nothing in history is accidental. History has meaning because behind the events of history is the plan of God. History, then, is purposely moving to a God-ordained and planned end, which includes God's plan of redemption for his greater glory. Indeed, all of God's works—creation, providence, history, and redemption—are due to God's free and purposed choice to be the theater for his extrinsic glory, which we, as his creatures, were created to enjoy, and which is the ultimate purpose of our redemption in Christ. The *Westminster Shorter Catechism* beautifully captures this truth in its first question: "What is the chief end of man?" Answer: "Man's chief end is to glorify God and enjoy him forever."

As God creates and relates to his creation, he does so as Creator and Lord. As Creator and Lord, he is fully present with us; he freely, purposely, and personally sustains and governs all things to his desired end (Ps 139:1–10; Acts 17:28; Eph 1:11; 4:6). In fact, God has created humans to know him in covenant relationship, *and* he has created the world to reveal his design, purposes, and glory (Ps 19:1–6), as we discussed in regard to natural/general revelation.[21] Also, God rules with perfect power, knowledge, and righteousness (Pss 9:8; 33:5; 138:1–4, 16; Isa 46:9–11) as the one true and living God. God is one, not only in singularity (there is only one God), but also simplicity (God is not composed of parts; all of his attributes are identical with his being); hence, he has fullness of life within himself apart from creation,

---

[19] Christensen, *What About Evil?*, 467.

[20] Christensen, 467.

[21] See part 2, chapter 6.

and he is not dependent on the world for his life or knowledge.[22] God knows and plans all things according to his will; *he* is the source and standard of truth. Furthermore, as the Holy One, he is the source and standard of goodness (Exod 3:2–5; Lev 11:44; Isa 6:1–3; 57:15; cf. Rom 1:18–23) since God alone has life "from himself" (*a se*, aseity).[23]

As the holy, independent, Creator and Lord, God is self-sufficient metaphysically (self-existent; *he* is "from himself"), epistemologically (self-attesting; *his* knowledge is "from himself"; *he* is the standard of truth), *and* morally (self-justifying; *his* will and nature is "from himself"; *he* is the absolute standard of goodness).[24] For this reason, as the absolute standard of goodness, God's holiness entails that he is "too pure to look on evil" and unable to tolerate wrong (Hab 1:12–13; cf. Isa 1:4–20; 35:8). When God confronts sin, he cannot overlook it; he *must* act in holy justice against it. Yet he is the God who loves his people with a holy, covenant love (Hos 11:9). God's holiness and love are never at odds (1 John 4:8; Rev 4:8); however, as sin enters the world, and God graciously promises to redeem us, a question arises as to how he will do so and remain true to himself—a question central to the Bible's unfolding redemptive story.

"Creation," then, first identifies the unique God of the Bible in all of his glory and splendor. And it is God's identity as the triune Creator-covenant Lord that gives a specific theistic shape to Scripture's theological framework, which is foundational for *all* doctrinal formulation. As we will note below, we cannot understand who humans are, the nature of our problem, the identity of our Lord Jesus Christ and the nature of his work, what salvation is, what eschatology is and the meaning of history, and so on without first identifying God correctly. Yet God is more than merely a concept central to the Christian worldview; he is our Creator, Lord, Redeemer, and our portion. This is *his* universe, and we are made for him. As Creator and Lord, he is the one who sets the terms of the covenant, and he is the one who deserves and rightfully demands all of our worship, praise, devotion, and obedience. As Asaph reminds us in Ps 73:25–28: "Who do I have in heaven but you? / And I desire nothing on earth but you.

---

[22] Van Til, *Apologetics*, 5 (see chap. 4, n. 81); cf. Bavinck, *Reformed Dogmatics*, 2:173–77.

[23] See Willem VanGemeren, *New International Dictionary of Old Testament Theology and Exegesis*, 3 vols. (Grand Rapids: Zondervan, 1997), 3:879; Muller, *Post-Reformation Reformed Dogmatics*, 3:497–503 (see chap. 3, n. 12); cf. Webster, *God without Measure*, 1:13–28.

[24] On this point, see Frame, *Doctrine of God*, 600–8.

/ My flesh and my heart may fail, / but God is the strength of my heart, / my portion forever. / Those far from you will certainly perish; / you destroy all who are unfaithful to you. / But as for me, God's presence is my good. / I have made the Lord God my refuge, / so I can tell about all you do."

From a worldview perspective, it is crucial to note how categorically different the biblical view of creation, origins, and ultimate reality is in comparison to all non-Christian thought. Watkin bluntly states it this way: "At bottom, reality is personal,"[25] in contrast to the "impersonal" understanding of most non-Christian worldviews. In rejecting the God of Scripture, non-Christian views reduce the most basic building blocks of reality to the "impersonal" or possibly finite conceptions of "god" (e.g., polytheism, animism). By contrast, Scripture argues that "God is personal in an original and irreducible way. Before anything existed, there was the personal God,"[26] the triune Lord who is fullness of life and perfection within himself.

John Frame captures this point as he contrasts the Christian worldview with all others. He notes that in non-Christian worldviews, both secular and religious,

> there has been a search for something *a se*: an ultimate cause of being, an ultimate standard of truth, an ultimate justification of right. In the realm of being (metaphysics), it may be a deity, a system of abstract forms, or natural law. In the realm of knowledge (epistemology), the standard may be a religious or secular authority, human subjectivity, sense experience, reason, or some combination. In the realm of ethics, it may be a system of duties, a calculation of consequences, or human inwardness. Ideally, the metaphysical absolute, the epistemological norm, and the ethical norm should all be grounded in one being, since these three are correlative to one another. But non-Christian thought has usually found it impossible to locate all these ultimates in a single principle. Part of the problem is that non-Christian thought is determined that its absolute be impersonal. But an impersonal being cannot serve as a norm for knowledge and ethics, nor can it be a credible first cause. So, many non-Christians have given up the quest for an absolute, preferring to embrace meaningless and chaos. The non-Christian substitutes for God have failed, just as the idols of Psalm 50 and

[25] Watkin, *Thinking through Creation*, 19.

[26] Watkin, 20.

> Isaiah 40 have failed. Only the *a se* God of Scripture can give unity and meaning to human thought and experience.[27]

Francis Schaeffer also repeatedly stressed this point in his speaking and writing.[28] Despite the diversity of worldviews, in terms of creation/origins, we start either with the Christian view of a personal beginning to everything, grounded in the triune God, or we affirm the impersonal. Much of Eastern thought is grounded in the impersonal (e.g., pantheistic: Hinduism, Taoism), along with some forms of Western rationalism and idealism (e.g., Baruch Spinoza, Georg Hegel) and New Age thought.[29] And now in the West, especially due to the embrace of evolutionary naturalism in contrast to Christian theism and even the deism of the Enlightenment, everything is reduced to the impersonal. But what consequences follow from these ideas/views?

Many consequences follow, but let us focus on three. First, the ground for human dignity and significance—indeed the "very notion of a person"[30]—is undermined if an impersonal view of creation/origins is embraced. Second, the warrant for objective truth and morality evaporates. For example, since humans and the world are not designed, ordered, and purposed, the "mind" of humans and the "facts" of the world are simply the product of randomness and chance. Even "laws" of science, logic, and morality are robbed of their universality, and anything that is "known" is not so because it corresponds to an objective reality that is planned and designed but solely due to a human subjective construction of an irrational world. Third, the meaning of history also vanishes. In our attempt to make sense of history, "without a personal

[27] Frame, *Doctrine of God*, 607–8. See Frame, *Apologetics*, 34–39, where he works out the implications. He also notes in the major religions of the world (pantheism, polytheism, dualism, animism, etc.), there is no way to speak of God's absolute *and* personal nature simultaneously. And in current scientific views tied to evolutionary naturalism, scientists seek to explain the universe, especially the personal elements "by the impersonal (matter, laws, motion), rather than the other way around" (38). And when scientists seek for absolutes—for example, the "origin of the universe"—they seek for an "elementary particle," a universal law ("theory of everything"), an initial motion (the "big bang"), or a combination of these" (38), but in the end, this reduces to the impersonal with disastrous consequences for grounding such things as human dignity, rationality, truth, moral norms, goodness, etc.

[28] See Schaeffer, *Complete Works of Francis A. Schaeffer*, 1:93–97, 227–344 (see chap. 1, n. 36); cf. Carson, *Gagging of God*, 222–32.

[29] See John W. Cooper, *Panentheism: The Other God of the Philosophers—From Plato to the Present* (Grand Rapids: Baker Academic, 2006); Herrick, *Making of the New Spirituality* (see chap. 2, n. 29).

[30] Watkin, *Thinking through Creation*, 21.

God whose providence governs history there can be no 'true' or 'objective' interpretation of history. The historian is then only the creator of fanciful illusions,"[31] which becomes nothing more than the will to power, as Friedrich Nietzsche stated over a century ago, and which postmodern "critical theorists" embrace with a vengeance.[32] In the end, we are left with two choices: impersonal chance and/or fate *or* the creation of the world by the absolute, personal triune Lord.

Think of the importance of this today. Our postmodern generation is lost and confused. Today we are caught up in chaos and confusion rooted in evolutionary and impersonal views of the universe. At the heart of the confusion is the question of origins and the nature of ultimate reality. Given an impersonal view of reality, it is impossible rationally to account for meaning, purpose, and human destiny unless we know where we have come from and who has made us. In fact, apart from the biblical view of creation/origins—indeed the biblical view of God—we have no epistemological warrant to ground rationality, meaning, design, order, morality, and justice. In the end, these concepts are robbed of their objective meaning and are reduced merely to subjective human constructions, which finally reduce to a mirage. Creation has to do with who God is and, by extension, who we are and why we are here. And wonderfully, creation affirms that existence has a purpose—we are not our own, we have been created to know God and to rule over creation, and now in Christ, we have been re-created to fulfill that very purpose, namely to know, love, obey, and glorify our triune Creator-covenant Lord (Rev 4:11; 5:12–14).

Humans

"Creation" also establishes the importance of humans, or a proper understanding of the "self." Although we will discuss theological anthropology in more detail later,[33] three points need to be stressed at this point as we think of the Bible's overall theological framework and worldview.

---

[31] Joseph Boot, *The Mission of God: A Manifesto of Hope for Society* (London: Wilberforce Publications, 2016), 112.

[32] On this point, see Trueman, *Rise and Triumph*, 163–92 (see chap. 1, n. 26); cf. Boot, *Mission of God*, 189–238.

[33] See volume 2.

First, creation identifies humanity, both male and female, as creatures of dignity, goodness, and responsibility. Although humans are creatures like the rest of creation, we alone are created in the image of the tri-personal God to rule over creation (Gen 1:26–28; cf. Ps 8). This entails that we are not the result of a cosmic accident or emanations from the impersonal, but personal creatures who have intrinsic value and significance. In fact, God has created and designed the world and humans in such a way that we can *know* God and the world since God has built into us the capacity to do so, and he has communicated to us, as we noted in our discussion of natural and special revelation.[34] Thus the knowledge of God *and* of the world is "natural" to us due to God's creation and revelation since humans were created to be in covenant relationship with our Creator and Lord and to carry out the creation mandate of subduing and ruling over all creation, which involves the task of knowledge and science. From a worldview perspective, the Bible's view of humans and our created value and inherent dignity is in direct contrast to most non-Christian worldviews since most of these views, apart from those who borrow from Scripture, locate humans in an ultimately impersonal environment.[35]

The complimentary creation accounts in Genesis 1–2 make this abundantly clear. Humans are the crowning act of God's creative activity. The *qualitative* difference between humans and the rest of creation is underscored in a number of ways. First, there is a solemn divine, intra-trinitarian counsel that precedes our creation (1:26).[36] Second, God directly acts in our creation, as evidenced in Gen 2:7, where we become "living beings" by the agency of God's Spirit.[37] Third, and most significant, although "man" (*adam*, i.e., humans collectively) is differentiated into male and female, both are created in the "image" and "likeness" of God to rule over creation as God's vice-regents, something not true of any other creature, even angels (Heb 1:14; 2:5–18).

[34] See part 2, chapters 5–7. For some helpful discussions of how "creation" impacts a Christian epistemology, accounting for how we know God and the world, see Frame, *Doctrine of the Knowledge of God* (see chap. 1, n. 11); and Alvin Plantinga, *Knowledge and Christian Belief* (Grand Rapids: Eerdmans, 2015).

[35] On this point, see Schaeffer, *Complete Works*, 1:93–118; Watkin, *Thinking through Creation*, 88–136.

[36] On the "us" language referring to intra-trinitarian deliberation, see part 4, chapter 18.

[37] See Michael S. Horton, *Rediscovering the Holy Spirit: God's Perfecting Presence in Creation, Redemption, and Everyday Life* (Grand Rapids: Zondervan, 2017), 52–56.

While the exact meaning of the terms *image* (*selem*) and *likeness* (*demut*) is disputed, and the words are not applied to humans often in Scripture,[38] the terms are foundational to a biblical understanding of human beings. Given their ancient Near East background, the concept of the "image of the god" conveys the idea of a physical representation of the "god," specifically the king who possessed the spirit of the "god." However, unlike the ancient Near East, where this concept is applied only to the king, Scripture teaches that *all* humans ("man," collectively) is created in the image of God, and under Adam's headship, *all* humans were created to be rulers over creation. Furthermore, although there is a semantic overlap for *image* and *likeness*, there is a fine distinction between the words that emphasizes a *dual* relationship that humans have first to God (likeness) and then to our rule over creation (image). *Likeness* specifies a covenantal relationship between humans and God, which parallels the idea of "sonship," while *image* specifies a covenantal relationship between humans and the world.[39] Thus, due to our creation in God's image-likeness, humans were created to know and love God in covenantal obedience *and* to rule over creation as we love our neighbors as ourselves. Although the great commandment is given specificity in the later covenants (Deut 6:4–5; Lev 19:18; Mark 12:28–29), it is what God requires of us from the moment of our creation as human beings.

Being made in God's image-likeness, then, signifies our *intrinsic* value before God and the representative role we play for the entire creation as God's royal sons. Gen 1:26c confirms this since it is best translated as a purpose clause: "in order that they [human beings] may have dominion" (author's translation), that is, function as royal kings and queens. Thus, our dominion over the world is *not* the definition of the image; instead, as Graeme Goldsworthy argues, it is "a consequence of" it.[40] The result: God deals with creation on the basis of how he deals with

---

[38] In terms of the biblical data, five texts designate humans as created as the "image of God" (Gen 1:27; 9:6; 1 Cor 11:7) or according to his "likeness" (Gen 5:1; Jas 3:9). Other texts refer to the renewal of humans to the "image" or "likeness" of God through redemption (Col 3:10; Rom 8:29; cf. Eph 4:24; 2 Cor 3:18). Also, there are crucial Christological texts that present the Son, our Lord Jesus Christ, as the true "image" of God, thus the archetype of our being created as God's image (Col 1:15; cf. Heb 1:3).

[39] See Peter J. Gentry and Stephen J. Wellum, *Kingdom through Covenant: A Biblical-Theological Understanding of the Covenants*, 2nd ed. (Wheaton: Crossway, 2018), 216–38; cf. Dan G. McCartney, "*Ecce Homo*: The Coming of the Kingdom as the Restoration of Human Viceregency," *WTJ* 56 (1994): 3–7.

[40] Graeme Goldsworthy, *According to Plan: The Unfolding Revelation of God in the Bible* (Downers Grove: InterVarsity, 1991), 96.

humans, which, as we will discuss in the next chapter, implies a unique covenantal relationship mediated through Adam. Goldsworthy confirms this when he writes,

> Although God commits himself to the whole of his creation for its good order and preservation, humanity is the special focus of this care. Creation is there for our benefit. Humanity is the representative of the whole creation so that God deals with creation on the basis of how he deals with humans. Only man is addressed as one who knows God and who is created to live purposefully for God. When man falls because of sin the creation is made to fall with him. In order to restore the whole creation, God works through his Son who becomes a man to restore man. The whole creation waits eagerly for the redeemed people of God to be finally revealed as God's perfected children, because at that point the creation will be released from its own bondage (Rom 8:19–23). This overview of man as the object of God's covenant love and redemption confirms the central significance given to man in Genesis 1–2.[41]

Given this understanding of image-likeness, it is not surprising that human rule over creation also conveys the idea of "kingdom." Although the phrase the "kingdom of God" is used later in Scripture, the concept is found in creation. As Goldsworthy notes,

> God's rule involves the relationships that he has set up between himself and everything in creation. In other words, God makes the rules for all existence. Both accounts of creation show mankind as the center of God's attention and the recipient of a unique relationship with him. Thus the focus of the kingdom of God is on the relationship between God and his people. Man is subject to God, while the rest of creation is subject to man and exists for his benefit. The kingdom means God ruling over his people in the material universe.[42]

Once again, this truth underscores our significance as humans, and it sets the stage for the Bible's unfolding covenantal story, a point we will develop in the next chapter. God created

---

[41] Goldsworthy, 96.

[42] Goldsworthy, 94–95. God's rule is key in the OT: "The idea of the rule of God over creation, over all creatures, over the kingdoms of the world, and in a unique and special way, over his chosen and redeemed people, is the very heart of the message of the Hebrew scriptures." Goldsworthy, "Kingdom of God" in *NDBT*, 618 (see chap. 1, n. 24).

us to rule over his world and to establish his kingdom. In fact, God made a *good* world (Gen 1:31) as the proper physical habitation for his kingdom people to live under his rule.[43] In contrast to non-Christian thought that often dichotomizes the physical and the spiritual, the biblical worldview insists that God created both good, and the task of Adam (along with all of humanity) was to expand the borders of Eden to the uttermost parts of the world, thus bringing God's rule to this world through the agency of humans.[44] But sadly, in Adam's disobedience, sin and death entered the world, which required God graciously and sovereignly to act to bring about a "new creation" and the consummation of an eternal kingdom by the work of a greater Adam and Son (see Isa 65:17–25; Rom 8:19–22; 2 Pet 3:13; Rev 21:1–4). All of these points are noteworthy to grasp a biblical view of the self, our intrinsic dignity and value, and our significant role in God's plan.

Second, creation also teaches that the only differentiation within "man" (*adam*, i.e., humans collectively) is male and female, both of whom are equally the image and likeness of God (Gen 1:26–28). This may seem like an obvious point, but today it is revolutionary. God's creation of "man" as male and female categorically denies all ideas of racial hierarchy *and* inseparably unites the concepts of sexuality and gender, as it speaks of a God-ordained and designed complementary distinction between male and female. God created male and female for each other, supremely reflected in marriage, to fulfill God's command to multiply and to rule over the earth (1:28). Scripture teaches that God's created order defines who we are and that our "essence (nature) precedes our existence."[45] In fact, any attempt to deny this truth only leads to futility, along with individual and societal breakdown, and divine judgment (Rom 1:18–32).

---

[43] On God's plan to have a people for himself in a place for themselves, see Dempster, *Dominion and Dynasty* (see chap. 4, n. 29).

[44] On this point see G. K. Beale, *The Temple and the Church's Mission: A Biblical Theology of the Dwelling Place of God*, NSBT 17 (Downers Grove: InterVarsity, 2004) and Benjamin L. Gladd, *From Adam and Israel to the Church: A Biblical Theology of the Church* (Downers Grove: InterVarsity, 2019), 5–21.

[45] "Essence precedes our existence" is a rejection of existentialism and postmodern thought that argues that our "existence," or autonomous choices, defines our individual "essence/nature." Existentialism is a worldview that embraces a naturalistic view of reality and a constructivist view of epistemology, thus rejecting that God has created and defined both the self and the world. For a description of current thought that rejects anything essential about human nature, which shows itself in the rise of the LGBT movement, critical theories, etc., see Trueman, *Rise and Triumph*, 271–382.

In Genesis 1–2, these truths are made evident. After Genesis 1 lays down the programmatic teaching regarding our creation in God's image-likeness, Genesis 2 focuses on our relationship to God in Adam and the creation of male and female for each other. What is striking in the account is that while God repeatedly declares creation good (1:31), there is something *not* good, namely, that Adam is alone. As such, God makes "a helper corresponding to him" (2:18). As the animals are paraded before Adam "to see what he would call [them]" (2:19), Adam finds "no helper . . . corresponding to him" (2:20), which means that there is a fundamental distinction between "man" and "animals." But in God's creation of woman, there is a fundamental, divinely-ordered compatibility between males and females. Although males and females are both image-bearers and equal in value; there is a complementary difference designed by God, which is specifically reflected in the establishment of marriage (Gen 2:24–25).

The significance of marriage is important in at least two ways. First, from a worldview perspective, God's creation of male and female not only establishes proper limits to the use of our sexuality, it also teaches us that the institution of marriage and the family are the most foundational building blocks in human society. Not surprisingly, as the biblical worldview is rejected, the first result is often a distortion of human sexuality and the dismantling of marriage and the family (Rom 1:18–32).[46] In its place, for example, as reflected in Marxist thought, when the family is dismantled, the state attempts to replace it, which has repeatedly led to societal collapse. God's created design of male and female, marriage, and the family must be protected, and anything that threatens these things must be strongly opposed in the church and in the larger society since the state is ordained by God to uphold what is right and good, which *minimally* is the protection of human life, marriage, and the family (Rom 13:1–7).[47] Second, from the perspective of the Bible's overall theological framework, as foundational as marriage is for the human society that continues until Christ returns, marriage also functions as a "type" that points beyond itself to a greater covenant relationship—God's relationship to his people. In this

---

[46] For example, Marxism, the Eugenic movement, the LGBT movement, and current "critical theories" all call for the destruction of the family, contrary to the biblical worldview. See Friedrich Engels, *The Origin of the Family, Private Property and the State* (1884; repr., New York: Penguin Classics, 2010); cf. Richard Weikart, *From Darwin to Hitler: Evolutionary Ethics, Eugenics, and Racism in Germany* (New York: Palgrave Macmillan, 2004); Trueman, *Rise and Triumph*, 225–382.

[47] See Boot, *Mission of God*, 401–56, for a helpful discussion of the importance of marriage and the family in a biblical worldview.

way, marriage is an important created means to a larger end, but in God's plan, it is not eternal (Matt 22:29–32). What is eternal is what marriage typifies—God's exclusive love for his people as shown in the new covenant relationship of Christ's love for his church (Eph 5:32). All of these truths are important in theological formulation, especially in the doctrinal areas of humans (theological anthropology), salvation (soteriology), the church (ecclesiology), and eschatology.

Third, creation also establishes the first Adam–last Adam typological relationship. As we will develop in the next chapter, God's creation of humans as his image-sons is first given *in Adam*. Scripture divides *all* people under the representative headship of either Adam or Christ (1 Cor 15:45; cf. Rom 5:14). Adam is not only the first human but also humanity's covenant head. To Adam, God first speaks and commands him to obey (Gen 2:15–17), and the significance of his role, including his disobedience, becomes apparent as history unfolds (Gen 3; Rom 5:12–21). From Adam (and all humans), God demands total devotion. The tree of the knowledge of good and evil tests whether Adam will be an obedient son. But sadly, Adam disobeys, and the result of his choice has cosmic consequences. Now, all people enter the world "in Adam"—fallen, guilty, and corrupt—and the entire creation is under God's curse. Our only hope is that *God* acts in grace to redeem, which not only drives the Bible's story forward to Christ; it also gives the rationale for why the divine Son assumed our human nature and why Christ alone is Lord and Savior.

From a worldview perspective, the significance of Adam as our covenant head is twofold. First, as Paul teaches in Acts 17:26, our common creation in Adam explains why *all* people have the same universal value. Second, Adam also explains why *all* people have the same universal problem (Rom 3:23). On both issues, the biblical teaching is the only view that can explain *why* humans have equal value *and* the same problem that only God can remedy.

From the perspective of the Bible's overall story, the image-son-Adam type is significant because it is developed along a trajectory that leads us to the true image-Son and last Adam. As Scripture unfolds, we discover the consequences of Adam's sin, which can only be remedied by Christ. In fact, crucial categories of Scripture emerge that are essential to grasp *who* Jesus is and *what* he does for us. For example, to be "in Adam" is to belong to the "old creation" and age characterized by sin, death, and judgment, while being "in Christ" is to belong to the "new creation" and an age characterized by life and salvation.[48] These crucial truths and categories

---

[48] See Douglas J. Moo, *The Epistle to the Romans*, NICNT (Grand Rapids: Eerdmans, 1996), 315.

are not mere window dressing; they are essential to grasp the Bible's story, and they are foundational for our doctrinal formulation of humans, sin, Christ, salvation, eschatology, and so on.

World

"Creation" also establishes at least two important truths about the "world." *First,* God creates a universe that is real and uniform within the structure of a controlled system (cf. Isa 45:18–19). As such, the universe does not operate outside of God's control and sustaining power, and God is free to act in his world. As Watkin notes, "if the universe is created by one God alone, it is a place of order, predictability and structure, not chaos, conflict and inexplicable change."[49]

From a worldview perspective, this is in direct contrast with either "open" or "closed" views of the universe.[50] For example, animism affirms an open universe where spirits control most things; there is no steady regularity to the world. On the other hand, naturalistic views insist on a closed view where everything is explained by the impersonal plus time and chance. Yet, the difficulty with such a view is holding together the ideas that the universe is random but governed by strict uniformity and regularity. By contrast, a Christian view of the world is able to maintain simultaneously that the world is objectively real, ordered, and designed and thus able to be studied and known—a foundational conviction that "motivate[ed] the birth of Western science."[51] At the same time, since "the cosmos is neither divine nor demonic but natural—pronounced 'good' by its triune Creator,"[52] God "is at perfect liberty to do things another way, with the result that miracles are possible."[53] As created, the universe is not necessary or the result of divine emanation or the product of an arbitrary will. Instead the world is the creation of the triune God who creates according to his plan and word and continues to sustain all things by his word, as he is active in the world in ordinary and extraordinary ways, an important point in the doctrinal formulation of divine providence and one that undergirds Scripture's overall theological framework.[54] This is why, as Nancy Pearcey notes,

[49] Christopher Watkin, *From Plato to Postmodernism* (London: Bristol Classical Press, 2011), 35.

[50] See Carson, *Gagging of God*, 201.

[51] Watkin, *From Plato to Postmodernism*, 35.

[52] Horton, *Rediscovering the Holy Spirit*, 61.

[53] Carson, *Gagging of God*, 201.

[54] See part 4, chapters 21–23.

"The divine word gives things their 'nature' or identity, governing both human life (moral law) and the physical universe (laws of nature) . . . [so that] God's law govern[s] every element in the universe, God's word constituting its orderly structure, God's truth discoverable in every field."[55]

Second, God creates the world *good*, which is repeatedly emphasized in Genesis 1 (vv. 12, 18, 21, 25), along with the final summary statement, "God saw all that he had made, and it was very good indeed" (1:31). From a worldview perspective, a biblical view of the world is in direct contrast to the pagan myths that viewed material reality as inferior or unclean.[56] Instead, Scripture teaches that God delighted in his creation and that it was good. Every aspect of God's creative work was consistent with his intention, and God delighted in his handiwork. Nothing comes from God's hand fallen, disordered, or evil, which is a vital point to note in answering questions about the nature of the human problem, the reality of sin and evil, the kind of Redeemer we need, the nature of salvation, and our future hope. Furthermore, a *good* world entails that both physical and spiritual realities were created good and that, in light of the fall, both are corrupted by sin and in need of redemption.[57] As Scripture later speaks of the Redeemer and his incarnation, it does so by stressing the need for Christ to become flesh (John 1:14; 1 John 1:1–3; 4:1–3) in order to redeem his people. In this light, it is important to remember that the first Christological heresy in the church did not deny Christ's deity but his humanity. Docetism (Gk. *dokeō*, "to appear"), which rejected the original goodness of the material world, also denied the reality of a true incarnation. The church, conversely, starting with a proper view of creation and its goodness, realized that without a real incarnation, the Redeemer could not fully redeem us.[58]

In summary, "creation," as the first plot movement of Scripture, is foundational to understand the Bible's overall framework and worldview. It begins by establishing the Bible's own content, categories, and intrasystematic structures, out of which doctrinal formulation arises. The Bible's view of origins is unique, grounded in a specific view of God, self, and the world, with theology proper grounding everything else. Creation establishes a specific theistic,

---

[55] Pearcey, *Total Truth*, 84; cf. Boot and his discussion on why a Christian worldview is foundational for a proper view of the world and our study of it. *Mission of God*, 442–51.

[56] See Watkin, *Thinking through Creation*, 46–87.

[57] See Pearcey, *Total Truth*, 82–95; cf. Pearcey, *Love Thy Body*, 17–46 (see chap. 11, n. 42).

[58] See volume 2.

eschatological, and covenantal framework from which we make sense of the world and grasp God's unfolding plan that begins in creation and culminates in the new creation. Creation also establishes the "original situation," prior to sin, in human history. Accordingly, it speaks of creation order and norms, proper relationships, and something of the ideal. Yet, we know from Scripture that creation is not an end in itself, but a means to a larger end. As the divine plan unfolds over time, we discover that God is bringing the goodness of his creation and the presence of his kingdom to its telos in a true and final image-Son-Adam, our Lord Jesus Christ, and a new creation for the good of his people and the supreme magnification of God's own glory (Ps 115:1; Isa 48:11; Rom 11:36; Eph 1:3–14; Phil 2:6–8). For this reason, a proper understanding of eschatology begins in creation and culminates in the new creation. But to get there, we need to turn to the other plot movements in order to grasp the Bible's overall theological framework and worldview.

The Fall

The second plot movement of the Bible's metanarrative and theological framework is the "fall." Every worldview must explain the nature of the human problem, and significantly, the answer given is always tied to one's understanding of creation/origins. No one can honestly examine human history, or even one human life, and not conclude that we have missed the mark, but what exactly is the problem? Without oversimplifying the matter, just as worldviews affirm either a personal or impersonal view of ultimate reality regarding "origins," so worldviews explain the human problem in two basic directions: intrinsic/metaphysical or moral-choice explanations.

Despite the variety of non-Christian worldviews, *all* of them view the human problem as *intrinsic* to the human condition or due to our metaphysical condition and finitude. If we are wicked and cruel, this is what we have always been from the beginning; it is "natural" or "intrinsic" to us. For example, think of evolutionary naturalism. Humans have evolved over time, but we have always been "fallen" given the impersonal environment we emerged from. Or think of Greek thought. It viewed evil and disorder as intrinsic to the material world, which has always been the case. In fact, Greek thought impacted heretical views such as Gnosticism, which were rejected by the early church because of their false views of creation and the fall.[59]

---

[59] Pearcey, *Total Truth*, 84; cf. Schaeffer, *Collected Works*, 1:109–14.

In the end, the human problem is intrinsic to us, tied to our evolutionary history, structure, genetics, and lack of knowledge and exacerbated by our environment. Yet such views offer little hope for change since our problem is *intrinsic*. Although many think that education, genetic engineering, environmental change through social action, redistribution of wealth, or what have you may help, human cruelty and evil is simply built into us.

The Bible, however, rejects such views and locates the human problem in a moral choice that occurred in *history*. God created us *good*, but in space-time history, Adam, as our covenant head, rebelled against God's command. The result: sin and death entered the world, our human nature was corrupted, and the entire world was placed under a curse (Gen 3:14–19; Rom 6:23; 8:20). Thus, "in Adam," humanity moved from an *original* state of goodness to our present *fallen* or *abnormal* state. On this point, the Bible's explanation of the human problem is categorically different from non-Christian thought. Conversely, the Bible's solution to the problem is also categorically different. Why? For this reason: since our problem is *not* tied to our creation but instead to a historical (and thus responsible) moral choice, sin and evil may be vanquished and perfectly eliminated. However, if the historicity of Genesis 3 is rejected, Scripture's explanation of the human problem becomes *intrinsic*, and its solution is undercut in at least three ways.[60]

First, apart from a historical fall, the responsibility for our sin and evil is ultimately traced back to our Creator, who made us "flawed" from the outset. However, in no uncertain terms, Scripture teaches that God created humans and the world "good" (Gen 1:31). All that is evil is not the Creator's fault, but tied to the responsibility of the creature, both human and angelic.[61]

Second, apart from Adam's representative choice in history, there is no true explanation for the *universality* of the human problem and why *all* people have the *same* problem before God. The Bible, unlike current "critical theories" that privilege various intersectional realities and

[60] For a defense of the historicity of Adam and the Fall, see Henri Blocher, *Original Sin: Illuminating the Riddle*, NSBT 5 (Downers Grove: InterVarsity, 2000); Madueme and Reeves, *Adam, the Fall, and Original Sin* (see chap. 11, n. 41).

[61] This is one of the problems with treatments of Genesis 3 that reject the historicity of the fall. For example, Paul Ricoeur does not want to equate finitude and sin, but apart from a historic fall, humans have always been "fallen" and thus structurally flawed. *The Symbolism of Evil*, trans. Emerson Buchanan (Boston: Beacon Press, 1986).

teach that some kinds of "oppression" are greater, makes *all* people equal in their fallenness: "For all have sinned and fall short of the glory of God" (Rom 3:23).[62]

Third, apart from a historical Fall, the hope for a solution to our present condition is undermined. Unlike non-Christian views, Scripture teaches that our *abnormal* condition can be reversed, not by scrapping us and starting over, but by God's own initiative to reverse what has occurred. In Christ, the divine Son has assumed our human nature, and as the incarnate Son, he has obeyed for us, paid for our sin, and secured the transforming work of the Spirit, who makes us new creations in Christ.[63] In Christ, our human nature is not destroyed, but renewed, transformed, and glorified. Herman Bavinck states it this way: "Grace serves, not to take up humans into a supernatural order, but to free them from sin. Grace is opposed not to nature, only to sin."[64] On these points, the biblical view is in a category all by itself; it alone explains our problem *and* offers a true solution to it.[65]

These truths are taught as we walk through the opening chapters of Genesis. Following on the heels of creation, Genesis 3 presents an epochal shift that changes everything.[66] After receiving every provision and the blessing of God to obey and enjoy him in royal service, Adam willfully disobeys God's command/law (Gen 2:15–17). It seems that Adam became dissatisfied with vice-regency under God and fell to Satan's temptation to rule without God by "be[coming] like God, knowing good and evil" (Gen 3:4–7). As noted, Genesis 3 teaches that the entrance of human sin into God's creation was *internal* or *moral*, but not *intrinsic* or original to creation. The temptation to sin came externally from Satan. The desire and will to

---

[62] Watkin argues that Western ideas of equality and the levelling of hierarchy have been borrowed from Christian theology. "If human beings are equal in bearing the image of God then they are also equal in sin, equal in a 'democracy of sin' in which everyone, regardless of their place in society, stands in need of God's mercy to forgive them." *From Plato to Postmodernism*, 37. On critical theories and intersectionality, see Lindsay and Pluckrose, *Cynical Theories*, 111–34 (see chap. 2, n. 116).

[63] On this point, see Blocher, *Original Sin*.

[64] Bavinck, *Reformed Dogmatics*, 3:577.

[65] Scripture never reduces the human problem to an issue of biology or social conditions, in contrast to Karl Giberson, *Saving the Original Sinner* (Boston: Beacon Press, 2015); Enns, *Evolution of Adam* (see chap. 11, n. 41). Without denying complex connections with our physical bodies and social interactions, our root problem is willful and responsible sin before God—a *moral* problem in need of a *moral* solution.

[66] This sense of timing is true from a narrative perspective. Regardless of the time lapse from the end of Genesis 2 to Genesis 3, the text emphasizes a drastic shift from goodness to corruption.

act in disobedience to God, however, was a moral choice that Adam made, thus underscoring the weight of human choice. Adam did not sin because he was created defective; instead, he sinned by choice, acting as the fool (Prov 1:7), thinking he, as the creature, could be like the Creator, indeed valuing created things more than God himself in all of his beauty and glory (Rom 1:18–25).

Once sin entered Eden, it did not remain there. The effects of sin corrupted everything due to Adam's covenant headship (Rom 5:12). Although Christian theology has differed on the precise effects of the transmission of Adam's sin to all human beings, Scripture clearly teaches that no one escapes the transmission.[67] This is evident in the subsequent narratives within Genesis and the entire Pentateuch. Beginning with murder in Adam's family (Gen 4:6–8), sin multiplied and expanded until "every inclination of the human mind was nothing but evil all the time . . . for every creature had corrupted its way on the earth" (Gen 6:5, 12). And the human problem of sin, with its corruption of all thoughts and desires, has continued to our day (Rom 3:23). In short, God's original vice-regent disobeyed God's command with tragic and universal consequences (Rom. 6:23). Furthermore, because all humanity was given dominion over the earth, the whole creation has been subjected to futility (Rom 8:18–23). Sin's effects not only alienate us from God but also bring alienation among ourselves and with creation itself. Humans, created to know, love, and obey God, now live under God's righteous condemnation (Eph 2:1–3).

However, there is a solution to our problem *if* God sovereignly and graciously chooses to make things right. Yet it is important to note that the fall introduces a *tension* into the Bible's story given God's promise to redeem us (Gen 3:15)—a *tension* between who God is *and* our sin before him. John Stott labels this tension the "problem of forgiveness."[68] What is

---

[67] See volume 2.

[68] John R. W. Stott, *The Cross of Christ*, 2nd ed. (Downers Grove: InterVarsity, 2006), 89–111. Stott describes the problem this way:

> The problem of forgiveness is constituted by the inevitable collision between divine perfection and human rebellion, between God as he is and us as we are. The obstacle to forgiveness is neither our sin alone, nor our guilt alone, but also the divine reaction in love and wrath towards guilty sinners. For, although indeed "God is love," yet we have to remember that his love is "holy love," love which yearns over sinners while at the same time refusing to condone their sin. How, then, could God express his holy love?—his love in forgiving sinners without compromising his holiness, and his holiness in judging sinners without frustrating his love?

this problem? Considering the divine response to human sin, it seems that God must do two things that appear to be mutually exclusive: fully judge sin *and* forgive it. On the one hand, God *must* fully judge sin because he is holy and just. On the other hand, God created and covenanted with us to glorify himself in the righteous rule of humans over creation, not in our destruction.

But the problem goes deeper, into the *nature* of God himself, as noted in our discussion of who God is in all of his glorious aseity. Whereas sin is an *internal* moral problem for humanity, divine forgiveness is an *intrinsic* moral problem for God due to God's own nature. God *is* holy and just, sin is against *him,* and sin *must* be punished. God cannot and will not overlook our sin, for *he* is the standard of goodness. All of his attributes are *essential* to him, including his holiness, righteousness, justice, and love. Regarding his justice, for example, God is *not* like a human judge, who adjudicates laws external to him; God *is* the law. Our sin, then, is not against an abstract principle or impersonal law; it is against *this* God, the triune Creator and Lord (Ps 51:4). So for God to forgive us, he *must* remain true to himself! That is why our forgiveness is possible only if the full satisfaction of *his* moral, holy demand is met. But this raises a crucial question: *Who* is able to satisfy God's righteous demand? Scripture's answer is that *God himself* must solve the problem. He must take the initiative to redeem us consistent with his own holy nature and true to his gracious promise to do so; otherwise, there is no hope for the human problem.

On these points, the biblical view stands in direct opposition to all non-Christian thought. Outside of the Bible, the biblical *tension* never arises since other worldviews deny the absolute-personal God of Scripture and the significance of human choice and thus trivialize sin. However, in doing so, non-Christian thought can never explain the human problem correctly, and thus it always underestimates the desperate condition that we find ourselves in. As a result, not only is the human problem misdiagnosed but the solutions proposed never satisfy, work, or result in lasting change of the human condition. It is only the biblical worldview, which takes God, humans, and sin seriously, that offers any hope of a solution, a point to which we now turn.

Confronted by human evil, how could God be true to himself as holy love? In Isaiah's words, how could he be simultaneously "a righteous God and a Savior" (45:21)? (90–91)

Redemption

"Redemption" is the third plot movement that gives shape to the broad contours of the Bible's interpretive framework and worldview. The question raised by "redemption" is whether there is a solution to the human problem. Just as most people admit that there is something wrong with humans and the world, so most people offer some kind of solution to the problem. Also, just as a worldview's diagnosis of the problem is organically related to its view of creation/origins, so a worldview's solution to the problem ("redemption") follows from its answers to these other areas. For this reason, if our problem is our lack of knowledge, our genetic structures, or various power/oppressive identity groups that oppress others, or what have you, then the solution to these problems is education, genetic engineering, political and social revolutions, and so forth. But if the problem is our sin before *God* and our having an *internal* moral problem that we are powerless to change, then "redemption" is not found, as it is in most non-Christian thought, either in individual humans or, more often, collectively in the state, but in *God alone*, who must sovereignly and graciously act.

In thinking about the categorical difference between the biblical view of "redemption" and non-Christian worldviews, at least three points require emphasis.

First, redemption is only possible if *God* unilaterally acts in sovereign grace to keep his promises to provide salvation for us (Gen 3:15). Salvation does not emerge from human initiative. The entirety of Scripture teaches that God *himself* must initiate to save: "Salvation belongs to the Lord" (Ps 3:8); "I—I am the Lord. / Besides me, there is no Savior" (Isa 43:11), which follows from the Bible's view of God and the serious nature of the human problem. After all, who can forgive sins; change the human heart; defeat sin, death, and Satan; and usher in a new creation other than God alone? If there is to be salvation at all, *God* must execute judgment and reveal his mighty arm in grace and power (Isa 51:9; 52:10; 53:1; 59:16–17; Ezek 34).

However, as we noted above, in the Bible's plotline, a *tension* arises between God and his promise to redeem and our sin before him. *God alone* must redeem us, but given who he is as the holy, just, *a se* God, how can he forgive our sins *and* simultaneously satisfy his own holy demand against us? Moreover, this *tension* is heightened when we remember the significance of Adam (and humans) in God's plan for creation. God has chosen to exercise his kingdom rule on earth through his image-sons, but given our sin, *all* humans stand condemned before God. Yet, as God's promise reminds us, *he* will redeem us and bring about a new creation *through* his provision of a *human*: "I will put hostility between you [Satan] and the woman, and between your offspring and her offspring. He will strike your head, and you will strike his heel" (Gen 3:15).[69] In this *protevangelium* (the first gospel),[70] God announces that his redemption will come through his provision of another Adam, a "seed" of the woman,[71] who unlike the first Adam, will fully obey God and restore humanity and creation. In this "seed," as Stephen Dempster notes, "human—and therefore divine—dominion will be established over the world. The realization of the kingdom of God is linked to the future of the human race."[72] Redemption depends on *God's* initiative *and* the provision of an obedient human. But here is the problem: given our sin, the human race cannot produce such a Redeemer or redemption. How, then, does God keep his promise, secure his rule in the world by a human, and justify sinners by satisfying his own holy demand against our sin? The answer to this question leads to the next point.

Second, redemption is only possible in *Christ alone* as the exclusive Lord and Redeemer.[73] Given the biblical teaching about God, humans, and sin, the only one who can fulfill all of God's promises and fully obey for us as our representative and substitute is the divine Son/Word become human (John 1:1, 14). Why? For this reason: given God's promise to redeem humans and to restore the world through a *human*, Christ must be fully human, the true image-son who keeps the covenant for us. Yet Christ must also be the *divine* Son, for the redemptive works that he does are the works *of God*: the establishment of *God's* kingdom and rule in this world, the securing and pouring out of *God's* Spirit (Ezek 36–37; Joel 2:28–32), the creation of

---

[69] See Goldsworthy, who connects creation and salvation as an unfolding drama by observing that "the background to God's work of rescuing sinners is his commitment to his creation." *According to Plan*, 112.

[70] See T. Desmond Alexander, *The Servant King: The Bible's Portrait of the Messiah* (Leicester: Inter-Varsity Press, 1998), 16–19; Vos, *Biblical Theology* (see chap. 1, n. 45).

[71] "Seed" (*zera*) is a key word in Genesis. It occurs 59 times, compared to 170 times in the rest of the OT. See Alexander, "Seed," 773 (see chap. 4, n. 64). Although the noun does not have distinctive singular and plural forms, one can make a strong case that it is singular, especially since the rest of Genesis focuses on a single line of seed, descended from Eve, to Noah, through Abram, and on to Christ (cf. Gal. 3:16); cf. C. John Collins, "A Syntactical Note (Genesis 3:15): Is the Woman's Seed Singular or Plural?" *TynBul* 48 (1997): 139–48; T. Desmond Alexander, "Further Observations on the Term 'Seed' in Genesis," *TynBul* 48 (1997): 363–67.

[72] Dempster, *Dominion and Dynasty*, 69.

[73] See volume 2 for Christology and the development of our Lord Jesus Christ's person and work.

a new creation (Isa 65:17), and the ratification of a new covenant bound up with the complete forgiveness of sin (Jer 31:34).

This last point is especially significant in thinking about the necessity and the nature of the atonement—a point central to our theological formulation of Christology and soteriology. God cannot overlook our sin since *he* is the standard of goodness. For God to be God, our sin *must* be punished. So for God to forgive us, *he* must satisfy his own righteous demand. But *who* is able to do so other than *God himself*? To be justified before God, we need a human image-son to be our perfect representative, but we also need the divine Son, the true image of the Father, to be our substitute by taking his own righteous requirements on himself, thus fully paying for our sins (Col 1:15–20; Heb 1:1–4; 2:5–18; 8:1–13). In the Bible's unfolding of redemption, salvation is only possible if the triune God acts to redeem and he does so in and through the person and work of the incarnate Son. For this reason, Christ alone (*solus Christus*) is Lord and Savior, and apart from him, there is no salvation (Acts 4:12).

Third, a biblical view of redemption warrants the truth that we live in a "moral universe." A moral universe affirms that there is an absolute standard of morality and that despite the horrors and injustices of this world, in the end, the scales of justice will be perfectly balanced. Although most people desire such a "balancing of the books" as cries for justice are daily heard, non-Christian views have little warrant to think such a universe exists. Again, despite the diversity of non-Christian thought, if ultimate reality is reduced to the impersonal, the warrant for objective, universal moral norms vanishes, along with any hope that true, universal, cosmic justice will result.[74] Even non-Christian "theistic" views, such as Islam, face a problem because of their rejection of the Trinity and because their concept of God is voluntaristic; that is, it uncouples the will from the nature of God, thus resulting in an arbitrary will. Moreover, Islam's view of salvation is works righteousness, which rejects any need for an atonement to pay for sin and to satisfy an absolute standard of divine goodness and justice in the forgiveness of sins. But such a view results in an arbitrary will. God "grades on the curve" as he weighs

[74] On this point, see Frame, *Apologetics*, 98–110. Frame argues that if the impersonal is ultimate, then "ethical" laws are the result of chance, carry no universal obligation, and become a matter of individual or societal "construction"; cf. Douglas Groothuis, *Christian Apologetics: A Comprehensive Case for Biblical Faith* (Downers Grove: IVP Academic, 2011), 330–63. Also see a critique of current non-Christian attempts to have "cosmic" justice apart from a Christian worldview in Sowell, *The Quest for Cosmic Justice* (see chap. 2, n. 114).

our good and bad deeds, but such views are unable to uphold an absolute, unchanging moral standard of goodness.[75]

Even within Christian theology, views that deny penal substitution face serious challenges in providing a strong warrant for a "moral universe."[76] At the heart of penal substitution is the truth that in Christ, God is just in declaring the ungodly just because the incarnate Son has fully satisfied divine justice. Yet views that reject penal substitution, such as the governmental or moral-example views, end up affirming what Garry Williams has called a kind of "moral naturalism." He states it this way: "God has created the world in such a way that sin has its punishment as a natural consequence,"[77] a kind of justice or righteousness that upholds the moral governing of the universe but does not treat sin as a personal affront against the holy God who will not let sin go unpunished. As such, God does not demand the full payment of our sin in our justification, and Christ's atoning work is not the full payment of our sin. What is at stake is a God who is the moral standard of the universe and who will not rectify anything apart from the satisfaction of his own righteous demand in Christ's cross. Our hope and longing that the horrors and injustices of this world will be fully dealt with is not warranted by a view that diminishes the demand for the full satisfaction of God's righteous demand; instead, it is only warranted in a God who demands the full satisfaction for sin either in the substitutionary work of the incarnate Son or, for those who stand outside of Christ, in an eternal judgment of their sin.

This is why the biblical view is categorically different from these views. First, the triune Creator and Lord is the absolute standard of goodness. His will and nature are "from himself" (*a se*). As such, we have confidence that God's holy justice will not overlook our sin but require its full satisfaction; we truly live in a moral universe. Second, in Christ and his work, we have the perfect Savior, who allows God to remain just *and* the justifier of sinners (Rom 3:21–26). In Christ's incarnation and obedient *human* life, he, as the mediator of the new covenant, obeys for us as our legal representative. And in his obedient death, the *divine* Son satisfies his

---

[75] See Groothuis, *Christian Apologetics*, 599–613. On Islam, see White, *What Every Christian* (see chap. 8, n. 51); Geisler and Saleeb, *Answering Islam* (see chap. 8, n. 51).

[76] See volume 2.

[77] Garry Williams, "The Cross and the Punishment of Sin" in *Where Wrath and Mercy Meet*, ed., David Peterson (Carlisle, UK: Paternoster, 2001), 95–96.

own righteous demand against us by bearing the penalty of our sin as our substitute (Rom 5:18–19; Phil 2:6–11; Heb 5:1–10). Through faith and union in Christ, his perfect obedience is imputed to us and the debt of our sin is fully atoned (Rom 4:1–8; 5:1–2, 9–11). Apart from Christ's life, death, and resurrection, for God to justify us would ultimately question his own integrity, justice, and moral character.[78] In the end, it is only the biblical worldview that warrants confidence that the world we live in is not ultimately immoral and amoral, but a true, moral universe.[79]

"Redemption," as with the previous two plot movements, not only provides the broad contours to the Bible's theological framework and worldview, it also lays the foundation on which our doctrinal formulations arise, especially Christology, soteriology, and eschatology.

New Creation

"New creation" or "consummation" is the last plot movement that gives overall shape to the Bible's theological framework and worldview. The question raised by "new creation" is, What may we hope? Where is history going? Is the future optimistic or pessimistic, utopian or dystopian? And on what grounds may we hope? As we have noted, Christian and non-Christian answers to these questions directly depend on answers given to the previous plot movements. The heart of the biblical answer to what we may hope is God's unfailing promises in Christ, grounded in his own initiative to redeem his people and to execute judgment on sin and evil according to his own perfect standard of righteousness and justice, thus making all things right in a consummated new creation (Isa 65:17; Matt 19:28; 1 Cor 15; 2 Pet 3:10–13; Rev 21–22).

In Scripture, the movement of history to the new creation is due to the outworking of God's eternal plan centered in Christ (Eph 1:9–10; Col 1:15–20). As we noted under "creation," God's intent for creation is for it to reach its *telos* in Christ, thus underlining Scripture's

---

[78] See the helpful discussion of this point in Moo, *Romans*, 240; cf. D. A. Carson, "Atonement in Romans 3:21–26: God Presented Him as a Propitiation," in *The Glory of the Atonement: Biblical, Historical and Practical Perspectives*, ed. Charles E. Hill and Frank A. James III (Downers Grove: InterVarsity, 2004), 119–39.

[79] On this point, see Schaeffer, *Collected Works*, 1:109–125, 293–304.

eschatological focus from creation to new creation. This is why a biblical understanding of "eschatology" is not a mere locus or simply one doctrinal area of theology; instead, it is a "lens" by which we view all doctrines, and it is central to the Bible's unfolding metanarrative and theological framework.[80]

In thinking about the plot movement of "new creation," it is important to note that Scripture presents the dawning of the new creation in terms of "inauguration and consummation." As we will develop more in the next chapter, the Bible divides history into two ages: "this present age" and "the age to come." The former age began when God created all things and continued through humanity's corruption of all things, and it remains until Christ's return. It is an age, especially now that we live in a post-fall world, which is characterized by sin, death, and opposition to God. The latter age, though it sounds entirely future oriented, is already here or inaugurated due to the incarnation and work of our Lord Jesus Christ. It is an age characterized by eternal life, the establishment of God's saving reign (kingdom) in this world, and the defeat of sin, death, Satan, and all opposition to God, which results in a new heavens and new earth. However, although "the age to come" is now here in Christ *in principle*, its final consummated end awaits Christ's glorious return, where *he* brings history to its appointed end (telos). Thus, "this present age" continues even with the decisive enthronement of Christ until he comes again. Between Christ's two comings, our Lord reigns over his creation-kingdom even though the full realities of life in "the age to come" await his return. But even now, due to our union in Christ, his people, both individually and corporately, participate in the new creation (2 Cor 5:17; Eph 2:11–22).

This two-age construction of redemptive history leads to an *already-not-yet* dynamic in the unfolding of God's plan, what is called *inaugurated eschatology*. Inaugurated eschatology and its already-not yet dynamic is not only important for understanding the Christo-centric and Christo-telic nature of Scripture; it is also significant for doctrinal formulation, especially in Christology, soteriology, ecclesiology, and obviously eschatology. In Christ, the final fulfillment of God's plan for humanity and all creation has begun: the way things will be forever has crashed into the way things are now temporarily.[81]

---

[80] On this point, see Horton, *Covenant and Eschatology*, 1–45 (see chap. 2, n. 147).

[81] For a discussion of inaugurated eschatology, see Schreiner, *New Testament Theology*, 41–116 (see chap. 4, n. 62); Herman Ridderbos, *Paul: An Outline of His Theology*, trans. John Richard de Witt (Grand Rapids: Eerdmans, 1975), 44–90.

Although more will be said about the significance of inaugurated eschatology in the next chapter, at this point, we want to focus on its importance for a biblical view of history and hope in contrast to non-Christian worldviews. Inaugurated eschatology not only reminds us that God governs history and that *he* is moving it to its consummated end in Christ but also that our hope for the future is sure. Most worldviews desire some kind of "utopia" or "ideal society."[82] However, the grounds for such a hope, especially if the worldview affirms that ultimate reality is impersonal, are unwarranted. In fact, non-Christian views, in rejecting the foreordination and sovereignty of God, which guarantees the certainty of *his* plan for the universe in Christ, foolishly locate hope in humans and supremely the state. In this way, hope for the future "is transferred from the transcendent to the immanent realm,"[83] and the result is often tyranny, as reflected, for example, in the utopian ideals of Marxism.[84] Judgment against perceived "social injustices" is not ultimately left to God, the judge of all the earth who always does what is right according to his perfect standard of justice (Gen 18:25; Rom 13:17–21). Instead, judgment is transferred from God's eternal order to the temporal according to human "constructivist" standards, which in the course of history has more often than not led to the destruction of freedom and liberty.

A biblical view of history is the opposite of non-Christian thought. Our hope for the future is grounded in what God has *already* done in Christ. The *not yet* is not a "fool's hope" but is tied to what God has done in *history*. Contrast this with the Marxist vision of reality. Marxism hopes for a better future, "when communism will triumph and conflict will vanish from the world,"[85] but there is nothing in the past or present that grounds their hope. Marxism truly is a "fool's hope," believing in a better world that has never existed. Furthermore, given their impersonal view of reality, they have no warrant to think that humans are evolving to a higher state since, after all, humans are simply the result of blind, impersonal forces. The only true hope is found in the God of Scripture, who in Christ Jesus our Lord has inaugurated *his* rule in this world, in contrast to the "secularized versions of the kingdom of God" that non-Christian thought offers.[86]

---

[82] See Thomas Molnar, *Utopia: The Perennial Heresy* (New York: University Press of America, 1990).

[83] Boot, *Mission of God*, 163.

[84] On this point, see Boot, 157–87; cf. Dennison, *Karl Marx* (see chap. 2, n. 127).

[85] Pearcey, *Total Truth*, 137.

[86] Pearcey, 137.

Applying the Bible's Theological Framework by Its Plot Movements

Thinking through the Bible's four plot movements has allowed us to begin the theological task by "putting together" Scripture's own interpretive framework as the lens by which we think about God, self, and the world. It also helps us make sure that our theological conclusions are true to the Bible's own categories and presentation, that is, its own biblical-theological framework, from which worldview formation and doctrinal formulation arises.

We want to conclude by sketching two application points. First, we want to illustrate how the Bible's plot movements are foundational for theological formulation as evidenced by Christology. Second, we want to illustrate how the Bible's plot movements are essential in a proper application of Scripture to the domain of ethics.

Christological Formulation and the Bible's Plot Movements

We began this chapter with the perceptive observation of David Wells: to understand correctly the *biblical* Jesus, we must first locate him within the interpretive framework of Scripture; otherwise, we are left with a Jesus of our own imagination. Essential to doing this is thinking through the Bible's plot movements.

For example, think of "creation" and the specific theistic and metaphysical framework it establishes, grounded in theology proper, and especially the Creator-creature distinction. Jesus's identity is tied to *this* God, and it is within *this* framework that Christ's identity is unveiled. Thus, for example, when the NT teaches Jesus's deity, it does so by identifying him with OT Yahweh texts and applying them directly to him (e.g., Rom 10:9; 1 Cor 12:3; Phil 2:11).[87] Also, when the NT applies *theos* texts to Jesus, when set within the Bible's theistic framework, this identifies Jesus with God, which entails trinitarian formulation *and* a two nature Christology.

Regarding the former, in biblical thought, no creature can share the attributes of God (Col 2:9), carry out the works of God (Col 1:15–20; Heb 1:1–3), receive the worship of God (John 5:22–23; Phil 2:9–11; Heb 1:6; Rev 5:11–12), and bear the titles and name of God

---

[87] See Wells, *The Person of Christ*, 21–81; Richard Bauckham, *Jesus and the God of Israel:* God Crucified *and Other Studies on the New Testament's Christology of Divine Identity* (Grand Rapids: Eerdmans, 2008).

(John 1:1, 18; 8:58; 20:28; Rom 9:5; Phil 2:9–11; Heb 1:8–9) unless *he* is God equal with God, and thus one who shares the one, identical divine nature. Regarding the latter, since Jesus is also human, and given the Creator-creature distinction, the only way we can think of the incarnation is in terms of a two nature Christology. Indeed, building on the last observation, Jesus also comes embedded in "creation's" teaching of Adam and humanity's role as image-sons, thus providing the theological rationale for the incarnation and Christ's work as the last Adam and our new covenant head. In fact, given God's promise in Gen 3:15, the entire redemptive plotline of Scripture anticipates another Adam who will undo the disastrous consequences of the first Adam, but thankfully someone who is far greater, thus underscoring Jesus as both a human son and *the* divine Son.

As we think of the fall, especially in regard to the *tension* created between who God is *and* our sin before him, another crucial point emerges for Christology. Given that God *is* the absolute standard of goodness, sin before him is a serious problem. As the *holy* one, God is "the Judge of all the earth" who always does what is right (Gen 18:25). But in promising to justify us *before him* (Gen 15:6; Rom 4:5), God *cannot* overlook our sin; *he* must remain true to his own righteous demand against sin. But how can God remain just *and* the justifier of the ungodly? In Scripture, *this* question drives the Bible's redemptive story. Ultimately, as God's plan unfolds, this question is answered in a specific person, namely, the Messiah, who is the Servant-Son, who alone can redeem us *because he is more than a mere human son*. He is also the divine Son, who becomes human to act as our representative and substitute (Rom 3:21–26). As *God the Son*, he is able to satisfy *his own righteous demand* against us, and as *human*, he is able to obey for us as our new covenant head.

In sum, it is *this* story, as given by the Bible's plot movements, that serves as the framework-theology-worldview for how Scripture identities Christ as God the Son incarnate and the nature of his work. We cannot understand the Jesus of the Bible apart from the Bible's own content, categories, and framework. In this way, the entire Bible speaks of Jesus as the *human son* (Gen 3:15; Matt 1:1), yet he is also the *eternal, divine Son* of the Father, identified with the LORD who has come to save his people from their sins (see Jer 31:34; Matt 1:21; John 1:1–3; 17:3). This last point is especially pertinent since Jesus can only save us from our sins if he is also the divine Son of the Father (Matt 11:25–30; John 5:16–30) who assumed our human nature so that he could bear our sin and make this world right by the ratification of a new covenant in his blood (Rom 3:21–26; 5:1–8:39; 1 Cor 15:1–34; Eph 1:7–10; Heb 8:1–13).

Out of the biblical teaching, Christological formulation arose, and what the church confessed at Nicaea and Chalcedon is simply a further reflection and theological "construction" of what the entire Bible teaches.

Drawing Ethical Application from Scripture

One of the theological challenges we face today is how to apply all that Scripture teaches in regard to God's moral commands. We also confront this challenge in thinking about a Christian's responsibility to the state. Since God has ordained the state to uphold what is right and good (Rom 13:1–7), what exactly is the "good" or "law" that the state is to uphold? Debates ensue within theology over what "law" is applicable to the state, but for our purposes, we want to illustrate how thinking through the Bible's plot movements helps answer these questions.[88]

Since "creation" is foundational to the Bible's story and theological framework, it gives us God's designed order for human life and thus moral norms prior to their distortion in the fall. As God unfolds redemption over time, especially in the coming of Christ and the new covenant, we discover a recovery of creation order/norms, which ultimately gives way to the consummated state in the new creation. As such, with a few nuances, creation establishes what is universal and "normal," sin describes what is "abnormal" and should be opposed, and redemption recovers God's created order and teaches us what *all* people, including the state, ought to value and uphold as good and right according to the standard of God's law.

So what do we find in creation that establishes God's designed order and moral norms that are universally applicable? Minimally, we find the following: the sanctity of human life; the proper use of our sexuality as male and female; the establishment and the protection of heterosexual, monogamous marriage; and the value of labor and property tied to the creation mandate (Gen 1:26–28). Not surprisingly, after the fall, all of these areas are distorted, but what God expects from his creatures, regardless of whether someone is a Christian or not, are these universal norms.

---

[88] For example, see Wayne G. Strickland, ed., *The Law, The Gospel, and the Modern Christian: Five Views* (Grand Rapids: Zondervan, 1993); Michael Hill, *The How and Why of Love: An Introduction to Evangelical Ethics* (Kingsford, Australia: Matthias Media, 2002); Boot, *Mission of God*, 293–359.

For example, think about the sanctity of human life. Given our creation as image-bearers, human life is precious (Gen 1:26–28; cf. Gen 9:6). Strife, anger, murder, and our inhumane treatment of others is a result of the fall. Throughout redemptive history, especially in the Mosaic covenant, these behaviors are explicitly forbidden and punished, but their prohibition is basically the outworking of who we are as created beings. In the NT, our Lord is clear that God's intent from the beginning was for his image-bearers to love God and their neighbors, which is precisely what the entire canon emphasizes (Lev 19:18; Deut 6:5; cf. Matt 22:34–40). Yet, in the new age, the full intent of how we are to love as God's people is now realized in a greater way. This is why Jesus stresses that it is not merely the absence of the act of murder, adultery, or lying that is forbidden, but our very heart-attitude toward one another (Matt 5:21–48). What God demands of his people is love. In the old era, the law covenant demanded it, but it also anticipated something more. Now, in Christ, what the old anticipated is here. This is why Paul can say that love *fulfills* the law (Rom 13:8–10; Gal 5:14)—not an amorphic love, but one governed by God's will and our renewal in Christ by the Spirit. As this understanding of humans and love is applied to ethical issues such as abortion, infanticide, and euthanasia, a sanctity of life ethic is foundational to a Christian ethic and consistent in all of Scripture.

Or think about sexual ethics. Creation gives us God's norm for human sexuality (Gen 1:26–30; 2:15–25). In the creation of male and female, God designed human sexuality to function within the permanent, covenant relationship of heterosexual marriage (Matt 19:4–9). All misuses of our sexuality, whether it is fornication, adultery, divorce, homosexuality, bestiality, or even polygamy, are distortions viewed against the backdrop of God's created order. Sadly, in light of the fall, all sexual distortions are introduced, viewed against God's creation order. Although the Mosaic law explicitly forbids specific sexual distortions (Lev 18:1–30), it is important to see that all of its prohibitions simply unpack the "one flesh" ideal of creation. In addition, given the prophetic function of the law covenant, as the law anticipates a greater righteousness to come, the ethical demand under the new covenant is greater, especially for the church. In Christ's coming and work, the new order has arrived, and the expectation for the church is to live out a proper use of our sexuality as grounded in creation and now what we are in Christ. Yet the creation order for human sexuality is still in place even for non-Christians, and as such, this is what the state is to encourage, uphold, and enforce.

Concluding Reflection

These are two brief examples of application that illustrate how the Bible's plot movements serve as the wide-angle lens that gives shape to the biblical worldview and from which doctrinal formulation arises. But complimentary to the plot movements for "putting together" the Scripture's interpretive framework is also the unfolding of God's eternal plan through the progression of the biblical covenants, which is the subject of the next chapter.

CHAPTER 14

Kingdom through Covenant: Progressive Covenantalism

Introduction

We continue to think through the Bible's long and layered story as we seek to capture the Bible's theological framework, out of which our doctrinal formulations arise. In addition to the Bible's plot movements that offer the "wide-angle" lens that gives shape to the Bible's overall worldview, we can add more specificity to Scripture's interpretive framework by thinking through the unfolding of God's eternal plan from creation to the new creation by the progression of the biblical covenants. Our goal is to "put together" Scripture according to its own presentation, content, and categories. As already noted, this is the task of biblical theology, which is neither presuppositionless nor beyond dispute. Christians differ on how best to construct the Bible's overall story, which we will discuss in the next chapter. Yet, given our conviction that Scripture is first-order and that it can correct our interpretations, we propose that "progressive covenantalism" is the best way of making sense of the Bible's own terms and how God's plan unfolds and reaches its culmination in Christ Jesus our Lord.

Scripture presents a *plurality* of covenants (Gal 4:24; Eph 2:12; Heb 8:7–13) that *progressively* reveal our triune God's *one* redemptive plan for his *one* people, which reaches its fulfillment, telos, and terminus in Christ and the new covenant. In Scripture, covenants are more than a unifying theme; they are the *backbone* to the Bible's entire storyline, the relational reality and architectural structure that moves history forward according to God's design and final plan for humanity and all creation. "Kingdom through the progression of the covenants" captures the fundamental dynamic at work as God's redemptive plan unfolds, which starts with Adam and creation and culminates in Christ. The "creation covenant" is the foundation that continues in *all* the covenants, and it is fulfilled in Christ and his obedient work. God's plan moves from creation in Adam to consummation in Christ, and each biblical covenant contributes to God's unified plan. To comprehend "the whole plan of God" (Acts 20:27), we must locate each covenant in its own context and then understand it in terms of what precedes *and* follows it. By the *progression* of the covenants, God's glorious plan and promises are unveiled, and we discover not only how all of God's promises are fulfilled in our Lord Jesus Christ (Heb 1:1–3; cf. Eph 1:9–10) but also how to live as God's new covenant people as we await the consummation at Christ's return.

Let us now add more detail to the Bible's overall covenantal framework by first saying something about *kingdom* before we explain how God's kingdom is progressively realized through the unfolding covenants, all of which is necessary to grasp for doctrinal formulation.[1]

"Kingdom" through Covenant

In the previous chapter, the concept of the kingdom was highlighted due to humanity's creation in God's image-likeness and our mandate to rule over the world (Gen 1:26–28). Now we want to summarize the idea of "God's kingdom" across the canon, adding detail to what was written. Graeme Goldsworthy correctly notes that, "The idea of the rule of God over creation, over all creatures, over the kingdoms of the world, and in a unique and special way, over his chosen and redeemed people, is the very heart of the message of the Hebrew scriptures."[2] Further, as Tom Schreiner demonstrates, God's kingdom is not only central to the OT but also "of prime importance in New Testament theology."[3] Four points need to be made to capture how the idea of the kingdom is understood in the OT before we see how the concept is brought to fulfillment in Christ.

---

[1] For a detailed treatment of this material, see Gentry and Wellum, *Kingdom through Covenant* (see chap. 13, n. 39).

[2] Graeme Goldsworthy, "Kingdom of God," in *NDBT*, 618 (see chap. 1, n. 24).

[3] Schreiner, *New Testament Theology*, 41 (see chap. 4, n. 62).

1. *The Triune God is the Universal Lord.* As outlined in the last chapter, Scripture begins with the declaration that God is the sovereign Creator, ruler, and King of the universe. From the opening verses of Scripture, God is identified as the Lord who created the universe by his word, while he himself is eternal and in need of nothing outside himself, thus having divine aseity (Pss 50:12–14; 93:2; Acts 17:24–25). God alone is God, utterly unique and complete within himself. As such, God alone is to be worshipped, trusted, and obeyed; he is the King and the entire universe is his kingdom. Psalm 103:19 states it this way: "The LORD has established his throne in heaven, and his kingdom rules over all" (cf. Ps 47:8; Dan 4:34–35).

Additionally, God's kingly work in creation is *not* an end in itself; instead, it is the beginning of God's eternal plan in time (Eph 1:11; Rev 4:11), which *he* directs toward a specific telos. Creation begins a drama that drives the course of history, what we call "redemptive history," to the end designed for it by its Creator and Lord. Creation, then, is *foundational* to the Bible's entire story. Creation leads to providence, and both creation and providence establish the eschatological direction of God's plan, purposely worked out in specific covenantal relationships God initiates, which, in the end, all lead to a specific goal centered in Christ (cf. Col 1:15–20). Although the *wording* "kingdom of God" is not found until much later in Scripture, the *idea* or *concept* is taught in Genesis 1–2.

2. *The Fall and God's Saving Reign.* Although our triune God is Creator and Lord, the fall changes everything from "very good" (Gen 1:31) to cursed and abnormal. Although the nature of creation's goodness is disputed, in light of Genesis 3, it minimally conveys the idea of moral goodness and purity.[4] Yet now, in light of human rebellion, God's rightful rule over the entire creation is rejected by his creatures. Sin is essentially rebellion against the claims of the King—moral autonomy—and so, as a result of our sin, we now stand under God's judicial sentence of condemnation, guilt, and death (Gen 2:16–17; Rom 3:23; 6:23).

[4] Some argue that "goodness" only refers to God's intention to bring about his purposes for creation, which does not necessitate a "perfect" world, thus allowing for death to exist before the fall. Adam and Eve were created mortal (like animals), but the penalty for their sin was a "new" kind of death. See William J. Dumbrell, *The Search for Order: Biblical Eschatology in Focus* (Grand Rapids: Baker, 1994), 20–22. A better view is to think of "goodness" as tied to moral realities, thus arguing that death and suffering did not exist prior to the fall; these realities are due to Adam's sin and divine judgment (see Gen 2:17; 3:19; Rom 5:12; 6:23). See Kulikovsky, *Creation, Fall, Restoration*, 204–20 (see chap. 5, n. 85).

Given the fall, the OT distinguishes between God's sovereign rule over creation and his coming *saving reign* to make all things right. For God to save, *he* must act, which sets the stage for the Bible's story of a coming Redeemer to set creation right and to usher in a new creation. As D. A. Carson reminds us, "Ultimately that plot-line anticipates the restoration of goodness, even the transformation to a greater glory, of the universe gone wrong (Rom 8:21), and arrives finally at the dawning of a new heaven and a new earth (Rev 21–22; cf. Isa 65:17), the home of righteousness (2 Peter 3:13)."[5] On the one hand, the kingdom of God will exclude all sin and rebellion. On the other hand, it will include all that is redeemed according to God's sovereign choice and action. Eventually, when all sin and evil is put down, we will see the fullness of God's kingdom in new covenant relationship—a new creation—in contrast to the old creation, which was lost due to Adam's sin and rebellion while acting as our representative head.

3. *The Coming of God's Redemptive Kingdom*. How does the *saving* kingdom of God come? As the OT unfolds, God's saving reign comes to this world *through* the covenants in two ways. First, it comes *through* (or "in," i.e., synchronically) the covenant relationship God establishes with his image-bearers, that is, his priest-kings. In this relationship, God's rule is extended through his people *and* to the entire creation, and we realize the purpose of our existence under God's rule. But, sadly, we have failed in our calling, which leads to the second use of *through*.

Second, God's kingdom comes *through* (or *over time*, i.e., diachronically) the covenants. *Through* the unfolding of the covenants, God has chosen to reverse the disastrous effects of sin and usher in his saving reign in this world. Following the loss of Eden, redemption is linked to the election of a people and by means of a promised human (Gen 3:15), which is given greater definition *through* Noah and his family, Abraham and his seed, the nation of Israel, and, uniquely, David and his sons/kings. These people, tied to the nation of Israel, are promised a land to dwell in; they will be the means of blessing to the nations. Moreover, *by* covenantal progression these promises, which stretch back to the *protevangelium* of Gen 3:15, are realized. In the exodus, which becomes a type/pattern of redemption, God reveals his redemptive plan. At Sinai, the people of God are constituted as a theocratic nation—a *kingdom* of priests and a holy nation called to serve the Lord (Exod 19:6), reveal God to the nations, and, *through* Israel as a nation, to usher in God's saving reign to this world (cf. Gen 12:1–3).

[5] Carson, *Gagging of God*, 202 (see chap. 2, n. 1).

Though rebellion leads to delay, the nation is eventually given possession of the land. Here the structures of government develop toward kingship under the dynasty of David in Jerusalem. Solomon builds the temple as the place where reconciliation and fellowship with God are established, a temple that stretches back to the garden-sanctuary of Eden itself.[6] The rule of the Davidic kings is representative of the rule of God over his kingdom. But Israel *and* the kings disobey; the kingdom divides and judgment falls. God's saving reign is not realized through these people and covenant heads; it is only typified, foreshadowed, and anticipated, as God had planned from eternity. In the end, it awaits the coming of the great antitype of Adam, Noah, Abraham, Moses, Israel, David, and his sons: Christ Jesus. It is only through this true, obedient image-Son that God's long-awaited kingdom is inaugurated in this world *through* the new covenant.

4. *The Promises Proclaimed by the Prophets*. In the OT, these promises, hopes, and expectations are announced by the prophets, who all write *after* the establishment of the Davidic covenant, an important point we will return to below. As the prophets look to the future, God announces through them hope for Israel and the Gentile nations. The prophets not only call Israel back to covenant loyalty but also proclaim an overall pattern of renewal by recapitulating the past history of redemption as developed through the typological patterns of the covenants.[7] They anticipate that in the "last days," the Lord will come to save his people through a new exodus, the establishment of a new temple and new Jerusalem, and a new Davidic king to rule in a glorious and eternal kingdom—all of which is tied to the coming of the new covenant age. In this way, the prophets anticipate the coming of the Lord and his Messiah-Son, specifically the Davidic king, who will usher in *God's* kingdom, making all things right and reversing the effects of sin and death (e.g., Pss 2; 45; 110; Isa 7:14; 9:6–7; 11:1–16; 42:1–9; 49:1–7; 52:13–53:12; Ezek 34:1–26). But this coming of *God's kingdom* will only occur *through* the ratification of a new covenant by the work of the Messiah, who is closely identified with the Lord, thus bringing to fulfillment all of God's promises as revealed through the covenants.

---

[6] See Gladd, *From Adam and Israel*, 5–57 (see chap. 13, n. 44); see also G. K. Beale and Mitchell Kim, *God Dwells Among Us: Expanding Eden to the Ends of the Earth* (Downers Grove: InterVarsity, 2016).

[7] On this point see Goldsworthy, *Christ-Centered Biblical Theology*, 111–49 (see chap. 1, n. 37).

This synopsis of the kingdom takes us to the end of the OT and the prophetic hope of God's future saving work—truths that the NT says have now come in Christ. At this point, it is vital to note that it is *this* OT teaching that serves as the backdrop for the NT's teaching on the kingdom and its inauguration in Christ and as *the* framework that structures our doctrinal formulations.

Kingdom *"through Covenant"*

In Scripture, *kingdom* and *covenant* are inseparable since it is *through* the covenants that God's saving reign comes to this world. This is why grasping the progression of the covenants is central to understanding how God's kingdom comes in Christ, how God's redemptive promise is realized, and how the Bible's metanarrative hangs together since the covenants constitute the framework and backbone for God's unfolding plan from creation to consummation.

Although Scripture refers to many covenants, our focus is on the six main covenants: creation, Noahic, Abrahamic, Mosaic, Davidic, and the new. In theology, the relationship between the covenants has been and is today disputed, especially between the two dominant biblical-theological systems of covenant and dispensational theology, which we will describe in the next chapter. Yet, despite differences between the views, there is probably more agreement than not. For example, minimally, both affirm that God has *one* plan of salvation, that history unfolds God's plan centered in Christ, and that Scripture moves from creation to fall, from Abraham to David, and finally to Christ. However, contrary to covenant theology that thinks of God's one redemptive plan in terms of *the* "covenant of grace" or "dispensational theology" that tends to partition history in terms of dispensations, it is better to think of God's *one* redemptive plan, grounded in the "covenant of redemption" (*pactum salutis*), revealed through a *plurality* of covenants (e.g., Gal 4:24; Eph 2:12; Heb 8:7–13), all of which reach their fulfillment in Christ and the new covenant. Post-fall and due to God's promise (Gen 3:15), God's *one* redemptive plan is revealed through the covenants *as the new covenant is progressively unveiled*. This allows us to think of the *continuity* of God's plan across time, now fulfilled in Christ, and it also helps us avoid "flattening" the *differences* between the covenants, which directly impacts a number of theological issues, specifically ecclesiology and eschatology. *Each* covenant, then, directs the life of those under it, but *each* covenant is also revelatory and prophetic of who and what is to come, namely Christ and the new covenant.

Before I summarize my understanding of the progression of the covenants, it is important to outline five hermeneutical points about the covenants that affect how I think the covenants fit together and that distinguish my view from covenant and dispensational theology.

Some Hermeneutical Points Regarding the Covenants

1. *The significance of progressive revelation for the unfolding of the biblical covenants.* As discussed in parts 1 and 2, Scripture comes to us over time. God's self-disclosure, alongside his redemptive work, unfolds by twists and turns, largely demarcated by the covenants. In this way, God's *one* plan unfolds step-by-step, culminating in Christ. The *progression* of the covenants is the primary means by which God's plan is unveiled, and God's promises *and* God-intended typological patterns are given, developed, and fulfilled in Christ and his people. For this reason, it is best to view *all* of the covenants as organically interrelated.

As God acts to redeem, the covenants disclose God's eternal plan and reveal many truths: who God is, the purpose of our creation, and how we are to live in relationship with God and each other. Most importantly, in light of the tragedy of human sin, the covenants teach us how God graciously chooses to redeem a fallen people for himself and set everything right, while also revealing a growing tension in the covenant relationship between God and his image-bearers. We discover how God is always faithful to his promises and obligations, while we are not, even though he demands total obedience from his responsible creatures. Through covenantal progression, we discover how God's promises to restore his elect from every nation to covenant relationship with him is ultimately achieved through the obedient work of God the Son incarnate, which was God's plan from eternity (Eph 1:4, 9–10; Col 1:17).

2. *The three contexts/horizons of biblical interpretation and their importance for understanding the progression of the covenants.* Since God's plan is revealed through the covenants, each covenant must be interpreted within three expanding contexts. First, the covenant must be understood within its own immediate context (i.e., textual context). Second, the covenant must be interpreted in light of what preceded it (i.e., epochal context) so we can see the unfolding nature of God's plan. Third, the covenant must be understood in terms of its fulfillment in Christ and the ratification of the new covenant (i.e., canonical context).

By tracing out the covenants in this fashion, we are able to see how the entire plan of God is *organically* related and how it reaches its culmination and fulfillment in Christ. Also, it is only when we do this that we rightly see how the *parts* of God's plan fit with the *whole* and that the theological conclusions we draw are truly *biblical* and thus warranted.

3. *The progression of the covenants is the primary means by which God's promises and typological patterns unfold and are fulfilled in Christ and his people.* In chapter 4, we noted that the "promise-fulfillment" motif is central to how Scripture glues the diverse epochs of his plan together. However, it is difficult to think of God's promises apart from the covenants. By covenantal progression, the biblical authors speak of the continuity of God's plan (tied to his promises) and its discontinuity (how fulfillment brings about God-intended changes). Also, *one* way that the promise-fulfillment motif is developed is via *typology*, which is unpacked through covenantal progression. This is why the progression of the covenants is the primary means by which we grasp how *all* of God's promises are "yes and amen" in Christ (2 Cor 1:20) and how *all* of the typological patterns find their fulfillment in Christ and his people. Thus, starting in creation and then unveiled *through* the covenants, we discover the full depth of the meaning of God's promises and how specific God-intended patterns, centered in specific persons, events, and institutions, reach their telos in Christ and the new covenant age.

For example, Adam, as the covenant head of the old creation, anticipates and looks forward to the coming of the "last Adam," our Lord Jesus Christ, who is the head of the new covenant (Rom 5:14). In the meantime, as the covenants are introduced and build on each other, "other Adams" appear on the stage of human history, who assume the role of the first Adam (e.g., Noah, Abraham, Israel, David). Yet none of these "other Adams" are the ultimate fulfillment, although they point beyond themselves in prophetic expectation of the "last Adam" to come. In this way, by the unfolding of the covenants, these typological patterns take on greater definition and clarity until the antitype arrives. What is true of Adam is also true of other typological patterns, whether they be various persons (e.g., Moses, Israel, David, prophets, priests, and kings), events (e.g., the exodus), or institutions (e.g., sacrificial system, tabernacle-temple). By this means, Scripture moves from lesser to greater and grounds the greater nature of Christ and the new covenant age.

4. *The new covenant is the fulfillment and telos of the biblical covenants.* Since *all* of the covenants are part of God's one plan, no covenant is unrelated to what preceded it, and no covenant makes sense apart from its fulfillment in Christ. No doubt, new covenant fulfillment involves an "already not yet," and until Christ comes again, creation order/structures continue

as promised in the Noahic covenant, an important point we will return to below. Yet, given Christ's coming, all of the previous covenants find their telos, or are "summed up," in him.[8]

For this reason, the new covenant is the *fulfillment* of the previous covenants; it has brought the other covenants to their God-intended end. *Fulfillment* in the NT primarily means that what the previous covenants revealed, anticipated, and predicted through instruction and various patterns is now here, albeit in inaugurated form.[9] This is why our Lord is presented as greater than Adam by undoing what Adam did and thus winning for us the new creation;[10] the true seed and offspring of Abraham, who brings blessings to the nations by his cross work; the true Israel, fulfilling all that she failed to be; and David's greater son, who rules the nations and the entire creation as King of kings and Lord of lords.

However, in *fulfilling* the previous covenants, this does not entail that the earlier covenants have no value for us today. The previous covenants are forever Scripture, and thus for our instruction and fully authoritative (2 Tim 3:16–17). But now that Christ has come, Christians are no longer under the previous covenants *as covenants* (except the Noahic until the end). This entails that we, as the church, obey *all* of Scripture, but now in light of Christ's coming and the new covenant age (1 Cor 9:19–21). This is an important point, especially in thinking about the proper application of the OT to believers today. This is consistent with the NT's presentation of our Lord who, as Carson notes in regard to Matt 5:17–20, is "the eschatological goal of the OT, and thereby its sole authoritative interpreter, the one through whom alone the OT finds its valid continuity and significance."[11]

5. *To categorize the covenants as either unconditional/unilateral (royal grant) or conditional/ bilateral (suzerain-vassal) is inadequate.*[12] By this distinction, some argue that the Abrahamic,

---

[8] In Christ, Paul argues, God's eternal plan is "summed up" (*anakephalaioō*) (Eph 1:9–10). This is another way of saying that Christ and his work is the telos (goal, end) of God's plan.

[9] See Carson for this understanding of fulfillment. *Matthew*, 117–26, 171–80 (see chap. 8, n. 71).

[10] We are using the word *undoing* in two ways. Christ, as the last Adam, "undoes" the fall by offering himself as a penal substitutionary sacrifice on our behalf. He also "does" what Adam failed to do; namely, as the true Son, he acts in complete devotion and obedience to his Father. These two ways correspond to what Reformed theologians have referred to as the "active and passive obedience" of Christ as our covenant head acting on behalf of his people.

[11] Carson, *Matthew*, 177.

[12] In contrast to Paul R. Williamson, *Sealed with an Oath: Covenant in God's Unfolding Purpose*, NSBT 23 (Downers Grove: InterVarsity, 2007), 17–43; Michael S. Horton, *God of Promise: Introducing*

Davidic, and new covenant are unconditional, while the covenant of works and the Mosaic Law are conditional. Or some draw "law-gospel" contrasts so that the covenant of works and the old covenant are "law" (bilateral), while the Abrahamic, Davidic, and the new covenant are "gospel" (unilateral).[13] This way of distinguishing the covenants is problematic since each covenant contains both elements. For example, God initiates each covenant, and each covenant is undergirded by sovereign grace. In this sense, the biblical covenants are "monergistic"; that is, God first acts to initiate and establish a covenant relationship with his people. However, God also demands from us complete loyalty, devotion, and obedience, hence God's demand for perfect obedience. This is not only true of the creation covenant, but it is also true of each covenant. In fact, because both of these elements are present in each covenant, there is a deliberate *tension* within the covenants—a tension that heightens as God's plan unfolds and is only resolved in Christ and his representative and covenantal obedience as the last Adam for us.[14] The *theological* categories of "Law" and "gospel" are correct, and a dismissal of them has serious consequences. To undermine these theological truths affects our understanding of God's total demand from his creatures, the nature of sin, the nature of Christ's work, and how sinners are justified before God by faith alone in Christ alone. However, Scripture does not derive these categories by simply dividing the covenants into either bilateral or unilateral covenants. This is too reductionistic.

Instead, on the one hand, the covenants gloriously reveal our triune Lord, who makes *and* keeps his promises, hence the emphasis on the unilateral. As God initiates covenant relationships with his creatures, he is always the faithful partner—true to his own nature and promises (Heb 6:17–18). Regardless of our unfaithfulness, God's promises, commencing in Gen 3:15, are certain and guaranteed. On the other hand, God, as our Creator and Lord, demands from us full devotion, which is true in every covenant. This is evident with Adam, as he is given commands and responsibilities to fulfill with the expectation and demand that he will do so in complete devotion. Obedience is also demanded from Noah, Abraham, Israel, David, and his

---

Covenant Theology (Grand Rapids: Baker, 2006), 23–110.

[13] See for example, Kline, *Structure of Biblical Authority* (see chap. 8, n. 770); Horton, *God of Promise*, 23–76.

[14] See A. B. Caneday, "Covenantal Life with God from Eden to Holy City," in Wellum and Parker, *Progressive Covenantalism*, 101–26 (see chap. 4, n. 34).

sons, but it is only in *the* Son that perfect covenant keeping results in his entire life and death (Phil 2:6–11).

However, as the covenants unfold, a *tension* grows between who God is in himself and his promise to redeem and our disobedience. Obedience is not an option for us. God is holy and just; he is the absolute standard of goodness, but we have sinned against *him*. But in light of Gen 3:15, God's promises are tied to the provision of an obedient son, who will undo Adam's disastrous choice. But where do we find such a son who fully obeys and meets God's moral demands? How can God remain in relationship with us unless our sin is removed? It is *through* the covenants that this tension increases, and it is through the same covenants that the answer is given: God himself—our covenant maker and keeper—must *unilaterally* act to keep his own promise by the provision of an *obedient* covenant partner, our Lord Jesus Christ.[15]

It is only by maintaining the dual emphasis of unilateral/bilateral in the covenants, leading us to their fulfillment in the unbreakable new covenant in Christ, that we grasp Scripture's glorious Christological focus. The Bible's storyline as unveiled through the covenants leads us to him. Jesus alone, who is God the Son incarnate and our great prophet, priest, and king, can secure our salvation. In Christ alone, the covenants are fulfilled and this built-in tension is resolved.

With these five hermeneutical points in place, let us now outline a biblical-theological summary of the relationship between the covenants and their fulfillment in Christ and the inauguration of the new covenant age, out of which our doctrinal formulations arise.

From Creation to the Promise of the New Covenant

Adam and the Covenant with Creation

Covenant theology refers to the covenant in Genesis 1–2 as the "covenant of works," and dispensational theologians rarely speak of a covenant with creation, or at least it does not

[15] Reformed theology rightly spoke of this in terms of Christ's active and passive obedience, which is foundational for soteriology, specifically the doctrine of justification. Active obedience refers to Christ's total obedience to the demands of the covenant/law in his life as our covenant representative, and passive obedience refers to his complete obedience in his death as our covenant, penal substitute. Both are necessary for our justification.

factor much into their theological system. For covenant theology, the "covenant of works" is made with Adam as the head/representative of the human race. To him and his entire posterity, eternal life is promised upon the condition of perfect obedience to God's law. But due to his disobedience, Adam, along with all humanity, was plunged into a state of sin, death, and condemnation. But God, by his sovereign grace and initiative, did not leave humans in this condition, but instead gave a saving promise, which is identified with "the covenant of grace," wherein God offered to sinners salvation through the last Adam, the covenantal head of his people, the Lord Jesus Christ. The covenant of grace commences in Gen 3:15, and all of the subsequent covenants (Noahic, Abrahamic, Mosaic, Davidic, and the new covenant) are subsets of it reflecting administrative differences throughout redemptive history, but each covenant is essentially the same.

Although this formulation is standard for covenant theology, some have questioned the validity of a "covenant of works" or any covenant in Genesis 1–2 due to the absence of the word *covenant* (*bĕrît*), which first occurs in Gen 6:18, and the idea of Adam *working* to merit the gift of eternal life. One must demonstrate caution regarding the notion of *works* in this context since Adam already stands in right relationship to God, yet Adam's state is not the glorified state we have in Christ, so the idea of probation and the need for covenantal obedience is legitimate.[16] Adam's task (and the task of humanity) was to extend "God's rule over the created order, so that his divine presence would radiate out from them. . . . God's aim is for humanity to spread [his] glorious presence over the entire earth, so it may be transformed into the new heaven and earth,"[17] resulting in a permanent and glorified state. Thus, it is legitimate to contend for a "covenant of creation" with Adam serving as the covenant mediator for at least three reasons.

First, the absence of the word *covenant* does *not* entail that there is no covenant; context and later Scripture are decisive (e.g., Hos 6:7; Gen 2:19–25 [marriage]). Exegetically, there is

---

[16] In light of the end of the Bible's story, it is best to affirm that Adam's original situation was temporary, which the tree of life seems to imply, as a fully obedient Adam, at some point, would have been granted eternal life. On this point, see Greg Nichols, *Covenant Theology: A Reformed and Baptistic Perspective on God's Covenants* (Birmingham: Solid Ground Christian Books, 2011), 321–58; Frame, *Systematic Theology*, 62–81 (see chap. 5, n. 1).

[17] Gladd, *From Adam and Israel*, 14, 20.

a distinction between cutting (for the first time) and establishing (continuing) a covenant.[18] In Gen 6:17–18 and 9:8–17, God "establishes" (Gen 6:18; 9:9, 11, 17) a covenant with Noah, which implies a preexisting *covenant* relationship, which can only be found in Adam and rooted in creation. Later Scripture confirms this point (Hos 6:7).

Second, contextually, when we turn to Genesis 2, it is a "covenant context." Although the word *covenant* is not used, all the elements of a Lord/vassal agreement are in the context, including conditions of obedience and sanctions of disobedience (Gen 2:16–17).[19] In addition, God identifies himself by his covenant name: Yahweh (Gen 2:4, 5, 7, 8; Exod 3:13–15). When the Israelites read the Pentateuch, they would have identified God's covenant name from Exodus 3 with Adam in creation. It is difficult to avoid the conclusion that Moses identifies the covenant God of Israel with Adam and creation. What we discover in Genesis 1–2 is an original and unique situation, which involved, especially in light of the rest of Scripture, Adam in a representative role on behalf of all humanity (cf. Rom 5:12–21; 1 Cor 15:20–21).

This point is further warranted by the truth that Adam (and all of humanity) is created as God's image and by the link between image and sonship, concepts tied to covenant relationships. As noted in the previous chapter, although people dispute the exact meaning of the *imago dei*—the terms *image* (*selem*) and *likeness* (*demut*) convey the idea that Adam is created to rule over creation as God's representative priest-king, which also extends to all humanity.[20] In fact, *image* speaks of Adam's relationship to the creation: he is vice-regent over it, while *likeness*

---

[18] See Gentry and Wellum, *Kingdom through Covenant*, 155–61; cf. William J. Dumbrell, *Covenant and Creation: A Theology of the Old Testament Covenants* (Carlisle, UK: Paternoster, 1984), 11–26, 31–39.

[19] God's demand upon Adam is stated in Gen 2:16–17. In Hebrew the infinite absolute is used to add great force—"eating you shall eat" and "dying you shall die." In the first case, the tone is that of fullness of permission. God is presented as the God of superabundance. God even *commands* this permission. On the other hand, disobedience to the command brings with it the threat of death. The use of the language underscores the importance of humanity's responsibility before God and the juridical aspect of the covenant. On the one hand, there is enjoyment of the Lord's gifts and the mandate to extend God's rule and glory to the entire creation as God's priest-kings, but on the other hand, is the condition of obedience by which Adam (and Eve) will fulfill their calling. Thus, it is best to think of this initial state as temporary, one in which if Adam and his progeny had obeyed and fulfilled their calling, it would have resulted in a glorified, consummated state. Sadly, Adam disobeyed, and it is only in Christ that humanity's calling is achieved by his covenantal obedience and work.

[20] See Gladd, *From Adam and Israel*, 5–21.

speaks of Adam's relationship to God.[21] Thus, there is a dual relationship of Adam and humans to God and to creation, confirmed by Gen 1:26c: we were created in order to have dominion over the world. A crucial text that buttresses this point is Psalm 8, which describes human beings in royal terms. Importantly, this text is applied to Christ in Heb 2:5–18, where Christ is not only the true "image of God" as the divine Son (see Col 1:15; cf. Heb 1:3) but also, by the incarnation, takes on our "image" and fulfills humanity's calling as the obedient incarnate Son. In all these ways, *image* and *likeness* are terms that signify our uniqueness, our dignity before God, and the representative role we play for the entire creation as God's servant priest-kings. This entails that God deals with creation on the basis of how he deals with humans, and all of this implies a covenantal relationship as mediated through Adam as our covenant head.

This truth is further underscored by the link between "image/likeness" and "sonship" and then "sonship" to the biblical covenants. Just as *image* carries a representational meaning, so does *son*.[22] In fact, the NT draws this connection by identifying Adam as the "son" of God (Luke 3:38). This makes sense because *sonship* is also representational in meaning. Adam is the "image" and "son" because he is the representative of God, as is the entire human race. He is to act and function in a way similar to God, under his sovereign rule, as a creature and vice-regent of God. As the covenants unfold, this same notion of "son" is applied to Israel (Exod 4:22; cf. Hos 11:1) and to the Davidic king(s) (2 Sam 7:14; Ps 2). In every instance, Israel as a nation and David and his sons are to represent the Lord by extending God's rule and presence to the entire creation. For this reason, *image* and *son* are terms tied to covenantal relationships, and they are crucial in making sense of Christ as the head of the new covenant. Scripture applies to the divine Son the expressions *image* and *Son* (as the original, archetype) and then describes how he is the antitypical fulfillment of Adam, Israel, and David. In this way, Scripture unpacks who Jesus is as the eternal Son in relation to the Father (and Spirit) *and* in relation to the incarnation, as the one who becomes the human image/son, thus revealing that he is both truly God and truly human.

Third, canonically and theologically, the Bible's entire story is centered on two foundational, representative individuals: Adam and Christ (Rom 5:12–21). It is difficult to think of Christ as the head of the new covenant without Adam as the head of a covenant in the original situation. What best explains this relationship is a "covenant with creation" where Adam stands in a unique

---

[21] See Gentry and Wellum, *Kingdom through Covenant*, 225–38.

[22] On this point see McCartney, "*Ecce Homo*," 3–7 (see chap. 13, n. 39).

and singular situation as head of humanity. As God's priest-king/son, Adam is given the mandate to rule over God's creation, to put all things under his feet (cf. Ps 8), and to establish the pattern of God's kingdom in this world, spreading God's glorious presence to the entire creation.[23] But, sadly, Adam, as our covenant head, disobeyed, and all humanity *and* creation is affected. Unless God acts in grace and power, in Adam, the original creation is under divine judgment. But thankfully God has promised that his purposes for humanity and creation will continue by his provision of a *human* seed (Gen 3:15), a Redeemer, which has to be understood as ultimately bringing about the reversal of the disastrous effects of Adam's sin and the achievement of our calling as humans in the world to see God's glorious presence fully realized in a new creation.

Theologically, the significance of the Adam-Christ typological relationship (Rom 5:12–21; 1 Cor 15:20–23; cf. Heb 2:5–18) for understanding the Bible's own categories, structures, and teaching is crucial. All humans fall under the representative headship of either Adam or Christ. Adam represents the "old creation" and "this present age," characterized by the "flesh," namely sin, death, and judgment.[24] Christ represents the "new creation," which from the perspective of the OT prophets is identified with the "age to come" (tied to a new covenant), characterized by the "Spirit" and thus salvation, life, and restoration. In fact, "Jew and Gentile" (all of humanity) are subsumed under Adam so that anyone who is "in Adam" now enters the world dead in their sins and under the judicial sentence of God (see Eph 2:1–3). Adam's headship, then, is more than ordinary fatherhood. It defines what it means to be human both in terms of our physical *and* covenantal head (1 Cor 15:49), and now, due to his sin, to be "in Adam" also speaks of the nature of the human problem of sin before God with all of its disastrous ramifications.

The Significance of the Creation Covenant. The value of starting with a "creation covenant" for understanding the Bible's story and *how* the covenants relate to each other cannot be overstated for at least two reasons.

---

[23] See Goldsworthy, *According to Plan*, 99 (see chap. 13, n. 40); cf. Gladd, *From Adam and Israel*, 5–21.

[24] In the NT, Paul can speak of being "in Adam" as being in the "flesh." Conversely, being "in Christ" is to be "in the Spirit" (Rom 8:1–17; Gal 5:16–26; Eph 2:1–3). These categories are not referring to "physical" vs. "spiritual" but to ages in redemptive history, one identified with the covenant headship of Adam and the other identified with the new covenant headship of Christ. Cf. Schreiner, *New Testament Theology*, 534–39; Ridderbos, *Paul*, 64–68, 100–7 (see chap. 13, n. 81).

First, the creation covenant is *foundational* for all future covenants since *all* later covenants unpack Adam's representative role in the world. Adam, and all humanity, is created as God's image-son, prophet-priest-king to rule over creation. Adam is created in relationship with God to mediate God's rule to the world with the goal of entering eschatological rest. And God demands from Adam, the creature, full devotion, obedience, and covenant loyalty, which he does not render. *All* subsequent covenant heads function as subsets of Adam, who, in God's plan, point forward to Christ, the last Adam, who by his obedience ratifies a new covenant, which is progressively revealed through the covenants. None of these covenant heads are the true "seed of the woman," and as such, none of them can fulfill humanity's calling. Instead, each one typifies in some way the true covenant keeper to come, and through their line, our Lord Jesus Christ comes as the true seed of Abraham and David's greater Son (Matt 1:1; Gal 3:16). In Christ alone, the original situation is recovered and God's intent for humanity is secured. For this reason, all the previous covenants find their fulfillment and telos in Christ and the new covenant, which underscores why the new covenant age is greater than what preceded it. Although the amount of space devoted to Adam is small, his role as the representative head of creation defines what comes after him and the entire work of Christ (Rom 5:12–21; 1 Cor 15:21–28; Heb 2:5–18).

Second, the creation covenant is foundational for establishing various typological patterns that eventually reach their telos in Christ and the new covenant. For example, think of the creation week, which culminates in God's rest on the seventh day after he declared everything "very good" (Gen 1:31). This not only speaks of God's entering into covenantal enjoyment of his creation and our enjoyment of God as we carry out our creation mandate as servant kings. It also lays down a structure/pattern for humanity. Adam is to "work" by fulfilling the creation mandate in order to enter into God's eschatological rest, ultimately in terms of the enjoyment of God's presence in a new creation (Rev 21–22). This structure/pattern is what grounds the later Sabbath law under the Mosaic covenant (Exod 20:8–11), which in turn functions as a type that looks back to creation and forward in redemption (Deut 5:15) to the new creation and a greater "rest" to come in Christ (Heb 3:7–4:13).[25] Or think of Eden as a garden-temple

---

[25] See Thomas R. Schreiner, "Good-bye and Hello: The Sabbath Command for New Covenant Believers," in Wellum and Parker, *Progressive Covenantalism*, 159–88; cf. D. A. Carson, ed., *From Sabbath to Lord's Day: A Biblical, Historical and Theological Investigation* (Grand Rapids: Zondervan, 1982).

mountain sanctuary, the emphasis on the land tied to creation, and how these patterns eventually find their fulfillment in our Lord Jesus, who is the antitypical fulfillment of the temple and who inaugurates the new creation, which both have a spillover effect and benefit for the church.[26] Or think of the establishment of marriage in Gen 2:24–25 and how, through the covenants, marriage pictures a greater reality, namely, God's relationship to his people and Christ's relationship to the church, which ultimately points forward to the consummation.[27] *All* of these patterns eschatologically terminate in Christ and his people and the consummated state. In these ways, the creation covenant in seed-form sows structures/patterns, which, through the covenants, reach their mature growth and full bloom in Christ, the church, and dawning of the new creation.

The Creation Covenant, the Fall, and the Promise. We cannot think of the "creation covenant" without mentioning the twofold emphasis on the entrance of sin into the world *and* God's first redemption promise—a promise that receives greater definition, clarification, and expansion in subsequent covenants. Let us highlight both of these emphases since they are central to the Bible's covenantal storyline.

First, Genesis 3 is crucial in describing how, in history, sin and evil came into the human realm—and thus the desperate nature of human depravity, which *God alone* can remedy.[28] Scripture, from beginning to end, takes the reality of sin and evil seriously. In moving from Genesis 1–2, we see how quickly humans move from a "very good" world (Gen 1:31) to an abnormal and cursed one (Gen 3:14–24), one now under God's judgment and under the sentence of death. Adam, after having received every blessing imaginable from God as well as the direct command not to eat of the tree of the knowledge of good and evil and with the warning still ringing in his ears—"for in the day that you eat of it you shall surely die" (Gen 2:17 ESV)—acts in willful, autonomous rebellion against God and thus, tragically, turns the created order upside down. Instead of ruling over the unclean serpent (Gen 3:1), keeping the temple sanctuary of Eden pure and undefiled, and obeying God's commands (Gen 2:15–17),

---

[26] See Beale, *Temple and the Church's Mission* (see chap. 13, n. 44).

[27] Raymond C. Ortlund Jr., *God's Unfaithful Wife*, NSBT 2 (Downers Grove: InterVarsity, 2003).

[28] My focus is primarily on human sin, not the entrance of sin into the angelic realm, which we will discuss later. Not much is said in Scripture about the time or the fall of the angels. It must have occurred before the fall of man, considering the arrival of the serpent in Gen 3:1. The texts that come closest to describing this event are possibly Jude 6 (cf. 1 Tim 3:6; 2 Pet 2:4) and Rev 12.

in the words of Paul, Adam (and Eve) chose to worship and serve "the creature rather than the Creator, who is blessed forever" (Rom 1:25 NKJV).[29] Adam failed in his task as God's priest-king, and the punishment, sadly, fits the crime: death. The human race is now under a death sentence, described in a variety of ways in Scripture—bondage to sin, dead in our trespasses, under the power of sin, death, and the Evil One, and so on (Jer 17:9; Rom 6:23; Eph 2:1–3). But worse than all of these terrible results is that humans, who were made to know, love, and serve God, are now enemies of God, living under his judgment and wrath, and no longer in a living relationship with him—spiritually dead unto God (Rom 8:7; Eph 2:1–3; 4:17–19). This in the end is death—physically and spiritually—for to live in relationship and fellowship with God is life, but to live apart from him is death.

As the text unfolds, the punishment of our sin is swift, leading to God's expulsion and exile of Adam and Eve from the garden, and God blocking entrance to the tree of life, signifying that we are no longer in life-giving fellowship with the Lord, living in his presence in terms of blessing, privilege, and relationship. In order to forbid access to the tree of life, God places the cherubim (cf. Ezek 1:5ff; 10:15; Rev 4:6ff) and adds "a flaming sword that turned every way to guard the way to the tree of life" (Gen 3:24 ESV). The flaming sword represents the justice and holiness of God at work in his judgments (cf. Jer 47:6; Ezek 21). By this description, Scripture is clear: as we move across redemptive history, the only way back to the presence of God is through God's way and God's provision, which eventually is seen through the biblical covenants and through the provision of the tabernacle, temple, and ultimately the coming of the one who is the replacement of the temple, our Lord Jesus Christ (see John 2:19–21; cf. Rev 21–22).

Furthermore, there is no doubt that Adam's sin is passed on to his progeny as evidenced in Cain's murderous action (Gen 4); the common refrain in the genealogical list in Genesis 5, "and he died . . ." (5:5, 8, 11, 14, 17, 20, 27, 31); and the flood (Gen 6–9). Paul's summary—"for all have sinned and fall short of the glory of God" (Rom 3:23)—is given by divine revelation, but it is also true to the Bible's entire story. From Genesis 3 on, Scripture teaches that *all* of us are under the condemnation of sin and that the only hope for our desperate condition is found in God's provision. The only hope for Adam's helpless race is found in the last Adam, who, unlike the first man (and the entire human race), does not fail, and who secures our

[29] See the helpful discussion of the fall in Gladd, *From Adam and Israel*, 22–34.

redemption. However, God unveils this truth over time, as the covenants reveal and anticipate, in instruction and type, the coming of our Lord Jesus Christ.

Second, Genesis 3 is also central in establishing God's first redemption promise, which drives the Bible's story through the covenants, leading us to Christ (Gen 3:15). Genesis 3 not only establishes the nature of the human problem; it also prepares us for God's provision. The effects of sin are comprehensive and disastrous, specifically our sin against God. This may seem like an obvious point, but today such an understanding is not obvious. We have a diminished view of God in all of his glory, and as such, we have embraced unbiblical views of humans and sin.[30] Whether it is the fallout of "modernism" or "postmodernism," the result is the same: sin and evil are not viewed first in relation to God but are reduced to "this world." Yet, without viewing sin and evil first in relation to God, the biblical concept of sin is misunderstood. As a result, we fail to grasp what is central to covenants, namely, how the triune God is going to provide a Redeemer that results in the full forgiveness of sin (see Jer 31:34; cf. Heb 8–10).

Also, after the fall, as we noted in the previous chapter, given who God is and who we are as fallen creatures, there is a *tension* in covenantal relations between God and humans. Covenants allow God to be present with his people, and his people to enjoy rest. Yet how can sinners dwell in his presence? How can God declare us just before him? Since God is holy, righteous, and just, he requires the punishment of our sin; we cannot dwell in his presence apart from our sin being vanquished. Sin cannot approach God, and God cannot tolerate it, but how can God be present and forgive our sins without denying himself? Or how can God be both *just and the justifier* of sinners (Rom 3:25–26)? How can God take the initiative *and* satisfy his own holy nature? Scripture's answer is that *God himself* must solve the problem. God himself must act to redeem, consistent with his perfect will and nature *and* provide a Redeemer true to his own promise.

The context of God's promise of redemption is God's "commitment to his creation,"[31] to reverse the effects of sin, to destroy the powers of "this present age," and bring about a new creation where God fully dwells with his people. In terms of the promise itself, God promises to put enmity between the "seed" of the woman and the seed of the serpent; the woman's seed will strike the serpent on the head, signifying defeat, while the serpent's seed will strike a blow

[30] See Wells, *Losing Our Virtue* (see chap. 1, n. 2).

[31] Goldsworthy, *According to Plan*, 112.

to the woman's seed on the heel, signifying some kind of battle and conflict. In the immediate context, Stephen Dempster is surely right that the promise entails that "the triumph of the woman's seed would suggest a return to the Edenic state, before the serpent had wrought its damage, and a wresting of the dominion of the world from the serpent."[32] Thus, through God's provision of a human, indeed a greater Adam, the Adamic/human role in creation will be restored, the curses will be removed, the serpent will be destroyed, and God's presence will be fully realized.

This promise makes sense given Scripture's description of the role of humans in creation as God's image-sons, priest-kings. In Adam, humans were created to represent God in creation. Not surprisingly, God deals with creation on the basis of how he deals with humans. When Adam sins and the creation is cursed, in order to restore creation, God promises to provide and work through a human to restore what was lost. The hope for the human race, then, is now found in God's provision of a "seed of the woman" that will restore the lost glory.

As the text unfolds, there is evidence that Adam lays claim on the promise. For example, Adam names his wife "Eve"—as the mother of all living (Gen 3:20), which implies more than a mere embrace of life. In this context, it is evidence that Adam is reclaiming dominion in faith "through *naming* his wife *the mother*, which cannot help but allude to the more specific role she will have as the one who will provide a seed who will strike the serpent."[33] However, at this point in the story, the promise is in "seed form," which will receive further clarity, definition, and development as God's plan unfolds through the covenants.

In this light, the church has correctly argued that Gen 3:15 is the *protevangelium*, namely, the first gospel proclamation.[34] God is promising that "someone out of the human race itself ('the woman's offspring'), although fatally 'wounded' himself in the conflict, would destroy the serpent (Satan)."[35] In fact, it is *this* promise that Scripture unfolds through the progression of the covenants, reaching their fulfillment and telos in Christ (see Rom 16:29; Gal 3:16). Also,

---

[32] Dempster, *Dominion and Dynasty*, 68 (see chap. 4, n. 29).

[33] Dempster, 68–69; cf. Gerhard von Rad, *Genesis: A Commentary*, trans. J. Marks (Philadelphia: Fortress, 1976), 96.

[34] For a discussion of this point, see Alexander, *Servant King*, 16–19 (see chap. 13, n. 70); Vos, *Biblical Theology*, 41–44 (see chap. 1, n. 45).

[35] Robert L. Reymond, *Jesus, Divine Messiah* (Fearn, Ross-shire, UK: Mentor, 2003), 69; see also Paul R. House, *Old Testament Theology* (Downers Grove: InterVarsity, 1998), 65.

we receive further confirmation that God's *unilateral* determination to redeem us is also tied to his provision of an obedient covenant partner, a greater image-son, priest-king than Adam. Yet, as history unfolds, God remains faithful to his promises, but we do not, which raises the question of precisely *who* this fully obedient covenant keeper will be. As each of the covenants progress, the identity of this promised one is unveiled, which finally culminates in God's provision of his own obedient Son, our Lord Jesus Christ, who alone brings redemption and the "age to come."

Should we view Gen 3:15 as the start of *the* "covenant of grace," as covenant theology teaches? No doubt, there is some truth in this since there are only two heads of the human race—Adam and Christ—and post-fall, all humans come into the world "in Adam" and redemption is only "in Christ." Thus, by faith alone in the covenant promises of God centered in Christ alone, we are justified before God, which has been true for God's people since Gen 3:15, even though over time more definition is given to Christ's precise identity as God's promised "seed" (Gen 15:6; Rom 4; Gal 3). Yet is Gen 3:15 the ratification of a *different* covenant? Or is it instead a gracious promise that despite Adam's sin and rebellion, God's purpose for humans and creation will stand and that from the human race, *God* will provide a Redeemer as the perfect covenant keeper, which is finally realized in Christ and the new covenant? In this sense, Gen 3:15 is a Christological promise that prophetically anticipates and predicts in seed form the ultimate provision of the new covenant, *which is progressively revealed through the covenants*. In the OT, believers are justified before God "in Christ" by believing God's covenant promises centered in him, even though the grounds for their justification awaits the finished work of Christ (Rom 3:21–26; Heb 9:15–28). But because the new covenant is a guaranteed certainty in God's plan (Rev 13:8), God justifies OT believers by grace through faith in Christ as they anticipate and long for his appearing (1 Pet 1:10–12).

Is this splitting hairs? Theologically, we both believe that there is only one salvific plan and Savior and that we are justified by grace alone through faith alone in Christ alone. But covenant theology affirms this by positing the *theological* concept of *the* covenant of grace, ratified or instituted in Gen 3:15, and then placing all subsequent covenants under this *one* theological covenant. As we will note in the next chapter, this "construction" of the Bible's story has doctrinal implications that are problematic. Instead of thinking of God's one plan unfolded through a plurality of covenants that progressively reveal, anticipate, and culminate in Christ and the new covenant, covenant theology tends to "flatten" the covenants and not account for how *all* of the OT covenants are revelatory-prophetic of the new covenant. Thus, they minimize the significant changes that have resulted in Christ's ratification of the new covenant as the fulfillment and telos of the covenants, specifically in ecclesiology, eschatology, and the application of the OT to Christians today.

The Noahic Covenant

The word *covenant* first appears with Noah (Gen 6:18; cf. 9:9–11), but it is a continuation of the prior creation covenant demonstrating God's commitment to creation, now in light of sin. Given sin, humans and creation are threatened, as evidenced by God's judgment in a universal flood, which becomes a typological pattern culminating in final judgment (Gen 6–8; 2 Pet 3:1–13). Yet, given God's promise in Gen 3:15 and now his promise to Noah, as "the earth remains" (8:22), the Noahic covenant reinforces God's intention that humans will fulfill their role as God's image-sons and priest-kings in creation. The "seed of the woman" will now come through Noah and his seed, and it is *he* who will reverse the effects of sin and usher in a "new creation." Noah is "another Adam" (Gen 9:1–7; cf. 1:26–30). He is given the same creation mandate, and the universal scope of the covenant reminds us that God's purposes include not just one people, but all nations and the entire creation. The universal emphasis of creation in Genesis 1–11 is not lost despite its narrowing focus in later covenants since a new creation is anticipated.

The Noahic covenant establishes three further points. *First*, God demands obedience from Noah (and all of us), but Noah's disobedience (Gen 9:18–28) demonstrates that our heart problem remains (see Gen 6:5–7 with 8:21–22) and that he is not the promised one. What we need is a greater heart transformation by the Spirit, tied to the forgiveness of sin, so that humans will fulfill their role as image-bearers. Yet at this point, the heart transformation of *all* the people is still in the future. Instead, what we see is the contrast between the rebellious human attempt to make their own name apart from God and God graciously electing/choosing and calling Abraham to make his name great (see Gen 11:4 with 12:1–3).

Second, the Noahic covenant explains why fallen humanity simultaneously exists alongside God's people *until* the consummation. Instead of continually wiping away fallen humanity and starting over again, two kingdoms emerge living side by side until the end: God's kingdom or saving reign, which is visible in his people through specific covenant relationships, as evidenced in Noah and then in Abraham, Israel, and David, *and* the kingdom of this world—identified with Satan—which stands in foolish opposition to God. Throughout the OT, there is a tension between these two kingdoms; this tension emerges in the NT in the larger church-state distinction. In fact, in the NT, given the Noahic promise, although Christ has *already* inaugurated the future age, an overlap of the ages continues until Christ returns and brings "this present age" to its end.

Third, the Noahic covenant also explains why creation order/structures, along with some typological patterns tied to creation, continue *until* the end despite the beginning of their transformation in the new covenant. For example, think of marriage. Marriage and family are part of the creation order that continues until the end (Gen 2:18–25; 8:22; 9:12–17). Yet, as the covenants unfold, we discover that marriage is also a type that ultimately reaches its fulfillment in the consummation, where there is no giving in human marriage (Matt 22:29–30; Eph 5:31–32). Although Christ has come, due to the Noahic covenant, creation structures continue to the end, while other types reach their fulfillment in Christ's first coming (e.g., various persons such as Adam, Moses, David, the tabernacle-temple, the sacrificial system, and the priesthood). Although Christ fulfills *all* the covenants, we still have to think carefully about *how* various aspects of the covenants are fulfilled due to Christ's two advents. But the truth that creation order/structures continue until the end (e.g., human dignity, male and female, monogamous heterosexual marriage, the family, work) is important in determining creation norms and what is still universally normative for all people and cultures.

The Abrahamic Covenant

Given its location in Scripture, the Abrahamic covenant plays a crucial role in the Bible's unfolding story. Abraham and his "seed" function as "another Adam" who is called to be God's true humanity; through them, salvation comes to the world and God's kingdom arrives. The hope for the world is found in Abraham and his seed (Israel, David, and ultimately Christ). In the NT, Paul underscores this point when he argues that the singular use of *seed* in Gen 12:3 (cf. Gen 22:17–18a; 24:60; Ps 72:17) is truly fulfilled in Christ Jesus (Gal 3:16).[36] Paul picks

---

[36] See Alexander, "Seed," 769–73 (see chap. 4, n. 64); Thomas R. Schreiner, *Paul: Apostle of God's Glory in Christ* (Downers Grove: InterVarsity, 2001), 73–85; Jason S. DeRouchie, "Counting Stars with

up the promise theme from Genesis 3 traced through a distinctive line of seed beginning with Adam, running through Noah, Abraham, Isaac, Israel, David, and finally fulfilled in Christ, the mediator of God's people and the one who fulfills all God's promises. In addition, Paul's argument in Gal 3:1–25 is that the Abrahamic covenant *preceded* the law covenant in redemptive history, thus demonstrating that the latter covenant does not set aside the former and that the former is foundational to the latter.

It is also significant that the Abrahamic covenant plays a distinctive role in the systems of covenant and dispensational theology, as we will note in the next chapter. Both systems appeal to the Abrahamic covenant to justify their core beliefs. Dispensational theology appeals to the role of national, ethnic Israel in God's plan tied to the unconditional land promise (Gen 15:18–21), while covenant theology appeals to the genealogical principle first given in Genesis 17, which remains unchanged across the covenants, including the new covenant. Given these differences within evangelical theology, four points will outline how I understand the nature of the Abrahamic covenant and its relationship to the other covenants.

First, the Abrahamic covenant is one covenant, not two.[37] It starts with God's electing and calling Abraham, God's giving of promises to him (Gen 12), and the cutting or inauguration of the covenant (Gen 15), with a further expansion of the initial promises throughout his life as greater definition and clarity of the covenant is given (see Gen 17, 22).

Second, in terms of its textual-epochal context, the Abrahamic covenant comes *after* Genesis 1–11. Similar to the Noahic covenant, the Abrahamic presents anew the plan of creation over against God's judgments on human sin (Gen 11). For this reason, elements from the creation covenant are repeated in the blessing to Abraham: God's promise of a great name and seed, the multiplication of progeny, the promise of the land, peaceful relations between God and humans, and blessing to the nations (Gen 12:1–3; cf. 15:4–5; 17:1–8; 18:18–19; 22:16–18). Furthermore, building on the Noahic covenant, God allows the nations to exist and then calls Abraham out of the nations to become a great nation (*gôy*), that is, a world political community, indeed, a kingdom. Despite God working through one family, because

---

Abraham and the Prophets: New Covenant Ecclesiology in OT Perspective," *JETS* 58, no. 3 (2015): 445–85.

[37] This is in contrast to Williamson, *Sealed with an Oath*, 77–93; cf. Gentry and Wellum, *Kingdom through Covenant*, 259–81.

the Abrahamic covenant is the answer to Adam's sin, it has a universal telos that will finally result in a new creation.

The Abrahamic covenant also develops the opposition between God's people and the world. On the one hand, we have the "kingdom" associated with Babel and all that stands in opposition to God (Gen 11). On the other hand, we have God's saving initiative in Abraham to fulfill the role of Adam, to bring salvation to the nations, and to reveal the kind of relationships that God originally intended for humanity. Throughout Scripture these two peoples are contrasted, but it is only through Abraham and his seed that God's saving rule will come, the resolution to sin and death will result, and the divine goal for humans and creation will result. This is finally realized in Christ, the new covenant, the church as God's royal priesthood and holy nation (1 Pet 2:9), and the consummated state of the new creation (Rev 21–22).

The Abrahamic covenant, then, *is the means* by which God will fulfill his promises for humanity, a subset of the "creation covenant." Abraham and his seed constitute "another Adam," a calling into existence of something new, parallel to creation, but in this case a "new creation" (see Rom 4:17). In Abraham and his seed, first in Isaac, then in Israel (Mosaic covenant), and then epitomized by the Davidic king (Davidic covenant), *all* of God's promises will be realized, promises that God unilaterally keeps, as revealed in the covenant ratification in Genesis 15.

Within Genesis, there is a hint that the fulfillment of the Abrahamic covenant will occur in two stages: first, in the nation of Israel, who will live in the promised land and serve as a kingdom of priests under the Mosaic covenant (Exod 19:4–6; Deut 4:5–8), and, second, in the Davidic king (Davidic covenant) which will ultimately result in the new covenant. In the Davidic covenant, Israel's king is the administrator of the Mosaic covenant, representing God's rule to the people and representing the people as a whole (2 Sam 7:22–24). Second, in Christ, Abraham's royal, *singular* seed will bless *all* nations (Gen 17:4–6; cf. 22:17–18a; 24:60; 49:8, 10; Ps 72:17; Isa 9:6). Even in Genesis, Abraham's "fatherhood" is expanded "beyond ethnic Israelites to include the nations."[38] This entails a promise of a global inheritance *and* the expansion of the land "to include the planet and its numerous people (Gen 1:28; Matt 5:5; Rom 4:13; cf. Eph 6:2–3; Heb 11:13–16)."[39] This point helps answer the question of what God

[38] DeRouchie, "Counting Stars with Abraham," 460.

[39] DeRouchie, 461.

intended by his promise of land to Abraham. Did God intend the land to be exhausted in a specific location, or did he intend for it to include much more? At this point in the story, there are hints that God intended the land to encompass the world, yet more revelation is needed to know precisely God's intent. But, as Jason DeRouchie notes, "This kind of expansion is suggested in Gen 22:17b–18 where we are told that the unique, male deliverer will not only bless 'all the nations of the earth' but will also possess 'the gate of his enemies,' claiming once-enemy territory, his kingdom expanding to fill the earth (cf. Gen 24:60)."[40] In the progress of the covenants, this makes sense since Abraham is the means God uses to fulfill his promises for humanity (Gen 3:15).

Third, the nature of the Abrahamic covenant is multifaceted. It encompasses spiritual aspects that link it to the new covenant; it also consists of national and typological elements that must be carefully unpacked through the covenants. For example, think about how Scripture speaks of Abraham and his seed.[41] First, the "seed of Abraham" refers to a *natural* (biological) seed: every person who descended from Abraham, such as Ishmael, Isaac, the sons of Keturah, and by extension Esau, Jacob, and so on. In each case, these children received the sign of the Abrahamic covenant, that is, circumcision, even though many of them were unbelievers, and it was only through Isaac that God's promises are realized (Gen 17:20–21; cf. Rom 9:6–9). Second, the "seed of Abraham" refers to a *natural but special* seed due to God's election: Isaac and, by extension, Jacob, the nation of Israel, and the Davidic king. God promised to Abraham a mighty nation (Israel) *and* the arrival of kings (realized in the Davidic covenant), which results in a singular royal seed (Gen 17:6–8; 22:17–18a; 24:60; 49:8–12, etc.). Yet, within this *special* seed, individuals and the nation are constituted as a "mixed" people, namely, believers and unbelievers. But unlike the mere natural seed (e.g., Ishmael), the special seed was God's chosen people under the Mosaic covenant. Also, this *special* seed functioned as a type of Abraham's singular, royal seed, namely Christ. Third, the *true* "seed of Abraham" is Christ (Gal 3:16), the antitype of the previous *special* seeds of Abraham. Thus, Christ *is* the *true* seed of Abraham, who is biologically from Abraham but greater than those who preceded him. Fourth, in Christ, all believers, regardless of nationality, are the

---

[40] DeRouchie, 461.

[41] See DeRouchie, 445–85; DeRouchie, "Father of a Multitude of Nations," in Wellum and Parker, *Progressive Covenantalism*, 7–38.

spiritual "seed of Abraham." This includes all believing Jews and Gentiles in the church (Eph 2:11–21), thus fulfilling the Abrahamic promise of blessing the nations. But only those who have experienced an internal "heart" circumcision by the Spirit's transforming power and who are united to Christ by faith are Abraham's *spiritual* seed (Gal 3:26–29). Under the new covenant, being a true member of Abraham's family, and thus part of the church, does *not* involve biological birth into a specific national lineage or merely receiving the external sign of circumcision, but believing in God's covenant promises centered now in Christ and being born of the Spirit.

Fourth, the Abrahamic covenant consists of unconditional/unilateral and conditional/bilateral elements; it is not reducible to one of these features alone. Although it is common to think of the Abrahamic covenant as an unconditional covenant (royal grant) or as two covenants due to the unilateral emphasis in Genesis 15 and the bilateral demands in Genesis 17,[42] both of these views are deficient. Instead, the Abrahamic covenant is *one* covenant, starting with divine promises in Genesis 12, ratification in Genesis 15, and further confirmation in Genesis 17 and 22. No doubt, there is an undeniable unilateral emphasis: God alone ratifies the covenant (Gen 15:12–21; cf. Jer 34:18–20). Regardless of Abraham's unfaithfulness, God will keep his promise, which Abraham receives by faith, and it is counted to him as righteousness (Gen 15:6). But in keeping his covenant promises, God still demands total devotion from his human covenant partners (Gen 17:1; 18:19; 22:16–18).[43] God's demand for obedience does not nullify God's promises and make the covenant bilateral; rather, it creates a *tension* within the covenant relation. God, as the covenant maker and keeper, always keeps his promises despite human disobedience. *And yet*, God demands devotion from a loyal human covenant partner that fallen humanity cannot create. This growing tension between God unilaterally keeping his promises *and* demanding an obedient covenant partner is not resolved here or in later covenants, as evidenced by Israel's and the Davidic kings' disobedience. Yet, within the Abrahamic covenant, there is a hint at how it will be resolved: "God himself will provide the lamb for the burnt offering" (Gen 22:8). But as the covenants unfold, God's provision will not merely be a lamb for us (or the priestly sacrificial system under the law covenant); God's provision will be his own Son, the true seed of Abraham, who, because he is God, can satisfy *God's*

---

[42] Horton, *God of Promise*, 77–110; and Williamson, *Sealed with an Oath*, 89–90.

[43] See Williamson, *Sealed with an Oath*, 84–91.

own righteous demand and, because he is human, can fully obey for us as the faithful *human* covenant partner.

The Old Covenant or the Covenant with Israel[44]

In the OT, the amount of space devoted to the "old covenant" is sizable, but Scripture teaches that it functions as a "means to an end" that results in the new covenant (Jer 31:29–34; Heb 8). This is why Scripture views the "old covenant" as *temporary* in God's plan; or better, it has an intended role to play, *as a covenant unit*, which reaches its telos in Christ and the new covenant. For this reason, Christians are no longer under it *as a covenant* (Gal 3:15–4:7). Unlike first-century Judaism, which viewed the law covenant as imperishable, immutable, and eternal, Paul argues that when the law covenant is located in its proper covenantal sequence, it is almost "a parenthesis (Gal 3:15–4:7)" in God's plan and, as such, that which precedes it, namely, the promise to Abraham (tied back to the creation covenant), "cannot be annulled by the giving of the law (3:17), regardless of how much space is given over to the law in the sacred text, or how large a role it played in the history of Israel."[45] As D. A. Carson notes, this inevitably leads to the question of Gal 3:19 (GNT): "What, then, was the purpose of the law?" Many answers could be given, but the main purpose of the law covenant was to reveal and intensify sin. In this way, the covenant functioned "in preparation for the coming of Christ 'when the set time had fully come' (Gal 4:4), which is itself the fulfillment of the promise."[46] Thus, to grasp the role of the old covenant in God's plan, one must think through what preceded it, how it advances the promise of Gen 3:15, and how it predicts and anticipates the coming of Christ and the dawning of the new covenant. Three points will capture its nature and its overall place and role in the covenants.

---

[44] The covenant with Israel goes by a number of names. Sometimes it is identified as the Mosaic covenant since Moses, in many ways, serves as its mediator. Moses functions in the role of prophet, priest, and king before those offices were separated in the life of Israel. It is also called the Sinai covenant given its location. In light of Christ, it is identified as the "old covenant" set over against the "new covenant."

[45] D. A. Carson, "Mystery and Fulfillment," 412 (see chap. 4, n. 40); see also Douglas J. Moo, "The Law of Christ as the Fulfillment of the Law of Moses," in Strickland, *Law, the Gospel, and the Modern Christian*, 319–24 (see chap. 13, n. 88).

[46] Carson, "Mystery and Fulfillment," 412.

First, by placing the old covenant in its textual and epochal/covenantal context, it is evident that God's establishing his covenant with Israel cannot be understood apart from his promises to Abraham (and through his sons Isaac and Jacob [Gen 26:3–5; 28:13–15; 35:9–12]). Due to the patriarchal promises, God calls Moses to deliver his people from Egypt (Exod 3:6; cf. 2:24–25; Deut 4:36–38; 2 Kgs 13:22–23; 1 Chron 16:15–19). God did not set his love on Israel because they were more numerous or better than the nations (Deut 7:7). Instead, God's election of Israel was by sovereign grace and due to his covenant loyalty to Abraham (Exod 19:4; Deut 7:8). The law covenant is directly linked to the Abrahamic, which in turn is linked to the creation covenant in Adam. By placing the old covenant vis-à-vis the previous covenants, we discover how the "seed" of Abraham is narrowed to the nation of Israel through Isaac and Jacob.

Also, building on the Abrahamic promise, God calls Israel to be a "kingdom of priests" and a "holy nation" (*gôy*, Exod 19:5–6), which speaks of the nation in *kingdom* and *Adamic* terms. Israel, *as a nation*, is "another Adam," a corporate image of God, called to exercise rule as priest-kings. As such, Israel was to demonstrate to the nations what God intended for humanity, to enjoy access to God's presence through the tabernacle-temple structures in the land. As such, the promised land is to Israel what Eden was for Adam. In that land, they were to know God, learn what it means to be fully obedient sons, and extend God's rule to the nations.[47]

Furthermore, given the location of the law covenant in Scripture, it is through Israel that God intends to fulfill his Gen 3:15 promise by resolving the problem of sin and death caused by the first Adam. This is why corporate Israel is identified as God's "son" (Exod 4:22–23) and the relationship between the Lord and Israel is a "Father-son" relationship. This is significant since this relationship not only looks back to Adam; it also looks forward to the Davidic covenant, where the Davidic kings are viewed in the same "Father-son" relationship with the Lord, thus linking these covenants together in God's overall redemptive plan. Israel, then, as a nation, was called to serve as God's image-son—servants, kings, priests—on the earth by demonstrating what true humanity was to look like, and through them God's redemptive promise was to be accomplished.

Second, the old covenant is best viewed as an entire unit. As an entire unit, one of its primary purposes is to reveal who God is and how we are to live before him (Lev 11:45). Scripture

[47] See Gladd, *From Adam and Israel*, 35–57.

does not partition the covenant into moral, civil, and ceremonial laws, although this is heuristically useful; instead, it is an entire unit/package that governed the life of Israel, and now, in Christ and the new covenant, it has been brought to fulfillment *as an entire covenant.*[48] Also, as an entire unit/package, the old covenant develops in greater detail a whole host of typological patterns that find their antitypical fulfillment in Christ and his people, the church.

For example, within the old covenant, Israel, as a kingdom of priests, needs Levitical priests to represent them before God. In fact, the Levitical priesthood serves as the foundation for the entire covenant relationship: covenant and priesthood are inseparable; hence, Christ's priestly work results in a change of covenant (see Heb 7:11–12). This makes perfect sense given the fact of sin. One cannot have a covenant relationship with the Lord without atonement for sin. Israel, as a kingdom of priests, is to enjoy access to God's presence as Adam did in Eden. But given that God is holy and just, how sinful people dwell in his presence is a burning issue that erupted in the Golden Calf disaster (Exod 32–34). So, given the problem of sin, Israel, as a kingdom of priests, needs specific priests to represent them before God and to offer gifts and sacrifices *for sins* (Heb 5:1). But as Israel's covenant will also reveal, God's righteousness did not come through the Levitical priesthood and law covenant (Rom 3:21). Instead, God's righteousness comes to us apart from the law covenant, in Christ, who is our great High Priest and by his cross work ratifies a better covenant (Rom 3:21–26; Heb 7–10).

Related to the priesthood is the tabernacle-temple-sacrificial system. All of these institutions allow for Israel to dwell in the land, enjoying God's presence as his king-priests, but they also anticipate their antitypical fulfillment in Christ and the full forgiveness of sin (Jer 31:34; Heb 10:1–18). In God's provision of his Son-Messiah, the Servant of the Lord (Isa 52–53), the role of the Levitical priest is fulfilled and transcended by Christ, who inaugurates an entirely different order (Heb 5:1–10; 7–10). In Christ, the entire tabernacle-temple typological pattern is fulfilled and then applied to us, the church, as God's new temple (see John 2:19–22; Eph 2:19–22). What is true about priests is also true of prophets and the anticipation of future kings—two other offices that reach their antitypical fulfillment in Christ with application to the church.[49] Or think of the paradigmatic events of the Passover and Exodus, which

---

[48] See Rosner, *Paul and the Law*, 26–44 (see chap. 4, n. 36); Moo, "Law of Christ," 336–37.

[49] Prophet: Deut 18:15–18; 34:10–12; Acts 3:22–26; Heb 1:1–3. King: Gen 17:6, 16; 49:8–12; Num 24:17–19; cf. 24:7; Deut 17:14–20; 2 Sam 7:8–16; Matt 1:1–17; Rom 1:3–4; Heb 1:5, 13; 5:4–6.

first established Israel in covenant relationship with God. Through the covenants, both events become patterns of a greater, new exodus/redemption to come, which is fulfilled by Christ and applied to his people.[50]

Third, although the Law covenant is bilateral and God rightly demands an obedient covenant partner, it is not reducible to it. As with all the covenants, God unilaterally keeps his promises, but Israel is to be a fully devoted, obedient son, and like Adam, they disobeyed. While the law covenant held out the promise of life (Lev 18:5), Israel broke the law and came under its curse of death and exile, as they served as a microcosm of the entire human race. The law was "holy and righteous and good" (Rom 7:12 ESV), but Israel was internally corrupt with sinful desires and thus incapable of keeping the law. God graciously provided a system of sacrifices to atone for the people's sin, but it was "impossible for the blood of bulls and goats to take away sins" (Heb 10:4). The entire priestly-sacrificial-temple system functioned as a type/pattern that anticipated its antitypical fulfillment in Christ. Human sin requires human death. God did not design the old covenant to secure a permanent solution to the problem of sin (Gal 3:10–12, 21–22; cf. Deut 27:26).[51] This is why the entire law covenant anticipated God's greater redemption in Christ since "apart from the law, the righteousness of God has been revealed" (Rom 3:21). In this sense, the entire law covenant was "prophetic" as it anticipated our full justification in God's provision of his obedient Son (Matt 11:13; cf. Rom 3:21–31; cf. Heb 2:5–18; 7–10).

The old covenant, then, is part of God's unfolding plan leading us to Christ. But, as with the other covenants, it continues and heightens the *tension* of how God's kingdom comes through fallen people. God *will* keep his promise to bring forth the offspring of Abraham, now through an Israelite. *And yet*, Israel cannot produce the obedient son and covenant partner that God demands. The law covenant holds out life, but due to sin, it cannot save. In fact, in Israel's history, the old covenant results in greater condemnation because it reveals more of Israel's sin; it increases sin by defining explicitly what is contrary to God's will (Rom 5:20), and it imprisons Israel under sin's power and condemnation (Rom 3:19–20; Gal 3:10, 13; Col 2:14).

---

[50] For example, see Exod 15:14–17; cf. Isa 11:15–16; 40:3–5; 41:17–20; 42:14–16; 43:1–3, 14–21; 48:20–21; 49:8–12; 51:9–11; 52:3–6, 11–12; 55:12–13; Jer 16:14–15; 23:4–8; 31:32; Hos 2:14–15; 11:1; 12:9, 13; 13:4–5.

[51] For the purpose of the law covenant, see Moo, "Law of Christ," 324–43.

Even God's provision of a sacrificial system only functioned as a "reminder of sins" (Heb 10:3), revealing the need for the new covenant tied to a full atonement (Jer 31:34) and the Spirit's internal transforming work (Ezek 36:25–27; cf. John 3:5–8). Thus, through the covenants, God teaches us that *he* alone redeems but that action also requires *his* provision of an obedient image-son-king, which is explicitly revealed in the Davidic covenant.

The Davidic Covenant

The Davidic covenant is the *epitome* of the OT covenants; it brings the previous covenants to a climax in the king, the representative of Israel, the seed of Abraham, and "another Adam."[52] In capturing the magnitude of the Davidic covenant in God's unfolding plan, two points are crucial. First, we must note the location of the Davidic covenant in the Bible's story to grasp its *organic* relationship to what *preceded* it and what *follows* it. Second, we must think about the unilateral-bilateral tension within the covenant to see how this tension, as with earlier covenants, contributes to the Bible's overall metanarrative and theological framework.

First, there are two main parts to the Davidic covenant: (1) God's promises concerning the establishment of David's house forever (2 Sam 7:12–16; 1 Chron 17:11–14), and (2) the promises concerning the "Father-son" relationship between the Lord and the Davidic king (2 Sam 7:14; 1 Chron 17:13; cf. Pss 2; 89:26–27). Given the Davidic covenant's location within the unfolding covenants, the meaning of this "sonship" is twofold. First, it inextricably ties the Davidic covenant to the previous covenants, and second, it anticipates in type the greater Sonship of the new covenant mediator to come. Regarding the former, the sonship applied to *corporate* Israel (Exod 4:22–23; cf. Hos 11:1) is now applied to the *individual* David king, who, in himself, is "true Israel." As such, the Davidic king is the administrator/mediator of Israel's covenant, representing God's rule to the people and creation and thus representing the people as a whole (2 Sam 7:22–24). The king is to be a devoted son, even functioning in priestly terms, instructing the nations in the righteousness of God and inviting them to come under the rule of the LORD.

Furthermore, given the epochal-covenantal location of the Davidic covenant, it is also inseparable from the Abrahamic covenant and the creation covenant under Adam. In

---

[52] On this point, see Goldsworthy, *Christ-Centered Biblical Theology*, 123–49.

regard to the Abrahamic, the great-name promise is passed to the Davidic king (2 Sam 7:9; 1 Chron 17:8; Ps 72:17) and the promise of a great nation (cf. Gen 12:2). The Davidic covenant serves to identify the promised line of "seed" that will mediate blessings to all nations. But the Davidic king also inherits the role of Adam *and* Israel as God's son to humanity. As Walter Kaiser has rightly argued, the expression in 2 Sam 7:19b should read, "This is the charter by which humanity will be directed," indicating David's own understanding of the implications of the Davidic covenant for all of humanity, namely, that his role as covenant mediator would effect divine rule in the entire world as God intended it for humanity in the original situation.[53] David's understanding of the implications of the Davidic covenant for the world not only becomes the basis for messianic expectation in Scripture but also links the Davidic to the Abrahamic covenant, which in turn is linked to God's earlier covenants. Thus, under the Davidic king, the Abrahamic promise of the great nation and great name unite. In fact, the final fulfillment of the Abrahamic covenant coincides with the fulfillment of the Davidic. The Abrahamic blessings, linked back to Adam and creation, are fully realized *only through the Davidic son*. The Davidic king becomes the mediator of covenant blessing tied back to Abraham and finally tied back to Adam as the covenant head of humanity.

This is not surprising if we link the covenants together. God's redemptive plan is to restore humanity's vice-regent role in creation through the seed of the woman. By the time we get to David, we know who will restore the lost fortunes of creation. In the OT, this truth is borne out in many places, especially in the Psalter, which envisions the Davidic son as ushering in a universal rule—psalms, importantly, that are applied to Jesus in the NT (e.g., Pss 2; 8; 45; 72; cf. Isa 9:6–7, 11, 53; Ezek 34) and the new covenant age. When David's greater Son finally comes, all of God's promises will be realized, and the roles of the previous mediator will be fulfilled. In the King, the role of Israel, tied to the role of Adam, will result, and ultimately, God's promise to reverse the effects of sin and death and to usher in a new creation will ensue.

But there is a major problem in this regard. As with the previous covenant heads—whether Adam, Noah, Abraham, or corporate Israel—God demands obedience, yet none of them are

---

[53] For a development of this point, see chapter 11. See also Walter C. Kaiser Jr., "The Blessing of David: The Charter for Humanity," in *The Law and the Prophets*, ed. John H. Skilton (Nutley: P&R, 1974), 311–14; cf. Dumbrell, *Covenant and Creation*, 151–52.

truly obedient. The same is true of David and his sons, which brings us to the larger discussion of the unilateral-bilateral *tension* built within the covenant.

Second, as in the previous covenants, God continues in his unilateral determination to keep his promise to bring forth the seed of Abraham, now identified as the Davidic king, who will reign under God over the whole world. Yet God also continues to demand perfect obedience from his covenant partners as represented by the covenant heads. Yet none of these covenant partners, including David and his sons, truly obey; they do not fulfill their role of bringing God's rule to this world, and they certainly do not overturn the effects of Adam's sin and death. All of the previous covenant heads only anticipate someone greater, identified as David's *greater* Son.

Regarding the Davidic covenant, it is common to view it solely as a "royal-grant" covenant, but this is inadequate.[54] No doubt, God's intention is to fulfill his promises for a lasting dynasty, kingdom, and throne (2 Sam 7:8–11a) despite the failure of the kings (see 1 Kgs 11:11–13, 34–36; 15:4–5; 2 Kgs 8:19; 2 Chron 21:7; 23:3). However, God demands obedience on the king's part (2 Sam 7:14–15)—an obedience which will effect divine rule in the world (2 Sam 7:18–19). Thus, God will keep his promises (i.e., unilateral action) but by a faithful son (i.e., the king obeying the Torah). For this reason, it is reductionistic to classify the Davidic covenant as either a royal-grant or a suzerain-vassal covenant: it includes elements of both.

Further evidence for this unilateral-bilateral tension within the Davidic covenant is found in Isa 55:3. As Peter Gentry has demonstrated, David is the subject of the phrase "*ḥasdê dāwîd*," which requires the translation the "sure mercies or faithfulness *performed by David*."[55] This is significant given the importance of Isaiah 55 in Isaiah's prophecy of the Messiah and the coming Davidic King. Alec Motyer has shown that the "servant of the LORD" in Isaiah is Davidic.[56] For example, the figurative language in which the Davidic king and kingdom are portrayed as a great tree cut down (Isa 6:13) and the reference to the shoot and root in Isa 53:2 link the servant of the Lord to the vision of a future king who is another David (Isa 11:1,

---

[54] See, e.g., Craig A. Blaising and Darrell L. Bock, *Progressive Dispensationalism* (Grand Rapids: BridgePoint, 1993), 159–65; Horton, *God of Promise*, 43–50. Blaising and Bock and Horton argue for the "royal-grant" nature of the Davidic covenant.

[55] See Gentry and Wellum, *Kingdom through Covenant*, 464–79.

[56] For example, see J. Alec Motyer, *The Prophecy of Isaiah: An Introduction and Commentary* (Downers Grove: InterVarsity, 1993).

10). In fact, the ongoing debate regarding the identification of Israel as the servant *and* an individual as the servant who delivers the nation is resolved if we realize that the Davidic king is a representative figure for the entire nation. As such, Isaiah presents us with a unified vision of a coming Davidic king who is the "servant of the Lord" and who, as a result of his victorious work, will restore Zion (Isa 2:1–5), delight in the fear of the Lord (11:1–10), perfectly act like the Lord in his righteous rule (11:3–5), become a banner to the nations (11:10), and, through his instruction, teach and rule the nations (42:1, 3–4; 49:1, 6), and so on. Then in Isaiah 55, the Davidic covenant is linked to the new covenant by the announcement that God will make an "everlasting covenant" grounded in the "faithfulness performed by David" (55:3). Thus, the Lord performs *his* covenant obligation, but David performs *his* too, which results in the ratification of a new covenant. This not only confirms that within the Davidic covenant, God demands total devotion from the king; it also prophetically anticipates the need for David's greater son. Why? For this reason: in OT history there is no faithful son-king who effects God's saving reign, yet the hope of salvation depends on such a king, which is precisely the message of the prophets.

The Promise of the New Covenant

The epochal/covenantal context of the OT writing prophets is post-Davidic. This is significant because their prophecies build on what God has already revealed through the covenants.[57] The prophets announce God's judgment on the nation due to their violation of the covenant, but they also proclaim an overall pattern of renewal by recapitulating the past history of redemption and projecting it into the future. The prophets announce that God will unilaterally keep his promises to save, but he will do so through a faithful Davidic king (Isa 7:14; 9:6–7; 11:1–10; 42:1–9; 49:1–7; 52:13–53:12; 55:3; 61:1–3; Jer 23:5–6; 33:14–26; Ezek 34:23–24; 37:24–28). In this king, identified as the "servant of the LORD," a new or everlasting covenant will come, and with it, God's saving reign among the nations, the forgiveness of sin (Jer 31:34), and a new creation (Isa 65:17). This king will have the Spirit in full measure (Isa 11:1–3; 49:1–2; 61:1–4), and due to his work, he will pour out the Spirit on his people

---

[57] Goldsworthy makes this point, but he does not tie it to the covenants. *Christ-Centered Biblical Theology*, 123–32.

(Ezek 36:24–38; 37:11–28; Joel 2:28–32). The future hope of the prophets is organically tied to the coming of the Messianic son-king and his establishment of a new covenant as the fulfillment of the previous covenants.[58]

Within the OT, the new covenant is viewed as *national* (Jer 31:31–40; 33:6–16; Ezek 36:24–38; 37:11–28) and *international.* It will include Jews *and* Gentiles, and its scope is universal, thus fulfilling the Abrahamic promise.[59] Isaiah projects the final fulfillment of the divine promises in the new covenant onto an "ideal Israel," that is, a community tied to the servant of the Lord, located in a rejuvenated new creation (Isa 65:17; 66:22). This "ideal Israel" picks up the promises to Abraham and is the fulfillment of the covenants that God established with Adam, the patriarchs, the nation of Israel, and David's son (Isa 9:6–7; 11:1–10; Jer 23:5–6; 33:14–26; Ezek 34:23–24; 37:24–28). Paul Williamson nicely captures this point: "Thus the new covenant is the climatic fulfillment of the covenants that God established with the patriarchs, the nation of Israel, and the dynasty of David. The promises of these earlier covenants find their ultimate fulfillment in the new covenant, and in it such promises become 'eternal' in the truest sense."[60]

What is *new* about the new covenant?[61] To answer this question, every OT new covenant text requires investigation.[62] However, one crucial text, Jer 31:29–34, speaks of *newness* in terms of a change in the *structure* and *nature* of God's people because of the work of its *greater* covenant head and mediator. Let us look at these respective changes.

First, the new covenant changes the *structure* of God's people. Under the old covenant, God dealt with his people in a mediated or "tribal-representative" structure, whereby God related to his people *through* specially called mediators.[63] The OT knows of individual believers, as

---

[58] See O. Palmer Robertson, *The Christ of the Covenants* (Phillipsburg: P&R, 1980), 280–81.

[59] See Isa 14:1–2; 19:23–25; 42:6, 20; 49:6; 55:3–5; 56:4–8; 66:18–24; Jer 16:19; 33:9; Ezek 36:36; 37:28; Amos 9:11–12; cf. Pss 47:9; 87:3–6; 67:2–3; 117:1.

[60] Paul Williamson, "Covenant," *NDBT*, 427 (see chap. 1, n. 24).

[61] Debate ensues over the meaning of the word *new* (Heb. *hadas*; LXX, *kainos*). Some argue that the word means "renewed" (e.g., Lam 3:22–23), while others argue for "new" in a qualitatively different sense (Exod 1:8; Deut 32:17; 1 Sam 6:7; Eccl 1:10). Ultimately, "newness" must be contextually determined. On this debate, see Dumbrell, *Covenant and Creation*, 175; James R. White, "The Newness of the New Covenant (Part 1)," in *Recovering a Covenantal Heritage: Essays in Baptist Covenant Theology*, ed. Richard C. Barcellos (Palmdale, CA: RBAP, 2014), 325–55; Robertson, *Christ of the Covenants*, 280.

[62] See Gentry and Wellum, *Kingdom through Covenant*, 161–643.

[63] See D. A. Carson, *Showing the Spirit: A Theological Exposition of 1 Corinthians 12–14* (Grand Rapids: Baker, 1987), 150–58.

evidenced in the remnant theme. But in general, the people's knowledge of God and their relationship with him depended on uniquely endowed leaders. As these leaders/shepherds acted righteously, the entire nation benefited, but also vice-versa, as Judges, Samuel, Kings, and Chronicles describe (see Ezek 34:1–25). On this point, the OT does not say that God's Spirit was poured out on every individual believer in the empowering/gifted sense. Instead, the Spirit anointed specific prophets, priests, kings, and other designated leaders (e.g., Bezalel). But Jeremiah signals a structural shift in the covenant community where *all* of God's people will know him, from the least to the greatest (Jer 31:29–30).[64] By this change, the new covenant raises *every member* of the covenant to the same relationship with God through the universal distribution of the Spirit (Joel 2:28–32; cf. Acts 2). The Messiah, being the first to be anointed with the Spirit (Isa 11:1–3; 49:1–2; 61:1–4), will pour out his Spirit on all flesh, namely, *everyone within the covenant community* (Ezek 11:19–20; 36:25–27; Joel 2:28–32; cf. Num 11:27–29).[65] Thus, already in the OT, the prophets anticipate a day when the new covenant people will be *structurally* different from Israel under the old covenant.[66]

Second, the new covenant changes the *nature* of God's people. We can think of this in two ways. First, the prophets anticipate that the new covenant people will consist of believing people from every nation, not merely the nation of Israel (e.g., Isa 14:1–2; 19:23–25; 42:6, 20; 49:6; 55:3–5; 56:4–8; 66:18–24; Jer 16:19; 33:9; Ezek 36:36; 37:28; Amos 9:11–12; cf. Pss 47:9; 87:3–6; 67:2–3; 117:1). In this international community, the Abrahamic promise is realized along with the universal focus that goes back to creation. Second, the prophets also announce that one will not enter this new covenant community by biological birth or by merely receiving the external sign of circumcision. Jeremiah distinguishes between the old and the new covenants based on the "heart" condition of its members (Jer 31:31–34). Whereas only a remnant under the old covenant truly knew the Lord, in the new covenant, on every member, "'[God] will write [his law] on their hearts. . . . And no longer will one teach his neighbor . . . for they

[64] Carson, 152. In context, the knowledge is a salvific knowledge. See Dumbrell, *Covenant and Creation*, 177–78.

[65] See Max Turner, "Holy Spirit," in *NDBT*, 551–58, and *pace* Derek Thomas, who argues that the "all flesh" of Joel 2:28/Acts 2:17 simply refers to "ethnic broadening." See Thomas, "Covenant, Assurance, and the Sacraments," in *Covenant Theology: Biblical, Theological, and Historical Perspectives*, ed. Guy P. Waters, J. Nicholas Reid, and John R. Muether (Wheaton: Crossway, 2020), 576.

[66] Within covenant theology, Robertson acknowledges this point. *Christ of the Covenants*, 290–97.

will all know me, from the least to the greatest of them,'—this is the Lord's declaration" (Jer 31:33–34). Describing the law as written on the "heart" picks up "circumcision of the heart" language (cf. Deut 30:6; cf. Deut 10:16; Jer 4:4; 9:25) that is closely tied to regeneration but also the transformation of the entire covenant community (Rom 2:29).[67]

This does not mean that there were no OT saints. Far from it. Instead, it anticipates that *all* within the covenant community will be regenerate, unlike Israel of old, hence a change in *scope*. Israel, under the old covenant, was constituted as a *mixed* people, but under the new covenant, the *entire* community will know God and obey from the heart because of the Spirit's work.[68] Within national Israel there were many believers saved by grace through faith in God's promises, but not all Israel was Israel (Rom 9:6), thus resulting in a distinction between the biological and spiritual seed of Abraham. Under the old covenant, both "seeds" were circumcised to identify them as God's covenant people, and both were full covenant members in the national sense. Yet it was only the *believers* within the nation who were the *spiritual* seed of Abraham, the "true Israel" in a salvific sense. But this is *not* what is anticipated of those under the new covenant.

Third, the new covenant changes the *sacrifice* made for God's people. The old covenant offered the forgiveness of sins through the priestly-sacrificial system. However, the OT believer, if spiritually perceptive, knew that this was not enough, as evidenced by the repetitive nature

[67] Covenant theologians often misunderstand what Jeremiah is anticipating in the arrival of the new covenant. For example, Kevin DeYoung thinks that the "law written on the heart" is no different than the old covenant since the OT knows of "interior piety" as does the new covenant. No doubt this is true, but the point is that the *entire community* will have circumcised hearts, not merely the elect within the nation. See DeYoung, "Afterword: Why Covenant Theology?," in Waters, Reid, and Muether, eds., *Covenant Theology*, 596. Also, DeYoung and Scott Swain minimize the regenerate nature of the new covenant church by arguing: if *all* the people *know* God, why do we still need teachers in the church? See DeYoung, "Afterword," 596; Scott Swain, "New Covenant Theologies," in Waters, Reid, and Muether, eds., *Covenant Theology*, 567. Again, this misses the point. Just because the *entire* community *knows* God, unlike Israel, this does not require that everyone has the same gifting (Eph 4:1–16; cf. 1 John 2:18–27). In the church, teachers are gifted to lead a church that consists of a *regenerate* people, who exercise their own gifts to build up the church. But under the new covenant, leaders do not function as prophets, priests, and kings did under the old, i.e., as those who uniquely mediate God's presence to the people. These roles are first fulfilled in Christ, who is the great prophet, priest, and king, with a spillover effect to the church, who takes up these roles due to its union in Christ.

[68] See House, *Old Testament Theology*, 317–21.

of the system and the sacrifice offered: "it is impossible for the blood of bulls and goats to take away sins" (Heb 10:4). The old covenant sacrifices were intended to remind the people of their sinfulness through repetition; the entire priestly-sacrificial system was typological. Yet God announces that in the new covenant, he "will remember their sins and their lawless deeds no more" (Heb 10:17 ESV; cf. Jer 31:33–34). In the OT, the concept of "remembering" is not simple recall (cf. Gen 8:1; 1 Sam 1:19). In the context of verse 34, for God "not to remember" means that no action will be needed in the new age against sin. Thus, under the new covenant, a *sacrifice* will occur that will result in the full payment of our sin, something the old covenant could only anticipate and point forward to.[69]

When other new covenant texts are considered, Jeremiah anticipates a glorious unfettered fellowship of God's people with the Lord due to the work of a *greater* priest-king and sacrifice (Ps 110; cf. Heb 5–10) and that harmony will be restored between creation and God in a new creation/new Jerusalem where God's dwelling is with his people and where heaven and earth are finally united (Ezek 37:1–23; cf. Dan 12:2; Isa 25:6–9; Rev 21:3–4).[70] With the arrival of the Messiah and the new covenant, the *protevangelium* will finally be realized and fulfilled.

Thus, in these three areas, the OT anticipates change in the arrival of the new covenant, grounded in the *greater* new covenant head/mediator. For the OT prophets, this was a future reality, but when it dawns, God's redemptive plan will reach its intended telos, and *God's* saving rule (kingdom) will come. God's plan is unveiled and accomplished through the covenants culminating in Christ and the new covenant as we discover how God alone must act by the provision of his Son; otherwise, there is no salvation. To undo Adam's disobedience and destroy sin, death, and Satan, an obedient human covenant partner must come through Noah, Abraham, Israel, and finally David's line. He must faithfully discharge his role and bring God's saving rule to this world by reversing the effects of sin and reconciling us to God.

---

[69] See Dumbrell, *Covenant and Creation*, 181–85. Again, DeYoung misses the point when he says that the promise of "iniquity forgiven" (Jer 31:34) is "not a new promise" because God forgave the sins of OT saints. See DeYoung, "Afterword," 596. No doubt this is true, but the *ground* for justification was not the sacrificial-priestly system of the old. Rather, the old typified and prophetically anticipated what was to come in Christ's work in the new covenant, which alone is the ground for God's justification of the ungodly and which fully pays for the sins of God's people in every era of redemptive history (see Rom 3:21–26).

[70] See Gladd, *From Adam and Israel*, 156–70.

This latter achievement is no small feat in light of who God is and the nature of our sin before God. As we have noted, after Genesis 3, a crucial tension *within* the covenant relationship is how humans can dwell before God, given his glory, holiness, and righteousness. God has created everything for himself, especially us. When God finishes his work of creation, he pronounces it "very good" and then rests, signifying his enjoyment of it and relationship with it. Everything is in its proper place and order. Yet due to Adam's sin, humans are cast out of God's presence and exiled. God will not and cannot tolerate sin in his holy presence; it must be punished and removed. How can humans be justified and reconciled before God? How can God dwell with his people without consuming them by the flame of his holiness? The nature of the covenant raises to new heights the problem of forgiveness.

As the OT unfolds, the only solution is found in the new covenant and its mediator. In the old covenant, God provided a sacrificial system that allowed for the forgiveness of sin (Lev 17:11), but as the OT teaches and the new covenant promise anticipates, it was purposely insufficient. The triune God was revealing the need for a more definitive provision, namely, a greater priest-king, the incarnate divine Son. Only in Christ alone and the new covenant is the Spirit of God poured out on the entire people, thus circumcising their hearts and ultimately restoring creation. However, at this point in the story, this is still future, but it is here that the curtain of the NT opens and announces that what God promised is now fulfilled in Messiah Jesus and his church.

The Fulfillment of the Covenants in Christ Jesus and the New Covenant

As the NT opens, *fulfillment* is in the air—what the OT predicted and anticipated is now here in Christ Jesus.[71] In fact, fulfillment begins with Jesus's conception, as the first man of the new creation, yet most significantly, fulfillment dawns in Christ's life and ministry, climaxing in his sacrificial death, glorious resurrection, ascension, and the outpouring of the Spirit at Pentecost. Our Lord's entire identity and work is framed by the OT; he is the one who fulfills *all* of God's promises as unveiled through the covenants, and by his obedience, he inaugurates God's promised "kingdom through [new] covenant." Jesus is the eternal Son of the Father *and* the promised king-priest-son who accomplishes God's plan to restore humanity's rule over

---

[71] For the meaning of "fulfillment," see Carson, "Matthew," 172–79; Schreiner, *New Testament Theology*, 70–79.

creation. Also, Jesus reminds us that his work is to redeem a *new* people for that kingdom, his church (Matt 16:18)—a people whose locus "is no longer national and tribal" but "international, transracial, transcultural."[72] Thus, in Messiah Jesus, God the Son incarnate, the triune God has acted in grace and power to save his people from their sins (Matt 1:21). In Jesus's life and work, the desperate plight begun in Eden now finds a solution as the new creation begins to dawn. In Christ alone, the prophetic anticipation of God's coming to save in and through David's greater Son is fulfilled. Carson states it this way:

> The promise that through Abraham's seed all the nations of the earth will be blessed, gradually expanded into a major theme in the OT, now bursts into the Great Commission, the mushrooming growth of the Jewish church into the Gentile world, the spreading flame reaching across the Roman Empire and beyond, in anticipation of the climactic consummation of God's promises in the new heaven and new earth.[73]

In Christ, *all* of God's promises are now being fulfilled; everything is now under his feet (Gen 1:26–28; Ps 8:6; 1 Cor 15:27; Heb 2:8), and as the victorious Davidic king and last Adam, he is "head" over creation for the benefit of his people, the church (*tē ekklēsia*) (Eph 1:22).

The *fulfillment* of God's promises may be explained in three steps: (1) how *Christ* fulfills the previous covenants, (2) the nature of fulfillment vis-à-vis inaugurated eschatology, and (3) how the church is *new* and receives *all* of God's covenant promises *in and through Christ.*

Christ Jesus Fulfills the OT Covenants

From the opening verse of the NT, Jesus is identified as "the son of David, the son of Abraham" (Matt 1:1), which is full of covenantal significance. Jesus, the eternal Word/Son made flesh (John 1:1–2, 14), has come, and in him, all of God's promises are "Yes and Amen" (2 Cor 1:20). In Christ's work, we see *God's* resolution to reverse the horrible effects of the fall and to satisfy his own demand against us, to make this world right by the inauguration of God's saving reign, and to do so by ratifying the new covenant in his blood. In Christ, the divine Son, who is one with the Father and Spirit, has become the first man and head of the new creation.

---

[72] Carson, *Gagging of God*, 254.

[73] Carson, 263.

In him, all of the previous covenant mediators and typological patterns have reached their fulfillment and telos.

Think about how the NT presents Jesus's identity, especially as tied to the covenants. Jesus *is* the divine Son and Lord who comes to save his people, *and* by his incarnation and work, he *becomes* the son, the antitypical fulfillment of the previous covenant mediators, securing our eternal redemption by his obedient life and death (Rom 1:3–4; Phil 2:6–11; Heb 1:1–3). In his incarnation and work, Jesus becomes David's greater Son; he inaugurates God's kingdom and is now seated as the Davidic king, leading history to its consummation at his return (Matt 28:18–20; Luke 1:31–33; Acts 2:32–36; Rom 1:3–4; Eph 1:9–10, 18–23; Phil 2:9–11; Col 1:15–20; Heb 1 [cf. Pss 2; 45; 110]). Jesus is also the true Israel; he fulfills Israel's role and brings Israel's exile to its end in a new exodus, and he obeys where Israel disobeyed (Matt 2:15 [Hos 11:1]; Matt 3:15–17 [cf. Isa 11:1–2; 42:1; 61:1]; Matt 4:1–11; John 15:1–6 [Isa 5:1–7]). Jesus is Abraham's true seed (Gal 3:16); he constitutes all those in faith union with him, the true children of Abraham and inheritors of *all* the Abrahamic promises (Rom 2:25–29; 4:9–22; Gal 3:6–9; Heb 2:14–18; Rev 5:9–10).

Moreover, Jesus, as the last Adam and the first man of the new creation, fulfills the foundational role of Adam and the creation covenant (Rom 5:12–21; 1 Cor 15:21–22; Heb 2:5–18; 8–10). In his conception, the Spirit, acting in parallel to the first creation (Gen 1:2), overshadows and brings about the beginning of the new creation (Luke 1:35; cf. Matt 1:18–25). In Jesus's baptism, he is identified as the promised Messiah (Mark 1:11; cf. Ps 2:7; Isa 42:1), who receives the Spirit in full measure (Isa 11:1–5; 61:1–2; Luke 4:14–21) *and* who pours out the Spirit on his people (Luke 3:16–17; John 20:21–23; Acts 2:1–36; 10:44–48; Gal 3:1–6; 3:26–4:7), fulfilling OT expectations of the new covenant. In his incarnation, Jesus is *not* "in Adam" as we are; instead, he is the beginning and head of the new creation. Moreover, in his work, Jesus fulfills Adam's role of ruling over the creation as the obedient royal son-priest (Heb 2:5–18 [Ps 8]), evidenced by his healings and miracles tied to the inauguration of *God's* kingdom (Matt 8–9). Notably, in Christ's *bodily* resurrection, the new creation is *now* visible *and physical*.[74] No wonder, in and through Christ, we are now the "new creation" by the Spirit, both individually (2 Cor 5:17; Eph 2:1–10) and corporately as the church (Eph 2:11–22).

---

[74] See G. K. Beale, *A New Testament Biblical Theology: The Unfolding of the OT in the New* (Grand Rapids: Baker, 2011), 227–354.

In every aspect of Jesus's life, ministry, and work, *he* fulfills all of the promises, instruction, and typological patterns of the previous covenants. Whether he is viewed as David's greater Son, the true obedient Israel, as greater than Moses (Heb 3:1–6; cf. Matt 5:17–20), or as the one who fulfills the temple (John 2:19–22) and ends all of the priestly sacrifices in his one-time offering of himself as our great High Priest (Heb 9:1–10:18), *all* of God's promises find their fulfillment and telos in him. What the OT prophets anticipated in the coming of the Lord and his Son/Messiah, tied to the dawning of the new covenant age, is *now* here in Christ Jesus. However, it is crucial to think about the nature of this fulfillment in terms of inaugurated eschatology.

Inaugurated Eschatology and the Nature of Fulfillment in Christ Jesus

The NT clarifies how Christ fulfills all of the OT promises and covenants. The OT prophets speak of the *one* coming of the Lord and Messiah to consummate all things. This one coming will result in the end of "this present age" (characterized by sin, death, and opposition to God) and the beginning of the "the last days" or "the age to come" (characterized by resurrection life, forgiveness of sin, the defeat of God's enemies, and the arrival of a new creation).[75]

Also, the OT prophets think of the "age to come" in terms of an *entire package*. Minimally, when the Lord and Messiah comes, we will see the following: the arrival of God's saving reign (kingdom), the pouring out of the Spirit, a new temple, the full forgiveness of sin, the judgment and defeat of God's enemies, resurrection life, eschatological rest, a restored eschatological Israel, a transformed people composed of believing Jews and Gentiles, and a new creation.[76]

As the NT opens, it never contravenes this OT expectation; rather, it clarifies the OT outlook in what is called "inaugurated eschatology." The NT announces that in Christ, the promised age is now here ("already") since *he*, in his life, death, resurrection, and ascension and in Pentecost, has inaugurated God's kingdom through the new covenant. Yet, the full consummation of what the OT prophets anticipated and predicted is "not yet" here in its fullness.[77] Inaugurated eschatology and the "already-not-yet" tension not only characterizes the basic

---

[75] See Schreiner, *New Testament Theology*, 41–116.

[76] See Anthony A. Hoekema, *The Bible and the Future* (Grand Rapids: Eerdmans, 1994), 3–22; cf. Beale, *New Testament Biblical Theology*, 88–116.

[77] For some helpful discussions of inaugurated eschatology, see Schreiner, *New Testament Theology*, 41–116; cf. Ridderbos, *Paul*, 44–90.

framework of NT eschatology; it also functions in two other important ways, both of which have significant doctrinal import.

First, inaugurated eschatology explains why and how OT promises, hopes, and covenants are *fulfilled* in Christ *and* applied to the church.[78] The *why* is due to *who* Jesus is as God the Son incarnate *and* his triumphant cross work for us. The *how* is both in terms of the "already-not-yet" relationship and underscoring that fulfillment has resulted in momentous epochal/covenantal changes due to the ratification of the new covenant. Although the NT continues the OT's basic timeline, once Christ comes, it is not surprising that many of the themes that were basic to the OT have now been transposed and transformed. Due to the epochal-covenantal shift Christ has inaugurated, Carson notes a few examples of the kind of transposition which has taken place:

> "Kingdom" no longer primarily conjures up a theocratic state in which God rules by his human vassal in the Davidic dynasty. It conjures up the immediate transforming reign of God, dawning now in the ministry, death, resurrection, ascension, and session of Jesus, the promised Messiah, and consummated at his return. Eschatology is thereby transformed. The locus of the people of God is no longer national and tribal; it is international, transracial, transcultural. If the OT prophets constantly look forward to the day when God will act decisively, the New Testament writers announce that God has acted decisively, and that this is "good news," gospel, of universal, eternal significance and stellar importance. Thus kingdom, Christology, eschatology, church, gospel, become dominant terms or themes. Temple, priest, sacrifice, law, and much more are transposed; national and tribal outlooks gradually fade from view.[79]

Second, inaugurated eschatology also explains how the NT clarifies the basic timeline of the OT to speak of *two* comings of Christ. The OT distinguished between "this present age"—an

---

[78] As noted above, *fulfillment* is used in its prophetic sense, i.e., Jesus "fulfills" the OT in that it points to him and, now that he has come, is fulfilled. In the NT, "fulfillment" can be *direct* in the sense of prophetic prediction (e.g., Mic 5:2; Matt 2:1–12), but it can also be more *indirect*, tied to typological patterns that are fulfilled in Christ. Both senses are prophetic, but not in exactly the same way. On "fulfillment," see Schreiner, *New Testament Theology*, 70–79; and Vern S. Poythress, *The Shadow of Christ in the Law of Moses* (Phillipsburg: P&R, 1995), 251–86.

[79] Carson, *Gagging of God*, 254.

age characterized by sin, death, and opposition to God as represented by earthy *kingdoms*—and "the age to come"—an age in which the LORD will come to rescue his people through his Messiah, the Davidic king, and inaugurate his kingdom through the new covenant. In the OT, these two ages are in chronological sequence. For this reason, the OT presents only *one* coming of the LORD and his Messiah to usher in the eschatological hope of the prophets, that is, the "age to come."

However, the NT modifies this basic timeline and now speaks of *two* comings of Christ and an overlap of the ages. In Christ's *first* coming, Jesus appears as Lord/Son in relation to his Father *and* as Messiah, who brings "the age to come" into "this present age" *in principle*. Yet the *consummation* of "the age to come" awaits Christ's *second* coming. Between these two advents, Jesus is reigning over his creation-kingdom. The realities of life in "the age to come" have *already* come into "this present age," but they are *not yet* here in full. "This present age," then, characterized by sin and death, continues until Christ's return even though he has already inaugurated the "age to come," hence the overlap of the ages.

Sometimes this overlap of the ages is illustrated by a World War II analogy using D-day and V-day.[80] In World War II, D-day brought about an important victory for the allied troops. As a result, the enemy was decisively defeated, and it was only a matter of time before final victory would be achieved, although the war was not yet over. D-day is analogous to Christ's first coming, which, in principle, has inaugurated the "age to come" but not yet in its fullness. In Christ's first coming, God's promise of redemption is now realized. God's saving reign has broken into this world and, along with it, the new covenant and the new creation. Sin, death, and the power of the Evil One have been destroyed. It is only a matter of time before final victory is won, but in principle, the victory has been won. Yet our D-day still awaits our V-day, that is, our final victory when Christ comes again and consummates what he began. In this overlap of the ages, although God's people are no longer identified with "this present age" since we have been transferred from being "in Adam" to being "in Christ" (Rom 5:12–21; Eph 2:1–10), and although we are now participants of the future age and have eternal life, justification before God, and the transforming power of the Spirit (everything associated with "the age to come"),

---

[80] Oscar Cullmann used this way of describing the different results achieved by Christ in his two advents. *Christ and Time*, trans. Floyd V. Filson (Philadelphia: Westminster, 1950). See also Hoekema, *The Bible and the Future*, 21.

we still await the arrival of his kingdom in consummated glory. But what Christ has won in his first advent is now our guarantee and pledge that the consummated age is not a vain hope, but a certainty.

In the NT, the already-not-yet tension is presented in a number of ways. For example, we see it in regard to the coming of God's kingdom and saving rule in Christ. The NT teaches that the God who rules over all (e.g., Pss 93:1; 97:1; 99:1; 103:19; Dan 4:34–35) has now brought his saving rule to this fallen world in Christ, as evidenced by the coming of the Spirit (Matt 12:28; Luke 11:20) and Christ's teaching and miracles (Luke 4:16–30; cf. Isa 61:1–2; 58:6; 29:18). In Christ, God's kingdom has broken into this world (Matt 4:17; Mark 1:14–15), but Jesus still teaches us to pray "Your kingdom come" (Matt 6:10) and of a future day when he will come "in his kingdom" (Matt 16:28; Luke 23:51), "which clearly refers to the future fulfillment of the kingdom promise."[81] This entails that because it is in "the present evil age" (Gal 1:4), Christ sits on the throne of heaven, "far above all rule and authority and power and dominion . . . not only in this age but also in the one to come" (Eph 1:21), there is continuity and discontinuity between his present and future rule. His future rule is here *in kind* (continuity), and the present kingdom of Christ will increase *unto completion* (discontinuity) at his return.

What is true about the already-not-yet dynamic of the inauguration of God's kingdom in Christ is also true of *the entire package* of prophetic anticipation of the "age to come." For example, think about how the pouring out of the promised Holy Spirit, tied to the new covenant age, is presented. Because Jesus is the risen and exalted Davidic king and Lord, *he* pours out the *promised* Spirit on his new covenant people in fulfillment of Joel's prophesy (Acts 2:32–36; cf. Luke 24:46–51; John 14:15–17). Yet the present gift of the Spirit is the *arrabōn,* the deposit and guarantee of our future inheritance in the consummation (Eph 1:13–14).[82] Thus, the reception of the Spirit signals that the OT restoration promises, first given to Israel, are *now* taking place in Christ *and* his people (the church), which entails that everyone *in Christ* has the

---

[81] Schreiner, *New Testament Theology*, 51. The "not-yet" reality of the kingdom is also seen in such texts as Matt 5:3–12; 8:11–12; 13:24–30, 36–43; 22:1–14; 25:1–13, 31–46; 26:29; etc.). See Schreiner, 50–68.

[82] As Anthony Hoekema summarizes, "we may say that in the possession of the Spirit we who are in Christ have a foretaste of the blessings of the age to come, and a pledge and guarantee of the resurrection of the body. Yet we have only the first fruits. We look forward to the final consummation of the kingdom of God, when we shall enjoy these blessings to the full." Hoekema, *The Bible and the Future*, 67.

Spirit and is *now* a participant and a partaker of the powers of the "age to come."[83] But the NT insists that what the Spirit gives is only a foretaste of far greater blessings to come.

Or think of other OT promises that are *now* here but still await their fullness in the *not yet*. In Christ, we are *now* justified, partakers of new covenant blessings (Jer 31:34; Rom 3:21–26; 8:1), yet we will still publicly stand before the judgment seat of Christ (2 Cor 5:10). Presently, in Christ, we are raised from spiritual death to life, adopted, redeemed, reconciled, and holy (Rom 8:9–17; 2 Cor 5:16–21; Eph 1:7–8; 2:1–10). But we still await our bodily resurrection, the full benefits of our adoption and inheritance, and our glorification at Christ's return (Rom 8:18–27; 1 Cor 15:35–58; Eph 1:13–14; 1 Pet 1:3–9). In Christ, we *now* experience salvation rest (Matt 11:28–30; Heb 3:7–4:11)—a rest that was first in creation, lost in the fall, typified in the Sabbath and entrance into the land, but *now* entered into by faith in Christ (Heb 4:1–11). But the fullness of our covenant rest waits the dawning of the new creation (Heb 11:16; 12:22–29). Related to our rest, *in Christ* (the antitype of the temple [John 2:19–22]), new covenant believers are *now*, individually and corporately, God's temple indwelt by the Spirit (1 Cor 3:16–17; 6:19; 2 Cor 6:16; Eph 2:21; Heb 3:6; 1 Pet 2:5). However, we still await the new creation where there is no temple "because the Lord God Almighty and the Lamb are its temple" (Rev 21:22 NIV).

Even the new creation promise is fulfilled in an *already-not-yet* way. Our Lord is the first man of the new creation in his incarnation and resurrection. G. K. Beale notes, "Christ's resurrection, however, placed him into the beginning of the new creation. The resurrected Christ is not merely spiritually the inauguration of the new cosmos, but he is literally its beginning, since he was resurrected with a physical, newly created body."[84] And, in union with Christ by the Spirit, we, individually and corporately, are *now* "new creation" (2 Cor 5:17; Eph 2:1–21), although we wait for a new creation where we will live forever and fulfill our role as image-sons.

Lastly, the already-not-yet dynamic also applies to the new covenant promise of a transformed people. The prophets predicted that Messiah's new covenant people (composed of

---

[83] See Alan J. Thompson, *The Acts of the Risen Lord Jesus: Luke's Account of God's Unfolding Plan*, NSBT 27 (Downers Grove: InterVarsity, 2011), 71–143.

[84] G. K. Beale, "The End Starts at the Beginning," in Benjamin L. Gladd and Matthew S. Harmon, *Making All Things New: Inaugurated Eschatology for the Life of the Church* (Grand Rapids: Baker Academic, 2016), 10. Also see the discussion in Thompson, *Acts of the Risen Lord Jesus*, 71–101, for the importance of the resurrection in prophetic hope and fulfillment.

believing Jews and Gentiles) would *not* be like Israel (Jer 31:29–34). Why? Because God will circumcise their hearts (Deut 30:1–6; Jer 31:33) by the Spirit (Ezek 36:25–27; 37), and as such, they will *all* know God and stand justified before God (Jer 31:34). Additionally, the Spirit will empower and gift the *entire* community (Joel 2:28–32; cf. Num 11:29). In Christ, *this* reality is *now* here in God's people, individually and corporately. A Christian is no longer "in Adam" but "in Christ," which entails that *all* new covenant blessings are ours *now*: we are born of and empowered by the Spirit and forgiven of our sin, and we know God. However, there is still more to come as we await our glorification, resurrection bodies, and a greater experience of the knowledge of God.

In sum, inaugurated eschatology and its relationship to consummated eschatology gives shape to the Bible's covenantal story, and it is the Bible's explanation of how Christ fulfills all the promises and expectations of the OT. One cannot understand the nature of the kingdom, eternal life, the gift of the Spirit, the church, salvation, eschatology, or, most significantly, Christology (tied to the Trinity) apart from this larger theological framework.[85] For example, to say that Jesus has *fulfilled* all of God's plans by inaugurating the promised "age to come" is another way of speaking of his total uniqueness, exclusivity, and sufficiency as the eternal Son made flesh. Furthermore, the framework of inaugurated eschatology also gives the warrant for *why* the new covenant is *greater* and thus the fulfillment and telos of the previous covenants. But although the concept of inaugurated eschatology is viewed as a "given" in evangelical theology, it is not always applied consistently in doctrinal construction, a point we will explain in the next chapter and throughout part 4, specifically in the doctrinal areas of ecclesiology and eschatology.

The Church Receives All of God's Promises in Christ

In the NT, "the church" is central to God's redemptive plan and our Lord's work. In fact, Jesus reminds us how central she is to his messianic mission when he says: "I will build my church" (Matt 16:18). By this time in his ministry, Jesus, as the true Israel (Matt 2:15; Hos 11:1) has begun to gather his messianic community by calling the twelve disciples and constituting them

---

[85] See David F. Wells, *God the Evangelist* (Grand Rapids: Eerdmans, 1987), 9–10; Schreiner, *New Testament Theology*, 41–116.

as the new Israel (Matt 4:18–22; 10:1–4).[86] The future tense of "I will build" (*oikodomēsō*) looks ahead to the time after Jesus's resurrection when the promised Spirit is poured out at Pentecost, thus signaling the arrival of the new covenant age. In fact, as Christ's mission unfolds in the book of Acts, Jesus's messianic people (*ekklēsia*) begins with the Twelve and with believing Jews (Acts 1–2), reunites Israel with the Samaritans' conversion (Acts 8), and then climaxes with the Gentiles; all of these *together* constitute the church (Acts 10; cf. Eph 2:11–21). In Christ, the church, as *his* people, has entered God's kingdom, and as a result, she lives, worships, and proclaims the gospel to all nations as she awaits Christ's return (Matt 28:18–20). Central, then, to Jesus's work is the fulfillment of his Father's will by redeeming, establishing, and building *his* church.

If the church is central to Christ's work, then it follows that she is also central to the entirety of our triune God's redemptive plan. This is why Paul can say that due to Jesus's triumphant work, the Father has "subjected everything under [Christ's] feet and appointed [Christ] as head over everything for the church" (Eph 1:22). Christ's lordship over all is for the benefit of his people; this certainly places the church at the center of God's redemptive purposes. In Eph 3:1–10, this same truth is taught. Paul identifies the "mystery" of God (i.e., God's eternal plan now revealed and made known in Christ) with the church.[87] As Paul proclaims the "incalculable riches of Christ" (v. 8), it results in the birth and growth of the church. The "mystery" is not an abstraction. In Christ and his church, it takes on concrete visible shape as a new, multiethnic humanity is formed and grows, consisting of believing Jews and Gentiles who display "God's multi-faceted wisdom" (v. 10). The church is the public display of God's power, grace and wisdom and is thus central to God's entire redemptive plan.[88]

Given the centrality of the church to God's plan and Christ's work as our new covenant head, there is an *inseparable, organic* relationship between Christ and his people, signified by our union with Christ. All that Christ has achieved is for the church's benefit, and as an entire church without distinction, she has received *all* of God's promises *in Christ*. Since the new

---

[86] See Andreas J. Köstenberger, "The Church According to the Gospels," in *The Community of Jesus: A Theology of the Church*, ed. Kendell H. Easley and Christopher W. Morgan (Nashville: B&H Academic, 2013), 35–63.

[87] Beale and Gladd, *Hidden but Now Revealed*, 159–73 (see chap. 4, n. 56).

[88] See John R. W. Stott, *The Message of Ephesians*, BST (Downers Grove: InterVarsity, 1984), 122–30.

covenant is the fulfillment of the previous covenants, the church, as God's *new* covenant kingdom people, is the only community that lasts forever, while all the kingdoms of this world fade away and ultimately come under divine judgment (Rev 18–22).

Two important theological entailments follow from the unbreakable Christ-church relation, which explains why the church receives *all* of God's promises *in Christ*. First, the church is part of the *one* people of God (elect) across time but is covenantally *new* and constituted *now* as a regenerate people and not a "mixed" people.[89] Second, the church is God's *new* creation that remains *forever*, consisting of believing Jews and Gentiles, who, in Christ, equally and fully receive *all* of God's promises. The church is *not* a parenthesis in God's plan or merely a *present-day* illustration of what national Israel and Gentile nations will be in the millennium and/or consummation as recipients of "distinct" blessings.[90] Three points will summarize these statements, but a full discussion awaits volume 2's treatment of ecclesiology.

First, God only has *one* elect people throughout time, all of which are saved by grace through faith in God's promises grounded in Christ. Proof of continuity between OT and NT saints is in the language used to describe both (Rom 1:1–2, 11; Phil 3:3, 7, 9). Descriptions of Israel as God's covenant people are applied to the church *through Christ*.[91] The language of "assembly" (Heb. *qāhāl*; Gk. *ekklēsia*) is also applied to Israel and the church (Deut 4:10; Isa 2:2–4; Matt 16:18; 1 Cor 11:18; Heb 10:25). But this does not mean that Israel and the church are by nature the same. Through Jesus, the last Adam and true Israel, the church is the "Israel of God" (Gal 6:16),[92] but there are major redemptive-historical differences due to the covenants.

Second, the church is covenantally *new* and constituted as a believing, regenerate people. Alongside Jeremiah's depiction of a transformed people, which the NT applies to the church (1 Cor 11:25; 2 Cor 3:7–18; Heb 8–10), are other truths that underscore the church's *newness*. For example, the church is viewed as an eschatological and "gathered" community—identified with the "age to come"—which has arrived in Christ and is consummated at his

---

[89] This is in contrast to Reformed, paedobaptist covenant theology, to be discussed in chapter 15.

[90] This is in contrast to dispensational theology, to be discussed in chapter 15.

[91] Exod 19:6; Deut 32:15; 33:12; Isa 43:20–21; 44:2; Jer 31:31–34; Hos 1:6, 9–11; 2:1, 23; see Rom 9:24–26; Gal 3:26–29; Eph 2:12, 19; 3:4–6; 1 Thess 1:4; Heb 8:6–13; 1 Pet 2:9–10.

[92] See Beale, *New Testament Biblical Theology*, 651–749. For a defense of Gal 6:16 as referring to the church, see Andreas J. Köstenberger, "The Identity of the ἸΣΡΑΗΛ ΤΟΥ ΘΕΟΥ *(Israel of God)* in Galatians 6:16," *Faith and Mission* 19 (2001): 3–24.

return. Her identity is not with "this present age" but with the saving reign of Christ that is now here.[93] Those who have placed their faith in Christ are *now* citizens of the new/heavenly Jerusalem, transferred from being "in Adam" to being "in Christ" with all the benefits of that union. This is the point of Heb 12:18–29. In contrast with the Israelites who assembled at Sinai (vv. 18–21), as new covenant believers, we have *already* gathered to meet God at the "heavenly Jerusalem" (vv. 22–24), associated with the dawning of the new creation.[94] As the church, we are beginning to enjoy by faith the privileges of that city still to come (Heb 13:14). But to participate in these realities *now* entails that the church is, by definition, part of the new creation, consisting of people who are raised and seated with Christ in the heavenly realms (Eph 2:5–6; Col 2:12–13; 3:3). This is only true of a regenerate people. Now that Christ has come, the NT knows nothing of someone who is *in Christ* (in the new covenant sense) who is not regenerate, effectually called by the Father, born of the Spirit, justified, holy, and awaiting glorification.

Furthermore, in Christ, the church is God's *new temple* (1 Cor 6:19; 2 Cor 6:16; Eph 2:21; Heb 3:6; 1 Pet 2:5). As God's temple, we now have direct access to the Father by the Spirit (Eph 2:18; Heb 10:19–22), something which is *new* in contrast to Israel. The OT does not describe Israel as God's temple in whom the Spirit dwells in each person (instead, they go to the temple), yet this is precisely what the church *is*. This is further proof that the church is *new* and a *regenerate* people. Why? For this reason: this description is only true of people who have been effectually called by the Father, experienced new birth by the Spirit, and been united to Christ in a permanent and secure covenantal union (Rom 8:28–39; Eph 1:13–14).

Third, the church is God's *new* creation/humanity that remains *forever*, constituted by believing Jews and Gentiles, who equally and fully receive *all* of God's promises in Christ. Ephesians 2:11–22 teaches this truth.[95] Gentiles, who were once outside of Israel's covenant

---

[93] See D. A. Carson, "Evangelicals, Ecumenism, and the Church," in *Evangelical Affirmations*, ed. Kenneth S. Kantzer and Carl F. H. Henry (Grand Rapids: Zondervan, 1990), 363–67.

[94] "You have already come" (*proselēluthate*) is in the perfect tense. This reminds us that believers *now* participate in new covenant realities as the gathered people of God, although we await the end. See Schreiner, *Commentary on Hebrews*, 394–402 (see chap. 4, n. 39); George H. Guthrie, *Hebrews*, NAC (Grand Rapids: Zondervan, 1998), 416–32.

[95] See Joshua Greever, "The Nature of the New Covenant: A Case Study in Ephesians 2:11–22," *SBJT* 20 (2016): 73–90; Andrews T. Lincoln, *Ephesians*, WBC 42 (Dallas: Word, 1990), 122–65.

(vv. 11–12), now *in Christ Jesus* are recipients of *all* of God's promises.[96] By Christ's work, the law covenant, which purposely separated Jews and Gentiles, is fulfilled. The result? *Both* Jews and Gentiles are now reconciled to God *and* each other by entering a new covenant and becoming God's new creation/humanity (vv. 14–18) and together inherit the same promises. Paul is forthright: the church is not merely the extension of Israel or an amalgam of Jews and Gentiles. The church is *new*—a third entity that is Christian (see Paul's view of himself in 1 Cor 9:19–23). The church transcends the old entities, although unbelieving Israel and disobedient Gentiles continue to exist. The church is not simply a replacement of Israel, or a "renewed" instantiation of it, or one phase in God's plan that will end in the future when God goes back to his previous plan for Israel and the nations. God's plan *always* anticipated the creation of *the church* (Eph 3:8–13). What makes this possible is Jesus, who fulfills God's promises and applies them to his people. One cannot understand the *identity, nature,* and *newness* of the church apart from Christ.

Further evidence that the church receives *all* of God's promises is how OT restoration promises for Israel are applied to the church *in Christ*. For example, in Acts, before Christ ascends, he teaches his disciples about the *kingdom* and tells them to wait in Jerusalem for *the promised* Spirit, tied to OT prophetic restoration hope. The disciples ask, "Lord, are you restoring the kingdom to Israel at this time?" (Acts 1:6). Jesus answers *not* by redirecting their attention to the church age, "implicitly postponing a restoration of Israel to the future" where she will finally receive promises "distinct" from believing Gentile nations.[97] This interpretation does not account for who Jesus is as "true Israel" and "last Adam" or how *he* fulfills *all* of the covenants *and* applies God's promises to the church.

Instead, Jesus answers their question by saying that Israel's restoration is about to occur at Pentecost (Acts 2) and in Jesus's reign, starting in Jerusalem with Jewish believers, extending to Judea and Samaria (Acts 8, thus a reconstituted Israel) *and* to the nations (Acts 10–11), thus creating a new humanity in Christ. Jesus responds to his disciples ("when the Holy Spirit has come on you," "you will be my witnesses," and "to the end of the earth") with language drawn

---

[96] See Beale and Gladd, *Hidden but Now Revealed*, 159–73.

[97] Thompson, *Acts of the Risen Lord Jesus*, 105; cf. Peterson, *Acts of the Apostles*, 108–13 (see chap. 1, n. 21).

from Isaiah (Isa 32:15; 43:12; 49:6), which anticipates the day when God will save *through his Servant*, bring about Israel's restoration, and include Gentiles in that restoration program. Jesus announces that what the OT prophets anticipated is now occurring in him and the church. Exactly *how* the Gentiles are included in God's people is yet to be shown (Acts 10–11, 15; cf. Eph 3); but there is no question that Gentiles will be included and that it is about to commence at Pentecost. The sequence of restoration is significant: first to Israel then to the nations (cf. Acts 3:26), which is precisely how the risen and exalted Christ builds his church.[98]

In Christ *and* the church, *all* of God's promises are now being fulfilled. Christ Jesus, who fulfills the previous covenants, applies his work to his people by triune agency. Moreover, as the OT anticipated and the NT teaches, God's people include believing Jews and Gentiles, who fulfill what Israel, indeed, Adam, only typified, as a transformed people who function as a royal priesthood and holy nation (1 Pet 2:9–10; Exod 19:6). Together they are the restored Israel as Abraham's children (Rom 4:9–22; Gal 3:6–9), true Jews because of their heart circumcision (Rom 2:25–29; Phil 3:3), the *one* new man (Eph 2:11–22), from the same olive tree (Rom 11:17–24), and part of the 144,000 who symbolically refer to the entire church (Rev 7:1–8; 14:3). Captured in Scripture's final vision, the church is Christ's bride, the heavenly Jerusalem, whose foundation is the twelve tribes of Israel *and* the twelve apostles (Rev 21:9–14), an international people (Rev 5:9–10) who inherit the new creation as God's covenant people (Rev 21–22).

Concluding Reflection

In the last two chapters, we have sought to think through the Bible's own theological framework. First, in terms of the Bible's major plot movements that ought to be the lens by which we view the world and critique other worldviews. Second, and complimentary to the plot movements, we have sought to add more specificity to Scripture's interpretive framework by thinking about how God's eternal plan unfolds through the covenants from creation to the new creation, what we have called progressive covenantalism. The reason for doing so is because our

[98] For a detailed treatment of OT restoration promises applied to the church, see Beale, *New Testament Biblical Theology*, 651–749; Thompson, *Acts of the Risen Lord Jesus*, 71–143.

theology is only biblical *if* it is true to Scripture's own presentation by following the Bible's own content, categories, and intra-systematic structures. Scripture is not a collection of isolated texts that we can organize at will. The Bible is God's own interpretation of his mighty acts, unfolding his eternal plan along a specific storyline centered in our Lord Jesus Christ, and it is out of the Bible's interpretive framework that our doctrinal formulation must arise.

However, Christians differ on how best to construct Scripture's theological framework. Although there is more agreement than not, disagreements arise at specific points that not only distinguish various theological systems but also lead to different doctrinal conclusions that continue to divide the church. If we are going to understand and resolve differences within Christian theology, we must first describe the biblical-theological constructions of other views on their own terms, which is the subject matter of the next chapter. Our goal is to understand why and where people differ so that Scripture is our final authority by which we evaluate our theological formulations and conclusions.

CHAPTER 15

Competing Biblical-Theological Systems in Evangelical Theology

Introduction

In the previous two chapters, we described the biblical-theological framework of Scripture. Why? For theology to be true to Scripture, our doctrinal formulations must be "constructed" from *within* the Bible's own interpretive framework (intratextual) so that our theological conclusions are true to the Bible's own presentation, content, and categories. However, the church has not always agreed on the specifics of the Bible's overall theological framework, which is one of the reasons for theological division among us.

Evangelical theology, as an heir of the Reformation, agrees on many points of doctrine,[1] and it agrees on the basic contours of the Bible's framework from creation to the new creation, which we must not minimize.[2] For example, evangelicals agree that "covenants" are central to the Bible's story and that God's redemptive plan unfolds over time, reaching its fulfillment in Christ. Most people also accept some form of redemptive epochs (or "dispensations") across

[1] See the "Mere Protestant" confession of a large swath of evangelicals, https://reformingcatholicconfession.com/.

[2] On this point, see Vanhoozer, *Biblical Authority After Babel* (see chap. 1, n. 34).

history demarcated by the biblical covenants, inaugurated eschatology, the fulfillment of God's plan in Christ and the church, and various changes in the administration of God's plan across redemptive history. But evangelicals also disagree on some of the specifics of God's plan and the exact relationships between the covenants. This is not a new debate. In the early church, the apostles wrestled with the implications of Christ's new covenant work (see Acts 10–11, 15; Gal 3–4; Eph 2:11–22).

And today, evangelicals still disagree on the precise relationships between the covenants, which has direct implications for other theological disputes, such as debates on the *newness* of what Christ has achieved; what moral law applies to the church today, as reflected in larger disagreements regarding the Decalogue, the Sabbath/Lord's Day observance, and the application of the civil laws of Israel to the state; and how previous OT promises are now fulfilled in Christ and the church, as tied to the larger discussion of the Israel-church relationship and the role of national Israel in God's plan. In these disputes, theological formulations are directly impacted, especially in ecclesiology, eschatology, aspects of soteriology, and the application of Scripture to ethics and political thought. How one "puts together" the Bible affects theological conclusions, and unless we see this, we will not resolve some of the disagreements among us.

In the last chapter, the theological framework of progressive covenantalism was described, which I believe best captures how God's eternal plan unfolds from creation to the new creation. However, not everyone agrees! But this should not deter us since we believe that Scripture is first-order, and as such, it can correct our interpretations as we "think God's thoughts after him" *and* interact with other ways that Christians have constructed the Bible's overall metanarrative. In this regard, within post-Reformation and evangelical theology, there are two dominant ways that the Bible's metanarrative and framework has been "constructed," namely, dispensational theology and covenant theology and varieties within each view. Since one's view of how Scripture is "put together" affects specific doctrinal conclusions, it is necessary to describe these other ways of making sense of the Bible's framework. In fact, unless we think carefully about where we agree and disagree with each other, we will not appreciate *why* and *where* the differences lie and thus make little headway in resolving our disagreements. Before a proper understanding and critique of views can take place, we must first know what the other theological views are saying, a point to which we now turn.

Dispensationalism and Its Varieties[3]

Dispensationalism is not a monolithic viewpoint. Over the years it has gone through a number of revisions although it remains united by a common core. As a movement, it first took shape in the Brethren movement in early nineteenth-century England. Originally it was associated with such names as John Darby (1800–82), Benjamin Newton (1807–99), and George Müller (1805–98) and, in North America, with such names as D. L. Moody (1837–99), J. R. Graves (1820–93), and C. I. Scofield (1843–1921) and the *Scofield Reference Bible*. Probably the most extensive systematic theology written from a dispensational view was Lewis Sperry Chafer's eight-volume *Systematic Theology*.[4] Presently, three forms of dispensationalism exist, which must be distinguished in order to grasp the development that has occurred within the view: "classic" (e.g., John Darby, Lewis S. Chafer, *Scofield Reference Bible*), "traditional" (e.g., John Walvoord, Charles Ryrie, J. Dwight Pentecost, revised *Scofield Bible*), and "progressive" (e.g., Craig Blaising, Darrell Bock, John Feinberg, Robert Saucy, Bruce Ware).

The term *dispensation* is a biblical term derived from *oikonomeō* (Eph 1:10; 3:2, 9; Col 1:25), which means "to manage, regulate, administer, and plan the affairs of a household."[5] Behind the word is the idea of God's plan or administration being accomplished in this world and how God arranges and orders his relationship to us. "Dispensation," as Glenn Kreider explains, refers to a "distinguishable period of time during which God administers His plan

---

[3] For summaries of dispensational theology, see D. Jeffrey Bingham and Glenn R. Kreider, eds., *Dispensationalism and the History of Redemption: A Developing and Diverse Tradition* (Chicago: Moody Publishers, 2015); John MacArthur and Richard Mayhue, eds., *Christ's Prophetic Plans: A Futuristic Premillennial Primer* (Chicago: Moody Publishers, 2012); Blaising and Bock, *Progressive Dispensationalism* (see chap. 14, n. 54); Craig A. Blaising and Darrell L. Bock, eds., *Dispensationalism, Israel, and the Church: A Search for Definition* (Grand Rapids: Zondervan, 1992); Robert L. Saucy, *The Case for Progressive Dispensationalism* (Grand Rapids: Zondervan, 1993); Herbert W. Bateman IV, ed., *Three Central Issues in Contemporary Dispensationalism: A Comparison of Traditional and Progressive Views* (Grand Rapids: Kregel, 1999); John S. Feinberg, ed., *Continuity and Discontinuity: Perspectives on the Relationship between the Old and New Testaments* (Wheaton: Crossway, 1988); Ron J. Bigalke Jr., ed. *Progressive Dispensationalism: An Analysis of the Movement and Defense of Traditional Dispensationalism* (Lanham: University Press of America, 2005).

[4] Lewis Sperry Chafer, *Systematic Theology* (1948; repr., Grand Rapids: Kregel, 1993).

[5] See Glenn R. Kreider, "What is Dispensationalism? A Proposal," in Bingham and Kreider, *Dispensationalism*, 20–21. *Dispensation* is the anglicized form of *dispensatio*, the Latin Vulgate rendering of *oikonomia*.

of redemption differently from other eras or periods. This change happens in history; God brings one economy or administration to an end, and then inaugurates a new one."[6] But dispensational theology does not view the progression of the covenants as *the* backbone to the Bible's story. Instead, the covenants are a major biblical theme, but structurally, they are not *the* central way God's plan unfolds across time, contrary to our discussion of the Bible's storyline in chapter 15.[7]

Dispensationalism is probably best known for its dividing the epochs of redemptive history into distinct "dispensations" and its claim that during each of these dispensations, God works out a specific phase of his overall plan. However, as Vern Poythress notes, there is a sense in which the word *dispensation* is *not* completely helpful for distinguishing dispensationalism from other theological systems since all Christians believe in distinct dispensations or epochs in the unfolding of God's plan: "The recognition of distinctions between different epochs is by no means unique to D[dispensational]-theologians."[8] Most current dispensationalists agree. For example, John Feinberg admits that one's defense of dispensationalism is *not* tied to the word. All Christians believe in some kind of "dispensational" change in the unfolding of God's plan so "it is no more distinctive to dispensationalism than talk of covenants is distinctive to covenant theology. Dispensationalists talk about covenants all the time."[9]

This observation raises an important question: What, then, is *distinctive* about dispensational theology? Within dispensationalism, various "essentials" have been proposed.[10] But an excellent case can be made that its *sine qua non* is the Israel-church distinction, which is largely tied to its understanding of the biblical covenants and the (inter)relationships between them. For *all* varieties of dispensationalism, *Israel* refers to an ethnic, national people, and it is *never* the case that the church is the transformed, restored eschatological Israel in God's plan or the people who fulfill Israel's role. For dispensationalists, the salvation of Gentiles is *not* part of the fulfillment of the promises made to Israel as a nation now realized in the church. God has

---

[6] Kreider, "What is Dispensationalism?," 21.

[7] For example, see Kreider, 20.

[8] Vern S. Poythress, *Understanding Dispensationalists*, 2nd ed. (Phillipsburg: P&R, 1994), 9–10.

[9] John S. Feinberg, "Systems of Discontinuity," in Feinberg, *Continuity and Discontinuity*, 69.

[10] See Craig A. Blaising, "Dispensationalism: The Search for Definition," in Blaising and Bock, *Dispensationalism, Israel, and the Church*, 13–34; and Michael Vlach, "What is Dispensationalism?," in MacArthur and Mayhue, *Christ's Prophetic Plans*, 19–38.

promised national Israel, first in the Abrahamic covenant and reaffirmed by the prophets, the possession of the land under Christ's rule as the Davidic king, which still awaits its fulfillment in the millennium and consummation. Since the OT promises to national Israel have *not yet* been realized, in the future, Israel, as a nation, will be restored and only then will she exercise her mediatorial role to the nations in the land, although some progressives downplay Israel's future *mediatorial* role.[11]

The church, then, is *never* viewed as the restored, eschatological Israel who receives *all* of God's promises in Christ, including OT promises to Israel, as described in the last chapter. Instead, the church is *new* in God's purposes, that is, *ontologically* different from Israel. Although in our present "dispensation" the church (composed of believing Jews and Gentiles) finds its origin in Christ and receives the *spiritual* blessings of the Spirit that were promised to OT Israel, this fact does *not* entail that the church fulfills the role of Israel. Rather, these blessings are only an inaugurated spiritual application to the church; they are not "a *replacement* of the specific hopes of Israel,"[12] only compatible with those hopes. In the future, Christ will rule over redeemed *nations*, not the church as another "people group." Believing Jews and Gentiles, who now compose the church, will join the redeemed of national Israel *and* the Gentile nations to live under Christ's rule "according to their different nationalities," and Israel specifically, *as a nation*, will finally receive all of God's outstanding promises made to her. In this present dispensation, then, the church serves as an illustration of what the redeemed *nations* will be like in the future as they experience the transforming work of the Spirit. But it is not the church as a *new covenant* people (i.e., *the* end-time forever people of God) that receives *all* of God's promises *equally* and *fully* in Christ. Rather, in the future, the redeemed *nations* will receive God's promises *according to their specific national identities*, hence the distinction between Israel as a nation and the church as a people who in an inaugurated form illustrate what is still to come.[13]

---

[11] For example, see Saucy, *Case for Progressive Dispensationalism*, 259, 306–23; and Craig A. Blaising, "God's Plan for History: The Consummation," in Bingham and Kreider, *Dispensationalism*, 195–218.

[12] Blaising and Bock, *Progressive Dispensationalism*, 267. *Replacement* is a loaded word in today's discussion. Nondispensational theology is often viewed as a "replacement" theology or a form of supersessionism, which is an unhelpful way of describing these views. The language should be dropped since it clouds the real debate.

[13] On this point, see Blaising, "God's Plan for History," 195–218; Blaising, "Biblical Hermeneutics," in *The New Christian Zionism: Fresh Perspectives on Israel and the Land*, ed. Gerald R. McDermott (Downers Grove: IVP Academic, 2016), 79–105; cf. Vlach, "What is Dispensationalism?," 27–33.

Dispensationalism also affirms that the church, as a people, began at Pentecost with the gift of the Holy Spirit. Thus, most insist that the salvation *experience* of the person in the church is *qualitatively* different from the salvation experience of the Israelite under the old covenant.[14] Furthermore, given the Israel-church distinction, dispensationalists see more *discontinuity* from the old to the new covenant vis-à-vis the *nature and structure* of the covenant communities, in contrast to covenant theology. Not surprisingly, given the Israel-church distinction and its outworking in dispensational theology, the major *theological* differences between dispensational and covenant theology often emerge in ecclesiology and eschatology.

Regarding ecclesiology, since the church is distinctively *new* due to Christ's coming and the *newness* of the Spirit's permanent indwelling in the believer, dispensationalists view the nature of the church, along with its structure and ordinances, as distinct from Israel. Regarding the *nature* of the church, for example, in contrast to covenant theology, dispensational ecclesiology views the church as constituted by a regenerate people and permanently indwelt by the Spirit, not as a "mixed" community of believers and unbelievers. Also, dispensational ecclesiology affirms credobaptism, contra paedobaptism, since one cannot equate the sign of the old covenant with the sign of the new given the fundamental Israel-church distinction and what the sign of baptism signifies for the church. By contrast, covenant theology rejects the Israel-church distinction of dispensational theology and argues for continuity between them both in terms of the nature of the covenant people (and similarity of salvation experience) and the meaning of the covenant signs of circumcision and baptism. On these points, dispensational ecclesiology differs from the ecclesiology of covenant theology.

Regarding eschatology, given the Israel-church distinction and God's unchanging promise to Israel of living in the land ruled by the Davidic king (i.e., Jesus), dispensational theologians affirm a distinct future for national Israel tied to her national identity in a future millennial age and continuing in the consummation. Much of the rationale for their form of premillennialism is their belief that specific promises to Israel from the OT are not yet fulfilled. For progressives, the kingdom is viewed as a multinational order of "redeemed peoples on a renewed earth."[15] Israel, as a redeemed nation, is guaranteed her "national and territorial identity" due

[14] See Feinberg, "Systems of Discontinuity," 71–85.

[15] Blaising, "God's Plan for History," 210.

to God's promise,[16] and redeemed Gentile nations will also live according to their national identities on a new earth. By contrast, covenant theology rejects this form of premillennialism mainly because they view all of God's promises as reaching their fulfillment in Christ and the dawning of the new creation, which the church, as the restored eschatological Israel, inherits and receives.[17]

In sum, the *theological* differences between dispensationalism and other views are largely due to different ways of "putting together" the Bible's overall story; hence, thinking through the Bible's framework is crucial for theology. Let us now turn to the varieties within dispensational theology to discover how these differences impact various theological conclusions.

Classic Dispensationalism

Central to *classic* dispensational theology is a dualistic conception of redemption linked to God's pursuit of two different purposes, one related to heaven and the other to earth, and tied to two different groups of people, a heavenly and an earthly humanity.[18] In terms of God's earthly purpose in redemption, it is God's plan to redeem the creation from its curse and to grant immortality to an earthly humanity, who will exist on the earth forever. This immortal earthly humanity first appears in the millennial age. It consists of those who are living on the earth when the Lord returns and reaches its completion in the new creation. They will not experience a final resurrection since they will not experience death, but they will continue to live on the earth forever. Alongside God's earthly purpose is his heavenly purpose, which is centered in a heavenly humanity. This heavenly people consist of all the redeemed from all dispensations (a transdispensational people) who have died prior to Christ's millennial return. They still await the final resurrection, and when they are resurrected, they will experience a "heavenly" inheritance.[19]

The classic view divides redemptive history into seven different dispensations: innocence (Eden), conscience (fall to flood), human government (Noah to Babel), promise (Abraham

---

[16] Blaising, 210.

[17] Covenant theology affirms a variety of millennial views, but dispensationalism affirms a distinctive dispensational form of premillennialism tied to its understanding of the Israel-church relationship.

[18] See Blaising and Bock, *Progressive Dispensationalism*, 23.

[19] See Lewis S. Chafer, "Dispensationalism," *BSac* 93 (1936): 390–449.

to Egypt), law (Moses to John the Baptist), grace (church age), and kingdom (millennium).[20] It views these dispensations as *different* arrangements under which humanity is tested. In the early dispensations, God gave promises about earthly life, but humans failed to obtain these promises. The present dispensation of the church is the first dispensation that presents God's "heavenly" purpose; unlike those in prior dispensations, the church knows that she is a heavenly people destined for an eternal inheritance, but the church is only a *parenthesis* in the history of God's earthly purpose of redemption. The primary purpose of the church is to pursue spiritual and not earthly matters and concerns.

Regarding the covenants, similar to *all* forms of dispensationalism, the classic view argued that the foundational covenant is the Abrahamic, not the creation covenant, since most rejected any covenant in creation.[21] In the Abrahamic covenant, God's earthly purpose was revealed as involving physical descendants who would become a great nation in a specific land, and Israel, as a nation, was given the role of mediating God's blessing to the Gentile nations. The classic view allowed for one to interpret the Abrahamic covenant *spiritually*, but it insisted that it must be interpreted "literally" for Israel, thus revealing God's early purpose for an earthly people. The same point is asserted in relation to the other covenants, which were all interpreted as "earthly" (e.g., the Palestinian [i.e., the land promise to Israel], the Mosaic, and the Davidic covenants). In fact, when the view applied its "literal" hermeneutic to Jeremiah 31, it insisted that the "new covenant" only applied to Israel and *not* to the church. Why? Because v. 31 states that the new covenant is made "with the house of Israel and with the house of Judah," and since Israel, as an earthly people, is *not* the church, it *cannot* apply to the church. But how is this possible if the NT applies Jeremiah 31 to the church (e.g., Heb. 8–10)? The classic view answered this question by positing *two* new covenants, one for Israel and one for the church, which, as critics noted, is highly problematic.[22] Ultimately, for the classic view, *all* of the biblical covenants, including the new covenant, find their fulfillment in an earthly people—first in the millennium and then in the final state—but they do *not* apply to the church.

---

[20] See *Scofield Reference Bible*, note on Gen 1:28.

[21] A notable exception is Lewis Sperry Chafer, *Systematic Theology*, vol. 1, 42. Most dispensationalists either reject a creation covenant or it does not play a central role in their overall theological system.

[22] See Blaising and Bock, *Progressive Dispensationalism*, 28–29. One has only to note how Jesus applies the new covenant to his death and thus to the church (Matt 26:27–28, par.), let alone the book of Hebrews (Heb 7–10).

The classic view of the covenants was also linked to its view of the kingdom. It distinguished between the "kingdom of heaven" (i.e., the fulfilment of the covenant made to David, in which God promised to establish the kingdom of his Son) and the "kingdom of God" (i.e., the moral rule of God in the hearts of his subjects). The kingdom of "heaven" begins to appear with Christ, but since Israel rejected it initially, the parenthesis age of the church was established. Ultimately, the kingdom of "heaven" will culminate in the millennium and the final state, where it merges with the kingdom of "God" in the hearts of his earthly people.

Traditional Dispensationalism

In the 1950s, dispensationalism rejected the earlier *eternal* distinction between the "earthly" and "heavenly" peoples of God. In its place, it argued for *two* peoples of God, namely, "Israel" as an ethnic, national people, and the "church" as a distinct international community. People belonged to either one or the other, but not to both at the same time, and each group was "structured differently, with different dispensational prerogatives and responsibilities."[23] Each group received the *same* salvation—eternal life in a resurrection state—yet they maintained an eternal distinction between the two groups since "the church is always church, Israel is always Israel."[24]

The traditional view also simplified the number of dispensations to three: God's purposes in the dispensations prior to grace (i.e., prior to the church), the dispensation of grace (i.e., the church age), and the kingdom viewed as the millennial reign of Christ on earth. In the era prior to grace, God worked through Israel to the Gentile nations. Through Israel, God achieved political, national, and spiritual purposes, but now in the church age, God's purpose is primarily spiritual. Although Israel and the church's spiritual experiences are similar, they are not the same; the church experiences the *new* reality of the baptism, sealing, and the permanent indwelling of the Spirit. Also, the church is a regenerate people in contrast to the "mixed" composition (i.e., believers and unbelievers) of the people of Israel. In these ways, traditional dispensationalists spoke of the differences between Israel and the church and thus of the discontinuity in God's plan of salvation.[25]

---

[23] Blaising and Bock, 32.

[24] Blaising and Bock, 32.

[25] See S. D. Toussaint, "Israel and the Church of a Traditional Dispensationalist," in Bateman, *Three Central Issues*, 227–52.

The traditional view also modified its understanding of the relationship of the new covenant to the church. Given that the NT applies Jeremiah 31 to the church (e.g., Luke 22:20 par.; Heb 7–10), it argued that the church was the "spiritual" seed of Abraham (Gal 3:26–29) and that the Abrahamic covenant was fulfilled *spiritually* in the church. But it maintained that the national, political terms of the OT covenants were *not* fulfilled in Christ's first coming but awaited a future fulfillment. Only when Christ establishes his millennial reign will the covenants be fulfilled in a "literal" way, that is, with Israel as a nation living in her land under Christ's rule, in the future millennial age and beyond. The traditional view allowed for OT promises and blessings to be *spiritually extended* to the church, but the covenants are *not* fulfilled in the church age. For example, the Davidic covenant is *not* partially fulfilled in Christ's first coming; rather, its fulfillment awaits Christ's return in his millennial kingdom. No doubt, Christ is enthroned in heaven now, but he is *not* on David's throne, and such texts as Psalm 110 only apply now to Christ's priestly role, not his rule as David's greater Son.[26] The OT covenants remain unfilled until Christ returns and establishes his millennial kingdom.

The traditional way of thinking about Israel and the church eventually led to the progressive view that argued that the church stood "in the line of a *historical* fulfillment of the new covenant promise to Israel" and not merely as a parenthesis in God's plan.[27] By this change, there was a move towards covenant theology's understanding of the Israel-church relation except that it maintained that Israel, as a nation, would still experience God's promises to her in terms of specific land promises that had not yet been realized in their fullness, in ways different from redeemed Gentile nations. In this revised trajectory, dispensationalists were now able to speak of the fulfillment of the promises made to Israel "literally" while simultaneously applying the Abrahamic and new covenant to the church "spiritually."[28] But significant differences still

[26] See John F. Walvoord, *The Millennial Kingdom: A Basic Text in Premillennial Theology* (repr., Grand Rapids: Zondervan, 1983), 197–207; Elliott E. Johnson, "Covenants in Traditional Dispensationalism," in Bateman, *Three Central Issues*, 130–31, 144.

[27] Blaising and Bock, *Progressive Dispensationalism*, 38.

[28] Progressive dispensationalists appeal to a "complementary hermeneutic" and inaugurated eschatology. The former refers to a "literal" reading of OT promises to national Israel that still await fulfillment in the future but also a *spiritual* application of these texts to the church. This hermeneutic is also linked to their view of inaugurated eschatology. For example, in the "*already*," only *spiritual* aspects of Jer 31:31–34 are applied to the church, while in the "*not yet*," the "literal" fulfillment will be applied

remain between dispensational and covenant theology. For dispensationalism, God's promise to Israel as a nation involves outstanding promises that have not yet been fulfilled, specifically the territorial land promise. For covenant theology, given its view of *continuity* between Israel and the church (that is, Israel *is* the church and the church *is* the transformed eschatological Israel), promises to Israel, including the land, are fulfilled in Christ and his church.

Finally, the traditional view modified its understanding of the "kingdom." It dropped the sharp distinction between the "kingdom of heaven" and the "kingdom of God." Though there were a number of alternative kingdom views proposed, most spoke of the "universal" kingdom (i.e., God's sovereignty over all things) and the "mediatorial" kingdom (i.e., God's rule over the earth through a God-chosen mediator, ultimately Christ). But in terms of the latter kingdom, it still insisted that since Christ is not presently on earth, the mediatorial kingdom is not present until Christ establishes his millennial reign and unites the universal and mediatorial kingdoms in the consummation. But Charles Ryrie and John Walvoord did speak of a *spiritual* kingdom here now in Christ's rule over the church, even though the political, national, and earthly fulfillment of the Davidic kingdom awaits Christ's return.[29] This allowed those holding this view to define "Christ's relation to the church as a kingdom,"[30] something not done by previous dispensationalists.

Progressive Dispensationalism

The progressive view modified previous dispensational thought by insisting that the church is more organically related to God's one plan of redemption. The appearance of the church, due to Christ's coming, does not signal a secondary redemption plan either to be fulfilled in heaven apart from the new earth or in a class of Jews and Gentiles who are forever distinguished from the rest of redeemed humanity.[31] Instead, the church today is a revelation/illustration of spiritual blessings that all of God's people throughout the ages will share in the future while preserving the distinctive national differences and roles within the one people of God.

---

to national Israel. See Bruce A. Ware, "The New Covenant and the People(s) of God," in Blaising and Bock, *Dispensationalism, Israel, and the Church*, 68–97.

[29] See Charles C. Ryrie, *Dispensationalism*, rev. ed. (Chicago: Moody, 2007), 182–83

[30] Blaising and Bock, *Progressive Dispensationalism*, 41.

[31] See Blaising and Bock, 46–48.

The term *progressive* is used in the progressive-revelation sense, that is, to underscore the unfolding nature of God's kingdom plan and the *successive* (not *different*) arrangements of the various dispensations as they lead to Christ and then the consummation. The progressive view, then, stresses the *continuity* of God's kingdom plan, but it also emphasizes that *each* dispensation reveals a different aspect of redemption that culminates in a final redemption in the final state.[32] But unlike covenant theology, it insists on a "*qualitative* progression in the manifestation of grace" that features a fundamental *discontinuity* in God's plan.[33] For this reason, dispensations are "not simply different historical expressions of the *same* experience of redemption (as in some forms of covenantalism), although they do lead to and culminate in one redemption plan."[34] This is also why progressives continue to view the church as *new* in God's unfolding plan and thus different from Israel but *not* new as previous dispensationalists thought. Blaising comments,

> Earlier dispensationalists viewed the church as a completely different kind of redemption from that which had been revealed before or would be revealed in the future. The church then had its own future separate from the redemption promised to Jews and Gentiles in the past and future dispensations. Progressive dispensationalists, however, while seeing the church as a new manifestation of grace, believe that this grace is precisely *in keeping with* the promises of the Old Testament, particularly the promises of the new covenant in Isaiah, Jeremiah, and Ezekiel. The fact that these blessings have been inaugurated in the church distinguishes the church from Jews and Gentiles of the past dispensation. But, only *some* of those blessings have been inaugurated. Consequently, the church should be distinguished from the next dispensation in which *all* of the blessings will not just be inaugurated, but completely fulfilled (which fulfillment will be granted to the saints of all dispensations through the resurrection of the dead).[35]

For progressives, then, the church should be viewed in light of its place in God's plan. It is *not* the same as Israel prior to Christ; it is *new*. It is the result of Christ's coming, and it consists

---

[32] See Blaising and Bock, 48.

[33] Blaising and Bock, 48 (emphasis mine).

[34] Blaising and Bock, 48.

[35] Blaising and Bock, 49.

of redeemed Jews *and* Gentiles (Eph 2:15), and it is part of the *one people of God.* But God's prophetic promises given to Israel and the Gentiles are still realized *according to their national identities.* For example, a Jewish Christian today does not lose his relationship to Israel's future promises. Both Jews and Gentiles, now and in the future, share the same salvation blessings, but "the same redeemed Jews and Gentiles will be directed and governed by Jesus Christ according to their different nationalities" and to distinct promises given to each nationality.[36] There is only one people of God and one plan of redemption, but there are also distinct roles for national Israel in the future alongside *different* roles for redeemed Gentile nations.[37]

To warrant these differences from previous dispensational thought, progressives argue that typology is more than a "spiritual" interpretation.[38] Instead, typology is viewed as that which "refers to patterns of resemblance between persons and events in earlier history to persons and events in latter history."[39] For example, the Davidic kingdom is a "type" of the future kingdom, or Israel is a "type" of the church but without losing a future for national Israel. By this view, progressives were able to affirm a more successive, unified unfolding of God's redemptive plan.

Regarding the covenants, progressives take seriously their unfolding nature, but they reject a creation covenant as *foundational* to *all* the covenants. Creation serves as the backdrop to God's work in the world, but it is the Abrahamic covenant that is foundational for future covenants.[40] Through the Abrahamic promise, we learn of God's promise to bless all life on earth, including the nations. Following a common way of categorizing the covenants today, progressives view the Abrahamic covenant as a "royal grant" (unconditional/unilateral) in contrast to a "suzerain-vassal" (bilateral/conditional) covenant. Abraham's obedience functions "as *the means*

---

[36] Blaising and Bock, 50.

[37] Blaising views the consummation as consisting of redeemed people living as *nations* according to their own identities "and assignments." Redeemed Israel has a different "assignment" than redeemed Gentile nations. See "God's Plan for History," 212. Although progressives strongly affirm *one* people of God (contrary to previous dispensational thought), one wonders how different "assignments" is not a return to *two* peoples, at least in the sense that God's promises are applied *differently* to redeemed national Israel and Gentile nations.

[38] See Blaising and Bock, *Progressive Dispensationalism*, 52–53.

[39] Blaising and Bock, 52.

[40] See Blaising and Bock, 134–35; Darrell L. Bock, "Covenants in Progressive Dispensationalism," in Bateman, *Three Central Issues*, 169–203.

by which he experiences God's blessing,"[41] along with the "*how* and the *when*" by which he receives the blessing,[42] but God's promise to bless the nations is unilaterally guaranteed despite human obedience.

Furthermore, given the foundational role of the Abrahamic covenant, *all* of the covenants must be viewed in relation to it *instead of Adam and a creation covenant.* God's blessing and the mediation of that blessing is passed to Abraham's descendants as they are chosen by God to inherit the covenant. In the old covenant, which is "bilateral/conditional," a new dispensation for blessing is established. The descendants of Abraham through Isaac and Jacob are constituted as a nation, which is to function as the means by which God's blessing is mediated to the nations. But given the bilateral nature of the covenant, it is possible for Israel to break it by her disobedience, which is precisely what occurred. Yet Israel's disobedience does not overturn God's unilateral promise to Abraham to bless the whole world through his seed, namely, Christ.

Similar to the Abrahamic covenant, the Davidic covenant is a "royal-grant" covenant. Under the Davidic king, its purpose was to mediate the Abrahamic blessing "to Israel and to all peoples and nations."[43] But given the failure of the Davidic kings, the prophets looked forward to the coming of a new dispensation in which a new covenant would replace the Mosaic and would bring the Abrahamic blessing to its ultimate consummation.

In the new covenant, God will bring about the full forgiveness of sin, the giving of the Spirit, and a transformation of the people of God culminating in resurrection life. It is this new covenant that Jesus inaugurates. But *not* all the promises and blessings of the new covenant are realized in Christ's first coming; its fulfillment involves an "already-not-yet" tension. "There are features promised in that covenant whose fulfillment has been delayed until the return of Christ (such as the national and territorial promises in Jer. 31:31, 36 and Ezek. 36:28 and 37:14)."[44] But since these latter features, specifically Israel's land promise, go back to the

---

[41] Blaising and Bock, *Progressive Dispensationalism*, 133.

[42] Blaising and Bock, 134.

[43] Blaising and Bock, 173. Blaising and Bock, in contrast to traditional dispensationalism, argue that the Davidic covenant has an inaugural fulfillment in Christ's first coming, although its complete fulfillment occurs at Christ's return (162–87). However, Saucy denies that Christ's present session involves an active Messianic rule. See Saucy, *Case for Progressive Dispensationalism*, 72–76, 80, 101, 106.

[44] Blaising and Bock, *Progressive Dispensationalism*, 202.

Abrahamic promise, they still await fulfillment at Christ's return. In this sense, the new covenant should be viewed as "*the form* in which the Abrahamic covenant has been inaugurated in this dispensation, and will be fulfilled in full in the future."[45] But the present form of the new covenant does not exhaust the Abrahamic promises, which still await their fulfillment in the future, when the specific national promises to Israel are finally realized in the millennium and in the consummated kingdom. It is only when this takes place that the Abrahamic covenant is truly and fully fulfilled.

What is the church in progressive dispensationalism? As in *all* forms of dispensationalism, the church is *not* the restored, eschatological Israel, which receives *all* of God's promises in Christ. Instead, the church is a people made up of Jewish and Gentile believers, who in this dispensation, "share a relational reality in Jesus" and "an inaugurated form of the salvific and pneumatological blessings that will, in their fullness, characterize the kingdom."[46] Thus, the church is an "inaugural form of the kingdom,"[47] which precedes the full establishment of redeemed nations at Christ's return, a kind of illustration of the "spiritual union of all redeemed peoples with Christ and with one another."[48] But, once Christ returns, the church as a *covenant* people gives way to the multinational worldwide kingdom composed of redeemed *nations*, who enjoy the same salvation but who also receive God's promises according to their *distinct* national identities. In this way, progressives continue to distinguish between Israel as a nation and the church as a people, thus maintaining the Israel-church distinction of dispensationalism.

Covenant Theology and Its Varieties[49]

Covenant theology, as a theological system, has its roots in the Reformation (Ulrich Zwingli [1484–1531], Heinrich Bullinger [1504–75], John Calvin [1509–64], Zacharius Ursinus

[45] Blaising and Bock, 53 (emphasis original).

[46] Blaising, "God's Plan for History," 211.

[47] Blaising, 211.

[48] Blaising, 211.

[49] On covenant theology, see Waters, Reid, and Muether, *Covenant Theology* (see chap. 14, n. 65); Frame, *Systematic Theology*, 55–84 (see chap. 5, n. 1); Horton, *God of Promise* (see chap. 14, n. 12); Bavinck, *Reformed Dogmatics*, 3:193–232 (see chap. 1, n. 9); Peter Golding, *Covenant Theology:*

[1534–1583]) and, in the post-Reformation era, was systematized by Herman Witsius (1636–1708) and Johannes Cocceius (1603–69). It has been taught among the English Puritans (John Owen [1616–83]), by Francis Turretin (1623–87), in Dutch Calvinism (Herman Bavinck [1854–1921], Geerhardus Vos [1862–1949], Louis Berkhof [1873–1957]), and in American Presbyterian theology as represented by old Princeton (Charles Hodge [1797–1878] and B. B. Warfield [1851–1921]) and the Westminster Theological Seminaries (John Murray [1898–1975] and Meredith Kline [1922–2007]). It is taught in the *Westminster Confession of Faith* (1643–49) and earlier Reformed confessions (*Belgic Confession* [1561]; *Heidelberg Catechism* [1563]). In Baptist theology, a nuanced version of it is reflected in the *Second London Baptist Confession* (1689).

Covenant theology views the covenants as more than a theme or concept of Scripture. Instead, covenants function as the Bible's own "architectonic structure . . . that provides the context within which we recognize the unity of Scripture amid its remarkable variety" and make theological conclusions.[50] As Michael Horton notes, "whenever Reformed theologians attempt to explore and explain the riches of Scripture, they are always thinking *covenantally* about every topic they take up."[51]

Covenant theology has taught that all of God's relations to humans are understood in terms of three covenants—the pre-temporal "covenant of redemption" (*pactum salutis*), between the triune persons; the "covenant of works" or "nature" (*foederus naturae*), made with Adam before the fall on behalf of the entire human race; and "the covenant of grace" (*foederus gratiae*), made "with Christ as the second Adam, and in him with all the elect as his seed,"[52] which, in history, is administered through a series of covenants from Adam to Christ.[53] Although covenant theology acknowledges *covenants*, it tends to subsume the plurality of covenants under the overarching

---

The Key of Theology in Reformed Thought and Tradition (Fearn, Ross-shire, UK: Mentor, 2004); Vos, "The Doctrine of the Covenant in Reformed Theology," in Gaffin, *Redemptive History and Biblical Interpretation*, 234–67 (see chap. 1, n. 45); Robertson, *Christ of the Covenants* (see chap. 14, n. 58).

[50] Horton, *God of Promise*, 13.

[51] See Horton, 14; cf. Horton, *Covenant and Eschatology* (see chap. 2, n. 147).

[52] *Westminster Larger Catechism*, q. 31.

[53] See R. Scott Clark, "Christ and Covenant: Federal Theology in Orthodoxy," in *A Companion to Reformed Orthodoxy*, ed. Herman J. Selderhuis (Boston: Brill, 2013), 406–7. Within covenant theology, there is a dispute regarding with whom the covenant of grace is made. Is it with the elect alone or with the elect and their children?

theological category of *the* covenant of grace. Thus, there is an overall continuity between the covenants since all of them are an expression of the *one* covenant of grace. Although there are *administrative* differences between the covenants, each covenant is *substantially* or *essentially* the same: "the emphasis [is] undeniably on the unity of *one* covenant of grace."[54]

For this reason, in contrast to dispensationalism, covenant theology insists on the *continuity* between Israel and the church, which directly impacts ecclesiology and eschatology. For example, it teaches that "Israel" and the "church" are *by nature* similar in the following ways—for example, both are "mixed" communities (constituted by believers/elect *and* unbelievers/non-elect);[55] the covenant signs (circumcision and baptism) signify the same gospel reality; and the salvation *experience* of believers in Israel and the church is basically the same. The only real difference is that the "church" is more racially mixed *and* a more knowledgeable version of "Israel." Since the salvation *experience* and the Spirit's *indwelling* is the same, the only difference is that Christians may experience a greater "consciousness and enjoyment" of salvation than OT saints.[56]

Let us now turn to a more detailed description of the view, with special focus on its overall construction of the Bible's framework, and its impact on specific doctrinal conclusions. Since covenant theology is not monolithic (e.g., there are differences between Presbyterian and Dutch Reformed, Federal Vision, etc.), our focus is on what unites paedobaptist covenant theology.[57]

---

[54] Poythress, *Understanding Dispensationalists*, 40; Richard L. Pratt Jr. applies this point to the ordinance/sacrament of baptism. He argues that "baptism administers the NT dispensation of the covenant of grace in ways that are analogous to the administration of the OT dispensation *of that same covenant*" (emphasis mine), although there are *different* covenants involved in redemptive history. "Reformed View: Baptism as a Sacrament of the Covenant," in *Understanding Four Views on Baptism*, ed. John H. Armstrong (Grand Rapids: Zondervan, 2007), 65.

[55] Israel-church as a "mixed" people entails that the locus of the covenant community and the locus of the elect are distinct, thus the distinction between the "visible" (elect and non-elect) and the "invisible" church (elect only).

[56] Bavinck, *Reformed Dogmatics*, 3:221. If one asks the question, When did the church begin? dispensational and covenant theology answer differently. For dispensationalism, the church is new and begins at Pentecost. For covenant theology, the church begins with the inauguration of the covenant of grace (Gen 3:15).

[57] For the Federal Vision view, see Douglas Wilson, *"Reformed" Is Not Enough: Recovering the Objectivity of the Covenant* (Moscow, ID: Canon Press, 2002).

Covenant Theology and the Biblical Covenants

For covenant theology, "covenant" is key to how Scripture fits together, but what is a covenant? Michael Horton defines it this way: "a covenant is a relationship of 'oaths and bonds' and involves mutual, though not necessarily equal, commitments."[58] The emphasis on "not necessarily equal commitments" is important since all of the biblical covenants are not exactly the same. So what is the relationship between the covenants? Covenant theology is unified in its answer: the historical *covenants* are placed under "the covenant of works" or "the covenant of grace," both of which are grounded in the eternal "covenant of redemption."[59]

The Covenant of Redemption

All Christian theology affirms that our triune God has an eternal plan, which he enacts by creation, providence, and redemption, although there are various debates about how God plans and the relationship between divine and human agency.[60] However, covenant theology has spoken of God's eternal plan of redemption in "covenant" categories, which J. V. Fesko defines in the following way:

> the covenant of redemption is the pre-temporal, intra-trinitarian agreement among Father, Son, and Holy Spirit to plan and execute the redemption of the elect. The covenant entails the appointment of the Son as surety of the covenant of grace who accomplishes the redemption of the elect through His incarnation, perfect obedience, suffering, resurrection, and ascension. The covenant of redemption is also the root of the Spirit's role to anoint and equip the Son for His mission as surety and apply His finished work to the elect.[61]

---

[58] Horton, *God of Promise*, 10; cf. Robertson, *Christ of the Covenants*, 3–15.

[59] See Bavinck, *Reformed Dogmatics*, 3:212–16; Vos, "Doctrine of the Covenant," 234–67; John Murray, "Covenant Theology," in *Collected Works*, 4 vols. (Carlisle: Banner of Truth, 1982), 4:216–40; and Robertson, *Christ of the Covenants*, 3–63.

[60] See the differences between a Reformed/Calvinist vs. Arminian view of divine providence, discussed in part 4.

[61] J. V. Fesko, *The Trinity and the Covenant of Redemption* (Fearn, Ross-shire, UK: Mentor, 2016), 131–32; cf. Vos, "Doctrine of the Covenant," 245–52.

Some have questioned the use of the term *covenant* to refer to the pact between the triune persons. No doubt, if one defines a covenant in terms of a kind of suzerain-vassal treaty, then we cannot apply the concept to the intratrinitarian relations since each person is equally divine: within God (*ad intra*) there are no lord-and-servant relations.[62] But, as Horton suggests, if one thinks analogically and we hold simultaneously to the Trinity and unconditional election, "it is unclear what objection could be raised in principle to describing this divine decree in terms of the concept of an eternal covenant between the persons of the Godhead."[63] In fact, this is what covenant theology has argued, and thus, most within covenant theology accept the legitimacy of speaking of God's redemptive plan in covenantal terms.[64] As such, the "covenant of redemption" is the "archetype for the historical covenants,"[65] and it serves as the foundation for the outworking of God's plan in history and our covenantal union with Christ as our mediator.

The Covenant of Works

For covenant theology, the first historical covenant is "the covenant of works" (or the "covenant of nature/life") made with Adam as the representative head of the human race prior to the fall.[66] To Adam and his posterity, eternal life was promised on the condition of perfect obedience to the law of God. But due to Adam's disobedience, he, along with all humanity, was plunged into

---

[62] On this point, see Horton, *God of Promise*, 81–82.

[63] Horton, *God of Promise*, 79; cf. Charles Hodge, *Systematic Theology*, 2:354–73 (see chap. 1, n. 13); Louis Berkhof, *Systematic Theology*, 4th ed. (Grand Rapids: Eerdmans, 1941), 265–83; David VanDrunen and R. Scott Clark, "The Covenant before the Covenants," in *Covenant, Justification, and Pastoral Ministry: Essays by the Faculty of Westminster Seminary California*, ed. R. Scott Clark (Phillipsburg: P&R, 2007), 167–96.

[64] On this point, I agree. Scripture teaches that God has *one* eternal plan, which is enacted in history (e.g., Ps 139:16; Isa 46:9–13; Eph 1:4–14; 1 Pet 1:20) and which involves the inseparable work of all three divine persons. In this plan, the Father gives a people to the Son (e.g., John 6:39; 10:29; 17:2, 6–10; Eph 1:4–12), the Son secures their redemption by his obedient life and death (John 6:37–40; 10:14–18; Heb 10:5–18), and the Spirit applies Christ's work to those same people (Rom 8:29–30; Eph 1:11–13; 1 Pet 1:5). Also, this eternal plan appoints Christ as covenant head and mediator, defines the nature of his mediation, and assigns specific roles to each person of the Godhead, which is accomplished through the unfolding of the covenants. Since Scripture teaches such a *divine plan*, roles, and promises, it is legitimate to think of God's eternal plan in *covenantal* terms.

[65] VanDrunen and Clark, "Covenant before the Covenants," 175.

[66] See Berkhof, *Systematic Theology*, 211–18; Bavinck, *Reformed Dogmatics*, 3:216–28.

a state of sin, death, and condemnation.[67] But solely due to God's free choice, "the covenant of grace" was established with the elect, by which salvation was offered to sinners through Christ. Although the covenant of works is vital to covenant theology, it has been disputed. Let us first describe its essential aspects before we mention some of the internal debates regarding it.

First, the covenant is between God and Adam—Adam not merely as a creature who by nature owes God perfect obedience, but as the appointed "head and representative of his whole race."[68] By God's positive command to Adam in Genesis 2 a covenant relationship is established by which Adam is constituted the legal, representative head of humanity.

Second, the promise of the covenant is eternal life (as represented by the tree of life), conditioned on Adam's perfect obedience to God's command. Although there is no explicit promise of eternal life to Adam, the threat of death "clearly implies such a promise."[69] Adam was created in a "state of integrity with the ability to render God complete obedience,"[70] but his covenant status at creation was not "the highest degree of holiness, nor did he enjoy life in all its fullness."[71] Instead, it was "provisional and temporary and could not remain as it was. It either had to pass on to higher glory or to sin and death."[72] Tragically, Adam, who had the ability to sin, broke God's law and plunged all of humanity into a state of death and condemnation.

Third, although Adam broke the covenant, its effects remain.[73] All humanity is born "in Adam," that is, under sin, death, and condemnation. God still demands perfect obedience from humanity; in theory, the conditional promise of "do this and live" (Lev 18:5; Rom 10:5; Gal 3:12) remains, but no human fully obeys and meets God's demand.

Fourth, the covenant of works sets the stage for the covenant of grace. Since Adam broke God's law, all humanity is now guilty and corrupt "in him." But God has acted in grace to establish a *second* covenant to redeem his elect from fallen humanity. In the covenant of grace, the Father appoints the Son to be our mediator, and in Christ's life and death, he perfectly obeys for us, thus meeting our legal demand before God and paying the debt of our sin. In this way, the

---

67 See *Westminster Confession of Faith* 7.2.

68 Hodge, *Systematic Theology*, 2:121; cf. Berkhof, *Systematic Theology*, 215–16.

69 Berkhof, 216; cf. Frame, *Systematic Theology*, 63–64.

70 Horton, *God of Promise*, 89.

71 Berkhof, *Systematic Theology*, 216.

72 Bavinck, *Reformed Dogmatics*, 2:564; cf. Bavinck, *Reformed Dogmatics*, 3:224–28.

73 Berkhof, *Systematic Theology*, 218; Vos, "Doctrine of the Covenant," 254–55.

covenant of works provides the warrant for our corporate solidarity either in Adam or Christ and is the grounding for Christ's active obedience and substitutionary work for us. It also establishes the "law-gospel" contrast that is essential to understanding the nature of Christ's work.

While the covenant of works is crucial for covenant theology, there are at least three disputes over its precise nature.[74] First, some question the existence of a covenant with Adam given the lack of "covenant" terminology and that "the word *covenant* in Scripture is always used in a context of redemption."[75] But this is a minority view in covenant theology.[76]

Second, some question the use of *works* since grace is fundamental to any divine-human relationship, including the relationship with Adam in the original situation.[77] Also, as O. Palmer Robertson notes, "works" language is inadequate since it has "tended to concentrate attention on one single element of the creational bond between God and man. . . . Rather than seeing the broader implications of man's responsibility to his Creator."[78] This is why Robertson suggests that the covenant with Adam is really a "covenant of creation."[79] But despite this objection, most retain the "works" language since it is foundational for grasping Christ's active and passive obedience and the "law-gospel" pattern of Scripture. *Law* refers to the covenant of works and *gospel* refers to the covenant of grace. Prior to the fall, God acts in "voluntary condescension,"[80] while after the fall, God acts in sovereign grace and mercy toward fallen humanity.

Third, there is a debate regarding the relationship between the covenant of works and the Mosaic covenant. For some, the Mosaic covenant is a *republication* of the covenant of works, thus viewing the Sinai covenant as a mixture of the covenant of works and grace. In fact, Horton, following Meredith Kline, categorizes the biblical covenants by the means of "law"

---

[74] See Horton, *God of Promise*, 83–104, for a helpful discussion of the debate within covenant theology. Cf. Anthony A. Hoekema, *Created in God's Image* (Grand Rapids: Eerdmans, 1986), 119–21; Frame, *Systematic Theology*, 65–66.

[75] Hoekema, *Created in God's Image*, 121; cf. Murray, *Collected Writings*, 2:49 (see chap. 11, n. 14); Williamson, *Sealed with an Oath*, 44–58 (see chap. 14, n. 12).

[76] See Frame, *Systematic Theology*, 63, who argues that minimally a covenant is *implicit*, although a stronger case can be made.

[77] See Murray, *Collected Writings*, 2:49–57; cf. Frame, *Systematic Theology*, 65; Hoekema, *Created in God's Image*, 119.

[78] Robertson, *Christ of the Covenants*, 56.

[79] See Robertson, 56.

[80] Michael Horton, *The Christian Faith: A Systematic Theology for Pilgrims on the Way* (Grand Rapids: Zondervan, 2011), 421.

(conditional-bilateral) and "gospel" (unconditional-unilateral), with the "law" associated with Adam and Sinai, and "gospel" associated with Abraham, David, and the new covenant.[81] In this view, the Mosaic covenant is a legal, conditional covenant that shares in the *substance* of the covenant of grace yet features a works principle like the covenant of works.[82] But within covenant theology, most reject the republication thesis since in *the* covenant of grace one cannot have a mixture of works and gospel. Cornelis Venema states the objection this way: "If what belongs to the substance of the covenant of works does not belong to the substance of the covenant of grace *in any of its administrations*, it is semantically and theologically problematic to denominate the Mosaic administration as *in any sense* a covenant of works."[83] Also, as Frame insists, the Mosaic covenant begins with God's grace, and similar to all covenants, obedience is demanded, but it is no more conditional than the Abrahamic covenant was, indeed, "the relation between God's grace and human obedience in the Mosaic covenant is the same as that in the other covenants."[84]

Despite these internal debates, covenant theology affirms a covenant of works or a creation covenant prior to the fall. But tragically, Adam, as our covenant head, disobeyed God, and his sin and guilt is now ours. After the fall, apart from God's initiative to redeem, we cannot achieve divine forgiveness by keeping God's commands. God must act in sovereign grace to redeem us from our sin, which is precisely what he has done in the covenant of grace.

The Covenant of Grace[85]

The "covenant of grace" begins immediately after the fall with the promise of Gen 3:15. This promise is progressively revealed and administered through the covenants with Noah,

---

[81] See Horton, *God of Promise*, 77–110; cf. Berkhof, *Systematic Theology*, 612.

[82] See Horton, *God of Promise*, 31–34, 47, 90, 94, 97–104, 130–31.

[83] Cornelis P. Venema, "The Mosaic Covenant: A 'Republication' of the Covenant of Works? A Review Article: *The Law is Not of Faith: Essays on Works and Grace in the Mosaic Covenant*," *MAJT* 21 (2010): 92 (emphasis original). Bavinck argues a similar point: "The covenant with Israel was essentially no other than that with Abraham. . . . The covenant on Mount Sinai is and remains a covenant of grace." *Reformed Dogmatics*, 3:220.

[84] Frame, *Systematic Theology*, 72–73.

[85] On the covenant of grace, see Berkhof, *Systematic Theology*, 272–83; Hodge, *Systematic Theology*, 2:362–77; Bavinck, *Reformed Dogmatics*, 3:216–32; Vos, "Doctrine of the Covenant," 252–67; Golding,

Abraham, Israel, and David and is finally realized in Christ and the new covenant. But though there are multiple *covenants*, each one is under the *one* covenant of grace, thus making the "substance" of each covenant the same. This is why the "new" covenant is only a more glorious "administration of the same covenant of grace."[86] Under the OT covenants, the covenant of grace was administered through various promises, prophecies, sacrifices, rites, and ordinances (e.g., circumcision) that typified and foreshadowed Christ's coming. Now, in light of Christ's work, the covenant of grace is administered through the Word and sacraments, but each covenant is "essentially" the same. Three further points are important to fully grasp the concept of "the covenant of grace."

First, a distinction between the *substance/essence* and the *administrations* of *the* covenant of grace allows covenant theology to account for its unity/continuity (the same essence) and the plurality of *covenants* over time (different administrations). No doubt, in Christ, a greater manifestation of the covenant of grace is revealed, but the essence of each covenant is the same. Bavinck states it this way:

> Although Christ completed his work on earth only in the midst of history and although the Holy Spirit was not poured out till the day of Pentecost, God nevertheless was able, already in the days of the Old Testament, to fully distribute the benefits to be acquired by the Son and Spirit. Old Testament believers were saved in no other way than we. There is one faith, one Mediator, one way of salvation, and one covenant of grace.[87]

Given this distinction, how does covenant theology determine the "accidental properties" of each covenant, or what exactly has and has not changed over time? Covenant theology follows the hermeneutical principle that given the underlying unity of the covenant of grace, unless God has specifically abrogated something from the OT, it is still in force in the NT era. In fact, this is how the continuity between circumcision and baptism is maintained. Circumcision, as a covenant sign, now carries over to baptism, but the *essence* of both signs is

---

Covenant Theology, 121–63.

[86] Robert R. Booth, *Children of the Promise: The Biblical Case for Infant Baptism* (Phillipsburg: P&R, 1995), 9; cf. Murray, "Covenant Theology," 223–34.

[87] Bavinck, *Reformed Dogmatics*, 3:215–16; cf. Berkhof, *Systematic Theology*, 277–80; Hodge, *Systematic Theology*, 2:364–73; Robertson, *Christ of the Covenants*, 45–52.

the same. Baptism, as the sign of the new covenant, reflects one of the several administrative changes that have resulted, but it signifies the same *spiritual* meaning as circumcision given the unity of the covenant. The form of the sign has changed, but the *substance* has not; thus, it is to be applied in the same way.

Given the substance/administration distinction, what, then, is *new* about the new covenant? The answer is not monolithic. Most insist that "promise fulfillment" highlights what is *new*, that is, what the older administration promised through types, ceremonies, and sacrifices, has now come to fulfillment in Christ.[88] But most think of *newness* in terms of *renewal* rather than replacement or fulfillment, thus downplaying discontinuity between the new and previous covenants.[89] This is why most insist that the new covenant merely expands the extent and application of the other covenants, while the *substance* remains the same. Minimally, covenant theology thinks of the "newness" of the new covenant in the following ways:[90]

1. On the basis of Christ's work and the Spirit's application of it, the new covenant results in a greater obedience, along with a greater consciousness and enjoyment of salvation blessings.
2. The knowledge of God is extended to all nations so that under the new covenant more people know God, which fulfills the Abrahamic promise of blessings to the nations.

---

[88] See Venema, "The Mosaic Covenant," 93. Venema argues that the Mosaic administration "includes everything that belongs to the substance of the covenant of grace, it communicated the same grace of Christ, albeit in the form of anticipatory types and shadows."

[89] See, Booth, *Children of the Promise*, 51; Jeffrey D. Niell, "The Newness of the New Covenant," in *The Case for Covenantal Infant Baptism*, ed. Gregg Strawbridge (Phillipsburg: P&R, 2003), 127–55. However, for those who think of the Mosaic covenant as a republication of the covenant of works, much more discontinuity is affirmed. For example, Horton and Kline argue that the "newness" of the new covenant is *qualitatively* different than the Mosaic. See Horton, *God of Promise*, 53. Where they establish the continuity of the covenant of grace is more in terms of the relation between the unconditional Abrahamic covenant and the new covenant.

[90] See Bavinck, *Reformed Dogmatics*, 3:223–24; Berkhof, *Systematic Theology*, 299–301; Hodge, *Systematic Theology*, 2:376–77; Robertson, *Christ of the Covenants*, 57–63, 275–86, 293–96; cf. David Gibson, "'Fathers of Faith, My Fathers Now!': On Abraham, Covenant, and the Theology of Paedobaptism," *Them* 40, no. 1 (2015): 14–34; Douglas Wilson, *To a Thousand Generations: Infant Baptism—Covenant Mercy for the People of God* (Moscow, ID: Canon, 1996), 22–34; Niell, "Newness of the New Covenant," 127–55; Richard L. Pratt Jr. "Infant Baptism in the New Covenant," in Strawbridge, *Case for Covenantal Infant Baptism*, 156–74.

3. The promise of redemption is now accomplished in Christ with the full payment of sin. The old Levitical administration, along with the ceremonial law, is now fulfilled. The types and shadows of the old (natural and temporal forms) have reached their fulfillment in what they pointed forward to (spiritual and eternal realities).
4. The new covenant is the final manifestation of the covenant of grace.

What is important to note, especially regarding the Israel-church relation and its implications for ecclesiology, is that covenant theology denies that presently the *nature* and *structure* of the church is different than Israel since Israel-church are *essentially* the same. For this reason, they affirm the "mixed" nature of the church, in contrast to Baptist theology (and the believers' church tradition), which leads to crucial *theological* differences in ecclesiology with numerous practical results.

Second, we must ask whether *the* covenant of grace is unconditional and/or conditional. Most contend that it is *unconditional* since God acts unilaterally to make the covenant and keep it.[91] Even God's demand from us to repent, believe, and obey is achieved by *God* by grace in Christ and the Spirit. As Cornelis Venema states,

> Not only are the covenant's obligations preceded by God's gracious promise, but these obligations are fulfilled for and in believers by the triune God—Father, Son, and Holy Spirit—in their respective operations. God's demands are born of grace and fulfilled in us by grace. In these respects, the covenant of grace is unconditional, excluding every possible form of merit, whereby the faith and obedience of God's people would be the basis for their obtaining life and salvation.[92]

However, within covenant theology, this issue is more complicated for two reasons. First, related to the republication discussion, some make a further unconditional/conditional distinction of the biblical covenants within *the* "unconditional" covenant of grace. Horton, for example, insists that the Mosaic covenant is mainly a "law"/conditional covenant, while the Abrahamic, Davidic, and new covenants are "gospel"/unconditional in nature. For this reason, now that the new covenant is here, the Sinai covenant is abrogated, while the other covenants

---

[91] See Bavinck, *Reformed Dogmatics*, 3:228–32.

[92] Cornelis P. Venema, "Covenant Theology and Baptism," in Strawbridge, *Case for Covenantal Infant Baptism*, 211.

remain, given their unconditional nature, and why, contrary to dispensationalism, the land promise has been forfeited by Israel's disobedience.[93] This is a minority position within covenant theology, but it illustrates a larger debate over the unconditional-conditional nature of the covenant of grace.

Second, although the covenant of grace is unconditional, it is also *conditional* in two ways. First, the blessings of the covenant of grace are completely dependent on the work of Christ, fulfilling the conditions of obedience first set down in the covenant of works. Second, to benefit from the covenant, we must fulfill the conditional obligations—repentance, faith, and obedience. These covenant obligations are not grounds for our justification; Christ is. Rather, they are "necessary responses to the covenant's promises."[94] In principle, then, the covenant of grace (which includes the new covenant) is *breakable* if the second condition is not met or kept. When combined with the "mixed" view of the covenant communities, like Israel, the church is constituted by covenant-keepers *and* breakers—"believers and their children"—who may not meet the conditions of the covenant; hence, for Israel *and* the church, the circle of the covenant community is larger than the circle of election.[95] As in Israel, so in the church people may be "*of* the covenant but not *in* the covenant."[96] Appealing to the often-cited parable of the weeds (Matt 13:24–30, 36–43), Horton argues that "not everyone who belongs to the covenant community will persevere to the end. Some are weeds sown among the wheat, seeds that fell on rocky soil or that is choked by the weeds. . . . Not everyone in the covenant of grace is elect."[97]

For covenant theology, it is this view of the covenant of grace and the "mixed" nature of the church that undergirds its practice of paedobaptism. If the church is "mixed" by nature, then there is nothing objectionable in applying the covenant sign to not-yet believers,[98] in contrast

---

[93] See Horton, *God of Promise*, 23–76.

[94] Venema, "Covenant Theology and Baptism," 211; cf. Horton, *God of Promise*, 182–86. Horton argues that the new covenant has a number of conditions attached to it for final salvation. These conditions involve not only initial repentance and faith, but perseverance in both, as well as holiness of life. However, within the new covenant, since it is a covenant of promise, "everything that God *requires* in this covenant is also *given* by God!" Horton, 184.

[95] See Venema, "Covenant Theology and Baptism," 214; cf. Horton, *God of Promise*, 182.

[96] Bavinck, *Reformed Dogmatics*, 3:232.

[97] Horton, *God of Promise*, 185, 182.

[98] See also Pratt, "Infant Baptism in the New Covenant," 170, for an affirmation of this point.

to Baptist theology, which insists that baptism must only be applied to those who profess faith in Christ. At the heart of these significant ecclesiological differences is a larger debate over the nature of covenants and the similarities and differences between Israel and the church.

Third, we must also ask, building on the last point: Who are the parties of *the* covenant of grace? Given its "conditionality" and the fact that not every one *of* the covenant is *in* it, who are the parties of the covenant of grace? Does God covenant with the elect only, or does he covenant with "believers and their children"—children who may not believe? Given covenant theology's view of "conditionality," it would seem that the answer is the latter, but there has been a major debate on this question. For example, the *Westminster Confession of Faith* (7.3) and *Larger Catechism* (31) insist that God covenants only with the elect in the covenant of grace: "In the strictest sense of the covenant as a saving communion with God, the parties of the covenant of grace are the triune God and his elect people."[99] One enters the covenant by repentance and faith. All those who reject the free offer of the gospel stand *outside* the covenant of grace and, it would also seem to imply, they are also *outside* the covenant community.

But if this is so, then how do covenant theologians insist that the covenant of grace includes "all believers and their children," even children who may never believe. To answer, an appeal to the "dual aspect" of the covenant of grace is made. Although the "life and salvation promised in the covenant of grace [is] inherited only by the elect . . . the covenant promise, together with its accompanying obligation, is extended to Abraham and his seed."[100] How do we make sense of this seemingly contradictory answer? This is not a minor point since, theologically speaking, the entire covenantal view of the church and its defense of paedobaptism depends on an answer to this question. In fact, a standard argument for paedobaptism is that "the children of believers were always included in the covenant of grace under the older covenant administrations . . . [as such,] *we must assume that, apart from explicit biblical warrant to the contrary*, the children of believers are still included in the covenant of grace" as members *of* the covenant community.[101]

However, to make this argument work, covenant theology must view *the* covenant of grace (an overarching theological category) through the lens of the Abrahamic covenant (a specific biblical covenant that includes within it national, typological, and spiritual aspects).

---

[99] Venema, "Covenant Theology and Baptism," 212.

[100] Venema, 214; cf. Berkhof, *Systematic Theology*, 272–89.

[101] Booth, *Children of the Promise*, 10.

This is why the genealogical principle ("to you and your children") given in the Abrahamic covenant and tied to circumcision continues *unchanged* across the covenants, including the new covenant. A common complaint against covenant theology is that it reduces the national and typological aspects of the Abrahamic covenant to the *spiritual,* which then becomes the grid by which *all* of the biblical covenants are viewed, especially the new covenant. This is why to really speak of *the* covenant of grace is to speak of the Abrahamic covenant reduced to its spiritual aspects alone. This is how covenant theologians can speak of the "dual aspect" of the covenant, even though "believers and their children" is a genealogical formula tied to the Abrahamic covenant.

Examples of the equation of *the* covenant of grace with the Abrahamic covenant abound.[102] Louis Berkhof, for example, acknowledges the national and spiritual aspects of the Abrahamic covenant, but in reality, the national aspects fall away and the *spiritual* aspects become primary. For this reason, he insists that circumcision is "the initiatory sign and seal of *the covenant of grace*" (when it is really the sign of the Abrahamic covenant, not every biblical covenant) and that "this covenant [Abrahamic] is still in force and is *essentially identical* with the 'new covenant' of the present dispensation" with little regard for the *distinctions* between the covenants.[103] Or John Murray argues that since "the new covenant is the fulfillment and unfolding of the Abrahamic covenant," and "the covenant made with Abraham included the infant seed, and was signified and sealed by circumcision," and "circumcision is the sign of the covenant in its deepest spiritual significance,"[104] we are under divine command, due to the unity of the covenant of grace, to baptize our infant children, thus constituting them as members *of* the new covenant. Again, to make this work, covenant theology must reduce the Abrahamic covenant to its spiritual aspects and then equate it one-to-one with the new covenant.

[102] See, e.g., J. V. Fesko, *Word, Water, and Spirit: A Reformed Perspective on Baptism* (Grand Rapids: Reformation Heritage Books, 2010), 342–43, 355–56. Fesko identifies the Abrahamic covenant with the new covenant. He then moves directly from circumcision to baptism and assumes that the genealogical principle continues without change.

[103] Berkhof, *Systematic Theology,* 633 (emphasis mine). Berkhof argues that what is normative for the church is not the Mosaic but the Abrahamic covenant (interpreted in light of its spiritual aspects) (296–97); cf. Horton, *God of Promise*, 40–57.

[104] Murray, "Baptism," in *Collected Writings*, 2:374.

But is this interpretation of the relationship between the covenants and *the* covenant of grace true to how Scripture relates the covenants together? Covenant theology's construction of the Bible's covenantal storyline directly impacts its *theological* conclusions in key doctrinal areas. Thus the arbitration of these doctrinal areas directly depends on the larger arbitration of how the Bible's entire metanarrative works. But before we move to this point, let us finish our discussion of covenant theology by looking at its view of the nature of the church.

Covenant Theology and the Nature of the Church

Covenant theologians insists that in the administration of the covenant of grace, there are numerous people who are *of* the covenant but not *in* the covenant or among the elect.[105] It is important to note how this view of the church is linked to such theologians' construction of the covenant of grace. Due to the unity of the covenant, God's people are by nature the *same*, especially viewed through the Israel-church relation, though there are nuances within the view.[106] For example, Berkhof states: "The New Testament Church is essentially one with the Church of the old dispensation. As far as their essential nature is concerned, they both consist of true believers, and of true believers only. And in their external organization both represent a mixture of good and evil."[107]

In stressing the unity of God's people over time, covenant theology views the church as the fulfillment and/or redefinition of Israel, not her "replacement."[108] The church, then, is the true, eschatological Israel, who receives all of God's promises in Christ.[109] Contrary to dispensational theology, even if Romans 11 teaches a mass conversion of Jewish people in the future, this does not require Israel's national restoration to receive some promises different than Gentile believers. The church, composed of believing Jews and Gentiles, is the one new man who

---

[105] See Venema, "Covenant Theology and Baptism," 214; Bavinck, *Reformed Dogmatics*, 3:228–32.

[106] For example, see Edmund P. Clowney, *The Church: Sacraments, Worship, Ministry, Mission* (Downers Grove: InterVarsity, 1995), 27–70; and Beale, *A New Testament Biblical Theology*, 651–772 (see chap. 14, n. 74).

[107] Berkhof, *Systematic Theology*, 571; cf. Hodge, *Systematic Theology*, 3:549–52; Murray, *Christian Baptism*, 31–44.

[108] See Horton, *Christian Faith*, 730.

[109] See Beale, *New Testament Biblical Theology*, 651–772.

lasts forever *as the church*. Also, given the unity of the covenant *and* God's people, a number of ecclesiological entailments follow, specifically the warrant for paedobaptism and a "mixed" view of the church. Since Israel included "believers and their children," the same is true for the new administration of the church.[110] Since Israel is constituted as a "mixed" people, so the church is similarly composed of "baptized believers and baptized unbelievers,"[111] thus making the circle of the church wider than the circle of true believers, or the elect.

At this juncture, covenant theology utilizes the "invisible-visible" distinction, which is important for their ecclesiology. The *invisible* church refers to God's elect through the ages. Thus, the church, whether under the old or the new covenant, is a spiritual entity, invisible to the physical eye, the one people of God over time.[112] However, the invisible church also shows itself in a *visible*, local form.[113] The church is a divinely created bond between God and his people and between other humans. It becomes visible in the ministry of the Word, in the practice of the sacraments, and in external organization and government.[114] But as a visible entity, it is a "mixture of regenerate and unregenerate people who are baptized."[115]

How does this view of the church warrant the practice of infant baptism? Since in the previous covenant administrations beginning with Abraham, infants of believing households were included in the *visible* church (Abraham's family, Israel) by their circumcision and *prior to a personal profession of faith* and, additionally, by that act were considered members *of* the covenant even though they were not yet regenerate members, the same is true for the church. This is the rationale for applying the covenant sign of baptism to infants of believing parents even though these infants have not yet exercised faith and even though this practice seems to disrupt the biblical order of baptism in the NT, namely, first repentance toward God and faith in Christ and then, secondly, a confession of that faith publicly in baptism.[116]

---

[110] See Booth, *Children of the Promise*, 73; cf. Gibson, "Fathers of Faith," 21–29.

[111] Pratt, "Reformed View," 68.

[112] See Berkhof, *Systematic Theology*, 566; cf. Pratt, "Reformed View," 68–72; Fesko, *Word, Water, and Spirit*, 351–56; and Murray, *Christian Baptism*, 31–33.

[113] See Murray, *Christian Baptism*, 32.

[114] See Berkhof, *Systematic Theology*, 566.

[115] Pratt, "Reformed View," 69.

[116] On this order, see G. R. Beasley-Murray, *Baptism in the New Testament* (Grand Rapids: Eerdmans, 1962), 93–305; and Robert H. Stein, "Baptism and Becoming a Christian in the New Testament," *SBJT* 2, no. 1 (1998): 6–17.

What evidence do covenant theologians give for their view of the church? There are at least four pieces of biblical and theological evidence often cited.[117]

First, the foundational evidence is the appeal to the *substantial* continuity of the covenant over time. For them, this entails that the "mixed" nature of the *one* people of God is the same.

Second, an appeal is made to the "already-not-yet" tension of inaugurated eschatology to explain the "mixed" nature of the church today. Though OT expectation seems to anticipate that Messiah's people will be a regenerate people at Christ's first coming, covenant theology's view of the church requires that this reality is only realized at Christ's return.[118] Richard Pratt and Greg Beale argue this point. They admit that Jeremiah 31 anticipates an *entire* new covenant people who are *regenerate*, but *presently* the church, although more "democratized" than Israel, remains a people constituted by true believers *and* sanctified unbelievers.[119] As such, the church *now* remains a "mixed" people; her *nature* as an entire regenerate people awaits the *not yet*.

Third, the warning passages are appealed to as further evidence that their "mixed" view of the church is correct, especially warnings that speak of the possibility of apostasy (e.g., Heb 6:4–6; 10:28–30). These texts seem to imply that the church is no different than Israel. Why? Because it seems that it is possible for a person to be a member *of* the covenant people (i.e., the visible church) but to depart, thus demonstrating that they were never truly *in* the covenant, although they were externally and objectively members of the covenant people. In this way, the warning passages function as evidence that "unregenerate members of the visible church can be covenant breakers in the new covenant" and that the new covenant is a breakable covenant like the old.[120] In commenting on the implications of the warning texts for understanding the nature of the church, Doug Wilson confidently asserts, "the *elect* and the *covenant members* are not identical sets of people."[121] Accordingly, the warning texts function as corroboratory

---

[117] See, for example, Fesko, *Word, Water, and Spirit*, 337–67; Beale, *New Testament Biblical Theology*, 651–832; Horton, *Christian Faith*, 715–871; Berkhof, *Systematic Theology*, 632–35; Murray, *Christian Baptism*, 31–68; and Wilson, *To A Thousand Generations*, 13–96.

[118] In chapter 14, we noted how Jer 31:31–34 anticipated a people who *knew* God and the *full* forgiveness of sin.

[119] See Pratt, "Infant Baptism in the New Covenant," 127–74; Beale, *New Testament Biblical Theology*, 728–49; cf. Fesko, *Word, Water, Spirit*, 351–56.

[120] See Gregg Strawbridge, introduction to Strawbridge, *Case for Covenantal Infant Baptism*, 4–5.

[121] Wilson, *To a Thousand Generations*, 34.

evidence supporting their view that the covenant community across the ages is a "mixed" community. But as Wilson notes, with the coming of Christ, "the *difference* between the covenants is that the promises in the New are much better—meaning that the ratio of believer to unbeliever will drastically change. The history of the New Israel will not be dismal like the Old Israel."[122]

Fourth, the promise of Acts 2:39 ("for you and your children"), "household" baptisms (Acts 16:15; 32–33; 18:8; 1 Cor 1:16), and the theme of households/families across the canon is given as further evidence that the "mixed" nature of the church continues. Covenant theology is not concerned by the fact that there is no explicit example of infant baptism in the NT. Instead, given the unity of the covenant of grace, the principle of continuity leads them to assume that infants are included in the church unless explicitly told they are not.[123] Of course, what is crucial to note is that covenant theologians' theological conclusions are dependent on their construction of the Bible's overall theological framework and that resolution to disagreements within ecclesiology are not dependent on a few texts but an entire understanding of how Scripture is "put together."

Covenant Theology and Covenant Signs

Given covenant theology's construction of the Bible's theological framework, it is not surprising that covenant theologians insist that the nature and function of the covenant signs (circumcision and baptism) are similar in that they both signify the same realities. In fact, this is what undergirds their overall defense of paedobaptism since now that Christ has come, baptism *replaces* circumcision. No doubt, in replacing circumcision, baptism signifies that the promised era of the OT is now here. In this sense, the new covenant *fulfills* the old. However, the basic *substantial* meaning and significance of circumcision and baptism is the same, namely, the covenant promise of God.[124]

What is the *essential* meaning of the two covenant signs? As *signs*, they signify the outward entrance into the covenant of grace and the covenant community. As *seals*, they confirm the

---

[122] Wilson, 35.

[123] See Murray, *Christian Baptism*, 48–50; cf. Gibson, "Fathers of Faith," 21–29.

[124] See Fesko, *Word, Water, and Spirit*, 337–67; Pratt, "Reformed View," 64–72; Booth, *Children of the Promise*, 96–119; Murray, *Christian Baptism*, 45–68; Wilson, *To a Thousand Generations*, 39–80.

binding nature of the covenant, grounded in God's promises to his covenant people. In the OT, circumcision was administered to all infant male children when they were eight days old. But circumcision was not effective on its own; it always had to be combined with faith. If it was not, one was shown to be only *of* the covenant but not truly *in* it. And what is true of circumcision is also true of baptism since now that Christ has come, baptism *replaces* circumcision as the covenant "sign and seal." In baptism, like circumcision, one enters the *visible* church, but baptism, like circumcision, does not effect a saving union. It is only by God's grace in conversion that we are united to Christ and become members of the *invisible* church.

Another important point to observe regarding covenant theology's discussion of circumcision is that most of their argument centers on the *spiritual* significance of the rite.[125] Why? Because central to their view is the *continuity* of the covenantal signs—a continuity that must speak of the significance of the signs in terms of *spiritual* realities, namely, regeneration, justification, union with Christ, and so on. Thus, for baptism to *replace* circumcision, it must be shown that both circumcision and baptism signify the same *spiritual* realities. No one disputes the fact that baptism signifies *spiritual* realities won by Christ and applied to us as his people. But the point of contention is whether circumcision, *in its OT covenantal context*, signifies *the exact same realities* as baptism does in the NT. After all, does not circumcision also convey national, typological, and spiritual realities that undercut the claim that circumcision and baptism signify the exact *same* realities? The only way to resolve this issue is to think through the relationships between the biblical covenants. As we do, we must exercise caution not to read new covenant realities into the old without first grasping the OT rite in its own covenantal context and then carefully thinking through the similarities and differences of the covenantal signs.

However, in covenant theology, the *spiritual* meaning of circumcision is understood in at least three ways—ways that ultimately link it to baptism under the new covenant.[126]

First, at the heart of the Abrahamic covenant is—"I will be your God, and you shall be my people"—which speaks to the blessing of union and communion with the Lord. As a sign of

---

[125] See Berkhof, *Systematic Theology*, 632–33; Booth, *Children of Promise*, 99–100; Murray, *Christian Baptism*, 46–47.

[126] See Murray, *Christian Baptism*, 45–68; Geerhardus Vos, *Reformed Dogmatics*, ed. and trans. Richard B. Gaffin Jr., 5 vols. (Bellingham: Lexham Press, 2016), 5:161–64.

the covenant, circumcision signifies and seals this blessing. Objectively, it makes one a member *of* the covenant community. The same is true of baptism, which signifies that the recipient has objectively entered into faith union with Christ in his redemptive work.[127] This is not to deny that the recipient must still exercise faith before covenant blessings may be appropriated. Failure to respond in faith to one's baptism brings covenant curses instead of blessings. But note: like circumcision, baptism is a sign that promises/anticipates gospel realities; it does *not* affirm or testify that these same gospel realities have already taken place in the recipient.

Second, circumcision, as a physical act, signified the removal of the defilement of sin, the cleansing from sin, and it pointed to the need for a circumcision of the heart (see Exod 6:12, 30; Lev 19:23; 26:41; Deut 10:16; 30:6; Jer 4:4; 6:10; 9:25). Likewise, baptism is an outward sign of the inward need for the grace of God in the heart of the covenant member—"it points to the necessity of spiritual regeneration";[128] it does *not* testify that regeneration has already occurred.

Third, circumcision was the seal of the righteousness Abraham had by faith while he was as yet uncircumcised (Rom 4:11). Circumcision is not a guarantee that Abraham has faith or even that Abraham (or anyone else, for that matter) has righteousness. Instead, "what circumcision guarantees is the word of God's promise: that *righteousness will be given on the basis of faith*."[129] The same is true of baptism, which testifies to God's promise to justify the ungodly by faith. One can circumcise or baptize an infant before faith is present because the sign is simply a promise that righteousness will be given when a person believes the covenant promises of God.

Thus, regarding the significance of circumcision and baptism, covenant theology insists that the two signs signify the same gospel truths, namely, regeneration (Col 2:11–12; Rom 2:29), union with Christ (Rom 6:4; Gal 3:27–29), and the blessings related to that union (Acts 2:38). Because the signs signify the realities and we are under the same covenant of grace, it is legitimate to apply the sign to "believers and their children."[130]

---

[127] See Booth, *Children of the Promise*, 107.

[128] Booth, 107.

[129] Mark Ross, "Baptism and Circumcision as Signs and Seals," in *The Case for Covenantal Infant Baptism*, ed. Gregg Strawbridge, 94 (emphasis original).

[130] If the signs signify the same truth, then why did circumcision end as a covenant sign, especially for the Jewish Christian? Most covenant theologians argue that the change was administrative due to the greater blessings of the new covenant, especially in extending more blessings to more people (e.g., Jew and Gentile, male and female). Also, within paedobaptist covenant theology, there is a debate on paedocommunion. Some insist that children should be included in communion since children are full

Preliminary Reflections on Competing Theological Systems

We have outlined the basic viewpoints of dispensational and covenant theology in terms of how each view seeks to "construct" the biblical-theological framework of Scripture and from which specific theological and doctrinal conclusions each system arises. The reason for doing so is twofold. First, we need to acknowledge that Christians differ regarding their understanding of the Bible's framework. This requires a critical examination of our theological systems, their assumptions, and our hermeneutical commitments in light of God's Word. Second, we cannot resolve our doctrinal differences without first understanding how theological systems work. Although evangelicals agree on more than we disagree on, and we can speak of a "mere" Protestant/evangelical theology, substantial disagreements remain. Resolution of these differences rarely occurs by appealing to one or two texts; instead, we have to do exegesis of texts in light of the entire canon. Specifically, we have to think through how each system "puts together" the Bible's metanarrative, specifically how each systems views the nature of the covenants and their (inter)relationships.

Often this point is forgotten in theological formulation and evaluation, and when it is, we tend to talk past each other. Frequently our critique of other views is by simple appeal to our own system and dismissing out of hand the other view without trying to understand it on its own terms. For this reason, I want to offer a few preliminary reflections on the theological systems of dispensationalism and covenant theology. My goal is to demonstrate why I think progressive covenantalism best captures the biblical framework and thus explain why on specific issues I draw different theological conclusions than the other systems.[131] For example, why do I think that a Baptist ecclesiology (i.e., the regenerate nature of the church, the practice of the ordinances, an elder-led but congregational rule of church government, etc.) is correct? Or why do I think that the Sabbath law from the old covenant has been fulfilled in Christ, which necessitates a more nuanced application of the Decalogue to the church? Why do I believe that

---

covenant members by baptism. See, e. g., Douglas Wilson, Peter Leithart, and Gregg Strawbridge, *The Case for Covenant Communion*, ed Gregg Strawbridge (Monroe, LA: Athanasius, 2006). For a view against paedocommunion, see Cornelis P. Venema, *Children at the Lord's Table?* (Grand Rapids: Reformation Heritage, 2009); and Fesko, *Word, Water, and Spirit*, 361–65.

[131] Also see my interaction with covenant and dispensational theology in *Covenantal and Dispensational Theologies: Four Views on the Continuity of Scripture*, ed. Brent E. Parker and Richard J. Lucas (Downers Grove: IVP Academic, 2022).

the church is God's final, new-creation people that last forever instead of merely a present-day illustration of what believing nations will be in the future? Or, to broaden it to areas other than ecclesiology and eschatology: Why do I affirm that Jesus is God the Son incarnate; that his work is absolutely necessary for our salvation; that for Christ to redeem us, he must obey for us in his life and death (active and passive obedience); and that the nature of his cross is best explained by penal substitution? No doubt, the answers to these questions are directly tied to specific biblical texts, but they are also tied to how these texts function in the Bible's overall theological framework. As such, it is important to offer some preliminary reflections on where progressive covenantalism differs from other "constructions" of the Bible's overall story and theological framework.

But before I do, I want to describe briefly the theological system of "1689 Federalism," a view similar to mine, but different at some key points. However, as a view, it constructs the Bible's theological framework in ways similar to progressive covenantalism.

Reformed Baptist Theology as "1689 Federalism"

Reformed Baptist theology arose in seventeenth-century England, and it is best summarized in the *Second London Baptist Confession* (1689).[132] In most doctrinal areas, Reformed Baptists embraced the theological commitments of the Reformation and of post-Reformed orthodoxy, such as pro-Nicene trinitarian theology; God's sovereignty over all things, including human free choices; Chalcedonian Christology; the active and passive obedience of Christ for our justification; penal substitution; the doctrines of grace; and the broad parameters of covenant theology—what many identify today as "Calvinism." However, as Baptists, they rejected specific aspects of covenant theology, namely, how covenant theology viewed *the* covenant of grace and its administrations, the mixed nature of the church, and the practice of infant baptism. Although Reformed Baptists held a variety of views on the covenant, Nehemiah Coxe (d. 1689) and Benjamin Keach (1640–1704) were key theologians who modified covenant

---

[132] See Nehemiah Coxe and John Owen, *Covenant Theology from Adam to Christ*, ed. Ronald D. Miller, James M. Renihan, and Francisco Orozco (Palmdale: Reformed Baptist Academic Press, 2005); Samuel D. Renihan, *From Shadow to Substance: The Federal Theology of the English Particular Baptists (1642–1704)* (Oxford: Centre for Baptist History and Heritage, 2018); Pascal Denault, *The Distinctiveness of Baptist Covenant Theology*, 2nd ed. (Birmingham: Solid Ground, 2017).

theology's understanding of the *one* covenant of grace expressed in different administrations, thus rejecting its understanding of the *essential/substantial* sameness of all the biblical covenants. Instead, they argued that the *one* covenant of grace is revealed progressively and formally concluded in the new covenant, thus modifying the essential-administration distinction in covenant theology.

Today, this view continues in what is known as 1689 Federalism.[133] The view is similar to progressive covenantalism although it differs at some key points, yet it offers a similar critique of dispensational and covenant theology. Here are some of its points of *agreement*:

1. The acceptance of Reformed theology in terms of Scripture, theology proper, creation and providence, humans and sin, Christology, soteriology, and eschatology.

2. The affirmation of a creation covenant with Adam, who functions as the covenant/federal head of all humanity. In 1689 Federalism, the language of "covenant of works" is retained, while I prefer "creation covenant" for reasons discussed in chapter 15. But there is agreement on the nature of the covenant: God's demand for perfect obedience, Adam's headship role and probationary state, and its foundational role for grasping the Bible's entire metanarrative.[134]

3. There is also basic agreement that "the covenant of grace" is revealed progressively from Gen 3:15 on, as it is announced and promised, but not formally concluded until Christ and the ratification of the new covenant.[135] However, I am more hesitant to use "the covenant of grace" language given its diverse use in theological systems, specifically covenant theology. Since "the covenant of grace" is *theological* language, we must make sure that it best explains the biblical teaching. But I am sympathetic with how 1689 Federalists employ the *concept* of the covenant of grace and their equating it with the new covenant even though I am hesitant to use the language. However we state it, we must preserve what Scripture teaches, namely, that our triune God has eternally planned our redemption in Christ, which is progressively

---

[133] For example, see Barcellos, *Recovering A Covenantal Heritage* (see chap. 14, n. 61); Samuel D. Renihan, *The Mystery of Christ: His Covenant and His Kingdom* (Cape Coral: Founders Press, 2019); also see http://www.1689federalism.com. Similar to 1689 Federalism is another version of Reformed Baptist theology: Earl M. Blackburn, ed., *Covenant Theology: A Baptist Distinctive* (Birmingham: Solid Ground, 2013); Nichols, *Covenant Theology* (see chap. 14, n. 16).

[134] On the creation covenant, see Pascal Denault, "By Farther Steps: A Seventeenth-Century Particular Baptist Covenant Theology," in Barcellos, *Recovering a Covenantal Heritage*, 71–75; Renihan, *The Mystery of Christ*, 59–77.

[135] Denault, "By Farther Steps," 78–91.

revealed through the covenants until it reaches its fulfillment in Christ. We must also preserve that after God's promise of redemption (Gen 3:15), *each* covenant, as part of the *one* plan of God, reveals, predicts, and anticipates in a whole host of ways who the "seed of the woman" will be, how God will redeem his people, and what the ultimate ground for our justification is in Christ, even though OT saints were forgiven their sins by grace through faith in Christ as they believed the covenant promises of God centered in Christ (Gen 3:15; 15:6).

4. There is agreement that we must account for important *biblical* differences between the OT covenants and the new covenant, thus allowing for discontinuity between Israel and the church and the covenant signs of both communities. Furthermore, there is basic agreement that *if* the language of a "covenant of grace" is used, one should identify it with the new covenant. Thus, as God's one redemptive plan unfolds through the covenants, the new covenant is progressively revealed, predicted, and anticipated. But again, I think the better way of stating this is in terms of how *each* covenant contributes to God's plan and how *each* covenant reaches its fulfillment, terminus, and telos in Christ and the new covenant.

5. There is agreement on the nature of the church as a believing, regenerate community, in contrast to Israel under the old covenant, and that the covenant signs of circumcision and baptism do not signify the same realities, hence our rejection of infant baptism.

However, here are some points of *disagreement*:

1. There is a tendency to think of the biblical covenants in unconditional or conditional terms. For example, the Mosaic covenant is viewed as a conditional/bilateral covenant that reaffirms the covenant of works, which Christ obeys.[136] Or the new covenant is solely unconditional due to God's initiative to save by sovereign grace and our Lord's keeping of it for us (so it is conditional for our Lord Jesus Christ).[137] Although I know what is being affirmed, the problem is that all of the covenants contain both aspects: *unconditional*, or better, "monergistic," due to God's gracious initiative and promises, and *conditional* due to his absolute demand on his creatures. As God's plan unfolds, it is precisely because the covenants contain both elements, tied to the larger Creator-creature relationship, that a *tension* is created in the Bible's storyline, which is only resolved in Christ. In the end, we agree on the end of the story, but we get there in a slightly different way.

[136] Denault, 98–104.

[137] Denault, 104–6.

2. Probably the greatest disagreement is over how we should view the Mosaic covenant in God's plan and especially how we should apply aspects of it to ourselves today. 1689 Federalists accept the tripartite division of the covenant (i.e., moral, civil, and ceremonial) and argue that the Decalogue is God's eternal moral law for all people as it is given in the covenant. Although we are not under the Mosaic covenant *as a covenant*, all people are directly under the Decalogue as it is given to Israel. In one sense, everyone agrees that the Decalogue reflects God's moral demand and thus his moral law. However, the problem arises in regard to the Sabbath command. If the Decalogue "comes over" to us as it is given in the covenant, then it follows that all people must obey the Sabbath command.[138] But the problem is how we justify such a position in light of the entire canon of Scripture. In the NT, there is little evidence that there is a continuation of the Sabbath command for the church or society, or even a transfer of the Sabbath to the Lord's Day.[139] Instead, the Sabbath is best viewed as a command *and* a type/pattern that looked back to the "creation rest" (and its loss as a result of sin) *and* forward to a greater salvation rest in Christ, which he has now accomplished and which we now enjoy (Matt 11:28–30; Heb 3:7–4:11). This may seem like a small point, but it reflects a larger hermeneutical debate regarding how to understand the law covenant and its role in God's plan and how to apply the entire OT to us now that Christ has come.[140]

Preliminary Reflections on Dispensational and Covenant Theology

We now turn to some of the points of disagreement between progressive covenantalism and the theological systems of dispensational and covenant theology. Let me describe *five* broad areas.

First, there is disagreement over some of the specifics of how God's plan unfolds through the covenants, which reach their fulfillment in Christ. In relation to covenant theology, before we mention our points of disagreement, it is important first to note our agreement. We agree

---

[138] See Richard C. Barcellos, *Getting the Garden Right: Adam's Work and God's Rest in Light of Christ* (Cape Coral: Founders Press, 2017), 99–272.

[139] See Carson, *From Sabbath to Lord's Day* (see chap. 14, n. 25); cf. Thomas R. Schreiner, "Goodbye and Hello: The Sabbath Command for New Covenant Believers," in Wellum and Parker, *Progressive Covenantalism*, 159–88 (see chap. 4, n. 34).

[140] See my "Progressive Covenantalism and the Doing of Ethics," in Wellum and Parker, *Progressive Covenantalism*, 215–34.

that foundational to the Bible's story is starting in creation with Adam and going to the new creation in Christ. We also agree that the covenants function as the backbone and framework of the Bible's story, unfolding God's plan of redemption *and his promises*, from Gen 3:15 to Christ. Creation, then, is the beginning rather than the goal of human existence, with Adam and Christ functioning as the two representative heads of humanity. This is in contrast to dispensational theology, which certainly believes in creation and Adam, but a creation covenant does not factor into their theological system. For dispensationalism, the Bible's plotline really starts in Genesis 12 with Abraham and is centered in the anticipation of Israel and the promises given to her as a nation.

However, in contrast to covenant theology, we reject that Scripture divides the covenants into two categories: the covenant of works ("law") and the covenant of grace ("grace/gospel"). Also, we deny that the *theological* category of "*the* covenant of grace" can be imposed on all of the covenants so that all of the covenants are *essentially* the same but only *administratively* different. No doubt, the *theological* categories of "law" and "gospel" are correct, but Scripture does not derive these categories by dividing covenants into either bilateral or unilateral covenants. Nor can we account for the differences between the covenants simply by administrative changes. Instead, it is best to think of God's plan unfolding through a *plurality* of covenants (Eph 2:12), with *each* covenant contributing to God's unified plan and *each* covenant being understood in its own textual/epochal context, before we think about how *each* covenant is fulfilled in Christ. In this way, we can affirm God's redemptive plan centered in Christ and how each covenant progressively reveals, predicts, and promises the coming of the new covenant. OT believers are "in Christ" as they look forward to him, and they live out their relation to God through the covenant they are under, as each covenant reveals and anticipates Christ. This also allows us to say that *all* of the OT covenants are revelatory-prophetic of the new covenant while accounting for the integrity of each covenant in its context and the *greater* nature of the new covenant.

Second, there is a disagreement over how we should think of the Israel-church relationship. On the one hand, in contrast to dispensational theology, Scripture teaches that God has *one* people and that the Israel-church relationship should be viewed *Christologically*. The church is not *directly* the "new Israel" or her replacement. Rather, in Christ, the church is God's new covenant people since *Jesus* is the fulfillment of Adam and Israel, the faithful seed of Abraham who inherits the promises by his work. The church is God's *new* creation/humanity, which remains *forever*, composed of believing Jews and Gentiles, who equally and fully receive *all* of God's promises in Christ, including the land promise realized in the new creation (Rom 4:13; Eph 6:3; Heb 11:10, 16; cf. Matt 5:5). Thus, as Eph 2:11–21 makes clear, the church is not merely the extension of Israel or an amalgam of Jews and Gentiles. The church is *new* as it transcends the old entities. The church is not one phase in God's plan that ends when God returns to his previous plan for Israel and the nations. God's eternal plan *always* anticipated the creation of *the church* (Eph 3:8–13)—Christ's bride who lasts forever (Rev 21:1–4).

On the other hand, in contrast to covenant theology, the church is *new* in the redemptive-historical sense because she is the people of the *new* covenant. In Christ, the church is God's new covenant people in continuity with the elect of all ages, but *different* from Israel. Under the old covenant, Israel, in its nature and structure, was a *mixed* community (Rom 9:6). But the church is constituted by people who are united to Christ by faith and partakers of the blessings of the new covenant, which minimally includes the forgiveness of sin, the gift of the Spirit, and heart circumcision. Thus, in contrast to Israel, the church is constituted as a believing, regenerate people. For this reason, baptism, the sign of the new covenant, is only applied to those who profess faith, and circumcision and baptism do *not* signify the same realities due to their respective covenantal differences. This view of the church is also confirmed by a number of other points. For example, the church is an eschatological and "gathered" (*ekklēsia*) people—identified with the "age to come." Her identity is not with "this present age" but with the saving reign of Christ that is now here. Those who have placed their faith in Christ are now citizens of the new/heavenly Jerusalem, no longer "in Adam" but "in Christ" with all the benefits of that union (Heb 12:18–29). As the church, we are beginning to enjoy by faith the privileges of that city still to come (Heb 13:14). Yet, to participate in these realities *now* is another way of saying that the church is, by definition, part of the new creation, consisting of people who are raised and seated with Christ in the heavenly realms (Eph 2:5–6; Col 2:12–13; 3:3). In biblical terms, this is only true of regenerate people. The NT knows nothing of one who is *in Christ* but who is not regenerate, effectually called by the Father, born of the Spirit, justified, holy, and awaiting glorification. On these points, covenant theology does not sufficiently account for how the previous covenants reach their fulfillment in Christ and the newness of Christ's people.

Third, there is disagreement over how we understand inaugurated eschatology. Although inaugurated eschatology is almost a "given" in evangelical theology, it is applied differently in theological systems. Specifically, we see this in the Israel-church relationship. On the one hand, dispensationalism distinguishes Israel from the church ontologically so that in the future, national/ethnic Israel must receive specific promises tied to the land and "distinct" from believing Gentile nations. The church is *not* viewed as the true, eschatological Israel, who receives *all* of the promises, including the inheritance of the land fulfilled in the new creation. So, when Jeremiah addresses "the house of Israel and Judah" (31:31) but in the NT this is applied to the church, many dispensationalists explain this by appealing to inaugurated eschatology. In the *already*, the new covenant is *spiritually* applied to the church, but in the *not yet*, the new covenant will be applied *literally* to national Israel in the land, thus receiving her "distinct" promises (tied to the land) different from those of believing Gentile nations.[141]

However, the *dispensationalist* view has at least *two* problems.

1. It does not properly understand the Israel-church relationship by working through the Bible's covenantal progression. In not starting with creation/Adam and then situating Israel within the covenantal storyline; it does not see how Christ, as David's greater Son, *is* the true Israel and last Adam and how *he* fulfills *all* of God's promises. In turn, it fails to view Messiah's people, the church, consisting of believing Jews and Gentiles, as the recipient of *all* of the OT promises equally *as the one new man* (Eph 2:11–21). No doubt, in Christ, people do not lose their ethnicity and gender; we are embodied creatures. Yet, the church is not merely a *spiritual* installment of the final state, which results in discrete believing nations receiving slightly different promises and privileges. Within God's covenant community, *all* are "co-inheritors" and "co-partakers" of God's promises in Messiah Jesus (Eph 3:6; cf. 2:12).[142] As Paul reminds us, God's promise, which includes our inheritance, "is by faith, so that it may be according to grace, to guarantee it to all the descendants—not only to those who are of the law but also to those who are of Abraham's faith. He is the father of us all. As it is written: 'I have made you the father of many nations'" (Rom 4:16–17a). In the church, Christ fulfills all of God's promises to Abraham because Christ—Abraham's true seed (Gal. 3:16), Israel's king, and the

---

[141] See Bruce Ware, "The New Covenant and the People(s) of God," in Blaising and Bock, *Dispensationalism, Israel and the Church*, 84–97; Michael J. Vlach, *Has the Church Replaced Israel? A Theological Evaluation* (Nashville: B&H, 2010), 157–58.

[142] On this point see Beale and Gladd, *Hidden but Now Revealed*, 159–73 (see chap. 4, n. 56); Sam Storms, *Kingdom Come: The Amillennial Alternative* (Fearn, Ross-shire, UK: Mentor, 2013), 177–227.

last Adam—has secured our salvation and every blessing for redeemed Jews and Gentiles alike, who together are Abraham's spiritual seed (Gal 3:29).

2. Regarding inaugurated eschatology, dispensationalism fails to see how *all* new covenant realities are *now* here in Christ *and* applied to the church *in principle*. We cannot simply apply spiritual blessings to the *already* and material/physical blessings to the *not yet*. Both are present *now*, although the fullness of both still awaits the consummation.[143]

In contrast to dispensationalism, covenant theology insists on the *continuity* between Israel and the church. The church, like Israel, is a mixed people, consisting of believers and unbelievers, *and* the covenant signs continue from circumcision to baptism, hence the warrant for paedobaptism. But how do we reconcile this view with the OT's expectation that Messiah's people will be a regenerate people because they will *all* be born/empowered/indwelt by the Spirit, *know* God, and receive *full* forgiveness of sin? Some covenant theologians admit that Jer 31:31–34 anticipates such a people, but to explain why the church is still "mixed," inaugurated eschatology is appealed to. Richard Pratt, for example, argues that Jeremiah 31's anticipation of an *entire* people who are *regenerate* is realized only in the *not yet*. *Presently*, the church remains a people constituted by true believers *and* sanctified unbelievers.[144] Beale argues that *presently* the church is different from Israel because she is more "democratized"; namely, there is no categorical distinction between priests and prophets and the rest of God's people. The church *now* remains a "mixed" people; her *nature* as an entire regenerate people awaits the *not yet*.[145]

However, covenant theology also has two problems:

1. It does not sufficiently account for the relationship of Christ to his people. Through covenantal progression, the genealogical principle, namely, the relationship between the covenant mediator and his seed, is transformed in the new covenant. In the previous covenants, the relationship is more biological (e.g., Adam, Noah, Abraham, Israel, and David), but now in Christ, the relationship is *spiritual*, that is, of the Spirit. One is *in Christ and the new covenant* not by physical birth, circumcision of the flesh, or the Torah, but by spiritual rebirth and faith. Only those in faith-union with Christ are *his* family and savingly know God.

---

[143] On this point, see Richard J. Lucas, "The Dispensational Appeal to Romans 11 and the Nature of Israel's Future Salvation," in Wellum and Parker, *Progressive Covenantalism*, 237–42.

[144] See Pratt, "Infant Baptism in the New Covenant," 127–74.

[145] Beale, *New Testament Biblical Theology*, 728–49.

2. Regarding inaugurated eschatology, covenant theology fails to see how *all* new covenant realities are *now* here in Christ *and* applied to the church *in principle*. Now that Christ has come, one is either in the new covenant or not, and to be *in* the new covenant entails that one *now knows* God, is *forgiven* of one's sins, and is *circumcised in heart*. Yes, the fullness of our salvation is future, but *already* the church is a believing, justified people. In other words, *all* of these new covenant blessings come to us as a unit fulfilled in Christ. It is no doubt true that the fullness of new covenant blessings is still future, but *already*, in Christ, both individually and corporately, we presently enjoy and partake of the blessings of the future age, which is now here. For the church, this entails that she is a regenerate people *now* since in Christ, *all* of God's promises are *here* (2 Cor 1:20). In fact, as James White notes, the author of Hebrews never argues that the new covenant is only partially here or that it "is only *partly* better now, and will get *much* better in the future."[146] Instead, the author argues that the new covenant "has been enacted" (*nenomothetētai*, perfect tense), which speaks of a completed action and a present reality.[147] The new covenant is here *now* in Christ's person and work; what has resulted is a *new* people who *all* savingly know God *and* the forgiveness of their sins. But if we argue that the new covenant is only partially *here* or partially *fulfilled*, then we have to bifurcate its blessings. But this does not account for how the author of Hebrews applies Christ's perfect once-for-all time work when he writes, "For by a single offering [Christ] has perfected [*teteleiōken*, perfect tense] for all time those who are being sanctified" (Heb 10:14 ESV). As Beale and others admit, this text demands that we acknowledge that our justification is *inaugurated*,[148] but if one blessing of the new covenant is *now* here, then on what basis do we argue that other blessings are still future, such as the reality of a transformed, regenerate people?

Instead, it is better to see that both new covenant blessings are *now* here, yet our glorification as a justified people, both individually and corporately, is still future. The church, as God's *new* covenant people, is different from Israel in her *nature*, *now* and *forever*. In fact, it is this *difference* that explains why baptism, as a new covenant sign, signifies something different from

---

[146] White, "Newness of the New Covenant (Part 2)," in Barcellos, *Recovering a Covenantal Heritage*, 380 (see chap. 14, n. 61).

[147] White, 379–81; cf. DeRouchie, "Counting Stars with Abraham," 481–85 (see chap. 14, n. 36).

[148] See Beale, *New Testament Biblical Theology*, 735.

circumcision under the Abrahamic and old covenant and why it is only to be applied to those who know God, have circumcised hearts, and are forgiven of their sins.

Fourth, there is disagreement over some hermeneutical issues, especially regarding how the Abrahamic covenant functions in relation to its fulfillment in the new and how specific typological structures unfold through the covenants.

Let us first think about how the Abrahamic covenant functions in *covenant theology*. Given the unity of the covenant of grace, covenant theology tends to identify the Abrahamic covenant one for one with the new covenant so that circumcision and the genealogical principle—"you and your future offspring" (Gen 17:7)—"comes over" to baptism and justifies a mixed view of the church. What also occurs is that the Abrahamic covenant is reduced to its *spiritual aspects* while its national and typological aspects are neglected. This is why covenant theology so easily views the church as the "new Israel" with the result that just as Israel was a "mixed" entity so is the church, and just as the genealogical principle and circumcision were operative in the Abrahamic covenant, so they also apply in exactly the same way to the church, now in relation to baptism.

But the problem is that covenant theology fails to do justice to the multifaceted nature of the Abrahamic covenant, and it reads *too fast* into the Abrahamic covenant many of the legitimate *spiritual* realities of the new covenant. In doing so, it fails to exegete the Abrahamic covenant first in its own immediate context before it thinks through how it reaches its fulfillment in the new covenant. For this reason, it fails to see that the genealogical principle of the Abrahamic covenant does *not* remain unchanged as the covenants unfold. At the heart of this principle is the relationship between the covenant head/mediator and his seed. In the previous covenants, the genealogical relationship is primarily *natural/biological* (e.g., Adam, Noah, Abraham, Israel, David). Yet the prophets anticipate a day when, in the new covenant, the relationship between its covenant mediator and his people is one born of the Spirit; this relationship is described diversely but uniquely as a circumcision of the heart (or a law written on the heart). Due to the *effective* nature of the new covenant (in contrast with the old), the *entire* community will become covenant keepers and know God immediately.[149] This is why the prophets speak of *all* those within the new covenant community as people who savingly know the Lord, who have the law written on their hearts, and have experienced the forgiveness

[149] On this point see White, "Newness of the New Covenant (Part 1)," 343–55.

of sins. This is in contrast with the "mixed" constitution of Israel as a nation.[150] Evidence for these kinds of changes in the new covenant is underscored by the prophetic anticipation of the unique work of the Spirit in the coming new age. Although a clear hypostatic distinction between God and his Spirit is not made until the coming of Christ, in the prophets there is an increased and heightened emphasis on the work of God's Spirit in the dawning of the new covenant, first poured out on the Messianic King (see Isa 11:1–3; 49:1–2, 61:1ff.) and then on Messiah's people (see Ezek 11:19–20; 36:25–27; Joel 2:28–32; cf. Num 11:27–29),[151] which entails that there will be a *universal* distribution of the Spirit upon God's people in this empowering/gifting sense (see Joel 2:28–32; Acts 2), which again is different than in Israel. By this change, the new covenant raises *every member* of the covenant to the same relationship with God through the universal distribution of the Spirit so that *all* those "under the new covenant" enjoy the promised gift of the eschatological Spirit (cf. Eph 1:13–14). As this OT anticipation is applied to the church, one cannot think of the church as other than a transformed, regenerate people from every people and nation (Eph 2:11–21; Rev 5:9)—the spiritual, believing seed of Abraham (Gal 3:26–29). As we place the Abrahamic covenant in relation to the other covenants, it is quite evident that the "new" covenant brings numerous changes.

On the other hand, *dispensationalism* appeals to the same Abrahamic covenant and the promise of land to Israel and argues that it "comes over" to the new covenant in exactly the same way. Like covenant theology, dispensationalism does not exegete the Abrahamic covenant first in its own immediate context, think through what preceded it, and then how it is picked up in later covenants before reaching its fulfillment in the new covenant. When one does this, one discovers that the "land" promise to national Israel is a promise *and* a typological pattern. Thus, God's intent in giving the promise tied to the Abrahamic covenant cannot be understood apart from a backward and forward look: backward to the archetype reality of Eden/creation and forward, through the covenants, to its antitypical fulfillment in the new creation that Jesus inaugurates. In Christ, as the first man of the new creation (last Adam) and the true Israel, and his people, the new creation is already here, and it will reach its fullness in the new

---

[150] For a development of this point, see Meade, "Circumcision of Flesh," 127–58 (see chap. 4, n. 34).

[151] On this point, see Max Turner, "Holy Spirit," in *NDBT*, 551–58 (see chap. 1, n. 24); Vos, "The Eschatological Aspect of the Pauline Conception of the Spirit," in *Redemptive History and Biblical Interpretation*, 91–125.

creation in the consummation. In the NT, then, built on the OT teaching and anticipation, the land promise is not fulfilled simply to national, believing Israel in a localized land somewhat "distinct" from believing Gentiles, but to the entire church, composed of believing Jews and Gentiles, in the glory of a new heavens and new earth. The new creation has "already" arrived in Christ, individual Christians (2 Cor 5:17; Eph 2:8–10), and the church (Eph 2:11–21), and at Christ's return, it will be consummated in a land that will be coextensive with the entire new creation (Rev 21–22). Minimally, two reasons lead us to this conclusion: first, the fact that the story of God's redemptive plan begins with creation, the land of Eden, and Adam's role to expand Eden's borders to the ends of the earth sets the context for the later promise given in the Abrahamic covenant. Yet, sadly, Adam disobeyed and was removed from Eden.[152] Second, as God's redemptive promise is given, starting in Gen 3:15, and is unpacked *through covenantal progression* from Adam to Christ, the old creation leads to the new creation, and the land, which functions as a microcosm of Eden, becomes a typological pattern that through the covenants reaches its inaugurated-consummated fulfillment in Christ and the new covenant age.[153]

Fifth, there is disagreement on how to categorize the covenants. Dispensational and covenant theology tend to categorize the covenants as either unconditional/unilateral (royal grant) or conditional/bilateral (suzerain-vassal). But this is problematic since each covenant contains both elements. In terms of God's initiative in the covenants, each covenant is unconditional, or better, monergistic. In relation to the creature, God demands from us complete loyalty, love, and obedience. Some covenants may emphasize one aspect more than the other, but both elements are found in all the biblical covenants. In fact, this is why there is a deliberate *tension* within the covenants—a tension that heightens as God's plan unfolds—and is only resolved in Christ.

On the one hand, the covenants gloriously reveal our triune Creator-covenant Lord who makes *and* keeps his promises. As God initiates covenant relationships with his creatures, he is always the faithful partner—true to his own character and promises (Heb 6:17–18). Regardless of our unfaithfulness, God's promises are certain. But God demands full devotion from us. In

---

[152] See Beale, *Temple and the Church's Mission*, 313–34 (see chap. 13, n. 44); cf. T. Desmond Alexander, *From Eden to the New Jerusalem* (Nottingham, UK: IVP, 2008).

[153] See Oren R. Martin, *Bound for the Promised Land: The Land Promise in God's Redemptive Plan*, NSBT 34 (Downers Grove: InterVarsity, 2015).

this sense, there is a bilateral aspect to the covenants. However, as the covenants progress, a *tension* grows between God's faithfulness to his promises and our disobedience. Obedience is not an option for us. God is holy and just; he is the moral standard of the universe, but we have sinned against *him*. And, in light of Gen 3:15, God's promises are tied to the provision of an obedient son who will undo Adam's disastrous choice. But where is such a son, who fully obeys and meets God's moral demands? How can God remain in relationship with us unless our sin is removed? It is *through* the covenants that this *tension* increases, and it is *through* the covenants that the answer is given: God himself—our covenant maker and keeper—must *unilaterally* act to keep his own promise by the provision of an *obedient* covenant partner.

It is only by maintaining the dual emphasis of the unilateral/bilateral elements in the covenants, which lead us to their fulfillment in the unbreakable new covenant in Christ, that we appreciate Scripture's glorious Christological focus. The Bible's story as told by the covenants leads us to him. Jesus alone, who is God the Son incarnate and our great prophet, priest, and king, can secure our salvation. In Christ alone, the covenants are fulfilled and this built-in tension is resolved.

Concluding Reflection

Evangelicals who are heirs of the Reformation agree on more than we disagree on. But our disagreements are not insignificant since behind them are entire ways of "constructing" the Bible's metanarrative and theological framework. As we turn to part 4, we will seek to work from within what we believe is Scripture's interpretive framework as we seek to think about the glory of the triune God and all things in relation to him for the life and health of the church.

PART 4

From Biblical Theology to Theological Formulation

CHAPTER 16

The God Who Is There: Contemporary Discussion

Introduction

We now turn from the Bible's metanarrative and overall theological framework to doctrinal formulation that arises from the entirety of Scripture. Where do we begin? We begin where Scripture begins: the glory of the triune God who has always existed in the self-sufficiency of his own being as Father, Son, and Holy Spirit. Genesis's opening words remind us that creation is not eternal, only God is, and before there was a universe, the eternal God was there in all of his perfection, love, holiness, and fullness of triune personal relations.

However, before we turn to the doctrine of God, we need to contextualize our discussion. Theology is never done in a vacuum. It is always done in a specific context as the church seeks faithfully to apply God's word to every area of life. Theology is not only the formulation of doctrine but also its defense in light of specific challenges, thus helping the church to know and to proclaim "the whole plan of God" (Acts 20:27) for God's glory and the church's good.

With this in mind, we will begin our discussion of theology proper by setting it in the context of contemporary discussions and challenges. Our goal is to demonstrate that our culture's embrace of modern/postmodern thought has not only created a rejection of, but also theological confusion regarding, the nature of the God of Scripture. Unfortunately, this confusion is also found within evangelical theology, a situation that requires that we avoid the current errors of our time by formulating a theology proper that is faithful to Scripture and to historic theology.

"God" in Contemporary Thought and Life: The "Problem" of God

"God" has become a problem for many today and the question, What God? helps us see something of why this is so. Given the corrosive effects of modern/postmodern thought, people either deny God's existence or, more commonly, they redefine who he is, especially in more "relational" terms. As a result, "God" is viewed as immanent and correlative with the world instead of the transcendent triune Lord who is perfect in himself. Let us look at three areas where God has become a "problem" for many today. As the church, we cannot ignore these areas if we are to remain true to Scripture and faithful in knowing, proclaiming, and enjoying the true and living God who is there.

The Religious-Pluralism Problem of God

In a pluralistic age, the exclusivity of God becomes a problem. Given pluralism, the Christian doctrine of God disappears but reemerges in a renewed interest in comparative religions. Repeatedly, we are told that "god" has many names and there is not one concept of him that is objectively true. Mahatma Gandhi represents this view. In speaking of religion and "god," he writes, "The soul of religion is one, but it is encased in a multitude of forms. My position is that all the great religions are fundamentally equal."[1] Or think of John Hick, who once identified as an evangelical, but as he worked with large Muslim and Hindu communities in Birmingham, England, he abandoned Christianity to affirm pluralism. For him, religion changed from being "God-centered" to "reality-centered," and he allowed for multiple concepts of "god" as equal.[2] In light of the religious-pluralism problem of God, Christian theology must expound, defend, and proclaim the triune God of Scripture as the *only* true God in all of his glory and beauty, in contrast to the false gods and idols of our age.

---

[1] Cited in Demarest, *General Revelation*, 255 (see chap. 6, n. 2).

[2] See John Hick, "A Pluralist View," in Okholm and Phillips, *Four Views on Salvation*, 29–59 (see chap. 6, n. 55).

The Philosophical Problem of God[3]

Ever since Immanuel Kant's phenomena-noumena dichotomy at the end of the Enlightenment, there has been an increased philosophical problem of God. Many follow Kant and think that our concepts are empty without experience to give them content, and as applied to God, since we do not experience God in our human experience, the "concept" of God is vacuous. Any talk about God is not in the realm of knowledge but "faith"—a "faith" divorced from objective truth. Hence the rise of classic liberal theology and its current iterations that talk of "God" by turning inward and analyzing our human religious feeling of absolute dependence. The end result of such a view is that God's holy transcendence is denied and he is relocated within the world.

In response, Ludwig Feuerbach, along with other "masters of suspicion," such as Sigmund Freud, Karl Marx, and Friedrich Nietzsche, argued that any talk of "God" is simply a projection or objectification of the ideals of humanity.[4] If "God" is not transcendent but only immanent, it is best to banish him entirely and admit that all theology is simply anthropology. As picked up by Marx, religion is simply the way unjust political systems perpetuate the system. Or, for those like Freud, "God" is simply an irrational, infantile illusion that needs to be banished from society in order to liberate us from our sexual taboos due to our belief in the Christian God. As Nietzsche's "death of God" philosophy has been embraced in our culture, the concept of God has become more problematic, with disastrous consequences. In such a context, Christian theology must reject all theologies "from below" for a theology "from above." We must proclaim the *known* triune Creator-covenant Lord who sustains and rules all things, and who acts by sovereign grace to redeem his people, and who demands and deserves our total love, devotion, and obedience.

---

[3] For a development of this "problem," see Thomas Joseph White, *The Trinity: On the Nature and Mystery of the One God* (Washington, DC: Catholic University of America Press, 2022), 32–49.

[4] See Feuerbach, *Essence of Christianity* (see chap. 2, n. 93); Sigmund Freud, *Civilization and Its Discontents*, trans. D. McLintock (London: Penguin, 2002); Karl Marx, "A Contribution to the Critique of Hegel's Philosophy of Right: Introduction," in *Karl Marx: Early Writings* (New York: Penguin, 1992); Friedrich Nietzsche, *"On the Genealogy of Morals" and Other Writings*, trans. C. Diethe (Cambridge: Cambridge University Press, 2018); cf. Trueman, *Rise and Triumph* (see chap. 1, n. 26); Vanhoozer, *Remythologizing Theology*, 13–23 (see chap. 2, n. 131).

The Cultural Problem of God

Although the church must theologically and apologetically address the above challenges that deny who God is and identify him with various human constructions, these "problems" tend to remain outside the church. But the cultural problem is different; it affects the church directly.

What exactly is the cultural problem of God? It is the effect that the growing secularization of our modern/postmodern world has had on theology, especially the doctrine of God. In chapter 2, we sketched the intellectual shifts that took place in the West and its impact on theology due to the disintegration of the "modern" world and its replacement by the "postmodern" mindset. As a gradual secularization and pluralization took place, the plausibility structures changed, which affected what Charles Taylor labels our "social imaginary" or worldview. The impact of this cultural revolution on the doctrine of God is not necessarily God's existence being denied (although some have done so). Instead, what has resulted is the marginalization of "God" to the periphery of our lives by relocating "God" to the part of our lives that is internal, subjective, and private, thus affirming God's immanence over his transcendent lordship.[5]

David Wells describes the "cultural problem of God" best in his *God in the Wasteland*.[6] His thesis is that modernity has blinded us to the truth and reality of God, and it has attempted to remove him from the center of all things. In a secular age, "God" is still affirmed, but not the God of the Bible. As Wells stated in an earlier work, "It is axiomatic that secularism strips life of the divine, but it is important to see that it does so by relocating the divine in that part of life which is private."[7] The consequence of such a relocation for theology proper is that the triune God of glory is now considered "weightless," that is, unimportant, so that "he rests upon the world so inconsequentially as not to be noticeable. He has lost his saliency for human life."[8] Although in various polls people affirm belief in God, "his truth is no longer welcome in our public discourse. The engine of modernity rumbles on, and [God] is but a speck in its path."[9]

---

[5] See Taylor, *A Secular Age* (see chap. 2, n. 4); cf. Trueman, *Rise and Triumph*, 35–102.

[6] Wells, *God in the Wasteland* (see chap. 1, n. 2).

[7] Wells, *No Place for Truth*, 79 (see Introduction, n. 1).

[8] Wells, *God in the Wasteland*, 88.

[9] Wells, 88–89.

Tragically, Wells argues that the evangelical church is not immune from this cultural influence since we have drunk deeply from the wells of modernity without realizing it. Wells writes: "The fundamental problem in the evangelical world today is not inadequate technique, insufficient organization, or antiquated music. . . . The fundamental problem . . . is that God rests too inconsequentially upon the church. His truth is too distant, his grace is too ordinary, his judgment is too benign, his gospel too easy, and his Christ is too common."[10] Similar to the churches in Revelation 2–3, the evangelical church in the West is in danger of becoming indistinguishable from its surrounding culture. Or, as Francis Schaeffer observed nearly two generations ago, what motivates the church is not knowing and proclaiming the glory of the triune God of sovereign power and grace, the truth of the gospel, and living under the lordship of Christ, but preserving our own "personal peace and affluence."[11]

What Wells (and Schaeffer) observe about the Western evangelical church, we cannot ignore. When our theology removes God from the center or, to use Wells' words, "when God becomes weightless . . . we lose the doctrinal signals that might otherwise warn us that some profound change has taken place—the sorts of signals that once warned of the threat of heresy. Too often in Our Time, there is only peace and quiet."[12] We may even affirm a classic view of God and hold to various confessional standards, but if we are not careful, the doctrine of God "no longer has the power to shape and to summon that it has had in previous ages."[13] Or, more likely, our view of God begins to embrace ideas from our culture and "what was once transcendent in the doctrine of God has either faded or been relocated to the category of the immanent, and then this diminished God has been further reinterpreted to accommodate modern needs."[14] But when this occurs, the entire meaning of Christian theology is turned on its head. As Wells notes, how "we think of [God's] love, his goodness, his saving intentions, what his salvation means, how he reveals himself, how his revelation is received, why Christ was incarnate. . . . All of this and much more [is affected] the moment that the formal categories of transcendence and immanence within the traditional doctrine of God are unsettled."[15] Wells

---

[10] Wells, 30.

[11] Schaeffer, *How Should We Then Live?*, 227 (see chap. 2, n. 27).

[12] Wells, *God in the Wasteland*, 89.

[13] Wells, 89.

[14] Wells, 90.

[15] Wells, 90.

concludes with this sobering observation: "Although weightlessness is not itself a doctrine, it has the power to hobble all doctrines. . . . Weightlessness tells us nothing about God but everything about ourselves, about our condition, about our psychological disposition to exclude God from our reality."[16] In the end, "a God who has thus lost weight is no longer the God of biblical faith or classical Christianity."[17]

The Glory of the Triune God in Scripture and Christian Theology

When we turn to Scripture, we find the opposite view of God from that of our culture. Instead of the "problem" of God, we are confronted with the glory and majesty of our triune Creator-covenant Lord, who alone is God and worthy of all of our thinking, love, and obedience.[18] From Genesis to Revelation, God is presented as the eternal, holy, simple, self-sufficient triune Lord, who by his own sovereign and gracious choice created all things for his own glory (Gen 1–2; Exod 3:14; Ps 50:12–14; John 1:1–3; Acts 17:24–25; Rom 11:33–36). For this reason, he alone is the Creator and Lord and utterly unique (sui generis); everything else is the finite, temporal creation, which is dependent on him for life and all things. He alone is the transcendent, holy One who is sovereign over all *and* the covenant Lord who is fully present with us and who freely, purposely, and effectually sustains and governs all things to *his* intended end (Ps 139:1–10; Isa 40:12–31; Dan 4:34–35; Acts 17:28; Eph 1:11). As the triune Lord, he rules with perfect knowledge and righteousness; his sovereign will cannot be thwarted (Pss 9:8; 33:5; 139:1–4, 16; Isa 46:9–11; Acts 4:27–28). Indeed, as the triune-personal God (Matt 28:18–20; John 1:1–18; 5:16–30; 17:1–5; 1 Cor 8:5–6; 2 Cor 13:14; Eph 1:3–14), he commands, loves, comforts, and judges consistent with himself and according to the covenant relationships that he establishes with his creatures.

Since this universe is *his*, not ours, and we were created to know, glorify, and obey him, he will not allow us to marginalize him to the periphery of our lives. God will not be robbed of his glory: "I am the LORD. That is my name, / and I will not give my glory to another / or my

---

[16] Wells, 90.

[17] Wells, 93.

[18] For a helpful summary of God's glory, see Christopher W. Morgan, "Toward a Theology of the Glory of God," in *The Glory of God*, ed. Christopher W. Morgan and Robert A. Peterson (Wheaton: Crossway, 2010), 153–87.

praise to idols" (Isa 42:8). Thinking about who the eternal triune God is in himself, his eternal plan, and the enactment of his plan for his own glory in creation, providence, redemption, and judgment is rightly called "theology proper" since *all* theological reflection is first about *him*! Theology, at its heart, seeks to know the incomparable God of Scripture in all of his beauty and to live before him according to his self-revelation in love, adoration, and obedience. In fact, to think wrongly about God is catastrophic. Ultimately, *all* false thinking in systematic theology is due to wrong ideas about God. For example, to misunderstand God's triune nature; how the divine persons relate to each other from eternity; the nature of God's attributes; and his works of creation, providence, redemption, and judgment will only lead to an impoverished theology that is disastrous for the church and in which God's name and glory will be dishonored.

What is our greatest need in the church? It is this: to remove from our thinking false ideas about God and to place *him* at the center of our thinking, preaching, and lives. If Wells is correct, one of the problems the evangelical church faces is not thinking rightly about God, thus making him "weightless" in our lives and churches. We must not only give God what he rightly deserves, namely, our complete love and devotion, but we must also never forget that wrong thinking about him leads to doctrinal error and our spiritual impoverishment. As J. I. Packer reminded us many years ago in his classic work *Knowing God*, the greatest need for the church is to be God-centered in our thinking and living.[19] This is an important place to begin our study of God. In our discussion of theology proper, we will examine many wonderful *and* difficult truths. After all, we are discussing the incomprehensible God, the Creator and sovereign Lord of history and salvation! Many people stumble over the God revealed in Scripture. In fact, sadly, within evangelicalism, one area where doctrine is being revised is in the doctrine of God, a point we will discuss below.

Conceptions of "God" in Worldview Collision

Why is the God of Scripture so different than the "gods" of our world? Scripture is clear in its answer. Since Genesis 3, humans have become idolaters, which, in truth, is the heart of human sin and rebellion. John Calvin famously identified fallen humanity as perpetual idol makers.[20]

---

[19] Packer, *Knowing God* (see chap. 1, n. 54).

[20] Calvin, *Institutes*, 1.11.8 (1:107–9) (see chap. 1, n. 3).

For this reason, there is always a worldview collision between who the true and living triune God is and our false constructions of "god" throughout the ages.

As we discussed natural revelation in chapter 6, we noted how Romans 1 teaches that in our sin, we attempt to make God small by "constructing" him after our image. In our suppression of the truth, we foolishly think we can dethrone God (Ps 14:1). What is true of pagan conceptions of "god" is no different than modern/postmodern conceptions of "god." Both construct "god" after some created thing, which results in an impotent deity who is no longer the self-sufficient, sovereign Creator and Redeemer of his people. In fact, Scripture views all attempts to define who God is apart from Scripture as idolatry. In intellectual history, there have been many conceptions of "god," all of which are a denial of the God of the Bible.

Various Reductions of God and His Glory

The most blatant rejection of God's glory is *atheism*, which denies that God exists and that this universe is the result of the blind naturalistic, impersonal forces over time. Such a view cannot account for the design and order of this world, human value and significance, universal moral norms, and objective truth. In the end, it elevates "nature" to the status of God while standing in midair since it cannot provide the basic preconditions for intelligibility and knowledge.

Agnosticism is seemingly a "humbler" version of atheism since it affirms that we cannot "know" whether or not God exists. But Scripture denies such a view and teaches the opposite: God is clearly known from what he has made and within our human constitution as image-bearers so that we are without excuse (Rom 1:18–31). In truth, agnosticism lives off the borrowed capital of the God of Scripture since agnostics reason, act morally, assume that truth is possible given their agnostic claim, yet have no transcendental warrant for their view.

Polytheism is the belief in a plurality of "gods." In the ancient world, the gods were believed to rule over specific areas. Such views continue today in various animistic religions, and they are also making a comeback in the West.[21] Such a view robs God of his glory and deifies creaturely things by making them some kind of finite deity. It rejects God's exclusivity, simplicity, and aseity and makes God to be a fellow genus and species along with other aspects of creation,

---

[21] See Herrick, *Making of the New Spirituality* (see chap. 2, n. 29).

thus denying the Creator-creature distinction and leading to worship of created things rather than God alone.

Deism, a dominant view in the Enlightenment, holds that there is only one God who is the Creator and transcendent but then argues that he is not involved in the world. Due to creation, God has established natural laws by which the universe operates on its own and moral laws by which humans order their lives, but it denies that God acts directly and effectually in the world (miracles). It affirms *methodological* naturalism in all the scientific and theological disciplines. As Herman Bavinck notes, "Deism creates a vast gulf between God and his creatures, cancels out their mutual relatedness, and reduces God to an abstract entity, a pure being, to mere monotonous and uniform existence."[22] Thus, deism robs God of his triune perfection and glory and denies his sovereign rule and active involvement in the world. It elevates the goodness of humans by denying our sin and depravity, and it rebelliously thinks we can save ourselves apart from God's sovereign grace and provision of Christ as our only Redeemer and Lord.

Pantheism identifies "god" with creation: "all things are divine."[23] In the East, it is identified with Hinduism; and in the West, with the thought of Baruch Spinoza, New Age spirituality, and various environmental movements. Although it brings "god" nearer to us by making all things divine, in truth, as Bavinck notes, it "erases the boundary line between the Creator and creature, robs God of any being or life of his own, thus totally undermining religion."[24] It depersonalizes God, and it robs God of the perfection of his being and his moral character, for in the end, it equates good and evil as one. Moreover, it destroys the warrant for objective truth and morality and denies that the triune God has "a blessed life of his own,"[25] thus robbing God of his glory within himself and denying that he alone is Creator, Lord, and Redeemer, who demands and deserves the devotion, love, and worship of his creatures.

The Postmodern Reduction of God: Panentheism

Although all of these views of "god" and denials of God's glory are with us today, *panentheism* uniquely captures the postmodern conception of "god," or what John Cooper has identified as

---

[22] Bavinck, *Reformed Dogmatics*, 2:331 (see chap. 1, n. 9).

[23] Letham, *Systematic Theology*, 52 (see chap. 5, n. 1).

[24] Bavinck, *Reformed Dogmatics*, 2:331.

[25] Bavinck, 2:331.

"the other God of the philosophers."[26] Unlike pantheism, which denies the Creator-creature distinction by identifying "god" and "nature," panentheism blurs the distinction by placing "all things"*(pan)* "in" (*en*) "God" so that God is neither fully distinct from his creation (contrary to historic theology) nor totally identified with it (contrary to pantheism). Instead, God encompasses the universe in such a way that "God is in the world and the world is in God,"[27] thus affirming a mutual correlation between God and the world, making both interdependent on each other. So while God is more than "nature," there is no clear ontological distinction between them, thus conceiving of the God-world relation as one of eternal mutual codependence.

In the twentieth century, *panentheism* was associated with process theism and the work of Alfred N. Whitehead and Charles Hartshorne. This version of it viewed all reality as a series of events each of which has two poles, including "God." The mental pole is all the possibilities that actual entities can become; the physical pole is the world, God's body, which is the progressive realization of the various possibilities. "God" is viewed as an event that is *in* everything, thus rejecting the Creator-creature distinction and making God correlative to the world. The world is a moment *within* the divine life, and since God is immanent to the world, he is not simple, *a se,* or immutable in his singular being but is undergoing a process of growth. God is not the transcendent, sovereign triune Creator and Lord. Instead, God is ("in") the natural processes of evolution by which the world and history takes shape as the one who "lures" and "shapes" the world by offering it various aims, but he cannot *guarantee* his will since he is incapable of unilateral and/or effectual agency, making him mutually dependent on the world.[28]

Although process theism is not the only version of panentheism, the basic understanding of the God-world relation is the same for all varieties of it. In many forms of postmodern theology, panentheism has become the given, especially given its compatibility with an evolutionary view of origins and an embrace of a process view of reality.[29] Given postmodern

---

[26] See Cooper, *Panentheism* (see chap. 2, n. 131).

[27] Letham, *Systematic Theology*, 52.

[28] See Cobb and Griffin, *Process Theology* (see chap. 2, n. 132).

[29] Panentheism is also hugely indebted to Georg Hegel. For Hegel, God is constituted by the dialectical unfolding of history so that God is not "above" history but located "within history." Although Hegel's overall philosophy is rejected by many, his historicizing of God's nature has influenced a number

theology's acceptance of panentheism, or what Kevin Vanhoozer labels "kenotic-perichoretic-panentheism,"[30] there has been a strong embrace of a "relational" and "social" understanding of God that has led to a recasting of historic theology's understanding of the God-world relation, along with a rejection of classical metaphysical categories regarding the nature of God. In this "new" view of God, the very existence of the world entails that God is essentially limited in power, knowledge, and agency, hence the emphasis on "kenosis," or God's emptying of himself in relation to the world. In contrast to historic theology, which affirms the Creator-creature distinction and two natures in Christ that were not mixed, panentheism blends God and the world, thus robbing God of his triune self-sufficiency within himself independent of the world, along with his ability to create, sustain, rule, and redeem in sovereign power and effectual grace.

Not surprisingly, panentheism reflects the character and mood of postmodernity.[31] Instead of the independent, self-sufficient, simple triune God who is the source of all existence, truth, and moral norms, the true, good, and the beautiful are now a conflation of God and the world, thus elevating the role of the self. Embracing an evolutionary view, panentheism is committed to *methodological* naturalism and to some version of panpsychism that views nature as "alive" with mind and purpose. God is no longer viewed as the transcendent Lord who can guarantee his plan; instead, God is essentially immanent, "the life force that moves history or the infinite pulsating ground that sustains the world order."[32] The world is not the creation of God *ex nihilo*; rather, it is the history of God, and "God himself is caught up in the evolutionary process, though at the same time he gives shape to evolution by guiding emergent possibilities toward the ideals of truth, beauty and goodness."[33] Given the God-world relation, God

---

of contemporary theologians, such as Paul Tillich, Jürgen Moltmann, Wolfhart Pannenberg, Karl Rahner, and some versions of social trinitarianism. On this point, see White, *Trinity*, 548–71; Cooper, *Panentheism*, 194–212, 237–300. For some theologians indebted to Karl Barth, there is also a tendency to historicize God's nature. For example, see Robert W. Jenson, *Systematic Theology*, vol. 1 (New York: Oxford University Press, 1997); Bruce L. McCormack, *The Humility of the Eternal Son: Reformed Kenoticism and the Repair of Chalcedon* (Cambridge: Cambridge University Press, 2021).

[30] See Vanhoozer, *Remythologizing Theology*, 130–38.

[31] See Donald G. Bloesch, *God the Almighty: Power, Wisdom, Holiness, Love* (Downers Grove: InterVarsity, 1995), 241–60.

[32] Bloesch, 244.

[33] Bloesch, 248.

works together with humanity to bring about a "better" world. Yet, if panentheism is true, the ground for objective truth and morality is undercut since, in contrast to historic theology, God is not in himself the absolute standard of truth and goodness, the norm by which all things are judged and evaluated.[34] At its heart, panentheism, in its conflation of God and the world, is a reduction of God's glory and the elevation of created things instead of the Creator who is to be praised forever (Rom 1:25).

The Reduction of God in Evangelical Theology: Open Theism

Unfortunately, evangelical theology has not escaped the reduction of God we have witnessed in postmodern thought, and its embrace of a relational, codependent, and historicized view of God's nature. This has occurred in a number of areas, but in theology proper, open theism is a clear example.[35]

At the end of the twentieth century, a movement known as open theism offered a radical rethinking of the doctrine of God within evangelical theology, a via media between classical theism and panentheism. In agreement with the latter, open theism embraced a relational theism that denied that God is the sovereign Lord, who, for his own glory, works out all things according to the counsel of his will. Instead, it viewed God as a loving parent and fellow-sufferer who chooses to relate to his creatures by coming to know events as they take place in history. Since God created humans to be free, God is not able to know the future in exhaustive detail before it occurs. But in contrast to panentheism, open theism argued that God's relation to his creation is by choice and, as such, self-limited. God, as the all-powerful one, not only creates *ex nihilo*, but, if necessary, he can act effectually in history, yet given his

---

[34] For a critique of process theology/panentheism, see Cooper, *Panentheism*, 319–46; Vanhoozer, *Remythologizing Theology*, 139–77; Feinberg, *No One Like Him*, 149–79 (see chap. 2, n. 51).

[35] For open-theist literature, see William Hasker, *God, Time, and Knowledge* (Ithaca: Cornell University Press, 1989); Pinnock et al., *Openness of God* (see chap. 2, n. 135); Pinnock, *Most Moved Mover: A Theology of God's Openness* (Grand Rapids: Baker Academic, 2001); David Basinger, *The Case for Free Will Theism* (Downers Grove: InterVarsity, 1996); Sanders, *God Who Risks* (see chap. 2, n. 135); Gregory Boyd, *God of the Possible* (Grand Rapids: Baker, 2000). More recently, Oord, *Uncontrolling Love of God* (see chap. 2, n. 135); Oord, "An Essential Kenosis View," in *God and the Problem of Evil: Five Views*, ed. Chad Meister and James K. Dew Jr. (Downers Grove: IVP Academic, 2017); Richard Rice, *The Future of Open Theism: From Antecedents to Opportunities* (Downers Grove: IVP Academic, 2020).

decision to create free creatures, other than in unique situations, he has chosen to limit his providential rule.[36]

Not surprisingly, open theism's recasting of the doctrine of God did not occur in a vacuum. It arose alongside postmodern theology's acceptance of a relational theism and major paradigm shifts in our *language* about God, sin, and salvation. Already, shifts had occurred away from speaking about God's holiness, wrath, and justice to that of relationships, self-fulfillment, and love.[37] Furthermore, alongside "relational" theism was the embrace of "social Trinitarianism."[38] Despite the term *social* being used in different ways, the common denominator of "social" views is to think of the Trinity as analogous to a "society or family of three human persons."[39] Most who affirm this "social" view define a divine person as a "distinct center of knowledge, will, love, and action,"[40] which allows them to speak of the Father, Son, and Spirit as distinct speech agents who exist in an I-Thou relationship, and who act harmoniously together. The divine persons' unity is not found in their equal subsisting in the one, simple divine nature, but in terms of a shared generic divine essence that constitutes a cooperative society of divine love,[41] or "the union of the three Persons by virtue of their perichoresis and eternal communion."[42]

In *this* context we see the rise of open theism. Without doubt, the debate over open theism within evangelical theology is a symptom of a growing fracture within evangelicalism at large. It is more than merely the perennial debate between Calvinists and Arminians over issues of

---

[36] An exception to this belief is Thomas Oord, who embraces a more panentheistic version of open theism.

[37] See Robert Brow, "Evangelical Megashift," *Christianity Today* 34, no. 2 (February 19, 1990): 12–17.

[38] We will discuss "social trinitarianism" in chapter 19. Since the term *social* covers multiple views, it is not always helpful, but I am using it to refer to views that redefine the classical view of "person" to include within it a distinct center of will, knowledge, and action. Those who embrace such a view usually reject a classical view of divine simplicity, inseparable operations, and in Christology endorse some form of kenoticism. For a discussion of the various views, see Thomas H. McCall, *Which Trinity? Whose Monotheism? Philosophical and Systematic Theologians on the Metaphysics of Trinitarian Theology* (Grand Rapids: Eerdmans, 2010), 11–55.

[39] McCall, *Which Trinity?*, 28.

[40] Cornelius Plantinga Jr., "Social Trinity and Tritheism," in *Trinity, Incarnation, and Atonement*, ed. Ronald J. Feenstra and Cornelius Plantinga Jr. (Notre Dame: University of Notre Dame Press, 1989), 22.

[41] See Plantinga Jr., "Social Trinity and Tritheism," 27–28.

[42] Leonardo Boff, *Trinity and Society* (Maryknoll: Orbis Books, 1988), 235.

divine sovereignty, foreknowledge, and providence. Instead, it is a debate that takes us to the heart of historic Christian theology. Since *all* theology is rooted and grounded in our view of God, different conceptions of God inevitably affect our *entire* theology. In fact, Clark Pinnock recognizes this point. He rightly notes that "no doctrine is more central than the nature of God. It deeply affects our understanding of the incarnation, grace, creation, election, sovereignty, and salvation."[43] For this reason, open theism is a major point of contention within evangelical theology, and if accepted, it will redefine Christian theology in disastrous ways.[44]

Thus, given its importance, in the remainder of the chapter, we will interact with open theism for two reasons. First, it continues to exert influence, and it reflects something of the current shifts away from a classical view that have occurred in the doctrine of God. Second, it also raises perennial issues in hermeneutics and theological method that are central to the *doing* of a doctrine of God. By discussing open theism, we are able not only to contrast it with the classic tradition of the church but also to introduce some key concepts that theology proper must address. In this way, we can learn from open theism by addressing crucial methodological matters that will inform our discussion in the following chapters, and we can also learn that the "older" theological formulation of classical theism is more faithful to Scripture.

Open Theism: What is it?

Two Key Components

Open theism attempts to chart a via media between classical theism and panentheism. There are two main components of the view that take us to the heart of it.

First, there is a very strong emphasis on divine relationality and divine love as God's defining and supreme attribute. Open theism rejects the classic view of God's triune self-sufficiency (aseity) and divine simplicity. Richard Rice states it this way:

> From a Christian perspective, *love* is the first and last word in the biblical portrait of God. According to 1 John 4:8: "Whoever does not love does not know God,

[43] Pinnock et al., *Openness of God*, 8.

[44] Open theism is an entire theology. For example, open theism redefines original sin, rejects penal substitution and eternal punishment, and embraces inclusivism.

> because God is love." The statement *God is love* is as close as the Bible comes to giving us a definition of the divine reality. . . . Love is not something God happens to do, it is the one divine activity that most fully and vividly discloses God's inner reality. Love, therefore, is the very essence of the divine nature. Love is what it means to be God.[45]

Given God's love and relationality, open theists insist that God's relation to the world is dynamic, that is, in a mutual give-and-take relationship. God does not act coercively, but instead he seeks to persuade humans to act freely in agreement with his intentions for them. For open theists, this is the opposite of classical theism, which they contend is a static, non-relational deity who "never experiences novelty, adventure, spontaneity, or creativity,"[46] an "aloof monarch, removed from the contingencies of the world, unchangeable in every aspect of his being, as an all-determining and irresistible power, aware of everything that will ever happen and never taking risks."[47] For them, the classical view is not the relational and loving God of Scripture, who influences us, and we influence him. God's love entails that he experiences the world, takes risks, and changes his mind in response to our choices. In contrast to classic theism, God has no eternal, comprehensive plan other than his eternal desires. Instead, God shares his rule of the world with humans, and in interaction with us, God comes to know what occurs as it happens. Thus, God's knowledge and experience are truly open, affected by new occurrences in the world.

Thomas Oord actually defines God's love as "essential kenosis," which means that God not only loves by nature but always in sympathetic response to his creatures. In contrast to other open theists, Oord rejects the idea that God *could* prevent evil. Instead, "God's loving nature requires God to create a world with creatures God cannot control."[48] For Oord, this also entails a rejection of *creatio ex nihilo* since it assumes that God has unlimited power, including his ability to coerce. But Oord insists that God has always been creating creatures to love and that he, by his very nature, cannot control others. On this point, Oord differs with most open

---

[45] Richard Rice, "Biblical Support," in Pinnock et al., *Openness of God*, 18–19; cf. Oord, *Uncontrolling Love of God*, 144.

[46] Boyd, *God of the Possible*, 128.

[47] Pinnock, "Systematic Theology," in Pinnock et al., *Openness of God*, 103.

[48] Oord, *Uncontrolling Love of God*, 146.

theists and is closer to panentheism.[49] Significantly, as Kevin Vanhoozer notes, for Oord "the ground of God's loving relationality is not his triune life *ad intra* but his everlasting creation of others *ad extra*."[50]

Second, open theism, similar to Arminianism, embraces a libertarian view of human freedom. Since the nature of freedom (both divine and human) intersects every doctrinal area, especially theology proper, let us carefully examine some of the current discussion regarding the nature of freedom before we describe how open theism's embrace of libertarian freedom impacts its overall theological viewpoint. This discussion will also set the stage for subsequent chapters, especially the chapters regarding God's attributes, the divine decree, and divine providence.

In the current theological and philosophical literature, there are two basic views of freedom: an indeterministic view known as libertarianism, and a deterministic view known as compatibilism.[51] Libertarianism, which falls under the broad category of "indeterminism,"

---

[49] See Rice, *Future of Open Theism*, 101–18.

[50] Kevin J. Vanhoozer, "Love without Measure? John Webster's Unfinished Dogmatic Account of the Love of God, in Dialogue with Thomas Jay Oord's Interdisciplinary Theological Account," *IJST* 19, no. 4 (2017): 512.

[51] Discussions regarding the nature of freedom are complicated. In theology, most of the discussion centers on the relationship between God's eternal plan, his knowledge of future free actions, and whether free choices are determined or not. *Indeterminism* is the view that "the state of the world up to a given point plus all existing natural laws are *not* sufficient to guarantee only one possible future. For example, even if one could specify all actions and events that precede a particular decision, all causal influences playing upon the agent's will, plus all laws of nature governing the decision, it would still be just as possible for the person to choose one option as opposed to any other." Feinberg, *No One Like Him*, 626. Indeterminism can be applied to the natural world (e.g., quantum physics) and to human actions (e.g., libertarian view of freedom). Theologically, open theism and Arminianism embrace a libertarian, or indeterministic, view of freedom.

Determinism is the view that "for everything that happens, there are conditions such that, given them, nothing else could occur." Feinberg, *No One Like Him*, 631; cf. Richard Taylor, "Determinism," in *Encyclopedia of Philosophy*, vol. 2, ed. Paul Edwards (New York: Macmillan, 1972), 359. Determinism too can be applied to the natural world and to human actions. In terms of the latter, "hard determinists" argue that since everything is causally determined, there is no human freedom. Most secular hard determinists are naturalists (physicalists) who reduce human freedom to natural causes, such as biochemistry, genetics, or psychological and social conditioning. By contrast, "soft determinists" insist that everything is causally determined but also that human actions are free and thus compatible with causal conditions that decisively incline the will as long as the will is not constrained (thus a compatibilistic view of freedom). In other words, "the causal conditions are sufficient to move the agent to choose one option over another, but the choice and resultant action are free as long as the person acts insists that a person is free if they are not causally determined by God or "any prior factors that influence our choices, including external circumstances, or motives, desires, character, and nature."[52] For this reason, libertarianism is "incompatible" with any form of "determinism," and as such, to be free requires that our choices are not causally determined by prior conditions or sufficiently inclined in one direction because we can always choose otherwise. This does not mean that our choices are arbitrary. Reasons or causes affect our choices, and libertarians acknowledge that many internal (genetics, nature, etc.) and external conditions (circumstances, culture, people, etc.) influence why we choose what we do. But in the end, we are only free if none of these reasons *sufficiently* incline or *causally determine* our wills in one direction.[53] Bruce Reichenbach emphasizes this point well: "Freedom is not the absence of

---

without constraint." Feinberg, *No One Like Him*, 637. Theologically, Calvinism and Reformed theology embrace *theological* determinism, which must be distinguished from *logical* determinism (i.e., all events are determined by logical necessities), *physical* determinism (i.e., every event is determined by prior physical laws), and *nomological* determinism (i.e., every event is determined by nonphysical events, such as mental and psychological laws). *Theological* determinism argues that "God determines all (not just some) events in the world, including human choices and actions." James N. Anderson and Paul Manata, "Determined to Come Most Freely: Some Challenges for Libertarian Calvinism" *Journal of Reformed Theology* 11 (2017): 275–76. But God determines all things by his free choice (i.e., decree), which includes the free actions and choices of his creatures (on this point see chapters 20, 22). Theological determinism also must be distinguished from "fatalism."

Fatalism argues that "everything that ever happens is set in advance, and no one can stop it," including God, which is a denial of the triune God of the Bible. Feinberg, *No One Like Him*, 633. Fatalism denies that God *freely* ordains all things, that what God ordains is *conditionally* necessary but not *absolutely* necessary, and that God's decree includes the reality of human secondary action and choices. Anderson and Manata, "Determined to Come," 276 n. 14; cf. Feinberg, *No One Like Him*, 633–35.

[52] Christensen, *What About Free Will?*, 6 (see chap. 4, n. 77); cf. Steve W. Lemke, "A Biblical and Theological Critique of Irresistible Grace," in Allen and Lemke, *Whosoever Will*, 150–51 (see chap. 4, n. 85).

[53] Often a distinction is made between *necessary* and *sufficient* conditions in our choices. A necessary condition is "a prior condition that is necessary in order for something to come about," but it is not sufficient since other conditions must also be met. Christensen, *What About Free Will?*, 18. For example, as Christensen notes, gasoline is necessary for your car to operate but not sufficient. A sufficient condition "is that which guarantees that something will come about, but this condition may not be necessary" (18). So, as Christensen illustrates, rain is sufficient for your lawn to get wet, but it is not necessary since you could water your lawn in other ways (18). In the case of human freedom, libertarians insist that

> some conditions (reasons, causes) may be necessary for a choice to be made, but they are never sufficient for that choice to be made; otherwise, we are not free. Nonconstraining

influences, either external or internal," but "we can still act contrary to those dispositions and choose not to follow their leading."[54] *Why* we choose something, then, is not due to God's decree but solely due to *our* choice (sometimes known as "agent causation"), and to be free requires the categorical ability to do otherwise (known as the "principle of alternative possibilities" or a "freedom of contrary choice").[55] Alvin Plantinga denotes both of these points in his definition of libertarian free will: "If a person is free with respect to a given action, then he is free to perform that action and free to refrain from performing it; no antecedent conditions and/or causal laws determine that he will perform the action, or that he won't. It is within his power, at the time in question, to take or perform the action and within his power to refrain from it."[56]

circumstances, internal desires, available options, persuasive actions of others, and so forth may be necessary conditions for a choice to be made, but they are not sufficient. Only our own power of willing is sufficient to guarantee feely made choices. Even if certain necessary conditions are present, it does not guarantee that a choice will be made. Christensen, 19.

[54] Bruce R. Reichenbach, "Freedom, Justice and Moral Responsibility," in *The Grace of God and The Will of Man*, ed. Clark H. Pinnock (Minneapolis: Bethany House, 1989), 286; cf. Feinberg, *No One Like Him*, 628–31.

[55] The ability to do otherwise is the "principle of alternative possibilities" (PAP). See Harry G. Frankfurt, *The Importance of What We Care About: Philosophical Essays* (Cambridge: Cambridge University Press, 1998), 1–10. For those who affirm libertarianism, there is a debate regarding the condition of freedom. For most libertarians, PAP is necessary for freedom and moral responsibility. For example, see Peter Van Inwagen, *An Essay on Free Will* (New York: Oxford University Press, 1983), 8; cf. Robert Kane, *The Significance of Free Will* (New York: Oxford University Press, 1998), 33; Kevin Timpe, *Free Will: Sourcehood and Its Alternatives*, 2nd ed. (New York: Bloomsbury, 2013). However, for "source" libertarians, PAP is not the necessary condition of freedom; rather, it is whether we are the *ultimate* source of our choices. See Linda Zagzebski, "Does Libertarian Freedom Require Alternate Possibilities?," *Philosophical Perspectives* 14 (2000): 245; Eleonore Stump, "Alternative Possibilities and Moral Responsibility: The Flicker of Freedom," *The Journal of Ethics* 3, no. 4 (1999): 324. In evangelical theology, William L. Craig affirms "source" libertarianism. See his "Response to Gregory A. Boyd," in *Four Views of Divine Providence*, ed. Dennis W. Jowers (Grand Rapids: Zondervan, 2011), 225. However, as Guillaume Bignon has shown, it is nigh impossible to affirm libertarianism without PAP. *Excusing Sinners and Blaming God: A Calvinist Assessment of Determinism, Moral Responsibility, and Divine Involvement in Evil* (Eugene: Pickwick, 2018), 124–28. In our discussion, we will assume that the condition of libertarian freedom is that the person or agent is both the ultimate source of their choices *and* that PAP is required.

[56] Alvin Plantinga, *God, Freedom, and Evil* (Grand Rapids: Eerdmans, 1977), 29. For others within Arminian theology and open theism who affirm a libertarian view of freedom *and* PAP as the condition

By contrast, compatibilism, which falls under the broad category of "determinism," insists that a person is free even though his actions are causally determined, or *sufficiently* inclined toward one option as opposed to another, if the following conditions are met: "(1) The immediate cause of the action is a desire, wish, or intention internal to the agent, (2) no external event or circumstances compels the action to be performed, and (3) the agent could have acted differently if he had chosen to."[57] If these three conditions are met, then our actions are free although they are causally determined and sufficiently inclined by previous reasons and causes. Theologically, such a view of freedom is viewed as *compatible* with God's decree of all things (i.e., *theological* determinism), including our free choices, and it affirms a strong view of dual agency. In evangelical theology, this view is embraced by Calvinism or Reformed theology.[58] For Reformed theology, dual agency means that in the same act, "God determines the choices of every person, yet every person freely makes his or her own choices. Thus, divine sovereignty is compatible with human freedom and responsibility."[59] For compatibilism, the condition of freedom is not the "ability to do otherwise" (i.e., the principle of alternative possibilities), but freedom to choose what we most want and desire without coercion; a "freedom of inclination" that "proceed[s] from the most compelling motives and desires we have, which in turn is conditioned on our base nature, whether good or evil."[60]

---

of freedom, see Roger E. Olson, "The Classical Free Will Theist Model of God," in *Perspectives on the Doctrine of God: 4 Views*, ed. Bruce A. Ware (Nashville: B&H Academic, 2008), 150; Norman L. Geisler, *Chosen but Free: A Balanced View of Divine Election* (Minneapolis: Bethany House, 1999), 30.

[57] Michael Peterson, et al. *Reason and Religious Belief* (New York: Oxford University Press, 1991), 59. John Feinberg states it this way: "If the agent acts in accord with causes and reasons that serve as a sufficient condition for his doing the act, and if the causes do not force him to act contrary to his wishes, then a [compatibilist] would say that he acts freely." Feinberg, "Diving Causality and Evil," *Christian Scholar's Review* 16 (1987): 400.

[58] Calvinism and Reformed theology will be discussed in more detail in chapter 20 (on the divine decree) and chapter 22 (on divine providence), where it will be compared and contrasted with a classic Arminian theology.

[59] Christensen, *What About Free Will?*, 6.

[60] Christensen, 6; cf. Feinberg, *No One Like Him*, 635–39. This does not mean that decision-making is not multifaceted and complex. Often in our decisions, we have conflicting desires due to internal motives and desires, along with external factors. But in the end, we choose based on sufficient reasons, in concrete situations, according to our strongest desires so that given those reasons or set of reasons (causes), we "cannot" do otherwise in the libertarian, contra-causal sense of the word. However, we "can" do otherwise if we had chosen to do so according to different desires and wants. There is nothing

In terms of open theism, along with Arminian theology, a libertarian view of human freedom is embraced and a compatibilist view of freedom is strongly rejected. This is not a minor point. Open theism's embrace of libertarian free will is central to its view. For open theism, along with Arminian theology, libertarianism is the only view that grounds moral responsibility,[61] absolves God from moral responsibility for the sin and evil that humans commit, and allows for a loving relationship with God. On this last point, Greg Boyd states it this way: humans "must possess the capacity and opportunity to reject love if they are to possess the genuine capacity and ability to engage in love."[62] Otherwise, if God unconditionally elects his people, then our love for God is coerced, and if it is coerced, it is not genuine love.

In fact, open theists are probably more *logically* consistent than Arminian theology in drawing two crucial entailments from their acceptance of libertarian free will: a redefinition of divine sovereignty *and* divine omniscience. Because God has chosen to create free creatures, he has also voluntarily chosen to limit himself in order to invite humans to have dominion over the world as fellow-partners with him, thus choosing to make himself vulnerable—that is, a risk-taker. For God's sovereignty this entails that God *cannot guarantee* that everything conforms to his will, but only that "God is able to deal with any circumstances that may arise,"[63] and if necessary, he is able to intervene by taking away our freedom. Thus, "by his decision to create a world like ours, God showed his willingness to take risks and to work with a history whose outcome he does not wholly decide."[64] Other than Thomas Oord, open theists insist that God has the ability to intervene in this way to "keep things on track."[65] But they deny that God will constantly do this given his commitment to create and uphold libertarian freewill.[66]

---

wrong with our ability to do so. Instead, the point is that our choices are made based on prior conditions that sufficiently incline our wills according to our wants and desires. On different senses of "can" and "cannot do otherwise" in the freedom debate, see Feinberg, 720–29.

[61] Jerry L. Walls and Joseph R. Dongell, *Why I Am Not a Calvinist* (Downers Grove: InterVarsity, 2004), 105.

[62] Gregory A. Boyd, *Satan and the Problem of Evil* (Downers Grove: InterVarsity, 2001), 52.

[63] Pinnock, "Systematic Theology," in Pinnock et al., *Openness of God*, 114.

[64] Pinnock, 116.

[65] For Oord, who is closer to panentheism, God *cannot* intervene to prevent human choices, even if he "wanted" to. In providence, God exerts persuasive influence, but he can *guarantee* nothing. Divine action is never efficacious, thus his redefinition of "miracles" to God working "persuasively" through the natural order. See Oord, *Uncontrolling Love of God*, 151–216.

[66] For a further discussion of these points, see Basinger, *Case for Free Will Theism*, 32–37.

In the end, God responds and adapts to the unexpected: "What God wants to happen does not always come to pass on account of human freedom. . . . There is no blueprint that governs everything that happens, it is a real historical project that does not proceed smoothly but goes through twists and turns. . . . There is no unconditional guarantee of success because there are risks for God and the creature."[67] But given that God is the superior power, open theists are confident that "God sets goals for creation and redemption and realizes them ad hoc in history. If Plan A fails, God is ready with Plan B."[68]

Open theists also redefine divine omniscience given their commitment to libertarian freedom. To say that God is omniscient means that he knows all that can be known. But since future free actions of creatures are not logically possible to know ahead of time, God cannot know them.[69] God's knowledge, then, includes all things past and present and the range of future possibilities, but it does not include the knowledge of what will actually happen in the future until it happens.[70] Thus, contrary to all forms of historic theology, open theists deny that God knows the future free actions of humans, which also entails a denial of divine aseity in regard to God's knowledge. God's knowledge is not completely "from himself"; instead, it is dependent on us, at least in terms of knowing our future choices. As David Basinger states, "It can no longer be said that God is working out his ideal, preordained plan. Rather, God may well find himself disappointed in the sense that this world may fall short of that ideal world God wishes were coming about."[71] Thus, to a large extent, reality is "open" rather than closed, and as Pinnock reminds us, "genuine novelty can appear in history which cannot be predicted even by God. If the creature has been given the ability to decide how some things will turn out, then it cannot be known infallibly ahead of time how they will turn out. It implies that the

[67] Pinnock, *Most Moved Mover*, 44–45.

[68] Pinnock, "Systematic Theology," in Pinnock et al., *Openness of God*, 113.

[69] For open theism's denial of divine foreknowledge of future free choices, see Boyd, *God of the Possible*, 120–23; Basinger, *Case for Free Will Theism*, 39–55. Given libertarian freedom, there are no antecedent sufficient conditions that decisively incline the will in one direction, hence God's inability *to know* what we will choose since we could always choose otherwise.

[70] See Boyd, *God of the Possible*, 15, where he states that "God knows it [the future] as a realm of possibilities, not certainties."

[71] David Basinger, "Divine Control and Human Freedom: Is Middle Knowledge the Answer?," *JETS* 36, no. 1 (1993): 58.

future is really open and not available to exhaustive foreknowledge even on the part of God."[72] But although God does not have exhaustive foreknowledge of future contingents, most open theists believe that his *ultimate* plans will come to pass. Since God knows the present causal tendencies and his own intent for the world, his ultimate desires will be realized even though the future remains open.[73]

Even in this brief description of open theism, it is obvious that it is a major departure from historic theology's view of God. With its denial of God's ability to know future free choices; its affirmation that God makes *ad hoc* plans in history in response to us as the "master chess player" or "ultimate psychoanalyst;"[74] and its over-emphasis on divine love at the expense of God's holiness, majesty, and glory, open theism, if adopted, presents a serious challenge to Christian theology. But what are the arguments for such a radical view? Especially, what are the *biblical* arguments? Let us now briefly outline its main arguments, biblical, philosophical, historical, and practical.

Arguments for Open Theism

First, how does open theism warrant its view biblically? They acknowledge that there are many biblical texts that present God as the sovereign and all-knowing God of history. Classical theism is correct on this point. But open theists insist that classical theism has too often de-literalized or anthropomorphized other biblical texts that present God as responsive to what happens in the world,[75] specifically texts that speak of God "changing" his mind or "repenting" of his actions. For example, God changes his intention to destroy Israel in response to the prayer of

---

[72] Clark Pinnock, "God Limits His Knowledge," in *Predestination and Free Will: Four Views of Divine Sovereignty and Human Freedom*, ed. David Basinger and Randall Basinger (Downers Grove: InterVarsity, 1986), 150; cf. Boyd, *God of the Possible*, 120–31.

[73] See Boyd, 21–87.

[74] Hasker unashamedly presents God as the "master chess player," who is able to predict what humans will choose with relative accuracy. Hasker, *God, Time, and Knowledge*, 195–96. Basinger says God is "the ultimate psychoanalyst or behaviorist," who can predict "with great accuracy what individuals will freely decide to do in the future in many cases." Basinger, *Case for Freewill Theism*, 40. But if God can predict with great accuracy what we will freely decide in most cases, it is also true that he is *mistaken* in other cases!

[75] This is Greg Boyd's charge. See *God of the Possible*, 53–87.

Moses (Exod 32:12–14) and in making Saul king (1 Sam 15:11, 35). Or, God changes his mind towards Ninevah after they repent (Jonah 3:10), or God tests Abraham to discover if he will obey him (Gen 22).[76] Also, there are texts that speak of God feeling joy, grief, anger, and regret (Jer 3:6–8; 7:31; 19:5; 32:35). If we take these texts "seriously," we must conclude that God's will "is not an irresistible, all-determining force,"[77] or that the future is settled, or that God does not "experience regret or unexpected disappointment" as he relates to his creatures.[78] Or appeal is made to God's love, which for open theists not only defines God's essence but also requires that God is in a reciprocal relationship with his creatures. Thus, the biblical argument for open theism is that it better explains the diversity of biblical teaching—the sovereignty and majesty texts, along with the texts that speak of God's vulnerability, suffering, and change of mind in response to humans.

What about predictive prophecy? How does open theism explain texts that declare that God is the true God precisely because he predicts the future (e.g., Isa 44–48)? Does this not require God's knowledge to include future free actions without an "open" future? Open theists have not ignored this problem. They respond by distinguishing three different kinds of prophecy—all of which do not require divine foreknowledge. First, there is conditional prophecy, which does not require a detailed foreknowledge of what will actually happen since the purpose of it is to call God's people back to covenant faithfulness and repentance.[79] In fact, conditional prophecy assumes that "what is foretold may *not* happen."[80] Second, other prophecies are "predictions based on foresight drawn from existing trends and tendencies,"[81] which do not require God to have foreknowledge of future contingents. For example, God predicts that Pharaoh will harden his heart. Richard Rice suggests that "the ruler's character may have

---

[76] See Rice, "Biblical Support," in Pinnock et al., *Openness of God*, 11–58; Boyd, *God of the Possible*, 53–87; and Sanders, *God Who Risks*, 39–139, for a discussion of these texts. For a similar non-evangelical approach to these texts, see Terence E. Fretheim, *What Kind of God? The Collected Essays of Terence E. Freithem*, ed. Michael J. Chan and Brent A. Strawn (Winona Lake: Eisenbrauns, 2015); Fretheim, *The Suffering of God: An Old Testament Perspective* (Philadelphia: Fortress Press, 1984); and Walter Brueggemann, *Theology of the Old Testament: Testimony, Dispute, Advocacy* (Minneapolis: Fortress Press, 1997).

[77] Rice, "Biblical Support," in Pinnock et al., *Openness of God*, 38.

[78] Boyd, *God of the Possible*, 86.

[79] Hasker, *God, Time, and Knowledge*, 194; cf. Pinnock, "God Limits His Knowledge," 158.

[80] Hasker, 194.

[81] Hasker, 194.

been so rigid that it was entirely predictable. God understood him well enough to know exactly what his reaction to certain situations would be."[82] Third, other prophecies include things that are foreknown because it is God's intention to bring them about regardless of human choices. Rice explains: "If God's will is the only condition required for something to happen, if human cooperation is not involved, then God can unilaterally guarantee its fulfillment, and he can announce it ahead of time. . . . God can predict his own actions."[83] In this category is placed God's prediction of the incarnation, the cross, and the second coming.[84]

Second, open theists offer a number of philosophical arguments for their view, especially regarding the nature of human freedom, divine omniscience, and the problem of evil. The issue of theodicy is of particular concern for open theists.[85] Most, if not all, adopt "the free will defense" to answer the problem. In fact, open theists believe that their solution to the problem of evil in turn justifies their reformulation of divine omniscience and sovereignty. Ultimately, open theists insist that their view has fewer philosophical difficulties than classical theism.[86]

Third, open theists also attempt to make an historical case for their view, but this is difficult since their view stands against the entire tradition. Open theism's explanation for this fact is the latest rendition of Harnack's "Hellenization of theology" thesis; that is, the tradition was distorted by the influence of Greek philosophy.[87] Instead of affirming the God of the Bible, theologians, such as Augustine, Anselm, Aquinas, and the Reformers, embraced the God of

[82] Rice, "Biblical Support," in Pinnock et al., *Openness of God*, 51.

[83] Rice, 51.

[84] Regarding the cross, open theists argue that God did not foresee it; instead, he declared that it was going to happen because he intended to bring it about. But open theists do not agree on the timing of this intention. For example, Boyd argues that "it was certain that Jesus would be crucified, but it was not certain from eternity that Pilate, Herod, or Caiaphas would play the roles they played in the crucifixion." *God of the Possible*, 45. Sanders does not think the cross was planned from the creation of the world; instead, it was planned as late as Gethsemane. *God Who Risks*, 98-104.

[85] Theodicy also drives much of current panentheistic thought along with most social-relational views of God. See Vanhoozer, *Remythologizing Theology*, 105–77.

[86] See the discussion of these issues in William Hasker, "A Philosophical Perspective," in Pinnock et al., *Openness of God*, 126–54. Also see Basinger, *Case for Freewill Theism*, 83–104. The charge that classical theism flounders on theodicy is not new, but it is especially strong in our day, and it drives much of the push towards an embrace of "relational theism."

[87] Adolf von Harnack, *History of Dogma*, 7 vols. (New York: Dover, 1961), 1:227–8; cf. Vanhoozer, *Remythologizing Theology*, 81–138.

the philosophers, thus distorting the "literal" and "natural" reading of the text. But, in our day, thanks to recent developments in philosophy and science towards a "relational" or "dynamic" view of reality, we are in a "better" position to read Scripture as it should have been interpreted.[88]

Fourth, the open view also insists that it explains better the practical aspects of the Christian life. For example, with respect to petitionary prayer, only the open view can make sense of why prayer makes any difference in the world. A classical view of prayer, they contend, only affects the person doing the praying; it does not change what God is going to do since he has already determined it ahead of time. Other examples could be provided, such as discerning God's will for our lives and our responsibility to evangelize and to change the world in terms of social action.[89] In the end, open theism claims that it better explains our Christian life and experience.

Open Theism: Biblical and Theological Problems

What is our evaluation of open theism? Given that our presentation of the doctrine of God awaits subsequent chapters, our evaluation will focus on five points that show open theism to be biblically and theologically untenable.[90] Specifically, we will highlight some crucial issues it raises regarding hermeneutics and theological method that doctrinal formulation of theology proper must address. In this way, our initial evaluation of open theism will serve as a negative example of theological formulation, and, in response to it, it will allow us to discuss how we ought to appeal to Scripture, speak rightly of God, and formulate a doctrine of God that is faithful to Scripture and the historical tradition of the church—points we will build on as we proceed.

---

[88] See John Sanders, "Historical Considerations," in Pinnock et al., *Openness of* God, 59–100; Boyd, *God of the Possible*, 17–18, 114–18.

[89] See David Basinger, "Practical Implications," in Pinnock et al., *Openness of God* , 155–76; cf. Boyd, *God of the Possible*, 89–112.

[90] For critiques of open theism, see Millard Erickson, *God the Father Almighty: A Contemporary Exploration of the Divine Attributes* (Grand Rapids: Baker, 1998), 67–92; John M. Frame, *No Other God: A Response to Open Theism* (Phillipsburg: P&R, 2001); John Piper, Justin Taylor, and Paul K. Helseth, eds., *Beyond the Bounds: Open Theism and the Undermining of Biblical Christianity* (Wheaton: Crossway, 2003); Steven C. Roy, *How Much Does God Foreknow? A Comprehensive Biblical Study* (Downers Grove: IVP Academic, 2006); Bruce A. Ware, *God's Lesser Glory: The Diminished God of Open Theism* (Wheaton: Crossway, 2000).

First, although open theism's argument that classical theism derives from Greek thought is incorrect, it does raise an important issue that must be addressed. It must be acknowledged that due to its cultural setting, Christian theology did utilize Greek language to describe immutability, impassibility, aseity, and so on. In fact, for theology to communicate well, it had to employ the language of its day. However, this fact does not entail that the tradition's *doctrine* of God was infected by the "Hellenistic virus" and that its concepts of simplicity, aseity, immutability, and so on are unbiblical.[91] If this was so, theology would never have affirmed the Creator-creature distinction, *creatio ex nihilo*, uncoupled *ousia* from *hypostasis* in trinitarian and Christological formulation, or taught the truth of the incarnation and resurrection—*all* concepts that are contrary to Greek thought! It is also false to claim that today, given our cultural embrace of "reality as dynamic and historical," we can now see things in Scripture that "we never saw before."[92]

The truth is that the church fathers, Augustine, Anselm, Aquinas, the Reformers, and the post-Reformed theologians transformed the language of their day to correspond to Scripture. The tradition's reading of Scripture is faithful so that the charge that "classical" theism has misread the Bible due to Hellenistic influences is not sustainable.[93] One reason why open theists get away with this charge, along with their caricature of classical theism, is due to a lack of knowing historical theology. Repeatedly, they use prejudicial language that portrays an inaccurate description of classical theism and then offer their view as the only

[91] See Pinnock, "Preface," in Pinnock et al., *Openness of God*, 8–9.

[92] Clark H. Pinnock, "From Augustine to Arminius," in Pinnock, *Grace of God*, 27. In Pinnock, "Systematic Theology," in Pinnock et al., *Openness of God*, 107, Pinnock wrongly asserts modern culture can actually assist us in this task because the contemporary horizon is more congenial to dynamic thinking about God than is the Greek portrait. Today it is easier to invite people to find fulfillment in a dynamic, personal God than it would be to ask them to find it in a deity who is immutable and self-enclosed. Modern thinking has more room for a God who is personal (even tripersonal) than it does for a God as absolute substance. We ought to be grateful for those features of modern culture which make it easier to recover the biblical witness.

[93] See Vanhoozer, *Remythologizing Theology*, 81–138; Craig A. Carter, *Contemplating God with the Great Tradition: Recovering Trinitarian Classical Theism* (Grand Rapids: Baker, 2021); cf. Paul Gavrilyuk, *The Suffering of the Impassible God* (Oxford: Oxford University Press, 2004), 21–36; Muller, *Post-Reformation Reformed Dogmatics*, vol. 3 (see chap. 3, n. 12).

alternative.[94] But their rejection of the entire tradition should make their view highly suspicious. Also, open theists quickly charge classical theism as unduly influenced by Hellenism, but they seem oblivious to the fact that the current *Zeitgeist* seems to have affected them, especially the current embrace of "relationality" and "panentheism." In fact, Pinnock insists that unless our view of God is changed to fit this "relational" turn, then belief in God will decline—an argument reminiscent of Friedrich Schleiermacher! Timothy George is correct in his observation:

> In their desire to defend "God's reputation," and to construct "plausible models" and "convincing conceptions" that would make it easier "to invite people to find fulfillment," they have devised a user-friendly God who bears an uncanny resemblance to a late-twentieth-century seeker. They need not be so concerned about "God's reputation." They only need to let God be God.[95]

Second, although open theism's hermeneutic and theological method is deeply flawed and it serves as a negative example of how to do theology, it does raise perennial methodological issues that require careful reflection, a point we will develop in *two* steps.

1. As an overall observation, open theists tend to emphasize one set of texts (e.g., divine repentance, God's love and relationality) to the exclusion of others (e.g., divine sovereignty, aseity, immutability, and omniscience).[96] No doubt, no one is exempt from doing this, but open theism reminds us that a sound theological method requires that we account for *all* of Scripture, starting with the Creator-creature distinction and God's triune self-sufficiency. If we do this, then, as Vanhoozer notes following the work of John Webster,

---

[94] For example, open theists caricature the classical view of God as "unaffected," "disengaged," "aloof Monarch," "distant king," "puppet-master," "a ventriloquist having a conversation with his dummy," etc. In contrast, only their view allows for a "real relationship with God," a God who is "truly personal," etc. This is simply incorrect.

[95] Timothy George, "A Transcendence-Starved Deity," *Christianity Today* 39, no. 1 (January 9, 1995): 34.

[96] In fact, Sanders admits this: "I am examining providence through the lens of divine risk-taking and am studying aspects of providence in order to see what should be said concerning a risk-taking God. This will lead some readers to judge the book 'imbalanced.'" *God Who Risks*, 14.

> The God who comes to save the world (economic Trinity) is able to save only because he has no need of and is perfectly independent of the world (immanent Trinity). God's perfect life in himself constitutes the ground of his self-communication to creation, and it is the triune character of God's perfect life . . . [that] is crucial for understanding the divine attributes or perfections, including love.[97]

By contrast, open theism begins with the divine economy and says little about God's perfect life in himself, thus making God dependent on the creature and, if one is not careful, making God's being that which is constituted by the world, which is one step away from panentheism.

2. In their reading of "divine repentance" texts (e.g., Gen 6:5–7; Exod 32:12–14; 1 Sam 15:11, 35), along with texts that express God's regret and surprise (e.g., Jer 3:6–8; 7:31), open theists not only fail to grasp why historic theology has always interpreted these texts analogically and not univocally; they also leave us with an inconsistent and incoherent hermeneutic. In this way, open theism serves as a negative example for us, yet they also help us to think through how we ought to read biblical language in reference to God and thus formulate a correct theology proper.

Contrary to the claim of open theists, classical theism has *not* ignored these important texts. Instead, historic theology, due to the Creator-creature distinction, has argued that *all* biblical language about God is analogical, accommodated, and God-chosen *human* speech to reveal who God is, but not exhaustively. For this reason, we must not equate "literal" speech about God with "univocal" speech (i.e., language that applies to God and humans in the *same* way, thus undermining the Creator-creature distinction) or "non-literal" speech with "analogical" speech (i.e., language that applies to God and humans in similar but different ways). Rather, under the larger category of *analogical* predication, we must locate both "literal" and "non-literal" speech about God. Thus, in "literal" speech, language is used in an ordinary and normal sense tied to convention unless some contextual clue suggests otherwise. For example, "God *is* love" or "God *is* holy" is a "literal" description of God. "Non-literal" speech, which includes figurative and metaphorical language, uses words in a non-ordinary way intended by the author. For example, "God *is* a rock" or "God has eyes" are "non-literal," or "metaphorical,"

---

[97] Vanhoozer, "Love without Measure?," 518.

descriptions of God. However, it is crucial to stress that both literal and non-literal speech about God is *analogical* and not univocal.

As this understanding of biblical language in reference to God is applied to divine-repentance texts, classic theism has consistently read these texts as an example of "non-literal" speech, specifically, as "anthropopathic" language that communicates truth about God but *analogically*.[98] Thus, we must *not* understand God's repentance like human repentance (univocal); God is not like us. Yet God has revealed himself to us so that the language *he* uses to describe himself is true but not exhaustive, analogical but not univocal. This is why we must let *all* of Scripture describe who God is and not privilege one set of texts over another. The entire canon must identify who God is according to Scripture's own presentation governed by the Creator-creature distinction and God's triune self-sufficiency.

However, this is not the hermeneutic of open theism. They claim to read Scripture "literally" or "according to common sense," but as critics have shown, their view of biblical language in reference to God is inconsistent in at least two ways.[99] First, they do not consistently maintain that *all* biblical language *in reference to God* is analogical, and second, they conflate "literal" with "univocal" so that when Scripture says that God repents, is surprised, asks questions, or what have you, they interpret this speech to mean that what is true for us is the same for God. Thus, when we repent or are surprised, it is either because we have made a mistake or did not anticipate the future. In the case of God, he does not make mistakes, but like us, his knowledge of future contingencies is not exhaustive, hence their argument for "open" theism.

Examples of this disastrous conflation of "literal" with "univocal" are not hard to find. For example, John Sanders approvingly quotes Herman Bavinck and his affirmation of analogical predication in reference to God,[100] but then conflates literal with univocal.[101] Greg Boyd makes

---

[98] Anthropopathism (Gk. *anthropos*, human; *pathos*, emotion) is metaphorical language that refers to God in terms of human emotional states, but analogically. Anthropomorphism (Gk. *anthropos*, human; *morphē*, form) is metaphorical language that refers to God in terms of human forms (e.g., eyes, arms, legs), but analogically.

[99] See A. B. Caneday, "Veiled Glory: God's Self-Revelation in Human Likeness—A Biblical Theology of God's Anthropomorphic Self-Disclosure," 149–99; and Michael S. Horton, "Hellenistic or Hebrew? Open Theism and Reformed Theological Method," 201–34, in Piper et al., *Beyond the Bounds*.

[100] Sanders, *God Who Risks*, 21–23.

[101] Sanders writes: "Even those who defend the doctrine of analogy presuppose that in *some* respects similarities between God and us are *univocal*. . . . Anthropomorphic language does not preclude *literal*

the same mistake. He seems to think that the classical view understands divine foreknowledge and sovereignty literally ("as he truly is"), while relational texts are read as mere "appearances" or "figures of speech." But this is mistaken since the classical view interprets *both* sets of texts *analogically*.[102] Or, Sanders and Boyd interpret the idiomatic use of "I thought" in Jer 3:6–8 univocally since they conclude that this text proves that God does not know future human choices.[103] But if such a reading is consistently applied, it means that God has amnesia since in the new covenant he promises that he will "never again remember our sin" (Jer 31:34)![104]

Ultimately, the open-theist hermeneutic cannot be applied consistently, and it results in internal contradictions. For example, other than Pinnock, who shockingly speculates that God as a person may mean that he has a body;[105] most open theists speak of God's eyes, hands, and so forth anthropomorphically. But when it comes to divine repentance, it is interpreted "literally," or better, univocally. This approach is inconsistent. Or, if we apply this hermeneutic consistently, when God asks, "Where are you?" (Gen 3:9), we will have to conclude that God does not know the *present*, let alone the future, and that God is *spatially located*.[106] This is why the classical interpretation of these texts is far better; that is, it reads *all* of them analogically.

Or think of 1 Sam 15, which is a very important test case for their view. Twice we are told that God "repented" that he made Saul king (vv. 11, 35). But sandwiched between these verses is the unequivocal statement that God does *not* repent (vv. 27–29). In fact, this text contrasts God and humans on this point. We change our mind, but God does not because God is *not* like us. Furthermore, if we locate this chapter in the Bible's unfolding covenantal story, it sets us up for the Davidic king—a king who in God's plan would come from Abraham's line (Gen

---

predication to God" (25, emphasis mine). Or he states, "Any God worth his salt must conform to *our* intuitive notion of deity or get out of the deity business" (33). Or he can say, "If God decides to disclose himself to us as a personal being who enters into relationship with us, who has purposes, emotions, and desires, and who suffers with us, then we ought to rejoice in this anthropomorphic portrait and accept it as disclosing to us *the very nature of God*" (38, emphasis mine).

[102] Boyd, *God of the Possible*, 14. He also says that "common sense tells us that we can only regret a decision we made if the decision resulted in an outcome other than what we expected" (56), which applied to God means that he does not know the future. This assumes that God's regret is understood univocally.

[103] Sanders, *God Who Risks*, 154; Boyd, *God of the Possible*, 60.

[104] For more examples, see Caneday, "Veiled Glory," 149–99.

[105] See Pinnock, *Most Moved*, 33–34.

[106] Boyd tries to respond but leaves us with no resolution. *God of the Possible*, 59.

17:6) and from the tribe of Judah (Gen 49:8–12; cf. Gen 3:15; Num 23:21; 24:17–19; Deut 17:14–20; Ruth 4:13–22), not from the tribe of Benjamin, as did Saul. Thus, in the Bible's overall metanarrative, 1 Samuel does not teach that God is making ad hoc plans in history based on the decisions of Saul or anyone else; instead, God is sovereignly working out his eternal plan to lead us to Christ. In the end, what open theism teaches us is that we need a consistent hermeneutic and that the way forward is the way of the past, namely, a consistent reading of biblical language in reference to God as analogical and gloriously true but not exhaustive.

Third, open theism cannot truly affirm that the triune God is the Creator and Lord of history. In our discussion of God's decree and his work of creation and providence,[107] we will discover that Scripture teaches that God ordains *and* knows all things, including the future free actions of his creatures (e.g., Gen 50:19–20; Ps 139:16; Isa 10:5–19; 40–48; Acts 4:27–28; Rom 11:33–36; Eph 1:11). The only way to account for *all* of this biblical data is to affirm God's lordship and dual agency in providence. But given open theists' embrace of libertarian freedom and its entailments for God's sovereignty and knowledge, this is not an available option for them. Open theists may offer a logically consistent view, but not a biblically faithful one. The strongest reason they offer for insisting on libertarian freedom is its perceived strength for solving the problem of evil. But as we will argue in subsequent chapters, this "perceived" advantage is not what it claims since it cannot even *guarantee* that God will triumph over evil. If a robust view of dual agency is rendered impossible, we have no assurance that God will destroy all sin and evil and make everything new, contrary to biblical teaching.[108]

Fourth, open theism cannot account for Scripture's teaching about predictive prophecy. As noted above, open theists claim that most predictive prophecies are conditional (Jer 18:7–10). But such a view cannot explain the *unconditional* predictions of Scripture where God declares what will certainly occur *through the means of future human choices*. In fact, Scripture teaches that these unconditional predictions demonstrate God's sovereign lordship over history (Isa 46:8–13), something open theism undercuts. What are some examples of these kinds of prophecies? The best examples are prophecies that predict the cross of our Lord Jesus Christ.

In Scripture, the cross is not the result of God's ad hoc plans in response to our choices. Instead, it is an event planned from eternity and accomplished in time (Acts 2:23; 4:23–30;

---

[107] See chapters 20–22.

[108] On this point, see Christensen, *What About Free Will?*, 84–116.

Rev 13:8). Nor can the cross be reduced to God's intentions independent of human actions.[109] God not only declared that Jesus would die, but he also declared the precise manner of his death and intricate details concerning all the humans who would freely bring it about, thus fulfilling many OT predictions and typological patterns (e.g., Pss 2; 22). Scripture's presentation of the cross requires more than God's general knowledge and strategies for the future; it requires God's detailed providence and a robust view of dual agency; that is, God sovereignly and effectually acts through the choices of free and responsible humans. D. A. Carson states this point well:

> It will not do to analyze what happened as an instance where wicked agents performed an evil deed, and then God intervened to turn it into good, for in that case the cross itself becomes an afterthought in the mind of God, a mere reactive tactic. All of Scripture is against the notion. The Biblical theology of sacrifice, the passover lamb, the specifications for *yom kippur*, the priestly/sacrificial system—all together anticipate and predict, according to the New Testament authors, the ultimate sacrifice, the sacrifice of the ultimate lamb of God. But neither will it do to reduce the guilt of the conspirators because God remained in charge. If there is no guilt attaching to those who were immediately responsible for sending Jesus to the cross, why should one think that there is guilt attaching to *any* action performed under the sovereignty of God? And in that case, of course, we do not need any atonement for guilt: The cross is superfluous and useless.[110]

Open theism simply cannot account for the Bible's presentation of the cross. In fact, when John Sanders tries to explain the cross, we quickly discover that open theism is impossible to reconcile with the biblical metanarrative. To think that the cross was *not* part of God's eternal plan but was only the mutual conclusion of the Father and Son reached in Gethsemane simply demonstrates that open theism is out of step with Scripture.[111] To argue such a point is not merely to reinterpret a few texts; it is to dismantle the Bible's entire plotline. In Christ, God's eternal plan and promises are fulfilled (Matt 5:17–20; Luke 24:25–27; 2 Cor 1:20). Scripture

---

[109] Contrary to Hasker, *God, Time, and Knowledge*, 195.

[110] D. A. Carson, "God, the Bible and Spiritual Warfare: A Review Article," *JETS* 42:2 (1999), 263.

[111] See Sanders, *God Who Risks*, 100–4.

does not present these events as contingent or uncertain. Indeed, from Adam to Christ, from creation to the new creation, God's redemptive plan was always to redeem his fallen people in Christ Jesus, which does not result in an "open" future but a certain one.

Fifth, open theism undercuts the *theological* warrant for an infallible, inerrant Scripture, which is serious indeed! In theology, we can evaluate theological views in at least two ways. First, does the view account for *all* of the biblical data? In this regard, we have given reasons why open theism fails, which will be further substantiated in subsequent chapters. Second, for sake of argument, does the view contradict other areas of our theology that we know to be true? As we argued in part 2, Scripture is the *transcendental* condition for objective truth and a normative theology. Without the triune God who speaks infallibly and inerrantly, theology in its historic sense is not possible.

However, on this point, open theism cannot provide a rational accounting for Scripture's view of itself. Why? Because open theism denies the dual agency required for the Bible's concursive view of divine inspiration. How can God *guarantee* that what *he* wants written is written through human authors who write freely in a libertarian sense? The only way to account for an infallible and inerrant Scripture is either to affirm a dictation theory of inspiration (which is patently not the case) or to appeal to paradox and say that somehow the authors "just happened" to do so (which offers no explanation).[112] Also, add to this predictive prophecy. How can God *guarantee* that his predictions will come to pass, especially when they involve the free decisions of humans? Is it possible that the prophets of Scripture could make predictions under the inspiration of the Spirit that actually turn out to be mistaken? Given open theism, this seems very likely. But if this is possible, then open theism cannot account for what Scripture *is*, which undercuts its authority and the possibility of a normative theology.

Open theists and others have responded to this criticism,[113] but much of it is off base. The argument is not that open theists cannot logically affirm inerrancy. After all, they could appeal to a "dictation theory of inspiration" or "paradox" to explain how Scripture is infallible/inerrant given their overall theology. Also, it is true that human error is only possible, not necessary. But

---

[112] See the argument by David Basinger and Randall Basinger, "Inerrancy, Dictation, and the Free Will Defense," *EvQ* 55 (1983): 177–80.

[113] See Jason A. Nicholls, "Openness and Inerrancy: Can They Be Compatible?," *JETS* 45, no. 4 (2002): 629–49.

this is not the point. Logical possibilities are one thing; reality is another. Instead, the argument is that open theism cannot offer a *theological* accounting for inerrancy from *within* its own view since the human authors' "just happening" to get things right is hardly a *theological* explanation. As we discussed in part 2, Scripture is not merely the record of God's mighty actions; it is also *God's* interpretation of his acts, which requires more than human knowledge and a robust view of dual agency. Instead, a proper theological accounting for an authoritative, infallible, and inerrant Scripture requires an omniscient and sovereign God and the ability for God to guarantee that what the human authors write *is* what he wants written. On its own terms, open theism cannot offer such a theological explanation for Scripture, and as such, it cannot account for what Scripture says about itself. Open theism undercuts Scripture as the *principium cognoscendi* for our theology. This is why most open theists do not hold to a traditional view of Scripture but instead affirm some iteration of a neo-orthodox view.

Concluding Reflection

Theology is never done in a vacuum, and our present day poses a number of challenges that theology must address. But we must not walk the path of embracing the postmodern direction of our culture that has only resulted in theological confusion regarding the identity and nature of God. Even within evangelical theology, as witnessed by open theism, instead of the glory of God, we have another example of the "weightlessness" of God, which must be rejected in the strongest of terms. However, learning from open theism's negative example and building on some crucial hermeneutical and methodological matters it legitimately raises, we now need to press on to formulate a theology proper that is faithful to Scripture and to historic theology. Indeed, more significantly, we need to formulate a theology proper that honors the "only Sovereign, the King of kings, and the Lord of lords, who alone is immortal and who lives in unapproachable light, whom no one has seen or can see, to him be honor and eternal power. Amen" (1 Tim 6:15–16).

CHAPTER 17

The Triune Covenant Lord: Theological Overview

Introduction

Who is the God of the Bible? One of the most beautiful theological summaries of God's identity and nature is given in the *London Baptist Confession* (1689), which builds on the *Westminster Confession of Faith* (1647).

> The Lord our God is but one only living and true God; whose subsistence is in and of Himself, infinite in being and perfection; whose essence cannot be comprehended by any but Himself; a most pure spirit, invisible, without body, parts, or passions, who only hath immortality, dwelling in the light which no man can approach unto; who is immutable, immense, eternal, incomprehensible, almighty, every way infinite, most holy, most wise, most free, most absolute; working all things according to the counsel of His own immutable and most righteous will, for His own glory; most loving, gracious, merciful, long-suffering, abundant in goodness and truth, forgiving iniquity, transgression, and sin; the rewarder of them that diligently seek Him, and withal most just and terrible in His judgments, hating all sin, and who will by no means clear the guilty.

> God, having all life, glory, goodness, blessedness, in and of Himself, is alone in and unto Himself all-sufficient, not standing in need of any creature which He hath made, nor deriving any glory from them, but only manifesting His own glory in, by, unto, and upon them; He is the alone fountain of all being, of whom, through whom, and to whom are all things, and He hath most sovereign dominion over all creatures, to do by them, for them, or upon them, whatsoever Himself pleases; in His sight all things are open and manifest, His knowledge is infinite, infallible, and independent upon the creature, so as nothing is to Him contingent or uncertain; He is most holy in all His counsels, in all His works, and in all His commands; to Him is due from angels and men, whatsoever worship, service, or obedience, as creatures they owe unto the Creator, and whatever He is further pleased to require of them.
>
> In this divine and infinite Being there are three subsistences, the Father, the Word or Son, and Holy Spirit, of one substance, power, and eternity, each having the whole divine essence, yet the essence undivided: the Father is of none, neither begotten nor proceeding; the Son is eternally begotten of the Father; the Holy Spirit proceeding from the Father and the Son; all infinite, without beginning, therefore but one God, who is not to be divided in nature and being, but distinguished by several peculiar relative properties and personal relations; which doctrine of the Trinity is the foundation of all our communion with God, and comfortable dependence on Him.

This statement is magnificent, but it is a lot to digest, so before we think through some of its specifics, namely the divine attributes (chapter 18) and the triune nature of God (chapter 19), I want to offer a theological overview of the triune God who is there. Why? For at least three reasons. First, it allows us not to get lost in the details but instead to present the "big picture" of who God is across the entire canon. Second, given that segments of evangelicalism are trending in the wrong direction, it is necessary to set forth who God is in all of his beauty, majesty, and lordship. Third, in a day of religious pluralism and its many conceptions of "God," focusing on the "big picture" of what distinguishes the true God from all others enables the church to know and to proclaim the only true God in all of his glory and uniqueness. Let us do so by summarizing who God is by the phrase "the triune Creator-covenant Lord" and then unpacking its worldview significance and why it distinguishes the God of the Bible from all others.

God: The Triune Creator-Covenant Lord

The LORD

In Scripture God identifies himself by a number of names that reveal who and what he is.[1] In fact, to speak of God's *name* is to speak of God himself (Exod 3:14; Pss 7:17; 9:2; 18:49; 29:2; 34:3). For example, God's name defends and saves us because *he* does so (Pss 20:1; 54:1). Or, God's name endures forever because God is eternal (Pss 72:17; 135:13). Or, when God reveals his glory to Moses, he reveals his name (Exod 33:18–19), which ultimately, in a greater way, is revealed in the glory and name of our Lord Jesus Christ (John 1:14–18). Although God is incomprehensible, he is also knowable, and God's self-revelation by his names is significant, and contrary to many extratextual theologies, we have no warrant to apply "other" names of God "from non-Christian religions, philosophies, and experience to describe him."[2]

In post-Reformation theology, God's names were categorized in the following way: God's *proper* or essential name (Yahweh/LORD, which applies to God alone); *common* names (analogical descriptions, such as King, Maker, Father, Redeemer, etc., that reveal who and what God is, which may also apply to creatures); and the *personal* names of the Father, Son, and Holy Spirit, which distinguish the divine persons from each other within the one God.[3]

For example, in terms of *common* names, God is identified as *'Elohim* (Gk. *theos*), which may also designate the "gods" of the nations (Pss 86:8; 95:3; 97:9; Isa 36:18) and sometimes humans in positions of authority (Ps 82:1, 6). However, in reference to God, it is often used in a creation context (Gen 1:1–2:4a) that describes God as the Creator, and when combined with Yahweh in Genesis 2, it describes God as the *covenant* God. Also, *'Elohim* is a plural noun that regularly takes singular verbs (Gen 1:1). Some have interpreted this as a plural of majesty. But it is better to see it as a hint of God's trinitarian nature, especially when combined with the "us" language of Gen 1:26 (cf. Gen 11:7; Isa 6:8). God is also identified as *'Adon* (Ruler, Lord),

---

[1] For discussions of God's names, see Muller, *Post-Reformation Reformed Dogmatics*, 3:246–70 (see chap. 3, n. 12); Frame, *Doctrine of God*, 343–86 (see chap. 3, n. 13); Beeke and Smalley, *Reformed Systematic Theology*, 1:549–65 (see chap. 1, n. 8); Bavinck, *Reformed Dogmatics*, 2:95–147 (see chap. 1, n. 9).

[2] Frame, *Doctrine of God*, 346.

[3] Muller, *Post-Reformation Reformed Dogmatics*, 3:254–70.

stressing God's rule of the created order (Mal 1:6). For the Jewish people who regarded *Yahweh* as too holy to pronounce, it became a substitute name, which was translated in the Greek by *kurios*. A similar meaning of *'Adon* is *'El* (Mighty One, Ps 68:4) and its various combinations (*'El Shaddai* [God Almighty, Gen 17:1–2; Exod 6:3; Num 24:4], *'El 'elyon* [God Most High, Gen 14:18–22; Num 24:16; Deut 32:8]).

However, God's *proper* name is Yahweh (Exod 3:14)[4]—"I AM who I AM"—which is then combined in a number of ways to speak of God as the only Creator and *covenant* Lord of his people (e.g., *Yahweh 'elohim* [Lord God, Gen 2:4b], *Yahweh tseva'oth* [Lord of hosts, 1 Sam 1:3]; *Yahweh yir'eh* [Lord will provide, Gen 22:14], *Yahweh rof'eka* [Lord who heals, Isa 35:5–6], *Yahweh tsidqenu* [Lord our Righteousness, Jer 23:6]).[5] Although people debate the precise meaning of *Yahweh*, the name reveals God's covenant lordship, and thus signifies both God's unique lordship and faithfulness to his covenant promises.[6] Regarding the former, "I AM" declares not only God's personal existence, but metaphysically, it reveals the singularity and uniqueness of his existence: God alone is independent, *a se*, and simple, and as such, he exists of himself and is not defined by anything outside of himself. He is the eternal one who is not subject to time, but sovereign over it and his entire creation, and as such, he is the unchanging God (Mal 3:6; cf. Rev 1:8). All things are from him, through him, and for him (Rom 11:36), which Moses witnessed firsthand in God's dealings with Egypt, and which is taught in all of Scripture. Regarding the latter, "I AM" declares that God is the covenant maker and keeper, which is confirmed by his self-identification as the God of Abraham, Isaac, and Jacob (Exod 3:14–15), and which is repeatedly taught as God's plan unfolds through the biblical covenants.

For this reason, John Frame is correct to suggest that in summarizing who God is, we are on firm ground to say that *he* is the Lord (Yahweh), picking up God's own naming of himself,

---

[4] Yahweh is referred to as the "tetragrammaton" because it is composed of four Hebrew letters (YHWH). It is derived from the verb "to be" (*hayah*), but its translation could be "I am he who is" or "I will be what I will be," but probably the best is "I am who I am." For a helpful discussion of the meaning of Yahweh in Exodus and the Pentateuch, see J. A. Motyer, "The Revelation of the Divine Name," *Theological Studies*, March 2005, https://theologicalstudies.org.uk/article_revelation_motyer.html. For an older discussion, see Turretin, *Institutes of Elenctic Theology*, 1:183–87 (see chap. 3, n. 55).

[5] See Bauckham, *Jesus and the God of Israel*, 7–11 (see chap. 13, n. 87).

[6] See Muller, *Post-Reformation Reformed Dogmatics*, 3:258–61; cf. Beeke and Smalley, *Reformed Systematic Theology*, 1:551.

which appears around "six thousand times in Scripture."[7] Yahweh is the Creator and sovereign Lord of creation, history, and nations (Job 38–41; Isa 40:12–31; 44:24; 45:18; 46:9–13; Jer 10:1–16). Throughout redemptive history, "God performs his mighty deeds so that people 'will know that I am the LORD.'"[8] Yahweh enters into covenant relationship with Adam, Noah, Abraham, Israel, and David and brings all of these covenants to fulfillment in Christ Jesus, who is Lord/Yahweh (Gen 2:15–17; 6:18; 9:8; 12:1–3; Exod 3:13–15; 6:1–8; 2 Sam 7:14; Heb 8–10). In fact, a crucial way that the NT teaches Christ's deity and unpacks the eternal Father-Son relation is by identifying Jesus with OT Yahweh texts and applying them directly to him (e.g., John 8:58; Acts 2:36; Rom 10:9; 1 Cor 12:3; Phil 2:11) as the Creator and Lord (John 1:1–3; Col 1:15–17; Heb 1:2–3) and the new covenant head of his people (Heb 8–10).[9]

The Covenant *LORD*

To identify God as the Lord (Yahweh), is also to identify him as the *covenant* God, an expression that beautifully captures much of what Scripture teaches regarding God's identity and nature.[10] As discussed in part 3, the biblical covenants are more than a unifying theme of Scripture; they are the backbone to the Bible's entire story, the relational reality that moves redemptive history forward according to God's plan and design for creation and humanity, ultimately to the praise of his glory and grace (Eph 1:3–14; Rev 5:12–14; 21–22).

In Scripture, the outworking of God's eternal plan or decree is through the progressive unfolding of six covenants (creation/Adam, Noahic, Abrahamic, Mosaic, Davidic), which all reach their fulfillment, telos, and terminus in Christ and the new covenant. God is not only the Creator and Lord of his universe; he is also the personal God who makes and keeps his promises. At the heart of the covenant is the staggering truth: "I am your God and you are my people." Although God is perfect in himself in all of his glorious triune self-sufficiency, he has chosen to create us for himself and to redeem us by his grace in Christ Jesus our Lord. The

[7] Beeke and Smalley, 550; cf. Frame, *Doctrine of God*, 21–35.

[8] Frame, *Doctrine of God*, 22. See Exod 14:4; Deut 4:35; 29:6; 32:39; Pss 83:18; 91:14; Isa 37:20; 41:4; 43:3, 10, 13; Jer 16:21, etc.

[9] See Bauckham, *Jesus and the God of Israel*, 18–59.

[10] See Frame, *Doctrine of God*, 30–35.

purpose of the covenant is for chosen creatures to share in the life, communication, and communion of the triune God (Rev 21:22–22:5).

*God in Himself (*ad intra*) and God in His Works (*ad extra*)*

In summarizing God as "the Creator-covenant Lord," we have primarily focused on the identity and nature of God in his works, or what is called the divine economy (e.g., creation, providence, redemption, and judgment). But as we will develop in chapter 19 in our discussion of the Trinity, it is crucial to distinguish God in himself (*ad intra*) from God in his works (*ad extra*), or God in the execution of his eternal plan. As we have noted in previous chapters, the opening verse of Scripture—"In the beginning God created the heavens and the earth" (Gen 1:1)—teaches that the creation is not eternal, only God is, hence the Creator-creature distinction, and that "before" the beginning, only the triune God existed in the perfection and fullness of his being.

For this reason, to understand all of God's works in redemptive history, we must first think of God's perfect life in himself since this not only makes sense of how God's external works are enacted but is also necessary to understand God's attributes. In other words, before we think of God in relation to the world, we must first think of God in himself apart from the world. In thinking about the eternal life of God, we are driven to reflect on the "eternal relations of origin" of the divine persons, Father, Son, and Holy Spirit (John 1:1; 5:26; 17:5). From eternity, the divine persons have subsisted in the one, identical divine nature, yet due to their mutual personal relations—the Father *begetting* the Son (paternity), the Son being *begotten* of the Father (eternal generation), and the Spirit *proceeding* from the Father and the Son (eternal spiration)—God's life in himself is full and perfect. To understand God's essential nature, we must first begin with God's eternal life in order to rightly understand God's external works. Apart from doing so, we run the danger of undermining the Creator-creature distinction and making God mutually dependent on the world, which occurs in some current forms of "relational theisms," such as panentheism and open theism.

Thus, when we think of God's free choice to act "outside of himself" (*ad extra*), God's external acts are inseparable and undivided as the one God. Also, God's choice to create, rule, redeem, judge, and communicate himself to us does not change him given his perfect internal life. Instead, creation is the theater of his glory, whereby he has chosen to share himself with us. But in light of sin, God has also acted to redeem; whereby in *grace* (i.e., undeserved and unmerited), God has chosen to justify sinners to know him forever. Yet in doing so, God remains what he has always been: the self-sufficient triune Lord, who is now working out all things for his own glory and the good of his people (Rom 8:28).

As we walk through the Bible's covenantal story from creation to Christ and the dawning of the new creation, this is precisely what Scripture teaches. The Bible's *primary* message is about the name and glory of our triune covenant God, who, from the perfection of his internal life, has planned in eternity and executed in time the judgment of sin and the making of all things new in Christ (Rom 11:33–36; Eph 1:9–10; Col 1:15–20), all of which is for his glory and the eternal benefit of his people (Eph 2:1–10).

Theological Significance: Divine Lordship

One entailment of saying that God is "the triune Creator-covenant Lord" is a strong affirmation of divine lordship as taught by classical theism and Reformed theology, in contrast to current versions of "relational theisms." Although divine lordship can be developed by focusing on God's aseity, simplicity, and triune internal blessedness, we will first develop it by following John Frame's formulation before we return to those other aspects under the heading of "world-view significance." Frame unpacks divine lordship under the helpful headings of "control," "authority," and "presence."[11]

First, God's being the covenant Lord means that he is in "control" and thus sovereign in creation, providence, redemption, and judgment. As we will develop in chapters 20–23, nothing occurs outside of God's eternal plan. From Genesis 1 on, God is the one who plans and knows all things and who effectually enacts his plan in history (Gen 1:1–2:3; 18:14; Job 38–40; Pss 33:10–11; 115:3; 135:6–7; 139:13–16; Isa 14:24–27; 43:13; 46:10; Dan 4:34–35; Acts 2:23–24; 17:24–26; Rom 8:28–29; 9:19–24; 11:33–36; Eph 1:3–14; Gal 4:4–5).

Second, God's being the covenant Lord means that he has all "authority," which is emphasized by the rhetorical question: "Who did [God] consult? / Who gave him understanding / and taught him the paths of justice? / Who taught him knowledge / and showed him the way

[11] See Frame, *Doctrine of God*, 47–102.

of understanding?" (Isa 40:14). God is the source and standard of truth and knowledge; his authority is absolute.

In characterizing the relationship between God's "control" and "authority," Frame describes it as "one between might and right." "Control means that God has the power to direct the whole course of nature and history as he pleases. Authority means that he has the right to do that."[12] As creatures, God's authority is his right to command and demand obedience from us. In addition, when God makes promises, "we can trust them without question, for they are infallibly right and true."[13] Also, "God is the supreme interpreter of both himself and the universe he has made. The world is what he says it is. His word can never prove false (John 17:17), because: (1) he is omniscient (Heb 4:12–13), (2) he never lies (Titus 1:2), (3) his word governs all creation, and . . . (4) he has the authority to declare what is the case."[14] In fact, without God's authoritative word, there would be no story of redemption since everything we know about God's plan, promises, and of our Lord Jesus Christ comes through such words. Without authoritative, divine words, divine lordship is robbed of its meaning, and in Christ, God gives us a reliable promise, without which we cannot be saved (Gen 3:15; John 3:16; Heb 6:13–20). As Frame notes, "Without words from God of absolute authority, there can be no gospel and no Christianity."[15] Divine authority entails self-attestation, infallibility, and inerrancy; God's word is beyond human criticism, and it is to be believed by his people, indeed, by every creature because God alone is God (Rom 3:4).

Third, God as the Lord also means that *he* is present in the entirety of his being *and* covenantally present with his people. God's presence is *not* a physical presence: God is spirit, immaterial, and simple. He is not "in" time/space as creatures are. God transcends time and space in the fullness of his triune being (Ps 139:7–12; 1 Kgs 8:27), but this does not mean that God is "absent" from the world. In fact, it is because God transcends time and space that *he*, in the entirety of his being, is wholly present, in contrast to pantheism or panentheism, which either identify the creation with God or place it "in" him, which results in God being correlative to the world and mutually dependent on it.

---

[12] Frame, *Doctrine of God*, 80.

[13] Frame, 80.

[14] Frame, 80–1.

[15] Frame, 92.

In fact, Scripture's view of God as the covenant Lord requires the ideas of control, authority, and presence (Ps 139; Jer 10:1–16; Dan 4:34–35). God is not Lord without having all authority and being fully present everywhere. For God to be Lord, his control must be an authoritative, omnipresent control, and his omnipresence means that he is Lord over creation, history, and the world (Isa 40:12–26). But Scripture also teaches that God's presence is not merely providential. It is true, as Paul reminded the Athenians, that "in him we live and move and have our being" (Acts 17:28), but this does not mean that God's presence is only to sustain, rule, and govern. Scripture teaches that God is fully present in the entirety of his immutable being but the *effects* of his actions differ in relation to his creatures. To humanity outside of saving grace, God is present in common grace and judgment (John 3:36; Rom 1:18–32). But to his people, God is *graciously* present due to the covenants; thus, we can speak of God's unique *covenantal* presence.

As Scripture walks through the progression of the covenants, this truth is unveiled. In creation, God is *with* Adam in Eden (Gen 2; 3:8), God's garden-temple sanctuary. After the fall, due to God's redemptive promise (Gen 3:15), God begins to redeem his people. For God's people, God is not merely *essentially* present but *graciously* and *covenantally* present. But even in the OT covenants, God's covenantal presence is limited and mediated through the structures of those covenants (e.g., tabernacle, temple, priesthood). But in Christ and the new covenant, what all the previous covenants anticipated, predicted, and foreshadowed in terms of a full restoration of God's covenantal presence has now come in Christ—Immanuel, God with us (Isa 7:14; Matt 1:23)—the divine Son incarnate (John 1:14–18). And as a result of Christ's new covenant work, what OT saints only knew and experienced in limited ways, we now know and experience in a greater way, which is a foretaste of even more to come (Rev 21:22–22:5).

Worldview Significance of the Triune Creator-Covenant Lord

Who is the God of the Bible? Our summary answer is that he is "the triune Creator-covenant Lord." Although this does not say everything that Scripture says about God, it captures something of the "big picture," a biblical theology of who God is across the entire canon.

We now want to think about the "worldview significance" of who God is by unpacking four truths that result from and expound further God as the triune covenant Lord.

Remember that our reason for doing so is the nature of theology as exposition and defense. In a day that denies objective truth and affirms that there are many "names" for "God," the church must proclaim and defend the God of the Bible as the only true God and do so by explaining why *he* is utterly unique and in a different category from all the false "constructions" of "God" in non-Christian thought and even from "reduced" views of God within segments of evangelical theology.

God Is Transcendent and Immanent

In theology and worldview discussion, everyone must wrestle with the "God-world" relation, often picked up in the language of transcendence and immanence. From the outset, Christian theology establishes a specific view of transcendence-immanence tied to the Creator-creature distinction, which sets it apart from all other views. The Christian worldview is a "two-level" view of reality; that is, the Creator and the creature are ontologically distinct, and due to God's creation "out of nothing" (*ex nihilo*), the creation, which is not eternal, has come to exist. Between God and everything else, there is no third category of being. In Christology this point is crucial to grasp. When the eternal Son assumed his human nature, the incarnation was neither a subtraction of his deity nor a divine-human mixture of natures. Instead, the divine Son added a human nature to himself so that *he* now has two natures that forever remain distinct, yet the Son is now able to live and act through both natures consistent with the attributes of each nature.

Christian theology diametrically rejects one-level views of reality that place God and the creation on "the same level" (e.g., naturalism, dualism, pantheism, and panentheism).[16] In all non-Christian thought independent of Scripture, "God" is viewed on the top of a continuum of a scale of being that God and the world both participate in. However these views are constructed, a biblical view of transcendence and immanence stands opposed to them. Unfortunately, even within Christian theology broadly conceived, the concepts of transcendence and immanence are often "ambiguous," thus, as Frame reminds us, requiring careful definition.[17]

---

[16] Frame, *Doctrine of God*, 217.

[17] Frame, 114.

First, God's *transcendence* means that, as Lord, he is exalted "above" all things, eternal, independent, and self-existent. "[God] is not a being within the universe but the sovereign Lord of all that exists."[18] Although Scripture communicates God's transcendence to us by descriptions of height, it is *not* a spatial concept.[19] Instead, biblical language is analogical in its referring to God as "high and lifted up" (Isa 6:1) or "Most High" (Gen 14:18–22; Deut 32:8; Pss 7:17; 9:2), in stating that "the Lord God is in heaven above" (Deut 4:39; cf. Pss 8:1; 57:5; 97:9; 113:5), in referring to the Son as coming "from heaven" or to Jesus as ascending to the "Majesty on high" (Heb 1:3; cf. Ps 110:1–2; Acts 2:33–34), or in stating that Jesus is now at God's right hand interceding for us (Rom 8:34).

By the use of analogical language, Scripture teaches that God is transcendent; that is, he is distinct from the world as its Creator and Lord. And this distinction between God and creation is "one of kind, not merely of degree."[20] God is "not on the same ontological plane as the universe, and not in any way limited by his universe."[21] God is omnipresent and transcendent; thus, he is not limited by space or time. "All points on the time line are equally and simultaneously present to God, and all places are equally and simultaneously present to him."[22] In the end, to affirm that God is transcendent is to say that he is the Creator and Lord, and thus utterly unique.[23]

Second, God's *immanence* means that he is present with his creation. God as the *covenant* Lord is not "locked out of his creation,"[24] and contrary to deism, God is active in the world even though he is not "in" time and space or limited by them (Deut 4:39; 10:14–15; Josh 2:11; Isa 57:15; Eph 4:4–6). Just as transcendence is not a spatial concept, the same is true of immanence. In the temple, God is uniquely present in the Holy of Holies, but, as Solomon knows, "the heavens, even the highest heaven, cannot contain you" (1 Kgs 8:27 NIV). In fact, God is supremely "with" us in Christ and his incarnation (Isa 7:14; Matt 1:23; John 1:14), yet even in

---

[18] Carter, *Contemplating God*, 67 (see chap. 16, n. 93).

[19] Various liberal theologians, such as Rudolf Bultmann, wrongly read biblical language of transcendence univocally, thus arguing that the Bible teaches a three-decker universe. This is a fundamental hermeneutical mistake.

[20] Carter, *Contemplating God*, 68.

[21] Carter, 68.

[22] Carter, 68.

[23] See House, *Old Testament Theology*, 59–64, 109–11 (see chap. 14, n. 35).

[24] Carter, *Contemplating God*, 69.

Christ's two natures, the Son is not "limited to" or "circumscribed" by his human nature since he continues to subsist in the divine nature in eternal relation with the Father and Son and is thus Lord over all of creation.[25]

When Scripture describes God's presence to us it does so analogically by placing God "in" the narrative. In the story, God interacts with people, asks questions, and acts. But we must not read these portions of Scripture univocally as if God is "in" time/space *as we are*. Open theism, along with other "relational theisms," mistakenly reads God's presence in the narrative univocally so that God actually is "in" time, or when he is "surprised" by his interactions with us, he actually learns and repents like we do. But this is to read the biblical language of immanence wrongly, which, if one is not careful, undermines the inviolable Creator-creature distinction. Instead, in Scripture, God is transcendent and immanent, but both descriptions are analogical.

Third, in Scripture, there is no tension between God's transcendence-immanence, but outside of historic Christian theology, this is not the case.[26] For example, some have understood God's transcendence as being "wholly other," thus importing some kind of univocal and spatial concept. Since God is "wholly other," it is argued that we can have no knowledge of him or make true statements about him. In Neoplatonic thought, whether in Philo or Plotinus, all that we can say about God is by negation. Gnosticism also represents this kind of false thinking. God is unknown and removed from this world, hence the need for intermediaries to create and interact with this world, which was a false idea behind many of the early heretical ideas of the Trinity and Christology. Or for those indebted to Immanuel Kant, language about God was viewed as a human construction by means of symbolic language. Or, more recently, some dialectical theologians have emphasized God's "wholly otherness" so much that God becomes unknowable.[27] In all these ways, a false view of transcendence is at work, contrary to the biblical teaching.

Outside of Christianity, monotheistic/unitarian religions, such as Islam, also employ an unbiblical concept of transcendence given their rejection of the triune God. In Islam, Allah is "transcendent" but conceived as "wholly other." For this reason, transcendence implies that

[25] In Christology, this is known as the *extra*, a point we will discuss in volume 2.

[26] On this point, see Frame, *Doctrine of God*, 107–15.

[27] On dialectical theology, see James C. Livingston et al., *Modern Christian Thought: The Twentieth Century*, 2nd ed. (Minneapolis: Fortress Press, 2006), 62–95, 140–64.

"language used in describing God has no *positive* connotation whatsoever; there is absolutely no relationship (or analogy) between the connotation of a word when predicated of God and its connotation when predicated of man."[28] It also implies that "God can never be really present in the world, or active in person, in the process of history; this would contradict His transcendence. He can only act upon the world from a distance by means of his creative word."[29] This is why the Qur'an as a holy book is not the same as a Christian view of Scripture.[30] The Qur'an is "sent down," a dictation from angels to the prophets, which is not a biblical view of inspiration.[31] Furthermore, God is absolutely free, "unrestricted even in the realm of truth and morality."[32] He is free to judge the same act as "good" in one situation and "evil" in another dependent on the situation and according to his divine will—a divine will that is divorced from his nature, and thus reflecting a form of voluntarism. But the Islamic view of transcendence is not the same as the Christian view. It denies God's knowability and personal nature, that humans are created in God's image to know him, and the revelatory importance of God's agency in history. Within Islam there are no covenants, only law given to be obeyed, and the incarnation of the divine Son is impossible given that their denial of the Trinity and view of transcendence renders it impossible.[33]

Likewise, in non-Christian thought, the concept of immanence is also contrary to Scripture. For example, in pantheism (Eastern religions, Baruch Spinoza), immanence makes "God" indistinguishable from the world, or in panentheism, "God" is virtually indistinguishable. The classic text for panentheists is Acts 17:28: "In him we live and move and have our being." However, biblically, "in" does not mean that the world is "in" God ontologically; instead, it means that human life and existence is totally dependent on God. Similarly, "in Christ" language does not refer to some kind of ontological "participation" in God; instead,

---

[28] Samuel P. Schlorff, "Theological and Apologetical Dimensions of Muslim Evangelization," *WTJ* 42 no. 2 (1980): 339; cf. Imad N. Shehadeh, *God With Us and Without Us: The Beauty and Power of Oneness in Trinity versus Absolute Oneness, Vol 1–2* (Carlisle, Cumbria, UK: Langham Publishing, 2020), 91–132; Geisler and Saleeb, *Answering Islam*, 131–45 (see chap. 8, n. 51); Robert Letham, *The Holy Trinity: In Scripture, History, Theology, and Worship*, 2nd ed. (Phillipsburg: P&R, 2019), 535–39.

[29] Schlorff, 339.

[30] See Schlorff, 354–59.

[31] See Schlorff, 339–40.

[32] Schlorff, 340.

[33] See Schlorff, 340–48.

it is to be understood in the Bible's own categories of covenant representative headship, blessing, and presence. In the end, all false views of immanence undermine the Creator-creature distinction and leave us with a God-world relation where God is no longer the triune Creator-covenant Lord.

God Is Absolute/Infinite and Personal

From a slightly different aspect than transcendence-immanence, we can think of God in the worldview categories of "absolute/infinite *and* personal." John Frame prefers the term "absolute personality," while Francis Schaeffer speaks of "infinite-personal,"[34] but regardless, God's absolute *and* personal nature must be affirmed simultaneously to capture the truth of who the God of the Bible is in all of his uniqueness and glory.

First, think of God's *absolute/infinite* nature. What these terms convey is that God is eternal, self-existent, and *a se*; thus, he is categorically different than any created being. As the absolute one, similar to the concept of transcendence, God is the Creator and the ground of all reality (Gen 1:1). He needs no other being for his existence; he always was (Pss 90:2; 93:2; John 1:1; Acts 17:25). Nor can anything destroy him; he always will be (Deut 32:40; Ps 102:26–27; 1 Tim 6:16; Heb 1:10–12; Rev 10:6). As the eternal one, he is the Lord of time (Ps 90:4; Gal 4:4; Eph 1:11; 2 Pet 3:8). His knowledge is total since he plans all things, including secondary agents and causes (Isa 41:4; 44:7–8; 46:9–13). Due to his creation of the world, the facts and laws of the world are according to his plan. In fact, God's knowledge of the facts and the laws of the world precede their existence. Indeed, his knowledge of human choices is not dependent on us; otherwise, his knowledge would be conditioned by the creature. Since God's power and knowledge are extensive, there is nothing that takes place apart from his plan and his providential rule (Isa 14:24–27; Dan 4:34–35; Rom 8:28; Eph 1:11). For this reason, God has all authority and he rightly deserves our total love and obedience (Exod 3:13–18; 20:2; Lev 18:2–5, 30; 19:37; Deut 6:4–9; Rom 4:16–22; 9:20; Heb 11:4, 7–8, 17). God's authority transcends all created authorities (Exod 20:3; Matt 8:19–22; 10:34–38; Phil 3:7–8), and it extends to every area of our lives (Exodus to Deuteronomy; Rom 14:23; 1 Cor 10:31; 2 Cor 10:5; Col 3:17, 23).

---

[34] See Frame, *Doctrine of God*, 21–35, 600–8; Schaeffer, *Francis A. Schaeffer Trilogy* (see chap 2., n. 27).

Second, as the *covenant* Lord, God is also *personal.* Indeed, as the triune God, before there was ever a world, God existed in the perfection of his divine life as Father, Son, and Holy Spirit. In Scripture, God is never presented as a power or abstract principle who is "infinitely distant" from the world; instead, God is a personal being who relates to his creatures with speech and action, yet he remains complete within himself apart from the world. Think of the Bible's story in this regard. The eternal triune God speaks and the world is created, and God's speech sustains, rules, and governs the world towards its appointed end (see Job 34:14–15; Ps 103:19; Neh 9:6; Dan 4:34–35; Acts 17:28; Rom 8:28–29; 11:36; Eph 1:9, 11; Phil 2:10–11; Col 1:17; Heb 1:3; 2 Peter 3:7). But God not only speaks to create; he also speaks *with* the personal beings he created in his image, and he enters into *covenant* relationship with them (Lev 26:12; cf. Exod 29:45; 2 Sam 7:14; Rev 21:27). God is the living and true God, as opposed to lifeless and powerless idols of this world. In the outworking of God's redemptive plan in history, God's *personal* responses to his creatures are stressed. In the context of human sin and/or repentance, there is a different experience of God, but God himself does not change (Mal 3:6; Jas 1:17). God's response to covenant keepers and/or breakers remains the same, and if we perceive a change in the way he works, it is because we have changed, not God (Jer 18:5–10).

Third, the worldview significance of God as the absolute/infinite-personal God reveals why he is utterly unique compared to all non-Christian thought. To use the words of John Frame, God is "self-contained fullness" (*a se*, "life from and in himself"). As noted in chapter 13, God's aseity is more than his self-existence; it also entails that his knowledge and goodness are "from himself" so that he is the source and standard of knowledge *and* moral norms.

Herman Bavinck states this well. He defines *aseity* as "all that God is, he is of himself,"[35] which he derives from God's self-identification as Yahweh. As Bavinck unpacks the implications of aseity, he writes, "By virtue of himself he is goodness, holiness, wisdom, life, light, truth, and so on."[36] God is "supreme (*summum*) in everything: supreme being (*esse*), supreme goodness (*bonum*), supreme truth (*verum*), supreme beauty (*pulchrum*). He is the perfect, highest, the most excellent being, 'than whom nothing better can exist or be thought.'"[37]

---

[35] Bavinck, *Reformed Dogmatics*, 2:151.

[36] Bavinck, 2:151.

[37] Bavinck, 2:151. The last phrase is from Anselm's *Proslogian* (Indianapolis: Hackett, 1995).

In terms of worldview significance, John Frame rightly points out that *all* non-Christian thought tries to ground its worldview in an absolute, but it inevitably ends up being impersonal (e.g., uncaused cause, ultimate physical particle, abstract unity in reality, abstract form, pure chance or randomness). Or, if a concept of the personal is taught, it is never absolute but finite (e.g., pagan religions such as animism and polytheism). But in Christian theology, the proper ground for metaphysics, epistemology, and ethics is the absolute *and* personal God. Thus, contrary to all non-Christian thought, the Bible locates the "ultimate cause of being, an ultimate standard of truth, an ultimate justification of right" in God himself.[38]

Moreover, this entails that the universe is not ultimately impersonal, governed by chance and/or fate, but personal since it is created by the absolute-personal God. For this reason, only the Christian worldview, grounded in who God is, has warrant for design, rationality, meaning, human dignity, morality, and justice. Apart from the triune covenant Lord, all of these concepts are robbed of their objective meaning and become the relativistic, subjective "constructions" of humans who themselves are only the product of impersonal forces. But thankfully, this is not what the world is. Instead, the triune God, who has perfect life in himself, is the one who has graciously and freely chosen to create the world and, specifically, to share with his people something of his own life, truth, and goodness to the praise of his glory and grace.

Furthermore, think of how other perfections of God are mutually related to God's absolute-personal nature, which distinguishes him from all other conceptions. Here are three examples.

1. *God's Unity*. In speaking of God's unity, we need to distinguish between God's unity of singularity and his unity of simplicity. Regarding the former, given that God is the triune Lord, he alone is the living and true God, and "all other beings exist only from him, through him, and to him" (see Deut 6:4; Isa 44:6; John 17:3; 1 Tim 1:17).[39] Regarding the latter, God's absolute-personal nature means that God in himself is absolute perfection, which entails that "every attribute of God is identical with his essence," "in God everything is one," and "God is everything he possesses."[40] Thus, unlike creatures, God is not composed of metaphysical parts that when added together make up God; he does not belong to a larger instance of being that we call "God"; his attributes are not accidental to him, nor is he experiencing change in himself.

---

[38] Frame, *Doctrine of God*, 607.

[39] Bavinck, *Reformed Dogmatics*, 2:170.

[40] Bavinck, 2:173–74.

Instead, God "is infinite and all that is in him is infinite. All of his attributes are divine, hence infinite and one with his being."[41] God alone is "perfect and infinite fullness of being,"[42] totally self-sufficient as the only one who has a perfect life in himself, with each of his attributes describing the entirety of his being. God is utterly unique and in a category all by himself. Furthermore, in relation to the Trinity, simplicity is crucial to understand correctly how each person subsists in and shares the same undivided divine nature and thus is fully and wholly God.

Due to God's aseity and simplicity, there is nothing in him that is independent of him. This is why, in contrast to Plato's Euthyphro problem, God's goodness is not an arbitrary act of will or something outside of him that he conforms to.[43] There is no abstract goodness outside of God that is more ultimate than him, for if there was, God would not be *a se* and goodness and moral norms would ultimately be arbitrary and impersonal. Instead, God's goodness is everything that God is since it is identical to his essence, which is also true of all of God's attributes.

2. *God's immutability*. God does not change in his being, plans, purposes, and character since there is nothing outside of him that he depends on (see Exod 3:14; Ps 102:26–28; Mal 3:6; 1 Tim 1:17; 6:16; Heb 1:11–12; Jas 1:7). Also, given that God's immutability is grounded in his triune self-sufficiency, to caricature immutability as giving us a static or immobile view of God is simply false.[44] God within himself is fullness of life, and in his works, he remains the same, whether in creation, revelation, or the incarnation. As Bavinck notes, "Without losing himself, God can give himself, and, while absolutely maintaining his immutability, he can enter into an infinite number of relations to his creatures."[45]

3. *God's omniscience*. God's knowledge is exhaustive because God fully knows himself and his plan for the world. There is nothing within him or outside of him that is independent of him. No doubt, God's knowledge is not mere introspection since God knows what takes place in the space-time world. Creation is genuinely "other" than God, and God knows it as "other" than himself. But even in knowing the world in its distinctness, God knows it as something that he has exhaustively interpreted prior to its existence. For this reason, God's knowledge is not dependent on the creature, a crucial point of division between Calvinism

---

[41] Bavinck, 2:176.

[42] Bavinck, 2:176.

[43] See Frame, *Doctrine of God*, 405–9, for a discussion of the famous Euthyphro problem.

[44] This is often the charge of open theists and panentheists against classical theism.

[45] Bavinck, *Reformed Dogmatics*, 2:159.

and Arminianism regarding divine sovereignty and omniscience, including discussions of middle knowledge and its implications for divine providence.[46] Reformed theology has always objected to Arminian theology since it undercuts God's aseity in knowledge, resulting in God being dependent on the creature and a world governed by choices independent of God's will.[47]

God Is Holy

Scripture presents God as the Holy One over his entire creation (Gen 2:1–3; Exod 3:2–5; Lev 11:44; Isa 6:1–3; 57:15). In the past, theologians stressed that God's holiness was an overarching description of God's sheer God-ness,[48] or God in his "consummate perfection and total glory."[49] Obviously, one must exercise extreme care in elevating one attribute over another, yet there is a sense in which holiness "pervades all of his actions and interprets all of his other attributes."[50] This is why whenever we combine God's holiness with love, justice, goodness, or what have you, we always say that it is a *holy* love, *holy* justice, and *holy* goodness.

The root meaning of the Hebrew noun for "holiness," *qōdeš*, and its related adjective (*qādôš*), along with the Greek *hagios*, is difficult to determine etymologically. The common view is that holiness means "to set apart," and thus it refers primarily to God's transcendence.[51] However, holiness means more than "to set apart." It conveys the idea of "consecration" or "devotion to," which then spills over into the moral realm since to be holy unto God, or devoted to him, means to honor what he honors and to love what he loves.[52]

---

[46] These issues will be discussed in chapters 18, 20, 22.

[47] For a discussion of Reformed theology's response to Arminian theology, see Muller, *Post-Reformation Reformed Dogmatics*, 3:397–432.

[48] See Bavinck, *Reformed Dogmatics*, 2:220, who describes God's holiness as the way of impressing on us his deity; or R. A. Finlayson, who describes holiness as "an attribute of attributes" that "lends unity to all the attributes of God." "Holiness, Holy Saints," in *New Bible Dictionary*, ed. J. D. Douglas et al., 2nd ed. (Downers Grove: InterVarsity, 1982), 487

[49] A. A. Hodge, *Outlines of Theology* (1879; repr., Grand Rapids: Zondervan, 1972), 163.

[50] Muller, *Post-Reformation Reformed Dogmatics*, 3:501.

[51] See VanGemeren, *NIDNTTE*, 3:879 (see chap. 13, n. 23).

[52] See H. Seebas, "Holy," *NIDNTTE* 2:224; Peter J. Gentry, "The Meaning of 'Holy' in the Old Testament," *BSac* 170 (2013): 400–17.

Within God himself (*ad intra*), holiness understood in the devoted sense is way of describing God's holy love.

> To say that "God is love" and that "God is holy" ultimately is to point to the same reality. Holiness is the intensity of the love that flows within the very being of God, among and between each of the three persons of the Father, Son, and Holy Spirit. It is the sheer intensity of that devotion that causes seraphim (whose holiness is perfect but creaturely) to veil their faces.[53]

For God, then, to be holy means that he is devoted to his own glory since he alone is God and thus the highest end of all things.[54] Geerhardus Vos picks up this point. Since God "knows Himself, seeks Himself, and loves Himself as the supreme embodiment of rational perfection," holiness is "that attribute of God by which He seeks and loves Himself as the highest good and demands as reasonable goodness from the creatures to be consecrated to him."[55]

As we tie holiness to God's essential nature, which is the primary and first sense of holiness, metaphysically it is associated with God's aseity and glorious majesty and utter uniqueness (Isa 6:1–3; 40:18–25).[56] As the triune Lord, God in himself has life from himself in the fullness of his being, and thus he is categorically different in nature and existence from everything he has made. God cannot be compared with the "gods" of the nations or be judged by human standards. God alone is God, the Holy One (1 Sam 2:2), hence the use of the superlative in reference to him—"Holy, holy, holy is the LORD of Armies; / his glory fills the whole earth" (Isa 6:3; cf. Rev 4:8).[57] For this reason, holiness is identified with God himself as the one who is "above," "high," "great," and "majestic," along with various other descriptions of God.[58]

---

[53] Sinclair Ferguson, *Devoted to God* (Carlisle: Banner of Truth Trust, 2016), 2.

[54] Beeke and Smalley define holiness as follows: "God's holiness means that *he is set apart by his glory, for his glory*." *Reformed Systematic Theology*, 1:569

[55] Vos, *Reformed Dogmatics*, 1:26–27 (see chap. 15, n. 126).

[56] Muller, *Post-Reformation Reformed Dogmatics*, 3:497–503.

[57] See Motyer, *Prophecy of Isaiah*, 76–77 (see chap. 14, n. 56).

[58] See Deut 26:15; Pss 3:4; 11:4; 20:6; 22:3; 28:2; 30:4; 33:21; 47:8; 48:1; 65:4; 87:1; 98:1; 103:1; 105:3, 42; 106:47; 108:7; 113:5; 145:3, 21; Isa 6:1; 10:17; 12:6; 17:7; 37:23; 40:12–26; 41:14, 16, 20; 43:3, 14, 15; 45:11; 47:4; 48:17; 52:10; 54:5; 55:5; 57:13–15; 60:9, 10; 63:10; Jer 25:30; Ezek 28:14; Joel 2:1; Amos 2:7; Zech 2:13.

In addition to the primary metaphysical sense of God's holiness is the *moral* sense: God is holy, and thus *he* is the objective moral standard of goodness, righteousness, and justice so that all that stands in opposition to *his* will and nature is sin. This is why Scripture reminds us that God is "too pure to behold evil"; he cannot tolerate wrongdoing (Hab 1:12–13; cf. Isa 1:4–20; 35:8). In fact, God *must* act in holy justice against sin precisely because God *is* holy.[59] God calls his creatures to be wholly devoted to him (Lev 19:2; 1 Pet 1:15–16), but our problem is that we are unholy. This is why Scripture strongly emphasizes the utter incompatibility of God's holiness and our sin.[60] For example, God is "Most High" (Isa 6:1; Pss 7:17; 9:2; 21:7; 46:4; 83:18) and thus inaccessible to sinners not because he is spatially removed, but because he is holy and we are not. Or God is presented as distant, or "far from us." Moses is not to come any closer to God, for he stands on holy ground (Exod 3:1–6). When God meets Israel at Mt. Sinai, limits are established so that they will not come too close (Exod 19). Or God's presence in the tabernacle-temple is limited and cordoned off; only the high priest may enter once a year, but not without atonement for his own sin and the sins of the people. Or God is described as "light and fire" (1 John 1:5; Heb 12:29), or his throne is surrounded by effects such as a thunder and lightning, a sea, other thrones, and so forth, which stresses his "distance" from us and the inaccessibility of our entering his presence. God's holiness and our sin are simply incompatible (Rev 4:4–8; cf. Isa 6:1–4).

In fact, a significant corollary of divine holiness in relation to our sin is divine *wrath*, that is, God's holy reaction to sin and evil.[61] Repeatedly, Scripture speaks of God's wrath against sin from Genesis 3 on. No doubt, God is forbearing and gracious, but he is also holy, and as such, he *cannot* deny himself by overlooking our sin. However, unlike God's holiness, love, justice, and so forth, God's wrath is not an *intrinsic* perfection. Instead, it is a function of God's entire holy being against sin. Where there is no sin, there is no wrath, but there is always the holy love of God. However, when sin is present, there *must* be divine wrath; otherwise, God is not holy.

Significantly, this truth creates a tension in the Bible's covenantal story. God is holy; we are not. Yet given God's choice to redeem us and to restore creation from the effects of sin (Gen

---

[59] See Muller, *Post-Reformation Reformed Dogmatics*, 3:501, who links God's holiness with God's exercise of retributive justice against human sin.

[60] On this point, see Stott, *Cross of Christ*, 107–11 (see chap. 13, n. 68).

[61] See D. A. Carson, *The Difficult Doctrine of the Love of God* (Wheaton: Crossway, 2000).

3:15), how can God demonstrate his holy justice and covenant love without denying himself? Ultimately the answer to this question is only resolved in the person and work of Christ, the divine Son incarnate, who alone is able to redeem us as our new covenant representative and substitute, while simultaneously upholding divine holy justice (Rom 3:21–26).

The worldview implications of divine holiness are important to consider since it too, along with transcendence-immanence and absolute-personal, distinguishes the God of the Bible from all other conceptions of "God." First, although due to divine simplicity, God *is* his attributes and we cannot elevate one attribute over another, there is a sense in which divine holiness is "the foundation of all [God's] other virtues . . . insofar as God must be characterized by his sacred self-regard or reflexive purity if he is to be perfect in wisdom, power, justice, and mercy and if he is to be properly regarded by his creation."[62] Thus to speak of God as the Holy One explains why God's own glory is the highest good and end of all things. For us, this entails that given who God is as the Holy One, he rightly demands exclusive loyalty, devotion, love, and obedience from us (Exod 20:1–3; Lev 19:2; 1 Pet 1:16; 1 John 2:15–17). In fact, sin must be seen in this light. Sin, first and foremost, must be viewed in light of the Holy One we have sinned against, which not only underscores the serious and hideous nature of sin, but it also leads to the next point.

Second, as we discussed in part 3, apart from a proper view of God's holiness in relation to sin, we will not understand the Bible's message of redemption and why we need a specific Redeemer (i.e., the divine incarnate Son) who does a specific work to save us (i.e., centrally a work of penal substitution). Also, we will never fully grasp why Christ alone can secure our justification, which only becomes ours by grace alone through faith alone in covenant union with Christ. In a day where many "saviors" and paths of salvation are affirmed, the Bible teaches that there is only one Lord and Savior tied to a specific view of who God is, including a specific understanding of God's essential holiness. Most worldviews believe in some kind of works righteousness, but Scripture teaches the opposite. Because of who God is, he *cannot* overlook our sin: he *is* holy. To be declared just *before* God, our sin must be paid for in full. And the only person who can do this is the divine Son, who takes on our humanity to obey for us *and* to satisfy *God's* own holy righteous demand against us. Apart from *this* view of

[62] Muller, *Post-Reformation Reformed Dogmatics*, 3:500.

God, the Bible's message will not be understood, and it will inevitably be replaced by some *extratextual* substitute.

In every age, but especially today, the church desperately needs to recapture a proper view of God so she can affirm and proclaim a correct view of the gospel. As we noted in chapter 16, we are surrounded by the weightlessness of God; what is needed is to know and proclaim the Holy One in all of his glory, beauty, and grace. David Wells states it this way:

> when we succeed in cloaking the holiness of God, in focusing on his love to the exclusion of his wrath, we unsettle the whole moral universe. We create a God who may be patient, kindly, and compassionate but who is without the will to resist what is wrong, without the will to judge it, and without the power to destroy it. Such a God lacks the moral earnestness to attract our attention, let alone inspire our belief or warrant our worship. Such a God is not the God of the Bible, is not the God of Jesus Christ. . . . When holiness slips from sight, so, too, does the centrality of Christ.[63]

God Is Triune

Although our entire discussion has assumed the triune nature of God, we are now making explicit its significance for our understanding the identity and nature of the God of the Bible. Within the one true and living God, there are eternal person-relations of holy love between the Father, Son, and Spirit, who equally subsist in the same divine nature so that God is not personal due to his relations with his creatures, but he is personal in respect to his own being; God from eternity has had "a blessed life of his own."[64] Why is this so crucial to understand?

First, the Trinity utterly distinguishes the God of the Bible from all other ideas of "God." In a day of rampant pluralism, this is no small point to emphasize.

Second, the Bible's message of redemption as revealed through the unfolding covenants cannot be made sense of apart from the one God who redeems us as three distinct persons who equally and fully possess the same divine nature: the Father who initiates, the Son who redeems, and the Spirit who applies Christ's work to us. In other words, apart from the

---

[63] Wells, *God in the Wasteland*, 143 (see chap. 1, n. 2).

[64] Bavinck, *Reformed Dogmatics*, 2:331.

Trinity, the Bible's story, along with who the Father, Son, and Spirit are as the one God, makes no sense.

Third, although the triune nature of God is given by special revelation and it is not the result of reasoning from natural revelation, given God's self-disclosure of himself, the Trinity can account for how God is transcendent, absolute, *a se*, and simultaneously personal. For example, without the Trinity, it is difficult to uphold Christian theology's denial of *correlativism*. What is correlativism? It is the view that makes God and the world mutually dependent. This point is often illustrated by referring to God's love. As a person, God loves the world. But does God need the world in order to satisfy his eternal love and be fully God? If so, then this has serious implications for Christian theology. At its heart, it undercuts the Creator-creature distinction and makes impossible the absolute, independent, and self-sufficient nature of God, especially in knowledge, ethics, and the expression of God's personal nature.

By contrast, since God is triune, his love is both self-contained and interpersonal apart from the world. He does not need the world to exist to know and to love since within God, due to his own personal life as Father, Son, and Spirit, "God is eternally, internally full."[65] Bavinck stresses this same point. He admits that we cannot demonstrate the truth of the Trinity from reasoning about divine love. However, given the truth that God is triune,

> The fact is that these attributes [of love and knowledge] as well as all the other attributes only come alive and become real as a result of the Trinity. Apart from it, they are mere names, sounds, empty terms. As attributes of the triune God they come alive both to our mind and to our heart. Only by the Trinity do we begin to understand that God as he is in himself—hence also, apart from the world—is the independent, eternal, omniscient, and all-benevolent One, love, holiness, and glory.[66]

For this reason, God's aseity, absolute-personal nature, and the Trinity are organically related and mutually require each other. God's triune nature grounds how he is *a se* and personal; otherwise, God would be relative to the world, which would undercut God as the one who has all glory in himself. The Trinity is not an esoteric doctrine, but essential to making sense of who God is as the "Creator-covenant Lord." As Bavinck notes, "The Trinity reveals

---

[65] Scott R. Swain, "B. B. Warfield and the Biblical Doctrine of the Trinity," *Themelios* 43 no. 1 (2018): 22.

[66] Bavinck, *Reformed Dogmatics*, 2:331.

God to us as the fullness of being, the true life, eternal beauty. In God, too, there is unity in diversity, diversity in unity. Indeed, this order and this harmony is present in him absolutely. In the case of creatures we see only a faint analogy of it."[67] As a result, the Bible's view of God is unique and incomparable, and it is no wonder that our only proper response to him is love, adoration, and total devotion.

Concluding Reflection

To say that God is the "triune Creator-covenant Lord" is to capture who the God of the Bible is over against the false constructions of non-Christian thought and even the "reduction" of God within some segments of evangelical theology. To unpack God's transcendence-immanence and absolute-personal and holy nature is to give a "big picture" view of God so that we are better able to know, proclaim, and defend who God is for the church and before a watching world. The purpose of this chapter was not to give specific details of the doctrine of God; instead, it was to focus on some key truths that distinguish the Christian view of God from all others, which is vitally important given our postmodern and religiously pluralistic context.

With this theological overview in place, we are now in a place to delve into the specifics by expounding further who God is in himself by first reflecting on God's perfections (chapter 18) and then turning to the doctrine of the Trinity (chapter 19). In so doing, we are following the order of Scripture and the traditional order of theological reflection by first thinking about "the one God" (*De Deo Uno*) who is also "the triune God" (*De Deo Trino*). Indeed, above all, we are seeking to describe him who is beyond compare (Isa 40:25)—the one who is worthy of our total trust, thought, life, and devotion (Rev 4:11; 5:9–10, 12–14).

---

[67] Bavinck, 2:331.

CHAPTER 18

The Attributes of Our Triune God

Introduction

We now turn to an exposition of the attributes or the perfections of God. As we do, we must pay close attention to Scripture since our knowledge of God's being is from his revelation, especially in his external works (*ad extra*) of creation, providence, redemption, and judgment. God is known in creation and supremely by his entire word-act revelation, namely Scripture. Furthermore, God's external works not only reveal who he is, but from these works, we also know something about God in himself (*ad intra*) apart from the world.[1]

In our discussion of God's attributes, we must remember two points. First, God, in himself and in his external works, is incomprehensible. What God reveals of himself in Scripture (and nature) is true, but it never exhausts his being. Second, biblical language in reference to God is analogical.[2] In our biblical and theological reasoning about God's attributes, we must account for all of the biblical data *and* preserve the Creator-creature distinction in our formulation of the divine attributes. Due to God's sovereign condescension, he has graciously chosen to reveal himself to us by speaking in ways that we can understand. However, in the end, biblical language about God is analogical and never univocal.

---

[1] See Duby, *God in Himself* (see chap. 1, n. 20).

[2] For a discussion of divine incomprehensibility and analogical language, see chapters 3 and 16.

In reflecting on God's nature, our goal is to think deeply about the glory and majesty of our triune covenant Lord in order to know, worship, trust, and obey God more. The perennial and greatest need of the church is to know God and to make him central in our thinking and lives. Today, the greatest problem the evangelical church faces is *not* thinking rightly about God in all of his aseity, holy love, justice, and transcendent glory. In a time that has sought to rob God of his glory and attempted foolishly to make him "weightless," our task is to know God in truth and to proclaim gladly his incomparable lordship. The reason for our creation as image-bearers and our re-creation in Christ Jesus is to know the only true God in all of his triune blessedness so we may properly fear him (Heb 12:28–29). As our Lord teaches: "This is eternal life: that they may know you, the only true God, and the one you have sent—Jesus Christ" (John 17:3).

As we turn to reflect on God's attributes, may our God fill us "with the knowledge of his will in all wisdom and spiritual understanding, so that [we] may walk worthy of the Lord, fully pleasing to him: bearing fruit in every good work and growing in the knowledge of God" (Col 1:9–10) so that in our theological reflections, Christ will "have first place in everything" (Col 1:18) and that "God may be all in all" (1 Cor 15:28).[3]

Preliminary Issues

What Is an Attribute?[4]

An attribute is *not* something we "attribute" to God as if it is a "part" of God. Instead, attributes are what God *is*, in his entire being and perfection as "the one God" (*De Deo Uno*). To

[3] For helpful works on theology proper, both historical and contemporary, see Muller, *Post-Reformation Reformed Dogmatics*, vol. 3 (see chap. 3, n. 12); Stephen Charnock, *Discourses upon the Existence and Attributes of God*, 2 vols. (repr., Grand Rapids: Baker, 1979); Packer, *Knowing God*, (see chap. 1, n. 54); C. Samuel Storms, *The Grandeur of God: A Theological and Devotional Study of the Divine Attributes* (Grand Rapids: Baker, 1984); Peter Sanlon, *Simply God: Recovering the Classical Trinity* (Nottingham: Inter-Varsity Press, 2014); Matthew Barrett, *None Greater: The Undomesticated Attributes of God* (Grand Rapids: Baker, 2019).

[4] On how historical theology in the West approached this question, see Muller, *Post-Reformation Reformed Dogmatics*, 3:195–226.

speak of God's attributes is to describe his "being" (Gk. *ousia*; Lat. *substantia, essentia*), or *what* God is in his one undivided essence. Also, in terms of God's trinitarian being, to speak of *God's* attributes is to think about what all three persons have in *common*. As we will discuss in the next chapter, the Father, Son, and Holy Spirit are *not* distinguished by divine attributes since they subsist in the same essence (Gk. *homoousios*); instead, they are only distinguished by their eternal, immanent, personal "relations of origin."

Historically, God's attributes have been viewed as his perfections that are *essential* to him. In contrast to creatures, God has no *accidental* attributes that attach to his being.[5] We have many accidental attributes that can be lost and new ones that can be gained while we remain what we are. For example, we could lose a leg in a car crash or our mental abilities due to a debilitating disease, but regardless, we remain *essentially* human. However, this is not true of God. God cannot "lose" or "gain" any attributes and still be God: God *is* who he is in the fullness of his being and life. For this reason, God's attributes are essential to him and thus necessary to his being. God *is* his attributes without loss or gain, a truth that totally distinguishes him from any created thing, thus underscoring the Creator-creature distinction.[6] In fact, the reason why God's attributes are essential to him is also due to his divine simplicity.

---

[5] An attribute is *essential* if it is necessary for a thing in question to be what it is. It is *accidental* if it can be lost (or added) and the thing remains what it is essentially. For example, it is essential for a triangle to have three sides. If one adds a fourth side, it is no longer a triangle. For humans, our being image-bearers is essential to us, but our hair, arms, and mental capacities are accidental since we remain human if those qualities are lost.

[6] Historically, Christian theology has viewed all of God's attributes as *essential* and not accidental or contingent. Today, however, the conceptual framework of "essentialism" makes a distinction between God's essential *and* contingent attributes. Essential attributes are necessary attributes, i.e., in every possible world (infinity, eternality, aseity, immutability, immensity, holiness), while accidental/contingent attributes are attributes that God has but not in every possible world (e.g., creator, redeemer, sustainer due to God's free decision to create, redeem, etc.). See Jay W. Richards, *The Untamed God: A Philosophical Exploration of Divine Perfection, Simplicity, and Immutability* (Downers Grove: InterVarsity, 2003). In our discussion of the divine attributes, we will follow the classic way of speaking of God's attributes as *essential* to him, indeed, as identical to him. When "essentialism" refers to God's contingent attributes, it is really identifying God's *ad extra* works (e.g., creator, redeemer, etc.), which are technically not attributes. Although one can speak of God's attributes within an "essentialist" framework, we will follow the older conceptual understanding of God's attributes.

Divine Simplicity

God is *one* (Deut 6:4), but as we briefly noted in chapter 17, there are two important senses to God's *oneness*. Let us develop this point in more detail.

First, God is one in terms of his singularity: God alone is the true God and there is no other (Gen 1:1; Isa 40:12–26; 44:6–8; 46:5, 9–11; Dan 4:34–35; Mark 12:29; John 17:3; Acts 17:24–26; 1 Cor 8:4–7; 1 Tim 1:17; Jas 2:19; Rev 4:1–5:14).[7] If God shared his being with another being, he would not be God, and if another being had the same perfections as God, God would not be the most perfect being that Scripture says he is. The Bible is forthright: the triune Creator-covenant Lord alone is God; thus, he alone is to be worshipped, trusted, loved, and obeyed.

However, God's *unity* is more than singularity; it is also *simplicity*. By simplicity, we mean that God is not divisible into parts; God's attributes are coexistent with who he is. Unlike creatures, God is not composed of metaphysical parts that when added together constitute God. God does not belong to a larger category of "God" (genus) that he is an instance of (species), nor is he simply the greatest instance of being that all beings participate in.[8] Instead, as Herman Bavinck states, God "is infinite and all that is in him is infinite. All of his attributes are divine, hence infinite and one with his being."[9] Indeed, as infinite, God alone is God; he is in a category all by himself, who in himself is fullness of perfection and transcends all limitations.[10]

---

[7] Scripture teaches a "strict monotheism," in contrast to those who think the OT does not. See Nathan MacDonald, *Deuteronomy and the Meaning of 'Monotheism'* (Tübingen: Mohr Siebeck, 2003). For a critique of MacDonald et al., see Bauckham, *Jesus and the God of Israel* (see chap. 13, n. 87).

[8] See Turretin, *Institutes of Elenctic Theology*, 1:192 (see chap. 3, n. 55).

[9] Bavinck, *Reformed Dogmatics*, 2:176 (see chap. 1, n. 9). Also see Augustine, *The Trinity*, trans. Stephen McKenna (Washington: Catholic University of America, 1963), 178–79 (5.4), 234–35 (8.5); Augustine, *Confessions*, trans. R. S. Pine-Coffin (Baltimore: Penguin Books, 1961), 7.11 (147), 9.4 (282); John of Damascus, *The Orthodox Faith*, 1.9; Thomas Aquinas, *Summa Theologica*, pt. 1, q. 3, in *Summa Theologica*, 1:14–20 (see chap. 2, n. 20). For a current defense of divine simplicity, see Steven J. Duby, *Divine Simplicity: A Dogmatic Account* (London: T&T Clark, 2016); James E. Dolezal, *God without Parts: Divine Simplicity and the Metaphysics of God's Absoluteness* (Eugene: Pickwick, 2011); cf. Dolezal, *All That Is in God: Evangelical Theology and the Challenge of Classical Christian Theism* (Grand Rapids: Reformation Heritage Books, 2017), 37–78.

[10] The exegetical case for divine simplicity is strong and related to other truths about God. See Duby, *Divine Simplicity*, 91–177. For example, Duby argues that divine simplicity follows from these

For this reason, God is the ground of his own existence. For creatures, we can distinguish *what* a thing is from the fact *that* it exists, but not so with God; he is the self-existent one. In fact, as triune, each person subsists in and wholly shares the one undivided divine essence so that "God has a distinct and infinite life of his own within himself."[11] For this reason, theologians rightly speak of God as "pure act" (Lat. *actus purus*) or "pure actuality" (Lat. *purus actua*). In God, there is the absolute fullness of life and being, of essence and existence. Again, unlike creatures, God has no "passive potency," which he needs to activate to be fulfilled. There is no potential for growth in God, either for better or worse, since in his fullness of triune life, God does not change; he is wholly complete within himself (Exod 3:14).

Related to God's simplicity is the fact that God's nature is not material but immaterial *spirit* (John 4:24; cf. Luke 24:36–40). No doubt, in the context of John 4, when Jesus says, "God *is* spirit," he is also unpacking a biblical theology of the "Holy Spirit" tied to the dawning of the new covenant era in his coming as the divine Messianic Son. But as our Lord speaks of the new age that he has inaugurated, he also reminds us that God's nature is *spirit*. God is not a material or corporeal being; he has no parts or dimensions, and we cannot perceive him by our bodily senses (in contrast to Mormonism).[12] The OT teaches this point in Isa 31:3. By juxtaposing creatures who are "flesh" (material) with God, who is "spirit" (immaterial), God is distinguished as utterly different; God is simple, *a se*, and immaterial. Paul stresses this point in Acts 17:29. Against the idolatry of Athens that constructs "gods" like creatures, Paul reminds

---

truths. First, simplicity follows from God's singularity, which entails God's uniqueness, that he transcends the categories of genus and species, and that God is not composed but identical with each of his attributes (Gen 1:1–2; Isa 40:25; 45:20–25; Dan 4:34–35; Acts 17:24–26; Rom 11:33–36; Rev 4:1–5:14). Second, simplicity follows from God's aseity, which entails that God is self-sufficient and not dependent on anything outside of himself (Exod 3:15; 33:19; Ps 50:12–13; John 5:26; Acts 17:24–26; Rom 9:1–24; 11:33–36). Third, simplicity follows from divine immutability, which entails the constancy of God's essence and the fullness of divine life within himself (Exod 3:15; Num 23:19; 1 Sam 15:29; Mal 3:6; Heb 6:13–18; 13:8; Jas 1:17). Fourth, simplicity follows from God's infinity, which entails God's limitless perfection and greatness (Exod 18:11; Deut 7:21; 11:7; Pss 86:10; 99:2; 135:5; 139:1–18; Isa 40:12–14; Rev 4:11).

[11] Bavinck, *Reformed Dogmatics*, 2:177.

[12] Mormon theology teaches that God the Father is a deified man and that creating humans in his image means that God has a physical nature. On this false teaching, see Travis S. Kerns, *The Saints of Zion: An Introduction to Mormon Theology* (Nashville: B&H Academic, 2018), 25–70; White, *Is the Mormon My Brother?*, 43–154 (see chap. 8, n. 55).

the Athenians that the true God is not like anything he has created; God's being is simple, eternal, self-sufficient, immaterial, infinite, omnipresent, and not susceptible to change.

The importance of divine simplicity for understanding God's attributes cannot be overstated. Let us consider four truths about God's attributes that follow from divine simplicity.

First, God's attributes are not abstract qualities existing independently of him. Instead, God's attributes are identical with his nature. The triune God is absolute perfection. For this reason, God is self-sufficient and not dependent on anything outside of himself. In contrast to Plato's eternal forms or ideas, there is no abstract goodness or knowledge outside of God; there is nothing more ultimate than him that he conforms to. God *is* his attributes, and each attribute *is* identical to God's essence. This is why God does not merely possess love, holiness, and justice; he *is* love, holiness, and justice. In fact, this is why, when sin stands in opposition to God, the triune Lord cannot deny himself: God's entire being in all of his glorious perfections upholds his own glory, opposes that which rebels against him, and remains true to himself in our salvation.[13]

Second, each attribute describes the entirety of God's being, not just a part of it; God is wholly and totally integrated. God is not a collection of attributes or a substance to which various properties attach. Instead, "there is nothing in God that is less than himself, less than the whole of who he is; neither can there be anything in him that is removable or adventitious. By the same token, the attributes are not only indivisible but also identical; the distinctions between them are for our benefit."[14]

Third, although God is simple and uncompounded, we distinguish God's attributes by "mode of signification" (*modus significandi*). Due to simplicity, God's attributes are not "really" distinct in him; rather, they are "formally" distinct. As Richard Muller notes, "The divine attributes all 'signify the one thing' (*unam rem*), namely, God, but 'they signify him under diverse and multiple concepts, which are not synonyms.'"[15] However, in our making distinctions between God's attributes, we must never think that God's attributes are distinct parts of his

---

[13] Scripture teaches that God *is* light, love, etc. (1 John 1:5; 4:8; Isa 6:3). God's attributes are God.

[14] Letham, *Systematic Theology*, 157 (see chap. 5, n. 1).

[15] Muller, *Post-Reformation Reformed Dogmatics*, 3:55. For Muller's entire discussion on this point, see pp. 53–58. Cf. Aquinas, *Summa Theologica*, part 1a, q. 13, art. 4. On the development of divine simplicity in the Patristic era, see Andrew Radde-Gallwitz, *Basil of Caesarea, Gregory of Nyssa, and the Transformation of Divine Simplicity* (Oxford: Oxford University Press, 2009).

nature. The divine nature is simple. Moreover, this entails that everything God does expresses his entire being, although by revelation, we distinguish his eternity from his power, his love from his holiness. Matthew Barrett illustrates this point by drawing an analogy between how light is refracted through a prism: "As the one, simple God is manifested to his creatures through human words and mighty acts, that one, undivided essence is displayed in a variety of ways."[16]

Fourth, some important *theological* applications follow from divine simplicity. Let us note three examples, all taken from Christology.

1. Think of the nature of the incarnation. As we will discuss in the next chapter, some social Trinitarians who embrace an ontological kenotic Christology propose that in the incarnation the divine Son "set aside" his non-essential divine attributes (e.g., omnipresence, omniscience, and omnipotence). As a result, the Son, either temporarily or permanently, no longer has specific attributes that the Father and Spirit have, but he also lives his life entirely circumscribed by his human nature. As such, the Son cannot continue to exercise those divine attributes that he has "set aside." For example, before the incarnation, the Son, along with the Father and Spirit, sustained the universe, but after the incarnation, the Son no longer does.[17]

This view is hugely problematic for a number of reasons. However, its core problem is its rejection of divine simplicity in its understanding of the divine essence. In redefining God's essence to include essential *and* accidental attributes, it veers in the wrong direction. God's essence is one and simple, and all of God's attributes are *essential* to him. The divine Son cannot "set aside" any attribute and still be God. In the end, this view undercuts biblical and theological orthodoxy, namely, that the Son is "of the same nature" (*homoousios*) with the Father and Spirit. Furthermore, the incarnation is not an act of subtraction but an act of assumption. The Son, from the Father and by the Spirit, takes to himself, or assumes, a human nature without change to his divine essence so that *he* now subsists, lives, and acts in both natures. The lesson is this: a denial of divine simplicity directly affects our trinitarian theology and Christology.[18]

---

[16] Barrett, *None Greater*, 82.

[17] For a detailed description of this view, see Stephen J. Wellum, *God the Son Incarnate: The Doctrine of Christ* (Wheaton: Crossway, 2016), 373–83.

[18] See Wellum, 395–419, for a developed critique of ontological kenotic Christology.

2. Divine simplicity is also important in understanding the nature of the atonement. When our triune God acts in love and displays his grace, he does not act contrary to his holiness and justice, as if his love overrides his holy opposition to our sin. God *is* love, holy, and just. No doubt, this creates an apparent "tension" in the Bible's redemptive story. Due to our sin, God is not obligated to redeem us, but due to his love and grace, he freely chooses to do so. But how does God forgive our sin and remain true to his holiness, justice, and righteousness? God *is* holy justice; he cannot deny himself. In fact, how does God uphold his own love, which is foremost God's love for himself within his eternal relations as the triune God? For God to remain true to his promises and true to himself, our justification demands that our sin be paid for in the death of a specific Redeemer, namely, God the Son incarnate. God himself, in his Son, must meet his own demand for us so that God can justify us by faith in him; yet the divine Son can only do so if he takes on our humanity and acts as our covenant representative and substitute. In the cross, we not only see God's love, grace, holiness, and justice on full display (Rom 3:21–26); we also see the significance of one's theology proper, specifically divine simplicity.[19]

3. Building on the previous example, divine simplicity also explains why some atonement theologies are less than theologically sound. For example, the "governmental theory" of the cross suggests that God is the ruler of the world, but it also suggests that God's moral law is only a function of his will and *not* an expression of his will tied to his nature. Thus, similar to a voluntarist and Socinian view, God can "relax" the demands of his moral law by an act of will. In other words, in God forgiving us of our sin, due to his "relaxed" demands, there is no necessity for God's moral demands to be fully satisfied, indeed paid in full, hence this theory's rejection of a penal substitutionary view of the atonement.

However, note how this view either denies or redefines simplicity. Instead of properly seeing that God's law is an expression of God's will *and* nature—God *is* holy, just, and righteous, and thus God *is* the law—the governmental view uncouples God's will from his nature. But simplicity reminds us that God *is* his attributes, and as the moral standard of the universe, nothing is "outside" of God that he conforms to. For this reason, God cannot

---

[19] For a development of this point, also see Stephen J. Wellum, *Christ Alone: The Uniqueness of Jesus as Savior* (Grand Rapids: Zondervan, 2017), 157–245. In volume 2, in our Christology section, we will develop the argument that what is at stake in atonement debates is fundamentally doctrine-of-God debates.

simply "relax" who he is or his holy demand against sin; God cannot deny himself. For God to justify us, God must provide a divine-human Redeemer who can represent us in his covenantal obedience, satisfying God's own moral demand against us as our substitute.[20] Again, what this illustration demonstrates is the *theological* significance of simplicity for understanding God's attributes.

Classical Theism and Classifying God's Attributes

Classical theism is the historic view of God identified with pro-Nicene trinitarian orthodoxy, Chalcedonian Christology, and the "Great Tradition."[21] In the West, it is associated with such theologians as Augustine, Thomas Aquinas, Anselm, the Reformers, and the post-Reformed tradition. It also includes various Baptist theologians, especially those identified with the *London Baptist Confession of Faith* (1689) and the *Abstract of Principles* (1858). As discussed in chapter 16, classical theism has been rejected by those outside of historic Christian theology (e.g., classic liberalism and postmodern panentheism) and from those within evangelical theology, such as open theism and some forms of Arminianism. From these diverse quarters, classical theism is criticized for not being "biblical" since, as the argument goes, it cannot account for God's loving and relational nature. In addition, many claim it is too dependent on Greek thought, thus the charge of the Hellenization of Christian theology. However, this latter charge is incorrect, as has been repeatedly demonstrated.[22]

Depending on the specific theologian, classical theism has sought to reflect rationally on God's attributes from Scripture *and* natural revelation. Given God's creation of the world, we know something of who God is by his created effects. The latter emphasis is often identified with *natural theology*, but as noted in chapter 6, there are different conceptions of natural theology. Historically, Christian theology has never sought to argue the nature of God from creation alone. It has always sought to interpret nature by the lens of Scripture: Scripture alone is our *final* authority in our theological formulations, which includes our theology proper. To

---

[20] See Wellum, *Christ Alone*, 173–92.

[21] See Carter, *Contemplating God* (see chap. 16, n. 93). For a definition of "pro-Nicene" trinitarianism, see chapter 19.

[22] See Gavrilyuk, *Suffering of the Impassible God*, 21–36 (see chap. 16, n. 93); Vanhoozer, *Remythologizing Theology*, 81–138 (see chap. 2, n. 131); Carter, *Contemplating God*, 15–46.

know God in a warranted way, we must ground our formulations in Scripture and all that God has revealed about himself across the entire canon. Yet this task is not completely divorced from what God has revealed about himself in creation.

For this reason, classical theism has employed three ways of thinking through natural *and* special revelation about God in our "faith seeking understanding": *via eminentiae* (by way of eminence; God is the most perfect being), *via causalitatis* (from effect to cause), and *via negationis* (by way of negation).[23] These three ways of reasoning about God are not contrary to Scripture; instead, they seek to understand the biblical teaching in light of what God has created. Obviously, one must exercise caution in one's use of these three ways. Scripture is our *final* authority; it alone warrants our conclusions. This is why our concept of perfection, omnipotence, and immutability must be true to Scripture and not merely the conclusion of rational reflection independent of Scripture. We must follow God's own description of himself in the unfolding drama of Scripture, yet this is never contrary to what God has revealed about himself in creation.

As these three ways are applied, by eminence, we unpack the biblical teaching that God is the "most perfect being," the Creator, not the creature, and that he is unique. As Scripture repeatedly reminds us: "'To whom will you compare me, / or who is my equal?' asks the Holy One" (Isa 40:25). Or, by causation, we know from Scripture that God is independent and self-sufficient, which allows us to say something about his simplicity and aseity. The universe is his creation; it did not create itself. God is the first cause from which all things come (Gen 1:1; Ps 100:3; John 1:1–3; Rom 11:33–36). Or, by negation, given that God alone is God, he is *not* like his creation since he has no imperfections. Repeatedly Scripture reminds us that God is not like us (Num 23:19; 1 Sam 15:29). Thus, if properly applied, these three ways helpfully allow us to reflect on Scripture as we think through God's being in all of its incomparable glory and majesty.

Furthermore, to grasp all that Scripture says about God's perfections, theologians have used various ways of classifying God's attributes.[24] For example, some have distinguished between God's "nature" attributes (e.g., simplicity, aseity, infinity, etc.) and "moral" attributes (e.g., love, holiness, goodness, etc.). The problem, however, with this classification system is that

---

[23] See Beeke and Smalley, *Reformed Systematic Theology*, 1:541–44 (see chap. 1, n. 8).

[24] See Storms, *Grandeur of God*, 39–45; Berkhof, *Systematic Theology*, 55–56 (see chap. 15, n. 63).

both sets of attributes constitute God's *nature*. Others distinguish between God's "absolute" attributes (e.g., attributes intrinsic to God) and "relative" attributes (e.g., attributes in relation to creation: creator, preserver, merciful). However, a helpful way of classifying God's attributes, often employed by the Reformed tradition, is to distinguish between God's "incommunicable" and "communicable" attributes. The former refers to attributes that God alone has that have no analogy in humans (e.g., simplicity, aseity, immutability, omniscience, omnipresence, etc.). The latter refers to attributes that God shares with his creatures (e.g., wisdom, righteousness, love, holiness) and in redemption by virtue of our regeneration by the Spirit, union with Christ, and our growth in grace.[25]

Although these classification systems differ, they have one thing in common. Each way of distinguishing God's attributes preserves the Creator-creature distinction and, by analogy, seeks to explain how God is like us and not like us. But, as John Frame cautions, even when we share something in common with God (i.e., communicable attributes), they are *not* shared equally![26] In this sense, *all* of God's attributes are incommunicable since God's holiness, love, goodness, and knowledge are unique (i.e., sui generis). For example, our love, at its best, is a faint image of God's love. God's love is identical to his essence and thus radically different from ours. Also, God is *not* merely quantitatively more holy; his holiness is qualitatively different! However, we classify God's attributes; we must preserve the Creator-creature distinction and the doctrine of analogy. God is not simply greater on a scale of being; God is utterly unique.

Our discussion of God's perfections will employ three categories: God's metaphysical, epistemological, and moral attributes.[27] Why? To emphasize that for Christian theology, in contrast to non-Christian worldviews, the proper—indeed the only ground for metaphysics, epistemology, and ethics—is the triune Creator-covenant Lord, a point we noted in chapter 17.

[25] Turretin, *Institutes of Elenctic Theology*, 1:190. This is important qualification. 2 Pet 1:4, "share in the divine nature" (*theias koinōnoi physeōs*) does not mean that we share God's essential nature, which is incommunicable to us, but that we share in him only by analogy due to our creation in God's image and re-creation in Christ (Col 3:10). In this sense, it refers to our regeneration, sanctification, and glorification. See Schreiner, *1, 2 Peter, Jude*, 293–96 (see chap. 4, n. 17).

[26] On this point, see Frame, *Doctrine of God*, 396 (see chap. 3, n. 13).

[27] This way of classifying God's attributes is indebted to Kevin Vanhoozer, who used it in his classes during my student days at Trinity Evangelical Divinity School. It also follows John Frame's development of God's self-contained nature and its importance for metaphysics, epistemology, and ethics. See Frame, *Doctrine of God*, 600–16.

Ultimately, all Christian theology is a reflection on the nature of God in himself and all things in relation to him. To underscore this point, we will employ these three categories to emphasize that our triune God is perfect in himself, and by his gracious choice and condescension, he has freely chosen to share himself with his creation, and especially his people.

Metaphysical Attributes of Our Triune Covenant Lord

Under this category, we will discuss attributes that entail an *absolute* distinction between God and humans. In many theologies, these attributes are classified as incommunicable since they underscore God's uniqueness, self-sufficiency, sovereignty, and lordship.

Independence-Aseity

We have briefly discussed the significance of divine aseity in chapter 17, related to God's absolute-personal nature as LORD (Exod 3:14).[28] There we noted that a biblical view of aseity is inseparable from God's triune nature as the one who has life *in* himself.[29] As Frame reminds us, our triune God is "self-contained fullness," which entails more than his self-existence since it also entails that God's knowledge and goodness are "from himself"; hence, God is the source and standard of existence, knowledge, and goodness. As Bavinck writes, "All that God is, he is of himself."[30] In many ways, everything we say about God's essence and attributes includes his aseity.

John Frame offers a helpful biblical argument for God's aseity.[31] By thinking through all that Scripture teaches, he makes the following four points. First, as Lord, God owns all things because he alone is God (Gen 14:19, 22; Exod 19:15; Deut 10:14; 1 Chron 29:11; Job 41:3; Pss 24:1; 50:10–12; 82:8; 89:11). Second, everything we have comes from God because of his free choice to create, rule, and provide for his creation (Exod 20:11; Neh 9:6; Ps 146:5–6; Jas 1:17). For this reason, God owes us nothing, and the only reason we have anything from him is due to his gracious choice to share himself with what he has made, tied to his covenant

---

[28] Aseity is from the Latin *a se*, which means that God has "life from himself."

[29] See Webster, *God without Measure*, 1:18–23 (see chap. 1, n. 6), who makes this point.

[30] Bavinck, *Reformed Dogmatics*, 2:151.

[31] See Frame, *Doctrine of God*, 603–8.

promises (Job 41:11; Luke 17:10; Acts 17:24–26; Rom 11:35–36). This is why when we give back to God, we give him only what he has first given us (Luke 12:42; 16:1–8; Titus 1:7). Third, building on these truths, Scripture teaches that God has no needs (Ps 50:8–15; Isa 40:19–20; cf. 41:7; 44:15–17; 46:6; Jer 10:3–5; Hab 2:18–20; Acts 17:24–30). Frame underscores this point by appealing to what Scripture teaches about worship. Unlike pagan worship, biblical worship does not meet the needs of God. Even in the sacrificial system, the purpose of the animal sacrifices was not to get God on our side; instead, the entire system was God-given to atone for human sin (Lev 17:11). The same is true regarding the foolishness of idolatry. Since the idol is dependent on its maker, it is silly for the maker to worship it. In contrast, Paul describes true worship: God is not worshipped because "he needs anything"; instead, God gives us "life, breath, all things" (Acts 17:25). Fourth, God is by nature *a se* (John 5:26; Rom 11:36). He needs nothing, but we need everything from him. In fact, Paul assumes this point in Gal 4:8–9, where he argues that those "who by nature are not gods" are not worthy of worship. By contrast, the true God deserves our worship because he is by nature self-existent and self-sufficient.

The importance of divine aseity for understanding the nature of God cannot be overstated. We can think of at least four points that underscore the significance of God's self-sufficiency.

First, divine aseity means that God's existence is grounded only in himself. God is the ground of his own being, and thus he needs nothing from us. However, we should not think of God's self-existence as "self-caused" (*causa sui*). Instead, as Bavinck reminds us, we should think of God "being from eternity to eternity who he is, being not becoming. God is absolute being, the fullness of being, and therefore also eternally and absolutely independent in his existence, in his perfections, in all of his works, the first and the last, the sole cause and final goal of all things."[32] Anselm captures this same point: "[God] alone has of himself all that he has, while other things have nothing of themselves. And other things, having nothing of themselves, have their only reality from him."[33]

Second, divine aseity reminds us that God did not create us because he was lonely or needed fellowship with other persons. This would imply that God needed to create us to be completely fulfilled in his existence. Rather, due to God's triune nature, God is self-sufficient.

---

[32] Bavinck, *Reformed Dogmatics*, 2:152. Webster, *God without Measure*, 1:22–23.

[33] Cited in Webster, *God without Measure*, 1:15.

In fact, as we have noted, divine aseity and the Trinity are organically related. "The life God has in himself is the relations of Father, Son, and Spirit."[34] Without creation, God would still be infinitely loving, just, eternal, omniscient, and so on (Exod 3:14; Ps 50:10–12; John 5:26; Acts 17:24–25; Rev 4:11). This is why the "God who comes to save the world (economic Trinity) is able to save only because he has no need of and is perfect independent of the world (immanent Trinity)."[35] Or, as John Webster reminds us, because God is perfect life from and within himself, "God's aseity, although it marks God's utter difference from creatures, does not entail his isolation, for what God is and has of himself is life, and that life includes a self-willed movement of love."[36]

Third, although God does not need us, the amazing truth is that we can glorify God and bring him joy. Although God has perfect life within himself, he has chosen to create us so that we would be meaningful to him (Isa 43:7; 62:3–5; Eph 1:11–12; Rev 4:11). But for us this entails that we will never understand the purpose of our existence apart from knowing God, and the attempt to do so will only result in futility and our inability to know ourselves!

In making these important points, we must still exercise caution. As we think about God's relation to his world, the creation has a real relationship to God; creation is dependent on God. However, we must not think that the creation's relation to God changes him.[37] Building on the classical tradition, Kevin Vanhoozer reminds us that "the only real relations that constitute God's eternal being are the *ad intra* trinitarian processions intrinsic to God's perfect life."[38] God does interact with his creatures, but these relations do not constitute God's being. Instead, as Vanhoozer continues, "It is precisely because God lacks nothing and needs nothing from the world that he can communicate his own good fullness to it. . . . The one who is present and active in human history is the one whose being is self-subsistent and wholly realized—perfect."[39]

---

[34] Vanhoozer, "Love without Measure?," 518 (see chap. 16, n. 50).

[35] Vanhoozer, 518; Webster, *God without Measure*, 1:23–27.

[36] Webster, *God without Measure*, 1:27.

[37] This is a controversial point. Aquinas argues that the relation is "real" (i.e., ontological) for the creature but only "conceptual" (i.e., notional) for God. Aquinas speaks of this as a "mixed relation" but not equal between God and the creation. See Webster, *God without Measure*, 1:115–26.

[38] Vanhoozer, "Love without Measure?," 522.

[39] Vanhoozer, 522–23.

Fourth, a corollary of aseity is God's infinite nature.[40] In theology and worldview discussion, the concept of infinity requires careful definition. As we apply this term to God positively, infinity suggests that God has qualities to the perfect degree. For example, God's holiness is the definition of what holiness is. Negatively, infinity means that there are no limitations on God's perfections. We can think of God's infinity expressed in a number of ways. God's being is infinite, absolute. In relation to time, he is eternal. In relation to space, he is immense, and to creation, he is omnipresent, a point we will discuss below.

Immutability

Aseity and immutability (i.e., God's *unchanging* nature) are inseparable. Our triune God has fullness of life within himself; he is *a se*. As such, God cannot change in his being, character, plans, and purposes since there is nothing outside of him that he depends on. Yet, although God does not need us, Scripture wondrously teaches, as Bavinck reminds us, "Without losing himself, God can give himself, and while absolutely maintaining his immutability, he can enter into an infinite number of relations to his creatures."[41] Both of these truths must be kept together to grasp all that Scripture teaches regarding God's immutability. Let us look at each of them in turn.

First, Scripture teaches that God is immutable in his nature, character, plans, and promises.

1. *God's nature is immutable*. God identifies himself as the eternal "I AM" (Exod 3:14), which entails his immutability. God will never be more powerful, knowing, loving, and holy. He is who he is and will always be (Deut 32:39; Ps 102:25–27; Mal 3:6; Heb 13:8; Jas 1:17). God is eternal and unchanging, the Alpha and the Omega, the first and the last (Isa 41:4; 43:10; 46:4; 48:12). He is incorruptible and alone immortal (Rom 1:23; 1 Tim 1:17; 6:16; Heb 1:11–12).

2. *God's character is immutable*. God can never become morally better or worse than he is (Mal 3:6; Jas 1:17). He will never be wiser or more loving; within him is fullness of life. God does not lie or repent; he is the absolute standard of moral perfection; and what God says he

[40] Bavinck, *Reformed Dogmatics*, 2:159–60.
[41] Bavinck, 2:159.

will do, he does (Num 15:28; 1 Sam 15:29). There is never a question that God cannot be trusted: God is unchanging in his character. Sam Storms states this well:

> If God could change (or become) in respect to His moral character, it would be either for the better or for the worse. If for the better, it would indicate that He had been morally imperfect or incomplete antecedent to the time of change, and hence never God. If for the worse, it would indicate that He is now morally less perfect or complete, i.e., subsequent to the time of change, and hence no longer God.[42]

3. *God's eternal plan and purposes are immutable* (Pss 33:10–11; 110:4; Isa 14:24; 46:8–11; Prov 19:21; Matt 13:35; 25:34; Eph 1:4, 11; 3:9, 11; 2 Tim 2:19; 1 Pet 1:20; Rev 13:8). As we will discuss in chapter 20, God's plan or decree is eternal and unconditional. Given this fact, the only way God could alter his plan is "(1) if He lacked the necessary foresight or knowledge to anticipate any and all contingencies; or, (2) assuming He had the needed foresight, He lacked the power or ability to effect what He had planned."[43] But in God's case, both conditions are not true. This does not mean that "changes" do not occur in God's plan as it unfolds in redemptive history. For example, the Mosaic covenant once governed the life of Israel, but now that Christ has ratified a new covenant, the old covenant is no longer in force *as a covenant*. However, this does not constitute a change in God's plan since God intended the temporary nature of the Mosaic covenant from eternity. These kinds of changes are simply the enactment in time of God's eternal decree; God's plan and purposes are immutable.

4. *God's promises are immutable* (Gen 3:15; 12:1–3; 2 Sam 7:8–16; Rom 11:1, 29; 2 Cor 1:20; Gal 3–4; Heb 6:16–18). Our God is the promise maker and keeper, a truth which is always tied to his covenant promises centered in Christ. Since God is unchanging, his promises are immutable; hence, we can trust him wholeheartedly. As our covenant God, he does what he promises, which is why each biblical covenant is undergirded by God's unilateral determination to keep his word (Ps 138:8; Phil 1:6).

As we reflect on the full scope of what Scripture teaches regarding God's immutability, classical, historic theology has spoken of God as "pure act" (*actus purus*). In the use of this

---

[42] Storms, *Grandeur of God*, 110–11.

[43] Storms, 111.

phrase, we must distinguish its theological use from its use in Greek thought. For Greek thought, "pure act" is impersonal, the "first mover," and thus a more static or impersonal concept. But in Christian theology, divine immutability speaks of God's fullness of life within himself, which is precisely why he cannot change.[44] Nothing outside of him can add to his glorious being since in himself, Father, Son, and Spirit are complete. Thomas Weinandy states it this way: "God is unchangeable not because he is inert or static like a rock, but for just the opposite reason. He is so dynamic, so active that no change can make him more active. He is act pure and simple."[45]

In fact, this is what distinguishes the Creator from the creature. All creation is in the process of becoming, but not God. God has life "in himself" and "from himself"; he does not change. Bavinck states it this way: "Becoming is an attribute of creatures, a form of change in space and time. But God is who he is, eternally transcendent over space and time and far exalted above every creature. He rests within himself and is for that very reason the ultimate goal and resting place of all creatures, the Rock of their salvation, whose work is complete."[46] However, if God truly is immutable, then how do we explain biblical language that seems to say that God changes in relation to his creatures? Let us answer this question by turning to the second point.

Second, many biblical texts seem to say that God changes in his interaction with creation. In our discussion of open theism, we noted how they appeal to these texts, especially texts that say God changes his mind to argue against God's immutability (e.g., Gen 6:6; Exod 32:10–14; 1 Sam 15:11, 35, etc.). After all, if God is immutable, why does Scripture speak this way? Although we addressed this issue in chapter 16, we offer three further reflections in order to account for what Scripture teaches regarding God's immutability *and* his interaction with his creation.

1. There are around thirty-five texts that say God "changes his mind." Yet, these texts do not overturn what Scripture teaches about God's immutability. For starters, as D. A. Carson notes, when one looks at these texts, much of God's repenting is *not* like human repenting, which requires us to interpret these texts carefully. For example, "human beings repent of

---

[44] See Bavinck, *Reformed Dogmatics*, 2:153–59; Berkhof, *Systematic Theology*, 59.

[45] Thomas G. Weinandy, *Does God Suffer?* (Notre Dame: University of Notre Dame Press, 2000), 79.

[46] Bavinck, *Reformed Dogmatics*, 2:158.

moral evil; God never does, since he performs no evil of which to repent. That is why most modern translations use words such as 'regret,' 'relent,' 'grieve over,' 'retract,' or the like."[47]

Moreover, as one looks at these texts, they are not all the same; thus, each text must be interpreted in its own context to determine what it is communicating. For example, "God can 'relent' over a step he has already taken (Gen. 6:6–7; 1 Sam. 15:11, 35). He may 'relent' over what he has said he would do or even started doing (Pss. 90:13; 106:44–45; Jer. 18:7–10; 26:3, 13, 19; Joel 2:13–14; Jon 3:9–10; 4:3), perhaps in response to the prayer of an intercessor (Exod. 32:12–14; Amos 7:3–6)."[48] But one cannot think of such prayer warriors, whether Moses or Amos, arising apart from God raising them up! To add to this observation, Scripture also teaches that unlike humans, God does *not* repent precisely because God is *not* like humans (Num 23:19; 1 Sam 15:29; Ps 110:4; Jer 4:28; 15:6; Ezek 24:14; Zech 8:14). And as we argued in chapter 16, in God's "repenting" that he made Saul king (1 Sam 15:11, 35), this was *after* he has already promised a coming king from Judah's line and not Benjamin's (Gen 49:10–12; Ruth 4:13–22), which means that God's "repentance" is utterly different than human repentance.

2. To reinforce the point that these "repentance" texts are not the same and that, if properly interpreted, they do not deny divine immutability, note how a number of these texts *presuppose* God's immutable nature, purposes, and promises! Jeremiah 18:7–10 is an example of this point. God seemingly "changes" his mind from "wrath to grace" in the case of Nineveh,[49] which does not please Jonah. But notice that God's "change" of mind in this context upholds immutability. Why? Because if God had destroyed Nineveh regardless of its repentance, he would have broken his promises and planned action in relation to sinners, thus showing himself to be mutable. For God to be immutable in his will, purposes, and promises, he must deal with us according to our actions. God's immutability requires that he acts consistent with the situation that exists, yet the change is on *our* side, not God's.

3. These texts also reflect the analogical nature of biblical language in reference to God. Historically, this has been the way to interpret these texts, and it is still the best option.[50] In fact, to do otherwise results in an inconsistent hermeneutic that, if one is not careful, undercuts

---

[47] Carson, *How Long O Lord?*, 197 (see chap. 4, n. 87).

[48] Carson, 197.

[49] See Storms, *Grandeur of God*, 114–16.

[50] For example, see Calvin, *Institutes*, 1.17.12 (1:225–27) (see chap. 1, n. 3).

the Creator-creature distinction. Anthropomorphic and anthropopathic descriptions are applied to God, but this language is analogical. When all of the biblical data is considered, we must affirm that God is immutable, yet from the fullness of his being, he relates to his creation without change to himself. The glory of our triune God is that he interacts with us, yet not in a way that he changes; we are the ones who change as he works out his eternal plan in history.

Third, in summary, in thinking about God's immutability, we must keep together the truth that God does not change but also that he interacts with his creation. Bavinck captures this point well: "There is change around, about, and outside of him, and there is change in people's relations to him, but there is no change in God himself."[51] Although God is immutable, eternal, and immeasurable in himself, he created us to relate to him, yet his nature, character, plan, and promises are immutable. God is able to give himself to us without losing himself. It is not easy to wrap our minds around these truths. Augustine illustrates them by appealing to the sun. The sun does not change, "whether it scorches or warms, hurts or animates."[52] Or Aquinas explains them by appealing to the concept of "mixed relations."[53] When we look at a fixed object, such as a pillar, on the side of my sense impressions, the relation is "real." Yet on the side of the pillar, it is not dependent on my sense of sight. Thus, the pillar remains the same "whether a person sees it on her right or on her left."[54] These illustrations are not perfect, yet they help us "make sense" of all that Scripture teaches about God's unchanging nature in relation to what he has created.

However, it is unhelpful to speak of God's unchanging nature ("ontological and ethical immutability") *and* his "relational mutability." No doubt, the reason for doing so is to uphold all of the biblical data. But to propose that, in God's relationship to the world, there is some kind of relational change *in* God is problematic.[55] Even if one affirms that these "real" changes

---

[51] Bavinck, *Reformed Dogmatics*, 2:158.

[52] Cited in Bavinck, 2:159.

[53] See Aquinas, *Summa Theologica*, pt. 1, q. 13, art. 7.

[54] Bavinck, *Reformed Dogmatics*, 2:159.

[55] See Bruce A. Ware, "An Evangelical Reformulation of the Doctrine of Immutability of God," *JETS* 29 (1986): 438–41. In fact, in *God's Greater Glory: The Exalted God of Scripture and the Christian Faith* (Wheaton: Crossway, 2004), Ware argues that post-fall, new qualities arose in God, such as anger, wrath, mercy, and grace, thus changing God forever (150–53). For a similar view, see Frame, *Doctrine of God*, 566–72. Frame affirms "Cambridge changes" vs. "real changes," which is consistent with the tradition. Then he says that not all changes in God are "Cambridge changes" since some "relational

do not change God's nature because he has ordained them before time, they still result in "real" change *within* God.[56] But how do these relational changes in God, then, not result in some kind of ontological change, especially if they result in "new qualities" within God? Furthermore, if God can will his own relational changes, then does this affect other attributes as well?[57] One must be careful that in trying to hold the biblical data together, one's understanding of biblical language does not slip into a univocal understanding versus a consistently analogical one.

The better formulation is the classical view, which upholds a consistent use of analogical language and rejects the idea of "relational" changes *within* God. Steven Duby represents this view by upholding God's unchanging nature *and* his interaction with creation. He writes: "If God's all-knowing, all-wise decree actively anticipates all the turnings of creaturely life and history, then it is appropriate to say that God does not change in relation to his creatures; rather, his creatures change in relation to him and begin accordingly to experience his constant holiness and love in different ways."[58] This allows us to affirm that creatures do not change God, but creatures change in relation to God, who is fullness of life within himself and who has ordained every detail of history. As God's plan unfolds, and when creatures act in different ways before God, there is change on the side of the creature, but not on the side of God. In relation to the world God has created, he remains who he has always been.

With this understanding, there is no need to say that the creation changes God; this creates more problems than it solves. Instead, as Augustine argued many years ago, God "makes changeable things without any change in [himself], and creates temporal things without any

changes" are "real" for God due to his "temporal omnipresence." For Frame, God exists in two modes: an atemporal existence in which he does not change, and a temporal existence in which he does change. In fact, Frame argues that God "views the passing of time as a process, *just as we do*" (571, emphasis mine). Frame does not consistently employ an analogical understanding; instead, at least in this context, he slips into a univocal understanding. The classical view is better: God is present in every moment of time and he only has one mode of existence. God does not need two different modes of existence to interact with creation.

[56] See Rob Lister, *God Is Impassible and Impassioned: Toward a Theology of Divine Emotion* (Wheaton: Crossway, 2012), 33, 167–68, 179.

[57] Dolzeal makes this point. See Dolezal, *All That Is in God*, 25.

[58] Steven J. Duby, "A Biblical and Theological Case for Divine Simplicity," in *The Lord is One: Reclaiming Divine Simplicity*, ed. Joseph Minich and Onsi A. Kamel (Leesburg: Davenant Press, 2019), 52.

temporal movement [in himself]."[59] The God who is fullness of life and unchanging creates a world he relates to but without change in himself. As Joel Beeke and Paul Smalley summarize, "God does relate to this world in love and mercy, wrath and judgment, and holy jealousy or zeal for the glory of his name (Ex. 34:6–7, 14). Yet these divine affections are manifestations at various points in time of God's eternal, immutable will, not a shifting pattern of oscillation or alteration in God himself."[60]

Impassibility

In historic theology, an important entailment of God's simplicity, aseity, and immutability is God's *impassibility*; that is, God is "without passions" (Gk. *apatheia*), or he cannot suffer. Divine impassibility has been consistently affirmed from the patristic era to our own, although recently, modern/postmodern theology has questioned its validity due to an embrace of social-relational views of God and especially more panentheistic conceptions of the God-world relationship.[61] One of the challenges raised is how to reconcile God's impassibility with biblical language about God's compassion, mercy, patience, rejoicing, pleasure, love, wrath, and jealousy. The charge is that classical theism has imbibed Greek thought, as we noted in our discussion of open theism (chapter 16). In addition, in recent discussion, impassibility is rejected because many think it renders the problem of evil more difficult.[62] If God is impassible, how does he care for us and identify with us in our suffering? Let us discuss divine impassibility in two steps: first, by describing various denials or the redefinition of impassibility and, second, by offering some reflections on what divine impassibility is and why we should continue to affirm it.

First, in the current discussion, there are at least three different reactions to impassibility that result in either a rejection or redefinition of it.[63]

---

[59] Augustine, *The Trinity* 1.1.3 (5–6).

[60] Beeke and Smalley, *Reformed Systematic Theology*, 1:706.

[61] Beeke and Smalley, 1:834. Impassibility has been affirmed by the Church Fathers, as well as Augustine, Anselm, Aquinas, the Reformed Confessions (e.g., *WCF* 2.1), and the *London Baptist Confession* (1689) (2.1).

[62] On this point, see Vanhoozer, *Remythologizing Theology*, 89–105.

[63] See Robert J. Matz and A. Chadwick Thornhill, *Divine Impassibility: Four Views of God's Emotions and Suffering* (Downers Grove: IVP Academic, 2019).

1. Process/panentheism, along with various social-relational views of God, rejects divine impassibility. In fact, consistent panentheistic views not only reject impassibility, but also divine aseity, simplicity, and immutability. These views redefine the Creator-creature distinction and, correspondingly, the God-world relationship. For them, the world is "in" God and God is a fellow sufferer with the world.[64]

2. Although open theism, Arminian theology, and "moderate classical theism" uphold the Creator-creature distinction, each of these views opts for a more social-relational view of God that makes God vulnerable in creating us with libertarian freedom. These views either deny or redefine divine simplicity, aseity, immutability, and impassibility.[65]

3. Some within Reformed, evangelical theology strongly affirm God's sovereignty and ontological immutability but claim that, in creating us, God has willed relational changes (i.e., relational mutability) that also involve changed emotional states.[66] This last option is closer to the historic view since it preserves God's sovereignty and embraces a qualified divine impassibility, yet, as noted in our discussion of immutability, this view is problematic if it results in some kind of relational change or the addition of "new qualities" *in* God.

Second, what is our response to these challenges? Should we reject, or minimally, redefine divine impassibility, or should we affirm what historic theology has consistently affirmed? Three points need to be made to affirm the historic view of divine impassibility as the best view.[67]

---

[64] Jürgen Moltmann, *The Crucified God* (London: SCM Press, 1974); Fretheim, *Suffering of God* (see chap. 16, n. 76); Fretheim, *God and World in the Old Testament: A Relational Theology of Creation* (Nashville: Abingdon Press, 2005); cf. John Polkinghorne, ed., *The Work of Love: Creation as Kenosis* (Grand Rapids: Eerdmans, 2001); Philip Clayton, *Adventures in the Spirit: God, World, Divine Action* (Minneapolis: Fortress, 2008); Robert W. Jenson, *Systematic Theology*, vol. 1 (see chap. 16, n. 29).

[65] See chapter 16 for the literature on open theism. For a "moderate classical theism," see John C. Peckham, *Divine Attributes: Knowing the Covenantal God of Scripture* (Grand Rapids: Baker Academic, 2021). Arminian theology is more difficult to categorize since classical Arminianism is more classical than current forms of Arminianism. On this point, see Thomas H. McCall and Keith D. Stanglin, *After Arminius: A Historical Introduction to Arminian Theology* (Oxford: Oxford University Press, 2021).

[66] Frame, *Doctrine of God*, 571, 609–11; Ware, "An Evangelical Reformulation," 440–41; Lister, *God Is Impassible and Impassioned*, 36, 150, 254.

[67] See the helpful discussion of divine impassibility in the following: Weinandy, *Does God Suffer?*; Gavrilyuk, *Suffering of the Impassible God*; Vanhoozer, *Remythologizing Theology*, 387–468; and Steven

1. We must first understand the historic view of impassibility. Two points are necessary to grasp what the historic view is. First, we must distinguish between "passions" and "affections."[68] Today, as Joel Beeke and Paul Smalley note, *passion* refers to any strong emotions or commitment, but historically this was not the use of the term.[69] In theology, *passion* was identified with *pathos*, which is tied to "inordinate affections" (e.g., sensual appetites, fear, anxiety, etc.) and "suffering," something inappropriate for God.[70] For this reason, classical theism has denied that God experiences "passions" in this way since God is never anxious, inwardly troubled, compulsive, and so on. God is not like us; he is impassible.

Second, and building on the first point, *passion* "implies experiencing an outside influence passively as it acts upon a person to change his life."[71] For this reason, the term was only applied to creatures or to finite "gods" who were susceptible to various mood swings as they were affected by the will of others. However, God is eternal, self-sufficient, and immutable. "Passions" are different from "affections." Affections are voluntary acts of the will, while passions are involuntary as they act upon us, thus rendering us passive. God has "affections," but he is "impassible"; God cannot be acted on. Thus, to affirm God's impassibility does not mean that God is not active or that he does not have affections: indeed, God is always active, but he is never passive.[72] Muller rightly describes the classical view: "The exclusion of 'passions' from the divine being never implied the absence of 'affections.'"[73] God loves, laughs (Ps 2:4–5), grieves over sin (Gen 6:6), and so forth, thus displaying a range of affections (Hos 11:8–9). Indeed, our historic confessional statements

---

J. Duby, *Jesus and the God of Classical Theism: Biblical Christology in Light of the Doctrine of God* (Grand Rapids: Baker Academic, 2022), 315–74.

[68] See Muller, *Post-Reformation Reformed Dogmatics*, 3:551–61; Beeke and Smalley, *Reformed Systematic Theology*, 1:838–40; Vanhoozer, *Remythologizing Theology*, 398–412. Sometimes "affections" are equated with "emotions," but since "emotions" today carry strong psychological overtones, we must define "emotions" carefully. On this point, see Thomas Dixon, *From Passions to Emotions: The Creation of a Secular Psychological Category* (Cambridge: Cambridge University Press, 2003).

[69] For a discussion of the historical use of "pathos," see Duby, *Jesus and the God of Classical Theism*, 326–30.

[70] Beeke and Smalley, *Reformed Systematic Theology*, 1:838.

[71] Beeke and Smalley, 1:839.

[72] See Vanhoozer, *Remythologizing Theology*, 400–4.

[73] Muller, *Post-Reformation Reformed Dogmatics*, 3:33.

reflect this truth: the same statements that affirm God's impassibility also speak of his affections.[74]

2. What does divine impassibility deny if not God's affections? It is this: God is *not* capable of being acted on from without or subjected to suffering imposed by an external force. In other words, God is not conditioned or dependent on the world for his emotional states. Although God relates to the world, he does not undergo successive, fluctuating emotional states that allow him to experience loss or growth in himself.[75] As the triune God, he is complete within himself. From eternity, he has always had fullness of divine life, love, and affections that never fluctuate: he alone has life and immortality.[76] This is why God's affections never need to be activated. Thus, divine impassibility positively affirms that the Father, Son, and Holy Spirit are impassible not because they are devoid of holy love but because they are constituted by their fully actualized relations of holy love. Thomas Weinandy nicely captures this truth: it is "precisely *because* [God] is impassible he is nonetheless loving and kind . . . *only* an impassible God, and not a passible God, is truly and fully personal, absolutely and utterly loving, and thoroughly capable of interacting with human persons in time and history."[77]

---

[74] For example, the *London Baptist Confession* (1689) states (2.1):

> The Lord our God is but one only living and true God; whose subsistence is in and of Himself, infinite in being and perfection; whose essence cannot be comprehended by any but Himself; *a most pure spirit, invisible, without body, parts, or passions*, who only hath immortality, dwelling in the light which no man can approach unto; who is immutable, immense, eternal, incomprehensible, almighty, every way infinite, most holy, most wise, most free, most absolute; working all things according to the counsel of His own immutable and most righteous will, for His own glory; *most loving, gracious, merciful, long-suffering, abundant in goodness and truth, forgiving iniquity, transgression, and sin; the rewarder of them that diligently seek Him, and withal most just and terrible in His judgments, hating all sin, and who will by no means clear the guilty*. (emphasis mine)

[75] Job 35:5–7 states this truth in this way: "Look at the heavens and see; / gaze at the clouds high above you. / If you sin, how does it affect God? / If you multiply your transgressions, what does it do to him? / If you are righteous, what do you give him, / or what does he receive from your hand?"

[76] Hugh Martin states is this way: "The blessedness of God! It is a great deep, it is a dazzling bright abyss. We can look into it only as with shaded eye. . . . The blessedness of God! It is the result of His possession of all perfections. . . . Inviolable repose and unhindered activity. . . . In him is no dark, no gloom, no shadow." "God's Blessedness and His Statutes," in *The Atonement: In Its Relations to the Covenant, the Priesthood, the Intercession of Our Lord* (London: James Nisbet & Co., 1870), 283–84.

[77] Weinandy, *Does God Suffer?*, 37–38.

When we think of God in his external works (*ad extra*), we cannot divorce God's affections from his will, knowledge, and power. If God chooses to create and share his love with us, it is due to his eternal plan. As we will discuss in chapter 20, God's eternal decree/plan includes created effects that begin in creation and unfold in history. In creating humans and allowing for human sin, God is not caught by surprise, and when sin occurs, the fullness of his being as the Holy One stands in opposition to it as expressed by divine wrath and a diverse range of affections. However, we must not think that God has changed or that his emotional states are conditioned by our actions. In planning all things from eternity, including our creation, sin, and salvation, his response to these effects is not passive but active. His entire being acts as the unchanging God to the change in us, not him. In holy love, he creates the world and shares himself with it. In our sin, he displays his same holy love, which shows itself in wrath and holy justice against all that opposes him. God is zealous for his own name and glory, which has always been the case. In grace, God graciously brings his people to repentance and faith, and his unchanging holy love is experienced by us in covenant relationship. God has affections, but he is not conditioned by the world. He sustains no "passion" that makes him vulnerable from the outside over which he has no control or which he has not foreseen. God does not become more holy or more loving in response to his creation; he *is* holy and he *is* love in absolute perfection. God is not indifferent to the world. Instead, God's action towards the world flows "from his eternal will outward to change the world, not from the world to change him."[78]

This is why we must consistently read biblical language about God analogically: God is not like us, which is good news! A God who is passible and suffers may sympathize with us, but he cannot help us. A God who is subject to emotional change raises doubt as to whether he can be trusted. In fact, it is only by affirming impassibility that we have hope. God is perfect in himself. His love is not constituted by the world, but within himself. God remains true to himself, and his love and grace are free. In his creation of the world, he does not change, but relates to the world according to his sovereign will and covenant promises to redeem a people for himself, which actually guarantees that he can do something to redeem us.

3. In thinking about divine impassibility, we should not allow any of this discussion to diminish the fact that God the Son took on our humanity and, in that humanity,

---

[78] Beeke and Smalley, *Reformed Systematic Theology*, 1:840.

experienced *human* suffering and emotions. However, this does not mean that the divine nature became passible.[79] As Scripture affirms and Chalcedon confesses, the *Word* became flesh (John 1:1, 14), not the divine nature or the other divine persons. The divine Son assumed a human nature that allowed him to live a fully human life and to experience suffering *as a man*. Yet the Son's two natures were not blended; the Son was not limited by his human nature since *he* continued to live and act in his divine nature. But "thanks to his humanity, then, the Son is able to 'feel' time. Such, I submit, is the implication of the *communicatio idiomatum*: the temporal experiences of Jesus Christ are to be assigned neither to an abstract human nature, nor to the divine nature, but rather to a divine person (viz., the Son) in his human mode of existence."[80] This is why the church has affirmed that in Christ, the impassible suffered. In our Lord Jesus Christ, the divine Son and our sovereign Lord died, but without change.[81]

Eternality

God's eternality does *not* simply mean that God is everywhere in time, as significant as this truth is. Instead, to say God is eternal is to affirm that our triune God transcends the very limitations of time: he is the absolute-infinite God in relation to time. This is why God is not subject to time; he has neither a beginning nor an end (Exod 3:14; Deut 33:27; Pss 90:2–4; 93:2; 102:12, 27; Isa 40:28; 41:4; 57:15; Rom 1:23; 1 Tim 1:16–17; 6:15–16; Rev 1:4, 8; 4:8–10). We may define God's eternity as "that perfection of God whereby he is elevated above all temporal limits and all succession of moments, and possesses the whole of his existence in one indivisible present."[82]

---

[79] See the helpful discussion in Duby, *Jesus and the God of Classical Theism*, 363–74.

[80] Vanhoozer, *Remythologizing Theology*, 425. We will discuss these points more in volume 2. The *communicatio idiomatum* affirms that what is true of each nature is true of the person. So, the Son, in his human nature, lived a full human life, and in his divine nature, he continued to experience his eternal divine life; hence, the divine nature did not change. What is also affirmed is the *extra*; i.e., due to the incarnation, the Son subsists in two natures, but *he*, as the Son, is not limited by his human nature since *he* continues to subsist in his divine nature and act "outside" (*extra*) of his human nature.

[81] On this point, see Weinandy, *Does God Suffer?*, 199–206.

[82] Berkhof, *Systematic Theology*, 60.

Trying to make sense of God's eternity is difficult; we are finite, space-time creatures who are limited in our thoughts and language. Scripture communicates to us something about God's eternality by saying that the number of God's years are unsearchable (Job 36:26) or that 1,000 years are nothing to him (Ps 90:4; 2 Pet 3:8). In the end, we must affirm that God transcends time and is not measured by it. He has no beginning, no end, and no "succession of moments."[83] For creatures, everything we know of these things is tied to the creation of the world of space and time, but God transcends these things. As Augustine wrestled with the exact nature of time,[84] time is best conceptualized as a "mode of existence" tied to creation.[85] Since God is from eternity and time is tied to creation, God is not in the process of becoming. God is the LORD, the eternal one (Exod 3:14; John 8:58).

Historically, theologians have conceptualized God's eternality in two ways: God's timeless eternity or his everlastingness, with divine timelessness being the predominant view.[86] Timeless eternality affirms that God is "outside" of time (e.g., Boethius, Aquinas, Calvin). On this view, God does not exist "in" time; there is simply no temporal location or duration in the life of God since he does not undergo any temporal succession. In other words, there is no past, present or future in God's own unique form of existence throughout the entirety of time; he exists wholly outside time, in the fullness of his eternal life.[87]

Usually some clarifications are given to explain God's timelessness. First, timelessness does not mean that God cannot distinguish where time is *in relation to us*. God always knows what time it is in *human* history. Instead, timelessness means that God "sees" the whole of time at once, and he sees it all at every moment. Second, timelessness does not mean that God cannot relate to time. God is not eternally static. He has fullness of life. As Bavinck explains: "Not only is God eternal; he is his own eternity. . . . God's eternity does not stand, abstract and transcendent, above time, but is present and immanent in every moment of time."[88] The advantage of this conception of God's eternality is that it accounts for biblical teaching that

---

[83] Bavinck, *Reformed Dogmatics*, 2:162.

[84] See Augustine, *Confessions* 11.14 (263–64).

[85] Bavinck, *Reformed Dogmatics*, 2:162.

[86] For a range of views on God's eternality and relation to time, see Gregory E. Ganssle, ed. *God and Time: Four Views* (Downers Grove: InterVarsity Pres, 2001).

[87] Boethius, *The Consolation of Philosophy* 5; Aquinas, *Summa Theologica*, pt. 1, q. 10, art. 1.

[88] Bavinck, *Reformed Dogmatics*, 2:163.

God is Lord over time. God is not a temporal being like us. Time has a way of "controlling" us, but not God.[89]

However, in recent days, some have rejected the concept of God's timeless eternity and replaced it with the idea of God's "everlastingness."[90] This latter view is *temporal* in orientation: God has always and always will exist, but his existence is temporally infinite in duration, unbounded in the past and future. There is in the life of God a past, present, and future, similar to the life of creatures, but unlike any of his creatures, God is everlasting, and necessarily so. Even though this conception of God's eternity "makes sense" to us since it allows us to think of God in terms of what we "know" of time, it is problematic to place God "in time." Usually, such a view entails a redefinition of divine aseity, immutability, impassibility, and so on.

Still others attempt to offer a "middle" option (via media) and speak of God's transcendence and immanence in relation to time parallel to God's relation to space. In this "middle" way, God transcends all spatial limitations and locations; hence, he is fully present (omnipresent), which is then applied to time. God transcends all temporal limitations but is fully present at every point of time in the fullness of his being.[91] Yet some conceptions of this, especially John Frame's formulation, seem to go further. Frame argues that God has two different "modes of existence" in relation to time and space. In his transcendence, his mode of existence is "atemporal," but in his immanence, he is "temporal." God exists *in* time as he exists *throughout* creation. But God also exists *beyond* time as he exists *beyond* creation. For Frame, it is not a choice between a "temporal" vs. "atemporal" view. Instead, it is a "both/and" so that as a result of creation, God now has two different "modes of existence,"[92] and as a result, God is even able to take on new properties.

Obviously, God's relation to time and space is not easy to conceive. Yet both "everlasting" notions of God's eternality and Frame's formulation are problematic. Thinking of the latter,

---

[89] For an exposition and defense of God's atemporality, see Paul Helm, *Eternal God* (Oxford: Clarendon Press, 1988); Helm, "Divine Timeless Eternity," in Ganssle, *God and Time*, 28–60.

[90] See the essays by William L. Craig and Nicholas Wolterstorff in Ganssle, *God and Time*, 129–60, 187–213.

[91] For example, see Frame, *Doctrine of God*, 553–59, 570–73; Erickson, *God the Father Almighty*, 114–40, 271–77 (see chap. 16, n. 90).

[92] See Frame, *Doctrine of God*, 558–59, 570–73. Also see Lister, *God Is Impassible and Impassioned*, 225–31.

Frame is not content to appeal to analogical language alone.[93] Furthermore, God's existence in two modes is hard to conceptualize. Beeke and Smalley state their concern this way: "It postulates a change in God's being when he created the world" and reads into the being of God "creaturely qualities when he created the world."[94] As difficult as these ideas are, the classical way is still best. God's eternal being and existence is such that he is able to relate to time without adding "properties" to his nature and changing the fullness of his triune being. Transcendence and immanence are helpful, but the idea of two different modes of existence is unnecessary. Creation is an eternal act of God that produces a temporal effect. However, as a result of creation, God is not now located "in" time; instead, he transcends what he has made, yet he can be immediately present to his creation. In addition, creation's absolute beginning is not a moment that follows a previous moment since time (and space) begins with creation, not prior to it. As Steven Duby notes, God's decretive act is "not located in the distant past; instead, its only temporal dimension is its execution, which takes place concurrently with the life and activity of creatures."[95] Or, as Bavinck states,

> God is the eternal One: in him there is neither past or future, neither becoming or change. All that he is is eternal: his thought, his will, his decree. Eternal in him is the idea of the world that he thinks and utters in the Son; eternal in him is also the decision to create the world; eternal in him is the will that created the world in time; eternal is also the act of creating as an act of God, an action both internal and immanent. For God did not *become* Creator, so that first for a long time he did not create and then afterward he did create. Rather he is the eternal Creator, and as Creator he was the Eternal One, and as the Eternal One he created. The creation therefore brought about no change in God.[96]

---

[93] Frame, *Doctrine of God*, 571: In reference to God's actions in time, he writes, "In my view, this is more than just anthropomorphic description. In these accounts, God is not merely *like* an agent in time; he really is *in* time, changing as others change. And we should not say that his atemporal, changeless existence is more real than his changing existence in time, as the term *anthropomorphic* might suggest. Both are real."

[94] Beeke and Smalley, *Reformed Systematic Theology*, 1:682.

[95] Steven J. Duby, "'For I Am God, Not a Man': Divine Repentance and the Creator-Creature Distinction," *Journal of Theological Interpretation* 12, no. 2 (2018): 157.

[96] Bavinck, *Reformed Dogmatics*, 2:429.

In the end, as finite creatures, we will never fully understand God's eternality, yet we must preserve a clear Creator-creature distinction in thinking about God's relation to time, which the classical view does better than its alternatives.

Immensity-Omnipresence

Due to creation, time and space are organically related, created realities that are best viewed as modes of existence. Since both are tied to creation, our triune Creator, who is eternal, *a se*, and self-sufficient, transcends both. Just as God is not "in" time, he also is not "in" space as if he were "somewhere." Instead, God is the Lord who is everywhere present.

Theologians use two words to refer to God's relation to space. The first word is "immensity"; that is, God is "without measure." It is a concept that applies to God alone and God within himself (*ad intra*), regardless of whether he created a world. It reminds us that God "transcends all space and location";[97] he is "not subject to its limitations."[98] Or, as Augustine wonderfully stated it: "Before God created heaven and earth, where did He dwell? . . . God dwelt in Himself, he dwelt with Himself, and God is with Himself."[99] The second word is "omnipresence." It communicates God's relation to the world he created. Instead of viewing God as "located" outside of space, it conveys the truth that God's entire being is simultaneously everywhere so that he fills every part of space. Immensity, then, speaks of God's transcendence, while omnipresence speaks of God's immanence. As Beeke and Smalley rightly summarize, "Taken together, God's immensity and omnipresence mean that all of God is in every place; he indwells creation fully and completely."[100]

Wayne Grudem offers a helpful definition of *omnipresence* that captures well the biblical teaching and even hints at some of the marvelous applications of the truth to our lives. He writes that omnipresence means that "God does not have size or spatial dimensions and is present at every point of space with his whole being, yet God acts differently in different places."[101] Let us develop this definition and draw some application of it for our lives by offering *six* points.

---

[97] Bavinck, *Reformed Dogmatics*, 2:167.

[98] Berkhof, *Systematic Theology*, 61.

[99] Augustine, *Expositions on the Book of Psalms* (*NPNF*[1], 8:597),

[100] Beeke and Smalley, *Reformed Systematic Theology*, 1:652.

[101] Grudem, *Systematic Theology*, 206 (see chap. 1, n. 14).

First, God is present everywhere with his whole being, not merely according to his operation. This is in contrast to deism, which only affirms God's presence by operation from a distance on the world. Rather, Scripture teaches God's entire being is present everywhere. We simply cannot think of God in spatial terms; God is present with his whole being in every part of space (Acts 17:28; Col 1:17).[102] David reminds us of this truth when he asks, "Where can I go to escape your Spirit? / Where can I flee from your presence? / If I go up to heaven, you are there; / if I make my bed in Sheol, you are there. / If I fly on the wings of the dawn / and settle down on the western horizon, / even there your hand will lead me; / your right hand will hold on to me" (Ps 139:7–10; cf. Jer 23:23–24).

Second, although God is wholly present in his entire being (Acts 17:28), he is also distinct from all things; that is, he is transcendent, in contrast to the view of pantheism and panentheism. As Storms reminds us, "It does not follow that because God is essentially *in* everything that everything *is* essentially God."[103] For example, "Pantheism asserts that God minus the world = 0; theism asserts that God minus the world = God. The universe is the creation of God and thus, in respect to essence, not part of Him. The creation is ontologically other than God, a product *ex nihilo* of the divine will, not an extension of the Divine Being itself."[104]

Third, God's presence "throughout the whole of space is not by local diffusion, multiplication, or distribution. Being wholly spirit, God is not subject to the laws of matter such as extension and displacement. He cannot be divided or separated such that one part of his being is here and not there, and another part there and not here."[105] God's entire triune being is simultaneously everywhere; God is not contained by space. In his building of the temple, Solomon acknowledges this point. Although God will uniquely "dwell" in the Holy of Holies, we must not think that God is contained by this space: "But will God indeed live on earth? / Even heaven, the highest heaven, cannot contain you, / much less this temple I have built" (1 Kgs 8:27; cf. Isa 66:1–2; Acts 17:24, 28).

Of course, related to this truth is the fact that God is *spirit* (John 4:24; cf. Luke 24:36–40; Acts 17:29), a truth we discussed in relation to God's simplicity. God's nature is immaterial,

---

102 Charnock, *Existence and Attributes of God*, 1:371–73.

103 Storms, *Grandeur of God*, 88.

104 Storms, 88.

105 Storms, 89; cf., Charnock, *Existence and Attributes of God*, 1:373–75.

not material; he has no form or body. Related to this truth is God's *invisibility* (John 1:18; cf. 6:46; Rom 1:20; Col 1:15; 1 Tim 1:17; 6:16; 1 John 4:12, 20). God in his essence will never be able to be seen by us; we only "see" God by his self-revelation through visible, created things (John 1:18; 1 Tim 1:17; 6:16; 1 John 4:12).

Fourth, "whereas the presence of a body in *a* place of space excludes the simultaneous and in all ways identical presence of another body in the same place of space, such is not true of the Divine Being. God *is*, in the whole of His being, *where* everything else *is* (including matter)."[106] In other words, the world was not spatially displaced by God's presence as if both cannot exist "in" the same space. Storms explains this idea well: "When God created all things out of nothing, He did not have to 'move out of the way' to make room for the world. He is where it is."[107] The Creator and the creation are not in competition with each other to take up space! Before creation, God in his immensity is not subject to space and location, and after his creation, *he* is everywhere without limit.

Fifth, biblical language in reference to God's relation to space is analogical. To forget this point means that we will misunderstand what Scripture teaches. For example, when the Spirit "indwells" Christians, this is not a denial of his omnipresence (Rom 8:11; John 14:23; Eph 2:22; 3:17; Col 1:27). Moreover, descriptions of the Spirit "descending" at Pentecost (Acts 2:17), or "falling on" believers (Acts 10:44–48), or even texts that refer to "heaven" as the place where God dwells (Deut 26:15; Pss 11:4; 33:13–14; 115:3) are not to be understood as "locating" God in a space. Two points are crucial for thinking through the Bible's use of analogical language in these areas.

1. The portrayal of God "in heaven" is not denying God's presence on the earth or anywhere else. Given what Scripture teaches about God's omnipresence, these descriptions emphasize God's *ontological* and *ethical* transcendence in relation to creation. It is God's holiness that is emphasized, both metaphysically and morally.[108] Alternatively, when God is described as present in the narrative, we must not think that he is limited by space, time, or creaturely freedom as open theism does. Instead, such a description is referring to God's interaction with creation as the God who also transcends all space and time.

---

[106] Storms, *Grandeur of God*, 89.

[107] Storms, 89.

[108] See Charnock, *Existence and Attributes of God*, 1:385–87.

2. Although biblical language about God is analogical, it also communicates the truth that the omnipresent God is present *in different ways in different places*, depending on the context. For example, sometimes God is present to punish (Amos 9:1–4), while he is constantly present in preserving and sustaining the universe (Acts 17:28; Col 1:17; Heb 1:3). Yet Scripture never speaks about God's presence in unbelievers in a direct way, thus reminding us that God is not responsible for our sinful choices. However, for God's people, whether OT or NT, God is present in covenant relationship and blessing (1 Sam 4:4; Exod 25:22; Matt 18:20). Thus, to be "far" from God (Eph 2:13) does not mean spatially distant but spiritually and covenantally separate from God. When God reconciles us and brings us "near" to the Father by the Son and in the Spirit, this does not require a journey, but repentance and faith (cf. Isa 57:15; 59:2; Prov 15:29; Eph 2:11–22; Heb 10:19–22).[109]

3. The same is true in reference to biblical language referring to God's invisibility/visibility. In Scripture we only "see" God due to his self-revelation through visible, created means, such as in theophanies; we do not see God's essence or spiritual being (Gen 18:1–33; 32:28–30; Exod 13:21–22; 24:9–11; Judg 13:21–22). In fact, when people see an outward manifestation of God, it is always hedged (Exod 33:11, 20–23). For example, Isaiah enters the temple and "sees" God, but it is only the "hem" of his garment; instead, what he sees is more the throne room of heaven (Isa 6). The same is true of Ezekiel (Ezek 1) or John (Rev 4). However, Scripture is also clear that in the incarnation of the divine Son, we now "see" God in and through him (John 1:14–18). But even here, we do not see God in his total being or essence. We come face to face with God in Christ, but we "see" God through Christ's humanity (John 14:9).

In discussions of eschatology, there has been much reflection on the "beatific vision."[110] The question is, What does Scripture mean when it says that we will "see" God in the eschaton (Matt 5:8; 1 Cor 13:12; Heb 12:14; 1 John 3:1–3; Rev 2:3–4)? Many have argued that in our glorified state, we will be able to see God without the mediation of created effects, yet since God is spirit and invisible, this "seeing" is not a physical vision. Instead, it is more of an intellectual vision due to God's grace that elevates our intellect and enables us to know God intuitively. In our glorification, God graciously and supernaturally enables us to understand beyond our natural abilities so that by this intellectual and intuitive vision, we are enabled

---

[109] See Charnock, 1:387–89.

[110] A more in-depth discussion of the beatific vision will be reserved for volume 2.

to see God in his essence. Nevertheless, we will never be able to comprehend all that God is.[111] Bavinck captures this point well: "Humanity's blessedness indeed lies in the 'beatific vision of God,' but this vision will always be such that finite and limited human nature is capable of it."[112] Yet, whatever the precise nature of the beatific vision is, we certainly know that we will experience the fullness of God's presence and see God with our eyes as we gaze on the glory of the God the Son in his glorified humanity, and it will be far greater than we can imagine.[113]

Sixth, the application of the truth of God's omnipresence to our lives is manifold, but we will apply it in terms of a warning, consolation and comfort, and an incentive to holiness.

Stephen Charnock first captures the application of God's omnipresence to warn us:

> How terrible should the thoughts of this attribute be to sinners! How foolish is it, to imagine any hiding-place from the incomprehensible God, who fills and contains all things, and is present in every point of the world. When men have shut the door, and made all darkness within, to meditate or commit a crime, they cannot in the most intricate recesses be sheltered from the presence of God. If they could separate themselves from their own shadows, they could not avoid his company, or be obscured from his sight. Hypocrites cannot disguise their sentiments from him; he is in the most secret nook of their hearts. No thought is hid, no lust is secret, but the eye of God beholds this, and that, and the other. He is present with our heart when we imagine, with our hands when we act. We may exclude the sun from peeping into our solitudes, but not the eyes of God from beholding our actions. "The eyes of the Lord are in every place, beholding the evil and good (Prov. 15:3).[114]

God's omnipresence should also function to give Christians consolation and comfort. Storms offers this reflection: "No matter what the trial, no matter the place of its occurrence, no matter the swiftness with which it assaults, no matter the depth of its power, *God*

---

[111] Turretin, *Institutes of Elenctic Theology*, 3:608–17.

[112] Bavinck, *Reformed Dogmatics*, 2:191.

[113] Calvin, *Institutes*, 3.25.10–11 (2:1004–7); cf. John Owen, "Meditations and Discourses on the Glory of Christ," in Owen, *Works of John Owen*, 1:378–89 (see chap. 4, n. 72).

[114] Charnock, *Existence and Attributes of God*, 1:397–98.

is ever with us! His loving protection ever abides. 'Even though I walk through the valley of the shadow of death, I will fear no evil, *for you are with me*; your rod and your staff, they comfort me' (Ps 23:4)."[115]

Finally, think of how God's omnipresence can also be incentive for us to grow in our Christian lives and to pursue holiness before the Lord. Again, Stephen Charnock states it well:

> What man would do an unworthy action, or speak an unhandsome word in the presence of his prince? The eye of the general inflames the spirit of the soldier. Why did David keep God's testimonies (Ps. 119:168)? because he considered that all his ways were before him; because he was persuaded his ways were present with God; God's precepts should be present with him. The same was the cause of Job's integrity (Job 31:4): "Doth he not see my ways?" To have God in our eye is the way to be sincere (Gen. 17:1); "walk before me" as in my sight, "and be thou perfect." Communion with God consists chiefly in ordering our ways as in the presence of him that is invisible. This would make us spiritual, raised and watchful in all our passions, if we considered that God is present with us in all our shops, in our chambers, in our walks, and in our meetings, as present with us as with the angels in heaven; who, though they have a presence of glory above us, yet have not a greater measure of his essential presence than we have.[116]

Omnipotence

To say that our triune God is omnipotent means that he is infinite in power and able to do all things consistent with his will and nature.[117] Six points will unpack this basic understanding.

First, we do not define omnipotence by philosophical definitions apart from Scripture. Scripture unequivocally teaches that God is omnipotent but also that his power is *not* the ability to do anything contrary to himself. This is why omnipotence is defined in terms of God's will and nature, contrary to various philosophical conundrums raised against divine

---

[115] Storms, *Grandeur of God*, 94.

[116] Stephen Charnock, *Existence and Attributes of God*, 1:404.

[117] On this point, see Charles Hodge, *Systematic Theology*, 1:409 (see chap. 1, n. 13).

omnipotence, such as, Can God do the logically impossible? Can God make stones so big that he cannot lift them? Can God sin, lie, or deny himself? The answer to all of these questions is that God's will and nature determines what is logically possible and morally right, and God's power is not contrary to who he is. For this reason, Scripture teaches that God cannot lie (Titus 1:2), break his promise (Heb 6:17–18), or do the logically impossible. God is able to do anything he chooses to do but it is never contrary to himself (Gen 18:14; Job 42:1–2; Ps 24:8; Isa 14:24, 27; 40:12; 46:10; 55:11; Jer 32:17–19; Dan 4:35; Mark 10:27; Luke 1:37; Rev 4:8; 11:17).

Second, God's infinite power is optional in its exercise. "Whereas God *is* power in His eternal being, it is not a necessary constituent of God's being that He always and in every way exercise His power."[118] For example, God did not have to create the world or plan our redemption from sin: those actions are free acts. But once God has planned a specific course, then his action is no longer optional. This is especially the case regarding his covenantal promises; once his promises are made, God is true to his word (Rom 4:20–21; Heb 6:17–18).

This truth is further underscored by an important distinction between God's "absolute power" (*potentia absoluta*) and his "ordained power" (*potentia ordinata*).[119] The former refers to God's ability to do *all* things consistent with his will and nature. However, the latter refers to that same power with respect to God's ability to do what he in fact plans to do. In this sense, God's power is greater than its external manifestation. For example, if God had so chosen, he could have raised up children for Abraham from stones (Matt 3:9) or ordered legions of angels to come to the aid of our Lord in Gethsemane (Matt 26:53), yet, in these cases, God chose not to exercise his power according to his larger plan and purposes.

Third, in speaking about God's "ordained power," which he freely exercises according to his plan and purposes, we must also speak about God's will. As the absolute-personal God, God plans, knows, and wills all things (Isa 46:9–10; Rom 11:36; Eph 1:11; Rev 4:11; 13:8). In defining God's will, Geehardus Vos states the following: God's will is "that perfection of God by which in a most simple act and in a rational manner, He goes out toward Himself as the

---

[118] Storms, *Grandeur of God*, 98.

[119] See Muller, *Dictionary of Latin and Greek*, s.v. "potentia absoluta," "potentia ordinate," 231–32 (see chap. 8, n. 37).

highest good and toward creatures outside Him for his own sake."[120] This definition is helpful because it has both an *ad intra* and *ad extra* focus.

In terms of the former, it reminds us that God alone is the supreme end of all things. As Bavinck rightly states, "Because he is God he cannot be blessed except in and through himself. His love is self-love and therefore absolute divine love. And that absolute self-love is nothing other than a willing of himself: the supreme and absolute divine energy of his will. Hence the object of God's will is God himself."[121] Not in the sense that God willed himself since God is eternal, self-existent, and simple, but in the sense that "God eternally wills himself with the will of delight, that he eternally loves himself with divine love and is completely blessed within himself."[122] However, in terms of the latter, it speaks of God's will with reference to his creation, yet not because God needs the world but because he has freely chosen to will things other than himself according to his own good pleasure (Eph 1:4–6), for the good of his people, and ultimately for his own glory (Rom 11:36).

Furthermore, in thinking about God's will *ad intra* and *ad extra*, we must also distinguish between God's *necessary* and *free* will. As Bavinck reminds us, "Although God wills himself and his creatures with one and the same simple act,"[123] we must distinguish between the different objects of that will. For example, in relation to himself, God wills himself, which is an eternal and necessary willing. But in relation to creation, God's will is free according to his own choices and good pleasure (Ps 115:3; Prov 21:2; Dan 4:35; Eph 1:4–6). In God's free choices in relation to creation, God plans all things, and as such, his will is the ultimate reason for all things.

In thinking about God's will toward his creatures, further distinctions are necessary. On the one hand, there is God's *decretive* will, sometimes known as his *secret* will (Pss 115:3; 135:6; Eph 1:11). On the other hand, there is God's perceptive will, sometimes known as his revealed will (Ps 143:10; Matt 6:10; Eph 6:6; 1 Thess 4:3). God's decretive will refers to what God has willed shall come to pass in history, a point we will discuss in more detail in chapter 20. God's perceptive will refers to what God has commanded of his creatures in terms of their lives and

---

[120] Vos, *Reformed Dogmatics*, 1:21 (see chap. 15, n. 126).

[121] Bavinck, *Reformed Dogmatics*, 2:232.

[122] Bavinck, 2:232.

[123] Bavinck, 2:233.

obedience to him. As we will discuss in subsequent chapters on the divine decree (chapter 20) and its outworking in providence (chapters 22–23), often "tensions" arise between what God has decreed and what he has revealed. In fact, sometimes God decrees what he disapproves of, specifically our sin, or he desires (2 Pet 3:9) what he has chosen not to decree (John 17:12). This does not lead to contradictory wills in God since God has *one* will, but it does mean that we must be careful not to pit biblical teaching against each other and maintain the entire breadth and depth of what Scripture teaches regarding God's will.

Fourth, God accomplishes his will and exercises his power in one of two ways. First, he acts in power directly or immediately, that is, without ordained means or secondary causes and agents. God's creation of the world *ex nihilo* is an example of God's immediate action. Second, God also acts by appointed means, or secondary causes and agents, both in terms of the creation itself—"laws of nature"—and human free agency (along with angelic beings). Providence is an example of this. But even in thinking of God's powerful acts of creation and providence, we should not think that these acts exhaust his divine power: "God could have created more than He has, if He so pleased. What God *has* done, therefore, is no measure of what He *could* have done or can do."[124]

Fifth, where do we see God's omnipotence? In God's mighty works of creation (Gen 1–2; Pss 19:1–6; 33:6; Isa 45:12; Rom 1:20), providence (Col 1:17; Heb 1:3), redemption (Rom 1:16; 2 Cor 1:22–24; Eph 3:20–21), judgment (Rom 9:22; 2 Pet 3:10–13; Rev 19; 20:11–15), and consummation (Rev 21–22). Supremely, God's powerful work is displayed in the incarnation of the divine Son and his entire work of redemption from conception (Luke 1:35–37) to his life (John 5:17–30; 11:25, 43), death (1 Cor 1:18), resurrection (1 Cor 15:1–3), ascension (Eph 1:20–23), and in his future return to consummate what he achieved in his first coming (Matt 24:29–31).

Sixth, knowing that our triune Creator-covenant Lord is omnipotent gives the Christian great comfort, assurance, confidence, and hope. When we face trials, persecution, and suffering, knowing that God is not a fellow sufferer but powerful to save gives us great hope. We are able to say with David, "The LORD is my light and my salvation—/whom should I fear? The LORD is the stronghold of my life—/whom should I dread?" (Ps 27:1). When beset by

[124] Storms, *Grandeur of God*, 99.

temptations, we remember that "God is faithful; he will not allow you to be tempted beyond what you are able, but with the temptation he will also provide a way out so that you may be able to bear it" (1 Cor 10:13). In our petitioning God in prayer, we are reminded that God is "able to do above and beyond all that we ask or think according to the power that works in us—to him be the glory in the church and in Christ Jesus to all generations, forever and ever. Amen" (Eph 3:20–21). In renewing our confidence in all that God has promised in Christ, we say with Jude: "Now to him who is able to protect you from stumbling and to make you stand in the presence of his glory, without blemish and with great joy, to the only God our Savior, through Jesus Christ our Lord, be glory, majesty, power, and authority before all time, now and forever. Amen" (Jude 24–25).[125]

Epistemological Attributes of Our Triune Covenant Lord

Under this category, we will discuss attributes that remind us that our triune God is Lord of knowledge, the absolute and final authority, because he is the source and standard of truth. In most theologies, these attributes are classified as both incommunicable (omniscience) and communicable (truthfulness, wisdom) since God is the archetype of knowledge, and humans, as God's image-bearers, are the ectype. Yet, God alone is the foundation of truth, and apart from him (*principium essendi*) and his speech (*principium cognoscendi*), there is no objective truth. Instead, "truth" becomes merely the arbitrary, subjective construction of finite, fallen humans.

Omniscience

The Meaning of Divine Omniscience

God's omniscience means that God knows everything that is possible to know. But what does this include? For open theists, God is only able to know what is past and present, but he is unable to know the future free actions of his creatures. In contrast, Scripture teaches that God knows all things past, present, and future—indeed, all things possible and actual, in a

[125] See Charnock, *Existence and Attributes of God*, 2:98–107.

comprehensive, certain, and immediate fashion.[126] Five truths will unpack what Scripture and historic Christian theology have meant by divine omniscience, especially in the Augustinian, Reformation, and post-Reformation tradition, including the Particular or Calvinist Baptists.[127]

First, God's knowledge is intuitive, not discursive.[128] Discursive knowledge is the result of observation, reasoning, induction, deduction, abduction, and so forth. This is how rational creatures learn and gain knowledge. However, God's knowledge is archetypal and intuitive. God does not learn from his creation, nor is his knowledge conditioned by our foreknown free choices, which is a key difference between Reformed and various forms of Arminian theology.[129] Instead, God knows in one simple, all-comprehensive act, and his knowledge of all things is "from himself" (*a se*). It is also important to distinguish between God's "necessary" and "free" knowledge. The former is God's exhaustive knowledge of himself and all things possible. The latter is God's knowledge of all actual things outside God, and even of what could have been, determined by God's own will, plan, and free choice to create for his own glory.[130]

Second, God's knowledge is immediate, instantaneous, and non-successive. God knows himself exhaustively and thus knows his own will, purposes, and plans. Otherwise, as Charnock rightly insists, without the knowledge of himself, "[God] could not be blessed. . . . The blessedness of God consists not in the knowledge of anything without him, but in the knowledge of himself and his own excellency, as the principle of all things; if, therefore, he did not perfectly know

---

[126] For example, see Job 37:16; Pss 139:1–4, 16; 147:5; Isa 40–48; cf. Isa 40:13–14; 41:21–23; 42:8–9; 43:9–12; 44:7; 45:21; 46:9–11; 48:3–7; Dan 11; cf. Dan 11:2, 4, 5–35; John 13:19–21 (cf. Isa 43:10); 13:38 with 18:19–27; 21:18–19; Rom 11:33–36; Heb 4:13; and predictive prophecy, which includes the future free actions of humans (cf. Deut 18:18–22; Isa 44:28–45:4; 1 Kgs 13:1–3; Acts 2:23–24).

[127] In the Augustinian-Reformed tradition, we are including the Particular or Calvinist Baptists as reflected by the *London Baptist Confession* (1689) and the *Abstract of Principles* (1858). This entire tradition parts company with Arminian theology on whether God's knowledge is dependent or conditioned on the creature. Arminian theology denies that God's knowledge is *a se* (from himself). We will discuss these two theological traditions in chapter 20 in our discussion of the divine decree and its outworking in God's external (*ad extra*) works.

[128] Berkhof, *Systematic Theology*, 66–67.

[129] For Arminian thought, see Richard Watson, *Theological Institutes* (New York: Phillips and Hunt, 1887), 2:392–449; John Lawson, *Introduction to Christian Theology* (Grand Rapids: Zondervan Academic, 1999), 206–35; cf. Roger Olson, *Arminian Theology: Myths and Realities* (Downers Grove: InterVarsity Press, 2006).

[130] Berkhof, *Systematic Theology*, 66–67.

himself and his own happiness, he could not enjoy a happiness; for to be, and not to know to be, is as if a thing were not."[131] However, divine blessedness not only assumes God's perfect knowledge of himself; it also assumes God's ability to create, rule, and govern. As Charnock continues, "Unless [God] knew his own power, he could not know how he created things; unless he knew his own wisdom, he could not know the beauty of his works; unless he knew his own glory, he could not know the end of his works; unless he knew his own justice, he could not know how to punish the crimes of his offending creatures."[132] In other words, nothing in his own nature is concealed from him; he knows himself and all things perfectly and comprehensively.

In fact, given God's eternality and atemporality, he "sees" things all at once and in their totality; he knows all things exhaustively and instantaneously. Technically, we cannot speak of his "foreknowledge" since God does not know things "in" time. As Storms reminds us, "The word *foreknowledge* is simply a way of expressing the nature and extent of God's knowledge from the vantage point of men on earth—in time. . . . But from God's perspective there is neither 'before' nor 'after.' God apprehends and knows all things (things which from our point of view may be past, present, and future) in one simultaneous act of cognition."[133]

Third, God's knowledge is independent, not dependent on the creature. This is another way of affirming God's aseity in relation to his exhaustive knowledge, which again, is a key point of division between Reformed and Arminian theology. When Isaiah asks, "Who did he consult? / Who gave him understanding / and taught him the paths of justice? / Who taught him knowledge / and showed him the way of understanding?" (Isa 40:14; cf. Job 38–41; Ps 139:6; Isa 46:10)—the answer is "no one!" God does not "gain" knowledge from anyone or anything external to himself. God does not know things by observation, "but from and of himself. . . . For that reason his knowledge is undivided, simple, unchangeable, eternal."[134]

Fourth, God's knowledge is infallible (Isa 40:13–14; 44:6–8; 46:5–13). Due to God's aseity and perfect knowledge of all things, our triune God is never wrong in what he knows. As we discussed in part 2, this is why Scripture is fully authoritative, infallible, and inerrant:

---

[131] Charnock, *Existence and Attributes of God*, 1:415.

[132] Charnock, 1:415.

[133] Storms, *Grandeur of God*, 63.

[134] Bavinck, *Reformed Dogmatics*, 2:196.

it is *his* word through human authors. God is the source and standard of truth; there is no higher authority. Just as God's being is immutable, so is his knowledge. Thankfully, God cannot change in what he knows. He does not increase or decrease in his understanding, nor does he learn things or suffer memory loss. God is completely trustworthy because he is never mistaken.

Fifth, God's knowledge is infinite, not partial. Since the triune God perfectly knows himself (Matt 11:27–27; 1 Cor 2:10–11), he knows everything that he has planned and created (Ps 139:2–3). Nothing in creation is hidden from him (Prov 15:3; Heb 4:13), including the recesses of our hearts (Ps 69:5; Jer 17:9–10). In the end, this is what gives us hope: God knows our situations and his people perfectly. As with Israel, God says to his new covenant people:

> Jacob, why do you say, / and, Israel, why do you assert, / "My way is hidden from the LORD, / and my claim is ignored by my God?" / Do you not know? / Have you not heard? / The LORD is the everlasting God, / the Creator of the whole earth. / He never becomes faint or weary; / there is no limit to his understanding. He gives strength to the faint / and strengthens the powerless. / Youths may become faint and weary, / and young men stumble and fall, / but those who trust in the LORD / will renew their strength; / they will soar on wings like eagles; / they will run and not become weary, / they will walk and not faint. (Isa 40:27–31)

The Divine-Foreknowledge–Human-Freedom Problem[135]

Given the biblical teaching that God knows all things exhaustively and infallibly, a legitimate question arises: If God *knows* all things,[136] including the future free actions of humans, it is true that those actions will necessarily happen. But if this is so, then the future is in some sense determined, and if the future is determined, how are humans free in their choices? This question is known as the divine-foreknowledge–human-freedom problem.

---

[135] In our discussion of the foreknowledge problem, we are discussing the main solutions but not the solution of Ockhamism. For a discussion of Okhamism, see Feinberg, *No One Like Him*, 752–59 (see chap. 2, n. 51). For a more detailed discussion of the foreknowledge problem, see James K. Beilby and Paul R. Eddy, *Divine Foreknowledge: Four Views* (Downers Grove: InterVarsity, 2001).

[136] We are defining knowledge as "justified true belief" (or, for some, "warranted" true belief). Knowledge requires more than true beliefs; it also requires justification or warrant for those true beliefs.

Proposed solutions to the problem go in one of two directions depending on one's view of the nature of human freedom. As discussed in chapter 16, currently in theology there are two basic views of freedom: an indeterministic view known as libertarianism and a deterministic view known as compatibilism.[137] Compatibilistic solutions argue that God infallibly knows all things "from himself" (*a se*) due to his own free choices but that our freedom is compatible with what God has decreed. Since our freedom involves sufficient conditions tied to our own wants and desires, and as long as our choices are not coerced by external factors, we act freely even though God has ordained our free choices.[138] For compatibilistic solutions, the problem is not really about *how* God foreknows our free actions since God knows all things due to his decree of all things. Instead, the real question is, *How* can God decree our choices while they remain free? This latter question is the divine sovereignty–human freedom problem, and we will discuss it in more depth and defend a Reformed view of it in chapters 20–22.

Libertarian solutions, on the other hand, wrestle with the foreknowledge-freedom problem for at least two reasons. First, libertarian views, especially in the Arminian tradition (including open theism), in contrast to Reformed theology, make God's knowledge conditional on what we choose. Second, libertarian views insist that a person is only free if they are not causally determined by "any prior factors that influence our choices, including external circumstances, or motives, desires, character, and nature,"[139] including God's unconditional plan. If both of these points are true, then the foreknowledge-freedom problem becomes a legitimate one.

Various libertarian solutions have been offered. We will discuss four proposed solutions, the first one falling outside of orthodoxy given its denial of God's knowing our future free actions, and the remaining three falling largely under the umbrella of Arminian theology. In the latter three solutions, foreknowledge is distinguished from foreordination. God knows all things in advance, but his "foreordination" is conditioned on what he foreknows we will freely

---

[137] As we will discuss in chapter 20, Arminian theology is usually associated with libertarianism, while Reformed theology is associated with compatibilism.

[138] Overall, this is the view of Augustinian-Reformed theology as represented by people such as Augustine, John Calvin, Francis Turretin, Jonathan Edwards, etc. See Bavinck, *Reformed Dogmatics*, 2:201–2; Berkhof, *Systematic Theology*, 67–68. Also see Paul Helm, "The Augustinian-Calvinist View," in Beilby and Eddy, *Divine Foreknowledge*, 161–89; Feinberg, *No One Like Him*, 740–41.

[139] Christensen, *What About Free Will?*, 6 (see chap. 4, n. 77).

choose, thus making God's decree dependent on the creature. Let us look at each of these views in turn. In the end, we will conclude that none of them sufficiently solves the problem.

First, there is the solution of "presentism."[140] Presentism defines God's knowledge as "knowledge of everything true which is logically possible to know." But what is logically possible to know? Presentism's answer: everything except future free actions of people. Why? Because of their embrace of a libertarian view of human freedom. Presentism argues that anything that is *indeterminate* cannot have a truth-value. Thus, statements about future undecided free actions are neither true nor false. It is impossible to foreknow the truth of future contingencies when they are still future since there is no truth-value to them, and thus, God cannot have foreknowledge about them until the specific choices are made. Future contingencies may be *guessed,* but presently there is no *knowledge* of them. This is why God's knowledge is always in the present tense. God has always known everything there is to know, but nobody—not even God—can *know* the indeterminate future. Presentism "solves" the divine-foreknowledge–human-freedom problem by upholding libertarian freedom but surrendering God's ability to know future free actions. The implications of such a view are not only a huge reduction in divine sovereignty but also a denial that God's plan is eternal and exhaustive. No doubt, God knows his own goals and purposes, but he does not know our future actions.

Presentism is unbiblical.[141] Scripture teaches that God eternally knows all things, including our future free actions. In fact, repeatedly, God reminds us that he alone knows the end from the beginning and that he is able to predict the future, much of which is tied to his entire redemptive plan centered in Christ (cf. Isa 40–48; Acts 2:23; 4:27–28). Presentism offers a *logical* solution to the problem, *but not a biblical solution.* Thus, it is not a viable option for Christian theology. In the end, it assumes a different view of God than Scripture teaches.

Second, God's "timeless knowledge" or "atemporal eternalism" is another solution.[142] Instead of denying that God can know future contingents, atemporal eternalism defends the

---

[140] Historically, Socinians argued for "presentism," and today it is the solution of open theists. See chapter 16 for our discussion of open theism. Also see Gregory A. Boyd, "The Open-Theism View," in Beilby and Eddy, *Divine Foreknowledge,* 13–47; Pinnock et al., *Openness of God* (see chap. 2, n. 135); Oord, *Uncontrolling Love of God* (see chap. 2, n. 135).

[141] For a thorough critique of presentism, see Feinberg, *No One Like Him,* 759–75.

[142] Norman Geisler, "God Knows All Things," in Basinger and Basinger, *Predestination and Free Will,* 61–84 (see chap. 16, n. 72). Classical theism consistently embraces atemporal eternalism (e.g.,

idea that God, as eternal, is outside of time. But how does this solve the problem? There are two steps to the solution. First, since God is outside of time, he sees all of time at once and as present. Thus, God knows all things without knowing the future since nothing is future to him. Thomas Morris states it this way: "God does not believe anything *in advance* of the occurrence of anything, because to hold a belief, or to do anything *prior to* or *in advance* of anything else is to be a temporal being subject to time."[143] Second, this means that whatever we do in the future (to us) is still left indeterminate. No doubt, God knows our future as present to himself. But from our perspective, our future is left open to us. As such, as Morris continues: "So when the time arrives for me, or for you, to make a decision or to choose one avenue of action over another, God has not *already* held a belief concerning exactly what will be done, and so it seems that there is nothing in our temporal circumstances to prevent our having a real array of options equally available to us."[144] The solution to the problem, then, is that given God's timeless knowledge, he can know all things, including "future" events, and we can exercise libertarian freedom.

Although atemporal eternalism is true, it does not work as a solution to the foreknowledge-freedom problem. John Feinberg is correct in his criticism:

> God is eternal and omniscient, and all things certainly are an eternal "now" to him. However, this does not mean that God does not know what time it is in *human history*. If he knows all things, he knows which things, though present to him, are future *from our perspective*. But, once that is admitted, the same old problem returns. How can God know even as *present* to him something which is *future* to us without that event being determined?[145]

In other words, when the time comes for me to choose, I still cannot refrain from choosing what God knows, which undermines the reality of libertarian freedom. Furthermore, even if

---

Boethius, Thomas Aquinas, John Calvin, Francis Turretin, etc.). However, those in the Augustinian-Reformed tradition do not appeal to atemporal eternalism to solve the divine-foreknowledge–human-freedom problem given their rejection of libertarian freedom.

[143] Thomas V. Morris, *Our Idea of God* (Downers Grove: InterVarsity, 1991), 97.

[144] Morris, 97–98.

[145] John S. Feinberg, "God Ordains All Things," in Basinger and Basinger, *Predestination and Free Will*, 33. Also cf. Feinberg, *No One Like Him*, 742–43.

God "sees" what we are doing, he cannot do anything about it; he must live with what he sees, thus greatly reducing God's ability to accomplish his eternal plan.

Third, "simple foreknowledge" is the solution widely held by Arminian theologians.[146] This view of divine foreknowledge teaches that "all *actual* free choices, including those that are yet to be made, but not (as in middle knowledge) those choices that *might have been* made but in fact never are."[147] In other words, simple foreknowledge is "knowledge at any given time t^1 of what will in fact happen in the actual world at any given time t^2."[148] For example, it is now true or false that "X *will* be elected President of the United States in 2024 in the actual world." No doubt, the relevant decisions have not yet been made. But X will either choose to continue to run or choose not to continue, he will either be nominated or not be nominated, and he will either be elected or not be elected. But, since God knows all true propositions, he knows now if X will be elected president in the actual world in November of 2024.

However, a legitimate question arises: How can God *know* our future choices without undermining libertarian freedom? God cannot know the future by knowing the *causal sufficient conditions* that will lead to the future events in question since that would deny libertarian freedom. Instead, God "*directly knows the actual future event;* that God's belief about the matter in question is somehow brought about *by the future event itself*."[149] In other words, God has some kind of "'direct vision' of the future as if in a crystal ball or a telescope."[150] But does such an explanation work? Let us focus on three problems with this view.

---

[146] See David Hunt, "The Simple-Foreknowledge View," in Beilby and Eddy, *Divine Foreknowledge*, 65–103. Historically, simple foreknowledge has been a common view held by many Arminian theologians. For example, see John Wesley (1703–91), Richard Watson (1781–1833), John Miley (1813–95), and Orton Wiley (1877–1961). Recently, Jack Cottrell, Thomas Oden, Robert Picirilli, and Roger Olson argue for the view.

[147] Hasker, *God, Time, and Knowledge*, 55–56 (see chap. 16, n. 35).

[148] David Basinger, "Divine Omniscience and Human Freedom: A 'Middle Knowledge' Perspective," *Faith and Philosophy* 1, no. 3 (1984): 291.

[149] Hasker, *God, Time, and Knowledge*, 56; also cf. Olson, "Classical Free Will," in Ware, *Perspectives on the Doctrine*, 156 (see chap. 16, n. 56).

[150] Hasker, *God, Time, and Knowledge,* 56; also cf. Jack W. Cottrell, "The Nature of the Divine Sovereignty," in *The Grace of God, the Will of Man: A Case for Arminianism*, ed. Clark H. Pinnock (Grand Rapids: Zondervan, 1989), 112.

First, if God *knows* what will happen in the future, then libertarian freedom must be rejected. Why? Because God's knowing this is part of the past and is now fixed, and since God is infallible, it is impossible that things will turn out differently than he now knows. This entails, of course, that the future event God knows is already unalterable, and given this fact, the agent will have to perform the action in question. But given libertarianism, if God *knows* that a person is going to perform an action and he will certainly perform it, then the person is not free.[151]

Second, for sake of argument, if one chooses to uphold libertarian freedom along with simple foreknowledge, then it is difficult to explain how God can really *know* that something will occur if it is *not* set or determined. If God cannot know the future in virtue of its causal antecedents, then on what basis does God know the future? We are told that God has a direct vision of the future or some kind of intuition of what we will do, but this seems to require an open future, similar to presentism.

Third, even if one grants simple foreknowledge, divine sovereignty is greatly reduced, which is difficult to reconcile with Scripture. God may know what a person will actually do, but he cannot do much about it. As Scott Christensen observes, "[God] would not be able to intervene and try to persuade you otherwise, since this would change the future that he already infallibly sees. God could never use his knowledge of the future to adjust his plans in response to anything that his creatures do, since what he will do is already fixed by way of his foreknowledge."[152] One could argue that God could intervene in human affairs and thus exercise control that is more sovereign. However, this option is problematic. Given simple foreknowledge, if God infallibly foreknows the future, then he cannot change it; otherwise, his foreknowledge is wrong. The end result is that God's sovereignty is greatly curtailed, and this is why many who affirm simple foreknowledge appeal to "mystery" in their explanation of *how* God can actually foreknow our indeterminate future choices.[153] As we will note in our discussion of the divine decree and its outworking in providence in later chapters, appeal to "mystery" is inevitable, but it is imperative that we locate the mystery in the correct spot, which we contend this view does not do.

---

[151] See William Hasker, "A Philosophical Perspective," in Pinnock et al., *Openness of God*, 147.

[152] Christensen, *What About Free Will?*, 48; cf. Feinberg who makes the same point. *No One Like Him*, 746.

[153] For a strong appeal to "mystery," see F. Leroy Forlines, *Classical Arminianism: A Theology of Salvation* (Nashville: Randall House, 2011), 74–76.

Fourth, the solution of Molinism, or "middle knowledge," is our last option, and probably the one that theoretically allows for more of God's sovereign control than the other views.[154] Central to the view is its belief that God has knowledge of propositions known as "counterfactuals of freedom." William Hasker explains what this is: "These propositions specify, concerning every possible free agent that God might create, exactly what the agent would freely choose to do in every possible situation of (libertarian) free choice in which the agent might find itself."[155] For middle knowledge, then, God possesses not only the knowledge of what *will* in fact happen in the actual world (i.e., simple foreknowledge), but also what *could* in fact happen in all worlds and "what *would* in fact happen in every possible situation, including what every possible free creature would do in every situation in which that creature could find itself."[156]

To understand the overall view better, we need to discuss how it thinks of God's knowledge. There are three logical moments in God's knowledge. The first moment is God's "natural knowledge": the knowledge that God has logically prior to any act of creation, concerning all necessarily factual truths and possibilities of creation. This is a knowledge of all that *is* or could *be*. William Craig states it this way:

> God's natural knowledge includes knowledge of all possibilities. He knows all the possible individuals he could create, all the possible circumstances he could place them in, all their possible actions and reactions, and all the possible worlds or orders which he could create. God could not lack this knowledge and still be God; the content of God's natural knowledge is essential to him.[157]

The third moment is God's "free knowledge": God's knowledge of the actual world that he has decided to create. In this moment, God freely and unchangeably wills all events in history to happen. Craig continues:

---

[154] From Luis de Molina (1535–1600), who was a Jesuit priest. See Alfred J. Freddoso's introduction to his translation of Luis De Molina, *On Divine Foreknowledge: Part IV of the Concordia* (Ithaca, NY: Cornell University Press, 1988), 1–81. Also see William L. Craig, "The Middle-Knowledge View," in Beilby and Eddy, *Foreknowledge and Freedom*, 119–43; Craig, *The Only Wise God: The Compatibility of Divine Foreknowledge and Human Freedom* (Grand Rapids: Baker, 1987); Kenneth Keathley, *Salvation and Sovereignty: A Molinist Approach* (Nashville: B&H Academic, 2010).

[155] Hasker, "A Philosophical Perspective," 143–44.

[156] David Basinger, "Middle Knowledge and Classical Christian Thought," *RelS* 22 (1986): 408.

[157] Craig, *Only Wise God*, 129.

> The third moment of God's knowledge is his knowledge of the actual world which he has created. This includes his foreknowledge of everything that will happen. The third moment is logically posterior to God's decision to create the world. Therefore, he has control over which statements are true and which are false in this moment. By willing to create another world, God would have brought it about that statements which are in fact true would be false and statements which are in fact false would be true.[158]

In between God's "natural" and "free" knowledge is the second moment, known as "middle knowledge." In this moment, God knows what every possible creature *would* do (as well as *could* do) in any possible set of situations.[159] For example, given middle knowledge:

> God knows whether Peter, if he were placed in certain circumstances, would deny Christ three times. By his natural knowledge God knew in the first moment all the possible things that Peter *could* do if placed in such circumstances. But now in this second moment he knows what Peter would in fact freely choose to do under such circumstances. This is *not* because Peter would be causally determined by the circumstances to act in this way. No, Peter is entirely free, and under the same circumstances he could choose to act in another way. But God knows which way Peter *would* freely choose. God's knowledge of Peter in this respect is not simple foreknowledge. For maybe God will decide not to place Peter under such circumstances or even not to create him at all. Middle knowledge, like natural knowledge, thus is logically prior to the decision of the divine will to create a world.[160]

How does middle knowledge "solve" the foreknowledge-freedom problem? Thomas Morris answers this way: "The story is basically very simple. Knowing how every individual he

---

[158] Craig, 129. Molinists affirm that God decrees the outcome of all things, but in contrast to a Reformed view, it denies that God is the primary cause of all things, thus making God conditioned on the creature for the outcomes that he chooses to enact.

[159] These are known as "counterfactuals of freedom." Scriptural texts such as Exod 13:17; 1 Sam 23:8–14; Jer 23:21–22; and Matt 11:21–24 are cited as examples of God's middle knowledge. However, God's natural and free knowledge also explain these texts. They are not determinative in warranting God's middle knowledge, especially when combined with libertarian freedom. On this point, see Christensen, *What About Evil?*, 104 n. 73 (see chap. 4, n. 86).

[160] Craig, *Only Wise God*, 130.

could possibly create would freely act in every complete set of circumstances he could possibly be placed in, God, by deciding who to create and what circumstances to create them in, completely provides himself with the knowledge of everything that will ever happen."[161]

What is the problem with this view? There are two major problems.[162] First, there is "the grounding objection."[163] Given Molinism's embrace of libertarian freedom, it cannot adequately "ground" how God can know the future. Let us explain this important objection a bit further. If one adopts libertarianism, then *how* does God *know* what we *would* do in any and all circumstances? Paul Helm offers an example to illustrate the problem. Let us suppose that among the propositions that God knows are the following conditional propositions:

> (A) Only if Jones were placed in circumstances C, and were free to choose between A and B, would he choose A.
>
> (B) Only if Jones were placed in circumstances C*, and were free to choose between A and B, would he choose B.
>
> Let us suppose that God wills that Jones chooses B. In that eventuality, clearly God will actualize circumstances C*.[164]

However, there is a problem with this scenario since Jones has libertarian freedom. If Jones has the power to choose any one of a number of alternatives open to him, then God cannot *know* that (A) or (B) is true. And because he cannot *know* that A is true, he cannot actualize (A) as a whole without removing libertarian free will. As Helm argues, "He [God] can actualize Jones, and he can actualize circumstances C; what he cannot do is actualize Jones's freely

---

[161] Morris, *Our Idea of God*, 96; cf. William Lane Craig, "God Directs All Things," in *Four Views on Divine Providence*, ed. Dennis W. Jowers (Grand Rapids: Zondervan, 2011), 83. Molinists distinguish between "feasible" and "possible" worlds. The latter is any logically possible world. The former is one of the possible worlds that God can actualize as long as it upholds libertarian freedom. If it does not, then it would be an "infeasible" world.

[162] See Bavinck, *Reformed Dogmatics*, 2:198–203; cf. Muller, *Post-Reformation Reformed Dogmatics*, 3:420–24; Henri A. G. Blocher, "'Middle Knowledge:' Solution or Seduction?," *Unio Cum Christo* 4, no. 1 (2018): 29–46; Feinberg, *No One Like Him*, 747–52.

[163] See the helpful discussion of the "grounding objection" in Blocher, "Middle Knowledge," 40–45; and Christensen, *What About Evil?*, 105–6.

[164] Paul Helm, *The Providence of God* (Downers Grove: InterVarsity, 1994), 58.

choosing A in circumstances C. For whether or not Jones does choose A when placed in circumstances C is up to Jones."[165] In other words, the "ground" for middle knowledge is gone if libertarian freedom is upheld, and conversely, if God actually does know, then it seems that libertarian freedom is removed. Ultimately, the *how* is not explained *on Molinism's own terms*. Inevitably, this results in mystery, but we are not convinced that this is where Scripture locates the mystery.

Second, Molinism undercuts God's aseity in knowledge. Why? Because God's decree is conditioned on the creature, similar to other libertarian views. In fact, Molinism's undercutting of God's aseity in knowledge was *the* crucial reason why Reformed theologians rejected it.[166] As Bavinck reminds us: for Molinism,

> God does not derive his knowledge of the free actions of human beings from his own being, his own decrees, but from the will of creatures. God, accordingly, becomes dependent on the world, derives knowledge from the world that he did not have and could not obtain from himself, and hence, in his knowledge, ceases to be one, simple, and independent—that is, God.[167]

Conversely, humans become both independent of God and the pivotal deciders on which God conditions his eternal plan. This is best seen in the Arminian view of "conditional" election, and if not careful, it opens the door for some kind of merit due to our human choice for God in contrast to those who do not choose the same way.[168]

---

[165] Helm, 58. Hasker makes the same point: "Insofar as an agent is genuinely free, there *are* no true counterfactuals stating what the agent would definitely do under various possible circumstances." *God, Time, and Knowledge*, 52.

[166] See Muller, *Post-Reformation Reformed Dogmatics*, 3:420–24; Blocher, "Middle Knowledge," 37–38.

[167] Bavinck, *Reformed Dogmatics*, 2:201.

[168] Middle knowledge offers no greater solution to the problem of evil than a Calvinist view, something we will discuss in chapter 23. One of the perceived strengths of Molinism is its affirmation of the "free will defense." However, in arguing that God decreed Adam's sin by creating our world out of a number of other possible options, it affirms what Reformed views also affirm, namely, that God intended and decreed for evil to occur. On this point, see Greg Welty, "Molinist Gunslingers: God and the Authorship of Sin," in *Calvinism and the Problem of Evil*, ed. David E. Alexander and Daniel M. Johnson (Eugene: Pickwick, 2016), 56–77.

In summary, the divine-foreknowledge–human-freedom problem has taxed the minds of many theologians throughout history. In our view, when libertarian freedom is embraced, it renders problematic a biblical view of God's omniscience and sovereignty. As we will discuss in the next section regarding God's decree and its outworking in providence, a better solution is to embrace a compatibilistic view, which allows us to uphold the glory of our triune Creator-covenant Lord.

As we conclude our discussion of God's omniscience, we offer four application points.

First, God's omniscience should lead us to humility. Stephen Charnock states this point well:

> There is nothing man is more apt to be proud of than his knowledge; it is a perfection he glories in; but if our own knowledge of the little outside and barks of things puffs us up, the consideration of the infiniteness of God's knowledge should abate the tumor: as our beings are nothing in regard to the infiniteness of his essence, so our knowledge is nothing in regard of the vastness of his understanding. We have a spark of being, but nothing to the heat of the sun; we have a drop of knowledge, but nothing to the Divine ocean. What a vain thing is it for a shallow brook to boast of its streams before a sea, whose depths are unfathomable! As it is a vanity to brag of our strength, when we remember the power of God, and of our prudence when we glance upon the wisdom of God, so it is no less a vanity to boast of our knowledge, when we think of the understanding and knowledge of God.[169]

Second, divine omniscience should incentivize us to pursue holiness of life. Again, Charnock captures this point well: "Can a man's conscience easily and delightfully swallow that which he [knows] falls under the cognizance of God, when it is hateful to the eyes of holiness, and renders the actor odious to him? . . . temptations have no encouragement to come near him, that is constantly armed with the thoughts that his sin is booked in God's omniscience."[170]

Third, God's omniscience should ground our comfort and assurance, especially in light of God's knowledge of our sin. Any one of us does not fool God; he knows the very depth of our hearts, but in spite of this, the triune God set his love on us, and in Christ Jesus, he has

---

[169] Charnock, *Existence and Attributes of God*, 1:474.

[170] Charnock, 1:495.

redeemed us by his grace. In fact, nothing in us merits God's choice of us; all we deserve is judgment, but while we were yet sinners, Christ died for us (Rom 5:6). John writes: "This is how we will know that we belong to the truth and will reassure our hearts before him whenever our hearts condemn us; for God is greater than our hearts, and he knows all things" (1 John 3:19–20).

Fourth, omniscience grounds our trust and hope. Once again, here are the words of Charnock:

> This perfection of God fits him to be a special object of trust. If he were forgetful, what comfort could we have in any promise? How could we depend upon him, if he were ignorant of our state? His compassion to pity us, his readiness to relieve us, his power to protect and assist us, would be insignificant, without his omniscience to inform his goodness, and direct the arm of his power. . . . You may depend upon his mercy that hath promised, and upon his truth to perform; upon his sufficiency to supply you, and his goodness to relieve you, and his righteousness to reward you; because he hath an infinite understanding to know you and your wants, you and your services. And without this knowledge of his, no comfort could be drawn from any other perfection; none of them could be a sure nail to hang our hopes and confidence upon.[171]

Truthfulness

Related to the fact of God's omniscience "from himself" is the affirmation of "truthfulness." Wayne Grudem offers a helpful definition: "God's truthfulness means that he is the true God, and that all his knowledge and words are both true and the final standard of truth."[172] This is why God is completely dependable and reliable, and his word is always true, a point we developed in part 2 in relation to Scripture. All that God is and says corresponds to reality since God is the one who has planned all things and enacted his plan by creation. Additionally, for God, the idea of his truthfulness is organically linked to his faithfulness (Heb.*'emeth*). God is

---

[171] Charnock, 1:484–85.

[172] Grudem, *Systematic Theology*, 233.

true, which means that he can be trusted; God remains true to his word and especially to his covenantal promises. As we expound on the senses in which God is truth, let us develop it in four ways.

First, God is the *true* God (Pss 96:5; 97:7; 115:4–8; Isa 44:9–10; John 17:3; 1 Thess 1:9). God alone is God, self-sufficient in himself, simple, eternal, and unchanging; everything else belongs to the realm of creation. Bavinck emphasizes this point by speaking of metaphysical truth; that is, "truth is a property of all being; it is identical with substance."[173] However, in the case of the creation, this is only because God, as "the supreme being, the supreme truth, and the supreme good,"[174] creates all things according to his will and plan and gives them being. Thus, God "does not possess but is the truth."[175] No wonder, in contrast to the idols, God is the true God, who alone is God, and nothing in all of creation compares to him.

Second, God is the *standard* of truth. In human thought, we often pit a coherence theory of truth against a correspondence theory. However, in Christian theology, this is a false dichotomy. God is the archetype of knowledge, and in him, these two theories are united. For example, truth is what coheres with God's will and plan. God is the absolute standard of truth and knowledge. Also due to creation, God has created a total correspondence between his thoughts and reality; hence, the correspondence theory of truth is true, and we are to "to think God's thoughts after him."[176] All of this entails that God's word is always true, reliable, and trustworthy. When God speaks, it is always true (Heb 6:18; Ps 12:6), and his word is the final standard by which we evaluate all truth claims (John 17:17). God's word is to be believed and obeyed over all human authorities. "Let God be true, even though everyone is a liar" (Rom 3:4). Furthermore, in our Lord Jesus Christ, who is the perfect image and exact correspondence of the Father (Col 1:15; Heb 1:3), we have a Redeemer who alone is the way, the truth, and the life (John 14:6).

Third, God is true in the *ethical* sense. This not only means that God is the standard of moral norms, but also that in God there is a perfect correspondence between his being and actions (Num 23:19; 1 Sam 15:29; Tit 1:2; Heb 6:18; 1 John 5:20–21). This is why God is

---

[173] Bavinck, *Reformed Dogmatics*, 2:208; cf. Berkhof, *Systematic Theology*, 69.

[174] Bavinck, *Reformed Dogmatics*, 2:209.

[175] Bavinck, 2:209.

[176] See Bavinck, 2:209; Berkhof, *Systematic Theology*, 69.

always true to his word; he is never a hypocrite, who says one thing and does another. In God, "there is a complete correspondence between his being and his revelation."[177]

Fourth, since divine truthfulness is a "communicable" attribute, we, as God's image-bearers created for a covenant relationship with him, are to imitate God in being people of truth. This means that we are to have a passion for the truth in every sphere of life. We are not to believe lies; our thinking must conform to God's word, both in natural and special revelation. In knowing the truth, we are to speak the truth by upholding what God has said (Col 3:10; Eph 4:25; 2 Cor 4:2), which means that we are also to hate falsehood (Exod 20:16; Ps 15:2; Prov 13:5; 12:22; Isa 59:3–4). In a day that denies the God of truth and makes humans the "standards" of truth, the church must stand against our culture for God's glory and for the sake of the truth. Believing lies and promoting them is always wrong. Christians are to be, in Francis Schaeffer's call for a new generation of Christians, people who are "radicals for truth."

Wisdom

Wisdom follows from God's knowledge and truthfulness since wisdom is the practical use of knowledge. Because God knows and plans all things and is the standard of wisdom, God always chooses the best means to bring about his ends. This is important in thinking about God's eternal decree or plan. God's plan was not "put together" arbitrarily but according to knowledge, truth, and wisdom. As Berkhof reminds us, God's wisdom is "that perfection of God whereby he applies his knowledge to the attainment of his ends in a way which glorifies him most."[178]

Scripture is replete with examples of God's infinite wisdom. In wisdom, our triune God created the world. Even in a fallen world, that wisdom is still wondrously evident (Pss 19:1–7; 104:1–34). In wisdom, God rules the world, which means that even in the midst of a fallen world in which we experience suffering and heartache, God is working out all things for the ultimate good of his people (Pss 33:10–11; 147:5; Rom 8:28). Although we may not know every detail of God's plan or why he has ordained what he has for our lives, for God's people, God's eternal plan enacted in providence is for his glory and our good, and it is supremely

---

[177] Bavinck, *Reformed Dogmatics*, 2:209.

[178] Berkhof, *Systematic Theology*, 69.

wise. Yet, it is probably in redemption that we see God's wisdom on display in a greater way (Rom 11:33–34; 16:27; Eph 3:10). In God's choosing of a people, establishing covenant relationships with us, and supremely in the sending of the divine Son, our Lord Jesus Christ, God confounds those who think they are wise. In his glorious plan of redemption, what is considered foolishness by the world is the very display of God's glorious wisdom in Christ (1 Cor 1:18–29). Indeed, the praise of heaven confirms it: "Worthy is the Lamb who was slaughtered / to receive power and riches / and wisdom and strength / and honor and glory and blessing!" (Rev 5:12).

As God's truthfulness is a communicable attribute, so is wisdom. Just as we are to be people of the truth, we are to be wise in our lives (Ps 19:7; Jas 1:5). Just think of the importance of the wisdom literature that reminds us that true wisdom is first found in knowing the God of wisdom and then in delightfully and joyfully obeying all that he has commanded (Prov 1:7).

Moral Attributes of Our Triune Covenant Lord

We now turn to the moral attributes of God. Under this category, we will discuss attributes that remind us that our triune God is not only the absolute standard of objective moral norms but also the God who upholds his own glory in the redemption of his people and in his judgment of all sin and evil. In most theologies, these attributes are classified as communicable since we, as God's image-bearers, were created to reflect God in these areas (Col 3:8–10; cf. Gen 1:26–31). Yet, as we have already noted, even God's communicable attributes are unique to him and not equally shared with us. God *is* holy, good, loving, and just but not quantitatively more than his creatures; God is *qualitatively* different. Communicable attributes only apply to us by analogy.

In classifying God's moral attributes, we will discuss them under the overarching attributes of *holiness* and *goodness* as we try to synthesize the biblical teaching regarding God's moral perfections. In addition, given God's triune nature and his fullness of life apart from the world, it is important to think about God's moral perfections first *ad intra* before we see them exercised in God's external works (*ad extra*). This is especially significant as we think about God's relation to a fallen world that he judges and to a people that he redeems by sovereign grace. In these relations, God does not change, but he does display the glory of *all* of his moral perfections, analogous to how we see light refracted through a prism.

Holiness and Goodness

As we discussed in our theological overview of our triune Creator-covenant Lord in chapter 17, holiness is the only attribute of God that is used in the superlative (Isa 6:3; Rev 4:8). This is not to say that it is more significant than other attributes, given divine simplicity, but it is to say that it functions as an overarching way of describing God's sheer God-ness, which also entails all of his other divine perfections. For this reason, divine holiness "pervades all of [God's] actions and interprets all of his other attributes."[179] This is why when Scripture describes God's love and justice, it is always God's *holy* love and *holy* justice.

Furthermore, we argued that holiness is more than being "set apart," although it does convey the idea of divine transcendence. At its core, holiness speaks of "consecration" or "devotion to," which then carries over to the moral realm. To be holy unto God is to honor and love what he loves, which demands specific moral entailments. Within God himself (*ad intra*), holiness is a way of describing God's holy *love*. As Sinclair Ferguson reminds us, "Holiness is the intensity of the love that flows within the very being of God, among and between each of the three persons of the Father, Son, and Holy Spirit. It is the sheer intensity of that devotion that causes seraphim (whose holiness is perfect but creaturely) to veil their faces."[180] Geerhardus Vos states it this way: holiness is "God's determination toward himself";[181] it is "that attribute of God by which He seeks and loves Himself as the highest good and demands as reasonable goodness from the creatures to be consecrated to him."[182]

Holiness, then, has a primary metaphysical sense that necessitates its secondary moral sense. Regarding the former, holiness is closely associated with God's aseity and uniqueness (Isa 6:1–3; 40:18–25). Regarding the latter, holiness is closely associated with God as the objective moral standard of goodness, justice, and righteousness so that all that stands in opposition to God's will and nature is sin. Since God *is* holy, in relation to the world (*ad extra*), especially a fallen one, God *must* act in holy justice against sin—he cannot overlook it. God *cannot* deny himself and still be God. God's holy love for himself, his name, and his glory is the supreme

---

[179] Muller, *Post-Reformation Reformed Dogmatics*, 3:501.

[180] Ferguson, *Devoted to God*, 2 (see chap. 17, n. 53).

[181] Vos, *Reformed Dogmatics*, 1:30.

[182] Vos, 1:27.

good. This is why Berkhof argues that God's justice is a "mode of his holiness,"[183] and Vos insists that God's righteousness is God working outwardly "to reveal and maintain his holiness."[184] It is also why divine holiness in relation to sin is revealed in divine *wrath*, that is, God's holy reaction to sin and evil. God within himself *is* holy; he is not wrath. But God in relation to the world *is* holy, *and* in relation to sin, God's holiness is expressed in wrath. Holiness, then, in an overarching way captures something of God's glorious triune being, metaphysically and morally, which then is inseparable from understanding other attributes, such as God's justice and righteousness, and why *his* name, honor, and glory are first and foremost and, for creatures, the chief end to pursue.

Goodness, similar to holiness, also functions as an overarching attribute, which inseparably relates to other moral attributes of God, both within God and in his external works. Again, this is not to say that "goodness" is more significant than other attributes; divine simplicity must govern our thinking in these matters. However, it is a way of capturing Scripture's glorious and diverse description of God's moral perfections. In fact, as Bavinck notes, "goodness" is also known from nature and in non-Christian thought, but sadly, due to sin, it is known in a distorted way.[185] For example, Plato spoke of the form of the Good, but he wrongly located this form outside of "god," thus making it impersonal. For Plato, the Creator-creature distinction was not foundational to his philosophy. By contrast, in Scripture, the Creator-creature distinction is foundational to our entire theology and worldview. The result: the absolute-tri-personal God *is good*; *he* is the objective standard of goodness, a truth that stands in antithesis to all non-Christian thought. God alone defines what is *good* according to *his* will and nature; goodness is not "outside" of God, something that he conforms to, nor is it defined by our human subjectivity. Because God *is* good, as Bavinck notes, "All virtues are present in [God] in an absolute sense,"[186] which is precisely what Scripture teaches: "No one is good except God alone" (Mark 10:18).

We can think of God's goodness in a number of ways, but Edward Leigh's definition is helpful: "God's *Goodness* is an essential property whereby he is infinitely and of himself good,

---

[183] Berkhof, *Systematic Theology*, 74.

[184] Vos, *Reformed Dogmatics*, 1:30.

[185] See Bavinck, *Reformed Dogmatics*, 2:210–11.

[186] Bavinck, 2:211.

and the author and cause of all goodness in the creature."[187] God *is* good within himself (*ad intra*) and in his external works (*ad extra*), and we see God's goodness displayed in a number of ways depending on whom it is directed towards. For example, in relation to those in distress and misery, God's goodness is revealed in his *mercy* and *compassion*. Towards those who are undeserving, God's goodness is displayed in his *grace*. When God's grace is towards all people, it is *common*; when it is displayed towards his people, it is *saving*. As God gives himself for his creation and especially the blessedness of his people, God's goodness is revealed in his *love*. God's goodness is especially revealed in God's covenant relations. In the biblical covenants, God reveals himself to be the promise maker and keeper—the God of covenant love (*hesed*) and faithfulness (*'emet*) (Exod 34:6–7)—all of which is supremely revealed and fulfilled in our Lord Jesus Christ and his new covenant work. What the OT discloses of God's goodness, love, grace, and covenant faithfulness is now fully unveiled in our Lord Jesus Christ, who is the epitome and embodiment of "grace and truth" (John 1:14–18). In Christ alone, fallen people are justified, reconciled, and re-created to be what God created us to be in the first place, yet now greater: those who know and reflect God's holiness and goodness in their lives (Luke 6:27, 33–35; Gal 6:10; 2 Tim 3:17; 1 Pet 1:15–16).

Justice and Righteousness

Justice and righteousness mean a "strict adherence to law,"[188] and they carry a forensic sense.[189] But unlike us, God *is* just and righteous,[190] and thus the standard of justice and righteousness—a

---

[187] Edward Leigh, *A Treatise of Divinity* (London, 1646), 2.10 (79), cited in Muller, *Post-Reformation Reformed Dogmatics*, 3:507. See Gen 1:31; Pss 34:8; 100:5; 104; 106:1; 107:1; 119:68; Luke 18:19.

[188] Berkhof, *Systematic Theology*, 74.

[189] See Moo, *Epistle to the Romans*, 79–90 (see chap. 13, n. 48); Schreiner, *Romans*, 66–77 (see chap. 6, n. 62).

[190] In Scripture, *justice* and *righteousness* belong to the same word group, in contrast to English usage, which can result in a number of misunderstandings of the words. In Hebrew (OT), *justice* and *righteousness* are from the *sdq* word group, while in Greek (NT), they are variations of the *dik-* root (e.g., Exod 9:27; 2 Chron 12:6; Ezra 9:15; Neh 9:8; Job 4:17; 35:2; 36:3; Pss 5:8; 31:1; 33:5; 40:10; 45:4, 7; 69:27; 71:2, 19; 89:16; 111:3; 116:5; 119:123; 143:1; 145:7, 17; Isa 46:13; 51:6, 8; 53:11; 54:17; 59:16–17; Jer 23:5; Lam 1:18; Dan 9:7, 16; Zech 8:8; 9:9; Matt 6:33; Rom 3:21; 5:18, 21; 1 Pet 3:18; 1 John 2:1).

law unto himself. In all of God's external works, he acts justly and righteously, consistent with his own will and nature. Righteousness may also be viewed as an outward expression of God's holiness and love.[191] As the righteous one, God requires moral conformity of his creatures to his moral demand. God is the Lord, indeed the "Judge of the whole earth" who always does what is right (Gen 18:25; cf. Ps 50:6; Zeph 3:5; 2 Tim 4:8). Justice, then, means that God deals with humans according to their adherence or lack of conformity to *his* laws (Deut 32:4; Pss 19:8; 36:6; 98:9; Isa 45:19–21; Acts 17:31). As the just and righteous one, God acts impartially, demanding that his creatures do likewise (Deut 10:17–18), something our secular-postmodern society misunderstands due to their rejection of God as the standard of what is just and right. As applied to humans, alongside its legal sense, *righteousness* can also describe what is "well pleasing" to God, or a godly person, and thus takes on strong ethical overtones, as it does in the NT, for example, in Matthew's Gospel.[192] Let us expound further on the meaning of God's justice/righteousness by focusing on four points.

First, let us outline what God's justice/righteousness is by the following distinctions.[193]

1. Within God (*ad intra*), God *is* holy, just, righteous, and the absolute moral standard. God's law is not external to him; God *is* the law because his will and nature determines what is right and just. Thus, a Christian view of justice, tied to our view of God, stands in total contrast to our secular-postmodern society, which views "justice" as a mere human social construct.

2. In God's external works (*ad extra*), we see the manifestation of God's justice-righteousness, which is the outworking of his holiness and the perfection "by which he maintains himself over against every violation of his holiness, and shows in every respect that he is the Holy One."[194] In God's works, he demands and acts in justice consistent with himself, and he does so for his own glory (Isa 45:22–23; 48; Rom 3:26; 15:5, 9–11; Rev 15:3–4; 19:2). Further, in God's external works, we can distinguish some different aspects of his justice/righteousness.

First, there is *rectoral* or *legislative* justice. God as our Creator and Lord establishes just laws for us to obey for his glory and our good. Given who God is, his demand on us is absolute, thus

---

[191] See Vos, *Reformed Dogmatics*, 1:30.

[192] Moo, *Romans*, 80–81; Schreiner, *Romans*, 66–77. For example, see Isa 5:7; Mic 6:8; Matt 5:6, 10, 20.

[193] See Frame, *Doctrine of God*, 448.

[194] Berkhof, *Systematic Theology*, 74–75.

requiring perfect obedience from us, first in Adam as our covenant head (Gen 2:16–17) and, by extension, to each one of us. God has established laws by which we are to live; specifically, God demands we love him and our neighbor, laws first given in creation (Ps 19:1–6; Rom 1:18–32) and then subsequently given further specificity in the biblical covenants. Depending on the covenant, God commands obedience to specific laws that later change due to the unfolding of God's plan and the fulfillment that results in Christ and the new covenant. For example, under the old covenant circumcision, food laws, hygiene laws, and so on were to be obeyed, but now that Christ has come, we are not directly under the old covenant *as a covenant* (Mark 7:17–23; Acts 10:9–16; 1 Cor 7:19; 9:19–23). Yet, from creation to Christ, God's universal moral demand is given in each covenant (Mark 12:29–31), and we are to obey all of God's commands in light of its fulfillment in Christ and through the lens of the new covenant (Gal 6:2). In addition, God has enacted his laws through God-ordained authorities, which operate in their own sphere: the family (Gen 2:18–25), the church (Matt 18:15–20), and the government (Matt 22:21; Rom 13:1–7).

Second, there is *distributive* justice, by which God administers rewards (i.e., *remunerative*) and punishments (i.e., *retributive*) for right and wrong action.[195] Much of God's administration of justice is done through the authorities that he has established, that is, the family, the church, and the government. In distributive justice, God demonstrates his holiness and righteousness.

Second, let us unpack God's *distributive* justice a bit more in two points.

1. In thinking about *remunerative* justice (Deut 7:9–13; 2 Chron 6:15; Ps 58:11; Mic 7:20; Matt 25:21, 34; Luke 17:10; Rom 2:7; 1 Cor 4:7; Heb 11:26), we must view it in light of God's covenant relationships and promises. God owes us nothing, but we owe him everything. God only rewards us due to his covenant promises and demands. In the creation covenant, God required perfect obedience from Adam with an attached reward, namely, to be confirmed in righteousness. However, given Adam's sin and its subsequent transmission to all of humanity, our problem is that we have broken God's commands and deserve nothing but his judgment. For this reason, our receiving any good from God is not due to us; it is solely due to God's grace, both common and saving.

---

[195] For *remunerative* justice, see Deut 27–28 (the blessing and curses of the covenant); Matt 10:41–42; 25:21, 34; Rom 2:6–7; 1 Pet 1:17; 2 Tim 4:8; 2 Thess 1:5; Heb 11:26; Rev 20:11–15. For *retributive* justice, see Ps 18:20, 24; Jer 18:20; Hos 12:2; Luke 14:14; 2 Thess 1:6–7; Heb 10:30.

In God's promise of redemption (Gen 3:15), he has graciously chosen to redeem us by the ultimate provision of a Redeemer who will render perfect covenant obedience, which, we now know is our Lord Jesus Christ. However, before Christ came and perfectly obeyed for us *and* paid for our sin, the biblical covenants unfolded God's promise as they prophetically anticipated Christ's coming. In the OT, the writers of Scripture constantly appealed to the "righteousness of God" as their ground of confidence and hope (Pss 4:1; 35:24; 143:1; Isa 45:8; 46:13; 51:6). In this use, "God's righteousness" may be understood as God's covenant faithfulness;[196] however, in the Bible's storyline, an apparent tension results. In the covenant, God demands perfect obedience to his commands tied to his own internal nature, but we do not render it. Yet God has promised to keep his promises. The resolution to how God keeps his promises and remains true to himself is ultimately only resolved in Christ and his cross (Rom 3:21–26). For it is only in Christ that God's absolute demand is met, and God's justice is satisfied. And now, due to our covenantal union with him, all of God's blessings are ours, which means that any reward we receive is solely due to God's provision and grace (Phil 2:13). No doubt, God disciplines his people (Prov 3:12; Heb 12:5) and rewards us (Matt 6:1–2, 5, 16; Luke 12:32; Heb 6:10), but undergirding all of God's rewards is his initiative and grace in Christ Jesus our Lord.

2. In thinking about *retributive* justice, given that God *is* holy and just, we need to understand that it means that God judges human conduct by an absolute moral standard, namely, *himself* and his revealed will to all people, known by natural and special revelation.[197] In other words, our triune God as the Judge condones no sin but judges all sin according to the absolute standard of his law.

In Scripture, related to God as the Judge of the world who always does what is right (Gen 18:25) is his holy wrath against our sin and all evil that stands in opposition to him. No doubt, God is patient, gracious, and merciful, but never in such a way that he denies himself; God will never "grade on the curve" or overlook our sin. From the very beginning, especially in light of sin, God's retributive justice is evident (Gen 2:17; 3:1–24). Indeed, the

[196] This point is rightly emphasized by the New Perspective on Paul, a point we will discuss below.

[197] See Gen 2:17; Exod 34:7; Deut 27:26; Pss 11:6–7; 96:13; Ezek 18:4; Dan 12:2; Hab 1:13; Matt 25:46; Acts 17:30–31; Rom 1:32; 2:9; 3:25–26; 6:23; 12:19; 2 Cor 5:10; 2 Thess 1:8; Heb 12:29; Rev 20:11–15.

reason for the incarnation of the divine Son and his cross is tied to a proper grasp of retributive justice (Rom 3:25–26).

Nevertheless, retributive justice is often questioned and disputed, especially by non-orthodox theology. In the post-Reformation era, the Socinians rejected retributive justice by arguing that God's "justice" "was not an essential property of God but rather a voluntary exercise of the divine righteousness *ad extra*—indicating, by extension, that God was under no necessity to punish sin."[198] For the Socinians, God's law is only a function of God's will and *not* of his will *and nature*, and as such, retributive justice is redefined. The result is that God may decide to punish sin, but there is no necessity for him to do so. He may choose to forgive us without an atonement, hence their denial of penal substitution.

However, the problem with the Socinian view is that God's execution of justice is uncoupled from his nature. Justice becomes a voluntary exercise of God's will that he may or may not choose to enact. In response, the Reformed tradition (e.g., Francis Turretin, John Owen) rightly argues that the justice/righteousness of God "is not a quality or accident in him, but his very nature, essential to him."[199] The reason why God must deal with sin is that it is against *him* and his moral character. God is *not* like a human judge, who adjudicates a law external to him; instead, the triune God *is* the law.[200] When God judges, he remains true to himself, and thus his own perfect moral demands; hence, there is a collision between our sin and God's holiness and justice, which is only resolved in the cross, and a cross that actually pays for our sin.

Like the Socinians, many today reject retributive justice for similar reasons. For those who do, Christian theology, specifically one's understanding of God, sin, Christology, the necessity and nature of the cross, and the nature of our justification before God, is forever changed.[201] Such rejections of retributive justice, whether old or new, ultimately undercut the warrant for objective morality grounded in God's own nature and leave us with a different theology.

---

[198] Muller, *Post-Reformation Reformed Dogmatics*, 3:481.

[199] Muller, 3:481.

[200] See Muller, 3:476–97.

[201] For example, see Fleming Rutledge, *The Crucifixion: Understanding the Death of Jesus Christ* (Grand Rapids: Eerdmans, 2017); Darrin W. Snyder Belousek, *Atonement, Justice, and Peace: The Message of the Cross and the Mission of the Church* (Grand Rapids: Eerdmans, 2012); Joel B. Green and Mark D. Baker, *Recovering the Scandal of the Cross: Atonement in the New Testament and Contemporary Contexts*, 2nd ed. (Downers Grove: InterVarsity, 2011).

Third, we cannot discuss righteousness/justice without mentioning the current debate regarding the expression the "righteousness of God" (*dikaiosynē theou*). Those who identify with the "New Perspective(s) on Paul" define "God's righteousness" as God's "covenant faithfulness." No doubt, there is some biblical warrant for this, but ultimately "the righteousness of God" cannot be reduced to "covenant faithfulness" alone.[202] Due to God's promise to save, the "righteousness of God" is inseparably related to his grace and faithfulness to his covenant promises (Pss 97:11–12; 98:2–3; 112:3–6; 116:5; 118:15–19). God's righteousness can refer to his saving activity, and it involves the fulfillment of his covenant promises (Pss 31:1; 36:10; 71:2; Isa 45:8; 46:13; 51:4–8).[203] But "righteousness/justice" and "salvation" are not interchangeable concepts despite the fact that they are closely related in God's redemptive plan. Why? For this reason: first and foremost, God's righteousness/justice refers to who God is in himself as the Holy One (Isa 40:25). God is true to his covenant promises and acts righteously *ad extra*, but in so doing, he does what is right and remains true to who he is *ad intra*. Scripture insists that God is "righteous in all his ways" (Ps 145:17), a "God who does no wrong" (Deut 32:4 NIV), because God's outward acts perfectly reflect his inward nature and will. As the righteous and just Judge, God punishes sin and holds people accountable for their actions (Exod 34:6–7; Deut 10:17–18; Pss 9:5–6, 15–20; 94:7–9; Prov 24:12; Amos 1:3–3:2; Rom 1:18–3:20).

As discussed in part 3, these crucial truths about God, especially in relation to our sin and due to his covenant promises to redeem, create an apparent tension in the Bible's redemptive story. God is the Judge of the universe, who always acts consistently with who he is. Yet, he cannot overlook our sin against him; he *must* act in holy justice/righteousness. But he is also the God of the covenant, who has promised to redeem us by his holy love and display his righteousness and remain true to his name (Pss 31:1–3; 79:9–13; 143:1, 11; Isa

[202] For example, see N. T. Wright, *What Saint Paul Really Said: Was Paul of Tarsus the Real Founder of Christianity?* (Grand Rapids: Eerdmans, 1997), 96, 103; cf. Wright, *Justification: God's Plan and Paul's Vision* (Downers Grove: IVP Academic, 2009). For a discussion and critique of the "New Perspective on Paul," see Robert J. Cara, *Cracking the Foundation of the New Perspective on Paul: Covenantal Nomism Versus Reformed Covenantal Theology* (Fearn, Ross-shire, UK: Mentor, 2017); Guy P. Waters, *Justification and the New Perspective on Paul: A Review and Response* (Phillipsburg: P&R, 2004); Stephen Westerholm, *Perspectives Old and New on Paul: The "Lutheran" Paul and His Critics* (Grand Rapids: Eerdmans, 2004), 297–340.

[203] Moo, *Romans*, 81–86.

43:7; 49:3). But how can he remain true to himself and justify the ungodly? Ultimately, for God to do so, he alone will have to take the initiative to provide a Redeemer who can act in perfect righteousness for us and fully meet God's own demand in the payment of our sin. On these points, namely, our justification requiring the active obedience of Christ and the imputation of his righteousness to us and the full payment of our sin (i.e., penal substitution), the New Perspective on Paul flounders. Why? There are probably a number of reasons, especially given the fact that the New Perspective is not a monolithic movement, but one of the key reasons is that many who embrace this view fail to think of God's righteousness/justice first in terms of God within himself (*ad intra*). Instead, God's righteousness is viewed more in terms of God's external works (*ad extra*) with a strong rectoral emphasis, namely, God making things right. But what is missing is the emphasis on God remaining true to himself and thus, in our justification, the need for the incarnate Son to meet God's own righteous demand against us by his perfect obedience imputed to us and the full payment for our sin. Unless we first think about divine righteousness/justice *ad intra*, we will define these concepts solely in terms of God's work of redemption (or the economy). By contrast, Muller, in describing how Reformed theology defines God's righteousness/justice, is on stronger biblical grounding when he defines these attributes this way: "Justice [is the attribute] by which God in all things wills that which is just; or it is the attribute whereby God is just in and of himself, and exercises justice toward all creatures, and giveth every one his due."[204]

Fourth, it is important to distinguish a biblical view of "justice" from a secular-postmodern understanding of "social justice." In the biblical covenants, God defines proper behavior, including how to relate to one another "justly/righteously," hence the concept of *social* justice.[205] In fact, one reason for the old covenant was for God to teach Israel how to relate rightly to him and to one another. In this way, Israel was to serve as a model nation, drawing the Gentile nations to know the LORD (Isa 2:1–4). Indeed, this ultimately is fulfilled in Christ Jesus, who is not only the last Adam but also the true Israel, who builds his church constituted by people from every tribe, nation, people, and tongue (Eph 2:11–22; Rev 5:9–10). Yet, even

---

[204] Muller, *Post-Reformation Reformed Dogmatics*, 3:481.

[205] See Gentry and Wellum, *Kingdom through Covenant* (see chap. 13, n. 39), especially Peter Gentry's discussion in part 2.

now in the church, as God's new creation in Christ, we are to display to the world what it truly means to act rightly and justly (Eph 3:10–11). But this understanding of "social" justice, tied to how we live in covenant relationship with God and each other, must *not* be confused with a distorted and false idea of "social justice" associated with our culture and current non-Christian thought.

As discussed in chapter 2, Western society, which was influenced largely by a Christian view, has thrown off that influence and moved steadily from a modern to a postmodern view. One of the defining marks of this worldview transformation is a rejection of the triune God as the source and standard of truth and his replacement with a human constructivist view of "truth." At its core, such a view is naturalistic, and even if some form of spirituality is embraced, it is usually thoroughly panentheistic. In the end, what results is a methodological naturalism that continues to place humans at the center of the universe as the "constructors" of reality. No longer is there the possibility of universal objective truth; in its place are simply the finite, subjective, human "identity" constructions of various groups vying for raw political power. In fact, in this "new" view of reality, everything is viewed in terms of the lens of race, gender, and intersectionality under the larger categories of the "oppressor" and the "oppressed." In this thoroughly non-Christian view of the world, the goal is to destroy the "traditional structures and systems deemed to be oppressive, and [redistribute] power and resources from oppressors to victims in pursuit of equality of outcome."[206] However, the epistemological ground on which the system stands is quicksand. As a result, even the determination of who the "oppressor" and "oppressed" are is relative, and without an objective basis to discern truth from error and good from evil, such a view, as history reminds us, ends in totalitarianism, statism, and the destruction of human life.

For this reason, we must not confuse our culture's desire for "social" justice with true biblical justice. Biblically, to act justly toward one another is always according to an objective standard,

---

[206] Allen, *Why Social Justice*, 43 (see chap. 11, n. 42). For a helpful discussion of the roots of this thinking, especially applied to the social construction of our identities in terms of sexuality, see Trueman, *Rise and Triumph* (see chap. 1, n. 26). Also see Sowell, *The Quest for Cosmic Justice* (see chap. 2, n. 114); Groothuis, *Fire in the Streets* (see chap. 11, n. 42); Ronald H. Nash, *Social Justice and the Christian Church* (Lima, OH: Academic Renewal Press, 2002); Yoram Hazony, *Conservativism: A Rediscovery* (Washington, DC: Regnery Gateway, 2022), 311–29.

namely, God's authoritative word. This is why our current cultural voices who cry for justice and then embrace abortion, deny a biblical view of sexuality and the family, who argue that mathematics and logical thinking is "racist," who endorse the destruction of private property, and who embrace the unlimited power of the state are not following biblical teaching. Instead, they are "constructing" their own system and their own view of "reality" ultimately built on a complete relativism. Today, there is probably no greater worldview clash than between a biblical view of justice and the so-called social justice of our secular-postmodern society.

Love, Grace, Mercy

We now turn to a discussion of God's moral attributes of love, grace, and mercy—all of which are an outworking of God's goodness and are consistent with God's holiness. In thinking through these attributes, it is important, as we did with justice/righteousness, to distinguish between God in himself (*ad intra*) and the exercise of these attributes in God's external works (*ad extra*).[207]

Why? For many reasons, but especially because, in the case of attributes associated with God's love, many mistakenly think that God's love necessitates a social-relational view that entails that God "needs" his creation to be completely satisfied. This is one of the errors of open theism, along with other "relational" views of God, such as panentheism. For these views, God's love means that he is in a mutual give-and-take relationship with the world; he takes risks, changes his mind in response to our choices, and his "rule" is only persuasive. God is not the sovereign Lord.

However, this view is unbiblical. God is triune, and from eternity, he has experienced a fullness of holy love between Father, Son, and Spirit that lacks nothing. As already noted, love and holiness are intrinsic to God and totally interrelated. If holiness conveys the idea of consecration and total devotion, then within God, holiness is the intensity of the love that flows within his being, as the divine persons are exhaustively devoted to each other, seeking their own glory, name, and honor. Within God, there is a perfection of life and love; God is *a se* and thus in need of nothing outside himself to satisfy himself.

Given this fact, it is earth shaking that God has chosen to share himself with what is external to him. In God's works, "God's love is his self-communicative activity by which he

[207] On this point, see Muller, *Post-Reformation Reformed Dogmatics*, 3:561.

communicates goodness—ultimately his own light and life—to others for the sake of consummation and communion."[208] By his own free decision, God has chosen to share his love and to give himself for the blessedness of his people.[209] But in giving himself for his creation, and especially his people, "God's love for what is not-God (i.e. creation/creatures) is 'a turning out of fullness, not out of lack.'"[210] God is love without creation. "Neither creation nor the cross constitute God as love; rather, they are events that establish and accomplish his loving purpose of holy fellowship with creatures."[211]

For this reason, in all of God's works, he freely chooses to share himself with his creation. In so doing, the *summum bonum* that God wills for his people is *himself*. Grace and mercy flow from this understanding. God's "grace" is an exercise of his love towards the undeserving, indeed, towards those who deserve judgment for their sin, which reveals in a greater way God's goodness. "Mercy," similar to grace, refers to God's having pity on those who are in distress regardless of the fact that no one deserves it. However, unless we distinguish between God's love *ad intra* and *ad extra*, we will not account for all that Scripture teaches about our triune God who is *a se*, but who also, out of the fullness of his divine life, chooses to share himself with us! With this point firmly in place, let us now expound further on God's love, grace, and mercy.

First, let us think about God's *love*.[212] J. I. Packer begins his discussion of God's love by first noting that Scripture twice states, "God is love" (1 John 4:8, 16), but then acknowledges how often this tremendous truth is misunderstood and distorted.[213] Packer suggests that a primary reason why this is so is that God's love is too often separated from other divine attributes, such as holiness, justice, and aseity. At work, at least implicitly, is a denial of divine simplicity, and unless we keep together all that Scripture teaches, inevitably distortions arise.

---

[208] Vanhoozer, "Love without Measure?," 519 (italics removed).

[209] Packer defines God's love as follows: "God's love is an exercise of his goodness toward individual sinners whereby, having identified himself with their welfare, he has given his Son to be their Savior, and now brings them to know and enjoy him in a covenant relation." *Knowing God*, 123 (italics removed).

[210] Vanhoozer, "Love without Measure?," 519.

[211] Vanhoozer, 520. Vanhoozer continues: "Our species is so self-centered that we easily forget that God *has* a life, quite apart from us, and always has" (520).

[212] My discussion is indebted to Carson, *Difficult Doctrine* (see chap. 17, n. 61). Also see Garry J. Williams, *His Love Endures Forever: Reflections on the Immeasurable Love of God* (Wheaton: Crossway, 2016); Packer, *Knowing God*, 117–27; Muller, *Post-Reformation Reformed Dogmatics*, 3:561–69.

[213] Packer, *Knowing God*, 117.

Furthermore, we must also account for the diverse ways Scripture speaks of God's love. God *is* love, but to grasp its breadth and depth, Scripture speaks of God's love in terms of different aspects, often reflected in the different ways God relates to the world. D. A. Carson is helpful on this point. He suggests that Scripture speaks of God's love in five distinguishable ways:[214] (1) the intra-trinitarian love of the Father, Son, and Holy Spirit;[215] (2) God's providential love for his creation often identified as *common* grace. God is pleased with what he has created (Gen 1:31) and cares for it (e.g., animals [Job 39; Matt 10:29] and humans [Matt 10:30–31; Acts 14:14–18; 17:24–29]). (3) God's salvific stance toward a fallen world (Ezek 33:11; John 3:16).[216] (4) God's selecting and effective love of his elect (e.g., Israel, church, individuals [Deut 7:7–8; 10:14–15; Mal 1:2–3; Eph 1:4–6; 5:25; 1 John 4:8–10]). (5) God's love of his people in a "conditional" way; that is, in covenant relationship with God, God requires our obedience. This last area is not about how we become Christians; instead, it is about our ongoing relationship with the Lord as his justified people (John 15:9–10; Jude 21).

After describing the diverse ways Scripture speaks about God's love, Carson astutely insists that to be *biblical*, we must not absolutize any one of these five ways. Instead, we must view them as complementary, and keep them together in their biblical proportion, which also requires our careful application of these truths to our lives. For example, if we absolutize God's *ad intra* love as *the* model for all of God's relations to the world, we have denied analogy and forgotten that within God there is a perfection of relations unlike anything in creation, and without sin. However, in God's love toward us, especially as fallen creatures, there is both love and wrath. This is not true of intra-trinitarian love. Or, if we absolutize God's providential love, then his love is no more than his care for creation. It says little about God's redemptive

---

[214] Muller discusses how this way of unpacking God's love was common in Reformed theology. Although slightly different from Carson's classification, Reformed theology spoke of: (1) God's intra-trinitarian love, (2) God's love for his creation, (3) God's love for humans, (4) God's love for his elect, and (5) God's love of the good. Muller, *Post-Reformation Reformed Dogmatics*, 3:562-64.

[215] Carson discusses a common exegetical mistake in thinking about God's love. Some argue that there are different "kinds" of love solely based on specific words for love (e.g., *eros*, *agapaō*, *phileō*). God's unique love, then, is always *agapē* love. This is incorrect. For example, *agapaō* (John 3:35) and *phileō* (John 5:20) both refer to the Father and Son's love for each other. Words have a range of meaning and but context is determinative for how an author uses the word.

[216] Carson argues that in John, "world" (*kosmos*) refers to the moral order in culpable rebellion against God.

love centered in our Lord Jesus Christ and God's love for his people. Alternatively, if God's love is only an inviting, yearning, sinner-seeking passion, then this does not account for God's justice, holiness, sovereignty, and glory. Or, if God's love exclusively refers to his love for the elect, we may wrongly conclude that God only loves the elect and no one else. Lastly, if God's love is exclusively tied to human obedience, then it might lead to some version of a merit theology and endless fretting about whether we have been good enough to enjoy the love of God. Instead, we must stress the entirety of what Scripture says about God's love and rightly apply it to our lives depending on the context. But in the end, as God's people, we must glory in God's love, which is necessary for our spiritual growth (Eph 3:17–19) and increases our faith and hope (Rom 5:5) and which we seek to emulate in our lives (Matt 22:37–38; John 13:35; 1 John 2:15; 4:11; 5:3).

Second, let us think about God's *grace*.[217] "Grace," at its heart, is the exercise of God's love toward the undeserving. Vos states it this way: Grace is "the undeserved love of God toward sinful beings who lie under the judgment of His righteousness."[218] In Scripture, grace involves two aspects: first, it is unmerited, and second, when it is at work in sinners, it is *monergistic*. As Vos notes, "If in its origin God's love toward sinners is without obligation and freely acting, it must therefore be sovereignly divine in its outworking, that is, an undivided work of God."[219] Also, Scripture can distinguish aspects of God's grace depending on its object. In relation to creation, and especially a fallen world, God's love toward the undeserving is *common* grace. In relation to his people, God's love is a unique and special *saving* grace.

Abraham Kuyper described *common* grace this way: it is "that act of God by which *negatively* he curbs the operations of Satan, death, and sin, and by which *positively* he creates an intermediate state for the cosmos, as well as for our human race, which is and continues to be deeply and radically sinful, but in which sin cannot work out its end."[220] In a similar way, John Murray describes common grace as "every favour of whatever kind or degree, falling short of salvation, which this undeserving and sin-cursed world enjoys at the hand of God."[221] In Scripture, common grace is evident in a number of ways. For example, God restrains sin so its effects are not as

[217] See Packer, *Knowing God*, 128–37; cf. Muller, *Post-Reformation Reformed Dogmatics*, 3:569–74.

[218] Vos, *Reformed Dogmatics*, 1:28.

[219] Vos, 1:29.

[220] Abraham Kuyper, *Principles of Sacred Theology* (Grand Rapids: Eerdmans, 1969), 279.

[221] John Murray, "Common Grace," in *Collected Writings*, 2:96 (see chap. 11, n. 14) (italics removed).

bad as they could be (Gen 6:3; Acts 17:30; Rom 2:4; 1 Pet 3:20; 2 Pet 3:9). In fact, the Noahic covenant is proof that God delays divine judgment and continues to give good gifts to this fallen order, including the upholding of many creation structures, such as marriage, the family, and government (Gen 6–9). Or Scripture reminds us that God pours out positive blessings on his creation due to the Noahic covenant, such as sun, rain, and harvest, so that we are able to live and function in the world (Gen 39:5; Pss 65:9–13; 104:10–30; 136:25; 145:1–16; Matt 5:44–45; Luke 6:35–36; 16:25; Acts 14:16–17). In fact, it is due to common grace that fallen people can perform "good" works (2 Kgs 10:30; 12:2; Matt 5:46; Luke 6:33; Rom 2:14–15), although never in such a way as to attain right standing before God. Scripture also reminds us that God is patient and kind to all people (Pss 36:5–9; 145:9; Matt 5:44–48; Luke 6:35–36; Acts 14:17), which is a display of his continued exercise of love to an underserving world.

Regarding God's *saving* grace, Bavinck defines it this way: "Ascribed to God, grace is the voluntary, unrestrained, and unmerited favor that he shows to sinners and that, instead of the verdict of death, brings them righteousness and life."[222] Bavinck continues, "grace" is a virtue and attribute of God (Rom 5:15; 1 Pet 5:10), which is demonstrated in the sending of Christ (John 1:14–18; 3:16) and the lavishing on God's people every spiritual blessing solely due to God's grace (Rom 5:20; Eph 1:3–14; 2:5, 8; Titus 3:7). As J. I. Packer reflects on the entirety of Scripture and God's glorious plan of redemption, which is nothing less than a display of God's grace, he writes, "The grace of God is love freely shown towards guilty sinners, contrary to their merit and indeed in defiance of their demerit. It is God showing goodness to persons who deserve only severity and had no reason to expect anything but severity."[223] For believers, when we understand this truth, this produces, by the Spirit's work (Rom 5:5), humility, gratitude, joy, and a love for our triune God that results in lives lived for his glory alone.

Third, let us think of God's *mercy* (Exod 34:6; Ps 103:8; 2 Cor 1:3; Heb 4:16).[224] Grace and mercy are closely related, but mercy focuses on God's attitude toward the undeserving, namely, "God's love and pity toward sinners, who are considered as wretched."[225] Ephesians 2 teaches this point. Paul describes what we were "in Adam," outside of Christ: spiritually dead,

---

[222] Bavinck, *Reformed Dogmatics*, 2:214.

[223] Packer, *Knowing God*, 132.

[224] See Muller, *Post-Reformation Reformed Dogmatics*, 3:574–81.

[225] Vos, *Reformed Dogmatics*, 1:29.

under the power and domain of sin, death, and the devil, and most serious of all, under God's wrath (vv. 1–3). Despite deserving nothing but judgment from God and being found in a helpless and pitiful condition, God, by sovereign grace and moved by his overwhelming mercy, took the initiative to save us in Christ Jesus. From the overflow of his love, God freely chose to take the initiative to redeem us in Christ (1:4–10), as Paul exclaims: "But God, who is rich in mercy, because of his great love that he had for us, made us alive with Christ even though we were dead in trespasses. You are saved by grace!" (2:4–5).

As magnificent as God's love, grace, and mercy are, some have thought that they are in conflict with retributive justice, which usually leads to a modification or rejection of the latter. At dispute is whether God can act in grace and mercy and forgive us of our sins apart from the payment of our sin, thus also denying penal substitution. If God is love, and he is so gracious and merciful, then why can he not simply forgive us? To demand the full satisfaction of his justice seems to conflict with God's grace and mercy. After all, when the prodigal son returned to his father and asked for his forgiveness, did not the father simply accept his repentance and forgive him without the need for any kind of atonement?[226] Let me offer three points in response.

1. Such a view misunderstands both love/grace/mercy and justice. Mercy is an expression of God's love, but God's love is first *ad intra* before it is *ad extra*. Regarding the former, God's holy love within himself means that God never denies himself. In relation to sin and God's external work of judgment, God's love always upholds his own holy name and glory. To think that God's love and mercy can overlook our sin or not demand full payment of our sin is to misunderstand them. In a similar way, God *is* holy and just, and as with his love, God cannot deny himself as the moral standard of goodness, which is good news as otherwise there is no ultimate justice in this world! In fact, in biblical thought, for God not to punish sin is an act of injustice and thus the opposite of love, especially since sin is first treason against God!

2. It is also crucial to stress the *optional, voluntary* nature of grace and mercy. God *is* holy love, and in all of his actions, he remains true to himself and to his will, plan, and promises. In God's relation to sin, he *must* judge it since it stands opposed to him, but to choose to redeem

---

[226] For this argument, see Green and Baker, *Recovering the Scandal of the Cross*, 174, who appeal to the work of Robin Collins.

us is a free choice on his behalf. God does not have to display his grace or mercy, for as Scripture reminds us, "I will show mercy to whom I will show mercy" (Rom 9:15; cf. Matt 11:26; Rom 11:33). What is shocking in Scripture is not that God judges our sin; instead, it is that he chooses to display his grace! As the Psalmist marvels: "But with you there is forgiveness!" (Ps 130:4).

3. To pit mercy against justice is incorrect. The opposite of mercy is not justice but cruelty, and the opposite of justice is not mercy but injustice. Justice is a function of God's holy love, which means that he does not act with indifference or indulgence toward us. To do so is not loving, but immoral. Furthermore, it is true that in our redemption, God justifies the ungodly without strict justice being applied to us (Rom 4:5). But this is only possible due to our Lord acting as our penal substitute and bearing God's strict justice in our place. In Christ, we receive abundant grace and mercy but not because justice was not met. For us, it was satisfied fully in Christ Jesus, our covenant head, representative, and substitute. The proof that mercy and justice are not mutually exclusive is the cross of Christ, where God's justice is on display alongside his love, grace, and mercy for us who did not deserve the precious gift of the divine Son, who loved us and gave himself for us (Gal 2:20). It is no wonder that John can point to the cross as the demonstration that God *is* love, not because he overlooks our sin, but because the Father has freely acted in grace and mercy to give us his Son to be the propitiation for our sins (1 John 4:9–10). Thus, in Christ's cross, we have a priestly act of justice in which the divine holiness comes against sin. In Christ, the Judge is judged in our place, thus upholding his own moral perfection and demonstrating the depths of divine mercy (Rom 3:21–26).

The Glory of Our Triune God[227]

It is fitting that we conclude our discussion of God's perfections by focusing on the glory of our triune God. In fact, God's *glory* is not really an attribute of God. Rather, it is a way of capturing God's *beauty*, *wonder*, *perfection*, and *blessedness*. In many ways, the glory of God refers to the integrated unity of the diversity of divine attributes in the single being of God. J. I. Packer helpfully speaks of God's glory as his "deity on display."[228]

---

[227] See Morgan, "Toward a Theology," in Morgan and Peterson, *Glory of God*, 153–87 (see chap. 16, n. 18).

[228] J. I. Packer, "The Glory of God," in Ferguson et al., *New Dictionary of Theology*, 272 (see chap. 7, n. 11).

In Scripture, *glory* (Heb. *kabod*; Gk. *doxa*) refers to the plenitude of God's perfections, along with God's "honor" and "excellent reputation" (Isa 43:7; John 17:5; Rom 3:23). *Kabod* connotes the idea of weight or heaviness.[229] When applied to God, it conveys the truth that God alone is God, the God of reality and *weight*, in contrast to the idols who are not real, and who blow in the wind like chaff. *Doxa* picks up the same truth, referring to "God's manifestation of his person, presence, and/or works, especially his power, judgment, and salvation."[230]

We must first think of God's glory *ad intra*. God as the triune Lord has fullness of life within himself as Father, Son, and Holy Spirit (Pss 24:7–10; 29:3; Acts 7:2; Eph 1:17). This means that if God had never created the world, he would still be the God of unimaginable glory (Isa 42:8). God's choice to create, then, is out of the fullness of his own divine life. In fact, even in creation, God did not exhaustively communicate his glory. Chris Morgan nicely makes this point: God's extrinsic display of his glory "is less than the intrinsic. As awe-inspiring as the extrinsic glory is, it never fully expresses the fullness of God's intrinsic glory that it communicates."[231]

But with this said, it is also true that we only know of God's glory by his external works.[232] In those works, the *blessed* (Gk. *makarios*) God (1 Tim 1:11; 6:15–16) displays his glory as "the King eternal, immortal, invisible, the only God," who alone demands and deserves all "honor and glory forever and ever. Amen" (1 Tim 1:17). No wonder Scripture teaches that God's entire plan for the universe, including his plan of redemption, is ultimately for the display of his glory! In God's works, his full display of attributes is seen, which we, as God's redeemed people, wonderfully experience, which allows us to ascribe to him all glory, honor, and praise (Pss 8:4–8; 29:2; Rom 11:36; 16:27; Phil 4:20; 2 Tim 4:18; Jude 24–25; Rev 1:5–6). Morgan captures these truths by the following statement: "The triune God who is glorious displays his glory, largely through his creation, image-bearers, providence, and redemptive acts. God's people respond by glorifying him. God receives glory and, through uniting his people to Christ, shares his glory with them—all to his glory."[233]

---

[229] Morgan, "Toward a Theology," 156.

[230] Morgan, 157.

[231] Morgan, 163–64.

[232] See Morgan, 155–56, who shows from creation to the new creation how God displays his glory.

[233] Morgan, 159 (italics removed).

As we see God's triune glory displayed across redemptive history through the covenants, God's "glory" in the OT is often associated with the ark of the covenant, the tabernacle, or the fiery manifestations of God associated with Mt. Sinai (Exod 3–4, 13–14; 16:7, 10; 20; 24; 29:43; 32–34; 40:34–38). In these cases, the glory of God is an indication of his transcendent *presence* on earth.[234] The verb *to dwell* (*shekin*) is used in connection with the glory and the tabernacle. The Shekinah is said to fill the tabernacle (Exod 40:34–35), the temple (1 Kgs 8:11), and the whole earth (Pss 6:3; 72:19). The idea of God dwelling with his people in covenant relationship pervades both Testaments. The purpose of our creation is to know the triune God of glory and to dwell in his presence forever. Indeed, the purpose of history is for God to display the full range of his attributes, which is nothing less than his glory.[235] In redemption, God has reconciled us to himself so that in the covenant, the supreme blessing is knowing *him* and experiencing *his* glorious presence. But as the OT people of God experienced firsthand, in a fallen world, God's presence is dangerous: sin must be dealt with, atonement must be made, and God must graciously provide redemption in order for us to experience the presence and glory of God.

As God's plan unfolds, all of the OT covenants prophetically anticipate God's provision of a greater Redeemer in the ratification of the new covenant, which occurs in the coming of the divine Son, who takes on our human nature in order to redeem us and to make all things new (John 1:1, 14). For this reason, in the NT, God's glory is supremely displayed in our Lord Jesus Christ (John 1:1–18) and his entire work (John 7:39; 12:16, 23–28; 13:31–32; 17:1–5; Phil 2:9–11; Heb 2:5–9; Rev 5:12–13). He is the Shekinah, the glory of God, in whom all of God's fullness dwells (Col 1:19). Christ is the "Lord of glory" (Jas 2:1 ESV) and as such, due to our union with him, we are justified before God, born and indwelt by the Spirit, re-created after the image of Christ, and God's new temple (Eph 2:19–22). As Christ's people, we are to reflect the glory of God. Indeed, the glory of God seen in the face of Christ is to be reflected in the church (2 Cor 4:3–6; 3:18). Until Christ returns, the mystery of this glory is that it is to be manifested above all in suffering, as the purpose of the church is to proclaim and confess the glory of God to the world.

---

[234] Morgan, 157.

[235] Isa 4:2–6; 40:5; 48:5; 55:5; 59:19; 60:1, 19; 66:12, 18–20, 21–24; cf. Rom 5:2; 2 Cor 4:17; Rev 4–5; 21–22.

Furthermore, in light of Christ's coming and work, we see more clearly how God's glory is fully trinitarian. In our redemption, the Father sends the Son, who glorifies the Father by his incarnation and work (John 17:1; Phil 2:5–11). The Father and the Son send the Spirit, who glorifies the Son (John 16:14). Because of Christ's work, the Father glorifies the Son (Acts 3:13–15; Rom 6:4; Phil 2:9–11), which results in all glory to the Father (Phil 2:11) and the triune God being all in all (1 Cor 15:28). As Jonathan Edwards beautifully captures these truths, "the whole is *of* God, and *in* God, and *to* God; and he is the beginning, middle, and end."[236]

Concluding Reflection

As we conclude our discussion of God's attributes, we have only scratched the surface. Trying to describe the incomprehensible God is no easy task, but it is the wondrous task that we will have the privilege of doing for all eternity; indeed, there is no higher calling for the church than to know and glorify our God.

As we have reflected on Scripture in light of historical theology, we have been reminded that the knowledge of God and the pursuit of his glory is the reason God created and redeemed us. In fact, the entire history of the world is the stage God created to display his glory, and in the end, history will be the story of God's self-celebration, which redounds to the good of his people. Indeed, after reflecting on the nature of God's being and thinking about God's self-sufficiency, simplicity, eternality, immutability, omnipresence, omnipotence, omniscience, trustworthiness, holiness, goodness, love, and grace, what higher end could we discover?

In 1973, J. I. Packer argued that the greatest need of the church in the twentieth century was to know, adore, trust, and glory in our triune Creator-covenant Lord. What he said then is still true today. After David reflects on God's majesty and glory, he turns to prayer and asks, "Search me, God, and know my heart; / test me and know my concerns. / See if there is any offensive way in me; / lead me in the everlasting way" (Ps 139:23–24). This ought to be our prayer as well.

---

[236] Jonathan Edwards, "The End for Which God Created the World," in *God's Passion for His Glory*, ed. John Piper (Wheaton: Crossway, 1998), 247.

We live in challenging days for both the church and our larger society. In our society, we are witnessing the end of the West as it increasingly implodes from within. In many ways, this is to be expected. Although God ordains the state, and it has an important task to fulfill, it is not the church. In biblical thought, the kingdoms of this world are passing away, but the kingdom of God will never fail. Yet, it is a sad fact that the implosion we see around us is largely due to the shift away from the influence of a broadly Christian worldview to the embrace of a secular-postmodern one. As is to be expected, this shift away from Christianity has not resulted in a flourishing society, but one that is bent on its own destruction. The dust of death is settling around us on every side. Interestingly, Friedrich Nietzsche predicted that this would occur. In his day, when he announced and celebrated the "death of God," he also said something profound: "When cultures lose the decisive influence of God, God dies. When God dies for a culture, they become weightless; there is a hollowing out."[237]

Nietzsche probably spoke better than he knew, but he was exactly right. With the loss of the influence of Christianity, and specifically the God of the Bible in the West (indeed in any society), eventually societies become "weightless." Remember that the Hebrew word for "glory" conveys the idea of God's "weightiness." What Nietzsche probably did not realize was that in his diagnosis of the problem of Western society, he was also pointing to its only hope and solution, which the church should already know. Ultimately, what is needed is for the God of glory to once again act in power and grace in true reformation and revival. Apart from his sovereign work in the life of the church, which then has a spillover effect on society, no society will ever last.

For the church, we must not forget this. In a day when we are often consumed by many "good" things but not primarily the glory of God, we need to turn from our self-absorption to the centrality of God and the lordship of Christ in every area of our lives. As the church, we need to once again call out to our God in repentance and faith and petition him to renew us, to continue to bring new life to the spiritually dead, and to turn us from our self-centeredness to love and adoration of the only true God, who alone is worthy of our devotion. We do not expect our society to last forever, but the church must learn to cry as Moses did in difficult days, "Show me your glory" (Exod 33:18 ESV). As God's new covenant people, Moses's prayer

---

[237] Cited in Os Guinness, "The Impact of Modernization," *Lausanne Movement*, May 21, 2018, https://lausanne.org/content/the-impact-of-modernization.

needs to be prayed again but, for us, with far greater understanding and urgency. Why? For this important reason: what Moses ultimately cried to see has come in Christ (John 1:14–18). In light of the fullness of the revelation of God's glory in Christ, we need to cry in a greater way, "Show us your triune glory in the face of our Lord Jesus Christ." In every age, our only hope is that God continues to visit his people with his grace, and revive his people to worship, love, obey, and glorify him more. "To the only wise God, through Jesus Christ—to him be the glory forever! Amen" (Rom 16:27).

CHAPTER 19

The Triune God of All Glory

Introduction

In our discussion of theology proper, we now turn our attention to the glory of our triune God. Building on our discussion of God's unity and attributes—what the Father, Son, and Holy Spirit equally and exhaustively have in common—we now contemplate God's triune being. There are at least three reasons why the doctrine of the Trinity is of vital significance.

First, the Trinity is the indispensable mystery at the heart of all of theology. Herman Bavinck states it this way: "The entire Christian belief system, all of special revelation, stands or falls with the confession of God's Trinity."[1] By God's self-revelation we discover that the Trinity is God's name (Matt 28:18–20) and that from eternity, the Father, Son, and Spirit have existed as the only true God in the blessed perfection of a fully shared life of love, joy, and communion. We get a sense of this when Jesus, the divine Son, prays to his Father and speaks of the glory and love he has shared with the Father (and Spirit) from eternity (John 17:5, 24; cf. 1:1–2, 18). Since God is complete within himself and in need of nothing (Acts 17:24–25), his choice to share himself with his creation, especially his people, is a free, sovereign, and gracious

[1] Bavinck, *Reformed Dogmatics*, 2:333 (see chap. 1, n. 9).

choice. In fact, the *summum bonum* God has willed for his church is to know *him* as Father, Son, and Spirit, and without the Trinity, we do not know who God truly is (John 5:22–23; 17:3). Bavinck is correct when he argues that what was at stake in "the development of the church's doctrine of the Trinity . . . was not a metaphysical theory or a philosophical speculation but the essence of the Christian religion itself."[2]

Second, the Trinity is what distinguishes the God of the Bible from all other ideas of "God." In some monotheistic views, especially those who borrow from Scripture, such as Islam and various unitarian conceptions (Socinianism, Jehovah's Witnesses, and now Judaism), there is a "formal" similarity in describing God's attributes, although without the Trinity, this description is "materially" different. But in all non-Christian thought, whether religious or philosophical, there is a uniform rejection of the Trinity. On this point, Christian theology is in total antithesis to *all* non-Christian thought—a significant point to remember in our pluralistic age. Also, given the centrality of the Trinity, it is not surprising that every heresy is, "in the last analysis, an attack upon the Trinity,"[3] which reminds us that the Trinity is not an insignificant point of doctrine.

Third, without the Trinity, we cannot make sense of God's self-description in Scripture and the Bible's gospel message as progressively revealed through the covenants centered in Christ. As Scripture begins, we are confronted by the eternal, independent, and self-sufficient God. As sin enters the world by human choice and rebellion, given who God is, we realize that sin is a major problem before him. Given God's gracious choice to redeem us, the question is how can he do so? Ultimately, we discover that we cannot solve the problem of sin; only *God* can do so. But in God's promise and provision of a Redeemer, we need more than a human deliverer (although we need an obedient, human covenant-keeper to obey for us); we need a

---

[2] Bavinck, 2:333. See Gregory of Nazianzus, *Orations* 40.41 (*NPNF*², 7:375):

> No sooner do I conceive of the One than I am illumined by the Splendor of the Three; no sooner do I distinguish Them than I am carried back to the One. When I think of any One of the Three I think of Him as the Whole, and my eyes are filled, and the greater part of what I am thinking of escapes me. I cannot grasp the greatness of That One so as to attribute a greater greatness to the Rest. When I contemplate the Three together, I see but one torch, and cannot divide or measure out the Undivided Light.

[3] Van Til, *In Defense of the Faith*, 5:223 (see chap. 3, n. 9).

divine Son to bear our sin and to satisfy *his* own righteous demand against our sin, along with a divine Spirit to raise us from spiritual death and apply the Son's work to us. In other words, the Bible's story of God, humans, sin, and salvation makes no sense apart from the Father, Son, and Spirit, who chooses to redeem us by grace and, from beginning to end, to accomplish what we need: a *divine* and *triune* work of redemption.

It is not surprising that all denials of the Trinity inevitably deny the Bible's view of God and salvation and substitute it for some humanistic "solution" that in the end cannot save. Without the Trinity, it is impossible to make sense of how the Bible describes who God is, the incarnation of the divine Son, the substitutionary nature of the atonement, and the work of the divine Spirit or to understand that the entire work of redemption is "Trinitarian through and through."[4]

Given these crucial truths, we now turn to the important task of expounding the doctrine of the Trinity from Scripture and in light of the confessional standards of the church. Unlike other doctrinal areas, there is widespread "catholic" agreement on the Trinity, which has been passed down since the fourth century. In what follows, we will unpack and develop the doctrine of the Trinity in five steps. We will (1) give a definition of the Trinity; (2) discuss the biblical evidence for the Trinity; (3) consider the historical development of pro-Nicene trinitarianism; (4) review some contemporary Trinitarian debates, especially within evangelical theology; and (5) conclude with some final reflections.

Definition of the Trinity

A basic working definition of the Trinity is as follows: "There is only one, true, and living God. There are also three persons in the Godhead: Father, Son, and Holy Spirit. These three persons are one true eternal God, the same in being, equal in power, glory, and authority although distinguished by their personal properties or eternally ordered relations."[5]

From the definition, a basic trinitarian theology may be given in five points.

First, there is only one, true, and living God, with God's "oneness" defined in terms of both singularity and simplicity. In terms of simplicity, God's one essence is not composed of

[4] Bavinck, *Reformed Dogmatics*, 2:334.

[5] The definition is a variation of *The Westminster Shorter Catechism*, questions 5 and 6.

parts: God is simple and unlike any created being. All of God's attributes are *essential* to him; indeed, God *is* his attributes. God is self-existent and self-sufficient (aseity).[6]

Second, this one God eternally exists as three "persons": Father, Son, and Holy Spirit. Within God (*ad intra*), each person subsists in the one divine essence, which means that each person is equal in all the divine attributes (e.g., eternity, aseity, omnipotence, omnipresence, omniscience, wisdom, authority, holiness, love, etc.). Thus, each person is *all* of God, not part of God. None of the persons are dependent on the others for their deity since each person *is* God himself (*autotheos*).[7]

Third, the persons are distinguished by their ordered (Gk. *taxis*) eternal "relations of origin" or personal "properties" (paternity, filiation, and spiration) that are unique and incommunicable. The Father alone has "paternity" because he is the Father of the Son and eternally generates the Son (i.e., active generation) and fully communicates to him the divine essence so that the Son has and is all that the Father essentially has and is. The Son alone has "filiation" because he is eternally generated or begotten from the Father (i.e., passive generation) and fully receives from the unbegotten Father the divine essence. The Spirit alone has "spiration" because he eternally proceeds from both the Father and the Son (i.e., active spiritation) and receives from both the Father and Son (i.e., passive spiration) the fullness of the divine essence, thus having a double procession.[8]

---

[6] We will discuss and develop this point in chapter 21.

[7] See Calvin, *Institutes*, 1.13.23–25 (1:149–54) (see chap. 1, n. 3); Webster says that the Son is *autotheos* "not in respect of his person (which is from the Father) but in respect of the common aseity which he has as a sharer in the one divine essence. The Father is *a se* in his person (as the *principium* of the triune life); the Son is *a se* only in his divine essence." *God without Measure*, 1:37 (see chap. 1, n. 6). Cf. Brannon Ellis, *Calvin, Classical Trinitarianism, and the Aseity of the Son* (Oxford: Oxford University Press, 2012).

[8] On the distinction of Father, Son, and Spirit according to their eternal relations of origin, see White, *Trinity*, 409–41 (see chap. 16, n. 3). The divine processions refer to God's inner life and eternal relations of the Father, Son, and Spirit. Within God, there are two processions: the eternal generation of the Son from the Father and the eternal spiration of the Spirit from the Father and Son. The divine processions are necessary and incommunicable so that "the Father alone is eternally characterized by paternity, is not generated, and does not proceed. The Son alone is eternally characterized by sonship/filiation and is eternally generated. The Holy Spirit alone eternally proceeds." Andreas J. Köstenberger and Gregg R. Allison, *The Holy Spirit* (Nashville: B&H Academic, 2020), 274.

Fourth, in all of God's external works (*ad extra*; e.g., creation, providence, and redemption), that is, in the divine economy, all three persons act inseparably and indivisibly as the one God but also according to their eternally ordered relations. Thus, the Father acts through the Son and by the Spirit; the Son acts from the Father by the Spirit; and the Spirit acts from the Father and the Son, yet it is one act (e.g., Gen 1:1–3; Matt 3:16–17; Luke 1:35; John 1:1–3; 5:19–23; Eph 1:3–14; Col 1:15–17; Heb 1:2–3; 9:14).

Fifth, although the divine persons act inseparably, specific acts are appropriated to one of the persons according to their eternally ordered relations. For example, the Father as unbegotten is the initiator, author, and planner of God's works (Eph 1:4–5) and is identified with creation (Eph 3:9; Rev 4:11); the Son, who is from the Father, accomplishes God's works and is identified with redemption (Eph 1:7; Rev 5:9–10); and the Spirit, who is from the Father and Son, brings to completion God's works and is identified with the application of Christ's work to us (Eph 1:13).[9]

With this basic theology in place, we can now ask: What is the biblical evidence for this? Let us now turn to Scripture and look at some of the biblical data for the triune God of glory.

Biblical Evidence for the Doctrine of the Trinity

Although the word *Trinity* is not found in Scripture, the *concept* is everywhere; we cannot make sense of God's self-revelation in redemptive history without recognizing that the Creator-covenant Lord is Father, Son, and Holy Spirit. Let us first look at how God's triune being is progressively revealed in the OT and then how it reaches its full disclosure in the NT with the coming of our Lord Jesus Christ and the new covenant work of the Spirit.

The Triune God Is Progressively Revealed in Scripture

God's triune being does not merely appear in the NT. There are hints of it in the OT, beginning in Genesis and reaching its fullness in the Father sending his Son and the Spirit, tied to Christ's incarnation and work. Although the OT does not yield a full trinitarian theology, it

[9] On points four and five, see White, 520–33; Scott R. Swain, *The Trinity: An Introduction* (Wheaton: Crossway, 2020), 105–20.

provides the foundation to do so. Here are some of the key points as we move from the OT to the NT.[10]

First, Gen 1:1–3 teaches that God's creation of the universe is by his word and Spirit, a truth that is tracked throughout the OT and that becomes a crucial way of distinguishing the divine persons from each other as the one God.

1. Think first of the relation between God and his "word," a point we discussed in chapter 5. In Genesis 1, God's word is not personified as it is later in the OT, but it is closely identified with God himself (Pss 18:30; 107:20; 147:15). In fact, God's *word* is God's own powerful, authoritative self-expression so that we cannot think of God apart from his word. For example, God's *word* has divine attributes: it is wonderful (Ps 119:129), righteousness (Ps 119:7), pure (Ps 119:40), faithfulness (Ps 119:86), uprightness (Ps 119:137), truth (Ps 119:142; cf. John 17:17), eternal (Ps 119:89, 160), omnipotent (Gen 18:14; Isa 55:11; Luke 1:37), perfect (Ps 19:7), and holy (Deut 31:26; 2 Tim 3:15). God's *word* is an object of worship (Pss 34:3; 9:2; 56:4, 10; 68:4; 119:48, 120, 161f; 138:2; Isa 66:5) closely related to his *name*, which is tied to God himself (Exod 3:14; 33:19; 34:6f; Pss 7:17; 9:10; 18:49; 68:4; 74:18; 86:12; 92:11; Isa 25:1; 26:8; 56:6; Zech 14:9; Mal 3:16). All of God's external acts are done by his word: creation (Gen 1:3ff; Pss 33:6, 9; 147:15–18; 148:5–6), revelation (Gen 3:8–19; 12:1; 15:1; 22:11; Isa 9:8; Jer 1:4; Ezek 33:7; Amos 3:1, 8), redemption (Ps 107:20; Isa 55:11), and judgment (Gen 3, etc.).

In the NT, John applies these truths to Jesus, the eternal Son of the Father.[11] "Word" (*logos*) is a summary title to identify the eternal Son ("In the beginning was the Word," 1:1a), who is distinct from God ("the Word was with God [*pros ton theon*]," 1:1b) but who *is* also God ("the Word *was* God [*theon ēn ho logos*]," 1:1c). *Word*, similar to *image* (Col 1:15) and *radiance* (Heb 1:3), speaks of the word's identity with and distinction from God "internal to God's being."[12] Also, through the word, God creates, rules, redeems (John 1:1–18; cf. Col 1:15–20; Heb 1:2–3), and fully reveals God precisely because he is the Father's "only begotten" Son who is God himself (*monogenēs theos*, John 1:18; cf. 8:58; 14:6–11).[13]

---

[10] For a helpful discussion of the biblical data, see Letham, *Holy Trinity*, 3–84 (see chap. 17, n. 28).

[11] On *logos*, see Carson, *Gospel According to John*, 111–39 (see chap. 5, n. 13).

[12] Swain, *Trinity*, 80.

[13] Historically, *monogenēs* (Gk. *monos* + *gennaō*) has been translated "only begotten" (KJV) and used to warrant the Son's "eternal generation" from the Father. Today, many think the etymology of *monogenēs* derives from *monos* + *genos* to mean "unique, only." See Carson, *Gospel According to John*,

2. The "Spirit of God" is also closely identified with God so that one cannot think of God's acts apart from his word *and* Spirit. For example, God's Spirit is identified with creation (Gen 1:2; 2:7; Job 33:4; Ps 33:6), providence (Ps 104:27–30; Isa 34:16; 40:7), revelation (Num 24:2; 2 Sam 23:2; Neh 9:30; Isa 61:1–4; Zech 7:12), and redemption (Ps 51:10–12; Isa 44:3; Ezek 11:19; 36:25–27; 37:14; Joel 2:28–29; Zech 12:10). Although the roughly 100 references to the "Spirit of God" in the OT do not require us to think of the Spirit as a distinct person of the Godhead (except possibly Isa 63:10),[14] as God's plan is unveiled, especially in the Prophets, the "Spirit of God" is inseparable from the future Davidic King/Son and the new covenant age he inaugurates. In other words, we cannot think of the Messiah/Son apart from the Spirit (Isa 11:1–5; 42:1–8; 61:1–3) or the Son apart from the Father/Yahweh (2 Sam 7:14; Pss 2; 110; Ezek 34:22–25). In the NT, the seeds sown in the OT regarding the Father-Son-Spirit relations come to full bloom as the Son can no longer be considered a mere human nor the Spirit merely God's "power" or "manifest presence," but both are distinct divine persons, who with the Father are the one God.

Second, the use of *'Elohim* is striking, especially when combined with the "us" language in Gen 1:26. *'Elohim* is a plural noun that often takes singular verbs (Gen 1:1). Grammatically, it may be called a plural of intensity, referring to the "fullness and richness of [God's] life."[15] In view of the strict monotheism of the OT, it is a striking linguistic use,[16] although it does not definitively demonstrate plurality within God. When it is used of angels, it is translated in the plural (cf. Ps 8:5 with Heb 2:7), and when it is used of the God of Israel, it often takes a singular verb or adjective, but it is also true that it can sometimes take plural verbs (Gen 20:13; 35:7; Exod 32:4; Neh 9:18; Isa 16:6). Also, there are texts where God is referred to as *'eloah*, the singular of *'Elohim* (Deut 32:15; Pss 18:32 [Heb]; 114:7; Hab 3:3; and most frequently in

---

111–39. However, a strong case can be made for the traditional meaning. For example, see Charles Lee Irons, "A Lexical Defense of the Johannine 'Only Begotten,'" in *Retrieving Eternal Generation*, ed. Fred Sanders and Scott R. Swain (Grand Rapids: Zondervan, 2017), 98–116. Cf. Letham, *Holy Trinity*, 193–201.

[14] Max Turner, "Holy Spirit," in *NDBT*, 551–58 (see chap. 1, n. 24); cf. Wells, *God the Evangelist*, 1–4 (see chap. 14, n. 85); Sinclair B. Ferguson, *The Holy Spirit* (Downers Grove: InterVarsity, 1996), 15–33.

[15] Bavinck, *Reformed Dogmatics*, 2:261.

[16] See Peter Toon, *Our Triune God: A Biblical Portrayal of the Trinity* (Wheaton: BridgePoint, 1996), 97–103.

Job). Since the singular is available and is used of God, the use of the plural may suggest more than a plural of intensity, especially when it is linked with the "us" language in Gen 1:26.

Historically, theologians have viewed the "us" language in Gen 1:26 (cf. Gen 3:22; 11:5–7; Isa 6:8) as a hint of plurality within God.[17] By contrast, others have argued that the language only refers to a "plural of majesty." Although linguistically this is possible, there are problems with this view. In the OT, there are no examples of a monarch using plural verbs or pronouns to refer to himself. Furthermore, if this is the obvious explanation, then why did the Jewish people struggle with this text?[18] For example, in *Jubilees* 2:14 (c. second century BC), the plural is omitted or altered. Moreover, Philo's discussion of Gen 1:26 demonstrates he is not sure what to do with it. His solution is to argue that God alone is the Creator, but that "he was assisted by subordinate powers in his creation of man. Since he was only able to create good, the evil in man must necessarily be created by others. So, when God is quoted as saying, 'Let us make man,' he was addressing these subordinates, who were his inferiors."[19] The Jerusalem Talmud argues that since Gen 1:27 "refers to one God, 1:26 must also."[20]

Another explanation is that the plurals refer to a divine council of angelic beings. But as Stephen Dempster notes, this interpretation has difficulty accounting for "the switch back to the singular, in which it is stated that God created in *his* own image and in *his* own likeness, and not in *our* own image and likeness."[21] Although the language does not demonstrate plurality in God, given later revelation, it is certainly legitimate to see a hint of trinitarian relations within God.

Third, there is also the messenger/angel of the Lord (*malak Yahweh*) who appeared to Hagar (Gen 16:6–13), to Abraham (Gen 18; 22:11–12), to Jacob (Gen 32:25–33), to Moses (Exod 3:2–6), to Joshua (Josh 5:14–15), to Gideon (Judg 6:11–14), and to David (1 Chr 21:16, 18, 27). Although much debate has occurred regarding this person's identity, it seems

[17] See Stephen G. Dempster, "The Trinity in the Old Testament," *Criswell Theological Review* 15, no. 1 (2017): 66–9.

[18] See the discussion in Millard J. Erickson, *God in Three Persons* (Grand Rapids: Baker, 1995), 166–71.

[19] Erickson, 168.

[20] Erickson, 168.

[21] Dempster, "Trinity in the Old Testament," 67.

to be a personal appearance of God, distinct from God (Exod 23:20–23; 33:14f; Isa 63:8–9), but also one with God in name, power, salvation, and blessing (Gen 16:10–13; 18:3; 22:12; 31:13; 32:28, 30; 48:16; Exod 3:2–8; 14:19; 23:20–23; Isa 63:8–9; Judg 6:21; 13:3).[22] As Dempster observes, "the Angel functions as almost a double of Yahweh, an alter ego, who can forgive, judge, deliver and be worshipped, and even be called God."[23] Here is another hint of plurality within the one God, which ultimately is disclosed with the coming of Christ and the giving of the Spirit.

Fourth, the primary way God's triune nature is revealed is by the Bible's unfolding storyline that unveils Messiah's identity. Starting in creation with God as the Creator and Lord, humans as image-sons created to know God, the entrance of sin into the world, and God's gracious promise to redeem his people by a greater Adam, the Father-Son-Spirit relations are gradually revealed. In other words, the triune nature of God is disclosed by the unveiling of Messiah as the divine Son of the Father who fully has the Spirit of God.[24] Here are some of the key points.

1. Scripture opens with the eternal God who is the Creator of all things, thus establishing the Creator-creature distinction. This God is also the covenant God, who after Adam's sin, promises a Messiah-son to come who will be human *and* one who is identified with God since he will fulfill all of God's promises, inaugurate God's saving reign, and share God's throne (Ps 110)—something no mere human or angelic being can do.[25]

In fact, one way that the NT teaches Christ's deity is by identifying Jesus with OT Yahweh texts (e.g., Rom 10:9; 1 Cor 12:3; Phil 2:11),[26] and applying *theos*, a word reserved for God, to Christ (John 1:1, 18; 20:28; Rom 9:5; Titus 2:13; 2 Pet 1:1; Heb 1:8).[27] But given the Bible's strict monotheism, no creature can share God's attributes (Col 2:9), do God's works

---

[22] See Malone, *Knowing Jesus* (chap. 5, n. 48); Vern S. Poythress, *Theophany* (see chap. 5, n. 48).

[23] See Dempster, "Trinity in the Old Testament," 73.

[24] For a more detailed description of this point, see our discussion of the Bible's covenantal story in part 3.

[25] Andrew Ter Ern Loke, *The Origin of Divine Christology*, SNTSNS 169 (Cambridge: Cambridge University Press, 2017), 48–99.

[26] David B. Capes, *The Divine Christ: Paul, the Lord Jesus, and the Scriptures of Israel* (Grand Rapids: Baker Academic, 2018); Chris Tilling, *Paul's Divine Christology* (Tübingen: Mohr Siebeck, 2012).

[27] Murray Harris, *Jesus as God: The New Testament use of* Theos *in Reference to Jesus* (Grand Rapids: Baker, 1992).

(Col 1:15–20; Heb 1:1–3), receive worship reserved for God alone (John 5:22–23; Heb 1:6; Rev 5:11–12), or bear God's name (John 8:58; Phil 2:9–11) unless he shares the divine nature as God.[28]

2. As God's plan unfolds in redemptive history, the identity of God's promised Messiah-son takes on greater clarity. He will be a human—the "seed of the woman" (Gen 3:15)—who comes through Noah, Abraham, Israel, and David, yet he will be greater than any human. Building on the typological pattern of image-son from Adam (Luke 3:38), through Israel (Exod 4:22–23), and then epitomized in the "Father-son" relation of Yahweh to the Davidic king (2 Sam 7:14; cf. Pss 2; 89:26–27), *the* promised son, especially in the Prophets, begins to break all human categories. David's promised son will not only effect God's rule in the world (2 Sam 7:19b; Ps 72),[29] he will also share God's name, rule, and throne, which places him on the side of the Creator and not merely the creature (Pss 45:6; 110; Isa 9:6–7; Dan 7:14; cf. Heb 1:5–14).[30]

Indeed, as the Prophets anticipate the future hope of the new covenant (Jer 31:31–34), they announce that God will keep his promises to redeem through *his* provision of a faithful Messiah-son-priest (Ps 110; Isa 7:14; 11:1–10; 42:1–9; 49:1–7; Ezek 34:23–24), the "servant of Yahweh" (Isa 52:13–53:12) who is human but also does what only God can do. In the coming of the Son of the Father, *he* will inaugurate God's saving rule, ratify a new covenant (Isa 55:3), forgive our sin (Jer 31:34), usher in a new creation (Isa 65), and bring about final judgment—all acts of God.

Isaiah pictures this well.[31] The future king will sit on David's throne (Isa 9:7) and bear the titles/names of God (9:6). Though this king is another David (Isa 11:1), he is also David's Lord, who shares the divine rule (cf. Ps 110:1; Ezek 34:23–25). He is the mediator of a new covenant; he will perfectly obey and act like Yahweh (Isa 11:1–5), yet he will suffer for our sin to justify many (Isa 53:11). Through him the forgiveness of sin will come, for he is "the LORD

---

[28] Matthew Levering, *Scripture and Metaphysics: Aquinas and the Renewal of Trinitarian Theology* (Oxford: Blackwell, 2004), 47–74; cf. Adonis Vidu, *The Same God Who Works All Things: Inseparable Operations in Trinitarian Theology* (Grand Rapids: Eerdmans, 2021), 1–51.

[29] Brandon Crowe, *The Last Adam: A Theology of the Obedient Life of Jesus in the Gospels* (Grand Rapids: Baker Academic, 2017), 199–215.

[30] Bauckham, *Jesus and the God of Israel* (see chap. 13, n. 87).

[31] See Dempster, "Trinity in the Old Testament," 74–76.

our righteousness" (Jer 23:5–6). In him, OT hope and expectation are joined: Yahweh must save but through his Messiah-Son—who is fully human yet also identified with God.

3. It is not only the Father-Son relation that is unveiled in the OT; it is also the Messiah/Son-Spirit relation as well. The Spirit of God is at work in creation (Gen 1:2) and poured out on various leaders in Israel, such as prophets, priests, and kings (Num 11:16–18; 1 Sam 16:13). But in the Prophets, David's greater son has the Spirit unlike anyone else. In fact, one cannot think of him apart from the fullness of the Spirit (Isa 11:1–3; 42:1; 61:1–3). Also, as a result of the Son's work, *he* will do what only Yahweh can do, that is, pour out the Spirit on his people (Ezek 36:25–27; Joel 2:28–32; cf. Acts 2). Already in the OT, in seed form, we have what blooms in the NT: the distinct yet shared identity of the Father, Son, and Spirit (Matt 28:18–20; John 1:1–2; 1 Cor 8:5–6; 2 Cor 3:18), which is the seedbed for trinitarian reflection.

4. As the NT opens, the triune nature of God is made explicit with the coming of Christ, the Son of the Father, who has and gives the Spirit. What was previously concealed is now revealed (Heb 1:1–3). Who is Jesus? *He* is the Son of the Father (John 5:16–30), who has the Spirit, the one who inaugurates *God's* kingdom and new covenant age, thus identifying him with Yahweh in all of his actions. In Jesus, God's act of forgiveness is achieved (Mark 2:5; 1 Cor 15:3), the eschatological Spirit is poured out (John 1:29–34; Acts 2), the new creation dawns (Luke 1:35; 1 Cor 15:16–28; 2 Cor 5:17; Eph 2:10, 15), and all of God's promises are fulfilled (Matt 5:17–20).

But we can only make sense of who Jesus is by affirming that he is both the eternal Son of the Father (due to his identification with Yahweh) and the obedient human son-king (due to his incarnation). Everywhere, Jesus is the *human* son (Matt 1:1) who fulfills all the typological roles of the previous sons for our salvation (e.g., Adam [Luke 3:38], Israel [Exod 4:22–23; Hos 11:1], David [2 Sam 7:14; Pss 2, 16, 72, 110]). By his incarnation and work, Jesus is the last Adam and the first man of the new creation (1 Cor 15:21–22; Heb 2:5–18). In his conception, the Spirit, who was at work in the first creation (Gen 1:2), overshadows Mary, which begins the new creation (Luke 1:35). In Jesus's baptism, he is identified as the promised Messiah, the Son of the Father, who receives the Spirit in full measure (Isa 11:1–5; 61:1–2; Luke 4:14–21) and who pours out the Spirit on his people (Luke 3:16–17; John 20:21–23; Acts 2:1–36; 10:44–48; Gal 3:26–4:7).

But Jesus can only do all of these actions if he is the *divine* Son of the Father (Matt 11:25–30; John 1:1–3; 5:16–30; 17:3) who assumed our humanity and lived, died, and was raised for our justification (Rom 4:25). For it is only as the eternal Word made flesh (John 1:1, 14) that he can fulfill all of the Law and the Prophets (Matt 5:17–20; Luke 24:44–49) and take on himself our sin and guilt by the ratification of a new covenant (Rom 3:21–26; Eph 1:7–10; Heb 7–10).

5. In the NT, then, due to Christ's coming and the giving of the Spirit, God's triune self-disclosure culminates. From Jesus's baptism to the Great Commission, the Creator-covenant Lord is identified as Father, Son, and Spirit (Matt 3:16–17; 28:18–20). In John's Gospel, the Father-Son-Spirit relations are made clear. Just as the Son is identified with the Father but is distinct (John 1:1–3, 18; 5:16–30; 17:5, 24; 20:28), so the Spirit is identified with the Father and Son but is distinct in his culminating work (John 14:16, 26, 31; 15:26; 16:12–15). Paul captures God's triune nature in his summary statement of redemptive history: "When the time came to completion, God sent his Son, born of a woman, born under the law, to redeem those under the law, so that we might receive adoption as sons. And because you are sons, God sent the Spirit of his Son into our hearts, crying '*Abba*, Father!'" (Gal 4:4–6). Or, as Paul restates the Shema of Deuteronomy 6 and closes in benediction, he does so by speaking of the glory of the triune God: "For us there is one God, the Father. All things are from him, and we exist for him. And there is one Lord, Jesus Christ. All things are from him, and we exist through him" (1 Cor 8:6), and "May the grace of the Lord Jesus Christ, and the love of God, and the fellowship of the Holy Spirit be with you all" (2 Cor 13:14 NIV; cf. Eph 1:3–14; 4:4–6). The God of the Bible is triune.

Explicit Biblical Teaching of the Triune God

The NT explicitly teaches that God is triune in at least two ways. First, specific texts teach that the Father, Son, and Spirit are the one God (e.g., Matt 28:19; 2 Cor 13:14; Eph 4:4–6). Second, by inference from biblical teaching, specifically that God is one and that the Father, Son, and Spirit are the one God but distinct from each other, we must conclude that God is triune. Let us briefly develop the second way that Scripture teaches God is triune.[32]

---

[32] For a helpful summary of the biblical data, see Vos, *Reformed Dogmatics*, 1:38–76 (see chap. 15, n. 126).

First, the Creator-covenant Lord is one. From Genesis to Revelation, Scripture teaches a strict monotheism grounded in the Creator-creature distinction: "Listen, Israel: The LORD our God, the LORD is one" (Deut 6:4).[33] God's oneness is both singularity and simplicity, and in terms of the latter, God is one with himself, the eternal self-sufficient God, who shares his glory with no one (Isa 48:11). This truth is also taught in God's proper name: Yahweh (Exod 3:13–15). God, as "I AM," declares his personal existence, and metaphysically it reveals the singularity and uniqueness of his existence. All things are from him, through him, and for him (Rom 11:36); hence, we are to know, love, and worship him alone (Mark 12:28–29). As the only true God (John 17:3; Rom 3:30; 1 Cor 8:4–6; 1 Tim 2:5; Jas 2:19), he alone is "the King eternal, immortal, invisible, the only God, [to whom] be honor and glory forever and ever. Amen" (1 Tim 1:17).

Second, the Father, Son, and Holy Spirit are the one God (Matt 28:18–20; 2 Cor 13:14; Eph 4:4–6) but are also distinct from each other. Three points will develop this biblical truth.

1. In terms of the one God, Scripture predicates of the Father, Son, and Spirit what they have in *common*; namely, all three equally and fully subsist in the same undivided divine nature, eternity, power, glory, and authority. Each person *is* the one God.

Biblical warrant for the Son's deity is abundant, a point we will return to in volume 2. For our present purposes, we simply note that building on the OT's covenantal storyline, starting with the Creator-creature distinction, the NT identifies the Son as Yahweh: the one who establishes the divine rule by inaugurating God's kingdom through a new covenant in fulfillment of OT promises, thus doing what only God can do (Isa 9:6–7; 11:1–10; Jer 31:31–34; Ezek 34:1–31). Also, with the Father and Spirit, the Son equally shares the divine name and nature (Matt 28:18–20; John 8:58; Phil 2:9–11; Col 2:9). The Son *is* identified as God (*theos*) (John 1:1, 18; 20:28; Rom 9:5; Titus 2:13; Heb 1:8; 2 Pet 1:1) because *he* is the word and the exact image, correspondence, and radiance of the Father (John 1:1; Col 1:15; Heb 1:3). As the Son, he inseparably shares with the Father and Spirit the divine rule, works, and receives divine worship (Ps 110:1; Matt 1:21; Mark 2:3–12; Eph 1:22; Phil 2:9–11; Col 1:15–20; Heb 1:1–3; Rev 5:11–12). Indeed, for Scripture to be fulfilled in him (Matt 5:17–19; 11:13) is to confess

---

[33] Bauckham, *Jesus and the God of Israel*, 1–126; Loke, *Origin of Divine Christology*, 12–78. See Exod 15:11; 20:2–3; Deut 32:39; Ps 95:3; Isa 44:6–8; 45:5–6, 22; Jer 10:10.

that he is *from* the Father *as the Son* and thus equal to him (Matt 11:25–27; John 5:16–30; 10:14–30; 14:9–13).

Biblical warrant for the Spirit's deity is also abundant, a point we will return to in volume 2. Here we will only mention a few crucial points. First, we cannot think of the work of the Father and Son apart from the Spirit, which locates the Spirit on the side of God and not the creature. For example, the Holy Spirit works alongside the Father and Son and is thus equal to them. In many places, the Son and Spirit work side by side: divine communion (Acts 9:31), divine indwelling (Rom 8:9–11), divine intercession (Rom 8:27, 34), Christian motivation (Rom 15:30; cf. Phil 2:1), and the work of justification (1 Cor 6:11). Also, there are numerous triadic passages that link the Father, Son, and Spirit together as the one God who brings about God's one plan of redemption (Matt 28:19; John 14:16–16:15; Rom 8; 1 Cor 12:4–6; 2 Cor 13:14; Eph 1:3–13; 2:18; 3:14–19; 4:4–6; 2 Thess 2:13–14; 1 Pet 1:2). Second, as with the Son, the Spirit is identified with Yahweh (2 Cor 3:17; 2 Thess 3:5).[34] For example, Yahweh is the "Holy One" (Isa 6:3; 40:25), which is repeatedly said of the Spirit. Or, God is the God of "glory" (Ps 29:3), which is applied commonly to the Father (Eph 1:17), the Son (1 Cor 2:8; Jas 2:1), and the Spirit (1 Pet 4:14). Or, "life" is what God alone gives, but the NT teaches that the Father, Son, and Spirit give "life" (John 5:21, 26; 6:32–33, 63; Rom 8:2; 2 Cor 3:6). Third, the Spirit bears the name/nature of God (Exod 17:7 [Heb 3:7–9]; Acts 5:3–4; 7:51; 28:25–27 [Isa 6:1–13]; Heb 10:15–17 [Jer 31:31–34]), does the works of God (e.g., creation, providence, extraordinary agency, redemption, and judgment [Gen 1:2; Ps 104:30; Matt 12:28; Luke 1:35; John 3:5; Rom 8:11; 1 Cor 2:10; 2 Thess 2:13; Heb 9:14; 1 Pet 3:18]), and receives the worship of God (Matt 28:19; 2 Cor 13:14).

2. In terms of distinction, the Father, Son, and Spirit are distinguished by their mutual relations, or what theology identifies as their eternal "relations of origin." Scott Swain recaps some of the biblical data that teaches these specific relations:

> The Father is the "Father of our Lord Jesus Christ" (Eph. 1:3; 1 Pet. 1:3). The Son is the Father's "beloved Son" (Matt. 3:17; Rom. 8:32; Gal. 4:4). The Holy Spirit is "the Spirit of God" (Matt. 3:16; 1 Cor. 2:11) and "the Spirit of Christ," "the Spirit of his

[34] On 2 Thess 3:5, see Basil of Caesarea, *On the Holy Spirit* 21.52.

Son" (Rom. 8:9; Gal. 4:6). What distinguishes the persons of the Trinity from each other are their relations to each other, not their relations to us.[35]

Also, in Scripture the mutual relations between the persons reflect a specific irreversible "order" (Gk. *taxis*). Within God (*ad intra*), the Father eternally begets (*monogenēs*) the Son (John 1:18; 3:16), and the Son is from the Father (John 1:1; 5:26). The Father and the Son eternally spirate the Spirit (John 14:26; 15:26). In God's external acts (*ad extra*), Scripture teaches us that the Father, Son, and Spirit inseparably and indivisibly act as the one God yet according to their eternally ordered relations so that the Father always acts through the Son by the Spirit (Luke 1:35 [Phil 2:6–7]; John 5:19; 14:16, 26; 15:26; 20:22; Acts 2:32–33; Col 1:15–17; Heb 1:2–3).

3. In God's *ad extra* works (i.e., the divine economy), and especially in the Father's sending of the Son and the Spirit for our redemption, we know and experience the one true God, who is Father, Son, and Spirit. In knowing the Father, we know him as the Father of the Son (Matt 3:16–17; 11:25–27; John 5:19–30), our Creator and Lord (Gen 1:1; Rev 4:11), and by grace, our Father in Christ and by the Spirit (Matt 6:9; Eph 1:3; 3:14–15). In knowing the Son, we know him as the Son of the Father (Matt 3:16–17; 11:25–27; John 5:19–30; Heb 1:1–14), our Creator and Lord (Gen 1:1; John 1:3; Col 1:15–17; Heb 1:3), and by grace, our Redeemer and the pattern of our sonship (Rom 3:21–26; 8:18–39; 1 Cor 15:45–49; Gal 4:4–7; Eph 1:4–10). In knowing the Holy Spirit, we know him as the Spirit of the Father and Son (John 15:26–27; 16:12–15; Rom 8:9; Gal 4:6), our Creator and Lord (Gen 1:1–2; Pss 33:6; 104:27–30), and by grace, the Spirit of grace and truth, who unites and applies Christ's work to us (John 3:3; 7:39; 16:12–15; Acts 2; Gal 4:6–7; Eph 1:13–14; Titus 3:3–7) and who brings glory to the Father and Son (John 16:14; 1 Cor 2:10–11; Gal 4:6).

In summary, to account for all of the biblical teaching, we must conclude that God is triune: the one glorious Creator-covenant Lord who subsists in three distinct persons who are truly, fully, and equally the one God. As the triune God, within himself, he eternally exists in the fullness of his personal relations so that God's life, love, and perfection are in and from himself. And in God's free and gracious choice to share his life with creatures, he has acted from himself to give himself to us not out of need or something lacking within himself, but due to his own choice to display his glory for the good of his people (Rom 8:28–39; 11:33–36; Eph 1:9–10).

---

[35] Swain, *Trinity*, 32–33.

The Formulation of Nicene Trinitarian Orthodoxy

The Bible's presentation of God is not the end of theological reflection; for the church, it is the beginning. As exegesis leads to biblical theology, it also leads to systematic theology—a "faith seeking understanding." In fact, the first 500 years of theological reflection in church history centered on the doctrine of God in two interrelated areas.

First, the church reflected on Trinitarian formulation. Given Jesus's self-identity as the divine Son in relation to the Father and the Spirit, how do we speak of their shared unity as the one God? Are the Son and the Spirit of the same essence as the Father (*homoousios*)? If so, then how do we speak of their distinctness from each other? As Fred Sanders notes, Trinitarian theology was born as the church clarified the relations between the Father, Son, and Spirit as the one God, specifically in clarifying that the Father's sending of his Son and the pouring out of the Spirit (i.e., the divine missions) "are the [temporal] manifestations of two eternal relations of origin" within God.[36] As such, "The Son is sent to be incarnate because he stands in an eternal relation of origin with regard to the Father, a relation called generation or begetting; and the Spirit is poured out because he stands in an eternal relation of origin with regard to the Father, a relation called spiration or breathing-out."[37] As the church clarified these relations and rejected false views, God's triune nature was given clarity and precision as expressed by the Nicene Creed.[38]

---

[36] Sanders, *Triune God*, 113 (see chap. 13, n. 16). The divine missions refer to the Father's temporal "sending" of the Son to be our redeemer *and* the Father and Son's temporal sending of the Spirit to apply Christ's work to us (John 3:16; 14:16, 26; 16:13–15; Gal 4:4–7). Specifically, the divine missions are extensions in time of the divine processions (i.e., the Father's eternal generation of the Son and the Father and Son's spiration of the Spirit) by which the Son and the Spirit become present to us in a new way in a created effect. Thus, for example, "as the Father eternally begets the Son, so he extends the Son's eternal relation of origin to us by sending him to dwell among us at the fullness of time," resulting in the Son's incarnation and his work as our Redeemer. Also, as the Father and Son eternally spirate the Spirit, "so they extend the Spirit's eternal relation of origin by sending him to dwell among us," resulting in the Spirit's outpouring at Pentecost, the application of Christ's work to his people, and his indwelling of us. Swain, *Trinity*, 114, 115. Cf. Köstenberger and Allison, *Holy Spirit*, 274–77.

[37] Sanders, *Triune God*, 112–13.

[38] The Nicene Creed represents the confessions of the first two councils of the church: Nicaea (325) and Constantinople (381). For a discussion of these councils, see Lewis Ayres, *Nicaea and its Legacy: An Approach to Fourth-Century Trinitarian Theology* (Oxford: Oxford University Press, 2004).

Second, the church, building on trinitarian doctrine, reflected further on questions centered on the nature of the incarnation of the divine Son, our Lord Jesus Christ. Although the church had rejected Arianism's denial of Christ's deity, further Christological questions remained that resulted in the Chalcedonian Definition (451), which we will discuss in volume 2.

As theological reflection birthed creedal formulation, it is important to remember that the church's confessional standards are not equal to Scripture. However, over the years, the church established orthodoxy in the laboratory of history, where ideas were tested for their biblical fidelity, and the Nicene Creed and Chalcedonian Definition have certainly passed the test. Contrary to the charge of early heretics that the creeds departed from Scripture by employing extrabiblical language or the charge of Adolf von Harnack that they were infected by acute Hellenization,[39] the Creeds confessed in theological language what Scripture teaches. As David Yeago insists, "the ancient theologians were right to hold that the Nicene *homousion* is neither imposed *on* the New Testament texts, nor distantly deduced *from* the texts, but rather describes a pattern of judgments present *in* the texts, in the texture of scriptural discourse concerning Jesus and the God of Israel."[40] Or, as C. Kavin Rowe states it, the doctrine of the Trinity was an "exegetical necessity" since "it is in fact the biblical text itself that necessitated the creedal formulations."[41] In fact, heresy arose when people reflected on the nature of God apart from the theology, concepts, and categories of Scripture. It was Greek philosophical categories that were unable to make the "person-nature" distinction or speak of shared relations within God, let alone account for the incarnation of the divine Son. Although the Nicene (and later Chalcedonian) Creed employed extrabiblical language, it correctly identified the God of the Bible from the Bible's storyline and framework, not an alien one. For this reason, the Nicene Creed accurately gives us the triune God in continuity with Scripture, not in continuity with Greek philosophy.[42] Thus, given the Nicene Creed's faithfulness to Scripture and its catholic consent, it, along with the Chalcedonian Definition, serves as a "rule of faith" and secondary

---

[39] See Adolf von Harnack, *What is Christianity?*, trans. T. B. Saunders (Philadelphia: Fortress, 1957), 211, 221.

[40] Yeago, "New Testament and the Nicene Dogma," 88 (see chap. 4, n. 78). In agreement with Yeago, see Bauckham, *Jesus and the God of Israel*, 57–58.

[41] C. Kavin Rowe, "Luke and the Trinity: An Essay in Ecclesial Biblical Theology," *SJT* 56 (2003): 4.

[42] The same can also be said of the Chalcedonian Definition in relation to correctly identifying who Jesus is.

standard for the church. Although the creeds could say more, given their biblical fidelity, they set the parameters and guardrails by which our doctrinal formulation ought to occur, and we ignore them to our peril.

Let us now turn to the development of trinitarian theology in historical theology that established "pro-Nicene" orthodoxy.[43] The amount of material is vast and complex; indeed, entire volumes have discussed this crucial era in church history, which we can only summarize.[44] But outlining the key points is necessary to accurate doctrinal formulation since we stand on the shoulders of theological giants. As we proceed, we will employ the image of a travelled road. Every road leads to a specific destination and every road establishes parameters within which to travel. Going too far on either side of the road leaves the traveler in the ditch. By analogy, the road to the Nicene Creed leads to the establishment of orthodoxy. Who is God? He *is* the Creator-covenant Lord, who is Father, Son, and Holy Spirit. As the church articulates this truth, she rejects heresies that cannot account for the biblical teaching about the triune God. In fact, two interrelated steps were crucial in this process. First, the church had to create a common theological language to make sense of the biblical data. Second, the church had to respond to false ways of "putting together" the biblical data. Let us look at each of these in turn.

The Person-Nature Distinction

As the church formulated the Trinity and responded to false views, a crowning achievement was the development of a common *theological* language, specifically the "person-nature" distinction. Scripture teaches that there is only one God. However within God's being there is a threeness: the Father, Son, and Spirit. To misconstrue God's oneness or threeness or to reduce them to the same thing is to deny biblical truth. But what language is appropriate to

[43] The term "pro-Nicene" refers to "those theologies, appearing from the 360s to the 380s, consisting of a set of arguments about the nature of the Trinity . . . and forming the basis of Nicene Christianity in the 380s." Ayres, *Nicaea and its Legacy*, 6. These theologies constituted arguments *for* Nicaea, hence "pro-Nicene," and they affirmed divine simplicity, the "person-nature" distinction, the eternal generation of the Son, and inseparable operations in God's external works. On these points, see Ayres, 273–429.

[44] For example, see Ayres, *Nicaea and its Legacy*; Khaled Anatolios, *Retrieving Nicaea: The Development and Meaning of Trinitarian Doctrine* (Grand Rapids: Baker Academic, 2011); Letham, *Holy Trinity*, 85–324.

conceptualize this? The answer to the question is the language of "person-nature": a theological distinction to account for the biblical teaching that God is triune. Thus, the church affirmed that there are three distinct "persons" who share the one divine "nature" or "essence" *and* that the one, undivided (simple) divine essence wholly subsists in each of the three persons so that each person *is* fully and equally God. Let us develop this in terms of five points.

First, the church employed the language of "essence" or "being" (i.e., "nature") to speak of God's oneness (Gk. *ousia*; Latin: *substantia, essentia*) and the language of "person" to speak of God's threeness (Gk. *hypostasis*; Latin: *persona, subsistentia*).[45] Yet even the use of this language took time since in Greek thought the words *ousia* and *hypostasis* were synonyms. In fact, it was not until the mid-fourth century that the words were conceptually distinguished by the church.[46] This fact illustrates that the church used extrabiblical language from the culture but then redefined the terms according to Scripture and not Greek thought. But what metaphysical content do we ascribe to these words?

Second, a "nature" is *what* a thing is, or in the words of Herman Bavinck, "that by which a thing is what it is."[47] The *divine* nature is *what* God *is* in his one undivided essence, which from Scripture and by "reason of analysis"[48] we describe in terms of God's attributes and what all three persons have in *common*. Historically, as we discussed in chapter 18, God's attributes have been viewed as *essential* and not accidental: God has his attributes eternally and necessarily. God's nature *is* simple, eternal, *a se*, immaterial, omnipotent, omniscient, and so forth and necessarily so.[49]

---

[45] Technically, the Greek for "nature" is *physis*. Although, there are nuances between the various terms, we are using the terms *being, essence*, and *substance* to refer to the broader category of "nature," or that which refers to the one being of God and what is common to the Father, Son, and Holy Spirit.

[46] This occurred at the Synod of Alexandria (AD 362).

[47] Bavinck, *Reformed Dogmatics*, 3:306.

[48] See Muller, *Dictionary of Latin and Greek*, s.v. "distinctio," 94 (see chap. 8, n. 37). Muller describes "reason of analysis" as follows: it makes a distinction between things but not in the sense that it is between things (i.e., a real distinction) or between formal aspects of the essence of a thing (i.e., a formal distinction). Instead, "reason of analysis" makes distinctions that are based in the thing and, as such, are not mere products of the mind. As applied to God's being, although God *is* his attributes (per divine simplicity), our distinguishing between attributes represents no distinction in God but a truth of reason about God.

[49] For a discussion of Medieval, Reformation, and post-Reformation ways of thinking about the divine attributes, see Muller, *Post-Reformation Reformed Dogmatics*, vol. 3 (see chap. 3, n. 12).

Third, what is a "person?" Before we answer this question, it is crucial to note that the *theological* use of *person* in trinitarian and Christological formulation is *not* the same as in contemporary usage. When we talk about "persons" today, we may mean an entire individual human being, or someone's personality traits, or something synonymous with one's soul. But in historic theology, when we speak of divine "persons," we do not use the word in any of these ways, nor is it even wise to speak of human persons in this way.[50] Instead, a divine "person" (and by analogy a human person) is the *who* or the *subject* that subsists in a nature, thus making an ontological distinction between "person" and "nature." No doubt, one cannot separate persons from their nature or essence, but also one must not reduce persons to their natures. Bavinck captures this point well when he states that a "person" is the subject of a rational nature, that which "exists in and for itself, the owner, possessor, the master of a nature, the subject that lives, thinks, wills, and acts through nature with all its abundant content [and] all its constituents, capacities, and energies."[51] In other words, a "person" is a subject who *does things* and *to whom things happen*, the subject or the subsistence of a nature that lives and acts in and through a nature.

Probably the most influential definition of a "person" is from Boethius: "an individual substance of a rational nature."[52] There is much debate regarding what Boethius meant by "individual substance," but it is best understood as a "subject," or a subsistence that acts in and through a "rational nature."[53] In such a definition, the intellect and will are located in the "essence" or "nature," which results in a distinction between the "person," or the subject who acts ("act of willing"), and the "nature" (which includes the capacities or faculties of intellect and will) in which the "person" subsists and by which the person acts.[54] This classical view of

---

[50] In our discussion of theological anthropology in volume 2, I will return to this point.

[51] Bavinck, *Reformed Dogmatics*, 3:306–7.

[52] Boethius, "A Treatise Against Eutyches and Nestorius," in *The Theological Tractates and The Consolation of Philosophy*, trans. H. F. Stewart and E. K. Rand, Loeb Classical Library (New York: G. P. Putnam's Sons, 1918), 85; cf. Gilles Emery, "The Dignity of Being a Substance: Person, Subsistence, and Nature," *NV* 9, no. 4 (2011): 994 (English edition); White, *Trinity*, 380–96, 442–55.

[53] See Boethius ("Treatise Against Eutyches," 85–91), who makes this point. Robert Spaemann, *Persons: The Difference between 'Someone' and 'Something,'* trans. Oliver O'Donovan (Oxford: Oxford University Press, 2006), 27–33, also makes this point.

[54] See Maximus the Confessor, *Disputatio cum Pyrrho*, in *The Disputation with Pyrrhus of our Father among the Saints, Maximus the Confessor*, trans. Joseph P. Farrell (South Canaan, PA: St. Tikhon's

person contrasts with more current views of persons unfortunately embraced by social trinitarianism. "Social" views place both the "acts of willing" *and* the "capacity or faculty of will" in the person, hence their embrace of three wills in God in contrast to the historic view of only one will, a point we will return to below.

Fourth, in defining a "person," we must now be more specific in distinguishing between *divine* and *human* persons. Given the Creator-creature distinction, divine persons are the archetype to the human ectype, and the relation between them is *not* univocal, but analogical; thus, they are similar but not the same. So what is a *divine* person? To build on our initial definition and to employ the definition of Thomas Aquinas, a *divine* person is a "subsisting relation" in the one divine essence,[55] unlike human persons, who subsist only in their own nature or essence. But if Father, Son, and Spirit each completely subsist in the divine essence, how are they distinct? The persons are *not* distinguished by the divine essence; each person subsists in the same divine essence fully and equally. Instead, the divine persons are distinguished by their eternal, immanent "relations of origin," which we know by special revelation.

Or, to state it another way, now utilizing the definition of John Calvin, the divine persons are "subsistent relations" that are distinguished by their own personal incommunicable "mode of subsisting" in the divine essence; or as John Owen states, a divine person is "nothing but the divine essence . . . subsisting in an especial manner."[56] The Father subsists in his "unique personal mode *as God* because he is the source of divine life for the Son and Spirit (by generation and spiration)."[57] The Son subsists in his "unique personal mode *as God* because he is eternally begotten of the Father and exists from the Father 'toward' the spiration of the Spirit with the Father."[58] The Spirit subsists in his "unique personal mode *as God* because he is eternally spirated from the Father and the Son, and no one proceeds from him."[59] In this way,

---

Seminary Press, 1990); cf. Bavinck, *Reformed Dogmatics*, 3:306–7.

[55] Thomas Aquinas, *Summa Theologica*, Pt. 1, q. 40, a. 2 ad 1 (see chap. 2, n. 20).

[56] Calvin, *Institutes*, 1.13.6 (1:128); Owen, *Works of John Owen*, 2:407 (see chap. 4, n. 72); cf. Richard of St. Victor, *On the Trinity*, trans. Ruben Angelici (Eugene: Cascade, 2011), 4.22 (163), who before Calvin stated that a divine person "is an incommunicable existence of the divine nature."

[57] White, *Trinity*, 446.

[58] White, 446.

[59] White, 446

the Father, Son, and Spirit each subsist as distinct persons according to their eternal relations that distinguish and constitute each person, with "each possessing fully the plenitude of divine nature and life (the divine essence)."[60]

By contrast, human persons are *not* subsisting relations in the same nature. For one thing, our relations are external to us and accidental. Each human person is created and finite, subsisting in its own concrete nature, which is constituted by a body and soul. Furthermore, no human person subsists in more than one concrete nature; no human person shares the same nature with another human person. Individual human beings are identified by both the "principle of subsisting" (i.e., the person or the subject or the subsistence of the nature) and the "principle of distinction" (i.e., a concrete human nature with *this* flesh and *this* soul). All concrete human natures are the same *kind* of nature, but not the same *instance* of it. Yet, a human person is analogous to divine persons because a human person is a personal *hypostasis*, or subject, that subsists in and acts through a nature, albeit a human nature.[61] This is an important point to remember in Christology since there is enough similarity between divine and human persons that the divine Son can assume a human nature without a human person (*anhypostatic*, contrary to Nestorianism) and be fully human although his person is the divine Son.[62]

Fifth, as applied to the doctrine of the Trinity, the Father, Son, and Spirit are distinguished by their eternally ordered (Gk. *taxis*), immanent relations. We know this due to God's special revelation and the Father's sending of the Son and the Holy Spirit to accomplish our redemption (i.e., the divine missions).[63] Even though God has not given us an exhaustive revelation of himself, we expect a continuity between the divine processions and the divine missions since the missions fittingly reveal the trinitarian processions "turned outside and in time,"[64] yet it is important to distinguish the two. As Matthew Levering reminds us: "The processions enable us to distinguish the persons [the Father, the Son, and the Holy Spirit] without eviscerating the

---

[60] White, *Trinity*, 446; cf. Gilles Emery, *The Trinitarian Theology of St. Thomas Aquinas* (Oxford: Oxford University Press, 2007), 51–150.

[61] See Emery, "Dignity of Being a Substance," 997–1001.

[62] We will discuss this point in volume 2.

[63] See Gilles Emery, *Trinity, Church, and the Human Person* (Naples: Sapientia Press, 2007), 115–53.

[64] Köstenberger and Allison, *Holy Spirit*, 276.

divine unity, while the missions add a 'specific relationship to the creature' without conflating the economy of salvation with the intratrinitarian life."[65]

Furthermore, in all of God's external works, it is the one God who acts but as triune. As such, all three persons inseparably act through the same divine nature, yet according to the person's eternally ordered relations and personal mode of existing.[66] Thus, every external act of God is one and undivided, but also triune.[67] As Scott Swain explains, "As the Father's distinct personal mode of existing is to exist from no one but to beget the Son and breathe the Spirit, so the Father's distinct personal mode of acting is to act from no one but to act through the Son and by the Spirit."[68] The same pattern follows for the Son and the Spirit. The Son, whose personal mode of existing or subsistence "is to exist from the Father as his only begotten and to breathe the Spirit,"[69] acts *from* the Father and *by* the Spirit. The Spirit, whose personal mode of subsistence "is to be eternally breathed forth by the Father and the Son," acts *from* the Father *and* Son, "bringing all of God's undivided external operations to their crowning fulfillment."[70] In this way, each of God's external works are one, indivisible, and common to all three persons yet also according to each person's mode of subsistence, "proceeding from the Father through the Son in the Spirit."[71]

However, Scripture also teaches that although all of God's external operations are common to Father, Son, and Spirit, various works have specific, but not exclusive, reference to one of the three persons, or to use more theological language, specific works are *appropriated* to one of the persons. For example, the Father is often identified as the author of the divine decree (Eph 1:4–6) and, as the Nicene Creed states, the "Maker of heaven and earth" (Eph 3:9; Rev 4:11), although

[65] Matthew Levering, *Engaging the Doctrine of the Holy Spirit: Love and Gift in the Trinity and the Church* (Grand Rapids: Baker, 2016), 169.

[66] At work here is a rule of trinitarian agency: natures do not act; only persons do. Yet, persons act through a nature, and it is in the one divine nature that the will is located. See John of Damascus, *On the Orthodox Faith* 3.3, 9, 11, (*NPNF*[2] 9:651–54, 666, 669–71). Or, as Thomas Joseph White describes Aquinas's thought on this point, "nature is the principle *through which* a subject or hypostasis acts, but it is always the subject *who* acts." "Dyotheletism and the Instrumental Human Consciousness of Jesus," *ProEccl* 17, no. 4 (2008), 403.

[67] Lat., *opera Trinitatis ad extra sunt indivisa*. See Vidu's discussion in *Same God Who Works*.

[68] Swain, *Trinity*, 109.

[69] Swain, 109.

[70] Swain, 109.

[71] Swain, 111.

the Son and the Spirit also decree and create as the one God (Gen 1:2; John 1:3; Col 1:15–17). Scripture identifies the Son as our Redeemer (Eph 1:7; Rev 5:9–10) and the Spirit as the one who applies Christ's work to us (Eph 1:13–14), although God's work of redemption is triune. The reason for these "appropriations" is that they reveal and reflect the eternal relations of the three persons. Since the Father is the one from whom the Son and Spirit proceed, Scripture appropriates to the Father the internal work of the decree and the external work of creation. In this sense, these works *terminate* on him, even though it is not exclusively his work. Or, in the case of the Son, the incarnation is a divine work appropriated to him (John 1:1, 14), or we can say that the incarnation terminates in him because he is the eternal Son of the Father, his perfect image (Col 1:15; Heb 1:3), who in assuming our human nature restores fallen, creaturely image-bearers to our sonship (John 1:12; Gal 4:5–6; Heb 2:5–18). Or, for the Spirit, as the one who proceeds from the Father and Son, Scripture *appropriates* to him the work of applying Christ's work to us by making us alive (John 3:6), uniting us to Christ (Rom 6:1–4; 8:9–17; Eph 1:13–14; 2:4–10), and conforming us to Christ (Eph 4:20–24; Col 3:9–10; 1 Pet 1:2).[72]

In summary, as the "person-nature" distinction was defined and clarified, trinitarian theology was formulated consistently with Scripture. Although the church assumed some kind of "person-nature" distinction from the outset, it took time to reach conceptual clarity. However, with this distinction in place, the church was able to confess coherently what Scripture teaches: the glorious Creator-covenant Lord is Father, Son, and Spirit. As the church did so, she had to also reject false ways of thinking about God. Let us now turn to this history and discover how trinitarian orthodoxy was formulated in "the mirror of heresy."[73]

Trinitarian Orthodoxy in the Mirror of Heresy

Ante-Nicene Developments

As the church conceptualized the biblical teaching of God's oneness of "nature" and threeness of "persons," false views were rejected, specifically views tied to Monarchianism and Arianism.

---

[72] See Swain, 110–13; Köstenberger and Allison, *Holy Spirit*, 282–84; White, *Trinity*, 520–33.

[73] "Orthodoxy in the mirror of heresy" is taken from Harold O. J. Brown, *Heresies: The Image of Christ in the Mirror of Heresy and Orthodoxy from the Apostles to the Present* (Garden City: Doubleday, 1984).

First, Monarchianism correctly emphasized God's unity (*monos*, "one"; *archos*, "ruler," "source"), but it denied the coequal deity of the Son (and Spirit). It took two forms.[74]

1. "Adoptionism" was one form of Monarchianism that denied Christ's deity. In this view, Jesus was a mere man, *not* the eternal Son made flesh. Due to Jesus's exemplary moral life, at his baptism, Jesus was "deified" or "adopted" to be God's son by the "Logos" coming on him and empowering him to do miraculous works. The Logos, then, is *not* a distinct person from the Father, but God acting in power on the man Jesus. Because God could not suffer, the Logos came off Jesus before he died on the cross, hence Jesus's cry of abandonment. This view was probably taught by Paul of Samosata (c. 200–275), and although rejected by the church in the third century, over a millennium later, it was taught by Socinianism and Unitarianism, and today many modern/postmodern theologians who deny the Trinity are adoptionistic in their Christology.[75]

2. "Modalism" (or "Sabellianism") was the more dominant form of Monarchianism. It affirmed God's unity, but it denied that the Father, Son, and Spirit were *distinct* persons who fully share the divine nature. Rather, these distinct person-names are only "modes" of the one God who reveals himself differently in history, thus making synonymous "person" and "nature" and resulting in Unitarianism. Another disastrous consequence of modalism is that the events of redemptive history become a charade. Not being a distinct person, the Son cannot represent us before the Father or die as our substitute. Also, modalism is necessarily docetic; that is, Christ only appeared to be human, unless one argues, which some did, that the Father suffered on the cross (Patripassianism) since the Son is not actually distinct from the Father.

Both of these forms of Monarchianism veered off the road into the ditch. God's unity was taught, but the *distinct* Son *as God* (and the Spirit) was denied, thus denying God's triune nature.

Second, the most significant heresy was Arianism, a view taught by Arius (c. 256–336), a presbyter in Alexandria, and then developed by others.[76] Arianism was condemned at the

---

[74] On Monarchianism, see J. N. D. Kelly, *Early Christian Doctrines*, 5th ed. (London: A&C Black, 1977), 115–23.

[75] For example, see Friedrich Schleiermacher; Albrecht Ritschl; John A. T. Robinson; and John Hick, ed., *The Myth of God Incarnate* (Philadelphia: Westminster Press, 1977).

[76] For a discussion of Arius, Arianism, and its development, see Ayres, *Nicaea and Its Legacy*; Rowan Williams, *Arius: Heresy and Tradition*, 2nd ed. (Grand Rapids: Eerdmans, 2002); Michel R. Barnes

Council of Nicaea (325) and Constantinople (381), but its influence continues today in Unitarianism and Jehovah's Witnesses. Despite its serious nature, Arianism helped the church define trinitarian and Christological orthodoxy and enabled the church to reject all forms of subordinationism.[77]

Arius affirmed God's absolute unity and transcendence, which for him denied any possibility of God sharing his being with another person.[78] However, contrary to modalism, he affirmed the *distinctness* of the Father and Son, but he did so by reducing the Son to a creature. For Arius, only the Father is eternal: the Son was created by God's will, thus distinguishing the will of the Father (Creator) from the will of the Son (creature).[79] Like the creation, the Son was "begotten" from God (or "created"), yet he is the firstborn in time and the highest of all created beings. But given God's absolute transcendence, in order to create, God first had to create the Son to act as a kind of Platonic demiurge. He is only God's "wisdom," "image," and "word" by grace and participation as a creature, not because he is the divine Son who shares fully the divine nature with the Father (and Spirit). The Son only "shares" God's will by agreement, not by unity of being.[80] The Son is not *homoousios* with the Father, for "there was a time when the Son was not." Thus, for Arius, the Father-Son relation is simply another aspect of the God-world relation.[81]

---

and Daniel H. Williams, eds., *Arianism After Arius: Essays on the Development of the Fourth Century Trinitarian Conflicts* (Edinburgh: T&T Clark, 2000); R. P. C. Hanson, *The Search for the Christian Doctrine of God: The Arian Controversy 318–381* (Edinburgh: T&T Clark, 1988).

[77] In terms of subordinationism, one must distinguish Origen (c. 185–254) from Arius. For Origen, the Son was eternal (not created) and divine but subordinate in his sharing of the divine nature with the Father. For Arius, the Son is subordinate as a creature since he is a product of God's will and external to God. See Letham, *Holy Trinity*, 100–7, 116–17; Williams, *Arius*, 131–48.

[78] See Aloys Grillmeier, *Christ in Christian Tradition*, vol. 1, *From the Apostolic Age to Chalcedon (451)*, trans. John Bowden, 2nd ed. (Atlanta: John Knox Press, 1975), 219–28.

[79] See Anatolios, *Retrieving Nicaea*, 41–79; cf. Ayres, *Nicaea and its Legacy*, 105–30; Letham, *Holy Trinity*, 110–14; cf. Williams, *Arius*, 95–116.

[80] See Gregory of Nyssa, *Against Eunomius* 2.14 (*NPNF*[2] 5:246–251), in which he writes against Arianism.

[81] Regarding biblical warrant, Arians appealed to texts that seem to say that Jesus is "less" than the Father in terms of his knowledge (Matt 24:36; Mark 13:32) and nature (John 5:19–29; 14:28), thus making him a created being (Col 1:15). However, the Arians failed to account for all of the biblical data that affirmed that Jesus is *God* the Son, that the first two texts refer to the *incarnate* Son in his mission to redeem his people as our new covenant head, and that "firstborn" in Col 1:15 is a reference to his

For Arianism and its later development in the Eunomians, Christ is the perfect creature and our "savior," but only quantitatively so. Jesus, as a creature, grows in his commitment to the good. He is our example of how we can attain perfection and partake of divinity as he did. But Jesus is *not* God the Son incarnate, worthy of our worship, or able to accomplish a *divine* work of redemption. In the end, Arianism leaves us with a "salvation" by human achievement, which is no salvation at all. Jesus is simply a creature, an intermediary figure—a "god" of lesser status than the Father—who is God's agent in creation, but mutable, imperfect in his knowledge, and unworthy of our worship. Arianism denies the triune God of the Bible, and the church had to reject it at Nicaea in no uncertain terms: the truth of the entire Bible and the gospel was at stake.

In 325, the Roman Emperor Constantine called 318 bishops, primarily from the East, to assemble at Nicaea to resolve the challenge of Arianism. The Arians presented a statement, drawn up by Eusebius of Nicomedia, that denied Christ's deity, which was resoundingly rejected by the majority of the bishops. The concern of the council was to confess belief in one God, the true Father and his Son, who both fully share the one divine nature. Not much was said about the Holy Spirit; that will come later at Constantinople (381), where the "third article" on the Spirit is added, and trinitarian orthodoxy is fully stated, what today we identify as the Nicene Creed.

Post-Nicene Developments to Constantinople (381)

Between Nicaea (325) and Constantinople (381), further developments occurred to establish trinitarian orthodoxy.[82] Although Arianism was officially rejected, its influence continued. The church also saw the rise of Macedonianism, or pneumatomachianism, which affirmed

---

supremacy over creation because he is the Creator and not a creature (Col 1:16). In our Christology section in volume 2, we will discuss these texts in more detail, but for a discussion of these texts, see Wellum, *God the Son Incarnate*, 159–62, 179–82, 455–59 (see chap. 18, n. 17); R. B. Jamieson and Tyler R. Wittman, *Biblical Reasoning: Christological and Trinitarian Rules for Exegesis* (Grand Rapids: Baker Academic, 2022), 167–70; 213–34; cf. Cyril of Alexandria, *Commentary on John* 10.1; Carson, *Gospel According to John*, 246–59, 506–8 (see chap. 5, n. 13).

[82] Between Nicaea and Constantinople, the church rejected Arianism as taught by the Eunomians (or Anomians); the homoian Arians (who affirmed that the Son is "like" the Father but from his will and not his nature); modalism (e.g., Marcellus of Ancyra); and a view similar to orthodoxy, namely, the

the Son's deity but refused to call the Spirit "God." In this era, Athanasius (c. 295–373) and the Cappadocians—Basil of Caesarea (329–79), his brother Gregory of Nyssa (335–95), and Gregory of Nazianzus (329–90)—were crucial in achieving linguistic clarity in regard to the "person-nature" distinction and conceptual clarity in regard to how the Father, Son, and Spirit are distinct persons yet subsist in the same identical nature. Here are some of the key points.

First, as noted above, during this time, linguistic clarity was achieved by uncoupling *person* (*hypostasis*) from *nature* (*ousia*) at the Synod of Alexandria (362). This allowed the church to gain conceptual clarity and speak coherently about how God is one and three simultaneously.

Second, regarding God's nature or essence, "one" included both the ideas of singularity and simplicity.[83] God *is* his attributes, he is not composed of parts, and he possesses one will and one activity. As such, the three persons subsist in the undivided divine essence not as three separate beings but as the one true and living God. Also, the divine essence does *not* belong to a general category that the persons belong to, parallel to how specific humans belong to the larger category of "humanity." By contrast, the divine essence "is identical with God, and subsists in and only in the three Persons. . . . The divine Persons are distinct, yet they cannot be separated from the godhead or from one another."[84] Thus, the Father, Son, and Spirit are identical in nature—they are one God.

Third, this one God is a plurality of three *hypostases* (persons). Because God acts with a single will toward the created world, it is only possible to know the distinctions of the divine persons due to the divine missions and by Scripture. Regarding the personal characteristics or "notions" of the divine persons, we can distinguish Father, Son, and Holy Spirit in the following way.[85] The personal property of the Father is "paternity." The Father

---

homoiousians, who affirmed that the Son is "like" the Father and fully God but with personal distinction (e.g., Basil of Ancyra).

[83] *Ousia* (and *homoousios*) conveys this truth. With the uncoupling of *hypostasis* and *ousia*, the concern of the "homoiousians" was met, i.e., the divine persons are equally God yet personally distinct. On this point, see Letham, *Holy Trinity*, 126–8.

[84] Brown, *Heresies*, 146; cf. Athanasius, *Against the Arians* 3.6.

[85] "Notions" identify what is proper to each divine person, thus allowing us to distinguish the persons in terms of their personal relations of origin and unique personal properties. On this point, see Muller, *Dictionary of Latin and Greek*, s.v. "Trinitas," 306–10; White, *Trinity*, 434–38. These "notions" were described by the Church Fathers, but came to full expression in Augustine and the later medieval tradition in Aquinas.

is characterized by three notions: unbegottenness, the active generation of the Son, and the active spiration of the Spirit. The personal property of the Son is "filiation." The Son is characterized by two notions: his passive generation from the Father and what he shares with the Father, namely, the active spiration of the Spirit. The personal property of the Spirit is "spiration." The Spirit is characterized by one notion: his passive spiration from the Father and the Son. All of this is to say, that although the Father, Son, and Holy Spirit are identical in essence, they are distinguished by their unique personal relations and properties, thus removing any hint of subordinationism while also upholding real ordered (*taxis*) relations between the persons.

Fourth, all of God's external works are inseparable, that is, indivisible and undivided. God alone creates, rules, and redeems, but he does so as the triune God. In other words, God's acts are one, but because God is three persons "the mutual relations between the persons of the Trinity exhibit themselves within God's indivisible external works. . . . The one God's distinct personal modes of existing as Father, Son, and Spirit are inflected in the Trinitarian shape of God's indivisible action: God's external actions proceed from the Father, through the Son, in the Spirit."[86] Keith Johnson explains it this way: "The Father acts with the other divine persons according to his mode of being 'from no one' (unbegotten). The Son acts with the other divine persons according to his mode of being 'from the Father' (generation). The Spirit acts with the other divine persons according to his mode of being 'from the Father and the Son' (procession),"[87] but as one undivided act. So God's one act of creation is the Father creating through the Son and by the Spirit, the Son creating from the Father and by the Spirit, and the Spirit creating from the Father and the Son.[88] Or God's one act of redemption is the Father redeeming by the sending of his Son and the Spirit, the Son redeeming by becoming the incarnate Mediator of his people by the Spirit, and the Spirit redeeming by applying the work of the Son to us to the praise and glory of the Father and the entire triune Godhead.[89]

Fifth, to explain further how the divine persons share or subsist in the same identical nature, the concept of *perichoresis* was introduced. Appealing to John 14:11 ("I am in the

---

[86] Swain, *Trinity*, 109–10.

[87] Johnson, *Rethinking the Trinity*, 119 (see chap. 6, n. 59).

[88] Gen 1:1–3; John 1:1–3; Col 1:15–16; Heb 1:2–3.

[89] Matt 1:20–23; 3:13–17; Luke 1:31–37; John 1:1–18; 3:16; 5:19–30; 15:25–26; 16:12–15; Rom 3:21–16; Eph 1:3–14.

Father and the Father is in me"), it was argued that the divine persons share the same nature by an exhaustive "indwelling" and "co-inherence."[90] As Donald Macleod explains,

> Taken temporally, *perichoresis* means that the Father, Son, and Holy Spirit occupy and fill the same time (or the same eternity). Each is unoriginated (*agenētos*), endless and eternal. Taken spatially, it means that each person and all the persons together occupy and fill the same space. Each is omnipresent while remaining unconfused with the others. Each fills immensity. Beyond that, each contains the other; each dwells in the other; each penetrates the other, and each conditions the mode of the existence of the other. None, not even the Father, would be what he is without the others.[91]

Furthermore, in our human experience, God comes toward us as one. However, as Macleod reminds us, "the one in whom he comes is the Father, the Son and the Holy Spirit. The coming is such that in the one the three come; and that in each the other comes."[92] Since the three persons subsist in and share the same identical divine essence, there is no relation with the divine essence that is not also a relation with the divine persons. Indeed, as Macleod correctly states, there is "no action of one person which does not also involve the action of the others; and yet no action of a person which does not have his own distinct mark upon it. The external acts of the triune God (the *opera ad extra*) are indeed common to all three persons, but that does not mean that each acts in the same way."[93]

With these conceptual distinctions in place, the church was able to formulate the Trinity with greater theological clarity, reaching its full confession at the Council of Constantinople

---

[90] Gk. *enperichoresis*; Lat., *circumincessio*. John of Damascus describes *perichoresis*:

"The subsistences dwell and are established firmly in one other. For they are inseparable and cannot part from one another, but keep to their separate course within one another, without coalescing or mingling, but cleaving to each other. For the Son is in the Father and the Spirit: and the Spirit in the Father and the Son: and the Father in the Son and the Spirit, but there is no coalescence or commingling or confusion. And there is one and the same motion: for there is one impulse and one motion of the three subsistences, which is not to be observed in any created nature." John of Damascus, *An Exact Exposition of the Orthodox Faith* 1.14 (*NPNF*[2] 9:17b)

[91] Donald Macleod, *The Person of Christ* (Downers Grove: InterVarsity, 1998), 141.

[92] Macleod, 142.

[93] Macleod, 142.

(381). This council ended the Arian controversy, and it crowned the efforts of Athanasius and the Cappadocians by rejecting all forms of modalism and subordinationism and by adding the "third article" about the Holy Spirit to the Nicene Creed. The full Nicene Creed reads as follows:

> We believe in one God, the Father Almighty, Maker of heaven and earth, and of all things visible and invisible.
>
> And in one Lord Jesus Christ, the only begotten (*monogenē*) Son of God, begotten of the Father before all worlds, Light of Light, very God of very God, begotten, not made, being of one substance (*homoousion*) with the Father; by whom all things were made; who for us men, and for our salvation, came down from heaven, and was incarnate by the Holy Ghost and the Virgin Mary, and was made man; he was crucified for us under Pontius Pilate, and suffered, and was buried, and the third day he rose again, according to the Scriptures, and ascended into heaven, and sitteth on the right hand of the Father; from thence he shall come again, with glory, to judge the quick and the dead; whose kingdom shall have no end.
>
> And in the Holy Ghost, the Lord and Giver of life, who proceedeth from the Father, who with the Father and the Son together is worshiped and glorified, who spake by the prophets. In one holy catholic and apostolic Church; we acknowledge one baptism for the remission of sins; we look for the resurrection of the dead, and the life of the world to come. Amen.[94]

Pro-Nicene Trinitarianism

The Nicene Creed results in what we now identify as pro-Nicene, or classical, orthodox trinitarian theology, which may be summarized by *five* important truths.

First, there is only one true and living God who is the Father Almighty, the only-begotten Son, and the Holy Spirit, the Lord and giver of life: the triune Creator-covenant Lord.

Second, the Father, Son, and Spirit are the one God and equally and fully share the identical divine nature. Nicaea (325) first taught this truth in regard to the Son. Against

[94] Schaff, *Creeds of Christendom*, 1:28–29 (see chap. 11, n. 64).

Arianism, the Son's full deity was affirmed: the Son is "of one substance (*homoousion*) with the Father," which meant that the being of the Son is identical to the being of the Father and that both equally possess all of the divine attributes, including the same will, thus placing "will" in the "essence" or "nature" and not in the "persons."[95] The Son is not merely from God's will; that is true of all creatures. Instead, the Son is "Light of Light, very God of very God" because his essence (*ousia*) is *identical* with the Father's nature.[96] Constantinople (381) later taught that the Spirit is not a creature but fully God by identifying him with God's proper name of "Lord," God's works ("Giver of life"), and worship ("with the Father and Son is worshipped and glorified"). Thus, all subordinationism is rejected since each person *is* God.[97]

Third, since the Father, Son, and Spirit share equally the same divine essence, they cannot be distinguished by divine attributes nor by a distinct will. Instead, they are only distinguished by their eternal "relations of origin" within the divine essence and their own unique personal property. Thus, the Father *as Father* is "unbegotten" and eternally and necessarily generates the Son and communicates to him the divine essence; the Son *as Son* is *from* the Father and receives from the Father the divine essence ("begotten of the Father"; "begotten, not made")

---

[95] See John of Damascus, *Exposition of the Orthodox Faith* 1.8 (*NPNF*[2] 9:558–69).

[96] See Athanasius, *De Decritis* 5.19–21 (*NPNF*[2] 4:162–64).

[97] Years later, John Calvin will emphasize this point by saying that each divine person is *autotheos* with specific emphasis on the Son in order to avoid any hint of subordinationism. See Calvin, *Institutes*, 1.13.23–25 (1:149–54). This does not mean that the Son is *autotheos* in respect of his person (because the Son is *from* the Father); instead, the Son is *a se* in respect to his divine essence that he shares fully and equally with the Father and Spirit. In historical theology, primarily due to Calvin, people differ regarding what is involved in the eternal generation of the Son from the Father (and correspondingly, the spiration of the Spirit from the Father and Son). Regarding eternal generation, the majority view is that it involves the communication of the divine essence from the Father to the Son, but given divine simplicity, this involves no subordinationism. On this point, see Ellis, *Calvin, Classical Trinitarianism*, 69–98; Duby, *Jesus and the God of Classical Theism*, 76–87 (see chap. 18, n. 67). Also see Turretin, *Institutes of Elenctic Theology*, 1:282–302 (see chap. 3, n. 55). The minority view, as represented by Calvin (and later by John Gill), speaks of eternal generation solely in terms of the Son's person *from* the Father, not the communication of the divine essence. Both views affirm that the divine persons are *autotheos* in respect to the divine essence but differ on whether eternal generation means that the Son's essence is communicated to him from the Father. If one maintains a proper view of divine simplicity, the majority view is the better way of thinking of eternal generation. We will discuss this point in more detail in volume 2.

and is *not* the Father (or Spirit); and, as Constantinople later adds, the Spirit *as Spirit* always *proceeds* from the Father "and the Son" and receives from the Father "and the Son" the divine essence and is thus distinct.

However, technically the original Nicene Creed does not say that the Spirit proceeds from the Father "and the Son" (*filioque*), a truth that the Western church added to the Creed at the Synod of Toledo (589) in Spain. The history surrounding the addition of the *filioque* is complicated, and it was one of the reasons for the first division in the church between East and West, known as the Great Schism (1054).[98] At issue was the proper way of distinguishing the divine persons. The Eastern Church argued that the Spirit's single procession was from the Father "through" the Son, while the West spoke of the double procession of the Spirit from the Father and the Son. Although these ideas are close, the West is on firmer ground for at least three reasons. First, Scripture teaches that the Spirit proceeds from the Father "and the Son" (John 14:26; 15:26; 16:7, 12–15; Acts 2:33). Second, without the *filioque*, it is difficult to distinguish the Son from the Spirit if they both proceed from the Father and relate to him in the same way.[99] Instead, the Son is *from* the Father (single relation of origin), and the Spirit is *from* the Father *and* the Son (double relation of origin).[100] Third, the *filioque* reminds us that the Spirit's work is not independent of the Son;[101] instead, his work is to apply Christ's work to us to the glory of the Father by making us alive and uniting us to Christ, not by acting outside of gospel realities.

Fourth, although the Creed does not use the word *perichoresis*, it is assumed given the influence of the Cappadocian Fathers. By this concept, the church sought to explain how the divine persons share the same nature and how to make sense of the tri-unity of God. Although the persons are distinct, "they are never separated from each other, but always coexist; wherever one is, there the other also really is."[102] Within the one Godhead, the three persons co-inhere

---

[98] See Letham, *Holy Trinity*, 229–51.

[99] See Aquinas, *Summa Theologica*, pt. 1, q. 36, art. 2–3. Remember "relations" are the only way to distinguish the divine persons, so the Spirit has to have a different relation to the Father than the Son. See Swain, *Trinity*, 92–103.

[100] See Köstenberger and Allison, *Holy Spirit*, 258–64.

[101] This is contrary to inclusivism's pneumatological proposal that separated the Spirit's work from Christ (see chap. 6).

[102] Turretin, *Institutes of Elenctic Theology*, 1:257.

in each other, interpenetrate each other, and as such, within God, independent of the world, there is fullness of life, communion, and holy love.

Fifth, a distinction is made between the triune God in himself (*ad intra*) apart from creation and God in his external works (*ad extra*). The former is called the "ontological" or "immanent" Trinity, while the latter is called the "economic" Trinity.[103] In God's works (i.e., creation, providence, redemption, consummation), the persons act inseparably and indivisibly but also according to their "ordered" (*taxis*) relations,[104] with specific acts appropriated to one of the divine persons, which fittingly reveal the eternal relations of the three persons.[105] Thus, for example, in regard to creation, the Father creates through the Son (Gen 1:3; John 1:3; Col 1:15–16; Heb 1:3) and by the Spirit (Gen 1:2; Ps 33:6), but the one act of creation is appropriated to the Father, who is the Maker of heaven and earth. We may even use the language of "termination," which means that "a work appropriated to one of the three persons terminates in that person in the sense of reaching the goal or end of that work."[106] In redemption, the Father plans our redemption and sends his Son (John 3:16; Gal 4:4; Eph 1:9–10); the Son alone becomes flesh and achieves our salvation as our obedient new covenant mediator (John 1:14; 5:16–30; 6:38; Heb 10:5–7); and the Spirit applies the benefits of Christ to us as he is sent from the Father and the Son (John 3:5–8; 14:26; 15:26; 16:7; 1 Pet 1:2). But as the creed notes, specific works are appropriated to one of the divine persons. For example, the incarnation is a divine work appropriated to the Son, which also means that the incarnation properly terminates in the Son. Although all three persons inseparably act in the incarnation, it is only the Son who assumes a human nature, not the Father or the Spirit. Also, it is fitting that the Son becomes incarnate because of his personal property of filiation. In the case of the Spirit, he is identified with giving us life by applying Christ's work to us, and as such Scripture appropriates the work of sanctification to him. This too is fitting since the Spirit proceeds from the Father and Son and thus is the person of the Godhead who brings everything to

---

103 "Economic" is from the Greek *oikonomia*, meaning "administration" or "ordering."

104 The triune persons' "mode of acting" is consistent with their eternal relations, or "mode of subsistence."

105 On "appropriation," see Gilles Emery, *The Trinity*, trans. Matthew Levering (Washington, DC: Catholic University of America Press, 2011), 164–68; Bavinck, *Reformed Dogmatics*, 2:319.

106 Köstenberger and Allison, *Holy Spirit*, 283; cf. Adonis Vidu, "Trinitarian Inseparable Operations and the Incarnation," *Journal of Analytic Theology* 4 (2016): 115.

completion.[107] The same pattern is also found in all of God's external works. This entails that all of God's actions are triune, effective, and unified since no person acts on their own apart from the others.[108]

In addition to how Scripture appropriates specific operations of the triune God to specific persons, which reveals and reflect the eternal relations of Father, Son, and Holy Spirit, the divine missions also reveal the trinitarian shape of God's external works.[109] In trinitarian theology, as Swain explains, the "divine missions" refers to "sendings," "specifically the Father's sending of the Son to redeem and the Father and Son's sending of the Spirit to sanctify (Gal. 4:4–7)."[110] As already noted, in the "missions," there is a specific sending of a triune person to us so that first, "missions are a mode of a divine person's presence" with us; second, they "terminate on creatures, in creatures"; and third, they "originate from God, in God."[111] In this way, "missions are extensions in time of a divine person's eternal relation of origin."[112] For example, the Father, who eternally generates the Son, sends him to become present with us in a new mode of presence by his incarnation, and as the incarnate Son, he accomplishes our redemption as our new covenant head and restores us to the purpose of our creation as God's image-sons. The Father and Son, who eternally spirate the Spirit, send him to be present with us, first to Christ's human nature so that "Christ's human nature is hypostatically united to the Son alone, but it is simultaneously filled with the presence of the Holy Spirit,"[113] and due to Christ's work, the Spirit is given to Christ's people to apply Christ's work to us and dwell within us. Indeed, as Swain correctly notes, "The missions of the triune God, more than anything else, manifest the grace of God the Father whereby he embraces us as his beloved children, at the cost of his only begotten Son, through the presence of his Holy Spirit, to the glory of his name."[114]

---

[107] See Horton, *Rediscovering the Holy Spirit*, 29–46 (see chap. 13, n. 37).

[108] To understand God's actions, this truth is important, but especially in soteriology, where the Father's election, the Son's accomplishment of our redemption, and the Spirit's application of Christ's work are effective and unified.

[109] See Emery, *Trinity*, 178–94.

[110] Swain, *Trinity*, 113.

[111] Swain, 114; cf. White, *Trinity*, 534–44.

[112] Swain, 114; cf. Köstenberger and Allison, *Holy Spirit*, 274–77.

[113] Dominic Legge, *The Trinitarian Christology of St. Thomas Aquinas* (Oxford: Oxford University Press, 2017), 153.

[114] Swain, *Trinity*, 115.

Here is the basic summary of pro-Nicene Trinitarianism that has functioned as established orthodoxy since the fourth century. Although debates occurred between the East and the West, until the Enlightenment, there has been basic "catholic" agreement on the Trinity. With the rise of modern/postmodern thought, the Trinity was rejected by deists and recast by forms of panentheism (e.g., various Hegelian reconstructions). Even with the resurgence of trinitarian theology in the twentieth century, there has not always been a return to a pro-Nicene view. In fact, today, there is an unmistakable appeal to a "social" view of the Trinity (that differs from the classical view), which has impacted the larger theological world and evangelical theology, a point to which we now turn.

Contemporary Debates within Evangelical Theology

In current theology, a "social" view of the Trinity has been embraced by many.[115] Despite the term covering diverse views, the common denominator is that the Trinity is viewed as a "society or family of three human persons."[116] Most who affirm a "social" view define a divine person as a "distinct center of knowledge, will, love, and action."[117] The Father, Son, and Spirit are distinct speech agents who exist in an I-Thou relationship and act harmoniously together. The divine persons' unity is not found in their sharing the one, undivided divine essence, but in sharing a generic divine essence that constitutes a cooperative society of divine love,[118] or "the union of the three Persons by virtue of their perichoresis and eternal communion."[119]

---

[115] Although the term *social* covers multiple views, here it refers to those views that redefine the classical view of "person" to include within it a distinct center of will, knowledge, and action, which usually also entails a rejection of divine simplicity, inseparable operations, and the embrace of a kenotic Christology. For some of the views, see McCall, *Which Trinity?*, 11–55 (see chap. 16, n. 38); Jason S. Sexton, ed., *Two Views on the Doctrine of the Trinity* (Grand Rapids: Zondervan, 2014).

[116] McCall, *Which Trinity?*, 28.

[117] Cornelius Plantinga Jr., "Social Trinity and Tritheism," in Feenstra and Platinga, *Trinity, Incarnation, and Atonement*, 22 (see chap. 16, n. 40); cf. William Hasker, *Metaphysics and the Tri-Personal God* (Oxford: Oxford University Press, 2013), 19–25.

[118] See Plantinga, "Social Trinity and Tritheism," 27–28.

[119] Boff, *Trinity and Society*, 235 (see chap. 16, n. 42).

For many, this view is attractive for three reasons. First, a social view is thought to warrant various social and political ideologies.[120] Second, a social view is seen as a "better" way to read Scripture. For example, in the Gospels, the Father, Son, and Spirit seem to act as distinct agents. If we follow Karl Rahner's rule that "the 'economic' Trinity is the 'immanent' Trinity,"[121] should we not view God as "three distinct centres of consciousness, volition, and agency, which stand as persons over against each other with faculties of their own,"[122] similar to how we think of human persons? The claim is that the social view accounts for the relationships between the divine persons better than the classical view, which unites the persons "in will, intellect, and essence."[123] Third, the social view also has perceived advantages for Christology given that the two doctrinal areas are inseparable. Social views tend to affirm a kenotic Christology, which C. Stephen Evans insists allows us to think of a God "who can fully empathize with us" and "fully shar[e] in the human condition," in contrast to a simple, immutable, and impassible God.[124]

But is this the case? The answer is no. A social view of the Trinity and its corresponding Christology is out of step with Scripture and the tradition. In its redefinition of a divine "person," it causes more theological problems than it solves. To substantiate this claim, we will describe current "social" views within evangelical theology by focusing on their redefinition of "person" and its consequences for the Trinity and Christology and then list some of the problems that result from such views and argue that classic trinitarianism is more faithful to Scripture.

Social-Relational Trinitarianism

Most "social" views of the Trinity define a divine "person" as a "distinct center of knowledge, will, and action." Thus, both the "act of willing" *and* the "faculty/capacity of willing," along

---

[120] For example, see Jürgen Moltmann, *The Trinity and the Kingdom of God* (London: SCM Press, 1981), 19–60, 191–222; Boff, *Trinity and Society*, 119, 151.

[121] Karl Rahner, *The Trinity* (New York: Herder & Herder, 1970), 22. Italics removed.

[122] Fred Sanders, "The Trinity," in *The Oxford Handbook of Systematic Theology*, ed. John B. Webster, Kathryn Tanner, and Iain Torrance (Oxford: Oxford University Press, 2009), 45.

[123] See Stephen R. Holmes, "Three Versus One? Some Problems of Social Trinitarianism," *Journal of Reformed Theology* 3 (2009): 81.

[124] C. Stephen Evans, "Introduction" in *Exploring Kenotic Christology: The Self-Emptying of God*, ed. C. Stephen Evans (Oxford: Oxford University Press, 2006), 7.

with the mind, is located in the "person" and not the "nature" or "essence."[125] For the Trinity, this entails that each person has a distinct will and mind and, for Christology, that the incarnate Son has one divine mind and will (monothelitism). But both of these entailments are contrary to pro-Nicene theology and Chalcedonian Christology, and they lead to serious problems. In evangelical theology, there are two versions of the "social" view. Let us look at each in turn.

Two Versions of the View

First, there is a more radical version that redefines the classical view of "essence/nature" and "person."[126] Such redefinition is thought necessary to account for the relational God of Scripture in contrast to the immutable and impassible God of classical theism.

Regarding God's essence, this view rejects divine simplicity and the notion that *all* of God's attributes are *essential* to him. It proposes that God's nature is a generic one that all three persons share. God's unity is not located in the one undivided nature that all three persons subsist in; instead, it is located in how the persons cooperate and function as one.[127] Each person has his own will, but they are one because "God is like a community,"[128] a perichoretic unity of persons by which the divine persons have "unity of purpose, fellowship, communion, hospitality, transparency, self-deference, or just simply the love among Father, Son, and Spirit."[129]

Also, in rejecting divine simplicity, this view applies an "essential-accidental" distinction to God's nature and attributes, something orthodox theology rejects. As this distinction is applied to the incarnation, this view embraces an ontological kenoticism: the divine Son "set aside" his accidental attributes but retained his essential ones in the incarnation.[130] But the accidental

---

[125] See Hasker, *Metaphysics and the Tri-Personal God*, 206–7.

[126] Social trinitarian-ontological kenotic Christology describes the view. See Feenstra and Plantinga, *Trinity, Incarnation, and Atonement*; Evans, *Exploring Kenotic Christology*; Stephen T. Davis et al., eds., *The Incarnation* (Oxford: Oxford University Press, 2002).

[127] Plantinga, "Social Trinity and Tritheism," 27–28.

[128] Stephen T. Davis, "Perichoretic Monotheism: A Defense of a Social Theory of the Trinity," in *The Trinity: East/West Dialogue*, ed. Melville Y. Stewart (Dordrecht: Kluwer Academic, 2003), 42.

[129] Thompson and Plantinga, "Trinity and Kenosis," in Evans, *Exploring Kenotic Christology*, 183–84.

[130] See Stephen T. Davis, "Is Kenosis Orthodox?," in Evans *Exploring Kenotic Christology*, 115–16. An *essential property* of x is an attribute that x has and cannot lose without ceasing to be x. An *accidental*

attributes the Son "set aside" were omniscience, omnipotence, and omnipresence since they are inconsistent with a human life![131] How, then, is Christ still truly God? In this way: Christ only "gives up" accidental attributes, but he retains all that is "essential" to deity.[132]

Regarding "person," this view defines it as a "distinct center of knowledge, will, love, and action."[133] As applied to the Trinity, within God there are *three* distinct wills, not one. As applied to Christology, Christ has only one will (monothelitism) since the will is located in the "person." Additionally, this view identifies "person" and "soul"—a significant departure from Chalcedon. The Chalcedonian Definition distinguished the two by teaching that the Son (person) assumed a human nature constituted by a body *and* a "rational soul," thus allowing for the Son to subsist and act in two natures. By contrast, this view insists that in the incarnation, the Son (person) *became* the soul of the human body.[134] By an act of *kenosis* (i.e., emptying) the Son freely "gave up" his accidental divine attributes and became a human soul and one consciousness that is now totally circumscribed within the limits of a human body and thus unable to act "outside" (*extra*) his human nature.

This last observation is important. As we will discuss in volume 2, classical Christology has argued for the *extra*;[135] that is, the Son subsists in two natures, and he continues to act "outside" of his human nature as he has always done, inseparably with the Father and Spirit. To deny this point not only renders inseparable operations impossible, but it also cannot account for biblical teaching that the incarnate Son continues to exercise cosmic functions (e.g., Col 1:15–17; Heb 1:3). Evans suggests that normally all three persons are involved in such cosmic functions, but given the incarnation, the Father and Spirit carry out the work *without* the agency of the Son. He writes: "In some way the activity of each person of the Trinity must involve the activity of each of the others. I see no reason why, if the second person of the Trinity became incarnate

---

property of x is an attribute that x has but can fail to have and still be x.

[131] See C. Stephen Evans, "Kenotic Christology and the Nature of God," in *Exploring Kenotic Christology*, 190–217.

[132] See Davis, "Is Kenosis Orthodox?," 118.

[133] Plantinga, "Trinity and Tritheism," 22; cf. Thompson and Plantinga, "Trinity and Kenosis," 165–89.

[134] See Thompson and Plantinga, "Trinity and Kenosis," 170. They make sense of this by positing "a strict identity between the Logos and Christ's human rational soul."

[135] The *extra* is shorthand for what is known as the *extra Calvinisticum*.

and divested himself of omnipotence and omniscience, what we might call the sustaining work of this person in creation could not be carried on by the other persons."[136]

What trinitarian consequences follow from this view? At least two. First, this view must reject the inseparable operations of the divine persons since there is a time when the incarnate Son is not doing any divine action; indeed, given the nature of the incarnation, he cannot do so.[137] Second, it also entails that the relations of the divine persons have changed. The *incarnate* Son now relates differently to the Father and Spirit since he has ceased to do any divine work. Also, his loss of accidental attributes now means that the Father and Spirit have different attributes than the Son, thus making problematic how the Son is *homoousios* with the Father.

Second, there is a more traditional version of the view.[138] It rejects applying the essential-accidental distinction to the divine essence or nature. The Son did not "set aside" any divine attribute in the incarnation; he is fully God and *homoousios* with the Father (and Spirit).[139] But for some who embrace this view, its understanding of the divine essence is not the classical view. Many reject divine simplicity and locate the "will" in the "person." For example, William L. Craig and J. P. Moreland deny that the divine essence is the common essence of the divine persons: "The divine persons of the Trinity are not divine in virtue of instantiating the divine nature."[140] Instead, the persons are divine because they are "parts of God."[141] In their view, God is a soul "endowed with three sets of cognitive faculties each of which is sufficient for personhood."[142] But the challenge for such a view is to account for divine unity and not to

---

[136] C. Stephen Evans, "The Self-Emptying of Love," in Davis et al., *The Incarnation*, 259.

[137] Thompson and Plantinga willingly concede this point: "To the objection that this sunders the *indivisa* of Trinitarian persons and their operations, we confess the transgression." "Trinity and Kenosis," 189.

[138] Social trinitarian-functional kenotic Christology identifies the view. See William L. Craig and J. P. Moreland, *Philosophical Foundations for a Christian Worldview* (Downers Grove: InterVarsity, 2003), 575–614; Garrett J. DeWeese, "One Person, Two Natures: Two Metaphysical Models of the Incarnation," in *Jesus in Trinitarian Perspective*, ed. Fred Sanders and Klaus Issler (Nashville: B&H, 2007), 114–53; Klaus Issler, *Living into the Life of Jesus* (Downers Grove: InterVarsity, 2012); and Gerald F. Hawthorne, *The Presence and the Power* (repr., Eugene: Wipf & Stock, 2003).

[139] See Moreland and Craig, *Philosophical Foundations*, 607.

[140] Moreland and Craig, 590.

[141] Moreland and Craig, 591.

[142] William Lane Craig, "Trinity Monotheism Once More: A Response to Daniel Howard-Snyder," *Philosophia Christi* 8 (2006): 101.

make the ultimate source of deity "the non-personal divine nature, which supports and enables their [the divine persons'] existence."[143]

However, this view's definition of "person" is the same as other "social" views; hence, it locates the "will" and "mind" in the "person" and *not* the nature.[144] Many also equate "person" with "soul" so that the Son (person) *becomes* the soul of Christ's human body.[145] Also, this view rejects the *extra*, which has serious consequences for our view of triune agency. In contrast to pro-Nicene and Chalcedonian theology, this view denies that the incarnate Son *continually* exercises his divine attributes, specifically in terms of ongoing cosmic functions.[146] By placing one divine will and mind in the "person," it renders problematic how the incarnate Son can act "outside" of his human nature inseparably with the Father and Spirit, which results in some kind of change in the relations of the divine persons due to the incarnation. Similar to Evans, Klaus Issler suggests that the Son, in a pre-incarnate decision, "temporarily delegated to the other members of the Trinity his usual divine duties, such as sustaining the universe (Col 1:17; Heb 1:3)."[147] This answer is consistent with their view of a "person"; namely, each person has an independent will, but this results in a rejection of a classic view of triune relations and agency, along with the self-identity of the divine Son.

Problems with the Two Views

First, regarding the first view, its redefinition of the divine nature renders pro-Nicene trinitarian theology impossible in at least three ways.

1. The application of the "essential-accidental" distinction to God's nature rejects divine simplicity and aseity. But a God who can still be God without omnipotence, omniscience, and omnipresence is not the biblical God.

---

143 Hasker, *Metaphysics and the Tri-Personal God*, 215.

144 DeWeese, "One Person, Two Natures," 144–49; Moreland and Craig, *Philosophical Foundations*, 611–12.

145 DeWeese, 147–48; Moreland and Craig, 608–10.

146 This view offers a spectrum of thought about how the incarnate Son uses his divine attributes. For example, some insist that Jesus *never* exercises them (e.g., Hawthorne), while others think he *occasionally* uses them (e.g., Issler and DeWeese). But the latter is hard to reconcile with their view of "person" and their denial of the *extra*.

147 Issler, *Living into the Life of Jesus*, 125, n. 31.

2. In its rejection of the *extra* as metaphysically impossible, it must also reject the inseparable operations of the divine persons *and* the cosmic functions of the incarnate Son. The problem is that Scripture teaches both (Col 1:17; Heb 1:3). To suggest that the Son temporarily ceased sustaining the universe contradicts Scripture and radically changes the triune personal relations.

3. Given the change in the triune personal relations, and that the Son "set aside" attributes that the Father and Spirit retain, how is the Son *homoousios* with the Father and Spirit? Not only is the continuity between the eternal Word (*Logos asarkos*) and the incarnate Word (*Logos ensarkos*) changed, but as the incarnate Son, he "gives up" his omniscience or omnipresence. This entails that the identity of the Son has radically changed, and even if this state is temporary, the Son does *not* share the same nature with the Father and Spirit. This not only flirts with semi-Arianism; it also, for a period of time, makes the Trinity more binitarian than trinitarian.

In summary, this view undercuts biblical teaching as upheld in pro-Nicene theology. Nowhere does Scripture distinguish the divine persons by their possession/non-possession or use/non-use of the divine attributes. Instead, Scripture teaches that the divine persons equally share the identical divine nature and inseparably act according to their eternal personal relations.

Second, regarding both views, their redefinition of "person" renders problematic pro-Nicene trinitarian theology in at least two ways.

1. "Social" views of "person" change how we think of triune relations and agency. Both views render problematic the *extra* in Christology, which entails that at least while the incarnate Son is on earth (and for some now permanently), the Father and Spirit sustain the universe (along with other divine actions) *apart* from the Son. Not only is such a view denied by Scripture, it also rejects inseparable operations and changes the ordered (*taxis*) personal relations in God's works. By contrast, a classical view of the person does not have any of these problems. In fact, it is able to account for the *extra*, and explain why there is consistency between the ordered personal relations within God and the mode of action in God's external works. It can explain how the Son acts as he has always acted, *from* the Father (John 5:19–30) and *by* the Spirit (John 3:34; Acts 10:38), and that in the incarnation, he is now able to act in both natures without confusion and change in either nature.

2. In Christology, "social" views of "person" render problematic Christ's humanity. By equating "person" and "soul" and locating "will" in the "person," this entails that the incarnate

Son only has one divine will and not a *distinct* human soul or human will. But if this is so, then how is he truly human: how can he act, think, and learn *as a man* apart from a distinct human soul, will, and mind (Luke 2:52)? Such a view is a repristination of the Apollinarian view that was rejected in the early church. Most significantly, how does he render *human* obedience to God *for us* apart from a human will (Phil 2:6–8; Heb 5:1–10; 10:5–10)? All of these implications are highly problematic and are not consistent with the teaching of Scripture.

Eternal Relational Authority Submission Trinitarianism (ERAS)

Although ERAS is similar to some versions of social-relational trinitarianism, it also differs on a number of points, thus making it difficult to categorize. However, since ERAS departs from pro-Nicene theology in its view of "person," we are examining it as a subset of social-relational views that warrants its own discussion. In recent years, ERAS has received a lot of attention within evangelical theology, and it is best represented by the work of Wayne Grudem and Bruce Ware.[148] Let us first look at the overall view before we evaluate it and argue that classic trinitarianism avoids the problems that ERAS unnecessarily creates.

ERAS: The View

The overall view may be summarized in four points.

First, regarding the divine essence, ERAS argues for a form of divine simplicity seemingly in agreement with pro-Nicene theology over against most "social" views. For example, Ware states: "The oneness of God explains why Father, Son, and Holy Spirit cannot rightly be conceived as three gods, for each possesses eternally and fully this one same and undivided divine essence."[149] Also, ERAS agrees with the classical view that the "will" is located in the essence and not the person, thus affirming that there is only one will in God and two wills in Christ.[150]

---

[148] For example, see Grudem, *Systematic Theology* (see chap. 1, n. 14); Bruce A. Ware, "Unity and Distinction of the Trinitarian Persons," in *Trinitarian Theology: Theological Models and Doctrinal Application*, ed. Keith S. Whitfield (Nashville: B&H Academic, 2019), 17–61; cf. Jonathan J. Routley, *Eternal Submission: A Biblical and Theological Examination* (Eugene: Wipf & Stock, 2019).

[149] Ware, "Unity and Distinction," 18; cf. Grudem, *Systematic Theology*, 211–14, 307–8.

[150] Ware, 47–49; Grudem, 307–8, 697–98.

Second, regarding how to distinguish the divine persons within God (*ad intra*), ERAS differs from the classical view. Historically, the *only* way to distinguish the divine persons is by the mutual *relations* between the Father, Son, and Holy Spirit. Although the personal relations are ordered (*taxis*) and irreversible—the Father is first and relates to the Son by his active generation of the Son and to the Spirit by his active spiration of the Spirit; the Son relates to the Father by his passive generation and with the Father to the Spirit by his active spiration of the Spirit; and the Spirit relates to the Father and Son by his passive spiration from both of them—these mutual relations do *not* entail an "authority-submission" *taxis* between the persons within the divine essence.[151] However, ERAS claims that it does and insists that the classical view does not go far enough, hence its redefinition of what a divine "person" is.

For ERAS, the persons are eternally distinguished by their ontological "relations" *and* by functional roles/relationships of "authority and submission," which is revealed in the economy. In fact, ERAS insists that the eternal relations of authority and submission "naturally flow from and are expressive of [the] eternal relations of origin."[152] Thus the Father is distinguished from the Son by his "unique hypostatic identity" of Father *and* his eternal possession of "the personal property of paternal authority," which entails his eternal relational authority over the Son. The Son is distinguished from the Father by his "unique hypostatic identity" as "the eternally begotten Son of the Father" *and* his possession of "the personal property of filial submission," which entails his eternal relational submission to the Father. The Spirit is distinguished by his "unique hypostatic identity" as "the One who eternally proceeds from the Father and the Son" *and* his possession of the personal property of "a submissive functional relation to both the Father and the Son."[153] In the economy, the Son's obedience/submission to his Father is true of his obedience/submission in eternity, which is also true of the Holy Spirit's relation to the Father and Son.[154]

What biblical evidence is given to warrant ERAS's view that the divine persons are eternally distinguished this way? Bruce Ware lists a number of texts that teach the primacy of the Father in relation to the Son and Spirit, which for him also entails an authority-submission

---

151 See Muller, *Dictionary of Latin and Greek*, s.v. "Trinitas," 309–10.

152 Ware, "Unity and Distinction," 51; cf. Ware, 19–25, 50–51, 56.

153 Ware, 21, 23, 56–57; cf. Grudem, *Systematic Theology*, 293–96.

154 See Ware, 35.

structure.[155] For example, in Heb 1:1–2, the Father is the subject of the verbs (e.g., God spoke, appointed, and created), which means that the Father has primacy and authority over the Son (and Spirit). In fact, in the Father's speaking through the Son (Heb 1:2a), this means that the Son's teaching did not originate in himself but in the Father, which assumes that the Father has primacy in both relation and authority. The same may be said of the Father's creation *through* the Son. For Ware, this demonstrates that the Father has an authority primacy vis-à-vis the Son; otherwise, the author could have simply said the Son created "with no mention of the Father."[156] Or, since Scripture teaches that the Father's appointment of the Son extends into the future eternally (Heb 1:2), this authority relation is not limited to the incarnation; instead, it requires that there is an *eternal* authority-submission relationship that distinguishes the Father from the Son.[157] In terms of the Spirit, a similar argument is made by appealing to texts that teach that the Spirit speaks from the Father (2 Pet 1:21) and says and does "what the Son gives him" (e.g., John 16:14–15).[158]

Third, given ERAS's redefinition of "person," its affirmation of one will is different than the classical view. Since authority-submission relationships eternally distinguish the persons, this seems to require three distinct wills, thus placing will in the persons. Although ERAS denies that this is so, their explanation is not always perspicuous. For example, ERAS affirms inseparable operations since each person's actions are always "through the one undivided nature."[159] Yet, inseparable action is explained more in terms of "harmonious unity" or that "the content of the divine will . . . is identically the same,"[160] which is not exactly the same as the classical view.[161] Also, ERAS explains the distinct acts of the persons by saying that each person exercises a distinct "inflection" or "expression" of the one divine will,[162] which entails "different and differing

---

[155] See Ware, 29–44; cf. Grudem, 299–318.

[156] Ware, 34.

[157] See Ware, 31–34. Other appointment texts that are used to warrant an eternal authority-submission relation that distinguishes the Father from the Son are Pss 2:7–9; 110:1; Matt 28:18–20; 1 Cor 15:25–28; Eph 1:20–23; Phil 2:8–11; Heb 2:8–9, 1 Pet 3:21–22.

[158] Ware, 41–44.

[159] Ware, 21; cf. pp. 45–46.

[160] Ware, 23 and 49 respectively. See Grudem, 307, 313. Grudem speaks of the unity of the will in terms of "complete agreement," or inseparable agency, as the persons are "in some way involved" (313).

[161] See Vidu, *Same God Who*, 91–125.

[162] Ware, "Unity and Distinction," 47–49; Grudem, *Systematic Theology*, 307–14.

roles and activities."[163] This is similar to the classical distinction between the "acts of the will" (person) and the "faculty of will" (nature) joined with the doctrine of appropriation, yet it is also different.[164] In fact, Ware thinks that the classical view of appropriation "falls short of expressing fully what Scripture indicates regarding the functional relations and operations of the trinitarian persons."[165] Why? Because *only* distinguishing the persons by their eternal relations of origin is not enough. It does not explain the Father's "personal planning, motives, purposes, and authority . . . in his sending of the Son,"[166] or the Father's "ultimate authority" in his relationship to the Son (and Spirit) *and* his "ultimate authority" in his action. The Father is the "the initiator, planner, designer, and architect of creation, who then assigns the building or crafting of this creation to his Son."[167] This statement goes beyond the classical view, which teaches that the Father *in relation to the Son* has priority, but priority does not entail authority-submission relationships; instead, it reveals relations of origin. ERAS, however, goes further by attributing to the Father distinct "purposes," "motives," "agency," and "authority." But in adding "authority-submission" relationships to the definition of a divine person and how they are distinguished, it seems as if three distinct wills are assumed. After all, a shared action is not the same as a singular one.

An example will illustrate this point. In God's act of creation, Ware rightly insists that all three persons create as the one God, yet he interprets the Father's action *through* the Son as demanding an authority-submission structure; it does not simply reveal an ordered "mode of acting" related to the triune persons' ordered "mode of subsistence."[168] In a classical view, however, creation is the singular act of God according to the ordered relations of the persons, but the Father, Son, and Spirit act through the same nature with the same will, power, *and authority*. For ERAS though, the ordered relations of the persons entail different properties of authority and submission for the persons.

---

[163] Ware, 24.

[164] The classical view distinguishes the "person" as the "principle which" (*principium quod*) acts, while the "nature" is the "principle by which" (*principium quo*) the person acts (see Duby, *Jesus and the God of Classical Theism*, 86). In contrast to ERAS, the classical view rejects three discrete actualizations of the divine will.

[165] Ware, "Unity and Distinction," 24.

[166] Ware, 24–25.

[167] Ware, 35, cf. 35–44.

[168] See Ware, 34–36.

Fourth, the ERAS redefinition of "person" requires that "authority" is not an attribute of the divine essence and thus *common* to all three persons, as taught by pro-Nicene theology.[169] Instead, "authority" is a personal property of the Father alone that eternally distinguishes him from the Son and Spirit. Yet, for Ware, since "authority and submission describe merely the manner in which these persons relate to each other, not what is true of the nature of the Father or the Son,"[170] although the Father has ultimate authority, the Son and Spirit's deity is not diminished. Why? Because for ERAS, "authority" is only a person property; it is "not essential (i.e., of the divine essence),"[171] and as such, the Father, Son, and Holy Spirit are equally God and identical in essence.

Problems with ERAS

Although ERAS is similar to the classical view, with its redefinition of "person," it creates more problems than it solves. Instead of distinguishing the persons only by their eternal relations of origin, ERAS adds another distinguishing factor, namely, eternal functional "authority-submission" relationships between the persons. Thus the Father alone has the property of "authority," while the Son alone has the property of "filial submission," and the Spirit alone the property of "submission" to the Father and the Son. For the Father-Son relationship, this results in the Son eternally submitting to the "ultimate authority" of the Father, both *ad intra* and *ad extra*. But, in contrast to the classical view, ERAS is problematic for at least two reasons.

First, in contrast to the classical view, "authority" is no longer *common* to all three persons; instead, it is only the personal property of the Father that eternally distinguishes him from the Son and Spirit in both immanent role(s) and external action. But once "authority"

---

[169] See Aquinas, *Summa Theologica*, pt. 1, q. 33, art. 1. Cf. Aquinas, *Summa contra Gentiles* 4.24.3, trans. Charles J. O'Neil (South Bend: University of Notre Dame Press, 1975). Aquinas writes: "the Son has an authority with respect to the Holy Spirit—not, of course, that of being master or being greater, but in accord with origin alone." Or, see Owen, *Works of John Owen*, 1:326. Owen writes: "He [the Son] was in the form of God—that is, he was God, participant of the divine nature, for God hath no form but that of his essence and being; and hence he was equal with God, in authority, dignity, and power."

[170] Ware, "Unity and Distinction," 52.

[171] Ware, 52.

is removed from the divine essence, all three persons no longer share the same authority, yet when Scripture speaks of divine "authority," it does so in terms of what God is *as God*. From Genesis 1 on, God is presented as the eternal, independent, self-sufficient, omnipotent, omniscient Creator and Lord (Gen 1–2; Ps 50:12–14; Isa 40–46; Jer 10:1–16; Acts 17:24–25), who has all authority (Exod 3:14; Deut 10:14; Job 40:1–5; Ps 24:1–2; Matt 5:17–20; John 14:6). In fact, to think of God's authority, we must first think of God within himself in all of his perfections, and then in his works, which is the outworking of his sovereign, authoritative will (Rev 4:11).

But when ERAS makes "authority" only a personal property of the Father, it is no longer common to all three persons. If one is not careful, it almost sounds like the Father has more authority because he has more knowledge, power, etc., which compromises the full deity of the Son and Spirit. No doubt, ERAS denies that this is the case. "Authority" is only a personal property and not an essential attribute,[172] and although this formulation preserves the full deity of the divine persons, one cannot speak of the authority of God *as God*. If ERAS wants to speak differently of the Father's authority versus an authority common to all three persons, it will need to speak of two different kinds of "authority," a personal property of the Father alone, *and* an essential attribute that is common to all three persons.[173] But all of this is unnecessary if one follows a classical view of persons and distinguishes the persons solely by their relations.[174]

In fact, John 5:16–20 is an important text that makes this point and shows why ERAS is not necessary. After his healing on the Sabbath, Jesus speaks of his relation to his Father. He states that as the Son, he "is not able to do anything on his own," but "whatever the Father does, the Son likewise does these things" (v. 19). To do "whatever" the Father does is equal power and authority, but the Son acts according to his filial "mode of agency" consistent with his "eternal relation" to the Father. The Son is not an independent agent acting on his own; he only acts as the Son *from* the Father, just as the Father always act *through* the Son (e.g., John 1:1–3; Col 1:15–17; Heb 1:1–3). Yet, the Son's relation *from* the Father (i.e., filiation, eternal

---

172 See Ware, 52.

173 See Routley, *Eternal Submission*, 83–86, who affirms two kinds of "authority" within God.

174 In pro-Nicene theology, "authority" has been attributed to the Father but only in terms of the ordered relations, not in terms of "authority-submission" structures. For example, see Aquinas, *Summa Theologica*, pt. 1, q. 33, art. 1.2.

generation) reveals itself in his "mode of action" *from* the Father, and it is the reason why he can do *all* things in common with the Father: creation, providence, revelation, redemption, and so on. In doing "whatever the Father does" (v. 19), the Son has equal authority and he receives equal honor as the Father (v. 23), but in all of his actions, he acts as the Son *from* the Father. What the ERAS view desires in terms of "ordered" relations is better explained and achieved by the classical way of distinguishing the persons, which avoids ERAS's accompanying problems.[175]

Second, for sake of argument, if we grant that the Father alone has the personal property of "authority," further problems arise. For example, if the Son eternally submits to the Father's authority, does this not entail three distinct wills? ERAS advocates respond by appealing to distinct "inflections" of the one will. But once those "inflections" are tied to "authority-submission" relationships that lead to "differing roles and activities" within God,[176] whereby the Father has distinct "purposes, motives, agency, and authority" from the Son or Spirit,[177] this is more difficult to maintain.[178] This is why ERAS is not clear on how it understands inseparable operations. It affirms inseparable operations, but interpreted as "harmonious unity" or "shared action" instead of singular action, which is problematic. Why is it problematic? Because in sharing the one divine essence, the Father, Son, and Spirit share *one* divine intellect, will, and power. This is confirmed by the Son's procession from the Father and the Spirit's procession from the Father and the Son. As the Father has "life in himself," so he has granted the Son to have "life in himself" (John 5:26), which per divine simplicity means that the Son (and Spirit) share the same identical divine essence. But this means that the divine persons do not have distinct intellects or wills or three discrete actualizations of the will that merely act in harmony. Instead, the divine persons act through the same intellect and will so that their action is one and singular yet also according to their eternally ordered relations. Furthermore, if authority-submission roles are immanent within God, what exactly is the Son submitting to in relation to the Father's authority? In Scripture, the Son's submission to the

[175] See Thomas Aquinas, *Commentary on the Gospel of John, Chapter 1–5*, trans. Fabian Larcher and James A. Weisheipl (Washington, DC: Catholic University of America Press, 2010), 282.

[176] Ware, "Unity and Distinction," 24.

[177] Ware, 24–25.

[178] Also see Routley, *Eternal Submission*, 94–102, who speaks of will as one in "nature" and three in "person."

Father is always tied to God's external work of redemption related to the divine missions, not the divine processions.[179]

But ERAS responds by arguing that Scripture is on its side. Appeal is made to the names of Father and Son, which ERAS believes requires an authority-submission structure. Or, as we noted, ERAS appeals to texts that refer to the priority of the Father (John 14:28; Heb 1:1–2), the Father's sending the Son (John 3:16–17), and the Father's appointing of the Son (Pss 2:7–9; 110:1; Matt 28:18–20; 1 Cor 15:25–28; Phil 2:9–11; Heb 1:3; 2:8–9), as proof of their position.

However, none of these texts demonstrate their point. First, all of these texts refer to God's decree, tied to the "covenant of redemption" worked out in the incarnation, and the obedience of the Son as our new covenant mediator. These texts do not refer to authority-submission within God, but instead the outworking of God's redemptive plan as unfolded through the progression of the biblical covenants centered in the coming of Christ and his work as the *incarnate* Son. Second, the classical view of persons that distinguishes the persons by their eternal relations of origin that are revealed in the divine economy explains these texts without the problems ERAS creates by adding properties to the divine persons.

Overall, the classical view avoids the problems that ERAS unnecessarily creates. By only distinguishing the persons by their ordered relations, the classical view allows for a common authority shared by all three persons, thus properly grounding *homoousios*, yet each person's "mode of action" follows from their "mode of subsistence." In this way, Father, Son, and Spirit have the same authority, but God's external action is according to an ordered *taxis* that avoids the appearance of three wills, or redefines inseparable operations, or opens the door to applying different authority, honor, and glory to the divine persons. In addition, the classical view rightly understands the Son's submission to the Father according to Scripture, that is, in terms of God's eternal plan of redemption worked out in the incarnation and in the human obedience of Christ as our covenant head, representative, and Redeemer. In all these ways, the

---

[179] Gregory of Nazianus, "The Fourth Theological Oration," in *Christology of the Later Fathers*, ed., Edward R. Hardy (Louisville: Westminster Press, 1954), 180. Gregory writes: "For in his character of the Word he was neither obedient nor disobedient. For such expressions belong to servants. . . . But, in the character of the form of a servant, he condescends to his fellow servants." Cf. Augustine, *Trinity* 1.22, 4.27 (33–34, 164–66); Owen, *Works*, 1:207, 326.

classical way is the better way to account for the biblical teaching and the theological entailments that follow.

Concluding Reflections

In this chapter, we have covered a lot of territory, but we conclude where we began: the Trinity is not an esoteric doctrine of little significance. Instead, the Trinity is who the God of the Bible is, and apart from knowing God as Father, Son, and Spirit, we do not know the true and living God. In fact, our concept of God is simply a human construct—an idol of our own making. As Bavinck noted: Christian theology "stands or falls with the confession of God's Trinity,"[180] and it is the Trinity that distinguishes Christianity from all non-Christian thought. All denials of the Trinity deny the God of the Bible and its entire gospel message.

Even more: God's being triune reminds us how and why God has all glory in himself. As the triune God, in the fullness of his personal relations, he lacks nothing; thus, "from him and through him and to him are all things" (Rom 11:36a). Within himself, he is perfect in his fully shared life of love, holiness, joy, and communion, and all of his external actions are freely chosen to glorify himself for the good of his people. Swain nicely captures this point: "Nothing enriches God; nothing adds to his glory; nothing increases his happiness (Job 22:2; 35:6–7; 41:11). God is not 'served by human hands, as though he needed anything' (Acts 17:25). God plus the world is not more sufficient, more glorious, or more blessed than God minus the world."[181] Not surprisingly, Scripture teaches that the ultimate end of God's plan in creation, providence, redemption, and consummation is God's own triune glory: the Father through the Son and by the Spirit (1 Cor 15:20–28; Eph 1:9–10; Phil 2:11; Col 1:18).

But Scripture also teaches that by God's free and sovereign grace, he has chosen to share himself with his creation, and specifically his people, the church. Due to God's plan, initiative, and grace, the church has the supreme privilege of knowing something of the love, communion, and fellowship of God within himself as redeemed creatures (John 15:9–11). Indeed, our Lord has prayed that his people will be with him to see his glory; a glory that he has always had

---

[180] Bavinck, *Reformed Dogmatics*, 2:333.

[181] Swain, *Trinity*, 127.

as the eternal and loved Son of the Father (John 17:3, 24–26). In the end, even in this fallen world, for God's people, God's entire plan is for his glory and our eternal good (Rom 8:28–39).

As we conclude, we offer three application reflections regarding trinitarian doctrine.

First, we must exercise care in trying to illustrate the Trinity by appealing to the created order. God's triune nature is unique, and the Creator-creature distinction must not be ignored. For this reason, all illustrations of the Trinity from creation fall short and end in error. For example, the egg as three (shell, yolk, and white) in one undercuts divine simplicity and wrongly thinks of the three as parts of God that can be separated from each other. Or using the analogy of a man who is a husband-father-son ends up affirming modalism. The triune God is unique and incomprehensible. Nothing in creation accurately captures the person-nature/essence distinction within God. Instead, we should describe the triune God by following the Bible's own grammar and description. As we do, we are able to understand at a created level the glory of the triune God and grasp more fully the Bible's presentation of him as the triune Creator-covenant Lord.

However, in understanding how the Trinity makes sense of how God is simultaneously absolute and *a se* but also personal, we should not wonder that the triune God is the only true foundation for metaphysics, epistemology, and ethics. As John Frame astutely observes, in non-Christian thought, there has been the attempt to

> search for something *a se*: an ultimate cause of being, an ultimate standard of truth, an ultimate justification of right. . . . Ideally, the metaphysical absolute, the epistemological norm, and the ethical norm should all be grounded in one being, since these three are correlative to one another. But non-Christian thought has usually found it impossible to locate all these ultimates in a single principle. [182]

Why? Part of the problem, as Frame continues, "is that non-Christian thought is determined that its absolute be impersonal. But an impersonal being cannot serve as a norm for knowledge and ethics, nor can it be a credible first cause."[183] But not so in Christian thought. The God of the Bible is not an impersonal being but the triune personal God who is *a se*. He who needs nothing is alone the ground for creation's existence, the source and standard of truth, and the

[182] Frame, *Systematic Theology*, 411 (see chap. 5, n. 1).

[183] Frame, 411.

objective norm for what is right. God is not dependent on anything outside of himself; as the triune God, he is perfect and glorious within himself. We cannot demonstrate the Trinity by observing nature; instead, due to God's special divine revelation, we learn that God is triune, which allows us to make sense of the world he has made. We understand in a greater way that, apart from him, there is no ultimate ground for reality, knowledge, and ethics.

Second, in speaking of the Trinity, the charge of contradiction often arises. In response, we must distinguish between "contradiction" and "mystery." The Trinity is not contradictory since God is one ("essence/nature") and three ("persons") at the same time but *not* in the same respect. Trinitarian theology has always made the person-nature distinction, which renders the doctrine logically coherent, but it has not removed the "mystery" or the unknowns.[184]

Third, in our worship, prayer, and lives, we must be thoroughly and consistently trinitarian. Too often our songs, prayers, and sermons are more unitarian than trinitarian. Or, often in our worship and prayer, we confuse the divine persons or do not think sufficiently about how the divine processions show themselves in the divine economy and missions and how we come to know, love, obey our triune God consistent with Scripture. In terms of worship, prayer, and our communion with God, one can do no better than learn from John Owen.[185] As Owen unpacks our communion and worship of God, he rightly notes that our worship of the one God is also the worship of all three persons. But given the ordered personal relations, our worship and prayer are to God the Father through the Son and by the Holy Spirit (Matt 6:9–13; Eph 2:18; 3:14–21). Each person may be worshipped and addressed, but ultimately we worship the *one* God who is triune.

Obviously, much more could be said, but in the next chapter, we begin a new section as we move from the triune God of glory within himself (*ad intra*) to the triune God in his external works (*ad extra*). As we do, we will continue to reflect on the majesty of our great and glorious God—the God who is perfect in himself and who is in need of nothing but, by his own sovereign grace and initiative, has chosen to become our Creator, Redeemer, and covenant Lord.

---

[184] See Anderson, *Paradox in Christian Theology* (see chap. 4, n. 89).

[185] For example, see John Owen, *Of Communion with God*, in *Works of John Owen*, 2:1–274.

CHAPTER 20

The Triune God Who Plans All Things: The Divine Decree

Introduction

In this chapter, we begin a new section. We move from the glory of God within himself (*ad intra*) in terms of God's attributes and triune nature to God's plan for the universe, which results in his external works (*ad extra*) in creation, providence, redemption, and consummation. In both areas (*ad intra* and *ad extra*), we speak of divine action; hence, we begin with the concept of divine action before we discuss God's eternal plan or decree.

Our goal in this chapter is to examine crucial theological issues regarding the nature of God's decree and its execution in his external works. Our purpose is to demonstrate that God's eternal plan for his creation is to display his own glory and, by grace, to benefit his people. Our triune Creator-covenant Lord has freely and graciously chosen to do this by sharing his fullness and perfection of life with his people in covenant relationship with the ultimate end that the church will glorify him and enjoy him forever.

Our discussion of God's display of his glory in his external works will proceed in four steps. First, we will reflect on the concept of divine action. Second, we will describe what Scripture teaches about God's eternal plan or decree. Third, we will outline two major theological views within evangelical theology regarding the divine decree: Arminianism and Calvinism. Fourth, we will offer a biblical-theological formulation of the divine decree and critique the Arminian view of the divine decree and its outworking in God's external works.

The Concept of Divine Action

Our Triune God Is a God of Action

From Scripture's opening verse, God is the one who acts for his own glory: "In the beginning God created the heavens and the earth" (Gen 1:1). God speaks and the universe comes to exist (Heb 11:3). And by that same speech, God sustains and governs the universe by acting in the world in ordinary and extraordinary ways (Col 1:17; Heb 1:3). In so doing, God reveals and demonstrates that he is the triune Creator-covenant Lord.

Repeatedly, Scripture celebrates that God is a God of action. For example, throughout the Psalter, Yahweh is praised because "The LORD's works are great, / studied by all who delight in them. / All that he does is splendid and majestic; / his righteousness endures forever. / He has caused his wondrous works to be remembered. / The LORD is gracious and compassionate" (Ps 111:2–4). Indeed, the author continues by saying that God has revealed his power in his works (v. 6), especially in the establishment of his covenant with his people (v. 9). This truth is also taught in Psalm 136. God is worshipped because he is "the God of gods" and the "Lord of lords" (v. 2–3), who demonstrates this truth by his acts. God alone does "great wonders" (v. 4) in creating the universe in wisdom (vv. 5–9), by acting in judgment on evildoers (v. 10), and in redeeming Israel from Egypt in faithfulness to his promises (vv. 11–26). Psalm 145 makes the same point. God's greatness and glory is exalted because of his "wondrous works" and "awe-inspiring acts" (vv. 1–7). Thus, from Genesis to Revelation, our triune covenant Lord is presented as the God who acts—first in creation, then in providence—as he alone rules and reigns over all, bringing his eternal purposes to pass, especially his glorious redemptive purposes for his people. Our Lord Jesus reminds us of this truth when says that the Father and he, as the divine Son, are constantly at work, sustaining and governing all things to their appointed end (John 5:17).

In thinking about divine action, we must distinguish between God's works within himself (*opera ad intra*, works that terminate within God's being) and God's works outside of himself toward his creation and creatures (*opera ad extra*, works that terminate outside of God's being).

God's *ad intra* works refer to the divine processions.[1] From eternity, within God, there is a shared fullness of divine life and action in the Father's generation of the Son and communication of the divine essence to him, the Son's procession from the Father and receiving from the Father the divine essence, and the Holy Spirit's eternal spiration from both the Father and Son and receiving from both the divine essence (John 1:1–2; 5:26; 14:26; 15:26; 16:5–11). Thus, by nature, "the Triune God eternally and necessarily delights in himself: God cannot fail to affirm his own perfect existence, nor can he will his nonexistence."[2] God is not static, inert, or immobile. Within his being, there is a shared fullness of life and love. "The Father knows and loves the Son eternally—from before the foundation of the world (Matt. 11:27; John 17:24)—and the Spirit searches the deep things of God (1 Cor. 2:10)."[3] As such, God is totally self-sufficient; he needs nothing external to himself to be made complete or satisfied (Acts 17:25).

Regarding God's *ad extra* works we must first think about God's decree/plan for all things. Because God's decree is eternal, in one sense it is an "internal work" of the triune God (*opera Dei interna*). However, since God's decree decides and directs all of his "external works" (*operationes Dei externae*), it pertains to that which is external to God. In other words, God's decree is eternal, but since it is his *free* act by which he plans all things "outside" of himself (*ad extra*), it is "completely tied to everything that pertains to created things."[4] In this way, God's decree links together God's perfect and complete immanent life to all of his external works. But God's immanent life

---

[1] On this point, see chapter 19 on the doctrine the Trinity.

[2] Scott R. Swain, "Covenant of Redemption," in Allen and Swain, *Christian Dogmatics*, 112 (see chap. 5, n. 91).

[3] Bavinck, *Reformed Dogmatics*, 2:342 (see chap. 1, n. 9).

[4] Vos, *Reformed Dogmatics*, 1:78 (see chap. 15, n. 126). Without God's decree being a free act, the world would be necessary to God and begin to collapse the Creator-creature distinction. Also, since God's decree is a free act, he could have planned things differently; what he has chosen is not due to necessity but due to his own choice and for his own good pleasure. Necessity (i.e., consequent necessity) only arises after God has chosen a specific course of action and he promises to keep his word. For example, God has chosen to create humans and to permit them to fall into sin, but it was not necessary for him to redeem us. It is only due to his gracious choice to redeem us in covenant relationship in Christ that it is now necessary for him to keep his promise. Likewise, in promising to redeem his people, God's redemptive work must also be consistent with God's nature. This is why God *cannot* simply justify sinners apart from the full satisfaction of his holy love and justice—a truth that is especially significant in our understanding of the atonement. On this point, see Turretin, *Institutes of Elenctic Theology*, 1:219, 313, 316 (see chap. 3, n. 55).

is not determined by his decree. Louis Berkhof captures well this truth: "God did not decree to be holy and righteous, nor to exist as three persons in one essence or to generate the Son. These things are as they are *necessarily*, and are not dependent on the optional will of God. That which is essential to the inner Being of God can form no part of the contents of the decree."[5] Instead, God's decree pertains to all the external acts of God that he freely chooses to enact.

Furthermore, it is important to note that God's decree "does not exhaust the riches of God's knowledge and wisdom. . . . With God all things are possible (Matt. 19:26), but they are not all actualized."[6] Yet what God has freely chosen is the reason why the world exists and all things in it. God's decree renders his plan for all things guaranteed, although God has not planned for all things to be made effective in the same way. For example, God has decided that "in the case of some things. . . . He Himself would bring them to pass, either immediately, as in the work of creation, or through the mediation of secondary causes, which are continually energized by His power."[7] Yet, "there are other things, however, which God included in His decree, and thereby rendered certain, but which He did not decide to effectuate Himself, as the sinful acts of His rational creatures."[8] Thus, it is important to distinguish between God's decree and its execution in time, history, and the entire created order.[9] God's decree is the "blueprint" for all things, and by creation, God enacts his plan by bringing all things into existence. By providence, God further enacts his plan by sustaining, ruling, and governing nature and history to its planned end, yet in different ways—a crucial point we will return to below in our biblical-theological formulation of the divine decree and in our discussion of divine providence.[10] But before we turn to our discussion of the divine decree, let us

---

[5] Berkhof, *Systematic Theology*, 103 (see chap. 15, n. 63). This understanding of the divine decree is in contrast both to Karl Barth's "eternalizing" of time and recent attempts, such as those of Robert Jenson, to "historicize" eternity. For a discussion of these views, see Horton, *Christian Faith*, 316–23 (see chap. 15, n. 80).

[6] Bavinck, *Reformed Dogmatics*, 2:342–43.

[7] Berkhof, *Systematic Theology*, 103. In chapters 21–22, we will discuss in more detail the distinction between primary and secondary causality. Primary cause refers to God as the cause of all things and secondary causes refer to created contingent causes, including the forces of nature and the free actions of humans and angels.

[8] Berkhof, 103.

[9] On this point, see Berkhof, 103; also see Feinberg, *No One Like Him*, 531 (see chap. 2, n. 51).

[10] On divine providence, see chapters 22 and 23.

reflect further on a biblical view of divine action in contrast to some current panentheistic reductions of it.

What Is a Divine Act?

In Scripture, God's action involves both "ordinary" and "extraordinary" action. But for many Christians, divine action is sometimes associated with extraordinary action alone—what we identify as "miracles"—forgetting that both forms are divine action. If we are thinking about extraordinary action, Scripture speaks of such acts as God's mighty "signs" (Gk. *sēmeion*), "wonders" (Gk. *teras*), and "power" (Gk. *dunamis*). They are "extraordinary" because they are not the normal/ordinary way that God sustains, rules, and governs all things. Yet, when God acts in this way, they are unique displays of his sovereign power and his covenant lordship.[11]

In historical theology, people have sometimes defined "miracles" in ways that are unhelpful. For example, a common but inadequate way to define a "miracle" is as a divine act that breaks "natural laws."[12] This is inadequate because it assumes "nature" can operate on its own except when God uniquely acts. This understanding has more in common with deism than Christian theology, a point we will return to in our discussion of divine providence. Instead, we must think of "nature" as metaphysically distinct from God but dependent on him and as something through which God continues to act. "Natural laws," then, reflect God's *ordinary* way of sustaining the created order. In fact, in the Noahic covenant, God confirms and promises that he will continue to sustain the universe in a uniform way until the end of the age (Gen 8:21–22). But these "natural laws" do not operate independently of God. Instead, they function as causes that he sustains and acts in and through, thus governing according to his plan and purposes.

For this reason, theologians make a distinction between "ordinary providence" (*providentia ordinaria*) and "extraordinary providence" (*providentia extraordinaria*) to emphasize that the workings of "nature," whether they be "ordinary" or "extraordinary," are both under God's

---

[11] Frame, *Doctrine of God*, 245–46, 258–60 (see chap. 3, n. 13).

[12] See David Hume, *An Inquiry Concerning Human Understanding* (repr., New York: Liberal Arts Press, 1957), 122, who wrongly defines "miracles" this way. Yet Hume's understanding is fairly common in people's thinking.

rule and both are properly viewed as God's action.[13] In terms of the former, the emphasis is on God's action through secondary causes "in strict accordance with the laws of nature."[14] In terms of the latter, God acts in a *different* way: either immediately or through secondary causes or agents but not in the regular, ordered way he normally sustains the universe. This is why miracles are "above nature" or "*super*-natural," but God is not "breaking" fixed, unalterable "laws" that function independently of him. Instead, God acts in a unique, *extra*-ordinary way, which demonstrates his sovereign lordship. For example, God delivers his people from Pharoah's grip by his mighty acts to demonstrate that he alone is God (Exod 7:5; cf. 8:19; 12:12; 15:6–11). Or Moses acknowledges that Yahweh alone is God due to his "deeds and mighty acts" (Deut 3:24). In the NT, this same point continues in the coming of our Lord Jesus Christ, who in his miracles demonstrates that he is more than merely David's greater son, but the divine Son, who has taken on our humanity and become our new covenant head and mediator (Mark 2:1–11; 4:35–41; 5:24–34; John 5:17–30; 11:1–44; 20:30–31). Thus, miracles do not simply attest revelation; they *are* revelation. They disclose God's character and perfections and demonstrate that he is the Creator, Lord, and covenant God of his people (Exod 15:1–19; Luke 5:1–10).

Miracles: Possibility and Probability

How *possible* are God's *extraordinary* actions or miracles? The answer depends on one's overall theology and worldview.[15] Within a biblical framework, miracles are possible because God is the Creator and Lord of his world. It is God who determines what is possible. Even the "regularities of nature" are an expression of this fact. There is no need to appeal to "quantum physics" to allow for the "possibility of miracles."[16] God has established a regularity and uniformity to creation, which is due to the purpose of the world and our human task to rule and subdue the earth for God's glory. But this does not entail that God cannot speak and act in extraordinary ways. Miracles are possible precisely because the triune God of Scripture exists. In performing

[13] See Berkhof, *Systematic Theology*, 176.

[14] Berkhof, 176.

[15] See Frame, *Doctrine of God*, 267.

[16] Contrary to Boyd, *God of the Possible*, 107–11 (see chap. 16, n. 35).

miracles, as Berkhof correctly states, "The forces of nature are not annihilated or suspended, but are only counteracted at a particular point by a force superior to the powers of nature."[17]

Furthermore, there is no evidence that God does not continue to act in extraordinary ways. We must distinguish God's extraordinary action from the question of whether God continues to give the church extraordinary gifts of the Holy Spirit, such as prophecy, tongues, healings. We will return to this question in our discussion of the doctrine of the church. Yet, setting that issue aside, we know that in every conversion, God has acted in an extraordinary way in bringing people from a state of spiritual death to life. Also, there is no reason to think that God does not act in extraordinary ways today, for example, in God's healing of the sick as the church prays for such an individual (Jas 5:13–16). No doubt, we should not expect miracles to occur as we see in specific periods of redemptive history. At specific turning points in redemptive history, we see a concentration of God's extraordinary activity to attest to and accomplish his redemptive plan, especially in the coming of Christ and the inauguration of the entire new covenant era. But as John Frame notes, "even in the biblical period, in which many miracles took place, these events were not evenly distributed over time. Many centuries went by (as for Noah to Abraham, Abraham to Moses, and Malachi to Jesus) without many miracles being recorded. . . . So God evidently reserves miracles for special occasions, including the attestation of his messengers."[18] This is why the normal pattern of God's action in the world is "ordinary" as he sustains, acts, and rules through secondary causes and agents, yet this does not preclude his extraordinary agency.

How *probable* are miracles? Since God acts in ordinary and extraordinary ways, we cannot identify everything as a miracle. To do so would destroy the uniqueness and extraordinary nature of God's act. Miracles are possible, but how probable are they? To answer this question, we must know something of God's intent and goals. God announced to Noah that the course of nature would normally proceed in a regular fashion (Gen 8:22), but God's higher intention is to redeem a people for himself. In order to do that, it is appropriate for him to perform unusual works—to accomplish redemption, to apply it, and to attest to it. Thus, given God's intention to redeem, and his promises to save, it is highly probable that he will identify himself in the natural order as its ruler and attest to his revelation so that we may know him as the "covenant Lord."

---

[17] Berkhof, *Systematic Theology*, 177.

[18] Frame, *Doctrine of God*, 263.

But how do we identify an event as a miracle? The surest way is to do so from Scripture. As Scripture identifies and interprets God's mighty acts, we know exactly which events are miracles. In fact, a miracle without an interpretative context is inherently ambiguous, both in terms of its meaning and significance. For example, how should we interpret the miraculous act of Christ's resurrection? Or how should we interpret the tongues of fire and the speaking of known languages that occurs in Acts 2? Apart from a word-revelation, we may interpret God's mighty actions wrongly, which unfortunately occurred in the case of Jesus's resurrection (Matt 28:11–15) and at Pentecost (Acts 2:13, 15). Also, one's worldview and presuppositions play an important role in identifying a "miracle." Furthermore, Scripture reminds us that not all unique events are necessarily miracles since some seemingly extraordinary events are the work of angelic and demonic hosts (Exod 7:22–23; 8:7; Matt 7:21–23). For this reason, Scripture exhorts us to "not believe every spirit, but test the spirits to see if they are from God, because many false prophets have gone out into the world" (1 John 4:1).

So how do we know if God has acted today, especially if we do not have a direct revelation that identifies it as a miracle? The answer is Scripture. Although the canon is now closed, the Bible still teaches us to discern what is from God versus what is not. For example, after John's exhortation to "test the spirits to see if they are from God," he then gives us a specific test: "This is how you know the Spirit of God: Every spirit that confesses that Jesus Christ has come in the flesh is from God, but every spirit that does not confess Jesus is not from God. This is the spirit of the antichrist, which you have heard is coming; even now it is already in the world" (1 John 4:2–3). In other words, we test whether a person or various events are from God by Scripture: Do they teach what Scripture teaches? Are their actions consistent with Scripture? If someone claims to do miracles from God yet denies the truth of God's word, we reject their claim. Conversely, when we witness a person's true conversion, Scripture tells us that we know God is at work since regeneration is not "natural" to us; it is the result of God exerting his mighty power—the same power that raised Christ from the dead—now applied to us by God's Spirit (Eph 1:18–2:10).

In addition, from Scripture, we also know what to expect in terms of what God has promised and not promised for his people. Nowhere in Scripture has God promised that he will heal every disease this side of Christ's return or that he will do "miracles" out of the blue that have nothing to do with his redemptive purposes and work. In evaluating some sensational claim, we are to judge in light of Scripture, knowing what God has promised for our time in redemptive history, as we live in the new covenant era awaiting the return of our Lord.

The Biblical View of Divine Action Contrasted with "the" Postmodern View of God

Although there are numerous conceptions of "god" in our pluralistic and postmodern world, as we discussed in chapter 16, the dominant view today is what John Cooper has identified as the "other God of the philosophers," namely, a "panentheistic" or process view of God.[19] This "new" view is in direct contrast to historic Christian theology or classical theism.[20]

Technically, process theism is a specific form of "panentheism" associated with Alfred N. Whitehead and Charles Hartshorne.[21] It is built on the idea of change rather than permanence. Rather than substances as the basic building blocks of reality, events are central. All reality is pictured as a series of events, each of which has two poles—a mental pole and a physical pole—including God.[22] For process theology, "God" is an event like all other beings, but "God" is the chief exemplification of other "actual entities." All reality is *in* God, yet God is "greater" than the world, hence the term "panentheism" (Gk. *pan*, "all"; *en*, "in"; *theos*, "God").

In other words, unlike pantheism, which outright rejects the Creator-creature distinction by identifying "God" and "nature," panentheism blurs the distinction and places all things "in" God so that God is neither fully distinct from his creation (contrary to Christian theology) nor totally identified with it (contrary to pantheism). But the result is that God *and* the world are eternal, correlative, and mutually dependent on each other. The world is a moment within the divine life, viewed as God's body, which is the progressive realization of various possibilities. Since God is immanent in the world, he is not *a se*, simple, or immutable but instead undergoing a process of self-development and growth in relation to the world. But God is "greater"

---

[19] See Cooper, *Panentheism* (see chap. 2, n. 131), and our discussion of panentheism in chapter 16. Also cf. Vanhoozer, *Remythologizing Theology*, 139–77 (see chap. 2, n. 131).

[20] See Carter, *Contemplating God* (see chap. 16, n. 93).

[21] On process theism, see Cobb and Griffin, *Process Theology* (see chap. 2, n. 132).

[22] In process theism, God's "mental pole" (or primordial nature) refers to the aspect of God's being that is eternal, permanent, and unchanging. God's "physical pole" (or consequent nature) refers to another aspect of God's being: his concreteness in relation to the world, which is constantly in development, growth, and change. It is this "part" of God where the world is "in" him and contributing to his consciousness.

than the world, and by virtue of his mental pole (which is permanent and unchanging),[23] he serves as the "ground of possibility in the processes of reality,"[24] which offers some kind of order, novelty, and direction for all things. Yet, given the "essential relatedness" of all reality "in" God and God's mutual dependence on the world, God's "direction" of the world is not effectual but only persuasive. God does not rule or govern the world, directing it to its appointed end. Rather, God "influences" the world according to his aims but never effectually or in a guaranteed way. Process theology, then, insists that process, change, and evolution are just as or more fundamental than substance, permanence, and stability. God, in a continuous and creative relationship of involvement with the world, is himself undergoing this same process of growth and development.

Although process theism is only one version of panentheism, the basic God-world relation is the same for all versions of it.[25] As noted in chapter 16, for many forms of postmodern theology, panentheism has become *the* view of God given its compatibility with an evolutionary view of origins and an embrace of a process metaphysic. What is common to all forms of panentheism is the rejection of the Creator-creature distinction and *creatio ex nihilo*, along with an embrace of a view of God who by nature is limited in power, knowledge, and agency.

For this reason, any talk of divine action is either rejected or redefined to fit within the limits of a process metaphysic, resulting in an adoption of methodological naturalism.[26] The Bible's view of God and divine agency is rejected as "mythological." For example, Schubert Ogden, an advocate of process theism, follows the demythologizing project of Rudolf Bultmann and insists that it is mythological to affirm that God "intervenes" in history. Ogden writes: "God's action, in its fundamental sense, is not an action in history at all . . . God's action as the Redeemer cannot be simply identified with any particular historical event or events."[27] For similar reasons, John Cobb and David Griffin also deny that God acts in the world in an

[23] Cobb and Griffin, *Process Theology*, 47.

[24] David A. Pailin, *God and the Processes of Reality: Foundations for a Credible Theism* (London: Routledge, 1989), 60.

[25] See Polkinghorne, *Work of Love* (see chap. 18, n. 64); Philip Clayton and Arthur Peacocke, eds., *In Whom We Live and Move and Have Our Being: Panentheistic Reflections on God's Presence in a Scientific World* (Grand Rapids: Eerdmans, 2004); Clayton, *Adventures in the Spirit* (see chap. 18, n. 64).

[26] For a thorough critique of process theism, see Feinberg, *No One Like Him*, 149–79.

[27] Schubert M. Ogden, "What Sense Does It Make to Say, 'God Acts in History'?," in Thomas, *God's Activity*, 90 (see chap. 5, n. 57).

"interventionist" sense. They believe that historic orthodox theology flounders on theodicy and the modern "scientific" view "that there are no events which happen without natural causes."[28]

How, then, does a panentheistic/process view of "God" think of divine action? Simply stated, such views think of divine action in terms of "persuasion" alone.[29] Panentheistic thought views God as the one who "lures" each actual entity with new possibilities to actualize, but he never does so in a "coercive," or better, effectual manner. In such a view of the God-world relation, God *cannot* control every detail of the world as the triune Creator and Lord. Instead, since each actual entity always has the freedom to choose otherwise (libertarian freedom), although God may present new possibilities to the entity that are attractive and persuasive, he cannot guarantee compliance. God is only able to "influence" and give teleological direction to the universe by providing the "initial aim" for each entity; he in no way can *guarantee* that his ends will be achieved. In fact, even if God wanted to, it is metaphysically impossible for him to guarantee anything, given the nature of reality.

For this reason, all iterations of panentheism reject efficient causation since every actual entity is in some measure self-determining and self-creating. The possibilities that God presents cannot override the inner decision of an emerging actual entity. God's power, like any other being, is limited, along with his knowledge of future events since they have not yet been determined.[30] Thus, for panentheism, "divine action" means that God acts in and is the *partial* cause of all events, but he is the *sole* cause of none.[31] God acts as a "divine, responsive final causation instead of an efficient causation,"[32] and his action in the world always involves risk.

[28] Cobb and Griffin, *Process Theology*, 50.

[29] James Keller confirms this when he states God "lacks the power to totally determine the behavior—more precisely, the concrescence—of any entity; God can only lure (attempt to persuade) the entity to develop in a certain way." "The Power of God and Miracles in Process Theism," *JAAR* 63, no. 1 (1995): 106. Also see Norman Pittenger, "The Divine Activity," *Enc* 47, no. 3 (1986): 257–65.

[30] See Cobb and Griffin, *Process Theology*, 52–53.

[31] See David Griffin, "Relativism, Divine Causation, and Biblical Theology," in Thomas, *God's Activity*, 132. Also see Ian Barbour, who describes the process view in terms of a "wise teacher who desires that students learn to choose for themselves and interact harmoniously, or a loving parent who does not try to do everything for the members of a family. God's role is creative participation and persuasion in inspiring the community of beings toward new possibilities of a richer life together." See *Religion in the Age of Science*, vol. 1, *The Gifford Lectures 1989–1991* (New York: Harper & Row, 1990), 260.

[32] Lewis S. Ford, "Evangelical Appraisals of Process Theism," *Christian Scholar's Review* 20 (1990–91): 153.

When such a view is compared with the biblical conception of divine action, the two are revealed as light-years removed. The "God" of panentheism and postmodern theology is not the triune Creator-covenant Lord of Scripture. The God of the Bible is the God who acts according to his eternal decree, and who acts sovereignly and effectively to accomplish all that he has planned, a point to which we now turn.

The Divine Decree

Our triune God is a God of action, but we must tie his temporal actions to his eternal plan, which Scripture and theology speak of as God's decree.[33] In common parlance, the term "decree" has fallen by the wayside. The term invokes visions of a king issuing arbitrary laws for his subjects. But when theology speaks of the divine decree, it refers to his *eternal* plan, whereby, before the creation of the world, God freely planned and determined all things. The *Westminster Shorter Catechism* nicely captures what is meant by God's decree by stating that it is "[God's] eternal purpose according to the counsel of His will, whereby, for His own glory, He hath foreordained whatsoever comes to pass."[34]

On the eternality and comprehensiveness of God's plan, Scripture is clear. For example, David rejoices that his entire life was planned "before a single one of them began" (Ps 139:16). Or, in Isaiah, Yahweh says that his plan is for the whole earth, that he alone "declare[s] the end from the beginning, / and from long ago what is not yet done, / saying: my plan will take place, / and I will do all my will" (Isa 46:10; cf. 14:24–27; 22:11; 37:26; Prov 16:4; 19:21). In the NT, we learn that our Lord's death was not an accident of history but "according to God's determined plan and foreknowledge" (Acts 2:23; cf. 4:27–28; Gal 4:4–5; Rev 13:8), and that the election of God's people was "before the foundation of the world" (Eph 1:4; cf. 1:11–12; 2:10; Rom 9–11).[35] Thus, the triune God within himself, from eternity, planned all things, and

---

[33] The word "decree" can be used in a singular and plural sense. The singular refers to God's one plan for creation. By one simple act, God decrees all things outside of himself. The plural emphasizes that in God's one decree and plan there are multiple effects that are disclosed in God's external works.

[34] G. I. Williamson, *The Shorter Catechism*, vol. 1, *Questions 1–38* (Phillipsburg: P&R, 1970), 25.

[35] Scripture speaks of God's plan as including the exact places we will live (Acts 17:26) and states that before time, God has even planned this fallen order for a greater good and ultimately for his glory (Rom 8:28–29).

what we see in history is the execution of his decree in all of his external works, starting with creation, unfolding through history, and leading to the consummation of the new creation.

In thinking about God's decree, a number of terms and concepts are utilized.[36] For example, the term *foreordination* is used to refer to God's decree with respect to his comprehensive plan, which includes within it all things. *Predestination*, although similar to foreordination, refers to God's decree with respect to the eternal condition of moral agents, specifically human beings, but it also includes angelic hosts. Under the category of "predestination," the terms *election* and *reprobation* are used. The former refers to God's positive choice of some individuals, that is, his elect, to salvation in Christ Jesus and all the glorious benefits that pertain to covenantal union in Christ. The latter refers to God's choice to leave some individuals, that is, the non-elect, to suffer eternal lostness due to their sin and rebellion against God. As we will discuss, the relationship of election and reprobation in God's decree is best viewed "asymmetrically." This means that God's positive and gracious choice of his elect out of a fallen humanity is more direct, while his choice to allow or permit some people to go their own way due to their sin is indirect. Both are planned by God from eternity, but in different ways. On this last point, Christians differ, along with their understanding how God's decree is formulated, which specifically is at dispute in debates between Arminian and Calvinist or Reformed theology. Before we discuss some of these important debates, let us first turn to the diverse biblical language that teaches us that our triune God from eternity has planned all things.

Biblical Terminology[37]

In the OT, a variety of terms are used to speak of God's eternal plan for all things. For example, David speaks of his entire life "ordained" or "planned" (*yāsar*) before he existed (Ps 139:16), which is also emphasized elsewhere to convey the idea of God's eternal purpose and prior determination of what occurs in history (Isa 22:11; 37:26; 46:11). In fact, in Isa 37:26, *yāsar* is used with *'ăsah* (from *yā'as*) to refer to God's prior determination to bring judgment on Israel's enemies: "Have you not heard? / Long ago, I ordained it (*'ăsah*). / In days of old I planned

[36] See Millard J. Erickson, *Christian Theology*, 2nd ed. (Grand Rapids: Baker, 1998), 372–77; Bavinck, *Reformed Dogmatics*, 2:374–77; Berkhof, *Systematic Theology*, 100–1, 109–11.

[37] See Erickson, *Christian Theology*, 373–77; Vos, *Reformed Dogmatics*, 1:79–81; Bavinck, *Reformed Dogmatics*, 2:343–47; Berkhof, *Systematic Theology*, 101–2; Feinberg, *No One Like Him*, 502–3.

(*yāsar*) it; / now I have brought it to pass" (NIV). In other places, *'ăsah* is used to convey the idea that God's plan is not arbitrary but has forethought and reason and that what he has "planned" will surely come to pass (Job 38:2; 42:3; Pss 33:11; 106:13; 107:11; Prov 19:21; 27:9; Isa 5:19; 14:26; 19:17; 28:29; 44:26; 46:10–11; Jer 32:19; 49:20; 50:45; Mic 4:12).

Scripture also speaks of God's "council" (*sôd*, from *yāsad*) by which he plans all things. For example, in Jeremiah, the Lord has planned by his "council" the future of Israel and the nations (Jer 23:18, 22; cf. Amos 3:7), in contrast to the "council" of foolish humanity who stands in opposition to God (Pss 2:2; 31:13). Or God's plan is spoken of in terms of his purposed "decisions" (*mĕzimmāh*, from *zāmam*), which cannot be thwarted (Jer 4:28; 51:12; cf. Prov 30:32). Nothing in God's plan is without thought, planning, and deliberation. God's plan is also according to his "good pleasure, desire, inclination, and will" (*haphēs* and *rasôn*). In regard to the death of the Suffering Servant, it was God's "will" or "desire" (*haphēs*) to bring it about for the salvation of his people (Isa 53:10). In restoring Israel, it was according to his "will" and "good pleasure" (*rasôn*) tied to his eternal plan (Ps 51:18; Isa 49:8). God's plan, determined by his "good pleasure," underscores the truth that it is not dependent on the choice and will of his creatures.

In the NT, we have corresponding terminology plus a strong emphasis on God's plan being from eternity tied to his own choice to glorify himself. For example, the NT speaks of God's "counsel" or "will" (*boulē*, *boulomai*) regarding his deliberate plan and choice of what comes to pass, especially in terms of *the* central event in all of history—Christ's death and resurrection (Acts 2:23; 4:28; 13:36). The planning of Christ's coming and work presupposes that in God's eternal "counsel," the entire history of creation, the fall, and our redemption was part of that plan. Elsewhere, *boulē* is used to refer to God's overall plan, which includes everything that has now been revealed to us and that we now proclaim (Acts 20:27; Eph 1:11; Heb 6:17). Similar to *boulē*, *thelēma* is another term for God's "will," but *thelēma* places the accent on God's actual willing of his plan (Matt 26:42; Acts 21:14; Eph 1:5, 11; 1 Pet 3:17; 4:19).

As in the OT, the NT teaches that God's plan is based on his own "good pleasure" (*eudokia*, *eudokeō*), thus underscoring God's free choice in making his plan and the independence or self-sufficiency of his plan tied to his purposes alone. For example, God's election of his people is "before the foundation of the world" and based on nothing but "the good pleasure of his will, to the praise of his glorious grace" (Eph 1:4–6). God's plan certainly benefits his people who are the recipients of it, but ultimately the end for which God has decreed all things is for the celebration of his own glory (Matt 11:26; Luke 3:22; 10:21; Eph 1:5, 9; Phil 2:13).

The NT also reminds us that God's decree or plan was eternal and comprehensive. Evidence for this truth is found in the use of such terms as *predestine* (*proorizō*: Acts 4:28; Rom 8:29–30; 1 Cor 2:7; Eph 1:5, 11); *to prepare beforehand* (*proētoimazō*: Rom 9:23; Eph 2:10); *to order or prescribe* (*prostassō*: Acts 17:26); *to appoint, determine*, and *decree* (*horizō*: Luke 22:22; Acts 2:23; 10:42; 17:26, 31; Heb 4:7); and *to foreknow* before time (*prognōsis, proginōskō*: Rom 8:29; 11:2; 1 Pet 1:2, 20). Regarding divine "foreknowledge," although it can refer to "knowing ahead of time," when it applies to God's foreknowing humans, it picks up the Hebrew use of *yada'*, which refers to a loving relationship and knowledge.[38] Thus when God "foreknows" people, especially in reference to election, the emphasis is on God's "fore-loving" his people from eternity, which is basically the same idea as election.[39]

Consistent with this understanding is the specific use of "election" language (*eklogē*). God's election of his people is before time, tied to God's "purpose and intent" (*prothesis, protithēmi*: Rom 8:28; 9:11; Eph 1:9, 11; 3:11; 2 Tim 1:9), and based on his will, grace, and good pleasure (Mark 13:20; Acts 9:15; 13:17; 15:7; Rom 9:11; 11:5, 28; 1 Cor 1:27–28; Eph 1:4–6; 1 Thess 1:4; 2 Pet 1:10; Jas 2:5). Of course, the classic text on election is Rom 9. Here we discover that God's purpose of election was before time and before people made any kind of choice (9:9, 11–12). As such, election is grounded in God's own gracious and free choice (15–18) to redeem the individuals that constitute his people for himself according to his will and for his ultimate glory. As Scripture makes clear, God's election does not remove the responsibility of the person, nor does it make God's choice dependent on what he foreknows people will choose. In Scripture, both truths are put side by side, thus reminding us of the need to maintain both truths together; otherwise, crucial biblical teaching is displaced and/or ignored.

---

[38] Walter Bauer, William F. Arndt, F. Wilbur Gingrich, and F. W. Danker, *A Greek-English Lexicon of the New Testament*, 2nd ed. (Chicago: University of Chicago Press, 1979), 703–4. "Foreknowledge" (noun and verb) is used seven times in the NT. Two times it refers to "knowing ahead of time" (Acts 26:5; 2 Pet 3:17). The other five times it speaks of God's actions toward others in the sense of "choosing beforehand" and "fore-loving" (Acts 2:23; Rom 8:29; 11:2; 1 Pet 1:2, 20). OT texts that speak of foreknowledge include 1 Chron 28:9; Job 28:24; Pss 139:1–4; 147:5; Isa 41:21–23; 42:9; 44:7; 45:21; 46:9–11; 48:3–7; Jer 1:5.

[39] Heb. *yada'*, "to know," refers to an intimacy of knowledge and love. In Gen 4:1, it is used to refer to Adam "knowing" his wife in terms of sexual relations. It also refers to God's election of a people (Gen 18:19; Amos 3:2; Hos 13:5; Rom 8:29; 11:2; 1 Pet 1:2). See S. M. Baugh, "The Meaning of Foreknowledge," in *Still Sovereign: Contemporary Perspectives on Election, Foreknowledge, and Grace*, ed. Thomas R. Schreiner and Bruce A. Ware (Grand Rapids: Baker, 2000), 183–200; cf. Feinberg, *No One Like Him*, 519–26.

The Covenant of Redemption and God's Decree

In thinking about God's decree, in the seventeenth century, Reformed theology began to develop in more detail what is known as the "covenant of redemption" (*pactum salutis*). It was viewed as part of the divine decree but conceptually distinguished "from God's decree regarding the creation and providential government of creatures, and also from God's decree regarding the election and reprobation of fallen human beings."[40] At its heart, the *pactum salutis* is about God's eternal determination and agreement among the divine persons to share their life in covenant relationship with the elect. In this eternal agreement, the Father appoints the Son to be the mediator of the new covenant and to accomplish our redemption by his incarnation, obedient representative headship, penal substitution, resurrection, and ascension. This covenant, then, becomes the means by which God brings about his people's redemption. Also, in this plan, the Son joyfully and voluntarily accepts his appointment along with its covenant stipulations and promises, which then are worked out in Christ's incarnation and work. Also, the Spirit is appointed to anoint and equip the incarnate Son to accomplish his new creation work and to apply Christ's finished work to us.[41] The *pactum* was rightly viewed as important because it not only established Christ as mediator; it also defined the nature of his mediation as our covenant representative and substitute, and it assigned specific roles to each divine person, consistent with their eternal divine processions. In this way, in God's plan of redemption, none of the triune persons are pitted against each other. All three persons equally subsist in and share the same divine essence and act inseparably according to their mode of subsistence, yet the one, unified work of redemption is appropriated to the Father, Son, and Spirit.

Theological Views of the Divine Decree and Its Enactment in History

In historical theology, there has been broad agreement on the divine decree. Historic Christian theology has agreed that God knows and plans all things from eternity and that in God's external works, God's eternal plan is enacted. However, there has been sharp disagreement regarding

---

[40] Swain, "Covenant of Redemption," 108.

[41] On this basic understanding of the covenant of redemption, see Fesko, *Trinity and the Covenant* (see chap. 15, n. 61); and Swain, "Covenant of Redemption," 108–9.

whether God's decree is *conditioned* on his foreknowing all that comes to pass, specifically dependent on the free actions of his creatures. Or, whether God's decree is *unconditional*, that is, based on God's own free choice that renders all things certain, including human free actions. Since the Reformation and post-Reformation eras, and especially today within evangelical theology, the former view is identified with Arminianism while the latter view is identified with Calvinism or Reformed theology. Let us now describe each view in terms of its overall theology before we offer what we consider the best biblical-theological formulation of God's decree.

Arminianism

Arminianism is associated with the theology of Jacob Arminius (1560–1609), who was professor of theology at the University of Leiden in the Netherlands. Arminius's views were systematized primarily due to the Synod of Dort (1618–19), where followers of Arminius, the Remonstrants, brought five charges against the Calvinist view of the Reformed Churches in the Netherlands. The Synod of Dort responded with what we now label as the "Five Points of Calvinism."[42]

Within evangelical theology, the debate over Arminianism and Calvinism is mostly located in the doctrine of salvation (or soteriology) given differences over the nature of sin (total depravity and whether sin's effects are alleviated by God's universal, prevenient grace), election (whether it is unconditional or conditional), grace (whether grace is effectual or resistible), the extent of the atonement (whether Christ makes possible the salvation of all people or whether he actually secures the salvation of his people), and whether believers are eternally secure (or whether they may possibly lose their salvation). However, it is crucial to understand that prior to the soteriology debates, there is a more foundational debate between the two views regarding the nature of God's decree tied to an entire theology proper, hence the discussion of these two theological viewpoints at this juncture.

---

[42] For a helpful discussion of the "Five Points of Calvinism," see Shawn D. Wright, *40 Questions about Calvinism* (Grand Rapids: Kregel, 2019), 25–38; cf. Michael Horton, *For Calvinism* (Grand Rapids: Zondervan, 2011). The "five" points are often stated by the acronym, TULIP: **T**otal depravity, **U**nconditional election, **L**imited or definite atonement, **I**rresistible or effectual grace, and the preservation and **P**erseverance of the saints. As we will discuss below, the term *Calvinism* is misleading since Calvin was not the only one who taught these "Five Points."

There is no pure form of Arminianism. Arminius's views continued with his followers, but it did not take long for them to go in different directions. For example, John Wesley (1707–88) and the Wesleyan tradition continued to uphold Arminius's theology. However, Hugo Grotius (1583–1645) departed from Arminius's commitment to the active obedience of Christ and the nature of the cross as penal substitution. In its place, Grotius and many in the Arminian tradition embraced a governmental theory of the atonement. For example, the governmental view continued in such Arminian theologians as John Miley, Philip Limborch, Charles Finney, H. Orton Wiley, and R. Larry Shelton. Today, open theism claims to be a form of Arminian theology; however, in key areas, such as total depravity, God's ability to foreknow future free actions of humans, and an embrace of inclusivism, open theists significantly depart from classical Arminian theology, a point we discussed in chapter 16. Given differences within Arminianism, we will outline the classical understanding of it.

Arminianism and Its View of the Divine Decree[43]

In agreement with all versions of historic Christian theology, Arminianism affirms that God has an eternal, comprehensive plan in the sense that God knows all things past, present, and future, including the future free actions of his creatures.[44] In terms of divine action, Arminianism also

---

[43] See Robert Letham, "Arminianism," in *NDT*, 64–66 (see chap. 2, n. 11); J. K. Grider, "Arminianism," in Treier and Elwell, *EDT*, 82–83 (see chap. 2, n. 18); Olson, *Arminian Theology* (see chap. 18, n. 129); Roger E. Olson, *Against Calvinism* (Grand Rapids: Zondervan, 2011); Roger E. Olson, "Classical Free Will," in Ware, *Perspectives on the Doctrine*, 148–72 (see chap. 16, n. 56); Clark H. Pinnock, ed., *Grace Unlimited* (Minneapolis: Bethany House, 1975); Pinnock, *Grace of God* (see chap. 18, n. 150); Jack Cottrell, *What the Bible Says about God the Ruler* (Eugene: Wipf & Stock, 1984); McCall and Stanglin, *After Arminius* (see chap. 18, n. 65); also see J. Arminius, *The Works of James Arminius*, 3 vols. (London, 1825, 1828, 1875).

[44] Although open theism identifies itself as a version of Arminianism, on this point it departs significantly from Arminian theology *and* the entire theological tradition of the church. Open theism denies that God has an eternal, comprehensive plan, and thus the language of divine decree is either dropped entirely or greatly modified. There is no eternal blueprint for history. God's plan is only his overall intent, desires, and aims for the world. God's will is not the ultimate explanation for everything that happens; human choices make an important contribution, too. In fact, as history unfolds, God's plan changes in response to our choices. Yet, God is able to accomplish his general goals, but God's specific desires are often thwarted by us, which requires new responses by God. Similar to panentheism, open theism greatly limits God's sovereignty and makes God's knowledge conditioned on the creature,

affirms God's ability to act unilaterally and effectually if he chooses to do so. However, since God has freely chosen to create humans with libertarian freedom, God has also chosen to limit himself in what he can and cannot do; a crucial point of distinction from panentheism or process theism.[45] Thus, to uphold human freedom, God cannot control our free actions if they are to remain free. God may have ultimate control, but he cannot direct every event exactly the way he wants. In other words, God cannot guarantee what he always wants or desires, and in this sense, God's will can be thwarted.[46]

Furthermore, given God's choice to create humans with libertarian freedom, God is not *a se* in his knowledge. Arminians affirm God's aseity in his existence; God has "life from himself." But when it comes to knowing what *free* creatures will do, he is "dependent" on the creature. For this reason, God's decree is "put together," conditioned on what he "foreknows" humans will do, and *based* on this foreknowledge, God plans all things from eternity. So, for example, before creation, God foreknew that humans would sin and that the effects of sin would be "total" or pervasive, thus rendering humans unable to respond to God apart from his gracious initiative.[47] Yet, God, in grace, took the initiative to offer a universal sufficient grace to all people (known as prevenient grace) that removes everyone's spiritual inability to respond to God. For Arminius, this offering of prevenient grace was tied to his view that God, in his decree, has an antecedent conditional will that offers to all people salvation on the condition that they repent of their sins, believe in Christ, and persevere in the faith.[48]

---

except most open theists believe that God can effectually act if he chooses, but if he does, this results in a temporary loss of our human freedom. God, then, cannot guarantee ahead of time how we will use our freedom, and so God is dependent on the world in a greater way than in classical Arminian theology.

[45] On the nature of libertarian freedom, see chapter 16. A libertarian view of freedom insists that a person is free if their choice is not sufficiently causally determined and the person could always choose otherwise.

[46] See Olson, *Arminian Theology*, 131.

[47] Classic Arminianism affirms "total" depravity: the effect of Adam's sin on all people includes *all* aspects of our human nature (e.g., our minds, wills, desires, and so on), thus rendering us spiritually unable to respond to God on our own. Today, some who identify as Arminians reject total depravity and affirm that sin's effects are only partial; thus, we are able to choose God on our own. This latter view is really semi-Pelagianism, not classic Arminianism.

[48] Arminians appeal to Ezek 18:23, 32; 33:11; Matt 23:37; John 3:16; 1 Tim 2:4; and 2 Pet 3:9 to demonstrate that God desires the salvation of all people and thus that he has made it possible for all

This is why Arminian theology affirms a "conditional" view of election. Before time, God foreknows who will respond to the gospel, and due to God's prevenient grace at work in all people, taking away their inability to believe, God chooses individuals on the basis of their foreknown faith. Thus, technically, "God does not choose anyone, but instead foresees that some will choose him."[49] Also, many Arminians embrace a "corporate" view of election, especially in their interpretation of Romans 9.[50] Instead of arguing that God elects specific individuals on the basis of their foreknown faith, God elects Christ and the corporate entity of the church, which we place ourselves into by faith. But in the end, the corporate view of election is a version of a conditional view of election based on God's foreknowing all that will come to pass. Similar to election, reprobation is also based on divine foreknowledge. In the case of reprobation though, God knows who will *not* believe, and as a result, they are properly judged for their sin.

But a legitimate question arises: If God has created humans with libertarian freedom, how does he exercise control over our world? Within Arminian theology, there are slightly different answers to this question, but mostly the claim is that God has general plans and goals that he wants to accomplish, but in his decree and plan, he incorporates our foreknown choices.[51] For some this means that God exercises very limited power, as evidenced by open theism. A more classic Arminian view is that God is just as sovereign as Reformed theology teaches, but to make room for libertarian freedom, God has chosen to forego exercising his power and control much of the time. Since it is a decision that God has made, it in no way limits his sovereignty. This is not to say that God does not work in our world. He may work directly in terms of miracles or more cooperatively in terms of prevenient grace. God is not idle, but humans are always free either to respond to God due to his enabling grace or reject him and go their own way.

How does God *guarantee* that any of his goals are achieved? Arminians answer this question by appealing to divine foreknowledge. In contrast to open theism, since God knows

---

people to repent and believe due to his prevenient grace, but all of this is conditioned on whether we repent and believe.

[49] Letham, "Arminianism," 65.

[50] See William Klein, *The New Chosen People* (Eugene: Wipf & Stock, 2001).

[51] For this reason, Arminian theology is rightly characterized as "synergistic" (Gk. *synergos*, "coworker") since God's decree is "put together" by God's own aims and goals *and* conditioned by our foreknown human choices.

the future exhaustively, he is not caught by surprise. But depending on whether one affirms God's timeless knowledge, simple foreknowledge, or middle knowledge and its relation to human freedom, the answer varies. As we discussed in chapter 19, for timeless knowledge and simple foreknowledge, God can know the future, but he cannot change it without changing the response of his creatures, which undercuts the reality of libertarian freedom. As such, God cannot guarantee everything he wants and desires; he can only guarantee his general goals and aims. For middle knowledge, God's sovereignty is greater, assuming the viability of the view. By God's free knowledge, he weakly actualizes the possible world that best serves his purposes, or which is most "feasible," based on his middle knowledge of counterfactuals.[52] As a result, God knows the future, and he is sovereign over which world he actualizes, thus allowing for more sovereign control. Thus, God can plan in advance how he will respond to our actions so as to accomplish his goals.

Biblical and Theological Arguments for Arminianism

There are numerous biblical and theological arguments given by Arminians for their view of the divine decree. Here are four main arguments.[53]

First, Arminianism insists that God has created humans with libertarian freedom and that this view of freedom is the only viable option to uphold a strong view of human responsibility. Often appeal is made to various texts that command humans to repent, believe, and respond to God, which requires the "ability to do otherwise." For example, Joshua calls the Israelites to "choose this day whom . . . [they] will serve" (Josh 24:15 ESV), which assumes they have the ability to do so.[54] In addition, coupled with these texts are various philosophical arguments

---

[52] William L. Craig, "God Directs All Things," in Jowers, *Four Views on Divine Providence*, 83 (see chap. 18, n. 161). A "possible world" refers to a world that is logically possible, but a "feasible world" is a possible world that God can decree or actualize because it upholds libertarian freedom.

[53] See McCall and Stanglin, *After Arminius*, 235–52; Keith D. Stanglin and Thomas H. McCall, *Jacob Arminius: Theologian of Grace* (Oxford: Oxford University Press, 2012), 47–188; cf. Feinberg, *No One Like Him*, 656–68.

[54] Other similar texts are 1 Kgs 18:21; Isa 55:1; Jer 33:3; Joel 2:32; Matt 7:13–14, 24; 10:32–33; John 6:40; 7:37–38; Rom 9:33; 2 Cor 9:7; Rev 22:17. Or think of various "whosoever will" texts that assume that people can freely respond to the call of the gospel (e.g., John 3:16). On this latter point, see

that contend that only libertarian freedom can provide this necessary condition of freedom and apart from it, freedom is a mirage.[55]

Second, building on the first point, evidence that God has created humans with libertarian freedom is that sometimes God's will and desires are thwarted due to our human choices, thus revealing the conditioned nature of God's decree. For example, similar to open theism, Arminian theology appeals to God's repentance in Scripture, which for them demonstrates God's *conditioned* response to our free choices (e.g., Gen 6:6; 1 Sam 15:11, 35). Or it appeals to texts that speak of God's will or desires being thwarted by our choices. For example, we read that God is "not wanting any to perish but all to come to repentance" (2 Pet 3:9) or that God "wants everyone to be saved and to come to the knowledge of the truth" (1 Tim 2:4), yet it is obvious that God's desires and wants are not realized due to our human choices and rebellion against God. In this sense, God's will is *not* guaranteed or effectually realized, at least in the case of people's salvation.[56] Or think of Christ's lament over Jerusalem: "Jerusalem, Jerusalem. . . . How often I wanted to gather your children together . . . but you were not willing" (Matt 23:37). All of these texts assume that God has created us with libertarian freedom and that we can thwart God's will.[57] In contemporary discussion, this point is underscored by appeal to God's relational and loving nature. Repeatedly, it is argued that a loving God entails that

---

Lemke, "A Biblical and Theological Critique," in Allen and Lemke, *Whosoever Will*, 122–27 (see chap. 4, n. 85).

[55] See Geisler, "God Knows All Things," in Basinger and Basinger, *Predestination and Free Will*, 64–65 (see chap. 16, n. 72); Bruce Reichenbach, "God Limits His Power," in Basinger and Basinger, *Predestination and Free Will*, 104; Olson, "Classical Free Will," 149–63.

[56] Reichenbach, "God Limits His Power," 117–18; Richard Rice, "Biblical Support for a New Perspective," in Pinnock et al., *Openness of God*, 54–55 (see chap. 2, n. 135); Olson, *Against Calvinism*, 67–68.

[57] Geisler, "God Knows All Things," 65; cf. Pinnock, "God Limits His Knowledge," in Basinger and Basinger, *Predestination and Free Will*, 149. Pinnock writes:

> According to the Bible, human beings are creatures who have rejected God's will for them and turned aside from his plan. This is another strong piece of evidence that God made them truly free. . . . We have actually deviated from the plan of God in creating us and set ourselves at cross-purposes to God. . . . Certainly our rebellion is proof that our actions are not determined but significantly free. . . . We may not be able to thwart God's ultimate plan for the world, but we certainly can ruin his plan for us personally and, like the scribes, reject God's purposes for ourselves (Lk 7:30).

God's divine power has been limited to make room for a loving relationship with free creatures. God, in creating us, has become vulnerable, and instead of exercising "control" over us, God interacts and responds to us conditioned on our choices.[58]

Third, Arminians argue that God's decree is conditional, not unconditional. God has general purposes for creation that are unconditional (e.g., to glorify himself, to share his goodness with us), but not specific unconditional purposes for each person. Why? For some of the reasons already noted. Arminians argue that God's creating us with libertarian freedom entails the following points.

1. God chooses to limit himself. Jack Cottrell states it this way:

> God limits himself not only by creating a world as such, but also and even further by the *kind* of world he chose to create. That is, he chose to make a world that is *relatively independent* of him. . . . man is free to act without his acts having been predetermined by God and without the simultaneous and efficacious coaction of God. . . . By not intervening in their decisions *unless* his special purposes require it, God respects both the integrity of their freedom he gave to human beings and the integrity of his sovereign choice to make free creatures in the first place.[59]

2. God's decree is conditioned on his foreknowledge of our future free actions. Again, Cottrell explains:

> [God's] foreknowledge is conditioned on the actual occurrence of events themselves (as foreknown); the entire plan of redemption, with all its many elements from Genesis to Revelation, is conditioned on (is a response to) man's sin; answers to prayer are conditioned by the prayers themselves (as foreknown). But in all of this God is *no less sovereign* than if he had unconditionally predetermined each specific component of the whole.[60]

3. Election in Scripture is conditional, not unconditional. Even Romans 9, which seems to affirm an unconditional election, is viewed as teaching a corporate view of election

[58] See Olson, "Classical Free Will," 149–58.

[59] Jack W. Cottrell, "The Nature of the Divine Sovereignty," in Pinnock, *Grace of God*, 108; cf. Olson, "Classical Free Will," 170–72.

[60] Cottrell, 107.

and not an individual view. For example, Cottrell insists that Romans 9–11 "shows that God's election and rejection of the Jews as a nation with regard to their role of service was a matter of God's sovereign choice, while his acceptance or rejection of individual Jews with regard to their salvation is conditioned on their belief or unbelief."[61] Thus, Romans 9 does not teach an unconditional election or rejection of individuals for salvation, but "simply setting [Israel] aside collectively—as a nation—as far as their service of preparation is concerned."[62]

Fourth, Arminians appeal to the doctrine of salvation and the problem of evil.[63] Building on the last point, if election is "unconditional," then why has God not saved everyone? Furthermore, if God decrees all things in a guaranteed way, including good and evil, then why has God not brought it about that there is no evil in the world? This last question looms large in Arminian argumentation for their view, and most insist that it is only their view that can adequately respond to questions regarding God's allowing evil in the world.

Calvinism and Reformed Theology

The terms "Calvinism" and "Reformed theology" require definition since they are used in a variety of ways in systematic theology.[64] In our present context, we are using the terms to refer to a specific view of the nature of God's decree and its outworking in creation, providence, and redemption. We are not using the terms to refer to a specific form of Reformed "covenant theology" as discussed in part 3, where we contrasted the biblical-theological systems of dispensational and covenant theology, although the terms can be used in that way. Instead, we are using the term *Calvinism* broadly to refer to the theological views associated with John Calvin (1509–1564) and Reformed theology's view of theology proper and the divine decree.[65]

---

[61] Cottrell, 114. See a similar argument in Olson, *Against Calvinism*, 67, 128–35.

[62] Cottrell, 114.

[63] See Cottrell, *God the Ruler*, 379–409; cf. Olson, "Classical Free Will," 158–63.

[64] On this point, see Wright, *40 Questions about Calvinism*, 17–31.

[65] Within "Reformed theology," there are differences regarding the "order" of the divine decree, reflected in debates over supralapsarianism, infralapsarianism, and sublapsarianism. We will discuss these differences below.

Furthermore, as Michael Horton rightly reminds us, "Calvin was not the first Calvinist," and "Calvin was not the only shaper of the Reformed tradition."[66] In fact, a "Reformed" view of predestination, election, and reprobation have been taught as early as Augustine and throughout the medieval era. As Horton rightly notes, "Calvin's views can scarcely be distinguished from that of Augustine, Bernard of Clairvaux, Archbishop Thomas Bradwardine, and Gregory of Rimini"; in fact, "Thomas Aquinas comes pretty close."[67] But this observation is only true of views regarding the nature of God's decree since differences quickly emerge when specific issues, such as "grace, merit, and justification,"[68] are discussed. In addition, after Calvin, the post-Reformed tradition continued to develop a robust theological understanding of God's decree and its relationship to creation, providence, and redemption. So, in this context, the terms *Calvinism* and *Reformed theology* refer to a specific view of the divine decree that has been taught since Augustine and especially by Reformed "covenant theology" churches along with various kinds of "Reformed" Baptist churches.[69]

Calvinism and Its View of the Divine Decree

Calvinism, like Arminianism and in agreement with all versions of historic Christian theology, affirms that God has an eternal, comprehensive plan for all things, which includes the future free actions of his creatures. Regarding divine action, similar to classic Arminianism, Calvinism affirms God's ability to act unilaterally and effectively, yet God's effectual agency plays a much more significant role in Calvinism than in Arminianism since God is not viewed as one who is self-limited by his choice to create free and responsible creatures.

---

[66] Horton, *For Calvinism*, 28–29. Italics removed.

[67] Horton, 28.

[68] Horton, 28. We will discuss these differences in volume 2, under the doctrine of salvation.

[69] For Reformed "covenant theology" churches, see the *Heidelberg Catechism* (1563) or the *Westminster Confession of Faith* (1646). For Reformed Baptist churches, see the *London Baptist Confession of Faith* (1689). In Southern Baptist life, see the *Abstract of Principles* (1859), which continues to serve as one of the doctrinal statements for the flagship seminary of the SBC, The Southern Baptist Theological Seminary. Also cf. Thomas J. Nettles, *By His Grace and for His Glory: A Historical, Theological, and Practical Study of the Doctrines of Grace in Baptist Life* (Grand Rapids: Baker, 1986).

For this reason, Calvinism denies that God has chosen to limit himself in his decision to create the world and significant creatures. Instead, God's decree or plan is grounded in his own choice and will, and as such, it is *not* dependent on the creature, as in Arminian theology. In Reformed theology, God is not only *a se* in his existence, but also in his knowledge since both God's existence and knowledge is "from himself." God's decree is not conditioned by what God foreknows humans will do. Rather, from eternity past, God has freely chosen and planned what will come to pass according to his will and purposes, and whatever he has chosen is guaranteed to occur infallibly. God's decretive will is not something that humans can thwart since God is sovereignly working out "everything in agreement with the purpose of his will" (Eph 1:11).

This is why, in contrast to Arminian theology, Reformed theology contends that election is unconditional, not conditional. In fact, unconditional election is argued for at least two reasons. First, election is unconditional since God's decree is unconditional and not "conditioned" by the creature. Second, election is also unconditional due to our sin. In fact, due to our identification with Adam as our covenant head and representative, along with our own sinful choices (Rom 5:12–21; Eph 2:1–3), apart from the Father's choice to elect us, the Son's work to accomplish our salvation, and the Spirit's work to apply Christ's work to us, there is no salvation for us. Indeed, apart from God's effectual grace, due to our sin, we will not and cannot respond to God in true saving faith.[70] For these two reasons, then, election is unconditional.

In terms of God's decree, a Reformed view is nicely summarized by the confessional statement of the *London Baptist Confession* (1689):

> God hath decreed in himself, from all eternity, by the most wise and holy counsel of his own will, freely and unchangeably, all things, whatsoever comes to pass; yet so as thereby is God neither the author of sin nor hath fellowship with any therein; nor is violence offered to the will of the creature, nor yet is the liberty or contingency of

---

[70] On this point, Calvinism is "monergistic" (Gk. *monos*, "alone;" *ergon*, "to work"), in contrast to the "synergism" ("co-worker") of Arminian theology. In Calvinism, God alone decrees all things, and in salvation, he alone must initiate by acting in effectual grace, by the Spirit's work bringing the spiritually dead to new life so that we are able to repent of our sins and believe in God's covenantal promises centered in our Lord Jesus Christ.

> second causes taken away, but rather established; in which appears his wisdom in disposing all things, and power and faithfulness in accomplishing his decree.[71]

From this statement a number of important points need to be noted regarding the Calvinistic view.

First, as the confessional statement affirms, although God has chosen all things, including sin and evil, God does not do any evil, nor is he morally responsible for it. In the decree, the relationship between God's decree of good and evil is asymmetrical. God is directly responsible for the good, but he has allowed or permitted sin "not for itself but because of its necessary connection with other things that he willed,"[72] which is tied to a greater good and ultimately for God's own glory. As we will discuss in chapters 22–23 in our discussion of divine providence, God does not always reveal to us what this greater good is, although ultimately it is related to the revelation and celebration of God's own glory and name. In both election and judgment, God's holy love, grace, mercy, and justice are revealed in a far greater way (Rom 9:22; Eph 1:3–14; 2:1–10; 3:10).

Second, God's decree includes within it both the ends and the means to bring about his plan. God's decree is the blueprint for all things, but it should not be viewed as a "causal agent." Instead, within God's decree, he has ordained various agents exerting causal power, which is another way of speaking about God's ordination of specific *means* to bring about his plan. Christian theology has always distinguished between God's *primary* causal agency and the reality of *secondary* causes and agents. God's decree ordains all things and guarantees the results; he is the ultimate cause of all human acts of choosing, but God acts in and through secondary causes and means. As the primary agent, God can act directly or immediately as in creation, or, more often, he acts through secondary means. Further, we can speak of God's "mediate" action in the categories of "remote" vs. "proximate." The remote category refers to God's causal agency through secondary means as more removed, such as in the case of allowing sin to occur. In this sense, God's decree of the good is direct and positive, but his decree of sin and evil is more remote and by permission. No doubt, as Geerhardus Vos reminds us, "The permissive decree is no less a certain decree than any other,"[73] yet sin is contrary to God's nature, and although he

[71] From "God's Decree" (3.1).

[72] Vos, *Reformed Dogmatics*, 1:94.

[73] Vos, 1:95.

permits it, he is not responsible for it (Jas 1:13; 1 John 1:5). We can also speak of God's action as closer or proximate, as in the case of the inspiration of Scripture (2 Pet 1:21) or the Spirit's work of sanctification in us (Phil 2:11–12). Yet, in both cases, in the same act, God is at work through secondary agents without removing their freedom and agency.[74] In a Reformed view, then, God's decree includes the "means to the ends," which is crucial in accounting for the reality of human freedom, how God can ordain sin and evil without being responsible for it, and how God can *guarantee* what he decrees without removing the reality of our free actions.

Third, a Reformed view of the divine decree employs a compatibilistic view of freedom, in contrast to Arminian theology.[75] A libertarian view of freedom necessitates some kind of self-limitation on God's part, but a compatibilist view does not. Human actions are causally determined by God, but they are free as long as the antecedent conditions that sufficiently incline the person's will does so without constraint and according to the person's desires and wants. There is no necessary contradiction between God decreeing all things, including our free choices, and the certainty of their occurring. Although there are plenty of unknowns involved as to how God can ordain all things in a guaranteed way without violating the reality of our choices, a compatibilistic view of human freedom helps make sense of it. It affirms that

> there is a dual explanation for every choice that we human beings make. God's sovereign determination serves as the sufficient *primary* (ultimate) but *remote* cause of our choices, while we serve as the *secondary* but *proximate* (the near or immediate) cause of our choices. . . . Yet . . . God's fixed providential direction is never coercive. He never moves people to act against their will.[76]

---

[74] See Calvin, *Institutes*, 3.23.8 (2:956–57) (see chap. 1, n. 3).

[75] Some have disputed this point. One problem is that "freedom" was not defined specifically as "compatibilistic," although the concept was present. As such, it can be shown that Reformed theology assumed what we now define as a "compatibilistic" view of freedom in contrast to a "libertarian" view. On this point, see Paul Helm, *Reforming Free Will: A Conversation on the History of Reformed Views of Compatibilism (1500–1800)* (Fearn, Ross-shire, UK: Mentor, 2020). Helm responds to the contrary view of Richard A. Muller, presented in Muller, *Divine Will and Human Choice: Freedom, Contingency, and Necessity in Early Modern Reformed Thought* (Grand Rapids: Baker Academic, 2017).

[76] Christensen, *What About Evil?*, 171 (see chap. 4, n. 86).

Thus, in the case of the divine decree, God ordains all things, including our free choices as actual means to bring about his purposed and planned ends.[77]

Thus, a Calvinistic view of God's decree affirms that from eternity, God freely foreordained all things, including our free actions, and as such, he knows all things infallibly and exhaustively. As a result, God *guarantees* that what he plans will actually come to pass, but through ordained means. In the difficult case of sin and evil, although God does not desire sin, it is part of his overall plan and contributes to his purposes (though we may not know what those purposes are) ultimately for his own glory and the eternal good of his people. In such a view, God is sovereign over his world, yet God's decree does not remove the liberty or contingency of secondary causes; indeed, it establishes them as part of his very plan.

Theological Formulation of the Divine Decree

Differences among Christians regarding the divine decree have been with us since the patristic era. Today, within evangelical theology, these differences are centered on the ongoing disputes between Arminianism and Calvinism. In what follows, we will first offer a Reformed theological formulation of the divine decree as the view that best reflects the entire sweep of the biblical teaching, followed by an evaluation and critique of the Arminian view as not fully accounting for all that Scripture teaches about the nature of God and his decree.

Biblical-Theological Formulation of the Divine Decree

Scripture teaches that the triune God from eternity has decreed or planned all things. We can speak of his decree as his eternal, comprehensive plan for the universe (Pss 136:6; 139:16; Prov 16:4; 19:21; Isa 14:24–27; 22:11; 37:26; 46:9–11; Dan 4:34–35; Acts 2:23; 4:27–28; 17:26; Rom 8:28–29; 9–11; Gal 4:4–5; Eph 1:4–6, 11–12; 2:10; Rev 13:8). In speaking of God's decree,

---

[77] Not everyone within the Reformed tradition embraces a compatibilistic view of human freedom. Some try to reconcile a libertarian view with a Calvinist view of the divine decree, but in my view, the attempt fails. For such an attempt, see Oliver D. Crisp, *Deviant Calvinism: Broadening Reformed Theology* (Minneapolis: Fortress Press, 2014), 71–96; and Crisp, *Freedom, Redemption, and Communion: Studies in Christian Doctrine* (New York: T&T Clark, 2021), 3–23. For a helpful (and correct) response to Crisp, see Anderson and Manata, "Determined to Come," 272–97 (see chap. 16, n. 51).

we must distinguish between the decree and its execution. God's decree is his eternal plan for all things, while its execution brings about what God has planned. God's decree is not a causal agent. God's decree is what he has planned, which includes within it the reality of secondary causes, which function as the means to bring about his planned ends in a guaranteed way.[78] God's decree is the *ultimate* reason why everything occurs, but it also includes within it secondary sufficient means to bring about his purposed ends. Ten statements summarize the nature of God's decree.

First, God's decree is eternal (Pss 33:11; 139:16; Isa 22:11; 37:26; Jer 31:3; Matt 25:34; Acts 15:18; 1 Cor 2:7; Eph 1:3–4; 3:11; 2 Tim 1:9–10; 2 Thess 2:13; 1 Pet 1:20). The triune God has planned all things before time regarding everything "outside" of himself (*ad extra*), which is then enacted in creation and providence. God's decree is one plan with multiple effects. As history unfolds, God's eternal plan is disclosed on the stage of the world he has created. All that happens in this world is the outworking of God's eternal plan/decree.

Second, God's decree is his free and sovereign choice (Ps 115:3; 135:6; Isa 40:12–14; Rom 11:33–36; 1 Cor 2:7; Eph 1:5–6, 9–11). God does "whatever he pleases" (Ps 135:6) according to his counsel, and his counsel is not dependent on anything outside of himself. This truth is stressed by Scripture's rhetorical questions: "Who did he consult? . . . Who taught him knowledge / and showed him the way of understanding?" (Isa 40:14). The answer, of course, is no one! God's decree is *a se* (i.e., "from himself"), the result of his own free choice and according to his own "good pleasure" (Eph 1:4–6, 11).

Third, the purpose of God's decree is his own glory (Rom 11:33–36; Eph 1:3–6, 12–14; 2:8–10; Col 1:15–18; Rev 4:11; cf. Isa 48:11; Ezek 20:9). God is perfect within himself and completely self-sufficient. Yet even though God lacks nothing, he has chosen to display his internal glory by his external actions of creation (Ps 19:1), providence, redemption (Eph 1:3–14), and consummation (1 Cor 15:28). For this reason, all of God's external acts are a display of his glory for the good of his people, uniquely centered in the glorification of the Father through the Son (Eph 1:9–10; Col 1:15–18), and by the Spirit (John 16:12–15; Eph 1:13–14).

Fourth, God's decree is founded in God's knowledge and wisdom (Rom 11:33–36; Eph 1:11). God's knowledge consists of his necessary knowledge, which includes his perfect knowledge of himself and all that is possible. From God's necessary knowledge, he chooses to make actual what he decides, thus resulting in his free knowledge. The decree, then, is "the foundation of

[78] On this point, see Feinberg, *No One Like Him*, 530–31.

His free knowledge or *scientia libera*. It is the knowledge of things as they are realized in the course of history,"[79] which is founded in his knowledge and wisdom (Ps 104:24; Prov 3:19; 8:22–31). Regarding God's plan of redemption, Paul reminds us that it is founded on divine wisdom (Eph 3:10), which we see unfold before us in Christ, the ratification of the new covenant, and the establishment of the church (Eph 3:1–7). Indeed, by Paul's heralding of Christ to the Gentiles, "the administration of the mystery [i.e., God's eternal plan] hidden for ages in God. . . . [is now made known] according to his eternal purpose accomplished in Christ Jesus our Lord" (Eph 3:9–11). God's decree may seem mysterious to us, but it is founded in knowledge, and as it is disclosed, we come to know more of God's glorious wisdom on display.

Fifth, God's decree is comprehensive and includes all things (Pss 119:91; 135:6; 148:5–6; Prov 16:33; 21:1; Dan 4:34–35; Acts 2:23; 17:26; Rom 9; Eph 1:10–11; Phil 2:12–13; 1 Pet 1:20). God's plan encompasses *all* things. Here are just a few examples.

1. God's decree includes everything in the natural world and the moral realm. Joel Beeke and Paul Smalley list some of the diverse aspects of God's plan, thus underscoring its totality:

> God decreed the distinguishing botanical characteristics of each kind of seed (1 Cor. 15:38); which woman Isaac would marry (Gen. 24:44); the flight of ravens to bring food to Elijah (1 Kings 17:4); the motions of clouds, tornadoes, rain, and lightning (Job 28:26; 37:12–13); the plans and victories of the king of Assyria (Isa. 10:6); and the time when Paul would be called and converted (Gal. 1:15).[80]

2. God's plan includes seemingly chance or contingent events (Gen 45:8; 50:20; Prov 16:33). This point is taught in the case of King Ahab (1 Kgs 22). Micaiah predicts Ahab's death based on God's word (v. 28), but it is fulfilled by a seemingly "chance" event: the misfire of a bow (v. 34). Although this "chance" event was random to us, it fulfilled the word of God, just as God had spoken ahead of time before the event even occurred (v. 38).

3. God's decree also includes specific details regarding *the* central event of history, that is, the death of our Lord. Christ's death was decreed before the foundation of the world; it was not an afterthought in God's plan (Rev 13:8; cf. Matt 26:54, 56; 27:9, 35; Mark 14:49; 15:28). Also, the specifics of Christ's death were predicted ahead of time by indirect typological patterns

[79] Berkhof, *Systematic Theology*, 102.

[80] Beeke and Smalley, *Reformed Systematic Theology*, 1:964 (see chap. 1, n. 8).

(e.g., Christ is the seed of Abraham, the son of David, the great prophet, priest, and king, the lamb of God, the manna, the temple, the vine, etc.) *and* direct verbal predictions (e.g., vinegar to drink, Ps 69:21 with John 19:28–29; no broken bones, Exod 12:46 with John 19:31–36; and the kind of death Jesus would die, John 12:32–33; 18:32). All of this underscores the fact that God's decree includes within it both general and specific foreordained truths.

4. God's plan includes both the good (Eph 2:10) and sinful acts of people (Gen 50:20; Job 1:21; 2:10; 12:7–10; Acts 2:23; 4:27–28; Rom 9:17–18; 1 Pet 3:17). But with reference to sin, God's decree is best viewed as "permissive," a point we will return to in our discussion of providence and the problem of evil in chapters 22–23. However, for our present purposes, in thinking about God's decree, including both the good and sinful actions of people, specifically sinful actions, Berkhof notes a number of crucial points. First, "by His decree God rendered the sinful actions of man infallibly certain without deciding to effectuate them by acting immediately upon and in the finite will."[81] Second, God does so by "decree[ing] to sustain [our] free agency, to regulate the circumstances of [our lives], and to permit that free agency to exert itself in a multitude of acts, of which some are sinful."[82] But although "for good and holy reasons He renders these sinful acts certain, He does not decree to work evil desires or choices efficiently in man. The decree respecting sin is not an efficient but a permissive decree."[83] These points are important. Scripture denies that God is responsible for sin or that he even delights in it, although he has decreed it. God's being is opposed to sin and evil, ultimately resulting in the entire work of Christ to defeat sin and evil and in a final judgment to bring all sin and evil to account.

5. God's decree includes the means to bring about his ordained ends, means that involve a number of causal relations depending on the nature of the thing involved. For "nature," God ordains what we identify as "natural" laws to bring about his purposes. For moral agents, God ordains various means, such as circumstances, events, evangelism, prayer, and so on, to achieve his ends. Indeed, by God's decree, "[he] establishes secondary causes and commits himself to empowering and directing them to their appointed ends by cooperating with them through his providence,"[84] which accomplishes his plan *and* upholds the reality of secondary causes/agents.

---

[81] Berkhof, *Systematic Theology*, 105.

[82] Berkhof, 108.

[83] Berkhof, 108.

[84] Swain, "Covenant of Redemption," 113.

Sixth, God's decree is efficacious (Job 42:2; Pss 33:10–11; 135:6; Isa 14:24–27; 46:10; 55:10–11; Jer 15:2; Dan 4:34–55; Hab 2:3; Matt 24:36; Luke 22:22; John 8:20; Eph 1:11). To say that God's plan is efficacious means that it is guaranteed to occur as planned. Nebuchadnezzar admits this truth. After his sanity is restored, he confesses that God "does what he wants with the army of heaven / and the inhabitants of the earth. / There is no one who can block his hand / or say to him, 'What have you done?'" (Dan 4:35). This does not mean that God causes all things in a direct or immediate manner, thus eliminating secondary causes and agents. God's decree renders his plan certain, but within God's decree are the planned means to bring about his ends, including the secondary causes of nature and the free acts of humans.[85]

Seventh, God's decree is immutable (Num 23:19; Job 12:13–16; Ps 33:11–12; Prov 19:21; Isa 14:24, 27; 43:13; 46:10; Mal 3:6; Luke 22:22; Acts 2:23; Rom 8:37; Heb 6:17; Jas 1:17). God does not alter his eternal plans; what he decrees, he carries out. As discussed in chapter 19, although Scripture speaks of God changing his mind, this has more to do with change in the creature. As Scripture repeatedly teaches: "the Eternal One of Israel does not lie or change his mind, for he is not man who changes his mind" (1 Sam 15:29).

Eighth, God's plan is unconditional, and it includes human free actions (Isa 44:28; 46:8–11; John 6:37, 44; cf. 15:16; Acts 2:23; Rom 9:11–13; Eph 2:8–10). The *unconditionality* of God's decree means that it is "based on nothing outside of God that moved him to choose one thing or another" given his triune self-sufficiency.[86] In reference to humans, God's plan includes both election and reprobation. Let us think about each of these significant concepts in turn.[87]

Election is the "eternal act of God whereby He, in His sovereign good pleasure, and on account of no foreseen merit in [us], chooses a certain number of [people] to be the recipients

---

[85] Berkhof lists some of the means that God decrees to guarantee his ends without removing the reality of secondary causes and agents. For example, in the case of humans, the decree ordains: "(a) That the agent shall be a free agent. (b) That his antecedents and all the antecedents of the act in question shall be what they are. (c) That all the present *conditions* of the act shall be what they are. (d) That the act shall be perfectly spontaneous and free on the part of the agent. (e) That it shall be certainly future. Ps. 33:11; Prov. 19:21; Isa. 46:10." *Systematic Theology*, 104.

[86] Feinberg, *No One Like Him*, 527.

[87] Election and reprobation will only be discussed briefly for sake of completion. In volume 2, in our discussion of soteriology, we will discuss them in more detail.

of special grace and of eternal salvation."[88] This definition of election, especially regarding its unconditional nature, is what we see in Scripture. Four statements will unpack this truth.

1. God's decree includes his *specific* choice of people to salvation while *permitting* others to go their own way and not to experience salvation in Christ (Deut 7:7–10; 10:14–15; Ps 33:12; Matt 22:14; 24:22, 24, 31; Luke 18:6–8; John 6:37–40; Rom 8:28–33; Col 3:12; 1 Thess 1:4; 5:9; 2 Thess 2:13; Titus 1:1–2; 1 John 4:19; Rev 17:14). The relation of election to reprobation in God's decree is an asymmetrical one. Furthermore, although election has a corporate element to it (e.g., God chose the nation of Israel for his redemptive purposes, Deut 4:37; 7:6–7; 10:15; Rom 9:1–5), election is first God's choice of a specific people to salvation (Rom 9–11, especially 9:6–9, 14–18; note 11:1–6 and the use of the singular and the distinction between the elect within Israel).[89]

2. Election is God's *gracious* choice of individuals to salvation. Election is found in God's eternal love and choice of a people for himself, hence the use of "foreknowledge" in relation to election (Rom 8:29). God, who is rich in mercy (Eph 2:4), "loved us and saved us not *because* but *despite* our being miserable."[90] Ephesians 1:3–14 beautifully teaches this truth, especially in verses 4–6. Paul teaches that "before the foundation of the world" (v. 4), the Father chose us (the elect), that is, specific individuals in Christ. Why did God elect us? What is his goal in doing so? The Father chose us to redeem us from our sin and guilt in Christ (1:7–10). Indeed, God chose us in our fallen state "to be holy and blameless before him" (v. 4 ESV) and to become his adopted sons in Christ Jesus (v. 5). But what is the *basis* of our election? It is not our foreknown faith but the Father's love for us—"In love he predestined us" (v. 5 ESV), which is *ultimately* based on "the good pleasure of his will, to the praise of his glorious grace" (vv. 5–6).

3. God's election of individuals is *unconditional*. Our election is not based on any foreknown faith or goodness in us (Rom 9:10–13, 15–16; 10:20; 1 Cor 1:26–29; Eph 1:11–12; 2:8–10; 2 Tim 1:8–10; 2 Thess 2:13–14; 1 Pet 1:1–2). Underneath this teaching are two biblical truths. First, God's plan is not dependent on the creature; it is the result of his free choice

---

[88] Berkhof, *Systematic Theology*, 114. Italics removed.

[89] See Vos, *Reformed Dogmatics*, 1:110–15; cf. Schreiner, *Romans*, 482–93 (see chap. 6, n. 62); Moo, *Epistle to the Romans*, 570–88 (see chap. 6, n. 67).

[90] Vos, *Reformed Dogmatics*, 1:133.

(Pss 115:3; 135:6; Isa 40:10–14; 46:9–11; Rom 11:33–36; Eph 1:5–6, 9, 11). Second, given the nature of human sin and its impact on us, apart from God's sovereign and gracious choice, we cannot *and* will not respond to God apart from his effectual grace at work in us (Gen 6:5–6; 8:21; Jer 17:9; Mark 7:21–23; John 3:3; Rom 8:7–8; Eph 2:1–3). Thus, given what Scripture teaches about our human inability and desire not to respond, either election, as Vos notes, "depends on God or it depends on man who will be saved. If one chooses the first, then one has accepted predestination."[91] But if one chooses the latter, humans either have an inherent ability that sin did not affect (Pelagianism) or God gives universal sufficient grace (i.e., prevenient) to all people. But both options result in humans becoming the *pivotal* appliers of Christ's work, which has no biblical warrant.[92]

It is on the *unconditional* nature of election that Calvinists and Arminians divide. Arminian theology appeals to the use of "foreknowledge" in Rom 8:28–30 to warrant their conditional view. But, as we discuss below, "foreknowledge" in Romans 8 is best understood as God fore-loving us. Thus, when God foreknows us, it means that he has chosen us on the basis of his grace (Rom 8:29; 11:2; 1 Pet 1:2, 20), not our foreknown faith. Attempts to deny the unconditional and individual nature of divine election, especially in Romans 9, is nigh impossible.[93] Let us make a number of points regarding Romans 9 given its importance in grasping the nature of election.

In context, as Paul wrestles with why many of his fellow Israelites did not believe in their Messiah (vv. 1–5), he unequivocally reminds us that God's word and promises have not failed. Instead, he offers two complimentary reasons why many Israelites did not believe: first, God never promised that every ethnic Israelite would be saved (9:6–23), and second, many Israelites did not respond to Christ due to their own responsible and culpable unbelief (9:30–10:21). In this way, Romans 9–10 does not pit divine sovereignty and human responsibility against each other; instead, it upholds both of them simultaneously, tied to God's ultimate plan and purposes.

As the first reason is developed, it is evident that God's election to salvation is *gracious* and *unconditional*. As Paul walks through redemptive history, he reminds us that God has always chosen a people for himself based on his sovereign grace alone. Although all of Abraham's

[91] Vos, 1:98.

[92] On this point, see Vos, 1:98.

[93] See Schreiner, *Romans*, 482–511; Moo, *Romans*, 570–609.

descendants benefited from God's covenant with him, this did not mean that each descendant was one of God's elect, as evidenced by God's unconditional choice of Isaac over Ishmael (vv. 7–9) and Jacob over Esau (vv. 10–13). In our discussion of the biblical covenants in part 3, we noted that the OT covenants were "mixed"; that is, they were constituted by believers/elect and non-believers/non-elect. God's historical election of Abraham and his family, and the nation of Israel, did not entail that every individual within the covenant community experienced salvation, thus Paul's reminder that "not all who are descended from Israel are Israel," (v. 6). What the OT covenants reveal is that God specifically chose his people from within the covenants, and it is these people that constitute God's elect/people throughout the ages. But Paul is also clear regarding the basis of God's choice: it is not based on any foreknown condition in us; instead, it is solely due to his own choice, grace, and mercy. In fact, we know this is so for the following two reasons.

First, Paul teaches that God's choice of the elect to salvation is not based on any foreknown condition in us. This is underscored by God's choice of Jacob over Esau before they were born and before they had done anything good or bad (v. 11). In other words, God's promise to bless Jacob and to overturn Esau's primogeniture status was prior to their existence and not based on any condition in them. Instead, it was based solely on "God's purpose according to election" (*kat' eklogēn prosthesis tou theou*, v. 11) and "God's calling" (*ek tou kalountos*, v. 12, author's translation). Tom Schreiner is correct when he asserts that "any attempt to explain the promise to Jacob on the basis of God's foresight of Jacob's good works turns the text upside down."[94]

Second, Paul's response to potential objections proves that election is unconditional. For example, after discussing God's gracious election of Isaac and Jacob over Ishmael and Esau, a potential question is raised: "Is there injustice with God?" (v. 14). But this question only makes sense if election is unconditional! Since God does not elect people on the basis of any condition in them but his free choice (vv. 11–12), this question naturally arises. Also, it is instructive to note Paul's answer to the question. Instead of appealing to divine foreknowledge of our future choices, he answers the question by quoting Exod 33:19: "I will show mercy to whom I will show mercy, and I will have compassion on whom I will have compassion" (v. 15). Paul then adds further commentary: "it does not depend on human will or effort but

[94] Schreiner, *Romans*, 488.

on God who shows mercy" (v. 16). Again, this answer only makes sense if election is unconditional. Schreiner is right to conclude that Paul's emphasis in Romans 9 is on "God's sovereign freedom" and that "what is fundamental for God is the revelation of his glory and the proclamation of his name, and he accomplishes this by showing mercy and by withholding it. God's righteousness is upheld because he manifests it by revealing his glory both in saving and in judging."[95] Thus, in Paul's answer, there is never a hint that God's election is based on foreknown faith or any condition in us; instead, it is based on God's own free, sovereign, and gracious choice.

The same point is taught in the second question raised in v. 19. After describing how God raised up Pharoah for his sovereign purposes, another question is asked: "Why then does he [God] still find fault? For who can resist his will?" Again, this question only makes sense if election is unconditional, since Paul could have simply appealed to our choices to reply to the question. But instead of doing so, he appeals to the image of the potter, which underscores God's sovereign right as the Creator and Lord to govern his world according to *his* prerogatives, which in the end, supremely display his own glory, power, and justice (vv. 20–23).

For these reasons, Romans 9 is best understood as teaching that God's election of a people for himself is gracious and unconditional. This does not entail that Paul rejects our responsible agency, since Rom 9:30–10:21 underscores this point. Nor should we think of God's election of some to salvation and his passing by others as on the same level. But it does underscore that in God's decree, including God's gracious election of his people to salvation, it is unconditional.

4. Scripture teaches that we only come to know God's election of us when we repent and believe (Acts 13:48; Rom 10:13–15a; 2 Thess 2:13; 2 Tim 2:10; 2 Pet 1:5–11; 1 John 4:19). Election does not negate the necessity for repentance and faith; it establishes the possibility of both. Also, in our Christian lives, God's election of us does not make us inactive but active as the Spirit works in us to conform us to Christ, our covenant head (Phil 2:12–13; cf. Rom 6:1–14).

Reprobation, on the other hand, is the theological term that refers to the "eternal decree of God whereby He has determined to pass some by with operations of His special grace, and to punish them for their sins, to the manifestation of His justice."[96] Three statements will unpack

---

[95] Schreiner, 496–97.

[96] Berkhof, *Systematic Theology*, 116. Italics removed.

God's passing by of some and allowing them to remain in their sin, which is technically known as "preterition" (Lat. *praeterire*, "to pass by").[97]

1. We must distinguish between God's decree of "preterition" and God's "condemnation" of our sin. Preterition is not the cause of our sin; we are. Our "condemnation" is due to our action; we are without excuse.[98] All people are justly responsible for their sin according to God's absolute moral demand, which is known in both natural and special revelation. Withholding of grace is due to God's choice, but God is not obligated to save anyone or display his saving grace. But again, God's decree is not the cause of our sin. What God has decreed will occur, but within his decree are the means to bring about God's ends, which includes our secondary agency. God's decree does not remove our choices; instead, it establishes them.

2. In the decree, we must stress the *asymmetrical* relation between election and preterition.[99] God does not have to save anyone; his display of grace is free and sovereign. But in the case of the non-elect, he has chosen to allow them to continue in their sin and fallen state, underscoring the permissive nature of "preterition." God does not delight in the death of the wicked (Ezek 33:11). But also God has not chosen to redeem all people, ultimately for reasons known only to him, but which are morally sufficient, wise, and for his own glory. Yet God's choice to "pass by" some is not exactly the same as his direct choice of some to salvation.[100]

3. What God decrees is always good and ultimately for his own name and glory. Given that sin and evil are always contrary to God's will and holy nature, Bavinck rightly insists that "[sin and evil] can therefore have been willed by God only as a means to a different, better, and

---

[97] On these points, see Turretin, *Institutes of Elenctic Theology*, 1:380–90.

[98] On this point, see Beeke and Smalley, *Reformed Systematic Theology*, 1:992.

[99] The asymmetrical relation of election to preterition is taught in Rom 9:22–23. By the use of the active voice in "he prepared beforehand" (*proētoimasen*) his elect for glory (v. 23) in contrast to those who "were prepared" (*katērtismena*, passive voice) for destruction (v. 22), God's election of some and non-election of others is not in the same way. On this point, see Schreiner, *Romans*, 509–11. Election *and* preterition are part of God's decree to display the full range of his attributes and glory, but as Schreiner notes, "God's ultimate purpose is to display his glory to all people. His glory is exhibited through both wrath and mercy, but especially through mercy" (*Romans*, 511).

[100] God's "passing by" of some is more indirect. Jesus speaks of his people in direct terms (John 10:14–15 NIV: "my sheep know me" or "I lay down my life for the sheep") and those who are not his people in indirect terms (John 10:26). Paul can distinguish between the "elect" and "others" (Rom 11:7), or a specific number of people in the book of life versus "everyone whose name was not written" (Rev 13:8), which is not exactly the same kind of relationship.

greater good. There is even a big difference between election and reprobation."[101] Thus, in election, God chooses for his own glory and name, and in it he takes great delight. But in allowing for sin and preterition, sin is never good; "it only becomes a good inasmuch as, contrary to its own nature, it is compelled by God's omnipotence to advance his honor. It is a good indirectly because, being subdued, constrained, and overcome, it brings out God's greatness, power, and justice,"[102] and ultimately for the glory of God's triune name (Rom 9:17, 22–23; 11:36; 1 Cor 15:28) in the face of our Lord Jesus Christ (1 Cor 15:24f; Eph 1:9–10; Phil 2:9; Col 1:16).

Ninth, God's decree arises from the fullness of life within himself. God's decree cannot be considered apart from the perfection and fullness of God's triune life. As Scott Swain reminds us, "The decree arises from the love of the Father for the Son in the Spirit, which is its sole principle, and directs all things to the love of the Father for the Son in the Spirit, which is their supreme end."[103] For this reason, in reference to creation, God's decree is unconditioned because he is the triune God who has perfect life and knowledge "from himself." Yet, as Swain continues, God's decree is only conditioned by God himself, who freely chooses to share his eternal life and glory with that which is outside of him. This means, then, that the ultimate end of God's decree is the display of "the Father's love for the Son in the Spirit,"[104] as well as God's display of his own glory and to share himself with his people.

This truth is crucial to remember, especially in understanding how God's eternal love can be displayed in the judgment of sin. The answer is that although God's condemnation of sinners is just and "may not be an exhibition of love *toward those sinners*, it is nevertheless an exhibition of the Father's love *for the Son* (Ps. 2) and *for those who are elect in the Son* (Ps. 36:10–12)."[105] The ultimate end of God's decree, which includes both salvation and judgment, is to display God's own glory within himself. The Father by the Spirit displays the glory of his Son among God's people and exalts in his preeminence over all things due to who he is and what he does as the incarnate Son and our new covenant head (Eph 1:9–10; Col 1:15–20; Heb 1:1–3). We simply cannot fully grasp the nature, purpose, and goal of the decree apart from this point.

---

[101] Bavinck, *Reformed Dogmatics*, 2:398.

[102] Bavinck, 2:398.

[103] Swain, "Covenant of Redemption," 113–14. Italics removed.

[104] Swain, 115 n. 37.

[105] Swain, 115 n. 37 (emphasis original); cf. Christensen, *What About Evil?*, 287–316, who argues the same point.

Tenth, God's decree includes within it the "covenant of redemption" (the pactum salutis).[106] Scripture teaches that in God's plan, especially in relation to redemption, the triune God is inseparably at work, but with specific tasks appropriated to the divine persons. For example, election is ascribed to the Father within the divine economy (John 6:37), and it is the Father who elects us in Christ (Eph 1:4–6), but this is not reversible. In other words, Scripture never says that the Son elects us in the Father. Instead, a specific ordering (*taxis*) is at work in the economy that reflects the personal mode of subsistence of the Father and Son. Or the work of the Spirit is described as the one who applies Christ's work to us (John 16:5–15) by giving us new life and uniting us to Christ as our new covenant head (John 3:5–8; Rom 6:1–14; 8:1–17; Eph 1:13–14). Again, never does our Lord Jesus Christ unite us to the Spirit as our new covenant head. Why? Are the works appropriated to the divine persons simply arbitrary or planned? Although every external work of God is one, why do we see these appropriated works in the divine economy?

Reformed theology has answered by appealing to the "covenant of redemption"—an eternal covenant between the divine persons as the means by which God's decree of redemption is accomplished. So when Scripture teaches that the Father has chosen a people for the Son (John 6:37), and that the Son has been appointed as covenant head of his people (Ps 2:7–12; Jer 31:31–34; Ezek 34:23–25; Luke 1:31–33; 22:20; Acts 2:22–36; Rom 1:3–4; Heb 8–10), this is not something arbitrary but part of God's decree. Also, in this covenant, the Son's appointment to be our new covenant head is joyfully accepted, and hence the reason that the eternal Son takes on our humanity and becomes our obedient covenant keeper (Heb 2:5–18; 5:1–10; 10:5–10), the greater and last Adam (Rom 5:12–21), who by his obedience in his representative life and substitutionary death accomplishes our eternal redemption and justification (Rom 3:21–26; Heb 5:8–10; 9:15–28). In addition, the Spirit is appointed to anoint and equip the incarnate Son to accomplish his work *and* to apply Christ's work to us (John 14:26; cf. 15:26).[107] These agreed on works are consistent with the personal modes of subsistence, but in terms of God's external work of redemption, the covenant of redemption

---

[106] Vos, *Reformed Dogmatics*, 1:132. In what follows, we will refer to the *pactum salutis* as simply the *pactum*.

[107] On this understanding of the covenant of redemption, see Fesko, *Trinity and Covenant of Redemption*, 129–41; Swain, "Covenant of Redemption," 108–9.

helps explain the precise works the divine persons accomplish in God redeeming a people for himself. In the covenant of redemption, we discover how God's decree results in God's own glory so the entire creation and history of the world is for the revealing of God's people in Christ (1 Cor 3:21–23).

Although many have questioned whether there is a "covenant of redemption" within God's decree, there are strong biblical and theological reasons to affirm it.[108] But at least two major challenges have been raised. First, some argue that "an intertrinitarian 'covenant' with terms and conditions between Father and Son mutually endorsed before the foundation of the world is to extend the bounds of scriptural evidence beyond propriety."[109] For Robert Letham, since there are only two kinds of covenants in Scripture, royal-grant or suzerain-vassal, neither of these kinds of covenants can be applied to intra-trinitarian relations.[110] If they could, Letham argues that the *pactum* would be too "contractual," which is not true of God's inner life.[111] Second, others, including Letham, also insist that the covenant of redemption requires three wills in God instead of one, thus opening the door to a social understanding of the Trinity.[112] Thus, instead of affirming the *pactum*, we simply need to affirm "the eternal Trinitarian counsel,"[113] which amounts to something similar to the *pactum* but without these two attending problems. Four observations may be given in response to these two criticisms.

1. Letham's positive statement of God's eternal counsel is very similar to the *pactum*, despite his protestations to the contrary. For example, Letham argues that God's eternal counsel is that "the Father . . . chose in Christ the Son, that he would be the Head of his church and to that end become incarnate as a man, make atonement for sin, rise from the dead, ascend, and reign with the Father and the Holy Spirit in the indivisible unity of the Trinity forever."[114] He continues, "Since the Trinity is indivisible, the Father's choice was inseparably the Son's and the Spirit's too, for they have one will."[115] As for the Spirit, he states that

---

[108] See Fesko, 51–124; cf. Swain, 118–21.

[109] Robertson, *Christ of the Covenants*, 54 (see chap. 14, n. 58).

[110] Letham, *Systematic Theology*, 435–36 (see chap. 5, n. 1).

[111] Letham, 437.

[112] See Letham, 436.

[113] Letham, 438. Italics removed.

[114] Letham, 438.

[115] Letham, 438.

> the undivided Trinity also determined that the Holy Spirit should bring into effect this plan in inseparable working with the Father and the Son, by upholding the incarnate Son in his earthly life and ministry, raising him from the dead, granting faith to those elected to salvation, sustaining them in the course of their lives, and energizing the renewal of the cosmos.[116]

But in reading Letham's alternative to the *pactum*, it amounts to the same truth, except that it drops the language of "covenant," a point we will return to. But overall, there is basic agreement that God's election of a people is effected by the means of our Lord Jesus Christ, who is appointed as our mediator and our new covenant head, and that the work of the Spirit is to uphold the Son in his work and apply that work to his people.

2. Does the *pactum* entail three wills in God? This is a strange charge since those who have affirmed the *pactum* have also affirmed classic, pro-Nicene trinitarian theology (e.g., John Owen, Herman Bavinck, Geerhardus Vos, Louis Berkhof, and current proponents, such as John Fesko and Scott Swain). These theologians, both past and present, affirm the *pactum* and one will in God. As we discussed in chapter 18, pro-Nicene trinitarianism affirms that there is one will in God yet the divine persons share and act through the one will according to their eternal personal relations or modes of subsistence. As Swain correctly insists,

> Far from undermining orthodox trinitarian theology, therefore, the doctrine of the covenant of redemption should be seen as an application of orthodox trinitarian principles to the locus of God's eternal decree. Because the Son is consubstantial with the Father, God's redemptive will cannot be limited to the Father; the Son too must be the agent of God's redemptive will. Moreover, because the Son eternally proceeds from the Father in his personal manner of subsisting, so too does his personal manner of willing proceed from the Father. The Son's willing submission to the Father in the *pactum salutis* is thus a faithful expression of his divine filial identity.[117]

3. What about the use of "covenant" language? Obviously, one must be careful in this regard. Analogy must be preserved, and speaking of intra-trinitarian relations in terms of the divine

[116] Letham, 438.

[117] Swain, "Covenant of Redemption," 122; cf. Fesko, *Trinity and Covenant of Redemption*, 167–93.

counsel is not easy. Yet it is hard to avoid covenant language, especially in reference to God's external work of redemption. Scripture teaches that the Father has appointed the Son to be our new covenant head and mediator. Indeed, this is the mission he has received from his Father from eternity and now worked out in time (Mark 12:1–12; John 4:34; 5:30; 6:38; Gal 4:4; Heb 10:5–10). All of Christ's work is tied to his specific office as the great prophet, priest, and king, which cannot be understood apart from the biblical covenants. No doubt these covenants are directly tied to the historical unfolding of God's covenantal plan, culminating in the new covenant. But it is hard to make sense of the new covenant apart from grounding it in God's eternal plan, and the specific relations and roles that the divine persons enact in the divine economy. For this reason, it is legitimate to refer to the divine decree, as applied to redemption, in covenantal terms while also realizing we do so analogically. Swain is on the right track when he writes,

> though the Scriptures are relatively reticent to speak of the Son's *eternal appointment* by the Father in covenantal terms, the Scriptures speak quite liberally about the Son's *historical execution* of that appointment in covenantal terms. And this language, when coupled with other biblical teaching about the eternal nature of the Son's messianic appointment, constitutes sufficient biblical warrant for the doctrine of the covenant of redemption.[118]

4. Why is it important to affirm the *pactum*? For this reason: it helps us grasp better how God's decree, specifically regarding redemption, is worked out in history and how all of God's triune purposes are uniquely centered in and fulfilled in our Lord Jesus Christ (Eph 1:10–12; Col 1:15–20). Apart from the *pactum*, it is difficult to make sense of Christ's appointment as our mediator, the nature of his mediation as our covenant representative and substitute, and the specific roles each person of the Godhead carries out in our salvation. And with the *pactum*, we can see better the Christological focus of God's triune works. The Son is not only Lord over all things as the *eternal* Son (Col 1:15–17), but by the *pactum*, the Father has appointed the *incarnate* Son to be Lord over all things due to his new covenant work on our behalf. The Father's eternal plan to "head up" all things in Christ (Eph 1:9–10) entails that

[118] Swain, 120.

God's ultimate glory is displayed in the Father's love for his Son in the Spirit so that God is all in all (1 Cor 15:28).

These ten statements have sought to condense the breadth of the biblical teaching regarding God's decree, which is captured well by Joel Beeke and Paul Smalley in their helpful definition: "The divine decree is the eternal and sovereign purpose of the triune God, based upon his will alone according to his incomprehensible wisdom and goodness, that determines all persons, things, events, and relationships outside of himself for his manifest glory in Jesus Christ."[119]

Critique of Arminianism and Its View of the Divine Decree

The Arminian view of the divine decree centers on two intertwined areas: the nature of divine foreknowledge and the nature of human freedom. In three steps, let us look at each of these in turn by beginning with the Arminian understanding of the nature of human freedom.

First, using current definitions of "free will," Arminian theology embraces a libertarian view of human freedom.[120] As we discussed in chapter 16 regarding open theism, a libertarian view of freedom is "indeterministic," while its alternative, "compatibilism," is deterministic. At its heart, a libertarian view insists that a person is free if they are not causally determined by God or "any prior factors that influence our choices, including external circumstances, or motives, desires, character, and nature."[121] This does not mean that a person's choices are arbitrary. Reasons or causes affect our actions, but we are only free if none of these reasons *sufficiently* inclines or causally determines our will in one direction. *Why* we choose something is solely due to *our* choice, and to be free requires the categorical ability to do otherwise. Alvin Plantinga captures this sentiment in his definition of free will: "If a person is free with respect to a given action, then he is free to perform that action and free to refrain from performing it; no antecedent conditions and/or causal laws determine that he

[119] Beeke and Smalley, *Reformed Systematic Theology*, 1:969.

[120] See Olson, "Classical Free Will," 150; Bruce Reichenbach, "God Limits His Power," in Basinger and Basinger, *Predestination and Free Will*, 102; Cottrell, "The Nature of the Divine Sovereignty," 103–6; Walls and Dongell, *Why I Am Not a Calvinist*, 105 (see chap. 16, n. 61).

[121] Christensen, *What About Free Will?*, 6 (see chap. 4, n. 77).

will perform the action, or that he won't. It is within his power, at the time in question, to take or perform the action and within his power to refrain from it."[122] But given such a view of human freedom, a number of problems emerge, the first one being whether the concept of libertarian freedom is even "rational"?

Two questions must be answered in discussing the nature of human freedom: *Who* chooses and *why* did we choose what we chose? Both libertarian and compatibilist views answer the *who* question the same: *you* choose. But the two views differ on the *why* question. A libertarian view with the condition of freedom as the "ability to choose otherwise" suggests "that to be free, people must have an indifference about the choices they make such that they could have equally made alternative choices, being under no compulsion to choose one way or another."[123] Thus, there is no *sufficient* reason for our choices; otherwise, our choices are determined and not free.

But the problem with libertarianism is that without giving sufficient reasons for our choices, they seem to be "irrational" (i.e., without *sufficient* reasons). But how are we accountable for our choices? As Frame reminds us, when we hold people accountable for their actions, we evaluate the *reasons* and *motives* for their choices. For example, we distinguish between pre-meditated murder and self-defense due to one's motives and *why* a person acted the way he did. Frame continues:

> civil courts normally assume the opposite of libertarianism, namely, that the conduct of criminals arises from motives . . . if [a person's] action was completely independent of his character, desires, and motives, one could well ask in what sense this action was really [the person's action]. And if it was not [the person's] action, how can he be held responsible for it?[124]

In many ways, a libertarian view not only makes our choices ultimately arbitrary; it also views humans contrary to how God has created us to make choices according to our nature.[125] Our choices are not independent of our desires and affections, and there are factors that incline

[122] Plantinga, *God, Freedom, and Evil*, 29 (see chap. 16, n. 56).

[123] Christensen, *What About Evil?*, 95.

[124] Frame, *Doctrine of God*, 141.

[125] On this point, see Frame, 142.

our wills sufficiently in one direction so that *we* choose what we *want*. By contrast, a compatibilistic view of freedom can account for *why* we choose what we do and for our choices being in accordance with what we most want. No doubt, alternative choices are presented to us, but those choices are made *only* because there are alternative *reasons* for them that did not apply to the other options. Different factors (e.g., influences, desires, wants, circumstances, etc.) generate specific reasons that lead us to choose specific choices. Thus, contrary to a libertarian view, compatibilism is a "freedom of inclination," not indifference. We always choose according to our strongest inclination (desires, i.e., reasons) and the combination of various *sufficient* reasons leads us to choose one thing over another. A compatibilistic view, then, can make sense of *why* we choose what we do and also hold us *responsible* for our choices precisely because *we* choose them according to who we are. Without such a conception of freedom, freedom becomes incoherent, hence the charge that the concept of libertarian freedom is "irrational."

But for sake of argument, let us assume that libertarian freedom is a coherent concept. The next problem is trying to "fit" it with biblical teaching and known theological conclusions. As we discussed in chapter 4 on theological method, in our use of extrabiblical concepts in theology, we must evaluate those concepts according to Scripture. In this case, we must evaluate which view of freedom accounts for *all* of the biblical data *and* is consistent with other theological truths that we know from Scripture. By this standard, we discover that libertarian freedom creates more problems than it solves, and as such, it ought to be rejected. Here are some examples.

1. God does not have libertarian freedom.[126] As we discussed in chapter 18, God's will is consistent with the perfection of his holy nature, so we cannot conceive of God's freedom as the freedom of indifference or the "ability to do otherwise" contrary to his nature and will. God is holy, just, and righteous and necessarily so. "God is light, and there is absolutely no darkness in him" (1 John 1:5). God is true to himself; "he cannot deny himself" (2 Tim 2:13). Indeed, as the triune God of aseity, his existence, knowledge, and goodness are all "from himself." In regard to goodness, something is good not merely because God wills it, but because what God wills is true to his nature. This is why God *cannot* sin (Heb 6:18; Jas 1:13); he is *essentially* holy, just, and good. There is no possible world in which God can sin and act contrary to his nature. Nor does God's love within himself allow for the possibility of the Father,

---

[126] Christensen, *What About Evil?*, 95–97; cf. Bignon, *Excusing Sinners and Blaming God*, 105–20 (see chap. 16, n. 55).

Son, and Spirit acting contrary to their love for each other. God would not be God if he could act contrary to his nature.[127] But all of these truths assume that God, as the freest and most morally praiseworthy being for all of his actions, does not have libertarian freedom, but instead has freedom consistent with his *inability* to do otherwise.

2. Most Christians affirm that in our glorified state, we will be unable to sin (*non posse peccare*). Due to Christ's entire new covenant work, our union with him by the Spirit, and our glorification by resurrection and transformation, we will experience perfect freedom and never sin again (Rom 8:29; 1 John 3:2). But if so, it is difficult to think that we will have libertarian freedom since we will no longer be able to do otherwise. But if libertarianism is true, does this mean that in our glorified state we are no longer "free"? Scripture views our glorified state as the epitome of creaturely freedom, where we will glorify and obey God in perfect conformity to Christ. Such freedom is not libertarian but compatibilistic. As Frame observes, "So the highest state of human existence will be a state without libertarian freedom."[128] If libertarian freedom is not true of our final state, then it is also not true of freedom in general.

3. Libertarianism is difficult to reconcile with the biblical data on God's decree that teaches that God foreordains and knows all things, including our free actions (e.g., Ps 139:16; Isa 40–48; Dan 4:34–35; Eph 1:11). Scripture teaches that God ordains all things, including such things as natural phenomena, historical events, and what humans will do. Although God's decree is not the cause of all things, it is the guarantee that it will occur. But how can God *guarantee* that our free choices will occur? This assumes a robust view of dual agency that libertarianism renders problematic. Libertarian freedom cannot account for how God is able to decree all things with certainty yet in his decree guarantee that our secondary choices are free and responsible. In fact, given libertarianism, no matter how much God inclines someone's will toward what he planned, such inclination can never be *sufficient* to bring about God's decreed action. In Arminianism, God is only able to *guarantee* his will if our freedom is removed or he makes his plan dependent on what he foreknows we will do. But either way, libertarian freedom cannot account for the comprehensive, effectual, and immutable decree of God that includes our free agency.[129]

---

[127] Frame, *Doctrine of God*, 142.

[128] Frame, 141; cf. Christensen, *What About Evil?*, 98.

[129] Christensen, *What About Evil?*, 91–92.

4. Scripture teaches that God can foreordain *free* and *responsible* human actions (Gen 50:19–20; Isa 10:5–19; Acts 2:23). Arminianism rejects this as impossible. It teaches that God is able to foreknow what we will do, then he enacts it, but this is not the same as God foreordaining our *free* actions and thus infallibly knowing what we will do because he has decreed it. Instead, Arminianism distinguishes God's antecedent conditional will from his consequent will, making God's eternal plan conditioned on the creature.[130] But as we note below, if foreknowledge is truly maintained, it also renders human choices certain, just as much as the divine decree. Yet there is a built-in inconsistency in trying to maintain that God can foreknow future libertarian choices, hence the debate within Arminian theology over open theism.

5. Classical Arminianism, in agreement with Calvinism, affirms total or pervasive depravity, yet this is hard to reconcile with libertarian freedom. From Adam's sin, all humans are morally corrupted and spiritually unable and unwilling to seek after God and to do what is good (John 8:34; Rom 3:23; 5:12–21). Specifically, Paul says that due to our sin, we are "hostile to God because [we do] not submit to God's law," thus focusing on our willful sin. But Paul also says that we are "unable" to do so (Rom 8:7–8). Apart from God's election and effectually drawing us by the Spirit (John 6:37, 44) in Adam (i.e., in the "flesh"), and apart from the Spirit's work, we are "unable" to understand the things of God (1 Cor 2:14). A bad tree cannot bear good fruit (Matt 7:15–20). But if this is so (which classical Arminianism acknowledges), then according to libertarianism, in our sin, we are no longer free and responsible since we cannot do otherwise, that is, not sin. But Scripture does not teach that "in Adam" we are not free and responsible. Even in our fallen state, God holds us responsible for our sin, despite our inability to do otherwise.

In light of this, many libertarians move in one of two directions. First, some weaken the effects of sin on the human will, resulting in a semi-Pelagian view that thinks that our wills are able on their own to choose God apart from his work of grace, which is contrary to

[130] Arminianism conceives of God's antecedent and consequent will differently than Reformed theology. For the latter, the distinction between the two refers only to a logical order in God's decrees whereby God makes one thing subject to another as a means to an end. But for Arminianism, God's *antecedent* will is "established by God in indeterminacy," while the *consequent* is a "determinate application of it after God has first taken note of free human choice." Vos, *Reformed Dogmatics*, 1:22. Thus, by God's antecedent will, God decrees to redeem all who believe. But it is only after he knows who will believe that he decrees with his consequent will to give them salvation.

Scripture.[131] As Guillaume Bignon rightly argues, it is not enough to say that "humans *can* avoid sinning but merely *don't*, or just *happen* not to," since Scripture and classic Arminian theology teach that *fallen* humans are unable and unwilling to seek God.[132] Second, classical Arminianism alleviates the effects of sin by introducing the concept of prevenient grace.

Prevenient grace is a universal, sufficient grace given by God universally to all people that alleviates the effects of our moral and spiritual inability due to Adam's sin. As a result, all people are now able to "choose otherwise," which means that they now have a restored ability to repent of their sins and believe the gospel. Apart from prevenient grace, our libertarian freedom is crippled by sin, but due to prevenient grace, all people now are free to choose, and in reality, "no human being actually exists in that natural state."[133] The result of prevenient grace is to allow humans to be able to respond to God, hence the synergistic nature of Arminian theology. However, there are at least three problems with this view.

First, if prevenient grace restores all humans to libertarian freedom, then it would seem that "humans have the theoretical potential through the force of their will to act contrary to any evil desire."[134] No doubt, the probability of such a situation is low, but "libertarianism does make it possible to act so that moral alternatives always present themselves as live possibilities; otherwise, freedom is curtailed as well as responsibility."[135] Thus, if prevenient grace is true, it allows for the possibility that some human being could always obey fully. But if this is so, this not only contradicts the teaching of Scripture that continues to affirm the ongoing sin and depravity of the human heart, but it also comes close to embracing a form of Pelagianism.[136] Of course, Arminian theology rejects both options, but in so doing, it remains inconsistent with its affirmation of libertarian freedom, prevenient grace, and the doctrine of human depravity.[137]

---

[131] This point is made by Martin Luther, *The Bondage of the Will*, trans. J. I. Packer and O. R. Johnston (Grand Rapids: Revell, 2009), 174; cf. Bignon, *Excusing Sinners and Blaming God*, 133–54.

[132] Bignon, *Excusing Sinners and Blaming God*, 151.

[133] Olson, *Arminian Theology*, 154.

[134] Christensen, *What About Free Will?*, 144.

[135] Christensen, 144.

[136] On this point, see Bignon, *Excusing Sinners and Blaming God*, 144–54.

[137] For example, Olson affirms that even in spite of prevenient grace, all humans are "dead in sin by *nature*." *Arminian Theology*, 149. But if this is so, then humans are no longer free, given that libertarian

Second, it is difficult to maintain the Reformation truth of "grace alone" (*sola gratia*) since ultimately what determines whether one person responds to God is our human choice. Given that all people equally experience prevenient grace, the pivotal factor in the application of Christ's work to us is the human subject. God's grace is *necessary* for humans to respond to God for salvation, but it is not *sufficient* since we must exercise our libertarian free choice.[138] But this is hard to reconcile with biblical teaching that salvation is by grace alone, through faith alone, and that the entire work of grace, including our faith, is a gift of God (Eph 2:8–10).[139] Nowhere does Scripture make our human choices the distinguishing factor or the ultimate reason why one person believes while another does not.[140]

Third, the biblical evidence for prevenient grace is lacking.[141] Texts such as John 1:9 and 12:32, along with Titus 2:11, do not teach prevenient grace. In context, John 1:9 does not refer to universal enlightenment of all people, but to the light that has come in Christ, which exposes and reveals the moral and spiritual state of our hearts. John 3:19–20 later makes this point: "This is judgment: The light has come into the world, and people loved darkness rather than the light because their deeds were evil. For everyone who does evil hates the light and avoids it, so that his deeds may not be exposed."[142] Nor is the "drawing of all people" by the cross (John 12:32) prevenient grace since in context, the "all" refers to Jews and Greeks (v. 20) and thus "all without distinction." Furthermore, the "drawing" language hearkens back to John 6:37 (and v. 44), where the emphasis is on the Father "drawing" those whom he has given the Son to salvation. In John, "drawing" does not make salvation possible; instead, it makes it effectual.[143]

---

freedom demands that we must be able to act contrary to our desires, wants, and even the effects of human sin.

[138] Paul Helm, "The Augustinian-Calvinist View," in Beilby and Eddy, *Divine Foreknowledge*, 169–70 (see chap. 18, n. 135).

[139] In volume 2, we will discuss this point further in the section on soteriology or the doctrine of salvation.

[140] On this point, see Christensen, *What About Evil?*, 93–94.

[141] See Thomas R. Schreiner, "Does Scripture Teach Prevenient Grace in the Wesleyan Sense?," in Schreiner and Ware, *Still Sovereign*, 229–46.

[142] See Carson, *Gospel According to John*, 121–24, 207–8 (see chap. 5, n. 13).

[143] Carson, 290–94, 442–47. Likewise, Titus 2:11 says nothing about a prevenient grace that gives to all people the ability to believe. This makes the text say much more than it does. Instead, minimally, it says that God's grace has been manifested through the cross, but one cannot then formulate an entire

6. Scripture and Chalcedonian Christology affirm that our Lord Jesus Christ, as the incarnate Son, was impeccable; that is, he was unable to sin.[144] Yet this theological truth is hard to reconcile with a libertarian view of human freedom. Impeccability assumes that Christ not only freely chose not to sin, but that his free choice was compatible with his being unable to sin, which is a denial of libertarian freedom. Obviously, one can deny Christ's impeccability in order to uphold libertarian freedom, but this results in serious implications for one's view of Christ's person and work. Our point here is that libertarian freedom results in a redefinition of classic Christology.

7. Libertarian freedom also undercuts the *theological* grounds for Scripture's view of itself; that is, Scripture *is* God's infallible and inerrant word. In chapter 16, we discussed this problem in relation to open theism. Unlike open theism, Arminian theology affirms that God foreknows the future free actions of his creatures. This allows God to know all things in a comprehensive way. However, such a view still runs into problems regarding the doctrine of Scripture. For example, given divine timeless knowledge or simple foreknowledge, God may know the future, but he can do little to guarantee what he wants; instead, God's knowledge is dependent or conditioned on the creature. Middle knowledge offers more sovereign control since God is able to choose the possible world that best corresponds to his desires, yet his knowledge is still dependent on the creature. However, a biblical view of inspiration is much stronger than God merely knowing ahead of time what authors will write. Instead, a concursive view of inspiration assumes a robust view of dual agency so that God is able to *guarantee* what he wants written, and human authors freely write *his* word. Given libertarian freedom, how God can *guarantee* what the authors write is exactly *his* word is not easy to account for. Only middle knowledge offers God a choice in which world he creates, but even here, what is the likelihood that finite and fallen authors get everything right (both in terms of facts and interpretation of the facts) apart from a stronger view of divine control? Not surprisingly, the historic view of Scripture is accounted for better within a Reformed view of the divine decree and its enactment in divine providence.

Second, we now turn to the nature of divine foreknowledge. For Arminian theology, God's decree is *conditioned* on his eternal foreknowing of our choices, which entails a denial of God's

---

doctrine of prevenient grace on this verse, especially given that "calling" language in Paul is always effectual, something Arminian theology denies (e.g., Rom 8:28–30; 1 Cor 9, 22–24, 26).

[144] In volume 2, we will discuss this point further in the section on Christology.

aseity in his knowledge of our free choices. Arminian theology argues that divine foreknowledge (*prognōsis*) means "to know beforehand," which is warranted by an appeal to Rom 8:29: "For those he foreknew he also predestined to be conformed to the image of his Son." From this text, it is argued that God's decree is *based* on his *foreknowledge* of who would choose to believe in Christ. But there are at least three problems with this view and interpretation of the text.[145]

1. Scripture can speak of divine foreknowledge as "to know beforehand" (Acts 26:5; 2 Pet 3:17), but that is not its meaning in this context. In Romans 8, God's foreknowledge is directly tied to his will, purpose, predestination, and election, which is always an act of his good pleasure (Eph 1:4–6; cf. Acts 2:23). In this text, it does not simply mean "to know beforehand" as it does in other contexts, a point we will return to below.[146]

2. If one assumes the Arminian interpretation of foreknowledge, then humans become the ultimate "deciders"; God's decree becomes conditioned on his creatures. Predestination, then, simply means that God ratifies in advance what he foreknows will occur, but this is not predestination in any meaningful sense of the word. Also, foreknown faith becomes the *basis* by which God chooses people, but Scripture does not teach this. In fact, when foreknowledge has the sense of knowing ahead of time, its object is never foreknown faith, especially in election. Instead, faith is the result of election, and a gift of God's initiative and effectual grace (John 6:44; Eph 1:4, 2:8–10; Acts 13:48; Phil 1:29; 1 Thess 1:2–4). For the Arminian interpretation to stand, a different view of God's aseity, divine grace, and acceptance of prevenient grace must be embraced, which on all three counts are problematic.

3. Specifically, Rom 8:29 speaks of God foreknowing *the person*, a concept that is rooted in the OT. In the OT, "to know" (Heb. *yada'*) a person speaks of a personal knowledge, and in reference to God, his covenant love for his people.[147] Thus, to foreknow is to set one's love on a person (cf. Gen 18:19; Exod 2:25; 33:17; Pss 1:6; 144:3; Jer 1:5; Hosea 13:5; Amos 3:2; Matt 7:23; 1 Cor 8:3; Gal 4:9; 2 Tim 2:19; 1 John 3:1). When God foreknows the person, it means that he has *chosen* individuals on the basis of his grace (Rom 8:29; 11:2; 1 Pet 1:2, 20).[148] The emphasis on God's choice is also in 1 Pet 1:20. Here Christ is the object of "foreknowledge"

---

[145] For a development of these points, see Baugh, "The Meaning of Foreknowledge," 183–200; Schreiner, *Romans*, 443–47.

[146] Feinberg, *No One Like Him*, 519–26.

[147] See Vos, *Reformed Dogmatics*, 1:105–6; cf. Feinberg, *No One Like Him*, 525.

[148] See Vos, 1:102–3, for a discussion of these texts.

(*proginōskō*), specifically according to his incarnation. Since the incarnation was decreed and planned from eternity, it makes no sense to say the Father "foreknew ahead of time" Christ's human nature independent of his will. Vos says it this way: "What is a result cannot at the same time be a ground or source. Therefore, it is certain that here this foreknowledge cannot be considered foresight of something that already existed for God outside His counsel."[149]

This understanding of foreknowledge fits the context of Romans 8. Paul's point is that for the elect, God is sovereignly working out everything for their good (v. 28), from his foreknowledge of them to their ultimate glorification (vv. 29–30). The focus, then, is on God's setting his love on specific persons and not merely a corporate body.[150] Verse 29 explains the purpose of God's foreknowledge and predestination of his people: "to be conformed to the image of his Son, so that he would be the firstborn among many," which, as Tom Schreiner rightly notes "signals the fulfillment of the Abrahamic covenant, in which 'all nations' are blessed in Abraham (Gen. 12:3)."[151] Now in Christ Jesus, God's firstborn Son, the last Adam and true Israel, by God's electing love, we have been brought into union with Christ, and restored to the purpose of our creation. In verse 30, after describing God's purpose in foreknowing and predestinating us, Paul then resumes "the golden chain" of verbs from verse 29, where God is the subject of each verb: God predestined, then called, then justified, and then glorified. Calling, in this context, is an effectual call, something Arminian theology denies. In fact, Arminian interpretation thinks of calling here solely as God's general call to salvation, to which we are to respond.

However, the entire chain of verbs denies such an interpretation. The point is that in eternity, God chose us to be in Christ, so it is guaranteed that in history we will be brought to saving faith and ultimately to our glorification. God's plan will not be thwarted, which grounds our confidence that "God works everything for good because the God who set his covenant love on them, predestined them to be like his Son, called them effectually to himself, and justified them will certainly glorify them."[152] Romans 8:28–30, in context, simply does not bear the weight that Arminian theology places on it for their view of the divine decree.

---

[149] Vos, 1:103.

[150] Schreiner, *Romans*, 444.

[151] Schreiner, 445.

[152] Schreiner, 447; cf. Vos, *Reformed Dogmatics*, 1:101–2, who makes this same point.

Third, as discussed in chapter 19 regarding the divine foreknowledge and human freedom problem, Arminian theology creates more problems than it solves. God's knowledge of the future renders it guaranteed and certain for both classic Arminian and Calvinist theology. Indeed, as Bavinck notes, "all Christian churches and theologians confess that all things exist, happen, and reach their destiny in accordance with God's eternal knowledge."[153] But the problem with the Arminian view is that in its embrace of libertarian freedom, it has a difficult time explaining *how* God is able to foreknow the future with certainty. No doubt, Arminian theologians rightly affirm God's exhaustive foreknowledge of future free actions, but their *theological* explanation as to *how* God does so is problematic. If God actually knows what *will* (not just might) occur in the future, the future must be set. No doubt, God's knowledge is not the *cause* of the future, but it *guarantees* that what God knows must occur, regardless of how it is brought about. But the options they provide (e.g., timeless knowledge, simple foreknowledge, and middle knowledge), as discussed in the previous chapter, do not succeed. At the heart of the problem is that they render the Creator dependent on the creature, which Scripture does not teach.

No doubt, questions remain regarding God's decree and *how* God is able to plan all things, including our free choices, while they still remain free. Questions also remain regarding God's decree of good and evil and how creatures are responsible for sin while God is not. In chapters 22–23, we will return to some of these questions in our discussion of divine providence, but at this juncture, our conclusion is that the Arminian view of the divine decree does not account for all of the biblical data, and theologically, it creates more problems than it solves.

The Order of the Divine Decree[154]

Before we conclude our treatment of the divine decree, there is one last theological issue to discuss. Is there a specific ordering of the decree? In historical theology, especially within Reformation and post-Reformation theology, this question has stimulated much debate. The focus of the debate centers on the "logical" ordering of God's plan and where

---

[153] Bavinck, *Reformed Dogmatics*, 2:379.

[154] See Berkhof, *Systematic Theology*, 118–25; Bavinck, *Reformed Dogmatics*, 2:382–92; Beeke and Smalley, *Reformed Systematic Theology*, 1:1024–29; Feinberg, *No One Like Him*, 531–36.

God's decree of election and reprobation stand in relation to the decree of the fall. Logical ordering speaks of what comes "first" in terms of priority but without reference to time. Temporal or chronological ordering refers to cause-and-effect relationships that occur in time.[155] Regarding God's decree, it is true that the effects of God's decree unfold in time. But logical ordering refers to what is logically "first" in God's "putting together" his eternal plan. God is eternal and not subject to time or succession of moments. God decrees all things in one simple act that is immediate, instantaneous, and comprehensive, but not successive.[156] Thus, what is at debate in this discussion is what has logical priority in God's eternal decree.

The discussion of the ordering of God's decree has been debated in soteriology and in discussions over the extent of the atonement. But since these doctrinal areas assume prior theological commitments, this discussion is first located in the nature of the divine decree. Basically, there are three different views within Reformed theology (supralapsarian, infralapsarian, and Amyraldian),[157] with Arminian theology serving as a fourth view. But since Arminian theology conditions the divine decree on divine foreknowledge, the ordering of the divine decree takes on a different cast than in Reformed thought.

Within Reformed theology, although there are three views, the two dominant ones are supralapsarianism and infralapsarianism, with the latter serving as the majority view.[158] The *supralapsarian* view argues that the decree of election and reprobation of individuals is

[155] In the doctrine of salvation, the question of *logical* priority also surfaces. Arminians and Calvinists differ on what is logically prior in the application of Christ's work to us. Does faith "precede" regeneration (Arminian view), or does regeneration "precede" faith (Calvinist view)? Since most acknowledge that regeneration and faith are simultaneous in time, the question is which has logical priority, which accents differences regarding the two views. Arminian theology affirms that the application of salvation is synergistic, while Calvinists affirm it is monergistic.

[156] On this point, see our discussion of divine omniscience in chapter 19.

[157] Muller, *Dictionary of Latin and Greek*, 292 (see chap. 8, n. 37).

[158] Many argue that Calvin was infralapsarian. For example, see Calvin's reasoning in *Institutes*, 3.23.9, 11 (2:957–58, 959–60). He views the elect and the non-elect as equally guilty, but God chooses to demonstrate his grace to the elect and to allow the non-elect to go their own way and thus receive just condemnation for their sin. Yet, in other places, he argues that God decreed sin, although he is not responsible for it, for a greater good and that God's willing of it was "prior" to the fall. The ultimate cause of election and reprobation, then, is God's will, which is similar to a supralapsarian view. See *Institutes*, 1.18.2 (1:231–32); 3.23.1–2, 7–8 (2:947–50, 955–57).

logically "prior" to or "above" (*supra*) the decree of creation and the decree to permit the fall (*lapsus*, "fall"), thus following a more teleological order in thinking about God's decree. The *infralapsarian* view insists that the decree of election and reprobation is "after" or "below" (*infra*) God's decree to create and allow the fall, thus following the Bible's redemptive-historical order of creation, fall, and redemption. In one sense, the *supra* view subsumes all of God's decrees under predestination to demonstrate God's virtues and glory in all of his external acts. It answers the question of why God allowed the fall by insisting that God has done so to display all of his glorious perfections in both salvation and judgment. By contrast, the *infra* view restricts predestination and the positive election of fallen creatures and the "passing by" of others to *below* God's decree to create and permit the fall. In so doing, it stresses that election and preterition are always viewed in terms of a *fallen* humanity, thus accenting God's free, sovereign, and gracious choice and choosing to leave unexplained why God has ordained the fall. But as Bavinck wisely notes, in the end, both the *supra* and *infra* view agree that ultimately God has decreed and planned all things, including the fall, for his own glory.[159]

The Amyraldian view is identified with Moïse Amyraut (1596–1664). This view follows the basic ordering of the *infra* view but gives logical priority to God's decree that all who believe in Christ will be saved. Within this "first" decree, God intends to provide a universal atonement for all people. But given our sin, God knows that he must graciously and unconditionally elect a people for himself and effectively bring them to saving faith by the Spirit's work. This view has direct implications for the extent of atonement debate, an issue we will discuss under Christology and the doctrine of Christ's work.

Supralapsarian View	Infralapsarian View	Amyrauldian View	Arminian View
Decree to reveal God's virtues in mercy, justice	Decree to create humans	Decree to create humans	Decree to create humans
Decree to elect some to salvation and to condemn others to judgment to show his mercy and justice	Decree to permit all humans to fall into sin	Decree to permit all humans to fall into sin	God foreknows humans will fall given their libertarian freedom

[159] Bavinck, *Reformed Dogmatics*, 2:385.

Decree to create both the elect and non-elect Decree to permit the fall	Decree to elect some fallen humans to salvation and to allow other fallen humans to go their own way	Decree that Christ's atonement makes possible the salvation of all people (universal, unlimited)	Decree that Christ's atonement makes possible the salvation of all people (universal, unlimited)
Decree to send Christ to redeem the elect by his work (particular, limited)	Decree to send Christ to redeem the elect by his work (particular, limited)	Decree to elect some fallen humans to salvation since no one believes apart from God's initiative and grace	God elects those he foreknows will cooperate with his universal, sufficient, prevenient grace
Decree to send the Spirit to apply Christ's work to the elect in regeneration, justification, glorification	Decree to send the Spirit to apply Christ's work to the elect in regeneration, justification, glorification	Decree to send the Spirit to apply Christ's work to the elect in regeneration, justification, glorification	God foreknows who will resist his prevenient grace, which results in their judgment

How should we evaluate this debate? Although this debate loomed large in historical theology, some today are more skeptical about it. For example, John Frame considers the entire discussion too speculative since Scripture does not give us a specific order of God's thoughts. Also, he fears that if we are not careful, we will think of God's decree as sequential, which it is not. Yet Frame admits that Scripture can refer to God's priorities in his decree. Minimally, we can say that God has decreed all things for "his own glory" and that the "eternal blessing of the elect in Christ is certainly an important means to that goal, and may itself be described as the goal of history."[160] As such, it is legitimate to think about God's ultimate purpose in his plan although God's has not exhaustively revealed this to us.

In reflecting on the debate, Berkhof's discussion is also helpful. He correctly points out that the *supra* and *infra* views are really answering different questions and considering the mystery of God's ways from different points of view, both of which are important.[161] As noted, the *supra* view thinks of God's decree by focusing on the "ideal or teleological," while the *infra*

[160] Frame, *Doctrine of God*, 338–39.

[161] Berkhof, *Systematic Theology*, 124, makes the point that each view considers the mystery of God's ways from a different aspect.

view focuses on "the historical, order of the decrees."[162] The *supra* view reminds us that God's decree is one with an ultimate goal, namely God's glory.[163] The *infra* view also reminds us that although God's decree is one, we can think of it as "differentiated with a view to [its] objects . . . that the purpose of creation and the fall is not exhausted by their being means to a final end; and that sin was above all and primarily a catastrophic disturbance of creation, one which of and by itself could never have been willed by God."[164] Thus, both views have something to contribute to our thinking about God's decree. Scripture is clear: God's ultimate goal is for his own glory, and he has chosen the means of creation, fall, redemption, and judgment to reveal this. But we must also be careful in saying "why he chose precisely this means and not another, why he planned the destruction of many and not the salvation of all."[165] We must learn to speak where Scripture speaks, but be silent where Scripture does not speak.

Recently, Scott Christensen has offered some helpful theological reflections on the debate.[166] Technically, his view is neither *supra* nor *infra*, although it incorporates truth from both views. Instead, he proposes that we think of God's decrees in terms of three truths of Scripture. First, "God's ultimate end is delighting in the magnificence of his own glory." Second, "God is in no way required to display his glory outside the intra-Trinitarian self-delight it elicits." Third, "God freely chose to create the world in order that he might have a theater to display and thus share the delight of his own glory with his intelligent creatures, especially human beings."[167]

As Christensen "puts together" these three truths, he then asks: "How did God deem it best to magnify his glory to those creatures?"[168] He answers: God deemed it best to magnify his own glory to his creatures by the redemption of his creation and his people in the incarnation and work of our Lord Jesus Christ. But as he points out, this entails that the fall, as horrendous as sin and evil are and contrary to God's being, was necessary to accomplish this goal for the greater good of displaying God's glory. In God's purposes, he decreed that his glory is best

---

[162] Berkhof, 124.

[163] Bavinck, *Reformed Dogmatics*, 2:391.

[164] Bavinck, 2:391; cf. Berkhof, *Systematic Theology*, 124, who makes the same point.

[165] Bavinck, 2:386.

[166] Christensen, *What About Evil?*, 461–71.

[167] Christensen, 466.

[168] Christensen, 466.

magnified "in the juxtaposition of creation, fall, and redemption."[169] But as Christensen notes, "the accent never rests on evil (the fall), but always on redemption's triumph over it."[170] Yet the fall is permitted by God; even the passing over of some is to magnify God's greater glory, although this in no way removes the responsibility of the creature. Thus, at the center of God's glorification of himself is the person and work of our Lord Jesus Christ so that the accent of God's plan is on redemption. In this way, Christensen suggests that

> the incarnation of Christ is the more proper focus of the traditional order of the divine decree, not the election of saints per se. This is a departure from the way that older supralapsarians have conceived of the decree, in which it appears that the accent is on election while the broader motif of redemption, and especially the cross and resurrection, appears as a secondary concern.[171]

Christensen concludes that God's triune glory is most magnified in Christ's glorious work, which results in the redemption of God's people. All of this requires that the fall and divine judgment were also ordained means by which God's ultimate glory in Christ is displayed. In stating it this way, Christensen proposes a way to think of the ordering of God's decree that does not fit nicely into either the *supra* or *infra* category but instead focuses on "the greater end of magnifying God's glory in the redemptive work of Christ whereby he brings about our rescue from evil's dark domain (Col. 1:13–14)."[172] In this way, God in himself and in all of his triune glory remains center stage, and all of God's plan and purposes are first to glorify himself, with the truly amazing benefit to his people, so that always and forever God is all in all (1 Cor 15:28).[173] To think otherwise is to make something created more ultimate than God, which is

---

[169] Christensen, 468.

[170] Christensen, 468.

[171] Christensen, 469.

[172] Christensen, 470.

[173] In our discussion of God's glory in chapter 19, we distinguished between God's intrinsic (*ad intra*) and extrinsic (*ad extra*) glory. For the former, it is not optional for God to pursue his own glory; his glory is who he is in himself. This is why God cannot deny himself; he must uphold his own name, glory, and fame. On this point, see Morgan, "Toward a Theology," in Morgan and Peterson, *Glory of God*, 153–87 (see chap. 16, n. 18). Morgan argues that although God's extrinsic glory that is displayed in his works is magnificent, "it never fully expresses the fullness of God's intrinsic glory that he

not only out of step with Scripture but the entire Christian tradition.[174] This is God's universe, and *he* is at the center of it, not humans or anything created. Yet God has chosen to display his glory to us, and to share his own life with his people. "Not to us, O LORD, not to us, / but to your name give glory" (Ps 115:1).

Concluding Reflection

In this chapter, we began to think of God's triune glory displayed in his external works, hence the emphasis on divine action. However, to think rightly about God's *ad extra* works, we must tie his temporal actions to his eternal decree and plan for all things, including his people.

We are now in a position to tie God's decree and eternal plan to his external works of creation and providence, which is the subject of the next two chapters. Creation is properly viewed as the temporal enactment of God's decree and the *origination* of God's good work with respect to the world and all things in it. This universe is not here by accident, nor is it merely an emanation or outflow of God. Instead, the world is real, and it has come to exist by the spoken word of the triune Creator and Lord, who has created a stage to serve as the theater of his glory. Providence is also an external act by which God *preserves* and *governs* all things subsequent to his having made them. Providence, then, properly understood is the outworking of God's eternal plan *in time* in relation to the world he has made. Providence reminds us that our triune Creator is also our *covenant* God as the one who is always present, active, and involved with the world that he has made, in contrast to deism and other false views of the God-world relationship. With this in mind, let us now turn to thinking through God as the triune Creator and providential Lord.

---

communicates" (163–64). And ultimately, God's triune glory is displayed and centered in Christ's entire person and work, which entails that God's decree is for the ultimate end of displaying his own glory.

[174] Bavinck argues that the church throughout the ages has "almost unanimously [taught] that the glory of God is the final goal of all God's works." *Reformed Dogmatics*, 2:433. This is true to Scripture. Repeatedly, God's glory is given as the ultimate reason for God's creation, rule, and redemption of the world (e.g., Pss 96:3; 108:5; 145:11–12; Isa 6:3; 40:5; 42:8; 48:11; Rom 11:36; 16:27; 1 Cor 8:6; Gal 1:5; Eph 3:21; Phil 4:20; Col 1:15–20; 1 Tim 1:17; 6:16; 2 Tim 4:18; Heb 13:21; 1 Pet 4:11; 2 Pet 3:18; Jude 25; Rev 1:6).

CHAPTER 21

The Triune God Who Creates: Creation

Introduction

We now turn to the first of God's external works (*ad extra*) that follow from his divine decree. Creation is the enactment of God's decree whereby he creates the universe as the stage on which his glory is displayed, or to use the words of John Calvin: "the theater of God's glory."[1] Following from creation is providence, that is, God's preservation of what he has created, along with his acting in the world and ruling over it, thus orchestrating all things to their appointed ends. In thinking about God's external works, often a further distinction is made between God's "work of nature" (*opus naturae*) and "work of grace" (*opus gratiae*), with the former "oriented to all creatures and their natural ends" (which includes creation and providence),[2] while the latter is oriented to God's elect as their Creator and Redeemer (which includes our election and redemption and the consummation). In this chapter, our focus is on God's work of "nature," specifically, God's creation of the entire space-time universe "out of nothing" (*ex nihilo*). In thinking about God's work of creation, two introductory points will frame our discussion.

---

[1] Calvin, *Institutes*, 1.5.8, 1.6.2, 1.14.20, 2.6.1 (1:61, 1:72, 1:179, 1:341) (see chap. 1, n. 3).

[2] John Webster, "Creation out of Nothing," in Allen and Swain, *Christian Dogmatics*, 128 (see chap. 5, n. 91). Also see Vos, *Reformed Dogmatics*, 1:156–57 (see chap. 15, n. 126).

First, although God has revealed himself in creation so that we are without excuse (Ps 19:1–6; Rom 1:18–32), the doctrine of *creatio ex nihilo* is sui generis (one of a kind), which entails that we only know *how* God created the universe by divine revelation.[3] Scripture's view of origins is unlike anything we know as creatures. We make things out of preexisting materials, but God creates out of nothing. Thus, the act of creation, as John Webster reminds us, "is not an object of experience or understanding but the precondition for all experience and understanding, functioning more like a category than a concept—something that we cannot get behind or look at from an independent vantage point."[4] On this point, Christian theology distinguishes itself from all other worldviews, other than those who borrow from it.

Furthermore, the causality involved in creation is also unique. As Webster notes, it "wholly exceeds any pattern of causality we are able to conceive." Why? For this reason: it "is not a change brought about in one entity by another, since in creation there is only the creator and his act, and no material cause."[5] Creation *ex nihilo* is an absolute beginning; it is not a "formation" from anything as if God works on primeval stuff and alters its shape. It is God acting and bringing about the reality and being of the created order; a created order that is totally dependent on him for its existence and continuation.

This is why there is an absolute distinction between the Creator and the creature in theology. God alone exists in all of his triune self-sufficiency, complete in himself apart from the world, but by an act of the will he speaks and brings into existence the entire created order. As such, the universe is not eternal; only God is, and there was a time when the world was not, yet God has always existed. Indeed, to begin to grasp this glorious truth, Webster reminds us that "what must be broken is our powerful attraction to the idea that created being is *necessary*, indeed more certain than the being of God."[6] The sheer marvel of God's question to Job must capture our thinking if we are to understand creation aright: "Where were you when

---

[3] On the formulation of *creatio ex nihilo* in patristic theology, see Gerhard May, *Creatio Ex Nihilo: The Doctrine of "Creation Out of Nothing" in Early Christian Thought* (Edinburgh: T&T Clark, 1994). However, May argues that *creatio ex nihilo* was not demanded by Scripture but only arose in the second century as early Christian apologists engaged with Greek thought and defended divine freedom and omnipotence (24, 180). This point is very debatable.

[4] Webster, "Creation out of Nothing," 130. Also see Webster, "Trinity and Creation," in *God without Measure*, 1:83–85 (see chap. 1, n. 6).

[5] Webster, "Creation out of Nothing," 130.

[6] Webster, 131.

I established the earth? / Tell me, if you have understanding" (Job 38:4). The doctrine of creation is unique, and it requires that we pay careful attention to what God has revealed in Scripture and not simply extrapolate from the created order back to God.[7]

Second, it is impossible to overestimate the significance of the doctrine of creation for theology and the Christian worldview. Creation is not only where the Bible's story begins, but it is also foundational to all theological formulation, starting most significantly with God himself. As discussed in chapter 13, creation establishes a unique theistic, covenantal, and eschatological framework by which we understand God and all things in relation to him. Joel Beeke and Paul Smalley capture this point when they write: "The doctrine of creation anchors our worldview in God, directs our lives to his glory, and protects us against idolatry (Acts 14:15; Rev. 4:11)."[8]

Creation first identifies God properly. As Louis Berkhof reminds us, "the doctrine of creation is not set forth in Scripture as a philosophical solution of the problem of the world,"[9] although it certainly is the answer as to why there is something rather than nothing. Instead, creation first reminds us that "God is the origin of all things, and that all things belong to Him and are subject to Him."[10] What distinguishes the God of the Bible from all others is that he is the Creator and the Lord of all (Jer 10:1–16; Rev 4:11).

Creation also establishes the proper interpretation and place of humans in the world. It reminds us that God is the covenant God who has created us for himself. Humans were created to know, love, and obey God; we are not products of impersonal forces and blind chance. If humans are now alienated from God, it was not always so. As finite, created beings, we are

---

[7] On this point, see Augustine, *City of God*, trans. Henry Bettenson (New York: Penguin, 1972), 2.11.4 (432). Augustine writes:

> For the belief that God made the world we can have no more trustworthy witness than God himself. Where do we hear this witness? Nowhere, up to the present time, more clearly than in the holy Scriptures, where his prophet said: "In the beginning God made heaven and earth." Are we to suppose that the prophet was there, when God made them? No: but the Wisdom of God was there, and it was through that Wisdom that all things were made; and that Wisdom "passes also into holy souls and makes them friends of God and prophets," and tells them, inwardly and soundlessly, the story of God's works.

[8] Beeke and Smalley, *Reformed Systematic Theology*, 2:55 (see chap. 1, n. 8).

[9] Berkhof, *Systematic Theology*, 126 (see chap. 15, n. 63).

[10] Berkhof, 126.

contingent and dependent on God for our existence and nature, along with our form and function. Creation also establishes creation order and moral norms, especially in relation to human dignity; sexuality (male and female); monogamous heterosexual marriage; and universal, objective moral norms. But creation is not an end in itself: it is the beginning of God's plan that moves forward in redemptive history to the consummation of all things, thus establishing a linear view of history and the theological grounding to the eschatological focus of God's unfolding covenantal plan, starting in the first Adam and leading to the last Adam, our Lord Jesus Christ.

In our secular-postmodern context, it is vital to emphasize the doctrine of creation. As noted in previous chapters, for a number of reasons, our society has turned from thinking that our world is created by an absolute, personal triune God to embrace an impersonal view of origins. Not surprisingly, this has led to disastrous consequences. All around us is the culture of death imploding from within, which is lost, confused, and self-destructive. Central to the confusion is a wrong view of origins. When the God of the Bible is rejected for an impersonal view of reality, such a rejection does not liberate us but rather enslaves us. Why? Because an impersonal view of origins cannot provide the preconditions rationally to account for meaning, truth, design, order, morality, and justice, let alone future hope. All that remains are finite human subjective constructions, which if worked out consistently, especially in light of sin, always result in the tyranny of the state as it sets itself as a rival to God and his rule (Ps 2:1–3).[11]

By contrast, creation begins with the glory of the triune God, which by extension has tremendous implications for us. Reality is not impersonal, reducible to impersonal forces. History is not a series of meaningless events that the human mind "constructs" at will. Instead, reality is created by God, who is fullness of life within himself, and history is the outworking of God's eternal plan, which he has ordained for his own glory. Existence has a purpose because it is grounded in the triune Creator-covenant Lord. For these reasons, we cannot overestimate the importance of creation, which the evangelical church must recapture if she is going to speak the truth to our society and provide *biblical* answers to the chaos and collapse we see around us.

How will we proceed? We will discuss the doctrine of creation in five steps. (1) We will discuss what creation is *not* by describing various false views of origins. (2) We will turn to what creation actually *is* by describing the triune God of creation, the act of creation, and

[11] In Scripture, especially Revelation, we see this in the contrast between Babylon and Jerusalem.

creatio ex nihilo. (3) We will discuss the biblical teaching on creation, with specific focus on Genesis 1–2. (4) We will unpack some of the theological implications of creation. (5) We will briefly discuss the "problem" of creation by addressing the challenge posed by the theory of evolution.

1. What Creation Is *Not*: False Views of the Origin of the Universe

Non-Christian Origin Views

Other than views that borrow from Christian theology,[12] all non-Christian views deny the Creator-creature distinction and *creatio ex nihilo*. In the end, although some may speak in dualistic terms, everything is reduced to "one-level" views of reality, making all things of a similar metaphysical reality, on some kind of "scale" of being.

Naturalism. This view reduces reality to one thing, namely, material stuff, and it denies that the triune God of Scripture exists. For naturalism, the material universe is eternal (at least self-generating) and independent of any act of supreme will or intelligence. The origin and existence of the universe can be explained by entirely immanent, natural, impersonal, and random factors over long periods of time. In Greek thought, naturalism was taught by Leucippus and Democritus (fifth century BC) and later Epicurus (341–270 BC). Presently, it is best represented by the naturalistic theory of evolution identified with Charles Darwin (1809–82) and his *Origin of the Species* (1859) and its various Neo-Darwinian modifications.[13] In such a view, what now exists has evolved by a slow, gradual process according to natural selection as mutations randomly produced changes without design or purpose. Currently, the origin of the universe is explained by the big bang theory, which argues that around fourteen billion years ago, from a point of inconceivable density and energy, the stars and planetary systems were formed as the universe expanded and cooled, with the earth forming around four billion years ago. From this, humans have evolved from animals, and as such, we are merely a stage of development in the evolutionary process.

---

[12] For example, Islam teaches a creation out of nothing, but it is dependent on Judaism and Christianity.

[13] Thomas Huxley (1825–95), Carl Sagan (1934–96), and Richard Dawkins (1941–) are well-known proponents of the evolutionary view.

Dualism. This is the view that there are two distinct, co-eternal substances, or self-existent principles, from which everything is derived, thus denying the Creator-creature distinction and *creatio ex nihilo*.[14] Instead, it affirms that "god," the good spirit, or the evil spirit is more of an "organizer/artisan" fashioning something out of preexisting matter. There are at least two forms of this view. First, God and matter (matter is viewed as imperfect and inferior) are co-eternal. "Creation," then, is "god," forming matter into a specific structure.[15] Second, good and evil are viewed as two eternally existing spirits that are constantly at war with one another.[16] In a popular way, this is picked up in the *Star Wars* movies. In their version of dualism, the "force" has a good/light and bad/dark side, and it is hoped that the good side will win in the end.

Pantheism. This view denies any distinction between the Creator and the creation: "all things are divine" and essentially "one."[17] The "world" is eternal, and it is explained by necessary "emanations" or spilling over of the divine being.[18] Yet metaphysically the world and "god" are one, resulting in a "one-level" view of reality. In the East, this view is identified with Hinduism, and in the West with the philosophy of Plotinus, Baruch Spinoza, forms of German idealism, and New Age spirituality.[19] In the end, it depersonalizes God and robs him of the perfection of his being, moral character, sovereignty, and triune glory.

Sub-Christian "Creation" Views

Under this category are views of "creation" that have been taught by those within the church, or at least who have identified with Christianity. But in each case, they either deny or undercut the Creator-creature distinction or *creatio ex nihilo*, thus giving us a less-than-biblical view.

Origen: Creation from eternity. Origen's view was an outlier in the early church and rejected. For Origen, God has been creating from eternity—indeed he has been creating a succession of worlds, ours being the most recent—so that creation, though finite and dependent, is eternal

---

[14] Berkhof, *Systematic Theology*, 138; Vos, *Reformed Dogmatics*, 1:180–81.

[15] For example, see Plato and some forms of Gnosticism.

[16] For example, see Zoroastrianism or Manicheanism.

[17] Letham, *Systematic Theology*, 52 (see chap. 5, n. 1).

[18] Berkhof, *Systematic Theology*, 138–39; Vos, *Reformed Dogmatics*, 1:181–82.

[19] For a discussion of the influence of pantheism in Western thought, see Bavinck, *Reformed Dogmatics*, 2:410–11 (see chap. 1, n. 9).

and not *ex nihilo*.[20] Why did he argue this view? For Origen, it was impossible to think of God apart from his being the Creator. He reasoned that such attributes as omnipotence and love must be expressed in specific acts that demonstrate them; otherwise, God would be mutable, thus necessitating that God has always been creating.

As noted, in the patristic era, Origen's view was rejected for a variety of reasons.[21] First, the concept of an eternal creation is difficult to reconcile with *creatio ex nihilo* since it assumes "a transition from nonbeing to being."[22] It also conflates creation with providence and makes providence either "a continuous creation, or creation eternal providence, which amounts to the same thing."[23] Second, it also conflicts with the idea that history has a beginning and an end, which is difficult to uphold if the world eternally exists. In the end, it conflates eternity and time. Bavinck states this crucial point this way:

> In eternity there is no "earlier" or "later." God *did* eternally create the world: that is, in the moment in which the world came into existence, God was and remained the Eternal One, and as the Eternal One he created the world. Even if the world *had* existed for an endless succession of centuries . . . it remains temporal, finite, limited, and therefore had a beginning.[24]

Third, Origen does not sufficiently distinguish between the triune God in himself (*ad intra*) and in his external works (*ad extra*). By failing to do so, he tends to collapse the divine processions within God into creation, which Nicene theology remedied. Thus, God is more than the Creator since creation is contingent and external to him. Within God, apart from the world, God is perfect within himself, and he does not need the world to express his attributes.[25]

Gnosticism. Gnosticism was part of a large and complex religious and philosophical movement that swept through the Hellenistic world at the beginning of the second century,

---

[20] See Origen, *On First Principles* 3.5.3.

[21] For example, it was rejected by Theophilus, Justin Martyr, Irenaeus, Tertullian, Clement of Alexandria, Athanasius, and Augustine.

[22] Vos, *Reformed Dogmatics*, 1:179.

[23] Vos, 1:179.

[24] Bavinck, *Reformed Dogmatics*, 2:428.

[25] On this point, see Letham, *Systematic Theology*, 272–73; Paul D. Molnar, "Classical Trinity: Catholic Perspective," in Sexton, *Two Views*, 84–90 (see chap. 19, n. 115).

and it was one of the first heresies the church addressed.[26] Unfortunately, it is still around today.[27] It was based on the Platonic dualism of matter and spirit. Gnostics argued that the material world was eternal and inherently evil, while the spirit world was potentially good. Also, Gnosticism offered people a detailed, secret knowledge (Gk. *gnosis*) of reality, claiming to know and to be able to explain things of which ordinary people, including Christians, were ignorant. It divided humans into various classes, and only those in the highest and most spiritual class could attain this secret knowledge. At every point, Gnosticism was antithetical to Christianity, and if it were mixed with biblical faith, the truth of the gospel would have been destroyed.

For example, Gnostics viewed God as one yet remote and unknowable—wholly other and thus removed from this fallen, material universe, which he did not create. Since in Gnostic thought there is a distance between God and the world, the "gap" is filled by a strange host of intermediaries. In fact, it was one of these intermediaries, a lesser power or god, the "demiurge," who created this material, fallen universe, including humans. Humans are composed of the same spiritual substance that God is, but we have become trapped in physical bodies, which are like tombs that must be escaped. Our "fall" into sin is not in history; rather, it is identical to our "fall" into matter and thus our becoming trapped in our physical bodies. In this way, creation and fall coincide due to the work of the demiurge. Sin is viewed as the alienation of our soul from the true God while we are in our bodies. As long as our souls are trapped in physical bodies, we will be subject to "sin." Salvation is an escape from the bondage of material existence and a journey back to the home from which our souls have fallen. This possibility is initiated by the great Spirit—"god"—who wishes to draw back into itself all the stray bits and pieces. "God" sends forth an emanation of himself—a spiritual redeemer—who descends through layers and layers of reality from pure spirit to dense matter and attempts to teach some of the divine sparks of Spirit their true identity and home. Once awakened by knowledge, we are able to begin the journey back.

---

[26] See Colin E. Gunton, *The Triune Creator: A Historical and Systematic Study* (Grand Rapids: Eerdmans, 1998); cf. Paul Gavrilyuk, "Creation in Early Christian Polemical Literature: Irenaeus against Gnostics and Athanasius against the Arians," *Modern Theology* 29, no. 2 (2013): 22–32; Robert M. Grant, ed., *Gnosticism: A Source Book of Heretical Writings from the Early Christian Period* (New York: Harper & Row, 1961).

[27] See Herrick, *Making of the New Spirituality* (see chap. 2, n. 29).

Jesus, in this view, is the human vehicle for this heavenly messenger, "Christ," who was sent by God to rescue the soul from the body. Gnostics denied that "Christ"—this heavenly, spiritual redeemer—became incarnate given the antithesis between spirit and matter. Instead, they argued that "Christ" either temporarily associated himself with the man Jesus (adoptionism) or he took the appearance of a physical body (Docetism; Gk. *dokeō*, "to appear"). At Jesus's baptism, the heavenly redeemer entered Jesus but left him before he died on the cross.

Gnosticism radically departed from the entirety of biblical teaching, starting with a flawed view of creation and creating an absolute dichotomy between creation and redemption. From this flawed view of God and creation, sin, salvation, and Christ were also radically redefined. At its heart, Gnosticism denied a proper Creator-creature distinction and the reality of the triune God and, correspondingly, the full deity of the Son and the reality of his incarnation. It also wrongly affirmed the eternality of matter, thus denying *creatio ex nihilo*. Not surprisingly, the church fathers, such as Ignatius, Irenaeus, and Tertullian, tirelessly argued against it. They correctly realized that Gnosticism was a heresy that had to be rejected *in toto*.

Process Theism ("panentheism").[28] As discussed in previous chapters, this view also denies the Creator-creature distinction. Instead, God and the world are seen as eternal; both are "actual entities" so that there is no absolute distinction of being between God and the world. Because this is so, "god" somehow has been creating from all eternity as he also develops from eternity. Today, process theists fully accept evolutionary theory. God creates, in their view, by presenting the world novel possibilities to actualize and then by luring them toward those he thinks are best, even though he cannot guarantee the results. For process theists, the universe is in a sense divine, but it is formed out of itself with help from God's primordial pole. In theology, Jürgen Moltmann is an example of such thinking, in which the Creator-creature distinction is flattened due to his flattening the distinction between God in himself (*ad intra*) and his external relations (*ad extra*). For Moltmann, "the idea of the world is already inherent in the Father's love for the Son,"[29] and thus, God "needs" the world, and "creation is a part of

[28] See Polkinghorne, *Work of Love* (see chap. 18, n. 64); Clayton and Peacocke, *In Whom We Live and Move* (see chap. 20, n. 25); cf. Oord, *Uncontrolling Love of God* (see chap. 2, n. 135).

[29] Jürgen Moltmann, *The Trinity and the Kingdom: The Doctrine of God* (New York: Harper & Row, 1981), 108.

the eternal love affair between the Father and the Son,"[30] thus making the world eternal and God's own being "dependent on the development of history for its own existence."[31] This view is rightly rejected as sub-biblical.

2. What Creation *Is*

Christian theology has always affirmed that our triune God is the Creator of the universe, which is taught in the early creeds and confessions. For example, the Apostles' Creed states: "I believe in God the Father, Almighty, Maker of heaven and earth." The Nicene Creed (AD 381) also confesses, "I believe in one God, the Father Almighty, Maker of heaven and earth, and of all things visible and invisible. . . . And in one Lord Jesus Christ, begotten, not made, being of one substance with the Father, by whom all things were made." The Chalcedonian Definition (AD 451) affirms the Nicene Creed, but it also goes on to speak of the incarnation of the divine Son for our salvation, thus linking together creation and redemption in the triune God.

What then *is* creation? Here is our working definition: Creation *is* the external work of the triune God by which he freely has produced heaven and earth (the universe) out of nothing (*ex nihilo*) and has imparted to all things their natures.[32] Let us unpack this definition in three steps.

Creation Is a Triune Act

To understand what creation *is*, we must first start with God in himself before we reflect on God's act of creation. Let us develop this point in *four* steps.

First, building on trinitarian theology, we affirm the following about trinitarian agency:[33]

1. Inseparable operations (*opera trinitatis ad extra sunt indivisa*). Creation is the *one* act of the triune God. This means that the Father, Son, and Holy Spirit act inseparably since they subsist in and share the one simple indivisible divine nature. As such, creation is one act of

---

[30] Moltmann, 59. Moltmann attempted to preserve the Creator-creature distinction and *creatio ex nihilo*, but given his panentheism, he could not do so consistently. On this point, see Molnar, "Classical Trinity," 88–90 n. 76.

[31] Molnar, "Classical Trinity," 89.

[32] The definition slightly modifies the one given by Vos, *Reformed Dogmatics*, 1:156.

[33] See chapter 18.

God, not three distinct acts. Thus, creation is not merely the work of the Father (Gen 1:1–31; Isa 40:12; 44:24; 1 Cor 8:6), it is also the work of the Son (John 1:3; 1 Cor 8:6; Col 1:15–17; Heb 1:1–3), and the Spirit (Gen 1:2; Job 33:4; cf. Ps 104:30). Creation is common to the three divine persons.

2. Although creation is the *one* act of God, it is also triune. As such, the Father, Son, and Spirit act according to their ordered modes of subsistence or their eternal relations of origin: paternity, filiation, and spiration. Thus, the Father acts through the Son and by the Spirit. Likewise, the Son acts from the Father and by the Spirit, and the Spirit from the Father and the Son.

3. Creation, as a *triune* act, is also appropriated to specific divine persons. This is why Scripture attributes creation to the Father (Eph 3:14–15), a point that is picked up in our creeds. But appropriation also affirms that creation is the one act of God that involves all three persons. We must not forget that "no divine person can be defined apart from the shared divine essence, since as a *modus essentis* (mode of being) each procession *includes* the divine nature."[34]

Second, creation as a triune act also requires us to distinguish between God in himself (*ad intra*) and God in his external works (*ad extra*). Let us explain why this is important to do.

1. God's *ad intra* works are intrinsic, internal, constitutive, and unceasing: in God there is unending, limitless life and complete self-satisfaction. Webster states it this way: "God the creator wholly exceeds the act of creation" since before creation God is perfect within himself.[35] "God's inner works (the relations of origin: paternity, filiation, and spiration) are wholly sufficient; God is entirely realized without potentiality."[36] Thus, when Scripture begins, "In the beginning God created the heavens and the earth," we must never forget that "before the beginning," the triune God existed perfect in himself. In God's eternal being, there was the fullness of holy love, life, and communion apart from creation. This is why Paul states in Acts 17:24–25 that God does not need us to add to the perfection of his own being.[37] In biblical

---

[34] Webster, "Trinity and Creation," 94.

[35] Webster, "Creation out of Nothing," 137.

[36] Webster, 137; cf. Webster, "Trinity and Creation," 89–92.

[37] Webster, "Trinity and Creation," 91: "Yet the triune God could be without the world; no perfection of God would be lost, no triune bliss compromised, were the world not to exist; no enhancement of God is achieved by the world's existence."

thought, the world cannot complete God as if he is deficient without it. God experiences no "codependency" on that which is external to him (in contrast panentheism and open theism).

2. Why is it important to affirm God's triune self-sufficiency *ad intra* apart from the world? For this reason: without doing so, we cannot understand creation in its full biblical sense. Bavinck argues this point well. He contrasts deism and pantheism with trinitarian theism. Against deism and pantheism, he argues that the "creation cannot be conceived as mere happenstance, nor as the outcome of divine self-development. It must have its foundation in God, yet not be a phase in the process of his inner life."[38] Only a proper view of the Trinity avoids these options. Why? Because within the self-contained triune God, the divine processions remind us of God's own fullness of life and productivity apart from the world: "He is life, blessedness, glory in himself."[39] Yet, if God "could not communicate himself inwardly (*ad intra*), then neither could there be any revelation of God *ad extra*, that is, any communication of God in and to his creatures."[40] This is why, "apart from the Trinity even the act of creation becomes inconceivable. For if God cannot communicate himself, he is a darkened light, a dry spring, unable to exert himself outward to communicate himself to creatures."[41] But the triune God who can communicate *ad intra* can *freely* communicate himself to his creatures. The God who can reveal himself "in an absolute sense to the Son and the Spirit" can do so "in a relative sense also to the world," and as such, "the self-communication that takes place within the divine being is archetypal for God's work in creation."[42] "All things come from the Father; the 'ideas' of all existent things are present in the Son; the first principles of all life are in the Spirit. Generation and procession in the divine being are the immanent acts of God, which make possible the outward acts of creation and revelation."[43]

3. Building on the previous points, we must also affirm that God's act of creation does not change God since whether it is before creation or after, God remains perfect in himself. Because

---

38 Bavinck, *Reformed Dogmatics*, 2:332.

39 Bavinck, 2:332.

40 Bavinck, 2:332.

41 Bavinck, 2:309. Bavinck (2:309 n. 118) cites Athanasius, *Against the Arians* 2.2; and John of Damascus, *Orthodox Faith* 1.8, as making the same point.

42 Bavinck, 2:333.

43 Bavinck, 2:333. Also see Josh Malone, "Eternal Generation: Pro-Nicene Pattern, Dogmatic Function, and Created Effects," in Sanders and Swain, *Retrieving Eternal Generation*, 278–80 (see chap. 19, n. 13).

of creation, there are now "two orders of being (uncreated and created)";[44] before, there was only one order of being, namely God himself. Why did God create? Not to satisfy himself as if he needed anything. Instead, creation is a free act whereby out of the fullness of his divine, holy love and life, he chooses to share himself with us. Webster states it this way: "Possessing unlimited blessedness, God does not have his being in competition, reserving being and life to himself. Beyond threat, God is also beyond envy, no other possible reality having the capacity to enhance or diminish his perfection. As the one who has life in himself he can give life to the world, he can be infinitely generous without self-depletion."[45]

Third, as an act of the triune God, the world was created *for his own glory*. Not only were human beings created for God's glory (Isa 43:7), but so was the entire creation (Ps 19:1–2; Rev 4:11). Creation serves many purposes, but first, at least for humans, creation is the stage on which God displays his glory, and we were created to know him and to enjoy him forever.

The Act of Creation

In thinking about God's *act* of creation, *three* further points will unpack what creation *is*.[46]

First, creation as an external act of the triune God entails that it is a *free* and *voluntary* act. This means that God's act of creation was not constrained or necessary. God did not have to make the world, but it was due to his sovereign will and for his own good pleasure (Eph 1:11; Rev 4:11). Yet God's *freedom* is tied to his nature so that his will is never indeterminate. As we discussed in the previous chapter, God chooses according to his decree, and thus with purpose, design, and planning. God, in his self-sufficiency, is "wholly self-determining."[47] But as Webster reminds us, God's "self-determination is not

---

[44] Webster, "Creation out of Nothing," 137.

[45] Webster, "Creation out of Nothing," 138. Also see Athanasius, *On the Incarnation*, in *Contra Gentes and De Incarnatione*, ed. R. W. Thomson (Oxford: Oxford University Press, 1971), 3: "God is good—or rather the source of goodness—and the good has no envy for anything. Thus, because he envies nothing its existence, he made everything from nothing through his own Word, our Lord Jesus Christ."

[46] See discussion in Webster, "Creation out of Nothing," 138–42; cf. Webster, "Trinity and Creation," 94–98.

[47] Webster, "Creation out of Nothing," 139.

arbitrary self-causation but simply God being the one he is, the one characterized by unrestricted goodness. 'Will' and 'goodness,' like 'freedom' and 'necessity' or 'nature,' are identical in God."[48]

Thus, in God's act of creation, he spoke the universe into existence (Gen 1:1), giving it an existence separate but dependent on him. Accordingly, the created world is intelligible *and* contingent—*intelligible* because God is the God of order, *contingent* because its Lord freely created according to his own will and plan. As we will note below, this *theological* view of creation was foundational for the rise of an empirical science in the West.

Second, creation as a free act of the triune God entails that he creates the universe *directly*, *immediately*, *instantaneously*, and *effortlessly* (Gen 1:1–2).

1. To say that God's act of creation is direct, immediate, and instantaneous reminds us that there was nothing that God acted on since only he existed. Creation is *not* an act in time or its first event. It involves no succession of moments; instead, God creates instantaneously the entire space-time order. God's act is from eternity that produces a temporal effect, but all succession of moments is within creation. This is why space and time are best conceptualized as "modes of existence" tied to creation.[49] Or, as Augustine observes: the world was created *with* time rather than *in* time.[50] Or, as Anselm states, creation is God acting "alone and through itself."[51]

2. Creation is also an *effortless* act. God's act of power is not merely quantitatively greater than creaturely power. It is qualitatively different. Nor is God's power some capacity he has in reserve that he needs to activate. Instead, God's power is what he is. Thus, when God speaks, the universe comes to exist without effort since "The LORD is the everlasting God, / the Creator of the ends of the earth. / He does not faint or grow weary" (Isa 40:28 ESV).

Furthermore, God's power to create is immediate, or direct. It is incommunicable and proper to God alone. Creatures make things, but not like God. In fact, as Webster reminds us, God's power to create "cannot be communicated to some instrument because

---

[48] Webster, 139.

[49] Bavinck, *Reformed Dogmatics*, 2:162; cf. Turretin, *Institutes of Elenctic Theology*, 1:436–41 (see chap. 3, n. 55).

[50] Augustine, *Confessions* 11.10–13; *City of God* 1.7.30; 1.11.4–6; 1.12.15–17.

[51] Anselm, *Monologion*, in Davies and Evans, *Anselm of Canterbury: The Major Works*, 7 (see chap. 8, n. 20).

any instrument is itself created."[52] No one is capable of creating but God alone.[53] This is why Gnosticism had to be rejected. God does not create through intermediaries; he creates directly as the triune God.

3. Given that creation is a triune act and that the persons are distinct, we can speak of the Son as both the "exemplary" and "efficient" cause of creation.[54] He is the "exemplary" cause because "as the Father's Word and Wisdom he is the reason for and the pattern of the production of creatures."[55] This is why the Son, as the true and exact image of the Father (Col 1:15; Heb 1:3) is the archetype for humans, with Adam functioning as a type (Rom 5:14), and the incarnate Son, as the last Adam, is able to restore us to the purpose of our creation as God's image-bearers (Heb 2:5–9; cf. Rom 8:29). Likewise, he is the "efficient" cause because in the one act of creation, the unbegotten Father creates "in him" and "through him" (Col 1:16 NIV), while the Spirit, as the Lord and giver of life, is creation's "perfecting" cause, "by whom created things are brought to their proper end."[56] Thus, originated by the Father and given form by the Word, created things are brought to life by the Spirit. In this way, "creation is a common work of the undivided Trinity; there are not three creators. But there are 'three who create'"[57] with respect to their eternal, immanent personal relations as Father, Son, and Holy Spirit.

Third, in creation, it is important to remember that there is no change or movement in God.[58] God is not acted on, or in his creation of the world, he does not take on new proper-

---

[52] Webster, "Creation out of Nothing," 142.

[53] See Thomas Aquinas, *Summa Theologica*, pt. 1a, q. 65, art. 3, resp (see chap. 2, n. 20).

[54] Discussions of causality are indebted to Aristotle. Aristotle argued that all things exemplify four different types of causes: material, formal, efficient, and final. The material cause of a thing is the material substance out of which the thing is made. The formal cause is the form or idea the thing exemplifies. The efficient cause is the means by which the thing is made. The final cause is the purpose for which the thing was made. See Muller, *Dictionary of Latin and Greek*, s.v. "causa," 61 (see chap. 8, n. 37).

[55] Webster, "Trinity and Creation," 97.

[56] Webster, 97; cf. Bavinck, *Reformed Dogmatics*, 2:423–26.

[57] Webster, 98.

[58] Vos, *Reformed Dogmatics*, 1:177–78. Vos distinguishes between "active" and "passive" creation. The former refers to the act of creating in God, while the latter refers to the universe as created. There is no change in God by the act of creation; instead, a new relationship results with creation, but it is best viewed as a "mixed" relation. On this point, see John Webster, "*Non Ex Aequo*: God's Relation to Creatures," in *God without Measure*, 1:115–26.

ties that result in some kind of "relational" change. As Thomas Weinandy explains, "The act of creation itself demands that God act by no other act than the pure act that he is as *ipsum esse* (i.e., existence itself) for no other act is capable of such a singular effect."[59] No doubt, the effect of his act is real, namely, the existence of the world. But God's act is out of the fullness of his divine life; in him there is no change. For this reason, theology has spoken of God as "pure act" (Lat. *actus purus*), but as noted in chapter 18, this means that in God there is the absolute fullness of life and being. Unlike creatures, God has no passive potency that he needs to activate. There is no potential for growth in God since in his fullness of triune life he is wholly complete in himself.[60]

When we put all of this together, Webster's summary about the act of creation is helpful: "God's act of creation is *sui generis*, and as we make our approach to it we have to check the impulse to think of it as one act of immeasurably great effectiveness in a field of other agents, acts, and objects. The act of creation is the beginning of all other being and action, not an act alongside or on them."[61]

*Creation Is "Out of Nothing" (*Creatio ex Nihilo*)*

Meaning of Creatio ex Nihilo

To affirm that God created "out of nothing" means that God did not begin with any previously existing materials when he created the universe, including space. God did not have planet-sized pieces of Play-Doh from which he formed the heavens and the earth. Before God began to create the universe, nothing existed except himself in all of his triune glory. Further, to affirm that God created *ex nihilo* means that there was no precedent for creating the heavens and earth, no blueprints for him to consult. Let us develop this important truth in six steps.

First, creation "out of nothing" reminds us that creation is not some kind of emanation or overflow of God's being, contrary to the view of pantheism or even panentheism.

Second, creation "out of nothing" entails that matter is not eternal (Ps 90:2), contrary to ancient Near East and Greek thought. As Anselm reminds us, to say "out of nothing" means

---

[59] Weinandy, *Does God Suffer?*, 132–33 (see chap. 18, n. 45).

[60] See Duby, *Divine Simplicity*, 168–69 (see chap. 18, n. 9).

[61] Webster, "Creation out of Nothing," 141.

that "while something has indeed been made, there is not some thing from which it was made."[62] God is all that is needed for creation to occur.

Third, creation "out of nothing" also reminds us that it is "not a causal relation or an act that brings about a change, for creation effects the coming-to-be of created reality rather than a passage from one state of being to another."[63] At this point, our understanding of causation in the world cannot be applied to the act of creation. "As 'first' cause, God is not first in a sequence but the one because of whom there is a sequence at all."[64] Nor is the act of creation a change since this would assume some kind of existing in the process of coming to exist. There is no process in creation, a movement of non-being to being. "Creation out of nothing means that there is God alone, and then by his will and goodness there is also created reality."[65]

Fourth, creation "out of nothing" further reminds us that creation has its being only from God, and it is totally dependent on him. In this sense, creation "participates" in God, but not in such a way as to remove the Creator-creature distinction. Instead, it means that created reality is dependent on God and because of God's act, shares in the goodness of being.

Fifth, creation "out of nothing" also means that we must distinguish the act of creation from providence, specifically preservation. In preservation, God sustains what he has made and brings it to its ordained end. But as Webster reminds us, the two works of nature, namely creation and providence, are related, but we must not confuse them. "Creation is a completed act . . . whereas conservation is a continuing activity of sustaining. . . . Creation introduces, and conservation governs and upholds."[66]

The distinction between creation and providence is important. The way God created the universe is different from the way he preserves, acts in, and governs it today. This is not only important theologically but also scientifically. In terms of the latter, we cannot assume that God's act in creation is the same as providence. In providence, God sustains the universe in a uniform way, but we must not embrace uniformitarianism. For example, in the debate over the age of the earth, radiometric dating and starlight are major arguments for an old earth. Yet, in both of these areas, there is a uniformitarian assumption that is generally true

---

[62] Anselm, *Monologion*, 22.

[63] Webster, "Creation out of Nothing," 145.

[64] Webster, 145.

[65] Webster, 146.

[66] Webster, 143.

of providence (except of God's extraordinary agency), but not true of the act of creation. The distant starlight argument is a case in point. It assumes that the light arrived on earth according to current laws of nature. Yet, in the act of creation, stars began giving off light. Current laws of nature describe ordinary providence, but they do not describe the act of creation, which is sui generis.[67] As Tim Chaffey and Jason Lisle note, "This is not to say that none of the laws of nature applied before God ended His work of creation. God was simultaneously sustaining the universe while continuing to create it. . . . But God was also working in a *different* way than He works today. . . .When God created the lights in the firmament (the sun, the moon, and the stars)," it suggests that they "fulfilled their purpose immediately, or at least on that day."[68]

Sixth, creation "out of nothing," is the historic view of the church, except for a few outliers like Origen. In second-temple Judaism, *creatio ex nihilo* was taught in 2 Macc 7:28. In the patristic era, it was also taught by Clement of Alexandria, the *Shepherd of Hermas*, Theophilus of Antioch, Irenaeus, Tertullian, and Augustine.[69] The same teaching continued in the medieval era, the Reformation, and until today, including all divisions of Christianity, which means that a denial of the doctrine is a rejection of a Christian view of creation.

Biblical and Theological Warrant

What is the biblical warrant for *creatio ex nihilo*? Doctrines are not usually established by one text alone; instead, they are warranted by multiple texts embedded in the entire teaching of Scripture. This is also the case for this doctrine. Here are *three* points that warrant the doctrine.

---

[67] On this point, see Beeke and Smalley, *Reformed Systematic Theology*, 2:107–11; Tim Chaffey and Jason Lisle, *Old-Earth Creationism on Trial* (Green Forest, AR: Master Books, 2008), 140–43.

[68] Chaffey and Lisle, *Old-Earth Creationism on Trial*, 142. We must remember this point as we interpret, for example, the evidence for the expansion of the universe. We must not assume that the universe has always been expanding the way it is today, given the distinction between the unique act of creation and the ongoing nature of providence. See Chaffey and Lisle, 143–45.

[69] See Allison, *Historical Theology*, 254–62 (see chap. 8, n. 9). See Clement of Alexandria, *Exhortation to the Heathen* 4 (*ANF* 2:189–90); *Shepherd of Hermas*, Vision 1.1 (*ANF* 1:20); Theophilus of Antioch, *Theophilus to Autolycus* 2.4 (*ANF* 2:95); Irenaeus, *Against Heresies* 2.10.4 (*ANF* 1:370); Tertullian, *Against Hermogenes* 21, 22 (*ANF* 3:489–90); Augustine, *Confessions* (12.8.8) (*NPNF*[1] 1:178).

First, the use of the verb *bārā'* (Gen 1:1). Although the verb *alone* does not warrant *creatio ex nihilo* since it may also be used to denote a secondary creation, in which God creates from the material he has already made,[70] its use in Scripture, especially Genesis 1, is unique.[71] For example, in the *qal* stem,[72] *bārā'* is used only of God, not of humans. The verb expresses the uniqueness of God's creative work as opposed to the "refashioning" that is characteristic of human creativity. Also, the verb never appears with an "accusative of material," that is, a direct object designating the material from which something else is made. The word tends to be used in places where there is no mention of the material ingredients from which something is made. Instead, Scripture teaches that God spoke the worlds into existence; he did not reshape preexisting material. Here are some further points to consider in relation to the use of the verb:[73]

1. In Gen 1:1, grammatically and contextually, the best translation is, "In the beginning God created the heavens and the earth," which takes "in the beginning" as an independent clause and thus as a reference to the absolute beginning of the space-time universe. This assumes that *bārā'* implies God's creation out of nothing.

2. Contextually, *bārā'* (in the *qal* stem) is used differently from other ancient pagan creation stories—e.g., the Babylonian *Enuma Elish* or the Greek poem by Hesiod, *Theogony*. Both of these ancient cosmogonies picture a "god" working on some sort of already existing primeval "stuff," which are all variations of a "relative" creation, not an "absolute" one.

3. Other verbs also may refer to a "relative" creation. For example, *bārā'* (Gk. *kitzō*) can do so in stems other than *qal* (Gen 1:21, 25; 5:1; Isa 45:7, 12; 54:16; Amos 4:13; Mark 13:19; 1 Cor 11:9; Rev 10:6). It can also refer to what comes under the providential control of God (Ps 104:30; Isa 45:7–8; 65:18; 1 Tim 4:4). The same is true of *'āśâ* (Gk. *poieō*, "to form something

---

[70] For example, *bārā'* is used in Gen 1:21, 27 to refer to God making sea creatures and humans, and in both cases, it assumes preexisting material (cf. Gen 2:7). Thus, *creatio ex nihilo* is not warranted by the verb alone.

[71] See John Oswalt, "*Creatio Ex Nihilo:* Is it Biblical, and Does it Matter?" *Trinity Journal* 39 (2018): 173–77.

[72] The *qal* stem is simple action that takes place in the active voice.

[73] On this point, see Douglas F. Kelly, *Creation and Change: Genesis 1:1–2:4 in the Light of Changing Scientific Paradigms* (Fearn, Ross-shire, UK: Mentor, 1997), 57–74; Frame, *Doctrine of God*, 298–302 (see chap. 3, n. 13); Berkhof, *Systematic Theology*, 128–29, 132–33; Oswalt, "*Creatio Ex Nihilo*," 171; Gordon J. Wenham, *Genesis 1–15*, WBC 1 (Waco: Word, 1987), 14; Kenneth A. Mathews, *Genesis 1–11:26*, NAC (Nashville: B&H, 1996), 128–29; Collins, *Genesis 1–4*, 50–55 (see chap. 4, n. 48).

that is already there"),[74] and *yāsar* (Gk. *plassein*), which conveys the idea of fashioning out of preexisting materials (Gen 2:7, 19; Ps 104:26; Amos 4:13; Zech 12:1; Rom 9:20).

Thus, on the basis of this data, Berkhof defines creation as including immediate (i.e., direct creation without means) and mediate creation (i.e., creation by the use of means), with the latter referring to God's creation by which he made use of what he already created. "Creation is that act by which God produces the world and all that is in it, partly out of nothing [immediate] and partly out of material [mediate] that is by its very nature unfit, for the manifestation of the glory of His power, wisdom, and goodness."[75] Yet the critical point in creation is in the first instance God's absolute creation of the universe *ex nihilo* (Gen 1:1).

Second, creatio ex nihilo is also taught in the NT. Two texts confirm this point. For example, Paul refers to God in Rom 4:17 as the one who "calls things into existence that do not exist" (*kalountos ta mē onta hōs onta*), which implies a creation out of nothing.[76] The same is true of Heb 11:3. The author reminds us that "by faith we understand that the universe was created by the word of God, so that what is seen was made from things that are not visible."[77] This text is consistent with *ex nihilo*, even though it still leaves open the possibility that God might have created the world out of something invisible, but this is highly unlikely given the entire teaching of Scripture grounded in the Creator-creature distinction.[78]

Third, building on the exegetical data, the following *theological* argument warrants *creatio ex nihilo*.[79] First, creation had a beginning and God is the Creator of all things.[80] Before the beginning, there was no universe, only God, thus there was no material stuff out of which the world was made.[81] Second, creation encompasses everything—"the heavens and the earth"—which includes all matter; matter is not eternal. Third, God creates as the triune self-sufficient

---

[74] See Gen 1:7, 16, 26; Matt 19:4.

[75] Berkhof, *Systematic Theology*, 129 (italics removed).

[76] Schreiner, *Romans*, 244–45 (see chap. 6, n. 62).

[77] "Not out of appearing things," i.e., visible things (*mē ek phainomenōn to blepomenon gegonenai*).

[78] Schreiner, *Commentary on Hebrews*, 343–44 (see chap. 4, n. 39). These texts imply *ex nihilo*, as they refer to the absolute beginning of the world (Matt 13:35; 24:21; Mark 10:6; Eph 1:4; 1 Pet 1:20; 2 Pet 3:4).

[79] This argument is from Frame, *Doctrine of God*, 301–2.

[80] Gen 1:1; Job 38:4; Pss 33:6, 9; 90:2; 102:25; Isa 40:21; 41:4; 46:10; Matt 19:4, 8; John 1:1–2; Acts 4:24; 14:15; 17:24–25; Eph 3:9; Col 1:16; Heb 1:10; Rev 1:8; 3:14; 4:11; 21:6; 22:13.

[81] See Oswalt, "*Creatio Ex Nihilo*," 171, who makes the same point.

Lord. In Scripture, the Creator-creature distinction is absolute, which means that the world is not the lower end of a continuum with God at the top. Creation is not an emanation of God's being. Thus to affirm that God is the Creator and Lord entails that he created *ex nihilo*.

3. Biblical Teaching on Creation

Creation is taught everywhere in Scripture.[82] As Berkhof correctly observes, "The Scriptural proof for the doctrine of creation is not found in a single and limited portion of the Bible, but is found in every part of the Word of God. It does not consist of a few scattered passages of doubtful interpretation, but of a large number of clear and unequivocal statements, which speak of the creation of the world as a historical fact."[83] But without doubt the *locus classicus* for creation is Genesis 1–2, where God's creation of the material universe *ex nihilo* is described in a straightforward historical narrative.

However, throughout church history, Genesis 1–2 has also been one of the most debated texts in Scripture, especially since the rise of historical criticism and the naturalistic evolutionary theory of origins.[84] In this work, we cannot discuss every issue. Instead, we will focus on two significant introductory issues before we offer a brief exposition of the text.

---

[82] Vos, *Reformed Dogmatics*, 1:160–61. Berkhof lists the basic biblical data on creation:

> (1) Passages which stress the omnipotence of God in the work of creation, Isa. 40, 26, 28; Amos 4:13. (2) Passages which point to His exaltation above nature as the great and infinite God, Ps. 90:2; 102:26, 27; Acts 17:24. (3) Passages which refer to the wisdom of God in the work of creation, Isa. 40:12–14; Jer. 10:12–16; John 1:3. (4) Passages regarding creation from the point of view of God's sovereignty and purpose in creation, Isa. 43:7; Rom. 1:25. (5) Passages that speak of creation as a fundamental work of God, 1 Cor. 11:9; Col. 1:16. *Systematic Theology*, 128.

Berkhof also lists such texts as Neh 9:6 along with Isa 42:5; 45:18; Rev 4:11; 10:6. *Systematic Theology*, 128.

[83] Berkhof, *Systematic Theology*, 127.

[84] Genesis 1–2 has been interpreted in a number of ways. *First*, the majority view is that Genesis 1–2 is an historical narrative describing God's creation of the world in six successive ordinary days (i.e., twenty-four-hour days), which usually requires a younger view of the age of the earth. *Second*, Augustine believed in a young earth but argued that God created the world instantaneously and not in six sequential days. For him, Genesis 1 was a theological allegory of God's creation in a moment. *Third*, some have argued that the "days" of creation are "unspecified" (e.g., Herman Bavinck

Genesis 1–2: Two Conflicting Accounts?

Since the Enlightenment and the rise of biblical criticism, many critical scholars have accepted some version of Julius Wellhausen's (1844–1918) "Documentary Hypothesis." Such a view argues that Genesis 1 and 2 are two different and conflicting accounts of creation. Genesis 1:1–2:3 is the "P," or priestly account, while Gen 2:4–3:24 is the "J", or Yahweh account. A number of reasons are given for this view, but three are often cited.[85] First, each account uses different names for God (e.g., *Elohim* in Gen 1; *Yahweh-Elohim* in Gen 2). Second, each account employs different verbs to describe the creation of humans (e.g., *bārā'* in Gen 1:27; *yāsar* in Gen 2:7–8). Third, there is a "contradiction" in the order of the creation of humans and the plants. In Gen 1:11–13, the plants are created on the third day while humans are created on the sixth. However, Gen 2:5 teaches that there were no plants in existence when Adam was created. What each point reveals is that Genesis 1–2 are two different and contradictory creation stories. In response, we offer the following three reflections.

[1854–1921], E. J. Young [1907–68]). This view argues that Genesis 1 is a sequential, historical account of creation, but we cannot determine from it the length of days or the age of the earth. *Fourth*, a number of interpretive options have been proposed for those who embrace an "old earth" view. (1) The "gap" or "restitution" view (e.g., Thomas Chalmers [1780–1847], *Scofield Reference Bible*). This view insists that Gen 1:2 gives us an unspecified period of time (i.e., billions of years) where angels fell and a previous world was judged, which resulted in a new start in Gen 1:3. (2) The "day-age" view (e.g., Benjamin Silliman [1779–1864], Hugh Miller [1802–1856], Charles Hodge [1797–1878], Hugh Ross [1945–]). This view argues that the six days of Genesis 1 are long periods of time parallel to geological ages. Genesis 1 presents us with a series of divine acts done over billions of years. (3) The "framework" view (e.g., Robert Grosseteste [ca. 1168–1253], Thomas Aquinas [1225–74], John Davis [1854–1926], Meredith Kline [1922–2007], Henri Blocher [1937–]). This view argues that Genesis 1 is not a chronological, sequential account of how creation occurred; rather, it is a theological account following a topical arrangement of six revelatory days of two triads that parallel one another. Also, given that Genesis 1 is a theological account, it says nothing about the length of days or the age of the earth. (4) The "analogical" day view (e.g., W. G. T. Shedd [1820–94], C. John Collins [1954–]) argues that the length of days is undefined, that there is an unspecified time gap in Gen 1:2, and that the creation account is analogous to human workdays. For a summary of interpretations of Gen 1–2, see Letham, *Systematic Theology*, 909–32; and Beeke and Smalley, *Reformed Systematic Theology*, 2:91–103.

[85] For a discussion and evaluation of the Documentary Hypothesis, see Wenham, *Genesis 1–15*, xxi-liii; Mathews, *Genesis 1–11:26*, 63–85.

First, Genesis 1–2 are not two conflicting accounts. Internally within Genesis, the accounts complement each other as they describe God's creation of the world, with special focus on the unique creation of humans and our role in creation. Genesis 1:1–2:3 is a complete literary unit that focuses on the "big picture" of creation. Genesis 2:4–3:24 then focuses on our creation and the establishment of Adam as humanity's covenant head and ultimately what goes wrong with humanity due to Adam's sin. Also, Gen 2:4–50:26 begins the *tôlĕdôt* formulas ("the generations of"), which links Adam to Noah, Abraham, the patriarchs, and the nation of Israel. Genesis 2:4 stands as a "signpost" pointing the way forward into the rest of Genesis; indeed, to the unfolding of God's redemptive plan in history. Not surprisingly, a narrowing takes place in Gen 2:4 since what is described in "overview" terms in Gen 1:26–28 is now given specific focus.[86] All of this is to say that, as Douglas Kelly reminds us,

> far from repeating (and internally contradicting) Genesis 1, Genesis 2:4–3:24 may be thought of as the bridge leading from the general creation of all things to the specific concern of the rest of the sixty-six books of the Bible: the redemption of mankind, chief image-bearer of the Creator of the entire cosmos. Hence it should not be surprising to find a somewhat different order of events in chapter 2 from those of chapter 1. The explanation is simple, once one understands the structure and purpose of these two earliest chapters. Chapter 1, the "headlines" or "whole picture" is meant to provide chronological sequence, whereas chapter 2 is there to develop one aspect of the picture or story . . . preparing the way for all the rest of divine revelation.[87]

Second, the uses of different names for God, or different verbs for our human creation, do not prove that the accounts are contradictory. First, *Elohim* is a name for God that focuses on his lordship as the Creator of all things, hence its exclusive use in Genesis 1. But *Yahweh* is the covenant name of God (Exod 3:14), which is used in Genesis 2 because the focus of the text is on God's creation of humans, his establishment of Adam as our covenant head, and God's personal relationship to his image-bearers. In fact, the rare compound of *Yahweh-Elohim* is used by Moses to remind Israel that the true and living God of creation is also their covenant Lord. In a similar way, the use of *bārā'* in Genesis 1 focuses on God as our Creator

[86] See Edward J. Young, *Studies in Genesis One* (Philadelphia: P&R, 1964), 1–14, 61–65.

[87] Kelly, *Creation and Change*, 48.

and Lord, while *yāsar* in Genesis 2 focuses on a different emphasis.[88] None of these differences prove contradiction.

Third, a "contradiction" between Gen 1:11–13 and 2:5 only results if we fail to read the text carefully and not see that 2:4–3:24 is one literary unit.[89] Let us develop this point.

1. In Gen 1:11, a general term is used for "vegetation" (*deše'*), which is divided into two classes, the "grasses" (*'ēśeb*) and "trees" (*'ēs*). But Gen 2:5 does *not* say that no vegetation existed prior to our creation; instead, it says that two specific types of vegetation did not yet exist, that is, the "shrub of the field" (*śîah haśśādeh*) and the "plant of the field" (*'ēśeb haśśādeh*). The former refers to any "non-edible, uncultivated plant growing in the wild, including thorns, thistles, and cacti,"[90] while the latter refers to "any non-woody, edible plant which requires human cultivation, including cereal crops, rice, vegetables and herbs."[91] The point of the text is that before humans were created, although vegetation existed, these two types of vegetation did not. In fact, two reasons are given for why this was so: God had not yet caused it to rain, and there were no humans to cultivate the ground (2:5), which, in the narrative, prepares us for the creation of Adam in v. 7, whose vocation will be to care for Eden and the entire earth.

2. The text also prepares us for what happens after the fall in Gen 3:8–24. In Gen 3:17–18 we are told that due to Adam's sin, he (and all of humanity) will have to work the ground "in painful toil" in order to produce "plants of the field" for food (NIV). This means that the "plants of the field" describe our diet that we eat only after the sweat of our labor due to sin (3:18–19), whereas the "seed-bearing" plants of Gen 1:11 "were provided by God for human and animal consumption (1:11–12, 29–30; 9:3). These plants reproduce themselves by seed alone, but 'plant,' spoken of in 2:5, requires human cultivation to produce the grains necessary for edible food; it is by such cultivation that fallen man will eat his 'food' (3:19)."[92] Likewise, the "shrub of the field" parallels Adam's "thorns and thistles," which are the result of God's

---

[88] See Mathews, *Genesis 1–11:26*, 191–93.

[89] For a full discussion of this point, see Umberto Cassuto, *A Commentary on the Book of Genesis*, trans. I. Abrahams, 2 vols. (Jerusalem: Magnes Press, 1961), 1:100–4; cf. Stephen Kempf, "Introducing the Garden of Eden: The Structure and Function of Genesis 2:4b–7," *JOTT* 7, no. 4 (1996): 33–53.

[90] Kulikovsky, *Creation, Fall, Restoration*, 181 (see chap. 5, n. 85). The term is also found in three other places in the OT (e.g., Gen 21:15; Job 30:4, 7).

[91] Kulikovsky, 180.

[92] Mathews, *Genesis 1–11:26*, 194.

curse on the ground (3:17–18). Ken Mathews correctly describes why there is no contradiction in the text: "[Genesis] 2:5–6 does not speak of the creation of overall vegetation but to specific sorts of herbage in the world to follow. The language of cultivation, 'work the ground' (2:5), anticipates the labor of Adam, first positively as the caretaker of Eden (2:15) but also negatively in 3:23, which describes the expulsion of the man and woman from the garden."[93]

3. Thus, there is no contradiction between Gen 1:11 and 2:5. Rather, the texts teach that God not only prepared the earth for Adam to work, but it also anticipates how the earth will be affected by Adam's sin and rebellion against God. On a side note, this is also strong evidence that Adam's sin not only brought about his physical and spiritual death; it also had effects that reverberated in the world. In fact, it also anticipates God's judgment against all humans for their sin in Noah's day. How so? Because one of the reasons why these two kinds of plants had not yet appeared was because no rain had yet appeared on the earth. It seems that the subterranean ground water described in 2:6 ("streams," *'ēd*) provided sufficient water for most types of vegetation, but not all. The "shrubs of the field" did not arise until after God announced he would send rain on the earth (7:4) due to humanity's sin in Noah's day, which may suggest that it did not rain until the advent of the global flood.[94] As Mathews notes, "Whereas in 2:5–6 rain is perceived as the welcomed welfare of God whereby herbage may survive, in the flood account the rains are the means of divine reparations for a morally depraved earth."[95]

What is our conclusion? If read properly, there is no contradiction between Genesis 1–2.

The Literary Form of Genesis 1–2

What kind of literature is Genesis 1–2? Depending on one's answer to this question, different conclusions will emerge as to the meaning of the text. If Genesis 1–2 is a historical narrative, then we ought to read it as giving a factual, historical, and truthful account of how God created the world. But if Genesis 1–2 is written as a poem, a parable, a work of fiction, or even as a "myth," then its correspondence to reality will differ greatly from a historical

[93] Mathews, 194.

[94] On this point, see Kulikovsky, *Creation, Fall, Restoration*, 181–82.

[95] Mathews, *Genesis 1–11:26*, 195.

narrative.[96] For example, think about the difference between the narrative account of the Exodus (Exod 14:5–31) and its more poetic description (Exod 15:1–21). Both are true, but they describe reality differently. What then is the literary form of Genesis 1–2? Here are four points to consider.

First, Genesis 1–2 must be read in its textual, literary, and historical context as we seek to discern Moses's intent in writing Genesis and the entire Pentateuch. When we do so, we discover that these chapters are part of the overall historical narrative of Genesis (and the Pentateuch), and there is no difference between the historical narrative of Genesis 1–11 and 12–50. In fact, specific genealogies structure Genesis—all of which are tied to historical people and events.[97] Although there are literary features in the text, such as symbolism and poetry, the text's form is narrative and not poetry.[98] No doubt, one must still determine whether the

[96] *Myth* is used in a number of ways. Broadly, it can refer to a story that functions as a larger worldview, but one still has to determine whether it is *true* story. But more commonly, *myth* refers to stories that are legends and fables, and thus works of fiction. Regarding Genesis 1–2, some try to argue that "myth" is also "mytho-history," that is, a story that functions as a worldview but also one that combines fiction and non-fiction in it. The majority view has not applied the category of "myth" to Genesis given the church's conviction that it is a true, historical narrative. But in recent days, some evangelicals insist that Genesis 1–11 is "mytho-history," which is highly problematic. Why? Because ultimately it requires an authoritative *extratextual* framework to determine what part of Genesis is fiction vs. non-fiction. But what exactly is that standard? As we discussed in part 1, this *extratextual* approach to Genesis is basically a return to some version of the historical-critical method. For some evangelicals who take this wrongheaded approach, see Enns, *Evolution of Adam* (see chap. 11, n. 41); and William Lane Craig, *In Quest of the Historical Adam: A Biblical and Scientific Exploration* (Grand Rapids: Eerdmans, 2021); Craig, "The Historical Adam," *First Things*, October 2021, https://www.firstthings.com/article/2021/10/the-historical-adam. For a helpful response to Craig, see Peter J. Leithart, "Doubts About William Lane Craig's Creation Account," *First Things*, November 1, 2021, https://www.firstthings.com/web-exclusives/2021/10/doubts-about-william-lane-craigs-creation-account; and the series of articles by Jason Lisle at https://biblicalscienceinstitute.com, starting with https://biblicalscienceinstitute.com/apologetics/the-historical-adam-part-1-an-introduction/.

[97] Genesis is divided into ten divisions, identified by the *tôlĕdôt* formulas ("these are the generations of") (Gen 2:4; 5:1; 6:9; 10:1; 11:27; 25:12; 25:19; 36:1; 36:9; 37:2). Within Genesis, there is no literary distinction in terms of historical narrative between Gen 1–11 and 12–50; it is one seamless whole starting in creation with Adam and continuing in the patriarchs.

[98] See Poythress, *Interpreting Eden*, 119–30 (see chap. 5, n. 85). Symbolism in narratives does not render it less historical. Narratives can include within them various literary forms (e.g., parables in the Gospels), but the fact that the text is a narrative communicates the author's intent on how it corresponds to reality.

narrative is a fictional or non-fictional account, but when these texts are located within Genesis and the Pentateuch, we have no evidence that Moses intends us to interpret these chapters as fiction, myth, or legend.[99]

But with this said, we must also locate the text in its historical context and not demand that it say more than it does. Moses is not giving us a "scientific" treatise about how God created the world. Instead, his account is a *theology* of creation, but it is still a historical narrative describing an actual state of affairs. Furthermore, as we discussed in part 2, Genesis is *God's* word through *human* authors. As such, its communication is authoritative and true but also "ordinary." God's speech through human authors is not intended to be a technical account, but a true, ordinary, and reliable account. As Bavinck reminds us, Scripture is a book "for the whole of humanity in all of its ranks and classes, in all of its generations and peoples. But for that very reason too it is not a scientific book in a strict sense. . . . It does not speak the exact language of science and the academy but the language of observation and daily life."[100] Scripture looks at the world in terms of observation or phenomena; hence, it speaks of the sun rising and setting. But this does not deny its truthfulness. In fact, if Scripture had spoken in the language of the science of its day, "it would have stood in the way of its own authority. If it had decided in favor of the Ptolemaic worldview, it would not have been credible in an age that supported the Copernican system. Nor could it have been a book for life, for humanity."[101]

---

[99] Some have strangely argued that since Genesis depicts God in anthropomorphic terms, it should be read in a figurative way (e.g., Ernest C. Lucas, Denis R. Alexander, R. J. Berry, G. Andrew D. Briggs, Colin J. Humphreys, Malcolm A. Jeeves). See also Anthony C. Thiselton, "The Bible, Science and Human Origins," *Science and Christian Belief* 28, no. 2 (2016): 83–84; and Craig, "The Historical Adam." This is a strange argument since all biblical language in reference to God is analogical (or anthropomorphic). As Leithart rightly notes,

> God, [Craig] claims, is "personal," but how does he know that this, too, is not an anthropomorphism? God "designed" the physical world, which sounds a lot like attributing human activities to God. The creation account, Craig says, teaches us to "set apart one day per week as sacred"; but while Genesis 2 tells us God rested, it actually says nothing about human rest. Craig's inference that we should rest one day a week depends on an analogy between God and man that he otherwise discounts. Perhaps Craig can filter legitimate from illegitimate anthropomorphism, but if so, he has not told us how to perform the trick. "Doubts About."

[100] Bavinck, *Reformed Dogmatics*, 1:445.

[101] Bavinck, 1:446; cf. Bavinck, 2:482–85.

In a recent work, Vern Poythress states this point well.[102] He observes that many recent treatments of Genesis follow the "vehicle-cargo" approach. This approach adopts a Socinian view of accommodation; that is, God communicates through the errors of ancient culture instead of following the classical view of accommodation. God speaks truthfully but in an ordinary way.[103] Poythress argues that if people follow the "vehicle-cargo" approach, they inevitably accept the "myth of scientistic metaphysics"; that is, "knowledge" from current science surpasses the knowledge of Scripture, thus undercutting God's ability to communicate truth in an ancient text. "Science" is then elevated to an extratextual authority over Scripture. However, such a view fails to account for Scripture as *God's* word, and it wrongly assumes that Scripture's ordinary descriptions are false. It views "science" as a neutral, objective discipline that yields greater knowledge than Scripture, and it embraces the false belief that "modern science exposes the way things 'really are,' as opposed to the mistaken character of appearances."[104] But this approach is deeply flawed and, if one is not careful, undercuts biblical authority.

Second, Genesis 1–2 is not "mytho-history" or dependent on the cosmogonies of the ancient Near East. Historical criticism has often argued that Genesis "borrows" from the stories of its surrounding culture, thus relativizing its uniqueness.[105] This is simply incorrect. No doubt, given its historical context, Genesis is both a *theological* and *polemical* account of *who* created the universe and *how* in contrast to the cosmogonies of its day (e.g., Mesopotamia's *Enuma Elish* or *Epic of Gilgamesh*, etc.). Thus, one should expect similar language and symbolism in order to set the biblical account over against the other accounts (e.g., "the deep," "waters," etc.).

However, it is not the similarities that are significant, but the *differences* in the accounts.[106] When Genesis is read on its own terms, it is *different* from its contemporary counterparts. For

---

[102] See Poythress, *Interpreting Eden*; cf. Berkhof, *Systematic Theology*, 130, 150–52.

[103] Poythress, *Interpreting Eden*, 67–69. We discussed the Socinian view of accommodation in part 2.

[104] Poythress, 75.

[105] For example, see Enns, *Inspiration and Incarnation* (see chap. 5, n. 39); John Walton, *The Lost World of Genesis One: Ancient Cosmology and the Origins Debate* (Downers Grove: IVP Academic, 2009); cf. Craig, *In Quest of the Historical Adam*, 35–203.

[106] On this point, see John Oswalt, *The Bible among the Myths* (Grand Rapids: Zondervan, 2009); Oswalt, "*Creatio Ex Nihilo*," 165–80; Berkhof, *Systematic Theology*, 150–51; Mathews, *Genesis 1–11:26*, 90–95.

example, all of the ancient Near Eastern accounts deny the Creator-creature distinction. They are polytheistic, as the "gods" struggle to bring order out of chaos and evil forces. Matter is evil and it preexists. As Michael Horton notes,

> In the Babylonian myth, Tiamat is the sea monster who represents chaos that must be overcome. In Genesis, the darkness and the void are called *tᵉhôm* ("the deep"), but unlike its namesake Tiamat, it is not personal and is not a threat to be overcome. It is itself the unformed matter that God had already brought into existence from nothing, the created stuff out of which he fashions the world.[107]

Also, in Genesis, totally unlike the other accounts, God alone is the subject of his creative work since he alone is the true God, who simply speaks and the universe comes to exist *ex nihilo* (Gen 1:1). Furthermore, it should not surprise us that all cultures have "origin" accounts. The issue is whether Genesis is the *true* account versus the sinful distortions of the surrounding cultures.[108]

Third, although Genesis 1–2 is a literary masterpiece (which includes within it symbolism and poetry)—even "exalted prose"[109]—it is a *true*, *historical*, and *chronological* narrative in continuity with Genesis and the entire Pentateuch. Throughout church history, there have been different interpretations of the historical nature of Genesis 1–2, as evidenced by Augustine and others. Yet the church has consistently interpreted these chapters as a true, historical narrative.

But since the rise of historical criticism and especially the Darwinian theory, people have sought to "fit" Scripture with the perceived truth of "science," which has resulted in a spectrum of thought regarding the historical nature of these chapters. Here is the basic spectrum.

1. "Classic liberal theology" interpreted Genesis 1–11 as mythical, legendary, and historically false. They rejected a historical Adam along with a space-time fall. Some tried to argue that despite Genesis's errors, we may allegorize the text to draw theological "truths" from it. But the problem with such a view is that Genesis is not an allegory and to read it as such is a major hermeneutical mistake. In fact, the only reason classical liberal theology interpreted

---

[107] Horton, *Christian Faith*, 325–26 (see chap. 15, n. 80).

[108] On this point, Rom 1:18–32 explains why and how all people, left to themselves apart from God's grace, distort the truth of creation and ultimately resort to myths.

[109] "Exalted prose" is C. John Collins's description of Genesis 1–3 (*Genesis 1–4*, 237–67). Yet, the literary structure of Genesis is a historical narrative consisting of *waw*-consecutives plus the imperfect.

Genesis in this way was due to their commitment to an *extratextual* framework more authoritative than Scripture. At first, this extratextual authority was deism, then panentheism, both of which embraced methodological naturalism and all of its metaphysical and epistemological entailments.

2. In the early twentieth century, "neo-orthodoxy" emerged as a reaction to "classic liberal theology." Neo-orthodoxy is largely identified with Karl Barth (1886–1968) and Emil Brunner (1889–1966). Barth argued that Genesis 1–2 was *not* a "myth"; instead, it was a "saga," that is, a story that includes in it theological "truth" but not necessarily "historical" truth. Genesis conveys universal theological "truths," and Adam was viewed as an archetypal figure that symbolically represented every person, but in the end, he did not actually exist or sin in space-time history.[110] Genesis, then, is more fiction than non-fiction, a product of the ancient Near East. For neo-orthodoxy, the findings of evolutionary "science" were viewed as "true" against the Genesis story. Thus, regardless of Barth's opposition to liberalism, his theology ends up interpreting Genesis through the extratextual lens of "science," which is perceived as more authoritative. Ironically, if Barth draws "theological" truth from Genesis, he can only do so by reading the text allegorically.

Although a majority in the church has always viewed the entirety of Genesis as a historical narrative, a number of evangelicals have recently embraced the view of neo-orthodoxy.[111] In doing so, they have also adopted a Socinian view of accommodation and argue that Genesis is a combination of legend, history, and truth. But what is "true" is inevitably determined by an "authoritative" standard "outside" of Scripture, thus rejecting a consistent intratextual approach to Scripture and Christian theology. For example, William Craig still affirms that Adam is a historical person, yet not as Genesis describes it. Instead, Adam is constituted as the first "human" from various pre-human ancestors, something that Genesis 1–2 (and the entire Bible) does not teach. One can only draw such a conclusion if one wrongly identifies the literary form of Genesis and reads the text allegorically, that is, by stating, "this text means *that*," where *that* is determined by an interpretive grid that does not arise from Scripture itself.

---

[110] Karl Barth, *CD* IV/1:508 (see chap. 2, n. 101).

[111] See Francis Collins, *The Language of God: A Scientist Presents Evidence for Belief* (New York: Free Press, 2006); Enns, *Evolution of Adam*; Denis Lamoureux, "No Historical Adam: Evolutionary Creation View," in Barrett and Caneday, *Four Views on the Historical Adam*, 37–65 (see chap. 5, n. 77); Craig, *In Quest of the Historical Adam*.

In the end, the early chapters of Genesis as a true and historical account is downplayed, if not outright rejected, and the "assured results" of evolutionary "science" are accepted seemingly without question.

3. In contrast to these other views, the majority view of the church from the first century to our present era is that Genesis is a true, historical, and chronological account of God's creation of the material universe. Specifically, it is an accurate account of God's creation of humans in his image, with the acceptance of an historical Adam and historical fall. The church has consistently argued that this is the *only* view that is true to Genesis and the entirety of Scripture.[112]

Fourth, here are some of the reasons for the historic view, which evangelical theology ought to affirm given biblical authority and the significance of these chapters to our entire theology.

1. Moses writes Genesis as a historical narrative within the Pentateuch, which the remainder of the OT and NT confirm. The only reason one would interpret it otherwise is due to something "outside" the text being read back on it. Yet, as we discussed in chapter 4, this hermeneutical approach and theological method is extratextual, not intratextual, which, if one is not careful, will undermine biblical authority and the priority of special revelation.

2. Within Genesis and the entire Bible, biblical genealogies signal that Moses intends for us to read Genesis as a historical narrative *and* to view Adam and Eve as historical people; indeed, the first human couple that all humans descend from (1 Chron 1:1; Luke 3:38). The same *tôlĕdôt* genealogical structure extends from Gen 2:4 through chapter 50, which sets the framework of human history (2:4; 5:1; 6:9; 10:1; 11:10; 11:27; 25:12; 36:1; 36:9; 37:2). There is nothing in Genesis (or the entire Bible) that allows us to think that Genesis is not presenting actual history. As Beeke and Smalley rightly state: "The Bible presents the Genesis accounts of creation as real history, of one piece with the history of God's redeeming acts in Jesus Christ."[113]

---

[112] See Allison, *Historical Theology*, 254–76; also see Francis A. Schaeffer, "Genesis in Space and Time" and "No Final Conflict," in *Complete Works of Francis A. Schaeffer*, 2:1–114, 2:119–48 (see chap. 1, n. 36). Schaeffer argues that there is flexibility in the Genesis account that allows for a young and old earth position but one breaks the text if one denies the historicity of Adam and the fall and embraces pre-hominid "humans."

[113] Beeke and Smalley, *Reformed Systematic Theology*, 2:81; cf. Vos, *Reformed Dogmatics*, 1:161; Kulikovsky, *Creation, Fall, Restoration*, 85–90; Young, *Studies in Genesis One*, 105; Poythress, *Interpreting Eden*, 131–34; Mathews, *Genesis 1–11:26*, 109–11.

3. Our Lord assumes that the early chapters of Genesis are history, along with the historical existence of Adam and Eve. In Jesus's teaching on divorce, he assumes the truthfulness of the Genesis account (Matt 19:4–6; Mark 10:6–8 [Gen 1:27; 2:24]). It is significant that when Jesus says that God created humans "from the beginning of creation" (Mark 10:6), the creation of Adam and Eve are closely tied to the absolute beginning described in Gen 1:1. The same point is taught in Luke 11:50–51 (Matt 23:35). Jesus not only refers to Abel as a historical person (Gen 4:1–16), he also places Abel in close proximity to the beginning of time—"since the foundation of the world." Jesus interprets Genesis as recording actual history, true and reliable for our understanding of how the generations have transpired from Adam, through Abel, to our present time, and the specific features of creation, especially the creation of Adam and Eve, as grounding marriage, the family, and other important truths and theological structures that are unpacked across the Bible's covenantal story. To say that Jesus is "accommodating" his teaching to the thought of the day, or worse, that Jesus was wrong in his understanding of creation, Adam, and human history, is ultimately to undermine his authority and the entire authority of Scripture.

4. The NT authors assume the truth of Genesis, creation, the historical existence of Adam and Eve as the first human couple, the covenant headship of Adam, and Adam's sinful action, which affects all of humanity along with creation itself. In this way, the NT builds on the OT covenantal story, which provides the background and framework for grasping the identity of Christ and his entire new covenant work. To deny these key points is to undercut and seriously undermine the Bible's entire theological framework. For example, Paul assumes the historical existence of Adam and Eve and the specific ordering of Genesis 2 in his grounding the complementary relationships between men and women, along with leadership in the family and the church (1 Tim 2:13–14 [Gen 2:15–25; 3:1–20]). At Athens, Paul grounds the unity of all humanity in "one man," which in the teaching of Scripture and Paul is a clear reference to Adam (Acts 17:26). There is no hint that Adam was the "first human" drawn from previous "pre-humans." To argue such a point is to impose on Scripture an extratextual lens that is not true to it on its own terms. In fact, the NT teaching regarding Christ as the last Adam is predicated on the fact that Adam is a historical person, and to deny this historical and theological type-antitype relation is to undermine the Bible's entire redemptive plan (Rom 5:12–21; 1 Cor 15:22–23, 45–47).[114]

---

[114] On this important point, see A. B. Caneday, "The Language of God and Adam's Genesis and Historicity in Paul's Gospel," *SBJT* 15, no. 1 (2011): 26–59; Caneday, "Already Reigning in Life

The same is also true of Peter and the author of Hebrews. Peter assumes the historical reliability of the Genesis account "since the beginning of creation" (2 Pet 3:4), which includes the reality of a global flood (2 Pet 3:3–7). In Hebrews, the creation account, specifically the reality of the seventh day, is assumed, as the author unpacks an important "rest" theme across the entire canon, which is now fulfilled in Christ (Heb 3:7–4:13). Overall, the NT assumes and teaches that Genesis and its recording of events are true, historical, and accurate.

5. Unless Adam and Eve were created morally good as historical people; Adam served as the covenant head of humanity; Adam's rebellious choice against God's command brought sin and death (spiritual and physical) into the world, so that now all humanity is fallen "in Adam"; the entire Christian position changes from what Scripture says it is. Why? Here are *three* reasons.

1. God would be linked with death, suffering, and evil and bear responsibility for it. What we identify as "natural" evil (e.g., death, suffering, etc.) would simply be a "normal" part of God's world that he created from the beginning. It would not be something abnormal due to Adam's sin and thus would not be God's judicial punishment for sin as it is in Scripture (Gen 2:16–17; 3:17–19; Rom 3:23; 6:23). In fact, an unbiblical wedge between creation and redemption would result. As Hans Madueme notes, "On the one hand, God *as Creator* uses suffering, pain, and death to advance the evolutionary process and to bring his creatures into being. On the other hand, God *as Redeemer* vanquishes sin and death, restores nature, and eradicates animal suffering. God's work of creation contradicts his work of redemption."[115]

2. There is also no hope for a solution to our problem. If physical "death" and "fallenness" is "normal" and not the result of a historic fall and our "fallenness" is tied to our metaphysical "makeup" as creatures, then our only hope is for God to scrap us and start all over again. This is why those who reject a historic Adam and fall also tend to reduce our human disposition

---

through One Man: Recovery of Adam's Abandoned Dominion (Romans 5:12–21), in *Studies in the Pauline Epistles: Essays in Honor of Douglas J. Moo*, ed. Matthew Harmon and Jay E. Smith (Grand Rapids: Zondervan, 2014), 27–43; J. P. Versteeg, *Adam in the New Testament: Mere Teaching Model or First Historical Man?*, trans. Richard B. Gaffin Jr., 2nd ed. (Phillipsburg: P&R, 2012); William VanDoodewaard, *The Quest for the Historical Adam: Genesis, Hermeneutics, and Human Origins* (Grand Rapids: Reformation Heritage, 2015).

[115] Hans Madueme, "The Theological Problem with Evolution," *Zygon* 56, no. 2 (2021): 484. Many who try to escape these conclusions tend to move in a more panentheistic direction, thus closely identifying God and the world.

to sin to genetic forces within us, thus relieving humans of their responsible agency.[116] But in Scripture, humans are treated as responsible creatures, who in Adam rebelled against God, which resulted in an *abnormal* situation that only God can remedy. In this case, not only is God not responsible for our sin: we are, but there is also hope for us. By the incarnation of the divine Son, and due to his moral obedience as our new covenant head, along with his payment of our sin, God can restore us to what we were first created to be; indeed, restore us to a greater situation. But in Scripture, our redemption in Christ is re-creation due to Adam's sin in history that changed a *good* world free of sin and death into a fallen, cursed world.

3. Apart from Adam's representative choice as our covenant head in history, there is no explanation for the origin of sin and its universality. In Scripture, sin and evil are due to the creature; they are not created by God or attributable to him. And the reason why *all* people sin is Adam's sin, along with our continued rebellion against God (Rom 3:23; 5:12–21; Eph 2:1–3). Also, the solution to the problem of sin "in Adam" is the incarnation of the divine Son. Inevitably, if one denies a historic Adam and fall, the biblical link between the first and last Adam is severed, and the rationale for the Bible's plan of redemption is rendered unnecessary. Only a *fallen* humanity needs a Redeemer, and the intelligibility of an "unfallen" Redeemer redeeming a fallen humanity and restoring us requires both a first and last Adam in history.

The bottom line is this: Genesis, read on its own terms, in the Pentateuch and the entire Bible, requires the affirmation of a historic Adam, historic fall, and the need for our triune God to provide the remedy to our problem in the last Adam, our Lord Jesus Christ. The only reason one would deny these points is due to a commitment to an "extratextual" view imposed on Scripture, and if one is not careful, this extratextual authority carries more authority than Scripture itself.

The Scriptural Account of Creation (Genesis 1:1–2:3)

Genesis 1–2 is not only the beginning of Genesis (and the Pentateuch); it is also the beginning of the Bible's unfolding covenantal storyline, which ultimately moves from creation to

[116] On this point, see Madueme, 491–92; cf. Hans Madueme, "All Truth is God's Truth: A Defense of Dogmatic Creationism," in *Creation and Doxology: The Beginning and End of God's Good World*, ed. Gerald L. Hiestand and Todd Wilson (Downers Grove: IVP Academic, 2018), 59–76.

the new creation, centered in the person and work of our Lord Jesus Christ. Our primary focus is on Gen 1:1–2:3, since Genesis 2–3 (along with 1:26–31) will be discussed in volume 2 in our exposition of the doctrine of humanity and sin. Let us look at Gen 1:1–2:3 in *four* steps.

First, verse 1: "In the beginning God created the heavens and the earth." The first exegetical decision to make is whether *bĕrēʾšît* ("In the beginning") is a dependent or independent clause. If the former, it is translated, "When God began to create," and it would not require that verse 1 is referring to the absolute beginning of the universe. Although this is grammatically possible, it is better to follow the majority view and argue that it is an independent clause and thus a reference to God's absolute creation of the world.[117] The context of the chapter, its placement in Genesis and the entire Bible, is explaining that God created the entire material, space-time universe.[118] In fact, apart from this verse referring to the absolute beginning, as Vos reminds us, "any reference to the first act of creation would be lacking,"[119] but its placement at the beginning of Scripture has the opposite effect. In addition, in contrast to the pagan myths, God is the only God—the transcendent and sovereign Lord who simply speaks all things into existence *ex nihilo*.

Verse 1 describes God's *immediate* creation of the universe, which is also confirmed by the use of the verb for "create" (*bārāʾ*), a point we have already discussed. Although *creatio ex nihilo* cannot be established by a single word, in the context of Genesis, it refers to God's

---

[117] Wenham, *Genesis 1–15*, 12–13; Oswalt, "*Creatio Ex Nihilo*," 171; Mathews, *Genesis 1–11:26*, 136–44; Young, *Studies in Genesis One*, 1–7; Kulikovsky, *Creation, Fall, Restoration*, 106–7.

[118] In contrast to John Walton, who insists that Gen 1–2 is not describing God's creation of the *material* universe. Walton argues that *bārāʾ* means that God creates "by assigning functions," which is problematic. To create does *not* mean to "assign a function." Also, the objects of *bārāʾ* in Gen 1 are all material: "the heavens and the earth" (1:1), the sea monsters (1:21), and humans (1:27). See Walton, *Lost World of Genesis.*

John H. Walton and N. T. Wright, *The Lost World of Adam and Eve: Genesis 2–3 and the Human Origins Debate* (Downers Grove: IVP Academic, 2015). For a critique of Walton, see Oswalt, "*Creatio Ex Nihilo*," 175–77; Noel K. Weeks, "The Bible and the 'Universal' Ancient World: A Critique of John Walton," *WTJ* 78 (2016): 1–28; Steve Ham, "What's Lost in John Walton's *The Lost World of Adam and Eve?*," in *Searching for Adam: Genesis and the Truth about Man's Origin*, ed. Terry Mortenson (Green Forest, AR: Master Books, 2016), 165–93.

[119] Vos, *Reformed Dogmatics*, 1:163.

unique act of the creation of the universe, which is confirmed by the phrase "the heavens and earth."[120]

Second, verse 2: "Now the earth was formless and empty (*tōhû* and *bōhû*), darkness covered the surface of the watery depths, and the Spirit of God was hovering over the surface of the waters." The syntax of the verse makes it clear that v. 2 is giving us background information for the narrative that begins in v. 3.[121] Its purpose is to explain the state of things, or better, the condition of the earth, after God's absolute creation of all things (v. 1) and before the narrative begins in v. 3, which then focuses on God's successive creation of a habitable earth.

1. The word order renders indefensible the "gap" or "restitution" theory.[122] The "gap" theory argues for a sequential reading of v. 2, which describes the recovery of the world from the chaos it had lapsed into between vv. 1–2. The view translates 1:2a as "and the earth became," arguing that v. 1 describes the original creation of the earth, while v. 2 refers to a judgment that

---

[120] See Exod 20:11; 2 Kgs 19:15; 2 Chron 2:12; Ezra 5:11; Neh 9:6; Pss 115:15; 121:2; 124:8; 134:3; Acts 14:15; 17:24; Col 1:16; Rev 10:6; 14:7. "The heavens and the earth" refers to the totality of the universe, but in contrast to some commentators, it does not necessarily mean "the completely ordered cosmos." Instead, as Wenham argues, "totality rather than organization is its chief thrust here." For this reason, as we will note in v. 2, Wenham correctly states: "It is therefore quite feasible for a mention of an initial act of creation of the whole universe (v 1) to be followed by an account of the ordering of different parts of the universe (vv 2–31)." *Genesis 1–15*, 15. Also, although "the heavens and earth" refers to the universe, the focus of the text moves from the "heavens" to the "earth" (v. 2; Gen 2:4), where God makes a suitable place for humanity.

[121] It is a *waw*-disjunctive clause (conjunction + subject + verb), which describes the condition of the earth before God speaks in v. 3. It cannot be translated as an independent sequential clause, which would mean that v. 2 relates to the next event in sequence. If that were the point, we would expect the *waw* consecutive + prefixed verbal form + subject. On this point, see Vos, *Reformed Dogmatics*, 1:164; Wenham, *Genesis 1–15*, 11–13, 15–17; Mathews, *Genesis 1–11:26*, 139–44; Kulikovsky, *Creation, Fall, Restoration*, 108–9. The structure of 1:1–3 is the following: v. 1 states God's absolute creation of the universe; v. 2 describes the condition of the earth at the point of creation; v. 3 begins the narrative of how God makes the earth suitable for habitation, especially culminating in human existence on the sixth day. A similar structure is given in 2:4–7: v. 4 is the overall statement; vv. 5–6 gives us background information regarding the state of the earth prior to the creation of man; and in v. 7 the narrative sequence begins with the creation of Adam, his placement in Eden, the establishment of the covenant, and then the creation of Eve.

[122] The "gap" or "restitution" theory was taught by Thomas Chalmers (1780–1847) and later popularized by the *Scofield Reference Bible*. Cf. Arthur C. Custance, *Without Form and Void* (Brockville, Ontario: n.p., 1970). For a helpful evaluation of the view, see Beeke and Smalley, *Reformed Systematic Theology*, 2:93–94.

reduced it to a chaotic condition. Verses 3–31, then, are the re-creation of the earth after an unspecified period. However, the disjunctive clause at the beginning of v. 2 is not sequential; thus, it does not narrate the next event in time.

One of the reasons for the "gap" theory was to reconcile the creation account with an old earth. By making v. 2 sequential in the narrative, it allowed for the potential of long geological ages, along with an emphasis on catastrophes that helped explain the fossil record. The view also speculated about when angels fell, something Scripture does not explicitly say. But this view is exegetically unsustainable given that v. 2 does not describe a time gap. In addition, as Beeke and Smalley rightly observe, the view

> is inconsistent with biblical teaching on creation. The tone of Genesis 1 runs entirely contrary to any idea of strife or judgment, but emphasizes the sovereign ease with which God acted in making the world in perfect harmony with his will. It is difficult to see how a world already marred by Satan's rebellion could be viewed as "very good" by God (v. 31). The entire work of creation took place in six days.[123]

2. In contrast to those who interpret "formless and empty" (*tōhû* and *bōhû*) as "uncreated" or as evidence of dependence on ancient Near Eastern myths,[124] the two nouns simply indicate the condition of the earth after God's absolute creation.[125] By the first circumstantial clause, we discover that the earth was not yet differentiated, separated, and habitable for human existence, let alone the existence of any other creature.[126] The second and third circumstantial clauses confirm this point. Not only was the earth "formless and empty," but "darkness was over the deep waters," and the "Spirit of God was hovering/brooding over the waters."[127]

Three points are emphasized: there was no light on the earth, the earth was not constituted as a firm body, and God, by his Word and Spirit, is the only one who can make the earth

---

[123] Beeke and Smalley, *Reformed Systematic Theology*, 2:94.

[124] See Bruce K. Waltke, *Genesis* (Grand Rapids: Zondervan, 2001); Walton, *Lost World of Genesis*.

[125] *Tōhû* (formless) and *bōhû* (empty) (Isa 34:11; Jer 4:23) refer to a "desolate and uninhabited place, rather than some chaotic state." See David T. Tsumaru, *The Earth and the Waters in Genesis 1–2* (Sheffield: Sheffield Academic Press, 1989), 326–28; Wenham, *Genesis 1–15*, 15–16; Kulikovsky, *Creation, Fall, Restoration*, 109–12.

[126] See Oswalt, "*Creatio Ex Nihilo*," 172–73.

[127] See Deut 32:11, where the same word for "hovering/brooding" is used for a bird who hovers over her young.

habitable for us.[128] In fact, as v. 3 begins with God's speech, we see a trinitarian hint that God by his word and Spirit is the Creator and Lord of all things. When God speaks, nothing resists his command and everything bows to his decree. Throughout the entirety of Genesis 1, God is the one who is the sovereign actor, speaker, and Creator. In this context, the "Spirit" is the bearer of God's presence by which he draws near (immanence), while remaining distinct from the elements of the universe (transcendence), thus preserving the Creator-creature distinction. In light of further revelation, it is legitimate to say that in the triune work of God, the Spirit is the "perfecting" cause, who along with the Father and Son, creates the world and makes it habitable for us.

3. Although the "gap" theory is indefensible, some argue that v. 2 does not specify how long the earth was in its uninhabitable condition.[129] For this view, the first day of creation starts in v. 3, not in v. 1, allowing for a potentially long period of time between God's absolute creation and the first day of creation. Historically, people have viewed v. 1 as the beginning of the first day, which Exod 20:11 seems to confirm.[130] Yet this view is exegetically possible, and it is one way that an older earth is defended from Genesis 1. But it is speculative since the text does not demand a time gap in v. 2. What drives this interpretation is the desire to reconcile Genesis 1 with contemporary science. This is legitimate, given that natural and special revelation are both God-given, but one must exercise caution. Scientific issues must be dealt with on their own terms, and as argued in chapter 6, Scripture must have priority in our interpretation.[131]

Third, verses 3–31 describe God's sequential acts of creation in six days. Discussion of these verses has resulted in a number of views of what is occurring. We offer *three* observations.

1. There is an obvious literary structure in the six days of creation, as many have argued.[132] Verses 3–31 present eight acts of creation occurring in the first six days if we exclude God's fiat act of creation in v. 1. The eight acts are divided into two groups of four acts (vv. 3–13, 14–31),

---

[128] "Spirit of God" best translates *rûach Elohim*, not the "wind/breath" of God. See Mathews, *Genesis 1–11:26*, 135–36; Young, *Studies in Genesis One*, 38–42.

[129] For example, see Collins, *Genesis 1–4*, 251–55; cf. Bavinck, *Reformed Dogmatics*, 2:478–79, 499.

[130] Turretin, *Institutes of Elenctic Theology*, 1:446–47.

[131] For me, the first day includes Gen 1:1–2, but this is a disputed point. For a defense of the first day starting with Gen 1:1, see Kulikovsky, *Creation, Fall, Restoration*, 123–29; Young, *Studies in Genesis One*, 87–89.

[132] Turretin, *Institutes of Elenctic Theology*, 1:446–52; Bavinck, *Reformed Dogmatics*, 2:478–82; Wenham, *Genesis 1–15*, 5–10; Collins, *Genesis 1–4*, 39–100; Mathews, *Genesis 1–11:26*, 144–81.

each group occurring within three days. The seventh day (2:1–3) is the climax of the preceding six days. In both groups, the movement is from the heavens to the waters to the earth. In the first three days, we see progressive *separations*: (1) light from darkness (day 1); (2) the waters above from the waters below (day 2); and (3) the waters below from the dry land (day 3). Then God *fills* his creation with essential life on the last three days: (1) God creates the luminaries to give light (day 4); (2) God creates the sea creatures and birds (day 5); and (3) God creates animals and humans to occupy the earth, with humans as the crowing act of his creation (day 6). On the seventh day, creation is complete and finished, which God's rest signifies.

2. Due to the literary structure, those who endorse "the framework view" argue that the successive days of creation are not chronological and that the days are not necessarily twenty-four-hour days.[133] However, two points require mention. First, the literary structure of Genesis 1 does not entail a non-chronological account. For example, as Beeke and Smalley point out, think of the structured accounts of the ten plagues on Egypt (Exod 7–12) or the six sets of seven in Christ's genealogy in Matthew 1.[134] Both of these examples are highly structured yet chronological and historical. Second, the proposed parallels between the days are not exact. For example, God sets the light bearers "in the expanse of the sky" on day four (1:14), but "the expanse" is created on day two, not day one. Also, day five is supposed to parallel day two, but the birds created on the fifth day "multiply on the earth" (1:22), which was made on the third day.[135] Beeke and Smalley's conclusion is sound: "Rather than collapsing days one and four, two and five, and three and six together into three nonchronological theological topics, it makes much more sense to read Genesis 1 as a chronological sequence of days in which each act of creation prepares for what follows it."[136]

3. Augustine argued that God instantaneously created the world. Thus, the description of creation given in vv. 3–31 is for our benefit, but the successive days of creation are not actual.

---

[133] In recent days, Meredith Kline (1922–2007) and Henri Blocher have argued for "the framework view." See Charles Lee Irons and Meredith G. Kline, "The Framework View," in *The Genesis Debate: Three Views on the Days of Genesis*, ed. David G. Hagopian (Mission Viejo: Crux Press, 2001), 217–56; Henri Blocher, *In the Beginning: The Opening Chapters of Genesis*, trans. David G. Preston (Downers Grove: InterVarsity, 1984).

[134] Beeke and Smalley, *Reformed Systematic Theology*, 2:98.

[135] Beeke and Smalley, 2:98. Also see Young, *Studies in Genesis One*, 68–73; Kulikovsky, *Creation, Fall, Restoration*, 155–62, who shows further discrepancies.

[136] Beeke and Smalley, *Reformed Systematic Theology*, 2:98.

The sequence of days, then, is God's way of describing what he did in a moment. We are then free to interpret the days of creation allegorically, which Augustine did. For example, he interpreted the light of v. 3 as a reference to angels. But Augustine did not think that the world was old.[137] Although he read Genesis 1 allegorically, he argued that the biblical genealogies were chronological and historically accurate, and thus he rejected an old earth.[138] Augustine's view is certainly interesting. It proves that prior to Darwin and the attempt to reconcile Genesis with current view of science, there had been different views of Genesis throughout church history.[139] But as interesting as his view is, the text gives no reason to think it is not a chronological and historical narrative of God's creation of the world in six successive days.

Fourth, the successive days of creation are presented in terms of our perspective of normal, ordinary days. No doubt, *day* (*yôm*) has a range of meaning, and it does not refer to a twenty-four-hour day in every context.[140] However, as Berkhof notes, we see in the creation account "a

---

[137] Augustine, *City of God* 12.11 (484). Augustine writes: "Those who hold such opinions are also led astray by some utterly spurious documents which, they say, give a historical record of many thousand years, whereas we reckon, from the evidence of the holy Scriptures, that fewer than 6,000 years have passed since man's first origin."

[138] Although Augustine is famous for his allegorical interpretation of Genesis 1, in his later works he took the literal meaning of the text more seriously, combining both readings. For example, he revisited his interpretation of the creation accounts in his *Literal Meaning of Genesis* and *Unfinished Literal Commentary on Genesis*. See *The Works of St. Augustine: A Translation for the 21st Century* (Hyde Park, NY: New City Press), I/13.

[139] Throughout church history there have been multiple interpretations of Genesis 1. But the majority view is that it is giving us a historical, sequential account of the six days of creation, mostly understood as twenty-four-hour days. On the history of interpretation, see Allison, *Historical Theology*, 254–76; Kulikovsky, *Creation, Fall, Restoration*, 59–84.

[140] See Vos, *Reformed Dogmatics*, 1:167–68; Beeke and Smalley, *Reformed Systematic Theology*, 2:95–103. For *day* (*yôm*) as long periods of time, see Hugh Ross and Gleason L. Archer, "The Day-Age View," in *The Genesis Debate*, 123–63. The following points are often given. (1) *Day* can refer to indefinite time periods (Gen 5:1; 2 Sam 21:12; Job 20:28; Ps 20:1; Prov 21:31; 24:10; 25:13; Eccl 7:14; Isa 11:16; 13:6, 9; Joel 1:15; 2:1; Amos 5:18; Zeph 1:14). In Gen 2:4, *day* refers to all six days of creation. (2) Since the sun, moon, and stars are not created until day 4, the first three days cannot be twenty-four-hour solar days. (3) Genesis is told from God's perspective and his calculation of time is not the same as ours (see Ps 90:4; 2 Pet 3:8). We must not limit the days to twenty-four hours. (4) The events on day 6 require a longer period than twenty-four hours to occur. (5) The seventh day is not twenty-four hours since there is no reference to "morning and evening." (6) Science has "demonstrated" that the earth is billions of years old.

definite gradation, the work of each day leads up to and prepares for the work of the next, the whole of it culminating in the creation of man, the crown of God's handiwork, entrusted with the important task of making the whole creation subservient to the glory of God."[141] This is why unless there are overwhelming reasons in the text why the days are not successive, ordinary days, this should be our default. In the context of Genesis 1, this is confirmed by the use of "morning and evening" in relation to *yôm*, along with the number designating each day. Later, Scripture also confirms this point (Exod 20:11; 31:17).[142] Here is a basic summary of days of creation.

Day 1 (1:1–5). After God's absolute creation of all things, he begins to make the creation habitable for human life by creating light and separating it from the darkness. By doing so, day and night are established, setting up a "rhythmic character by which they follow each other."[143] Light is not something that emanates from the sun, but it is the condition of all life. Later the sun is described as a "light-bearer," but the sun is not light. As Vos notes, "Only of God is it said

---

For *day* referring to twenty-four-hour days, see Kulikovsky, *Creation, Fall, Restoration*, 145–76; Kelly, *Creation and Change*, 107–35. Here are some of the arguments for this view. (1) Mostly, *day* refers to twenty-four hours. In Gen 1, there are no contextual indicators that a "day" is not 24 hours. (2) In Gen 2:4, *day* refers to all six days and thus is longer than a normal day (cf. Job 20:28; Ps 20:1; Prov 21:31; 24:10; 25:13; Eccl 7:14). Yet, in these contexts, *day* is given in a compound or bound expression, different than its use in Gen 1. (3) The repeating phrase "it was evening and morning, the __ day" communicates that the days are normal days. The seventh day does not have the formula for a variety of reasons, but foremost, it emphasizes that God's creative acts have ceased, and God now enters into enjoyment with what he created. Exodus 20:9–11; 31:17 confirm this since these texts assume that the days are normal days. Regarding the first three days, the fact that the sun and moon, as measures of time, were not present does not mean there was no time. The earth was still revolving on its axis according to a set rhythm, thus even if the sun, moon, and stars are not in place until the fourth day, the events of the first three days could still have taken place within a twenty-four-hour period. (4) The events of the sixth day could have occurred on one day. (5) The "appearance" of old age requires interpretation. We must distinguish God's work of creation that resulted in some kind of maturity from providence. We must also factor in the effects of global flood (Gen 6–9) on the geological "facts." (6) Scripture teaches that prior to the fall, there was no death (physical and spiritual) in the world. Due to Adam's sin, death entered the world, which affects the entire created order (Rom 5:12–21; 8:18–22; cf. Gen 2:15–16; 3:17–19). But an old earth requires that suffering and physical death began with God's absolute creation of the world, which also seems to contradict God's creation of a "good" world (Gen 1:31).

[141] Berkhof, *Systematic Theology*, 155.

[142] See Allen P. Ross, *Creation and Blessing: A Guide to the Study and Exposition of Genesis* (Grand Rapids: Baker, 1988), 109; Kulikovsky, *Creation, Fall, Restoration*, 123–76; Kelly, *Creation and Change*, 107–35.

[143] Vos, *Reformed Dogmatics*, 1:167.

that He is light."[144] Also, the emphasis of the text is this: By God's word, light is created, which is also true in redemption and our re-creation. God brings light and life to us. The description of the day concludes: "There was an evening, and there was a morning: one day."

Day 2 (1:6–8). It begins with God's work of separation. The firmament is established by dividing the "waters above" (clouds and expanse, not some solid dome) from the "waters below," that is, seas, rivers, lakes, and subterranean aquifers (Ps 148:4, 8).[145]

Day 3 (1:9–13). On this day, God does two works. First, he separates the water and the dry land on the earth. Second, he brings forth vegetation of "seed-bearing" plants and trees according to their kinds. Nothing in the text says that these plants evolved from each other. God created different species of plants that each bring forth seed after their "kind," and thus only reproduce their kind.

Day 4 (1:14–19). God now creates the light bearers, that is, the sun, moon, and stars, to divide the day from the night, to be signs for seasons, and to serve as lights for the earth, thus allowing for organic life on earth to continue to exist. Nothing in the text says that these "lights" would not have been visible on day 4, which demands that the act of creation is different than the normal processes of divine providence. In providence, light travels at a specific speed, and we can measure how far various light bearers are from us. But this kind of calculation does not apply to the singular and unique event of creation, which is another way of distinguishing an "origin" from an "operational" science.

Day 5 (1:20–23). On this day, God creates animals for the air (birds, etc.) and for the water (e.g., fish), according to their "kind." Again, nothing in the text hints of evolution or distinct species evolving from each other. God's creation is direct and specific to each "kind."

Day 6 (1:24–31). Everything in the narrative leads us to the crowning action of God on the sixth day. In fact, the works of the first five days are preparatory to the creation of humans. On the sixth day, God first creates land animals (1:24–25). These land animals (or "living creatures") are divided into three basic kinds: "cattle," "creeping things," and "beasts of the earth."

---

[144] Vos, 1:166.

[145] In contrast to those who argue that, the "firmament" (*raqiya'*) is a "solid dome," thus "proving" that Genesis teaches an ancient, mythological cosmology. See Lamoureux, "No Historical Adam," 47–54. This is incorrect. The "waters which were above the firmament" refer to clouds (Judg 5:4; 1 Kgs 18:44–45; Job 26:8; 36:27–28; Pss 77:16; 147:8; Eccl 11:3). The basic meaning of the word is to "spread out," tied to God stretching out the skies. See Kulikovsky, *Creation, Fall, Restoration*, 129–32.

Then we have the creation of "man," speaking of humans as male and female, along with God's giving of the creation mandate to us.

Day 7 (2:1–3). The entire account concludes with God's rest not because God is tired, but because his work is complete. This day makes a clear distinction between God's work of creation and providence, although God's sustaining of the universe has occurred since 1:1. These verses also serve to complete the story of creation presented as six successive days concluding in the seventh. In the text, the seventh day is not only special but also unending since, in contrast to the previous days, there is no refrain of "evening came and then the morning."

Many people appeal to this fact as proof that *yôm* on the seventh day is not a twenty-four-hour day, and thus the other days of creation are also not twenty-four-hour days. This is an interesting observation, but it misses the point. Obviously, the seventh day ended; otherwise, we would never have arrived at our present day. Instead, by reading the text in context, Moses intends the reader to grasp an important *theological* point: God rests due to his satisfaction with what he has made; thus, the seventh day becomes the context in which humans are to relate to God in covenant relationship, something unpacked in more detail in Genesis 2. But tragically, Adam did not obey God. He did not complete his work like God did, and thus he did not fully enter into God's rest, that is, into a permanent, glorified state in God's presence. Instead, Adam and Eve were cast from Eden and God's covenantal presence. How they are able to return to Eden to enjoy fully God's presence in covenant relationship waits further unfolding. But due to God's promise (Gen 3:15), Adam is not the last word for God's people; instead, a new creation will come by God's own provision of a greater, last Adam, our Lord Jesus Christ. Christ alone, unlike the first Adam, is the perfect covenant keeper, and by his obedience pays for our sin and secures our eternal-salvation rest in a new heavens and new earth (Heb 3:7–4:14; Rev 21–22). In this way, in the opening chapters of Genesis, there is an organic link between the old creation and the new, along with God's plan for creation and redemption in Christ Jesus.

4. The Theological Significance of Creation.[146]

Much could be said regarding the theological significance of creation. In chapter 13, we have already highlighted some important points in this regard. Here we simply want to focus on

[146] See Carson, "Genesis 1–3," 143–63 (see chap. 13, n. 10).

what creation teaches us about the glory of our triune God, the significance of ourselves, and the world God has created for us to enjoy and explore.

God: The Triune Creator-Covenant Lord

First, from creation, we know that our triune God is utterly incomparable and glorious. Not only is he the source of all there is, but he alone is the true God who needs nothing other than himself. Think of how *creatio ex nihilo* confirms God's aseity, simplicity, and self-sufficiency.[147] Since God is the cause of all that is other than himself, this entails that "God is really identical with each of his attributes."[148] Otherwise, as Steven Duby correctly insists, "if the perfections were other than God himself, God would cause or create his own nature (and thus himself), which is logically untenable and subversive of the freedom of God in the work of creation."[149] Creation, then, not only establishes God's singular uniqueness but also makes the Creator-creature distinction absolute. The biblical presentation of God as Creator stands in direct opposition to all naturalistic, dualistic, deistic, polytheistic, pantheistic, and panentheistic views and establishes a God-world relation that is unique to Christian theology. This is God's universe, not ours. We are here for his glory, not our own.

Second, creation underscores God's sovereign authority over all that he has created. God is independent and self-sufficient, but creation is totally dependent on him. As the triune God, he does not need his creation, nor was he compelled to create; creation is a free, gracious, and sovereign act of God.[150] In addition, creation reminds us that there is nothing that mediates God's relation to the world. Bavinck captures this truth this way: "It is God who posits the creature, eternity which posits time, immensity which posits space, being which posits becoming, immutability which posits change. There is nothing intermediate between these two classes of categories: a deep chasm separates God's being from that of all creatures."[151]

---

[147] See Duby, *Divine Simplicity*, 167–77, for a defense of God's simplicity and aseity from *creatio ex nihilo*.

[148] Duby, 171.

[149] Duby, 171.

[150] See Vos, *Reformed Dogmatics*, 1:158–59.

[151] Bavinck, *Reformed Dogmatics*, 2:158–59.

God's sovereign authority is repeatedly taught in his act of creation. Think of how the eternal God simply speaks and all things come to exist. In fact, ten times we are told, "God said . . . and it was so" (Gen 1:3, 6, 9, 11, 14, 20, 24, 26, 28, 29). All of this underscores God's perfect freedom, power, and authority over all that he has made. In reflecting on God's speech, Stephen Dempster astutely comments: God's "ten divine commands literally create the world (Genesis 1)."[152] As Creator and Lord, God has all authority, and our joy as creatures is to know God and gladly and willingly to obey his commands. This is important to remember, especially when God gives specific commands to Adam in Genesis 2. Obedience to God's word is not an option while disobedience results in sin and death (Gen 2:16–17; 3:1–6, 17–19; Rom 6:23). As Scripture's story unfolds, ultimately what is needed is a greater Adam who will obey God's covenant commands for us, thus fulfilling the purpose of our existence and securing our eternal redemption and justification (Rom 5:12–21; Phil 2:6–11; Heb 5:1–10).

Third, creation reminds us that our triune God is our covenant God. Our transcendent, self-sufficient Lord is also involved in his creation. As Creator, he does not stand aloof from what he has made. God is living and active; he not only creates the world and humans, but he continually preserves, acts in, and rules over his creation. God's purpose in creation is to display his glory and freely to share himself with us in covenant relation. God's rest on the seventh day paves the way for his enjoyment of what he has made, especially of his image-bearers, whom he created to know, love, and obey him. Creation is not an end in itself but the stage he created to display his triune glory. Creation, then, leads to providence; protology anticipates eschatology; and history is the linear unfolding of God's decree. In fact, the purpose of creation is tied to Christ (Eph 1:9–10), who is both the efficient and exemplary cause of creation (Col 1:15–16; Heb 1:3).

Fourth, creation underscores God's holiness, goodness, and moral perfection. In contrast to ancient Near Eastern myths, evil is not part of the natural order that God struggles to control. God creates all things "good" (Gen 1:4, 10, 12, 18, 21, 25, 31). There is no dualism between spirit and matter such that spirit is good and matter is evil. When sin and evil come to exist, it is due to the creature and not God. God is absolutely holy and good, and everything

---

[152] Dempster, "Extraordinary Fact: Part 1," 49 (see chap. 9, n. 25).

that he creates is good. Creation reminds us that physical *and* spiritual realities are both good, which is crucial for a proper view of creation and redemption.

Humans: God's Image-Bearers and Creatures of Dignity and Value

Creation also teaches us about ourselves. We have already discussed the significance of creation for understanding ourselves in chapters 13–14, and in volume 2, we will discuss in more detail the doctrine of humanity, or better, a "theological anthropology." Here we simply list a few theological implications from creation for establishing a proper view of ourselves, in direct contrast to the thought of our day.

First, although we are creatures, due to our creation in God's image, humans are in a different category than all other created things. We were created to know God in covenant relation, to rule over his world, and to be responsible to him as our Creator and Lord. Nothing in the creation account suggests that we have evolved from pre-hominids or the animal kingdom. This truth is taught in Gen 1:26–31; reiterated in Gen 2:7, where God directly acts in our creation; and confirmed in the unique creation of Eve. All of this substantiates that humans, despite being creatures, are qualitatively different than animals. Biblical warrant for the unity of humanity and our inherent dignity is our creation in God's image. Any view that denies this point undercuts the metaphysical and epistemological warrant for human significance and value. Evolutionary theories, including theistic evolution, cannot fully account for the biblical presentation of our human uniqueness, which, sadly, our secular postmodern culture of death makes evident on a daily basis.

Second, in our creation as male and female (Gen 1:26–28), along with the ordaining of heterosexual marriage (Gen 2:18–25), God establishes the proper boundaries and use of our sexuality, and the foundational building block for all human society—marriage and the family. Creation order, tied to God's commands, is the foundation for ethics and human responsibility. All departures from God's created norm are viewed as sin, idolatry, and self-destruction.

Third, our creation in God's image ensures that true knowledge of God is not only possible but also normal. It also reminds us that we are endlessly restless if we suppress or deny the truth of creation. In denying the triune God of glory who created us for himself, we live in a catch-22 situation. To deny him is to rob us of our significance and our raison d'être (reason to exist).

But to affirm the truth of our creation means that we must admit we are creatures, not our own creators, and that we are responsible to God for our life, breath, and all things (Acts 17:28).

Fourth, creation is also our home and environment. As vice-regents and stewards of God's world, we are responsible for the correct use of its resources. We are to follow God's instructions for using and cultivating the world, and we are to apply wisdom to the task. A proper basis for creation care is grounded in our doctrine of creation, and apart from a Christian view, the warrant for a responsible stewardship of the earth is lacking, despite protestations to the contrary.[153]

It is crucial to note that all of these important theological implications are predicated on the historicity of the creation account. If Genesis 1–2 is simply "mytho-history," these conclusions are hanging in mid-air. If Adam and Eve are not created uniquely as the first couple, then the unity of the human race, our inherent dignity, and our qualitative difference from the animals is undercut. In addition, if the creation account did not happen as presented, it is difficult to have a strong warrant for sexual ethics, the significance of the family as the foundational unit of human society, and Adam's role as our covenant head. In addition, the universal nature of the human problem will be different than Scripture describes. This will directly impact what is necessary to redeem a created but now fallen humanity by the incarnation of the divine Son, our Lord Jesus Christ, by his obedient life and penal substitutionary death for us.

World: The Ordered Stage and Theater of God's Glory

In chapter 13, we noted some of the worldview implications of creation for our understanding of the world. Here we reiterate three theological implications.

First, since *creatio ex nihilo* is the result of the free choice of our triune sovereign God, the world is designed, ordered, mathematically precise, and law governed. But in its structure the creation is never merely mechanistic, independent of God's preservation and his action in the world. A Christian view of creation rejects both *open* and *closed* views of the world. In its place, we affirm a *controlled* universe.[154] God created a world that is objectively real, ordered, and designed and thus able to be studied and known but that is also dependent on him. In

---

[153] For example, see Schaeffer, *Pollution and the Death of Man*, in *Collected Works*, 5:1–76.

[154] Carson, *Gagging of God*, 201 (see chap. 2, n. 1).

providence, God's preserving action is "ordinary," but this does not preclude his "extraordinary" action. On this account, an empirical science is possible, God's ordinary and extraordinary agency is upheld, and methodological naturalism is rejected.

Second, creation reminds us that the material world and all that is in it has value. When God evaluates his work of creation as "very good" (Gen 1:31), this means more than it accomplished what he purposed (although that is true); it also conveys the idea of worth, value, beauty, and a world free of disorder, sin, suffering, and death. In many ways, God is saying "yes!" to what he created. On this point, it is not surprising that a consistent theology of creation rejects ancient Near Eastern thought, Platonism, Gnosticism—indeed, any view that elevates the spiritual over the physical.[155] Creation teaches us that every aspect of God's creative work is good, including the spiritual and the physical, which provides the warrant for a proper respect for the world, our enjoyment of it, and our care of it in our daily work.

Third, creation also provides the foundation for the Bible's view of redemption. In creation, God made the physical and the spiritual good. But tragically, in Adam's sin, both the physical and spiritual are affected. Not only does sin render us spiritually dead before God, but spiritual death is inseparable from physical death. For this reason, in our redemption, we need a Redeemer who is not "docetic." Instead, the divine Son *must* assume our human nature and as the *incarnate* Son redeem us (John 1:14; Heb 2:5–18). In addition, our redemption requires more than a mere "spiritual" resurrection; it also requires a physical resurrection (1 Cor 15) and the making of a new creation (Rev 21–22). The Bible's view of redemption depends on its view of creation and the effects of the fall on it, and if creation is misunderstood, inevitably our understanding of our Redeemer and his work of redemption will also be distorted.

Only a Christian theology offers a proper view and perspective on creation. As Bavinck states, in a proper theological understanding of creation, "there is room for love and admiration of nature, but all deification is excluded. Here a human being is placed in the right relation to the world because he has been put in the right relation to God."[156]

---

[155] Watkin, *Thinking through Creation*, 46–87 (see chap. 13, n. 13).

[156] Bavinck, *Reformed Dogmatics*, 2:438.

Creation as Foundational to the Bible's Covenantal Story

As we previously noted, creation is not an end in itself but a stage on which God's glory is displayed. Thus, creation leads to providence as God's eternal decree is enacted in history. In fact, in insisting on the goodness of God's original creation, the Bible also sets the stage for what goes wrong—Adam's sin, which leads to our spiritual and physical death, and God's judgment, which results in an abnormal, fallen order. But in the midst of judgment, there is hope due to God's sovereign initiative to redeem us and to restore what was affected by Adam's sin. By God's promise to provide a Redeemer (Gen 3:15)—out of humanity but ultimately greater than Adam—the Bible's covenantal metanarrative unfolds until it leads us to the last Adam, our new covenant head, our Lord Jesus Christ.

Apart from creation and all that transpires in the opening chapters of Genesis, the rest of the Bible makes little sense. For this reason, creation is foundational to the entire Bible as it sets the backdrop and framework for the rest of the story. As Scripture's plotline moves from creation to providence, from the original creation to the fall, and to God's unfolding plan of redemption, what is anticipated is the restoration of goodness, even the transformation to a greater glory, which finally arrives at the dawning of a new heaven and a new earth (Rev 21–22), the home of righteousness (2 Pet 3:13). As God's plan unfolds, after the fall, redemption is viewed in terms of creation, but now a "new creation" (2 Cor 4:6; 5:17; Eph 2:1, 10). In God's plan, the new creation was not intended to replace an original creation that God somehow failed to keep on course. Instead, in God's decree, redemption was always part of God's plan before the world was created (1 Cor 2:7; Eph 1:5–11; 2 Tim 1:9; Titus 1:2) so that by creation, fall, redemption, and new creation, God's triune glory would be fully displayed to the praise of his glory. In this sense, the new creation represents the goal of the old. As God's plan unfolds over time, God is bringing the goodness of his creation and the presence of his kingdom to its purposed end in a true and final image-Son-Adam, our Lord Jesus Christ, and the dawning of a new creation.

But for *this* theology to be true, it requires that Genesis is true, that the events recorded are real, that there was an actual Adam (and Eve) who fell into sin, and that the God of creation is also the sovereign Lord of redemption. However, all of these points were challenged by the acceptance of Darwin's theory of evolution—a theory that rejected the Bible's view of creation, God, humans, sin—indeed, rejected the Bible's entire metanarrative from creation to Christ.

Given the significant challenge of the evolutionary view to a biblical view of creation, let us now offer some reflections on how theology should respond to it.

5. The "Problem" of Creation: Science and the Metanarrative of Evolution.

Introducing the "Problem"

In our day, the main alternative to the doctrine of creation is the naturalistic theory of evolution. Charles Darwin's *On the Origin of Species* (1859) changed the way people viewed God, the self, and the world, and it functioned as a competing vision of reality. In many ways, the competing visions of what humans are in our modern/postmodern era are largely the outworking of the evolutionary view.

From a Christian view, evolutionary theory was not a "neutral" theory; instead, it was a *direct* assault on the Bible's view of creation. As Greg Bahnsen rightly notes, it "challenged the existence of the personal, transcendent, sovereign God of Christianity. If man emerged from some supposed primordial slime, the eventual implication could be nothing less than the death of biblical theism,"[157] and ironically, also the "death" of humans in terms of their value and significance. By denying the Creator-creature distinction and *creatio ex nihilo*, the evolutionary theory had worldview significance far beyond biology since it affected every area of thought—philosophy, anthropology, sociology, culture, and science in general. In fact, Darwin knew this to be the case. He was not an "innocent" discoverer of a new theory of origins. In one of Darwin's early notebooks, J. C. Greene reminds us that Darwin predicted that his evolutionary theory would affect the entire study of *metaphysics*.[158] Josiah Royce expressed the same point: "With the one exception of Newton's 'Principia,' no single book of empirical science has ever been of more importance *to philosophy* than this work of Darwin."[159]

---

[157] Greg L. Bahnsen, "On Worshipping the Creature Rather than the Creator," *Journal of Christian Reconstruction* 1, no. 1 (1974): 81.

[158] See J. C. Greene, *The Death of Adam* (Ames: Iowa State University Press, 1959), 307 (emphasis mine).

[159] Josiah Royce, *The Spirit of Modern Philosophy*, 2nd ed. (New York: Braziller, 1955), 286 (emphasis mine).

Darwin's theory called people away from the common view of a fiat, a mature creation by God, which had also experienced catastrophes, such as a global flood. In its place, Darwin proposed his macro-theory of evolution of gradual ascent from the simple to the complex solely based on random, impersonal processes over time. Darwin's theory, as we discussed in chapter 2, resulted in a worldview shift of seismic proportions as both modern and post-modern thought "has definitively turned to the metaphysical model of process and alteration instead of substance and permanence, to becoming instead of being."[160] In fact, evolutionary/process thought is now a given in our institutions, along with its commitment to methodological naturalism. As such, the biblical view of creation is viewed as highly implausible, if not impossible.[161] At best, it is viewed as merely another origin "myth," on par with the myths of the ancient world. Evolution, then, is more than a "scientific" theory; it now functions as the "metanarrative" for the secular modern/postmodern worldview of the West.

Why has the metanarrative of evolution been so widely accepted? Our society offers a simple answer: evolution is a "fact," and to deny it is to deny "science." Yet today, this answer is problematic since the arguments against evolutionary naturalism are strong and growing.[162] However, the biblical answer to this question is ultimately Romans 1. If we take Scripture seriously, we must acknowledge that no humans post-fall are innocent in their suppression of the truth and turning from their Creator to created things. Evolutionary thought promises to secure our human autonomy, which Richard Dawkins candidly admits: evolution allows one to be "an intellectually fulfilled atheist."[163] So who is right? Given that creation and evolution function as two entirely different metanarratives, how should theology respond to the

---

[160] Bahnsen, "On Worshipping the Creature," 82.

[161] See Robert C. Neville, *God the Creator* (Chicago: University of Chicago Press, 1968), 7: "Whereas in past centuries a theory of creation would be more expected than not, the present situation is dominated by an antimetaphysical bias, on the one hand, and by the antitranscendence bias of many of the leading metaphysicians, on the other. A theory of creation is now an anomaly." Cited in Bahnsen, "On Worshipping the Creature," 82.

[162] Groothuis makes this point in *Christian Apologetics*, 268–69 (see chap. 13, n. 74). He notes that in Darwin's day there were many who rejected his view, which has continued to our present day. In fact, many non-Christians reject the theory, a point made by Michael Denton, *Evolution: A Theory in Crisis* (Bethesda: Alder & Ader, 1985). In 2001, many scientists signed a published statement questioning the truthfulness of the Darwinian theory. See www.dissentfromdarwin.org and https://www.discovery.org/m/securepdfs/2021/07/Scientific-Dissent-from-Darwinism-List-07152021.pdf

[163] Richard Dawkins, *The Blind Watchmaker* (New York: W. W. Norton, 1986), 6.

theological and apologetic challenge of evolution? Obviously, the literature on this subject is legion, and given the limits of this book, we cannot fully engage evolutionary theory. Instead, we will offer some reflections on what a theological-apologetic response would look like, and along the way offer some resources for further study.

Approaching the "Problem": Getting Our Bearings

First, the naturalistic theory of evolution must first be viewed as a philosophical/religious theory, not merely a "scientific" one. People too often pit "science" against "religion," but this is a false dichotomy. The truth of the matter is that "evolution" is just as much a philosophical theory as any creation view. In fact, the discipline of "science" is not a purely "neutral" or "objective" discipline. As a discipline, it assumes prior philosophical/worldview commitments, which it cannot operate apart from. For example, the statement "only what can be known by science or quantified and empirically tested is rational and true" is self-refuting. As J. P. Moreland has pointed out, this statement itself is not a statement *of* science; rather, it is a philosophical statement *about* science.[164] This is why the aims, methodologies, and presuppositions *of* science cannot be validated *by* science. The validation of science is a philosophical issue, not a scientific one, and any claim to the contrary is ultimately self-refuting.

Furthermore, it is important to distinguish between "origin" and "operational" science.[165] The latter involves observation and experimentation, and for it to work, it assumes specific preconditions that are worldview dependent. Once again, this reminds us that even an operational science depends on specific philosophical commitments. But this is even more so when it comes to "origin" science since the question of origins is not answered directly by observation and experimentation. This is why on the issues of origins, entire worldview frameworks look at the same "facts" but interpret them differently, again confirming that "science" is not "neutral."

Second, we need to drill down on the fact that the discipline of science is not neutral but worldview dependent, and specifically dependent on Christian *theology*. This statement may seem strange since we are constantly told that "science" is against "theology," but this is simply

---

[164] J. P. Moreland, *Scaling the Secular City: A Defense of Christianity* (Grand Rapids: Baker Academic, 1987), 197–98. Also see Moreland, *Scientism and Secularism* (Wheaton: Crossway, 2018), 49–69, 135–57.

[165] Groothuis, *Christian Apologetics*, 299–300.

not true. In fact, historically, many great scientists in the West were committed to *theology*.[166] But even more: many philosophers of science have argued that it was Christian *theology* that provided the necessary presuppositions for science to be conceived as a possible discipline.[167] Let us spend some time explaining why this critical point is the case.

Historians and philosophers of science have noted that science is not "natural" to humanity. Inquisitiveness about the world is natural to humans, but institutional science is different from being inquisitive. Loren Eiseley makes this exact point.

> It [science] has rules which have to be learned, and practices and techniques which have to be transmitted from generation to generation by the formal processes of education . . . [it] is an *invented* cultural institution, an institution not present in all societies, and not one that may be counted upon to arise from human instinct. . . . [science] demands some kind of unique soil in which to flourish . . . [apart from that soil, it is] "as capable of decay and death as any other human activity, such as a religion or a system of government.[168]

---

[166] For example, consider Isaac Newton, Galileo, Johannes Kepler, Blaise Pascal, Robert Boyle, Michael Faraday, James C. Maxwell.

[167] See Reijer Hooykaas, *Religion and the Rise of Modern Science* (Grand Rapids: Eerdmans, 1972); Stanley Jaki, *The Road of Science and the Ways to God*, The Gifford Lectures (Chicago: University of Chicago Press, 1978); A. N. Whitehead, *Science and the Modern World* (New York: Macmillan, 1946); Herbert Butterfield, *The Origins of Modern Science* (New York: Free Press, 1957); E. H. Hutten, *The Origins of Science: An Inquiry into the Foundations of Western Thought* (London: Allen & Unwin, 1962); Harold P. Nebelsick, *Circles of God: Theology and Science from the Greeks to Copernicus* (Edinburgh: Scottish Academic Press, 1985); Nebelsick, *Renaissance, Reformation and the Rise of Science* (Edinburgh: T&T Clark, 1992); T. F. Torrance, *Space, Time, and Incarnation* (Oxford: Oxford University Press, 1969); Christopher Kaiser, *Creation and the History of Science* (Grand Rapids: Eerdmans, 1991); Peter Harrison, *The Bible, Protestantism, and the Rise of Natural Science* (Cambridge: Cambridge University Press, 1998); Harrison, *The Fall of Man and the Foundations of Science* (Cambridge: Cambridge University Press, 2007); Peter E. Hodgson, *The Roots of Science and Its Fruits: The Christian Origin of Modern Science and Its Impact on Human Society* (London: Saint Austin, 2002); Hodgson, *Theology and Modern Physics* (New York: Routledge, 2005); Rodney Stark, *For the Glory of God: How Monotheism Led to Reformations, Science, Witch-Hunts and the End of Slavery* (Princeton: Princeton University Press, 2004); Meyer, *Return of the God Hypothesis*, 13–66 (see chap. 5, n. 79); Pearcey and Thaxton, *Soul of Science* (see chap. 2, n. 53).

[168] Loren Eiseley, "Francis Bacon," in *The Horizon Book of Makers of Modern Thought*, ed. Bruce Mazlish (New York: American Heritage Publishing, 1972), 95–96, cited in Pearcey and Thaxton, *Soul of Science*, 17.

This raises the question: What is the unique soil that allows for science to arise, operate, and flourish? Along with other historians, Eiseley identifies the "soil" with Christian theology, but he does so reluctantly. He states, "In one of those strange permutations of which history yields occasional rare examples, it is the Christian world which finally gave birth in a clear, articulate fashion to the experimental method of science itself."[169]

Eiseley's observation is important, although it pains him to make it. The truth is that science is not against theology; rather, theology provides specific metaphysical and epistemological preconditions that science requires for it to be possible, and apart from these preconditions, science, as a discipline, is not sufficiently warranted. To make this point, let us discuss nine such preconditions that arise from theology, and specifically a Christian view of creation, which allows for an operational science to be possible as a rational discipline.[170]

1. *Nature is real.* This truth seems too obvious to mention, but not all worldviews can account for the objective reality of nature. For example, pantheism and idealism teach that the material world is an "appearance" of the absolute, thus undercutting the reality of finite things. In the East, Hinduism views the world of material objects as *maya* (i.e., "illusion"), and in the West, Spinoza and others make the world ultimately a manifestation of the infinite. By contrast, a Christian view of God and the Creator-creature distinction gives metaphysical reality to the world distinct from God: a world that he designed and ordered and thus possible to study.

2. *The goodness of creation.* For science to be possible, it requires specific metaphysical views *and* "convictions about value."[171] A society must be persuaded that the study of "nature" is of value, but not all worldviews agree. For example, the Greeks often equated the material world with evil and disorder; Gnosticism grew from this view. This is probably why the Greeks did not develop an *empirical* science since doing so requires a belief that the world is good. By contrast, Scripture views the material world as having value. Especially in the Renaissance and Reformation, where an empirical science began in earnest, the entire culture was influenced by Christian theology that gave dignity to work and the study of the

---

[169] Loren Eiseley, *Darwin's Century* (Garden City: Doubleday, 1958), 62, cited in Pearcey and Thaxton, *Soul of Science*, 18.

[170] The following discussion is taken from Pearcey and Thaxton, *Soul of Science*, 17–42. But also see Meyer, *Return of the God Hypothesis*, 13–49; Moreland, *Scientism and Secularism*, 49–157.

[171] Pearcey and Thaxton, *Soul of Science*, 22.

world. Johannes Kepler viewed his work as a scientist as a vocation from God to be used for his glory.[172]

3. *The non-deification of nature.* The Creator-creature distinction reminds us that nature is created, designed, and good, but it is not "god." Pagan religions, however, view the world as either "the abode of the divine or as an emanation of God's own essence."[173] Animism believes that spirits reside in nature, but this view undercuts the warrant for an empirical science, uniform causal relationships that can be studied, and a proper "de-deification" of nature.[174] As Pearcey and Thaxton note, "As long as the world is charged with divine beings and powers, the only appropriate response is to supplicate them or ward them off," but "the monotheism of the Bible exorcised the gods of nature, freeing humanity to enjoy and investigate it without fear. When the world was no longer an object of worship, then—and only then—could it become an object of study."[175]

4. *A rational God, an orderly world.* A crucial precondition for the possibility of an empirical science is the inductive principle. Induction assumes that cause and effect relations in the world are uniform, real, and predictable. But not all worldviews, including naturalism, can provide the epistemological warrant for induction and science's conviction that the universe is ordered.[176] However, a biblical view of God and creation does so. God has created the universe according to his plan, and he has promised to sustain it in an orderly, predictable way. But apart from the Christian view, where does this conviction arise? Copernicus illustrates the importance of this point in practice. As Pearcey and Thaxton remind us, in his search for a better cosmology than Aristotle or Ptolemy, Copernicus first went back to the writings of the ancient philosophers, but he discovered disagreement among them regarding the metaphysical makeup of the universe. Copernicus was bothered by this inconsistency since he was convinced that the universe was "wrought for us by a supremely good and orderly Creator."[177] Note that his quest for a better cosmology was driven by his conviction that God had created a universe

---

[172] Pearcey and Thaxton, 23.

[173] Pearcey and Thaxton, 23.

[174] See Hooykaas, *Religion and the Rise of Modern Science*, 17.

[175] Pearcey and Thaxton, *Soul of Science*, 24.

[176] On this point, see James N. Anderson, "The Laws of Nature and of Nature's God: The Theological Foundations of Modern Science," *Reformed Faith & Practice* 4, no. 1 (2019): 11–13.

[177] Pearcey and Thaxton, *Soul of Science*, 25.

of "regularity, uniformity, and symmetry that befitted the work of God."[178] For Copernicus, *theological* convictions about God and the nature of the world provided the warrant to think that the universe was designed, orderly, and understandable.

5. *Laws of nature.* The concept of the "laws of nature" arose due to the *theological* truths of God, creation, and providence. Due to the influence of Christianity in the West, we forget how unique the concept of "natural law" is.[179] As Pearcey and Thaxton remind us, "People in pagan cultures who see nature as alive and moved by mysterious forces are not likely to develop the conviction that all natural occurrences are lawful and intelligible."[180] In fact, A. R. Hall points out that the concept of "laws of nature" was not indigenous to ancient Western or Asian cultures. However, when the concept arose in the medieval era, the source of it was Christian theology. Hall argues that the concept of "law" in the context of natural events "would have been unintelligible in antiquity, whereas the Hebraic and Christian belief in a deity who was at once Creator and Law-giver rendered it valid."[181] Note the order of reasoning in this development. As Pearcey and Thaxton observe, "The early scientists did not argue that the world was lawfully ordered, and *therefore* there must be a rational God. Instead, they argued that there was a rational God, and *therefore* the world must be lawfully ordered."[182] The concept of "natural" law and induction was not first derived from empirical observation; instead, it was derived from prior *theological* commitments that then were confirmed by the investigation of the world.

6. *Mathematical precision.* Another distinctive feature of our understanding of operational science is its use of math and the conviction that mathematical formulas correspond to reality in an exact and precise way. Again, we often take this idea for granted, but not all cultures assume it given their denial of the Creator-creature distinction. Other worldviews that reject *creatio ex nihilo* generally affirm that the world began with some kind of preexisting stuff that has its own recalcitrant nature. Such views do not affirm the self-sufficient triune Creator

---

[178] Kaiser, *Creation and the History of Science*, 109; cf. Meyer, *Return of the God Hypothesis*, 22–25.

[179] In this context, "natural law" does not refer to its usual sense of moral laws; instead, it refers to "laws of nature" that view the world as a law-governed realm that we can observe and study.

[180] Pearcey and Thaxton, *Soul of Science*, 26.

[181] A. R. Hall, *The Scientific Revolution, 1500–1800: The Formation of the Modern Scientific Attitude* (Boston: Beacon Press, 1954), 171–72; cf. Meyer, *Return of the God Hypothesis*, 36–40.

[182] Pearcey and Thaxton, *Soul of Science*, 26–27.

who creates the universe perfectly consistent with his eternal plan. Instead, a finite "artisan" struggles to bring order out of chaos but never does so perfectly.

Pearcey and Thaxton illustrate this point from Platonic thought. For Plato, the world consists of eternal matter structured by eternal forms (ideas), but in Plato's creation myth, the creator-demiurge is a finite deity who "merely inject[s] reason (Ideas) into reason-less matter,"[183] but imperfectly. The end result, as Hooykaas reminds us, is that the finite "creator," who does not create "out of nothing," is limited in at least two ways: "He had to follow not his own design but the model of the eternal Ideas; and second, he had to put the stamp of the Ideas on a chaotic, recalcitrant matter which he had not created himself."[184] For this reason, the Greeks did not expect the metaphysical nature of the world to be precise; instead, they "expected a level of imprecision in nature, a certain fuzziness at the edges. If some facts did not fit their theories, well, that was to be expected in an imperfect world. Individual things were, after all, only rough approximations to the rational Ideas or Forms."[185] Dudley Shapere states this point well: in Greek philosophy the world "contains an essentially irrational element: nothing in it can be described *exactly* by reason, and in particular by mathematical concepts and laws."[186]

By contrast, Christian theology affirms God created the universe *ex nihilo*, which means that he was not limited by preexisting matter that he struggled to conform to his will. Rather, "nature" perfectly and precisely corresponds to his will, which entails no imprecision in God's creation of the world. Pearcey and Thaxton illustrate this point from the work of Kepler. They note how Kepler "struggled for years with the slight difference of eight minutes between observation and calculation of the orbit of the planet Mars. Eventually this slight imprecision drove him to abandon the idea of circular orbits and to postulate elliptical orbits."[187] Their conclusion: "If Kepler had not maintained the conviction that nature must be precise, he would not have agonized over those eight minutes and would not have broken through a traditional belief in circular orbits that had held sway for two thousand years. Kepler spoke gratefully of those

---

[183] Pearcey and Thaxton, 27.

[184] Hooykaas, *Religion and the Rise of Modern Science*, 3–4.

[185] Pearcey and Thaxton, *Soul of Science*, 28.

[186] Dudley Shapere, *Galileo: A Philosophical Study* (Chicago: University of Chicago Press, 1974), 134–36, cited in Pearcey and Thaxton, *Soul of Science*, 28; cf. Meyer, *Return of the God Hypothesis*, 36–40, 47–48; Moreland, *Scientism and Secularism*, 59–69, 141–49.

[187] Pearcey and Thaxton, *Soul of Science*, 28.

eight minutes as a 'gift of God.'"[188] R. G. Collingwood states this point well: "The possibility of an applied mathematics is an expression, in terms of natural science, of the Christian belief that nature is the creation of an omnipotent God."[189]

7. *Humans created in God's image.* Science operates with a correspondence theory of truth and the belief that our minds correspond to the world so that we can discover the objective order and design of the world. In philosophy, this is known as the subject-object relation, but why is it so? How did science come to believe that the world is ordered and that it can be known objectively by rational minds? This question is crucial because it illustrates that "science cannot proceed without an epistemology, or theory of knowledge, guaranteeing that the human mind is equipped to gain genuine knowledge of the world."[190] The answer: it came from the *theological* conviction that God created an ordered and designed world *and* that he created humans to study the world in order to exercise dominion over it.

8. *Empirical investigation.* As an *empirical* discipline, science not only assumes that the order of creation is intelligible by humans; it also requires a specific kind of intelligibility. But in Western thought, as Pearcey and Thaxton note, various conceptions of intelligibility have competed for acceptance. For example, the Aristotelian concept of intelligibility is tied to an object's rational goal and purpose, not its material base. Thus, in analyzing a saucepan, it does not matter whether it is made of aluminum or cast iron; what matters is the purpose of the saucepan. Once we know its purpose, we may logically deduce many of its properties.

As applied to the study of "nature," Aristotle argued that nature consists of matter structured by purposes, essences, and forms. Scientists know the *nature* of an object by discerning its purpose; they do not need to make further empirical observations about the object. Once the purpose is known, the essential properties of the object may simply be deduced. Thus, for Aristotelian science, the emphasis is on "rational intuition of purposes or Forms followed by deduction, rather than observation and experiment."[191]

---

[188] Pearcey and Thaxton, 28.

[189] R. G. Collingwood, *An Essay on Metaphysics* (Chicago: Regnery, 1972), 253–57, cited in Pearcey and Thaxton, *Soul of Science*, 28–29. On this point, see Anderson, "Laws of Nature," 13–15.

[190] Pearcey and Thaxton, *Soul of Science*, 29. For a development of this point, see Anderson, "Laws of Nature," 8–11.

[191] Pearcey and Thaxton, *Soul of Science*, 31.

In the medieval era, Aristotle's influence was introduced into Western thought. At this time, science continued to emphasize rational intuition of forms rather than empirical observation, and it was only when people moved away from Aristotelian thought that an *experimental* science resulted. But what brought about this shift? The cause was *theological*. Over time, Christians became concerned that Aristotle's forms "appeared to limit God's creative activity, as though God had to make do with the prescribed properties of matter."[192] In fact, some Christian Aristotelians argued that the "nature" of the heavens *required* circular motion "by its inner law of rational necessity—as though God's hand were restrained by some inherent necessity in the structure of things."[193] In 1277, Etienne Tempier, Bishop of Paris, condemned those who thought that God could only create circular orbits, a view solely based on Aristotelian thought. His action was one reason for the rise of *voluntarism*—a theology that emphasized God's free choice, and which did not predetermine ahead of time what God *had* to choose.

The result for science was that voluntarism argued that "natural laws" are not due to forms inherent within nature—something "outside" of God's will and control—instead, they were due to God's will, which is free to create according to his choices. As such, "voluntarism insisted that the structure of the universe—indeed, its very existence—is not rationally necessary but is contingent upon the free and transcendent will of God."[194] For science, this meant that we cannot discern what God has created by logical deduction; instead, we must investigate the world by empirical observation. One important consequence of *creatio ex nihilo* is that the creation is dependent on God's free and sovereign act. If God had so chosen, he could have created "nature" in a different way. Thus, in creating the world, God was only bound by his own will, plan, and purposes. The world does not have its own inherent rationality independent of God. To know the *nature* of things, we must "look and see" what God has actually created. This *theological* reason provided a crucial warrant for the rise of the experimental method of science.[195]

---

[192] Pearcey and Thaxton, 31.

[193] Pearcey and Thaxton, 31.

[194] Pearcey and Thaxton, 31. Robert Boyle and Isaac Newton are examples of scientists who rejected Aristotelian thought based on voluntarism. Interestingly, this discussion was important in the geocentric vs. heliocentric debate. Aristotle argued for geocentricism based on rational deduction, but Copernicus rejected this argument based on a voluntaristic understanding that necessitated that he discover what God had created by empirical investigation.

[195] Pearcey and Thaxton illustrate this point from Roger Cotes's preface to the second edition of Newton's *Principia*. They write, quoting Cotes: "Cotes argued that the world 'could arise from nothing

9. *Science and technology*. Science has also given birth to modern technology, yet specific beliefs were required to make this possible. Specifically, it required the belief that it was morally acceptable to intervene in natural processes for the good of humanity. Yet not all worldviews believe this. For example, animism and pantheism are more interested in conforming to nature than "using" it for specific ends. But in Christianity, God created us to rule over the world as his image-bearers, not merely to conform to nature. Part of our creation mandate is to study the world and to harness its resources for God's glory and our good. In fact, Francis Bacon (1561–1626) argued that one of the purposes of science is to alleviate the destructive effects of the fall: man "fell at the same time from his state of innocency and from his dominion over creation," yet "both of these losses can, even in this life, be in some part repaired; the former by religion and faith, the latter by arts and sciences."[196]

Much more could be said, but the point is this: theology is not against science; instead, it gives to science the metaphysical, epistemological, and moral warrant for its development. This point is nicely summarized by Pearcey and Thaxton:

> To begin with, Christian teachings have served as *presuppositions* for the scientific enterprise (e.g., the conviction that nature is lawful was inferred from its creation by a rational God). Second, Christian teachings have *sanctioned* science (e.g., science was justified as a means of alleviating toil and suffering). Third, Christian teachings supplied *motives* for pursuing science (e.g., to show the glory and wisdom of the Creator). And fourth, Christianity played a role in *regulating* scientific methodology (e.g., voluntarist theology was invoked to justify an empirical approach in science).[197]

Third, further proof that our disagreement with the evolutionary theory is at the worldview level is the observation that even in Darwin's day, evolutionary thought was nothing new. For example, deism was already waning, while idealism and pantheism/panentheism were on the rise. One thinks of the thought of Baruch Spinoza, Georg Hegel, Johann Fichte, and Friedrich Schelling, which in some form argued for evolutionary views. But the reason why

---

but the perfectly free will of God directing and presiding over all.' In all of creation, Cotes wrote, there is 'not the least shadow' of logical necessity—and '*therefore,*' he concluded, we must learn 'from observations and experiments.'" *Soul of Science*, 33; cf. Meyer, *Return of the God Hypothesis*, 22–29.

[196] Cited in Pearcey and Thaxton, *Soul of Science*, 36.

[197] Pearcey and Thaxton, 36–37.

Darwin was so significant is that he proposed a "mechanism" of evolution to explain how species originated, namely, natural selection. For Darwin, all species were *not* created by God but evolved over a long period of time via unintelligent, purposeless natural causes. In their struggle for survival, the fittest survive and replace the less fit. By this mechanism, all of life evolves from the simple to the complex, and given enough time, new species emerge, which appear over time and incrementally. By this explanation, he made Genesis superfluous, but it is important to remember that an evolutionary way of thinking was not new to Darwin. Thus, what began to occur was that evolution began to serve as a *paradigm* for our thinking so that it is not the "facts" that are leading us to the theory; rather, the evolutionary theory is a way of interpreting the "facts." This observation has been confirmed in recent days.[198]

Fourth, with these points in mind, how should we approach the naturalistic theory of evolution? First, we need to evaluate it and critique it as an entire worldview that seeks to offer a comprehensive explanation for metaphysics, epistemology, and ethics.[199] On this point, our argument against the view is the same as our argument against naturalism. Second, we are then in a position to deal with specific scientific issues as they relate to Scriptural teaching.[200]

---

[198] See for example, Denton, *Evolution: A Theory in Crisis*, 356f; Phillip E. Johnson, *Darwin on Trial* (Downers Grove: InterVarsity, 1991); Johnson, ed., *Evolution as Dogma: The Establishment of Naturalism* (Mesquite: Haughton, 1990); Jonathan Wells, *Icons of Evolution: Science or Myth?* (Washington, DC: Regnery, 2002).

[199] See Alvin Plantinga, *Where the Conflict Really Lies: Science, Religion, and Naturalism* (Oxford: Oxford University Press, 2011). Plantinga argues that the conflict is ultimately at the worldview level. The conflict is not between science and theology but science and naturalism since naturalism cannot provide the transcendental preconditions for the intelligibility of science.

[200] The amount of literature questioning the naturalistic theory of evolutionary is legion. For example, see Johnson, *Darwin on Trial*; Johnson, *Reason in the Balance: The Case Against Naturalism in Science, Law, and Education* (Downers Grove: InterVarsity, 1995); Denton, *Evolution: A Theory in Crisis*; Michael Pitman, *Adam and Evolution* (London: Rider, 1984); Michael J. Behe, *Darwin's Black Box: The Biochemical Challenge to Evolution* (New York: Free Press, 1996); Behe, *The Edge of Evolution: The Search for the Limits of Darwinism* (New York: Free Press, 2007); J. P. Moreland, ed., *The Creation Hypothesis: Scientific Evidence for an Intelligent Designer* (Downers Grove: InterVarsity, 1994); Thomas Woodward, *Doubts about Darwin: A History of Intelligent Design* (Grand Rapids: Baker, 2003); Groothuis, *Christian Apologetics*, 171–417; Norman C. Nevin, ed., *Should Christians Embrace Evolution? Biblical and Scientific Responses* (Phillipsburg: P&R, 2009); Charles B. Thaxton et al., *The Mystery of Life's Origin: The Continuing Controversy* (Seattle: Discovery Institute, 2020); Stephen C. Meyer, *Signature in the Cell: DNA and the Evidence for Intelligent Design* (San Francisco: HarperOne, 2009); Meyer, *Darwin's Doubt:*

A Summary Critique of the Naturalistic Theory of Evolution

We must carefully define the term *evolution* to know where the debate really lies.

First, there is "microevolution." This refers to small developments within one species, something we observe repeatedly. For example, peppered moths change color so they are less vulnerable as prey, flies become immune to insecticides, horses come in different varieties, humans are diverse, and varieties of plants are developed. No one disputes microevolution. Yet examples of microevolution must not warrant what is at dispute, namely, macroevolution.[201]

Second, the debate is really over "macroevolution," or the "general theory of evolution." When combined with naturalism, both metaphysically and methodologically, this is the view that around fourteen billion years ago, the universe came to exist as a result of the "big bang." As the universe cooled, subatomic particles formed, followed by atoms and molecules of the basic chemical elements (e.g., hydrogen, helium, etc.). By the force of gravity, physical matter collected into lumps, eventually resulting in solar systems, galaxies, and stars. Around four billion years ago, organic molecules were formed on earth, which became the building blocks for organic life. Once these molecules became self-replicating lifeforms, the Darwinian processes "kicked in." Over millions of years, by random genetic mutations and natural selection, single-celled organisms evolved into multicelled organisms, asexual organisms evolved into sexually differentiated organisms, and so forth so that eventually primitive mammals appeared on the earth, which became the ancestors of primitive apes, which became the ancestors of primitive humans. Thus, nonlife resulted in life, unconsciousness resulted in consciousness, and the perceived "order" of "nature" is explained solely by the impersonal plus time and chance.[202]

Creation rejects macroevolution, especially the naturalistic, blind-watchmaker variety since it attempts to account for the origin of the world and humans apart from God as the triune Creator. In a real sense, naturalistic evolution abandons the attempt to discover our origins insofar as this term connotes ultimate purpose. Instead, it is content to inquire after the

---

The Explosive Origin of Animal Life and the Case for Intelligent Design (San Francisco: HarperOne, 2013); Meyer, *Return of the God Hypothesis*; and Moreland et al., *Theistic Evolution* (see chap. 5, n. 79).

[201] On this point, see Wells, *Icons of Evolution*, 156–75. Wells identifies many of these microevolution "icons" and rightly argues they do not demonstrate the truth of macroevolution. Cf. Groothuis, *Christian Apologetics*, 280–85; Johnson, *Darwin on Trial*, 26–28, 160–61.

[202] In contrast to Darwin, the emphasis today is neo-Darwinism, which stresses beneficial random genetic mutations that natural selection conserves, which result in the development of new species.

beginnings of humanity as a species among other species. Humans are viewed as products of purely natural processes. As organisms evolved that were capable of surviving on earth by random mutations and natural selection, they left "fitter" offspring. As a result, there is a gradual "upgrading" of the species. Eventually, human beings appeared on the scene, an organism of great complexity, not because someone planned us this way, but because these features enabled us better to survive.

The naturalistic theory of evolution functions as the metanarrative for our age. However, like previous false "origin" stories, it faces serious challenges.[203] Here are *five* serious problems.

1. The Absolute Beginning: The Origin of the Universe.[204]

Everything we know about the universe is that it had a beginning. But the explanation for its origin on naturalistic grounds alone is highly unlikely if not impossible. In fact, the evolutionary explanation of impersonal processes over time by natural selection producing all that we see must explain two things: first, the origin of the universe and, second, how living systems came from nonliving systems (abiogenesis). In terms of the second point, it is important to remember that natural selection does not work on nonliving systems since it requires living systems already existing and functioning. However, the naturalistic explanation faces serious problems in trying to explain both of these areas. To explain the ultimate origin of living systems from nonliving systems, appeal is often made to the work of Harold Urey and Stanley Miller in 1953 since they supposedly "created" organic compounds from inorganic material. But there are serious problems with this experiment and their so-called proof for abiogenesis.[205]

First, the experiment assumed that the earth's early atmosphere was non-reducing; that is, it lacked oxygen. But the evidence shows that the early earth's atmosphere contained oxygen, yet the organic reactions thought necessary for the build-up of complicated organic molecules will not occur in the presence of oxygen.

---

[203] What follows are only some of the problems with the naturalistic theory of evolution. For various summaries of the issues, see Berkhof, *Systematic Theology*, 162–63; Groothuis, *Christian Apologetics*, 266–329; and the literature cited in chap. 21, n. 200.

[204] See Thaxton et al., *Mystery of Life's Origin*; Meyer, *Return of the God Hypothesis*; Groothuis, *Christian Apologetics*, 207–39, 316–22.

[205] For a developed critique of abiogenesis, see Thaxton et al., *The Mystery of Life's Origin*.

Second, in recent experiments that have attempted to synthesize organic compounds under the conditions that supposedly existed on the early earth, there are at least two problems.

1. Our best synthesis of compounds has only resulted in the complexity and information of the word *me*. But the jump from this to the information of a DNA code is mathematically implausible. Information uses a language or code to transmit a message, "but the code is *not* defined by the material on which it is written or the medium through which the communication is made," and the "message expressed using a language or code is *not* defined by the code used."[206] In other words, the message transcends the code or language used, which "demonstrates that there must be intelligence involved in such a system."[207]

2. Any progress we have made is due to "illegitimate spectator interference." The reactants at a certain stage of a synthesis experiment must be quickly withdrawn, isolated from the environment, cooled, and added to a new environment. But all of these steps have occurred due to a *person* intervening at just the right time. How can natural, impersonal processes do this?

Third, the evolution of life from nonlife also runs into thermodynamic problems. As Andy McIntosh argues, information is closely related to thermodynamics. Natural selection has no power to create new functional structures since it only works on systems that are already in place. Given the first law of thermodynamics, that is, that "no energy is either created or destroyed," and the second law, namely, that "in an isolated system the entropy will always increase in any non-equilibrium process,"[208] in order to make new functional structures, we need more than energy added. Instead, we need intelligence from the start. In other words,

---

[206] Andy McIntosh, "Information and Thermodynamics," in Nevin, *Should Christians Embrace Evolution?*, 160.

[207] McIntosh, 161. Also see Michael Polanyi, "Life's Irreducible Structure," in *Knowing and Being*, ed. Marjorie Grene (Chicago: University of Chicago Press, 1969), 229, who argues the same point. As Polanyi argues, the information in DNA "cannot be explained by the lower level chemical laws or properties any more than the information in a newspaper headline can be explained by reference to the chemical properties of the ink." Stephen Meyer, "The Difference It Doesn't Make: Why the 'Front-End Loaded' Concept of Design Fails to Explain the Origin of Biological Information," in Moreland et al., *Theistic Evolution*, 224–27, underscores this point. He argues that building a cell requires assembly instructions stored in DNA or some equivalent molecule that assumes huge about of information, which nonliving chemicals cannot generate.

[208] McIntosh, "Information and Thermodynamics," 161.

raw energy does not result in order or information out of chaos. Raw energy needs a blueprint (such as DNA) to direct it and an energy-converting mechanism (such as a digestive system) to convert the form of energy so it will be usable. But blueprints and energy-converting mechanisms are produced only by life.

Fourth, there are insurmountable mathematical problems. In 1967, Murray Eden argued that the chance emergence of life from nonlife was statistically impossible.[209] Eden argues: "It is our contention that if 'random' is given serious and crucial interpretation from a probabilistic point of view, the randomness postulate is highly implausible and that an adequate scientific theory of evolution must await the elucidation of new natural laws—physical, physico-chemical and biological."[210] That is quite a statement! If we think that everything happened randomly, we must calculate the probability of all of these things coming together in a random way. The naturalistic theory says the universe came to exist around fifteen billion years ago. But assuming the randomness postulate, one would need hundreds of more billion years. This is why Eden says that we would need "new natural laws"!

Michael Denton explains some of these mathematical difficulties. He argues that to get *one* cell from chance would require at least 100 functional proteins to appear simultaneously in one place. The probability of each is 10^{20} for each of the 100 functional proteins. But you also need 100 functional proteins, so we need to add another 10x. Now the number is 10^{2000}. Denton summarizes:

> The Darwinian claim that all the adaptive design of nature has resulted from a random search, a mechanism unable to find the best solution in a game of checkers, is one of the most daring claims in the history of science. But it is also one of the least substantiated. No evolutionary biologist has ever produced any quantitative proof that the designs of nature are in fact within the reach of chance.[211]

Due to these mathematical problems, Francis Crick, a codiscoverer of DNA, confessed that "the origin of life appears to be almost a miracle, so many are the conditions which would

---

[209] Murray Eden, "Inadequacies of Neo-Darwinian Evolution as a Scientific Theory," in *Mathematical Challenge to the Neo-Darwinian Interpretation of Evolution*, ed. Paul S. Moorhead (Philadelphia: Wistar Institute, 1967), 109–10.

[210] Eden, 109.

[211] Denton, *Evolution: A Theory in Crisis*, 324.

have to be satisfied to get it going."[212] To explain the origin of the universe *and* the origin of life from nonlife apart from intelligent, directed processes is highly implausible. However, instead of turning to the triune Creator-covenant Lord, Crick proposed the theory of "directed panspermia," which claimed that the earth had been seeded for life by aliens who injected earth with the seeds of life that then evolved over time. Thus, by "kick-starting" life from this outside source (with no explanation for the existence of these aliens), Crick thought he could reduce the mathematical odds against evolution, but in the end, he had to resort to myth to do so.

2. Irreducible Complexity

Even if one grants that the naturalistic evolutionary theory can explain the origin of the universe (which it cannot), it must still explain how life evolved from nonlife and how the simple evolved into the complex. We have already mentioned the sheer impossibility of abiogenesis, but we have also discovered at the molecular level what Michael Behe has described as the "irreducible complexity" of the smallest of living cells. Darwin knew little about microbiology. But due to technological advances and the discovery of DNA, we now know how complex living cells actually are, something evolution cannot explain apart from God's design of creation. At the smallest level, we discover systems that are composed of many parts that are all required for the system to function.[213] Given such *irreducible* complexity, cells could not have evolved from the simple to the complex since all the parts are required for the system to function from the start. Behe states it this way,

> In summary, as biochemists have begun to examine apparently simple structures like cilia and flagella, they have discovered staggering complexity, with dozens or even hundreds of precisely tailored parts. . . . As the number of required parts increases, the difficulty of gradually putting the system together skyrockets, and the likelihood of indirect scenarios plummets. Darwin looks more and more forlorn. New research on

---

[212] Francis Crick, *Life Itself: Its Origin and Nature* (New York: Simon & Schuster, 1981), 88.

[213] Behe points out that Darwin knew little of microbiology and thus thought that the building blocks of life were relatively simple. But as molecular biology has developed in recent decades, Darwin's "black box" is now open. For a development of Behe's argument applied to DNA and the complexity of the cell, see Meyer, *Signature in the Cell.*

> the roles of the auxiliary proteins cannot simplify the irreducibly complex system. The intransigence of the problem cannot be alleviated; it will only get worse. Darwinian theory has given no explanation for the cilium or flagellum. The overwhelming complexity of the . . . systems push us to think it may never give an explanation.[214]

In other words, the incredibly complex structures of living systems not only rule out gradual evolution by mutation and natural selection, they also require an absolute creation, that is, being made "full grown" or fully functional. As Behe rightly insists,

> The conclusion of intelligent design for physically interacting systems rests on the observation of highly specified, irreducible complexity—the ordering of separate, well-fitted components to achieve a function that is beyond any of the components themselves. . . . Clearly, if something was not put together gradually, then it must have been put together quickly or even suddenly.[215]

But if this is so, then it requires intelligent design to write the program by which these systems operate. The naturalistic theory of evolution cannot account for the complexity of the cell.[216]

3. The Fossil Record.[217]

The fossil record is also a problem for the evolutionary theory. If the Darwinism was true, one would expect at least two patterns of fossil evidence. First, "the earliest strata of paleontological evidence should disclose simple and scarce organisms followed by more and more organisms of increasing complexity."[218] Second, given that evolution proceeds in small increments, "there

---

[214] Behe, *Darwin's Black Box*, 73.

[215] Behe, *Darwin's Black Box*, 187, 223.

[216] For a summary of Behe's conclusions from molecular biology, see Groothuis, *Christian Apologetics*, 305–12.

[217] For a helpful treatment of how the fossil record does not prove the naturalistic evolutionary theory, see Wells, *Icons of Evolution*; and Marvin L. Lubenow, *Bones of Contention: A Creationist Assessment of Human Fossils*, 2nd ed. (Grand Rapids: Baker, 2004). Also see Günter Bechly and Stephen C. Meyer, "The Fossil Record and Universal Common Descent," in Moreland et al., *Theistic Evolution*, 331–61; and Casey Luskin, "Missing Transitions: Human Origins and the Fossil Record," in Moreland et al., *Theistic Evolution*, 437–73.

[218] Groothuis, *Christian Apologetics*, 285.

should be a substantial record of transitions between species."[219] The problem is that we do not see either of these patterns of fossil evidence. Interestingly, even Darwin admitted that the absence of "transitional" forms weakened his theory, but he thought that over time more fossils would be discovered to prove his theory. However, the fossil record continues to remain silent in this regard. In fact, paleontologist David Raup admits that even though our knowledge of the fossil record is greater, "we have even fewer examples of evolutionary transition than we had in Darwin's time."[220] Yet many evolutionists still claim that there are a number of examples that support the theory even though these examples are highly questionable.[221]

Proof of this fact is the need to propose an alternative explanation to account for why we do not find a gradual transition but sudden jumps to new life forms. For example, Stephen Jay Gould (1941–2002) proposed an alternative explanation known as "punctuated equilibrium." Gould argued that macroevolution is not a gradual process; instead, it took place in sudden jumps to new life forms, not leaving any fossil record.[222] He argued this way to account for the fact that in the fossil record we see two things: (1) *Stasis*, that is, "most species exhibit no directional change during their tenure on earth. They appear in the fossil record looking much the same as when they disappear; morphological change is usually limited and directionless."[223] (2) *Sudden appearance*, that is, "in any local area, a species does not arise gradually by the steady

[219] Groothuis, 286.

[220] David Raup, "Conflicts Between Darwin and Paleontology," *Field Museum of Natural History Bulletin* 30, no. 1 (1979): 25, cited in William Dembski and Jonathan Wells, *The Design of Life: Discovering Signs of Intelligence in Biological Systems* (Dallas: Foundation for Thought and Ethics, 2008), 68.

[221] One noted example is archaeopteryx, the supposed missing link between reptiles and birds. For a discussion of why this is not a missing link, see Groothuis, *Christian Apologetics*, 290; Wells, *Icons of Evolution*, 111–36. Also, in terms of humans, various prehistoric candidates have been suggested as the missing link between humans and their apelike ancestors, such as Piltdown man, Java man, and Wadjak man. However, on closer look, none of these examples demonstrate missing links. On this point, see Lubenow, *Bones of Contention*, 73–134.

[222] Niles Eldredge and Stephen Jay Gould, "Punctuated Equilibria: An Alternative for Phyletic Gradualism," in *Models in Paleobiology*, ed. Thomas Schopf (San Franciso: Freeman, Cooper, 1972), 82–115; Stephen Jay Gould, *The Structure of Evolutionary Theory* (Cambridge: Harvard University Press, 2002). Gould tried to explain "the Cambrian explosion" (dated by evolutionists to around 500 million years ago), where the fossil record shows that the major animal groups appear suddenly and fully formed, which seems contrary to the Darwin theory.

[223] Stephen Jay Gould, "Evolution's Erratic Pace," *Natural History* 86 (1977): 14.

transformation of its ancestors; it appears all at once and 'fully formed.'"[224] The problem, however, with Gould's explanation is that it runs counter to the entire theory. No wonder many rejected his view, yet either way, the fossil record does not prove evolutionary theory.

4. The Mechanism of Natural Selection

Evolution also faces difficulties in terms of mutations and the mechanism of natural selection. Central to evolution is natural selection, that is, a random process whereby life-forms that are the fittest will be the most successful in reproducing themselves and surviving. Natural selection functions so that over time advantageous genetic tendencies (i.e., qualities that will help the life-form survive better than others of its species) will accumulate so that eventually a large-scale change in life-forms will occur, thus resulting in new species that are better adapted to their environment and able to survive and reproduce.

However, the problem is that over more than a century of experimental breeding of various kinds of plants and animals, the amount of variation that can be produced (even with *intentional* breeding) is extremely limited. Why? Because there is a limited range of genetic variation in each type of living thing, which means that species remain stable over time. In fact, natural selection, which is supposed to account for the survival of new organisms, is a conservative force that works to preserve the genetic fitness of populations, not to generate new species. It is hard to see how small changes could be beneficial to an organism. Most mutations are destructive and do not bring about major changes in organisms.[225] We simply do not see cases "where a genetic mutation has resulted in an increase in genetic information for an organism. But that is precisely what is needed for species to change into other species instead of remaining what they are."[226]

Also, most structures (e.g., eye, heart, the cell) are useful only when the whole structure is in place, a point made by the concept of irreducible complexity. In the end, we do not see

---

[224] Gould, "Evolution's Erratic Pace," 14. See the discussion of this point in Johnson, *Darwin on Trial*, 50.

[225] Interestingly, Dawkins admits this, but he wrongly thinks it is not a problem. *Blind Watchmaker*, 233.

[226] Groothuis, *Christian Apologetics*, 289; cf. Andy McIntosh, "Information and Thermodynamics," 158–59.

natural selection working on random mutations that result in a change in species over time. Sometimes appeal is made to artificial selection when breeders breed for certain characteristics and thereby dramatically change the traits of certain life-forms. Yet the problem is that artificial selection is governed by intelligent design, that is, the breeder. By contrast, in evolutionary theory, natural selection is supposed to work apart from intelligent design, which renders it problematic.

5. Homology and Genetic Information

Evolution also appeals to the similarity of structures (homology) and genetic code between humans and their apelike predecessors as proof of common descent and the overall theory. However, on both accounts the case has not been made.

First, regarding homology, we can observe similarities of structures, but this does not prove evolutionary theory. In fact, most who appeal to homology to prove evolution are guilty of a circular argument. Why? Because if homology is defined as "similarity due to a common descent," then homology automatically proves the theory.[227] But this does not follow. In fact, as we look closer, we discover that these "similarities" result in entirely different functions, which entails that these similarities "cannot be traced back to homologous cells or regions in the earliest stages of embryogenesis."[228] Instead, a better explanation is an appeal to creation. Given creation, why creatures are similar is due to their common creation and living on earth. This interpretation of the "facts" explains the data better than the evolutionary alternative. Furthermore, the "common" structures that prove common descent have often been demonstrated to be false. For example, various vestigial organs have been proposed to prove that humans have organs or structural remnants from our common descent that no longer serve any purpose. Yet a closer look demonstrates that these "vestigial" organs do serve a purpose and thus are not proof of common descent (e.g., human coccyx, appendix, pineal gland, thymus gland).[229]

---

[227] See Norman C. Nevin, "Homology," in Nevin, *Should Christians Embrace Evolution?*, 137–41; Wells, *Icons of Evolution*, 63.

[228] Denton, *Evolution: A Theory in Crisis*, 146.

[229] Groothuis, *Christian Apologetics*, 294–95.

Second, the same is true regarding the similarity between the genetic codes of humans and their supposed ancestors. No doubt, there is similarity in the genetic code between humans and chimpanzees, but this argument does not prove common descent.[230] As Vern Poythress argues, it only "proves" common descent if Darwinism is true, but this is what is at dispute. Given creation, God designed us for a common world, and there is every reason to think that our DNA would be similar, but we must also acknowledge the differences.[231] Thus, the claim that the DNA of humans and chimps is 99 percent similar is false. In fact, "there is at least a 5% difference in our DNA, and that does not count rearrangements in the DNA, or where one segment of human DNA is in a different location than in chimpanzees."[232] Also, we must note other substantial differences, such as our brain size, thyroid hormone metabolism, immune system, language, and cultural and behavioral differences.[233] And just as so-called vestigial organs in homology have been shown to be functional in humans, so has so-called junk DNA that "proved" our common descent been shown not to be "junk" after all. Further research has uncovered many positive functions of what was formerly viewed as "junk."[234]

What about Theistic Evolution?

Although we have found the naturalistic theory of evolution problematic, first as a worldview and, second, in terms of the actual evidence, some theologians and scientists think that the

---

[230] See the essay by Ann K. Gauger, Ola Hössjer, and Colin R. Reeves, "Evidence for Human Uniqueness," in Moreland et al., *Theistic Evolution*, 475–502; and "An Alternative Population Genetics Model," in Moreland et al., *Theistic Evolution*, 503–21. Also see the essays by Geoff Barnard, "Chromosomal Fusion and Common Ancestry," in Nevin, *Should Christians Embrace Evolution?*, 151–57; and "Does the Genome Provide Evidence for Common Ancestry?," in Nevin, *Should Christians Embrace Evolution?*, 166–86; Nathaniel Jeanson and Jeffrey Tomkins, "Genetics Confirms the Recent, Supernatural Creation of Adam and Eve," in Mortenson, *Searching for Adam*, 287–330.

[231] Vern Poythress, "Adam Versus Claims from Genetics," *WTJ* 75 (2013): 65–82.

[232] Gauger, Hössjer, and Reeves, "Evidence for Human Uniqueness," 481.

[233] See Gauger, Hössjer, and Reeves, 491–92, for a list of these differences.

[234] Poythress states this fact well: "The ENCODE project (the 'Encyclopedia of DNA Elements') has endeavored to catalog systematically the noncoding DNA, and reports that more than 80 percent 'have now been assigned at least one biochemical function.' The leader of the ENCODE project accordingly called for retiring the word 'junk.'" "Adam Versus Claims from Genetics," 74. Also see Barnard, "Does the Genome Provide Evidence?," 166–86, who makes this same point.

problematic features of the view, specifically its lack of intelligent design, can be remedied by embracing *theistic* evolution. This is the view that God began the process of evolution (thus explaining the origin of the universe), implanting within creation the laws that its development has followed (thus avoiding the "blind watchmaker" aspect of evolution). In this sense, God is the "ultimate" cause of the world, and evolution is the "means" by which God has "created" the world in its present form. By making evolution *theistic*, one can account for more direction and teleology in the evolutionary process, which includes the evolution of humans.

What should we think about theistic evolution? There are at least two problems. First, on the science front, we must be convinced that the evidence for evolution is in fact true, which we have questioned. The plausibility of theistic evolution assumes the truthfulness of the larger theory of evolution, which is the issue at dispute. Second, on the biblical and theological front, we must ask whether such a view fits with Scripture given the authority of God's word and the priority of special revelation over natural revelation. However, one of the problems in evaluating theistic evolution, or what some identify as "evolutionary creation," is properly defining what it is.[235] For example, if theistic evolution is defined as "God created matter and after that did not guide or intervene or act directly to cause any empirically detectable change in the natural behavior of matter until all living things had evolved by purely natural processes,"[236] then it is difficult to reconcile with Scripture. However, not all theistic evolutionists accept this definition. Deborah Haarsma objects to this definition since it is too deistic; instead, she, along with many at BioLogos, affirm a broad definition, such as "God creates all living things through Christ, including humans in his image, making use of intentionally designed, actively-sustained, natural processes that scientists today study as evolution."[237] This definition seeks to avoid any deistic overtones, yet it still affirms ideas that are hard to reconcile with Scripture. For example, this definition of "evolutionary creation" affirms that God used the mechanisms

[235] On this point, see Stephen C. Meyer, "Scientific and Philosophical Introduction: Defining Theistic Evolution," in Moreland et al., *Theistic Evolution*, 33–58.

[236] See Wayne Grudem, "Biblical and Theological Introduction," in Moreland et al., *Theistic Evolution*, 67. This definition of theistic evolution is consistent with the work of Karl Giberson and Francis Collins, *The Language of Science and Faith* (Downers Grove: InterVarsity, 2011), 115; also see Collins, *Language of God*, 200 (see chap. 21, n. 111).

[237] See Deborah Haarsma, "A Flawed Mirror: A Response to the Book 'Theistic Evolution,'" *BioLogos*, April 18, 2018, https://biologos.org/articles/a-flawed-mirror-a-response-to-the-book-theistic-evolution/. Also see "What We Believe," BioLogos, https://biologos.org/about-us/what-we-believe.

of evolution to generate novelty, a point that is at dispute. Furthermore, and most significantly, it rejects "the traditional *de novo* view of human origins (in which God miraculously creates the first pair roughly 10,000 years ago, with this pair as the sole genetic progenitors of all humans today)."[238] Such a view is consistent with either archetypal or symbolic views that deny a historical Adam and Eve or an affirmation of a historical Adam and Eve within a larger population of humans. However, both options are difficult to reconcile with the biblical teaching that views Adam and Eve as uniquely created as the sole genetic progenitors of the human race.[239]

Much could be said in response to the various understandings of theistic evolution, but we offer the following brief points in terms of its basic fit with the Scriptural teaching.[240]

First, minimally, if theistic evolutionists are going to be consistent with Genesis 1–2, they would have to argue that God intervened in the evolutionary process at least in three areas: (1) the absolute creation of the universe *ex nihilo* (Gen 1:1); (2) the creation of the simplest life form; and (3) the unique creation of a younger historic Adam and Eve not from prehominids. They will also need to accept the existence of a historic fall (Gen 1:26–31; 2:7; 3:1–6). If these minimal points are denied, it is difficult for someone to say they are taking the Genesis account seriously. But depending on the specific version of theistic evolution, (2) and especially (3) is either rejected or redefined.[241]

Second, overall, it is very difficult to "fit" theistic evolution with Genesis 1–2 on other areas. Let me list a number of these areas, building on the first point.

1. In our exposition of Genesis 1–2, we noted how God is active in every aspect of creation, especially in the unique creation of Adam and Eve, a point that is difficult to reconcile with most versions of theistic evolution. There is no evidence in the text that God is "overseeing"

---

[238] Haarsma, "Flawed Mirror."

[239] For a theistic evolutionary view that argues that Adam and Eve are uniquely created and the sole genetic progenitors of the human race, see Craig, *In Quest of the Historical Adam*, 330–80. However, Craig has to interpret Genesis 1–11 under the larger category of "mytho-history," and he must distinguish the "literary Adam" from the "historical Adam," which on both counts is difficult to reconcile with Scripture.

[240] For more detailed discussions and evaluation of theistic evolution and its fit with Scripture, see Berkhof, *Systematic Theology*, 162–63; Grudem, *Systematic Theology*, 366–83 (see chap. 1, n. 14); and the entire work by Moreland et al. *Theistic Evolution*, especially section 3 (783–952), which includes a biblical and theological critique.

[241] For an admission of a revision of these points, see Haarsma, "Flawed Mirror."

natural processes that he has established, such as allowing mutations to occur randomly on their own. Instead, God is acting intentionally and directly so that at every point, "intelligent design" is at work, not "randomness."

2. Ten times Genesis speaks of God's creative word bringing forth an immediate response. This does not fit with the idea of millions of years and random mutations in living things.

3. God creates "according to their kinds" (Gen 1:11, 24). This suggests that God created many different types of plants and animals, and although there would be variety among them, there is no evidence for evolutionary change via genetic mutations across species.

4. God creates humans as his image-bearers directly, not from other creatures. Not only is this evident in Gen 1:26–28, but it is even more so in Gen 2:7. God makes Adam from the dust of the ground and then adds the "breath of life" (*nᵉšāmâ ḥay*). As a result, Adam becomes a "living being" (*nepeš ḥay*). But what is significant about this point is that animals and humans are both "living beings" (Gen 6:17), but only humans have the "breath of life," thus underscoring the qualitative difference between humans and animals. This point is confirmed in God's creation of Eve and later Scripture that speaks of Adam and Eve as historical people who did not originate from pre-human hominids.[242] On this point, most versions of theistic evolution deny what Genesis teaches, rendering it "mytho-history" instead of a true, historical narrative.

4. All versions of theistic evolution must acknowledge that "death," "pain," and "suffering" are "normal" to God's world, even if they affirm that there was a historic fall (which most do not) that resulted in sin and death in the human realm. But this is difficult to reconcile with Scripture, which links sin, death, and a cursed world to Adam's sin (Gen 1:31; 2:15–17; 3; Rom 6:23; 8:18–25; Rev 21–22).

5. Most theistic evolutionists reject a global flood in Genesis 6–9 and opt for a local one. This position is very difficult to reconcile with Scripture and later NT authors who assume that the flood in Noah's day was global (e.g., 2 Pet 3:3–7).[243]

On these points and many others, we reject the view of theistic evolution and argue that it is incompatible with a biblical view of creation and the teaching of Scripture.

---

[242] See Craig, *In Quest of the Historical Adam*, who argues this point. Nowhere does Craig address Gen 2:7.

[243] Beeke and Smalley, *Reformed Systematic Theology*, 2:117–121. For example, see Craig, *In Quest of the Historical Adam*, 47–157, who rejects a global flood.

Concluding Reflections

Without a correct doctrine of creation framing our entire theology, most, if not all, doctrinal areas will be detrimentally affected. This is why we began the chapter by saying that it is impossible to overestimate the significance of the doctrine of creation for theology and the Christian worldview. Creation establishes the Bible's unique theistic, covenantal, and eschatological framework, by which we understand God and all things in relation to him.

Given the theological significance of creation, it is not surprising that it has been challenged, along with the early chapters of Genesis. The church must certainly respond to these challenges both in exposition of the doctrine and its defense. But as we do, we must never forget that creation reminds us first about the glory of our triune Creator-covenant God, who deserves all of our worship, trust, devotion, and obedience. In all of our theological reflection about creation and its application to our lives, we must never forget this point: "Our Lord and God / you are worthy to receive / glory and honor and power, / because you have created all things, / and by your will / they exist and were created" (Rev 4:11).

CHAPTER 22

The Triune God Who Sustains and Rules: Providence (Part 1)

Introduction

The doctrine of providence has fallen on hard times in our day. Naturalism, both metaphysical and methodological, has taken deep root, and people do not view their lives as ordered and governed by the triune Creator-covenant Lord. Paul confronted at Athens (Acts 17:16–34) two impersonal Greek views of "providence," namely, the randomness worldview of Epicureanism and the fatalism of Stoicism, and these two views are still with us today, albeit in different forms. Naturalism is alive and well, along with various versions of pantheism/panentheism, which in the end leaves us with an impersonal view of the universe: in its origins, history, and "providence."

In Christian theology, by contrast, a correct understanding of providence is not a minor issue: it is of crucial significance. Without a *doctrine* of providence, the idea of the triune God and his involvement with his creation is largely irrelevant to what is actually happening in the world. Providence reminds us that the triune God of glory is not only the sovereign Creator, but also the covenant Lord. Providence undergirds the Bible's story and the progressive unfolding of God's eternal plan through the biblical covenants centered in our Lord Jesus Christ. Providence reminds us that we are creatures of God, whose lives are not random and meaningless, and that history is God himself working out his sovereign purposes for his own glory and the good of his people.

"Providence" (Lat. *providentia*, from *pro*, "ahead," and *videre*, "to see") is a *theological* term. It is not found directly in Scripture; instead, it is a concept used to capture all that Scripture teaches regarding God's ongoing preservation of, ruling over, and active relationship to his creation. It conveys the basic meaning of "to act with foresight," thus emphasizing God's prior knowledge of and plan for the world, along with his sovereign power to accomplish what he has decreed. Louis Berkhof offers a helpful working definition of the concept: "Providence may be defined as that continued exercise of the divine energy whereby the Creator preserves all His creatures, is operative in all that comes to pass in the world, and directs all things to their appointed end."[1]

A Brief History of the Doctrine of Providence[2]

In the patristic era, the church countered the Greco-Roman views of Stoicism and Epicureanism, similar to Paul's encounter at Athens. In the former, there is little or no distinction between God and the world, no *creatio ex nihilo*, and no absolute-personal triune God who sustains, rules, and governs all things to his planned end. In the latter, there is no *creatio ex nihilo* or providence other than the chance configuration of atoms and the randomness of the course of nature. In both views, all reality is reduced to the impersonal, with no room for God's primary agency and the reality of secondary causes. Also, the possibility of miracles evaporates, along with human significance, freedom, justice, and the possibility of covenant relationships with the triune Lord.

In response, the church underscored the foundational metaphysical truth of the Creator-creature distinction and its corollary, the reality of primary and secondary agency and causes.[3]

---

[1] Berkhof, *Systematic Theology*, 166 (see chap. 15, n. 63). Italics removed.

[2] See the helpful summary in Berkhof, 165–66; Allison, *Historical Theology*, 277–97 (see chap. 8, n. 9).

[3] Christian theology has universally distinguished between God's will as primary and creaturely wills as secondary. For example, in discussing God's planning of evil, Tertullian says: "Though some things seem to savor of the will of God, seeing that they are allowed by him, it does not necessarily follow that everything which is permitted proceeds out of the mere and absolute will of him who permits

The triune Creator who made all things continues to sustain and rule over all.[4] Indeed, God is so active that he enters into covenant relationships, ultimately culminating in the new covenant centered in Christ Jesus, the divine Son who has taken on our humanity and lived among us. Yet, many in the patristic era did not fully develop God's decree in terms of his foreordaining all things according to his will, which includes within it secondary agency. Instead, God's plan was tied to God's foreknowledge of all things, including God's knowledge of who would believe.[5]

However, Augustine (354–430) ties God's control of all things to God's foreordination and predestination. God foreknows all things because he foreordains/predestines all things. But in emphasizing the reality of secondary causes and dual agency, he protects God's goodness and holiness, especially in relation to evil, along with the truth of human freedom and responsibility.[6] Election is based on God's unconditional and gracious choice, yet sin and evil are

---

[it]." Tertullian, *On Exhortation to Chastity* 3 (*ANF* 4:51); cf. Origen, *Against Celsus* 7.68 (*ANF* 4:638); Clement of Alexandria, *Stromata* 1.17; 4.12 (*ANF* 2:320, 424).

[4] For example, Irenaeus says that "God does exercise a providence over all things . . . and arranges the affairs [events] of our world." Irenaeus, *Against Heresies* 3.25.1 (*ANF* 1:459). Or Origen affirms that "Of those events which happen to men, none occur by accident or chance, but in accordance with a plan so carefully considered, and so stupendous, that it does not overlook even the number of hairs of the heads, not merely of the saints, but perhaps of all human beings, and the plan of which providential government extends even to caring for the sale of two sparrows for a denarius." Origen, *First Principles* 2.11.5 (*ANF* 4:299). Also see Justin Martyr, *Dialogue with Trypho*, 102.

[5] For example, Justin Martyr speaks of God creating humans and angels with free will and foretelling that humans and angels who sin against God will be punished, but he does so "because [he] foreknew that they would be unchangeably [wicked], but not because God had created them so." Justin Martyr, *Dialogue with Trypho*, 141. In a similar way, Irenaeus ties God's plan to his foreknowledge: "God, knowing the number of those who will not believe, since He foreknows all things, has given them over to unbelief, and turned away His face from men of this stamp." Irenaeus, *Against Heresies* 4.29.2. Cf. Tertullian, *Against Marcion* 2.23.

[6] In reflecting on the relationship between God's will and our choices, Augustine rejects the either/or of Cicero: either God foreknows all things and humans have no freedom, or we have freedom and God does not foreknow all things. Instead,

> [God] knows unalterably all that is to happen and what he himself is going to do. . . . Now if there is for God a fixed order of all causes, it does not follow that nothing depends on our free choice. Our wills themselves are in the order of causes, which is, for God, fixed, and is contained in his foreknowledge, since human acts of will are the causes of human activities.

also willed by God differently than election to salvation is willed.[7] Thus, God plans all things, including sin and evil, but his willing of good and evil is asymmetrical.[8] The Augustinian position was reaffirmed by Thomas Aquinas (1225–74) and the magisterial Reformers, specifically Martin Luther (1483–1546), Ulrich Zwingli (1484–1531), and John Calvin (1509–64), but in the later Lutheran tradition, it was modified to include God's antecedent and consequent will—a theological formulation similar to later Arminian theology.[9]

In the medieval era, Thomas Aquinas continued the Augustinian view. He affirmed a universal providence: God preserves in existence everything that he has created,[10] and directs everything to their purposed end.[11] Along with the entire Christian tradition, Aquinas

---

> Therefore he who had prescience of the causes of all events certainly could not be ignorant of our decisions, which he foreknows as the causes of our actions.

Augustine, *The City of God* 5.9 (192) (see chap. 21, n. 7).

[7] Augustine, *The City of God* 5.9 (193), writes: "Just as [God] is the creator of all natures, so he is the giver of all power of achievement, but not of all acts of will. Evil wills do not proceed from him because they are contrary to the nature which proceeds from him. . . . But all bodies are subject above all to the will of God." Also, in 5.10 (195), Augustine continues: "The fact that God foreknew that a man would sin does not make a man sin; on the contrary, it cannot be doubted that it is the man himself who sins just because he whose prescience cannot be mistaken has foreseen that the man himself would sin. A man does not sin unless he wills to sin; and if had willed not to sin, then God would have foreseen that refusal" (cf. 14.11, [568–70]). Or, in terms of Augustine's affirmation of dual agency, he writes: "We are in no way compelled either to preserve God's prescience by abolishing our free will, or to safeguard our free will be denying (blasphemously) the divine foreknowledge. We embrace both truths" (5.10, [195]).

[8] For a helpful discussion of Augustine's view of providence, see Bavinck, *Reformed Dogmatics*, 2:350–51 (see chap. 1, n. 9).

[9] For example, see Philip Melanchthon (1497–1560). In his *Loci Communes*, he changed his chapter, "Human Powers, Especially Free Will," from 1521 to 1535. Although the Formula of Concord continued to affirm total depravity, unconditional election, and the need for effectual grace, it agreed with the Augsburg Confession in its equation of election with predestination but reprobation with foreknowledge. This allowed for God's antecedent will to desire the salvation of "all without exception" (universal salvific will), but God's consequent will to elect those whom he foresaw would believe in Christ. This formulation is similar to the Arminian view regarding God's antecedent and consequent will and the role of foreknowledge in the divine decree.

[10] Thomas Aquinas, *Summa Theologica*, pt. 1, q. 104, art. 1 (see chap. 2, no. 20): "For the being of every creature depends on God, so that not for a moment could it subsist, but would fall into nothingness were it not kept in being by the operation of the Divine power."

[11] Aquinas, pt. 1, q. 22, art. 2: "all things are subject to divine providence, not only in general, but even in their own individual selves. . . . For since every agent acts for an end, the ordering of the effects

strongly emphasized the distinction between God's primary agency and creation's secondary causality and humanity's secondary agency, thus absolving God from evil and affirming the reality of the created order, especially human freedom and responsibility. In God's eternal decree, he has ordained the reality of secondary causes and agents to bring about his ordained ends.[12]

In the Reformation, John Calvin is the key theologian. Following Augustine, he taught that God rules over all things by controlling *and* caring for all that comes to pass in a purposeful and deliberate manner. Calvin insisted that God does not sit idly by; God "govern[s] all events" in a deliberate manner,[13] and not merely according to a "bare foreknowledge,"[14] but by his active determination to bring about his eternal decree in history.[15] For Calvin, God's will is personal, good, and wise, and God's providential rule over the world is exhaustive and extensive. All of creation, even seemingly "chance" occurrences, along with human actions are under God's providential rule: nothing falls outside of God's decree and rule. As with Augustine and Aquinas, Calvin distinguished between primary and secondary causality, thus emphasizing that God is *not* the author of evil and that humans act freely and responsibly before God.[16] As we noted in chapter 20, Calvin's view of the divine decree and its outworking was foundational for the development of the Reformed tradition and what today is identified as "Calvinism."

In the beginning of the post-Reformation era, the view of Jacob Arminius (1560–1609) arose, which modified the Augustinian-Aquinas-Calvin trajectory regarding the decree and providence. As we discussed in chapter 20, Arminius was professor of theology at the University of Leiden in the Netherlands. His views were systematized into what is known today as "Arminianism." Although Arminius held much in common with the

---

towards that end extends as far as the causality of the first agent extends. . . . But the causality of God, Who is the first agent, extends to all being. . . . Hence all things that exist in whatsoever manner are necessarily directed by God towards some end."

[12] Aquinas, pt. 1, q. 19, art. 5, reply obj. 2; pt. 1, q. 19 art 7, reply obj. 2; pt. 1, q. 19, art. 8, answer; pt. 1, q. 22, art. 4, reply obj. 2; pt. 1, q. 23, art. 5, answer; pt. 1, q. 23, art. 8, answer.

[13] Calvin, *Institutes*, 1.16.4 (1:202) (see chap. 1, n. 3). For Calvin's entire discussion of providence, see 1.16–18 (1:197–237).

[14] Calvin, 1.16.4 (1:202).

[15] See Calvin, 1.16 (1:197–210).

[16] Calvin, 1.17.1–5 (1:210–17).

magisterial Reformation, he and his followers (the Remonstrants) departed significantly from the Augustinian-Calvinist view of the divine decree and its outworking in providence. Arminius was concerned that the Reformed tradition floundered on the issue of *theodicy*. In agreement with historic Christian theology, he affirmed that God has an eternal plan due to his perfect knowledge. However, since God has freely chosen to create humans with freedom (which is best understood as libertarian), God has also chosen to limit himself in what he can and cannot do. In fact, since God has chosen to give us human freedom, he cannot control our free actions or always guarantee what he desires will occur unless he eliminates our freedom. Furthermore, as discussed in chapter 20, Arminius and classical Arminian theology insist that God's decree is "put together" conditioned on what he foreknows humans will do, thus entailing that God's rule over creation is more general in scope. God has ultimate control, but given that his eternal plan is dependent on what he foreknows the creature will do, he cannot direct every event exactly the way he wants. In fact, depending on the specific kind of knowledge God has (e.g., timeless knowledge, simple foreknowledge, or middle knowledge), his sovereign control will vary. Ultimately, God will accomplish his overall plan, but his plan is dependent on human choices. Foreordination, and especially predestination in reference to moral agents, does *not* apply to every individual activity; instead, it refers "to the comprehensive purpose of God which is *the structural context* in which history moves and from which it receives its meaningful form and direction."[17] In terms of providence, Arminians teach that God preserves *and* governs all things, but he does not directly rule over the human will. As such, dual agency is not exactly the same as in the Reformed tradition; that is, in every action, God acts and humans act simultaneously so that God's will is guaranteed and human freedom and responsibility is also upheld, a point we will return to below in our discussion of *concursus*.[18]

From the post-Reformation era to our day, within evangelical theology, Arminianism and Calvinism continue to dominate the discussion regarding the nature of divine providence.[19] In

---

[17] Clark H. Pinnock, "Responsible Freedom and the Flow of Biblical History," in Pinnock, *Grace Unlimited*, 102 (see chap. 20, n. 43).

[18] See *The Arminian Confession of 1621*, trans. and ed. Mark A. Ellis (Eugene: Pickwick, 2005), 58–63.

[19] See Jowers, *Four Views on Divine Providence* (see chap. 18, n. 161); Basinger and Basinger, *Predestination and Free Will* (see chap. 16, n. 72).

addition, due to the influence of social and relational views and the concerns of panentheism, open theism has gone further than Arminianism, a point we discussed in chapter 16. Outside of evangelical theology, in the Enlightenment, due to the influence of deism and then Darwinian evolution, the doctrine of providence faded. In fact, as classic liberalism morphed into postmodern theology, panentheism arose as the dominant view, which ultimately identifies "God" with the world and its natural processes. As a result, theistic evolution and methodological naturalism is embraced, and God's action in the world is viewed as immanent, cooperative, and non-effectual.[20] In all of these latter views, we no longer have a biblical and Christian view of divine providence.

The Three Components of Divine Providence

In light of historical theology, and more significantly Scripture, a correct biblical-theological doctrine of providence involves at least three intertwined and necessary components or aspects: preservation, concurrence, and government. Before we discuss each of these components, we must remember that all of God's *ad extra* acts, including providence, are triune: "For from him and through him / and to him are all things. / To him be the glory forever. Amen" (Rom 11:36).

As we have discussed in previous chapters, God's external acts are undivided (*opera trinitatis ad extra indivisa sunt*) yet specific actions terminate or are appropriated by the divine persons. Thus, God acts as the one true and living God, yet the Father acts through the Son and by the Spirit; the Son acts from the Father and by the Spirit; and the Spirit acts from the Father and the Son. By appropriation, Scripture can speak of the Father as the Creator (Matt 6:9; Eph 3:14), the Son as our Redeemer (Acts 4:12; Eph 1:7), and the Spirit as the Sanctifier (1 Cor 6:11), yet all of God's external works are without division.

As applied to divine providence, it is God who sustains, acts in, and rules over his creation. Yet God's work of providence is triune: the Father is the one who creates, sustains, and rules in and through the Son (John 1:1–2; 5:17–19; Col 1:16–17); the Son, from the Father and by

[20] For a helpful overview of panentheism, see John W. Cooper, *Panentheism—The Other God of the Philosophers: From Plato to the Present* (Grand Rapids: Baker Academic, 2006).

the Spirit, creates and "[sustains] (*pherō*) all things by his powerful word" (Heb 1:3); while the Spirit, from the Father and the Son, is the one who gives life, makes effective, and brings to completion the work of the Father and the Son (Gen 1:2; Ps 104:30; cf. Job 33:4).[21] Thus, in providence, all three persons act as the one God yet according to their ordered personal mode of subsistence due to their eternal relations of origin (the divine processions). Divine providence, then, is not merely the work of the Father or even the Son, but the *one* act of the Father, Son, and Holy Spirit: the triune God at work displaying his own internal, immanent glory in his external acts. With this crucial point in place, let us now unpack the nature of divine providence by expounding on preservation, concurrence, and government.

Preservation

Preservation is God's continuous activity, his active supervision by which he maintains in existence all things that he has created consistent with their designed and ordered nature.[22] In contrast to deism, preservation does not mean that God is passive; he does not merely create the world and let it operate on its own. Rather, preservation is God's active upholding and sustaining all things; the created order is not self-sufficient. Apart from God's presence and sustenance, life would cease to exist. This is what Paul emphasizes to the Athenians: God is the Creator and providential Lord—"For in him we live and move and have our being" (Acts 17:28). Paul is not denying the Creator-creature distinction and affirming some version of panentheism, nor is he saying that the universe is continually created.[23] Instead, Paul is reminding the Athenians that the world is created, distinct from God, and not self-sustaining. John Webster nicely captures the difference between creation and providence: "Creation bestows being and does not merely tantalize with the possibility of being. Once bestowed, the being of

---

[21] See Horton, *Rediscovering the Holy Spirit*, 29–80 (see chap. 13, n. 37); cf. Beeke and Smalley, *Reformed Systematic Theology*, 1:1064–65 (see chap. 1, n. 8).

[22] Deut 33:25–28; Neh 9:6; Job 34:14–15; Pss 104:30; 107:9; 127:1; 145:14–15; Matt 10:29; John 5:17; Acts 17:28; Rom 11:36; Col 1:17; Heb 1:3; 2 Pet 3:7.

[23] This is the view of Jonathan Edwards. For a critique of "continuous creation," see Bavinck, *Reformed Dogmatics*, 2:607; and Berkhof, *Systematic Theology*, 171. Such a view has difficulty accounting for the reality of secondary causes, and if one is not careful, it moves in the direction of panentheism by not upholding sufficiently the Creator-creature distinction.

creation has its own relative independence; it needs no further creating (for to create is to call into existence) but does need to be sustained by providential care."[24]

Against today's naturalistic "scientific" worldview, God's creation of the world *and* his preserving activity is the metaphysical and epistemological ground for the possibility of an objective empirical science. God has not only created an ordered and designed universe that can be objectively studied, but also one that functions in predictable ways due to his metaphysical preservation. Due to creation, the universe consists of things with real natures with their own abilities and capacities distinct from God's existence. Yet none of these created things, whether the things of nature or rational moral creatures, exist on their own; they are preserved by God according to their created nature. For this reason, as Michael Horton observes, it is Christian theology that provides the rational ground for the "pure *naturalness* of nature."[25] Indeed, as Horton continues, "even the methodological naturalism of the hard sciences is a product of a biblical distinction between the Creator and creation. Philosophical naturalism is the kind of heresy that could only have arisen in the milieu of a biblically informed culture."[26] Thus, due to God's creation *and* preservation of the world, theology accounts for the objective and uniform nature of the world *and* God's continuous preservation of it through natural or secondary causes. Yet, given that God sustains all things by his word, he is also able to act in "extraordinary" ways, hence the distinction between "ordinary" and "extraordinary" providence.

In addition to metaphysical preservation,[27] there is also covenantal/redemptive-historical preservation.[28] In fact, God's promise to sustain our present created yet fallen order until the end is due to the Noahic covenant. As discussed in part 3, the Noahic covenant is a creation

---

[24] John Webster, "Providence," in Allen and Swain, *Christian Dogmatics*, 159 (see chap. 5, n. 91).

[25] Horton, *Rediscovering the Holy Spirit*, 60.

[26] Horton, 60.

[27] Frame, *Doctrine of God*, 279 (see chap. 3, n. 13).

[28] Regarding "covenantal" preservation, Bavinck astutely notes that "preservation" is "greater" than the act of creation. Why? Because God created the world, and especially humans, to grow in its dependence on God and thus to realize true freedom and its created purpose. Bavinck writes: "A creature is the more perfect to the degree that God indwells it more and permeates it with his being." But creation "only initiated the beginning of existence"; preservation, especially tied now to redemption and our covenant union in Christ, "is the progressive and ever increasing self-communication of God to his creatures." *Reformed Dogmatics*, 2:608.

covenant but ratified in the post-fall context. Due to God's promises, starting in Gen 3:15, it ultimately anticipates the dawning of a new creation in the Last Adam, our Lord Jesus Christ. However, until Christ returns and consummates what he inaugurated in his first coming, it remains in force (Gen 8:21–22; 2 Pet 3:5–7). As John Frame notes, "God's preservation of the natural order, then, is characteristic of the time between the two great judgments: the typical judgment of the Flood and the antitypical judgment of the final catastrophe. The time in between is the time of God's patience."[29] In fact, this is one of the reasons why common grace is operative. Until all of God's redemptive purposes are brought to their consummated fullness, especially the salvation of God's people, this present order remains. Seedtime and harvest, summer and winter remain, along with the order and structures of creation (e.g., human dignity, male and female, the family, universal moral norms, etc.), until all of God's covenant people are born and brought to saving faith. In the meantime, God's elect and non-elect live side by side in a common order as God's plan of redemption and judgment eschatologically moves forward to its appointed end.

Concurrence

God's work of providence is more than preservation. It also involves what is known as "concurrence," or "co-working," namely, "the cooperation of the divine power with all subordinate powers, according to the pre-established laws of their operation, causing them to act and to act precisely as they do."[30] Due to creation, God has created all things, including humans, with their own nature, which includes their own abilities, capacities, and powers. As Bavinck observes, "Every creature received a nature of its own, and with that nature an existence, a life, and a law of its own. Just as the moral law was increated in the heart of Adam as the rule

---

[29] Frame, *Doctrine of God*, 281.

[30] Berkhof, *Systematic Theology*, 171; cf. Muller, *Dictionary of Latin and Greek*, 76–77 (see chap. 8, n. 37). In part 2, we discussed *concursus* in relation to the doctrine of Scripture and the "concursive theory of inspiration." We noted that in the production of Scripture, the triune God by the appropriated work of the Holy Spirit was the primary agent, while human authors, in their freedom and integrity, were secondary agents. Yet, in the case of Scripture, God's act of inspiration was an "extraordinary" act of *concursus*, not merely an "ordinary" one. For this reason, Scripture is *God's* authoritative and inerrant word written through the agency of human authors.

for his life, so all creatures carried in their own nature the principles and laws for their own development."[31] But although God gives to all things their own nature, no created thing is *a se*, self-sustaining, and explained by finite causes alone. For this reason, God not only preserves all things; he also acts as the primary cause in and through all things, which function as secondary causes, but in such a way that he upholds each thing's created integrity. This is what is meant by concurrence.[32]

Scripture teaches this truth. Paul's statement that in God "we live and move and have our being" (Acts 17:28) involves more than preservation; it also involves concurrence. Just as nothing in creation is explained by finite causes alone, this is also true of our human actions. Even our human choices are under the rule of God's sovereignty and foreordained before the foundation of the world (Prov 19:21; 21:1; Eph 1:11; Phil 2:12–13). In addition, Scripture teaches that God sustains nature but also acts in and through it down to the smallest details (Ps 104:21; Matt 5:45; 10:29; Acts 14:17). Indeed, the teleology of nature and history cannot be explained merely by finite causes alone (Dan 4:34–35).

Thus, in providence and especially concurrence, God not only sustains what he has created but also acts in and through it as the primary cause, yet without violating the integrity of nature or of rational creatures. Bavinck states it this way: "[God's] will, his power, his being is immediately present in every creature and every event. All things exist and live together in him (Acts 17:28; Col. 1:17; Heb. 1:3). Just as he created the world by himself, so he also preserves and governs it by himself,"[33] but in such a way that God's primary agency is not in competition with secondary causes and/or agency. As Bavinck continues, "God respects and develops—and does not nullify—the things he called into being in creation."[34] Or, as Aquinas states the same truth: "it belongs to Divine providence, not to destroy but to preserve the nature of things."[35]

---

[31] Bavinck, *Reformed Dogmatics*, 2:609; cf. Webster, "Providence," 162–63, who makes a similar point. To say that the moral law was "increated" in Adam refers to God "implanting" within us a natural knowledge of his moral demand, which is written on the conscience and to which we are accountable before God.

[32] Frame properly locates the discussion of concurrence in terms of "the relationship between the divine primary cause and the natural secondary causes of events in the world," with the principal focus on the relationship between divine and human agency. *Doctrine of God*, 287.

[33] Bavinck, *Reformed Dogmatics*, 2:610.

[34] Bavinck, 2:610.

[35] Aquinas, *Summa Theologica*, pt. 1–2, q. 10, art. 4.

This is another reason why miracles are best understood as God's acts of "extraordinary" providence and not violations of "natural laws," as if natural laws can be viewed independently of God's preservation and concurrence. In other words, God is not more directly the cause of miracles than he is the cause of any ordinary event. Rather, "in miracles God only puts into effect a special force that, like any other force, operates in accordance with its own nature and therefore also has an outcome of its own."[36] Thus, in concurrence, God preserves and rules his creation according to each creature's nature so that the objective nature of his creation is upheld.

On these points, Christian theology is in basic agreement. However, when it comes to the specifics of concurrence, especially the relation between divine and human agency, differences within theology begin to emerge. For example, Reformed theology has affirmed a robust sense of dual agency, while Arminian theology has not. As discussed in chapter 20, for Arminianism, God has created humans with capacities and abilities that are able to act independently of God; this view is due to its commitment to libertarian freedom. Thus, if God acts, especially in an effectual way, our human freedom is reduced, and conversely, if humans are truly free, then God must choose to limit himself in terms of his ability to guarantee what he desires and wants.[37]

By contrast, a Reformed view of dual agency affirms that in the same act, God, as the primary agent, acts according to his decreed will, and humans, as secondary agents, also act but not in the same sphere or on the same level. In *concursus*, then, as Geerhardus Vos notes, "we encounter two spheres into which one and the same object falls without the one limiting the other."[38] In every event and action, God acts and humans act without excluding the other: God's action is primary while human action is secondary. In terms of primacy of order, God preserves the creature both in their nature and capacities and works through their actions to bring about his purposes, while humans also act according to their own will and desires, thus upholding their free and responsible agency. Hence,

---

[36] Bavinck, *Reformed Dogmatics*, 2:610.

[37] On this point, see Bavinck, 2:601–4, 608–15. Carter identifies this false assumption as thinking that divine and human action result in a "zero-sum game" so that either God acts or the creature acts but not simultaneously in a proper sense of dual agency. *Interpreting Scripture*, 56 (see chap. 4, n. 2).

[38] Vos, *Reformed Dogmatics*, 1:192 (see chap. 15, n. 126).

> in relation to God the secondary causes can be compared to instruments (Isa. 10:15; 13:5; Jer. 50:25; Acts 9:15; Rom. 9:20, 23); in relation to their effects and products they are causes in the true sense. And precisely because the primary and secondary cause do not stand and function dualistically on separate tracks, but the primary works through the secondary, the effect that proceeds from the two is one and the product is one[39]

yet the integrity of each is preserved. As applied to the relationship between divine and human agency, Bavinck notes that "human persons speak, act, and believe, and it is God alone who supplies to a sinner all the vitality and strength he or she needs for the commission of a sin. Nevertheless the subject and author of the sin is not God but the human being."[40]

Government

Government emphasizes another component of divine providence: our triune Creator-covenant Lord has a purpose in all that he does in the world. As such, God not only preserves and acts in the world but also continually governs, rules, and directs all things to their appointed end.[41] In other words, government reminds us that God's rule through secondary causes and agents is teleological and eschatological: history is moving from creation to new creation according to God's eternal plan (Ps 103:19; Dan 4:35; Rom 11:36; Eph 1:11; Phil 2:10–11; Rom 8:28–29). Vos states it this way: "The governing of God is the action of His providence by which, everywhere it is necessary, He gives to *causae secundae* [second causes], maintained by Him in their existence and in their powers while they are working under His concursus, a specific direction or combines them in a certain way for reaching the end intended by Him."[42]

Often in Scripture, "government" is closely associated with God's rule as Father, Lord, and King (Matt 11:25; Acts 17:24; Eph 3:15; 1 Tim 1:17; 6:15; Rev 1:6; 19:6). Since God alone is

---

[39] Bavinck, *Reformed Dogmatics*, 2:614.
[40] Bavinck, 2:615.
[41] Berkhof, *Systematic Theology*, 175.
[42] Vos, *Reformed Dogmatics*, 1:199.

sovereign over all, any creaturely rule tied to various created spheres, such as marriage, family, the church, and government, are under God's rule. As Bavinck rightly asserts,

> The government of the universe is not democratic, nor aristocratic, nor republican, nor constitutional, but monarchical. To God belongs the one undivided legislative, judicial, and executive power. His sovereignty is original, eternal, unlimited, abundant in blessing. He is the King of kings and the Lord of lords (1 Tim. 6:15; Rev. 19:6). His royal realm is the whole of the universe.[43]

Furthermore, under the heading of "government," theologians often distinguish between different aspects of God's *one* will.[44] Some have objected to making these distinctions; however, to account for all of the biblical teaching, it is necessary to do so.[45] When Scripture says that God wills something or wants something, biblical language is used in different ways. For example, as we discussed previously, God's will can refer to his *decree* (i.e., decretive will), which includes within it his entire plan for the universe, which cannot be thwarted (Pss 115:3; 135:6; Isa 42:8; 46:10; 48:9; Acts 2:23; Eph 1:11; Rev 13:8).[46] Related to the decree is God's *secret* will, namely, what God has not revealed to us regarding his providential governing of all things (Deut 29:29). Although God has disclosed much to us about his plan, he has not revealed everything, and as such, we must learn to trust his providential hand even in the midst of trials, difficulties, and suffering (Job 1–2, 38–42; Rom 8:18–39). Scripture also refers to God's will in terms of his *revealed* will and his specific *commands* (i.e., moral, perceptive will). In these areas, God is not silent; he has given us specific instructions for us to obey. God's moral, perceptive will is revealed across the entire canon of Scripture and through the unfolding of the biblical covenants. In light of God's revealed will, we pray with David to do God's will (Ps 143:10), to be holy (1 Thess 4:3), and for God's will to be done on earth as it is in

---

[43] Bavinck, *Reformed Dogmatics*, 2:616.

[44] See Turretin, *Institutes of Elenctic Theology*, 1:220–21 (see chap. 3, n. 55); Calvin, *Institutes*, 1.16.3–4 (1:200–3). Also see Carson, *How Long O Lord?*, 198–200 (see chap. 4, n. 87); John Piper, "Are There Two Wills in God? Divine Election and God's Desire for All to be Saved," in Schreiner and Ware, *Still Sovereign*, 107–31 (see chap. 20, n. 39).

[45] Many open theists (even some Arminians) object to making distinctions within God's one will in order to capture the nuances of the biblical teaching. For example, see Pinnock, *Flame of Love*, 185–214 (chap. 6, n. 57).

[46] For a discussion of God's will, see chapters 18 and 20.

heaven (Matt 6:10). Also related to God's revealed will is his will in terms of his *desires* and what he *permits*. God's desire is for everyone to be saved (1 Tim 2:4) and for no one to perish (2 Pet 3:9), but this is not the same as his decretive will, at least if one is convinced that the triune God of aseity is not thwarted. Lastly, Scripture also speaks of God's will in terms of *permission*. This is significant in thinking about God's ordination of both good and evil. Regarding the latter, God permits sin and evil to occur (Job 1–2; Rom 1:24, 26, 28), and humans (along with angels) are directly responsible for their sinful actions, even though it is part of his eternal plan centered in Christ.

In thinking about the way Scripture speaks of these different aspects of God's will, we must not conclude that God has different wills and that these aspects of God's will are contradictory. God only has *one* will, but these different aspects are the way that God reveals to finite creatures his diverse relations to us so that we may understand something of the glory of the triune God. For example, think of God's command for Abraham to sacrifice Isaac (Gen 22:2). From the overall story, we know that God did not intend for Isaac to die (i.e., decretive will), but God commanded Abraham to sacrifice him (i.e., moral will), not only to test Abraham but also to reveal a greater purpose and through type and shadow to point forward to the need for God's provision of a greater sacrifice in our Lord Jesus Christ.[47] This illustration from Scripture reminds us that the diverse aspects of God's will are not contradictory. In fact, related to God's plan of redemption, God decrees what he disapproves of, namely, our sin. In doing so, God remains opposed to sin and anything contrary to his will and nature, but he does so for a greater good and purpose. There is no contradiction here, but certainly many tensions and unknowns.

All of these components together—preservation, concurrence, and government—give us a complete *theology* of providence. Each component is a necessary part of the entire doctrine, and each one offers a different and essential aspect of the whole. Our triune God's providential rule over his creation, history, and our lives should be a great source of confidence, hope, and trust for God's people. This world is not governed by chance, but sustained and ruled by our sovereign God, specifically related to his covenant promises in Christ. In part 3, we outlined how God's eternal plan has unfolded across time through the biblical covenants. In the present age, we live between the first and second advents of our Lord, where this fallen order continues

[47] On this point, see Beeke and Smalley, *Reformed Systematic Theology*, 1:764.

("this present age") even though he has inaugurated the "last days" and the "age to come" (2 Tim 3:1; Heb 1:1–3). But, although we live in the light of the dawning of the new creation, until Christ returns, the church will experience opposition and suffering, but our confidence is found in our triune Creator-covenant and providential Lord, who is working out his eternal purposes in Christ (Eph 1:9–10) for the good of his people (Rom 8:28) and the glory of his name (1 Cor 15:28; Rev 5:13).

Indeed, all of redemptive history is the theater of God's glory, the stage on which God is working out his plan for the ultimate good of his people. In our Lord Jesus Christ, we have seen God's extraordinary providence at work, and by the work of the Spirit, we have been born, united to Christ, justified, adopted, and sanctified and are now awaiting our glorification in a new heavens and new earth. In reflecting on the comfort of providence and God's redemptive work in Christ, Bavinck captures the sentiment of Scripture and of the Christian: "The Christian believer now surveys the whole of existence and the entire world and discovers in all things, not chance or fate, but the leading of God's fatherly hand."[48] Bavinck continues: "It is above all by faith in Christ that believers are enabled—in spite of all the riddles that perplex them—to cling to the conviction that the God who rules the world is the same loving and compassionate Father who in Christ forgave them all their sins, accepted them as his children, and will bequeath to them eternal blessedness."[49] What this means then is that "God's providence is no illusion, but secure and certain; it rests on the revelation of God in Christ and carries within it the conviction that nature is subordinate and servicable to grace, and the world [is likewise subject] to the kingdom of God. Thus, through all of its tears and suffering, it looks forward with joy to the future."[50]

The Key Issue in Providence: The Relationship Between Divine and Human Agency

Within Christian theology, although there is broad agreement on what divine providence is, as discussed in chapter 20, there are different views regarding the specifics of both the nature

[48] Bavinck, *Reformed Dogmatics*, 2:594.

[49] Bavinck, 2:594.

[50] Bavinck, 2:594–95.

of God's decree and its outworking in history. Within evangelical theology, the two dominant views are reflected by classical Arminianism and Calvinism/Reformed theology.

Both views agree on preservation but disagree on the exact relationship between divine and human agency, which results in a different understanding of concurrence and government. Most of the discussion of these specific disagreements centers on perennial debates regarding the relationship between divine sovereignty and human freedom, or from the Arminian view, the divine-foreknowledge–human-freedom relationship. Arminianism contends that God has freely chosen to limit himself due to his decision to create humans with libertarian freedom. As such, God's decree/plan is *conditioned* or dependent on God's foreknowledge of our choices, which results in a redefinition of divine aseity in relation to God's knowledge. This is why Arminian theology wrestles with the relationship between divine foreknowledge and human freedom and how God is able to foreknow our future free actions while they remain free. In chapter 19, we discussed the divine-foreknowledge–human-freedom problem and offered reasons why the Arminian view does not adequately provide a sufficient theological answer. In chapter 20, we offered an overall critique of the Arminian view of the divine decree and concluded that the view was biblically and theologically unwarranted.

In what follows, we now offer a biblical-theological exposition and defense of a Reformed view of divine providence. In agreement with historic Christian theology, a Reformed view affirms that God knows all things, but unlike an Arminian view, God knows everything that will happen, including our future free actions, because he has foreordained all that comes to pass. God's decree and knowledge is not conditioned on creation or the creature. Yet, in God's decree, he has ordained both the ends and the means to the ends, including our free and responsible choices. Additionally, God has decreed both good and evil, yet asymmetrically: God is not responsible for sin; we are. For this reason, a Reformed view affirms a robust view of dual agency, tied to primary and secondary causality and agency, and thus a different view of concurrence (and also government) than Arminian theology. The Reformed view of the relationship between divine and human agency affirms that in every action, God and humans simultaneously act. However, God acts as Creator and Lord, the primary cause and agent, while humans act as responsible creatures and secondary agents yet according to what God has eternally decreed/planned will come to pass.

As we turn to Scripture, we are convinced that a Reformed view accounts for the biblical teaching, both in terms of specific texts and the Scripture's entire storyline, especially the Bible's view of theology proper. From Genesis to Revelation, the triune Lord is not dependent on his creation, either in terms of his existence, knowledge, or goodness. It is simply not the case that God's decree and the outworking of it in providence is dependent on what he foreknows we will do. This is why the accent of Scripture is more on the divine-sovereignty–human-freedom relationship than on the divine-foreknowledge–human-freedom relationship, which already favors a Reformed view more than an Arminian one.

So what is the specific biblical data that warrants a Reformed view of providence, especially its view of concurrence? Although much could be discussed, minimally, we must think through and put together four biblical truths in order to account for all that Scripture teaches:[51] (1) God is completely sovereign in his providential rule of creation, including his rule of sin and evil so that nothing in his world is done outside of his foreordained plan and/or permission. God does all things for his own glory and for the benefit and good of his people. (2) God is perfectly good, holy, righteous, and just. God is not responsible for sin and evil nor an accomplice of it; God's goodness is non-negotiable. (3) Humans (and angels) are free and morally responsible for their choices and actions—we choose, rebel, obey, believe—but our freedom never limits God's rule over the universe. And (4) sin and evil are real and due to the creature and not God, yet both are ordained by God for a greater and more ultimate good.

Let us now turn to each of these four biblical truths in order to offer a biblical exposition of a Reformed view of divine providence. After we expound on these truths, we will conclude with some initial theological reflections of how to "put together" the puzzle of providence as we move from biblical exposition to theological formulation. Then in the next chapter, we will offer a theological exposition and defense of a Reformed view of providence before we conclude by applying a theology of providence to the problem of evil and to aspects of our Christian lives.

The Overall Biblical Teaching

First, let us think about God's sovereignty over all things, a truth that accents God's aseity and reminds us that nothing occurs in this world outside of God's decree or foreordained plan.

---

[51] My discussion is indebted to Carson, *How Long O Lord?*, 177–203; Frame, *Doctrine of God*, 21–182; Feinberg, *No One Like Him*, 625–796 (see chap. 2, n. 51).

Three points will be expounded on to unpack this biblical truth, moving from the general to the specific.

1. God's complete, universal, and efficacious sovereignty is taught throughout Scripture by a number of *general*, or broad-sweeping, texts that identify God as the Creator and sovereign Lord. For example, the Psalmist can ask: "Why should the nations say, / 'Where is their God?'" and the answer is immediate: "Our God is in heaven / and does whatever he pleases" (Ps 115:2–3), whether that is "in heaven and on earth, / in the seas and all the depths" (Ps 135:6). In fact, as the Psalmist continues, God's sovereignty extends over the natural world and the human world, including within it human actions and choices (Ps 135:7–12).[52] Nothing occurs outside of God's eternal plan and purposes; nothing is done apart from his will—a lesson Nebuchadnezzar had to learn firsthand. In his memorable words, Nebuchadnezzar lifts his eyes to heaven after his sanity is restored and he praises the sovereign Lord by confessing, "For his dominion is an everlasting dominion, / and his kingdom is from generation to generation. / All the inhabitants of the earth are counted as nothing, / and he does what he wants with the army of heaven and the inhabitants of the earth. / There is no one who can block his hand / or say to him, 'What have you done?'" (Dan 4:34–35; cf. Ps 33:10–11). This is the same sentiment that is taught throughout Isaiah as the nation of Israel is encouraged by the fact that Yahweh is on his throne, bringing about his plans and purposes in such a way that no one can or will thwart him (Isa 14:24–27; 40:1–31). Think of Isa 46:8–13, where this point is strongly emphasized. God is presented as the one who knows the end from the beginning *because* it is rooted in his purpose and plan, not his foreknowledge of future free actions. In other words, God's foreknowledge is true because God has planned all things. As v. 10 emphasizes: "I declare the end from the beginning, / and from long ago what is not yet done, / saying: my plan will take place, / and I will do all my will," which includes within it both the natural order and the plans and actions of humans.

One of the most sweeping statements of God's complete sovereignty over the world is Eph 1:11. In the larger context of this text, Paul is rejoicing in the triune God of sovereign grace: the Father, who has unconditionally chosen a people for salvation in Christ in eternity past according to his grace (Eph 1:4–6); the Son, who, in history, has accomplished our redemption and who is now bringing all things "in heaven and on earth" under his headship (Eph 1:7–10);

[52] Ps 139:16; cf. 33:11; Job 42:2; Jer 23:20; Zech 1:6.

and the Spirit, who as the precious seal, deposit, and guarantee of our inheritance, is keeping us to the end as we await the consummation of God's redemptive plan in Christ. In the midst of this glorious long sentence, running from vv. 3–14, Paul again returns to our predestination in Christ as part of God's decree—a plan that God "works out everything in agreement with the purpose of his will" (Eph 1:11). It is difficult to deny that Paul is teaching the universal and efficacious sovereign rule of God over his universe—a teaching that is found from Genesis to Revelation.[53]

2. Scripture not only makes general, sweeping statements about God's complete, universal, and efficacious sovereignty; it also teaches that God has *specific* sovereignty over all creation, including the natural world and the human realm. For example, God not only assigns time and places to all people so that where we live is according to his plan, rule, and appointment (Acts 17:26), but even the most mundane natural processes are ascribed to him, thus underscoring divine providence in both preservation and concurrence (Gen 8:22; Job 38–40; Pss 65:9–11; 104:14; 148:8; Matt 5:45; 6:26, 30; Acts 14:17). This truth does not minimize the reality of secondary causes, but Scripture never views these natural processes as independent of God's providential activity and will. D. A. Carson makes this point: "The writer of Ecclesiastes knows of the water cycle, but biblical authors prefer to speak of God sending the rain than to say, 'It is raining.'"[54] In Scripture both statements are true: "God sends the rain" and "it is raining" but the latter statement is never independent of the first.

Scripture also teaches that God's specific sovereignty pertains to everyday affairs of life, including our human choices. So, kings come and go (Ps 33:10–11; Isa 45:1–46:13); wombs are closed and opened (Gen 17:15–22); the hairs of our head are numbered (Matt 10:29–30); family misfortune (Ruth 1:13, 20) and unintentional manslaughter (Exod 21:13) are tied to God's will; and the "chance" events of people's lives (Prov 16:33), including the random shot of an arrow that wounds Ahab, fulfill the word of the Lord (1 Kgs 22:1–28, esp. v. 28 and

---

[53] For a fine treatment of this text and its implications for understanding God's complete sovereignty, see John S. Feinberg, "God Ordains All Things," in Basinger and Basinger, *Predestination and Free Will*, 29–32. Feinberg rightly notes that "this verse, then, indicates that what occurs is foreordained by God, and nothing external to God such as the foreseen actions or merits of God's creatures determines his choices. God deliberates, chooses and accomplishes all things on the basis of his purposes" (30). Cf. Feinberg, *No One Like Him*, 683–93.

[54] Carson, *How Long O Lord?*, 180.

22:34, 38). All of these events are under God's will and rule. Even human choices cannot thwart God's plan and purposes (Prov 16:9; 21:1, 30–31). We plan our course, but it is the Lord's purpose that prevails: "Many plans are in a person's heart, / but the LORD's decree will prevail" (Prov 19:21).

These kinds of statements are taught repeatedly in Scripture.[55] In the OT, God announces ahead of time his purposes and raises up leaders to fulfill his plan (Cyrus, Isa 45:1) without a hint that his purposes and promises can ever be thwarted. Or, in the NT, Jesus predicts Peter's denial, and Peter does exactly what the Lord says he will do, yet freely and responsibly (Luke 22:34). This data teaches that God's sovereignty is *universal* and *efficacious* because God's decree includes all things and it will occur. John Frame nicely makes this overall summary statement:

> God never fails to accomplish what he sets out to do. Nothing is too hard for him (Jer. 32:27); nothing seems marvelous to him (Zech. 8:6); with him nothing is impossible (Gen. 18:14; Matt. 19:25; Luke 1:37). His purpose always prevails (Isa. 14:24–27; Job 42:2; Jer. 23:20). . . . Creatures may oppose him, to be sure, but they cannot prevail (Isa. 46:10; Dan. 4:35). For his own reasons, he has chosen to delay the fulfillment of his intentions for the end of history and to bring about those intentions through a complicated historical sequence of events. In that sequence, his purposes appear sometimes to suffer defeat, sometimes to achieve victory. But each apparent defeat actually makes his eventual victory all the more glorious.[56]

3. What about God's sovereignty over evil? No doubt this subject is a bit more complicated. Scripture teaches that God decrees both good and evil, but it *never* ascribes to God responsibility for sin, even though it is part of his eternal plan. It is difficult to make sense of "the Lamb (Jesus Christ) who was slain from the creation of the world" (Rev 13:8 NIV); the typological relation between Adam and Christ (Rom 5:14); and Peter's statement in Acts 2:23, "Though he [Jesus] was delivered up according to God's determined plan (*hōrismenē boulē*) and foreknowledge (*prognōsei*)"; without affirming that Adam's fall (and thus sin) and Christ's cross were part of the foreordained plan of God. In addition, God's plan encompasses human

[55] Ezra 1:1; 6:22; Ps 105:25; Jer 10:23–24; cf. Jas 4:15.

[56] John M. Frame, "The Problem of Evil," in *Suffering and the Goodness of God*, ed. Christopher W. Morgan and Robert A. Peterson (Wheaton: Crossway, 2008), 143.

decisions and not just good ones; it also includes our sinful choices without removing our responsibility for our choices (Gen 45:5–8; Isa 44:28; Luke 22:22; Acts 2:23–24; 4:27–28; 13:27; Rev 17:17).

Regarding the latter point, read together Josh 10:8, 40 with 11:20 (cf. Judg 1:4, 7; 4:23; 20:35). As Joshua enters the promised land and is commanded to wage war and destroy the people of the land, not only does the Lord assure him of success (10:8), which he and the nation achieved by their actions (10:40), but the text also tells us that God is actively involved in the battles. "For it was the LORD's intention to harden their hearts, so that they would engage Israel in battle, be completely destroyed without mercy, and be annihilated, just as the LORD had commanded Moses" (11:20). Yet there is no evidence that the hardening of the people's hearts removed their free and responsible action. Instead, what we have is dual agency: God and humans simultaneously act. This is important: Scripture teaches that in the same act, that is, the warfare waged, God foreordained the event (given his eternal plan and knowledge of all things, including future free actions of his creatures) and acted in it while humans simultaneously acted in a free and responsible manner. In fact, the same phenomenon is also found before this incident in God's interaction with Pharoah via Moses. Prior to Pharoah's hardening his own heart in rebellion against God (Exod 8:15, 32; 9:34), God says to Moses, "When you go back to Egypt, make sure you do before Pharoah all the wonders that I have put within your power. But I will harden his heart so that he won't let the people go" (4:21)—a pattern that is emphasized repeatedly in the narrative (Exod 7:3; 9:12; 10:20; 14:4, 8)—alongside the emphasis on Pharoah freely and responsibly hardening his own heart. Paul also emphasizes this point as he discusses dual agency in the unbelief and disobedience of the nation of Israel in their rejection of Christ. The reason many ethnic Jews rejected their Messiah was not only due to God's choice in election but also their culpable unbelief (Rom 9–10).[57]

---

[57] Examples could be multiplied. If Naaman enjoyed military victory, it is God's doing (2 Kgs 5:1). The sinful king Nebuchadnezzar and Cyrus are both God's servants (Jer 25:9; 27:6; 2 Chron 36:22–23) in chastening or releasing the covenant people who have rebelled. God himself raises up the Assyrians (Isa 10:5–15), as well as the Babylonians (2 Chron 36:17; Hab 1:6). In Job, Satan is given permission to bring harm to Job's possessions and children, and though this harm comes through secondary agents (Job 1:12, 15, 17, 19), Job can see behind it the hand of God (Job 1:21). But although Job says that the Lord has done it, he does not blame God for the evil or attribute wrong to God. Repeatedly, in the book of Revelation, the authority of the dragon and of his beasts is "given" to them (Rev 17:17), which, similar to Job, speaks of the evil one not being able to do anything apart from God's sovereign permission.

In thinking about what we identify as "natural" evil, that is, famines, droughts, diseases, and so forth, Scripture teaches that God is sovereign over it. When these events occur, they are not merely the result of natural secondary causes apart from God's primary causality and divine intent. Scripture teaches that natural causes are real, but God also acts with intent for a greater good through these events to accomplish his plan either in terms of salvation or judgment. For example, in judgment God acts through famines (Deut 32:23–24; 2 Kgs 8:1; Ps 105:16; Ezek 5:16–17), plagues (Exod 7–11), droughts (Deut 28:22; 1 Kgs 8:35; Isa 3:1; Amos 4:6–8), disease (Lev 26:16, 25; Deut 28:21–22, 27; 2 Chron 21:14, etc.), wild animals (Lev 26:22; Deut 32:23–24; 2 Kgs 17:25; Ezek 14:15, 21), various natural forces (Pss 65:9–11; 77:18; 83:13–15; 135:6–7; 148:7–8), and death (Deut 32:39; 1 Sam 2:6–7) to accomplish his will. Natural evil is under God's sovereign rule.

The same is also true in regard to "moral" evil. God sovereignly acts through our wicked choices to accomplish his will for a greater good and purpose. For example, it was not accidental that Eli's sons died due to their sin: God was actively involved in executing judgment (1 Sam 2:23–25 with 1 Sam 4:11). Or think of Samson. His sinful desire for a wife from the Philistines was also from the Lord, but God's holy and good purpose in it was for the judgment of the Philistines (Judg 14:1–4). Repeatedly, Scripture teaches that in the same act, God is at work for good, but humans are choosing their own destruction.[58] All of this is to say that Scripture teaches that God's decree includes within it human decisions, even decisions which are sinful, without a hint that as those decisions are made there is a reduction of human responsibility for those actions.

After looking at this data, we conclude that Scripture teaches that our triune God ordains all things, and thus is completely sovereign over his universe. Nothing occurs in this world outside of God's decree, including the reality of both good and evil. But alongside God's sovereignty, Scripture also teaches that God is good, holy, and just, a point to which we now turn.

Second, alongside Scripture's teaching about God's sovereignty and his foreordination of all things, including evil, Scripture also unequivocally insists that God is perfectly holy and good.

Or see Isa 45:7; cf. Lam 3:37–38. In Isa 45, the word for "create" is *bara'*. *Evil* (*ra'*) can mean disaster, woe, or calamity, but it does not just refer to natural disasters, for the word is common for "evil" in general (see Gen 2:9; 6:5; 13:13; Ps 34:14; Isa 5:20; 59:7; Amos 3:6; etc).

[58] Absalom and Rehoboam are examples of this. They both freely reject sound counsel, but in their free choice God is also at work bringing about his ordained purposes (2 Sam 17:14; 1 Kgs 12:1–15).

To affirm God's goodness is another way of describing God's perfect moral character. God, as the absolute moral standard, always acts consistently with himself. Scripture describes God's goodness as his perfect righteousness, kindness, love, grace, covenant faithfulness, compassion, and much more. One of the defining texts of the OT that teaches God's goodness and covenant faithfulness—a text that Scripture repeatedly echoes—is Exod 34:6: "The LORD, the LORD, the compassionate and gracious God, slow to anger, abounding in love and faithfulness." This text becomes a bedrock description of God throughout the entire canon, and it reminds us that God's ways and works are perfect and just (Deut 32:4). God does not take pleasure in sin and evil (Ps 5:4); in fact, his eyes are too pure to even look on evil (Hab 1:13). In God's plan and work in redemptive history, our triune God acts to destroy sin and evil finally and definitively, which is precisely what he has done in our Lord Jesus Christ and his entire new covenant work. No doubt in God's plan he decrees sin and evil, but God is not responsible for it, and his entire redemptive plan is to bring good out of evil for his own glory (Ps 145:8–9, 13–16; Jas 1:17).

For this reason, extreme care must be exercised in thinking through the relation between God and sin/evil since Scripture will not allow us to question either God's sovereignty or his goodness. In Scripture, as Carson rightly states, "God is *never* presented as an accomplice of evil, or as secretly malicious, or as standing behind evil in exactly the same way that he stands behind good."[59] The goodness, holiness, and justice of God are non-negotiables (see Deut 32:4; Hab 1:13; 1 John 1:5; Rev 15:3–4) and alongside God's absolute sovereignty, including his decree of both good and evil, we must also equally and simultaneously affirm God's goodness.

No doubt, tensions and mystery results in holding these truths together, but these truths must never be severed from each other. In fact, as we will discuss in the next chapter, the problem of evil arises in Christian theology due to the biblical teaching that God, who is sovereign over all, has also ordained good and evil, yet evil is attributed to the creature and not to God. As theology wrestles with how these truths cohere in a noncontradictory way, precise distinctions and clarifications are required to account for the depth and breadth of the biblical teaching. For example, as we will develop more in the next chapter, Carson, building on the entire Christian tradition, helpfully distinguishes between God's standing "behind" good and evil in a *different* way. This is why Scripture and theology use the language of "permission"; it reminds

---

[59] Carson, *How Long O Lord?*, 182.

us that God ordains good and evil but in an *asymmetrical* manner. However, "permission" never means that God is less sovereign; hence, Frame speaks of God's "*efficacious* permission."[60] But *permission* is a helpful term because it allows us to uphold simultaneously God's sovereignty and goodness, as well as human responsibility. God foreordains all things, including sin, but sin is always attributed to the creature and not to God.

Third, Scripture also teaches the freedom and responsibility of humans. Humans, as God's image-bearers, are created free and morally responsible—we significantly choose, rebel, obey, believe, defy, and so on—and God rightly holds us accountable for our choices.[61] In fact, human choices are so significant that Adam's rebellious decision to disobey God as the covenant head of the human race has brought sin and evil into the world, resulting in God's curse and judgment, which has affected the entire universe (Gen 3:17–19; cf. Rom 5:12–21). This is why moral evil precedes natural evil, and natural evil is a consequence of creaturely sin and rebellion against God (see Gen 3; Rom 8:19–22), which only Christ can remedy and rectify.

Moreover, even after the fall, although Adam's sin has been transmitted or passed on to all people so that no one escapes its disastrous consequences (Rom 3:23; 5:12–21), Scripture still treats humans as responsible for their actions. Although humans are now sinners by nature and choice (Eph 2:1–3), our human responsibility before God is not diminished. In our fallenness, we delight in our sin and willingly oppose God's rightful rule over us, which is understood as our total depravity and spiritual inability (Rom 8:7). We stand under God's judgment and wrath (Rom 8:1; Eph 2:1–3), but as free and responsible creatures. Final judgment is proof of this.

As we think about humans as free and responsible creatures, it is true that Scripture does not define the nature of our freedom. Definitions of freedom are "extrabiblical" and the result of theological (and philosophical) reflection, thus the debate between libertarian and compatibilistic definitions. Our choice of which view of freedom is more "biblical" is based on which view best accounts for all of the biblical data and does not contradict it. In this regard, if we take seriously the Bible's teaching on the divine decree, divine sovereignty, and dual

---

[60] Frame, "Problem of Evil," 161.

[61] Humans are tested by God to find out what is in their hearts (Gen 22:12; Exod 16:4; 2 Chron 32:31). Joshua calls on the people to choose (Josh 24:14–15; Rom 10:9–11). God utters moving pleas for human repentance and finds no pleasure in the death of the wicked (Isa 30:18; 65:2; Lam 3:31–36; Ezek 18:30–32; 33:11; Hos 11:7–12).

agency (concurrence), it is best to embrace a compatibilistic view. In our critique of open theism (chapter 16) and classic Arminianism (chapter 20), we noted how libertarian freedom renders it nigh impossible to affirm simultaneously a biblical view of God's decree and divine sovereignty. Why? Because by definition libertarianism demands that our choices are not determined in advance by God since we always have the freedom to choose otherwise, even contrary to our character and desires. But such a view cannot be reconciled with God's universal and efficacious sovereignty. Furthermore, Scripture never presents the human will as independent of God's plan as libertarianism does, thus rendering a biblical concept of dual agency and concurrence problematic.

Instead, human freedom is best viewed compatibilistically because it allows us to uphold both Scripture's view of God's decree and divine sovereignty *and* human freedom. Furthermore, a compatibilistic view also makes better sense of how our choices are not separated from our own character and nature. In other words, we choose for sufficient, non-constraining reasons, and thus according to our desires and wants, a point we will return to in the next chapter.

Fourth, Scripture teaches that sin and evil are real and that human (and angelic) creatures are to blame for it, not God. This last point almost seems unnecessary to state, but given the larger pluralistic world we operate within, composed of multiple worldviews that deny the reality of sin and evil, it is a crucial point to stress. In fact, Scripture, in the strongest of terms, affirms the reality of sin and evil so much so that the only way to eradicate them is by our triune Creator-covenant Lord acting in sovereign grace and power. On this point, the Bible's entire storyline, from Genesis to Revelation, is clear: for sin, evil, and death to be destroyed, the Father must send his Son to assume our humanity, to live our life, die our death, and be raised for our justification; and the Spirit of God must act in extraordinary power to apply all that Christ has achieved for us in his new covenant and new-creation work.

Thus, in contrast to all non-Christian thought that ultimately minimizes the reality of sin and evil in different ways depending on its overall worldview, the Bible alone takes sin seriously. This is one of the reasons why we, in our sin, see no need for a Savior to do what we could never do, namely, defeat, destroy, and eradicate sin and evil in the universe and in ourselves. Despite having to wrestle with why God has allowed sin and evil into his world and thinking through the relationship between God's sovereignty, our freedom, and sin/evil, Christian theology has no problem affirming the reality and horrendous nature of sin, evil, and death. This is important to remember, especially in thinking about the "problem of evil."

We do not "solve" the problem by dispensing with evil. Unfortunately, as Doug Groothuis reminds us, this is the route "taken by various forms of pantheism, such as Advaita Vendanta Hinduism, Zen Buddhism, assorted New Age worldviews and mind-science churches such as Christian Science, Religious Science and Unity. Since all is ultimately divine, evil is unreal; it is only a problem of perception, and not a problem of objective reality."[62] But, thankfully, this is not the route taken by Christian theology. Instead, we affirm the reality and power of sin/evil *and* the greater reality and power of the triune God of sovereign grace, who is able to destroy it and make all things new.

Initial Formulation of the Biblical Teaching

The above summary of the basic biblical data that warrants a Reformed view of providence, especially its view of concurrence, is not exhaustive. Nevertheless, a *biblical* view of providence must account for these four truths. It is difficult to account for the Bible's entire storyline from creation to new creation without each of these truths being affirmed. In fact, if each truth is upheld in its full force without any reduction of what Scripture teaches, legitimate questions arise regarding *how* to put together the truths and *how* to affirm all that Scripture teaches without contradiction, but faithful *theological* formulation requires us to do this.

However, before we turn to theological formulation, defense, and application in the next chapter, we want to make one further observation of the biblical teaching that is essential in our theological formulation. It is not enough merely to affirm these four truths; we must affirm them *simultaneously*. In other words, in our theological formulation we must uphold together each biblical truth without diminishing, redefining, or eliminating any of the other truths.

This may seem like an "obvious" point, but it is often neglected. Divine sovereignty, for instance, is sometimes affirmed but then redefined in such a way that human freedom "limits" God's sovereignty. In this case, biblical truths are not upheld simultaneously in their full force. Moreover, concurrence, tied to "dual" agency is affirmed, but not in such a way that in the same event, God, as the primary agent, acts to bring about his decreed will, and humans, as secondary agents, also act according to God's decree but freely and responsibly. As we noted, with an Arminian view of dual agency, a robust view of *concursus* is not upheld. Thus, if

---

[62] Groothuis, *Christian Apologetics*, 620 (see chap. 13, n. 74).

God acts, human freedom is reduced; or if humans act, God's sovereignty is self-limited. But the problem with the Arminian view is that it is not upholding the biblical truths fully *and* simultaneously.

In fact, Scripture often puts together these four truths without qualification or reduction. Our theological formulation of concurrence (and government) must do likewise in order to be *biblical*. So, before we turn to theological formulation in the next chapter, we want to finish our biblical exposition of providence by illustrating how Scripture simply places these four truths side by side without explanation or commentary by investigating a number of illustrative texts. No doubt, this raises legitimate questions that theology seeks to reflect on, especially regarding the relation between divine and human agency. But in doing so, Scripture actually moves us in the direction of a Reformed view of concurrence, in contrast to an Arminian understanding. Let us see how this is the case by turning to these sample texts taken from the entire canon.[63]

First, Genesis 50 illustrates well how these four truths are placed side by side, thus moving us toward a Reformed view of concurrence and dual agency. After Jacob's death, Joseph's brothers approach him to plead for their lives fearing that he would enact revenge on them. Joseph's response is that he will not do so: "Am I in the place of God?" (v. 19). Furthermore, Joseph sees in their actions the plan and purpose of God: "You planned evil against me; God planned it for good to bring about the present result—the survival of many people" (v. 20). What is significant about Joseph's response is how he affirms a robust view of dual agency. In the same act of selling Joseph into slavery, his brothers acted in a wicked manner, while God acted for good according to *his* intended end. But note: God's intention was *not* a "clean-up" operation *ex post facto*. The God of the Bible is the Creator and Lord who plans and knows all things, and even in the narrative, through Joseph's dreams (Gen 37), God was orchestrating history to bring about this very event to preserve Abraham's family ultimately for Christ to come. Thus, here we see God sovereignly at work bringing about his foreordained plan for good, while humans are freely and responsibly acting, and sadly in this case, in a sinful way, all in accordance with God's plan. Precisely *how* God foreordained the free actions of Joseph's brothers is left unexplained, but Scripture teaches that God did so without diminishing his sovereignty, reducing our free and responsible action, or making himself responsible for the evil actions of his creatures.

---

[63] Also see Carson, *How Long O Lord?*, 183–88, for a discussion of some of these texts.

Second, Isaiah 10 is another example of this same point, but now in terms of God's sovereign rule of entire nations. God chooses to use the Assyrians as his agents of judgment against Israel; Assyria is completely under his authority and power. God calls Assyria "the rod of *my* anger" and says, "the staff in their hands is *my* wrath" (v. 5, emphasis mine). The intensive use of the verbs in v. 6 emphasizes God's sovereign initiative and action: "I will send" and "I will command."[64] Interestingly, when God finishes with Assyria, he does not let them off the hook; instead, they are brought to judgment for their wicked and evil actions even though their actions are God's foreordained means to execute judgment on Israel (v. 12)! Just because they are instruments in God's hand, their human responsibility is not removed. In addition, the text assumes the reality of human freedom and responsible choices. The Assyrians plan, scheme, and boast to destroy Israel without any idea that they are instruments in God's hand. They act according to their evil desires; they have no idea that they are acting on God's behalf (vv. 7–11, 13–14). But alongside these truths, the text also reminds us that God's actions in salvation and judgment are good, while the actions of the Assyrians are wicked, even though their very actions are part of God's plan. As in Genesis 50, *how* we make sense of the relationship between divine and human agency is not explained, yet a Reformed view of dual agency is at work. In the same event, God is acting to bring about his good purposes, and Assyria is acting in sinful ways that God will judge. No doubt, it is not easy to "keep together" these truths, but Scripture demands that we do so. Any *theological* formulation of providence (especially concurrence) must account for this data.

Third, Acts 2:22–24 (cf. 4:23–31) is another example of how God's sovereignty and human responsibility are placed side by side, thus giving us a robust view of dual agency. Significantly, in this text, we move from the domain of God's sovereign action within a family (Gen 50:19–20) and among nations (Isa 10:5–19) to *the* central event in all of human history, namely, the cross of our Lord Jesus Christ. Contrary to the perception of many, our Lord's death was

[64] See J. Alec Motyer, *Isaiah: An Introduction and Commentary*, TOTC (Downers Grove: InterVarsity, 1999), 95. As Motyer introduces this important text, he makes the astute comment: "this passage asserts a philosophy of history, how the historical facts arise from hidden supernatural causes, and how the human actors who are the hinges on which history outwardly turns are themselves personal and responsible agents within a sovereignly ordered and exactly tuned moral system" (95).

not an accident of history.[65] Instead, the cross was decreed by God from eternity; thus, it was certain to occur. But God's decree of the cross included the free and, in this case, sinful actions of humans: "You used lawless people to nail him to a cross and kill him" (Acts 2:23). In other words, God foreordained the cross as a guaranteed event by the secondary means of human choices; those who crucified Christ "could not do otherwise" than what God had planned before the foundation of the world. Thus, in the same event, God was at work accomplishing his decreed *good* ends, while humans were doing precisely what God had decreed, yet in a free and responsible manner, and by *evil* actions. In one sense, those who crucified Christ should not have done so, and they will be held responsible for their actions. Yet, in another sense, those who crucified our Lord were doing exactly what God had ordained for them to do, but freely and responsibly! *How* exactly we "put together" these truths is not easy, but a *biblical* view of providence demands that we do so.

Fourth, there are a variety of texts pertaining to our salvation, election, and our Christian lives that also illustrate a robust view of concurrence and dual agency. For example, think of Job's life. Job knows that the calamities that he is experiencing are from God (Job 1:21), yet these trials, difficulties, and even the death of his children are also the result of the secondary causality of nature (Job 1:16, 18–19) and the agency of humans (Job 1:13–15, 17). God's intent in allowing Job to suffer is for a greater good tied to *his* purposes that Job is unaware of (Job 1–2). But what happens to Job is due to secondary causes and agency and, especially in regard to human agency, was done freely and responsibly. Within the entire book of Job, there is no hint that God's primary agency is in competition with secondary causality and agency or that God is not good and just, although Job is never told why God has sovereignly permitted all that he experiences from God's providential hand. God's revealed will for Job does not fully explain or exhaust God's decretive will, yet Job sees that God is the good Creator and sovereign Lord. In the end, Job learns to place his full confidence and trust in the providential Lord who works out all things, including his suffering, for his ultimate good and the glory of God's name (Rom 8:28).

---

[65] In the prophetic revelation this point is made. As Isaiah 53 reminds us, as people looked on the suffering servant (vv. 1–3), they had no idea that he was suffering due to Yahweh's will and foreordained plan (v. 10; cf. vv. 4–9). Yet, the death of the suffering servant was no accident; it was the outworking of God's eternal plan (Rev 13:8).

Or think of John 6:37–40, which places side by side God's sovereignty, goodness, and grace in our election along with our human responsibility, thus underscoring the reality of dual agency. On the side of divine sovereignty, Jesus says: "Everyone the Father gives me will come to me, and the one who comes to me I will never cast out" (v. 37). This is part of the biblical data that teaches that God unconditionally chooses a people for himself before the foundation of the world (Eph 1:4–6), grounded in his grace, good pleasure, and eternal plan. The emphasis in this text, as Carson rightly states, is that all those whom the Father has chosen and given to the Son will be kept until the end.[66] But at the same time, v. 40 stresses our human responsibility to believe even though God has chosen us: "For this is the will of my Father: that everyone who sees the Son and believes in him will have eternal life, and I will raise him up on the last day." Thus, even God's unconditional election does not set aside our human responsibility to believe. Apart from people placing their faith in Christ, we are not assured that we are the elect. Both divine sovereignty and human responsibility are placed side by side without reduction or full explanation.

Romans 9–10 teach the same point. As Paul wrestles with why his fellow countrymen did not believe in their Messiah, two answers are given that are both true. First, they did not believe due to God's unconditional election of a people for himself: "not all who are descended from Israel are Israel" (Rom 9:6). Being an ethnic Israelite and part of the covenant nation did not automatically make a person a "true Israelite" in the salvific sense. From eternity, and worked out on the stage of history, God's election shows itself by some believing and others not. We know that this is what Paul is teaching given how he responds to the potential objections to his teaching (vv. 14, 19, 22). All of his responses to potential objections assume an unconditional view of election.[67] Yet we must immediately add that Paul can also give another reason, *which is equally true*, for why many Israelites did not believe in their Messiah; namely, they refused to believe, thus underscoring their free and responsible choice (Rom 9:30–10:21). *How* can both of these be true simultaneously? No answer is given, but both are taught, which necessitates that we affirm both equally as part of the fabric of God's providential rule and reign over this world.

---

[66] See Carson, *How Long O Lord?*, 185–86.

[67] On this point, see Schreiner, *Romans*, 466–562 (see chap. 6, n. 62).

One last text, Phil 2:12–13, also teaches God's sovereign action and our responsible choices side by side in our sanctification. How does a Christian grow in grace? Paul answers with a twofold response. First, we grow in grace by our own choices and action—"work out your own salvation with fear and trembling" (v. 12). If we are not growing in holiness and godliness, it is *our* fault, and we are held responsible for it. But this is not all that is involved in the Christian life. We also grow in grace due to God's sovereign and gracious work in us by his Spirit, which brings about our transformation—"For it is God who is working in you both to will and to work according to his good purpose" (v. 13). Without the *effectual* work of the Spirit, first in new birth and then in sanctification, no one would be conformed to the image of Christ. However, this point does not entail that we are not active in our sanctification and that we merely "let go and let God." Instead, the very evidence that the Spirit of God is at work in us is that *he* effectually makes *us* active in our sanctification. Once again, divine sovereignty and human responsible action are placed side by side without qualification or complete explanation. Dual agency in providence, and especially concurrence, is affirmed, a dual agency that moves more in a Reformed understanding than an Arminian one.

Concluding Reflection

In this chapter, we have discussed what historic Christian theology has affirmed regarding a biblical understanding of divine providence by unpacking its three intertwined and necessary components: preservation, concurrence, and government. In addition, we began to move from broad agreement on what divine providence is within historical theology to an exposition of a Reformed view of providence, especially in regard to concurrence and the relationship between God's primary and human secondary agency. As we developed the four biblical truths that are essential to account for all that Scripture teaches about the nature of God's sovereign rule over the world, we argued that a Reformed view of concurrence and dual agency results. Repeatedly, side by side, Scripture teaches God's complete, universal, and efficacious sovereignty; that God is at work in everything accomplishing his eternal plan through nature's secondary causes and the secondary agency of rational, moral creatures (humans and angels); that God's action is always good and that sin and evil is always attributed to the creature despite the fact that God has decreed both good and evil; and that sin and evil are sovereignly permitted by God not because he is secretly malicious, but for a greater good ultimately tied to a full display of God's glory.

However, many questions remain, especially questions regarding *how* to "put together" and "keep together" all that Scripture teaches regarding divine providence in a noncontradictory way. This is the task of *theological* formulation—"faith seeking understanding"—as we move from whole-Bible exposition to doctrinal construction. Such theological formulation is necessary since Christians inevitably wonder *how* to make sense of all that Scripture teaches, and if careful theological conclusions are not made, the life and health of the church will be affected. It is often in the doctrine of providence that many questions arise both within and outside the church. Believers often struggle with how to live in light of God's sovereign hand, especially when we confront suffering and difficulties in our lives. In our witness to unbelievers, we are often challenged to make sense of how God is sovereign yet evil exists in the world he has made, what is famously known as the "problem of evil." For reasons such as these, plus many more, it is not enough merely to affirm the four biblical truths of divine providence; we must also seek "to understand" how they cohere with each other and, more significantly, how to live in light of what God has revealed of his sovereign rule and lordship. As such, we now turn to more explicit theological formulation, defense, and application, which is the subject of the next chapter.

CHAPTER 23

The Triune God Who Sustains and Rules: Providence (Part 2)

Introduction

Although the doctrine of providence has fallen on hard times in our day due to an embrace of metaphysical and methodological naturalism and various iterations of panentheism, a correct understanding of providence is of crucial significance for Christian theology. Without a *theology* of divine providence, the relationship between the triune God in himself (*ad intra*) and his external works (*ad extra*) and involvement with his creation is severed. Providence reminds us that the triune God of glory, the Creator of the universe, is also the covenant Lord. Providence undergirds the Bible's metanarrative and the progressive unfolding of God's eternal plan through the biblical covenants centered in our Lord Jesus Christ. Providence reminds us that we are creatures of God, whose lives are not random and meaningless, and that history is God himself working out his sovereign purposes for his own glory and the good of his people (Rom 11:36).

In the last chapter, after looking at a brief history of the doctrine, we described and developed providence's three components: preservation, concurrence, and government. Although within Christian theology, there is broad agreement on what divine providence is, there are significant differences, especially reflected in the ongoing debates between Arminianism and Calvinism. We argued that to account for all of the biblical data, we must affirm four truths simultaneously: God has complete sovereignty so that nothing in this world is done outside of his foreordained plan and/or permission; God is perfectly good, holy, righteous, and just, and he is not responsible for sin and evil; humans are free and morally responsible creatures, but our freedom does not make God dependent on us for his knowledge; and sin and evil are real and due to the creature and not to God even though both are ordained by God for a greater and more ultimate good. In offering the biblical warrant for these truths, we began an exposition of a Reformed view, especially in regard to concurrence and the relationship between God's primary and humans' secondary agency.

We now turn from biblical warrant to theological construction, defense, and application. Scripture places these four truths side by side, but legitimate questions arise: *How* do we best "put together" and "keep together" all that Scripture teaches without contradiction? And *how* do we apply a biblical view of providence to such issues as the problem of evil and our daily lives?

From Canon to Concept: Theological Formulation of Providence

Review of the Task of Theology

As theology moves from canon to concept as an exercise in "faith seeking understanding," it involves the twofold task of "construction" and "defense." Regarding the former, theology seeks to bring our lives and thought into conformity with God's word under Christ's lordship. Regarding the latter, theology helps the church bear witness to the truth of the gospel to the world and to defend it against various challenges both within and outside the church.

In theology's constructive work, we seek to "put together" and "make sense" of all that Scripture teaches in terms of application, logical coherence, and metaphysical entailments. We do so in light of the church's tradition and contemporary questions but faithful to and consistent with the Bible's own teaching and presentation. In the case of providence, theology's task is to "put together" *all* of the biblical teaching by wrestling with the relation between God's decree, his primary agency in all things, and the reality of our secondary agency and how sin and evil are a part of God's eternal plan. In doing so, we draw logical conclusions from Scripture in order to understand *how* all of the biblical data "fits" together with proper application to our lives. The epistemological warrant for our theology of providence is Scripture (*sola Scriptura*), but given that Scripture is not an exhaustive revelation, inevitably we are left with many "unknowns." This means that in our theologizing about divine providence, we *know* that our theological formulation is warranted *if* it remains true to Scripture, but in the end, since God has not fully disclosed everything to us, we will not be able to answer every *how* and *why* question.[1]

But since Scripture is *God's* word and objectively true, we know it does not contradict itself. Thus, in our theological construction of providence, it is incumbent on us to demonstrate that there is no *necessary* contradiction in what Scripture teaches, even if we cannot fully explain every *how* and *why*. How do we do this? Building on the biblical data without eliminating any of it, we now demonstrate its logical coherence by the employment of careful definitions and precise distinctions that uphold the biblical teaching and by locating "mystery" in its correct place. After this "constructive" task is done, we are then in a position to "defend" our theology of providence against various criticisms, both within and outside the church. Regarding our defense within the church, the main debate within evangelical theology is with Arminianism and its various iterations. Since we have already offered a critique of Arminian theology in chapter 20, our task now is to argue that our understanding of the biblical teaching presented in the last chapter is logically consistent. Regarding our defense of providence outside the church, we must address the apologetic challenge raised against Christian theology known as "the problem of evil." Let us now turn to both of these tasks before we finish with how providence applies to our daily lives.

Definitions, Distinctions, and Clarifications in "Constructing" Providence

Our epistemological warrant for our theology of providence is Scripture. *How* do we show that there is no necessary contradiction in what Scripture teaches? First, we begin by employing a specific *definition* of freedom. Then, we will offer six *distinctions* that are true to Scripture and that allow us to "make sense" of the biblical data in a logically consistent way.

---

[1] As discussed in part 1, this truth is due to the Creator-creature distinction, and it builds off the archetype-ectype distinction in terms of our knowledge of God. Due to God's revelation, we *know* objective truth, but God's self-disclosure to us is not exhaustive; hence, there are plenty of unknowns or mysteries in our formulations.

Definitions: The Nature of Human Freedom

To make sense of the biblical data in a noncontradictory manner, two points need to be made regarding a proper definition of human freedom.

First, a compatibilistic view of freedom must be employed, in contrast to a libertarian view. In previous chapters, we discussed the differences between these two views of freedom. A libertarian view insists that a person is free only if nothing sufficiently inclines his will in one direction or the other. The condition of freedom, in other words, is the "principle of alternate possibilities" (PAP). As already argued, if one accepts *this* definition of freedom, which requires an overall indeterminism, we cannot logically reconcile the biblical teaching on God's decree and sovereignty, especially the biblical data regarding *concursus* and dual agency. This is why theologies that adopt a libertarian view inevitably make God's knowledge dependent on the creature, embrace some concept of God's self-limitation, and redefine dual agency.

However, by contrast, a compatibilistic view allows one to logically affirm a robust view of divine sovereignty *and* human freedom and moral responsibility. Why? Because such a view is consistent with our freedom being determined by sufficient conditions or causes that incline our choices in one direction as long as those conditions do not coerce us.[2] For a compatibilist, the condition of freedom is not PAP; rather, it is our ability to choose what we most desire and to act free of constraint. Freedom means that I choose what I want, but since my choices are *mine*, they are *sufficiently* influenced by my own internal dispositions and various external influences (e.g., immediate circumstances, upbringing, education, culture, etc.). In fact, as creatures, we are not self-sufficient; we are created and sustained by God. God has created us as free creatures who choose according to our strongest motives and desires. Although compatibilism denies PAP as a condition of freedom, it does not deny that we would be able to make "contrary" choices if the antecedent factors were different and provided a sufficient motive that appeals to our self-interested inclinations. We choose what we *most* want to choose, and biblically, all of our moral and spiritual decisions are circumscribed by our "hearts" (Matt 6:21).

The significance of this point is that if one adopts a compatibilistic view of freedom, despite many unknowns regarding human freedom, it is *not* a logical contradiction to affirm

---

[2] Feinberg, *No One Like Him*, 714–34 (see chap. 2, n. 51); Christensen, *What About Evil?*, 170–74 (see chap. 4, n. 86).

that God can *guarantee* that his goals will be accomplished through our free agency. Why? Because God's decree includes both his chosen ends and the means to such ends, and the means include whatever conditions are necessary to convince us (without constraint) to freely choose what we want *and* what God has decreed will occur. The only way this formulation is necessarily contradictory is if one embraces a libertarian view of human freedom.

Second, assuming a compatibilist view of human freedom, we must still answer the charge that such a view is inconsistent with a true understanding of moral responsibility. The objection raised against a compatibilist view goes something like this. Given a Calvinist view of the divine decree and its outworking in divine providence, it is certain in advance that we will do "x." But if we cannot do other than "x," then we are not responsible for "x." Of course, this objection assumes the libertarian condition of freedom, namely, PAP. In other words, unless we have the "ability to do otherwise," we are not free or responsible for our acts.

What is our response to this objection? First, in previous chapters, we have already given reasons to reject PAP as a condition of freedom due to the biblical and theological problems it creates. Second, to say that we cannot do other than "x" must be carefully defined. No doubt, we cannot do other than God has decreed, but the objection assumes that we "cannot" do other than "x" in *any* sense, which is not true. For example, compatibilism affirms that if antecedent conditions were different, we "could" have chosen differently according to different desires that sufficiently inclined our will. In this case, God's decree would have included those different conditions. The condition of freedom is not PAP; rather, we choose what *we* want. And in the case of God's decree, there is no reason to think that God's ordination removes our freedom by "forcing" us to do something against our wants and desires. Instead, God's decree includes all the necessary and sufficient means to accomplish his ends by our free and responsible choices.[3]

Of course, demonstrating that God's decree is logically consistent with our free choices does not explain the entire *how* question. It is still legitimate to ask: *How* is God able to foreordain our free choices so that they will occur *and* so that we do them without compulsion? For creatures, we do not have this ability. For example, think of a parent. No parent is able to guarantee that their child will always do what they want unless some kind of coercion results. So how can

[3] Feinberg, 714–29. Also see Christensen, 208–10; cf. Bignon, *Excusing Sinners and Blaming God*, 75–77, 155–65 (see chap. 16, n. 55); Frame, *Doctrine of God*, 125–38 (see chap. 3, n. 13).

God do it? The short answer is that we do not exactly know. But this should not surprise us since for most of the things that God does, we do not know precisely how he does them. For example, we do not know exactly how God is able to speak the universe into existence *ex nihilo* other than the fact that he can do so *as God*. Creatures cannot render certain what other creatures will do in advance without coercion, but God, as the Creator and Lord, is able to do so.

But how do we *know* that God has this kind of metaphysical ability? The answer: Scripture says so. What is possible for God, or what God can or cannot do, is not determined by our reason independent of Scripture; instead, it is revealed by God. Our answer, then, to this metaphysical question must come from Scripture. As we have previously argued, Scripture teaches that God is able to foreordain our free actions so that they will occur without coercion. Scripture teaches us that God is *able* to decree all things, including our free and responsible choices (e.g., Gen 50:19–20; Isa 10:5–19; Acts 2:23). Although we cannot fully explain how he can do so, since Scripture teaches that he can, it is at *this* point that we properly locate the "unknowns" or "mysteries" in our formulation of divine providence. But mystery is not the same as logical contradiction.[4]

Various Distinctions and Clarifications

We now turn to *six* distinctions and clarifications that both are true to Scripture and enable us to affirm a Reformed view of providence without contradiction, although "unknowns" remain.

First, in our construction of the relation between God's decree and its enactment in history, we must distinguish between the "necessity of infallibility" and the "necessity of compulsion."[5] The former refers to the truth that God's decree makes all things certain; what God has

---

[4] The issue of "mystery" is inevitable for all theological formulations of divine providence, whether they be Arminian or Calvinist. However, the proper location of mystery is where people differ since where one places the mystery will affect other areas of one's theology. For example, the Arminian locates the "mystery" in *how* God can foreknow our future free actions while they are still free. The Calvinist locates the "mystery" in *how* God can foreordain our human choices while they remain free. Although both appeal to "mystery," the Arminian view entails a compromise of God's aseity, while a Calvinist view does not, and on this issue, Scripture is on the Calvinist side.

[5] Samuel D. Renihan, *Deity and Decree* (np: Kindle Direct Publishing, 2020), 123–24; see Turretin, *Institutes of Elenctic Theology*, 1:319–22 (see chap. 3, n. 55); cf. Muller, *Divine Will and Human Choice* (see chap. 20, n. 75).

planned from eternity will occur in a guaranteed fashion. However, God's decree does not result in a "necessity of compulsion" since it does not force or "compel the will of creatures."[6] Humans are true secondary agents, and we choose according to our wants and desires but also according to God's plan. Humans choose but not due to a natural or inherent necessity compelling us to do so. As already noted, there is nothing logically contradictory about this construction of dual agency. But without such a distinction, it is more difficult to maintain simultaneously the biblical teaching on God's decree, his complete sovereignty, and our free and responsible agency.

Second, to make sense of a biblical view of concurrence and dual agency, Reformed theology has also distinguished between God as "the sufficient *primary* (ultimate) but *remote* cause of our choices," and humans as "the *secondary* but *proximate* (the near or immediate) cause of our choices."[7] Why? To remove any possible contradiction between the two. In fact, apart from such a distinction, it is difficult to account for how God is able to ordain all things (including evil) and remain *good* and allow creatures to act in a free and responsible manner. If there is no secondary agency, God would necessarily be the direct cause of all things, including our sin, but given secondary agency, we can make sense of how God can ordain all things (including evil) while we remain responsible for our choices. No doubt, God is the ultimate sufficient cause of all things, yet given the distinction between primary and secondary agency, *God's* intent and *our* intent are not the same. For example, think of Saul's death. Saul took his own life for reasons different than God's, yet in the same act of Saul's death, both God and Saul intended a specific outcome (1 Chron 10:4, 13–14). Indeed, sometimes God acts "directly" without secondary means (1 Chron 13:10; 2 Chron 26:19–20), while most times he works through them (e.g., John 9:1–3). Again, such a distinction does not answer every question we have about dual agency, but it does allow us to affirm that there is no necessary contradiction.

Third, further clarifications can be made to help account for a Reformed view of dual agency, tied to the larger Creator-creature distinction.[8] To affirm that God ordains all things

---

[6] Renihan, *Deity and Decree*, 124.

[7] Christensen, *What About Evil?*, 171.

[8] On this point, my discussion is indebted to James N. Anderson, "Calvinism and the First Sin," in Alexander and Johnson, *Calvinism and the Problem of Evil*, 200–32 (see chap. 18, n. 168).

is to say he is the first cause of every event and that his decree is the *ultimate* sufficient cause of every event. But we must remember that *divine* causation is *not* the same as *intramundane* causation (i.e., causation within the world). For starters, divine causation does not have spatial or temporal location, and as such, it is of a "wholly" different order than creaturely causation. Divine causation is not like causation in nature; it is sui generis, or totally unique, and thus only *analogically* related to any kind of creaturely causation in this world.[9]

For this reason, we must not think of divine causation in terms of what James Anderson identifies as the "Domino Model of Providence." [10] In this model, lines of causation are entirely "horizontal" and intramundane; they operate on the same "ontological" plane. But this view assumes that God and the world are related by an arrangement of "univocal causal chains."

The Domino Model of Providence

God $\rightarrow E_1 \rightarrow E_2 \rightarrow E_3 \rightarrow E_4$

causation
$\rightarrow$

Instead, Anderson suggests that we think of divine causation along the lines of an "Authorial Model of Providence."[11] In this model, God's acts of creation and providence are analogous to the human authoring of a book. At the ultimate level, the author *determines* everything that takes place in the book, but the author himself does not do the actions of the characters in the book. The author is the first and ultimate sufficient cause, but authorial causation operates at a *different* level than the intranarrative causes.

---

[9] Helm makes this point. First, Helm makes the important distinction between God's primary agency and our secondary agency: "The primary cause [God] is an enabling and sustaining cause, making possible secondary causes and setting bounds to them." But we must not forget that God as the primary cause is not an event in time, while secondary causes are. Instead, God is the "eternal cause which has the whole of the creation as its effect" (86), while secondary causes are in time and wholly dependent on God. *Providence of God*, 86–87 (see chap. 18, n. 164).

[10] Anderson, "Calvinism and the First Sin," 207–10. The diagrams are from Anderson, 208–9.

[11] The discussion and diagram are from Anderson, 209. John Frame, *Doctrine of God*, 156–59, uses the authorial illustration. Also, see Vanhoozer, *Remythologizing Theology*, 297–386 (see chap. 2, n. 131).

In a similar way, divine providence conceived in light of this model distinguishes between God's causation (α-causation) and intramundane causation (ß-causation) since they operate at different ontological levels. Thus, as Anderson suggests, we are able to affirm the following: "For every creature C: (1) God α-causes C to exist in the first place; (2) God α-causes C to *continue* to exist (i.e., α-causally sustains C's existence); and (3) God α-causes C to have the ß-causal powers that he has."[12] But given that α-causation (divine) and ß-causation (intramundane) are not on the same level, Anderson correctly insists that "we should avoid saying 'God caused C to cause E.'"[13] Why? Because it assumes a univocal, horizontal causal chain, which is incorrect. Instead, we should say "'God α-caused C's ß-causing of E.'"[14]

The Authorial Model of Providence

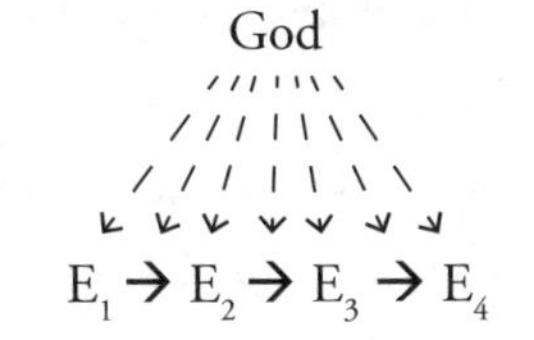

God

E_1 → E_2 → E_3 → E_4

--> α-causation (divine causation)

→ ß-causation (intramundane causation)

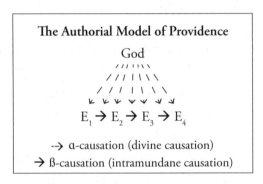

Why is this important? Because it allows us to uphold the Creator-creature distinction, and it helps make sense of the distinction between primary and secondary agency and how God acts as the primary sufficient cause as the Creator and Lord, while humans act as real secondary causes as creatures. Obviously, the limitation of the author model, as Anderson admits, is that "God 'really exists' whereas the world created by the human novelist doesn't,"[15] but as an analogy it helps make sense of divine providence by demonstrating its logical consistency.

Fourth, Reformed theology has also argued that in God's decree, he has ordained "good" and "evil" *asymmetrically* (i.e., not in the same way). This distinction is necessary in order to make sense of God's direct ordination of the good and his indirect "permission" of sin

[12] Anderson, "Calvinism and the First Sin," 209.

[13] Anderson, 209.

[14] Anderson, 209.

[15] Anderson, 210.

(Job 1–2; Rom 1:24, 26, 28). Sin does not occur outside the bounds of God's decree and sovereignty, yet "good" is directly chargeable to God and derivatively to creatures, while sin is alone chargeable to the creature. This understanding of divine permission is different than in Arminianism. For Arminian theology, God leaves it up to us what we will choose, and by foreknowing it, God incorporates it as part of his plan. By contrast, a Reformed view of permission argues for what Frame calls an "efficacious permission."[16] Christensen states it this way: "God specifically permits his creatures to choose evil that he has ordained by not preventing it and by ensuring the circumstances in which the evil comes about."[17] Yet, although God's decree encompasses everything, God "stands behind" good and evil differently, thus allowing us to uphold simultaneously God's sovereignty, absolute goodness, and human responsible agency without contradiction.

Fifth, given our embrace of a compatibilistic view of freedom, we must address the question, If humans were created "good," that is, in a state of moral uprightness, then how could they have sinned? This is an important question since compatibilism teaches that our choices arise from our nature, which gives rise to specific desires and the reasons why we choose. But how does a good nature give rise to sinful choices? After the fall, we can make perfect sense of this, but how do we account for Adam's choice before the fall? Does Adam have a different kind of freedom pre-fall versus post-fall? Although these questions are difficult to answer, here are some points to consider that remove any necessary contradiction but still leaves us with various unknowns.

1. One answer to this question is to posit that Adam had libertarian freedom before the fall and compatibilistic freedom thereafter. Thus, pre-fall, Adam could "choose otherwise," while post-fall, he could only choose consistent with his fallen nature. However, the problem with this answer is twofold. First, it assumes that libertarian freedom is a coherent view, which in previous chapters we have questioned. Human freedom, whether it is pre-fall or post-fall, must be the same kind of freedom, which entails that we always choose for sufficient reasons. In fact, though we are not told everything about Adam and Eve's reasons for rebelling against God, some motives are given: the tree was "good for food," "delightful to look at," and most

---

[16] Frame, *Doctrine of God*, 178; cf. Turretin, *Institutes of Elenctic Theology*, 1:516–17.

[17] Christensen, *What About Evil?*, 221 n. 59.

significantly, "desirable for obtaining wisdom" (Gen 3:6). At first glance, this description fits better with a compatibilism than libertarianism. Second, libertarian freedom requires indeterminism, which necessarily rules out the biblical data regarding the divine decree and God's foreordination of all things, including our free actions and Adam's free and morally responsible decision to sin.[18]

2. Given a compatibilistic view for both pre-fall and post-fall, can we say anything further about where the "desire" to sin arises? John Feinberg offers some helpful comments in response to this question.[19] He reflects on Jas 1:13–15, which teaches that we are tempted when we are "drawn away and enticed by [our] own evil desire. Then after desire has conceived, it gives birth to sin" (v 14). Feinberg notes that our choices are tied to our "desires," and that "morally evil actions ultimately stem from human desires."[20] But, he also notes that some "desires" in themselves are not necessarily evil nor do evil.[21] Instead, as "desires" are "drawn away and enticed to the point of bringing us to choose to disobey God's prescribed moral norms, we have sinned."[22] Given this understanding, all that we need to say is that God did not create Adam with a positive inclination toward sin. No doubt, God would have established the conditions that resulted in Adam's sin, but "temptation to evil and the actual willing of evil stem not from God but from man."[23] More needs to be said, yet this explanation is helpful in making some sense of how a good creature could actually sin.

3. We must also distinguish between Adam as a "good" versus "glorified" creature. Christian theology has rightly insisted that Adam's pre-fall state is not the same as our future "glorified" state. As early as Augustine, Adam's pre-fall state was characterized as "able to sin" (*posse peccare*), while our post-fall state is "not able not to sin" (*non posse non peccare*), and our final glorified state due to Christ's work, our covenantal union in him, and the transforming

---

[18] See Christensen, 220–22. See debate between Muller, *Divine Will and Human Choice*; and Paul Helm, *Reforming Free Will* (see chap. 20, n. 75).

[19] John S. Feinberg, *The Many Faces of Evil: Theological Systems and the Problems of Evil*, 2nd ed. (Wheaton: Crossway, 2004), 169–72; cf. Feinberg, *No One Like Him*, 654, 789–90.

[20] Feinberg, *Many Faces of Evil*, 169.

[21] It is important to note that *some* desires are sinful, especially those contrary to creation order, such as a "desire" for another person's spouse or homosexual desire.

[22] Feinberg, *Many Faces of Evil*, 170.

[23] Feinberg, 171.

work of the Spirit is "not able to sin" (*non posse peccare*).[24] These distinctions are helpful and necessary in order to make sense of Adam's pre-fall state and why he was able to sin.

How so? It helps explain how Adam was created good, morally upright, but able to sin. Adam was not created in a "glorified" or "perfected state" as we will be in the future. In fact, Adam as our covenant head was created in a good state, but one which had to be tested in order to be confirmed in righteousness. God's demand on Adam, along with his demand on all of his creatures, was to obey him perfectly in love, devotion, and covenant loyalty. But unfortunately, Adam disobeyed, thus plunging all of humanity into sin and death (Rom 5:12–21). However, thankfully and gloriously, in our Lord Jesus Christ, the last Adam, God has taken on our humanity, obeyed perfectly in his life and death as our new covenant head, and secured our eternal salvation and glorification by the Spirit (Heb 5:1–10).[25] Again, this explanation does not answer all of our questions, yet it helps make sense of how God can create a "good" creature so that nothing from his hand is fallen but also why a "good" creature is able to sin. This combination of "good" but not "tested" is helpful, especially when coupled with the next point.

4. In Adam, God created humans "good," but we must never forget that as finite creatures, we are dependent on God for everything, including our ability to obey God perfectly. On this point, we must deny that Adam sinned *because* he was finite since this would make our creatureliness the primary explanation for our sin. Ultimately, responsibility for our sin would be chargeable to God since he created us as finite creatures. In fact, Scripture tells us that our finitude is not the primary problem since in our glorified state we will forever remain finite but unable to sin. Instead, we must affirm that God created us finite but good, with the possibility of sinning, but Adam did not have to sin; it was a free choice on his part. Yet, as finite creatures, we are wholly dependent on God for our entire existence; we are not self-sufficient (Acts 17:28). As we discussed in the last chapter under "preservation," God must sustain us at every moment of our existence; otherwise, we would cease to exist. We are creatures and not the Creator.

---

[24] See the discussion in Christensen, *What About Evil?*, 218–19. There is a fourth state that refers to those in Christ prior to our glorification, namely, "able not to sin" (*posse non peccare*).

[25] Hoekema, *Created in God's Image*, 130–32, 231 (see chap. 15, n. 74); also see Donald Macleod, "Original Sin in Reformed Theology," in Madueme and Reeves, *Adam, the Fall, and Original Sin*, 131–36 (see chap. 11, n. 41).

Given this fact, a number of theologians have suggested that God provided Adam with *sufficient* grace to act correctly according to his good nature, but God did not provide him with *efficacious* grace to positively endure.[26] Thus, at the moment of the fall, Adam was good, God sustained his existence, yet apart from God positively enabling him to endure, he chose to rebel against God. We can then legitimately affirm that "God withdrew his grace so that the finite Adam would succumb to temptation,"[27] in contrast to our glorified state. In the future, due to Christ's perfect covenantal work for us and the Spirit's application of his work to us, in our final state, "God never withdraws his grace, which will sustain his glorified but finite creatures in an immutable state of righteousness."[28] But, in reference to Adam, it is crucial to note, as Donald Macleod correctly argues, that God's withholding of an efficacious grace "was neither an excuse for man nor a ground of accusation against God."[29] Adam alone was responsible for his choice. He was not compelled or forced to do it, either internally or externally; he acted freely and responsibly. Francis Turretin captures this point well: Adam "willingly sinned and freely and of his own accord without any compulsion or external force transgressed the command of God, though he was furnished with such strength and helps that he might easily have avoided sin, if he had wished."[30] In other words, Adam willingly sinned on his own accord. He was not coerced by God or Satan; he alone is to be blamed for his choice. God did not infuse Adam with evil thoughts or desires.[31] However, God did withhold his efficacious grace, thus allowing Adam to sin according to his decreed plan for a greater good and ultimately the display of God's triune glory in and through our Lord Jesus Christ, which is to the eternal good of God's people.[32]

---

[26] See Christensen, *What About Evil?*, 223. This distinction is also found in Turretin, *Institutes of Elenctic Theology*, 1:611; Bavinck, *Reformed Dogmatics*, 3:66–67 (see chap. 1, n. 9); Macleod, "Original Sin in Reformed Theology," 136; Bignon, *Excusing Sinners and Blaming God*, 221–22.

[27] Christensen, *What About Evil?*, 223.

[28] Christensen, 223.

[29] Macleod, "Original Sin in Reformed Theology," 136.

[30] Turretin, *Institutes of Elenctic Theology*, 1:608.

[31] Turretin, 1:514; cf. Christensen, *What About Evil?*, 223.

[32] We can also add to the above points James Anderson's appeal to *akrasia*, i.e., weakness of Adam's will (see Anderson, "Calvinism and the First Sin," 216–20). From Aristotle, Anderson suggests that Adam performed a weak-willed action that was freely chosen against his better judgment, but such an action does not require a "design" flaw in Adam's original created constitution. Adam, in performing such an action, does not necessitate him to have a "weak-willed character" (217). Instead, Adam had

Sixth, although there are plenty of reasons to think that there is no necessary contradiction in what Scripture teaches regarding divine providence, and especially regarding the relationship of concurrence, there is still plenty of mystery surrounding the fall, whether in the human or angelic realm. For this reason, theologians legitimately refer to the irrationality of sin and evil's origin.[33]

However, Scripture will not allow us to say either that God's knowledge of the fall was "conditioned" by the creature or that God "forced" humans to sin to accomplish his decreed end. Instead, Scripture teaches that God has foreordained all things, including sin and evil, but we are responsible for it, not God. In fact, God has foreordained all things, including our free choices, so that his decreed ends will occur and our freedom is upheld. *That* God is able to do so is not the question if we uphold all that Scripture teaches. But exactly *how* he is able to do so is where the "unknowns" or "mystery" arises. In the end, how we reconcile all that Scripture teaches goes back to our theology proper and what Scripture teaches God can and cannot do. To claim that the Bible's description of God's decree, his sovereign rule over the universe, and dual agency are *necessarily contradictory* cannot be demonstrated. Following Scripture, defining our terms, and making the necessary distinctions lead us to conclude that there is no contradiction in what Scripture teaches, although there are plenty of unknowns. God has revealed much to us about divine providence, but he has not disclosed everything to us. Our knowledge on these matters is the knowledge of redeemed creatures, but it is ectypal and finite. As such, we must remain true to all that Scripture teaches without eliminating any of the data, and when we do, we affirm in the strongest terms that our triune God has the ability to foreordain our free human actions.

The bottom line is this. We must uphold the four truths discussed in the last chapter that function as the biblical givens for formulating a biblical view of divine providence. This is especially the case regarding the relationship between divine and human agency and a biblical view

---

a "misalignment of evaluations and motivational strengths" that arose "in the normal course of events (albeit exacerbated by a diabolical temptation)" that should not be "regarded as a design flaw, as though God were guilty of suboptimal engineering" (218). Why is this point helpful? Because it helps demonstrate that there are explanations that allow us to affirm God's creation of Adam as good, but also explain how a "good" creature with compatibilistic freedom could sin without making God responsible for Adam's sin.

[33] Hoekema, *Created in God's Image*, 130–32; Christensen, *What About Evil?*, 224; Bavinck, *Reformed Dogmatics*, 3:69; G. C. Berkouwer, *Sin* (Grand Rapids: Eerdmans, 1971), 130–48.

of concurrence. Our "putting together" of the biblical teaching must remain within the biblical data without eliminating any of it, regardless of the tensions and unknowns that result. Especially as we work through the biblical teaching that God has ordained both good and evil, we must never conclude that God is not perfectly good, or that his sovereignty is weakened, or that humans are not responsible for their actions. In our "constructing" a theology of providence, we must remain faithful to Scripture and also demonstrate the noncontradictory nature of the biblical teaching, which we have sought to do. Our epistemological warrant for our theological formulation of divine providence is Scripture, but how we put the pieces together matters. In the end, having unknowns or "mysteries" in theology is inevitable, especially in the doctrine of providence, but mysteries are not the same as contradictions. Yet, it is crucial to locate "mystery" in its proper place, which ultimately is in the Bible's presentation of the God-world relationship. Specifically, the "mystery" is located in *how* God can foreordain all things, including our free human actions, and by doing so guarantee his decreed will *and* establish our secondary agency. Although we cannot fully explain *how* God can do this, Scripture teaches us that he can.

With our construction of a Reformed view of providence complete, let us now apply it in at least two directions. First, we need to defend it against the charge that it cannot answer the problem of evil. Second, we need to reflect on how we apply God's sovereign and providential rule to our Christian lives in such practical areas as prayer and evangelism.

Theological Application of Providence: The Problem of Evil

Introduction to the Problem of Evil

The problem of evil is one of the most difficult problems in theology. Non-Christians often appeal to it, especially in its logical or philosophical form, as a crucial reason for denying God's existence, thus placing Christians in a defensive posture that necessitates an apologetic answer. In its logical form, it is a serious challenge to the Christian faith since it seeks to demonstrate the *internal* inconsistency of our theological beliefs.[34] Often called the "Achilles' heel"

---

[34] In apologetics, there are two categories of arguments against Christianity: internal and external arguments. *Internal* arguments employ our own beliefs and argue that they are logically inconsistent. If such arguments are true, then our theology is contradictory from the start. The problem of evil is an example of an internal argument since it utilizes our own beliefs (e.g., God is omnipotent, omniscient,

of theology, the problem of evil seeks to demonstrate that it is contradictory to affirm simultaneously belief in the God of the Bible, who is omnipotent, omniscient, and perfectly good, *and* the existence of evil in the world. If God is good and omnipotent, then why is there evil and suffering in the world? Sadly, the fact of evil is not difficult to document. Regardless of whether we are talking about *moral* evil, that is, the sin of rational creatures, or *natural* evil, that is, pain and suffering that are the result of such things as earthquakes, floods, and diseases, if the Christian God exists, how can there be sin, evil, and suffering in the world?[35]

The problem of evil, however, is not just an issue that non-Christians raise and that rightly requires a full theological answer; it is also a problem for Christians in at least two ways.

First, in our daily lives, we often struggle with what is known as the "emotional problem of evil." Christians too live in a fallen world ravaged by sin. Although we may not question how God and evil can exist together in exactly the same way as non-Christians do, we often

---

and good) and then seeks to demonstrate that if such a view of God is true, evil should not exist. *External* arguments appeal to an "external" authority or another worldview "outside" of Christianity and argue that Christian theology is inconsistent with that external "authority." For example, an external argument is if someone denied the Bible's view of miracles *because* it contradicts their metaphysical and/or methodological naturalism. External arguments are easier to answer since they inevitably "beg the question," i.e., they assume the authority of the "external" worldview in their rejection of Christian theology, often forgetting that *this* is precisely what is at dispute. For their argument to work, they must demonstrate that the Christian view is false *on its own terms* and that the external view is correct *on its own terms*.

[35] "Moral evil" arises from personal agents (humans and angels). It assumes moral ability and responsibility. It is tied to intention, motive, and action. It includes deliberate actions and also not acting, what is known as sins of commission and sins of omission. "Natural evil" refers to conditions that arise in the world that do not necessarily arise from human choices that cause pain and suffering, for example, natural disasters, such as earthquakes, tsunamis, tornadoes, and famine; or accidents, such as blown tires while driving that result in death; or illnesses, such as cancer, leprosy, viruses, or various physical handicaps. Usually, something is considered natural evil if it causes pain and suffering to humans. A tornado hitting your house and you is different than a tornado reaching land but never harming anyone. Also, one must not forget that some destructive things in "nature" are *good* in terms of their results. Forest fires clear out dead trees and unleash new growth. A crucial question is the relationship between moral and natural evil. In Scripture, they are linked due to a historic Adam and fall (Gen 2:15–17; 3:13–19; Rom 8:19–22; cf. Rom 5:12–21). Natural evil is part of a post-fall, cursed, abnormal world. For those who affirm an old earth, some aspects of "natural" evil have been here from the beginning and are not tied to Adam's sin alone.

wrestle with the relationship of God's sovereignty to evil and wonder why specific evils happen to us and to others. We also cry with God's people in Scripture—"How long, O Lord?"—and if we are not careful, we may even doubt God's providential rule over the world. If we live long enough, *all* of us will experience some form of suffering. For this reason, Christians too struggle with the problem of evil, which requires that we think through the issue biblically and theologically so that we place ourselves in a better position to respond to evil and suffering when it occurs.

Second, the problem of evil must also be answered from *within* Christian theology since there are different conceptions of God's decree, sovereignty, and human freedom in theology. As we have discussed, Arminianism and Calvinism theologize about God and his relationship to sin and evil differently. Although both views have much in common, they differ on God's decree and its outworking in providence. They disagree on how to think of God's sovereignty over evil, and thus their answer to the problem of evil differs. For example, Arminian theology appeals to the "free will defense," but since this defense incorporates a libertarian view of freedom (along with its various theological entailments), a Calvinist cannot fully embrace it. A Reformed view appeals to human freedom as an important reason for evil, but not as the sole explanation. For this reason, both views answer the problem of evil but according to their specific theology. Although we have already critiqued Arminianism in chapter 20, we will discuss some further inadequacies of the free will defense since it is considered a key strength of the Arminian view. For many, Calvinism flounders on theodicy, so it is important to demonstrate that a Reformed view of divine providence is able to answer the problem of evil in a way consistent with its view of God's decree and divine providence.

Preliminary Observations in Our Response to the Problem of Evil

Before we respond to the problem of evil, we need to offer two preliminary observations.

First, given our embrace of a Reformed view of providence, our response to the problem of evil must be consistent with the four biblical truths outlined in chapter 22. This entails that some "solutions" to the problem of evil are eliminated as viable *biblical* solutions. For example, we cannot respond to the problem of evil by questioning God's sovereignty, power, or knowledge.

As Frame rightly notes, "Given what the Bible teaches about God's sovereignty, then, the various attempts to show that God is too weak to prevent evil do not seem promising."[36]

Nor is it enough, as most Arminian theology claims, to think that the entire problem of evil is explained by the abuse of human freedom as argued in the "free will defense." No doubt, Scripture teaches that a crucial reason why moral evil exists is due to human (and angelic) rebellion and choice. God created the world good (Gen 1:26, 31); he did not create evil nor is he responsible for it. It is only due to Adam's sin, rooted in an historic fall, that moral evil, and then natural evil, results (Gen 3). Moreover, evil is not metaphysically necessary as if it were part and parcel of God's creation of a world. Evil is the result of creaturely rebellion. God did not directly cause or create evil in the same way he created the universe.[37] Yet, sin and evil are decreed by God, and our answer to the problem of evil must include this fact. Furthermore, it is also not enough, on the Calvinist side, to explain evil in terms of "God's will" without qualification. The biblical data leads to the conclusion that God stands behind good and evil asymmetrically no matter how difficult it is to wrap our minds around all of the biblical teaching.

Thus, in our response to the problem of evil, to be *biblical*, we must hold *all* of the biblical teaching together, which, in the end, entails that "mystery" is inevitable. Our task is not to explain every *how* since that would require an *archetypal* knowledge we do not have. How does God foreordain our free human actions? How does God foreordain evil in such a way that he is not responsible and he remains perfectly good, while we, as creatures, are responsible for it? As noted above, we may not be able to answer this question fully, but we are warranted in affirming that God is able to do so because Scripture teaches it. Our task, given that Scripture is objectively true and unified but not exhaustive, is to demonstrate that there is no necessary contradiction in the biblical data. We cannot eliminate mystery in our response to the problem

---

[36] Frame, "Problem of Evil," 144 (see chap. 22, n. 56). Frame gives the example of Harold Kushner, *When Bad Things Happen to Good People* (New York: Schocken, 1981), and also the solution of process theology, such as David Ray Griffin, *God, Power, and Evil* (Philadelphia: Westminster, 1976). I would also add the literature of open theism since it operates with an unbiblical understanding of God's sovereignty, power, and knowledge. See Pinnock et al., *Openness of God* (see chap. 2, n. 135); Sanders, *God Who Risks* (see chap. 2, n. 135); Boyd, *Satan and the Problem of Evil* (see chap. 16, n. 62). In addition, see the two essays by William Hasker and Thomas Oord in Meister and Dew, *God and the Problem of Evil*, 57–97 (see chap. 16, n. 35), who offer a weakened view of God.

[37] See Groothuis, *Christian Apologetics*, 626–27 (see chap. 13, n. 74), who makes this point.

of evil. D. A. Carson rightly makes this point: "The problem looks neater when, say, God is not behind evil in any sense. But quite apart from the fact that the biblical texts will not allow so easy an escape, the result is a totally nonmysterious God."[38] He continues with the helpful observation that "after reading some neat theodicies that stress, say, that all suffering is the direct result of sin, or that free will understood as absolute power to contrary nicely exculpates God, I wonder if their authors think Job or Habakkuk were twits. Surely they should have seen that there is no mystery to be explained, and simply gone home and enjoyed a good night's sleep."[39] Our response to the problem of evil must demonstrate that there is no necessary contradiction in the biblical teaching, but this does not require that we explain the full scope of God's providence.

Second, it is crucial to note that there is no *the* problem of evil but a number of *problems* that have to be answered on their own terms. In *The Many Faces of Evil*, John Feinberg argues this point.[40] In fact, he insists that there are *three* different problems of evil that require a slightly different response: the logical, the evidential, and the emotional or practical problem of evil.

Probably the most famous is the *logical* problem. It is a deductive argument that seeks to demonstrate that our theology is internally contradictory. The *evidential* problem is different. It is an inductive argument that insists that the *amount* and *kinds* of evil in the world renders it *implausible* that God exists. Lastly, there is the *emotional* problem. The questions raised by it are *not*, Why is there evil in the world? or, How can God be omnipotent and good and allow evil to exist? Instead, the questions it asks are more personal: Why is this specific evil happening to me? Why did God allow my loved one to die? In the midst of this tragic event, can I trust God? The emotional problem is one which many Christians experience, and the answer to it is not exactly the same as the answer given to the other forms of the problems of evil.

In the end, our response to the *problems* of evil will depend upon the specific nature of the problem addressed, but whatever specific problem of evil we are addressing, we must do so from *within* the full range of the biblical teaching. Let us now turn specifically to the logical, evidential, and emotional problems of evil and respond to each one respectively.

---

[38] Carson, *How Long O Lord?*, 200 (see chap. 4, n. 87).

[39] Carson, 200.

[40] See Feinberg, *Many Faces of Evil*, 17–30.

The Logical Problem of Evil

The logical problem of evil charges Christian theology with an "internal" logical contradiction in the biblical teaching regarding God's sovereignty, human freedom, and the reality of evil.[41] It is a deductive problem; given the truth of its premises, the conclusion necessarily follows. The argument has been stated in numerous places, and it takes the following form:

1. God's power means God can prevent any evil since God can do absolutely anything.
2. God's goodness means he would prevent any evil.
3. But there is evil.
4. So God *cannot* exist.[42]

What response can we give to this challenge that upholds Scripture and removes the contradiction? Before we respond, it is important to note that in answering *logical* problems, all that is required is to demonstrate that the conclusion does not follow from the premises.[43] How do we do this? By adding a premise to the argument that is consistent with the biblical teaching *and* that renders the conclusion of the argument a non sequitur, that is, one that does not logically follow.

Is there such a premise? Yes, but before we give it, let us note two beliefs that the logical problem assumes without argument. Douglas Groothuis nicely describes both of these beliefs: "(1) God can prevent any evil, since God can do absolutely anything, and that (2) there is never a sufficient reason for God to allow evil."[44] But the problem with these beliefs is that they are highly debatable. For example, as Groothuis continues, for (1), "it may be that God can

---

[41] The "logical" problem of evil is also identified as the "philosophical" problem. The argument can be found all the way back to Epicurus (341–270 BC). In the Enlightenment era, it is argued by David Hume (1711–76), and more recently by J. L. Mackie, Antony Flew, George Smith, and Michael Martin.

[42] Groothuis, *Christian Apologetics*, 629.

[43] Often a distinction is made between a "defense" vs. a "theodicy." For this distinction, see Plantinga, *God, Freedom, and Evil* (see chap. 16, n. 56). A defense responds by proposing a possible solution that renders the argument a non sequitur, i.e., the conclusion does not *logically* follow from the premises. However, a defense does not answer the entire *how* question; it simply demonstrates that there is no necessary contradiction in maintaining the four biblical truths simultaneously. A theodicy is the grander attempt of seeking to justify God's ways to us, of demonstrating the goodness of all of his actions.

[44] Groothuis, *Christian Apologetics*, 630.

only bring about certain goods by letting some evils exist, and that God therefore cannot just do *anything*."[45] However, as Groothuis notes, God's omnipotence does not mean that God is able to bring about contradictory states of affairs since contradictions are not possible things.[46] Similarly, Feinberg argues that (1) is possible only if God contradicts other valuable things he has decided to do, directly contradicts what Scripture reveals about his attributes, and/or performs actions that we would not desire since they would result in a greater evil.[47] Whether we agree with Feinberg's entire solution is not the point. Instead, the point is that (1) cannot be assumed. The same is true of (2). In fact, to warrant (2) as true would require an *archetypal* knowledge that we do not have. Also, Scripture gives us reasons to believe that God has morally sufficient reasons for allowing evil. Minimally, the entire plan of redemption is one of those reasons, even though Scripture does not give us an exhaustive explanation.

What premise can we add to the argument to make it a non sequitur? Groothuis suggests the following premise, which is both consistent with Scripture and removes the contradiction.

1. God is omnipotent and omniscient.
2. God is omnibenevolent.
3. There is objective evil.
4. For any evil that God allows, God has a morally sufficient reason for allowing this evil, even if we do not know what this morally sufficient reason is in some cases.[48]

When the argument is restated in this way—if God has a morally sufficient reason for evil—then it does *not* logically follow that there is a contradiction between God and evil existing. In fact, to insist that there is *no* morally sufficient reason for God allowing evil is contrary to Scripture, and it would require the critic to argue a universal negative, which is impossible to do. Thus, with this added premise, the *logical* problem of evil is resolved in a biblically faithful and logically consistent way.

But despite this solution, a question is often asked: What *is* the morally sufficient reason? Technically, for logical problems we do *not* have to answer this question to resolve the problem.

---

[45] Groothuis, 630.

[46] See Groothuis, 630.

[47] See Feinberg, *Many Faces of Evil*, 167–80.

[48] Groothuis, *Christian Apologetics*, 630.

All we need to demonstrate is that the added premise in question is *possibly* true, which certainly is the case. Scripture gives us many reasons to think that God's planning and permission of evil, given his perfect goodness and in light of our human choices, is for a morally sufficient reason, although God has not given us an exhaustive answer. Yet, Christians throughout the ages have sought to say something more about God's reasons for allowing sin and evil. But in offering these *possible* answers, we should not forget that none of these possible answers are necessary to solve the logical problem of evil and that none of them offer a complete answer. Ultimately, our warrant for believing that God has a morally sufficient reason for allowing evil is Scripture, and as such, we have ample reason to trust what God has disclosed about his character and ways. With that said, what are some of the morally sufficient reasons that Christians have proposed? Let us look at two options.

The Free Will Defense[49]

Many Christians, especially Arminians (and open theists) contend that "free will" is *the* morally sufficient reason that explains why God has permitted evil. Usually, this defense is also combined with the "natural law defense."[50] Let us look at each of these in turn before we evaluate whether this is the best *biblical-theological* explanation for God's permission of evil.

First, the "free will defense" insists that God created us with libertarian freedom, which is "morally" valuable and superior to having no freedom at all. However, in choosing to create us with libertarian freedom, God cannot *guarantee* that we will always choose the good over evil. Thus, it is logically possible for God and evil to exist simultaneously, for God to have a morally sufficient reason to permit evil, and for creatures to be the ones responsible for evil.

Second, the "natural law defense" argues that in addition to creating humans with libertarian freedom, God has created a stable environment and natural order for humans to live within. This natural order is good and valuable, but it allows for the possibility of evil. For example, if I walk on the edge of a cliff and slip, I cannot escape the law of gravity, and normally God is not going to repeal the law of gravity in such a case. Or when I abuse my freedom and misuse the natural laws God has created, it is not God's fault. Thus, a world governed by

---

[49] For a contemporary defense of the "free will defense," see Plantinga, *God, Freedom, and Evil.*

[50] See C. S. Lewis, *The Problem of Pain* (New York: Macmillan, 1962).

gravity, inertia, plate tectonics, and so on can result in pain and suffering; hence, there are various "natural" evils.

Third, these two defenses combined explain God's morally sufficient reason for permitting moral *and* natural evil and why God is not responsible for it.[51] The perceived advantage of these defenses is that God does *not* intend that evils come to pass or that evils are God's intended means to bring about specific goods. Rather, moral and natural evil are the *unintended* by-product of God's desire to give us two great goods, namely, libertarian freedom and a stable world to exercise our free will. Of course, the assumption of both of these defenses is that God's goodness is more apparent if we are assured that God *does not intend* that any evils come to pass. God only makes it *possible* that evil may occur after he has decided to create these two "goods." Thus, in choosing to give us these "goods," God limits himself and takes a risk that *moral* evil could result from our abuse of our free will and that *natural* evil could occur in the stable world he has placed us in. This is why God *cannot* give us free will *and* guarantee that we will not abuse it nor create a stable world *and* guarantee it will not cause us pain. Combined together, these two defenses offer a "general" greater-good defense instead of a "particular" one, which means that God created a universe in which we have free will and a stable environment, but he *does not intend* for any specific evil to occur. Moral and natural evil are due to *general policies* God pursues rather than *specific* choices he makes to ensure their occurrence. In fact, God hopes that the goods will occur without the evils, but he cannot guarantee that this is the case.

Fourth, what is our overall evaluation of these two defenses, which attempt to explain why God has permitted evil for a morally sufficient reason and a "greater good"? Two points of criticism.

1. There is truth in what these two defenses argue, but they do not account for all of the biblical teaching. For example, human freedom is responsible for sin and evil, a point that the "free will defense" rightly stresses. Also, God has created the world in a regular way that helps explain some aspects of "natural evil," and it is true that when humans violate these natural laws, it can result in pain and suffering. However, these defenses are not the *total* explanation, and as such, they cannot account for all of the biblical teaching. For example, libertarian

[51] My discussion of this point is indebted to Greg Welty, *Why Is There Evil in the World (And So Much of It)?* (Fearn, Ross-shire, UK: Christian Focus, 2018), 41–46, 155–78.

freedom is inconsistent with the Bible's view of divine sovereignty. Also, Scripture teaches that God's foreordination and our free actions are compatible, which means that the "free will defense" can never be a complete *biblical* answer to the logical problem of evil.[52] Human freedom is part of the reason God allowed evil, along with his creation of the natural order, but it is not the only reason, and as we have argued, libertarian freedom results in more problems than it solves.

2. We must question the perceived strengths of these two defenses. For the sake of argument, let us assume the truthfulness of these defenses within the framework of classic Arminian theology. The problem is that even on their own terms, these defenses do not fully explain why God has permitted moral and natural evil. Remember the perceived advantage of these defenses: moral and natural evil are the *unintended* by-product of God's desire to give us two great goods, namely, libertarian free will and a stable world in which to exercise our free will. But is this really so? And do they stand up to biblical scrutiny? For example, think of the "natural law defense." Why is it that a stable environment *always* requires the possibility of natural evil? This may be true of a post-fall world, but what about Eden (Gen 1–2) and the final new creation (Rev 21–22), both of which reflect a stable environment without natural (or moral) evil?[53]

Moreover, most people who affirm these defenses believe that God can effectively act in the world, in contrast to panentheism.[54] But this raises a serious problem. In Scripture, God has acted many times to prevent moral and natural evil by either suspending or ending altogether a person's exercise of free will and/or directly intervening in nature in an extraordinary way.[55] For example, think of the following actions by God in which he intentionally intervened in human history to stop human sin:[56] the flood (Gen 6–7), the Exodus and destruction of

---

[52] See Feinberg, *No One Like Him*, 777–96, who makes this point.

[53] On this point, see Christensen, *What About Evil?*, 112–15; Welty, *Why is There Evil in the World?*, 164–67.

[54] Open theists also believe that God can effectively act in the world if he so chooses. To guarantee his will, God may have to remove our freedom, but open theism does not deny effectual agency. However, Thomas Oord seems to be an exception among open theists. As noted in chapter 16, Oord's view is closer to panentheism with his denial of creation *ex nihilo* and effectual action and his affirmation of an "essential kenotic" view of God.

[55] On this point, see Welty, *Why is There Evil in the World?*, 164–67.

[56] See Welty, 171–75.

Pharoah and his army (Exod 14), the taking of Nadab and Abihu's life for their disobedience (Lev 10), the preservation of Jonah's life by a great fish (Jonah 1:17), our Lord's protection of his disciples on the Sea of Galilee (Matt 8:23–27; Mark 4:35–41), and God's judgment of Herod by ending his life (Acts 12:20–23). In all of these cases, God overrode "free will" *and* the stability of "natural laws" to *eliminate* these specific evils. God decided that his "general" policies of upholding human freedom and a stable environment would be removed in these cases. But note: for God to *intervene* is just as much a decision on God's part as to *permit* things to occur. Even when God permits, he is still making a decision.

What is the point? It is this: the perceived strength of these two defenses evaporates as the *sole* explanation for why God has permitted evil. Even for these defenses, each and every case of moral and natural evil is due to a decision on God's part to allow them to exist. Why? For this reason: if God had not decided to *permit* it, he would have *prevented* it. So, even for these defenses, God makes specific decisions that ensure that specific cases of evil (pain, suffering) come to pass. Thus, the ultimate reason why specific moral and natural evils occur is still due to God's individual decision that they actually occur. This is why these two defenses do not fully explain why God has permitted moral and natural evil. The only alternatives are to take these views further than Arminian theology wants to go, namely, to embrace either panentheism, which further limits God's ability to act in an extraordinary or effectual way, or to embrace a Reformed view and argue that God has a morally sufficient reason for allowing evil, tied to his *intended* purposes, a point to which we now turn.

God's-Greater-Glory Defense

Are there other "morally sufficient" reasons that are more faithful to Scripture and that affirm all of the biblical data, especially God's sovereignty and lordship? There are, and most of them are associated with some form of "the greater-good defense" against the problem of evil. Here are some key points regarding this argument and some of these morally sufficient reasons.[57]

---

[57] Frame, "Problem of Evil," 152. William Wainright, *Philosophy of Religion*, 2nd ed. (Belmont: Wadsworth, 1999), 75, explains the "greater-good defense" this way: "This defense attempts to show (roughly) that (1) evil . . . is logically necessary to some good, that (2) this good outweighs the evil, and that (3) there are no alternative goods not involving those evils that would have been better." In other words, all evils serve some justifiable purpose in God's plan. For a further discussion of the strategy of

First, central to "greater-good" defenses is that God has multiple *good* purposes for allowing evil, and that *greater* goods result from such evils, which otherwise would not have come. Also, God *intends* for these *goods* to outweigh these evils, hence morally sufficient reasons for God to allow evil exist. Although the "free will defense" is a form of a "greater-good" argument, it only thinks that God is pursuing "general" goods, such as free will, that allow for the *possibility* of evil, which God did not intend. But the "greater-good" argument here denies this point. Instead, we contend that God allows no evils in the world that do not contribute to his overall good purposes, which is more consistent with the biblical teaching regarding God's sovereignty. This explains why God sometimes exercises judgment on some sins immediately (e.g., the flood [Gen 6–9]; Sodom and Gomorrah [Gen 19]), while for other sins, he delays (judgment of nations under Joshua [Gen 15:15–16]) due to his working out his overall good purposes for the world.

Second, Scripture reveals some of God's good purposes for allowing evil but not all of them. But just because God has not revealed all his purposes to us, it does not mean they do not exist. Divine revelation is the foundation of our knowledge, and God has given us enough reasons why he has allowed evil to trust him. In fact, Scripture speaks repeatedly of the positive uses of evil for various "greater goods." For example, God uses evil to test his servants (Job; 1 Pet 1:7; Jas 1:3), to teach them patience and perseverance (Jas 1:3–4), to get people's attention so that they will repent and avoid final judgment (Luke 13:1–5), to judge evildoers now and in the age to come (Deut 28:15–68; Matt 25:41–46), to discipline us (Heb 12:7–11), to give us greater joy when our present suffering is replaced by the consummated state (1 Pet 4:13), to display God's glory (John 9:3; Rom 9:17), and so on. All of these reasons and many more underscore the fact that evil is truly evil, but God ordained evil to achieve his good purposes, and our triune God is completely good, just, righteous, and trustworthy in all that he does.

Third, Frame also offers some helpful reminders from Scripture in thinking about God's "greater-good" reasons for planning and permitting evil.[58] First, we must define the "greater good" theistically. It is not our pleasure that is the greater good but God's glory, even though it is true that what brings God glory also benefits his people (see Rom 8:28). Second, if we are

---

"greater-good" defenses, see Groothuis, *Christian Apologetics*, 637–46; Welty, *Why is There Evil in the World?*, 41–73; Christensen, *What About Evil?*, 78–82.

[58] Frame, "Problem of Evil," 154–57.

to evaluate God's actions correctly, we must evaluate them over the full extent of human history. As Frame reminds us, "The Christian claim is not that the world is perfect as it is now; in fact, Scripture denies that it is. But the full goodness of God's plan will be manifest only at the end of redemptive history."[59] For reasons that God only knows, he has chosen to work out his sovereign purposes over millennia. Evil would not be such a problem if it were resolved in a short period of time. But God has chosen to work patiently over time, which prolongs God's consummating work and reminds us that in the long haul God does work out all things, including our suffering, for the good of his people (Rom 8:28). With Paul, we learn to say that "our momentary light affliction is producing for us an absolutely incomparable eternal weight of glory" (2 Cor 4:17). Third, God often surprises us by the ways in which he brings good out of evil. Whether it is in the case of the patriarchs, Joseph, Job, the nation of Israel, or, most significantly, the cross of Christ, we have ample reason to say that God does all things well.

Fourth, Scripture teaches that the *ultimate* morally sufficient reason that God has allowed evil is for his *greater glory* tied to his eternal plan of redemption in our Lord Jesus Christ. Scott Christensen argues this point well.[60] God's ultimate purpose in freely creating the world is to supremely magnify his own triune glory to all his creatures, especially humans, who alone bear his image. God did not need to create the world; the triune God within himself needs nothing due to the perfection and blessedness of his own divine life. But once God freely, graciously, and sovereignly chose to share himself and to create the world, he also chose to maximize his own glory as the goal of creation, centered in his entire plan of redemption.[61] Indeed, what else could serve as the ultimate reason for creation, providence, redemption, and judgment but God's own glory? (Rom 11:33–36; Eph 1:9–10; Col 1:15–17) Thus, in God's plan of redemption, his glory is supremely magnified in the incarnation of the divine Son and his entire work as the sole means of accomplishing our redemption.[62] But note: redemption and God's desire to glorify himself by the display of his grace are unnecessary without our fall into sin. In other words, the goods God pursues in the face of evil are dependent on those evils, and the goods pursued in the face of evil are important enough to justify the evils that produce

---

[59] Frame, 155.

[60] Christensen, *What About Evil?*, 7–8 (and the entire book).

[61] See the development of this point in Christensen, 279–316.

[62] See Christensen, 317–460.

those goods. This is why the fall of humanity, although freely chosen by Adam, is necessary to God's ultimate purpose in creating the world, which is to display and maximize God's glory in the salvation of his people and the judgment of sin and evil. In this light, the phrase *felix culpa* ("fortunate fault") is key. In God's plan, the fall was not a mistake, and it did not catch God by surprise. Adam freely chose to rebel against God (which continues for all humans), but God decreed the fall to result in the greater good of our salvation and supremely a display of *his* greater glory. A fallen-but-being-redeemed world is better than an unfallen-not-needing-redemption world. Such a world brings greater glory to God and as such is the ultimate morally sufficient reason for allowing evil.

Given these reasons and many more, the burden of proof is on the critic to demonstrate that there is *no* morally sufficient reason for God's allowing evil and bringing good out of it (a universal negative). Scripture teaches otherwise, and thus a Reformed view of providence can answer the *logical* problem of evil if done within the parameters of the biblical teaching.

The Evidential Problem of Evil[63]

The *evidential* problem of evil differs from the logical, deductive form of the problem. By contrast, it is an inductive argument claiming that God's existence is improbable due to the existence of evil in the world. The evidential problem treats theism as a large-scale hypothesis or explanatory theory that implies specific consequences for the way the world ought to be, or at least how *we* think it ought to be. Thus, if Christian theism is true, we expect that the world will not contain evil, or at least not contain the *amount* and various *kinds* of evil that are in the world. As such, the reality of evil does not necessarily render belief in God impossible, but rather implausible.

What is our response to the evidential form of the problem? It is twofold. First, it is nigh impossible to demonstrate what the world *ought* to be if God exists. What epistemological warrant do we appeal to? Apart from the objective standard of God and his word, it reduces to *our* finite perceptions, which is hardly a sufficient warrant. Second, the argument assumes that there is no morally sufficient reason for God to allow a specific amount

---

[63] For an excellent discussion and response to the evidential problem of evil from within Calvinist theology, see Feinberg, *The Many Faces of Evil*, 207–391.

of evil to exist rather than a lesser amount. However, as argued in our response to the logical problem of evil, this is an unbiblical assumption. Scripture gives us ample reasons to affirm that God is sovereign *and* good, and that he has a morally sufficient reason for evil existing. If this is so, then arguing either from the *fact* of evil (i.e., the logical argument) or from the *amount* and *variety* of evil (i.e., the evidential argument) equally assumes that the critic has grounds for knowing that God does *not* have a morally compelling reason for permitting the existence of evil. But on what grounds? What we discover is that although the evidential problem of evil is different than the logical problem, the theological answer to both of them is similar.

The Personal-Emotional Problem of Evil

As we must distinguish the logical from the evidential problem of evil, so we must distinguish the *personal-emotional* problem of evil from the other forms.[64] In regards to the latter, wrestling with the problem of evil is often more felt than thought. Even Christians, who know that sin and evil exist due to Adam's sin and our ongoing rebellion against God, struggle with suffering, tragedies, and evil in their lives. We cry from the depths of our heart, "How long O Lord?" and "Why?" By these questions we do not necessarily want to know *how* it is logically possible to reconcile God's existence with the existence of evil. Instead, we want to know why suffering and evil has come into our lives and the lives of others. Our response to these kinds of questions may overlap with the previous responses, but mostly it will consist of bringing people back to the glorious triune God in all of his sovereignty, grace, and beauty. We will seek to remind people of God's great plan of redemption across the Bible's covenantal storyline and ultimately lead them to Christ and his cross, which alone is the ground of our trust, confidence, and hope. For it is in the gospel that we see how horrendous sin and evil are to God, how they have been defeated in our Redeemer's work, and that the consummated state consists in a new heavens and earth where righteousness dwells and God is all in all. In other words, we respond to this form of the problem of evil by taking people back to the gospel and thinking through Scripture's presentation of

[64] Christensen calls it the "existential or emotional" problem of evil, while Feinberg labels it the "religious" problem of evil. Christensen, *What About Evil?*, 78; Feinberg, *The Many Faces of Evil*, 447–87.

the God-human-evil relationship. With this in mind, we will conclude with five biblical-theological reflections that attempt to capture important points that are essential to remember as we live in a fallen world, under God's sovereignty, and in light of the cross work of our Lord Jesus Christ.[65] A Reformed view of providence and response to the problem of evil would not be complete without thinking about these issues in terms of a "whole Bible" centered in the outworking of God's decree in redemptive history as the ultimate display of his glory for the good of his people.

Biblical-Theological Reflections on the Problem of Evil

First, to make a significant apologetic point, it is not only Christians who must answer questions surrounding the problem(s) of evil; *every* worldview must also answer questions about evil, albeit differently depending on one's view.[66] For example, naturalistic worldviews must first explain *on their own terms* how they can *warrant* the distinction between good and evil. For the sake of argument, if naturalism is true, what objective grounds does it offer for universal moral standards? Naturalism often raises the problem of evil against Christian theism, but in so doing, it must *assume* an objective distinction between good and evil, which their own view cannot warrant.[67] Thus, in order to get the argument off the ground, naturalists parasitically borrow from Christianity. Given our view of God and Scripture, Christians have no problem making an absolute distinction between good and evil and knowing what good and evil are. But naturalism, on its own terms, cannot do so apart from implicitly assuming the Christian position. In this way, Frame notes that many non-Christian worldviews, including naturalism, have a "'problem of good.' Without God, there is neither good nor evil."[68]

---

[65] For a very helpful and moving discussion of the *emotional* problem of evil, see John S. Feinberg, *Where is God? A Personal Story of Finding God in Grief and Suffering* (Nashville: B&H, 2004); also John S. Feinberg, "A Journey in Suffering: Personal Reflections on the Religious Problem of Evil," in Morgan and Peterson, *Suffering and the Goodness of God*, 165–237 (see chap. 22, n. 56).

[66] Contra Welty, *Why is There Evil in the World?*, 26–27, who seems to downplay this point.

[67] See Groothuis, *Christian Apologetics*, 617; and Frame, "Problem of Evil," 155, who make this point. Also see C. S. Lewis, *Mere Christianity* (San Francisco: HarperSanFrancisco, 2001), who made this argument famous.

[68] Frame, "Problem of the Evil," 155.

The same could be said about other non-Christian views but the point is that everyone has to wrestle with the problem of evil in light of their own worldview claims.[69] In terms of Christian thought, our problem is not *accounting* for the distinction between good and evil. We can make sense of our moral revulsion and condemnation of wicked actions. In fact, the Bible takes sin very seriously. From Genesis to Revelation, the Bible affirms the reality of sin and evil. In fact, the entire plan of redemption, centered in the incarnation of the divine Son, the cross, and so on, is meant to deal with the problem of evil and sin. In Scripture, the subject of sin and evil is not simply an intellectual discussion, something to be treated in a cavalier manner. Evil is real. Evil is ugly. And we are to take sin/evil seriously because God takes it seriously. God's entire plan is his unfailing determination to stamp evil out of his universe. One cannot make sense of Genesis 3, the cross, and final judgment without it. One cannot grasp the truth of the Gospel without seeing this point. The reality of sin and evil does not undermine the Christian view, it validates it.

However, our challenge is to make sense of *why* God plans and permits sin and evil, pain and misery. In answering these questions, we are driven back to Scripture and the entire covenantal story of God's eternal plan worked out in redemptive history in our Lord Jesus Christ.

Second, the Bible's metanarrative takes seriously the distinction between creation and the fall and thus the present fallenness and abnormality of this world. As we discussed in part 3, a helpful way of thinking through the Bible's story is by its own internal theological framework: creation, fall, redemption, and new creation. When thinking about the problem of evil, and specifically the thorny question of the origin of evil and its relation to God's plan, the distinction between creation and the fall is essential to maintain. God created the universe "good" (Gen 1:10, 12, 18, 21, 25, 31); everything that *he* made comes from his creative hand

---

[69] See Groothuis, *Christian Apologetics*, 617–25, who gives further examples of non-Christian worldviews which have a difficult time accounting for the distinction between good and evil, including Buddhism, Hinduism, and other religious viewpoints. I would also argue that even though Islam can claim a standard for good and evil rooted in Allah's will, Islam has a major problem in accounting for the distinction between good and evil. Their view of God is fairly arbitrary and God's will is not rooted in his perfect moral character. In addition, they teach a works righteousness view of salvation which requires that God does not enforce moral standards perfectly and justly, thus questioning how their concept of God can serve as an absolute, universal, unchanging moral standard.

as morally good. No doubt, as we have discussed, sin and evil are part of God's foreordained plan, but Scripture *never* concludes that God is responsible for evil, although it is part of his eternal plan.

Instead, Scripture distinguishes creation and fall, and it grounds this distinction in history. Sin entered the world by our creaturely act of rebellion, first in the angelic realm and then in the human world. Sin is not here because it is a metaphysical necessity tied to our finitude, nor is it here because that is just the way things are. Instead, sin is here due to our rebellion against God, which is chargeable to the creature and not the Creator. In fact, Scripture takes sin and evil so seriously that the entire plan of redemption is to destroy it and to remove it from God's universe! And, thankfully, because sin and evil are not metaphysically necessary, in removing sin and evil, God does not have to scrap us and start over again. Instead, God must remove our sin by paying for it in Christ and then transforming us by the Spirit in order to restore us and make us new creations in Christ.[70] What this demonstrates is that the triune God stands totally opposed to sin and evil. Thus, the same Scripture that teaches God foreordains all things, including sin and evil, also teaches that sin and evil are an abnormality, an intrusion and a distortion of this good world, which God alone can remedy in Christ's work of redemption and by the work of the Spirit. Also, although God ordains evil to bring about a greater good, Scripture never concludes that sin and evil are less than what Scripture says they are. Evil remains evil: totally, radically, and absolutely, and God stands in complete opposition to it, as the entirety of Scripture teaches.

Many applications could be drawn from these points, especially regarding how we are to confront the reality of sin, evil, and suffering in this world. Since Eden and on this side of the consummation, we live in an abnormal and fallen world, and none of us escape it. Any suffering we experience is due to the present condition of this world. This does *not* mean that all suffering is tied to a specific sin, as the book of Job makes abundantly clear, although some suffering may be due to specific sins (e.g., Acts 5; 1 Cor 11; cf. Heb 12). But suffering is first part of the present condition of this world, now awaiting the consummation, which requires that we have realistic expectations when suffering faces us head on. We often do not know why specific suffering comes our way; that is tied to the sovereign plan of God. Yet we do know that we will face sin and evil, and when we do, God is not to blame.

---

[70] See Groothuis, *Christian Apologetics*, 625–29, who emphasizes these points.

Third, in God's plan of redemption, God not only demonstrates that he is sovereign over sin and evil but also that he is destroying sin and evil by Christ's work, thus demonstrating that he is perfectly good and trustworthy. Scripture teaches that in redemption, God is not indifferent to our suffering and plight. Although we do not deserve anything from him but judgment, God has displayed his grace and sovereignly acted to defeat sin and evil. In fact, it is precisely because he is the sovereign and gracious Lord that we can have real hope, help, relief, and comfort since he is able not only to sympathize with us; he is also able to save.

Does not the entirety of Scripture teach this point? In the coming of Christ, the promised "age to come" has dawned. In Christ's life, death, and resurrection as our new covenant head, he has defeated sin, death, and Satan and won for us our salvation (e.g., Rom 3:21–25; Col 2:13–15; Heb 2:14–15; 1 Cor 15:56–57; Rev 5). In Christ, the triune God has demonstrated that he is utterly trustworthy, faithful, and good. We might not know all the mysteries of his ways, including exactly how all the biblical data fits together. Yet, we do know that the truth of God's sovereignty and goodness is beyond question. In our redemption, God is not sitting idly by, without care or concern for his people. In Christ's cross and resurrection, we have the greatest demonstration of God's sovereignty over evil and his willingness to identify with us in order to save us from sin, evil, and death. In our facing suffering, there are many questions. But as we think of our sufferings in light of Christ and his cross, we learn how to trust. God himself has suffered unjust suffering, and when we remember this, we learn that God is for us and not against us, that he is completely trustworthy, and that he stands opposed to sin and evil in a far greater way than we can even imagine. After all, what does the incarnation of God's Son, his life, death, and resurrection, teach us if not that God hates sin and evil and that he sovereignly acts to destroy it even though it is part of his foreordained plan (Acts 2:23)? Thus, if we can trust God in using evil for good purposes in the cross, we can certainly trust him in all other events, even though we may not know all the morally sufficient reasons behind those events.[71]

Fourth, given the biblical teaching of God's sovereignty over sin and evil, our responsibility for it, and God's goodness and total determination to destroy evil, we must fight against sin and evil in line with what God is doing. Interestingly enough, this conclusion is the opposite of critics of a Reformed view of providence. For example, Bruce Little contends that a Reformed

[71] For an excellent discussion of how the problem of evil must be viewed in light of the cross, see Henri Blocher, *Evil and the Cross*, trans. David G. Preston (Downers Grove: InterVarsity, 1994).

view of divine sovereignty entails that "Christians should not be engaged in standing against social injustice (that which the Bible calls evil)" since "if God is really sovereign and He ordains the evil, it would be impossible for mere humans to stop it, so standing against social injustice would be an exercise in futility."[72] But this conclusion is a non sequitur. The Bible teaches both God's sovereignty over evil and his complete opposition to it.

In this regard, John 11:33–35 is an important text. As Jesus approaches the tomb of Lazarus in sovereign power to raise him, he is "deeply moved in spirit and troubled."[73] Jesus, as God the Son incarnate, is outraged at the death of his friend, and the sin that brought death into this world. Jesus is not outraged with himself as the Lord even though sin, evil, and death are part of his eternal plan and the reason he is going to the cross in the first place. Instead, he is outraged by what sin has wrought by creaturely actions, that which he has come to defeat and destroy. Jesus, as the sovereign Lord, stands in complete opposition to sin and evil, and we must do likewise. When moral evil takes place, we do not blame God or respond in a laissez-faire manner. Rather, we fight sin and evil by proclaiming the gospel and, by God's grace, seeing people made new, and by standing for justice by upholding what is good and punishing evil through the appropriate authorities that God has established. We never justify sin and wrong actions by appealing to divine sovereignty at the expense of human responsibility, nor do we reduce God's sovereignty in light of human choices. We hold the biblical teaching in tension as we fight with all our might against sin and evil in line with what God himself is doing.

Fifth, what about specific suffering in our lives? Often when we go through suffering, we wish that God would have allowed us to go through something else. Why do we experience specific suffering? Why do some escape specific tragedies while others do not? In response to such questions, many points could be made, but we conclude with these reflections. John 21:15–23 reminds us that God calls each of us to different callings in life. When Peter asked about John's future, Jesus never answered him directly but instead said, "Follow me." Our lives are part of God's sovereign plan, and most of the time, we do not know what the Lord has ordained for our lives. As we live before the Lord, we must maintain simultaneously the biblical data without denying, minimizing, or marginalizing it. For the Christian, we are assured that even in our suffering in this life, which is part of the fallenness of this world

---

[72] Little, "Evil and God's Sovereignty," in Allen and Lemke, *Whosoever Will*, 284 (see chap. 4, n. 85).

[73] See Carson, *Gospel According to John*, 415 (see chap. 5, n. 13).

order, God never allows us to experience anything we cannot bear by his grace and power (1 Cor 10:12–13). Sometimes the suffering we experience is due to persecution for the Lord's name, which we should consider joy (Mark 8:34–38; 2 Tim 3:12; 1 Pet 4:12–16). Other times it may be due to the discipline of the Lord (Hebrews 12). Yet in many cases, we experience difficulties related to the abnormality of this world, not knowing why the specific events beset us. But what we are assured of is this: our God is sovereign, and the defeat of sin and evil is accomplished. We live our lives in full conviction that in Christ, we have every assurance that God is Lord over evil and that until the end we can live confidently, trusting God's promises and word.

As we conclude, it is certainly the case that the relationship of God to sin and evil is one of the most difficult questions in theology. In this chapter, we have sought to defend a Reformed view of divine providence, which we believe more accurately reflects the biblical teaching. We have also sought to demonstrate how a Reformed view applies the biblical teaching to the problem of evil. Although many questions remain, one thing is sure: our sovereign and gracious triune God is worthy of all of our confidence and trust. Solutions to the problem of evil, such as the free will defense, are not only biblically inadequate, but in the end, they rob us of our confidence in our sovereign God, who is working out all things in this world for his glory and our good. We only have knowledge of God's plan and actions as creatures, but in light of God's actions in creation and redemption, in light of God's glorious plan of redemption, centered in the coming of our Lord Jesus Christ and his majestic triumphant cross work for us, we have every reason to trust what God has said and to live in confident expectation of our Creator-covenant God's consummating what has already begun in Christ in a mind-blowing new creation (Rev 21–22). While we continue to live between the ages as we await the return of our Lord, our calling as the church is to trust God's promises, proclaim Christ as our only hope and salvation, and stand with our triune God against sin and evil as we await the consummation.

Theological Application of Providence: Prayer and Evangelism

We must also apply God's providential rule to our lives. Our theology of providence must never remain merely theoretical; it is meant to be lived out as we grow in our knowledge, love, and obedience to our triune covenant Lord and learn to trust him in our daily lives. However, as we do, we must hold together the four biblical truths that constitute the Bible's view of providence without redefinition or reduction, as we discussed in the previous chapter. As in our theological formulation, so in our daily lives, we must learn to live with the tension between God's total sovereignty and our free and morally responsible choices without explaining the tension away. In fact, Carson suggests a principle that we should follow as we apply providence to our daily lives: we must let each biblical truth *function* as it does in Scripture. Carson states it this way: "We must do our best to ensure that these complementary truths function in our lives in the same ways they function in the lives of believers described in Scripture."[74] In this way, we live out a biblical view of concurrence and dual agency consistent with and faithful to the biblical teaching. Let us now apply this principle to the important topics of prayer and evangelism.

Providence and Prayer[75]

In the application of providence to prayer, two extremes must be avoided. Both are unbiblical because they do not allow the four truths to function together in their full biblical force.

One extreme is the view that our prayers change God's mind, and his plan is ultimately dependent on what he foreknows we will pray. Those who affirm this view of prayer often ask: "What is the point in praying to God if he has already decreed all things?"[76] The assumption of such a question, as Graeme Goldsworthy suggests, is "that there is no point in praying if we cannot change God's mind, or at least influence it in some way, by praying."[77] But of course, this question can be turned on its head, as Goldsworthy does: "What is the point in praying to God if he is not in control of all things?"[78] The problem with this view of prayer is that it emphasizes the significance of our human choices at the expense of God's sovereign rule over the world. Goldsworthy captures this point well: "the human element fills the scene almost entirely: it is the conditions which *we* must meet, the promises *we* must claim, the things *we*

---

[74] D. A. Carson, *A Call to Spiritual Reformation: Priorities from Paul and His Prayers* (Grand Rapids: Baker Academic, 1992), 160.

[75] See Carson, 145–66. Also see Graeme Goldsworthy, *Prayer and the Knowledge of God: What the Whole Bible Teaches* (Downers Grove: InterVarsity, 2003), 53–67.

[76] See David Basinger, "Practical Implications," in Pinnock et al., *Openness of God*, 156–62.

[77] Goldsworthy, *Prayer and the Knowledge of God*, 53–54.

[78] Goldsworthy, 54.

must do, in order to get our requests granted; and *God's* claims, *God's* right, *God's* glory are often disregarded."[79] In fact, in elevating human freedom and downplaying divine sovereignty, it operates with a false view of dual agency. It assumes that if God is sovereign, then our freedom is lessened, or conversely, if our freedom is upheld, then God must choose to limit his sovereignty, a point we have argued is not warranted by Scripture.

On the other hand, the other extreme is to emphasize God's complete sovereignty at the expense of our free choices. Since God has decreed all things, why pray at all? Or such a view may encourage people to pray, "Your will be done," and leave it there. For such a view, there is really nothing specific we can petition God with since we cannot "change" God's will. But similar to the first option, this view also eliminates biblical data. It opts for a strong view of divine sovereignty, but it does not account for the significance of our choices in God's plan.

In other words, both views draw inferences about prayer that Scripture does not draw. They permit one component of the biblical teaching to function in unbiblical ways, and as such, they fail to understand how prayer functions in Scripture. God's sovereignty is never a disincentive to pray; rather, it encourages us to pray.[80] Furthermore, prayer is always done in light of God's revelation of himself and his entire plan. Another way of saying this is that our prayers function in light of God's revealed will. Prayer in Scripture, as Goldsworthy rightly insists, is "inescapably concerned with God as he acts and reveals himself in the world. We do not worship or praise or petition God in the abstract."[81] For this reason, Goldsworthy continues, "Christians at prayer have only one option: to pray towards the fulfillment of God's revealed purposes for the whole universe. Anything else would be an act of idolatry or of total rebellion against God. All Christian prayer, then, will be oriented towards the gospel and its God-ordained outcome."[82] What this entails for a proper understanding of prayer, then, is that we learn to pray consistent with God's revelation of himself and his plan. As Carson reminds us, we pray "in line with what God has already disclosed he is going to do."[83] This means that our prayers will not only be specifically tied to God's revealed will but will also function as

---

[79] Goldsworthy, 54.

[80] On this point, see Carson, *Call to Spiritual Reformation*, 161.

[81] Goldsworthy, *Prayer and the Knowledge of God*, 60.

[82] Goldsworthy, 60.

[83] Carson, *Call to Spiritual Reformation*, 162.

God's ordained means to bring about his planned ends.[84] As we discovered in a proper view of dual agency, in every act, God is at work bringing about his planned ends while humans are also acting. Prayer, then, is one of God's ordained means that we freely engage in, consistent with his eternal plan.

This view of prayer in relation to God's providence is repeatedly illustrated in Scripture. For example, think of Daniel. Daniel prays for the end of the exile precisely because he knows that according to God's word from Jeremiah, the time for the end of the exile has arrived (Dan 9:1–2). Knowing that God *will* sovereignly keep his promise, instead of simply waiting for the seventy years to pass, Daniel turns to God in prayer and petitions him to keep his covenant promises so that *God's* name will be glorified (Dan 9:4–19). For Daniel, God's sovereignty leads him to prayer, and his prayers are in line with God's revealed will, thus holding together God's sovereignty and our human responsibility to pray.[85]

David is another example of prayer at work under the hand of God's providential rule. In 2 Samuel 7, God ratifies the Davidic covenant. As discussed in part 3, the Davidic covenant is the epitome of the OT biblical covenants; it is through David's greater Son, our Lord Jesus Christ, that all of God's promises will be fulfilled. David is assured that God will keep his promises and they will not fail. As David turns to prayer, he not only thanks God for his sovereign and gracious action towards him and his entire family, but he also petitions God in line with what God has promised he will do: "Now, LORD God, fulfill the promise forever that you have made to your servant and his house. Do as you have promised, so that your name will be exalted forever" (2 Sam 7:25–26a). As Goldsworthy correctly notes, "It is inconceivable that David prays like this because he is nervous that God might go back on his word."[86] Instead, David prays in line with what God has revealed and promised, and his prayer functions as God's ordained means to bring about God's planned and purposed ends.

---

[84] See Carson, 164–65; Goldsworthy, *Prayer and the Knowledge of God*, 61–65.

[85] See Carson, 162. Something similar occurs in Jeremiah 29. After God tells the exiles that they will be in Babylon for seventy years and they are to go about their lives in faithfulness to the Lord (vv. 4–7), he reminds them that he will keep his promises to them and return them to the land (vv. 10–14). But in making this promise, God also expects the Israelites to petition him: "You will call to me and come and pray to me, and I will listen to you. You will seek me and find me when you search for me with all your heart" (vv. 12–13). See Goldsworthy, *Prayer and the Knowledge of God*, 63–64.

[86] Goldsworthy, *Prayer and the Knowledge of God*, 63.

In the NT, our Lord exemplifies this same view of prayer in light of God's sovereignty. In John 17, Jesus knows that his "hour" is now here. In John's gospel, the "hour" refers to the Father's appointed time for Jesus's death for us (John 12:23–24; 17:5).[87] Christ's cross is not an event planned *ad hoc* in history but foreordained before the foundation of the world. But now with the cross immediately impending, what does Jesus pray? Does he merely resign himself to whatever will happen? Does he conclude that there is no reason to pray since God's will is guaranteed to occur? No. Instead, our Lord turns to prayer and specifically petitions the Father in line with God's sovereign plan. Jesus prays, "Father, the hour has come. Glorify your Son so that the Son may glorify you" (v. 1). As Carson notes, "Jesus' logic runs like this: My Father's appointed hour for the 'glorification' of his Son has arrived; so then, Father, glorify your Son."[88] Thus, our Lord's prayer not only reflects God's revealed will, but it functions as the very means to bring about what God has decreed from eternity. In this way, God's sovereignty and human responsibility are upheld.

Something similar also occurs in texts that refer to God "changing his mind." For example, think of Exodus 32–33. Due to the sin of Israel, God has threatened to destroy Israel and start over again with Moses (Exod 32:9–10). Instead of resigning himself to this situation, Moses turns to the Lord in prayer and petition. Moses appeals to God's covenant promises to Abraham and the immutability of his own declared purposes (32:12–13). In other words, Moses is not only praying in light of God's revealed word; he is also appealing to the fact that God does not change and he is true to his word. As a result of Moses's prayer, God relents. As Carson notes, a casual reader may think that this is evidence that prayer actually changes God's sovereign purposes, but "such a conclusion would be both one-sided and premature."[89] Instead, what is unfolding before our eyes is the fact that God always remains true to his covenant promises, and Moses knows this right well. Moses petitions God in line with what he has promised, and in this way, Moses's prayer functions as the means to bring about God's ordained ends. Both divine sovereignty and human responsible agency are upheld so that in the very same act of prayer, God is at work fulfilling his purposes, and Moses is at work.[90]

---

[87] See Carson, *Gospel According to John*, 553–54.

[88] Carson, *Call to Spiritual Reformation*, 162.

[89] Carson, 163.

[90] Carson, 164–65, also illustrates this point from Ezekiel 13 and 22 and Amos 7. In both cases, prayer functions as God's means to bring about his ordained ends. As Carson rightly observes, "God

Prayer is part of our Christian lives and a true test of our spiritual life and growth in Christ. Under God's providential rule, prayer does not function to "get" us our way or as a mere resignation to God's decree. Instead, prayer functions to allow us to know God according to his word and to grow in trust in his promises as we commune with him. We petition God in light of his revealed word, and as we do, our prayers function as significant means to bring about God's ordained ends.

Providence and Evangelism

What is true of how prayer functions under God's sovereign hand is also true for evangelism. As with prayer, we need to avoid two extremes. On the one hand, we can so emphasize our freedom that God's ability to save his people apart from us is thwarted as if God is dependent on us. On the other hand, we can so emphasize God's sovereignty that our proclamation of the gospel is unnecessary for God to save his elect. Once again, the problem with these two extremes is that they uphold some of the truths of divine providence at the expense of all of the data. Inferences are drawn that Scripture does not allow. As with prayer, the solution is to make sure evangelism *functions* in our lives and thinking as it does in Scripture in relation to God's sovereign rule.

For example, think of how God's sovereignty in election functions in relation to evangelism in Acts 18. In a night vision, the Lord speaks to Paul and says: "Don't be afraid, but keep on speaking and don't be silent. For I am with you, and no one will lay a hand on you to hurt you, because I have many people in this city" (vv. 9–10). Paul is reminded that God has sovereignly and graciously chosen a people for himself, yet Paul is the means by which those people will come to repentance and faith. In other words, God's sovereignty in election does not remove the need for evangelism since our proclaiming the gospel is God's ordained means to bring about the salvation of God's elect. In this way, Paul is assured that his work is not in vain,

---

expects to be pleaded with; he expects godly believers to intercede with him. Their intercession is his own appointed means for bringing about his relenting" (164). But if we do not pray, we do not conclude that God is "frustrated" because he cannot find someone to pray. Instead, this simply means that the entire situation has changed, which reflects God's planned intention in another way, by ensuring deliverance from another place, which reflects his ordained purposes (cf. Esth 4:14).

yet he must still proclaim the gospel to know who God's elect actually are. Divine sovereignty and human responsibility work hand in hand, and what is underscored here is dual agency.[91]

The same truth is taught in Romans 9–10. In chapter 20, we discussed how Romans 9 teaches God's unconditional, gracious election of his people. Yet, God's sovereignty in election does not remove the need for humans to repent, believe, and respond to the gospel. Both are true. In fact, the reason why many Israelites did not receive their Messiah is explained by both of these truths.

As we conclude our discussion of how to apply divine providence to our lives, Scripture will not allow us to choose one biblical truth and pit it against other biblical truths. What is crucial in our theological application of doctrine is that we allow the doctrine to function in our lives as it does in Scripture, regardless of the tensions that result. We must remember that biblical tensions are God-given, due to our ectypal knowledge, and yet are not contradictions. The biblical data must be maintained both in our construction of doctrine and its application to our lives.

Concluding Reflection

This chapter concludes this section, where we have discussed the glory of our triune God in his external works. As we have discussed issues surrounding God's decree and its outworking in creation and providence, we have sought to capture something of the majesty, beauty, and self-sufficiency of our triune God as our Creator-covenant Lord. Indeed, we have reflected on the one of whom Paul rightly says: "Oh, the depth of the riches / and the wisdom and of the knowledge of God! / How unsearchable his judgments / and untraceable his ways! . . . For from him and through him / and to him are all things. / To him be the glory forever. Amen" (Rom 11:33, 36).

Obviously, much more could be said; we have only scratched the surface on these profound truths, but in the end, we are reminded anew that this universe is *his* and that *he* alone deserves all of our worship, love, trust, obedience, and total devotion. In reflecting on the

---

[91] On this point, see Carson, 160. Historically, it is important to remember that the modern mission's movement began with a Reformed view of providence (cf. William Carey, George Whitefield, Howell Harris, and so on).

wonder of God's eternal plan and its enactment—first, by God creating the world to be the stage on which he displays his glory, and second, by his preserving, acting, and ruling over history—we must respond the same as the angelic hosts who surround God's throne. As John heard the praise of heaven, as the angels bowed before the Holy One, so must we sing on earth: "Our Lord and God, you are worthy to receive glory and honor and power, because you have created all things, and by your will they exist and were created" (Rev 4:11). And as John later heard the song of redemption, centered in the glory of our Lord Jesus Christ, which we will unpack and develop more in volume 2, so we also must sing: "Blessing and honor and glory and power be to the one seated on the throne, and to the Lamb, forever and ever!" (Rev 5:13).

NAME INDEX

A

Abraham, William, 96
Adam, Karl, 63
Alexander, Archibald, 62
Alexander, Denis R., 811
Amyraut, Moïse, 780
Anderson, James, 902–3, 907
Anselm, 43, 194, 198, 260, 601, 605, 798, 800
Aristotle, 799, 842–43, 907
Arius, 695–96
Arminius, Jacob, 741, 743, 865–66
Athanasius, 43, 193, 365, 382, 387, 698, 701, 791
Augustine, 40, 43, 45, 193, 259–61, 318, 325, 333, 361, 369–70, 382, 601, 611–12, 619, 622, 749, 787, 791, 798, 802, 813, 824, 863–65, 905

B

Bacon, Francis, 844
Bahnsen, Greg, 268, 321, 834
Balthasar, Hans Urs von, 198
Barbour, Ian, 735
Barrett, Matthew, 178, 278–79, 283, 298, 599
Barr, James, 139, 184, 251–52, 273–74, 277, 286, 371
Barth, Karl, 24, 63, 77, 174, 197, 208, 225, 233, 236–37, 239–41, 244, 246–48, 258, 305, 545, 814
Bartholomew, Craig G., 396
Barton, John, 251–52
Basil of Caesarea, 698
Basinger, David, 555
Baur, F. C., 58
Bavinck, Herman, 7, 27, 40, 62, 87, 139, 167, 171, 181–83, 193, 214, 220, 244, 263–64, 268, 279, 298, 347, 416, 500, 507, 543, 563, 583, 585, 591–92, 596, 604–5, 607, 609, 611, 619, 621, 626, 629, 643, 646, 650, 663, 671–72, 689, 721, 766, 778, 780, 784, 791, 811, 828, 832, 869, 871, 873–74, 876
Baxter, Richard, 262
Beale, Greg, 112–13, 477, 515, 527–28
Beckwith, Roger, 365, 380
Beeke, Joel, 328, 613, 615, 621–22, 755, 768, 787, 815, 821, 823
Behe, Michael, 850–51
Belshazzar, 316
Ben Sira, 375
Berkeley, George, 46
Berkhof, Louis, 500, 512–13, 647, 650, 728, 731, 756–57, 766, 781, 787, 804–5, 824, 862
Berry, R. J., 811
Bignon, Guillaume, 773
Bird, Michael, 313
Blaising, Craig, 487, 496–98
Blocher, Henri, 306, 806, 823
Bock, Darrell, 487, 498
Boethius, 619, 690
Botta, Paul Emile, 316
Bousset, Wilhelm, 58
Boyce, J. P., 263
Boyd, Greg, 239, 242, 248, 554, 563–64
Boyle, Robert, 843
Briggs, G. Andrew D., 811
Brunner, Emil, 63, 814
Bullinger, Heinrich, 499
Bultmann, Rudolf, 58, 63–64, 95, 174, 579, 734

C

Calvin, John, 5, 40, 44–45, 69, 74, 111, 195, 257–58, 266, 325, 370, 499, 541, 619, 691, 702, 748, 779, 785, 864–65
Caneday, Ardel, 114, 128, 282
Carson, D. A., 16, 75–76, 116, 125, 155, 255, 281, 284, 361, 388–89, 394, 434, 439, 458, 471, 474, 566, 609, 661, 880, 884, 913, 930, 933
Carter, Craig, 872
Chafer, Lewis Sperry, 487
Chaffey, Tim, 802
Chalmers, Thomas, 806
Charnock, Stephen, 195–96, 627, 633, 644–45
Chase, Mitchell L., 128, 133
Childs, Brevard, 25
Christensen, Scott, 401, 639, 782–83, 904
Churchill, Winston, 18
Cleanthes, 379
Clement of Alexandria, 386–87, 791, 802
Clement of Rome, 259
Clowney, Edmund, 121–22
Cobb, John, 734–35
Cocceius, Johannes, 500
Cole, Zachary, 324
Collingwood, R. G., 842
Collins, C. John, 806
Cooper, John, 543–44, 733
Copernicus, 839–40, 843
Copleston, Frederick, 51
Cotes, Roger, 843
Cottrell, Jack, 747–48
Coxe, Nehemiah, 520
Craig, William, 640–41, 710, 814
Crick, Francis, 849–50
Cullmann, Oscar, 174, 475

D

Darby, John, 487
Darwin, Charles, 48, 61, 90, 789, 824, 834, 845, 850
Davis, John, 806
Dawkins, Richard, 789, 835, 853
Democritus, 789
Dempster, Stephen G., 119, 377, 420, 450, 678–79, 829
Denton, Michael, 849
DeRouchie, Jason, 456
Derrida, Jacques, 70–71, 90
Descartes, René, 46, 66, 70
DeYoung, Kevin, 468–69
Duby, Steven, 142, 248, 612, 621, 828
Dulles, Avery, 153

E

Eck, Johannes, 261
Eden, Murray, 849
Edwards, Jonathan, 668, 868
Ehrman, Bart, 317, 367
Eiseley, Loren, 837–38
Enns, Peter, 243–44, 246, 249, 313, 328, 348
Epicurus, 789, 914
Epimenides, 379
Epiphanius, 376
Erasmus, Desiderius, 261, 353
Eusebius of Caesarea, 384, 387
Eusebius of Nicomedia, 697
Evans, C. Stephen, 53, 707, 710–11

F

Farley, Edward, 35, 186–88, 300
Feinberg, John, 71, 73, 487–88, 637, 880, 905, 913, 915
Feinberg, Paul, 293–94, 296, 314, 327
Ferguson, Sinclair, 274, 276, 301, 649
Fesko, J. V., 502, 512, 766
Feuerbach, Ludwig, 62, 537
Fichte, Johann, 844
Finney, Charles, 742
Flew, Antony, 914
Foucault, Michel, 71
Fountain, Andrew, 381
Frame, John, 8, 27, 54, 87, 154–55, 157–58, 161, 163–64, 169, 181–82, 185, 216–17, 233, 247–48, 275, 280, 325, 330, 337–38, 340–41, 344–45, 351, 403, 421, 506, 572, 575–76, 582–84, 603–5, 611–12, 620, 722, 731, 769, 771, 781, 870–71, 881, 885, 912, 920–21
Franke, John, 96, 235, 247, 249, 294–95, 313
Frei, Hans, 44, 77
Freud, Sigmund, 62, 537
Fuller, Andrew, 263
Funk, Robert, 84

G

Gabler, Johann Philipp, 23
Gaffin, Richard, 372
Gandhi, Mahatma, 536
Garner, David, 336, 355
Gentry, Peter, 381, 464
George, Timothy, 561
Gibson, David, 227
Gill, John, 263, 702
Gogarten, Friedrich, 63–64

Goheen, Michael W., 396
Goldsworthy, Graeme, 121–22, 407–8, 432, 465, 930–32
Gould, Stephen Jay, 852
Graves, J. R., 487
Greene, J. C., 834
Gregory of Nazianzus, 698
Gregory of Nyssa, 698
Grenz, Stanley, 43, 96, 235, 249, 294–95
Griffin, David, 734–35
Groothuis, Douglas, 887, 914–15
Grosseteste, Robert, 806
Grotius, Hugo, 742
Grudem, Wayne, 8–9, 146, 622, 645, 713, 715
Gunton, Colin, 95

H

Haarsma, Deborah, 856
Hall, A. R., 840
Harnack, Adolf von, 36, 58, 60, 139, 558, 687
Hartshorne, Charles, 544, 733
Harvey, Van A., 56–57
Hasker, William, 640
Hays, Richard, 118
Hebert, Gabriel, 121
Hegel, Georg, 60, 544, 844
Heidegger, Martin, 64
Helm, Paul, 642, 902
Herrmann, Wilhelm, 60
Hick, John, 536
Hodge, A. A., 62, 220, 256, 258, 263
Hodge, Charles, 8–9, 62, 256, 264, 500, 806
Hoekema, Anthony, 476
Hooykaas, R., 841
Horton, Michael, 78, 116–17, 200, 249, 305, 500, 502–3, 505, 508–10, 749, 813, 869
Hoskins, Paul, 127
Hume, David, 46–47, 729, 914
Humphreys, Colin J., 811
Huxley, Thomas, 789

I

Ignatius, 385, 793
Irenaeus, 259, 361, 385–86, 791, 793, 802, 863
Issler, Klaus, 711

J

Jeeves, Malcolm A., 811
Jensen, Peter, 176, 280
Jerome, 376, 382
John of Damascus, 193
Johnson, Keith, 699
Josephus, 317, 366, 375–76
Jowett, Benjamin, 52
Junius, Franciscus, 195
Justin Martyr, 259, 385, 791, 863

K

Kaiser, Walter, 463
Kant, Immanuel, 43, 46–47, 64, 66–68, 70, 73, 90, 537, 580
Keach, Benjamin, 263, 520
Kelly, Douglas, 194, 807
Kepler, Johannes, 839, 841
Kline, Meredith, 275, 500, 505, 508, 806, 823
Knight, George W., 294
Krahmalkov, Charles, 316
Kreider, Glenn, 487
Kruger, Michael, 269, 370, 383–84
Kuyper, Abraham, 10, 62, 220, 263–64, 319, 662

L

Ladd, George, 175
Lake, Kirsopp, 256, 265
Lane, William, 114–15
Leibniz, Gottfried, 46
Leigh, Edward, 650–51
Lessing, Gotthold, 53
Letham, Robert, 765–66
Leucippus, 789
Levering, Matthew, 692–93
Lewis, C. S., 18
Lienhard, J. T., 369
Limborch, Philip, 742
Lindbeck, George, 60, 77, 116
Lints, Richard, 126–27, 129
Lisle, Jason, 802
Little, Bruce, 927–28
Locke, John, 46
Lucas, Ernest C., 811
Luther, Martin, 34, 40, 257, 261, 308, 353, 374, 864
Lyotard, Jean-François, 66, 71

M

Machen, J. Gresham, 63, 76, 220, 263, 265
Mackie, J. L., 914
Macleod, Donald, 700, 907
Macrobius, 317
Madueme, Hans, 817
Maier, Gerhard, 362
Manly, Basil Jr., 263
Marcion, 384–85
Martin, Michael, 914

Marx, Karl, 62, 71, 537
Mathews, Ken, 809
May, Gerhard, 786
McCormack, Bruce L., 198
McGowan, Andrew T. B., 294
McGrath, Alister, 43
McIntosh, Andy, 848
McKim, Donald, 256–58, 260, 264
Melanchthon, Philip, 864
Menander, 379
Miley, John, 742
Miller, Hugh, 806
Miller, Stanley, 847
Mohler, R. Albert, Jr., 313
Moltmann, Jürgen, 545, 793–94
Moo, Douglas, 388
Moody, D. L., 487
Moreland, J. P., 710, 836
Morgan, Christopher, 666, 783
Morris, Leon, 388
Morris, Thomas, 637, 641–42
Motyer, Alec, 464, 889
Muhammad, 271
Müller, George, 487
Muller, Richard, 598, 615, 657, 661, 689
Murray, John, 220, 363, 500, 512, 662

N

Nabonidus, 316
Nash, Ronald, 214
Newton, Benjamin, 487
Newton, Isaac, 50, 843
Nietzsche, Friedrich, 62, 70, 90, 405, 537, 669

O

Ogden, Schubert, 734
Olson, Roger, 773
Oord, Thomas, 549, 554, 918
Origen, 376, 382, 386–87, 696, 790–91, 802, 863
Owen, John, 29, 257, 500, 655, 691, 723, 766

P

Packer, J. I., 16, 82, 179, 222, 250, 360, 370, 541, 660, 663, 665, 668
Pagels, Elaine, 367
Pannenberg, Wolfhart, 94, 174, 545
Papias, 385
Parker, Brent, 131
Paul of Samosata, 695
Pearcey, Nancy, 412–13, 839–42, 844
Pentecost, J. Dwight, 487
Philo, 366, 375, 380, 580, 678
Pictet, Benedict, 337
Pinnock, Clark, 189, 202, 555, 561, 564
Plantinga, Alvin, 90, 552, 768, 845
Plato, 585, 598, 650, 841
Plotinus, 580, 790
Polycarp, 385
Poythress, Vern, 488, 812, 855
Pratt, Richard L., Jr., 501, 515, 527
Preus, Robert, 261
Provan, Iain, 355, 371

R

Rahner, Karl, 545, 707
Ramsay, William, 316
Raup, David, 852
Rauschenbusch, Walter, 60
Reid, Thomas, 264
Reimarus, Herman, 43, 53, 55, 58
Rice, Richard, 548–49, 557–58
Ritschl, Albrecht, 49, 58, 60
Robertson, O. Palmer, 505
Robinson, Donald, 121
Rogers, Jack, 256–58, 260, 264
Rosner, Brian, 22
Ross, Hugh, 806
Rousseau, Jean-Jacques, 51
Rowe, C. Kavin, 687
Royce, Josiah, 834
Ryrie, Charles, 487, 495

S

Sagan, Carl, 789
Sandeen, Ernest, 258
Sanders, Fred, 686
Sanders, John, 563–64, 566
Sargon, 316
Saucy, Robert, 370, 487, 498
Schaeffer, Francis, 41, 81–82, 395, 404, 539, 582, 647
Schelling, Friedrich, 844
Schleiermacher, Friedrich, 7, 49, 60, 92, 174, 197
Schreiner, Tom, 291, 432, 760, 777
Schweitzer, Albert, 58
Scofield, C. I., 487
Sennacherib, 316
Shapere, Dudley, 841
Shedd, W. G. T., 806
Shelton, R. Larry, 742
Silliman, Benjamin, 806
Simon, Richard, 53, 262–63

Sire, James, 50
Smalley, Paul, 328, 613, 615, 621–22, 755, 768, 787, 815, 821, 823
Smith, George, 914
Sonderegger, Katherine, 233–35
Sparks, Kenton, 190, 241, 246, 249, 296, 328
Spinoza, Baruch, 46, 53, 543, 581, 790, 844
Spurgeon, Charles, 28
Storms, Sam, 608, 623–24, 633
Strauss, David, 58
Swain, Scott, 468, 693, 705, 721, 763, 766–67

T

Tacitus, 317
Talshir, Ziporah, 376
Tatian, 385
Taylor, Charles, 32–33, 66, 68–69, 538
Tempier, Etienne, 843
Tertullian, 193, 259, 791, 793, 802
Thaxton, Charles, 839–42, 844
Theophilus of Antioch, 791, 802
Thomas Aquinas, 43, 194, 261, 268, 361, 601, 611, 619, 691, 806, 864–65
Thompson, Mark, 245–46, 337, 350–52, 354, 363
Tiessen, Terrance, 211
Tillich, Paul, 545
Trobisch, David, 386
Troeltsch, Ernst, 56–57, 76
Trueman, Carl, 18–19
Turretin, Francis, 257, 262, 298, 500, 655, 907

U

Urey, Harold, 847
Ursinus, Zachary, 499

V

Vanhoozer, Kevin, 68, 74, 110, 126, 128, 178, 184, 186, 231, 297, 312–13, 324–25, 359–60, 545, 550, 561–62, 606
Van Til, Cornelius, 84–85, 101–2, 220, 323, 348
Venema, Cornelis, 506, 508–9
Vos, Geerhardus, 25, 62, 121–22, 175, 220, 500, 587, 628, 649, 662, 751–52, 759, 766, 777, 799, 819, 872–73

W

Waltke, Bruce, 323–24
Walton, John, 819
Walvoord, John, 487, 495
Ware, Bruce, 487, 611, 713–17
Warfield, B. B., 6, 62, 220, 223–24, 256, 258, 263, 287, 292–93, 296, 298–99, 304, 500
Waters, Guy, 245, 313
Watkin, Christopher, 399, 403, 412, 416
Watson, Francis, 93
Webb, William J., 243, 342
Webster, John, 6, 8, 178, 180, 296, 299, 561–62, 606, 674, 786, 795, 797–98, 800–801, 868–69
Weinandy, Thomas, 616, 800
Wellhausen, Julius, 806
Wells, David, xvi, 32, 79, 394, 426, 538–41, 590
Wesley, John, 742
Whitaker, William, 261–62
Whitehead, Alfred N., 544, 733
White, James, 528
Wiley, H. Orton, 742
Williams, Garry, 422
Williams, Michael D., 113
Williamson, Paul, 466
Wilson, Doug, 515
Winckler, Hugo, 315
Witsius, Herman, 500
Wolterstorff, Nicholas, 96–97, 237, 305–6
Woodbridge, John, 258, 260
Wrede, William, 58
Wright, David, 308
Wright, G. E., 174
Wright, N. T., 36, 245

Y

Yeago, David, 687
Young, E. J., 220, 311, 321–22

Z

Zwingli, Ulrich, 40, 499, 864

SUBJECT INDEX

A

Abel, 331, 379, 816
Abraham, 123–24, 158, 434, 453–57, 459, 518, 875
    children of, 124, 472, 483
accommodation, 166, 240, 244–45, 257, 260, 325–26, 337, 562–63, 812, 814
actualism, 197–98, 227
Adam, 131–32, 158, 170, 203, 217, 410–11, 416–17, 438, 440, 447–48, 450, 503–4, 506, 524, 531, 827, 904–7
    headship, 407, 411, 415, 417, 434, 442–44, 504, 750, 807, 816–18
    historicity, 181, 813–18, 858
adoption, 190, 477, 682, 734
adoptionism, 695, 793
affection, 615–17
agnosticism, 46, 542
allegory, 128, 361, 805, 813
already-not-yet, 132, 424, 438, 473–74, 476–78, 498
Amyrauldianism, 779–81
analogical language, 103–4, 329, 562–64, 579, 593, 610, 612, 617, 624–25
analogy of Scripture, 355
analytic theology, 27
Angel of the Lord, 167, 678–79
angels, 64, 67, 99, 381, 406, 447, 570, 581, 627–28, 677–78, 728, 806, 821, 824, 863, 875, 878, 892, 910, 936
animism, 403–4, 412, 584, 839, 844
Anselm, ontological argument, 194
anthropology, 51, 61–63, 92, 197–98, 328, 405, 411, 537, 690, 830, 834
Apocrypha, 38, 366–67, 374, 376, 379–82
apologetics, 20, 26–27, 266, 269, 396, 909
apophatic theology, 98–99
apostles, 159, 168, 178, 222, 279–80, 283–85, 383
Apostles' Creed, 794
apostolic letters, 385
apostolic succession, 37–38, 40, 343, 347, 361–62
application, 8, 10, 13–14, 17, 21, 28, 137, 146, 148, 341–42
appropriated discourse, 96–97, 237
Arianism, 687, 694–97, 701–2
Arians, 138–39, 143, 696–97
Aristotle, 799, 839, 842–43, 907
Arius, 695–97
ark of the covenant, 667
Arminianism, 40, 554, 614, 741–48, 759, 768–81, 866, 872, 877
Arminius, Jacob, 741–42, 865–66
assurance, 146, 565, 630–31, 644–45
atemporal eternalism, 636–37
Athanasius, 43, 193, 365, 382, 387, 698, 701, 791
atheism, 24, 542
atonement, 37, 421, 423, 460, 462, 600, 673, 741
    governmental theory, 742
    satisfaction theory, 39
attribute
    accidental, 595, 599
    essential, 418, 585, 595, 599
attributes of God, 14, 86, 160, 212, 398, 418, 589, 593–96, 598, 648, 668, 674, 689
    aseity, 14, 87, 151, 162, 399, 548–49, 563, 583, 585, 587, 604–7, 633, 649

classification of, 602–3
eternality, 618–22
immanence, 86, 538, 544–45, 578–81, 620, 822
immensity, 622
immutability, 585, 607–13
impassibility, 613–18
incomprehensibility, 98–102
omnipotence, 627–31
omnipresence, 620, 622–27
omniscience, 87, 91, 554–56, 558, 585–86, 631–34, 644–45
self-sufficient, 402, 585, 598, 605, 683, 786, 796
simplicity, 14, 87, 212, 401, 548–49, 584–85, 596–601, 673–74, 683
singularity, 14, 401, 584, 596, 673, 683
transcendence, 86, 540, 578–81, 586, 620, 623, 822

audience, 12
Augustine, 259–60
epistemological argument, 333
authorial intent, 111, 118, 128, 237, 296, 325, 328
authority, 18–19, 36–38, 83, 158, 168, 249, 269–73, 337, 360, 718

B

baptism, 490, 501, 507–8, 516–18, 525, 528–29
credobaptism, 490
paedobaptism, 490, 510–11, 514, 516
Baptist, xvii, 220, 265, 500, 509, 511, 519–20, 601, 749
Baptist Faith and Message, The, 221, 264, 312
Barth, Karl, 24, 63–65, 197–200, 225–33
beatific vision, 625–26
Belgic Confession, 102, 263, 500
belief, 32–34, 46, 50, 60
Bible, 154–55
storyline, 11–12, 17, 116, 120, 134, 393–96, 424, 431, 484, 679, 818, 833–34, 886, 925
biblical criticism, 52–55, 57, 806
biblical exposition, 28, 878, 888
biblical theology, 8, 17, 22–25, 108, 115–16, 184, 394, 431
evangelical, 25
Biblical Theology Movement, 24, 139, 174
biblicism, 19
Boyd, Gregory, 239–41

C

Cain, 448
calling, 156, 443, 760
Calvinism, 40, 741, 748–53, 759
Calvinist-Arminian debates, 143–44
canon, 22, 103, 111, 117, 125, 127, 168, 275, 277, 341, 365–68
closed, 340, 346, 367, 374, 376, 378, 382
criteria, 387–88
recognition of, 368–69, 372–73, 382–88
canonical self-consciousness, 274, 277, 286, 373, 386
causation, 187–88, 550–51, 553, 602, 638, 751, 756, 786, 799, 801, 865, 883, 890, 902–3
Chalcedonian Definition, 135, 687, 709, 794
Chicago Statement on Biblical Inerrancy, 220, 312
Christ
fulfillment in, 129–32, 134, 171, 175, 245, 278, 280–84, 330, 339–40, 342, 355, 400, 424, 432, 436–38, 441, 446–47, 450, 453, 455, 460, 468, 470–78, 485, 524, 526, 528, 531–32, 577, 653, 657, 681, 817
Redeemer, 420–21, 445, 449
two natures, 545, 580, 618, 709
type, 131–32
Christian life, 21, 28–29, 134, 148, 559, 627, 890–91
Christocentric theism, 197, 226–27
Christology, 10, 16, 20, 37–38, 40, 44, 51, 54–55, 84, 92–95, 135, 140–43, 179, 242, 246, 271, 305, 345, 394, 420–21, 423–24, 426–27, 474, 478, 520–21, 578, 580, 599–600, 655, 692, 695, 697, 706–9, 712, 775, 780
church, xv, 5, 7, 19, 28–29, 35, 37, 39, 41, 78, 81, 105, 132, 137, 284–85, 347, 352, 369–71, 384–85, 439, 455, 457, 460, 468, 471–72, 474, 476, 478–83, 486, 488–89, 492–97, 499, 501, 510, 527, 529, 538–39, 669, 721
beginning, 490, 501
bride of Christ, 483
invisible, 514, 517
nature of, 513–16, 522, 525, 527
visible, 514, 517
church councils, 20, 36, 38
circumcision, 123–24, 341, 456, 490, 501, 507, 516–17, 525, 529
heart, 457, 468, 478, 483, 518
classical foundationalism, 46, 362
classical theism, 546, 549, 556, 558, 560–62, 601–4
moderate, 614
classic liberalism, 24, 49, 59–65, 76, 92, 200
comfort, 630–31, 644–45
common grace, 141, 172, 210, 651, 661–63, 870
compassion, 613, 645, 651, 760, 884
compatibilism, 553, 635, 644, 752, 768, 770, 886, 898–99, 904
complementary hermeneutic, 494
concurrence, 870–73, 887–89, 901

concursus, 188, 299–300, 304, 775, 866
condemnation, 15, 193, 417, 448, 461, 504, 762–63
confessions, xvi, 20, 42, 70, 268, 309, 356, 500, 686, 794
confidence, 630–31, 777, 876, 929
conscience, 192, 195–97, 206–7
constructivism, 47–48, 66, 68, 74, 185, 334, 362, 658
consummation, 423–24, 447, 472, 489, 497, 531, 630
context, 12, 32, 79–80, 117–18, 125–26, 341, 437, 810
continuity, 438, 476, 480, 490, 496, 501, 507, 515–17, 527
contradictions, 47, 78, 145, 147, 229, 243, 328, 362, 564, 909, 915, 935
correlativism, 591
Council of Chalcedon, 139, 346
Council of Constantinople, 686, 696, 702
Council of Jamnia, 373
Council of Nicaea, 139, 346, 686, 696
Council of Trent, 347, 382
covenant community, 467–68, 501, 510–11, 516, 518, 526, 529, 760
covenant Lord, 86, 99
covenant mediator, 442, 458, 462–63, 466–67, 472, 503–4, 767
covenant of grace, 442, 451, 500, 504, 506–12, 516, 521–22, 524, 529
covenant of redemption, 156, 400, 436, 500, 502–3, 740, 764–68
covenant of works, 441–42, 500, 503–6, 510, 521, 524
covenants, xvii, 23, 103, 120–21, 123, 127, 131, 133, 172, 274–76, 373, 431–32, 434, 436–43, 449, 471–73, 485–86, 488, 497, 500, 502, 507, 524, 531–32, 573–74, 577, 653, 760, 767
  Abrahamic, 123, 133, 158, 341, 436, 453–57, 459, 462–63, 492, 494, 497–98, 511–12, 517, 529–30
  book of the, 277
  conditionality, 439–40, 457, 509–10, 522, 531
  creation, 432, 436, 441–52, 454, 459
  Davidic, 377, 436, 455, 459, 462–65, 494, 498
  fulfillment in new, 439
  Law, 124–25, 158, 170, 175, 341, 429, 454, 458–59, 461, 482
  Mosaic, 123–24, 133, 341, 436, 446, 455–56, 458, 505–6, 523, 608
  new, 7, 121, 123–24, 133, 277, 284, 341, 383, 411, 421–22, 435–39, 451, 455, 465–70, 474, 492, 494, 498–99, 507–9, 516, 522, 524, 527–30, 577, 608, 653, 683
  Noahic, 436, 439, 452–53, 663, 729, 869–70
  old, 458–62
  Sinai, 458
covenant signs, 123–24, 341, 501, 516–18, 528
covenant theology, 436, 441–42, 454, 486, 490, 499–502, 507, 509, 513, 519, 523–32
creation, 14, 31, 87, 141, 160, 164, 192–93, 200, 203–4, 208–9, 396–405, 412–14, 417, 450, 524, 577, 606, 621, 630, 660, 676, 785–88, 794–800, 833–34
  analogical day view, 806
  day-age view, 806, 824
  ex nihilo, 786, 800–805, 819–20, 828, 831, 841
  framework view, 806, 823
  gap view, 806, 820–22
  Genesis 1-2, 805–16, 818–27, 857–58
  goodness, 413, 433, 832, 838, 905–6
  historical narrative, 810–17
  mytho-history, 812–13
  old earth, 806
  young earth, 805
creation mandate, 406, 409, 443, 445–46, 452, 831
creator-creature distinction, 14, 61, 86, 138, 144, 162, 299, 398–99, 427, 544–45, 563, 578, 593, 609, 679, 683, 722, 727, 786, 801, 822, 828, 838–39, 901–3
crisis theology, 63
critical theory, 34, 71, 185
cross, the, 240, 565–66, 665, 927
cultural relativism, 185
culture, 21, 538–39

D

David, 120, 122–23, 131–33, 167, 203, 271, 277–78, 295, 316, 328, 331–32, 377, 434–36, 438–40, 444, 446, 453–54, 462–66, 469, 471–73, 493–94, 506–7, 526–27, 529, 573, 623, 627, 630, 668, 678, 680–81, 687, 730, 736–37, 756, 874, 932
Davidic king, 132–33, 276, 377, 435, 444, 455–57, 459, 462–65, 471–72, 475–76, 489–90, 498, 564, 677, 680
Dead Sea Scrolls, 323, 367, 380
death, 409, 415, 448, 461, 504, 817
Decalogue, 224, 486, 519, 523
deconstruction, 68
defense, xvii, 6, 10, 13, 134, 138–39, 147–48, 184, 215, 267, 272, 311, 488, 511, 516, 535, 558, 578, 877–78, 887, 893, 896–97, 911, 914, 916–20, 929

deism, 50–52, 83, 86, 543, 796
Derrida, Jacques, 70–71
Descartes, René, 45–46
desires, 51, 69, 140, 158, 202, 207, 212–13, 417, 461, 549, 551–54, 556, 564, 630, 635, 719, 735, 742–43, 745–46, 752, 756, 768–70, 774–75, 866, 872, 875, 886, 889, 898–99, 901, 904–5, 907
determinism, 550–51, 553
  theological, 551, 553
dialectical presence, 153, 173
dialectical theology, 63–64, 580
Diatesseron, 385
disciples, 5, 282, 284, 478–79, 482, 919
discontinuity, 132, 438, 476, 490, 493, 496, 508, 522
dispensationalism, 487–93, 495, 498–99, 501, 510, 519, 524, 526–27, 530
  classic, 491–93
  progressive, 494–99
  traditional, 493–95
dispensational theology, xvii, 137, 436–37, 454, 486–88, 490–91, 513, 519, 523–32
dispensations, 436, 485, 487–88, 491–93, 496
divine economy, 189, 192, 285, 347, 354, 562, 574, 675, 685, 764
divine freedom, 199, 230, 233, 247
divine missions, 202, 686, 692, 698, 705, 720
divine permission, 875, 882, 884–85, 903–4, 916
divine processions, 177, 606, 674, 686, 692, 699, 719, 727, 740, 796, 868
divine speech, 7, 87–89, 101, 152, 154, 158, 160, 166–70, 217, 294, 829
docetism, 413, 793
doctrine, 17, 135, 138, 153
Documentary Hypothesis, 806
dogmatic theology, 6
dual agency, 189, 224, 299, 553, 565–66, 866, 872, 882, 887, 889, 891–92, 901, 903, 908
dualism, 578, 790, 792, 829

E

Eastern Orthodox Church, 36
ectypal theology, 99
Eden, 122, 170, 409, 417, 434–35, 446–47, 459–60, 471, 491, 530–31, 577, 808–9, 827, 918, 926
efficient causation, 300, 735, 799
election, 434, 459, 554, 661, 737–41, 757–62, 776, 779–81, 863, 890–91, 934–35
  conditional, 643, 744, 747
  unconditional, 750, 758–59, 761, 891
elect, the, 480, 501, 661
Elohim, 571–72, 677–78, 806–7
empirical investigation, 842–43, 869
empiricism, 46–47
Enlightenment, the, 23–24, 31–33, 41–54, 57–59, 79, 83, 110, 196
Enns, Peter, 243–44
Epicureanism, 861–62
epistemology, 45–49, 67–71
  revelational, 44, 67, 88–89
Esau, 315, 456, 760
eschatology, 414, 424
  consummated, 478
  inaugurated, 424–25, 473–78, 486, 494, 515, 525–28
eternal generation, 574, 702, 718–19
eternal life, xi, 39, 177, 335–36, 424, 442, 475, 478, 493, 503–4, 574, 594, 619, 763, 891
eternal relational authority submission trinitarianism (ERAS), 713–20
eternal security, 741
ethics, 13, 17, 26–27, 42, 50, 67, 84, 90, 137, 185–86, 241, 334, 349, 396, 403, 426, 428–29, 486, 584, 591, 603, 722–23, 830–31, 845
Eunomians, 697
evangelicalism, xvi, 63, 235, 389, 541, 547, 570
evangelicals, xv, 3, 25, 96, 108, 121, 200, 220, 235, 255–56, 265, 311, 485–86, 519, 532, 814
Evangelical Theological Society, 312
evangelical theology, 20, 29, 73, 81, 85, 97, 105, 116, 121, 189, 220, 225, 235–36, 311, 313, 368, 454, 478, 485–86, 519, 525, 536, 546–48, 553, 568, 578, 592, 601, 614, 673, 706–8, 713, 725, 741, 753, 815, 866–67, 877, 897
evangelism, 216, 756, 909, 930, 934–35
Eve, 331, 348, 448, 450, 815–17, 827, 830–31, 833, 857–58, 904
evil, 434, 447, 751, 762, 817, 829, 863, 878, 881, 884, 886, 905
  moral, 883, 885, 910
  natural, 817, 883, 885, 910
evolution, 72, 181–82, 544–45, 789, 826, 830, 833–36, 845–51, 853–58, 867
evolutionary theory, 61, 72, 348, 789, 793, 833–36, 844–47, 850–51, 853–54
exegesis, 20, 22, 82, 97, 108, 111–12, 118, 126, 134, 147, 237–38, 249, 295, 302, 519, 686
exegetical theology, 22
existentialism, 409
exodus, 170, 174, 434, 460–61
extrabiblical language, 138–42, 687, 689

F

faith, 40, 123–24, 158, 195, 339, 423, 451, 457, 477, 510, 518, 537
    saving, 202, 211, 213–14, 344, 750, 780, 870
faith seeking understanding, xi, 10, 20, 108, 134, 194, 198, 602, 686, 893, 896
fallenness, 246, 416, 541, 885
fall, the, 101–2, 178, 191, 217, 246, 397, 411, 413–18, 433–34, 447–50, 471, 505, 577, 808–9, 817–18, 858, 904, 907–8
    historicity, 415–16, 815
fatalism, 551, 861
figures of speech, 327, 329, 564
filiation, 177, 674, 699, 704, 718, 795
filioque clause, 37–38, 202, 703
flood, 131, 271, 331, 448, 452, 491, 809, 817, 825, 835, 858, 870, 910, 918, 920
foreknowledge, 556, 633–45, 739, 743–44, 747, 758–59, 775–78, 863, 877
    simple, 638
foreordination, 425, 635, 737, 753, 771–72, 863, 866, 908
forgiveness, 52, 417–18, 421, 449, 452, 460, 465, 468, 470, 473, 498, 506, 515, 525, 527–29, 664–65, 680–81
fossil record, 821, 851–53
Franke, John, 235–39
Fuller Seminary, 63, 312
Fundamentalist-Modernist controversies, 62–63, 256

G

genealogical principle, 454, 512, 527, 529
genealogies, 377, 448, 810, 815, 824
genetic code, 854–55
Gentiles, 123–25, 203–7, 212, 352, 457, 466, 473, 478–83, 488–89, 495–97, 513, 525–27, 531, 755
glorification, 171, 213, 306, 477–78, 481, 525, 528, 603, 625–26, 754, 771, 777, 781, 783, 876, 906, 933
Gnostic Gospels, 367
Gnosticism, 414–15, 580, 790–93, 799, 832, 838
God
    absolute, 582–86
    actions, 17, 164–65, 170, 174–75, 177–78, 726–30, 751–52, 797–98, 867
    authority, 575–76, 582
    being, 160
    character, 15, 332, 607–8
    conceptions of, 541–46
    creator, 86, 156, 401–2, 433, 540
    decree, 400, 553, 573, 725, 727–28, 736–37, 740, 750, 753–57, 762–64, 767, 771, 778–84, 833, 865, 874, 880–81, 899–901, 908
    decree, conditional, 747
    doctrine of, 535, 540–41
    eternal, 535, 582, 673, 679, 829
    existence, 542, 597, 621, 922–23
    faithfulness, 231, 532, 645
    glory, 171, 399, 542–43, 575, 606, 665–70, 682, 721, 754–55, 783, 797, 829, 919–22
    goodness, 585, 649–51, 664, 829, 878, 883–85
    holiness, 402, 427, 586–90, 624, 649–51, 659, 829
    identity, 17, 402, 569, 573, 680
    invisible, 625
    judge, 156, 207, 422, 652, 654
    king, 433–34
    knowledge, xi, 204–5, 546–47, 549, 555–56, 582, 754–55, 862
    law, 428–29
    Lord, 401–2, 433, 540, 565, 571–73, 575–77
    love, 212, 411, 548–49, 557, 587, 600, 603, 649, 651, 659–62, 664–65, 758, 763, 776–77
    name, 160, 571–72, 671, 807
    nature of, 152, 162, 177, 332, 418, 574–75, 594, 607, 689, 698
    perfection, 584, 598, 602, 617, 829
    personal, 86, 156, 221, 403–4, 573, 582–86, 722
    presence, 166–67, 212–13, 576–77, 579–80, 667, 868
    "problem" of, 536–40
    promises, 116, 123, 127, 172, 176, 248, 280, 330, 419–20, 423, 438, 440–41, 447, 449–50, 457, 480–82, 524, 573, 608, 654
    providence, 136, 160, 178–79, 292, 296, 304, 372, 565, 586, 630, 785, 801, 827, 833, 867–68
    pure act, 608–9
    relationality, 548–49
    repentance, 556–57, 562, 564, 609–10, 746
    rest, 827
    righteousness, 203, 457, 460–62, 518, 650–57, 761
    sovereignty, 14, 86, 99, 136, 145–46, 156–57, 165, 171, 180, 247, 401, 434, 476, 540, 554, 566, 575, 586, 614, 744, 754, 761, 828–29, 862, 873–74, 878–84, 887–92, 908, 927
    spirit nature, 597, 623–24
    supremacy, xvi, 697

truthfulness, 645–47
will, 157, 188, 402, 421, 628–30, 738, 750, 754, 770, 797, 862–63, 874–75, 931
wisdom, 647–48, 754–55
works, 162, 335, 617, 699, 726–27, 795
wrath, 16, 203–5, 448, 547, 588, 613, 650, 661, 664, 762, 885, 889
God-world relationship, 179–81, 186–90, 224, 246–47, 303–4, 398, 578, 614, 734, 828, 909
Goldsworthy, Graeme, 121–22, 407–8, 432, 930–32
gospel, 12, 14, 28–29, 39, 175–76, 339, 344, 358, 505–6, 524
Gospels, 53, 59, 93, 175, 260–61, 271, 301, 326, 328–29, 352–53, 384–87, 707, 810
government, 193, 343, 422, 435, 491, 514, 519, 600, 653, 663, 740, 742, 837, 867–68, 873–75, 877, 888, 892, 895
grace, 15, 38, 40, 61, 209, 419, 451, 459, 575, 651, 659–60, 662–65, 741, 759, 762, 774, 907
prevenient, 743–44, 759, 773–74
saving, 165, 178, 193, 202, 577, 662–63
grammatical-literary-historical exegesis, 111, 118
great commandment, 205–7, 407
Great Commission, 5, 471, 682
Great Schism (1054), 35, 38, 703
Greek, 15, 139–40, 154, 319, 324, 329–30, 365, 375, 414, 558, 560, 572, 586, 601, 609, 613, 687, 689, 774, 789, 800, 803, 838, 841, 861
Grenz, Stanley, 235–39

H

harmonization, 326
heart transformation, 452
Hebrew, 119, 139, 154, 319, 323, 376, 378–79, 408, 432, 443, 572, 586, 651, 669, 739
Heidelberg Catechism, 500, 749
hermeneutical non-realism, 74
hermeneutical realism, 74
hermeneutics, 52–57, 73–75, 295–96, 324–26, 357–58
historical criticism, 55–57, 83, 182–85, 362, 813
historical theology, 19, 25–26, 345–46, 356
history, 18–19, 54, 56, 80, 153, 164, 401, 425, 788, 791
holiness, 16, 21, 217, 298, 402, 417–18, 448, 470, 504, 510, 535, 547, 556, 583, 586–91, 595, 598–600, 602–3, 607, 612, 624, 626–27, 644, 648–53, 655, 659–60, 662, 665, 668, 674, 721, 829, 863, 884, 892
Holy Spirit, 97, 136, 157, 159, 178, 195, 209, 213, 238–39, 278–79, 284–85, 290–92, 299, 346, 352, 354, 357–60, 383, 420, 462, 465, 467, 472, 476–79, 481–83, 490, 530, 597, 624, 673, 677, 681, 684
homology, 854–55
homoousios, 138, 384, 595, 599, 686, 696, 698, 710, 712, 720
homosexuality, 21, 205, 210, 429
hope, 423, 425, 435, 466, 630–31, 645
human depravity, 15, 62, 447, 773
human dignity, 51, 206, 217, 272, 404, 406, 453, 584, 788, 830–31, 870
human dominion, 407–9, 444, 450
human experience, 8, 49, 60, 75, 96, 176, 251, 537, 700
human freedom, 140–41, 145–46, 157, 188, 248, 550–51, 553–56, 558, 566, 634–45, 743, 752–53, 768–73, 863, 866, 877–78, 882, 885–92, 898, 904–5, 912, 916–19
humanity, 405–11, 692
difference from creation, 406, 830
male and female, 409–10, 830
human nature, 10, 26, 48, 68, 84, 99, 135, 140, 162–63, 179, 197, 242, 246, 280, 409, 411, 415–16, 427, 578, 580, 599, 618, 626, 667, 692, 694, 704–5, 709, 711, 743, 777, 832
human problem, 11, 14, 21, 83, 397, 413–19, 445, 449, 831
human responsibility, 14–15, 415, 443, 552, 554, 745–46, 770, 818, 885, 899, 907, 928
human sexuality, 21, 185, 410, 429
humility, 644, 663
hypostatic union, 99, 179, 246

I

identity thesis, 187, 221
idolatry, 12, 203, 205–6, 209, 542, 597, 605, 787, 830, 931
illumination, 85, 136, 178, 196, 215, 297, 300, 302, 343, 346, 351–52, 357–60, 372
image of God, 14–15, 91, 99, 165, 336, 406–7, 409, 429, 443–44, 678, 830–31, 842, 858
inauguration, 121, 125, 133, 284, 424, 436, 441, 454, 471–72, 476–77, 501, 731
inclusivism, 39, 172, 200–202, 211–14, 548, 703, 742
indeterminism, 550–51, 898, 905
inductive principle, 839
inerrancy, 96, 225, 229, 236, 256–63, 269, 283, 311–15, 324–34, 567
definition, 314–15
precision, 327–28
infallibility, 187, 221, 225, 229, 232, 252, 257, 263, 311–13, 327, 333, 336, 356, 567, 576, 900

infralapsarianism, 748, 779–81
inheritance, 455, 476–77, 491–92, 526, 880
inner experience, 153
inspiration, 111–12, 173, 176, 178, 182, 219, 232–34, 240, 252, 283, 285–86, 289–310, 319, 333, 338, 359, 370, 775
  concursive, 188–89, 224, 298–300, 303
  dictation, 298, 303–4
  dynamic, 298
  illumination, 298
  intuition, 298
  verbal-plenary, 223–24, 283, 301, 311
interpretation, 9, 11, 109, 111, 115–26, 134, 291, 302, 324–26, 342, 353, 355
  allegorical, 113, 360–61
  authorial-discourse, 237
  literal sense, 361
  textual-sense, 237–38
interpretive framework, 9, 13, 113, 134, 142, 177, 344, 348, 393–94, 426, 431, 483, 485
irreducible complexity, 850–51
Isaac, 133, 454–56, 459, 498, 572, 755, 760, 875
Ishmael, 456
Islam, 143, 200, 270–72, 367, 421, 580–81, 672, 789, 925
Israel, 131–32, 158, 163, 275, 434–35, 444, 454–56, 459–60, 462, 465–66, 468, 479–80, 482, 488–89, 492–93, 496, 498–99, 501, 510, 513–14, 530, 759–60
  national, 489–90
Israel-church relationship, 486, 488–91, 497, 499, 509, 522, 524–26, 528

J

Jacob, 167, 456, 459, 498, 572, 634, 678, 760, 888
Jesus
  ascension, 630
  baptism, 472, 681
  death, 422, 630, 738, 755, 889–90
  divinity, 420, 427, 679, 683, 695, 697
  first coming, 475
  fulfillment in, 114–15, 117–19, 122–23, 125, 128, 130–32, 134, 158, 160, 167, 175, 274, 283, 301, 340–42, 355, 400, 431–32, 436–37, 441, 446–47, 450, 461, 491, 494, 498–99, 522–23, 525, 531, 573, 653
  historical, 44, 54, 58–59
  humanity, 413, 416, 420, 427, 617–18, 681
  identity, 16, 53–54, 76, 84, 281, 426–27, 470, 472, 683
  incarnate Word, 31, 65, 103, 115, 155, 158, 160, 162, 167, 170, 174, 227, 243, 274, 280, 283–84, 335, 383, 420, 471, 667, 676
  incarnation, 99, 178, 244, 413, 422, 427, 444, 472, 578–79, 599, 630, 673, 681, 687, 704, 777, 818
  last Adam, 167, 411–12, 427, 438, 448–49, 471–72, 799, 816, 827
  life, 422, 471, 630
  mediator, 422
  miracles, 476
  obedience, 505
  prophet, 167
  resurrection, 15–16, 54, 94, 472, 477, 630, 732, 738, 832
  return, 424, 472, 475, 477, 479, 491, 495, 499, 515, 630
  sayings, 59
  sinless, 246, 775
  Son of God, 471, 676, 681
  sufficient work, 40
  teaching, 166, 278, 350–51, 378–79, 476, 816
  temptation, 278
  true Israel, 472
  works, 284, 470–72, 510, 667, 681
Jews, 12, 123–25, 262–63, 365, 375, 380, 457, 466, 473, 478–83, 489, 495–97, 513, 525–27, 531, 748, 774, 882
John the Baptist, 281, 492
Judaizers, 121, 123–25
judgment, 15, 158, 160, 165, 171, 192, 207, 212, 418–19, 423, 448, 452, 465, 630, 664, 763, 809, 883, 885
  final, 15, 203
justice, 213, 588–89, 651–57, 664–65
  distributive, 653
  legislative, 652
  remunerative, 653–54
  retributive, 654–55, 664
justification, 39, 123, 344, 421–22, 451, 469, 477, 510, 589, 600, 657, 665

K

Kant, Immanuel, 47–48
kenosis, 545, 549, 709
kingdom, 122–23, 351, 408, 432, 436, 454–56, 459, 474, 480, 482, 490, 492–95, 497, 499, 669, 701, 830
kingdom of God, 12, 61, 133, 325, 408–9, 414, 419–20, 424–25, 432–36, 445, 452–53, 461, 464, 469–76, 478–79, 493, 495–96, 669, 681, 683, 833, 876, 879
kingdom of heaven, 281, 493, 495

kingdom of this world, 453
knowledge, 5, 54, 66–67, 88, 91, 100, 144–47, 151, 222, 344–45, 406
 of God, 5, 7, 14, 27–28, 35, 91, 99, 101, 103–4, 148, 151, 162, 197–200, 208–9, 217, 339, 344, 354, 478, 594, 667, 685, 830
 saving, 192–93, 201–2, 210–14

L

land, 120, 434–35, 447, 455–56, 459–60, 477, 492, 494–95, 526, 530–31, 823, 826, 882
land promise, 119, 454, 456, 489–90, 494–95, 498, 510, 525–26, 530–31
Law, 207, 275, 350, 429, 461, 505–6, 524, 655
law-gospel, 440, 505
laws of nature, 50, 299, 413, 550, 630, 729–30, 756, 802, 840, 843, 916
Lessing, Gotthold, 53–55
Lessing's ugly ditch, 54, 76–78, 88
libertarianism, 550–52, 554, 565, 635–36, 639, 735, 743, 745–46, 752, 768–73, 775, 778, 872, 886, 898
logic, 26, 91, 138, 142, 144, 211, 271–72, 404, 933
logocentrism, 68, 70, 90
love, xv, xvii, 21, 98, 103–4, 136, 158, 177, 188, 198, 205, 212, 216, 399–400, 402, 405, 408, 411, 417–18, 429, 448, 459, 531, 535, 537, 539–41, 543, 547–49, 554, 556–57, 561–62, 582, 586–92, 594, 598–600, 603, 606, 612–13, 616–17, 629, 644, 648–49, 651–53, 656, 659, 661, 663–64, 668–71, 674, 682–83, 685, 704, 706, 708–9, 721, 723, 727, 739, 751, 758, 763, 768, 770–71, 776–77, 787, 791, 794–95, 797, 829, 832, 884, 906, 929, 935
 for God, 7, 27–28, 30, 105, 134, 143, 206–7, 407, 429, 554

M

Macedonianism, 697–98
marriage, 17, 21, 28, 39, 159, 206, 209–10, 341–42, 409–11, 428–29, 442, 447, 453, 663, 788, 816, 830, 874
Marxism, 410, 425
Masoretic text, 323
masters of suspicion, 62, 537
mathematics, 659, 840–42
McKim, Donald, 256–58, 260, 264
mental pole, 544, 733–34
mercy, 201, 211, 416, 505, 589, 611, 613, 645, 651, 659–60, 663–65, 751, 758, 760–62, 780, 882
Messiah, 12–13, 135, 175, 213, 273–74, 279–82, 291, 332, 388, 400, 427, 435, 460, 464, 467, 469–75, 477, 515, 526–27, 530, 677, 679–81, 759, 882, 891, 935
messianic expectation, 463
methodological naturalism, 24, 49–50, 56, 61, 68, 72, 83, 184, 253, 362, 543, 545, 658
middle knowledge, 586, 638, 640–43, 745, 775, 778, 866
millennium, 480, 489, 491–94, 499
miracles, 24, 48, 53, 55, 63–64, 165, 172, 187, 272, 412, 472, 543, 554, 729–32, 744, 862, 872, 910
missions, 216, 705
modalism, 140, 695–97, 701, 722
modernism, 42, 65–68, 71, 74–75, 77, 79, 235, 313, 449
modernity, 42, 46, 65, 73, 226, 364, 538–39
Molinism, 640–43
Monarchianism, 694–95
monergism, 37, 40, 440, 662, 750
monothelitism, 708–9
Montanists, 384–85
moral agents, 299, 737, 756, 866
moral subjectivism, 185
moral theology, 47
Mormon theology, 597
Moses, 120, 122, 125, 132–33, 160, 167–68, 271, 273, 275, 277–78, 295, 318–20, 331, 349, 351, 373, 376–78, 435, 438, 443, 453, 458–59, 473, 492, 557, 571–72, 588, 610, 669, 678, 730–31, 807, 810–11, 815, 827, 882, 933
Mt. Sinai, 163, 166, 588, 667
Muratorian list, 386–87
mystery, 37, 129, 145–47, 358, 479, 639, 643, 667, 671, 723, 755, 781, 884, 897, 900, 908–9, 912–13
myth, 58, 64, 181, 809–14, 835, 841, 850

N

Nag Hammadi Library, 367
nations, xv, 5, 29, 107, 125, 148, 396, 434–35, 439, 452, 454–57, 459, 462–63, 465, 471, 479–80, 482–83, 489, 491–94, 497–99, 508, 520, 525–26, 571, 573, 587, 657, 738, 777, 879, 889, 920
naturalism, 14, 24, 48–50, 56, 61, 64, 66, 68, 70–72, 75, 83, 184, 196, 251, 273, 362, 422, 543, 545, 578, 658, 734, 789, 814, 832, 835, 839, 845–46, 861, 867, 869, 895, 910, 924
naturalism, evolutionary, 66–68, 70, 83, 89–90, 253, 404, 414, 835
natural law, 71, 207, 215, 403, 729, 840, 843, 849, 872, 916–19
natural selection, 789, 845–48, 851, 853–54

natural theology, 52, 173, 195–98, 200, 214–16, 601
neo-Darwinism, 846
neo-liberal theologies, 76
neo-orthodoxy, 62–63, 153, 163, 173, 221, 225, 244–48, 250–51, 255, 303, 814
new awareness, 153
new creation, 133, 397, 409, 414, 421, 423–25, 434, 446, 455, 471–72, 477, 481, 531, 832, 870
new heavens and new earth, 424, 531, 827, 833, 876
New Perspective on Paul, 654, 656–57
New Testament, 154, 280, 283–86, 321, 324, 339, 351, 366, 370–72, 378–79, 382–88, 432, 474, 513, 566, 682, 687
    historical reliability, 316–17
Nicene Creed, 38, 686–88, 693, 697, 701, 703, 794
Nicodemus, 350
1689 Federalism, 520–23
Noah, 120, 123, 131, 133, 158, 271, 274, 331, 420, 434–35, 438, 440, 443, 452–54, 463, 469, 491, 506, 527, 529, 573, 680, 731, 807, 809, 858
non-foundationalism, 96, 235–39

O

obedience, 5, 158, 209, 287, 357, 389, 440–41, 452, 457, 461, 463–64, 504, 510, 532, 653–54, 661, 829
Old Testament, 112–13, 122–23, 276–84, 291, 293, 321, 339, 350, 366, 370, 373–82, 387, 496, 507, 675–76
    fulfillment, 113, 278–79, 283, 470
    historical reliability, 315–16
    quotation in the New, 301, 329, 331–32, 379
open theism, 73, 189, 240, 546–68, 574, 580, 601, 609, 613–14, 624, 635–36, 659, 742, 744, 746, 768, 772, 775, 796, 867, 886, 912, 918
Origen, 376, 380, 382, 386–87, 696, 790–91, 802, 863
original sin, 39, 51–52, 143, 349, 548
origins, 181–82, 348, 396, 405, 788–93, 836, 847–50

P

panentheism, 24, 61, 67, 72–73, 179, 196–97, 251–52, 267, 300, 362, 543–46, 548, 550, 554, 561–62, 574, 576, 578, 581, 601, 614, 623, 659, 706, 733–36, 742, 793–94, 796, 800, 814, 844, 861, 867–68, 895, 918–19
panpsychism, 545
pantheism, 14, 87, 404, 543–46, 576, 578, 581, 623, 733, 790, 796, 800, 838, 844, 861, 887
parables, 200, 223, 351–52, 810
passion, 38, 206, 569, 613, 615–17, 627, 647, 662
Passover, 460–61
paternity, 177, 574, 674, 698, 795
Patripassianism, 695
Paul, 5, 11–16, 21, 28–29, 77–78, 83, 102, 108, 118, 120, 123–25, 128, 203–7, 211–12, 215, 229, 274, 279–80, 283, 286, 292–95, 298, 321, 332, 339–42, 348, 352, 354, 357–58, 369, 379, 385–88, 396, 411, 429, 439, 445, 448, 453–54, 458, 479, 482, 526, 577, 597, 605, 654, 656–57, 663, 682, 755, 758–62, 772, 775, 777, 795, 804, 816, 861–62, 868, 871, 879–80, 882, 891–92, 921, 934–35
Pelagianism, 759, 773
penal substitution, 37, 40, 422, 439, 520, 548, 589, 600, 655, 657, 664, 740, 742, 831
Pentateuch, 53, 118, 125, 224, 275, 278, 295, 318, 373, 377, 379, 417, 443, 572, 810–11, 813, 815, 818
Pentecost, 12, 165, 178, 285, 327, 470, 473, 479, 482–83, 490, 501, 507, 624, 686, 732
people of God, 132, 169, 251–52, 349, 408, 434, 467, 474, 477–78, 480–81, 489, 495, 497–98, 514–15, 667, 923
perichoresis, 547, 699–700, 703–4, 706
personal experience, 7–8, 251, 363
perspicuity, 253, 302, 336, 349–63
phenomenological language, 327–28
philosophy, 11, 13, 25–28, 45–48, 64, 67–68, 70, 74, 82, 92, 137–38, 141, 159, 264, 267, 333–34, 344, 537, 558–59, 650, 687, 790, 834, 836, 841–42
plan, eternal, 8, 86, 88, 110, 114, 136, 152, 156, 171, 335, 395, 400–401, 423, 433, 437, 502–3, 541, 573, 608, 617, 725, 736–39, 753, 866, 879, 921–22
plan, redemptive, 113, 119, 121, 340, 431, 434, 436, 755, 807
plan, unfolding, 114–15, 119, 129
pluralism, 32–33, 61, 64, 76, 79, 96, 185, 536, 570, 590
pneumatological proposal, 202, 213
pneumatomachianism, 697–98
polytheism, 403, 542, 584
post-conservative theology, 77, 163, 185, 226, 235
post-liberalism, 77–78, 163, 233–35, 241, 260, 296, 312
postmodernism, 42, 62, 64–79, 83, 449, 538, 545
postmodern theology, 76, 153, 163, 179, 225, 244, 251–53, 322, 359, 544–45, 547, 613, 734, 736, 867

pragmatism, xvi, 68
prayer, xviii, 136, 235, 382, 556, 559, 610, 631, 668–69, 723, 747, 756, 909, 929–34
preaching, 12, 28, 179, 214, 228, 230, 247, 286, 541
predestination, 737, 749, 759, 776–77, 780, 863, 866, 880
premillennialism, 490–91
presentism, 636, 639
preservation, 408, 785, 801, 831–32, 862, 867–72, 875, 877, 880, 892, 895, 906, 919
presuppositions, 23–27, 52, 57, 83, 186–87, 396, 732, 836–37, 844
preterition, 762–63, 780
priesthood, Levitical, 460
priesthood of believers, 41
priests, kingdom of, 434, 455, 459–60
principle of alternative possibilities, 552–53
problem of evil, 143, 157, 188–89, 242, 300, 558, 565, 613, 643, 748, 756, 878, 884, 886–87, 893, 896–97, 909–29
process theism, 544, 733–35, 743, 793
progressive covenantalism, xvii, 120–21, 123, 431–32, 436, 451, 483, 486, 519–21, 523–32
promise fulfillment, 103, 127, 175, 178, 280, 438, 455, 466, 471, 508, 681, 683
promises, 331, 339, 434–35, 459, 477
promises, restoration, 476, 482–83
prophecy, 291–92, 330, 374, 557–58, 565, 567, 756
prophets, 158, 166, 168, 222, 275–77, 283, 383, 435, 465, 473, 530
Prophets, the, 122, 213, 330, 350, 373, 375, 377
propitiation, 665
Protestant Reformation, 39
protevangelium, 127, 420, 434, 450, 469
providence (doctrine), 140, 157, 180, 188–89, 412–13, 433, 729–30, 751, 784, 861–62, 864–67, 875–78, 887–92, 895–96, 902
Pseudepigrapha, 374, 380–81

Q

quests for the historical Jesus, 57–59, 61, 93

R

rationalism, 45–47, 52, 68, 169, 404
rationality, 27, 34, 43–44, 52, 66, 68, 87, 93, 194, 404–5, 584, 843
reason, 43, 90, 102, 142–43, 146, 195–97, 200, 209
rebellion, 15–16, 69, 170, 206, 381, 417, 433–35, 447, 451, 541, 661, 672, 737, 746, 809, 818, 821, 882, 885, 912, 923, 926, 931
reconciliation, 228, 435, 469
redemption, 15, 156–57, 160, 165, 171, 174, 178, 397, 401, 417, 419–23, 434, 446, 449, 462, 472, 491, 577, 589, 630, 654, 663, 668, 672–73, 699, 704, 731, 818, 827, 832, 927
redemptive history, 86, 99, 103, 119–20, 122, 127, 165, 274–75, 340–41, 433, 448, 486, 488, 608, 682, 788, 876
redemptive plan, 463, 469, 478–79, 485, 495, 503, 522, 524, 531, 583, 684
Reformation *solas*, xvi, 39
Reformed Baptist theology, 520–23
Reformed theology, xvi–xvii, 441, 553, 614, 748–53, 764, 877–78
regeneration, 37, 51, 136, 196, 299, 358–60, 372, 468, 517–18, 603, 732, 779, 781
relational theism, 546–47, 558, 574–75, 580
relativism, 145, 185, 334, 659
repentance, 14–15, 364, 510–11, 514, 557, 561–64, 583, 610, 617, 625, 664, 669, 746, 761, 885, 934
replacement, 489, 513
reprobation, 737, 740, 744, 749, 757–58, 761–63, 779–81, 864
rest, 477, 523, 811, 817, 823, 827, 829
resurrection, bodily, 15–16, 44, 63–64, 94, 472, 477–78, 491
retrieval theology, 20
revelation, 8–9, 14, 26, 31, 64, 86, 88–105, 152–54, 170–71, 354, 796
    general, 153, 172, 192
    human constitution, 165, 192
    inclusivism, 172
    locus of, 102–3, 153
    modes, 163–69, 297, 303
    natural, 13, 88, 102, 141, 153, 170, 172, 180, 191–218, 344, 347–48
    ongoing, 367
    progressive, 23, 112–14, 117, 174, 240, 275, 301–2, 340, 351, 355, 436–37, 524
    propositional, 221–23, 235
    special, 88, 102, 153, 165–66, 172–74, 180, 196, 214, 217
    specific, 14
    universal, 203–4
    word-act, 9, 113–17, 173–77, 222, 296, 373, 383, 394
Rogers, Jack, 256–58
Roman Catholic Church, 19, 37–38, 261, 264, 266, 342, 352–53, 355, 369, 380
Roman Catholic theology, 195, 296, 347, 356, 361, 369

ruled rules, 20, 107, 169, 225, 346
rules of faith, 19, 154, 347, 355, 361, 365, 371–72, 388, 687

S

Sabbath, 121, 446, 477, 486, 519, 523, 718
Sabellianism, 695
sacraments, 37–39, 41, 507, 514
sacrificial system, 132, 438, 453, 457, 460–62, 468–70, 566, 605
salvation, 15, 37, 39–40, 158, 193, 197, 201, 307, 421, 589, 656, 661, 748, 758–59, 890–91
  initiated by God, 419
salvation history, 187
salvation, natural, 164
sanctity of life, 429
Satan, 278, 309, 328, 416, 419–20, 424, 450, 453, 469, 662, 821, 882, 907, 927
satisfaction, 39, 418, 422, 664, 727, 795, 827
Savior, 13–15, 76, 201, 285, 308, 411, 418–19, 421–22, 451, 589, 631, 660, 886
science, 49–50, 71–73, 181–82, 811, 813, 836–44
scientific method, 50, 74
Scripture, xi–xii, 4, 7–13, 16–17, 22–23, 31, 38, 57, 79, 83, 102–4, 109–34, 136, 141–42, 144–48, 152, 154–55, 168–69, 171–81, 186–90, 195–97, 218–19, 335, 395, 732, 897, 900
  apostolicity, 387
  authority, xii, 40, 74–75, 169, 176, 189–90, 219–53, 261, 265–66, 269, 278–80, 285–87, 290, 307–8, 320, 333, 336, 346, 361–63, 368–71, 384, 601–2, 812, 815
  canonical unity, 110–11, 296, 355
  catholicity, 388
  clarity, 283, 336–37, 349–63
  clarity (external), 353
  clarity (internal), 353
  composition, 295
  covenant document, 176, 275
  doctrine of, 153, 162, 180, 186, 389, 775
  dual authorship, 292, 298–300, 304, 359, 775
  fallible, 228–29, 231–34, 239–41, 246–48, 252–53
  human authors, 110–11, 115, 163, 169, 174, 176, 178–79, 189, 222, 224, 229, 278–79, 283, 285, 287, 289–92, 297–98, 303, 307, 383, 811
  importance, 228
  limitations, 344–45
  nature of, 96–98, 182, 337
  necessity, 336
  original autographs, 317–24
  orthodoxy, xii, 388
  purpose, 343
  received view, 220–21, 255–69, 294
  reliability, 92–94, 184–85, 189
  self-attestation, 255, 265–69, 273–74, 287, 306, 315, 330, 369, 388
  sufficiency, 283, 293, 336–49, 363–64
  sufficiency (formal), 338
  sufficiency (material), 338
  translation, 319
  transmission, 319, 322–23
Scripture Principle, 35, 186
Second London Baptist Confession, 263, 268, 309, 343, 500, 520, 569, 750–51
secularism, 32–33, 538
secularization, 32–33, 42, 538
seed, 127, 279, 420, 445, 449–50, 453–54
  of Abraham, 124, 133, 439, 455–57, 464, 468, 494
semi-Pelagianism, 743, 772–73
sensus plenior, 112
Septuagint, 319, 380, 382
serpent, 331, 447, 449–50
servant, 131, 156, 229, 444, 446, 459, 465, 503, 680, 720, 882, 890, 920, 932
servant of the Lord, 460, 464–66
Shekinah, 667
signs, 165, 516–18, 522, 527, 729
sin, 14, 37–38, 40, 102, 157, 171–72, 192, 197, 200, 205–7, 209–10, 212, 409, 413, 415–16, 418, 433–34, 447–49, 452, 460–61, 470, 504, 518, 588–89, 600, 649–50, 662, 664, 672, 741, 750, 756, 762, 772, 817–18, 832, 858, 878, 884–86, 904, 906
  noetic effects, 172, 195
  sexual, 205, 429
  universality, 417, 419
skepticism, 41–42, 45, 47, 66, 81, 315, 372
slavery, 241, 342, 888
social imaginary, 33–34, 41, 66–68, 79, 538
social justice, 334, 657–59
social Trinitarianism, 545, 547, 691, 706–13
Socinians, 139, 143, 636, 655
sola Scriptura, xvi, 18, 33, 39–40, 42, 52, 60–61, 74, 79, 85, 92, 105, 107, 134, 136, 141, 225, 236, 238, 261, 266, 269, 307–8, 333–34, 342, 356, 360–61, 363, 370, 897
Solomon, 120, 122, 295, 316, 331, 435, 579, 623
sonship, 400, 407, 443–44, 459, 462, 674, 685, 694
Southern Baptist Convention, conservative resurgence, 63, 312
Sparks, Kenton, 241–43

speech-act, 156, 305, 312
speech-act theory, 159
spiration, 177, 574, 674, 686, 691, 699, 702, 714, 727, 795
spiritual gifts, 346, 468, 731
state, the, 28, 42, 67, 210, 397, 410, 419, 425, 428–29, 486, 659, 669, 788
Stoicism, 14, 861–62
subjectivism, 88–91, 97, 185, 239, 334
subordinationism, 696, 699, 701–2
suffering, 28, 282, 340, 433, 502, 557, 569, 613, 615–16, 618, 630, 647, 667, 817, 825, 832, 844, 858, 874, 876, 890, 893, 910–11, 913, 917, 919–21, 923, 926–29
supralapsarianism, 748, 779–81
syncretism, 12, 33, 42, 76, 80, 83
synergism, 37, 39–40, 744, 750, 773
Synod of Dort, 741
systematic theology
  definition, xi, 4–6, 8
  foundation, 85–104, 107
  goal, 27–29, 393
  importance, 137
  nature, 17–21
  nature of, 134, 139
  possibility, 35–36, 85

T

tabernacle, 132–33, 160, 438, 448, 453, 459–60, 577, 588, 667
technology, 844
temple, 120, 122, 132–33, 167, 320, 326, 331, 375, 435, 438, 446–48, 453, 459–61, 473–74, 477, 481, 577, 579, 588, 623, 625, 667, 756, 802
textual criticism, 263, 301, 318, 322–24, 344
theism, 14, 51, 56, 64, 72, 86, 197, 227, 267, 362, 404, 544, 546–49, 556, 558, 560–63, 575, 585, 601–2, 613–15, 623, 636, 708, 733, 796, 834, 922, 924
theistic evolution, 242, 830, 855–58, 867
theodicy, 188, 558, 735, 866, 911, 914
theological categories, 15–16, 116, 440, 524
theological framework, xvii, 11–15, 17, 44, 83, 94, 126, 345, 348, 389, 394–95, 402, 405, 410, 412, 414, 423–24, 426, 428, 431, 462, 478, 483–86, 516, 519–20, 532, 535, 816, 925
Theological Interpretation of Scripture, 25
theological method, 8–9, 33, 57, 80, 105, 109, 116, 148, 197, 264, 367, 389, 548, 559, 561, 770, 815
theology
  apologetic, 11, 134, 137–38
  constructive, 135
  contextual, 11–12
  definition, xv, 4–5, 7–9, 57–65
  extratextual, 33–34, 60, 76, 79, 83, 138
  foundation, 81, 104–5
  importance, xv–xvi, 5–6, 10, 107
  intratextual, xvii, 13, 23, 33, 77, 82–84, 113, 116, 393
  liberal, 7, 813–14
  nature of, 3–4, 82, 84, 91, 535, 541
  normative, 92–98, 151, 250
  possibility, xvi, 75–78, 81
  practice, 17, 108
  purpose, 11
  relation to science, 836–44
  task, 107, 137, 146, 148, 198, 896–97
theology proper, xvi, xviii, 135, 140, 142, 152, 179–80, 186–89, 221, 252, 269, 300, 303–4, 332, 353, 399, 413, 426, 521, 535–36, 538, 541, 546, 548, 550, 559, 562, 568, 594, 600–601, 671, 741, 748, 878, 908
theophany, 167, 172–73
theosis, 37
Third Council of Carthage, 384, 387
timelessness, 619
tolerance, 67
Torah, 271, 319–20, 373, 375–77, 379, 464, 527
total depravity, 37, 40, 349, 741–43, 772, 864, 885
tradition, 19–20, 36, 38, 345–47, 356
trajectory hermeneutic, 243
transcendental condition, 31, 90, 96, 151, 250, 253, 360, 567
tree of life, 442, 448, 504
tree of the knowledge of good and evil, 102, 411, 447
Trinity, 37–38, 40, 86–87, 135, 140, 157, 160–61, 178, 202, 336, 399–400, 590–92, 606, 661, 668, 671–75, 682–88, 700–706, 721–23, 763–64, 794–97, 867
  economic, 704
  eternally ordered relations, 675, 692–93, 702
  ontological, 704
  person-nature distinction, 688–94, 698
  relations of origin, 674, 684–85, 795
triune creator-covenant Lord, 27, 31, 61, 67, 83, 86, 94, 105, 134, 151, 397–99, 402, 405, 531, 537, 540, 570–71, 574–75, 577, 582, 592, 596, 603, 630, 644, 649, 668, 701, 722, 725–26, 736, 788, 828–29, 850, 861, 873, 886
trust, 53, 103, 110, 136, 158, 222–23, 278, 308, 576, 592, 594, 608, 634, 645, 668, 859,

874–75, 890, 913, 916, 920, 923, 927, 929, 934–35
truth, 12, 16–17, 21, 34, 60, 66–67, 70, 77–78, 80–81, 86, 89–91, 100–101, 105, 151, 192, 235–36, 334, 646
defense of, 29, 647
suppression of, 195, 203–5, 207, 209, 217
typology, 119, 123, 127–33, 438, 445–46, 497, 755, 799
union with Christ, 37, 132, 423, 468, 472, 477, 479–80, 503, 517–18, 527, 589, 603, 777

U

Unitarianism, 695–96
universalism, 61, 213
universe, 7, 14–15, 50–51, 70–72, 87–88, 145, 151, 156–57, 162, 171, 181–82, 184, 195–96, 208, 215, 290, 329, 335, 348, 399, 402, 404–5, 408, 412–13, 422, 425, 433–34, 532, 535, 540, 542–44, 573, 576, 579, 584, 590, 599–600, 602, 623, 625, 656, 658, 666, 676, 711–12, 725–26, 729–30, 735, 753, 784–86, 789, 792–94, 798–805, 812–13, 815, 819–20, 822, 827–28, 831, 839–41, 843, 846–47, 849–50, 856–57, 861, 868–69, 874, 878, 880, 883, 885–86, 895, 900, 908, 912, 917, 925–26, 931, 935
moral, 421–23

V

Vatican II, 38–39, 347
voluntarism, 581, 843
warning passages, 515

W

Westminster Confession of Faith, 263, 268, 343, 401, 500, 511, 569, 736, 749
Westminster Theological Seminary, 63, 220, 312, 500
wisdom literature, 223, 276, 297, 648
women, 81, 281, 342, 816
word of God, xiii, 8, 64, 110, 153–63, 170–71, 178, 199, 226–33, 239, 245, 278–79, 285, 339, 349–50, 366, 389, 507, 676
works, 61, 87, 123, 211–12, 283, 309, 400, 421, 442, 505–6, 589, 663, 683, 693–94, 704, 764–65
worldview, 11, 13, 33, 81–85, 137, 182, 272, 395–96, 403–4
biblical, 11, 13, 16, 21, 185, 401, 403–4, 413
worship, xvii, 27, 160, 200–201, 206, 209, 234, 343, 402, 426, 448, 479, 543, 570, 590, 594, 605, 670, 676, 680, 683–84, 697, 702, 723, 839, 859, 931, 935
wrath, 185, 203–4, 211, 417, 448, 588, 610, 617, 650, 654
Writings, the, 373, 375, 377, 379

Y

Yahweh, 426, 443, 571–73, 583, 677–81, 683–84, 726, 730, 736, 806–7, 879, 890

SCRIPTURE INDEX

Genesis

1 *382, 410, 413, 575, 676, 803, 805–7, 819, 821–25, 829*
1:1 *100, 156, 161, 290, 398, 571, 574, 582, 596, 602, 677, 685, 726, 798, 803–4, 813, 816, 819–20, 822, 827, 857*
1:1–2 *88, 136, 597, 685, 798, 820, 822*
1:1–2:3 *274, 575, 806–7, 818–19*
1:1–2:4a *571*
1:1–3 *88, 675–76, 699, 820*
1:1–5 *825*
1:1–31 *795*
1–2 *86, 398–99, 406, 408, 410, 433, 441–43, 447, 540, 630, 718, 789, 805–7, 809–10, 812–14, 818–19, 831, 857, 918*
1:2 *157, 159, 161, 472, 677, 681, 684, 694, 704, 795, 806, 820–22, 868*
1:2–3 *352*
1:2–31 *820*
1:2a *820*
1–3 *131, 133, 398, 813*
1:3 *100, 156, 160, 704, 806, 820, 822, 824, 829*
1:3–13 *822*
1:3–31 *821–23*
1:3ff *676*
1:4 *820, 829*
1:5 *157*
1:5–6 *820*
1:6 *100, 829*
1:6–8 *826*
1:7 *820*
1:8 *157*
1:9 *100, 156, 160, 829*
1:9–13 *826*
1:10 *157, 829, 925*
1–11 *123, 452, 454, 810, 813, 857*
1:11 *156, 160, 808–9, 829, 858*
1:11–12 *808*
1:11–13 *806, 808*
1:12 *413, 829, 925*
1:14 *100, 823, 829*
1:14–19 *826*
1:14–31 *822*
1:18 *413, 829, 925*
1:20 *100, 829*
1:20–23 *826*
1:21 *413, 803, 819, 829, 925*
1:22 *156, 160, 823*
1:24 *100, 829, 858*
1:24–25 *826*
1:24–31 *826*
1:25 *413, 803, 829, 925*
1:26 *156, 406, 571, 677–78, 829, 912*
1:26–28 *165, 210, 406, 409, 428–29, 432, 471, 807, 830, 858*
1:26–30 *429, 452*
1:26–31 *648, 819, 830, 857*
1:26c *407, 444*
1:27 *205, 278, 407, 678, 803, 806, 816, 819*
1:27–28 *157*
1:28 *101, 409, 455, 492, 829*
1:29 *829*
1:29–30 *808*
1:31 *409–10, 413, 415, 433, 446–47, 651, 661, 821, 825, 829, 832, 858, 912, 925*

2 *410, 416, 443, 504, 571, 577, 806–8, 811, 816, 827, 829*
2:1–3 *586, 823, 827*
2–3 *819*
2:4 *443, 807, 810, 815, 820, 824*
2:4–3:24 *806–8*
2:4–7 *820*
2:4–50:26 *807*
2:4b *572*
2:5 *443, 806, 808–9*
2:5–6 *809*
2:6 *809*
2:7 *406, 443, 677, 803–4, 808, 830, 857–58*
2:7–8 *806*
2:8 *443*
2:9 *883*
2:15 *101, 809*
2:15–16 *825*
2:15–17 *170, 217, 411, 416, 447, 573, 858, 910*
2:15–25 *429, 816*
2:16 *166*
2:16–17 *158, 433, 443, 653, 817, 829*
2:17 *433, 447, 654*
2:18 *410*
2:18–25 *453, 653, 830*
2:19 *410, 804*
2:19–25 *442*
2:20 *410*
2:24 *278, 816*
2:24–25 *410, 447*
3 *172, 203–5, 381, 411, 415–16, 433, 447–49, 454, 470, 541, 588, 676, 858, 885, 912, 925*
3:1 *447*
3:1–6 *829, 857*
3:1–20 *816*
3:1–24 *654*
3:4–7 *416*
3:6 *905*
3:8 *577*
3:8–19 *676*
3:8–24 *808*
3:9 *564*
3:13–19 *910*
3:14–19 *156, 415*
3:14–24 *447*
3:15 *123, 125, 127, 158, 160, 172, 214, 332, 340, 417, 419–20, 427, 434, 436, 440–42, 445, 449–52, 456, 458–59, 501, 506, 521–22, 524, 531–32, 565, 576–77, 588, 608, 654, 680, 827, 833, 870*
3:17 *102*
3:17–18 *808–9*
3:17–19 *817, 825, 829, 885*
3:17ff *160*
3:18 *203*
3:18–19 *808*
3:19 *433, 808*
3:20 *450*
3:22 *678*
3:23 *809*
3:24 *448*
4 *379, 448*
4:1 *739*
4:1–16 *816*
4:6–8 *417*
5 *448*
5:1 *407, 803, 810, 815, 824*
5:1–2 *133*
5:5 *448*
5:8 *448*
5:11 *448*
5:14 *448*
5:17 *448*
5:20 *448*
5:27 *448*
5:31 *448*
6:3 *663*
6:5 *417, 883*
6:5–6 *759*
6:5–7 *452, 562*
6:6 *609, 615, 746*
6:6–7 *610*
6–7 *918*
6:7 *156, 160*
6–8 *452*
6–9 *448, 663, 825, 858, 920*
6:9 *810, 815*
6:12 *417*
6:17 *858*
6:17–18 *443*
6:18 *442–43, 452, 573*
7:4 *809*
8:1 *469*
8:21 *759*
8:21–22 *156, 452, 729, 870*
8:21f *160*
8:22 *452–53, 731, 880*
9:1–7 *452*
9:1–17 *133*
9:3 *808*
9:6 *210, 407, 429*
9:8 *573*

9:8–17 *443*
9:9 *443*
9:9–11 *452*
9:11 *443*
9:12–17 *164, 453*
9:17 *443*
9:18–28 *452*
10:1 *810, 815*
10:15 *315*
11 *454–55*
11:4 *452*
11:5–7 *678*
11:6f *160*
11:7 *571*
11:10 *815*
11:27 *810, 815*
12 *454, 457, 524*
12:1 *676*
12:1–3 *133, 158, 160, 279, 434, 452, 454, 573, 608*
12:2 *463*
12:3 *453, 777*
12:7 *154, 167*
12–50 *810*
13:13 *883*
14 *125*
14:18–22 *572, 579*
14:19 *604*
14:22 *604*
15 *123–24, 454–55, 457*
15:1 *676*
15:3 *332*
15:4–5 *454*
15:6 *123–24, 214, 427, 451, 457, 522*
15:12–21 *457*
15:15–16 *920*
15:17 *167*
15:18–21 *454*
16:6–13 *167, 678*
16:10–13 *167, 679*
17 *123, 454, 457*
17:1 *154, 167, 457, 627*
17:1–2 *572*
17:1–8 *454*
17:1–22 *133*
17:4–6 *455*
17:6 *460, 564*
17:6–8 *456*
17:7 *529*
17:8 *332*
17:15–22 *880*
17:16 *460*
17:20–21 *456*
17:22 *167*
18 *167, 678*
18:1 *154*
18:1–33 *625*
18:3 *167, 679*
18:14 *156, 160, 575, 628, 676, 881*
18:18–19 *454*
18:19 *457, 739, 776*
18:25 *100, 425, 427, 652, 654*
19 *920*
19:23 *327*
20:3 *167*
20:13 *677*
21:15 *808*
22 *454, 457, 557*
22:2 *875*
22:8 *457*
22:11 *676*
22:11–12 *167, 678*
22:12 *167, 679, 885*
22:14 *572*
22:16–18 *454, 457*
22:17–18a *453, 455–56*
22:17b–18 *456*
22:18 *332*
24:44 *755*
24:60 *453, 455–56*
25:12 *810, 815*
25:19 *810*
26:2 *154*
26:3–5 *459*
26:24 *154, 167*
28:12ff *167*
28:13–15 *459*
31:13 *167, 679*
31:24 *167*
32:25–33 *678*
32:28 *167, 679*
32:28–30 *625*
32:29–30 *167*
32:30 *167, 679*
35:7 *154, 677*
35:9 *167*
35:9–12 *459*
36:1 *810, 815*
36:9 *810, 815*
36:20 *315*
37 *888*
37:2 *810, 815*
39:5 *663*
45:5–8 *882*

45:8 *755*
48:16 *167, 679*
49:8 *455*
49:8–12 *456, 460, 565*
49:10 *455*
49:10–12 *610*
50 *815, 888–89*
50:19 *888*
50:19–20 *304, 565, 772, 889, 900*
50:20 *755–56, 888*

Exodus

1:1–7 *133*
1:8 *466*
2:24–25 *459*
2:25 *776*
3 *443*
3:1–6 *588*
3:1–15 *86*
3:2 *167*
3:2–5 *402, 586*
3:2–6 *167, 678*
3:2–8 *167, 679*
3–4 *667*
3:6 *345, 459*
3:13–15 *443, 573, 683*
3:13–18 *582*
3:14 *160, 540, 571–72, 585, 597, 604, 606–7, 618–19, 676, 718, 807*
3:14–15 *107, 135, 572*
3:15 *597*
4:10–16 *168, 245*
4:21 *882*
4:22 *444*
4:22–23 *131, 133, 459, 462, 680–81*
6:1 *329*
6:1–8 *573*
6:2 *167*
6:3 *572*
6:6 *329*
6:12 *518*
6–15 *174*
6:30 *518*
7:3 *882*
7:5 *165, 730*
7–11 *883*
7–12 *823*
7:22–23 *732*
8:7 *732*
8:15 *882*
8:19 *329, 730*
8:32 *882*
9:12 *882*
9:16 *279*
9:27 *651*
9:34 *882*
10:20 *882*
12:12 *730*
12:46 *330, 756*
13–14 *667*
13:17 *641*
13:21–22 *625*
14 *919*
14:4 *573, 882*
14:5–31 *810*
14:8 *882*
14:18 *165*
14:19 *167, 679*
14:31 *165*
15 *165*
15:1–18 *175*
15:1–19 *730*
15:1–21 *810*
15:6–11 *730*
15:11 *683*
15:14–17 *133, 461*
16:4 *885*
16:7 *667*
16:10 *667*
17:7 *684*
18:11 *597*
19 *166–67, 175, 588*
19:4 *459*
19:4–6 *455*
19:5–6 *459*
19:6 *434, 480, 483*
19:15 *604*
19–20 *133, 163, 166*
20 *166, 175, 667*
20:1–3 *589*
20:1–4 *245*
20:2 *582*
20:2–3 *683*
20:3 *582*
20:8–11 *446*
20:9–11 *825*
20:11 *604, 820, 822, 825*
20:16 *647*
21 *175*
21:13 *880*
23:20–23 *167, 679*
24 *133, 667*
24:3–4 *245*
24:7 *176, 277*

24:9–11 *625*
24:12 *275*
25:22 *625*
29:43 *667*
29:45 *583*
31:17 *825*
31:18 *275, 303*
32:4 *677*
32:9–10 *933*
32:10–14 *609*
32:12–13 *933*
32:12–14 *557, 562, 610*
32:15–16 *224, 275, 320*
32:19 *320*
32–33 *933*
32–34 *133, 320, 460, 667*
33:11 *166, 625*
33:14f *167, 679*
33:17 *776*
33:18 *160, 669*
33:18–19 *571*
33:19 *597, 676, 760*
33:20–23 *625*
33–34 *160*
34:1 *275, 320*
34:5–7 *160*
34:6 *332, 663, 884*
34:6–7 *613, 651, 656*
34:6f *676*
34:7 *654*
34:14 *613*
34:27–28 *320*
40:34–35 *667*
40:34–38 *667*

Leviticus

8–9 *133*
9:23 *154*
10 *919*
11:13–19 *328*
11:44 *86, 402, 586*
11:45 *459*
17:11 *470, 605*
18:1–30 *429*
18:2–5 *582*
18:5 *461, 504*
18:6–19 *154*
18:30 *582*
19:2 *588–89*
19:18 *407, 429*
19:23 *518*
19:37 *582*
20:11 *154*
26:12 *583*
26:16 *883*
26:22 *883*
26:25 *883*
26:41 *518*

Numbers

11:16–18 *681*
11:25 *157, 352*
11:27–29 *467, 530*
11:29 *352, 478*
12 *168, 377*
12:6–8 *166*
14:10 *154*
15:28 *608*
16:19 *154*
22:31 *154*
22:35 *277*
23:5 *277*
23:12 *277*
23:16 *277*
23:19 *311, 332, 597, 602, 610, 646, 757*
23:21 *565*
24:2 *677*
24:3–4 *157*
24:4 *572*
24:7 *460*
24:16 *572*
24:17–19 *460, 565*
33 *316*
33:45b–50 *316*

Deuteronomy

2:12 *315*
2:22 *315*
3:24 *730*
4:1–2 *338*
4:2 *275, 286, 308, 321*
4:5 *286*
4:5–8 *159–60, 349, 455*
4:10 *480*
4:13 *275*
4:14 *286*
4:15 *166*
4:26 *164*
4:35 *86, 573*
4:36–38 *459*
4:37 *758*
4:39 *86, 579*
4:40 *286*
5:15 *446*

5:22 *103, 274–75*
5:28–31 *166*
5:32 *103, 274–75*
6 *158, 682*
6:1–8 *107*
6:4 *135, 584, 596, 683*
6:4–5 *407*
6:4–9 *349, 582*
6:5 *429*
6:6ff *169*
6:24–25 *275*
7:6–7 *758*
7:7 *459*
7:7–8 *661*
7:7–10 *758*
7:8 *459*
7:9–13 *653*
7:21 *597*
8:3 *278, 339*
8:11 *275*
8:11–18 *165*
10:2 *320*
10:4 *275, 320*
10:14 *604, 718*
10:14–15 *579, 661, 758*
10:15 *758*
10:16 *468, 518*
10:17–18 *652, 656*
11:7 *597*
12:32 *275, 286, 308, 321, 338*
13:1–2 *276*
13:1–5 *168, 245, 276, 330*
17:14–20 *460, 565*
17:18 *319–20*
17:18–19 *339*
18 *377*
18:14–22 *133, 275*
18:15–18 *377, 460*
18:15–22 *158, 168, 245*
18:18–22 *168, 632*
18:20 *276, 339*
18:20–22 *276, 330*
18:22 *276*
25:4 *286, 382*
26:15 *587, 624*
27:26 *461, 654*
27–28 *653*
28:15–68 *920*
28:21–22 *883*
28:22 *883*
28:27 *883*
29:6 *573*
29:9 *103, 274–75*
29:29 *144, 154, 353, 874*
30:1–6 *478*
30:6 *468, 518*
30:9–10 *275*
30:11–14 *160, 350*
30:15–16 *103, 274–75*
30:19 *164*
31:9–13 *349*
31:19 *275*
31:19–22 *275*
31:24–29 *275*
31:26 *160, 275, 676*
31:28 *164*
32 *275*
32:1 *164*
32:4 *304, 652, 656, 884*
32:8 *572, 579*
32:11 *821*
32:15 *480, 677*
32:17 *466*
32:23–24 *883*
32:39 *573, 607, 683, 883*
32:40 *582*
32:43 *345*
33:12 *480*
33:25–28 *868*
33:27 *618*
34 *295, 318, 377–78*
34:10–12 *133, 168, 460*

Joshua

1:1–9 *378*
1:5 *379*
1:6–9 *339*
1:7 *275*
1:7–8 *103, 274–75*
1:7–9 *350*
1:8–9 *158*
2:11 *579*
5:14–15 *167, 678*
8:34 *275*
10:8 *882*
10:40 *882*
11:20 *882*
24:14–15 *304, 885*
24:15 *745*
24:25–28 *275*

Judges

1:4 *882*
1:7 *882*

3:4 *319*
4:23 *882*
5:4 *826*
6:11–14 *167, 678*
6:21 *167, 679*
13:3 *167, 679*
13:21–22 *625*
14:1–4 *883*
20:35 *882*

Ruth
1:13 *880*
1:20 *880*
4:13–22 *565, 610*
4:18–22 *378*

1 Samuel
1:3 *572*
1:19 *469*
2:2 *587*
2:6–7 *883*
2:23–25 *883*
2:27 *154*
3:4–14 *166*
3:21 *154*
4:4 *625*
4:11 *883*
6:7 *466*
15 *564*
15:11 *557, 562, 564, 609–10, 746*
15:27–29 *564*
15:29 *311, 332, 597, 602, 608, 610, 646, 757*
15:35 *557, 562, 564, 609–10, 746*
16:13 *681*
23:8–14 *641*

2 Samuel
7 *932*
7:5–16 *133*
7:8–11a *464*
7:8–16 *460, 608*
7:9 *463*
7:12–14 *277*
7:12–16 *462*
7:14 *400, 444, 462, 573, 583, 677, 680–81*
7:14–15 *464*
7:18–19 *464*
7:19b *463, 680*
7:22–24 *455, 462*
7:25–26a *932*
17:14 *883*
21:12 *824*
23:2 *677*
24:1 *328*

1 Kings
2:3 *319*
3:5 *167*
8:10 *167*
8:11 *667*
8:27 *86, 576, 579, 623*
8:35 *883*
9:2 *167*
9:28 *316*
11:11–13 *464*
11:34–36 *464*
12:1–15 *883*
13:1–3 *632*
15:4–5 *464*
17:1 *168*
17:4 *755*
18:21 *745*
18:24 *160*
18:26 *160*
18:29 *160*
18:36 *160*
18:44–45 *826*
22 *755*
22:1–28 *880*
22:19ff *167*
22:28 *755, 880*
22:34 *755, 881*
22:38 *755, 881*

2 Kings
5:1 *882*
8:1 *883*
8:19 *464*
10:30 *663*
12:2 *663*
13:22–23 *459*
17:25 *883*
19:15 *820*
22 *320*
22:8 *320*
22:13 *320*
23:2–3 *277*
23:21 *277*

1 Chronicles
1:1 *815*
10:4 *901*
10:13–14 *901*

13:10 *901*
16:15–19 *459*
17:8 *463*
17:11–14 *277, 462*
17:13 *462*
21:1 *328*
21:16 *167, 678*
21:18 *167, 678*
21:27 *167, 678*
28:9 *739*
29:11 *604*
29:29 *276*

2 Chronicles
2:12 *820*
6:15 *653*
7:1 *167*
9:29 *276*
12:6 *651*
20:34 *276*
21:7 *464*
21:14 *883*
23:3 *464*
24:20–22 *379*
26:19–20 *901*
32:31 *885*
34 *320*
34:3–7 *320*
34:14 *320*
34:14–31 *176, 277*
36:17 *882*
36:22–23 *378*
36:22ff *882*

Ezra
1:1 *881*
5:11 *820*
6:22 *881*
7:10 *355*
7:14 *319*
9:15 *651*

Nehemiah
8:8 *319*
9:6 *583, 604, 805, 820, 868*
9:8 *651*
9:18 *677*
9:30 *677*

Esther
4:14 *934*

Job
1–2 *874–75, 890, 904*
1:12 *328, 882*
1:13–15 *890*
1:13–19 *328*
1:15 *882*
1:16 *890*
1:17 *882, 890*
1:18–19 *890*
1:19 *882*
1:21 *328, 756, 882, 890*
2:10 *756*
4:17 *651*
12:7–10 *756*
12:13–16 *757*
20:28 *824–25*
22:2 *721*
26:8 *826*
28:24 *739*
28:26 *755*
30:4 *808*
30:7 *808*
31:4 *627*
33:4 *677, 795, 868*
33:11f *160*
34:14–15 *583, 868*
35:2 *651*
35:5–7 *616*
35:6–7 *721*
36:3 *651*
36:26 *619*
36:27–28 *826*
37:12 *156, 160*
37:12–13 *755*
37:16 *632*
38:1–42:6 *100–101*
38:2 *738*
38:4 *787, 804*
38–40 *575, 880*
38–41 *171, 267, 573, 633*
38–42 *874*
39 *661*
40:1–5 *718*
41:3 *604*
41:11 *605, 721*
42:1–2 *628*
42:2 *757, 879, 881*
42:3 *738*

Psalms
1 *158, 276, 339*

1:1–2 *277*
1–2 *377–78*
1:2 *350*
1:6 *776*
2 *135, 400, 435, 444, 462–63, 472, 566, 677, 680–81, 763*
2:1–3 *788*
2:2 *738*
2:4–5 *615*
2:7 *280, 472*
2:7–9 *156, 715, 720*
2:7–12 *764*
3:4 *587*
3:8 *419*
4:1 *654*
5:4 *884*
5:8 *651*
6:3 *667*
7:17 *86, 160, 571, 579, 588, 676*
8 *125, 133, 406, 444–45, 463, 472*
8:1 *579*
8:4–8 *666*
8:5 *677*
8:6 *471*
9:2 *86, 160, 571, 579, 588, 676*
9:5–6 *656*
9:8 *86, 401, 540*
9:10 *160, 676*
9:15–20 *656*
11:4 *587, 624*
11:6–7 *654*
12:6 *646*
12:6–7 *277*
14:1 *203, 542*
15:2 *647*
16 *345, 681*
16:10 *279–80*
18:15 *156, 160*
18:20 *653*
18:24 *653*
18:30 *676*
18:32 *677*
18:49 *160, 571, 676*
19 *99, 164*
19:1 *754*
19:1–2 *203, 797*
19:1–6 *86, 88, 208, 401, 630, 653, 786*
19:1–7 *647*
19:7 *338, 648, 676*
19:7–11 *277, 339, 350*
19:7ff *160*
19:8 *652*
20:1 *571, 824–25*
20:6 *587*
21:7 *86, 588*
22 *566*
22:3 *587*
22:18 *330*
23:4 *627*
24:1 *604*
24:1–2 *345, 718*
24:7–10 *666*
24:8 *628*
27:1 *630*
28:2 *587*
28:3–9 *160*
29 *161*
29:2 *571, 666*
29:3 *666, 684*
30:4 *587*
31:1 *651, 656*
31:1–3 *656*
31:13 *738*
33:5 *86, 99, 401, 540, 651*
33:6 *157, 159–61, 630, 676–77, 685, 704, 804*
33:9 *160, 676, 804*
33:9–11 *86*
33:10–11 *575, 608, 647, 757, 879–80*
33:11 *156, 738, 754, 757, 879*
33:11–12 *757*
33:12 *758*
33:13–14 *624*
33:21 *587*
34:3 *160, 571, 676*
34:8 *651*
34:14 *883*
35:24 *654*
36:5–9 *663*
36:6 *652*
36:7–9 *350*
36:10 *656*
36:10–12 *763*
40:10 *651*
45 *400, 435, 463, 472*
45:4 *651*
45:6 *680*
45:7 *651*
46:4 *588*
46:6 *160*
46:8–10 *164*
47:8 *433, 587*
47:9 *466–67*

48:1 *587*
50 *403*
50:6 *652*
50:8–15 *605*
50:10–12 *604, 606*
50:12–13 *597*
50:12–14 *86, 398, 433, 540, 718*
51:4 *418*
51:10–12 *677*
51:18 *738*
54:1 *571*
56:4 *160, 676*
56:10 *160, 676*
57:5 *579*
58:11 *653*
65 *164*
65:4 *587*
65:9–11 *880, 883*
65:9–13 *663*
66:5–7 *165*
67:2–3 *466–67*
68:4 *160, 572, 676*
68:17 *167*
69:5 *634*
69:21 *756*
69:27 *651*
71:2 *651, 656*
71:19 *651*
72 *400, 463, 680–81*
72:17 *453, 455, 463, 571*
72:19 *667*
73:25–28 *402*
74:2 *167*
74:18 *160, 676*
77:11–20 *165*
77:16 *826*
77:18 *883*
79:9–13 *656*
82 *332*
82:1 *571*
82:6 *278, 331, 571*
82:8 *604*
83:13–15 *883*
83:18 *573, 588*
86:8 *571*
86:10 *597*
86:12 *676*
87:1 *587*
87:3–6 *466–67*
89:11 *604*
89:16 *7, 651*
89:26–27 *462, 680*
90:2 *582, 800, 804–5*
90:2–4 *618*
90:4 *582, 619, 824*
90:13 *610*
91:14 *573*
92:11 *676*
93:1 *476*
93:2 *86, 398, 433, 582, 618*
94:7–9 *656*
95 *125*
95:3 *571, 683*
96:3 *784*
96:5 *646*
96:10–13 *86*
96:13 *654*
97:1 *476*
97:7 *646*
97:9 *86, 571, 579*
97:11–12 *656*
98:1 *587*
98:2–3 *656*
98:9 *652*
99:1 *476*
99:2 *597*
100:3 *602*
100:5 *651*
102:12 *618*
102:25 *804*
102:25–27 *607*
102:26 *805*
102:26–27 *582*
102:26–28 *585*
102:27 *618, 805*
103:1 *587*
103:8 *663*
103:19 *433, 476, 583, 873*
104 *164, 651*
104:1–34 *647*
104:10–30 *663*
104:14 *880*
104:21 *871*
104:24 *155, 208, 755*
104:26 *804*
104:27–30 *677, 685*
104:30 *684, 795, 803, 868*
105:1 *160*
105:3 *587*
105:16 *883*
105:25 *881*
105:42 *587*
106 *165*
106:1 *651*

106:13 *738*
106:44–45 *610*
106:47 *587*
107:1 *651*
107:9 *868*
107:11 *738*
107:20 *676*
108:5 *784*
108:7 *587*
110 *125, 135, 156, 278, 332, 400, 435, 469, 472, 494, 677, 679–81*
110:1 *331, 680, 683, 715, 720*
110:1–2 *579*
110:4 *608, 610*
111:2–4 *726*
111:3 *651*
111:6 *726*
111:9 *160, 726*
112:3–6 *656*
113:5 *579, 587*
114:7 *677*
115:1 *171, 414, 784*
115:2–3 *304, 879*
115:3 *575, 624, 629, 754, 759, 874*
115:4–8 *646*
115:5–9 *160*
115:15 *820*
116:5 *651, 656*
117:1 *466–67*
118:15–19 *656*
118:22–23 *278*
119 *158, 339*
119:7 *160, 275, 676*
119:18 *357*
119:19–20 *278*
119:27 *357*
119:31 *278*
119:34 *357*
119:40 *676*
119:41–42 *278*
119:43 *332*
119:46–48 *278*
119:48 *160, 676*
119:68 *651*
119:73 *357*
119:86 *160, 278, 676*
119:89 *160, 275, 278, 676*
119:89–91 *160*
119:91 *755*
119:105 *338, 350*
119:120 *160, 676*
119:123 *651*
119:129 *160, 275, 676*
119:130 *350*
119:137 *160, 676*
119:140 *160, 275, 278*
119:142 *160, 275, 332, 676*
119:151 *332*
119:160 *160, 275, 332, 676*
119:161–68 *160*
119:161f *676*
119:168 *627*
121:2 *820*
124:8 *820*
127:1 *868*
130:4 *665*
132:13 *167*
134:3 *820*
135 *165*
135:5 *597*
135:6 *629, 754–55, 757, 759, 874, 879*
135:6–7 *575, 883*
135:7–12 *879*
135:13 *571*
135:15–18 *160*
135:21 *167*
136 *165, 726*
136:2–3 *726*
136:4 *726*
136:5–9 *726*
136:6 *753*
136:10 *726*
136:11–26 *726*
136:25 *663*
138:1–4 *401*
138:2 *160, 676*
138:8 *608*
138:16 *401*
139 *577*
139:1–4 *86, 99, 332, 540, 632, 739*
139:1–10 *86, 99, 401, 540*
139:1–18 *597*
139:2–3 *634*
139:6 *100, 633*
139:7–10 *623*
139:7–12 *576*
139:13–16 *575*
139:16 *86, 99, 304, 332, 503, 540, 565, 632, 736–37, 753–54, 771, 879*
139:23–24 *668*
143:1 *651, 654, 656*
143:10 *629, 874*
143:11 *656*
144:3 *776*

145 *726*
145:1–7 *726*
145:1–16 *663*
145:3 *100, 587*
145:4 *165*
145:7 *100, 651*
145:8–9 *884*
145:9 *663*
145:11–12 *784*
145:12 *165*
145:13–16 *884*
145:14–15 *868*
145:15f *160*
145:17 *651, 656*
145:21 *587*
146:5–6 *604*
147:5 *332, 632, 647, 739*
147:8 *826*
147:15 *155, 676*
147:15–18 *155–56, 164, 676*
147:18 *155*
148:4 *826*
148:5 *160*
148:5–6 *676, 755*
148:5–8 *164*
148:7–8 *883*
148:8 *160, 826, 880*

Proverbs

1:7 *5, 276, 417, 648*
2:6–8 *276*
3:12 *654*
3:19 *755*
8:22–31 *755*
9:10 *276*
11:13 *154*
12:22 *647*
13:5 *647*
15:3 *626, 634*
15:29 *625*
16:4 *736, 753*
16:9 *304, 881*
16:33 *755, 880*
19:21 *304, 608, 736, 738, 753, 757, 871, 881*
20:19 *154*
21:1 *304, 755, 871, 881*
21:2 *629*
21:30–31 *881*
21:31 *824–25*
24:10 *824–25*
24:12 *656*
25:9 *154*
25:13 *824–25*
27:9 *738*
30:5 *277*
30:5–6 *276, 332, 338*
30:6 *275, 321*
30:32 *738*

Ecclesiastes

1:10 *466*
7:14 *824–25*
11:3 *826*
12:13–14 *276*

Isaiah

1:4–20 *402, 588*
2:1–4 *657*
2:1–5 *465*
2:2–4 *480*
2:4 *276*
2:21 *167*
3:1 *883*
4:2–6 *667*
5:1–7 *131, 472*
5:7 *652*
5:19 *738*
5:20 *883*
6 *167, 625*
6:1 *86, 579, 587–88*
6:1–3 *402, 586–87, 649*
6:1–4 *588*
6:1–13 *684*
6:3 *587, 598, 649, 684, 784*
6:8 *571, 678*
6:9–10 *351*
6:13 *464*
7:14 *320, 435, 465, 577, 579, 680*
8:1 *320*
8:1–2 *276*
9:6 *455, 680*
9:6–7 *135, 435, 463, 465–66, 680, 683*
9:7 *680*
9:8 *676*
9:11 *463*
9:53 *463*
10 *889*
10:5 *889*
10:5–15 *882*
10:5–17 *304*
10:5–19 *565, 772, 889, 900*
10:6 *755, 889*
10:7–11 *889*
10:12 *889*

10:13–14 *889*
10:15 *873*
10:17 *587*
11 *400*
11:1 *464, 680*
11:1–2 *472*
11:1–3 *135, 213, 465, 467, 530, 681*
11:1–5 *472, 677, 680–81*
11:1–10 *465–66, 680, 683*
11:1–16 *435*
11:3–5 *465*
11:9 *7, 276*
11:10 *465*
11:15–16 *133, 461*
11:16 *824*
12:6 *587*
13:5 *873*
13:6 *824*
13:9 *824*
14:1–2 *466–67*
14:24 *608, 628, 757*
14:24–26 *304*
14:24–27 *575, 582, 736, 753, 757, 879, 881*
14:26 *738*
14:27 *628, 757*
16:6 *677*
17:7 *587*
19:17 *738*
19:23–25 *466–67*
20:1 *316*
22:11 *736–37, 753–54*
25:1 *160, 676*
25:6–9 *469*
26:8 *160, 676*
28:29 *738*
29:18 *476*
30:8 *320*
30:8–11 *276*
30:18 *885*
30:30 *156, 160*
31:3 *597*
32:15 *483*
34:11 *821*
34:16 *159, 677*
34:16–17 *276*
35:5–6 *572*
35:8 *402, 588*
36:18 *571*
37:20 *573*
37:23 *587*
37:26 *736–37, 753–54*
40 *404, 805*
40:1–31 *879*
40:3–5 *133, 461*
40:5 *667, 784*
40:6–8 *277*
40:7 *677*
40:8 *169, 245, 248*
40:10–14 *759*
40:12 *628, 795*
40:12–14 *597, 754, 805*
40:12–26 *577, 587, 596*
40:12–31 *99, 540, 573*
40:13–14 *86, 632–33*
40:14 *576, 633, 754*
40:17–29 *86*
40:18–25 *587, 649*
40:19–20 *605*
40:21 *804*
40:25 *592, 597, 602, 656, 684*
40:26 *161, 805*
40:27–31 *634*
40:28 *332, 618, 798, 805*
40–46 *718*
40–48 *100, 565, 632, 636, 771*
40:68 *171*
41:4 *573, 582, 607, 618, 804*
41:7 *605*
41:14 *587*
41:16 *587*
41:17–20 *461*
41:20 *587*
41:21–23 *632, 739*
42 *400*
42:1 *135, 213, 465, 472, 681*
42:1–8 *677*
42:1–9 *435, 465, 680*
42:3–4 *465*
42:5 *805*
42:6 *466–67*
42:8 *398, 541, 666, 784, 874*
42:8–9 *632*
42:9 *739*
42:14–16 *461*
42:20 *466–67*
43:1 *156, 160–61*
43:1–3 *461*
43:3 *573, 587*
43:7 *606, 656, 666, 797, 805*
43:9–12 *632*
43:10 *573, 607, 632*
43:11 *419*
43:12 *483*
43:13 *573, 575, 757*

43:14 *587*
43:14–21 *461*
43:15 *587*
43:20–21 *480*
44:2 *480*
44:3 *278, 677*
44:6 *584*
44:6–8 *171, 276, 596, 633, 683*
44:7 *632, 739*
44:7–8 *582*
44:9–10 *646*
44:15–17 *605*
44:24 *573, 795*
44:26 *738*
44:28 *757, 882*
44:28–45:4 *632*
44–48 *557*
45 *883*
45:1 *881*
45:1–46:13 *880*
45:5–6 *683*
45:7 *803, 883*
45:7–8 *803*
45:8 *654, 656*
45:11 *587*
45:12 *630, 803*
45:18 *573, 805*
45:18–19 *412*
45:18–22 *86*
45:19–21 *652*
45:20–25 *597*
45:21 *418, 632, 739*
45:22 *683*
45:22–23 *652*
45:48 *652*
46:4 *607*
46:5 *596*
46:5–13 *633*
46:6 *605*
46:8–10 *5, 151*
46:8–11 *608, 757*
46:8–13 *565, 879*
46:9–10 *628*
46:9–11 *86, 99, 304, 401, 540, 596, 632, 739, 753, 759*
46:9–13 *86, 107, 136, 503, 573, 582*
46:10 *575, 628, 633, 736, 757, 804, 874, 879, 881*
46:10–11 *332, 738*
46:11 *737*
46:13 *651, 654, 656*
47:4 *587*
48:3–7 *632, 739*
48:5 *667*
48:9 *874*
48:11 *414, 683, 754, 784*
48:12 *607*
48:17 *587*
48:20–21 *461*
49:1 *465*
49:1–2 *465, 467, 530*
49:1–7 *435, 465, 680*
49:3 *657*
49:6 *465–67, 483*
49:8 *738*
49:8–12 *461*
51:4–8 *656*
51:6 *651, 654*
51:8 *651*
51:9 *419*
51:9–11 *461*
51:16 *276–77*
52:3–6 *461*
52:10 *419, 587*
52:11–12 *461*
52:13–53:12 *435, 465, 680*
52–53 *460*
53 *890*
53:1 *154, 419*
53:1–3 *890*
53:2 *464*
53:4–9 *890*
53:10 *738, 890*
53:11 *651, 680*
54:5 *587*
54:16 *803*
54:17 *651*
55 *464–65*
55:1 *278, 745*
55:3 *279–80, 464–65, 680*
55:3–5 *466–67*
55:5 *587, 667*
55:8–9 *100*
55:10–11 *350, 757*
55:11 *157, 160, 171, 628, 676*
55:12–13 *461*
56:4–8 *466–67*
56:6 *160, 676*
57:13–15 *587*
57:15 *402, 579, 586, 618, 625*
58:6 *476*
58:11 *278*
59:2 *625*
59:3–4 *647*

59:7 *883*
59:16–17 *419, 651*
59:19 *667*
59:21 *159, 276–77*
60:1 *667*
60:9 *587*
60:10 *587*
60:19 *667*
61 *400*
61:1 *472*
61:1–2 *213, 278, 472, 476, 681*
61:1–3 *135, 465, 677, 681*
61:1–4 *359, 465, 467, 677*
61:1ff *530*
62:2 *156, 160–61*
62:3–5 *606*
63:8–9 *167, 679*
63:10 *587, 677*
65 *680*
65:2 *885*
65:15 *156, 160–61*
65:17 *421, 423, 434, 465–66*
65:17–25 *409*
65:18 *803*
66:1–2 *103, 623*
66:2 *159, 245, 287*
66:5 *160, 676*
66:6 *156, 160*
66:12 *667*
66:18–20 *667*
66:18–24 *466–67*
66:21–24 *667*
66:22 *466*

Jeremiah

1:4 *676*
1:4–12 *168*
1:5 *739, 776*
1:6–19 *158, 168, 245*
1:9 *276–77*
1:14 *277*
3:6 *276*
3:6–8 *557, 562, 564*
4:4 *468, 518*
4:23 *821*
4:28 *610, 738*
5:14 *276*
6:10 *518*
7:31 *557, 562*
9:25 *468, 518*
10:1–16 *135, 160, 573, 577, 718, 787*
10:3–5 *605*
10:10 *683*
10:12–16 *805*
10:23–24 *881*
11:20 *86*
15:2 *757*
15:6 *610*
16:14–15 *461*
16:19 *466–67*
16:21 *573*
17:9 *448, 759*
17:9–10 *634*
18:5–10 *583*
18:7–10 *565, 610*
18:20 *653*
19:5 *557*
23:4–8 *461*
23:5 *651*
23:5–6 *465–66, 681*
23:6 *572*
23:18 *738*
23:20 *879, 881*
23:21–22 *641*
23:22 *738*
23:23–24 *623*
25:9 *882*
25:13 *276*
25:30 *587*
26:3 *610*
26:13 *610*
26:17–18 *276*
26:19 *610*
27:6 *882*
29 *932*
29:4–7 *932*
29:10–14 *932*
29:12–13 *932*
30:2 *276*
31 *125, 492, 494, 515, 527*
31:3 *754*
31:29–30 *467*
31:29–34 *277, 458, 466, 478*
31:31 *132, 492, 498, 526*
31:31–34 *125, 467, 480, 494, 515, 527, 680, 683–84, 764*
31:31–40 *466*
31:32 *461*
31:33 *478*
31:33–34 *468–69*
31:34 *421, 427, 449, 460, 462, 465, 469, 477–78, 564, 680*
31:34a *7*
31:36 *498*

32:17–19 *628*
32:19 *738*
32:27 *881*
32:35 *557*
33:3 *745*
33:6–16 *466*
33:9 *466–67*
33:14–26 *465–66*
34:18–20 *457*
36:28 *320*
47:6 *448*
49:20 *738*
50:25 *873*
50:45 *738*
51:12 *738*
51:60–61 *276*

Lamentations

1:18 *651*
3:22–23 *466*
3:31–36 *885*
3:37–38 *883*

Ezekiel

1 *167, 625*
1:1 *160*
1:5ff *448*
3:4 *277*
3:22 *160*
3:26 *276*
5:16–17 *883*
10:15 *448*
11:19 *677*
11:19–20 *467, 530*
13 *933*
13:2f *158*
13:17 *158*
14:15 *883*
14:21 *883*
18:4 *654*
18:23 *743*
18:30–32 *304, 885*
18:32 *743*
20:9 *754*
21 *448*
22 *933*
24:14 *610*
28:14 *587*
33:7 *676*
33:11 *661, 743, 762, 885*
34 *419, 463*
34:1–25 *467*
34:1–26 *435*
34:1–31 *683*
34:22–25 *677*
34:23–24 *465–66, 680*
34:23–25 *680, 764*
36:24–38 *466*
36:25–27 *213, 462, 467, 478, 530, 677, 681*
36:28 *498*
36:36 *466–67*
36–37 *420*
36:37 *478*
37:1–23 *469*
37:11–28 *466*
37:14 *277, 498, 677*
37:24–28 *465–66*
37:28 *466–67*

Daniel

2:22 *154*
4:34–35 *99, 136, 304, 433, 476, 540, 575, 577, 582–83, 596–97, 753, 755, 771, 871, 879*
4:34–55 *757*
4:35 *628–29, 757, 873, 881*
5 *316*
7:14 *680*
9:1–2 *276, 932*
9:2 *276*
9:4–19 *932*
9:7 *651*
9:16 *651*
11 *632*
11:2 *632*
11:4 *632*
11:5–35 *632*
12:2 *469, 654*

Hosea

1:6 *480*
1:9–11 *480*
2:1 *480*
2:14–15 *133, 461*
2:23 *480*
6:5 *160*
6:7 *442–43*
11:1 *131, 133, 444, 461–62, 472, 478, 681*
11:7ff *885*
11:8–9 *615*
11:9 *402*
12:2 *653*
12:9 *461*

12:13 *461*
13:4–5 *461*
13:5 *739, 776*

Joel

1:15 *824*
2 *213*
2:1 *587, 824*
2:13–14 *610*
2:28 *352, 467*
2:28–29 *677*
2:28–32 *420, 466–67, 478, 530, 681*
2:32 *745*

Amos

1:3–3:2 *656*
2:7 *587*
3:1 *676*
3:2 *739, 776*
3:6 *883*
3:7 *154, 738*
3:8 *676*
4:6–8 *883*
4:13 *803–5*
5:18 *824*
7 *933*
7:3–6 *610*
9:1–4 *625*
9:11–12 *466–67*

Jonah

1:17 *919*
3:9–10 *610*
3:10 *557*

Micah

3:12–13 *276*
4:1–5 *276*
4:12 *738*
5:2 *474*
6:8 *652*
7:20 *653*

Habakkuk

1:5 *280*
1:6 *882*
1:12–13 *402, 588*
1:13 *304, 654, 884*
2:3 *757*
2:4 *277*
2:14 *276*
2:18–20 *160, 605*
3:3 *677*

Zephaniah

1:14 *824*
3:5 *652*

Zechariah

1:6 *879*
1:8–12:3 *167*
2:13 *587*
7:12 *677*
8:6 *881*
8:8 *651*
8:14 *610*
9:9 *651*
12:1 *804*
12:10 *330, 677*
13:7 *330*
13:7–9 *278*
14:8 *278*
14:9 *160, 676*

Malachi

1:2–3 *661*
1:6 *572*
3:1 *167*
3:6 *572, 583, 585, 597, 607, 757*
3:16 *160, 676*
4:4–6 *378*

Matthew

1 *120, 122, 823*
1:1 *427, 446, 471, 681*
1:1–17 *460*
1:2–6a *120*
1:6b–11 *120*
1:12–17 *120*
1:18 *167*
1:18–25 *472*
1:20–23 *699*
1:21 *427, 471, 683*
1:22 *279, 320*
1:23 *165, 577, 579*
2:1–12 *474*
2:3 *329*
2:5 *279*
2:15 *131, 279, 472, 478*
2:16 *317*
2:17 *279*
2:23 *279*

3:3 *279*
3:9 *628*
3:13–17 *699*
3:15–17 *472*
3:16 *684*
3:16–17 *675, 682, 685*
3:17 *166, 684*
4:1–11 *278, 472*
4:4 *100, 110, 278, 320, 339, 350*
4:4–10 *277*
4:5–10 *328*
4:7 *351*
4:10 *351*
4:17 *476*
4:18–22 *479*
5:3–12 *476*
5:5 *455, 525*
5:6 *652*
5:8 *625*
5:10 *652*
5:17–18 *133, 169, 330*
5:17–19 *683*
5:17–20 *158, 245, 281, 330, 350–51, 371, 439, 473, 566, 681–82, 718*
5:20 *652*
5:21–48 *429*
5:43 *321*
5:44–45 *663*
5:44–48 *663*
5:45 *327, 871, 880*
5:46 *663*
6:1–2 *654*
6:5 *654*
6:9 *685, 867*
6:9–13 *723*
6:10 *476, 629, 875*
6:16 *654*
6:21 *898*
6:26 *880*
6:30 *880*
6:33 *651*
7:13–14 *745*
7:15–20 *772*
7:21–23 *732*
7:21–27 *156*
7:21–29 *284*
7:21ff *158*
7:23 *776*
7:24 *745*
7:28f *158*
8:4 *277*
8–9 *472*
8:11–12 *476*
8:19–22 *582*
8:23–27 *919*
8:27 *156, 160*
8:28–34 *326*
10:1–4 *479*
10:1–15 *284*
10:26 *154*
10:29 *661, 868, 871*
10:29–30 *880*
10:30–31 *661*
10:32–33 *745*
10:34–38 *582*
10:41–42 *653*
11 *281*
11:10 *277*
11:11 *281*
11:11–15 *133*
11:13 *461, 683*
11:21–24 *641*
11:25 *873*
11:25–27 *156, 684–85*
11:25–28 *167, 245*
11:25–30 *427, 681*
11:26 *665, 738*
11:27 *167, 352, 727*
11:27–27 *634*
11:28–30 *477, 523*
11:29 *167*
12:1–8 *350*
12:3 *278*
12:3–4 *331*
12:5 *278*
12:28 *476, 684*
12:40–41 *331*
12:42 *331*
13:24–30 *476, 510*
13:31–32 *325*
13:35 *608, 804*
13:36–43 *476, 510*
15:4 *277*
15:7 *277*
16:18 *372, 471, 478, 480*
16:24 *167*
16:28 *476*
17:5 *166, 291*
18:15–20 *653*
18:20 *625*
19:3–9 *350*
19:4 *804*
19:4–5 *277*
19:4–6 *278, 331, 816*

19:4–9 *429*
19:7 *321*
19:8 *277, 804*
19:25 *881*
19:26 *728*
19:28 *423*
21:3 *277*
21:12–17 *326*
21:13 *351*
21:16 *279*
21:42 *277–78*
22 *331*
22:1–14 *476*
22:14 *758*
22:21 *653*
22:29–30 *453*
22:29–32 *345, 411*
22:31 *278*
22:31–32 *350*
22:32 *331*
22:34–40 *429*
22:35 *331*
22:36–40 *98*
22:37 *143*
22:37–38 *27, 107, 662*
22:37–40 *7*
22:43 *277*
22:43–45 *277–78, 331*
22:44 *352*
22:45 *279*
23:25 *331*
23:35 *378–79, 816*
23:37 *743, 746*
24:4–8 *326*
24:15 *277*
24:21 *804*
24:22 *758*
24:24 *758*
24:29–31 *630*
24:31 *758*
24:36 *696, 757*
24:37–38 *331*
25:1–13 *476*
25:21 *653*
25:31–46 *156, 476*
25:34 *608, 653, 754*
25:41–46 *920*
25:46 *654*
26:27–28 *492*
26:29 *476*
26:31 *277, 351*
26:34 *277*
26:42 *738*
26:53 *628*
26:54 *278, 755*
26:54–56 *330*
26:56 *755*
27:9 *755*
27:35 *755*
28:2–3 *326*
28:11–15 *732*
28:18–20 *5, 29, 86, 107, 399, 472, 479, 540, 671, 681–83, 715, 720*
28:19 *135, 682, 684*

Mark

1:2 *279*
1:11 *472*
1:14–15 *476*
1:15 *175*
2:1–11 *730*
2:3–12 *683*
2:5 *681*
2:10–12 *165*
3:13–19 *284*
4:11–12 *351*
4:22 *154*
4:35–41 *730, 919*
5:24–34 *730*
7:1–13 *321*
7:5–13 *346*
7:6 *277*
7:6–7 *378*
7:10–13 *378*
7:17–23 *653*
7:21–23 *759*
8:34–38 *929*
8:38 *158, 284*
9:7 *291*
10:3 *278*
10:6 *331, 804, 816*
10:6–8 *816*
10:18 *650*
10:27 *628*
11:17 *378*
12:1–12 *767*
12:10 *277*
12:10–11 *378*
12:24 *378*
12:26 *277*
12:28–29 *407, 683*
12:29 *596*
12:29–31 *653*
12:36 *277*

13:19 *803*
13:20 *739*
13:32 *10, 696*
14:27 *330*
14:49 *279, 755*
15:15 *317*
15:28 *279, 755*

Luke

1:1–4 *295, 297*
1:2 *384*
1:31–33 *472, 764*
1:31–37 *699*
1:35 *472, 675, 681, 684–85*
1:35–37 *630*
1:37 *156, 160, 628, 676, 881*
1:67 *157*
1:70 *279*
1:79 *154*
2:1–4 *317*
2:9 *167*
2:25–32 *157*
2:52 *99, 713*
3:1–2 *317*
3:16–17 *472, 681*
3:22 *738*
3:38 *444, 680–81, 815*
4:5–12 *328*
4:14–21 *213, 472, 681*
4:16–19 *278*
4:16–21 *319, 378*
4:16–30 *476*
4:17–20 *286*
4:17–21 *167*
4:21 *175, 277, 279*
4:25–26 *331*
4:27 *331*
4:40 *327*
5:1–10 *730*
6:12–16 *284*
6:27 *651*
6:33 *663*
6:33–35 *651*
6:35–36 *663*
7:1–10 *156, 160*
7:7–9 *156*
7:30 *746*
8:21 *158, 284*
8:26–39 *326*
9:26ff *158, 284*
9:35 *166, 291*
10:7 *286, 382*
10:21 *738*
10:26 *278*
11:20 *476*
11:50–51 *816*
12:32 *654*
12:42 *605*
12:56 *32*
13:1–5 *920*
14:14 *653*
16:1–8 *605*
16:19–31 *351*
16:25 *663*
17:10 *605, 653*
17:26–32 *331*
18:6–8 *758*
18:19 *651*
20:17 *278*
22:20 *494, 764*
22:22 *157, 739, 757, 882*
22:34 *881*
22:37 *279*
23:51 *476*
24 *282, 351*
24:25 *287, 350*
24:25–27 *167, 283, 371, 566*
24:32 *282*
24:36–40 *597, 623*
24:44 *277, 279, 284, 330–31, 340, 370–71, 378*
24:44–49 *682*
24:46 *351*
24:46–51 *476*

John

1:1 *10, 86, 155, 158, 160–62, 167, 277, 335, 384, 400, 420, 427, 574, 582, 618, 667, 679, 682–83, 685, 694*
1:1–2 *88, 155, 167, 280, 471, 671, 681, 727, 804, 867*
1:1–3 *156–57, 274, 427, 540, 573, 602, 675, 681–82, 699, 718*
1:1–4 *86*
1:1–18 *99, 135, 165, 399, 540, 667, 676, 699*
1:1a *676*
1:1ac *155*
1:1b *155, 161, 400, 676*
1:1c *161, 400, 676*
1:3 *160, 167, 685, 694, 704, 795, 805*
1:9 *774*
1:10 *167*

1:12 *694*
1:14 *10, 155, 158, 162, 167, 277, 280, 335, 413, 420, 471, 579, 618, 667, 682, 694, 704, 832*
1:14–18 *133, 160, 274, 571, 577, 625, 651, 663, 670*
1:18 *384, 427, 624, 671, 676, 679, 682–83, 685*
1:29–34 *681*
1:32–34 *213*
2:11 *154, 165*
2:12–25 *326*
2:19–21 *448*
2:19–22 *460, 473, 477*
2:21–22 *351*
3:3 *685, 759*
3:5 *684*
3:5–8 *462, 704, 764*
3:6 *694*
3:10 *350*
3:14 *331*
3:16 *576, 661, 663, 685–86, 699, 704, 743, 745*
3:16–17 *720*
3:19–20 *774*
3:34 *712*
3:34–35 *157*
3:34ff *167*
3:35 *661*
3:36 *577*
4 *597*
4:3 *610*
4:24 *597, 623*
4:34 *156, 767*
5:16–20 *718*
5:16–30 *86, 400, 427, 540, 681–82, 684, 704*
5:17 *726, 868*
5:17–19 *867*
5:17–30 *630, 730*
5:19 *685, 718–19*
5:19–23 *675*
5:19–29 *696*
5:19–30 *171, 685, 699, 712*
5:19–47 *245, 284*
5:20 *156, 167, 661*
5:21 *684*
5:21–30 *160*
5:22–23 *426, 672, 680*
5:23 *214, 719*
5:26 *177, 574, 597, 605–6, 684–85, 719, 727*
5:30 *767*
5:39 *319, 330*
5:39–40 *282, 351*
5:45 *277*
5:45–47 *167, 283*
5:46–47 *330*
6:32–33 *684*
6:37 *757, 764, 772, 774, 891*
6:37–40 *503, 758, 891*
6:38 *704, 767*
6:38f *156*
6:39 *503*
6:40 *745, 891*
6:44 *757, 772, 774, 776*
6:45 *351, 378*
6:46 *624*
6:63 *156, 158–59, 284, 684*
6:68 *156, 158*
6:68–69 *284*
7:16 *167*
7:19 *331*
7:21–24 *278*
7:37–38 *745*
7:37–39 *351*
7:38 *277*
7:38–39 *278*
7:39 *213, 667, 685*
8:12–30 *245*
8:17 *278, 351*
8:20 *757*
8:28 *167*
8:34 *772*
8:47 *158, 284*
8:56 *331*
8:58 *160, 384, 427, 573, 619, 676, 680, 683*
9:1–3 *901*
9:3 *920*
10 *332*
10:14–15 *762*
10:14–18 *503*
10:14–30 *171, 684*
10:26 *762*
10:29 *503*
10:34–35 *278, 330–31, 378*
10:35 *110, 159, 169, 277, 321*
11:1–44 *730*
11:25 *630*
11:33–35 *928*
11:43 *630*
12:16 *667*
12:20 *774*
12:23–24 *933*

12:23–28 *667*
12:27ff *284*
12:28 *166*
12:32 *774*
12:32–33 *756*
12:38–41 *331*
12:47–49 *167*
12:47–50 *158, 284*
12:48 *156*
13–17 *284*
13:18 *279*
13:19–21 *632*
13:31–32 *667*
13:35 *167, 662*
13:38 *632*
14:6 *167, 214, 245, 277, 646, 718*
14:6–11 *676*
14:9 *162, 167, 625*
14:9–13 *684*
14:11 *699*
14:15 *158, 284*
14:15–17 *476*
14–16 *99*
14:16 *201, 682, 685–86*
14:16–16:15 *684*
14–18 *86*
14:21 *158, 284*
14:23 *624*
14:23–24 *284*
14:23–26 *159, 168*
14:23f *158*
14:25 *154*
14:25–26 *245*
14:26 *168, 284, 352, 383, 682, 685–86, 703–4, 727, 764*
14:28 *696, 720*
14:31 *682*
15:1–6 *472*
15:1–17 *131*
15:7 *158, 284*
15:9–10 *661*
15:9–11 *721*
15:10 *158, 284*
15:11 *154*
15:14 *158, 284*
15:16 *757*
15:25 *279, 378*
15:25–26 *699*
15:26 *284, 682, 685, 703–4, 727, 764*
15:26–16:16 *159*
15:26–27 *168, 245, 284, 685*
16:1 *154*
16:5–11 *727*
16:5–15 *284, 764*
16:7 *703–4*
16:7–11 *213*
16:12–15 *245, 383, 682, 685, 699, 703, 754*
16:13 *159, 168*
16:13–14 *297*
16:13–15 *352, 686*
16:13f *168*
16:14 *668, 685*
16:14–15 *715*
17 *933*
17:1 *668, 933*
17:1–5 *86, 99, 400, 540, 667*
17:1–26 *156*
17:2 *503*
17:3 *xi, xv, 5, 7, 427, 584, 594, 596, 646, 672, 681, 683, 722*
17:5 *177, 400, 574, 666, 671, 682, 933*
17:6 *154, 158, 284*
17:6–10 *503*
17:8 *167*
17:12 *279, 630*
17:17 *158, 160, 171, 284, 287, 332, 338, 372, 576, 646, 676*
17:24 *400, 671, 682, 727*
17:24–26 *722*
18:19–27 *632*
18:31–33 *324*
18:32 *756*
18:37–38 *324*
19:23–24 *330*
19:24 *167, 279*
19:28 *279*
19:28–29 *756*
19:31 *167*
19:31–36 *756*
19:36 *279*
19:36–37 *330*
20:21 *383*
20:21–23 *472, 681*
20:22 *685*
20:28 *384, 427, 679, 682–83*
20:30–31 *730*
20:31 *103, 339*
21:15–23 *928*
21:18–19 *632*
21:25 *174, 328*

Acts

1–2 *479*
1:6 *482*

1:16 *278–79, 352*
2 *213, 280, 359, 467, 482, 530, 681, 685, 732*
2:1–4 *159*
2:1–36 *472, 681*
2:13 *732*
2:14–41 *285*
2:15 *732*
2:17 *331, 467, 624*
2:22 *156, 165*
2:22–24 *889*
2:22–36 *175, 764*
2:23 *155, 157, 304, 565, 636, 736, 738–39, 753, 755–57, 772, 776, 874, 881, 890, 900, 927*
2:23–24 *99, 575, 632, 882*
2:25–32 *345*
2:30–31 *278*
2:32–33 *685*
2:32–36 *285, 472, 476*
2:33 *703*
2:33–34 *579*
2:33–36 *156*
2:34–35 *332*
2:36 *573*
2:38 *518*
2:39 *156, 516*
2:42 *284*
3:11–26 *175*
3:12–26 *285*
3:13–15 *668*
3:18 *279*
3:22 *331*
3:22–23 *284*
3:22–26 *460*
3:22ff *167*
3:26 *483*
4 *280*
4:12 *214, 421, 867*
4:23–30 *565*
4:23–31 *304, 889*
4:24 *804*
4:24–26 *279*
4:25 *278, 352*
4:27–28 *86, 540, 565, 636, 736, 753, 756, 882*
4:28 *157, 738–39*
5 *926*
5:3–4 *684*
5:37 *317*
6:2 *285*
6:7 *285*
7:1–53 *120, 327*
7:2 *666*
7:2–16 *120*
7:2–53 *165*
7:17–45a *120*
7:37 *167, 331*
7:38 *279*
7:45b–53 *120*
7:51 *684*
8 *479, 482*
8:4 *285*
8:25 *285*
8:30–31 *356*
8:32 *331*
8:35 *293*
9:4 *166*
9:15 *739, 873*
9:31 *684*
10 *479*
10:9–16 *653*
10–11 *121, 482–83, 486*
10:19 *166*
10:34–48 *175*
10:36 *285*
10:38 *712*
10:42 *739*
10:44 *285*
10:44–48 *472, 624, 681*
11:1 *285*
11:27–28 *168*
12:20–23 *317, 919*
12:24 *285*
13:1–3 *168*
13:2 *166*
13:5 *12, 285*
13:7 *317*
13:14–41 *12*
13:15 *286*
13:16–41 *175, 285, 327*
13:16–52 *280*
13:17 *739*
13:27 *882*
13:32–33 *127*
13:32–35 *294*
13:34–35 *279*
13:35 *279*
13:36 *738*
13:44–45 *12*
13:44–49 *285*
13:46 *285, 352*
13:48 *761, 776*
14:1 *12*
14:14–18 *661*
14:15 *787, 804, 820*

14:15–18 *203*
14:16–17 *663*
14:17 *164, 195, 208, 663, 871, 880*
15 *121, 483, 486*
15:7 *739*
15:13–17 *321*
15:18 *754*
15:21 *286*
15:25 *285*
15:36 *285*
16:15 *516*
16:32 *285*
16:38 *317*
17 *21*
17:2 *12, 319*
17:2–3 *378*
17:6 *317*
17:10 *12*
17:11 *319, 378*
17:13 *285*
17:16–32 *11*
17:16–34 *861*
17:17 *12*
17:20 *154*
17:22–31 *203, 208*
17:24 *623, 805, 820, 873*
17:24–25 *86, 107, 398, 433, 540, 606, 671, 718, 795, 804*
17:24–26 *304, 575, 596–97, 605*
17:24–27 *208*
17:24–28 *86, 99*
17:24–29 *661*
17:24–30 *605*
17:24–31 *171*
17:25 *582, 605, 721, 727*
17:26 *411, 736, 739, 753, 755, 816, 880*
17:26–28 *164*
17:28 *86, 99, 379, 401, 540, 577, 581, 583, 623, 625, 831, 868, 871, 906*
17:28–29 *216*
17:29 *597, 623*
17:30 *663*
17:30–31 *654*
17:31 *652, 739*
18 *934*
18:6 *352*
18:8 *516*
18:9–10 *934*
18:11 *285*
18:28 *378*
19:10 *285*
19:20 *285*
19:31 *317*
20:27 *22, 32, 432, 535, 738*
21:9–14 *168*
21:14 *738*
21:17–18 *317*
22:21 *352*
24:14–15 *378*
24:24 *317*
26:5 *739, 776*
26:22 *378*
27:15 *292*
28:7 *317*
28:25 *279*
28:25–27 *684*
32–33 *516*

Romans

1 *13, 193, 203, 211, 215, 542, 835*
1:1–2 *480*
1:1–5 *759*
1–2 *211*
1:2 *366*
1–3 *212*
1:3–4 *280, 460, 472, 764*
1:4 *165*
1:6–7 *156*
1:11 *480*
1:16 *29, 156, 160, 630*
1:16–17 *284*
1:17 *203, 279*
1:18 *203, 205*
1:18–3:20 *203, 656*
1:18–20 *208*
1:18–21 *26*
1:18–23 *402*
1:18–25 *417*
1:18–31 *542*
1:18–32 *86, 88, 99, 105, 164, 171–72, 208, 210, 409–10, 577, 653, 786, 813*
1:19–20 *204*
1:20 *102, 195, 204–5, 208, 624, 630*
1:20–23 *209*
1:21 *204, 206*
1:21–22 *205*
1:22 *206*
1:22–23 *205*
1:23 *607, 618*
1:23–31 *206*
1:23–32 *205*
1:24 *14, 204–5, 875, 904*
1:24–32 *209*
1:25 *14, 205, 448, 546, 805*

1:25–26 *14*
1:26 *15, 204–5, 875, 904*
1:26–29 *14*
1:28 *14, 204–6, 875, 904*
1:29–31 *15*
1:30–31 *15, 206*
1:31 *15*
1:32 *206–7, 209, 216, 654*
2:4 *663*
2:6–7 *653*
2:7 *653*
2:9 *654*
2:14–15 *206, 663*
2:14–16 *211–12*
2:16 *159, 284*
2:25–29 *472, 483*
2:26 *207*
2:29 *468, 518*
3:1–2 *172, 378*
3:2 *204, 279, 294, 371*
3:4 *279, 332, 576, 646*
3:9–20 *205*
3:19–20 *461*
3:21 *133, 460–61, 651*
3:21–16 *699*
3:21–25 *927*
3:21–26 *422, 427, 451, 460, 469, 477, 589, 600, 654, 665, 682, 685, 764*
3:21–31 *461*
3:23 *185, 203, 411, 416–17, 433, 448, 666, 772, 817–18, 885*
3:25–26 *449, 654–55*
3:26 *652*
3:30 *329, 683*
3:31 *133*
4 *123, 158, 279, 451*
4:1–8 *423*
4:3 *279*
4:5 *427, 665*
4:9–22 *472, 483*
4:11 *518*
4:13 *455, 525*
4:16–17a *526*
4:16–22 *582*
4:17 *455, 804*
4:17b *156*
4:18 *279*
4:20–21 *628*
4:25 *682*
5:1–2 *423*
5:1–8:39 *427*
5:2 *667*
5:5 *662–63*
5:6 *645*
5:9–11 *423*
5:12 *417, 433*
5:12–13 *120*
5:12–21 *120, 133, 203, 348, 411, 443–46, 472, 475, 750, 764, 772, 816–18, 825, 829, 885, 906, 910*
5:14 *102, 128, 131–32, 411, 438, 799, 881*
5:14–17 *120*
5:15 *663*
5:18 *651*
5:18–19 *423*
5:18–21 *120*
5:20 *461, 663*
5:21 *651*
6:1–4 *156, 694*
6:1–14 *761, 764*
6:4 *518, 668*
6:23 *415, 417, 433, 448, 654, 817, 829, 858*
7:12 *461*
8 *684, 759, 776–77*
8:1 *477, 885*
8:1–17 *445, 764*
8:2 *684*
8:4 *207*
8:5–11 *143*
8:7 *448, 885*
8:7–8 *759, 772*
8:9 *685*
8:9–11 *684*
8:9–17 *477, 694*
8:11 *624, 684*
8:14–17 *359*
8:18–22 *825*
8:18–23 *417*
8:18–25 *858*
8:18–27 *477*
8:18–39 *685, 874*
8:19–22 *203, 409, 885, 910*
8:19–23 *408*
8:20 *415*
8:21 *434*
8:27 *684*
8:28 *156, 372, 575, 582, 647, 739, 777, 876, 890, 920–21*
8:28–29 *575, 583, 736, 753, 873*
8:28–30 *759, 775, 777*
8:28–33 *758*
8:28–39 *146, 481, 685, 722*
8:29 *407, 739, 758–59, 771, 776–77, 799*
8:29–30 *503, 739, 777*

8:30 *777*
8:32 *684*
8:34 *579, 684*
8:37 *757*
9 *739, 744, 747–48, 755, 759, 761, 935*
9:1–5 *758*
9:1–24 *597*
9:5 *384, 427, 679, 683*
9:6 *468, 525, 760, 891*
9:6–9 *456, 758*
9:6–23 *759*
9:7–9 *760*
9:9 *739*
9–10 *759, 882, 891, 935*
9:10–13 *758, 760*
9–11 *121, 736, 748, 753, 758*
9:11 *739, 760*
9:11–12 *739, 760*
9:11–13 *757*
9:12 *760*
9:14 *760, 891*
9:14–18 *758*
9:15 *665, 760*
9:15–16 *758*
9:15–18 *739*
9:16 *761*
9:17 *279, 294, 763, 920*
9:17–18 *756*
9:19 *761, 891*
9:19–24 *575*
9:20 *582, 804, 873*
9:20–23 *761*
9:22 *630, 751, 762, 891*
9:22–23 *762–63*
9:23 *739, 762, 873*
9:24–26 *480*
9:30–10:21 *759, 761, 891*
9:33 *745*
10:5 *504*
10:6–8 *160, 350*
10:9 *426, 573, 679*
10:9–11 *885*
10:11 *279*
10:13–15a *761*
10:13–17 *339*
10:17 *154*
10:20 *758*
11 *513*
11:1 *608*
11:1–6 *758*
11:2 *279, 739, 759, 776*
11:5 *739*
11:7 *762*
11:17–24 *483*
11:28 *739*
11:29 *608*
11:33 *28, 665, 935*
11:33–34 *648*
11:33–36 *5, 86, 88, 99, 171, 393, 540, 565, 575, 597, 602, 632, 685, 754, 759, 921*
11:35–36 *605*
11:36 *28, 414, 572, 583, 605, 628–29, 666, 683, 763, 784, 867–68, 873, 895, 935*
11:36a *721*
12:1–2 *137, 143*
12:2 *11, 34, 80*
12:19 *654*
13:1–7 *410, 428, 653*
13:8–10 *429*
13:17–21 *425*
14:23 *582*
15:3–6 *379*
15:4 *280, 339, 370*
15:5 *652*
15:9–11 *652*
15:30 *684*
16:22 *321*
16:25–27 *284*
16:27 *648, 666, 670, 784*
16:29 *450*

1 Corinthians

1:2 *156, 352*
1:9 *99*
1:16 *516*
1:18 *357, 630*
1:18–25 *358*
1:18–29 *648*
1:18–31 *107, 137*
1:20 *358*
1:24 *156*
1:26 *156, 358*
1:26–29 *758*
1:27–28 *739*
2 *357–58*
2:2–16 *357*
2:6 *358*
2:6–7 *400*
2:6–10a *358*
2:6–16 *284*
2:7 *358, 739, 754, 833*
2:7–13 *300*
2:8 *684*
2:9–10 *359*

2:9–12 *346*
2:9–16 *100*
2:10 *358, 684, 727*
2:10–11 *634, 685*
2:10–13 *159, 168, 245*
2:10–16 *359*
2:10b–13 *358*
2:11 *88, 684*
2:11b *336*
2:12 *358*
2:13 *298, 358*
2:14 *352, 354, 772*
2:14–16 *358*
3:1–3 *357*
3:16–17 *477*
3:21–23 *765*
4:1 *159, 168*
4:7 *653*
5:7 *331*
6:11 *684, 867*
6:16 *279*
6:19 *477, 481*
7:19 *124, 653*
8:3 *776*
8:4–6 *683*
8:4–7 *596*
8:5–6 *86, 540, 681*
8:6 *135, 167, 682, 784, 795*
9 *775*
9:19–21 *439*
9:19–23 *482, 653*
9:22–24 *775*
9:26 *775*
10:1–12 *339*
10:1–13 *284*
10:4 *167, 331*
10:6 *128, 370*
10:11 *128, 379*
10:12–13 *929*
10:13 *631*
10:25–26 *345*
10:31 *582*
11 *926*
11:1 *167*
11:7 *407*
11:9 *803, 805*
11:18 *480*
11:25 *480*
12:2 *160*
12:3 *426, 573, 679*
12:4–6 *684*
13:12 *625*
14:37 *245, 369*
14:37–38 *383*
15 *279, 423, 832*
15:1–2 *383*
15:1–3 *29, 344, 630*
15:1–34 *427*
15:2f *169*
15:3 *681*
15:3–4 *279*
15:3–8 *327*
15:3–11 *175*
15:12–19 *307*
15:16–28 *681*
15:20–21 *443*
15:20–23 *445*
15:20–28 *721*
15:21–22 *472, 681*
15:21–28 *348, 446*
15:21–49 *131*
15:22–23 *816*
15:24f *763*
15:25 *332*
15:25–28 *715, 720*
15:26–28 *171*
15:27 *471*
15:28 *594, 668, 754, 763, 768, 783, 876*
15:29 *355*
15:33 *379*
15:35–58 *477*
15:38 *755*
15:45 *411*
15:45–47 *816*
15:45–49 *685*
15:49 *445*
15:56–57 *927*
16:21 *321*

2 Corinthians

1:3 *663*
1:13 *352*
1:20 *174, 245, 248, 280, 283, 438, 471, 528, 566, 608*
1:22–24 *630*
3 *284*
3:6 *176, 383, 684*
3:7–18 *480*
3:14 *176, 352*
3:14–16 *357*
3:17 *352, 684*
3:18 *407, 667, 681*
4:1–6 *159*
4:2 *321, 647*

4:3–4 *357*
4:3–6 *667*
4:6 *833*
4:17 *667, 921*
5:10 *477, 654*
5:16–21 *477*
5:17 *424, 472, 477, 531, 681, 833*
6:16 *477, 481*
9:7 *745*
10:3–5 *107, 308*
10:4b–5 *xi, 4*
10:5 *27, 29, 32, 76, 108, 137, 143, 582*
10:9 *286*
12:1 *159*
12:7 *159*
12:12 *165*
13:2–3 *287*
13:14 *86, 135, 400, 540, 682–84*

Galatians

1:1 *159, 168, 245, 383*
1:2 *352*
1:4 *476*
1:5 *784*
1:6–9 *284, 344*
1:6–10 *29*
1:8–9 *388*
1:11–16 *159*
1:11–17 *166*
1:11f *168*
1:15 *755*
1:16 *168, 329*
2 *294*
2:2 *168*
2–3 *121*
2:20 *665*
3 *279, 378, 451*
3:1–6 *124, 472*
3:1–25 *454*
3–4 *124, 486, 608*
3:6–9 *124, 158, 472, 483*
3:8 *279, 293–94, 329*
3:10 *461*
3:10–12 *461*
3:12 *504*
3:13 *331, 461*
3:15–4:7 *125, 458*
3:15–29 *124*
3:16 *124, 133, 279, 321, 332, 420, 446, 450, 453, 456, 472, 526*
3:17 *125, 458*
3:19 *458*
3:21–22 *461*
3:21–24 *125*
3:22 *279, 294*
3:25–29 *125*
3:26–4:7 *132, 472, 681*
3:26–29 *457, 480, 494, 530*
3:27–29 *518*
3:29 *132–33, 527*
4:4 *175, 458, 582, 684, 704, 767*
4:4–5 *575, 736, 753*
4:4–6 *682*
4:4–7 *339, 685–86, 705*
4:5–6 *694*
4:6 *685*
4:6–7 *685*
4:8–9 *605*
4:9 *776*
4:21 *331*
4:24 *431, 436*
4:24–26 *128*
4:30 *279*
5:14 *429*
5:16–26 *445*
6:2 *653*
6:10 *651*
6:11 *321*
6:16 *132, 480*

Ephesians

1:3 *684–85*
1:3–4 *754*
1:3–6 *754*
1:3–13 *684*
1:3–14 *86, 99, 171, 284, 400, 414, 540, 573, 575, 663, 675, 682, 699, 751, 754, 758, 880*
1:4 *437, 608, 736, 758, 776, 804*
1:4–5 *675*
1:4–6 *146, 629, 661, 693, 738–39, 753–54, 758, 764, 776, 879, 891*
1:4–10 *664, 685*
1:4–12 *503*
1:4–14 *503*
1:5 *738–39, 758*
1:5–6 *754, 758–59*
1:5–11 *833*
1:7 *675, 694, 867*
1:7–8 *477*
1:7–10 *427, 682, 758, 879*
1:9 *583, 738–39, 759*

1:9–10 *111, 171, 174, 393, 395, 423, 432, 437, 439, 472, 575, 685, 704, 721, 754, 763, 767, 829, 876, 921*
1:9–11 *754*
1:10 *487*
1:10–11 *755*
1:10–12 *400, 767*
1:11 *67, 86, 99–100, 136, 151, 155–57, 213, 304, 311, 332, 372, 401, 433, 540, 565, 582–83, 608, 628–29, 738–39, 750, 754, 757, 759, 771, 797, 871, 873–74, 879–80*
1:11–12 *606, 736, 753, 758*
1:11–13 *503*
1:12–14 *754*
1:13 *675*
1:13–14 *476–77, 481, 530, 685, 694, 754, 764*
1:17 *666, 684*
1:17–19 *143*
1:18–2:10 *732*
1:18–23 *472*
1:20 *332*
1:20–23 *630, 715*
1:21 *476*
1:22 *471, 479, 683*
2 *663*
2:1 *833*
2:1–3 *417, 445, 448, 664, 750, 759, 818, 885*
2:1–7 *156*
2:1–10 *171, 393, 472, 475, 477, 575, 751*
2:1–21 *477*
2:4 *758*
2:4–5 *664*
2:4–10 *694*
2:5 *663*
2:5–6 *481, 525*
2:8 *663*
2:8–10 *531, 754, 757–58, 774, 776*
2:10 *681, 736, 739, 753, 756, 833*
2:11–12 *172, 203, 482*
2:11–21 *457, 479, 525–26, 530–31*
2:11–22 *121, 424, 472, 481, 483, 486, 625, 657*
2:12 *431, 436, 480, 524, 526*
2:13 *625*
2:14–18 *482*
2:15 *497, 681*
2:17 *285*
2:18 *481, 684, 723*
2:19 *480*
2:19–22 *460, 667*
2:20 *284, 286, 346, 383*
2:21 *477, 481*
2:22 *624*
3 *483*
3:1–7 *755*
3:1–10 *479*
3:2 *487*
3:2–6 *280*
3:3 *168*
3:4 *352*
3:4–6 *480*
3:6 *526*
3:8 *479*
3:8–13 *482, 525*
3:9 *487, 608, 675, 693, 804*
3:9–11 *755*
3:10 *479, 648, 751, 755*
3:10–11 *658*
3:11 *608, 739, 754*
3:14 *867*
3:14–15 *161, 685, 795*
3:14–19 *684*
3:14–21 *723*
3:15 *873*
3:17 *624*
3:17–19 *662*
3:20–21 *630–31*
3:21 *784*
4:1–16 *468*
4:4–6 *579, 682–84*
4:6 *86, 99, 401*
4:7–16 *356*
4:8 *279*
4:12–13 *28*
4:13 *137*
4:14 *xi, xv, 28, 108*
4:17 *196*
4:17–19 *207, 448*
4:20–24 *132, 694*
4:24 *217, 407*
4:25 *647*
5:25 *661*
5:31–32 *453*
5:32 *411*
6:1–3 *352*
6:2–3 *455*
6:3 *525*
6:6 *629*
6:17 *154*

Philippians

1:1 *352*

1:6 *608*
1:29 *776*
2:1 *684*
2:5–11 *668*
2:6–7 *685*
2:6–8 *414, 713*
2:6–11 *10, 384, 423, 441, 472, 829*
2:8–11 *715*
2:9 *763*
2:9–11 *135, 284, 426–27, 472, 667–68, 680, 683, 720*
2:10–11 *583, 873*
2:11 *426, 573, 668, 679, 721*
2:11–12 *752*
2:12 *892*
2:12–13 *755, 761, 871, 892*
2:13 *654, 738, 892*
2:16 *156, 160*
3:3 *480, 483*
3:7 *480*
3:7–8 *582*
3:9 *480*
4:20 *666, 784*

Colossians

1:9–10 *594*
1:9–13 *143*
1:13–14 *783*
1:15 *167, 407, 444, 624, 646, 676, 683, 694, 696, 799*
1:15–16 *161, 699, 704, 829*
1:15–17 *384, 573, 675, 685, 694, 709, 718, 767, 795, 921*
1:15–18 *754*
1:15–20 *171, 284, 393, 401, 421, 423, 426, 433, 472, 575, 676, 680, 683, 763, 767, 784*
1:16 *167, 697, 763, 799, 804–5, 820*
1:16–17 *156, 867*
1:17 *173, 437, 583, 623, 625, 630, 711–12, 726, 868, 871*
1:18 *594, 721*
1:19 *667*
1:25 *487*
1:27 *624*
1:28–29 *xv, 29, 107*
2:3 *xi*
2:6–8 *26, 80*
2:6–10 *107*
2:7 *108*
2:8 *33, 137, 388*
2:8–9 *78*
2:8–10 *76, 308, 344, 346*
2:9 *167, 277, 426, 679, 683*
2:11–12 *518*
2:12–13 *481, 525*
2:13–15 *927*
2:14 *461*
3:3 *481, 525*
3:8–10 *648*
3:9–10 *694*
3:10 *407, 603, 647*
3:12 *758*
3:17 *582*
3:23 *582*
4:16 *284, 286, 385*
4:18 *321*

1 Thessalonians

1:2–4 *776*
1:4 *383, 480, 739, 758*
1:5 *157, 159, 161, 286, 359*
1:9 *646*
2:13 *286, 359, 370, 383*
4:2 *159, 284*
4:3 *629, 874*
4:8 *286*
5:9 *758*
5:27 *284, 286*

2 Thessalonians

1:5 *653*
1:6–7 *653*
1:8 *654*
2:2 *159*
2:13 *684, 754, 758, 761*
2:13–14 *684, 758*
2:15 *169, 248*
3:5 *684*
3:6 *169, 248*
3:14 *245, 284, 286–87*
3:17 *321*

1 Timothy

1:11 *666*
1:16–17 *618*
1:17 *584–85, 596, 607, 624, 666, 683, 784, 873*
2:4 *202, 743, 746, 875*
2:5 *683*
2:11–15 *342*
2:13–14 *816*
3:2 *356*
3:6 *447*

3:9 *206*
4:2 *207*
4:4 *803*
4:13 *286, 352*
4:16 *5*
5:18 *279, 286, 382*
6:3 *158, 284, 388*
6:15 *873–74*
6:15–16 *568, 618, 666*
6:16 *107, 582, 585, 607, 624, 784*
6:20 *169*

2 Timothy

1:3 *206*
1:8–10 *156, 758*
1:9 *739, 833*
1:9–10 *754*
1:10 *160*
1:12ff *169*
1:13–14 *340*
2:2 *169*
2:10 *146, 761*
2:13 *248, 770*
2:15 *5, 108*
2:19 *608, 776*
2:25 *356*
3 *292, 297*
3:1 *293, 876*
3:10–14 *293*
3:12 *929*
3:14–15a *352*
3:14–17 *379*
3:15 *159–60, 293, 339, 366, 676*
3:15–16 *177, 319, 370*
3:15–17 *110, 168, 176, 245, 280, 371, 381*
3:16 *160–61, 232, 274, 283, 289–90, 294–95, 298, 302, 311, 319–20, 335, 339, 346, 352, 359, 365, 383*
3:16–17 *285, 290, 292–93, 306, 340, 352, 439*
3:17 *651*
4:1–5 *28, 107*
4:2 *340*
4:5 *340*
4:6–8 *340*
4:8 *652–53*
4:18 *666, 784*

Titus

1:1–2 *758*
1:1–3 *400*
1:2 *248, 332, 576, 628, 646, 833*
1:7 *605*
1:9 *5, 29, 137, 356*
1:12 *379*
1:15 *207*
2:11 *154, 774*
2:13 *679, 683*
3:3–7 *685*
3:7 *663*

Hebrews

1 *472*
1:1–2 *25, 87, 103, 111, 114, 154, 274, 284, 715, 720*
1:1–3 *78, 130–31, 133, 161, 168, 171, 174, 281–82, 284, 301, 340, 355, 371, 383–84, 426, 432, 460, 472, 680–81, 683, 718, 763, 795, 876*
1:1–4 *421*
1:1–14 *685*
1:2 *160, 167, 282, 715*
1:2–3 *573, 675–76, 685, 699*
1:2a *715*
1:3 *156, 160, 173, 332, 407, 444, 579, 583, 625, 630, 646, 676, 683, 685, 694, 704, 709, 711–12, 720, 726, 799, 829, 868, 871*
1:4–14 *284*
1:5 *460*
1:5–14 *279, 680*
1:6 *345, 426, 680*
1:7–10 *279*
1:8 *679, 683*
1:8–9 *427*
1:10 *804*
1:10–12 *582*
1:11–12 *585, 607*
1:13 *332, 460*
1:14 *406*
2:1–4 *165*
2:3 *384*
2:5–9 *667, 799*
2:5–18 *125, 131, 133, 406, 421, 444–46, 461, 472, 681, 694, 764, 832*
2:7 *677*
2:8 *471*
2:8–9 *715, 720*
2:14–15 *927*
2:14–18 *472*
2:17–18 *284*
3:1–6 *133, 284, 473*
3:6 *477, 481*
3:7 *279, 352*
3:7–4:11 *125, 477, 523*
3:7–4:13 *446, 817*

3:7–4:14 *827*
3:7–9 *684*
3:15 *279*
4:1–11 *477*
4:3 *279*
4:5 *279*
4:7 *739*
4:12 *161, 337*
4:12–13 *161–62, 576*
4:13 *161, 632, 634*
4:14–10:18 *284*
4:16 *663*
5:1 *460*
5:1–10 *423, 460, 713, 764, 829, 906*
5:4–6 *460*
5:6 *279*
5:6–10 *332*
5:7 *279*
5:8–10 *764*
5–10 *469*
5:11–6:12 *357*
5:12 *279*
6:4–6 *515*
6:10 *654*
6:13 *267*
6:13–18 *597*
6:13–20 *277, 576*
6:16–18 *608*
6:17 *738, 757*
6:17–18 *176, 440, 531, 628*
6:18 *248, 311, 332, 646, 770*
7 *125*
7:2 *331*
7–8 *331*
7–10 *460–61, 492, 494, 682*
7:10–28 *332*
7:11 *125*
7:11–12 *460*
7:21 *279*
7:28 *125*
8 *125, 458*
8:1 *332*
8:1–13 *421, 427*
8:5 *128, 279*
8:6–13 *480*
8:7–13 *431, 436*
8:8 *279*
8–10 *449, 472, 480, 492, 573, 764*
9:1–10:18 *473*
9:14 *675, 684*
9:15–28 *451, 764*
9:24 *128*
10:1–18 *460*
10:3 *462*
10:4 *461, 469*
10:5–7 *704*
10:5–10 *713, 764, 767*
10:5–18 *503*
10:12–13 *332*
10:14 *528*
10:15–17 *352, 684*
10:16 *279*
10:17 *469*
10:19–22 *481, 625*
10:25 *480*
10:28–30 *515*
10:30 *279, 653*
11:3 *156, 160, 726, 804*
11:4 *582*
11:7–8 *582*
11:8–19 *158*
11:10 *525*
11:13–16 *455*
11:16 *477, 525*
11:17 *582*
11:26 *653*
11:32 *379*
11:39–40 *379*
12 *926, 929*
12:2 *332*
12:5 *654*
12:7–11 *920*
12:14 *625*
12:18–21 *166, 481*
12:18–29 *481, 525*
12:22–24 *481*
12:22–29 *171, 477*
12:26 *279*
12:28–29 *594*
12:29 *588, 654*
13:5 *279, 379*
13:8 *597, 607*
13:14 *481, 525*
13:18 *206*
13:21 *784*

James

1:1 *352*
1:3 *920*
1:3–4 *920*
1:5 *648*
1:7 *585*
1:13 *752, 770*
1:13–15 *905*

1:14 *905*
1:17 *583, 597, 604, 607, 757, 884*
1:22–25 *17, 352, 357*
1:25 *279*
2:1 *667, 684*
2:5 *739*
2:8 *279*
2:19 *596, 683*
2:21–24 *158*
3:9 *407*
4:15 *881*
5:13–16 *731*

1 Peter

1:1 *352*
1:1–2 *758*
1:2 *684, 694, 704, 739, 759, 776*
1:3 *684*
1:3–9 *477*
1:5 *503*
1:7 *920*
1:10–12 *115, 283–84, 339, 379, 451*
1:15–16 *588, 651*
1:16 *589*
1:17 *653*
1:19–20 *400*
1:20 *503, 608, 739, 754–55, 759, 776, 804*
2:2 *339, 352*
2:5 *477, 481*
2:9 *455*
2:9–10 *480, 483*
2:21 *167*
3:15 *6, 32, 80*
3:15–16 *29, 107, 137*
3:16 *206*
3:17 *738, 756*
3:18 *651, 684*
3:18–22 *131*
3:19 *355*
3:20 *331, 663*
3:21 *128, 206*
3:21–22 *715*
4:11 *279, 784*
4:12–16 *929*
4:13 *920*
4:14 *684*
4:19 *738*
5:10 *663*

2 Peter

1 *297*
1:1 *679, 683*
1:3 *339*
1:4 *339, 603*
1:5–11 *761*
1:10 *739*
1:16 *291*
1:16–21 *339*
1:17 *167*
1:19 *281, 291, 352*
1:20 *291*
1:20–21 *110, 285, 290–91, 298, 371, 383*
1:21 *160–61, 168, 176–77, 180, 232, 245, 274, 291–92, 335, 352, 359, 715, 752*
2:4 *447*
2:5–6 *331*
2:21 *169*
3 *160*
3:1–13 *452*
3:2 *285, 339–40, 383, 385*
3:3–7 *817, 858*
3:4 *804, 817*
3:5–7 *160, 870*
3:7 *156, 583, 868*
3:8 *582, 619, 824*
3:9 *202, 213, 630, 663, 743, 746, 875*
3:10–13 *423, 630*
3:13 *409, 434, 833*
3:15–16 *245, 286, 355, 385*
3:16 *284, 354, 370, 382*
3:17 *739, 776*
3:18 *784*

1 John

1:1 *156, 160, 167*
1:1–3 *413*
1:3 *178*
1:5 *304, 588, 598, 752, 770, 884*
2:1 *651*
2:3–5 *158*
2:15 *662*
2:15–17 *589*
2:18–27 *468*
2:27 *359*
3:1 *776*
3:1–3 *625*
3:2 *771*
3:16 *167*
3:19–20 *645*
3:22 *158*
4:1 *732*
4:1–3 *413*
4:2–3 *29, 732*
4:8 *402, 548, 598, 660*

4:8–10 *661*
4:9–10 *665*
4:11 *662*
4:12 *624*
4:13 *178*
4:16 *660*
4:19 *758, 761*
4:20 *624*
5:2f *158*
5:3 *662*
5:5–10 *29*
5:9 *359*
5:13 *339, 352*
5:20–21 *646*

2 John
6 *158*

Jude
3 *xv, 19, 109, 169, 248, 357*
6 *447*
7 *331*
9–10 *381*
14–15 *379, 381*
17–19 *159*
21 *661*
24–25 *631, 666*
25 *784*

Revelation
1:3 *286*
1:4 *618*
1:5–6 *666*
1:6 *784, 873*
1:8 *572, 618, 804*
2:2–5 *21*
2–3 *539*
2:3–4 *625*
3:14 *804*
4 *625*
4:1–5:14 *596–97*
4:3 *86*
4:4–8 *588*
4–5 *667*
4:6ff *448*
4:8 *402, 587, 628, 649*
4:8–10 *618*
4:11 *99, 135, 398, 405, 433, 592, 597, 606, 628, 675, 685, 693, 718, 754, 787, 797, 804–5, 859, 936*
5 *927*
5:9 *530*
5:9–10 *472, 483, 592, 657, 675, 694*
5:11–12 *426, 680, 683*
5:12 *648*
5:12–13 *667*
5:12–14 *405, 573, 592*
5:13 *876, 936*
7:1–8 *483*
10:6 *582, 803, 805, 820*
11:17 *628*
12 *447*
12:17 *158, 284*
13:7–8 *400*
13:8 *156–57, 451, 566, 608, 628, 736, 753, 755, 762, 874, 881, 890*
14:3 *483*
14:7 *820*
14:12 *158, 284*
15:3–4 *652, 884*
17:14 *758*
17:17 *882*
18–22 *480*
19 *630*
19:2 *652*
19:6 *873–74*
20:11–15 *160, 171, 630, 653–54*
21:1–4 *409, 525*
21:3–4 *469*
21:6 *804*
21:9–14 *483*
21–22 *99, 171, 423, 434, 446, 448, 455, 483, 531, 573, 630, 667, 827, 832–33, 858, 918, 929*
21:22 *477*
21:22–22:5 *574, 577*
21:27 *583*
22:13 *804*
22:17 *745*
22:18–19 *286, 308, 321, 341*
22:19–20 *275*